To Nana & Grandad   1976

GW00363717

To Nana & Grandad   1976

Philips'
New
WORLD
ATLAS

Philips'
New
WORLD
ATLAS

Edited by **Harold Fullard,** M.Sc.,
Cartographic Editor

George Philip and Son Limited
London

ISBN
0 540 05316 3

Printed in Great Britain by
George Philip Printers Limited, London

Acknowledgment is made to the following for providing the photographs used in this atlas.
Air India, Australian Information Service, Brazilian Embassy, London, British Aircraft Corporation, British
Airways, British Leyland, British Petroleum, British Rail, British Steel Corporation, British Tourist Authority,
Central Electricity Generating Board, D. Chanter, Danish Embassy, London, Egypt Air, Fiat (England) Ltd.,
Finnish Tourist Bureau, Freightliners Ltd., H. Fullard, M. H. Fullard, Gas Council Exploration Ltd.,
Commander H. R. Hatfield/Astro Books, H. Hawes, Israeli Govt. Tourist Office, Japan Air Lines, Lufthansa,
M.A.T. Transport Ltd., Meteorological Office, London, Moroccan Tourist Office, N.A.S.A. (Space Frontiers),
National Coal Board, London, National Maritime Museum, London, Offshore Co., Pan American World
Airways, Royal Astronomical Society, London, Shell International Petroleum Co. Ltd., Swan Hunter Group,
Ltd., Swiss National Tourist Office, B. M. Willett, Woodmansterne Ltd.

Preface

Philips' **New World Atlas** has been specially planned to meet the need for an atlas of convenient size and yet of sufficient proportions to provide adequate maps for normal reference purposes. This is essentially an atlas that a busy person requires in our modern world changed as it is by the increasingly rapid means of communications, the development of new organizations of many kinds and the ever faster pace of international events brought to our television screens every night by satellite.

An overall view of the earth in space, the composition of the earth and its surrounding atmosphere open the Atlas by diagrams, charts, tables and illustrations, followed by physical, demographic, economic and political maps. Further regional maps, designed for detailed reference, have an emphasis on the inclusion of a large number of place names on a physical background which also includes political and administrative divisions.

The style of colouring takes advantage of new developments in cartographic design and map production. Lighter yet cleaner layer colours have made possible the inclusion of a hill shading to bring out clearly the character of the landscape without impairing the detail of names, settlements and communications. The opportunity of new reproduction was also taken to revise topographical and cultural details from the new surveys of recent years, and to express measures in metric form.

Attention is drawn to the policy adopted where there are rival claims to territory: international boundaries are drawn to show the *de facto* situation. This does not denote international recognition of these boundaries: it shows the states which are administering the areas on either side of the line.

Spellings of names are in the forms given in the latest official lists. Generally, they agree with the rules of the Permanent Committee on Geographical Names and the United States Board on Geographical Names. This index contains over 44 000 entries.

HAROLD FULLARD

Contents

Preface

Contents

Principal Countries of the World

The Universe, Earth and Man

1	Chart of the Stars
2-3	The Solar System
4	The Earth
5	The Moon
6-7	Time
8-9	The Atmosphere and Clouds
10-11	Climate and Weather
12-13	The Earth from Space
14-15	The Evolution of the Continents
16-17	The Unstable Earth
18-19	The Making of Landscape
20-21	The Earth: Physical Dimensions
22-23	Distances
24-25	Water Resources and Vegetation
26-27	Population
28	Language
29	Religion
30-31	The Growth of Cities
32-33	Food Resources: Vegetable
34	Food Resources: Animal
35	Nutrition
36-37	Mineral Resources I
38-39	Mineral Resources II
40-41	Fuel and Energy
42	Occupations
43	Industry
44-45	Transport
46-47	Trade
48	Wealth

Maps 1–128

1	General Reference	
1	The World–Physical	1:150M
2-3	The World Political	1:80M
4-5	The Polar Regions	1:35M
6-7	The Atlantic Ocean Equatorial Scale	1:50M
8-9	Europe Physical European Organisations	1:17½M 1:40M
10	Europe Political	1:20M
11	The British Isles Political	1:4M
12-13	England and Wales	1:2M
14	Scotland	1:2M
15	Ireland	1:2M
16	The Netherlands, Belgium and Luxembourg	1:2½M
17	France	1:5M
18-19	Northern France	1:2½M
20-21	Southern France	1:2½M
22-23	Central Europe	1:5M
24-25	Germany and Switzerland	1:2½M
26-27	Austria, Czechoslovakia and Hungary	1:2½M
28	Poland	1:2½M
29	Spain and Portugal	1:5M
30-31	Western Spain and Portugal	1:2½M
32-33	Eastern Spain	1:2½M
34-35	The Mediterranean Lands	1:10M
36-37	Italy and the Balkan States Malta	1:5M 1:1M
38-39	Northern Italy and Western Yugoslavia	1:2½M
40-41	Southern Italy	1:2½M
42-43	Yugoslavia and Bulgaria	1:2½M
44-45	Greece and Albania	1:2½M
46	Rumania	1:2½M

Contents

47	**Southern Norway**	1:2½M
48–49	**Denmark and Southern Sweden**	1:2½M
50–51	**Scandinavia and the Baltic Lands** Iceland	1:5M 1:5M
52–53	**The U.S.S.R. in Europe**	1:10M
54–55	**European Russia** Central	1:5M
56–57	**European Russia** South	1:5M
58–59	**The Union of Soviet Socialist Republics**	1:20M
60	**Asia** Physical	1:50M
61	**Asia** Political	1:50M
62	**Palestine**	1:1M
63	**Arabia and The Horn of Africa**	1:15M
64–65	**The Near and Middle East**	1:10M
66–67	**South Asia**	1:10M
68–69	**The Indo-Gangetic Plain** S. Asia - Irrigation	1:6M 1:40M
70	**Southern India and Sri Lanka**	1:6M
71	**Mainland South-East Asia** Malaya & Singapore	1:10M 1:6M
72–73	**The East Indies** Java & Madura	1:12½M 1:7½M
74	**Japan** Southern Japan	1:10M 1:5M
75	**China**	1:20M
76–77	**Eastern China and Korea**	1:10M
78	**Africa** Physical	1:40M
79	**Africa** Political	1:40M
80–81	**Northern Africa**	1:15M
82–83	**North-West Africa**	1:8M
84–85	**West Africa**	1:8M
86–87	**The Nile Valley** The Nile Delta	1:8M 1:4M
88–89	**Central and South Africa**	1:15M
90–91	**East Africa**	1:8M
92–93	**Southern Africa** Malagasy Republic	1:8M 1:8M
94–95	**The Pacific Ocean** Equatorial Scale	1:60M
96–97	**Australia** Australasia–Political	1:12M 1:80M
98–99	**Eastern Australia** Papua New Guinea	1:7½M 1:12M
100	**South-East Australia**	1:4½M
101	**New Zealand** Samoa Fiji and Tonga New Zealand and Dependencies	1:6M 1:12M 1:12M 1:60M
102–3	**North America** Physical Political	1:30M 1:70M
104–5	**Canada** Alaska	1:15M 1:30M
106–7	**Eastern Canada**	1:7M
108–9	**Western Canada**	1:7M
110–11	**The United States** Hawaii	1:12M 1:10M
112–13	**North-Eastern United States**	1:2½M
114–15	**The Eastern United States**	1:6M
116–17	**The Middle United States**	1:6M
118–19	**The Western United States**	1:6M
120	**Mexico** Panama Canal	1:12M 1:1M
121	**The West Indies** Bermuda Leeward Is. Windward Is. Trinidad and Tobago Jamaica	1:12M 1:1M 1:8M 1:8M 1:8M 1:8M
122	**South America** Physical	1:30M
123	**South America** Political	1:30M
124–25	**Central South America**	1:8M
126–27	**South America** North	1:16M
128	**South America** South	1:16M
	Index	

Principal Countries of the World

Country	Area in thousands of square km	Population in thousands	Density of Population per sq. km	Capital Population in thousands
Afghanistan	647	18 796	29	Kabul (534)
Albania	29	2 416	84	Tiranë (175)
Algeria	2 382	16 275	7	Algiers (943)
Angola	1 247	5 812	5	Luanda (475)
Argentina	2 777	25 050	9	Buenos Aires (8 353)
Australia	7 687	13 339	2	Canberra (185)
Austria	84	7 528	90	Vienna (1 859)
Bangladesh	144	74 991	521	Dacca (1 132)
Belgium	31	9 804	321	Brussels (1 075)
Belize	23	136	6	Belmopan (3)
Benin	113	3 029	27	Porto-Novo (85)
Bhutan	47	1 146	24	Thimphu (10)
Bolivia	1 099	5 470	5	Sucre (107) La Paz (605)
Botswana	600	661	1	Gaborone (18)
Brazil	8 512	104 243	12	Brasilia (517)
Brunei	6	144	25	Bandar Seri Begawan (41)
Bulgaria	111	8 679	78	Sofia (937)
Burma	677	30 310	45	Rangoon (3 189)
Burundi	28	3 678	132	Bujumbura (107)
Cameroon	475	6 282	13	Yaoundé (178)
Cambodia	181	7 888	44	Phnom Penh (2 000)
Canada	9 976	22 479	2	Ottawa (619)
Central African Rep.	623	1 716	3	Bangui (187)
Chad	1 284	3 949	3	Ndjamena (193)
Chile	757	10 405	14	Santiago (3 069)
China	9 597	824 961	86	Peking (5 000)
Colombia	1 139	23 952	21	Bogotá (2 978)
Congo	342	1 313	4	Brazzaville (250)
Costa Rica	51	1 921	38	San José (395)
Cuba	115	9 090	79	Havana (1 755)
Cyprus	9	641	69	Nicosia (116)
Czechoslovakia	128	14 686	115	Prague (1 096)
Denmark	43	5 045	117	Copenhagen (1 378)
Dominican Republic	49	4 562	94	Santo Domingo (671)
Ecuador	284	6 951	25	Quito (597)
Egypt	1 001	36 417	36	Cairo (4 961)
El Salvador	21	3 980	186	San Salvador (337)
Equatorial Guinea	28	305	11	Rey Malabo (37) Bata (27)
Ethiopia	1 222	27 239	22	Addis Ababa (1 083)
Fiji	18	560	31	Suva (80)
Finland	337	4 682	14	Helsinki (845)
France	547	52 507	96	Paris (9 108)
French Guiana	91	58	1	Cayenne (25)
Fr. Terr. Afars & Issas	22	104	5	Djibouti (62)
Gabon	268	520	2	Libréville (57)
Gambia	11	510	45	Banjul (48)
Germany, East	108	17 166	159	East Berlin (1 089)
Germany, West	248	62 041	250	Bonn (283)
Ghana	239	9 607	40	Accra (738)
Greece	132	8 962	68	Athens (2 540)
Greenland	2 176	49	0·02	Godthaab (4)
Guatemala	109	5 540	51	Guatemala (707)
Guinea	246	4 312	18	Conakry (197)
Guyana	215	774	4	Georgetown (195)
Haiti	28	4 514	163	Port-au-Prince (494)
Honduras	112	2 933	26	Tegucigalpa (302)
Hong Kong	1	4 249	4 066	Victoria (675)
Hungary	93	10 458	112	Budapest (2 044)
Iceland	103	215	2	Reykjavik (98)
India	3 280	586 056	179	Delhi (3 630)
Indonesia	1 904	127 586	65	Djakarta (4 576)
Iran	1 648	31 955	19	Tehran (3 774)
Iraq	435	10 765	25	Baghdad (2 969)
Irish Republic	70	3 086	44	Dublin (650)
Israel	21	3 299	159	Jerusalem (326)
Italy	301	55 361	184	Rome (2 833)
Ivory Coast	322	4 765	15	Abidjan (420)
Jamaica	11	1 998	182	Kingston (573)
Japan	372	109 671	295	Tokyo (11 612)
Jordan	98	2 646	27	Amman (583)
Kenya	583	12 912	22	Nairobi (630)
Korea, North	121	15 439	128	Pyongyang (1 500)
Korea, South	98	33 459	340	Seoul (5 536)
Kuwait	16	929	52	Kuwait (295)
Laos	237	3 257	14	Vientiane (174)
Lebanon	10	2 784	268	Beirut (710)
Lesotho	30	1 016	33	Maseru (29)
Liberia	111	1 669	15	Monrovia (110)
Libya	1 760	2 346	1	Tripoli (332)
Luxembourg	3	342	132	Luxembourg (78)
Malagasy Republic	587	7 100	12	Tananarive (378)
Malawi	118	4 900	41	Zomba (20)
Malaysia	330	11 700	35	Kuala Lumpur (452)
Mali	1 240	5 561	4	Bamako (197)
Malta	0·3	323	1 024	Valletta (14)
Mauritania	1 031	1 290	1	Nouakchott (100)
Mauritius	2	872	426	Port Louis (137)
Mexico	1 973	58 118	29	Mexico (10 767)
Mongolia	1 565	1 403	1	Ulan Bator (282)
Morocco	447	16 880	38	Rabat (534)
Mozambique	783	9 029	12	Maputo (384)
Nepal	141	12 319	87	Katmandu (333)
Netherlands	41	13 541	332	Amsterdam (1 002)
New Zealand	269	3 027	11	Wellington (142)
Nicaragua	130	2 084	16	Managua (399)
Niger	1 267	4 476	4	Niamey (102)
Nigeria	924	61 270	66	Lagos (1 477)
Norway	324	3 987	12	Oslo (469)
Oman	212	743	3	Muscat (25)
Pakistan	804	68 214	85	Islamabad (77)
Panama	76	1 631	22	Panamá (393)
Papua New Guinea	462	2 652	6	Port Moresby (76)
Paraguay	407	2 572	6	Asunción (388)
Peru	1 285	15 383	12	Lima (3 158)
Philippines	300	41 457	138	Quezon City (896)
Poland	313	33 691	108	Warsaw (1 377)
Portugal	92	8 735	95	Lisbon (1 612)
Puerto Rico	9	3 031	341	San Juan (695)
Rhodesia	391	6 100	16	Salisbury (502)
Rumania	238	21 029	89	Bucharest (1 529)
Rwanda	26	4 123	157	Kigali (54)
Saudi Arabia	2 150	8 706	4	Riyadh (300)
Senegal	196	4 315	22	Dakar (581)
Sierra Leone	72	2 707	38	Freetown (214)
Singapore	0·6	2 219	3 819	Singapore (2 147)
Somali Republic	638	3 090	5	Mogadishu (230)
South Africa	1 221	24 920	20	Pretoria (562) Cape Town (1 096)
S. W. Africa	824	692	1	Windhoek (60)
Spain	505	35 225	70	Madrid (3 146)
Sri Lanka	66	13 679	208	Colombo (618)
Sudan	2 506	17 324	7	Khartoum (648)
Surinam	163	411	3	Paramaribo (182)
Swaziland	17	478	28	Mbabane (14)
Sweden	450	8 161	18	Stockholm (1 350)
Switzerland	41	6 481	157	Berne (285)
Syria	185	7 121	38	Damascus (923)
Taiwan	36	14 990	417	Taipei (1 922)
Tanzania	945	14 763	16	Dar-es-Salaam (344)
Thailand	514	41 023	80	Bangkok (1 867)
Togo	56	2 171	39	Lomé (193)
Trinidad and Tobago	5	1 064	207	Port of Spain (68)
Tunisia	164	5 641	34	Tunis (648)
Turkey	781	38 270	49	Ankara (1 554)
Uganda	236	11 172	47	Kampala (331)
United Arab Emirates	84	215	3	Dubai (70)
U.S.S.R.	22 402	252 064	11	Moscow (7 528)
United Kingdom	244	56 113	229	London (7 168)
United States	9 363	211 909	23	Washington (2 861)
Upper Volta	274	5 897	22	Ouagadougou (125)
Uruguay	178	3 028	17	Montevideo (1 376)
Venezuela	912	11 632	13	Caracas (2 175)
Vietnam, North	159	23 244	146	Hanoi (920)
Vietnam, South	174	19 367	111	Saigon (1 825)
Yemen (Sana)	195	6 477	33	Sana (120)
Yemen (South)	288	1 633	5	Aden (285)
Yugoslavia	256	21 151	83	Belgrade (1 204)
Zaïre	2 345	24 222	10	Kinshasa (2 008)
Zambia	753	4 751	6	Lusaka (348)

Chart of the Stars

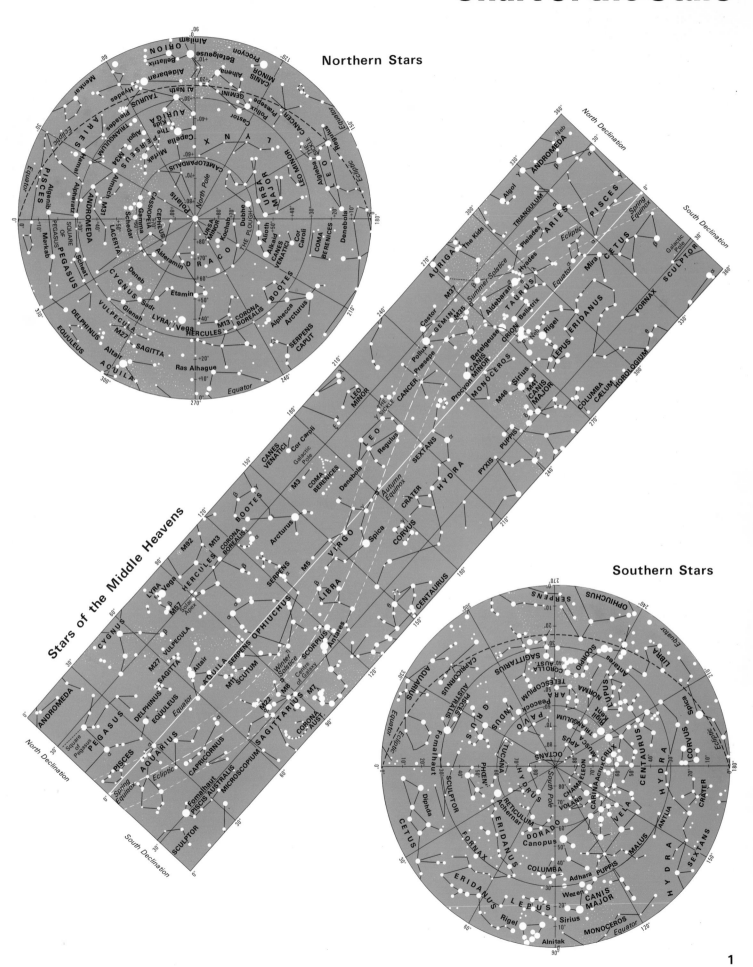

Northern Stars

Stars of the Middle Heavens

Southern Stars

The Solar System

The Solar System is a minute part of one of the innumerable galaxies that make up the universe. Our Galaxy is represented in the drawing to the right and The Solar System (S) lies near the plane of spiral-shaped galaxy, but 27 000 light-years from the centre. The System consists of the Sun at the centre with planets, moons, asteroids, comets, meteors, meteorites, dust and gases revolving around it. It is calculated to be at least 4 700 million years old.

The Solar System can be considered in two parts: the Inner Region planets- Mercury, Venus, Earth and Mars - all small and solid; the Outer Region planets - Jupiter, Saturn, Uranus and Neptune - all gigantic in size, and on the edge of the system the smaller Pluto.

Our galaxy

Inner region planets

Outer region planets

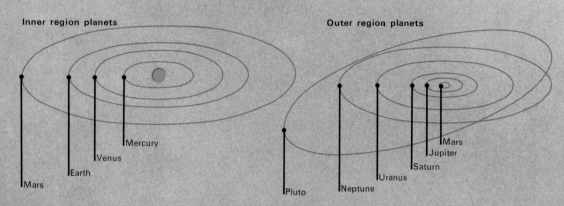

Mars
Earth
Venus
Mercury

Pluto
Neptune
Uranus
Saturn
Jupiter
Mars

The planets

All planets revolve round the Sun in the same direction, and mostly in the same plane. Their orbits are shown (left) - they are not perfectly circular paths.

The table below summarizes the dimensions and movements of the Sun and planets.

The Sun

The Sun has an interior with temperatures believed to be of several million °C brought about by continuous thermo-nuclear fusions of hydrogen into helium. This immense energy is transferred by radiation into surrounding layers of gas the outer surface of which is called the chromosphere. From this "surface" with a temperature of many thousands °C "flames" (solar prominences) leap out into the diffuse corona which can best be seen at times of total eclipse (see photo right). The bright surface of the Sun, the photosphere, is calculated to have a temperature of about 6 000 °C, and when viewed through a telescope has a mottled appearance, the darker patches being called sunspots - the sites of large disturbances of the surface.

Total eclipse of the sun

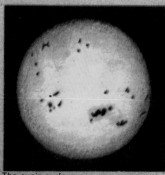

The sun's surface

	Equatorial diameter in km	Mass (earth=1)	Mean distance from sun in millions km	Radii of orbit (earth=1)	Orbital inclination	Sidereal period	Period of rotation on axis	Number of satellites
Sun	1 392 000	333 434	—	—	—	—	25 days 9hrs	—
Mercury	4 840	0·04	58	0·39	7°	88d	59 days	0
Venus	12 300	0·83	108	0·72	3°24'	225d	244 days	0
Earth	12 756	1·00	150	1·00	—	1 year	23 hrs 56m	1
Mars	6 790	0·11	228	1·52	1°51'	1y 322d	24 hrs 37m	2
Jupiter	143 200	318	778	5·20	1°18'	11y 315d	9 hrs 50m	12
Saturn	119 300	95	1 427	9·54	2°29'	29y 167d	10 hrs 14m	10
Uranus	47 100	15	2 870	19·19	0°46'	84y 6d	10 hrs 49m	5
Neptune	51 000	17	4 497	30·07	1°46'	164y 288d	15 hrs 48m	2
Pluto	5 900	0·06	5 950	39·46	17°06'	247y 255d	6d 9 hrs 17m	—

The Sun's diameter is 109 times greater than that of the Earth.

Distances from sun in millions km

58	Mercury
108	Venus
150	Earth
228	Mars
778	Jupiter
1427	Saturn
2870	Uranus
4497	Neptune
5950	Pluto

Mercury is the smallest planet and nearest to the Sun. It is composed mostly of metals and probably has an atmosphere of heavy inert gases.

Venus is similar in size to the Earth, and probably in composition. It is, however, much hotter and has a dense atmosphere of carbon dioxide which obscures our view of its surface.

Earth is the largest of the inner planets. It has a dense iron-nickel core surrounded by layers of silicate rock. The surface is approximately ⅜ land and ⅝ water, and the lower atmosphere consists of a mixture of nitrogen, oxygen and other gases supplemented by water vapour. With this atmosphere and surface temperatures usually between −50°C and +40°C. life is possible.

Mars, smaller than the Earth, has a noticeably red appearance. Recent photographs sent back by satellite show clearly the cratered surface and the ice areas at the poles made from condensed carbon dioxide.

The Asteroids orbit the Sun mainly between Mars and Jupiter. They consist of thousands of bodies of varying sizes with diameters ranging from yards to hundreds of miles.

Jupiter is the largest planet of the Solar System. It shines brightly in the sky (magnitude −2·5), and is notable for its cloud belts and the Great Red Spot.

Saturn, the second largest planet consists of hydrogen, helium and other gases. Its density is less than that of water. It is unique in appearance because of its equatorial rings believed to be made of ice-covered particles.

Uranus was discovered in 1781 by Herschel. It is extremely remote yet faintly visible to the naked eye. Methane in its atmosphere gives it a slightly green appearance.

Neptune, yet more remote than Uranus and larger. It is composed of gases and has a bluish green appearance when seen in a telescope. As with Uranus, little detail can be observed on its surface.

Pluto No details are known of its composition or surface. The existence of this planet was firstly surmised in a computed hypothesis, which was tested by repeated searches by large telescopes until in 1930 the planet was found.

The Earth

Seasons, Equinoxes and Solstices

The Earth revolves around the Sun once a year and rotates daily on its axis, which is inclined at $66\frac{1}{2}°$ to the orbital plane and always points into space in the same direction. At midsummer (N.) the North Pole tilts towards the Sun, six months later it points away and half way between the axis is at right angles to the direction of the Sun (right).

Earth data

Maximum distance from the Sun (Aphelion) 152 007 016 km
Minimum distance from the Sun (Perihelion) 147 000 830 km
Obliquity of the ecliptic 23° 27′ 08″
Length of year - tropical (equinox to equinox) 365.24 days
Length of year - sidereal (fixed star to fixed star) 365.26 days
Length of day - mean solar day 24h 03m 56s
Length of day - mean sidereal day 23h 56m 04s

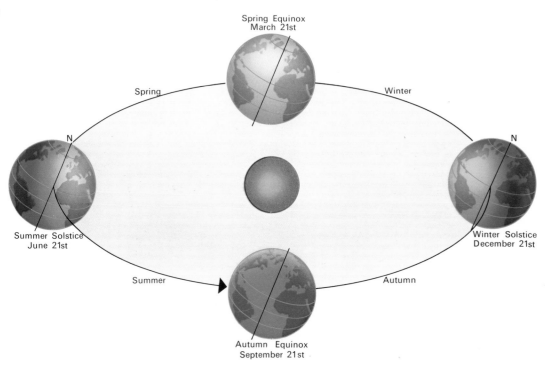

Length of day and night

At the summer solstice in the northern hemisphere, the Arctic has total daylight and the Antarctic total darkness. The opposite occurs at the winter solstice. At the equator, the length of day and night are almost equal all the year, at 30° the length of day varies from about 14 hours to 10 hours and at 50° from about 16 hours to 8 hours.

Apparent path of the Sun

The diagrams (right) illustrate the apparent path of the Sun at A the equator, B in mid latitudes say 45°N, C at the Arctic Circle $66\frac{1}{2}°$ and D at the North Pole where there is six months continuous daylight and six months continuous night

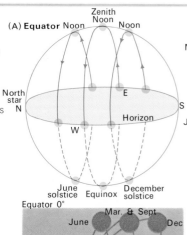

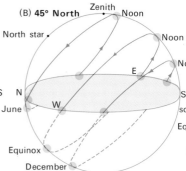

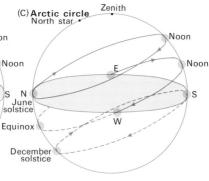

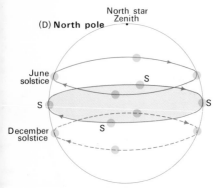

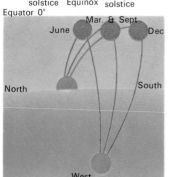

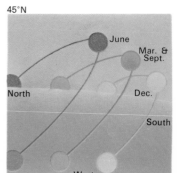

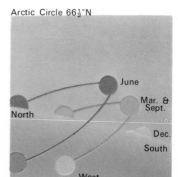

4

The Moon

The Moon rotates slowly making one complete turn on its axis in just over 27 days. This is the same as its period of revolution around the Earth and thus it always presents the same hemisphere ('face') to us. Surveys and photographs from space-craft have now added greatly to our knowledge of the Moon, and, for the first time, views of the hidden hemisphere.

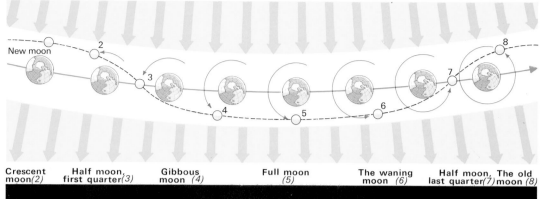

Phases of the Moon

The interval between one full Moon and the next is approximately $29\frac{1}{2}$ days - thus there is one new Moon and one full Moon every month. The diagrams and photographs (right) show how the apparent changes in shape of the Moon from new to full arise from its changing position in relation to the Earth and both to the fixed direction of the Sun's rays.

| Crescent moon(2) | Half moon, first quarter(3) | Gibbous moon (4) | Full moon (5) | The waning moon (6) | Half moon, last quarter(7) | The old moon (8) |

Moon data

Distance from Earth 356 410 km
to 406 685 km
Mean diameter 3 473 km
Mass approx. $\frac{1}{81}$ of that of Earth
Surface gravity $\frac{1}{6}$ of that of Earth
Atmosphere - none, hence no clouds, no weather, no sound.
Diurnal range of temperature at the Equator +200°C

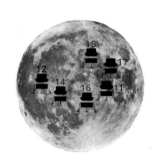

Landings on the Moon

Left are shown the landing sites of the U.S. Apollo programme.
Apollo 11 Sea of Tranquility (1°N 23°E) 1969
Apollo 12 Ocean of Storms (3°S 24°W) 1969
Apollo 14 Fra Mauro (4°S 17°W) 1971
Apollo 15 Hadley Rill (25°N 4°E) 1971
Apollo 16 Descartes (9°S 15°E) 1972
Apollo 17 Sea of Serenity (20°N 31°E) 1972

Eclipses of Sun and Moon

When the Moon passes between Sun and Earth it causes a partial eclipse of the Sun *(right 1)* if the Earth passes through the Moon's outer shadow *(P)*, or a total eclipse *(right 2)*, if the inner cone shadow crosses the Earth's surface.

In a lunar eclipse, the Earth's shadow crosses the Moon and gives either total or partial eclipses.

Partial eclipse (1)

P *P* *P*

Total eclipse (2)

Lunar eclipse

Tides

Ocean water moves around the Earth under the gravitational pull of the Moon, and, less strongly, that of the Sun. When solar and lunar forces pull together - near new and full Moon - high spring tides result. When solar and lunar forces are not combined - near Moon's first and third quarters - low neap tides occur.

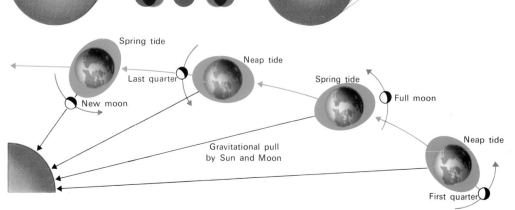

Spring tide
Neap tide
Last quarter
New moon
Spring tide
Full moon
Gravitational pull by Sun and Moon
Neap tide
First quarter

Time

Time measurement
The basic unit of time measurement is the day, one rotation of the earth on its axis. The subdivision of the day into hours and minutes is arbitrary and simply for our convenience. Our present calendar is based on the solar year of $365\frac{1}{4}$ days, the time taken for the earth to orbit the sun. A month was anciently based on the interval from new moon to new moon, approximately $29\frac{1}{2}$ days - and early calendars were entirely lunar.

Rotation of the Earth
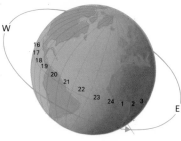

The International Date Line
When it is 12 noon at the Greenwich meridian, 180° east it is midnight of the same day while 180° west the day is only just beginning. To overcome this the International Date Line was established, approximately following the 180° meridian. Thus, for example, if one travelled eastwards from Japan (140° East) to Samoa (170° West) one would pass from Sunday night into Sunday morning.

Time zones
The world is divided into 24 time zones, each centred on meridians at 15° intervals which is the longitudinal distance the sun appears to travel every hour. The meridian running through Greenwich passes through the middle of the first zone. Successive zones to the east of Greenwich zone are ahead of Greenwich time by one hour for every 15° of longitude, while zones to the west are behind by one hour.

Night and day
As the earth rotates from west to east the sun appears to rise in the east and set in the west: when the sun is setting in Shanghai on the directly opposite side of the earth New York is just emerging into sunlight. Noon, when the sun is directly overhead, is coincident at all places on the same meridian with shadows pointing directly towards the poles.

Greenwich Observatory

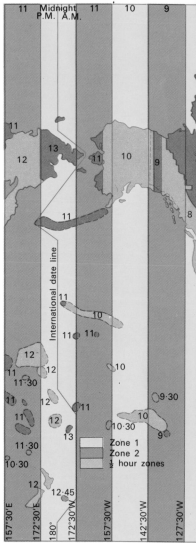

Prime Meridian

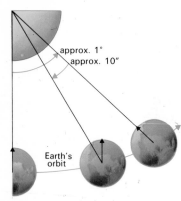

Solar time
The time taken for the earth to complete one rotation about its own axis is constant and defines a day but the speed of the earth along its orbit around the sun is inconstant. The length of day, or 'apparent solar day', as defined by the apparent successive transits of the sun is irregular because the earth must complete more than one rotation before the sun returns to the same meridian.

Sidereal time
The constant sidereal day is defined as the interval between two successive apparent transits of a star, or the first point of Aries, across the same meridian. If the sun is at the equinox and overhead at a meridian on one day, then the next day the sun will be to the east by approximately 1°; thus the sun will not cross the meridian until about 4 minutes after the sidereal noon.

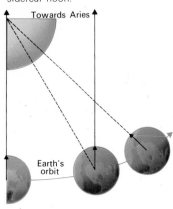

Astronomical clock, Delhi

Sundials
The earliest record of sundials dates back to 741 BC but they undoubtedly existed as early as 2000 BC although probably only as an upright stick or obelisk. A sundial marks the progress of the sun across the sky by casting the shadow of a central style or gnomon on the base. The base, generally made of stone, is delineated to represent the hours between sunrise and sunset.

Kendall's chronometer

Chronometers
With the increase of sea traffic in the 18th century and the need for accurate navigation clockmakers were faced with an intriguing problem. Harrison, an English carpenter, won a British award for designing a clock which was accurate at sea to one tenth of a second per day. He compensated for the effect of temperature changes by incorporating bi-metallic strips connected to thin wires and circular balance wheels.

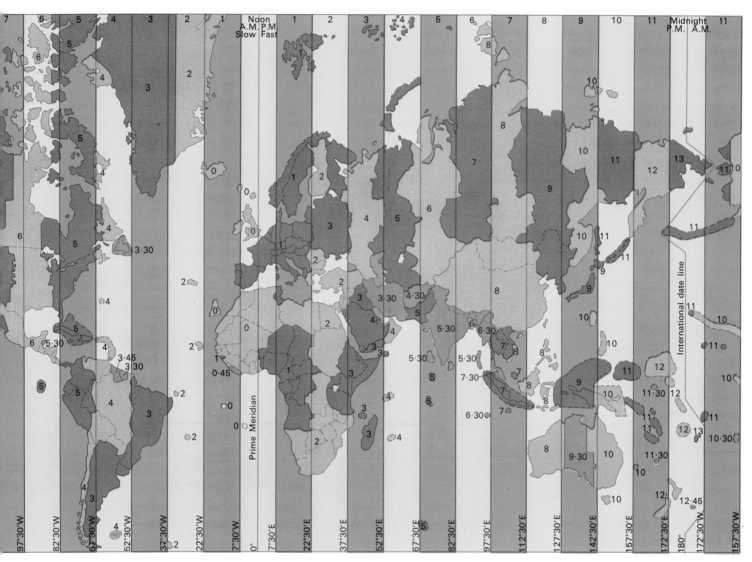

International date line

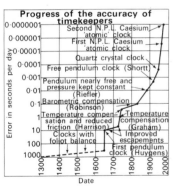

Progress of the accuracy of timekeepers

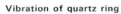

Vibration of quartz ring

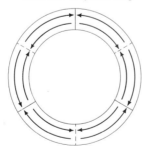

Time difference when travelling by air

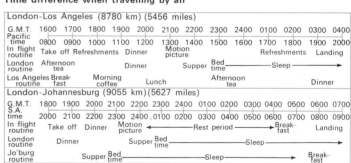

London-Los Angeles (8780 km) (5456 miles)															
G.M.T.	1600	1700	1800	1900	2000	2100	2200	2300	2400	0100	0200	0300	0400		
Pacific time	0800	0900	1000	1100	1200	1300	1400	1500	1600	1700	1800	1900	2000		
In flight routine	Take off	Refreshments	Dinner		Motion picture						Refreshments		Landing		
London routine	Afternoon tea			Dinner			Supper	Bed time		Sleep					
Los Angeles routine	Break-fast		Morning coffee		Lunch				Afternoon tea				Dinner		

London-Johannesburg (9055 km) (5627 miles)															
G.M.T.	1800	1900	2000	2100	2200	2300	2400	0100	0200	0300	0400	0500	0600	0700	
S.A. time	2000	2100	2200	2300	2400	0100	0200	0300	0400	0500	0600	0700	0800	0900	
In flight routine	Take off		Dinner		Motion picture		Rest period					Break-fast		Landing	
London routine		Dinner			Supper	Bed time		Sleep							
Jo'burg routine				Supper	Bed time			Sleep					Break-fast		

Chronographs

The invention of the chronograph by Charles Wheatstone in 1842 made it possible to record intervals of time to an accuracy of one sixtieth of a second. The simplest form of chronograph is the stopwatch. This was developed to a revolving drum and stylus and later electrical signals. A recent development is the cathode ray tube capable of recording to less than one ten-thousanth of a second.

Quartz crystal clocks

The quartz crystal clock, designed originally in America in 1929, can measure small units of time and radio frequencies. The connection between quartz clocks and the natural vibrations of atoms and molecules mean that the unchanging frequencies emitted by atoms can be used to control the oscillator which controls the quartz clock. A more recent version of the atomic clock is accurate to one second in 300 years.

International date line

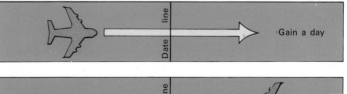

Gain a day

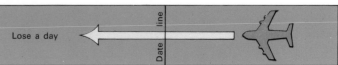

Lose a day

The Atmosphere and Clouds

Earth's thin coating *(right)*
The atmosphere is a blanket of protective gases around the earth providing insulation against otherwise extreme alternations in temperature. The gravitational pull increases the density nearer the earth's surface so that 5/6ths of the atmospheric mass is in the first 15 kms. It is a very thin layer in comparison with the earth's diameter of 12 680 kms., like the cellulose coating on a globe.

Exosphere*(1)*
The exosphere merges with the interplanetary medium and although there is no definite boundary with the ionosphere it starts at a height of about 600 kms. The rarified air mainly consists of a small amount of atomic oxygen up to 600 kms. and equal proportions of hydrogen and helium with hydrogen predominating above 2 400 kms.

Ionosphere*(2)*
Air particles of the ionosphere are electrically charged by the sun's radiation and congregate in four main layers, D, E, F1 and F2, which can reflect radio waves. Aurorae, caused by charged particles deflected by the earth's magnetic field towards the poles, occur between 65 and 965 kms. above the earth. It is mainly in the lower ionosphere that meteors from outer space burn up as they meet increased air resistance.

Stratosphere*(3)*
A thin layer of ozone contained within the stratosphere absorbs ultra-violet light and in the process gives off heat. The temperature ranges from about -55°C at the tropopause to about -60°C in the upper part, known as the mesosphere, with a rise to about 2°C just above the ozone layer. This portion of the atmosphere is separated from the lower layer by the tropopause.

Troposphere*(4)*
The earth's weather conditions are limited to this layer which is relatively thin, extending upwards to about 8 kms. at the poles and 15 kms. at the equator. It contains about 85% of the total atmospheric mass and almost all the water vapour. Air temperature falls steadily with increased height at about 1°C for every 100 metres above sea level.

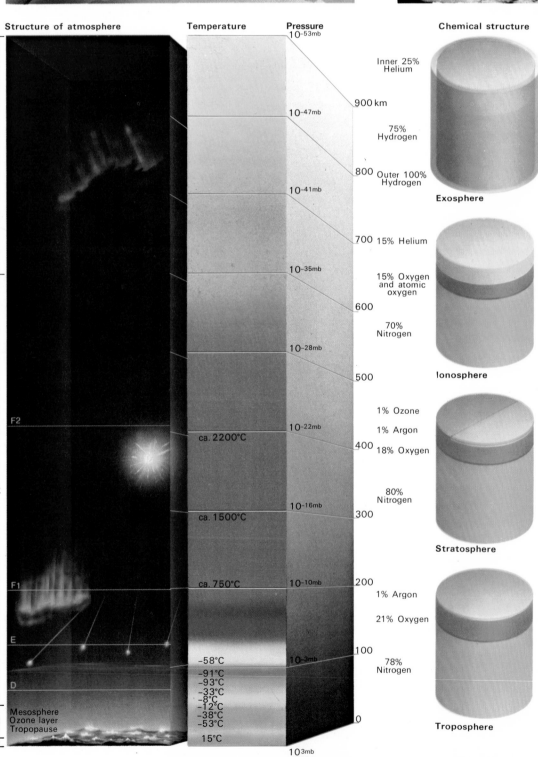

Structure of atmosphere

Temperature

Pressure

Chemical structure

600 km

15 km

10⁻⁵³mb

Inner 25% Helium

900 km

75% Hydrogen

800 — Outer 100% Hydrogen

Exosphere

700 — 15% Helium

15% Oxygen and atomic oxygen

600

70% Nitrogen

500

Ionosphere

1% Ozone

1% Argon

400 — 18% Oxygen

80% Nitrogen

300

Stratosphere

200

1% Argon

21% Oxygen

100

78% Nitrogen

Troposphere

ca. 2200°C

ca. 1500°C

ca. 750°C

-58°C
-91°C
-93°C
-33°C
-8°C
-12°C
-38°C
-53°C

15°C

10⁻⁴⁷mb
10⁻⁴¹mb
10⁻³⁵mb
10⁻²⁸mb
10⁻²²mb
10⁻¹⁶mb
10⁻¹⁰mb
10⁻³mb

Mesosphere
Ozone layer
Tropopause

10³mb

F2

F1

E

D

Pacific Ocean
Cloud patterns over the Pacific show the paths of prevailing winds.

Circulation of the air

Circulation of the air
Owing to high temperatures in equatorial regions the air near the ground is heated, expands and rises producing a low pressure belt. It cools, causing rain, spreads out then sinks again about latitudes 30° north and south forming high pressure belts.

High and low pressure belts are areas of comparative calm but between them, blowing from high to low pressure, are the prevailing winds. These are deflected to the right in the northern hemisphere and to the left in the southern hemisphere (Corolis effect). The circulations appear in three distinct belts with a seasonal movement north and south following the overhead sun.

Cloud types

Clouds form when damp air is cooled, usually by rising. This may happen in three ways: when a wind rises to cross hills or mountains; when a mass of air rises over, or is pushed up by another mass of denser air; when local heating of the ground causes convection currents.

Cirrus *(1)* are detached clouds composed of microscopic ice crystals which gleam white in the sun resembling hair or feathers. They are found at heights of 6 000 to 12 000 metres.

Cirrostratus *(2)* are a whitish veil of cloud made up of ice crystals through which the sun can be seen often producing a halo of bright light.

Cirrocumulus *(3)* is another high altitude cloud formed by turbulence between layers moving in different directions.

Altostratus *(4)* is a grey or bluish striated, fibrous or uniform sheet of cloud producing light drizzle.

Altocumulus *(5)* is a thicker and fluffier version of cirro cumulus, it is a white and grey patchy sheet of cloud.

Nimbostratus *(6)* is a dark grey layer of cloud obscuring the sun and causing almost continuous rain or snow.

Cumulus *(7)* are detached heaped up, dense low clouds. The sunlit parts are brilliant white while the base is relatively dark and flat.

Stratus *(8)* forms dull overcast skies associated with depressions and occurs at low altitudes up to 1500 metres.

Cumulonimbus *(9)* are heavy and dense clouds associated with storms and rain. They have flat bases and a fluffy outline extending up to great altitudes.

High clouds

Middle clouds

Low clouds

Thousands of metres

1 Cirrus

2 Cirrostratus

3 Cirrocumulus   4 Altostratus

5 Altocumulus   6 Nimbostratus

7 Cumulus

8 Stratus

9 Cumulonimbus

9

Climate and Weather

All weather occurs over the earth's surface in the lowest level of the atmosphere, the troposphere. Weather has been defined as the condition of the atmosphere at any place at a specific time with respect to the various elements: temperature, sunshine, pressure, winds, clouds, fog, precipitation. Climate, on the other hand, is the average of weather elements over previous months and years.

Climate graphs *right*
Each graph typifies the kind of climatic conditions one would experience in the region to which it is related by colour to the map. The scale refers to degrees Celsius for temperature and millimetres for rainfall, shown by bars. The graphs show average observations based over long periods of time, the study of which also compares the prime factors for vegetation differences.

Development of a depression *below*
In an equilibrium front between cold and warm air masses (i) a wave disturbance develops as cold air undercuts the warm air (ii). This deflects the air flow and as the disturbance progresses a definite cyclonic circulation with warm and cold fronts is created (iii). The cold front moves more rapidly than the warm front eventually overtaking it, and occlusion occurs as the warm air is pinched out (iv).

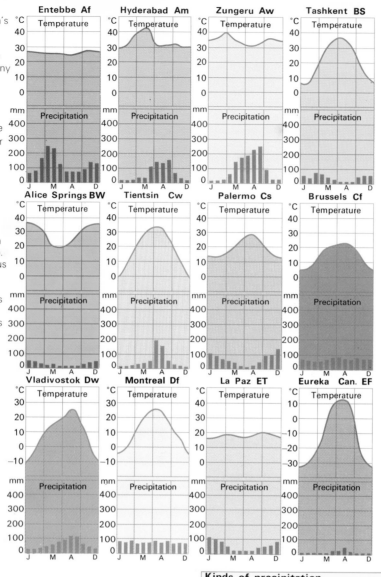

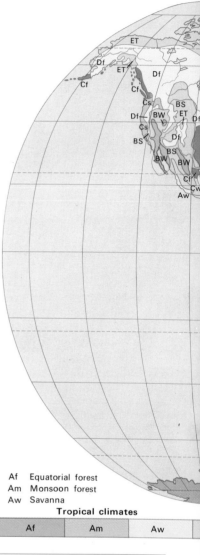

Af   Equatorial forest
Am   Monsoon forest
Aw   Savanna

Tropical climates

Af	Am	Aw

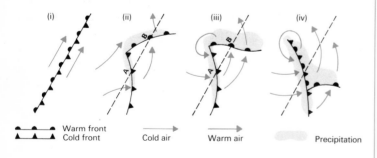

Warm front
Cold front   Cold air   Warm air   Precipitation

Frontal cloud

Precipitation

The upper diagrams show in plan view stages in the development of a depression.
The cross sections below correspond to stages (ii) to (iv).

Kinds of precipitation
Rain The condensation of water vapour on microscopic particles of dust, sulphur, soot or ice in the atmosphere forms water particles. These combine until they are heavy enough to fall as rain.

Frost Hoar, the most common type of frost, is precipitated instead of dew when water vapour changes directly into ice crystals on the surface of ground objects which have cooled below freezing point.

Hail Water particles, carried to a great height, freeze into ice particles which fall and become coated with fresh moisture. They are swept up again and refrozen. This may happen several times before falling as hail-stones.

Snow is the precipitation of ice in the form of flakes, or clusters, of basically hexagonal ice crystals. They are formed by the condensation of water vapour directly into ice.

10

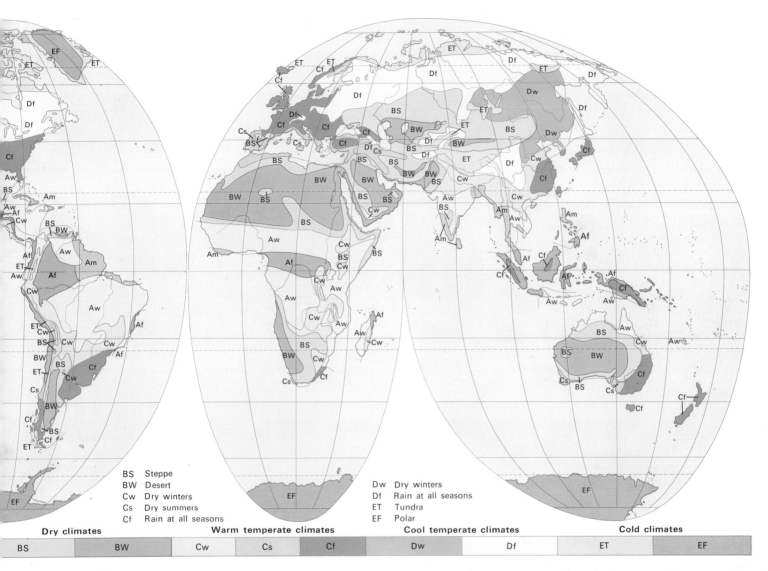

BS   Steppe
BW   Desert
Cw   Dry winters
Cs   Dry summers
Cf   Rain at all seasons

Dw   Dry winters
Df   Rain at all seasons
ET   Tundra
EF   Polar

Dry climates			Warm temperate climates			Cool temperate climates		Cold climates	
BS	BW	Cw	Cs	Cf	Dw	Df	ET	EF

Tropical storm tracks *below*

A tropical cyclone, or storm, is designated as having winds of gale force (60 kph) but less than hurricane force (120 kph). It is a homogenous air mass with upward spiralling air currents around a windless centre, or eye. An average of 65 tropical storms occur each year, over 50% of which reach hurricane force. They originate mainly during the summer over tropical oceans.

Extremes of climate & weather *right*

Tropical high temperatures and polar low temperatures combined with wind systems, altitude and unequal rainfall distribution result in the extremes of tropical rain forests, inland deserts and frozen polar wastes. Fluctuations in the limits of these extreme zones and extremes of weather result in occasional catastrophic heat-waves and drought, floods and storms, frost and snow.

Hurricane devastation

Hot desert

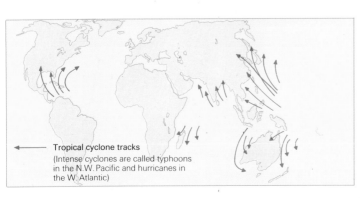
← Tropical cyclone tracks
(Intense cyclones are called typhoons in the N.W. Pacific and hurricanes in the W. Atlantic)

Tornado

Arctic dwellings

The Earth from Space

Mount Etna, Sicily *left*
Etna is at the top of the photograph, the Plain of Catania in the centre and the Mediterranean to the right. This is an infra-red photograph; vegetation shows as red, water as blue/black and urban areas as grey. The recent lava flows, as yet with no vegetation, show up as blue/black unlike the cultivated slopes which are red and red/pink.

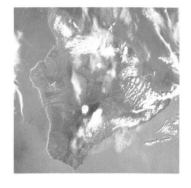

Hawaii, Pacific Ocean *above*
This is a photograph of Hawaii, the largest of the Hawaiian Islands in the Central Pacific. North is at the top of the photograph. The snowcapped craters of the volcanoes Mauna Kea (dormant) in the north centre and Mauna Loa (active) in the south centre of the photograph can be seen. The chief town, Hilo, is on the north east coast.

River Brahmaputra, India
left
A view looking westwards down the Brahmaputra with the Himalayas on the right and the Khasi Hills of Assam to the left.

Szechwan, China *right*
The River Tachin in the mountainous region of Szechwan, Central China. The lightish blue area in the river valley in the north east of the photograph is a village and its related cultivation.

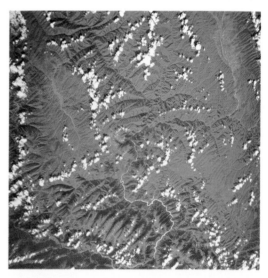

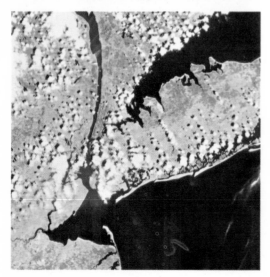

New York, U.S.A. *left*
This infra-red photograph shows the western end of Long Island and the entrance to the Hudson River. Vegetation appears as red, water as blue/black and the metropolitan areas of New York, through the cloud cover, as grey.

The Great Barrier Reef, Australia *right*
The Great Barrier Reef and the Queensland coast from Cape Melville to Cape Flattery. The smoke from a number of forest fires can be seen in the centre of the photograph.

Eastern Himalayas, Asia
above left
A view from Apollo IX looking
north-westwards over the
snowcapped, sunlit mountain
peaks and the head waters of
the Mekong, Salween,
Irrawaddy and, in the distance,
with its distinctive loop, the
Brahmaputra.

Atacama Desert, Chile
above right
This view looking eastwards
from the Pacific over the
Mejillones peninsula with the
city of Antofagasta in the
southern bay of that peninsula.
Inland the desert and salt-pans
of Atacama, and beyond, the
Andes.

The Alps, Europe *right*
This vertical photograph shows
the snow-covered mountains
and glaciers of the Alps along
the Swiss-Italian-French
border. Mont Blanc and the
Matterhorn are shown and, in
the north, the Valley of the
Rhône is seen making its sharp
right-hand bend near Martigny.
In the south the head waters
of the Dora Baltea flow
towards the Po and, in the
north-west, the Lac d'Annecy
can be seen.

The Evolution of the Continents

The origin of the earth is still open to much conjecture although the most widely accepted theory is that it was formed from a solar cloud consisting mainly of hydrogen. Under gravitation the cloud condensed and shrank to form our planets orbiting around the sun. Gravitation forced the lighter elements to the surface of the earth where they cooled to form a crust while the inner material remained hot and molten. Earth's first rocks formed over 3500 million years ago but since then the surface has been constantly altered.

Until comparatively recently the view that the primary units of the earth had remained essentially fixed throughout geological time was regarded as common sense, although the concept of moving continents has been traced back to references in the Bible of a break up of the land after Noah's floods. The continental drift theory was first developed by Antonio Snider in 1858 but probably the most important single advocate was Alfred Wegener who, in 1915, published evidence from geology, climatology and biology. His conclusions are very similar to those reached by current research although he was wrong about the speed of break-up.

The measurement of fossil magnetism found in rocks has probably proved the most influential evidence. While originally these drift theories were openly mocked, now they are considered standard doctrine.

The jigsaw
As knowledge of the shape and structure of the earth's surface grew, several of the early geographers noticed the great similarity in shape of the coasts bordering the Atlantic. It was this remarkable similarity which led to the first detailed geological and structural comparisons. Even more accurate fits can be made by placing the edges of the continental shelves in juxtaposition.

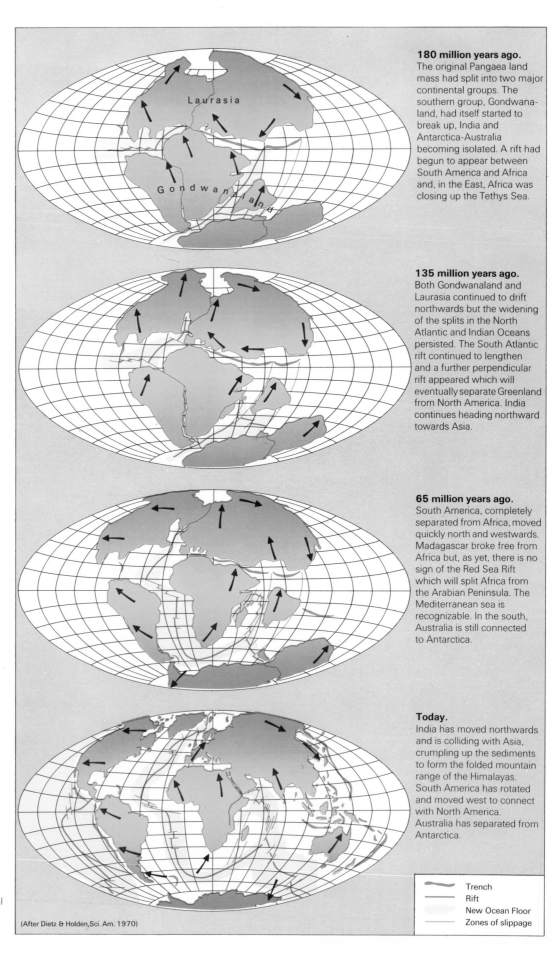

(After Dietz & Holden, Sci. Am. 1970)

180 million years ago.
The original Pangaea land mass had split into two major continental groups. The southern group, Gondwanaland, had itself started to break up, India and Antarctica-Australia becoming isolated. A rift had begun to appear between South America and Africa and, in the East, Africa was closing up the Tethys Sea.

135 million years ago.
Both Gondwanaland and Laurasia continued to drift northwards but the widening of the splits in the North Atlantic and Indian Oceans persisted. The South Atlantic rift continued to lengthen and a further perpendicular rift appeared which will eventually separate Greenland from North America. India continues heading northward towards Asia.

65 million years ago.
South America, completely separated from Africa, moved quickly north and westwards. Madagascar broke free from Africa but, as yet, there is no sign of the Red Sea Rift which will split Africa from the Arabian Peninsula. The Mediterranean sea is recognizable. In the south, Australia is still connected to Antarctica.

Today.
India has moved northwards and is colliding with Asia, crumpling up the sediments to form the folded mountain range of the Himalayas. South America has rotated and moved west to connect with North America. Australia has separated from Antarctica.

~~	Trench
	Rift
	New Ocean Floor
	Zones of slippage

14

Plate tectonics

The original debate about continental drift was only a prelude to a more radical idea; plate tectonics. The basic theory is that the earth's crust is made up of a series of rigid plates which float on a soft layer of the mantle and are moved about by convection currents in the earth's interior. These plates converge and diverge along margins marked by earthquakes, volcanoes and other seismic activity. Plates diverge from mid-ocean ridges where molten lava pushes upwards and forces the plates apart at a rate of up to 30mm. a year. Converging plates form either a trench, where the oceanic plate sinks below the lighter continental rock, or mountain ranges where two continents collide. This explains the paradox that while there have always been oceans none of the present oceans contain sediments more than 150 million years old.

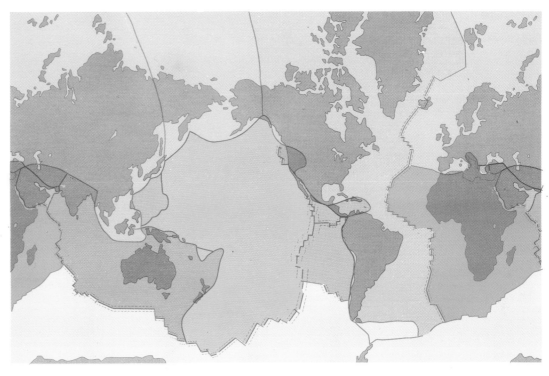

Trench boundary

The present explanation for the comparative youth of the ocean floors is that where an ocean and a continent meet the ocean plate dips under the less dense continental plate at an angle of approximately 45°. All previous crust is then ingested by downward convection currents. In the Japanese trench this occurs at a rate of about 120mm. a year.

Transform fault

The recent identification of the transform, or transverse, fault proved to be one of the crucial preliminaries to the investigation of plate tectonics. They occur when two plates slip alongside each other without parting or approaching to any great extent. They complete the outline of the plates delineated by the ridges and trenches and demonstrate large scale movements of parts of the earth's surface

Ridge boundary

Ocean rises or crests are basically made up from basaltic lavas for although no gap can exist between plates, one plate can ease itself away from another. In that case hot, molten rock instantly rises from below to fill in the incipient rift and forms a ridge. These ridges trace a line almost exactly through the centre of the major oceans.

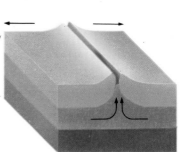

Destruction of ocean plates.

As the ocean plate sinks below the continental plate some of the sediment on its surface is scraped off and piled up on the landward side. This sediment is later incorporated in a folded mountain range which usually appears on the edge of the continent, such as the Andes. Similarly if two continents collide the sediments are squeezed up into new mountains.

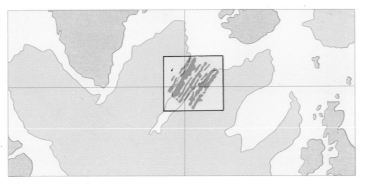

Sea floor spreading

Reversals in the earth's magnetic field have occured throughout history. As new rock emerges at the ocean ridges it cools and is magnetised in the direction of the prevailing magnetic field. By mapping the magnetic patterns either side of the ridge a symmetrical stripey pattern of alternating fields can be observed (see inset area in diagram). As the dates of the last few reversals are known the rate of spreading can be calculated.

The Unstable Earth

The earth's surface is slowly but continually being rearranged. Some changes such as erosion and deposition are extremely slow but they upset the balance which causes other more abrupt changes often originating deep within the earth's interior. The constant movements vary in intensity, often with stresses building up to a climax such as a particularly violent volcanic eruption or earthquake.

The crust *(below and right)*
The outer layer or crust of the earth consists of a comparatively low density, brittle material varying from 5 to 50 kilometres deep beneath the continents. Under this is a layer of rock consisting predominately of silica and aluminium; hence it is called 'sial'. Extending under the ocean floors and below the sial is a basaltic layer known as 'sima', consisting mainly of silica and magnesium.

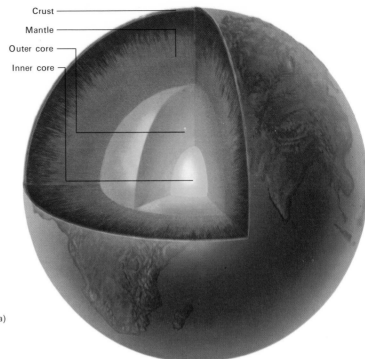

Crust
Mantle
Outer core
Inner core

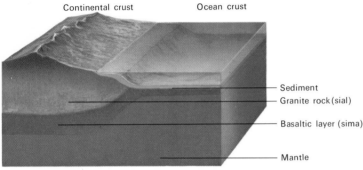

Continental crust
Ocean crust

Sediment
Granite rock (sial)
Basaltic layer (sima)
Mantle

Volcanoes *(right, below and far right)*
Volcanoes occur when hot liquefied rock beneath the crust reaches the surface as lava. An accumulation of ash and cinders around a vent forms a cone. Successive layers of thin lava flows form an acid lava volcano while thick lava flows form a basic lava volcano. A caldera forms when a particularly violent eruption blows off the top of an already existing cone.

The mantle *(above)*
Immediately below the crust, at the mohorovicic discontinuity line, there is a distinct change in density and chemical properties. This is the mantle - made up of iron and magnesium silicates - with temperatures reaching 1 600°C. The rigid upper mantle extends down to a depth of about 1 000 km., below which is the more viscous lower mantle which is about 1 900 km. thick.

The core *(above)*
The outer core, approximately 2 100 km. thick, consists of molten iron and nickel at 2 000°C to 5 000°C possibly separated from the less dense mantle by an oxidised shell. About 5 000 km. below the surface is the liquid transition zone, below which is the solid inner core, a sphere of 2 740 km. diameter where rock is three times as dense as in the crust.

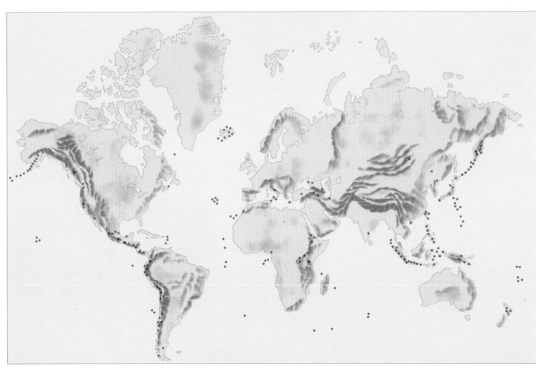

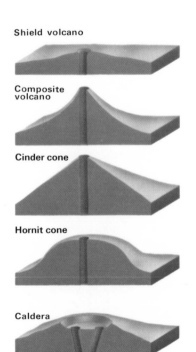

Shield volcano

Composite volcano

Cinder cone

Hornit cone

Caldera

Major earthquakes in the last 100 years	numbers killed
1896 Japan (tsunami)	22 000
1906 San Francisco	destroyed
1906 Chile, Valparaiso	22 000
1908 Italy, Messina	77 000
1920 China, Kansu	180 000
1923 Japan, Tokyo	143 000
1930 Italy, Naples	2 100
1931 Napier	destroyed
1931 Nicaragua, Managua	destroyed
1932 China, Kansu	70 000
1935 India, Quetta	60 000
1939 Chile, Chillan	20 000
1939/40 Turkey, Erzincan	30 000
1948 Japan, Fukui	5 100
1956 N. Afghanistan	2 000
1957 W. Iran	2 500
1960 Morocco, Agadir	12 000
1962 N.W. Iran	10 000
1963 Yugoslavia, Skopje	1 000
1966 U.S.S.R., Tashkent	destroyed
1970 N. Peru	66 800
1972 Nicaragua, Managua	7 000
1974 N. Pakistan	10 000
1975 Turkey, Lice	2 300
1976 China, Tangshan	650 000
1976 Turkey, Van	3 800

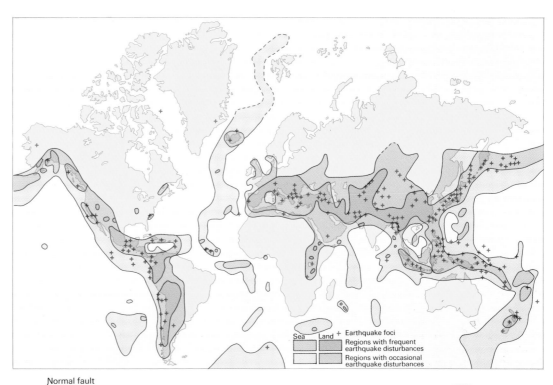

Sea Land + Earthquake foci
Regions with frequent earthquake disturbances
Regions with occasional earthquake disturbances

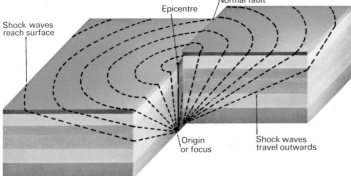

Epicentre
Normal fault
Shock waves reach surface
Origin or focus
Shock waves travel outwards

Earthquakes (right and above)

Earthquakes are a series of rapid vibrations originating from the slipping or faulting of parts of the earth's crust when stresses within build up to breaking point. They usually happen at depths varying from 8-30 km. Severe earthquakes cause extensive damage when they take place in populated areas destroying structures and severing communications. Most loss of life occurs due to secondary causes i.e. falling masonry, fires or tsunami waves.

Alaskan earthquake, 1964

Tsunami waves (left)

A sudden slump in the ocean bed during an earthquake forms a trough in the water surface subsequently followed by a crest and smaller waves. A more marked change of level in the sea bed can form a crest, the start of a Tsunami which travels up to 60 kph with waves up to 60 metres high. Seismographic detectors continuously record earthquake shocks and warn of the Tsunami which may follow it.

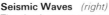
Wave travel times in hours

Seismic Waves (right)

The shock waves sent out from the epicentre of an earthquake are of three main kinds each with distinct properties. Primary (P) waves are compressional waves which can be transmitted through both solids and liquids and therefore pass through the earth's liquid core. Secondary (S) waves are shear waves and can only pass through solids. They cannot pass through the core and are reflected at the core-mantle boundary taking a concave course back to the surface. The core also refracts the P waves causing them to alter course, and the net effect of this reflection and refraction is the production of a shadow zone at a certain distance from the epicentre, free from P and S waves. Due to their different properties P waves travel about 1·7 times faster than S waves. The third main kind of wave is a long (L) wave, a slow wave which travels along the earth's surface, its motion being either horizontal or vertical.

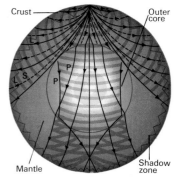

Crust
Outer core
Mantle
Shadow zone

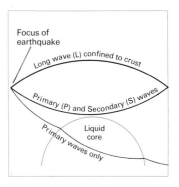

Focus of earthquake
Long wave (L) confined to crust
Primary (P) and Secondary (S) waves
Primary waves only
Liquid core

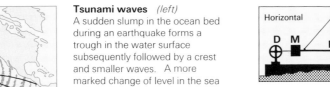

Horizontal
D M P

Vertical
D M S P

Principles of seismographs (left)
M = Mass
D = Drum
P = Pivot
S = Spring

P S L

Seismographs

are delicate instruments capable of detecting and recording vibrations due to earthquakes thousands of miles away. P waves cause the first tremors. S the second, and L the main shock.

The Making of Landscape

The making of landscape

The major forces which shape our land would seem to act very slowly in comparison with man's average life span but in geological terms the erosion of rock is in fact very fast. Land goes through a cycle of transformation. It is broken up by earthquakes and other earth movements, temperature changes, water, wind and ice. Rock debris is then transported by water, wind and glaciers and deposited on lowlands and on the sea floor. Here it builds up and by the pressure of its own weight is converted into new rock strata. These in turn can be uplifted either gently as plains or plateaux or more irregularly to form mountains. In either case the new higher land is eroded and the cycle recommences.

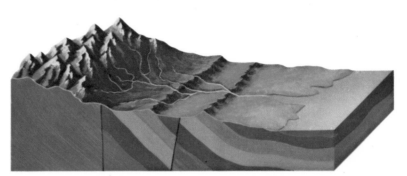

A Peneplain

Uplifted peneplain

Rivers

Rivers shape the land by three basic processes: erosion, transportation and deposition. A youthful river flows fast eroding downwards quickly to form a narrow valley (1) As it matures it deposits some debris and erodes laterally to widen the valley (2). In its last stage it meanders across a wide flat flood plain depositing fine particles of alluvium (3).

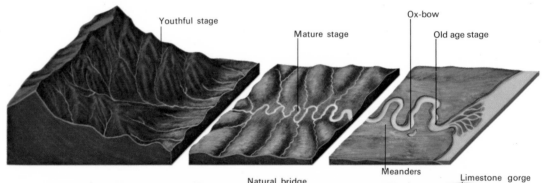

Youthful stage

Mature stage

Ox-bow

Old age stage

Meanders

Underground water

Water enters porous and permeable rocks from the surface moving downward until it reaches a layer of impermeable rock. Joints in underground rock, such as limestone, are eroded to form underground caves and caverns. When the roof of a cave collapses a gorge is formed. Surface entrances to joints are often widened to form vertical openings called swallow holes.

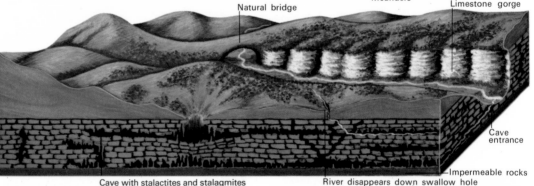

Natural bridge

Limestone gorge

Cave entrance

Impermeable rocks

Cave with stalactites and stalagmites

River disappears down swallow hole

Wind

Wind action is particularly powerful in arid and semi-arid regions where rock waste produced by weathering is used as an abrasive tool by the wind. The rate of erosion varies with the characteristics of the rock which can cause weird shapes and effects (right). Desert sand can also be accumulated by the wind to form barchan dunes (far right) which slowly travel forward, horns first.

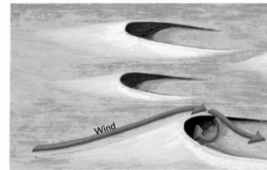

Wind

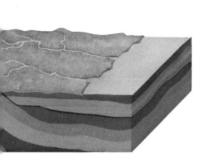

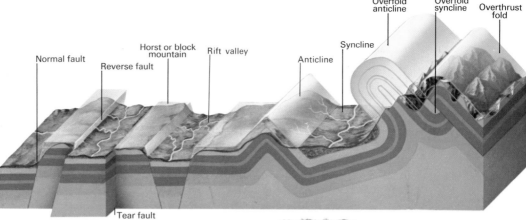

Normal fault

Reverse fault

Horst or block mountain

Rift valley

Tear fault

Anticline

Syncline

Overfold anticline

Overfold syncline

Overthrust fold

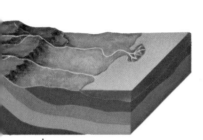

Folding and faulting

A vertical displacement in the earth's crust is called a fault or reverse fault; lateral displacement is a tear fault. An uplifted block is called a horst, the reverse of which is a rift valley. Compressed horizontal layers of sedimentary rock fold to form mountains. Those layers which bend up form an anticline, those bending down form a syncline : continued pressure forms an overfold.

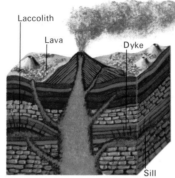

Laccolith

Lava

Dyke

Sill

Volcanic activity

When pressure on rocks below the earth's crust is released the normally semi-solid hot rock becomes liquid magma. The magma forces its way into cracks of the crust and may either reach the surface where it forms volcanoes or it may collect in the crust as sills dykes or lacoliths. When magma reaches the surface it cools to form lava.

Waves

Coasts are continually changing, some retreat under wave erosion while others advance with wave deposition. These actions combined form steep cliffs and wave cut platforms. Eroded debris is in turn deposited as a terrace. As the water becomes shallower the erosive power of the waves decreases and gradually the cliff disappears. Wave action can also create other features (far right).

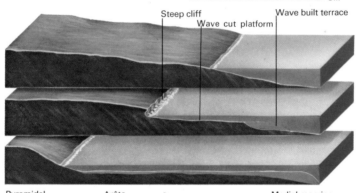

Steep cliff

Wave cut platform

Wave built terrace

Ice

These diagrams (right) show how a glaciated valley may have formed. The glacier deepens, straightens and widens the river valley whose interlocking spurs become truncated or cut off. Intervalley divides are frost shattered to form sharp aretes and pyramidal peaks. Hanging valleys mark the entry of tributary rivers and eroded rocks form medial moraine. Terminal moraine is deposited as the glacier retreats.

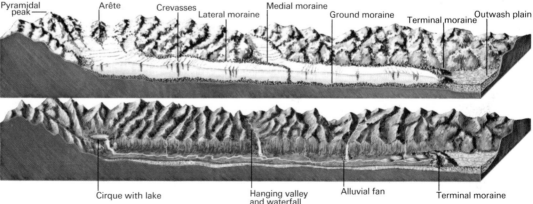

Pyramidal peak

Arête

Crevasses

Lateral moraine

Medial moraine

Ground moraine

Terminal moraine

Outwash plain

Cirque with lake

Hanging valley and waterfall

Alluvial fan

Terminal moraine

Subsidence and uplift

As the land surface is eroded it may eventually become a level plain - a peneplain, broken only by low hills, remnants of previous mountains. In turn this peneplain may be uplifted to form a plateau with steep edges. At the coast the uplifted wave platform becomes a coastal plain and in the rejuvenated rivers downward erosion once more predominates.

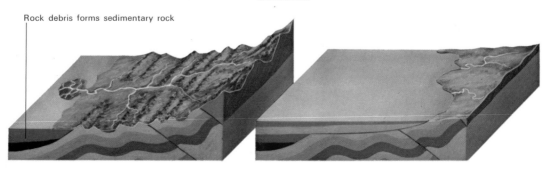

Rock debris forms sedimentary rock

The Earth: Physical Dimensions

Its surface

Highest point on the earth's surface: Mt. Everest, Tibet - Nepal boundary 8 848 m
Lowest point on the earth's surface: The Dead Sea, Jordan below sea level 395 m
Greatest ocean depth,: Challenger Deep, Mariana Trench 11 022 m
Average height of land 840 m
Average depth of seas and oceans 3 808 m

Dimensions

Superficial area	510 000 000 km^2
Land surface	149 000 000 km^2
Land surface as % of total area	29·2 %
Water surface	361 000 000 km^2
Water surface as % of total area	70·8 %
Equatorial circumference	40 077 km
Meridional circumference	40 009 km
Equatorial diameter	12 756·8 km
Polar diameter	12 713·8 km
Equatorial radius	6 378·4 km
Polar radius	6 356·9 km
Volume of the Earth	1 083 230 x 10^6 km^3
Mass of the Earth	5·9 x 10^{21} tonnes

The Figure of Earth

An imaginary sea-level surface is considered and called a geoid. By measuring at different places the angles from plumb lines to a fixed star there have been many determinations of the shape of parts of the geoid which is found to be an oblate spheriod with its axis along the axis of rotation of the earth. Observations from satellites have now given a new method of more accurate determinations of the figure of the earth and its local irregularities.

Land and Sea Hemispheres.

About 85% of the total land area is contained in the hemisphere centred on a point between Paris and Brussels.

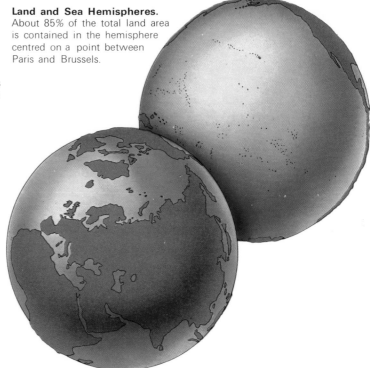

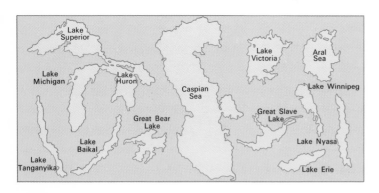

Oceans and Seas
Area in 1000 km²

Pacific Ocean	165 721	North Sea	575
Atlantic Ocean	81 660	Black Sea	448
Indian Ocean	73 442	Red Sea	440
Arctic Ocean	14 351	Baltic Sea	422
Mediterranean Sea	2 966	Persian Gulf	238
Bering Sea	2 274	St. Lawrence, Gulf of	236
Caribbean Sea	1 942	English Channel & Irish Sea	179
Mexico, Gulf of	1 813	California, Gulf of	161
Okhotsk, Sea of	1 528		
East China Sea	1 248		
Hudson Bay	1 230		
Japan, Sea of	1 049		

Lakes and Inland Seas
Areas in 1000 km²

Caspian Sea, Asia	424·2	Lake Ontario, N.America	19·5
Lake Superior, N.America	82·4	Lake Ladoga, Europe	18·4
Lake Victoria, Africa	69·5	Lake Balkhash, Asia	17·3
Aral Sea (Salt), Asia	63·8	Lake Maracaibo, S.America	16·3
Lake Huron, N.America	59·6	Lake Onega, Europe	9·8
Lake Michigan, N.America	58·0	Lake Eyre (Salt), Australia	9·6
Lake Tanganyika, Africa	32·9	Lake Turkana (Salt), Africa	9·1
Lake Baikal, Asia	31·5	Lake Titicaca, S.America	8·3
Great Bear Lake, N.America	31·1	Lake Nicaragua, C.America	8·0
Great Slave Lake, N.America	28·9	Lake Athabasca, N.America	7·9
Lake Nyasa, Africa	28·5	Reindeer Lake, N.America	6·3
Lake Erie, N.America	25·7	Issyk-Kul, Asia	6·2
Lake Winnipeg, N.America	24·3	Lake Torrens (Salt), Australia	6·1
Lake Chad, Africa	20·7	Koko Nor (Salt), Asia	6·0
		Lake Urmia, Asia	6·0
		Vänern, Europe	5·6

Longest rivers

	km.
Nile, Africa	6 690
Amazon, S.America	6 280
Mississipi - Missouri,N.America	6 270
Yangtze, Asia	4 990
Zaïre, Africa	4 670
Amur, Asia	4 410
Hwang Ho (Yellow), Asia	4 350
Lena, Asia	4 260
Mekong, Asia	4 180
Niger, Africa	4 180
Mackenzie, N.America	4 040
Ob, Asia	4 000
Yenisei, Asia	3 800

The Highest Mountains and the Greatest Depths.

Mount Everest defied the world's greatest mountaineers for 32 years and claimed the lives of many men. Not until 1920 was permission granted by the Dalai Lama to attempt the mountain, and the first successful ascent came in 1953. Since then the summit has been reached several times. The world's highest peaks have now been climbed but there are many as yet unexplored peaks in the Himalayas some of which may be over 7 600 m.

The greatest trenches are the Puerto Rico deep (9 200m). The Tonga (10 822 m) and Mindanao (10 497 m) trenches and the Mariana Trench (11 022 m) in the Pacific. The trenches represent less than 2% of the total area of the sea-bed but are of great interest as lines of structural weakness in the Earth's crust and as areas of frequent earthquakes.

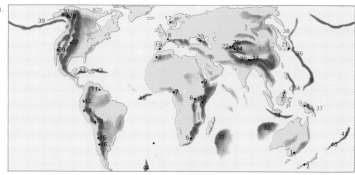

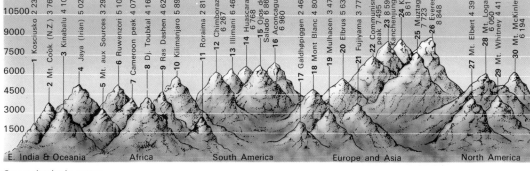

Mountain heights in metres

1 Kosciusko 2 230 · 2 Mt. Cook (N.Z.) 3 764 · 3 Kinabalu 4 101 · 4 Jaya (Irian) 5 029 · 5 Mt. aux Sources 3 299 · 6 Ruwenzori 5 109 · 7 Cameroon peak 4 070 · 8 Dj. Toubkal 4 165 · 9 Ras Dashen 4 620 · 10 Kilimanjaro 5 895 · 11 Roraima 2 810 · 12 Chimborazo 6 267 · 13 Illimani 6 462 · 14 Huascaran 6 768 · 15 Ojos del Salado 6 863 · 16 Aconcagua 6 960 · 17 Galdhøpiggen 2 469 · 18 Mont Blanc 4 807 · 19 Mulhacen 3 478 · 20 Elbrus 5 633 · 21 Fujiyama 3 776 · 22 Communism peak 7 495 · 23 Kanchenjunga 8 598 · 24 K2 8 611 · 25 Muztagh 7 723 · 26 Everest 8 848 · 27 Mt. Elbert 4 399 · 28 Mt. Logan 6 050 · 29 Mt. Whitney 4 418 · 30 Mt. McKinley 6 194

E. India & Oceania · Africa · South America · Europe and Asia · North America

Ocean depths in metres

Sea level

31 Mauritius basin 6 400 · 32 W. Australian basin 6 459 · 33 Java trench 7 450 · 34 Mindanao trench 10 497 · 35 Mariana trench 11 022 · 36 Japan trench 10 554 · 37 Bougainville deep 9 140 · 38 Kuril trench 10 542 · 39 Aleutian trench 7 822 · 40 Kermadec trench 10 047 · 41 Tonga trench 10 822 · 42 Cayman trough 7 680 · 43 Puerto Rico trough 9 200 · 44 S. Sandwich trench 8 428 · 45 Romanche deep 7 758

Indian Ocean · Pacific Ocean · Atlantic Ocean

High mountains

Bathyscaphe

Waterfall

Dam

Notable Waterfalls
heights in metres

Angel, Venezuela	980
Tugela, S. Africa	853
Mongefossen, Norway	774
Yosemite, California	738
Mardalsfossen, Norway	655
Cuquenan, Venezuela	610
Sutherland, N.Z.	579
Reichenbach, Switzerland	548
Wollomombi, Australia	518
Ribbon, California	491
Gavarnie, France	422
Tyssefallene, Norway	414
Krimml, Austria	370
King George VI, Guyana	366
Silver Strand, California	356
Geissbach, Switzerland	350
Staubbach, Switzerland	299
Trümmelbach, Switzerland	290
Chirombo, Zambia	268
Livingstone, Zaïre	259
King Edward VIII, Guyana	256
Gersoppa, India	253
Vettifossen, Norway	250
Kalambo, Zambia	240
Kaieteur, Guyana	226
Maletsunyane, Lesotho	192
Terui, Italy	180
Murchison, Uganda	122
Victoria, Rhodesia-Zambia	107
Cauvery, India	97
Stanley, Zaïre	61
Niagara, N.America	51
Schaffhausen, Switzerland	30

Notable Dams
heights in metres
Africa

Cabora Bassa, Zambezi R. (under construction)	168
Akosombo Main Dam, Volta R.	141
Kariba, Zambezi R.	128
Aswan High Dam, Nile R.	110

Asia

Nurek, Vakhsh R., U.S.S.R.	317
Bhakra, Sutlej R., India	226
Kurobegawa, Kurobe R., Jap.	186
Charvak, Chirchik R., U.S.S.R.	168
Okutadami, Tadami R., Jap.	157
Bhumiphol, Ping R., Thai.	154

Australasia

Warragamba, N.S.W., Australia	137
Eucumbene, N.S.W., Australia	116

Europe

Grande Dixence, Switz.	284
Vajont, Vajont, R., Italy	261
Mauvoisin, Drance R., Switz.	237
Contra, Verzasca R., Switz.	230
Luzzone, Brenno R., Switz.	208
Tignes, Isère R., France	180
Amir Kabir, Karadj R., U.S.S.R.	180
Vidraru, Arges R., Rum.	165
Kremasta, Acheloos R., Greece	165

North America

Oroville, Feather R.,	235
Hoover, Colorado R.,	221
Glen Canyon, Colorado R.,	216
Daniel Johnson, Can.	214
New Bullards Bar, N. Yuba R.	194
Mossyrock, Cowlitz R.,	184
Shasta, Sacramento R.,	183
W.A.C. Bennett, Canada.	183
Don Pedro, Tuolumne R.,	178
Hungry Horse, Flathead R.,	172
Grand Coulee, Columbia R.,	168

Central and South America

Guri, Caroni R., Venezuela.	106

Distances

Kms

Upper-right triangle = miles; lower-left triangle = kilometres.

Kms	Berlin	Bombay	Buenos Aires	Cairo	Calcutta	Caracas	Chicago	Copenhagen	Darwin	Hong Kong	Honolulu	Johannesburg	Lagos	Lisbon	London
Berlin		3907	7400	1795	4370	5241	4402	222	8044	5440	7310	5511	3230	1436	5…
Bombay	6288		9275	2706	1034	9024	8048	3990	4510	2683	8024	4334	4730	4982	44…
Buenos Aires	11909	14925		7341	10268	3167	5599	7498	9130	11481	7558	5025	4919	5964	69…
Cairo	2890	4355	11814		3541	6340	6127	1992	7216	5064	8838	3894	2432	2358	21…
Calcutta	7033	1664	16524	5699		9609	7978	4395	3758	1653	7048	5256	5727	5639	49…
Caracas	8435	14522	5096	10203	15464		2502	5215	11221	10166	6009	6847	4810	4044	46…
Chicago	7084	12953	9011	3206	12839	4027		4250	9361	7783	4247	8689	5973	3992	39…
Copenhagen	357	6422	12067	9860	7072	8392	6840		8017	5388	7088	5732	3436	1540	5…
Darwin	12946	7257	14693	11612	6047	18059	15065	12903		2654	5369	6611	8837	9391	86…
Hong Kong	8754	4317	18478	8150	2659	16360	12526	8671	4271		5543	6669	7360	6853	59…
Honolulu	11764	12914	12164	14223	11343	9670	6836	11407	8640	8921		11934	10133	7821	72…
Johannesburg	8870	6974	8088	6267	8459	11019	13984	9225	10639	10732	19206		2799	5089	56…
Lagos	5198	7612	7916	3915	9216	7741	9612	5530	14222	11845	16308	4505		2360	31…
Lisbon	2311	8018	9600	3794	9075	6501	6424	2478	15114	11028	12587	8191	3799		9…
London	928	7190	11131	3508	7961	7507	6356	952	13848	9623	11632	9071	5017	1588	
Los Angeles	9311	14000	9852	12200	13120	5812	2804	9003	12695	11639	4117	16676	12414	9122	87…
Mexico City	9732	15656	7389	12372	15280	3586	2726	9514	14631	14122	6085	14585	11071	8676	89…
Moscow	1610	5031	13477	2902	5534	9938	8000	1561	11350	7144	11323	9161	6254	3906	24…
Nairobi	6370	4532	10402	3536	6179	11544	12883	6706	10415	8776	17282	2927	3807	6461	68…
New York	6385	12541	8526	9020	12747	3430	1145	6188	16047	12950	7980	12841	8477	5422	55…
Paris	876	7010	11051	3210	7858	7625	6650	1026	13812	9630	11968	8732	4714	1454	3…
Peking	7822	4757	19268	7544	3269	14399	10603	7202	6011	1963	8160	11710	11457	9668	81…
Reykjavik	2385	8335	11437	5266	8687	6915	4757	2103	13892	9681	9787	10938	6718	2948	18…
Rio de Janeiro	10025	13409	1953	9896	15073	4546	8547	10211	16011	17704	13342	7113	6035	7734	92…
Rome	1180	6175	11151	2133	7219	8363	7739	1531	13265	9284	12916	7743	4039	1861	14…
Singapore	9944	3914	15879	8267	2897	18359	15078	9969	3349	2599	10816	8660	11145	11886	108…
Sydney	16096	10160	11800	14418	9138	15343	14875	16042	3150	7374	8168	11040	15519	18178	169…
Tokyo	8924	6742	18362	9571	5141	14164	10137	8696	5431	2874	6202	13547	13480	11149	95…
Toronto	6497	12488	9093	9233	12561	3873	700	6265	15498	12569	7465	13374	8948	5737	57…
Wellington	18140	12370	9981	16524	11354	13122	13451	17961	5325	9427	7513	11761	16050	19575	188…

Los Angeles	Mexico City	Moscow	Nairobi	New York	Paris	Peking	Reykjavik	Rio de Janeiro	Rome	Singapore	Sydney	Tokyo	Toronto	Wellington	
785	6047	1000	3958	3967	545	4860	1482	6230	734	6179	10002	5545	4037	11272	**Berlin**
700	9728	3126	2816	7793	4356	2956	5179	8332	3837	2432	6313	4189	7760	7686	**Bombay**
122	4591	8374	6463	5298	6867	11972	7106	1214	6929	9867	7332	11410	5650	6202	**Buenos Aires**
580	7687	1803	2197	5605	1994	4688	3272	6149	1325	5137	8959	5947	5737	10268	**Cairo**
52	9494	3438	3839	7921	4883	2031	5398	9366	4486	1800	5678	3195	7805	7055	**Calcutta**
612	2228	6175	7173	2131	4738	8947	4297	2825	5196	11407	9534	8801	2406	8154	**Caracas**
742	1694	4971	8005	711	4132	6588	2956	5311	4809	9369	9243	6299	435	8358	**Chicago**
594	5912	970	4167	3845	638	4475	1306	6345	951	6195	9968	5403	3892	11160	**Copenhagen**
888	9091	7053	6472	9971	8582	3735	8632	9948	8243	2081	1957	3375	9630	3309	**Darwin**
232	8775	4439	5453	8047	5984	1220	6015	11001	5769	1615	4582	1786	7810	5857	**Hong Kong**
558	3781	7036	10739	4958	7437	5070	6081	8290	8026	6721	5075	3854	4638	4669	**Honolulu**
362	9063	5692	1818	7979	5426	7276	6797	4420	4811	5381	6860	8418	8310	7308	**Johannesburg**
713	6879	3886	2366	5268	2929	7119	4175	3750	2510	6925	9643	8376	5560	9973	**Lagos**
668	5391	2427	4015	3369	903	6007	1832	4805	1157	7385	11295	6928	3565	12163	**Lisbon**
442	5552	1552	4237	3463	212	5057	1172	5778	889	6743	10558	5942	3545	11691	**London**
	1549	6070	9659	2446	5645	6251	4310	6310	6331	8776	7502	5475	2170	6719	**Los Angeles**
		6664	9207	2090	5717	7742	4635	4780	6365	10321	8058	7024	2018	6897	**Mexico City**
			3942	4666	1545	3600	2053	7184	1477	5237	9008	4651	4637	10283	**Moscow**
				7358	4029	5727	5395	5548	3350	4635	7552	6996	7570	8490	**Nairobi**
					3626	6828	2613	4832	4280	9531	9935	6741	356	8951	**New York**
493						5106	1384	5708	687	6671	10539	6038	3738	11798	**Paris**
769	10724						4897	10773	5049	2783	5561	1304	6557	6700	**Peking**
544	14818	6344						6135	2048	7155	10325	5469	2600	10725	**Reykjavik**
936	3364	7510	11842						5725	9763	8389	11551	5180	7367	**Rio de Janeiro**
085	9200	2486	6485	5836						6229	10143	6127	4399	11523	**Rome**
060	12460	5794	9216	10988	8217						3915	3306	9350	5298	**Singapore**
936	7460	3304	8683	4206	2228	7882						4861	9800	1383	**Sydney**
155	7693	11562	8928	7777	9187	17338	9874						6410	5762	**Tokyo**
188	10243	2376	5391	6888	1105	8126	3297	9214						8820	**Toronto**
123	16610	8428	7460	15339	10737	4478	11514	15712	10025						**Wellington**
073	12969	14497	12153	15989	16962	8949	16617	13501	16324	6300					Miles
811	11304	7485	11260	10849	9718	2099	8802	18589	9861	5321	7823				
492	3247	7462	12183	574	6015	10552	4184	8336	7080	15047	15772	10316			
814	11100	16549	13664	14405	18987	10782	17260	11855	18545	8526	2226	9273	14194		

Water Resources and Vegetation

Water resources and vegetation

Fresh water is essential for life on earth and in some parts of the world it is a most precious commodity. On the other hand it is very easy for industrialised temperate states to take its existence for granted, and man's increasing demand may only be met finally by the desalination of earth's 1250 million cubic kilometres of salt water. 70% of the earth's fresh water exists as ice.

The hydrological cycle

Water is continually being absorbed into the atmosphere as vapour from oceans, lakes, rivers and vegetation transpiration. On cooling the vapour either condenses or freezes and falls as rain, hail or snow. Most precipitation falls over the sea but one quarter falls over the land of which half evaporates again soon after falling while the rest flows back into the oceans.

Distribution of water

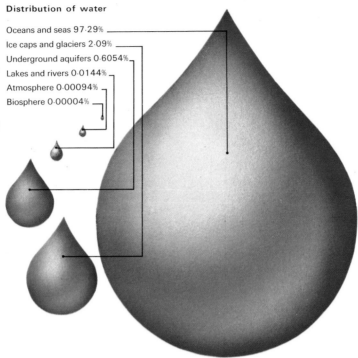

Oceans and seas 97·29%
Ice caps and glaciers 2·09%
Underground aquifers 0·6054%
Lakes and rivers 0·0144%
Atmosphere 0·00094%
Biosphere 0·00004%

Tundra

Mediterranean scrub

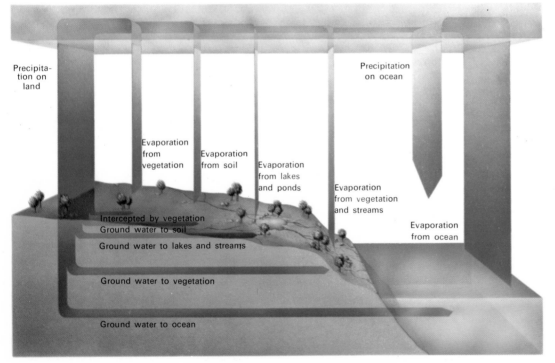

Precipitation on land

Precipitation on ocean

Evaporation from vegetation

Evaporation from soil

Evaporation from lakes and ponds

Evaporation from vegetation and streams

Evaporation from ocean

Intercepted by vegetation
Ground water to soil

Ground water to lakes and streams

Ground water to vegetation

Ground water to ocean

Domestic consumption of water

An area's level of industrialisation, climate and standard of living are all major influences in the consumption of water. On average Europe consumes 636 litres per head each day of which 180 litres is used domestically. In the U.S.A. domestic consumption is slightly higher at 270 litres per day. The graph (right) represents domestic consumption in the U.K. in 1970.

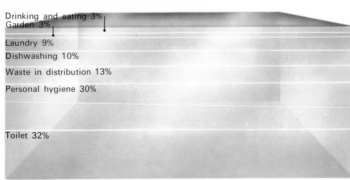

Drinking and eating 3%
Garden 3%
Laundry 9%
Dishwashing 10%
Waste in distribution 13%
Personal hygiene 30%
Toilet 32%

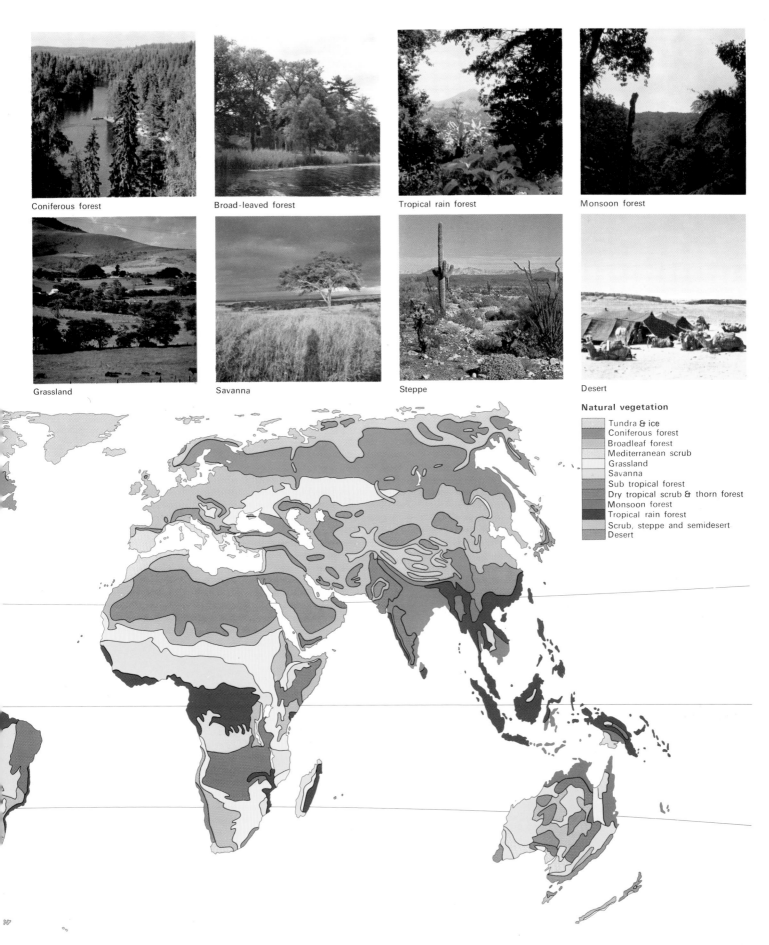

Coniferous forest

Broad-leaved forest

Tropical rain forest

Monsoon forest

Grassland

Savanna

Steppe

Desert

Natural vegetation

Tundra & ice
Coniferous forest
Broadleaf forest
Mediterranean scrub
Grassland
Savanna
Sub tropical forest
Dry tropical scrub & thorn forest
Monsoon forest
Tropical rain forest
Scrub, steppe and semidesert
Desert

Population

Population distribution
(right and lower right)

People have always been unevenly distributed in the world. Europe has for centuries contained nearly 20% of the world's population but after the 16-19th century explorations and consequent migrations this proportion has rapidly reduced. In 1750 the Americas had 2% of the world's total: in 2000 AD they are expected to contain 16%.

The most densely populated regions are in India, China and Europe where the average density is between 100 and 200 per square km. although there are pockets of extremely high density elsewhere. In contrast Australia has only 1·5 people per square km. The countries in the lower map have been redrawn to make their areas proportional to their populations.

U.S.A. (1972)
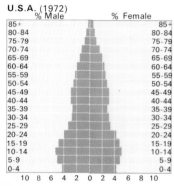

France (1972)
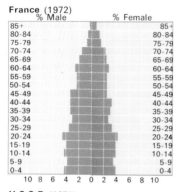

Brazil (1971)

U.S.S.R. (1970)
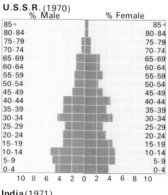

Ghana (1970)
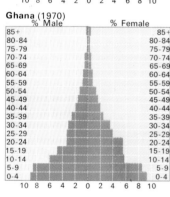

India (1971)
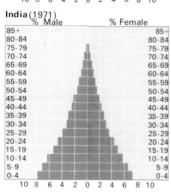

Age distribution
France shows many demographic features characteristic of European countries. Birth and death rates have declined with a moderate population growth - there are nearly as many old as young. In contrast, India and several other countries have few old and many young because of the high death rates and even higher birth rates. It is this excess that is responsible for the world's population explosion.

World population increase
Until comparatively recently there was little increase in the population of the world. About 6000 BC it is thought that there were about 200 million people and in the following 7000 years an increase of just over 100 million. In the 1800's there were about 1000 million; at present there are over 3500 million and by the year 2000 if present trends continue there would be at least 7000 million.

1650   1700   1750   1800

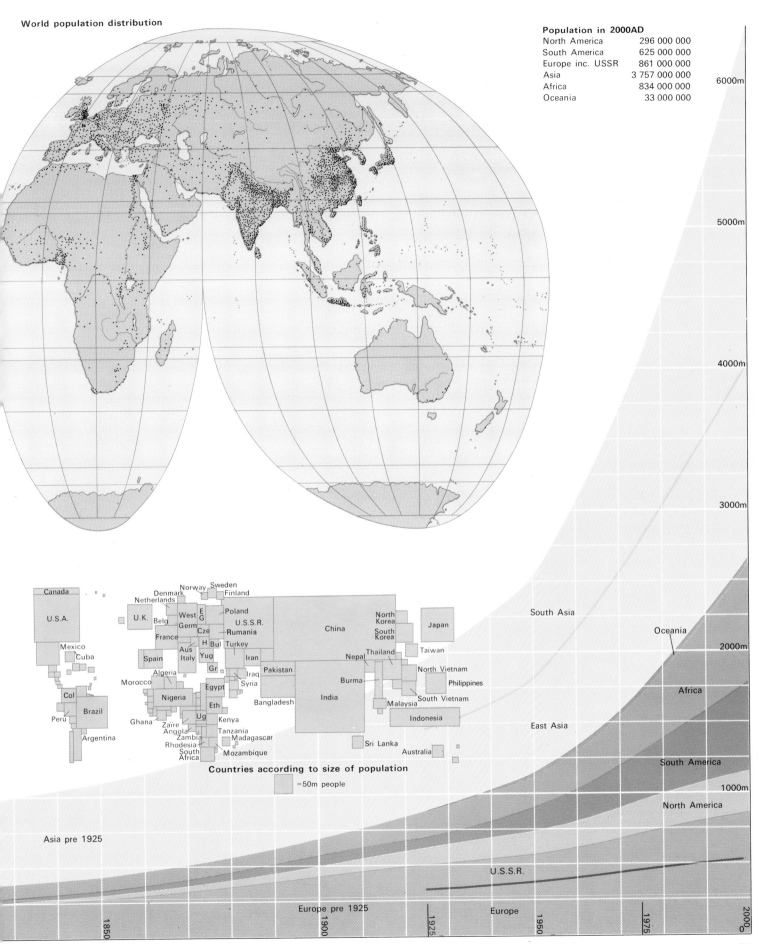

World population distribution

Population in 2000AD
North America	296 000 000
South America	625 000 000
Europe inc. USSR	861 000 000
Asia	3 757 000 000
Africa	834 000 000
Oceania	33 000 000

Countries according to size of population
= 50m people

6000m
5000m
4000m
3000m
2000m
1000m

South Asia
Oceania
Africa
East Asia
South America
North America

Asia pre 1925
U.S.S.R.
Europe pre 1925
Europe

1850
1900
1925
1950
1975
2000

Language

Languages may be blamed partly for the division and lack of understanding between nations. While a common language binds countries together it in turn isolates them from other countries and groups. Thus beliefs, ideas and inventions remain exclusive to these groups and different cultures develop.

There are thousands of different languages and dialects spoken today. This can cause strife even within the one country, such as India, where different dialects are enough to break down the country into distinct groups.

As a result of colonization and the spread of internationally accepted languages, many countries have superimposed a completely unrelated language in order to combine isolated national groups and to facilitate international understanding, for example Spanish in South America, English in India.

Assyrian (carved)

Ancient Hebrew (painted)

Egyptian hieroglyphic (painted)

Some modern non-latin type faces

Greek
ΑΒΓΔΕΖΗΘΙΚΛΜΝΞΟΠΡΣΤΥΦΧΨΩς

Cyrillic
АБВГДЕЖЗИЙІКЛМНОПРСТУФХЦЧШ

Arabic
فى عام ١٨٩٧ وصل إلى إنجلترا أ نموذج

Bengali
১৮৯৭ খ্রীস্টাব্দে আধুনিক মডেলের একটি

Telugu
నిన్న సాయింటకి వచ్చిన యాతిథ యేమియు

Japanese
国 土 の 位 置 と 地 形

Chinese
父 獨 子 出 有 之 限 地 位 司，
司 在 提 印 芬 刷 奧 業 司 上 有 能

Related languages

Certain languages showing marked similarities are thought to have developed from common parent languages for example Latin. After the retreat of the Roman Empire wherever Latin had been firmly established it remained as the new nation's language. With no unifying centre divergent development took place and Latin evolved into new languages.

Calligraphy

Writing was originally by a series of pictures, and these gradually developed in styles which were influenced by the tools generally used. Carved alphabets, such as that used by the Sumerians, tended to be angular, while those painted or written tended to be curved, as in Egyptian hieroglyphics development of which can be followed through the West Semitic, Greek and Latin alphabets to our own.

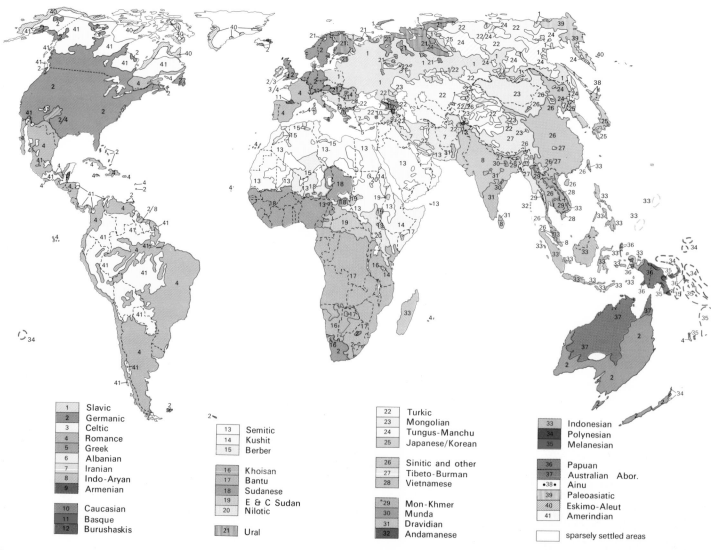

1	Slavic
2	Germanic
3	Celtic
4	Romance
5	Greek
6	Albanian
7	Iranian
8	Indo-Aryan
9	Armenian
10	Caucasian
11	Basque
12	Burushaskis

13	Semitic
14	Kushit
15	Berber
16	Khoisan
17	Bantu
18	Sudanese
19	E & C Sudan
20	Nilotic
21	Ural

22	Turkic
23	Mongolian
24	Tungus-Manchu
25	Japanese/Korean
26	Sinitic and other
27	Tibeto-Burman
28	Vietnamese
29	Mon-Khmer
30	Munda
31	Dravidian
32	Andamanese

33	Indonesian
34	Polynesian
35	Melanesian
36	Papuan
37	Australian Abor.
•38•	Ainu
39	Paleoasiatic
40	Eskimo-Aleut
41	Amerindian
	sparsely settled areas

Religion

Throughout history man has had beliefs in supernatural powers based on the forces of nature which have developed into worship of a god and some cases gods.

Hinduism honours many gods and goddesses which are all manifestations of the one divine spirit, Brahma, and incorporates beliefs such as reincarnation, worship of cattle and the caste system.

Buddhism, an offshoot of Hinduism, was founded in north east India by Gautama Buddha (563-483 BC) who taught that spiritual and moral discipline were essential to achieve supreme peace.

Confucianism is a mixture of Buddhism and Confucius' teachings which were elaborated to provide a moral basis for the political structure of Imperial China and to cover the already existing forms of ancestor worship.

Judaism dates back to c. 13th century B.C. The Jews were expelled from the Holy Land in AD70 and only reinstated in Palestine in 1948.

Islam, founded in Mecca by Muhammad (570-632 AD) spread across Asia and Africa and in its retreat left isolated pockets of adherent communities.

Christianity was founded by Jesus of Nazareth in the 1st century AD The Papal authority, established in the 4th century, was rejected by Eastern churches in the 11th century. Later several other divisions developed eg. Roman Catholicism, Protestantism.

Christian monastery

Jewish holy place

Hindu temple

Mohammedan mosque

Buddhist temple

- ▲ Roman Catholicism
- Orthodox and other Eastern Churches
- • Protestantism
- Sunni Islam
- Shiah Islam
- Buddhism
- Hinduism
- Confucianism
- Judaism
- Shintoism
- Primitive religions
- Uninhabited

The Growth of Cities

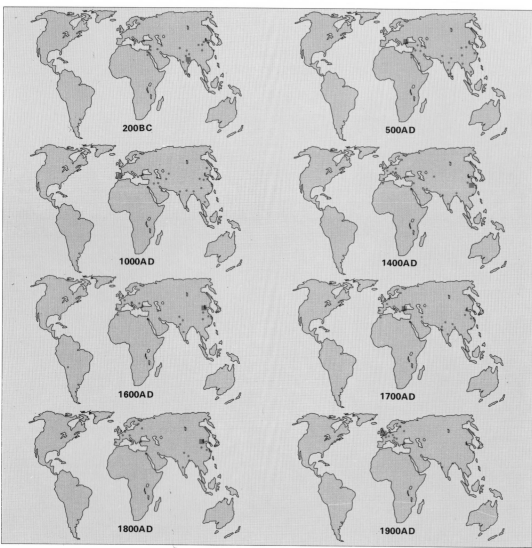

200BC

500AD

1000AD

1400AD

1600AD

1700AD

1800AD

1900AD

Cities through history
The evolution of the semi-perm anent Neolithic settlements into a city took from 5000 until 3500 BC. Efficient communications and exchange systems were developed as population densities increased as high as 30 000 to 50 000 per square kilometre in 2000BC in Egypt and Babylonia, compared with New York City today at 10 000.

- ▪ The largest city in the world
- · The twenty five largest cities in the world

Sao Paulo

Increase in urbanisation
The increase in urbanisation is a result primarily of better sanitation and health resulting in the growth of population and secondarily to the movement of man off the land into industry and service occupations in the cities. Generally the most highly developed industrial nations are the most intensely urbanised although exceptions such as Norway and Switzerland show that rural industrialisation can exist.

Increase in urbanisation
1 Norway
2 Japan
3 Switzerland
4 Sweden
5 Canada
6 England and Wales
7 U.S.A.

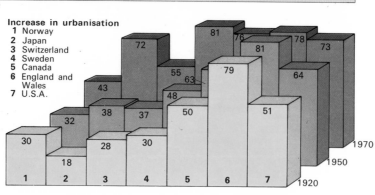

Metropolitan areas
A metropolitan area can be defined as a central city linked with surrounding communities by continuous built-up areas controlled by one municipal government. With improved communications the neighbouring communities generally continue to provide the city's work-force. The graph (right) compares the total populations of the world's ten largest cities.

City populations

1	Shanghai (1973)	12 000 000
2	Tokyo (1973)	11 612 000
3	New York (1970)	11 571 000
4	Mexico City (1974)	10 767 000
5	Paris (1975)	9 108 000
6	Peking (1973)	7 570 000
7	Moscow (1975)	7 528 000
8	London (1974)	7 168 000
9	Los Angeles (1970)	7 032 000
10	Calcutta (1971)	7 031 000

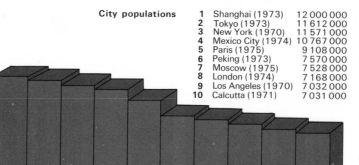

Major cities
Normally these are not only major centres of population and wealth but also of political power and trade. They are the sites of international airports and characteristically are great ports from which imported goods are distributed using the roads and railways which focus on the city. Their staple trades and industries are varied and flexible and depend on design and fashion rather than raw material production.

w York

Sydney

Moscow

Tokyo

Hong Kong

Bombay

London

Cairo

Rio de Janeiro

Rome

Cities over 5 000 000 inhabitants

2 000 000-5 000 000 inhabitants

1 000 000-2 000 000 inhabitants

250 000-1 000 000 inhabitants

Food Resources: Vegetable

Cocoa, tea , coffee

These tropical or sub-tropical crops are grown mainly for export to the economically advanced countries. Tea and coffee are the world's principal beverages. Cocoa is used more in the manufacture of chocolate.

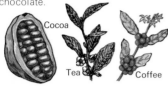

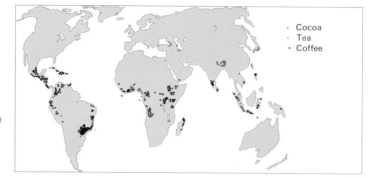

- Cocoa
- Tea
- Coffee

Sugar beet, sugar cane

Cane Sugar - a tropical crop - accounts for the bulk of the sugar entering into international trade. Beet Sugar, on the other hand, demands a temperate climate and is produced primarily for domestic consumption.

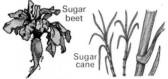

- Sugar beet
- Sugar cane

World production 1973 million tons

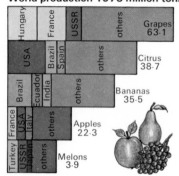

Hungary, France, USSR, others — Grapes 63·1
USA, Brazil, Spain, others — Citrus 38·7
Brazil, Ecuador, India, others — Bananas 35·5
France, USA, Italy, others — Apples 22·3
Turkey, USSR, Japan, others — Melons 3·9

Vegetable oilseeds and oils

Despite the increasing use of synthetic chemical products and animal and marine fats, vegetable oils extracted from these crops grow in quantity, value and importance. Food is the major use- in margarine and cooking fats.

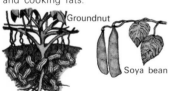

Groundnuts are also a valuable subsistence crop and the meal is used as animal feed. Soya-bean meal is a growing source of protein for humans and animals. The Mediterranean lands are the prime source of olive oil.

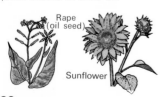

Fruit, wine

With the improvements in canning, drying and freezing, and in transport and marketing, the international trade and consumption of deciduous and soft fruits, citrus fruits and tropical fruits has greatly increased. Recent developments in the use of the peel will give added value to some of the fruit crops.

Over 80% of grapes are grown for wine and over a half in countries bordering the Mediterranean.

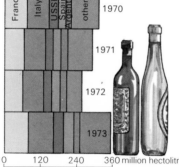

France, Italy, USSR, Spain, Argentina, others
1970
1971
1972
1973
0   120   240   360 million hectolitres

- Groundnuts
- Soya beans

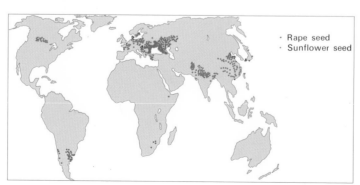

- Rape seed
- Sunflower seed

Cereals

Cereals include those members of the grain family with starchy edible seeds - wheat, maize, barley, oats, rye, rice, millets and sorghums.

Cereals and potatoes (not a cereal but starch-producing) are the principal source of food for our modern civilisations because of their high yield in bulk and food value per unit of land and labour required. They are also easy to store and transport, and provide food also for animals producing meat, fat, milk and eggs. Wheat is the principal bread grain of the temperate regions in which potatoes are the next most important food source. Rice is the principal cereal in the hotter. humid regions. especially in Asia. Oats, barley and maize are grown mainly for animal feed; millets and sorghums as main subsistence crops in Africa and India.

Maize (or Corn)

 Needs plenty of sunshine, summer rain or irrigation and frost free for 6 months. Important as animal feed and for human food in Africa, Latin America and as a vegetable and breakfast cereal.

U.S.A. China Brazil

World production 320·6 million tonnes

Barley

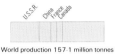 Has the widest range of cultivation requiring only 8 weeks between seed time and harvest. Used mainly as animal-feed and by the malting industry.

U.S.S.R. China France Canada

World production 157·1 million tonnes

Oats

Widely grown in temperate regions with the limit fixed by early autumn frosts. Mainly fed to cattle. The best quality oats are used for oatmeal, porridge and breakfast foods.

U.S.S.R. U.S.A. Canada W.Germany Poland

World production 50·5 million tonnes

Rice

 Needs plains or terraces which can be flooded and abundant water in the growing season. The staple food of half the human race. In the husk, it is known as paddy.

China India Indonesia

World production 342·9 million tonnes

Wheat

 The most important grain crop in the temperate regions though it is also grown in a variety of climates e.g. in Monsoon lands as a winter crop.

U.S.S.R. U.S.A. China India

World production 362·6 million tonnes

Rye

 The hardiest of cereals and more resistant to cold, pests and disease than wheat. An important foodstuff in Central and E. Europe and the U.S.S.R.

U.S.S.R. Poland W.Germany

World production 26·0 million tonnes

Millets

 The name given to a number of related members of the grass family, of which sorghum is one of the most important. They provide nutritious grain.

India China U.S.A.

World production 52·3 million tonnes

Potato

An important food crop though less nutritious weight for weight than grain crops. World production is over 300 million tonnes.

U.S.S.R. Poland China

World production 301·6 million tonnes

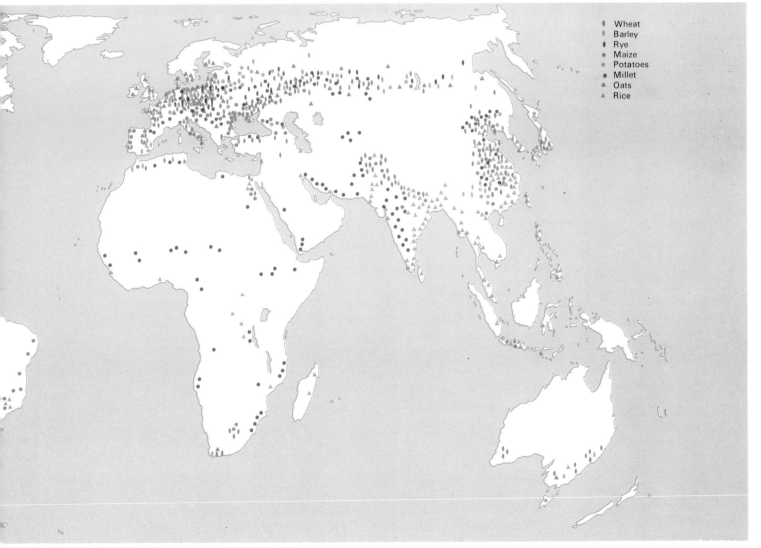

Wheat
Barley
Rye
Maize
Potatoes
Millet
Oats
Rice

Food Resources: Animal

Food resources: Animal
Meat, milk and allied foods are prime protein-providers and are also sources of essential vitamins. Meat is mainly a product of continental and savannah grasslands and the cool west coasts, particularly in Europe. Milk and cheese, eggs and fish - though found in some quantity throughout the world - are primarily a product of the temperate zones.

Beef cattle Australia, New Zealand and Argentina provide the major part of international beef exports. Western U.S.A. and Europe have considerable production of beef for their local high demand.

World production 978·8 million head

Dairy Cattle The need of herds for a rich diet and for nearby markets result in dairying being characteristic of densely-populated areas of the temperate zones - U.S.A., N.W. Europe, N.Zealand and S.E. Australia.

World production 200·0 million head

Cheese The principal producers are the U.S.A., India, W. Europe, U.S.S.R., and New Zealand and principal exporters Netherlands, New Zealand, Denmark and France.

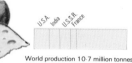
World production 10·7 million tonnes

Sheep Raised mostly for wool and meat, the skins and cheese from their milk are important products in some countries. The merino yields a fine wool and crossbreds are best for meat.

World production 1 046·2 million head

Pigs Can be reared in most climates from monsoon to cool temperate. They are abundant in China, the corn belt of the U.S.A. N.W. and C. Europe, Brazil and U.S.S.R.

World production 674·3 million head

Fish Commercial fishing requires large shoals of fish of one species within reach of markets. Freshwater fishing is also important. A rich source of protein, fish will become an increasingly valuable food source.

World catch 65·7 million tonnes

Butter The biggest producers are U.S.S.R., W. Europe, U.S.A., New Zealand and Australia.

World production 6·3 million tonnes

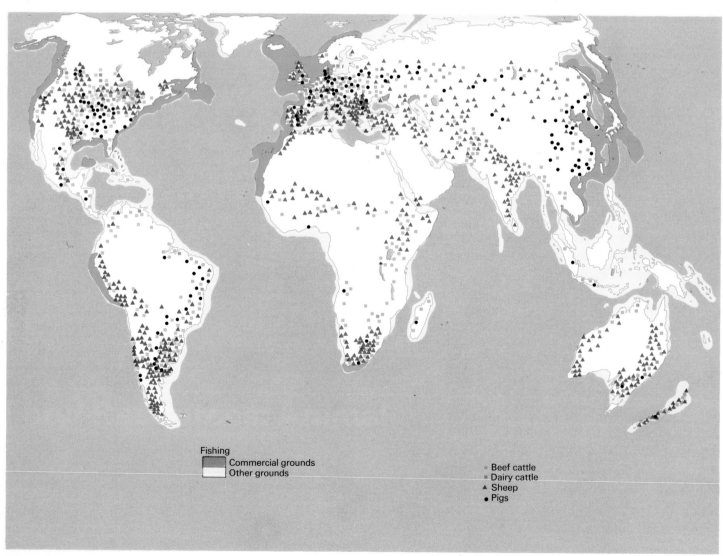

Fishing
Commercial grounds
Other grounds

- Beef cattle
- Dairy cattle
- ▲ Sheep
- ● Pigs

34

Foodstuffs fall, nutritionally, into three groups - providers of energy, protein and vitamins. Cereals and oil-seeds provide energy and second-class 'protein'; milk, meat and allied foods provide protein and vitamins, fruit and vegetables provide vitamins, especially Vitamin C, and some energy. To avoid malnutrition, a minimum level of these three groups of foodstuffs is required: the maps and diagrams show how unfortunately widespread are low standards of nutrition and even malnutrition.

Comparison of daily diets

Supplies Require-ments — Far East, Near East, Africa & Latin America

Supplies Require-ments — Europe, Oceania & North America

Vitamin deficiencies

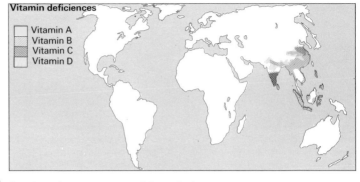

- Vitamin A
- Vitamin B
- Vitamin C
- Vitamin D

Proportions of calories

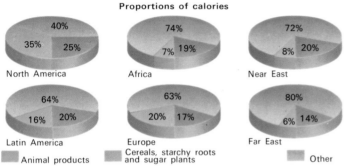

North America 40% 35% 25%

Africa 74% 7% 19%

Near East 72% 8% 20%

Latin America 64% 16% 20%

Europe 63% 20% 17%

Far East 80% 6% 14%

- Animal products
- Cereals, starchy roots and sugar plants
- Other

People and tractors engaged in agriculture

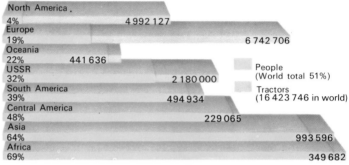

North America 4% — 4 992 127
Europe 19% — 6 742 706
Oceania 22% — 441 636
USSR 32% — 2 180 000
South America 39% — 494 934
Central America 48% — 229 065
Asia 64% — 993 596
Africa 69% — 349 682

People (World total 51%)

Tractors (16 423 746 in world)

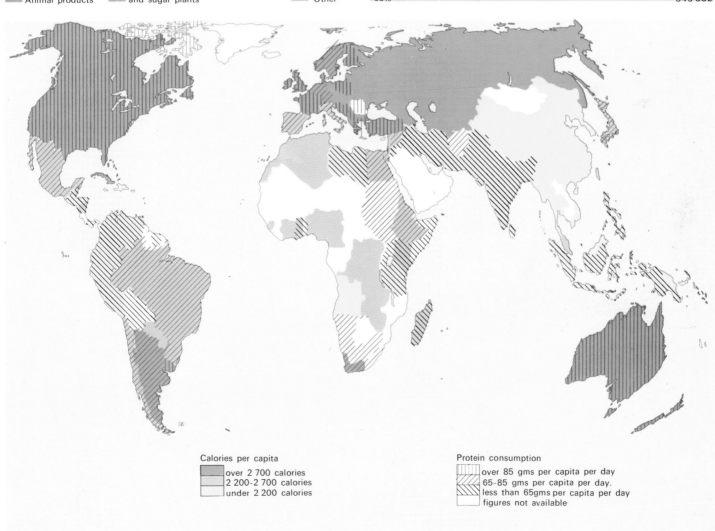

Calories per capita
- over 2 700 calories
- 2 200-2 700 calories
- under 2 200 calories

Protein consumption
- over 85 gms per capita per day
- 65-85 gms per capita per day
- less than 65gms per capita per day
- figures not available

Mineral Resources I

Primitive man used iron for tools and vessels and its use extended gradually until iron, and later steel, became the backbone of the Modern World with the Industrial Revolution in the late 18th Century. At first, local ores were used, whereas today richer iron ores in huge deposits have been discovered and are mined on a large scale, often far away from the areas where they are used; for example, in Western Australia, Northern Sweden, Venezuela and Liberia. Iron smelting plants are today increasingly located at coastal sites, where the large ore carriers can easily discharge their cargo.

Steel is refined iron with the addition of other minerals, ferro-alloys, giving to the steel their own special properties; for example, resistance to corrosion (chromium, nickel, cobalt), hardness (tungsten, vanadium), elasticity (molybdenum), magnetic properties (cobalt), high tensile strength (manganese) and high ductility (molybdenum).

Production of Ferro-alloy metals

Molybdenum World production 83 040 tonnes
U.S.A. | Canada U.S.S.R. Chile

Chromium World production 3.3 million tonnes
U.S.S.R. | S. Africa | Albania Rhodesia | Turkey — Philippines

Nickel World production 736 500 tonnes
Canada | New Caledonia | U.S.S.R. — Australia

Cobalt World production 25 600 tonnes
Zaire | Zambia U.S.S.R. Canada Cuba

Tungsten World production 48 230 tonnes
China | U.S.S.R. U.S.A. | Bolivia Thailand | Canada — S. Korea N. Korea

Manganese World production 9.2 million tonnes
U.S.S.R. | S. Africa Brazil Gabon India — Australia

Vanadium World production 19 250 tonnes
S. Africa | U.S.A. | U.S.S.R. Chile Finland

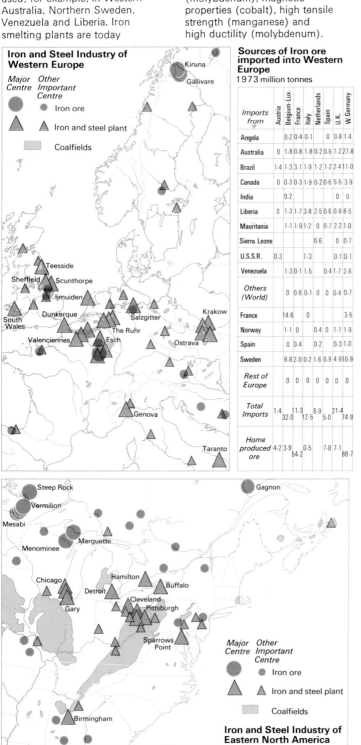

Iron and Steel Industry of Western Europe

Major Centre	Other Important Centre	
● (large)	● (small)	Iron ore
▲ (large)	▲ (small)	Iron and steel plant
▮		Coalfields

Kiruna, Gällivare, Teesside, Sheffield, Scunthorpe, Ijmuiden, Dunkerque, South Wales, Valenciennes, Salzgitter, The Ruhr, Esch, Krakow, Ostrava, Genova, Taranto

Sources of Iron ore imported into Western Europe
1973 million tonnes

Imports from	Austria	Belgium-Lux.	France	Italy	Netherlands	Spain	U.K.	W. Germany
Angola	0.2	0.4	0.1		0	0.8	1.4	
Australia	0	1.8	0.8	1.8	0.2	0.6	1.2	27.8
Brazil	1.4	1.3	3.1	1.9	1.2	1.2	2.4	11.0
Canada	0	0.3	0.3	1.9	0.2	0.6	5.5	3.9
India	0.2					0	0	
Liberia	0	1.3	1.7	3.8	2.5	0.6	0.9	8.5
Mauritania	1.1	1.9	1.2		0	0.7	2.2	1.0
Sierra Leone			0.6			0	0.7	
U.S.S.R.	0.3		1.3			0.1	0.1	
Venezuela	1.3	0.1	1.5		0.4	1.7	2.6	
Others (World)	0	0.6	0.1	0	0	0.4	0.7	
France	14.6	0					3.5	
Norway	1.1	0		0.4	0	1.1	1.9	
Spain	0	0.4		0.2		0.3	1.0	
Sweden	8.8	2.0	0.2	1.6	0.9	4.9	10.9	
Rest of Europe	0	0	0	0	0	0	0	
Total Imports	1.4	32.0	11.3	12.5	6.9	5.0	21.4	74.9
Home produced ore	4.2	3.9	54.2	0.5		7.0	7.1	88.7

Iron and Steel Industry of Eastern North America

Steep Rock, Vermilion, Mesabi, Menominee, Marquette, Gagnon, Chicago, Hamilton, Detroit, Buffalo, Gary, Cleveland, Pittsburgh, Sparrows Point, Birmingham

Major Centre	Other Important Centre	
● (large)	● (small)	Iron ore
▲ (large)	▲ (small)	Iron and steel plant
▮		Coalfields

Structural Regions

- Pre-Cambrian shields
- Sedimentary cover on Pre-Cambrian shields
- Palæozoic (Caledonian and Hercynian) folding
- Sedimentary cover on Palæozoic folding
- Mesozoic folding
- Sedimentary cover on Mesozoic folding
- Cainozoic (Alpine) folding
- Sedimentary cover on Cainozoic folding

World production of Pig iron and Ferro-alloys

Total World production 1972: 461·9 M tonnes

Lux.	1%
Rumania	1%
S. Africa	1%
Brazil	1%
Spain	1%
Australia	1%
India	1·5%
Poland	1·5%
Czech.	2%
Canada	2%
Italy	2%
Belg.	2·5%
U.K.	3%
France	4%
China	6%
W. Germany	7%

Others 8·5%
U.S.S.R. 20%
U.S.A. 18%
Japan 16%

Growth of World production of Pig iron and Ferro-alloys

M tonnes

1938
1946
1951
1956
1961
1966
1974

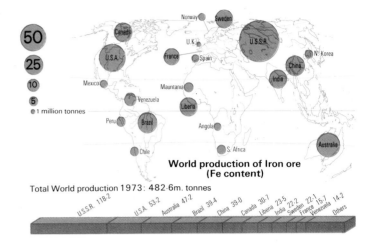

World production of Iron ore (Fe content)

Total World production 1973: 482·6m. tonnes

U.S.S.R. 118·2 U.S.A. 53·2 Australia 47·2 Brazil 39·4 China 39·0 Canada 30·7 Liberia 23·5 India 22·2 Sweden 22·1 France 15·7 Venezuela 14·2 Others

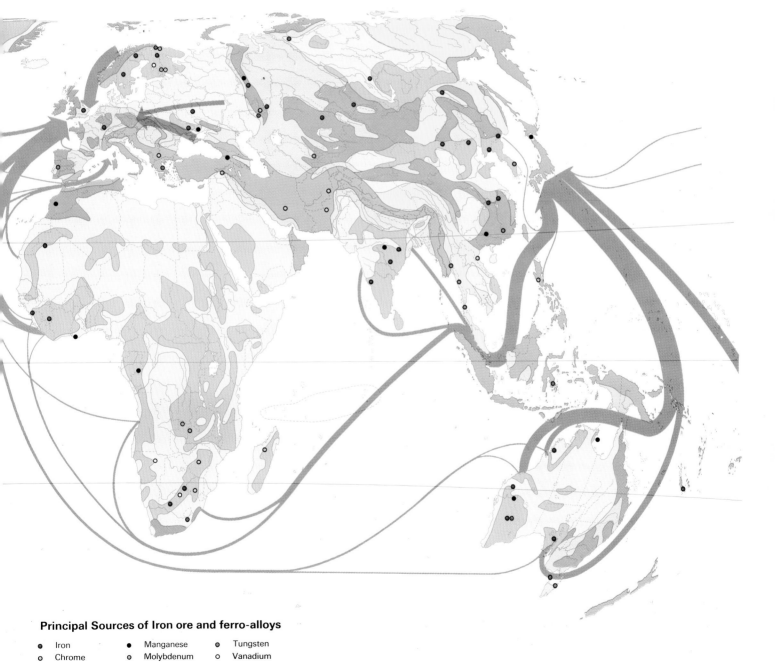

Principal Sources of Iron ore and ferro-alloys

- Iron
- Chrome
- Cobalt
- Manganese
- Molybdenum
- Nickel
- Tungsten
- Vanadium
- Iron ore trade flow

Mineral Resources II

Antimony – imparts hardness when alloyed to other metals, especially lead.
Uses: type metal, pigments to paints, glass and enamels, fireproofing of textiles.

World production 78 478 tonnes

S. Africa China Bolivia U.S.S.R. Turkey Thailand

Lead – heavy, soft, malleable, acid resistant.
Uses: storage batteries, sheeting and piping, cable covering, ammunition, type metal, weights, additive to petrol.

World production 3·57 million tonnes

U.S.A. U.S.S.R. Australia Canada

Tin – resistant to attacks by organic acids, malleable.
Uses: canning, foils, as an alloy to other metals (brass and bronze).

World production 217 200 tonnes

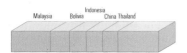

Malaysia Bolivia Indonesia China Thailand

Aluminium – light, resists corrosion, good conductor.
Uses: aircraft, road and rail vehicles, domestic utensils, cables, makes highly tensile and light alloys.

World production 81·22 million tonnes (of Bauxite)

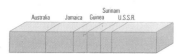

Australia Jamaica Guinea Surinam U.S.S.R.

Gold – untarnishable and resistant to corrosion, highly ductile and malleable, good conductor. The pure metal is soft and it is alloyed to give it hardness.
Uses: bullion, coins, jewellery, gold-leaf, electronics.

World production 1 135 tonnes

S. Africa U.S.S.R.

Copper – excellent conductor of electricity and heat, durable, resistant to corrosion, strong and ductile.
Uses: wire, tubing, brass (with zinc and tin), bronze (with tin), (compounds) – dyeing.

World production 7·89 million tonnes

U.S.A. U.S.S.R. Chile Canada Zambia Zaire

Mercury – the only liquid metal, excellent conductor of electricity.
Uses: thermometers, electrical industry, gold and silver ore extraction, (compounds) – drugs, pigments, chemicals, dentistry.

World production .8932 tonnes

U.S.S.R. Spain China Italy Mexico

Zinc – hard metal, low corrosion factor.
Uses: brass (with copper and tin), galvanising, diecasting, medicines, paints and dyes.

World production 5·89 million tonnes

Canada U.S.S.R. Australia U.S.A. Peru

Diamonds – very hard and resistant to chemical attack, high lustre, very rare.
Uses: jewellery, cutting and abrading other materials.

World production 44·63 million carats

Zaire U.S.S.R. S. Africa Ghana Botswana

Silver – ductile and malleable, a soft metal and must be alloyed for use in coinage.
Uses: coins, jewellery, photography, electronics, medicines.

World production 9306 tonnes

U.S.S.R. Canada Peru Mexico U.S.A Australia

World consumption of non-ferrous metals

These diagrams show the average yearly world consumption of certain refined metals for 1949/51, 1963/65 and 1971/73 and also the percentage of the latter produced from scrap. The figures beneath each diagram show estimates made in 1950, 1964 and 1973 of reserves in the Western World.

While indicating that the reserves are by no means infinite the figures show how widely these estimates have differed over 10 years and take no account of unknown reserves, particularly in the sea-bed, or advances in mining technology which will make it economic to mine low-content ores.

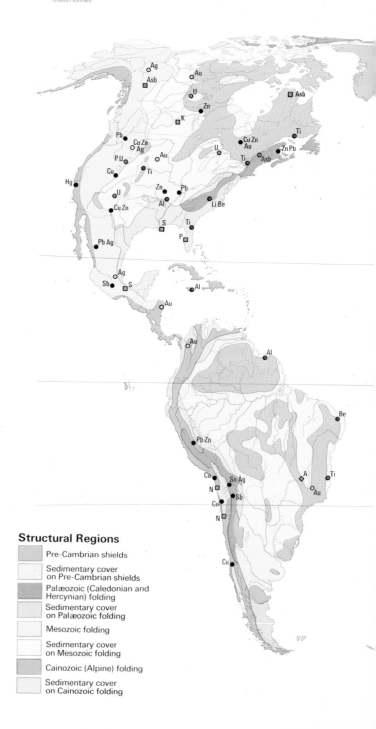

Structural Regions

- Pre-Cambrian shields
- Sedimentary cover on Pre-Cambrian shields
- Palæozoic (Caledonian and Hercynian) folding
- Sedimentary cover on Palæozoic folding
- Mesozoic folding
- Sedimentary cover on Mesozoic folding
- Cainozoic (Alpine) folding
- Sedimentary cover on Cainozoic folding

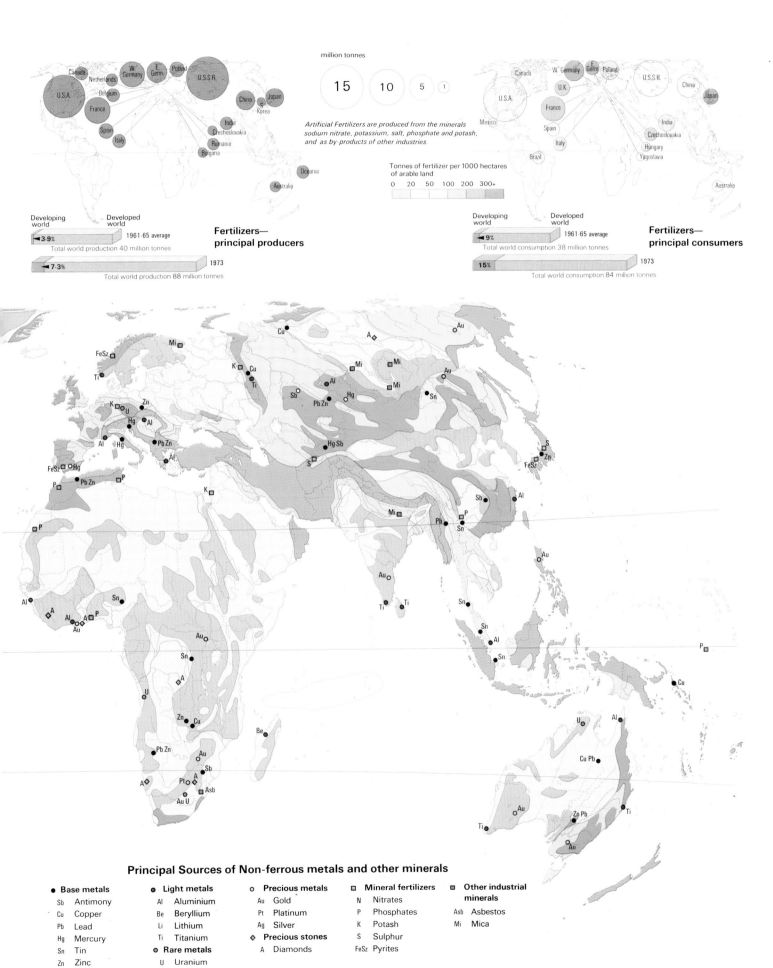

million tonnes

| 15 | 10 | 5 | 1 |

Artificial Fertilizers are produced from the minerals sodium nitrate, potassium, salt, phosphate and potash, and as by-products of other industries.

Tonnes of fertilizer per 1000 hectares of arable land

0   20   50   100   200   300+

Fertilizers— principal producers

Developing world — Developed world

◄3·9% 1961-65 average
Total world production 40 million tonnes

◄7·3% 1973
Total world production 88 million tonnes

Fertilizers— principal consumers

Developing world — Developed world

◄9% 1961-65 average
Total world consumption 38 million tonnes

◄15% 1973
Total world consumption 84 million tonnes

Principal Sources of Non-ferrous metals and other minerals

● Base metals
- Sb Antimony
- Cu Copper
- Pb Lead
- Hg Mercury
- Sn Tin
- Zn Zinc

● Light metals
- Al Aluminium
- Be Beryllium
- Li Lithium
- Ti Titanium

◉ Rare metals
- U Uranium

○ Precious metals
- Au Gold
- Pt Platinum
- Ag Silver

◇ Precious stones
- A Diamonds

□ Mineral fertilizers
- N Nitrates
- P Phosphates
- K Potash
- S Sulphur
- FeSz Pyrites

▣ Other industrial minerals
- Asb Asbestos
- Mi Mica

39

Fuel and Energy

Coal

Coal is the result of the accumulation of vegetation over millions of years. Later under pressure from overlying sediments, it is hardened through four stages: peat, lignite, bituminous coal, and finally anthracite. Once the most important source of power, coal's importance now lies in the production of electricity and as a raw material in the production of plastics, heavy chemicals and disinfectants.

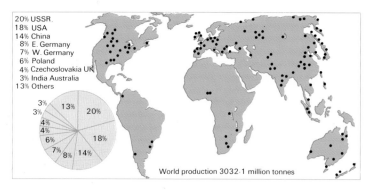

20% USSR.
18% USA
14% China
8% E. Germany
7% W. Germany
6% Poland
4% Czechoslovakia UK
3% India Australia
13% Others

World production 3032·1 million tonnes

Coal mine

Oil

Oil is derived from the remains of marine animals and plants, probably as a result of pressure, heat and chemical action. It is a complex mixture of hydrocarbons which are refined to extract the various constituents. These include products such as gasolene, kerosene and heavy fuel oils. Oil is rapidly replacing coal because of easier handling and reduced pollution.

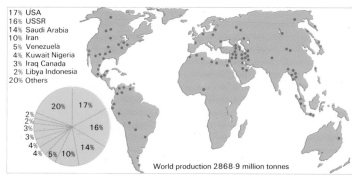

17% USA
16% USSR
14% Saudi Arabia
10% Iran
5% Venezuela
4% Kuwait Nigeria
3% Iraq Canada
2% Libya Indonesia
20% Others

World production 2868·9 million tonnes

Oil derrick

Natural gas

Since the early 1960's natural gas (methane) has become one of the largest single sources of energy. By liquefaction its volume can be reduced to 1/600 of that of gas and hence is easily transported. It is often found directly above oil reserves and because it is both cheaper than coal gas and less polluting it has great potential.

48% USA
20% USSR
7% Canada Netherlands
3% UK
2% Rumania Iran
Mexico
W. Germany
7% Others

World production 1280 million cubic metres

North sea gas rig

Water

Hydro-electric power stations use water to drive turbines which in turn generate electricity. The ideal site is one in which a consistently large volume of water falls a considerable height, hence sources of H.E.P. are found mainly in mountainous areas. Potential sources of hydro-electricity using waves or tides are yet to be exploited widely.

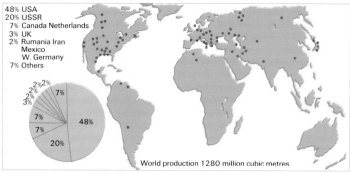

22% USA
16% Canada
10% USSR
6% Norway
5% Japan Sweden
4% France Brazil
3% Italy
25% Others

World production 1 226 210 million kWh

Water power

Nuclear energy

The first source of nuclear power was developed in Britain in 1956. Energy is obtained from heat generated by the reaction from splitting atoms of certain elements, of which uranium and plutonium are the most important. Although the initial installation costs are very high the actual running costs are low because of the slow consumption of fuel.

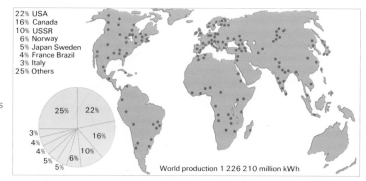

46% USA
15% UK
8% Canada France
6% W. Germany
2% USSR Italy
1% India Sweden
11% Others

World production 181 300 million kWh

Nuclear power station

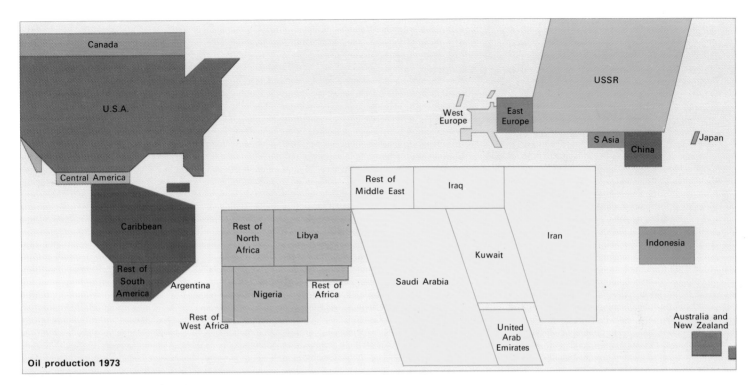

Oil production 1973

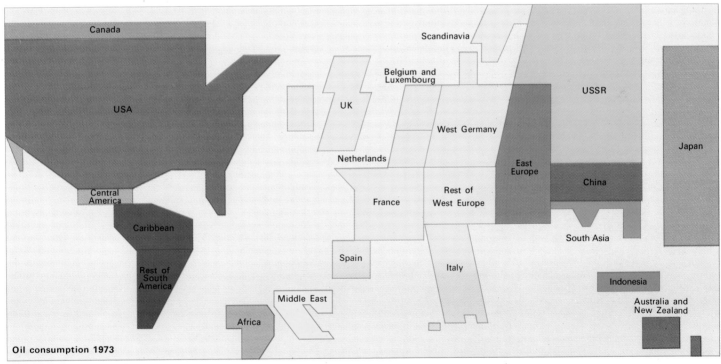

Oil consumption 1973

Oil's new super-powers *above*
When countries are scaled
according to their production and
consumption of oil they take on
new dimensions. At present, large
supplies of oil are concentrated in
a few countries of the Caribbean,
the Middle East and North Africa,
except for the vast indigenous
supplies of the U.S.A. and U.S.S.R.
The Middle East, with 55% of the
world's reserves, produces 37% of
the world's supply and yet
consumes less than 3%. The U.S.A.,
despite its great production, has
a deficiency of nearly 300 million
tons a year, consuming 30% of the
world's total. Estimates show that
Western Europe, at present
consuming 747 million tons or 27%
of the total each year, may by
1980 surpass the U.S. consumption.
Japan is the largest importer of
crude oil with an increase in
consumption of 440% during the
period 1963-73.

Index of
energy balance
▨	-500
■	-100 to -500
■	-50 to -100
▨	-15 to -50
□	-1 to -15
□	+1 to +15
▨	+15 to +50
■	+50

Occupations

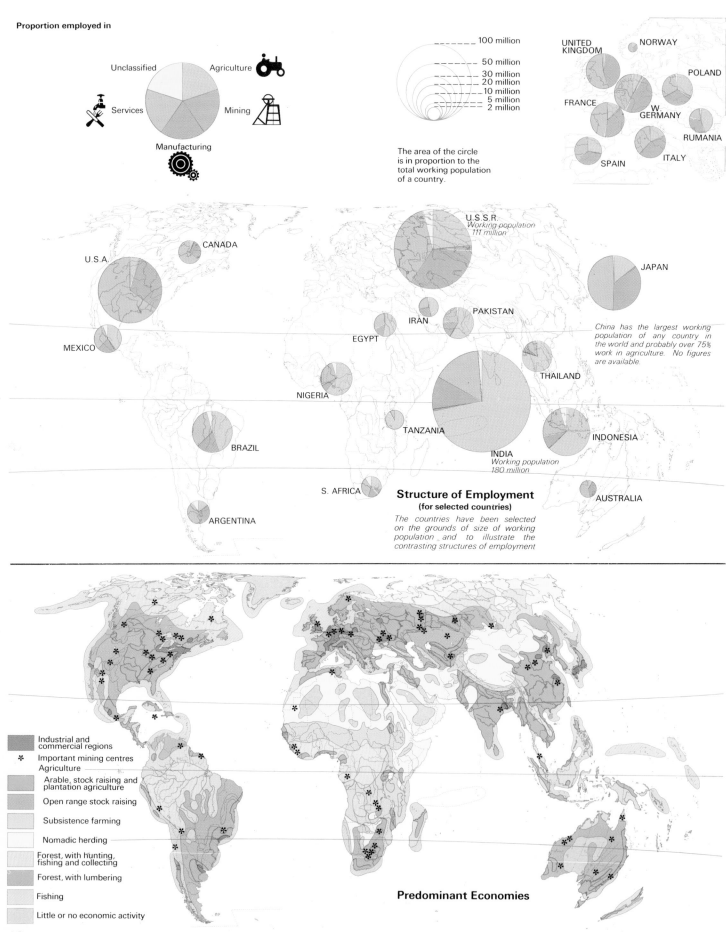

Proportion employed in

- Unclassified
- Agriculture
- Services
- Mining
- Manufacturing

_____ 100 million
_____ 50 million
_____ 30 million
_____ 20 million
_____ 10 million
_____ 5 million
_____ 2 million

The area of the circle is in proportion to the total working population of a country.

UNITED KINGDOM
NORWAY
POLAND
FRANCE
W. GERMANY
RUMANIA
SPAIN
ITALY

CANADA
U.S.A.
MEXICO

U.S.S.R.
Working population 111 million

JAPAN

IRAN
PAKISTAN
EGYPT

China has the largest working population of any country in the world and probably over 75% work in agriculture. No figures are available.

NIGERIA
THAILAND

BRAZIL

TANZANIA

INDIA
Working population 180 million

INDONESIA

S. AFRICA

ARGENTINA

AUSTRALIA

Structure of Employment
(for selected countries)

The countries have been selected on the grounds of size of working population and to illustrate the contrasting structures of employment

- Industrial and commercial regions
- * Important mining centres

Agriculture
- Arable, stock raising and plantation agriculture
- Open range stock raising
- Subsistence farming
- Nomadic herding
- Forest, with hunting, fishing and collecting
- Forest, with lumbering
- Fishing
- Little or no economic activity

Predominant Economies

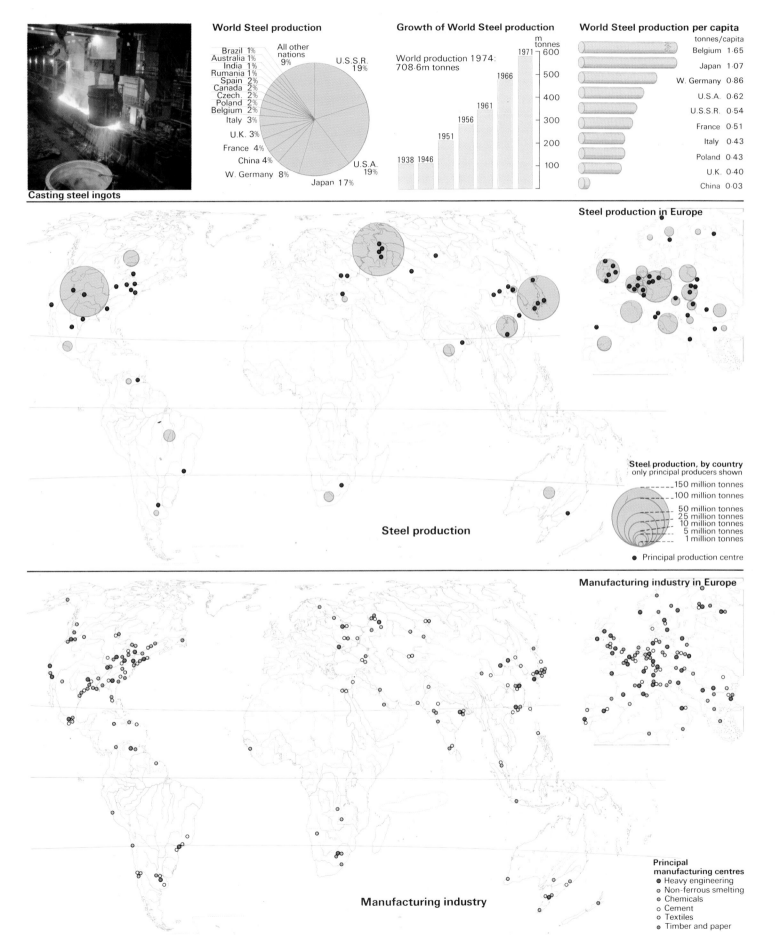

World Steel production

Brazil 1%
Australia 1%
India 1%
Rumania 1%
Spain 2%
Canada 2%
Czech. 2%
Poland 2%
Belgium 2%
Italy 3%
U.K. 3%
France 4%
China 4%
W. Germany 8%
Japan 17%
U.S.A. 19%
Japan 17%
U.S.A. 19%
U.S.S.R. 19%
All other nations 9%

Growth of World Steel production

World production 1974: 708·6m tonnes

m tonnes
1971 600
1966 500
1961 400
1956 300
1951 200
1938 1946 1951 100

World Steel production per capita

tonnes/capita
Belgium 1·65
Japan 1·07
W. Germany 0·86
U.S.A. 0·62
U.S.S.R. 0·54
France 0·51
Italy 0·43
Poland 0·43
U.K. 0·40
China 0·03

Casting steel ingots

Steel production in Europe

Steel production

Steel production, by country
only principal producers shown

- - - - - 150 million tonnes
- - - - - 100 million tonnes
- - - - - 50 million tonnes
- - - - - 25 million tonnes
- - - - - 10 million tonnes
- - - - - 5 million tonnes
- - - - - 1 million tonnes

● Principal production centre

Manufacturing industry in Europe

Manufacturing industry

Principal manufacturing centres
- ● Heavy engineering
- ◉ Non-ferrous smelting
- ◑ Chemicals
- ○ Cement
- ◐ Textiles
- ● Timber and paper

43

Transport

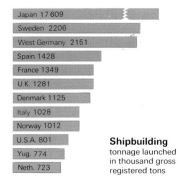

Japan 17 609	
Sweden 2206	
West Germany 2151	
Spain 1428	
France 1349	
U.K. 1281	
Denmark 1125	
Italy 1028	
Norway 1012	
U.S.A. 801	
Yug. 774	
Neth. 723	

Shipbuilding
tonnage launched
in thousand gross
registered tons

Shipyards

Aircraft Industry

In 1975 there were approximately
10 000 civil passenger airliners in
service. This diagram shows where they
were built.

U.S.A. 53%	U.S.S.R. 33%		U.K. 6% Netherlands 3% France 2%

Trade in Aircraft and Aircraft Engines
1973   *million U.S. $.*

	Exports			Imports	
	Aircraft	Engines		Aircraft	Engines
U.S.A.	4143	714	U.S.A.	563	218
U.K.	605	591	Canada	438	108
France	360	150	France	400	250
Canada	325	132	U.K.	389	393
W. Germ.	200		Australia	342	20
Neth.	192	89	W. Germ.	279	
Italy	137		Japan	236	107

Concorde and Boeing 747

• Principal shipbuilding centres

• Principal aircraft manufacturing centres

Motor vehicles

Production 1973 thousand units	Exports 1973	Imports million U.S. $.
U.S.A. 12 638	6076	1005
Japan 7088	4899	193
W. Germany 3949	9107	996
France 3596	3779	1903
U.K. 2164	2701	1599
Italy 1960	1963	1263
Canada 1604	4814	5349
U.S.S.R. 1604	611	240
Belgium 938	2215	1457

Railway vehicles

Exports 1973		Imports million U.S. $.	
U.S.A.	219·2	Yugoslavia	109·2
France	210·2	Brazil	65·8
Japan	186·3	S. Africa	48·4
W. Germany	157·7	W. Germany	47·4
Canada	76·1	U.S.A.	39·0
Yugoslavia	59·6	Belg.-Lux.	34·9
Italy	42·2	Netherlands	34·4
Spain	42·2	France	31·3
U.K.	38·6	Canada	30·0
Sweden	24·2	Argentina	25·7
Belg.-Lux.	22·0	Italy	22·9
Portugal	14·4	Sweden	19·4
Austria	11·8	S. Korea	18·8

Locomotive works

Car assembly line

• Principal locomotive building centres

• Principal motor vehicle plants

Merchant Shipping

Gross Registered Tonnage of merchant fleets registered in each country

2 5 10 20 30 40
Millions of G.R.T.

Weight of goods loaded and unloaded in each country's external trade, per inhabitant

Dry cargo only, petroleum excluded

1 2 3 4 5 6 7 8 9
Metric tons/inhabitant

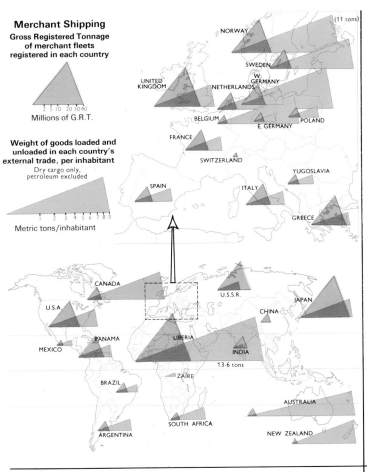

Density of Transport Networks

Density of network in km/100 km²

Road: 100 / 75 / 50 / 25 / 0
Rail: 20 / 15 / 10 / 5 / 0
Inland Waterway: 10 / 5 / 4 / 3 / 2 / 1 / 0

Road **Rail** **Inland Waterway**

Strict comparisons between the transport networks of different nations cannot be made due to differences in the gauges of railways, sizes of inland waterways and in the criteria used to designate roads

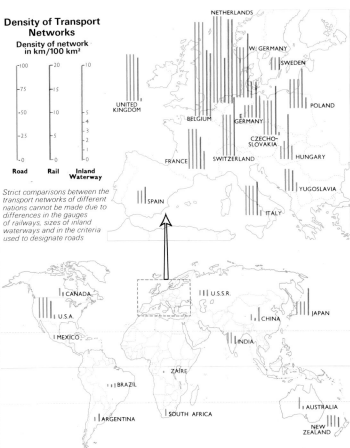

Motor Vehicles and Passenger Transport

Private vehicles per 1000 inhabitants
250 / 200 / 150 / 100 / 50 / 0

Commercial vehicles per 1000 inhabitants
100 / 75 / 50 / 25 / 0

Passenger-km. travelled by air and by rail, per 100 inhabitants

Air: 75 000 / 50 000 / 25 000 / 10 000 / 5000 / 1000
Rail: 250 000 / 150 000 / 100 000 / 50 000 / 25 000

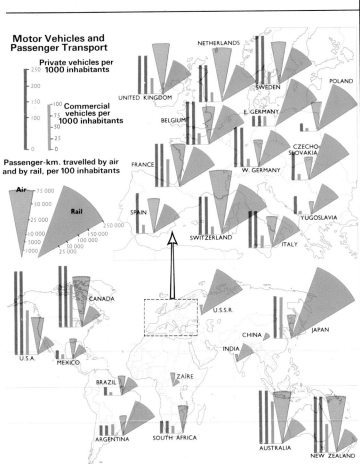

Freight Carried

Freight carried by air
3000 / 2000 / 1000 / 500 / 100 ton—km /100 inhabitants

Freight carried by rail
750 000 / 500 000 / 250 000 / 100 000 / 50 000 / 25 000 ton—km /100 inhabitants

Freight carried by inland waterway
300 000 / 200 000 / 100 000 / 50 000 / 25 000 ton—km /100 inhabitants

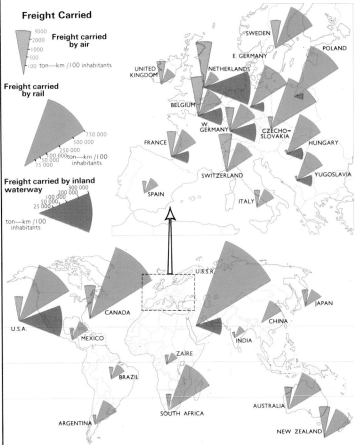

45

Trade

Road container lorry.

Oil tanker.

Airfreight.

Road/rail container depot.

The Trade of Europe

The semi-circles on this map are at the same scale as those on the World map below. See the legend to the latter.

Norway Sweden Finland
Ireland
U.K. Netherlands Denmark W. Germany
Belgium E. Germany Poland
France Switzerland Austria Czechoslovakia
Hungary Rumania
Portugal Spain Yugoslavia
Italy Bulgaria
Greece

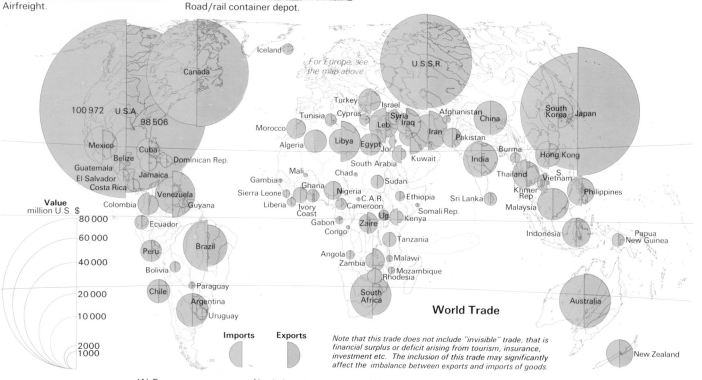

Iceland
Canada
U.S.S.R.
For Europe, see the map above
Turkey Israel
Tunisia Cyprus Syria Iraq Afghanistan China South Japan
100 972 U.S.A. Morocco Leb. Iran Korea
98 506 Algeria Libya Egypt Jor. Pakistan Burma Hong Kong
Mexico Cuba Kuwait India Thailand S. Vietnam
Belize Dominican Rep. South Arabia Khmer Philippines
Guatemala Jamaica Mali Chad Sudan Rep. Malaysia
El Salvador Gambia Ghana Nigeria Sri Lanka
Costa Rica Sierra Leone C.A.R. Ethiopia
Venezuela Liberia Ivory Cameroon Somali Rep. Indonesia Papua
Colombia Guyana Coast Zaire Ug. Kenya New Guinea
Ecuador Gabon
Congo Tanzania
Peru Brazil Angola Malawi
Bolivia Zambia Mozambique
Paraguay Rhodesia Australia
Chile South
Argentina Africa **World Trade**
Uruguay New Zealand

Value
million U.S. $

80 000
60 000
40 000
20 000
10 000
2000
1000

Imports Exports

Note that this trade does not include "invisible" trade, that is financial surplus or deficit arising from tourism, insurance, investment etc. The inclusion of this trade may significantly affect the imbalance between exports and imports of goods.

These diagrams show the destination of exports from each of the regions of the World.

= 20 000 million U.S. $

The total exports are in million U.S. $

	W. Europe	North America	Asia	Soviet bloc	Latin America	Africa	Australasia
Exports to:-	Australasia, Africa, Latin America, Soviet bloc, Asia, N. America, Exports within W. Europe	Australasia, Africa, Latin America, Soviet bloc, Asia, Exports within N. America, W. Europe	Australasia, Africa, Latin America, Soviet bloc, Exports within Asia, N. America, W. Europe	Africa, Latin America, Exports within Soviet bloc, Asia, N. America, W. Europe	Africa, Exports within Latin America, Soviet bloc, Asia, N. America, W. Europe	Exports within Africa, Latin America, Soviet bloc, Asia, N. America, W. Europe	Exports within Austr., Africa, Latin America, Soviet bloc, Asia, N. America, W. Europe
Total exports	337 250	131 440	196 490	70 910	48 610	38 810	14 280

46

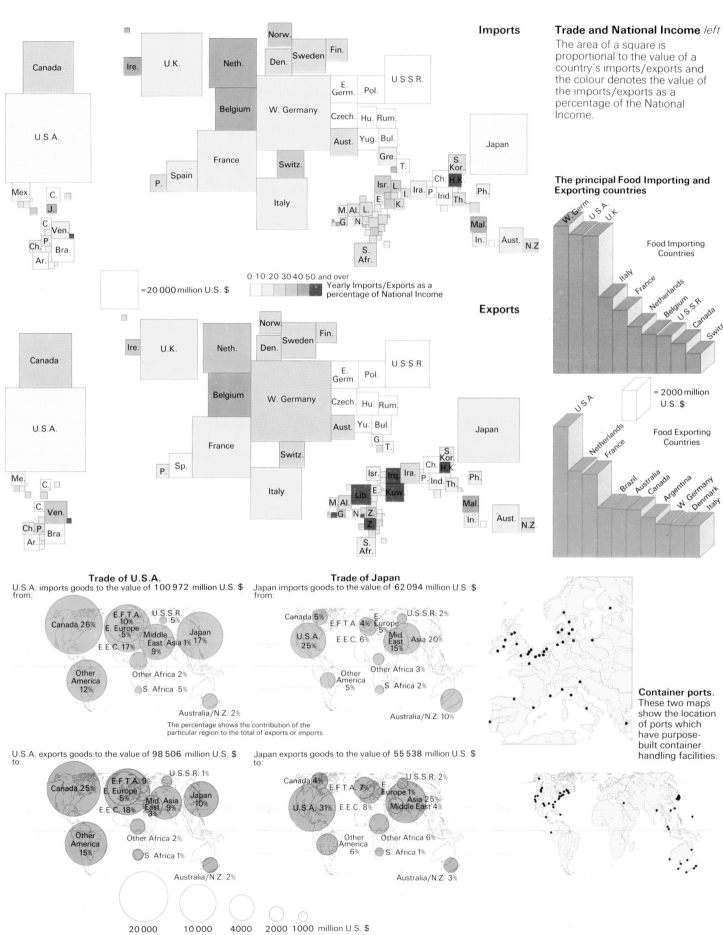

Imports

Trade and National Income *left*
The area of a square is proportional to the value of a country's imports/exports and the colour denotes the value of the imports/exports as a percentage of the National Income.

Canada
U.S.A.
Mex.
C.
J.
C.
Ven.
Ch.
P.
Bra.
Ar.

Ire.
U.K.
Neth.
Norw.
Den.
Sweden
Fin.
E. Germ.
Pol.
U.S.S.R.
Belgium
W. Germany
Czech.
Hu.
Rum.
Aust.
Yug.
Bul.
Gre.
T.
France
Switz.
Isr.
L.
Ch.
S. Kor.
H.K.
Ira.
P.
Ind.
Th.
Ph.
Japan
P.
Spain
E.
K.
Italy
M.
Al.
L.
G.
N.
Mal.
In.
Aust.
N.Z.
S. Afr.

0 10 20 30 40 50 and over
= 20 000 million U.S. $ Yearly Imports/Exports as a percentage of National Income

The principal Food Importing and Exporting countries

W. Germ.
U.S.A.
U.K.
Italy
France
Netherlands
Belgium
U.S.S.R.
Canada
Switz.

Food Importing Countries

= 2000 million U.S. $

U.S.A.
Netherlands
France
Brazil
Australia
Canada
Argentina
W. Germany
Denmark
Italy

Food Exporting Countries

Exports

Canada
U.S.A.
Me.
C.
C.
Ven.
Ch.
P.
Bra.
Ar.

Ire.
U.K.
Neth.
Norw.
Den.
Sweden
Fin.
E. Germ.
Pol.
U.S.S.R.
Belgium
W. Germany
Czech.
Hu.
Rum.
Aust.
Yu.
Bul.
France
Switz.
G.
T.
P.
Sp.
Italy
Isr.
Irq.
Ira.
S. Kor.
H.K.
E.
Kuw.
P.
Ind.
Th.
Ph.
Japan
M.
Al.
Lib.
G.
N.
Z.
Mal.
In.
Aust.
N.Z.
S. Afr.

Trade of U.S.A.
U.S.A. imports goods to the value of 100 972 million U.S. $ from:

Canada 26%
E.F.T.A. 10%
E. Europe 5%
U.S.S.R. 5%
Middle East 9%
Asia 1%
Japan 17%
E.E.C. 17%
Other America 12%
Other Africa 2%
S. Africa 5%
Australia/N.Z. 2%

The percentage shows the contribution of the particular region to the total of exports or imports

Trade of Japan
Japan imports goods to the value of 62 094 million U.S. $ from:

Canada 5%
E.F.T.A. 4%
E. Europe 5%
U.S.S.R. 2%
U.S.A. 25%
E.E.C. 6%
Mid. East 15%
Asia 20%
Other Africa 3%
Other America 5%
S. Africa 2%
Australia/N.Z. 10%

U.S.A. exports goods to the value of 98 506 million U.S. $ to:

Canada 25%
E.F.T.A. 9%
E. Europe 5%
U.S.S.R. 1%
Mid. East 3%
Asia 9%
Japan 10%
E.E.C. 18%
Other America 15%
Other Africa 2%
S. Africa 1%
Australia/N.Z. 2%

Japan exports goods to the value of 55 538 million U.S. $ to:

Canada 4%
E.F.T.A. 7%
E. Europe 1%
U.S.S.R. 2%
U.S.A. 31%
E.E.C. 8%
Middle East 4%
Asia 25%
Other America 6%
Other Africa 6%
S. Africa 1%
Australia/N.Z. 3%

20 000   10 000   4000   2000 1000 million U.S. $

Container ports.
These two maps show the location of ports which have purpose-built container handling facilities.

Wealth

The living standard of a few highly developed, urbanised, industrialised countries is a complete contrast to the conditions of the vast majority of economically undeveloped, agrarian states. It is this contrast which divides mankind into rich and poor, well fed and hungry. The developing world is still an over-whelmingly agricultural world: over 70% of all its people live off the land and yet the output from that land remains pitifully low. Many Africans, South Americans and Asians struggle with the soil but the bad years occur only too frequently and they seldom have anything left over to save. The need for foreign capital then arises.

National Income *see right*
The gap between developing and developed worlds is in fact widening eg. in 1938 the incomes for the United States and India were in the proportions of 1:15; now they are 1:35.

Islands *see map right*
a Antilles   h Mauritius
b Martinique   j Solomon
c Barbados   k New Hebrides
d Cape Verde   l Fiji
e Bahrein   m New Caledonia
f Comoro   n Tonga
g Reunion

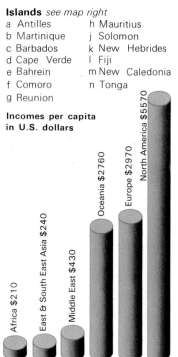

Incomes per capita in U.S. dollars

Africa $210
East & South East Asia $240
Middle East $430
Oceania $2760
Europe $2970
North America $5570

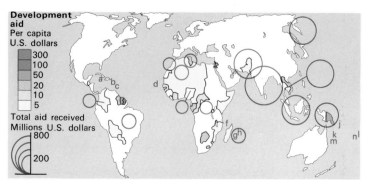

Development aid
Per capita U.S. dollars

300
100
50
20
10
5

Total aid received
Millions U.S. dollars
800
200

Development aid
The provision of foreign aid, defined as assistance on con-cessional terms for promoting development, is today an accepted, though controversial aspect of the economic policies of most advanced countries towards less developed countries. Aid for development is based not merely on economic considerations but also on social, political and historical factors. The most important international committee set up after the war was that of the U.N.; practically all aid however has been given bi-laterally direct from an industrialised country to an under-developed country. Although aid increased during the 1950's the donated proportion of industrialised countries GNP has diminished from 0·5 to 0·4%. Less developed countries share of world trade also decreased and increased population invalidated any progress made.

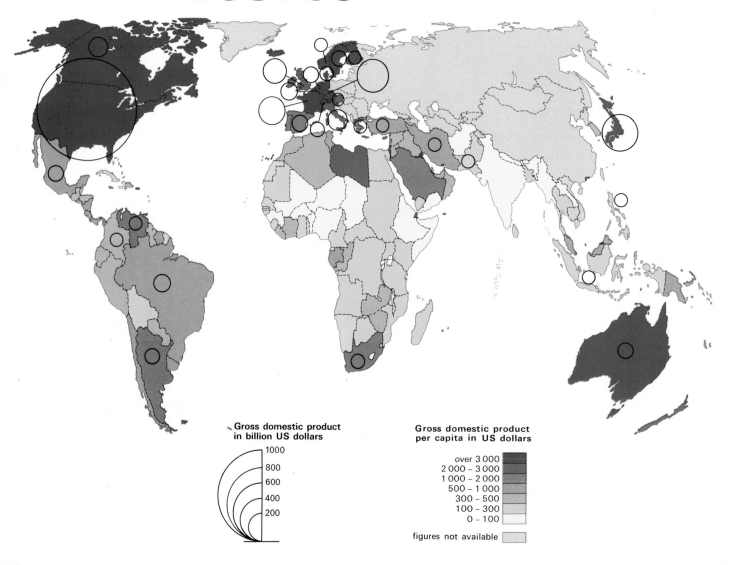

Gross domestic product in billion US dollars

1000
800
600
400
200

Gross domestic product per capita in US dollars

over 3 000
2 000 – 3 000
1 000 – 2 000
500 – 1 000
300 – 500
100 – 300
0 – 100

figures not available

GENERAL REFERENCE

Abbreviations of measures used — ft Feet; mm {Millimetres / Millimeters}: cm {Centimetres / Centimeters}: m {Metres / Meters}, Km {Kilometres / Kilometers}: mb Millibars

City and Town symbols in order of size

⬡ ⬡ ◼ ◉ ⦿ ◎ ○ ∘

⋰ Sites of Archæological or Historical Importance

▬▬▬ International Boundaries

▬ ▬ ▬ International Boundaries (Undemarcated or Undefined)

▬▬ ⋯⋯ Internal Boundaries

⌇ Principal Roads

╌╌╌ Tracks, Seasonal and other Roads

⌐−−−⌐ Road Tunnels

∿ Principal Railways

∿ Other Railways

╌╌╌ Railways under construction

⌐−−−⌐ Railway Tunnels

⊥⊥⊥⊥⊥ Principal Canals

⊢⊥⊥⊢ Principal Oil Pipelines

───── Principal Air Routes

✧ Principal Airports

3386 ╌╌╌ Principal Shipping Routes (Distances in Nautical Miles)

∿ Perennial Streams

╌╌╌ Seasonal Streams

⬭ Seasonal Lakes, Salt Flats

⁖ Swamps, Marshes

⌣ Wells in Desert

▱ Permanent Ice

⤡ Passes

▲ 8848 Height above sea-level ⎫
▼ 8050 Depth below sea-level ⎬ in metres
1134 Height of lake-level ⎭

CONVERSION SCALE

ft	m
30 000	9000
	8000
24 000	7000
	6000
18 000	5000
12 000	4000
9000	3000
6000	2000
3000	1000
	500
Sea-Level 0	0 Sea-Level
	500
	1000
1000	2000
2000	3000
	4000
3000	5000
	6000
4000	7000
	8000
5000	9000
6000	10 000
	11 000
	12 000
7000 fathoms	m

THE WORLD
Physical
1:150 000 000

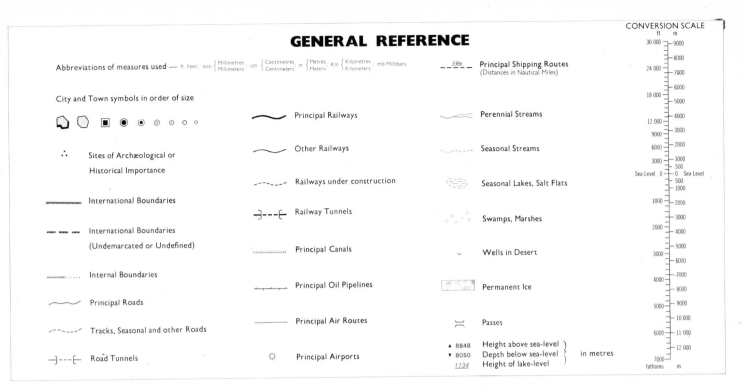

m	4000	2000	200	0	200	2000	4000	m
ft	12 000	6000	600	0	600	6000	12 000	ft

Projection: Hammer Equal Area

Projection: Hammer Equal Area

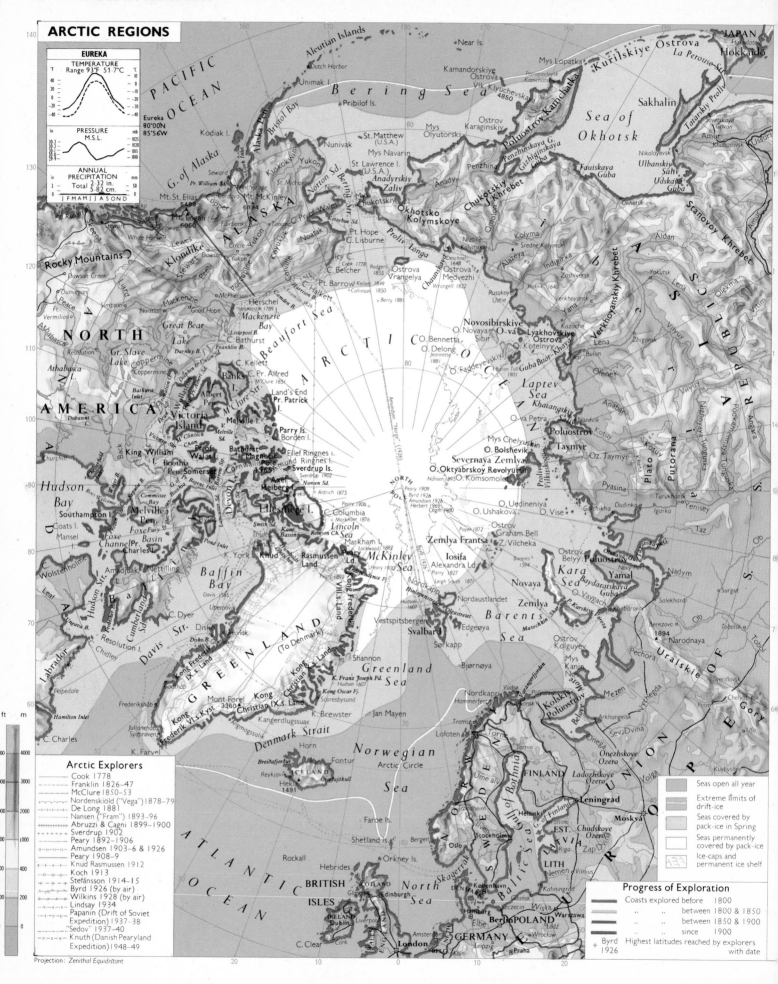

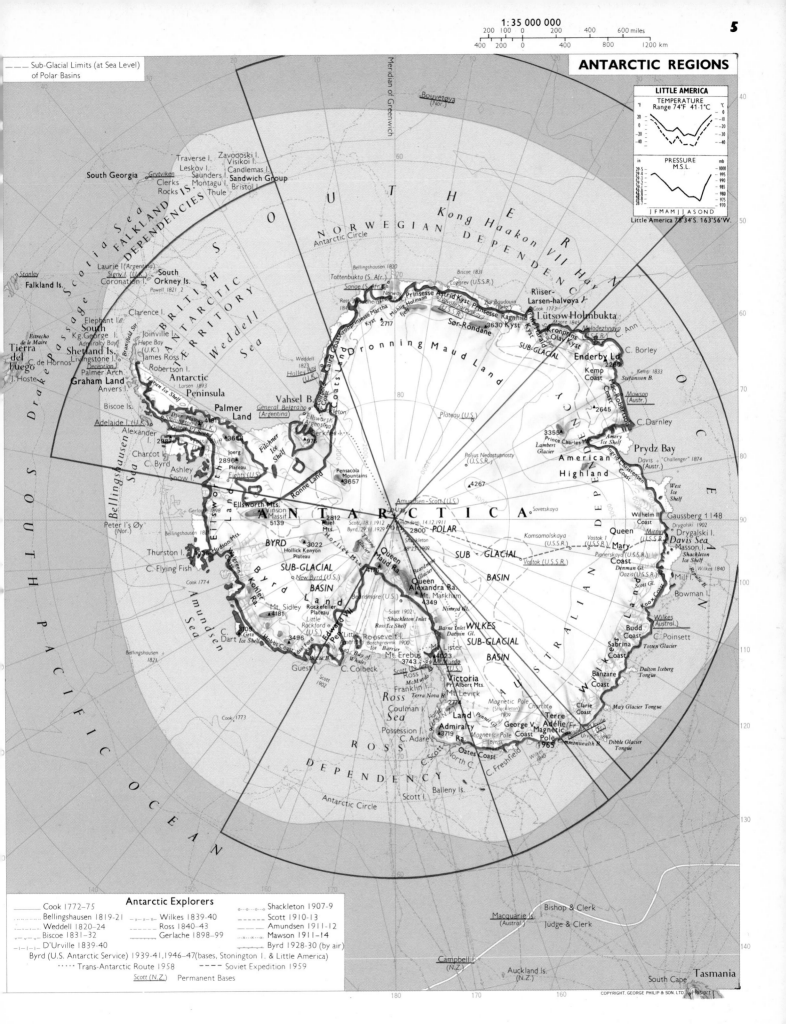

1:35 000 000

200 100 0 200 400 600 miles

400 200 0 400 800 1200 km

ANTARCTIC REGIONS

Sub-Glacial Limits (at Sea Level) of Polar Basins

LITTLE AMERICA

TEMPERATURE
Range 74°F 41·1°C

°F / °C

J F M A M J J A S O N D

PRESSURE M.S.L.

in. / mb

J F M A M J J A S O N D

Little America 78°34′S. 163°56′W.

SOUTHERN

OCEAN

Bouvetøya (Nor.)

Meridian of Greenwich

NORWEGIAN DEPENDENCY

Kong Haakon VII Hav

Antarctic Circle

South Georgia   Grytviken

Traverse I. Zavodoski I.
Leskov I. Visikoi I.
Candlemas I.
Saunders I.
Clerks Montagu I.
Rocks Is. Thule   Bristol I.
Sandwich Group

Scotia Sea   FALKLAND DEPENDENCIES

Bellingshausen 1830

Tottenbukta (S. Afr.)
Sange (S. Afr.)
Norway

Biscoe 1831
Lazarev (U.S.S.R.)

Prinsesse Astrid Kyst   Prinsesse Ragnhild
Prinsesse Martha   Kyst   2717   Kyst

Riiser-Larsen-halvøya

Lützow Holmbukta

Kronprins Olav Kyst

Melodezhnaya (U.S.S.R.)

C. Ann

Stanley

Falkland Is.

Laurie I (Argentina)
Signy I. (U.K.)   South
Coronation I.   Orkney Is.
Powell 1821   Is.

BRITISH   ANTARCTIC   TERRITORY

Dronning Maud Land

Sør-Rondane

3630 Kyst

Cook 1773

C. Borley

Enderby Ld.

Kemp Coast   Kemp 1833

Stefansson B.

Estrecho de la Maire
C. de Hornos
Tierra del Fuego
I. Hoste

Drake Passage

Clarence I.
Elephant I.
South   Kg.George I.
Shetland Is.   Admiralty Bay
Livingstone I.   Hope Bay (U.K.)
Deception I.   James Ross I.
Palmer Arch.   Robertson I.
Graham Land   Anvers I.   Antarctic   Larsen 1893   Larsen Ice Shelf
Peninsula
Biscoe Is.   Palmer Land

Weddell Sea

Weddell 1823
Halley (U.K.)

Coats Land

Vahsel B.
General Belgrano (Argentina)
Berkner I.

Filchner Ice Shelf

2645

3355

Mac-Robertson Coast

Mawson (Austr.)

C. Darnley

Prince Charles
Lambert Glacier   Amery Ice Shelf

Prydz Bay

Davis (Austr.)   "Challenger" 1874

Bellingshausen Sea

Adelaide I. (U.K.)
Alexander I.   2987

Charcot I.
C. Byrd
Ashley Snow (U.S.)

Joerg
Dyer Plateau   4101
3618
2896
Plateau
Eights (U.S.)

Ronne Land

Ellsworth (Argentina)
976

Pensacola Mountains
3657

Plateau (U.S.)

Pôlius Nedostupnosty (U.S.S.R.)

4267

American Highland

West Ice Shelf

Wilhelm II Coast   Gaussberg 1 148

Peter I's Øy (Nor.)   Bellingshausen 1821

Thurston I.
C. Flying Fish

Cook 1774

Amundsen Sea

Bellingshausen 1821

Hudson (U.S.)

Ellsworth Land

Ellsworth Mts.
Vinson Massif   2812
5139   Thiel Mts.

Byrd, 29.11.1929   Amundsen-Scott (U.S.)

Scott, 18.1.1912

POLAR

Sovetskaya

Amundsen, 14.12.1911

2800

Drygalski 1902

Komsomolskaya (U.S.S.R.)

Queen Mary Coast

Mirnyy (U.S.S.R.)
Davis Sea
Masson I.

ANTARCTICA

BYRD   3022   Hollick Kenyon Plateau

New Byrd (U.S.)

SUB-GLACIAL BASIN

Byrd Land

Kohler Ra.
Mt. Sidley   4181

Rockefeller Plateau
Little Rockford (U.S.)
3105
Dart Ice Shelf   3496
Hobbs Coast

Getz Ice Shelf

Edward

Horlick Mts.
476

Thorne Glacier

Shackleton

Queen Maud Ra.

Queen Alexandra Ra.
Mt. Markham   4349

Beardmore (U.S.)
Scott 1902
Shackleton Inlet

Ross Ice Shelf

QUEEN   Byrd 23.1.1909

SUB-GLACIAL BASIN

Vostok (U.S.S.R.)

Pionerskaya (U.S.S.R.)

Denman Gl.   Scott Gl.
Oazis (U.S.S.R.)
Knox Coast

Wilkes 1840

Shackleton Ice Shelf

Mill I.   Bowman I.

Budd Coast

Sabrina Coast   C. Poinsett

Totten Glacier

WILKES   SUB-GLACIAL BASIN

AUSTRALIAN DEPENDENCY

Roosevelt I.
Bay of Whales
Little America

Borchgrevink 1900
Ross Ice Barrier

Bjaa I.

Lister
4023   Mt. Erebus   3743

McMurdo (U.S.)

Nimrod Gl.

Barne Inlet
Darwin Gl.

WILKES

Bellingshausen 1821

Dalton Iceberg Tongue

Banzare Coast

May Glacier Tongue

Guest I.
C. Colbeck

Scott 1902

Ross Sea

Coulman I.

Franklin I.

Scott (N.Z.)
McMurdo
Terra Nova Bay
Mt. Levick   2774
Pr. Albert Mts.

Victoria Land

Admiralty Ra.   3719

Magnetic Pole (Shackleton) 1909

George V Coast
Magnetic Pole (Byrd) 1963

Terre Adélie (Fr.)
Magnetic Pole 1965

Clarie Coast

Dibble Glacier Tongue

Possession I.
C. Adare

Oates Coast

C. Scott   North C.   C. Freshfield
Commonwealth B.
Dumont d'Urville 1840

ROSS   DEPENDENCY

Antarctic Circle

Scott I.

Balleny Is.

SOUTH   PACIFIC   OCEAN

Antarctic Explorers

——— Cook 1772–75	○—○—○ Shackleton 1907–9	
——— Bellingshausen 1819–21	—·—·— Wilkes 1839–40	——— Scott 1910-13
——— Weddell 1820–24	——— Ross 1840–43	——— Amundsen 1911–12
—·—·— Biscoe 1831–32	——— Gerlache 1898–99	——— Mawson 1911–14
—·—·— D'Urville 1839–40		——— Byrd 1928–30 (by air)

Byrd (U.S. Antarctic Service) 1939–41, 1946–47 (bases, Stonington I. & Little America)

········ Trans-Antarctic Route 1958   — — — Soviet Expedition 1959

Scott (N.Z.)   Permanent Bases

Bishop & Clerk

Macquarie Is. (Austral.)

Judge & Clerk

Campbell I. (N.Z.)

Auckland Is. (N.Z.)

South Cape   Tasmania

Hobart

COPYRIGHT. GEORGE PHILIP & SON LTD.

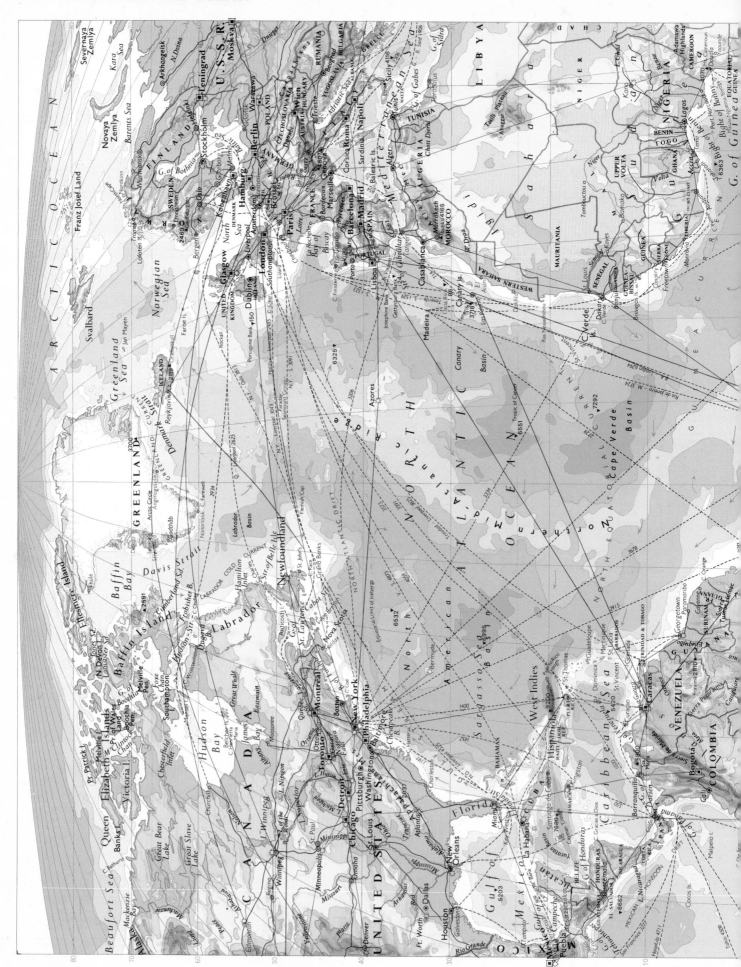

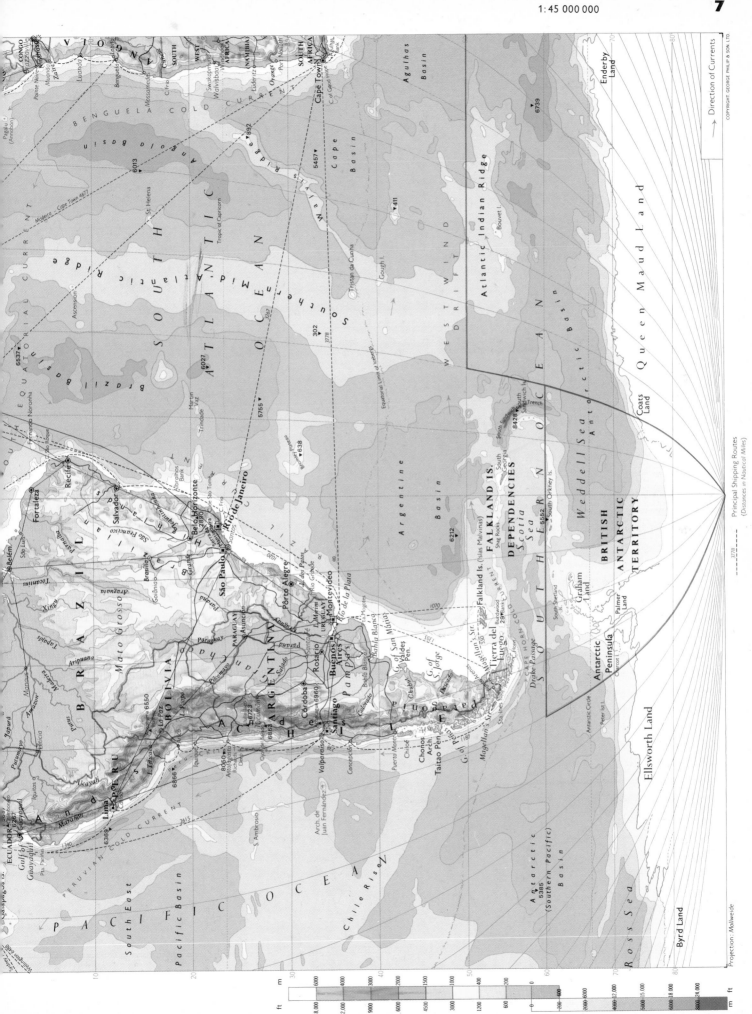

Direction of Currents

COPYRIGHT GEORGE PHILIP & SON, LTD.

CONGO
Brazzaville
ANGOLA
Pointe Noire
Muanda
Luanda
Zaire
SOUTH
WEST
AFRICA
NAMIBIA
Swakopmund
Walvis Bay
Lüderitz
Orange
Port Nolloth
SOUTH AFRICA
Cape Town
C. of Good Hope
Agulhas Bank

Pagalu
(Annobon)
Benguela
Mossamedes
C. Frio

Madeira – Cape Town 4877

BENGUELA COLD CURRENT

Angola Basin
6013

Walvis Ridge
892

Agulhas Basin

6739

Enderby Land

St. Helena

Ascension

Cape
Basin

5457

Mid Atlantic Ridge

SOUTH ATLANTIC OCEAN

Tropic of Capricorn

411
Bouvet I.

Atlantic Indian Ridge

Queen Maud Land

Fernando de Noronha
6537
São Roque

Brazil Basin

Martin Vaz
Trindade
6027

Gough I.

Tristan da Cunha

Southern Winds

302
3778
5755

WEST WIND DRIFT

Coats Land

Equatorial Limit of Icebergs

8428
South Sandwich Trench

SOUTH

Antarctic Basin

SOUTH EQUATORIAL CURRENT

BRAZIL

Recife
Fortaleza
São Luís
Belém

Salvador
Abrolhos Bank
5467

São Francisco
Belo Horizonte
Rio de Janeiro
2890
C. Frio
638

Santos

Argentine Basin
6212

FALKLAND IS.
(Islas Malvinas)
South Georgia
Shag Rocks

DEPENDENCIES
Scotia Sea
5552
South Orkney Is.

Weddell Sea

BRITISH
ANTARCTIC
TERRITORY

ATLANTIC OCEAN

São Paulo
Pôrto Alegre

Brasília
Goiânia
Tocantins
Araguaia
Xingu
Tapajós
Araguaia

Mato Grosso

PARAGUAY
Asunción
URUGUAY
Montevideo
Rio de la Plata

Pará
Paraná
Uruguay

1070

South Shetland Is.

Graham Land

Antarctic Circle

Peter I Is.

Ellsworth Land

BRAZIL
Peru
Amazon
Iquitos
Manaus
Ucayali
Marañón
Purus
Madeira
Juruá

BOLIVIA
La Paz
6550
6723
6960

Córdoba
ARGENTINA
Santiago
CHILE
Valparaíso
Concepción
8050
6864

ANDES
Andes de Chile
Tucumán

Rosario
Buenos Aires
Bahía Blanca
Blanca
Pampas
Colorado

G. of San Matías
Valdés Pen.
Chubut
G. of S. Jorge
Deseado
1355

Magellan's Str.
Tierra del Fuego
CAPE HORN COLD CURRENT
Drake Passage
Antarctic
Peninsula
Palmer
Land

ECUADOR
Guayaquil
Gulf of Guayaquil
Lima
PERU
6389

PERUVIAN COLD CURRENT

Chiloé
Chonos Arch.
Taitao Pen.
Puerto Montt
Arch. de Juan Fernández
S. Ambrosio

2615
1340

Galápagos Is.

PACIFIC OCEAN

South East Pacific Basin

Chile Rise

Antarctic
(Southern Pacific) Basin
5385

Ross Sea

Byrd Land

SOUTH INDIAN OCEAN

Principal Shipping Routes
(Distances in Nautical Miles)
3778

Projection: Mollweide

m ft
6000 18,000
4000 12,000
3000 9000
2000 6000
1500 4500
1000 3000
600 1800
400 1200
200 600
0 0
200 – 600
2000 6000
4000 12,000
5000 15,000
6000 18,000
8000 24,000
m ft

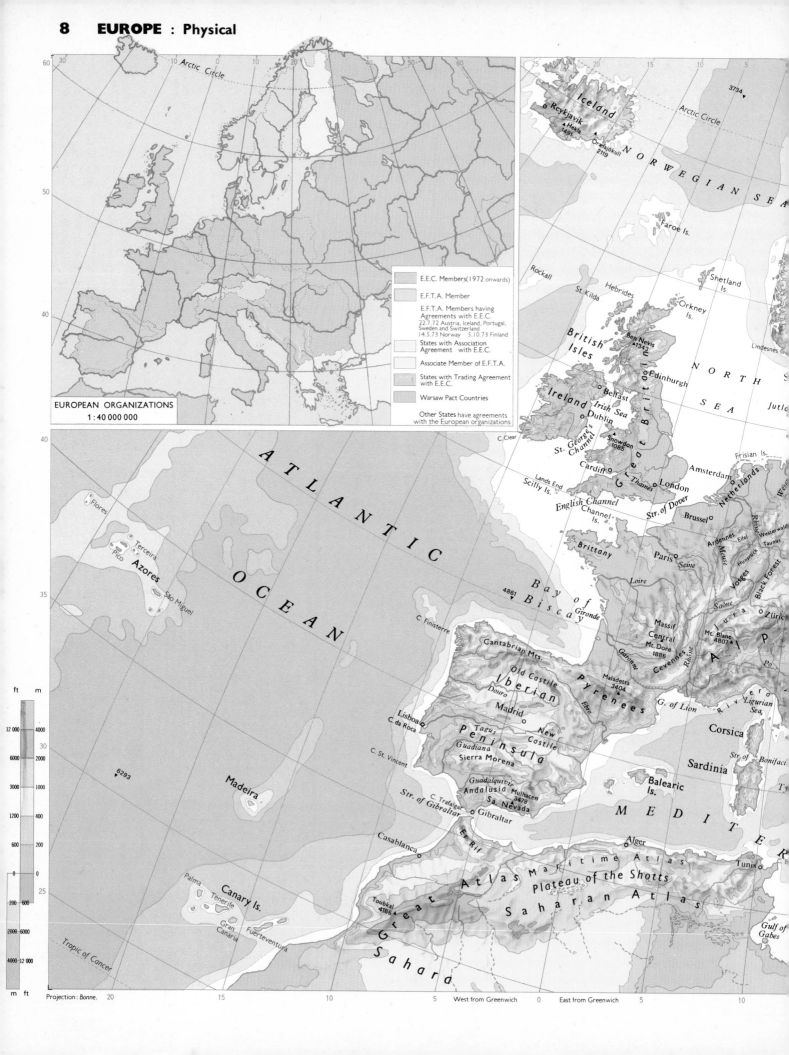

ATLANTIC

OCEAN

EUROPEAN ORGANIZATIONS
1 : 40 000 000

E.E.C. Members (1972 onwards)

E.F.T.A. Member

E.F.T.A. Members having
Agreements with E.E.C.
22.7.72 Austria, Iceland, Portugal,
Sweden and Switzerland
14.5.73 Norway   5.10.73 Finland

States with Association
Agreement with E.E.C.

Associate Member of E.F.T.A.

States with Trading Agreement
with E.E.C.

Warsaw Pact Countries

Other States have agreements
with the European organizations

NORWEGIAN SEA

Iceland
Reykjavik
Hekla
1491
Öræfajökull
2119
3734

Arctic Circle

Faroe Is.

Rockall

Shetland
Is.

St. Kilda

Hebrides

Orkney
Is.

Lindesnes

British
Isles

Ben Nevis
1343

NORTH

SEA

Edinburgh

Jutla

Great Britain

Belfast

Ireland

Irish Sea

Dublin

St. George's
Channel

Snowdon
1085

Frisian Is.

Amsterdam

Netherlds

Cardiff

Thames

London

C. Clear

Lands End
Scilly Is.

English Channel

English Channel
Is.

Str. of Dover

Brussel

C. Finisterre

Cantabrian Mts.

Iberian

Old Castile

Douro

Madrid

Tagus
New
Castile
Peninsula

Guadiana

Lisboa
C. da Roca

Sierra Morena

C. St. Vincent

Guadalquivir
Andalusia
Mulhacen
3478
Sa. Nevada

C. Trafalgar
Str. of Gibraltar
Gibraltar

Cantabrian Mts.

Pyrenees

Maladetta
3404

Ebro

Garonne

G. of Lion

Brittany

Paris

Seine

Loire

Massif
Central
Mt. Dore
1886

Cevennes

4861
Gironde

Bay of
Biscay

Ardennes
Eifel

Meuse
Hunsrück

Vosges

Saône

Rhine

Black Forest

Taunus

Westerwald

Jura

Mt. Blanc
4807

Zürich

ALPS

Po

Ligurian
Sea

Corsica

Str. of
Bonifacio

Sardinia

Balearic
Is.

MEDITER

Ty

Casablanca

Er Rif

Alger

Maritime Atlas

Plateau of the Shotts

Tunis

Palma

Canary Is.

Tenerife

Gran
Canaria

Fuerteventura

Toubkal
4165

Great Atlas

Saharan Atlas

Gulf of
Gabes

Sahara

Tropic of Cancer

Madeira

6293

Azores

Flores

Terceira
Pico
Sao Miguel

ft	m
12 000	4000
6000	2000
	1000
1200	400
600	200
	0
200	600
2000	6000
4000	12 000
m	ft

30

30

25

Projection: Bonne.   20   15   10   5   West from Greenwich   0   East from Greenwich   5   10

1:17 500 000

100   0   100   200   300   400   500 miles
100   0   200   400   600   800 km

Nordkapp   Nordkinn

Lofoten

Kebnekaise 2123

Scandinavia

L. Inari

Lappland

Kola Peninsula

Kanin Peninsula

Tundra

Pechora

Ob

Narodnaya 1894

Ural Mountains

West Siberian Plain

Irtysh

Umeälv

Torne älv

Indalsälven

Gulf of Bothnia

Finland

White Sea

Mezen

N. Dvina

Telpos Iz. 1617

Onega

Tobol

Gldhøpiggen 2469

Oslo

Stockholm

Vänern

Måleren

Vättern

Gotland

Åland Is.

Helsinki

Gulf of Finland

Neva Leningrad

L. Chudskoye

Lake Ladoga

Svir

L. Onega

Dvina

Rybinsk Res.

Gorkiy

Volga

Kama

Obshchi Syrt

Ural

Kirgiz Steppe

Valdai Hills

Volga

Moskva

Oka

Volga Heights

Skaw

Katte-gat

København

BALTIC SEA

North European Plain

Central Russian Uplands

Neman

Berlin

Oder

Vistula

Warszawa

Pripet

Pripet Marshes

Kiyevo Dnieper

Ukraine

Tsimlyansk Res.

Volga

Ust Urt Plateau

Karagiye Depression -132

Ore Mts. Prahao

Sudetes

Bohemian Forest

Moravian Hts.

Tatra 2655

Carpathians

Dniester

Bug

Don

Caspian Sea

-28

Kara Bogaz

Inn

Wien

Bakony Forest

Budapest

Plain of Hungary

Dráva

Sava

Tisza

Mureş

Transylvanian Alps

Prut

Odessa

Dnieper

Sea of Azov

Crimea

Kuban

Terek

Elbrus 5633

Caucasus

Transcaucasia

Kura

Baku

Dinaric Alps

Dalmatia

Beograd

Morava

Bucureşti

Wallachia

Danube

2211

Black Sea

Strait of Kerch

Pontine Mts.

Ararat 5165

L. Van

Kura

Araks

L. Urmia

Elburz Mts.

Tehran

Adriatic Sea

Apennines

Gran Sasso 2914

Roma

Str. of Otranto

Sofiya

Balkans

Rhodope

Balkan Peninsula

Istanbul

Bosporus

Sea of Marmara

Dardanelles

Pindus

Aegean Sea

Ankara

Kizil

Anatolia

Kurdistan

Mesopotamia

Calabria

Strait of Messina

Etna 3263

Sicily

C. Spartivento

Ionian Sea

Ionian Is.

Morea

Athinai

L. Tuz

Erciyas 3770

Taurus Mts.

Halab

Euphrates

Tigris

Baghdad

nian

Pantelleria

Malta

5121

C. Matapan

Rhodes

Crete

Cyprus

Bayrut

Levant

Syrian

Desert

Tripoli

MEDITERRANEAN SEA

Gulf of Sidra

Nile Delta

Tel Aviv-Yafo

Dead Sea -395

Persian Gulf

COPYRIGHT. GEORGE PHILIP & SON. LTD.

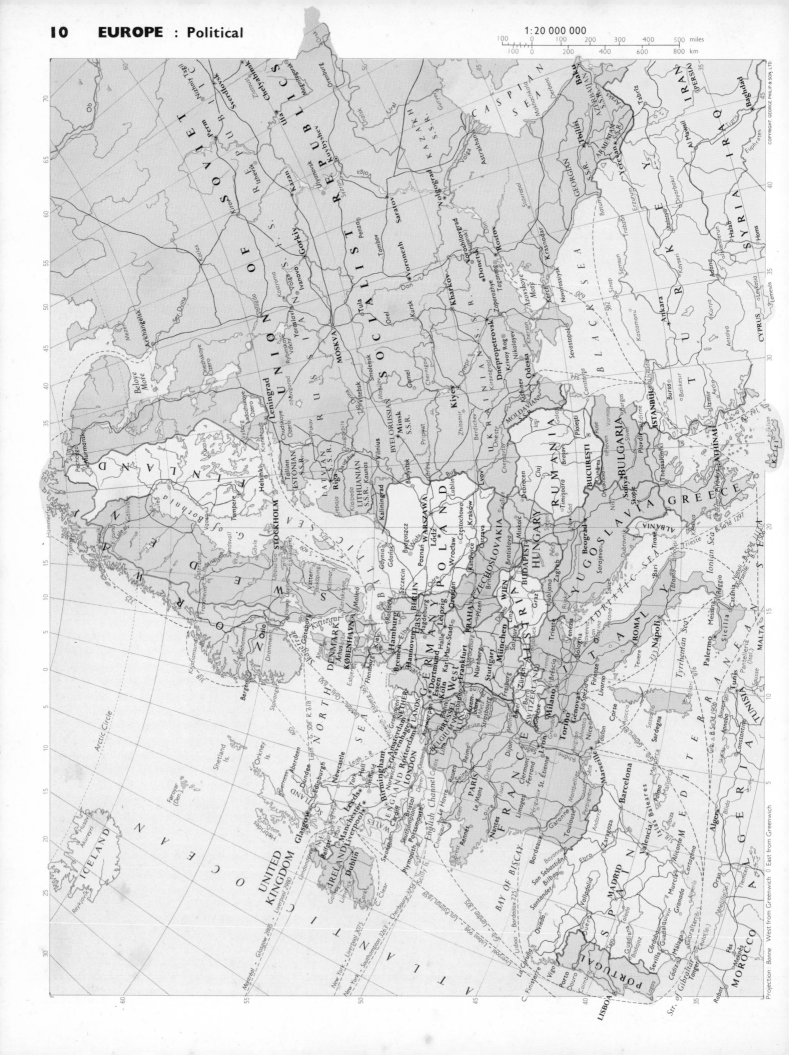

1:20 000 000

100   0   100   200   300   400   500 miles

100   0   200   400   600   800 km

COPYRIGHT GEORGE PHILIP & SON, LTD.

Projection: Bonne   West from Greenwich   0   East from Greenwich

1 : 4 000 000

20 0 20 40 60 miles
20 0 20 40 60 80 km

The DISTRICTS of Northern Ireland have been numbered and can be identified by reference to this table.

1	Londonderry	14	Craigavon
2	Limavady	15	Armagh
3	Coleraine	16	Newry & Mourne
4	Ballymoney	17	Banbridge
5	Moyle	18	Down
6	Larne	19	Lisburn
7	Ballymena	20	Antrim
8	Magherafelt	21	Newtownabbey
9	Cookstown	22	Carrickfergus
10	Strabane	23	North Down
11	Omagh	24	Ards
12	Fermanagh	25	Castlereagh
13	Dungannon	26	Belfast

Orkney Is. / Shetland Is.

1 Merseyside
2 Greater Manchester
3 West Yorkshire
4 South Yorkshire
5 West Glamorgan
6 Mid Glamorgan
7 South Glamorgan

ATLANTIC OCEAN — NORTH SEA — IRISH SEA — ENGLISH CHANNEL — St. George's Channel — Bristol Channel — Cardigan Bay

SCOTLAND — IRELAND — WALES — HIGHLAND — GRAMPIAN — TAYSIDE — CENTRAL — STRATHCLYDE — BORDERS — DUMFRIES AND GALLOWAY — NORTHUMBERLAND — CUMBRIA — DURHAM — CLEVELAND — NORTH YORKSHIRE — LANCASHIRE — HUMBERSIDE — LINCOLN — NORFOLK — SUFFOLK — WALES — CORNWALL — DEVON — SOMERSET — DORSET — HANTS — WEST SUSSEX — EAST SUSSEX — KENT — SURREY — LONDON — ESSEX

1:2 000 000

ORKNEY IS.
On same scale

SHETLAND IS.
On same scale

Projection: Conical, with two standard parallels.

West from Greenwich

COPYRIGHT. GEORGE PHILIP & SON, LTD.

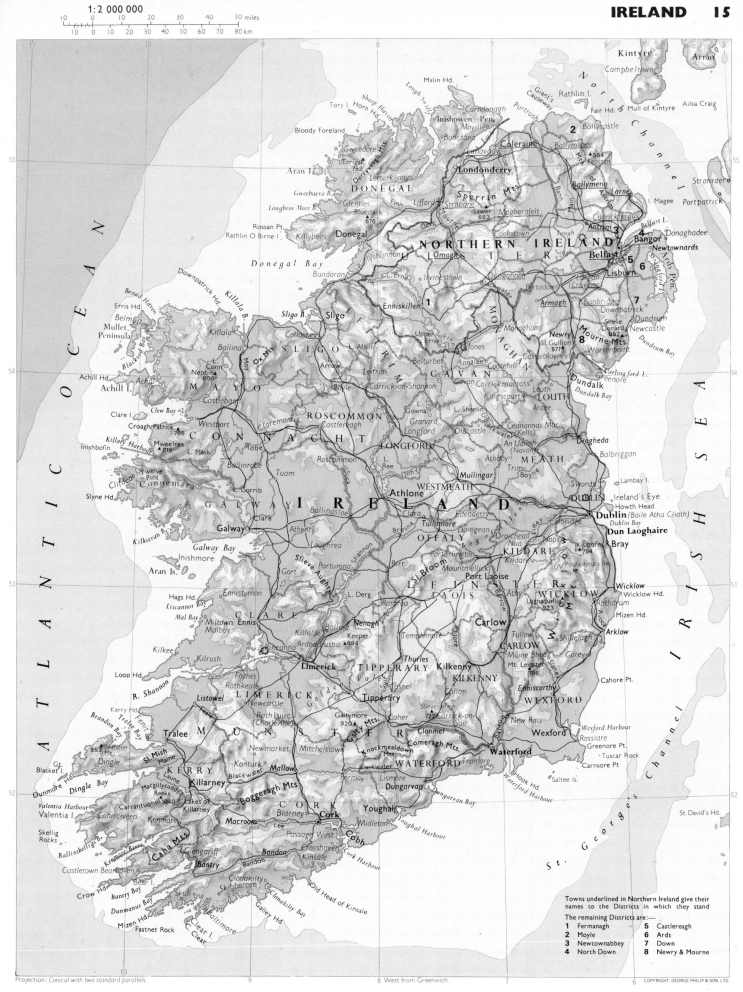

1:2 000 000

Towns underlined in Northern Ireland give their
names to the Districts in which they stand
The remaining Districts are:—

1	Fermanagh	5	Castlereagh
2	Moyle	6	Ards
3	Newtownabbey	7	Down
4	North Down	8	Newry & Mourne

1 : 2 500 000

10   0   10   20   30   40   50 miles
10   0   10 20 30 40 50 60 70 80 km

NORTH

SEA

ENGLAND

NETHERLANDS

BELGIUM

FRANCE

LUXEMBOURG

GERMANY

Major cities and places:

Bremerhaven, Wilhelmshaven, Nordenham, Oldenburg, Groningen, Emden, Leeuwarden, Assen, Emmen, Ostfriesland, Cloppenburg, Meppen, Lingen, Nordhorn, Osnabrück, Münster, Almelo, Hengelo, Enschede, Zwolle, Deventer, Apeldoorn, Amersfoort, Amsterdam, Haarlem, Leiden, 's-GRAVENHAGE (The Hague), ROTTERDAM, Utrecht, Arnhem, Nijmegen, Dordrecht, Breda, Tilburg, Eindhoven, Venlo, Krefeld, Düsseldorf, Mönchengladbach, KÖLN (Cologne), Bonn, Duisburg, ESSEN, Bochum, DORTMUND, Gelsenkirchen, Oberhausen, Mülheim, Wuppertal, Remscheid, Solingen, Leverkusen, Aachen, Maastricht, Liège, Hasselt, Antwerpen, BRUSSEL (Bruxelles), Gent, Brugge, Oostende (Ostend), Roeselare, Kortrijk, Tournai, Mons, Charleroi, Namur, Dinant, LUXEMBOURG, Bastogne, Arlon, Trier, Koblenz, Wiesbaden, Mainz, Saarbrücken, Metz, Nancy, Strasbourg

Dover, Calais, Boulogne-sur-Mer, Dunkerque, Lille, Roubaix, Arras, Amiens, Reims, Châlons-sur-Marne, Épernay, St. Dizier, PARIS, Versailles, St. Germain

Texel, Den Helder, Alkmaar, Hoorn, Enkhuizen, IJsselmeer, Noordoost Polder, Kampen, Harlingen, Sneek, Heerenveen, Hoogeveen, Terschelling, Ameland, Schiermonnikoog, Borkum, Juist, Norderney, Langeoog, Spiekeroog, Wangerooge

Projection: Conical with two standard parallels

East from Greenwich

COPYRIGHT. GEORGE PHILIP & SON, LTD.

ft   m
1200 400
600   200
0   0
50   150
m   ft

1:5 000 000

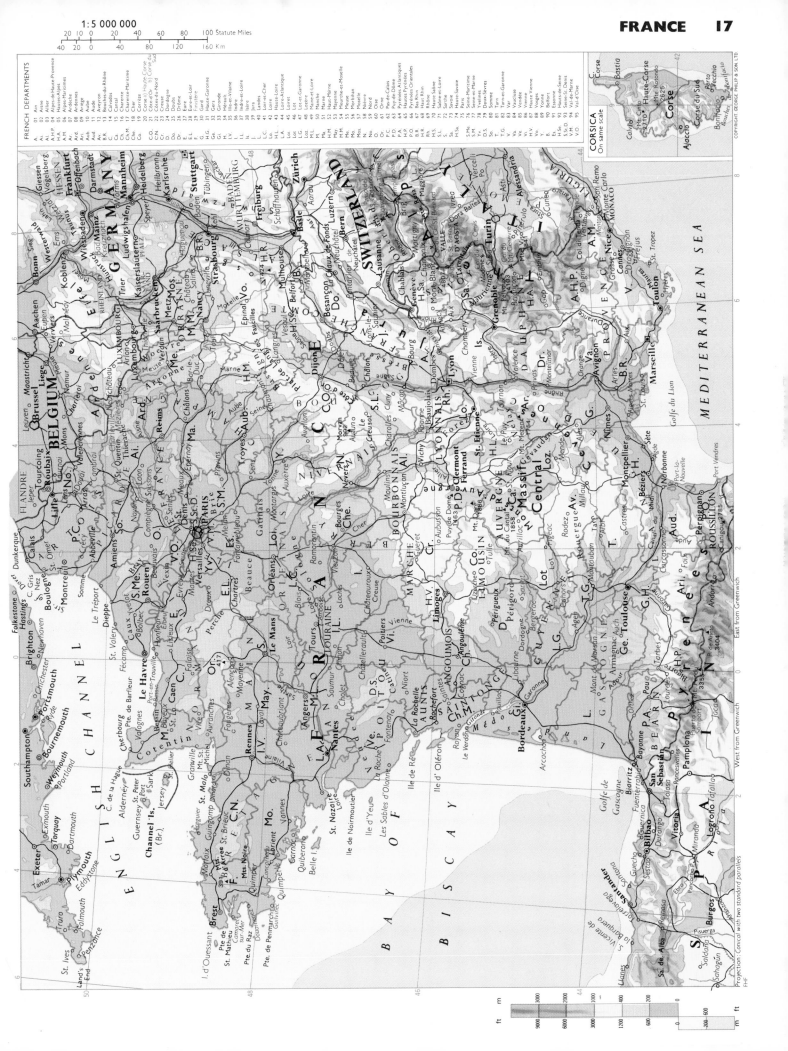

FRENCH DEPARTMENTS

A.	01 Ain
Ai.	02 Aisne
A.H.P.	04 Alpes-de-Haute-Provence
H.A.	05 Hautes-Alpes
A.M.	06 Alpes-Maritimes
Ard.	07 Ardèche
Ar.	08 Ardennes
Ari.	09 Ariège
Aub.	10 Aube
Aud.	11 Aude
Av.	12 Aveyron
B.R.	13 Bouches-du-Rhône
C.	14 Calvados
Ca.	15 Cantal
Ch.	16 Charente
Ch.M.	17 Charente-Maritime
Cr.	18 Creuse
D.S.	19 (Corse) Haute-Corse
	20 b) Corse-du-Sud
C.O.	21 Côte-d'Or
C.N.	22 Côtes-du-Nord
Do.	25 Doubs
Dr.	26 Drôme
E.L.	27 Eure-et-Loir
F.	29 Finistère
Gi.	33 Gironde
H.G.	31 Haute-Garonne
Ge.	32 Gers
H.L.	43 Haute-Loire
I.V.	35 Ille-et-Vilaine
I.	36 Indre
I.L.	37 Indre-et-Loire
Is.	38 Isère
Ju.	39 Jura
La.	40 Landes
L.C.	41 Loir-et-Cher
Lo.	42 Loire
L.A.	44 Loire-Atlantique
Lt.	45 Loiret
L.	46 Lot
L.G.	47 Lot-et-Garonne
Loz.	48 Lozère
M.L.	49 Maine-et-Loire
Ma.	50 Manche
M.	51 Marne
H.M.	52 Haute-Marne
May.	53 Mayenne
M.M.	54 Meurthe-et-Moselle
Me.	55 Meuse
Mo.	57 Moselle
N.	59 Nord
O.	60 Oise
Or.	61 Orne
P.C.	62 Pas-de-Calais
P.D.	63 Puy-de-Dôme
P.A.	64 Pyrénées-Atlantiques
H.P.	65 Hautes-Pyrénées
P.O.	66 Pyrénées-Orientales
B.R.	67 Bas-Rhin
H.R.	68 Haut-Rhin
Rh.	69 Rhône
S.L.	71 Saône-et-Loire
Sa.	72 Savoie
H.Sa.	73 Haute-Savoie
P.	75 Paris
S.Me.	76 Seine-Maritime
S.M.	77 Seine-et-Marne
Y.	78 Yvelines
D.S.	79 Deux-Sèvres
So.	80 Somme
T.	81 Tarn
T.G.	82 Tarn-et-Garonne
Va.	83 Var
Ve.	85 Vendée
Vi.	86 Vienne
H.V.	87 Haute-Vienne
Vo.	88 Vosges
B.	90 Belfort
Es.	91 Essonne
H.Se.	92 Hauts-de-Seine
S.S.t.D.	93 Seine-St.-Denis
V.M.	94 Val-de-Marne
V.O.	95 Val-d'Oise

CORSICA
On same scale

Corse

Projection: Conical with two standard parallels

ft m

12 000 4000

9000 3000

6000 2000

4500 1500

3000 1000

1200 400

600 200

0

200 600

2000 6000

m ft

DÉPARTEMENTS IN THE PARIS AREA
1 Ville de Paris   3 Val-de-Marne
2 Seine-St. Denis   4 Hauts-de-Seine

Projection: Conical with two standard parallels

West from Greenwich   East from Greenwich

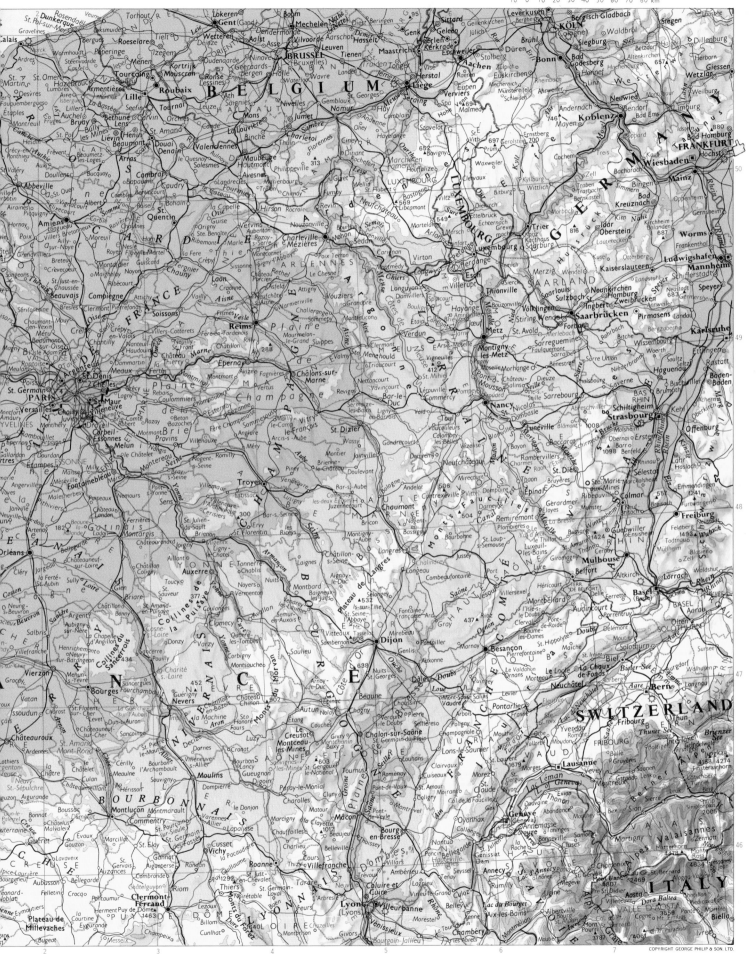

BELGIUM

FRANCE

LUXEMBOURG

GERMANY

SAARLAND

SWITZERLAND

ITALY

BRUSSEL
(Bruxelles)

Liège

Köln

Bonn

FRANKFURT

Wiesbaden

Mainz

Worms

Ludwigshafen

Mannheim

Speyer

Karlsruhe

Baden-Baden

Strasbourg

Mulhouse

Basel

Bern

Freiburg

Colmar

PARIS

Reims

Châlons-sur-Marne

Nancy

Metz

Saarbrücken

Troyes

Dijon

Besançon

Lyon
(Lyons)

Clermont-Ferrand

Genève
(Geneva)

Lausanne

1:2 500 000

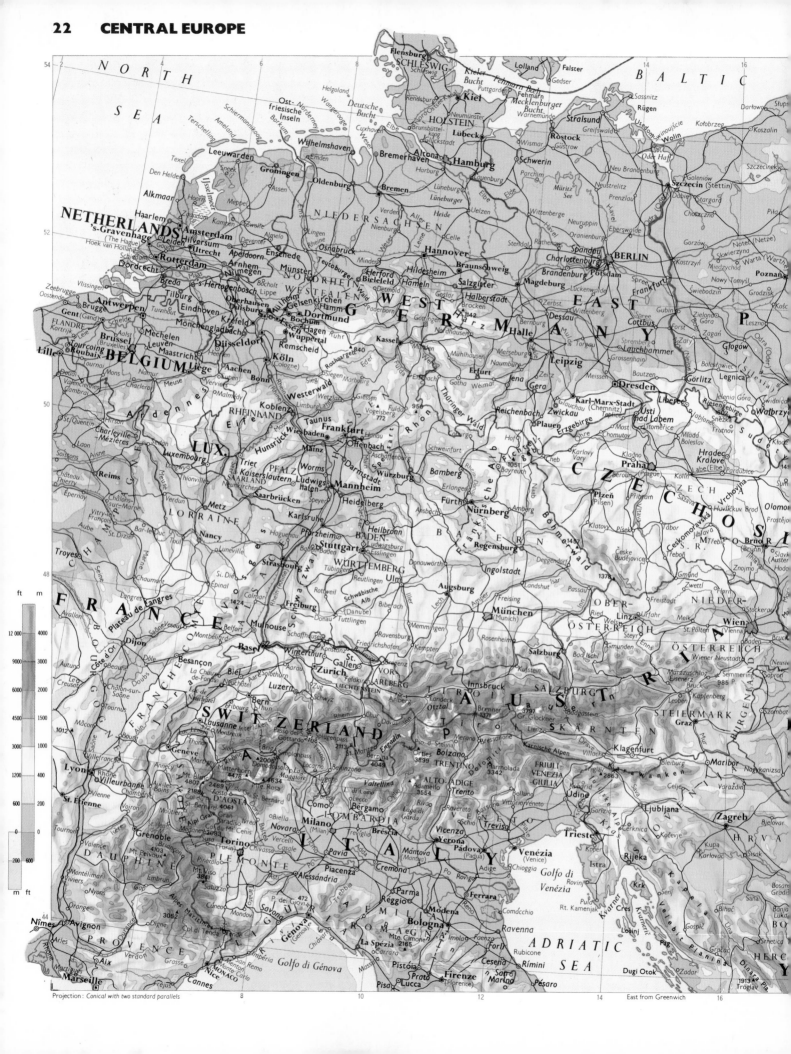

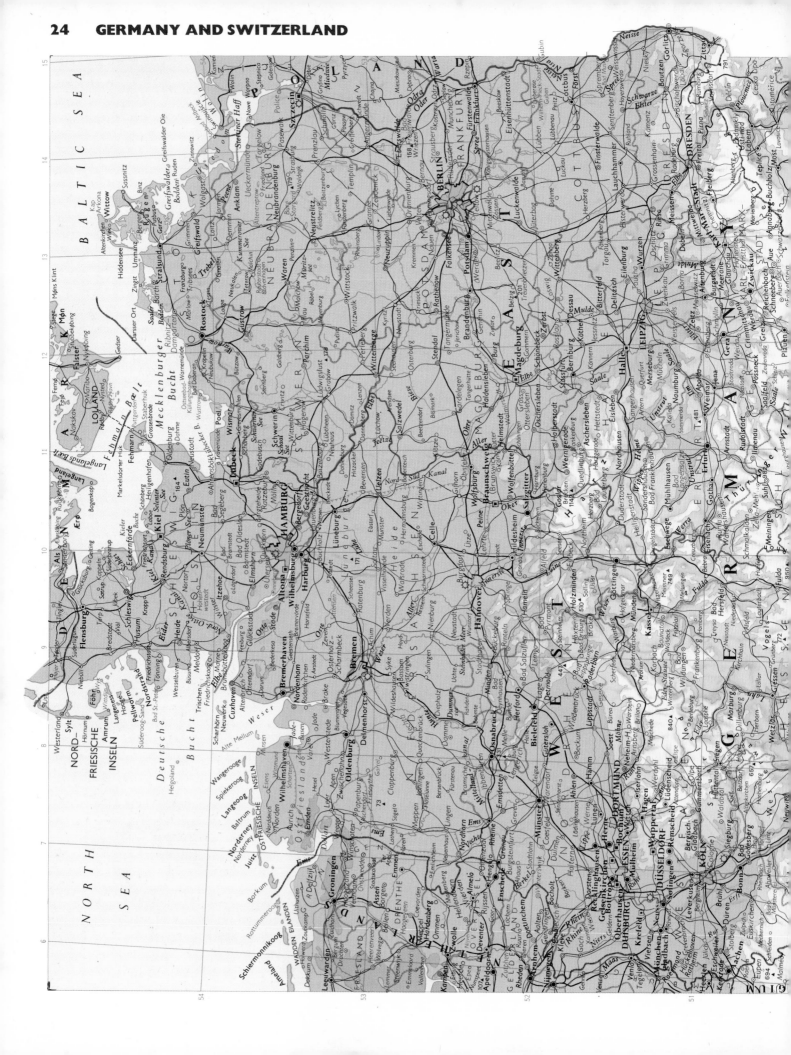

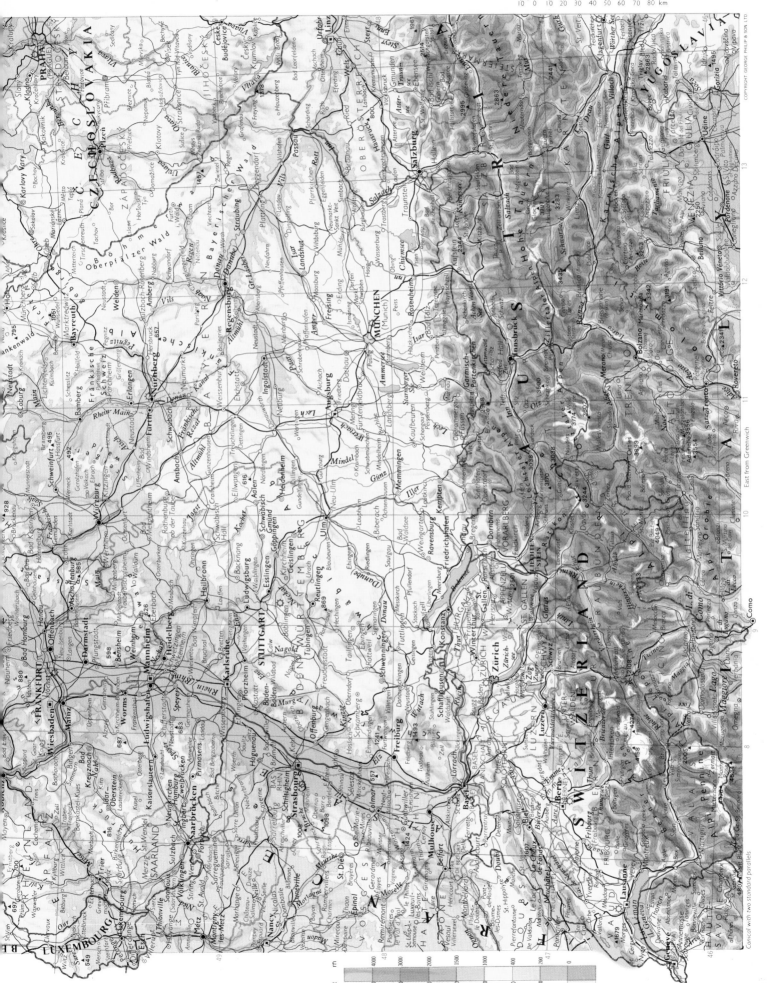

1:2 500 000

1:2 500 000

East from Greenwich

COPYRIGHT GEORGE PHILIP & SON LTD

POLAND

CZECHOSLOVAKIA

HUNGARY

YUGOSLAVIA

Wrocław (Breslau) · Opole · Częstochowa · Kielce · Katowice · Bytom · Gliwice · Kraków · Tarnów · Rzeszów · Przemyśl

Ostrava · Olomouc · Brno · Žilina · Bratislava · Košice · Uzhgorod

Wien (Vienna) · Budapest · Miskolc · Debrecen · Szeged · Pécs · Timişoara · Arad · Oradea

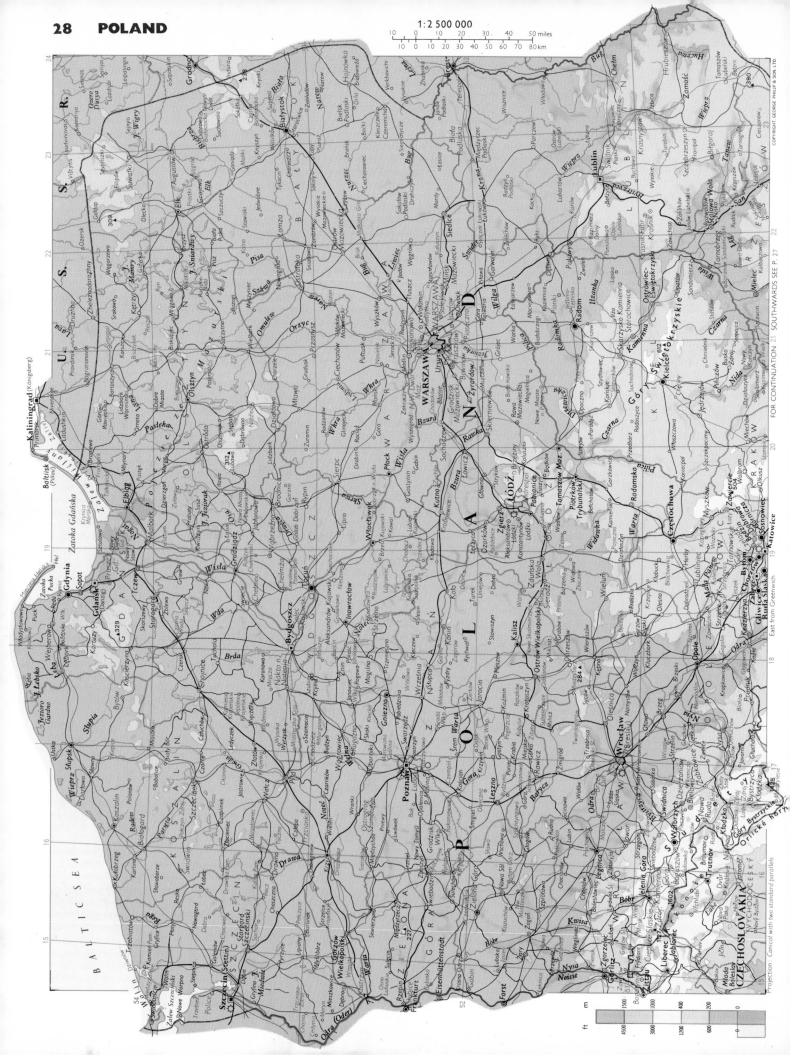

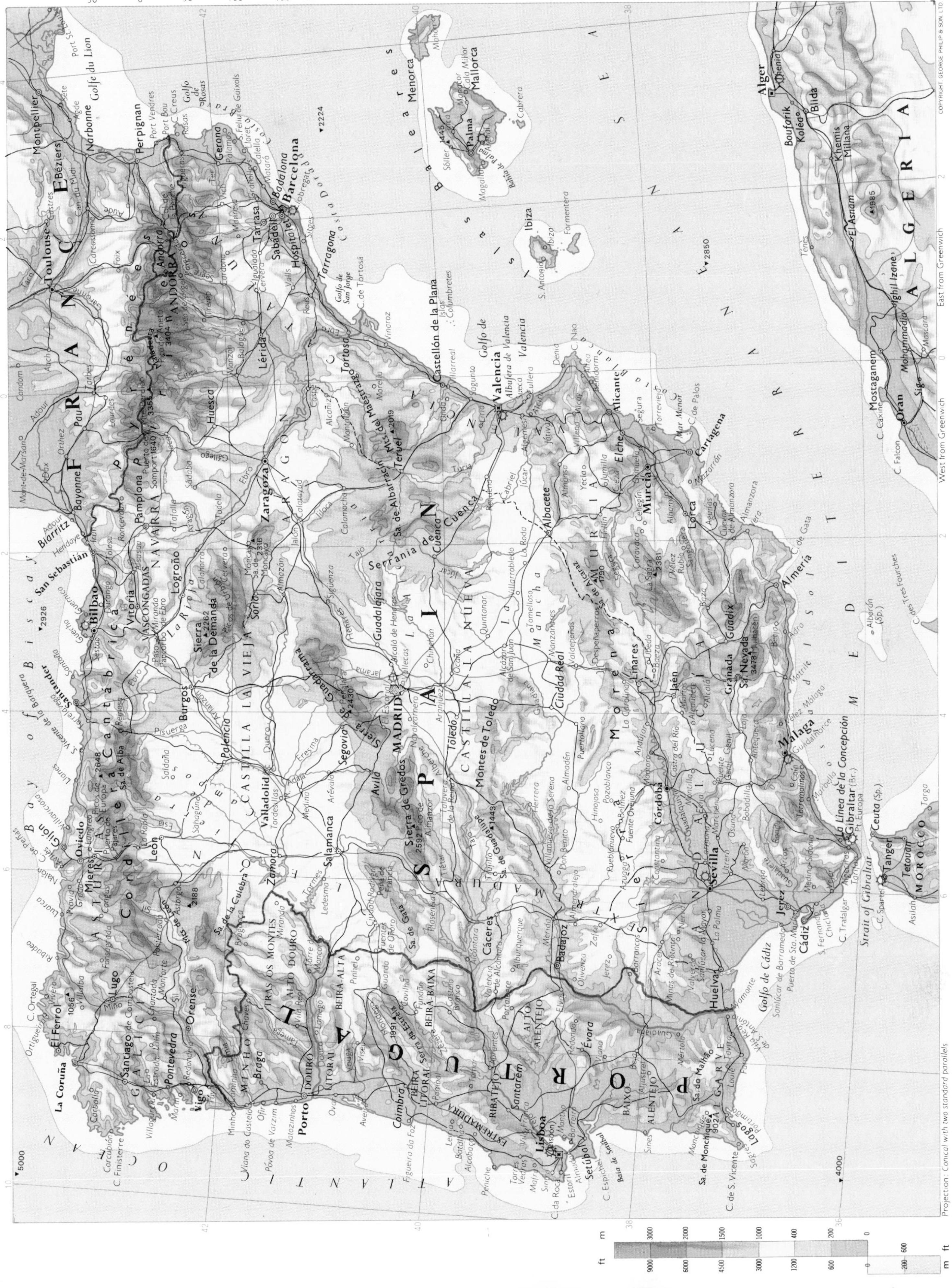

1:5,000,000

50 0 50 100 miles

50 0 50 100 150 km

COPYRIGHT GEORGE PHILIP & SON LTD

East from Greenwich

West from Greenwich

Projection : Conical with two standard parallels

FRANCE

ANDORRA

SPAIN

PORTUGAL

ALGERIA

MOROCCO

Bay of Biscay

ATLANTIC OCEAN

MEDITERRANEAN SEA

Baleares

Mallorca

Menorca

Ibiza

Pyrénées

Cordillera Cantábrica

Sierra de la Demanda

Serrania de Cuenca

Montes de Toledo

Sierra Morena

Sierra Nevada

Sierra de Gredos

Guadalquivir

Ebro

Tajo

Duero

Guadiana

MADRID
Barcelona
Valencia
Sevilla
Málaga
Zaragoza
Bilbao
Lisboa
Porto

m ft

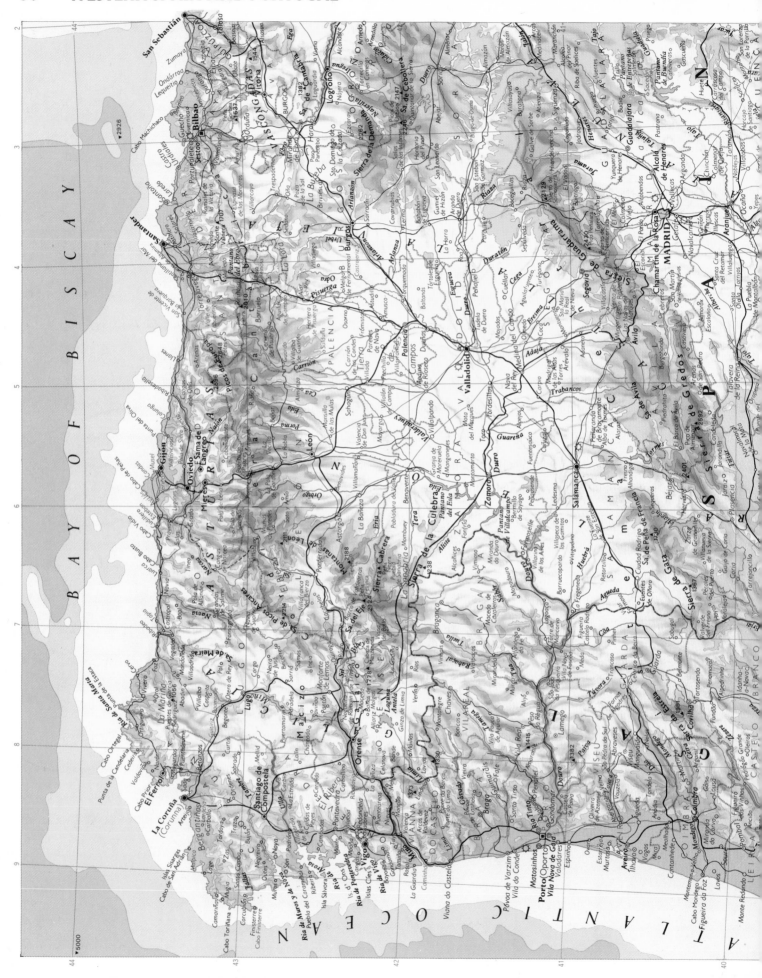

1:2 500 000

MEDITERRANEAN

SEA

MOROCCO

Golfo de Cádiz

Sierra Nevada

Córdoba

Sevilla

Granada

Málaga

Cádiz

Badajoz

Mérida

Cáceres

LISBOA

Setúbal

Évora

Beja

Faro

Huelva

Jaén

Tetouan

Tangier

Ceuta (Sp.)

Melilla (Sp.)

Algeciras

Strait of Gibraltar

Gibraltar (Br.)

ALGARVE

PORTALEGRE

ALENTEJO

West from Greenwich

Projection: Conical with two standard parallels

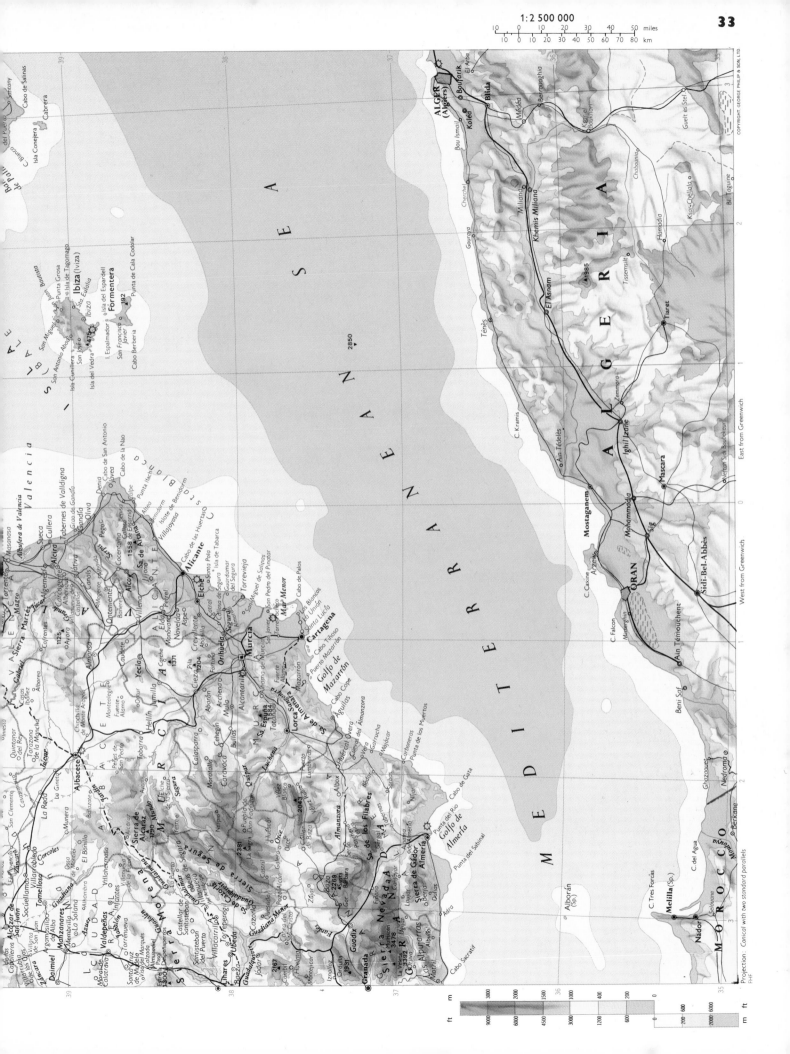

1:10 000 000

50 0 50 100 150 200 miles
50 0 100 200 300 km

POLAND
Poznań, Płock, Warszawa, Łódź, Radom, Lublin, Legnica, Wrocław, Chorzów, Kielce, Kraków, Tarnów, Przemyśl, Ostrava, Jablunkovský Pr. 550, Košice, Bratislava, Banská Stiavnica, Miskolc

Brest, Pinsk, Polesye, Chernigov, Konotop, Sumy, Belgorod
Kiyev, Zhitomir, Vinnitsa, Poltava, Kharkov
Kamenets-Podol'skiy, Uman, Pervomaysk, Kirovograd, Krivoy Rog, Dnepropetrovsk, Zaporozhye, Donetsk, Makeyevka, Gorlovka, Shakhty, Rostov, Novocherkassk, Volgograd, Voroshilovgrad

U. S. S. R. **U K R A I N I A N S. S. R.**

HUNGARY
Budapest, Kecskemét, Szeged, Hódmezővásárhely, Arad, Pécs, Subotica, Timişoara, Novi Sad, Beograd

RUMANIA
Oradea, Cluj, Braşov, Sibiu, Galaţi, Brăila, Ploieşti, Bucureşti, Craiova, Constanţa

MOLDAVIAN S.S.R.
Iaşi, Kishinev, Bendery, Tiraspol, Odessa, Kherson, Nikolayev, Melitopol, Berdyansk

Sea of Azov, Kerch, Krasnodar, Maykop, Armavir, Stavropol
Crimea, Simferopol, Sevastopol, Yalta, Feodosiya, Novorossiysk, Tuapse, Sukhumi, Batumi, Poti

B L A C K   S E A

BULGARIA
Sofiya, Plovdiv, Varna, Burgas, Ruse, Tolbukhin, Turnovo, Pleven, Stara Planina

YUGOSLAVIA
Zagreb, Banja Luka, Sarajevo, Mostar, Dubrovnik (Ragusa), Skopje, Niš

ALBANIA
Tirana, Durrës, Vlora, Elbasan

GREECE
Thessaloníki, Lárisa, Vólos, Athínai, Piraiévs, Patrai, Kórinthos, Pelopónnisos, Spárti, Kalamáta, Iráklion, Kríti

Ionian Sea, Aegean Sea

TURKEY
İstanbul, Üsküdar, İzmir, Bursa, Eskişehir, Ankara, Kayseri, Sivas, Konya, Adana, Antalya, Gaziantep, Antakya, İskenderun, Trabzon, Samsun

ISTANBUL — Karadeniz Boğazı (Bosporus), Marmara Denizi

CYPRUS — Levkosía (Nicosia), Lemesós, Larnaca

SYRIA — Halab, Hamā, Homs, Tarabulus
LEBANON — Bayrūt (Beirut), Dimashq (Damascus)
ISRAEL — Haifa, Tel Aviv-Yafo, Jerusalem
JORDAN — Ammān

EGYPT — El Qâhira, El Iskandariya, El Mahalla el Kubra, Tanta, Bûr Saîd, El Suweis, El Faiyûm

LIBYA — Banghāzī, Al Marj (Barce), Cyrene, Derna, Tobruq

M E D I T E R R A N E A N   S E A

Bari, Brindisi, Táranto, Golfo di Táranto, Reggio, Str. di Messina

COPYRIGHT. GEORGE PHILIP & SON. LTD.

MALTA
1:1 000 000
0   5   10 miles
0   5   10   15 km.

S.E. EUROPE
POLITICAL
1:25 000 000
Projection: Conical with two standard parallels

LIGURIAN SEA

Golfo di Génova

CORSE
(CORSICA)

ILES D'HYÈRES

CORSE

CORSICA

CORSE-DU-SUD

Golfo dell'
Asinara

SARDEGNA

SARDEGNA

SARDINIA

Golfo di
Oristano

Golfo di
Cágliari

TYRRHENIAN

SEA

ROMA
(Rome)

Golfo di
Gaeta

Isole
Ponziane

Ischia
(Naples)

Ustica

PALERMO

Trápani
Erice

Isole Égadi

Marsala

SICI

Sicilian Channel

Iles de la
Galite

TUNISIA

TUNIS

Golfe de Tunis

Pantelleria
(It.)

MEDITE

1:2 500 000

10   0   10   20   30   40   50 miles
10 0 10 20 30 40 50 60 70 80 km

ADRIATIC

SEA

IONIAN

SEA

MEDITERRANEAN SEA

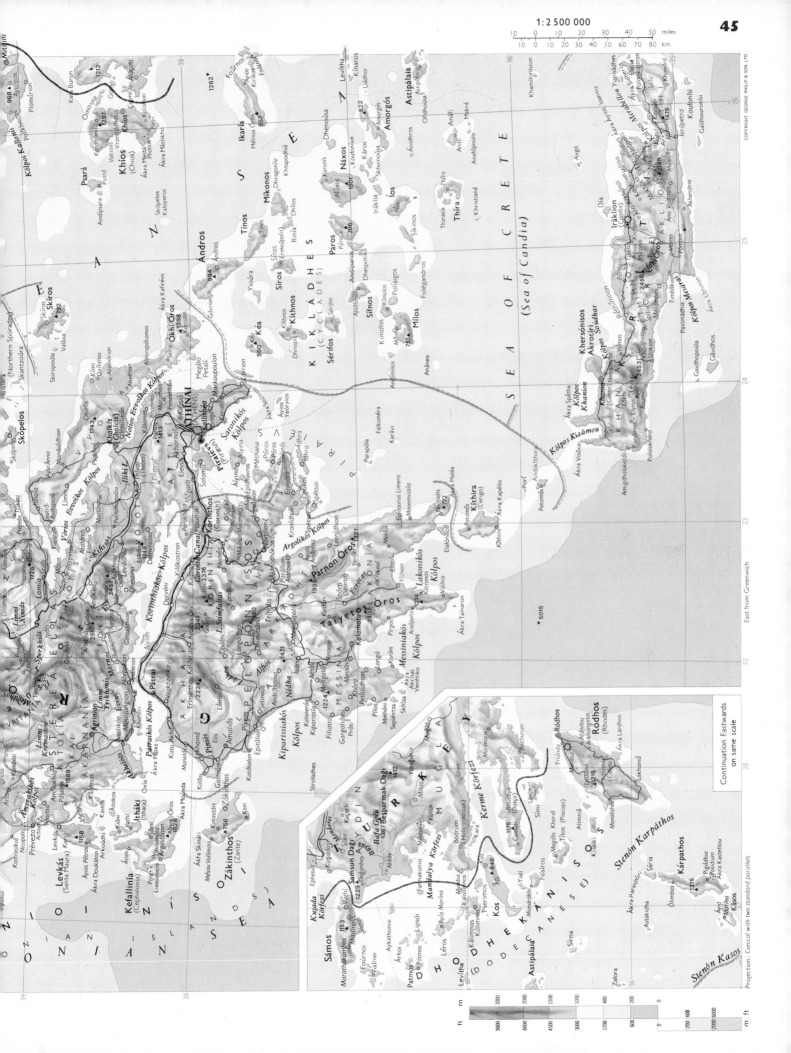

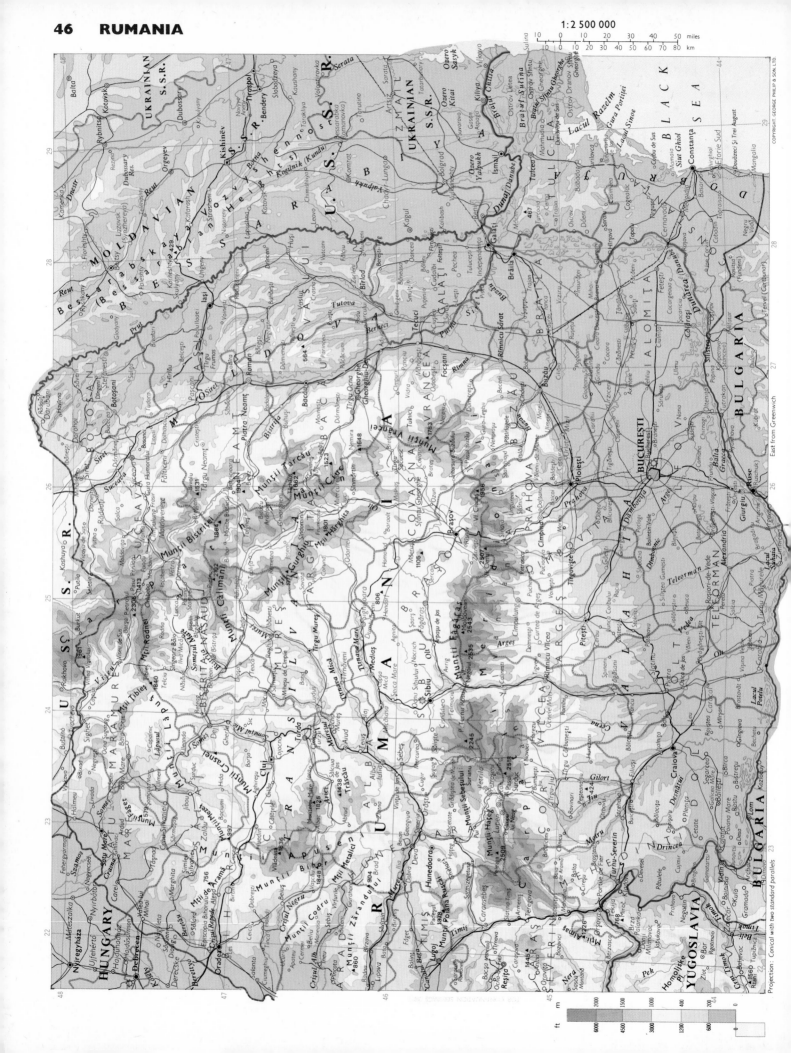

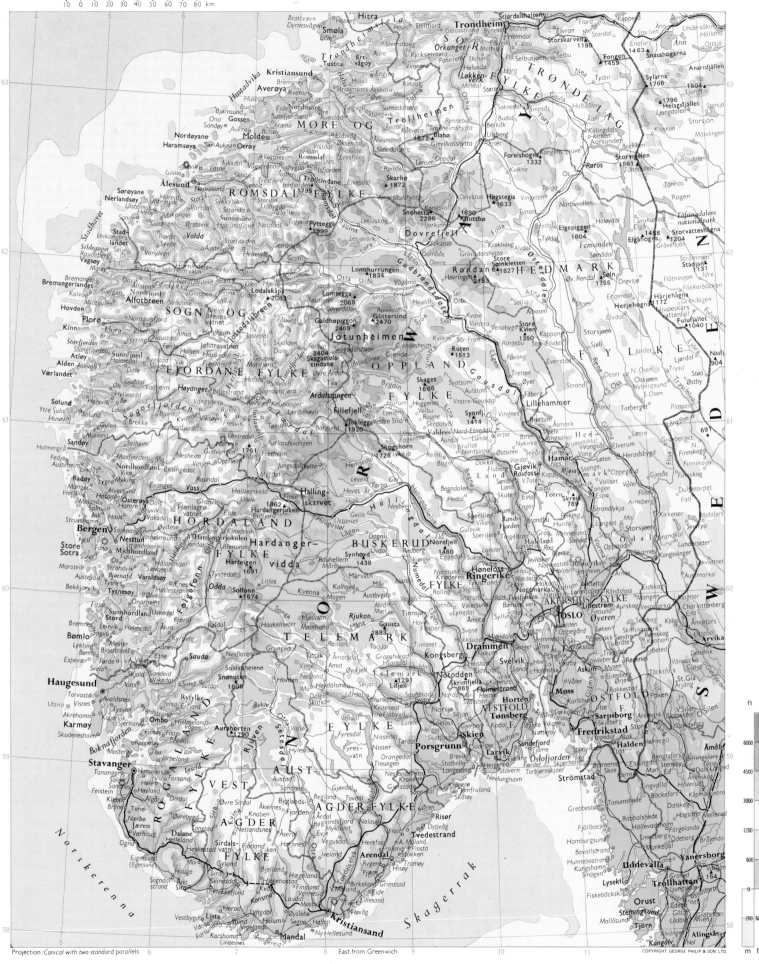

Projection: Conical with two standard parallels

East from Greenwich

COPYRIGHT. GEORGE PHILIP & SON. LTD.

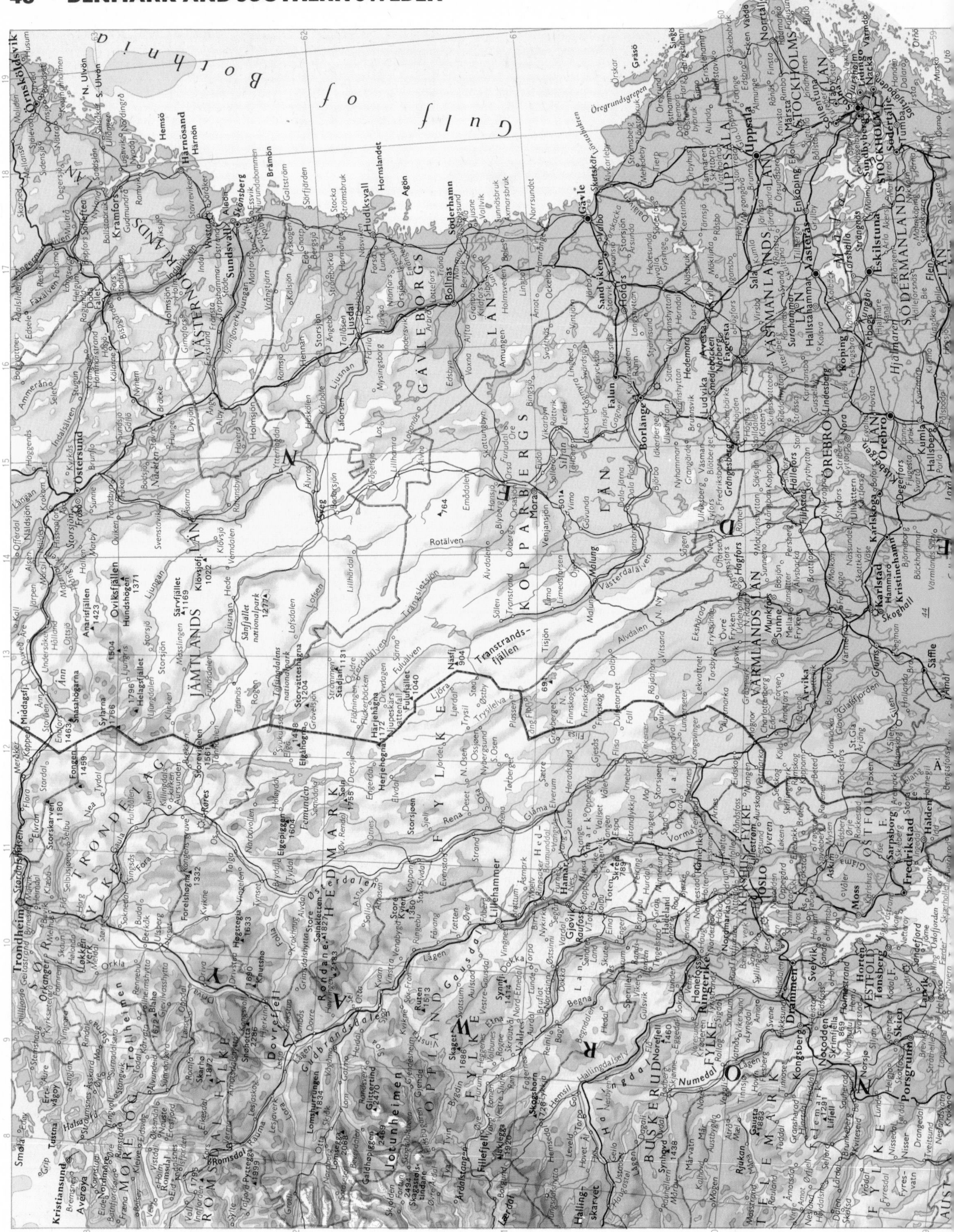

Gulf of Bothnia

VÄSTERNORRLANDS LÄN

JÄMTLANDS LÄN

GÄVLEBORGS LÄN

KOPPARBERGS LÄN

VÄSTMANLANDS LÄN

SÖDERMANLANDS LÄN

UPPSALA LÄN

STOCKHOLMS LÄN

ÖREBRO LÄN

VÄRMLANDS LÄN

SØR-TRØNDELAG FYLKE

NORD-TRØNDELAG FYLKE

MØRE OG ROMSDAL FYLKE

OPPLAND FYLKE

HEDMARK FYLKE

BUSKERUD FYLKE

AKERSHUS FYLKE

ØSTFOLD FYLKE

OSLO

VESTFOLD FYLKE

TELEMARK FYLKE

AUST-

Trondheim
Östersund
Härnösand
Sundsvall
Hudiksvall
Söderhamn
Bollnäs
Ljusdal
Gävle
Sandviken
Falun
Borlänge
Mora
Uppsala
STOCKHOLM
Södertälje
Eskilstuna
Västerås
Köping
Arboga
Örebro
Kumla
Karlstad
Kristinehamn
Säffle
Arvika
Hamar
Lillehammer
Gjøvik
Oslo
Drammen
Kongsberg
Hønefoss
Horten
Tønsberg
Sandefjord
Larvik
Skien
Porsgrunn
Fredrikstad
Sarpsborg
Moss
Halden
Kristiansund
Averøya

Dovrefjell
Jotunheimen
Rondane
Transtrandsfjällen
Härjehågna
Syljätfjäll
Helagsfjället 1796
Oviksfjällen
Sylarna 1766
Snasahögarna
Fongen 1459
Glittertind 2470
Galdhøpiggen 2469
Skagastølstindane 2405
Nuvkegga 1920
Storsjön
Siljan
Runn
Rotälven
Vänern
Fulufjället 1040
Städjan 1131
Klövsjöfjället 1169

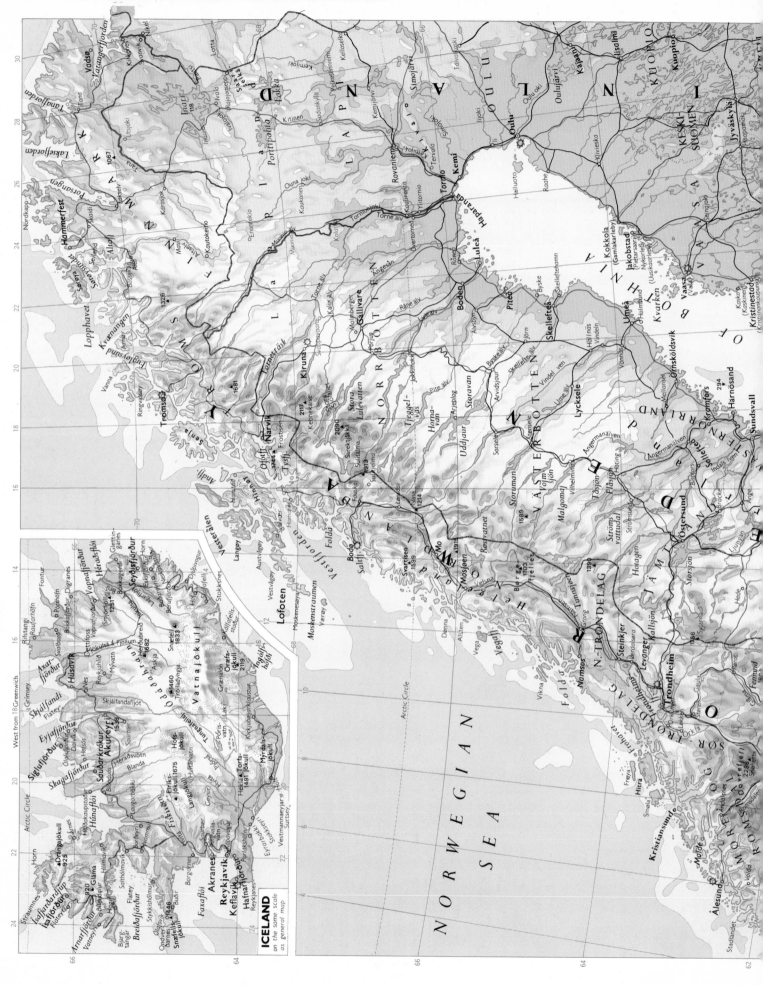

NORWEGIAN SEA

ICELAND
on the same scale
as general map

1:5 000 000

20 10 0 20 40 60 80 100 miles
40 20 0 40 80 120 160 km

BALTIC SEA

GULF OF FINLAND

GULF OF BOTHNIA

Gulf of Riga (Rīgas Jūras Līcis)

Skagerrak

Kattegat

The Sound

FINLAND

Helsinki (Helsingfors), Tampere, Turku (Åbo), Rauma, Pori, Uusikaupunki, Hämeenlinna, Lahti, Heinola, Kotka, Lovisa, Porvoo, Hangö (Hanko), Ekenäs, Kokemäenjoki

HÄME, UUSIMAA, TURKU JA PORI, KYMI

Åland (Ahvenanmaa), Mariehamn (Maarianhamina)

ESTONIAN S.S.R.
Tallinn, Pärnu, Haapsalu, Valga, Viljandi, Kingisepp, Hiiumaa (Dagö), Saaremaa (Ösel), Ruhnu

LATVIAN S.S.R.
Rīga, Jelgava, Liepāja, Ventspils, Valmiera, Cēsis, Tukums, Kuldīga

LITHUANIAN S.S.R.
Vilnius, Kaunas, Klaipėda, Telšiai, Šiauliai

R.S.F.S.R.
Kaliningrad, Sovetsk, Chernyakhovsk

POLAND
Gdańsk, Gdynia, Szczecin (Stettin), Bydgoszcz, Toruń, Grudziądz, Białystok, Grodno, Łomża, Ostrołęka, Olsztyn, Elbląg, Zatoka Gdańska, Słupsk, Koszalin, Kołobrzeg

GERMANY
Hamburg, Lübeck, Kiel, Rostock, Schwerin, Bremen, Bremerhaven, Wilhelmshaven, Oldenburg, Flensburg, Warnemünde, Greifswald, Stralsund, Rügen, Usedom, Wolin

NETHERLANDS
Groningen

DENMARK
København, Odense, Århus, Ålborg, Esbjerg, Randers, Kolding, Vejle, Horsens, Fredericia, Viborg, Herning, Silkeborg, Holstebro, Thisted, Frederikshavn, Hjørring, Roskilde, Korsør, Slagelse, Svendborg, Nykøbing, Abenrå, Sønderborg, Helsingør, Sjælland, Fyn, Lolland, Falster, Bornholm, Rønne, Store Bælt, Lille Bælt, Limfjorden

SWEDEN
STOCKHOLM, Uppsala, Västerås, Örebro, Norrköping, Linköping, Eskilstuna, Södertälje, Nyköping, Oxelösund, Nynäshamn, Göteborg, Malmö, Helsingborg, Landskrona, Trelleborg, Ystad, Kristianstad, Karlskrona, Karlshamn, Kalmar, Västervik, Oskarshamn, Nybro, Växjö, Jönköping, Värnamo, Ljungby, Halmstad, Falkenberg, Varberg, Borås, Alingsås, Mölndal, Trollhättan, Vänersborg, Uddevalla, Lidköping, Skövde, Mariestad, Karlstad, Kristinehamn, Filipstad, Arvika, Åmål, Falun, Borlänge, Ludvika, Avesta, Hedemora, Fagersta, Sala, Köping, Arboga, Gävle, Sandviken, Hudiksvall, Söderhamn, Bollnäs, Mora, Gällivare

ÖLAND, GOTLAND, Visby, Fårö, Gotska Sandön, Slite, Burgsvik, Hemse

Provinces/Counties: GÄVLEBORG, KOPPARBERG, VÄSTMANLAND, UPPSALA, SÖDERMANLAND, ÖSTERGÖTLAND, ÖREBRO, VÄRMLAND, ÄLVSBORG, GÖTEBORG OCH BOHUS, SKARABORG, HALLAND, JÖNKÖPING, KRONOBERG, KALMAR, BLEKINGE, SKÅNE, DALARNA

Lakes: Vänern, Vättern, Hjälmaren, Mälaren, Siljan

NORWAY
Oslo, Bergen, Stavanger, Kristiansand, Drammen, Skien, Tønsberg, Larvik, Sandefjord, Fredrikstad, Sarpsborg, Halden, Moss, Horten, Kongsberg, Hønefoss, Hamar, Lillehammer, Gjøvik, Kongsvinger, Haugesund, Egersund, Flekkefjord, Mandal, Arendal, Grimstad, Lillesand, Risør, Kragerø, Notodden, Rjukan

Counties: HORDALAND, ROGALAND, VEST-AGDER, AUST-AGDER, TELEMARK, BUSKERUD, VESTFOLD, ØSTFOLD, AKERSHUS, OPPLAND, HEDMARK, SOGN OG FJORDANE

Hardangerfjorden, Sognefjorden

Projection: Conical with two standard parallels

m ft elevation scale: 6000 4500 3000 1500 600 0 -200 ft / 2000 1500 1000 400 200 0 -600 m

1:5 000 000

50 0 50 100 miles

50 0 50 100 150 km

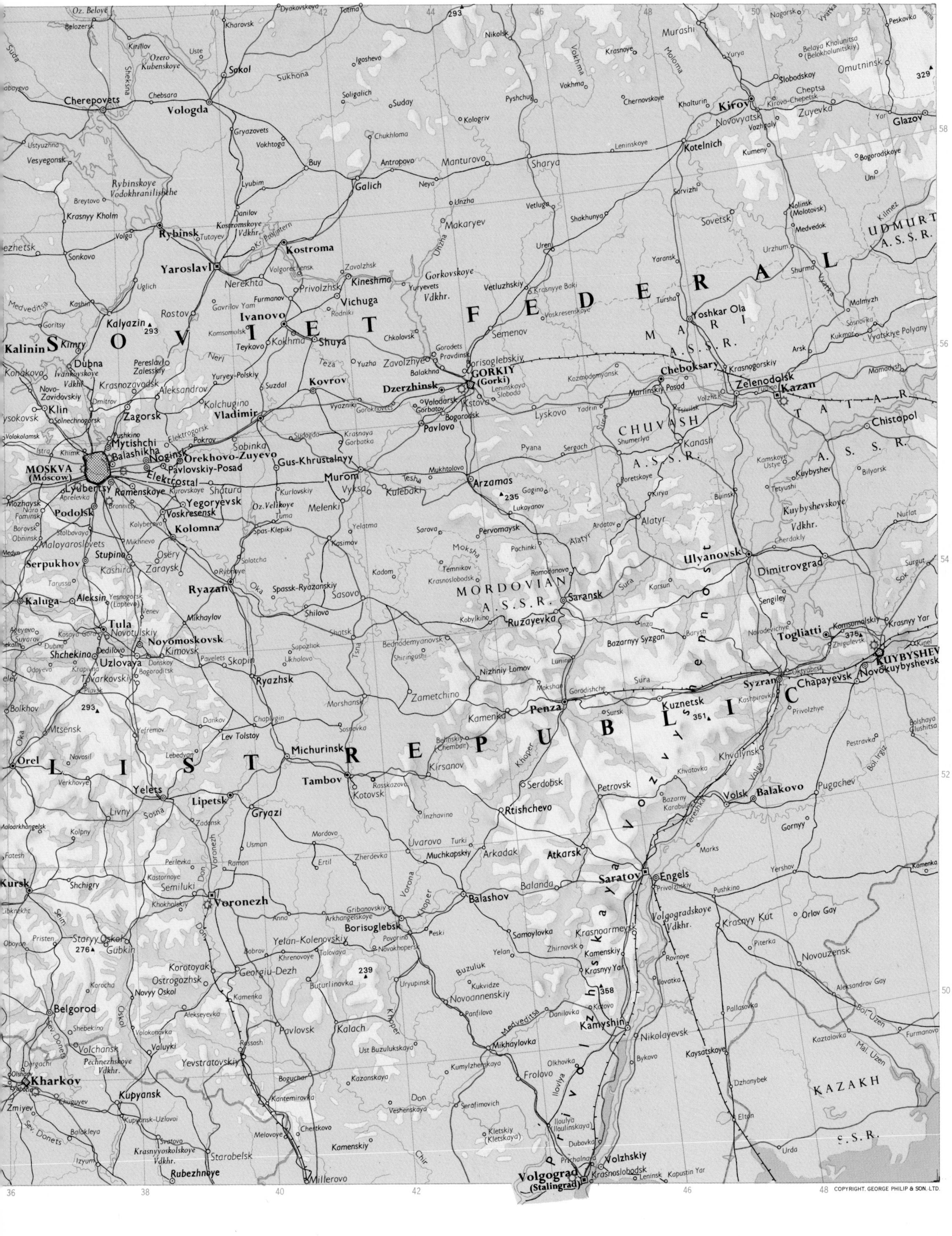

S O V I E T   F E D E R A L

. . . L I S T   R E P U B L I C

Moskva (Moscow)

GORKIY (Gorki)

Kazan

KUYBYSHEV

Volgograd (Stalingrad)

Saratov

Voronezh

Kharkov

Kirov

Cheboksary

Ulyanovsk

Penza

Tambov

Ryazan

Tula

Kaluga

Orel

Kursk

Belgorod

Lipetsk

Yelets

Vologda

Cherepovets

Yaroslavl

Kostroma

Ivanovo

Vladimir

Murom

Kolomna

Serpukhov

Podolsk

Kalinin

Rybinsk

Kalyazin

CHUVASH A.S.S.R.

MARI A.S.S.R.

MORDOVIAN A.S.S.R.

TATAR A.S.S.R.

UDMURT A.S.S.R.

KAZAKH S.S.R.

Zelenodolsk

Dzerzhinsk

Arzamas

Saransk

Ruzayevka

Syzran

Togliatti

Novokuybyshevsk

Chapayevsk

Dimitrovgrad

Kuznetsk

Balakovo

Volsk

Engels

Kamyshin

Nikolayevsk

Volzhskiy

Krasnoslobodsk

Yoshkar Ola

COPYRIGHT. GEORGE PHILIP & SON. LTD.

Projection: Conical with two standard parallels

1:5 000 000

50   0   50   100 miles
50   0   50   100   150 km

East from Greenwich

KAZAKH S.S.R.

Prikaspiyskaya Nizmennost

Ergeni Vozvyshennost

Povolzhskaya Vozvyshennost

KALMYK A.S.S.R.

CHECHENO-INGUSH A.S.S.R.

DAGESTAN A.S.S.R.

KABARDINO-BALKAR A.S.S.R.

N. OSETIN A.S.S.R.

ABKHAZ A.S.S.R.

ADZHAR A.S.S.R.

GEORGIAN S.S.R.

ARMENIAN S.S.R.

AZERBAIJAN S.S.R.

CASPIAN SEA

Bolshoi Caucasus

Maly Caucasus

Daglar Mountains

Volgograd (Stalingrad) Volzhskiy Krasnoslobodsk Kamyshin Nikolayevsk Novouzensk

Astrakhan Guryev Elista (Stepnoi)

Rostov Batalysk Azov **Novocherkassk** **Shakhty** Gukovo **Krasnodar** **Armavir** Maykop **Stavropol** Nevinnomyssk Cherkessk Mineralnyye Vody Pyatigorsk Yessentuki Kislovodsk Karachayevsk **Nalchik** **Ordzhonikidze** **Groznyy** Gudermes **Makhachkala** Kaspiysk Derbent Mozdok Prokhladnyy Kizlyar

Sochi Adler Gagra Sukhumi Ochamchire Poti Kobuleti **Batumi** **Kutaisi** Samtredia Tskhinvali Gori **Tbilisi** Rustavi Telavi

Kirovakan Leninakan Kars **Yerevan** Echmiadzin Kirovabad Mir-Bashir Mingechaur Shemakha Sumgait **BAKU** Kazi Magomed

Elbrus 5633 Kazbek 5047 Tebulos 4492 Bazar Dyuzi 4466 Aragats 4090 Baba dag 3629

Ozero Sevan Mingechaurskoye Vdkhr. Oz. Manych-Gudilo Tsimlyanskoye Vdkhr.

COPYRIGHT. GEORGE PHILIP & SON. LTD

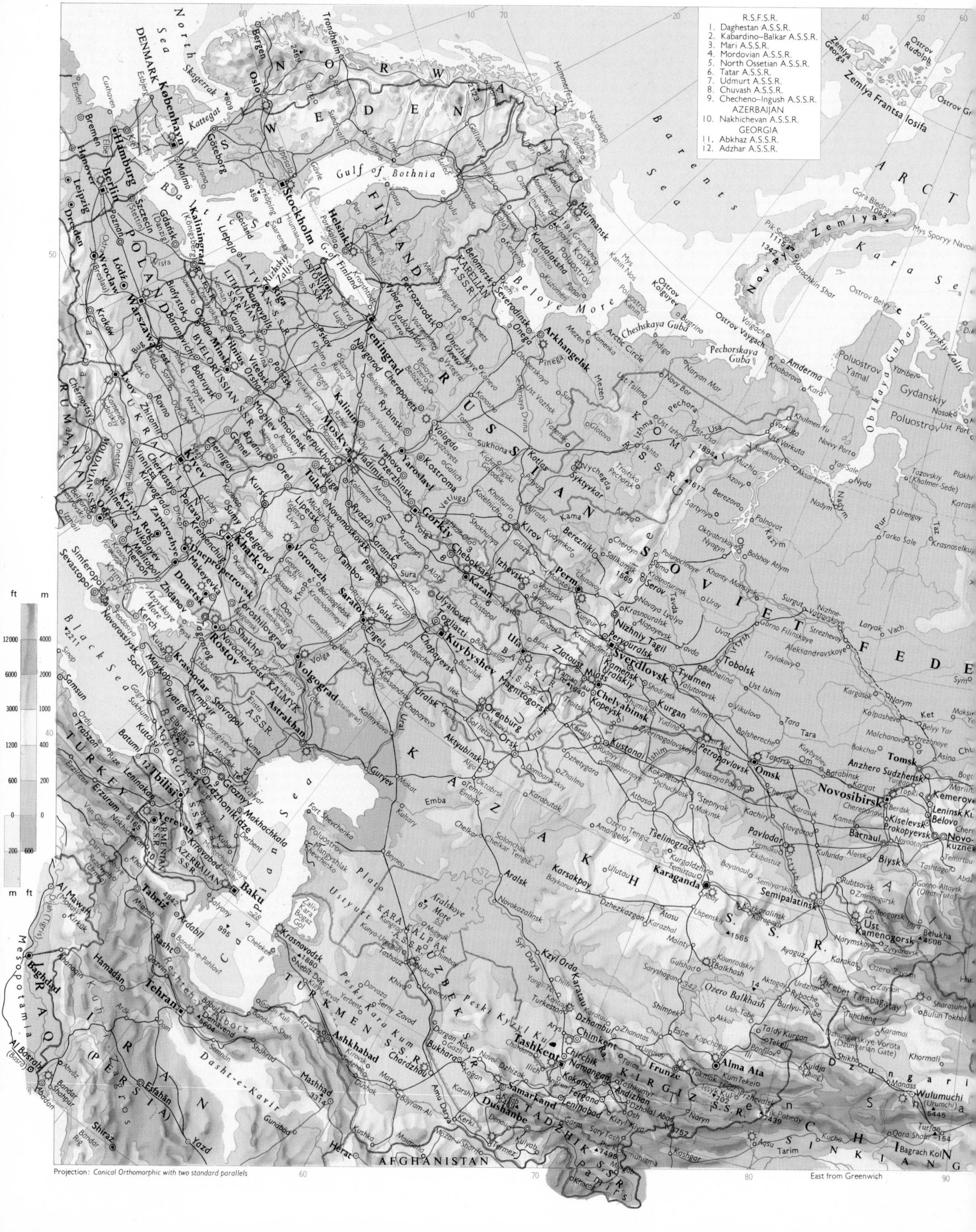

R.S.F.S.R.
1. Daghestan A.S.S.R.
2. Kabardino-Balkar A.S.S.R.
3. Mari A.S.S.R.
4. Mordovian A.S.S.R.
5. North Ossetian A.S.S.R.
6. Tatar A.S.S.R.
7. Udmurt A.S.S.R.
8. Chuvash A.S.S.R.
9. Checheno-Ingush A.S.S.R.
AZERBAIJAN
10. Nakhichevan A.S.S.R.
GEORGIA
11. Abkhaz A.S.S.R.
12. Adzhar A.S.S.R.
ft m
12000 4000
6000 2000
3000 1000
1200 400
600 200
0 0
200 600
m ft
North Sea
NORWAY
SWEDEN
FINLAND
DENMARK
POLAND
Barents Sea
Kara Sea
ARCTIC
Zemlya Frantsa Iosifa
Novaya Zemlya
Gulf of Bothnia
Baltic Sea
Beloye More
Black Sea
Caspian Sea
Aralskoye More
RUSSIAN SOVIET FEDERATIVE
KAZAKH S.S.R.
UKRAINIAN S.S.R.
BYELORUSSIAN S.S.R.
TURKMEN S.S.R.
UZBEK S.S.R.
KIRGIZ S.S.R.
TADZHIK S.S.R.
TURKEY
IRAQ
IRAN (PERSIA)
AFGHANISTAN
SINKIANG
Moskva
Leningrad
Kiyev
Kharkov
Gorkiy
Kuybyshev
Sverdlovsk
Novosibirsk
Tashkent
Alma Ata
Baku
Tbilisi
Yerevan
Tehran
Baghdad
Stockholm
Helsinki
Oslo
København
Berlin
Hamburg
Warszawa
Projection: Conical Orthomorphic with two standard parallels
East from Greenwich

59

1:20 000 000

100   0   100   200   300   400   500 miles
100   0   200   400   600   800 km

COPYRIGHT. GEORGE PHILIP & SON. LTD.

Boundaries of U.S.S.R.
Boundaries of S.S.R.
Boundaries of A.S.S.R.

1:50 000 000

250   0   250   500   750   1000 miles
250   0   500   1000   1500 km

COPYRIGHT. GEORGE PHILIP & SON LTD.

PACIFIC OCEAN

ARCTIC OCEAN

INDIAN OCEAN

North Pole

Aleutians

Bering Str.
C. Dezhnev
Bering Sea
Kamchatka Peninsula
Kryucevskaya Vol. 4750
Sea of Okhotsk
Kurile Is.
Sakhalin
I. de Perouse Str.
Hokkaido
Honshu
Bonin Is.
Japan
Kyushu
Korea Str.
Korea
Formosa
Ryukyu Is.
East China Sea
Guam
Caroline Is.
Pelew Is.
New Guinea
Halmahera
Moluccas
Ceram
Celebes Sea
Celebes
Banda Sea
Flores Sea
Timor
Arafura Sea
Australia
Flores
Bali
Java Sea
Java
Sunda Is.
Str. of Malacca
Sumatra
Borneo
Palawan
Sulu Sea
Philippine Is.
Luzon
Mindanao
Cape Johnson Deep 10,497
Hainan
G. of Tonkin
Malay Peninsula
G. of Siam
Menam
Mekong
Salween
Irrawaddy
Andaman Is.
Nicobar Is.
Bay of Bengal
Ceylon
Palk Strait
Chagos Arch.
Maldive Is.
Laccadive Is.
Amirantes
Seychelles
Socotra
G. of Aden
Somali Peninsula
Ras Asir (C. Guardafui)
Red Sea
Arabian Sea
Gulf of Oman
Persian Gulf
G. of Oman
Ar Rub al Khali
Arabia
Gulf of Suez
Suez Canal
Sinai Pen.
Nile
Libyan Desert
Mediterranean Sea
Adriatic Sea
Rhine
Elbe
Oder
Danube
Vistula
Carpathians
North Sea
British Isles
Iceland
Greenland
Baltic Sea
Scandinavia
Finland
North Cape
Arctic Circle
Kola Pen.
White Sea
N. Dvina
Kolguyev I.
Novaya Zemlya
Barents Sea
Kara Sea
Svalbard
Narodnaya 1894
Ural Mountains
Ural
Volga
Don
Black Sea
Bosporus
Anatolia
Taurus Mts.
Cyprus
Dead Sea
Syrian Desert
Tigris
Euphrates
Mesopotamia
Ararat 5156
Elburz Mts.
Demavend 5603
Caspian Sea
Caucasus
Elbruz 5633
North European Plain
Central Russian Uplands
West Siberian Plain
Ob
Irtysh
Tobol
Aral Sea
Syr Darya
Amu Darya
Turan Plain
Balkhash L.
Ili
Chu
Steppes
Plateau of Iran
Great Salt Desert
Zagros
Hilmand
Seistan
Helmand
Baluchistan
Thar
Indus
Sulaiman Ra.
Solaiman Ra.
Hindu Kush
Karakoram Ra.
Pamirs
Communism Pk. 7495
Tien Shan
Tarim
Tarim Basin
Takla Makan
Turfan Basin
Lop Nor
Altai
Belukha 4506
Sayan Mts.
Plateau of Mongolia
Selenga
Angara
L. Baikal
Yablonovy Ra.
Lena
Aldan
Stanovoy Ra.
Verkhoyansk Range
Central Siberian Plateau
Lower Tunguska
Yenisei
Taimyr Peninsula
C. Chelyuskin
Severnaya Zemlya
Laptev Sea
New Siberian Is.
Wrangel I.
Indigirka
Kolyma
Gydan Ra. (Kolyma)
Srednny Ra.
Amur
Manchurian Plain
Sungari
Great Khingan Mts.
Sikhote Alin Ra.
Sea of Japan
Port Arthur
Yellow Sea
Great Plain of China
Hwang Ho
Hwang
China
Koko Nor
Kunlun Shan
Plateau of Tibet
Everest 8848
Tsangpo
Brahmaputra
Himalaya
Ganges
Godavari
Kistna
Western Ghats
Eastern Ghats
Deccan
India
Narmada
Tapti
Yamuna
C. Comorin
Gulf of Cambay
Si-kiang
Yangtse Kiang
Lake Rudolf
Tropic of Cancer
Equator
East from Greenwich

Land (m / ft)
6000 / 18 000
4000 / 12 000
2000 / 6000
1000 / 3000
600 / 1200
400 / 600
200 / 0
0
Sea (m / ft)
200 / 600
2000 / 6000
4000 / 12 000
6000 / 18 000
8000 / 24 000

Projection: Bonne

1:50 000 000

250 0 250 500 750 1000 miles
250 0 500 1000 1500 km

Projection: Bonne

PACIFIC OCEAN

ARCTIC OCEAN

INDIAN OCEAN

U. S. S. R.

CHINESE REPUBLIC

MONGOLIA

INNER MONGOLIA

MANCHURIA

SINKIANG - UIGUR

TIBET

INDIA

PAKISTAN

AFGHANISTAN

IRAN (PERSIA)

IRAQ

SAUDI ARABIA

TURKEY

SYRIA

EUROPE

AFRICA

AUSTRALIA

INDONESIA

PHILIPPINES

MALAYSIA

BURMA

THAILAND (SIAM)

VIETNAM

LAOS

NEPAL

KASHMIR

OMAN

YEMEN

SOUTH YEMEN

JORDAN

ISRAEL

LEBANON

KUWAIT

EGYPT

LIBYA

SUDAN

ETHIOPIA

SOMALI REP

KENYA

TANZANIA

ZAIRE

ZAMBIA

UGANDA

RWANDA

BURUNDI

MALAWI

UNITED KINGDOM

ICELAND

SRI LANKA (CEYLON)

BANGLADESH

HONG KONG (Br.)

Tokyo
Yokohama
Osaka
Kyoto
Nagasaki
Shanghai
Nanking
Peiping
Tientsin
Wuhan
Canton
Chungking
Chengtu
Kunming
Foochow
Soochow
Tsingtao
Harbin
Vladivostok
Khabarovsk
Moskva
Leningrad
Warszawa
Berlin
Paris
London
Roma
Wien
Istanbul
Ankara
Baghdad
Tehran
Esfahan
Shiraz
Karachi
Bombay
Delhi
Calcutta
Madras
Hyderabad
Ahmadabad
Lahore
Kabul
Tashkent
Samarkand
Novosibirsk
Omsk
Sverdlovsk
Chelyabinsk
Magnitogorsk
Irkutsk
Krasnoyarsk
Tomsk
Barnaul
Alma Ata
Ulaanbaatar (Ulan Bator)
Rangoon
Mandalay
Hanoi
Saigon
Bangkok
Singapore
Manila
Kuala Lumpur
Colombo
Makkah
Al Madinah
El Qâhira
El Iskandarîya
Addis Abeba
Nairobi
Mogadishu

Equator

Tropic of Cancer

Arctic Circle

East from Greenwich

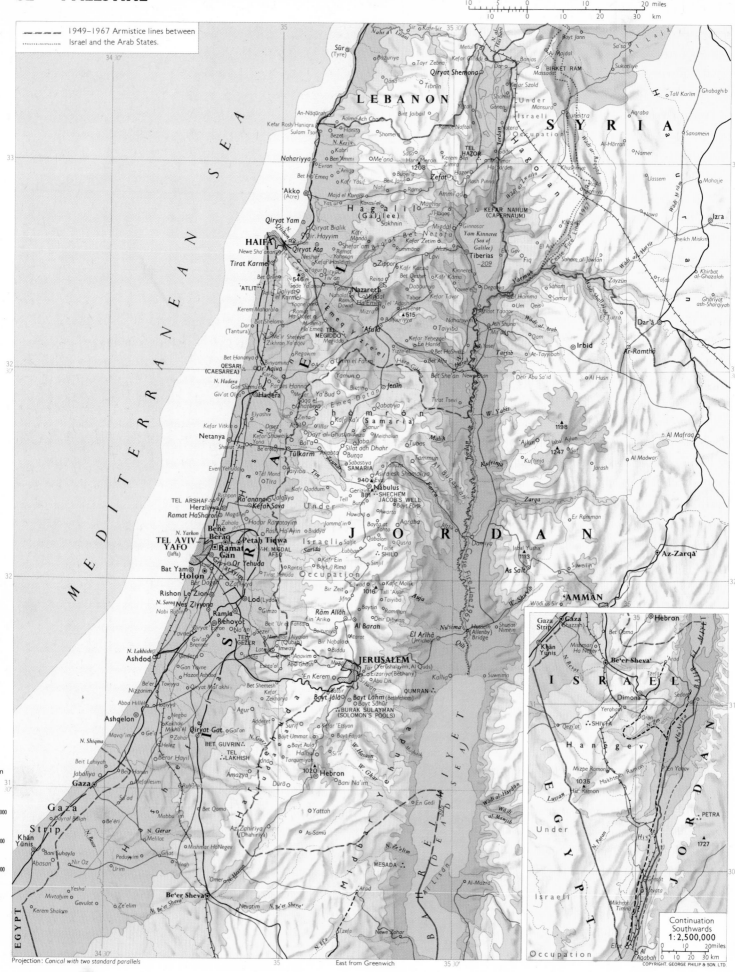

1 : 1 000 000

1:15 000 000

100   0   100   200   300   400 miles
150   0   150   300   450   600 km

Countries and regions

LEBANON
SYRIA
IRAQ
IRAN (PERSIA)
AFGHANISTAN
ISRAEL
JORDAN
EGYPT
SAUDI-ARABIA
KUWAIT
NEUTRAL TERR.
UNITED ARAB EMIRATES
TRUCIAL STATES
OMAN
YEMEN
SOUTH YEMEN
HADHRAMAWT
SUDAN
ETHIOPIA
FR. TERR. AFARS & ISSAS
SOMALI REP.
KENYA
ZAIRE
UGANDA
EL ISTWA'YA
KORDOFAN
EQUATORIA

Selected places

Bayrût, Dimashq (Damascus), Haifa, Tel Aviv-Yafo, Jerusalem, Amman, Baghdad, Al Basrah, Esfahan, Yazd, Shiraz, Kermān, Bam, Bandar 'Abbās, Muscat (Masqat), Matrah, Ar Riyâd (Riyadh), Al Kuwayt (Kuwait), Bahrain, Ad Dammâm, Doha, Abū Zabī, Abu Dhabi, Makkah (Mecca), Jiddah, Al Madinah, Ta'if, Asmera (Asmara), Addis Abeba (Addis Ababa), Al 'Adan (Aden), Madinat al Shaab, Djibouti, Berbera, Hargeisa, Mogadiscio (Mogadishu), El Khartûm (Khartoum), Omdurmân, Bûr Sûdân (Port Sudan), Aswân, Bûr Safâga, Quseir

Physical features

An Nafûd, Es Sahra' esh Sharqiya, Es Sahrâ en Nûbia (Nubian Desert), Ar Rab' al Khâli, RED SEA, PERSIAN GULF, Gulf of Oman, Gulf of Aden, INDIAN OCEAN, Dasht-e Lût, Tropic of Cancer, L. Tana, L. Turkana, L. Nasser (Buheiret en Naser), Bab el Mandeb, Socotra (South Yemen), 'Abd al Kûrî, Al Masirah

Elevation key (ft / m)

ft	m
12 000	4000
9000	3000
6000	2000
4500	1500
3000	1000
1200	400
600	200
0	0
600	200
6000	2000
12 000	4000

Projection: Sanson-Flamsteed's Sinusoidal
East from Greenwich

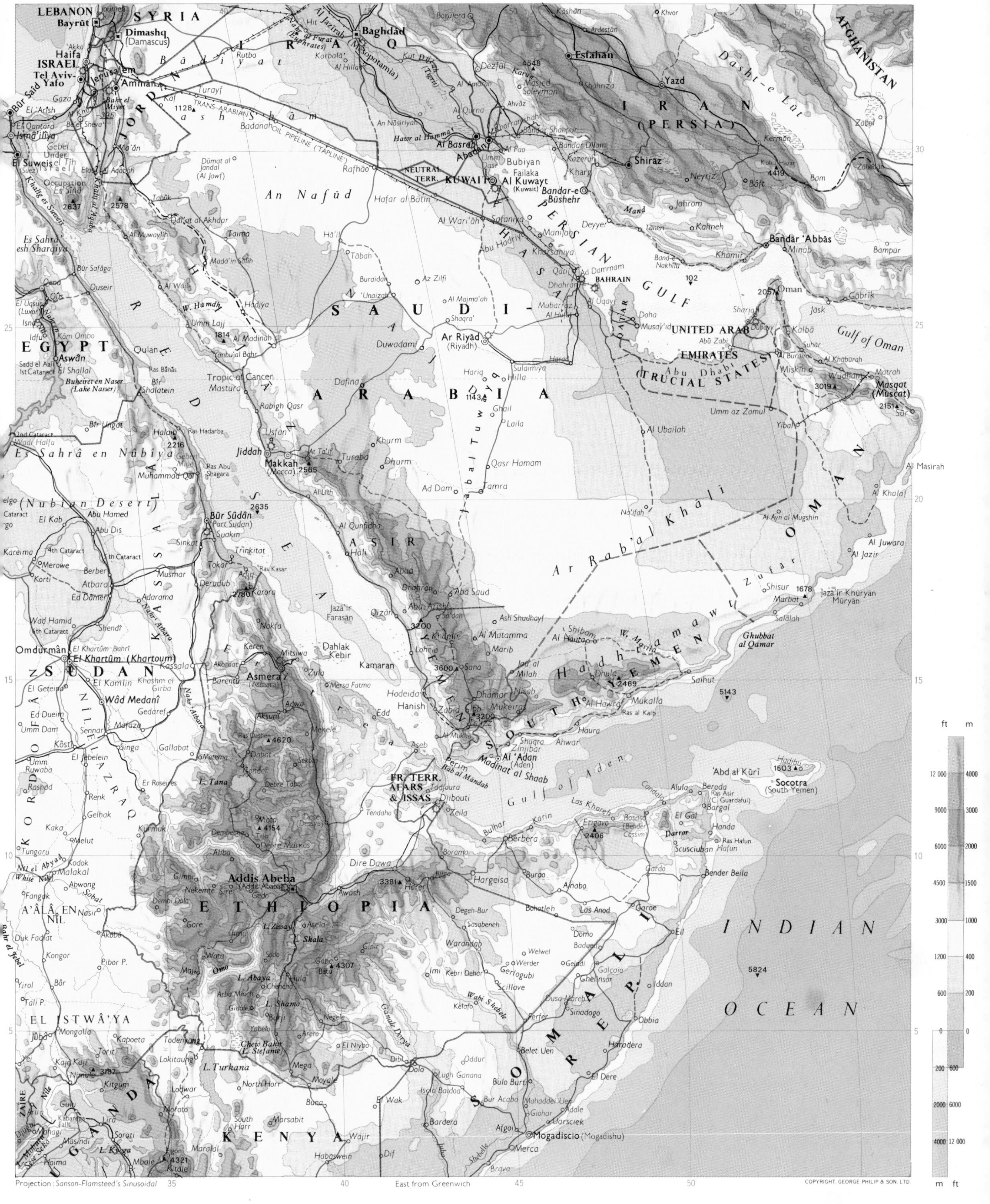

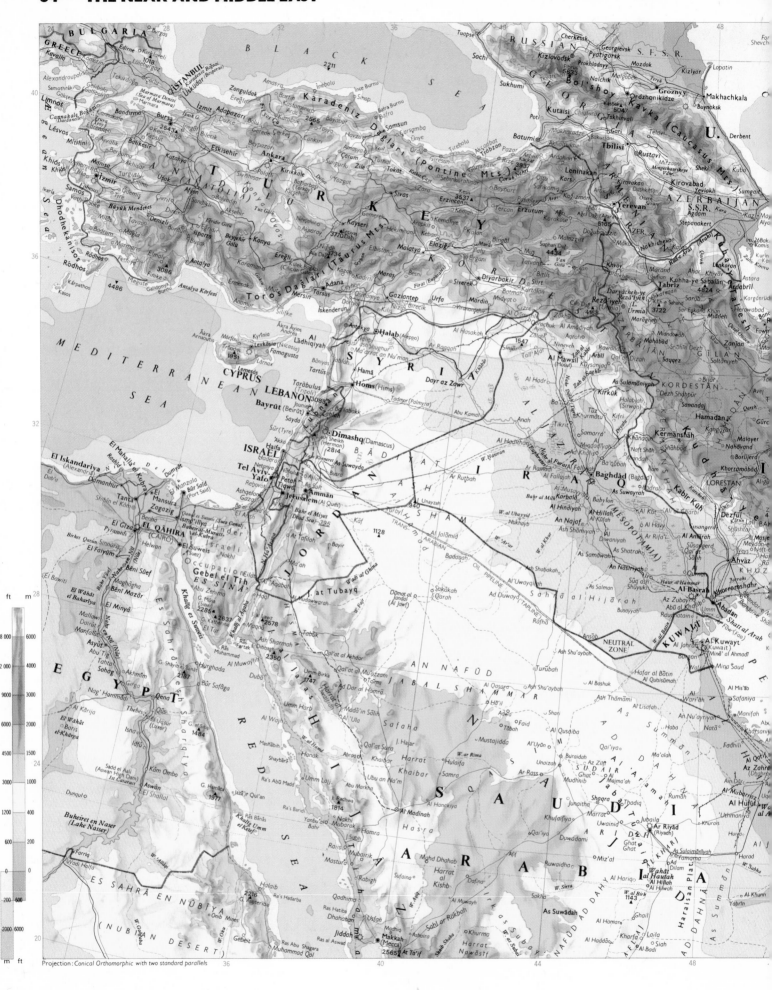

Projection: Conical Orthomorphic with two standard parallels

100   0   100   200   300 miles
100   0   100   200   300   400   500 km

East from Greenwich

KAZAKH S.S.R.

Plato Ustyurt

Aralskoye More
Muynak

KARA-KALPAKISCHE A.S.S.R.

PESKI KYZYL KUM

KAZAKH S.S.R.

Turkestan
Chimkent
Arys
Dzhambul
Talass

Kazakhskiy Zaliv

Shevchenko

Ozero Sudoche
Kungrad
Chimbal
Nukus
Khiva
Urgench
Turtkul

Sr Darya
Chirchik
Tashkent
Angren
Kokand
Namangan
Andizhan
Leninsk
Margelan
Osh
Fergona

KIRGIZ S.S.R.

Tien Shan
Kashgar

CHINA

Sartass

Kara Bogaz Gol

U Z B E K   S. S. R.

Tashaus
Darganata

Amu Darya
Gizhduvan

Bukhara
Kagan
Katta Kurgan
Samarkand

Dushanbe
TADZHIK S.S.R.

Pamir

Krasnovodski Poluostrov

Krasnovodsk

T U R K M E N   S. S. R.

K A R A   K U M

Chardzhou

Karshi
Guzar
Denau
Kurgan-Tyube
Kulyab
Khorog

Nebit Dag
Kizyl Arvat

K o p p e h   D a g

Ashkhabad

Muhammadābād

Mary (Mery)
Bairam Ali
Iolotan

Karakumskiy Canal

Termez
Aq Chah (Balkh)
Mazār-i-Sharīf

BADAKHSHAN

Faizabad

Kizyl Atrek

Shāhābād
Gonbad-e Kāvūs
Bojnurd
Qūchān

Dushak
Tedzhen
Serakhs
Tashkepri

Andkhui
Shibarghan

Sheberghan
BALKH
TAKHAR

PESHAWAR

CASPIAN SEA

Gorgān
Shāhī
Sārī
Bābol

Kuh-e Binalud
Mashhad (Meshed)

Kuh-e Kubūd Gumbī

FARYAB
Maimana

Band-i-Turkistan

HINDU KUSH

Kabul
NANGARHAR
Jalalabad
Peshawar
RAWALPINDI
Rawalpindi

Resteh-Ye Kūkhā-Ye Alberz

Dāmghān
Shāhrūd
Mazinān
Sabzevār
Neyshābūr

Kuh-e Sorkh

Tūran
Kāshaf

Torbat-e Heydārīyeh
Torbat-e Jām

Herat
Obeh
Safed Koh

BĀDGHĪS

Kohi

WARDAK
Gardez

SEMNAN
Diz Chah

Herat
Ghūrīān
Tulak

URUZGAN
GHAZNI
Ghazni

Damāvand

Garmsār
Semnan
Torūd

KHORASAN
Gonābād
Ferdow

Daryācheh-i-Namakzar

Yazdan
Shin Dand

A F G H A N I S T A N

PAKTIA
URGUN

Qom
Kāshān

DASHT-E KAVĪR
(Great Salt Desert)

Nagineh
Bashrūyeh
Khvor
Tabas
Deyhūk

Birjand
Tabas
Sarbisheh

FARAH
Farah
Qala-i-Kirta

KANDAHAR
Kandahar

Toba Kakar
Quetta

Natanz
Zavāreh
Ardestān
Anārak
Bayāzd
Khūr

Mūzhan
Shūsf
Darvācheh-ye-Sīstān
Nehbandan

Juwain
Chakhansur
Khash

Khugiani

Gīrishk
Kandahar

Khojak
Chaman

R A N   (P E R S I A)

Esfahān
Kūhpāyeh
Nā'īn

HELMAND
KANDAHAR

Dasht-i-Margo
Registan

Quetta

Sibi

Shahrezā
Yazd

Hamun Helmand
Zabol
Kang

Seistan

CHAKHANSUR

Chagai Hills
Gaud-i-Zirreh

Baghato

Kuh-e Dinar
Abādeh
Abarqū

Rāvaro
Zerand
Rafsanjān
Shahdād

Nostatābād

Zāhedān (Duzdab)

Gaud-i-Zirreh
Chagai Hills

Nushki

Kalat

Shiraz
FARS

Kermān
Bāghīn

KERMAN

Mirjāveh
Nok Kundi

Dashti-Tahlab

Sīstān
Bam
Fahraj

Lādīz (Vasht)

Hamun-i-Mashkel

Dalbandin
Kharan Kalat

Jahrom

Kūh-e Furgun

Kuh-e Hazārān

Sabzvāran

Bampūr
Īrānshahr
Zāboli

Dāvar Panāh

Siahan Range

Panjgur

BALUCHISTAN

KALAT

Lārestān

Hormoz

Kūhhā-ye Bashākerd
Qasr-e Qand

Central Makran Range
Turbat

Jhal Jhao

KARACHI

Qeshm
Bandar Abbās
Mīnāb

Remeshk
Bent
Nikshahr
Pishin

Makran Coast Range

Hyderabad

Strait of Hormuz

Oman
Khasab
Ras al Khaima

OMAN
Jāsk

Gwadar
Pasni
Ormara

Mouth of the Indus

KARACHI

GULF

BAHRAIN
Doha
QATAR

Dubayy
Sharjah
Ajman
Fujaira

Gulf of Oman

A R A B I A N   S E A

UNITED ARAB EMIRATES
(TRUCIAL STATES)

ABU DHABI
DHAFRA

Al Wāḩāt al Buraimi

Masqat (Muscat)
Matrah

Tropic of Cancer

Gulf of Kutch

O M A N

Ras al Hadd

INDIA

Porbandar
Dwarka

Jamnagar

Continuation Southwards
on same scale

Projection: Conical with two standard parallels

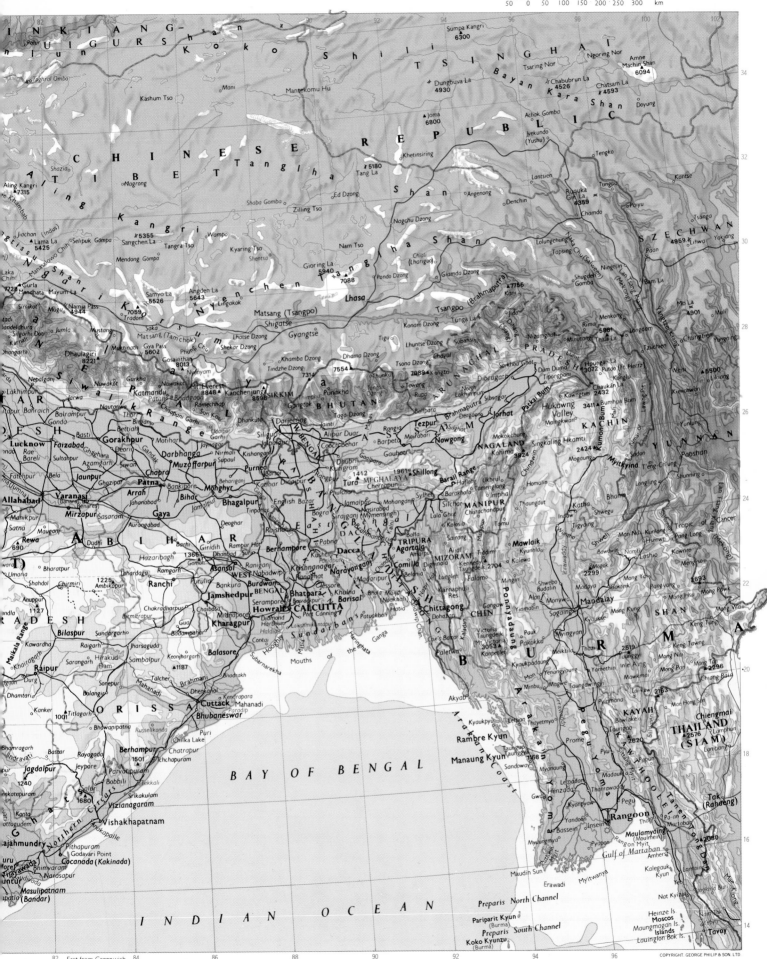

1:10 000 000

50   0   50   100   150   200 miles
50   0   50 100 150 200 250 300 km

I N K I A N G –
n l i u n g U R S K h a n

S i n g k i a n g U R S K h a n
Koko Shili

Sumpa Kangri
6300

T S I N G H A I

Tsaring Nor   Ngoring Nor
Amne
Machin Shan
6094

Toghrol Ombo

Mani

Dungbuva La
4930

Ji Chaburun La
4526   Chatsam La
4593

Ngoring Nor

Bayan Kara Shan

Doyung

C H I N E S E   R E P U B L I C

Kashum Tso

Mantekomu Hu

Khetinsiring

S Z E C H W A N

Jyekundo
(Yushu)

Tengko

Tsanga

Kantse

Aling Kangri
7315

B E T

T a n g l h a   S h a n

Joma
6800

Lantsien

Tungpo

Yingkiang

Nagrong

5180
Tang La

Angenong   Denchin

Ruoka
Gia La
4359

Paiyu

4959
Lihua

Chungtren

Shazia

Ed Dzong

Zilling Tso

Nogchu Dzong

Tapsing Chu (Salween)
Chamdo

Ningtsin
Mo La
4901

Chungtren

Lama La
5425

Sangchen La
5355

Wampo

Kyaring Tso
Shentsa

Nam Tso

Chiali
(Lhariguo)

Giamda Dzong

Lolungchung La
Shugden Gomba

Bam La

Muli

Mendong Gompa

Gioring La
5940

Tanglha Shan
7088

Pondo Dzong

7756

Jido   Rima
5881
Minutang Thala La   Longdam

Longgu

Gurla
7728

Mayum La

Namla Pass
4944

Tradom
7059

Saka
(Tamchok)

Matsang (Tsangpo)

Lhasa

Shigatse

Gyangtse

Tsangpo (Brahmaputra)

Konam Dzong

Tunga Lian

Subansiri

Nizamghat   Menkong

Chayul

A R U N A C H A L   P R A D E S H

Hpungan La
3072   Putao (Ft. Hertz)

Weisi
5500

Liki̇ang

Dhaulagiri
8221

Muktinath
5602

Gya Pass

Gosainthan
8013

Khamba Dzong

Dhama Dzong

7554

Tsona Dzong

Towang
7089   Kangto

North Lakhimpur

Sarkhoa Ghat

Dum Duma

Tipongpani

Chaukan La
2432

Kawngtun
Bumhpa Bum

Lhatse Dzong   Shekar Dzong

Tindzhe Dzong

Thunkar

Dibrugarh

Pakhi Bum

Kawngtung

Dhankuta

Mt Everest
8848

Kanchenjunga
8598

S I K K I M

Gangtok

B H U T A N

Taga Dzong

Rupa
Ballpara

Brahmaputra
Bergaong

Sibsagar

Jorhat

Hukawng Valley

3411
Mingkwan

K A C H I N

Katmandu
Patan   Bhadgaon

Ramechhap

Sun Kosi

Darjeeling

Jainti
Alipur Duar

Rangia

Cooch Behar

A S S A M

Barpeta

Mairabari

Tezpur
Silghat   Nowgong

Mokokchung

N A G A L A N D

Kohima
3924

Singkaling Hkamti

2424

Maopung

Myitkyina

Teng-chung

Longling

Yunlung

Paoshan

BAY OF BENGAL

INDIAN OCEAN

East from Greenwich

COPYRIGHT GEORGE PHILIP & SON, LTD

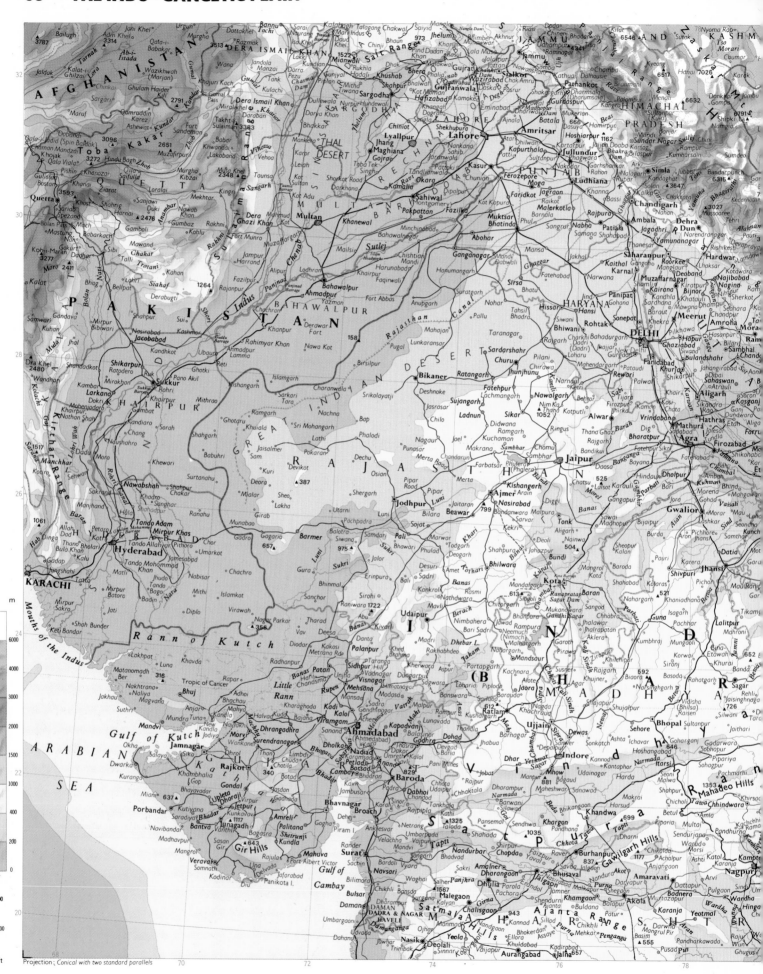

1 : 6 000 000

50 0 50 100 150 miles

50 0 50 100 150 200 250 km

CHINESE REPUBLIC

TIBET

AFGHANISTAN KASHMIR

PAKISTAN

NEPAL

INDIA

BANGLA-DESH

BURMA

Tropic of Cancer

SRI LANKA

S. ASIA: IRRIGATION
1 : 40 000 000

Irrigated Areas

CHINESE REPUBLIC

KAILAS RANGE

KANGRI

Manasalowo Chih

Laka Chih

Kailas 7315

Gurla Mandhata 7728

Nanda Devi 7817

Dhaulagiri 8172

Annapurna 8078 Manaslu 8156

Gosainthan 8013

Mt Everest 8848 Makalu 8481

Kanchenjunga 8598

HIMALAYA

SIKKIM

Gangtok

BHUTAN

Darjeeling

Katmandu

Patan Bhadgaon

NEPAL

Biratnagar

ASSAM

Gauhati

MEGHALAYA

Khasi Hills

Garo Hills

Brahmaputra

UTTAR PRADESH

Lucknow

KANPUR

Faizabad

Gorakhpur

Bettiah

Motihari

Darbhanga

Muzaffarpur

Chapra

Patna

Hajipur

Monghyr

Bhagalpur

BIHAR

Allahabad

Varanasi (Banaras, Benares)

Mirzapur-cum-Vindhyachal

Gaya

Ganges

Son

English Bazar

Malda

RAJSHAHI

Bogra

Mymensingh

BANGLADESH

DACCA

Jabalpur

Narmada

MADHYA PRADESH

Panna Hills

Kaimur Hills

Maikala Range

Rihand Dam

Ranchi

Jamshedpur

Hazaribagh

Dhanbad

Bokaro Steel City

Jharia

Asansol

Durgapur

Burdwan

Raurkela

Bilaspur

Raipur

Durg

Bhilainagar

Raigarh

Sambalpur

Hirakud Dam

Mahanadi

ORISSA

Cuttack

Bhubaneswar

Chilka Lake

Puri

Konarak

Brahmani

Balasore

Midnapore

Kharagpur

Howrah

CALCUTTA

Hoogly-Chinsura

Khulna

Barisal

Sundarbans

Mouths of the Ganga

The Sandheads

BAY OF BENGAL

East from Greenwich

COPYRIGHT GEORGE PHILIP & SON LTD.

1:6 000 000

SRI LANKA
On same scale

1:10 000 000

50   0   50   100   150   200 miles
50 0 100   200   300 km

CHINA

INDIA

BANGLADESH

CHIN

BURMA

NORTH VIETNAM

SHAN

Mandalay

Hanoi

Haiphong

Gulf of
Tongking

Hainan

LAOS

Luang Prabang

Vientiane

THAILAND
(SIAM)

Chiengmai

KAYAH

KAREN

Rangoon

Pegu

Gulf of Martaban

Krung Thep
(Bangkok)

Thonburi

ANDAMAN
SEA

North
Andaman

Middle
Andaman

Andaman
Islands

South
Andaman

Little
Andaman

ANNAM

SOUTH VIETNAM

Hué

Da Nang (Tourane)

Khorat

Nakhon
Ratchasima
(Khorat)

Phanom Dang Raek

CAMBODIA

Tonle Sap

Angkor
Siem Reap

Phnom Penh

Saigon

Gulf of Siam

Kho Khot Kra
(Isthmus of Kra)

Chumphon

Ko Samui

Surat Thani

Nakhon Si Thammarat

Phuket

SOUTH CHINA SEA

WESTERN

MALAYSIA

MALAYA

Kuala Lumpur

George Town
Pulau Pinang

Kelang

Seremban

Melaka

SUMATERA

INDONESIA

Singapore

Johor Baharu

MALAYA AND SINGAPORE

1:6 000 000

50   0   50 miles
50 0 50 km

THAILAND
(SIAM)

PERLIS

Alor Setan

KEDAH

PINANG

George Town

Butterworth

PERAK

Ipoh

Taiping

MALAYA

KELANTAN

Kota Baharu

TERENGGANU

Kuala
Terengganu

PAHANG

Kuantan

SELANGOR

Kuala Lumpur
Petaling Jaya

Kelang

NEGERI SEMBILAN

Seremban

MELAKA

Melaka

JOHOR

SUMATERA

INDONESIA

SINGAPORE

Strait of Malacca

Projection: Conical with two standard parallels

East from Greenwich

COPYRIGHT GEORGE PHILIP & SON LTD

ft   m

9000   3000
6000
4500
3000   1000
1200
600   200
0
200   600
2000 6000

m   ft

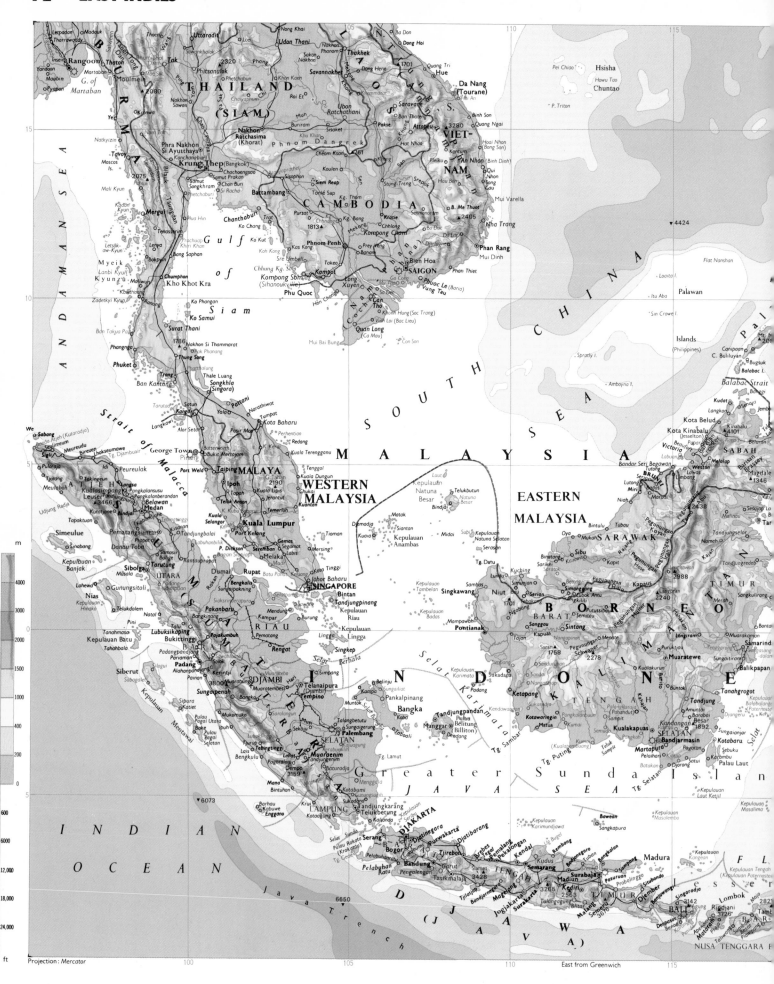

SEA OF JAPAN

PACIFIC OCEAN

SEA OF JAPAN

Sea of Okhotsk

CHŪGOKU

SHIKOKU

KYŪSHŪ

HOKKAIDŌ

TŌHOKU

KANTŌ

CHŪBU

KINKI

SOUTH KOREA

Major cities and places (clockwise/by region):

Suzu-misaki, Wajima, Suzu, Nanao, Toyama-wan, Naoetsu, Takada, Takamachi, Kitaibaraki, Kanazawa, Toyama, Nagano, Ueda, Matsumoto, Kiryū, Utsunomiya, Mito, Maebashi, Takasaki, Kumagaya, Omiya, Urawa, Kawaguchi, Kawasaki, TOKYO, Hachiōji, Funabashi, Chiba, Ichihara, YOKOHAMA, Hiratsuka, Fujisawa, Yokosuka, Odawara, Atami, Tateyama, Nojima-Zaki

Matsue, Izumo, Yonago, Tottori, Fukui, Komatsu, Maizuru, Ayabe, Fukuchiyama, KYŌTO, Ōtsu, NAGOYA, Gifu, Ichinomiya, Toyota, Okazaki, Shizuoka, Shimizu, Numazu, Mishima, Itō, Ō-Shima, Nii-Jima, Miyake-Jima

Hamada, Masuda, Hagi, Shimonoseki, KITAKYŪSHŪ, Hiroshima, Kure, Fukuyama, Kurashiki, Okayama, Himeji, KOBE, OSAKA, Sakai, Amagasaki, Nishinomiya, Higashiōsaka, Nara, Wakayama, Kishiwada, Izumi-sano, Kushimoto, Shio-no-Misaki

Fukuoka, Karatsu, Saga, Kurume, Ōmuta, Omura, Sasebo, Nagasaki, Isahaya, Shimabara, Kumamoto, Yatsushiro, Minamata, Sendai, Kagoshima, Makurazaki, Kanoya, Miyazaki, Nobeoka, Hyūga, Nichinan, Miyakonojō, Ōita, Beppu, Usuki, Saiki

Ōsumi-Kaikyō, Ōsumi-Shotō, Tane-ga-Shima, Yaku-shima, Yakushima

Wakkanai, Rishiri-Tō, Rebun-Tō, Sōya-Misaki, Asahikawa, Abashiri, Shiretoko-Misaki, Nemuro-Kaikyō, Rumoi, Otaru, Sapporo, Obihiro, Kushiro, Muroran, Hakodate, Tomakomai, HOKKAIDŌ, Daisetsu-zan 2290, Poroshiri-Dake 2052, Tsugaru-Kaikyō

Aomori, Hirosaki, Hachinohe, Towada-Ko, Morioka, Miyako, Akita, Kamaishi, Sakata, Ishinomaki, Yamagata, Sendai, Niigata, Nagaoka, Fukushima, Kōriyama, Iwaki, Mito, Utsunomiya, Sado

Scale bars:

1:5 000 000
Projection: Conical with two standard parallels

1:10 000 000
Projection: Bonne

East from Greenwich

ft	m
9000	3000
6000	2000
4500	1500
3000	1000
1200	400
600	200
0	0
600	200
6000	2000
12,000	4000
18,000	6000
24,000	8000
m	ft

Continuation Southwards on same scale

Tokara-Kaikyō, Tokara-Shima, Suwanose-Jima, Nansei-Shotō, Amami-Ō-Shima, Toku-no-Shima, Ōsumi-Shotō, Tane-ga-Shima, Yaku-Shima

REFERENCE TO PREFECTURES

HOKKAIDŌ DISTRICT
1 Hokkaidō

TŌHOKU DISTRICT
2 Aomori
3 Akita
4 Iwate
5 Yamagata
6 Miyagi
7 Fukushima

CHŪBU DISTRICT
8 Niigata
9 Ishikawa
10 Toyama
11 Fukui
12 Gifu
13 Nagano
14 Yamanashi
15 Aichi
16 Shizuoka

KANTŌ DISTRICT
17 Gumma
18 Tochigi
19 Saitama
20 Ibaraki
21 Tōkyō
22 Chiba
23 Kanagawa

KINKI DISTRICT
24 Hyogo
25 Kyōto
26 Shiga
27 Ōsaka
28 Nara
29 Mie
30 Wakayama

CHŪGOKU DISTRICT
31 Tottori
32 Okayama
33 Shimane
34 Hiroshima
35 Yamaguchi

SHIKOKU DISTRICT
36 Kagawa
37 Tokushima
38 Ehime
39 Kōchi

KYŪSHŪ DISTRICT
40 Fukuoka
41 Saga
42 Nagasaki
43 Kumamoto
44 Ōita
45 Miyazaki
46 Kagoshima

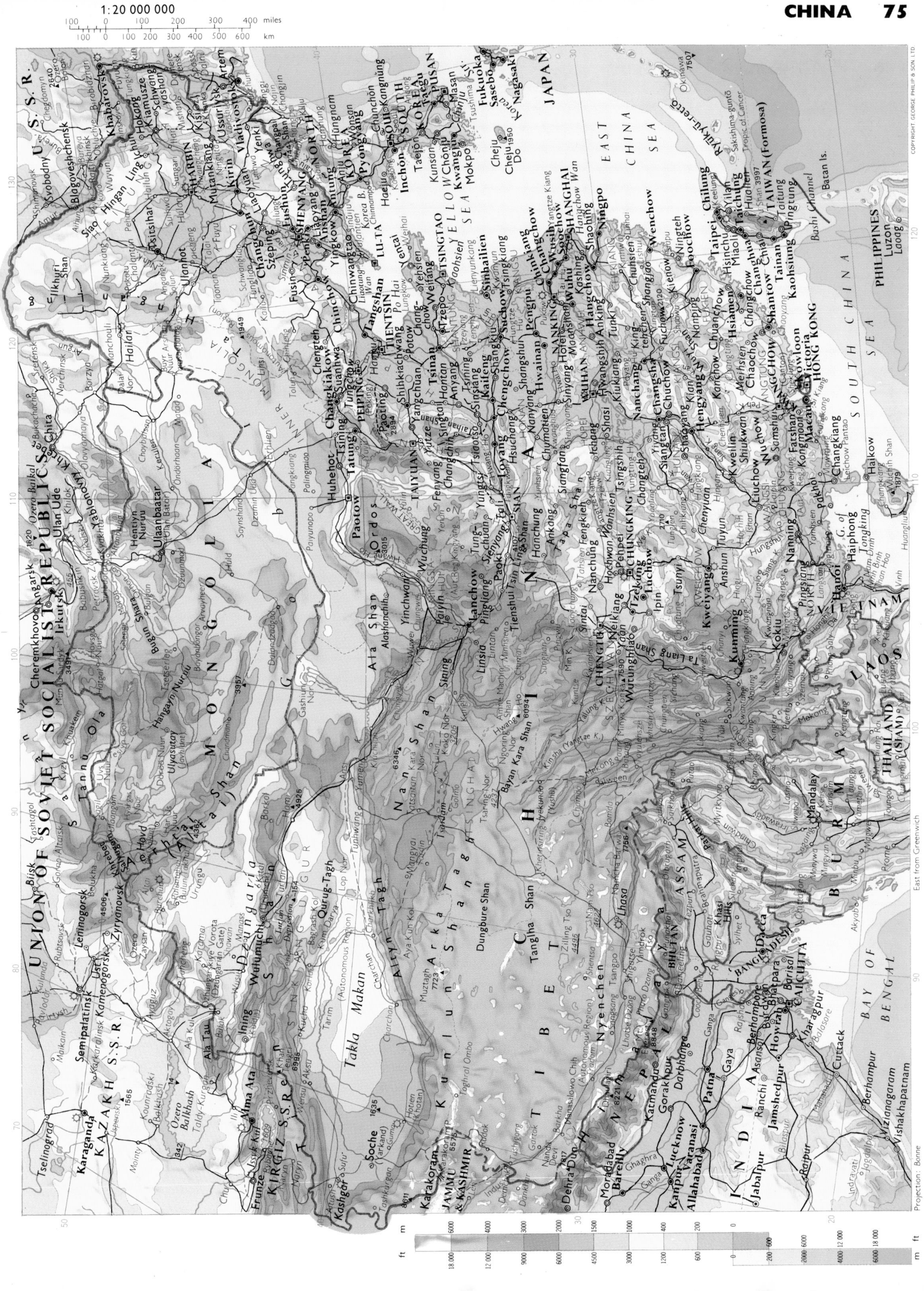

1:20 000 000

miles
km

U.S.S.R.

UNION OF SOVIET SOCIALIST REPUBLICS

KAZAKH S.S.R.

KIRGIZ S.S.R.

MONGOLIA

INNER MONGOLIA

SINKIANG UIGUR (Autonomous Region)

Takla Makan

Kunlun Shan

Nan Shan

TIBET (Autonomous Region)

Lhasa

NEPAL

BHUTAN

INDIA

BANGLADESH

ASSAM

BURMA

THAILAND (SIAM)

LAOS

VIETNAM

NORTH VIETNAM

YUNNAN

SZECHWAN

KWEICHOW

KWANGSI

KWANGTUNG

HONG KONG

Macao

SOUTH CHINA SEA

CHINA

CHEKIANG

FUKIEN

KIANGSI

HUNAN

HUPEH

ANHWEI

HONAN

SHENSI

KANSU

NINGSIA

SHANSI

HOPEI

SHANTUNG

KIANGSU

SHANGHAI

NANKING

PEIPING

TIENTSIN

HARBIN

SHENYANG

NORTH KOREA

SOUTH KOREA

Seoul

Pyongyang

JAPAN

Fukuoka

Nagasaki

EAST CHINA SEA

YELLOW SEA

RYUKYU-retto

TAIWAN (Formosa)

Taipei

Kaohsiung

PHILIPPINES

Luzon

BAY OF BENGAL

CALCUTTA

Tropic of Cancer

East from Greenwich

Projection: Bonne

ft m   6000 4000 3000 2000 1500 1000 600 400 200 0   ft m

18 000 12 000 9000 6000 4500 3000 1200 600 0   6000 12 000 18 000

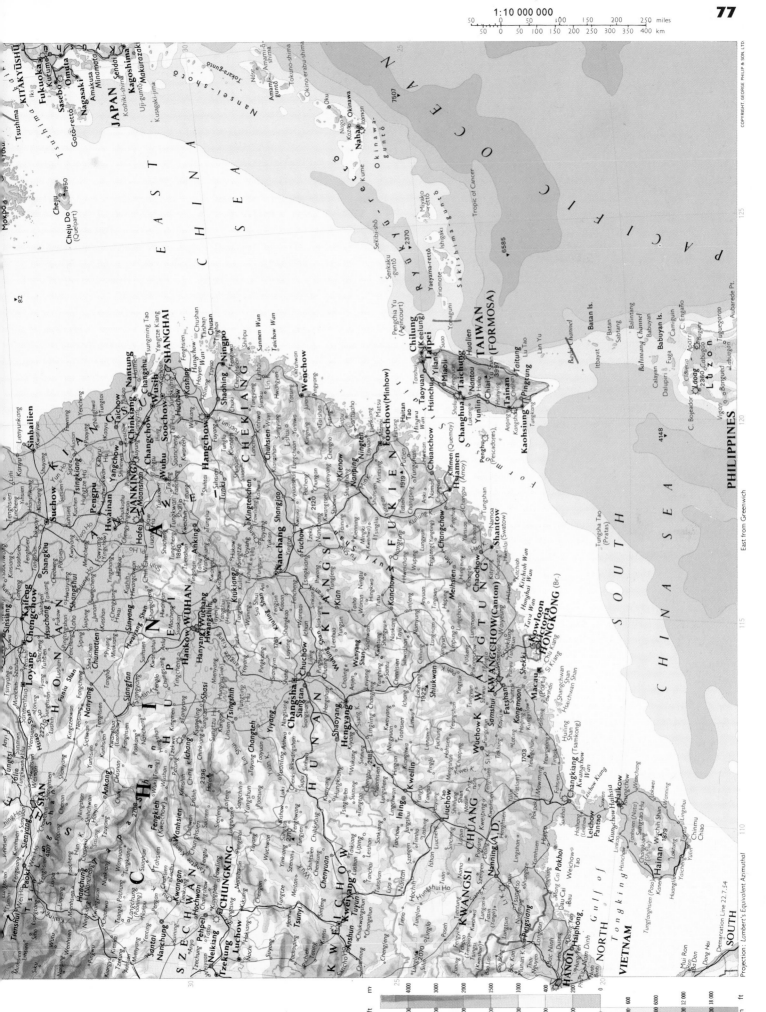

1:10 000 000

50   0   50   100   150   200   250 miles
50   0   50   100   150   200   250   300   350   400 km

PACIFIC   OCEAN

KITAKYŪSHŪ
Fukuoka
Kurume
Omuta
Sasebo   Kumamoto
Nagasaki   Amakusa   Sendai
Minamata
Makurazaki   Kagoshima
JAPAN
Goto-retto
Koshiki-shima
Uji-guntō   Tanega-shima
Tsushima

Cheju Do   1950
(Quelpart)

MOKPO

EAST   CHINA   SEA

Nansei-shoto

Tokara-guntō

Amami-gunto
Amami-ō-shima
Tokuno-erabu-shima

Okino-erabu-shima
Okinawa
Naha   Okinawa-guntō
Itoman
Kozo   Kume

Okinawa-guntō

Sekibi-shō   Miyako
Senkaku gunto   Miyako-rettō   Yonaguni
Yaeyama-rettō
Iriomote   Ishigaki
Sakishima-guntō

7507

2370

6585

Tropic of Cancer

RYŪKYŪ

Batan Is.
Batan   Sabtang
Bashi Channel
Balintang
Bulintang Channel
Calayan   Babuyan Is.
Dalupiri   Fuga
Camiguin
Babuyan

Aparri   C. Engaño
Vigan   Laoag   2360
Cabugao   Tuguegarao   Aubarede Pt.

PHILIPPINES

Luzon

TAIWAN
(FORMOSA)
Chilung (Keelung)
Chilung   Hualien
Taipei
Yilan
Taoyuan
Miaoli   Taichung
Hsinchu   Nantou   3997
Changhua
Chiai   Yunlin   Taitung
Tainan   4148
Anping   Hsinying
Kaohsiung   Pingtung

Penghu
(Pescadores)

SOUTH   CHINA   SEA

SHANGHAI
Nantung
Changshu
Wusih   Kashing
Soochow   Hangchow   Ningpo
Changchow   Shaohing
Chinkiang   Huchow
NANKING   Wuhu

KIANGSU

ANHWEI

CHEKIANG
Wenchow

KIANGSI

FUKIEN
Foochow (Minhow)
Nanping
Kienow
Changchow
Kinmen (Quemoy)
Hsiamen (Amoy)
Shantow (Swatow)

KWANGTUNG
KWANGCHOW (Canton)
Macau (Port.)
HONGKONG (Br.)
Kowloon
Victoria

HONAN
Kaifeng
Loyang   Chengchow
Sinsiang
Hsuchang

HUPEH
WUHAN
Hankow   Wuchang
Hanyang

HUNAN
Changsha
Siangtan
Hengyang
Shaoyang

KWANGSI-CHUANG (AD)
Nanning
Wuchow
Kweilin

KWEICHOW
Kweiyang
Tsunyi
Tuyun

SZECHWAN
CHUNGKING
Neikiang
Luchow
Nanchung

VIETNAM
HANOI
Haiphong

NORTH

SOUTH

Gulf of   Tongking

Hainan
Haikow
Kiungchow
Leichow

East from Greenwich

Projection: Lambert's Equivalent Azimuthal
Demarcation Line 22.7.54

ft   m
12 000   4000
9000   3000
6000   2000
4500   1500
3000   1000
1200   400
600   200
0   0
200   600
2000   4000
4000   6000
6000   18 000
m   ft

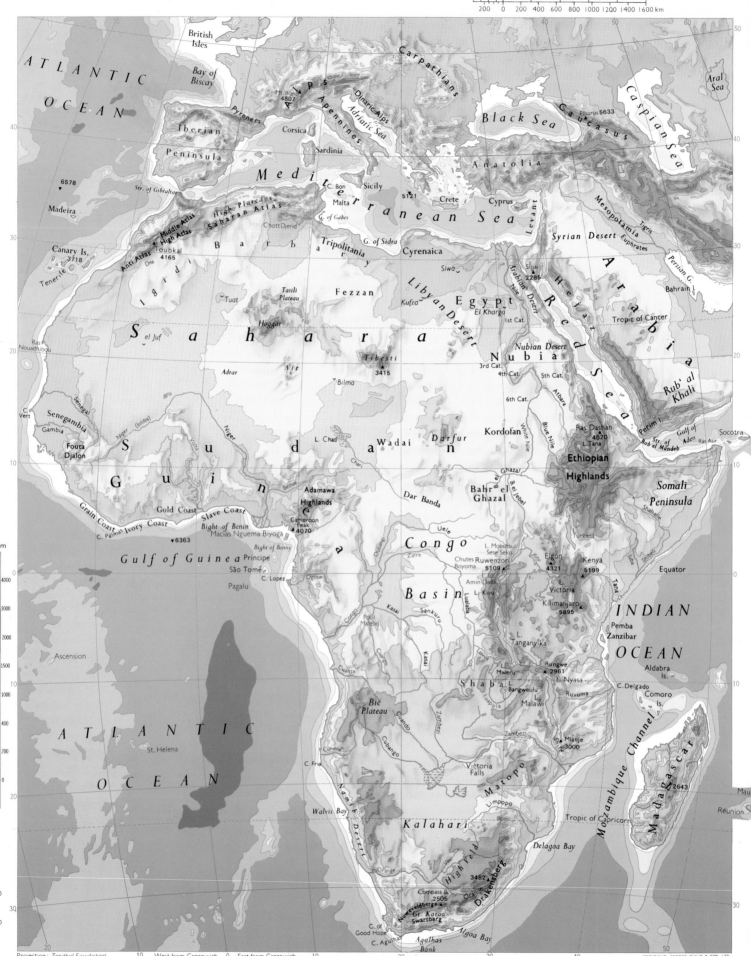

1:40 000 000

200   0   200   400   600   800   1000 miles
200   0   200 400 600 800 1000 1200 1400 1600 km

ATLANTIC OCEAN

British Isles

Bay of Biscay

ALPS
Carpathians
Mt. Blanc 4807
Pyrenees
Apennines
Dinaric Alps
Adriatic Sea
Black Sea
Caucasus
Elbruz 5633
Caspian Sea
Aral Sea

Iberian Peninsula

Corsica
Sardinia
Anatolia

6578

Madeira

Str. of Gibraltar
Middle Atlas
High Atlas
High Plateaus
Saharan Atlas
Barbary
C. Bon
Sicily
Malta
G. of Gabes
Crete
Cyprus
5121
Mediterranean Sea
Levant
Mesopotamia
Tigris
Euphrates
Syrian Desert

Canary Is. 3718
Tenerife
Anti Atlas
Toubkal 4165
Dra
Igidi
Barbary
Tripolitania
G. of Sidra
Cyrenaica
Siwa
Libyan Desert
Egypt
El Kharga
1st Cat.
Arabian Desert
Sinai 2285
Red Sea
Hejaz
Tropic of Cancer
Persian G.
Bahrain I.
Arabia

C. Vert
Ras Nouadhibou

S. el Juf
Sahara
Adrar
Tasili Plateau
Fezzan
Hoggar
Air
Tibesti 3415
Bilma
Kufra
Nubian Desert
3rd Cat.
4th Cat.
5th Cat.
Nubia
Rub' al Khali

Senegal
Senegambia
Gambia
Fouta Djalon
Niger (Joliba)
Volta
Niger
L. Chad
Chari
Wadai
Darfur
Kordofan
6th Cat.
White Nile
Blue Nile
Atbara
Ras Dashan 4620
L. Tana
Ethiopian Highlands
Str. of Bab el Mandeb
Gulf of Aden
Perim I.
Ras Asir
Socotra

Sudan
Guinea
Benue
Adamawa Highlands
Cameroon Peak 4070
Macias Nguema Biyoga
Dar Banda
Bahr el Ghazal
Bahr el Jebel
Uele
Turkana
Somali Peninsula
Shabelle

Gold Coast
Slave Coast
Ivory Coast
Grain Coast
C. Palmas
Bight of Benin
6363
Bight of Bonny
Principe
São Tomé
Pagalu

Gulf of Guinea
C. Lopez
Ogoué
Ubangi
Zaire
Congo Basin
L. Mobutu Sese Seko
Chutes Boyoma
Ruwenzori 5109
Amin Dada
L. Kivu
Elgon 4321
L. Victoria
Kenya 5199
Kilimanjaro 5895
Tana
Equator
INDIAN OCEAN

ft   m
12 000   4000
9000   3000
6000   2000
4500   1500
3000   1000
1200   400
600   200
0   0
200   600
1000   3000
2000   6000
4000   12 000
6000   18 000
m   ft

Ascension

ATLANTIC OCEAN
St. Helena

Congo
Kasai
Pool Malebo
Kwango
Kasai
Sankuru
Lualaba
L. Tanganyika
Rungwe 2961
Mweru
L. Nyasa
Pemba
Zanzibar
INDIAN OCEAN
Aldabra Is.
C. Delgado
Comoro Is.

Cuanza
Shaba
Bangweulu
L. Bangweulu
Lualaba
Malawi
Ruvuma
Mlanje 3000

Bié Plateau
Cuango
Cuando
Zambezi
Zambezi

Victoria Falls
Matopo
Madagascar
2643
Mozambique Channel

C. Fria
Cunene
Cubango
Kalahari
Limpopo
Namib Desert
Tropic of Capricorn
Delagoa Bay
Maur
Réunion

Walvis Bay

High Veld
3482
Drakensberg
Compass B. 2505
Nuweveldberge
Gt. Karoo
Swartberg
C. of Good Hope
C. Agulhas
Agulhas Bank
Orange
Vaal
Oranje
Algoa Bay

1:40 000 000

200 0 200 400 600 800 1000 miles
200 0 200 400 600 800 1000 1200 1400 1600 km

ATLANTIC OCEAN

UNITED KINGDOM London NETH. GERMANY POLAND Warszawa
BELG. Praha CZECHOSLOVAKIA Kiyev
Paris Wien AUSTRIA HUNGARY RUMANIA Volgograd
FRANCE SWITZ. Odessa U. S. S. R.
Bay of Biscay ITALY YUGOSLAVIA Black Sea Aral Sea
Corse Roma Adriatic Sea BULGARIA İstanbul Caspian Sea
Madrid SPAIN Sardegna ALB. GREECE TURKEY Ankara Baku
Lisboa PORTUGAL Sicilia Kriti Athínai CYPRUS SYRIA Halab Al Mawsil Tehrān
Tanger Gibraltăr (Br.) Alger Annaba Tunis MALTA Tel Aviv-Yafo Dimashq Baghdād Esfahān
Casablanca Tetouan Oran Constantine TUNISIA Tarābulus El Iskandaríya Jerusalem ISRAEL JORDAN Al Basrah IRAN
Rabat Fès Sfax Djerba Bûr Sa'îd Syrian Desert KUWAIT
MOROCCO Marrakech Tûnis El QÂHIRA El Suweis Persian Gulf
Essaouira Ghadames Banghāzī Al Bayda EGYPT El Faiyûm Sîwa SAUDI- Bahrein QATAR
Madeira (Port.) Ifni ALGERIA LIBYA Asyût Al Madînah ARABIA Tropic of Cancer
Islas Canarias Tenerife El Aaiun In Salah Ghat Marzûq Aswân Makkah
Dra WESTERN SAHARA Sahara Al Jawf Wadi-Halfa Es Sahrâ En Nûbiya
P'Dérik S a h a r a Dongola Bûr Sûdân
Ras Nouadhibou Nouakchott Esh Shimâliya Atbara Mitsiwa YEMEN Socotra (South Yemen)
MAURITANIA Tombouctou Agades Omdurmân El Khartûm Kassala Asmera SOUTH YEMEN Ras Asir
St. Louis Gao NIGER CHAD El Fâsher SUDAN Kordofan Madinat al Shaab Aden G. of Aden
C. Vert Dakar SENEGAL Kayes MALI Niamey Sokoto Nguru Abéché El Obeid Dârfûr Nîl el Azraq Djibouti (Fr.) Berbera Hafun
GAMBIA Banjul Bamako Kano Maiduguri Ndjamena (Ft.-Lamy) Bousso Nîl el Abyad Addis Abeba Harer Hargeisa
GUINEA BISSAU Bissau UPPER VOLTA Ouagadougou Kaduna Bauchi Chari Malakâl L. Tana ETHIOPIA SOMALI REP.
GUINEA Konkan NIGERIA Sarh Waw Bahr el Ghazal A'Âla en Nîl Mongalla Shebele
Conakry Freetown SIERRA LEONE Tamale Ibadan Benue Ngaoundéré Bangui Mongalla CENTRAL AFRICAN REPUBLIC El Istwâ'ia L. Turkana Mogadishu
LIBERIA Bouake IVORY COAST GHANA Kumasi Lagos Enugu CAMEROON Ngaoundéré Oubangi Zaire UGANDA KENYA INDIAN
Monrovia Tamale Abidjan Accra Lomé Porto Novo Port Harcourt Yaoundé Douala Bangui Kisangani L. Idi Amin Dada L. Mobutu Sese Seko Kampala Equator
Sekondi-Takoradi Bight of Benin Rey Malabo Macias Nguema Biyogo ZAIRE Lulaba L. Victoria Kisumu Nairobi OCEAN
Gulf of Guinea Príncipe Rio Muni Libreville GABON Zaire Mbandaka RWANDA Kigali Nyanza Tana
São Tomé EQUATORIAL GUINEA C. Lopez Brazzaville Kinshasa Kasai Ilebo L. Kivu Bujumbura BURUNDI Mombasa
Pagalu Pointe Noire Boma Kigoma Tabora Pemba
Cabinda ZAIRE S h a b a Kalemie TANZANIA Dodoma Zanzibar
Ascension (Br.) Luanda Bukama L. Tanganyika Dar-es-Salaam
Cuanza Likasi Lubumbashi L. Mweru L. Nyasa Cabo Delgado Aldabra Is. (Br.)
ATLANTIC Benguela Lobito ANGOLA Kitwe Lilongwe Ruvuma Arch. des Comores Diego-Suarez
OCEAN Huambo Lubumbashi ZAMBIA L. Malawi Mozambique Majunga
St. Helena (Br.) Moçâmedes Cuando Lusaka Zambeze Zomba Blantyre Quelimane Chinde
Cunene Cubango Kafue Livingstone Salisbury Sofala MALAGASY
Swakopmund Windhoek Zambezi Limpopo RHODESIA Tananarive REPUBLIC
SOUTH WEST AFRICA (NAMIBIA) Walvis-baai BOTSWANA Bulawayo MOZAMBIQUE Tropic of Capricorn MAURITIUS Réunion (Fr.)
Lüderitz Kalahari Gaborone TRANSVAAL Pretoria Maputo (Lourenço Marques) Tuléar Fianarantsoa
Johannesburg SWAZ. Durban-Mauritius
Oranje Kimberley O.V. Bloemfontein NATAL Durban
SOUTH AFRICA CAPE PROVINCE East London
Cape Town Kaap die Goeie Hoop (Cape of Good Hope) Port Elizabeth

LES. Lesotho
O.-V. Oranje-Vrystaat
SWAZ. Swaziland
T.A.I. Territory of Afars and Issas

Projection: Zenithal Equidistant.   West from Greenwich   East from Greenwich   COPYRIGHT. GEORGE PHILIP & SON. LTD.

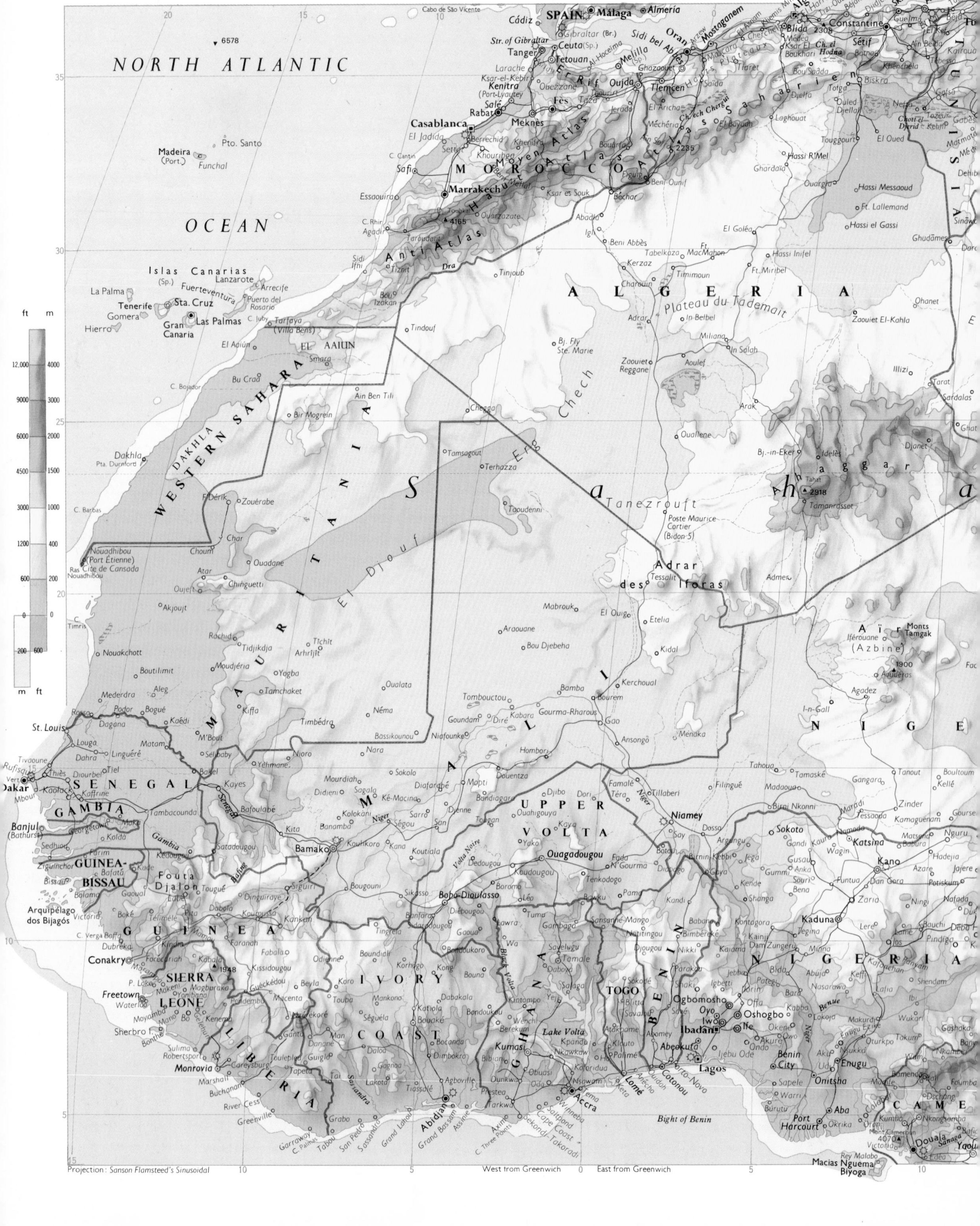

NORTH ATLANTIC

OCEAN

SPAIN

Str. of Gibraltar
Gibraltar (Br.)
Tanger
Ceuta (Sp.)
Tetouan

Cádiz · Málaga · Almería · Oran · Alger (Algiers) · Constantine · Annaba · Skikda

Casablanca
Rabat
Salé
Meknès
Fès
Marrakech
Essaouira
Agadir

MOROCCO

Haut Atlas · Moyen Atlas · Anti Atlas

Madeira (Port.)
Funchal
Pto. Santo

ALGERIA

Plateau du Tademait

Islas Canarias (Sp.)
Lanzarote
Fuerteventura
La Palma
Tenerife
Gomera
Hierro
Gran Canaria
Las Palmas
Sta. Cruz

WESTERN SAHARA

El Aaiun
Smara
Bu Craa
Dakhla

MAURITANIA

Nouadhibou (Port Étienne)
Atar
Chinguetti
Nouakchott
Tidjikdja
Akjoujt

M A L I

Tombouctou
Gao
Tanezrouft

A h a g g a r
Tamanrasset

N I G E R

Agadez
Aïr
Monts Tamgak
(Azbine)

SENEGAL
St. Louis
Dakar
GAMBIA
Banjul (Bathurst)
GUINEA-BISSAU
Bissau

GUINEA
Conakry

SIERRA LEONE
Freetown

LIBERIA
Monrovia

IVORY COAST

GHANA
Accra
Kumasi
Lake Volta

UPPER VOLTA
Ouagadougou
Bobo-Dioulasso

Bamako

TOGO
Lomé

BENIN
Cotonou
Porto-Novo

NIGERIA
Kano
Kaduna
Zaria
Katsina
Sokoto
Ibadan
Lagos
Benin City
Enugu
Port Harcourt

Niamey

Bight of Benin

CAME

Projection: Sanson Flamsteed's Sinusoidal

West from Greenwich   East from Greenwich

ft   m
12,000   4000
9000   3000
6000   2000
4500   1500
3000   1000
1200   400
600   200
0   0
200   600
m   ft

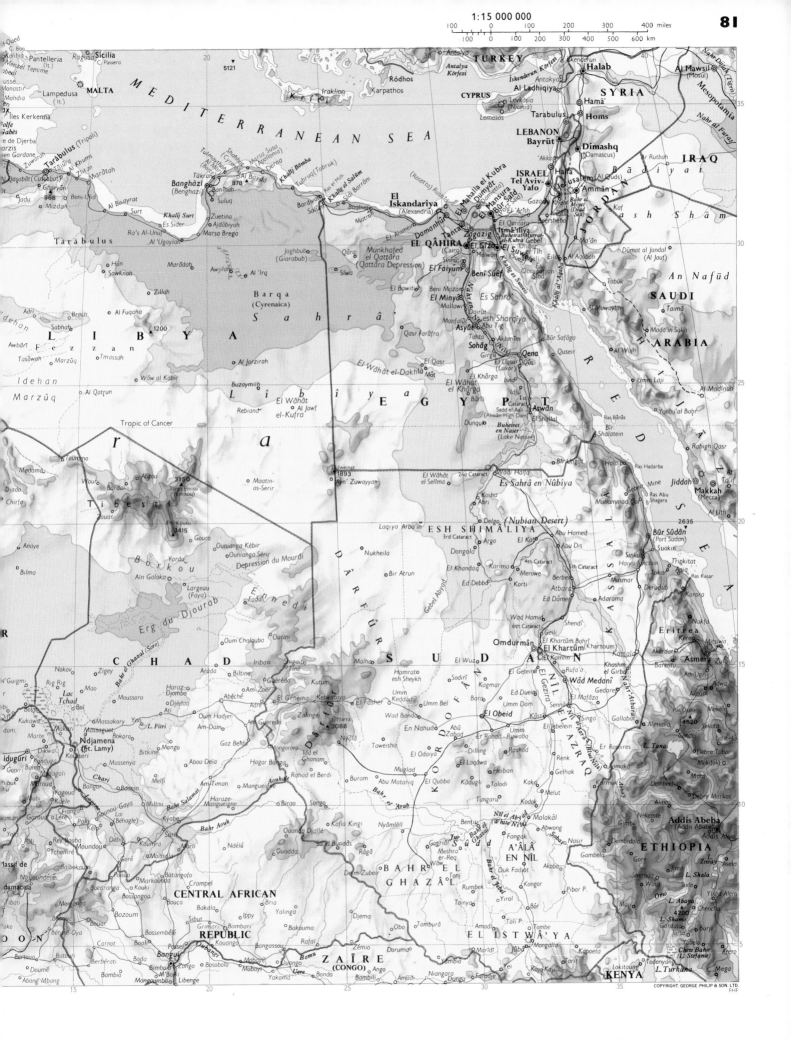

1:8 000 000

50　0　50　100　150　200 miles
50　0　50　100　150　200　250　300 km

MEDITERRANEAN SEA

SICILY
Marsala　Agrigento　Caltanissetta　CATANIA　Etna 3340　C. Spartivento
Ragusa　Siracusa　C. Passero
Valletta　MALTA

Linosa I. (Italian)
Lampione I.　Lampedusa (Italian)
Pantelleria (Italian)

Bizerte (Binzert)
Menzel Bourguiba　Menzel-Temime
Galite Is.　Tabarka
TUNIS　Hammamet　Nabeul
G. de Hammamet　Kelibia
Zaghouan　Soliman　C. Bon
Kairouan　**Sousse**　Monastir　Moknine
Msaken　Mahdia
Sfax　Iles Kerkenna
Maharès　Kneiss Is.
G. de Gabès
Gabès　Djerba I.
Zarzis　Djerba　El Kantara
Bahiret el Bibane

CONSTANTINE　Guelma
Skikda　Annaba
Sétif　El Eulma
Batna　Khenchela　Tébessa
Biskra
Chott Melrhir
Gafsa
Nefta　Chott el Fedjadj
Tozeur　Chott Djerid
El Oued　Kebili　Hamma
Touggourt　Douz　Matmata
Médenine
Ouargla
Ben Gardane
Zuwārah　**Tarābulus (Tripoli)**　Tājūrā
Nālūt　Jabal Nafūsah　Tarhūnah
Gharyān　Mizdah
Ghudāmis
Daraj
AL JABAL AL GHARB
Al Qaryah ash Sharqīyah
Ash Shuwayrif

Banghāzī (Benghazi)
Khalij Surt (Gulf of Sidra)
Misurata
Surt
AL KHUMS
MISRĀTAH
Al Hufrah
Marādah　'Ayn Zaqqūt
Waddān
Jabal Waddān
Hūn
Zillah
SABHAH
Jabal as Sawdā　840
Al Harūj al Aswad　1200
Brāch　Wādī ash Shāṭi
Sabhah (Sebha)
Awbārī
Marzūq
Idehan Marzūq
Al Qaţrūn
Madrūsah
Waw an Nāmūs
583
Tropic of Cancer

Grand Erg Oriental
Plateau du Tinrhert
In Amenas
Edjeleh
Illizi
Ghat　1428
Djanet
Tassili n' Ajjer
Erg d'Admer
Hamada de Tinrhert
Tamanrasset　2918
Mt. Tahat
Massif de l'Ahaggar
Adrar 2254

Ténéré
Sarīr Tibasti
Tibesti
Emi Koussi 3415
Tarso Emissi 3150
Pic Touside 3265
Zouar
Bardaï
Aozou
Massif de Kemet 2286
Pic Bette

Plateau du Djado
Chirfa
Djado

NIGER
Massif de Terazit

CHAD

COPYRIGHT GEORGE PHILIP & SON LTD.

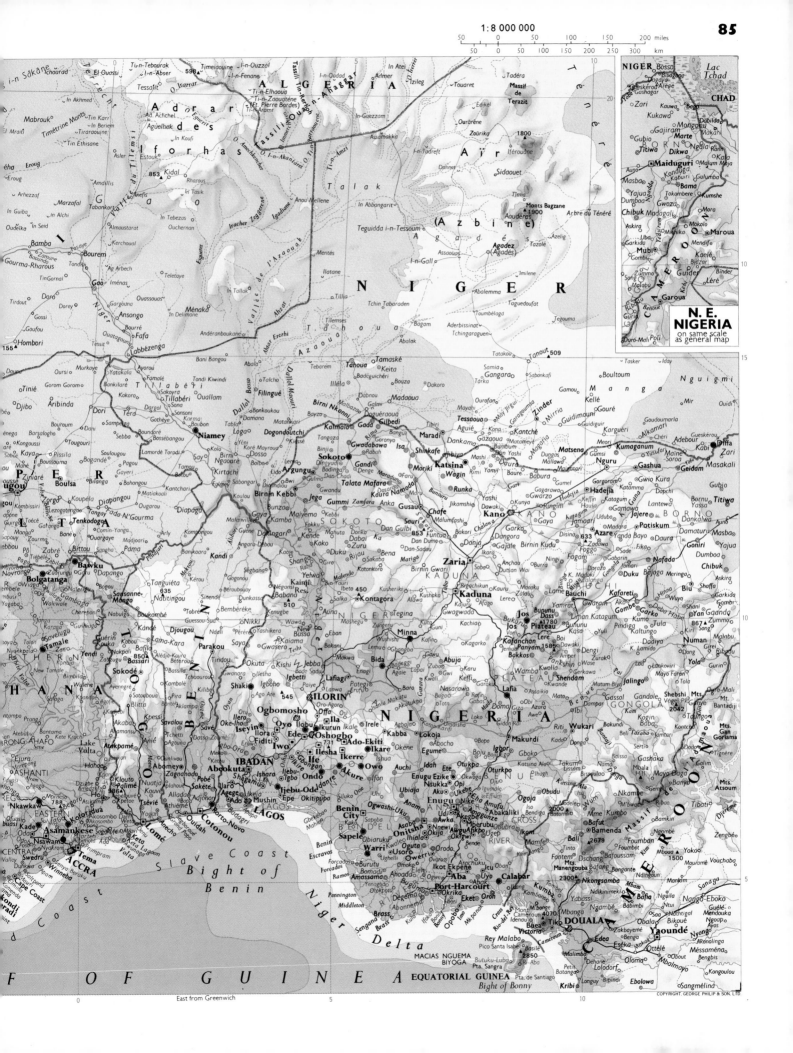

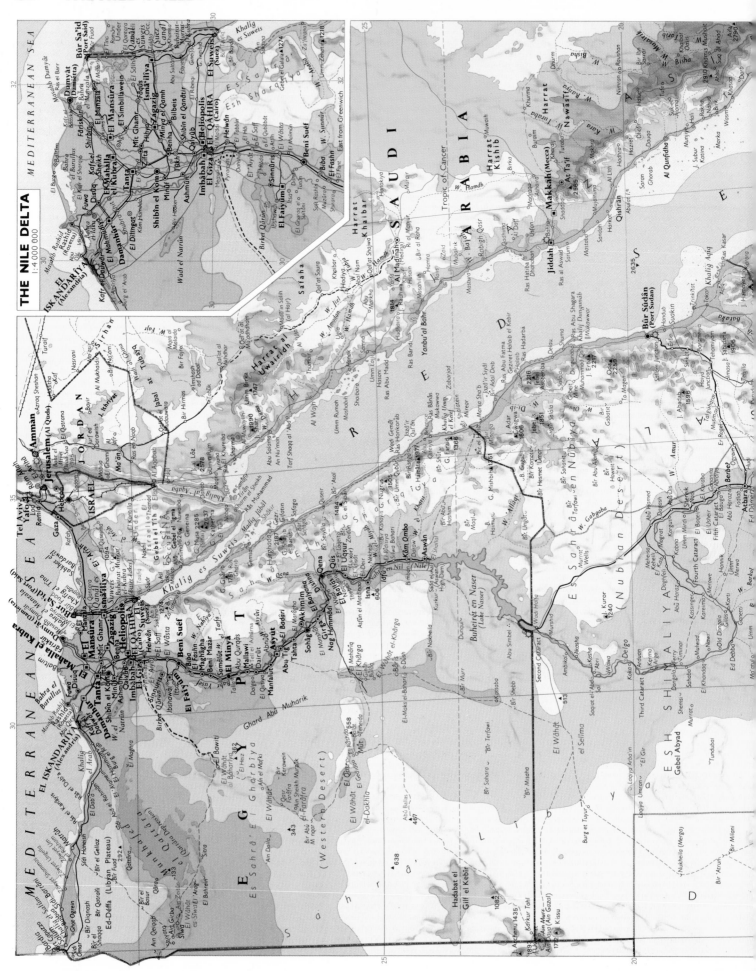

THE NILE DELTA
1:4 000 000

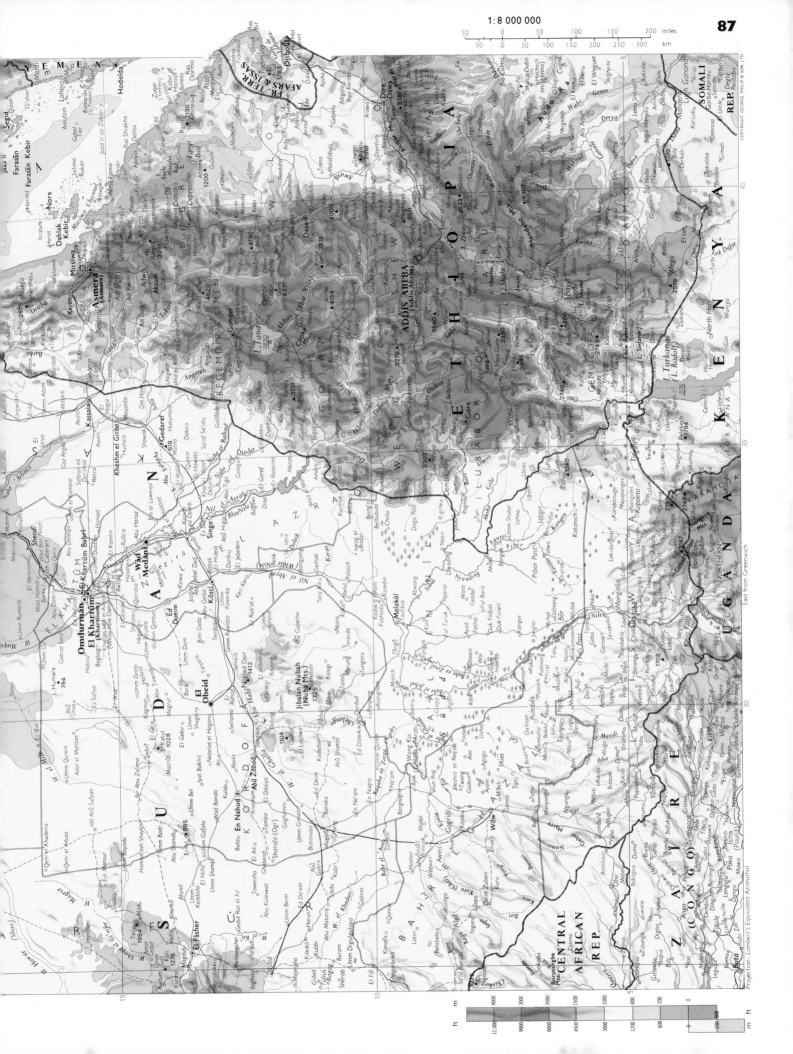

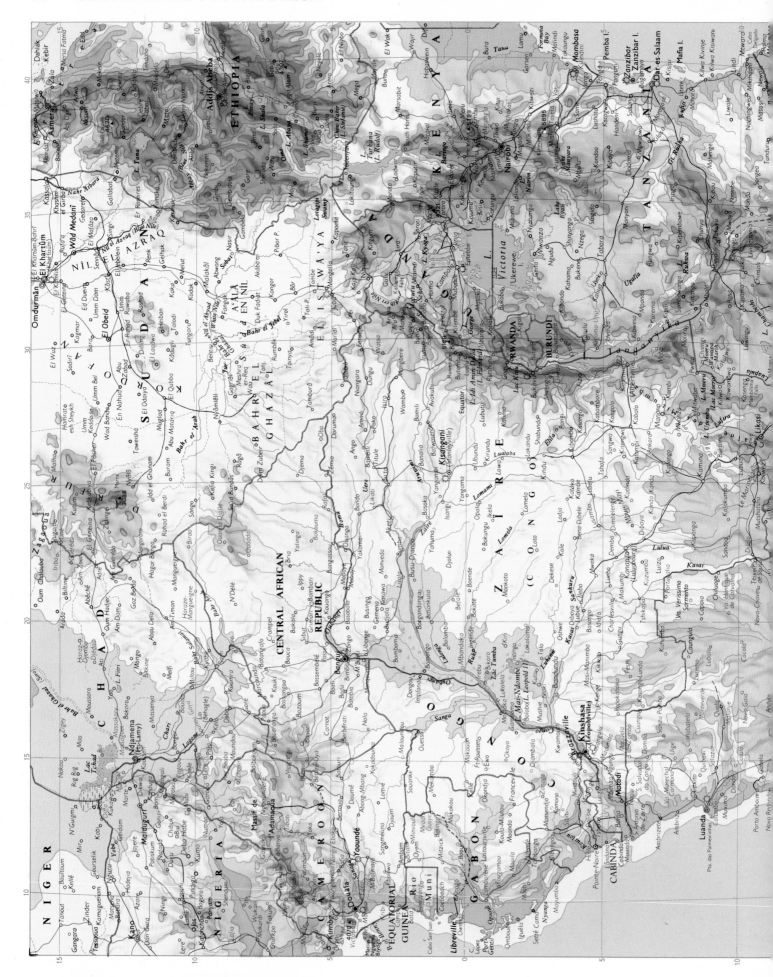

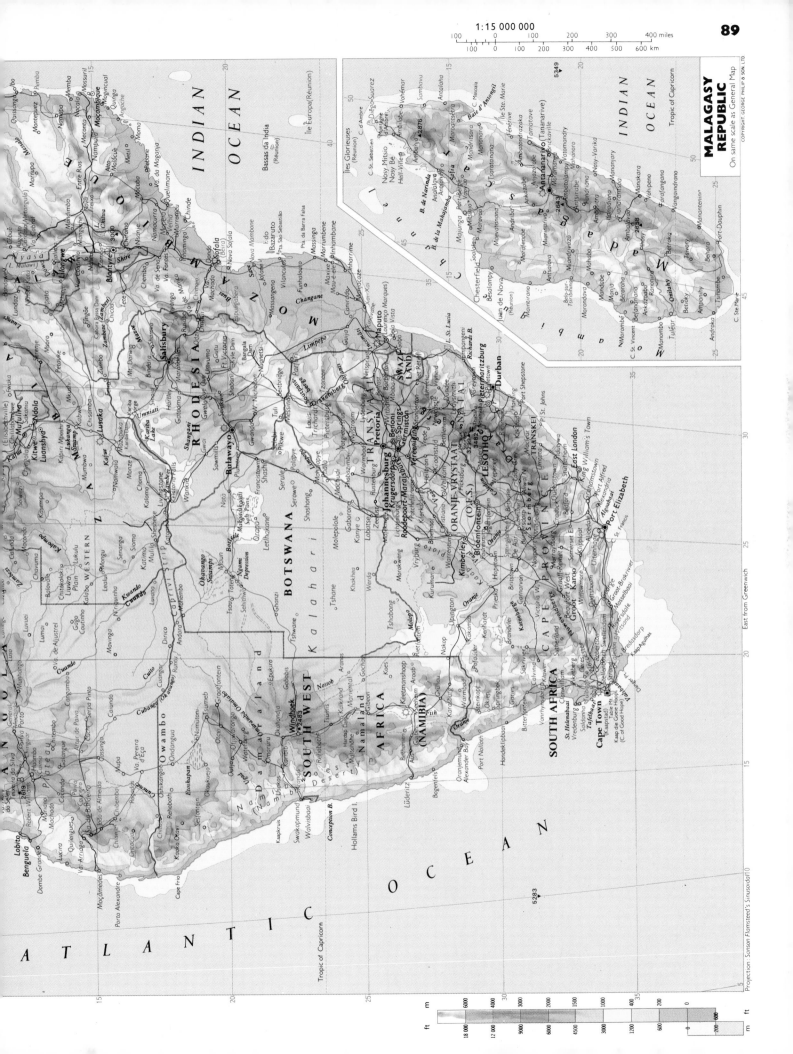

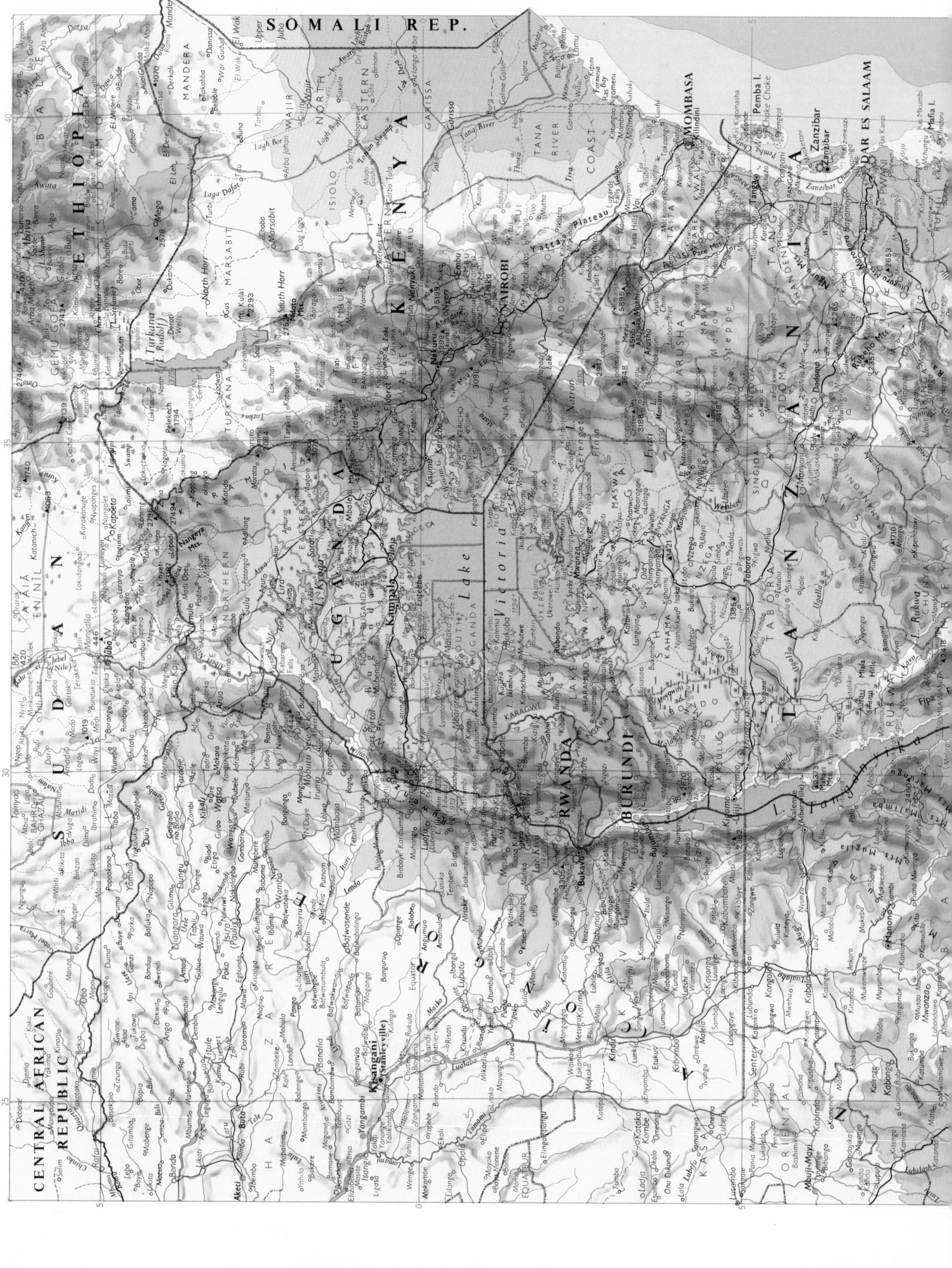

SOMALI REP.

ETHIOPIA

KENYA

UGANDA

TANZANIA

SUDAN

CENTRAL AFRICAN REPUBLIC

RWANDA

BURUNDI

MOMBASA

DAR ES SALAAM

ZANZIBAR

Pemba I.

Lake Victoria

L. Turkana (L. Rudolf)

NAIROBI

Kampala

Entebbe

Jinja

Bukavu

Stanleyville

EQUATOR

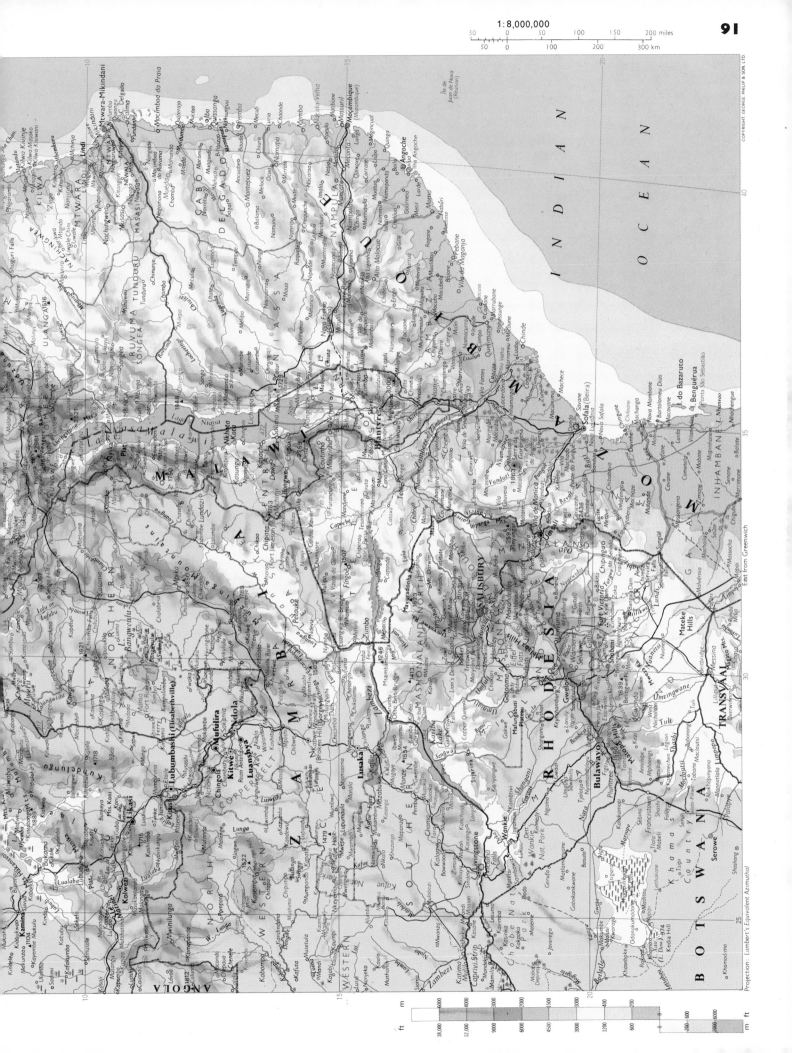

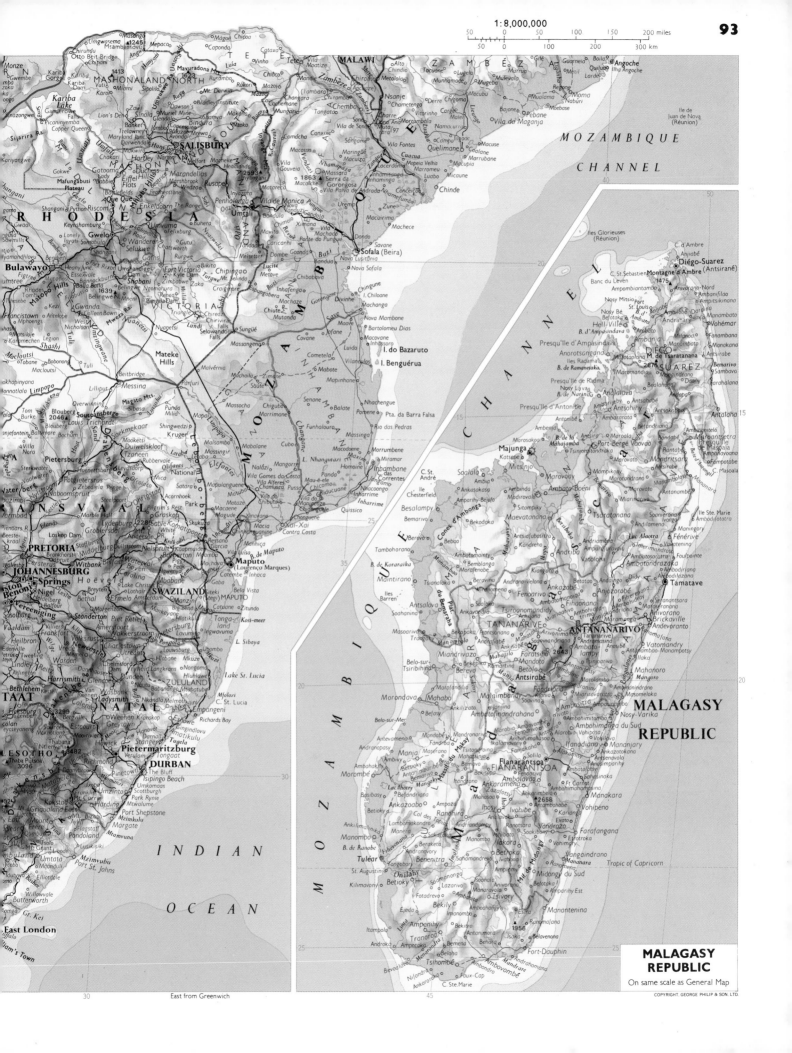

1:8,000,000

50   0   50   100   150   200 miles
50   0   100   200   300 km

MALAWI

ZAMBÉZIA

MOZAMBIQUE
CHANNEL

Ile de
Juan de Nova
(Réunion)

MASHONALAND NORTH

Kariba
Lake

RHODESIA

SALISBURY

MASHONALAND

Bulawayo

Matopo Hills

VICTORIA

Mateke
Hills

M O Z A M B I Q U E

Sofala (Beira)

Iles Glorieuses
(Réunion)

C. d'Ambre

Diégo-Suarez
(Antsirané)

Montagne d'Ambre

Banc du Leven

Nosy Mitsioa

Nosy Bé

Hell-Ville

Presqu'île d'Ampasindava

DIÉGO
SUAREZ

Messina

I. do Bazaruto

I. Benguérua

Presqu'île d'Antonibe

Majunga

Mitsinjo

15

TRANSVAAL

PRETORIA

JOHANNESBURG
Springs

Maputo
(Lourenço Marques)

SWAZILAND

MAPUTO

I N D I A N
O C E A N

M O Z A M B I Q U E   C H A N N E L

Morondava

MALAGASY

REPUBLIC

PIETERMARITZBURG

DURBAN

NATAL

LESOTHO

TANANARIVE

ANTANANARIVO
(Tananarive)

Antsirabé

FIANARANTSOA

Tamatave

Tuléar

Tropic of Capricorn

Fort-Dauphin

East London

C. Ste. Marie

30

East from Greenwich

45

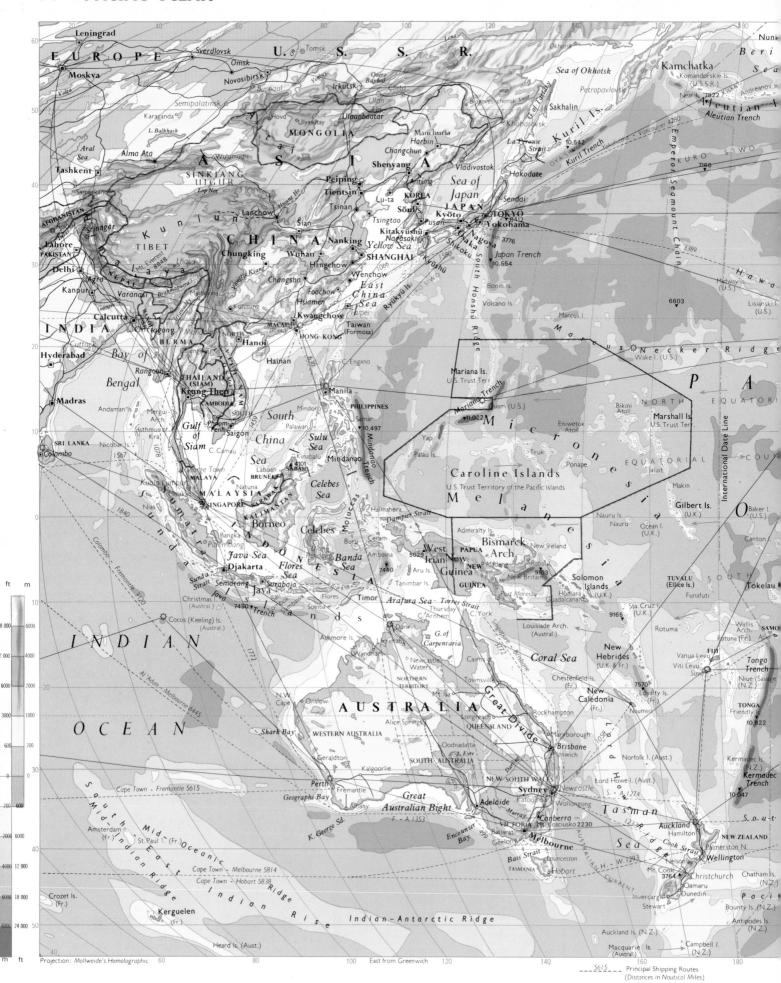

Projection: Mollweide's Homolographic   East from Greenwich

------5615------ Principal Shipping Routes
(Distances in Nautical Miles)

ALASKA
6050
Bristol Bay
Gulf of Alaska
Juneau
Prince of Wales I.
Prince Rupert
Kitimat
Queen Charlotte Is.
Vancouver
Vancouver I.
Victoria
Seattle
Tacoma
Portland
C. Blanco
Mendocino Seascarp
C. Mendocino
Sacramento
Oakland
San Francisco
4418
Los Angeles
San Diego

CANADA
Churchill
L. Athabaska
Dawson Creek
Edmonton
Prince Albert
Saskatoon
L. Winnipeg
Winnipeg
Regina
Medicine Hat
Spokane
Helena
Butte
Boise
Salt Lake City
Denver

NORTH AMERICA

Hudson Bay
Lynn Lake
James Bay
Belcher Is.
Schefferville
Hamilton Inlet
Labrador
Strait of Belle Isle

GREENLAND
C. Farewell

NORTH

BRITISH ISLES

Bismarck
Missouri
Cheyenne
Des Moines
Kansas
UNITED STATES
Santa Fe
Oklahoma

Duluth
L. Superior
St. Paul
Minneapolis
Milwaukee
L. Michigan
CHICAGO
Indianapolis
St. Louis
Memphis
Little Rock
Dallas
Austin

Sault Ste. Marie
Montréal
Québec
Toronto
L. Ontario
Detroit
Erie
Pittsburgh
Cincinnati

St. Lawrence
Anticosti
G. of St. Lawrence
Fredericton
Pr. Edward I.
St. John
C. Breton I.
Sable I.

Newfoundland
C. Race
Southampton 3091

NEW YORK
Philadelphia
Baltimore
Washington
Richmond
Norfolk
C. Hatteras

New York
New York – Recife 3078
Bermuda (U.K.)

ATLANTIC

OCEAN

Mendocino Seascarp
Murray Seascarp
2491

6741

2091

Guadalupe
6225
Pto. Eugenia
C. S. Lucas

GULF OF CALIFORNIA
CALIFORNIAN CURRENT

Tropic of Cancer

Hawaiian Is.
(U.S.A.)
Oahu
Honolulu
Hawaii

Clarion Fracture Zone

Ridge
(U.S.)

PACIFIC

CURRENT

OCEAN

EQUATORIAL
CURRENT

Palmyra Is. (U.S.)
Washington I. (U.K.)
Fanning I. (U.K.)
Christmas I.
Jarvis I. (U.S.)
Christmas Island Ridge

CURRENT

Malden I.
Starbuck I.

Tongareva
Penrhyn Is.
Manihiki
Suwarrow Is. (Suvorov)
Vostok I.
Flint I.
Caroline I.

Phoenix Is.
(U.K. & U.S.)

Equator

Clipperton Fracture Zone
Clipperton I. (Fr.)

4711
3666

Revilla Gigedo Is.
(Mexico)

MEXICO
SIERRA MADRE
Torreón
Monterrey
3277
Aguascalientes
Guadalajara
San Luis Potosí
México
Puebla
3700
Acapulco

Ciudad Juárez
El Paso
San Antonio
Houston
Galveston
New Orleans
Mobile
Tampico
Veracruz
Mérida
Yucatán Channel
Gulf of Mexico
Miami
Florida Strait
BAHAMAS
CUBA
La Habana

Savannah
Jacksonville
Tampa

Appalachian Mts.
Atlanta

NYC 1972

Panamá 4530

West Indies
Hispaniola
HAITI
9200
DOM. REP.
Santo Domingo
JAMAICA
Kingston
PUERTO RICO
St. Thomas (U.S.)
Virgin Is.
Guadeloupe (Fr.)
Martinique (Fr.)
BARBADOS
Leeward Is.

Caribbean Sea
BELIZE
S.E. MONSOON DRIFT
GUATEMALA
Guatemala
HONDURAS
Tegucigalpa
SALVADOR
NICARAGUA
Managua
San José
COSTA RICA
CENTRAL AMERICA
PANAMA
Panamá Canal

Barranquilla
Curaçao (Ne.)
Maracaibo
Windward Is.
TRINIDAD & TOBAGO
Caracas
Orinoco
VENEZUELA

Cocos I.

Galápagos
(Ecuador)

Guayaquil
ECUADOR
Chimborazo 6267
Cuenca
C. Pariñas
Lobos I.
Chiclayo
Trujillo

Medellín
Bogotá
Cali
COLOMBIA
835
Quito

C. S. Francisco
Manaus
Amazon
Iquitos

BRAZIL
SOUTH

706

6369
Lima
Callao
Cuzco
PERU
AMERICA

PERUVIAN CURRENT

Marquesas Is.
(Fr.)

Society Is. (Fr.)
Cook Islands
Tahiti (Fr.)
Windward Is.
Leeward Is.
Tuamotu Archipelago
(Fr.)

Tuamotu Ridge

Hervey Is.
Rarotonga

Seamount Chain

Tubuai Is.
(Austral Is.)
(Fr.)

Rapa Iti
(Fr.)

AUSTRAL

Pitcairn I. (U.K.)
Ducie I. (U.K.)

Tahiti – Panamá 4570

Auckland – Panamá 6510

EAST PACIFIC RIDGE

Tropic of Capricorn

Sala-y-Gomez
(Chile)
Easter Is.
(Chile)

San Félix (Chile)
San Ambrosio (Chile)

Southeast

Pacific Basin

La Paz
BOLIVIA
Illampu & Ancohuma
6550
L. Titicaca
Arequipa
6866
Iquique

8050
Antofagasta
Trench
Chile

ANDES

Salta
Tucumán
Asunción
PARAGUAY
Corrientes

Arch. de Juan Fernández
(Chile)
Alejandro Selkirk
Robinson Crusoe

Chile Rise

Aconcagua 6960
Valparaíso
Santiago
Concepción
Neuquén
Córdoba
Rosario
Buenos Aires
La Plata
Río de la Plata
Santa Fe
URUGUAY
Montevideo
Paysandú
Pto. Alegre

P.A.–Valparaíso
1414
1355
795
PATAGONIA
Paraná

ARGENTINA

Mar del Plata

G. of San Matías

SOUTH
ATLANTIC
OCEAN

PACIFIC

ANTARCTIC RIDGE

WEST WIND DRIFT

CAPE HORN CURRENT

Pacific–
Antarctic
Basin

Chonos Arch.
G. of Penas
Wellington
Sta. Cruz
Punta Arenas
P. Deseado
G. of San Jorge
Argentine Basin
6212
Buenos Aires – Montevideo
P.A.
Falkland Is. (U.K.)
Stanley
Str. of Magellan
Tierra del Fuego
C. Horn
South Georgia

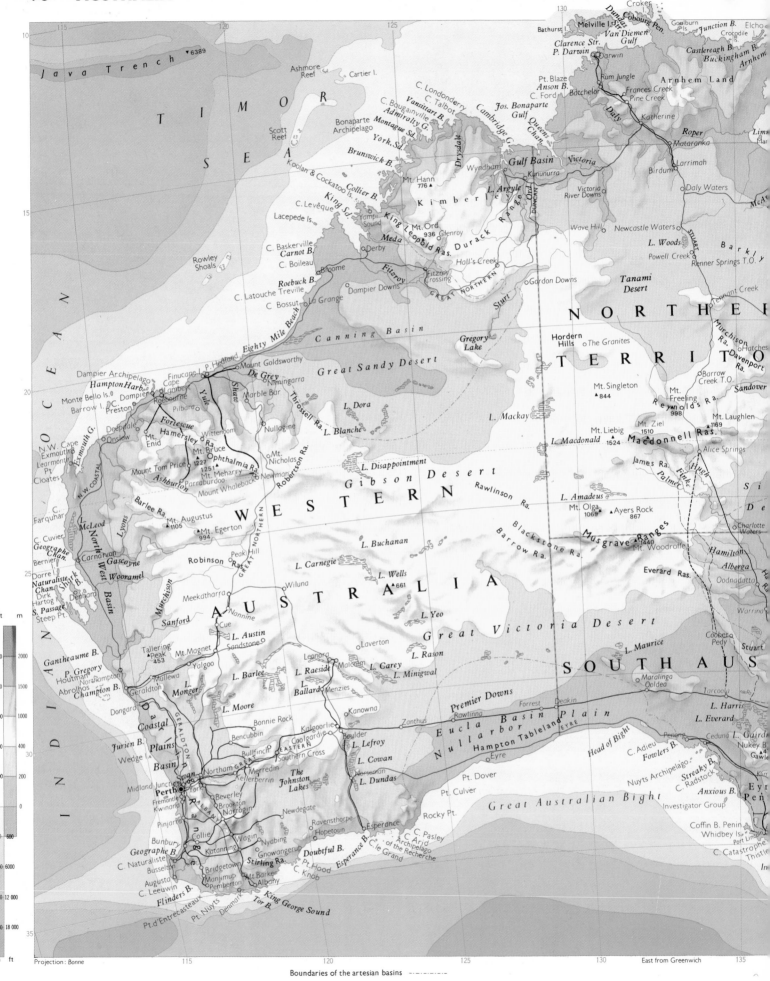

Projection: Bonne

Boundaries of the artesian basins ‑‑‑‑‑‑‑‑

East from Greenwich

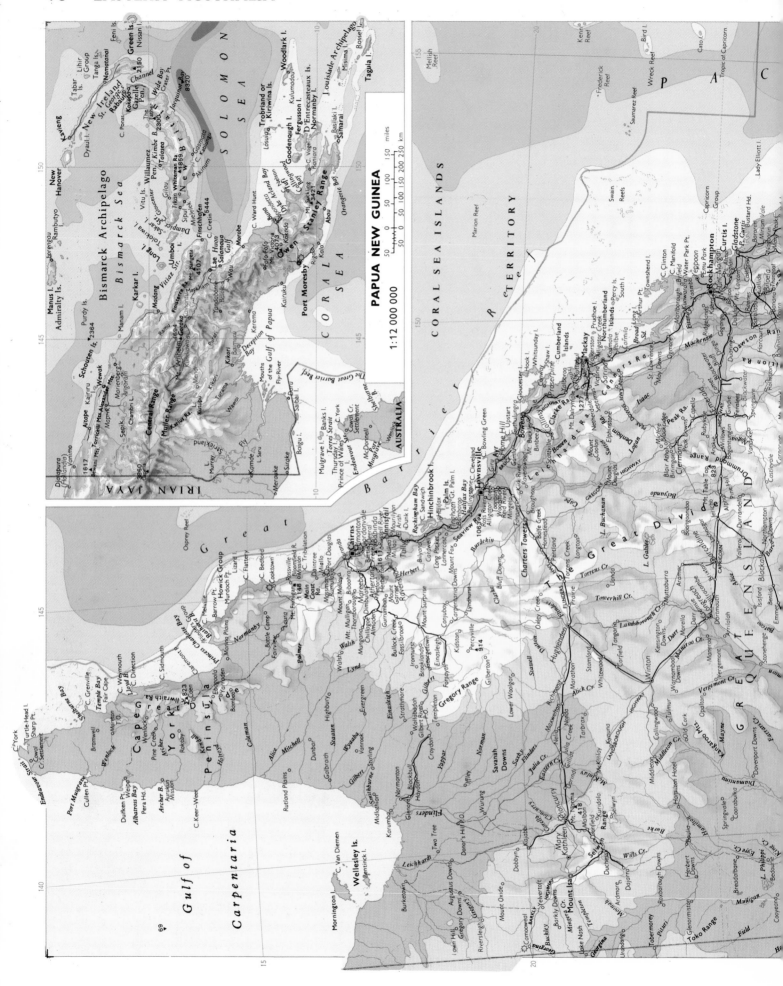

PAPUA NEW GUINEA

1:12 000 000

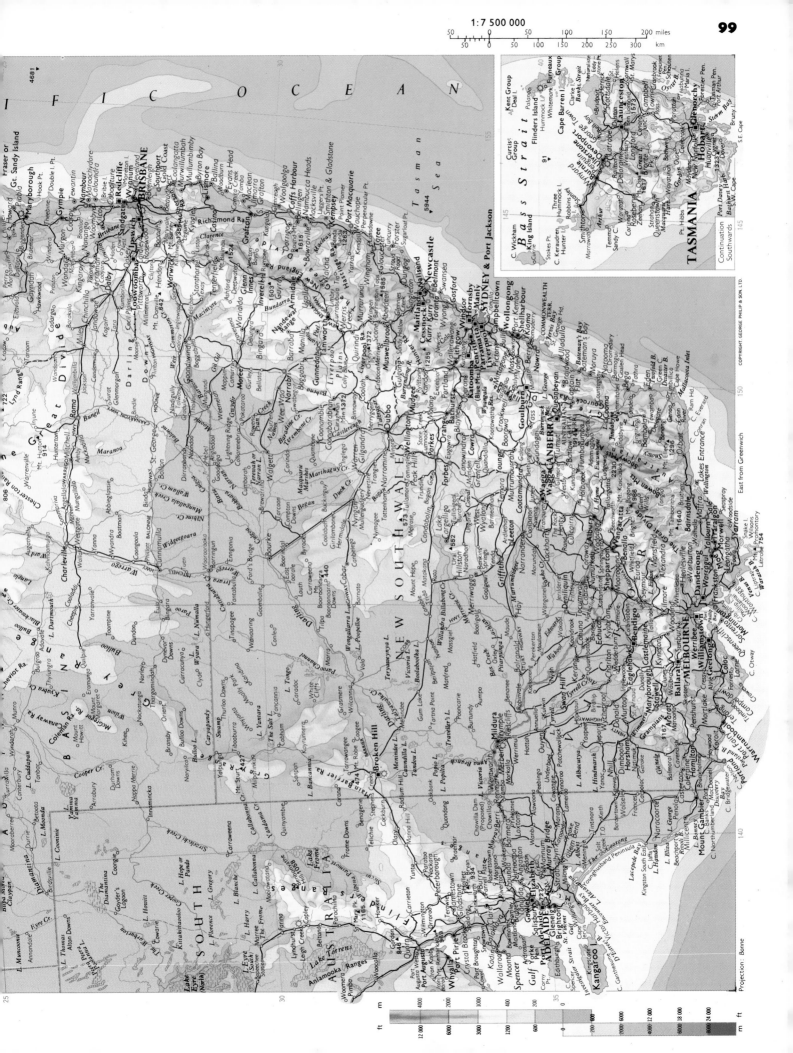

1 : 4 500 000

20 0 20 40 60 80 100 miles
20 0 40 80 120 160 km

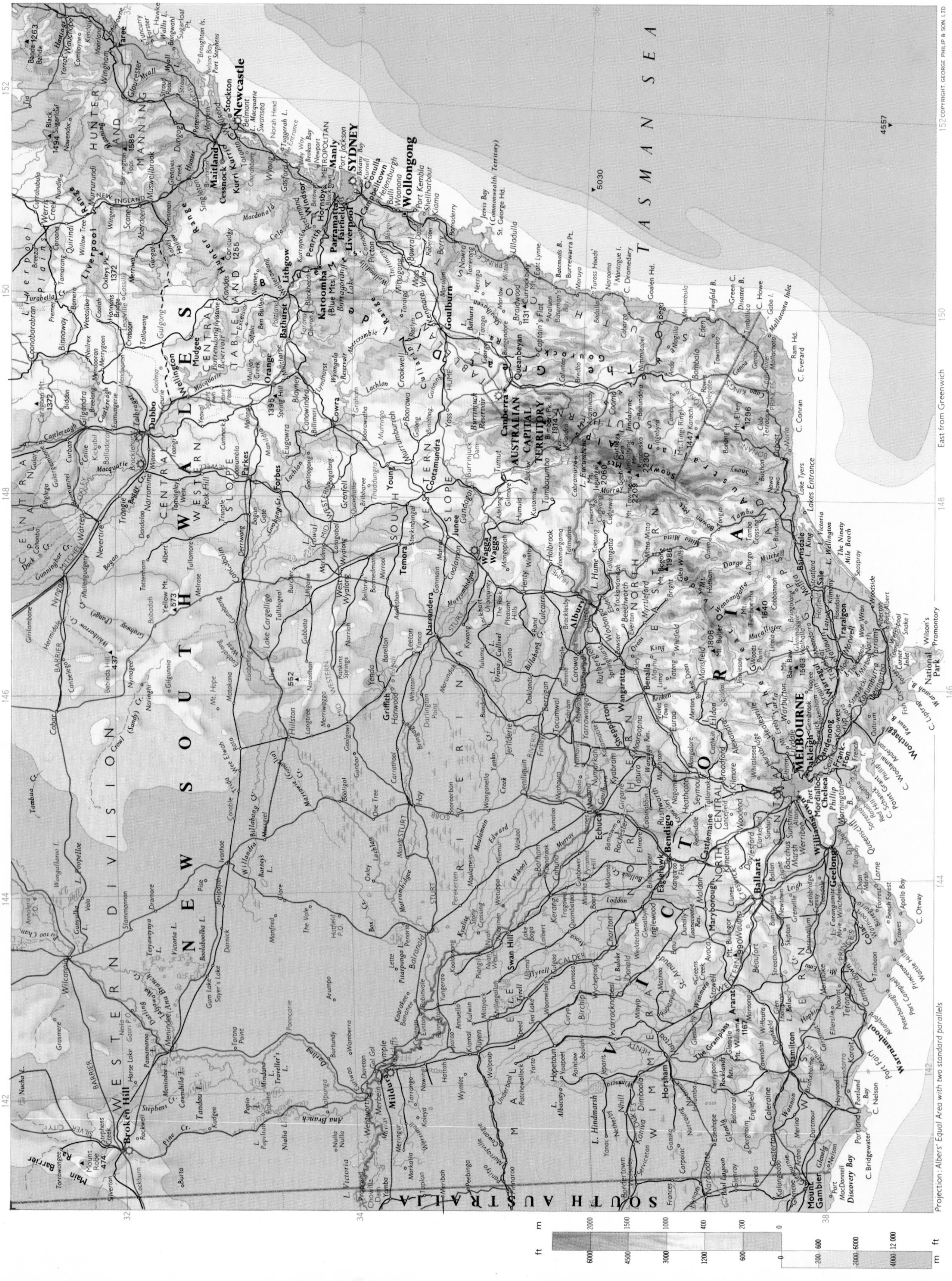

COPYRIGHT GEORGE PHILIP & SON LTD.

T A S M A N   S E A

S O U T H   W A L E S

N E W   S O U T H   W A L E S

V I C T O R I A

S O U T H   A U S T R A L I A

WESTERN DIVISION

CENTRAL WESTERN SLOPE

WESTERN SLOPE

RIVERINA

EASTERN HIGHLANDS

WIMMERA

MALLEE

NORTH CENTRAL

CENTRAL

WESTERN

SYDNEY
Newcastle
Wollongong
Maitland
Cessnock
Katoomba (Blue Mts.)
Lithgow
Bathurst
Orange
Dubbo
Parkes
Forbes
Cowra
Goulburn
Canberra
AUSTRALIAN CAPITAL TERRITORY
Queanbeyan
Wagga Wagga
Albury
Griffith
Temora
Junee
Cootamundra
Young
Narrandera
Leeton
Broken Hill
Mildura
Swan Hill
Bendigo
Ballarat
Geelong
MELBOURNE
Sale
Traralgon
Warrnambool
Hamilton
Horsham
Mount Gambier
Penrith
Parramatta
Liverpool
Fairfield
Manly
Taree

Liverpool Range
Liverpool Plains
HUNTER
MANNING
NEW ENGLAND
CENTRAL TABLELAND
Great Dividing Range
SNOWY MTS.
Mt. Kosciusko 2230
Mt. Bogong 1986
Wilson's Promontory
National Park

Projection: Albers' Equal Area with two standard parallels

East from Greenwich

m 6000 4500 3000 1500 1000 400 200 0
ft
ft 0 200 600 1200 2000 4000 12000
m

152   150   148   146   144   142

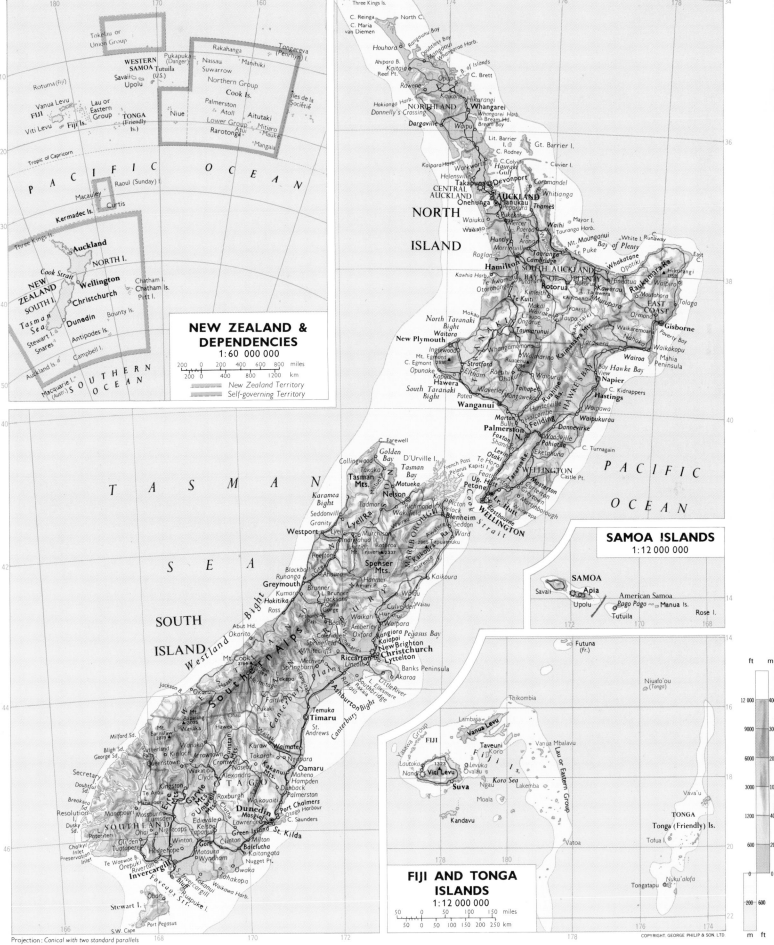

1:6 000 000

20 0   20   40   60   80   100 miles
20 0   40   80   120   160 km

NEW ZEALAND & DEPENDENCIES
1:60 000 000

200   0   200   400   600   800 miles
200   0   400   800   1200 km

␣␣␣␣␣␣␣␣ New Zealand Territory
␣␣␣␣␣␣␣␣ Self-governing Territory

SAMOA ISLANDS
1:12 000 000

FIJI AND TONGA ISLANDS
1:12 000 000

50   0   50   100   150 miles
50   0   100   150   200   250 km

Projection: Conical with two standard parallels

COPYRIGHT. GEORGE PHILIP & SON. LTD.

1:30,000,000

100 0 100 200 300 400 500 600 700 miles

100 0 200 400 600 800 1000 km

Tropic of Cancer

Bahama Islands

Milwaukee Deep
Puerto 3200
Rico

Hispaniola

Cuba

La Habana

Greater Jamaica

Florida Strait

C. Sable

C. Catoche

Gulf of Mexico

New Orleans

Mississippi Delta

Houston

Rio Grande del Norte

Monterrey

Eastern Sierra Madre

México Popocatepetl Orizaba

Western Sierra Madre

Guadalajara Sanago

Mexican Plateau

Puebla

Chilatepel

Mazatlan

Gulf of California

California

C. San Lucas

C. Corrientes

Revilla Gigedo Is.

Clarion Fracture Zone

Yucatán Strait

Yucatán Peninsula

Yucatan Basin

Gulf of Campeche

Gulf of Honduras

C. Catoche

Guatemala

Isthmus of Tehuantepec

G. of Tehua

Guatemala Trench
6662

Antilles Sea

Porto
Prince

Trough
7880

Cayman

C. Gracias à Dios

Colombian Basin

Venezuelan Basin

Sierra Madre

Maracaibo Bogotá

Caribbean

Caribbean Sea

G. of Venezuela

G. of Darién

G. of Panama

Panama Canal

Nicaragua

Panama
3837

5300

Cordillera Occidental
Cordillera Central
Cordillera Oriental
Magdalena

Quito Cotopaxi 5897
Chimborazo 6267

Napo

Maranon

Ucayali

Putumayo

Orinoco

A n d e s

Bolivian Plateau

La Paz

Peru Trench

Chile

Lima

Chincha Is.

C. de San Francisco

G. de Guayaquil

Pta. Parina

Pta. Agua

Lobos Is.

Tropic of Capricorn

Galapagos

P A C I F I C   O C E A N

POLITICAL 1:70,000,000

GREENLAND (Denmark)

Denmark Str.

Godthaab

C. Farewell

ARCTIC OCEAN

Ellesmere I.

Queen Elizabeth Islands

Patrick I.

Banks I.

Victoria I.

Baffin Island

Hudson Strait

Hudson Bay

Labrador

Davis Strait

Beaufort Sea

C. Barrow

Arctic Circle

Mackenzie

Gt. Bear L.

Gt. Slave L.

Athabasca L.

Churchill

Reindeer L.

Lake Winnipeg

C A N A D A

Yukon

Dawson

Skagway

Juneau

ALASKA

Anchorage

Pr. Rupert

Queen Charlotte Is.

Vancouver

Victoria

Seattle

Portland

Spokane

Fraser

Edmonton

Calgary

Lethbridge

Medicine Hat

Regina

Saskatoon

Winnipeg

Minneapolis

St Paul

Milwaukee

Chicago

Omaha

Missouri

Platte

Denver

Salt Lake City

Snake

Gt. Salt L.

San Francisco

Oakland

Los Angeles

El Paso

Dallas

Houston

Galveston

Kansas City

St. Louis

Memphis

Cincinnati

Pittsburgh

Detroit

Buffalo

Toronto

Montreal

Ottawa

Quebec

Timmins

New York

Philadelphia

Baltimore

Washington

Boston

Nova Scotia

U N I T E D   S T A T E S

Atlanta

New Orleans

Florida

C. Hatteras

Bermuda (Br.)

ATLANTIC OCEAN

Tropic of Cancer

BAHAMAS

CU-BA

La Habana

Gulf of Mexico

Red

Monterrey

Tampico

Veracruz

Mexico

Guadalajara

Acapulco

Baja California

M E X I C O

Coatzacoalcos

Mérida

GUATEMALA
BELIZE
EL SALVADOR
HONDURAS
NICARAGUA
COSTA RICA

CENTRAL AMERICA

PANAMA

Caribbean Sea

Kingston

HAITI
DOM.

Puerto Rico (U.S.)

Cartagena

Maracaibo

Caracas

COLOMBIA

VENEZUELA

SOUTH AMERICA

TRINIDAD & TOBAGO

Guadeloupe (Fr.)

Martinique (Fr.)

Revilla Gigedo (Mex.)

Valparaiso 5138

PACIFIC OCEAN

Bering Sea

Aleutian Is. (U.S.)

West from 90 Greenwich

Projection: Bonne

m 4000 3000 2000 1500 1000 400 200 600

ft 12 000 9000 6000 4500 3000 1200 600 200 600 2000 6000 12 000 18 000 24 000 ft

ft m

Projection: Bonne

ALASKA
1:30 000 000

100 0   100 200 300 miles
100 0   200   400 km

1:15 000 000

100 50   0   100   200   300   400 miles
100   0   100   200   300   400   500   600 km

GREENLAND

ATLANTIC

Baffin Bay

Devon Island
Lancaster Sound

Arctic Bay
Brodeur
Peninsula
Bylot I.
Pond Inlet
Milne Inlet
Milne
Mary River
Fury & Hecla Str.
Igloolik Island
Melville
Peninsula
Hall
Lake
Prince
Charles
Foxe
Basin
C. Dorchester
Foxe
Penin.
Amadjuak
Cape Dorset
Lake Harbour
Frobisher Bay

Home B.
C. Hewett
Clyde
Broughton Island
Pangnirtung Island
Cumberland Peninsula
C. Dyer
Cape Dyer
Hoare B.
Cumberland Sd.
C. Mercy
Resolution I.
C. Chidley

Davis Strait

Disko
Christianshåb
Sukkertoppen
Godthåb
Frederikshåb
Ivigtut
Julianehåb
Nanortalik
Kap Farvel

Angmagssalik

Kong Frederik VI's Kyst

Sendre Strømfjord
Holsteinsborg

Svartenhuk Halvø

Disko B.

Hudson Strait

Ungava Bay

Ungava
Peninsula
Payne
Payne L.
Portland Promontory
Inoutcjouac (Port Harrison)

Hudson

Bay

Ottawa Is.

Sleeper Is.
King George Is.
King George Is.
Baker's Dozen
Belcher Is.

Clearwater
Gr. Whale
Poste de la Baleine
(Great Whale River)

LABRADOR

QUEBEC

NEWFOUNDLAND

St. John's

Gulf of
St. Lawrence

PR. EDWARD I.
Charlottetown
Summerside

NOVA SCOTIA

Halifax
Dartmouth

NEW BRUNSWICK
Moncton
Saint John
Fredericton

MONTRÉAL
Québec
Ottawa
TORONTO

Thunder Bay

Lake Superior

Sudbury

Lake Huron

L. Ontario

Buffalo
Rochester
Syracuse
Albany

Boston

NEW YORK

CHICAGO

DETROIT
Toledo
Cleveland
Akron

Milwaukee

West from Greenwich

COPYRIGHT. GEORGE PHILIP & SON. LTD.

PACIFIC OCEAN

YUKON TERRITORY

NORTH WEST

GREAT SLAVE LAKE

WOOD BUFFALO NATIONAL PARK

BRITISH COLUMBIA

ALBERTA

ALASKA

VANCOUVER ISLAND

QUEEN CHARLOTTE ISLANDS

WASHINGTON

IDAHO

Projection: Lambert's Equivalent Azimuthal   West from Greenwich

1:7 000 000

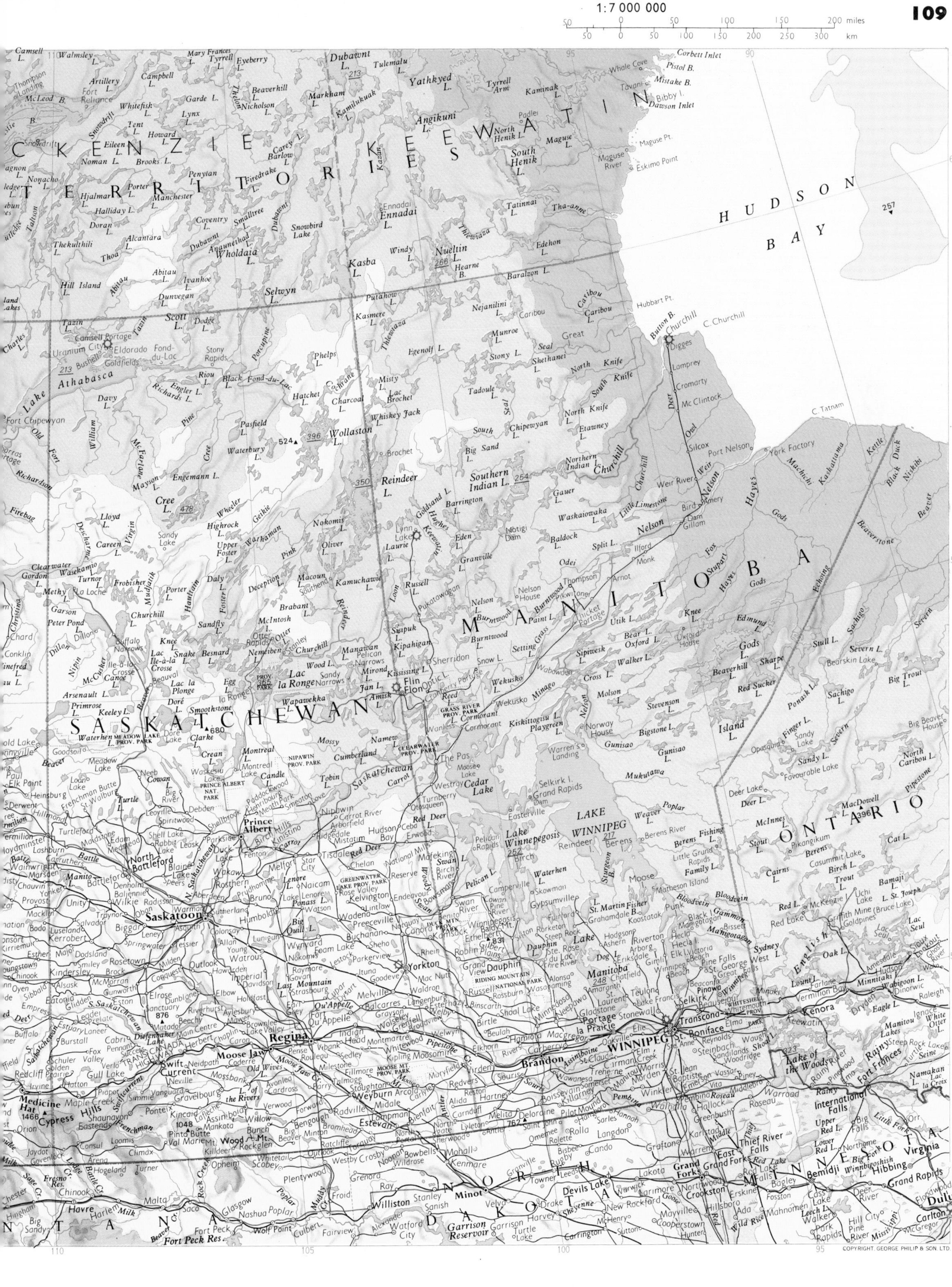

50 0 50 100 150 200 miles
50 0 50 100 150 200 250 300 km

HUDSON BAY

MACKENZIE / TERRITORIES / KEEWATIN

SASKATCHEWAN

MANITOBA

ONTARIO

NORTH DAKOTA

MINNESOTA

MONTANA

Lake Athabasca

Cree L.

Reindeer L.

Wollaston L.

Southern Indian L.

LAKE WINNIPEG

Lake Winnipegosis

Lac la Ronge

Churchill

Saskatoon

Prince Albert

North Battleford

Regina

Moose Jaw

Swift Current

Medicine Hat

Cypress Hills

Yorkton

Dauphin

Brandon

WINNIPEG

St. Boniface

Portage la Prairie

Selkirk

Kenora

Lake of the Woods

Flin Flon

The Pas

Churchill

Nelson

Minot

Williston

Fort Peck Res.

Garrison Reservoir

Devils Lake

Grand Forks

Bemidji

Duluth

COPYRIGHT. GEORGE PHILIP & SON LTD.

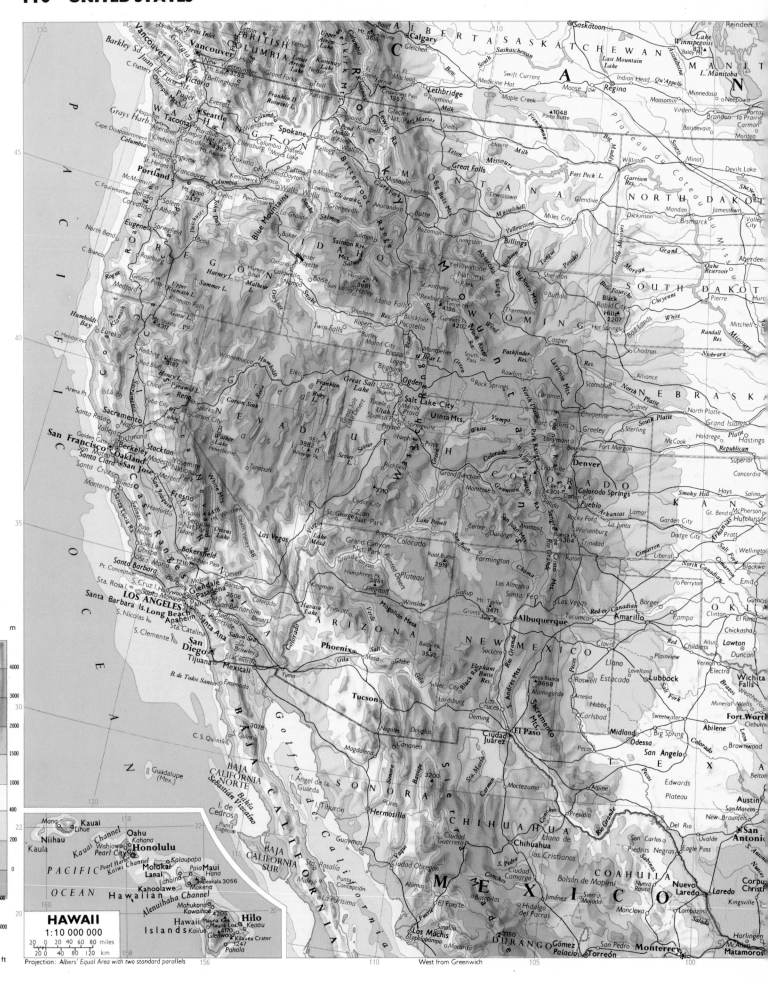

HAWAII
1:10 000 000

Projection: Albers' Equal Area with two standard parallels

1:12 000 000

50   0   50   100   150   200   250   300 miles
50   0   50 100 150 200 250 300 350 400 450 km

COPYRIGHT: GEORGE PHILIP & SON, LTD

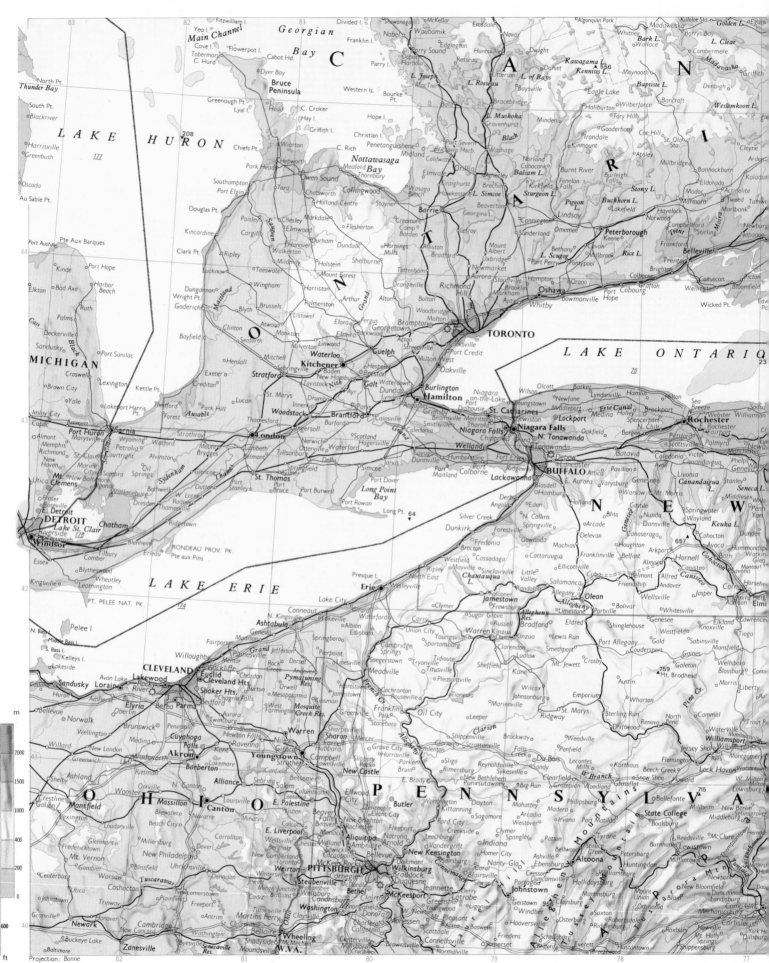

Projection: Bonne

Interstate Highways (U.S.A.), Superhighways (Canada)

Interstate Highways and Superhighways under Construction

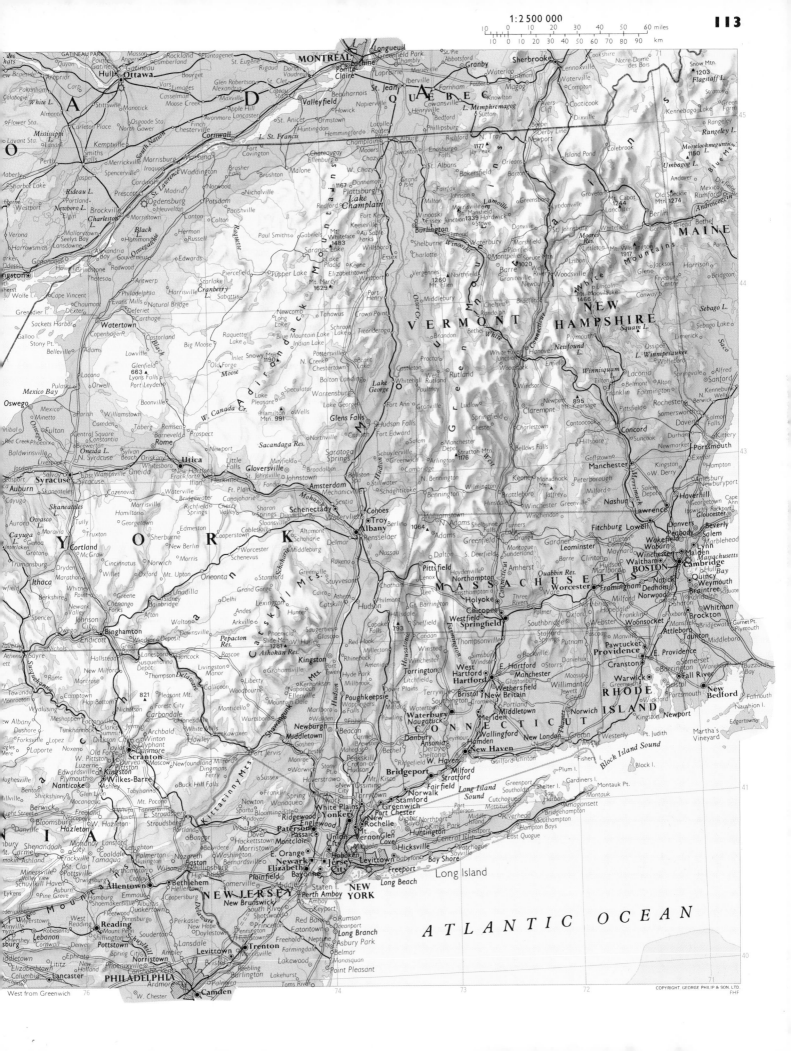

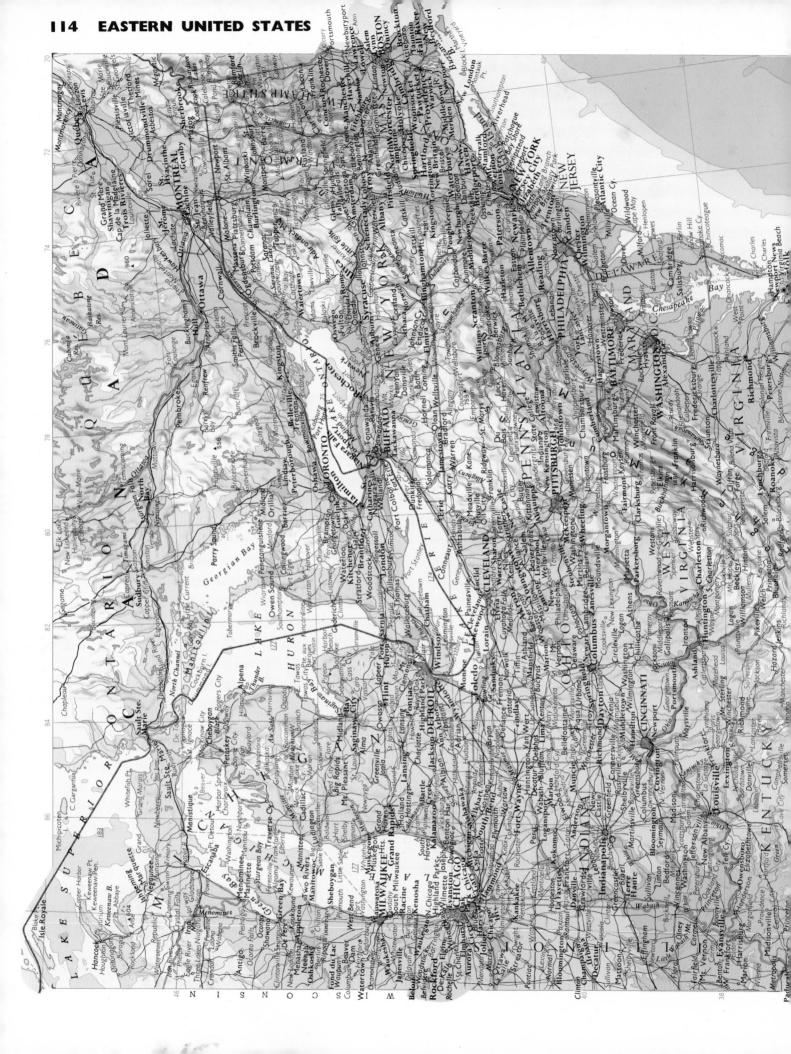

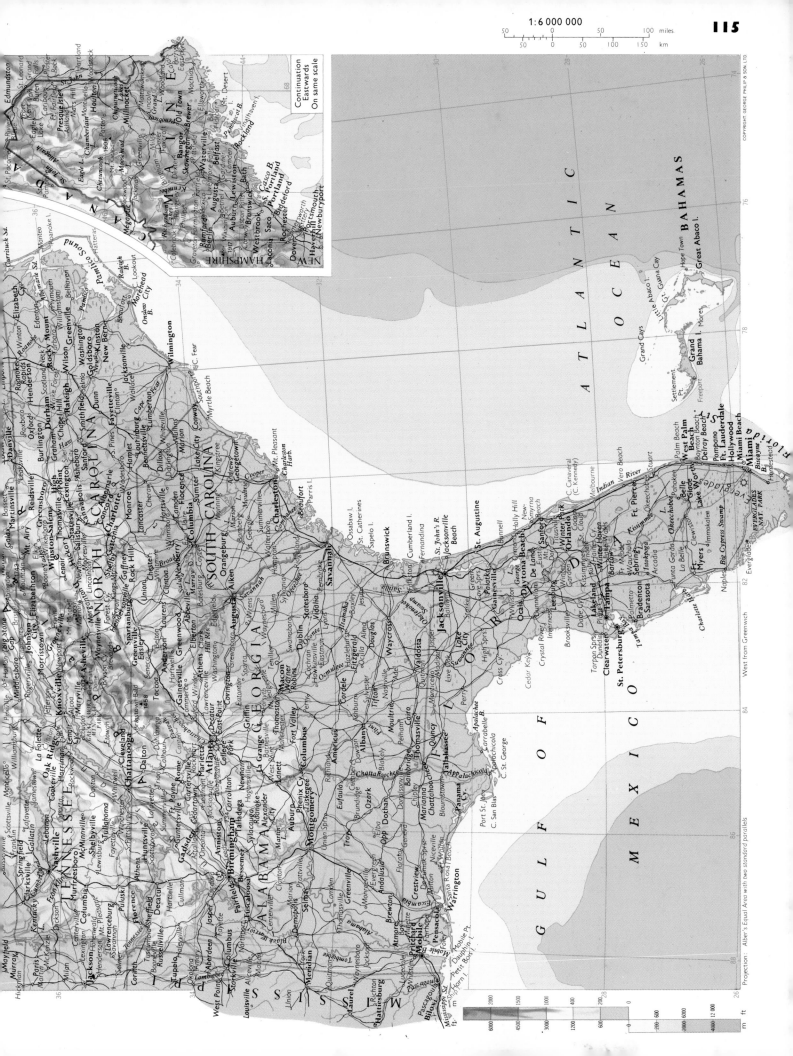

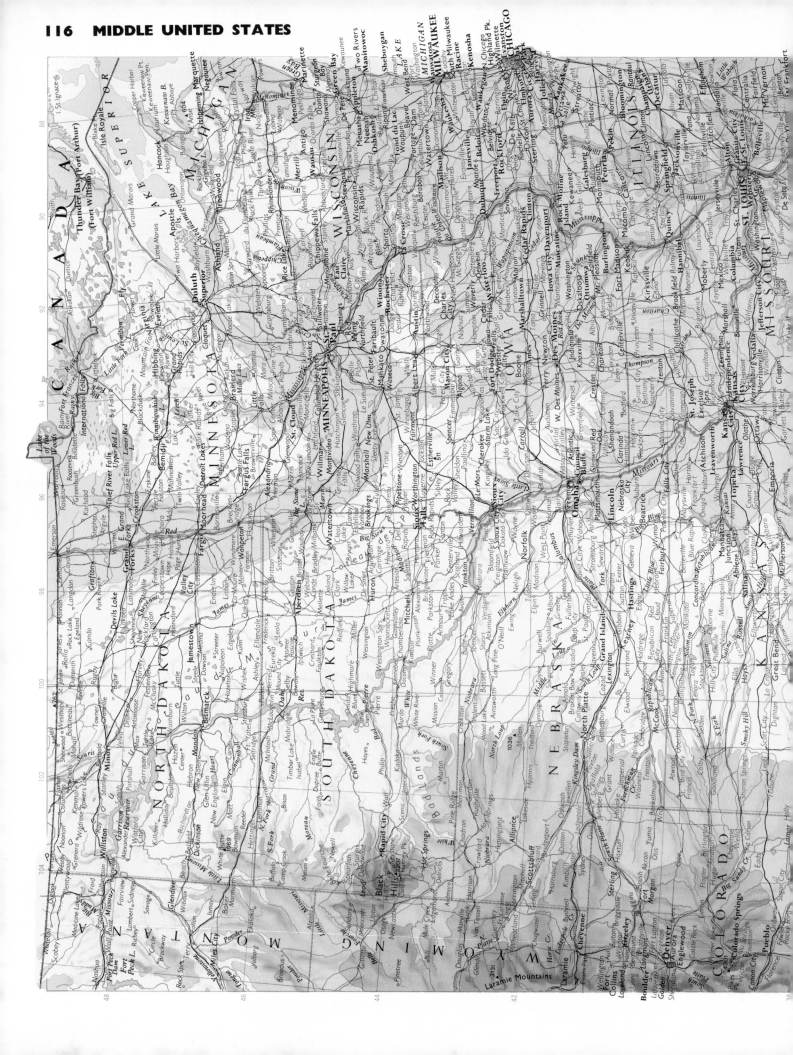

1:6 000 000

50　　　0　　　50　　　100 miles
50　0　50　100　150 km

SASKATCHEWAN

ALBERTA

BRITISH COLUMBIA

M O N T A N A

W Y O M I N G

Bighorn Mountains

Medicine Bow Range

U T A H

I D A H O

GREAT SALT LAKE

Salt Lake City

Great Salt Lake Desert

Uinta Mountains

Ogden

Provo

Pocatello

Idaho Falls

Blackfoot

N E V A D A

Lewis Range

GLACIER NAT. PARK

Cabinet Mountains

Bitterroot Range

Clearwater Mountains

Salmon River Mountains

Lemhi Range

Sapphire Mts.

Big Belt Mts.

Little Belt Mts.

Crazy Mts.

Great Falls

Helena

Butte

Anaconda

Bozeman

Billings

Sheridan

Casper

YELLOWSTONE NAT. PARK

Wind River Range

Absaroka Range

Green River

Rock Springs

Flaming Gorge Res.

W A S H I N G T O N

O R E G O N

C A L I F O R N I A

Blue Mountains

Wallowa Mts.

Coast Range

Cascade Range

Seattle

Tacoma

Olympia

Spokane

Walla Walla

Pendleton

La Grande

Baker

Portland

Vancouver

Salem

Albany

Eugene

Bend

Klamath Falls

Medford

Grants Pass

Roseburg

Olympic Mts.

Mt. Rainier 4392

Mt. Baker 3285

Mt. Adams 3751

Mt. Hood 3427

Mt. Jefferson 3200

Three Sisters 3166

Mt. Shasta 4317

Lewiston

Moscow

Pullman

Boise

Nampa

Caldwell

Twin Falls

Reno

Carson City

Lake Tahoe

Pyramid L.

Humboldt River

Shoshone Mountains

Independence Mts.

Ruby Mts.

Diamond Mts.

Elko

Winnemucca

Lovelock

VANCOUVER

New Westminster

Victoria

Juan de Fuca Strait

Bellingham

Everett

Bremerton

Aberdeen

Longview

Astoria

Redding

Eureka

Sacramento

Yakima

Wenatchee

Ellensburg

Kennewick

Pasco

Richland

Columbia River

Snake River

Missouri

Fort Peck Reservoir

Fort Peck Dam

Glasgow

Havre

Lewistown

Miles City

Glendive

Buffalo

Thermopolis

Riverton

Lander

Rawlins

Laramie

Coeur d'Alene

Sandpoint

Kalispell

Pend Oreille

Flathead L.

South Pass

Jackson L.

Yellowstone L.

Klamath Mts.

1:12 000 000

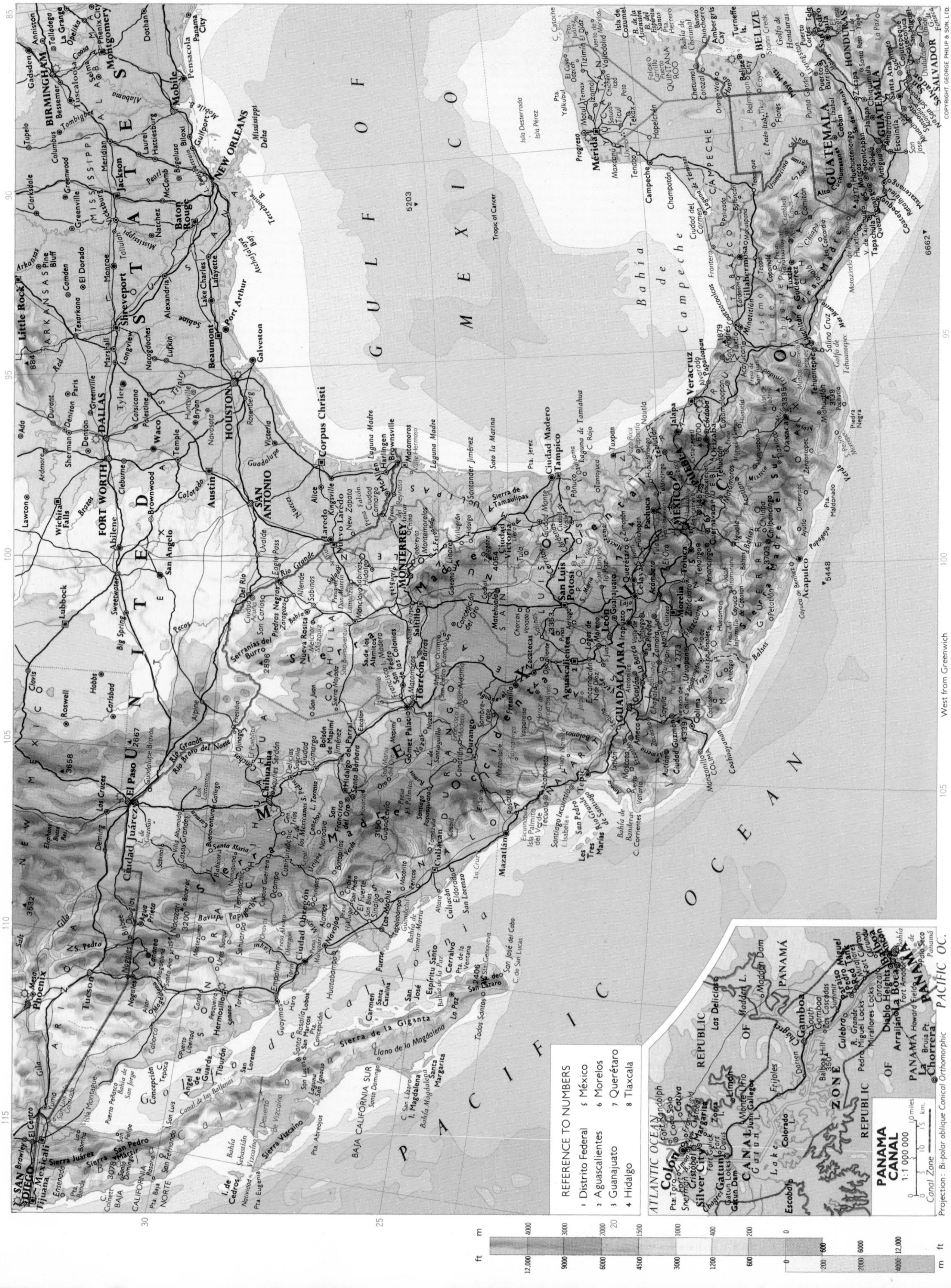

100   0   100   200 miles
100   0   100   200   300 km

West from Greenwich

REFERENCE TO NUMBERS

1 Distrito Federal   5 México
2 Aguascalientes   6 Morelos
3 Guanajuato   7 Querétaro
4 Hidalgo   8 Tlaxcala

PANAMA CANAL
1:1 000 000
0   5   10   15   20 miles
0   5   10   15   20   25   30 km
Canal Zone

Projection: Bi-polar oblique Conical Orthomorphic

UNITED STATES

GULF OF MEXICO

PACIFIC OCEAN

ATLANTIC OCEAN

PACIFIC OC.

m
4000
3000
2000
1000
600
200
0

ft
12,000
9000
6000
4500
3000
1500
600
200
0

1:12 000 000

100   0   100   200 miles
100   0   100   200   300 km

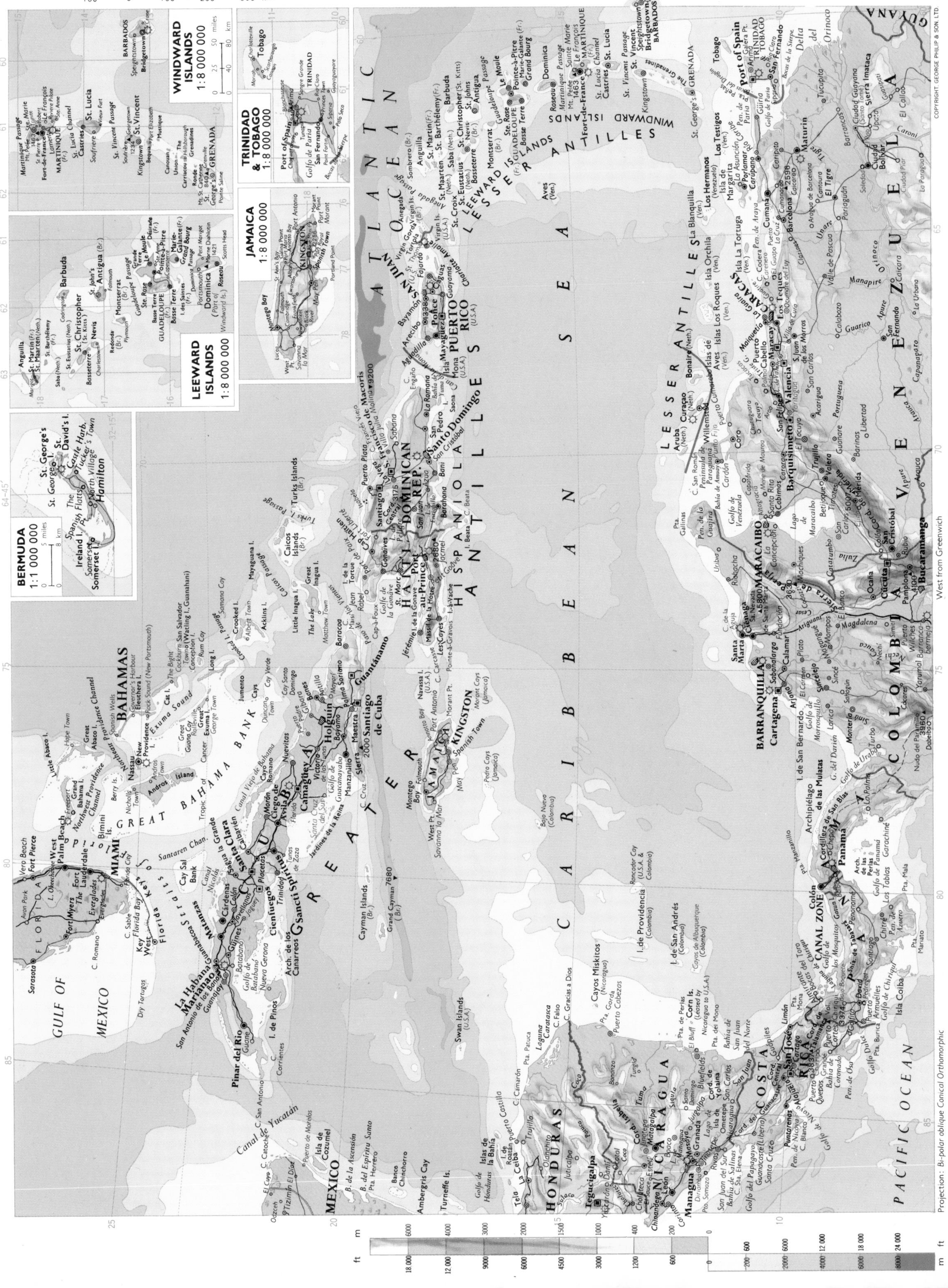

WINDWARD ISLANDS
1:8 000 000

TRINIDAD & TOBAGO
1:8 000 000

JAMAICA
1:8 000 000

LEEWARD ISLANDS
1:8 000 000

BERMUDA
1:1 000 000

ATLANTIC OCEAN

CARIBBEAN SEA

GREATER ANTILLES

LESSER ANTILLES

WINDWARD ISLANDS

LEEWARD ISLANDS

BAHAMAS

GREAT BAHAMA BANK

CUBA

JAMAICA

HAITI

DOMINICAN REP.

HISPANIOLA

PUERTO RICO

GULF OF MEXICO

MEXICO

FLORIDA

MIAMI

HONDURAS

NICARAGUA

COSTA RICA

PANAMA

CANAL ZONE

COLOMBIA

VENEZUELA

GUIANA

PACIFIC OCEAN

CARACAS

MARACAIBO

BARRANQUILLA

Cartagena

Port of Spain

TRINIDAD
TOBAGO

GRENADA

BARBADOS

St. Vincent

St. Lucia

MARTINIQUE

DOMINICA

GUADELOUPE

Montserrat

Antigua

Barbuda

St. Christopher (St. Kitts)

Nevis

Anguilla

Santo Domingo

Port-au-Prince

Santiago de Cuba

La Habana

Kingston

Managua

Tegucigalpa

San José

Panama

Copyright GEORGE PHILIP & SON, LTD.

West from Greenwich

Projection: Bi-polar oblique Conical Orthomorphic

m   ft

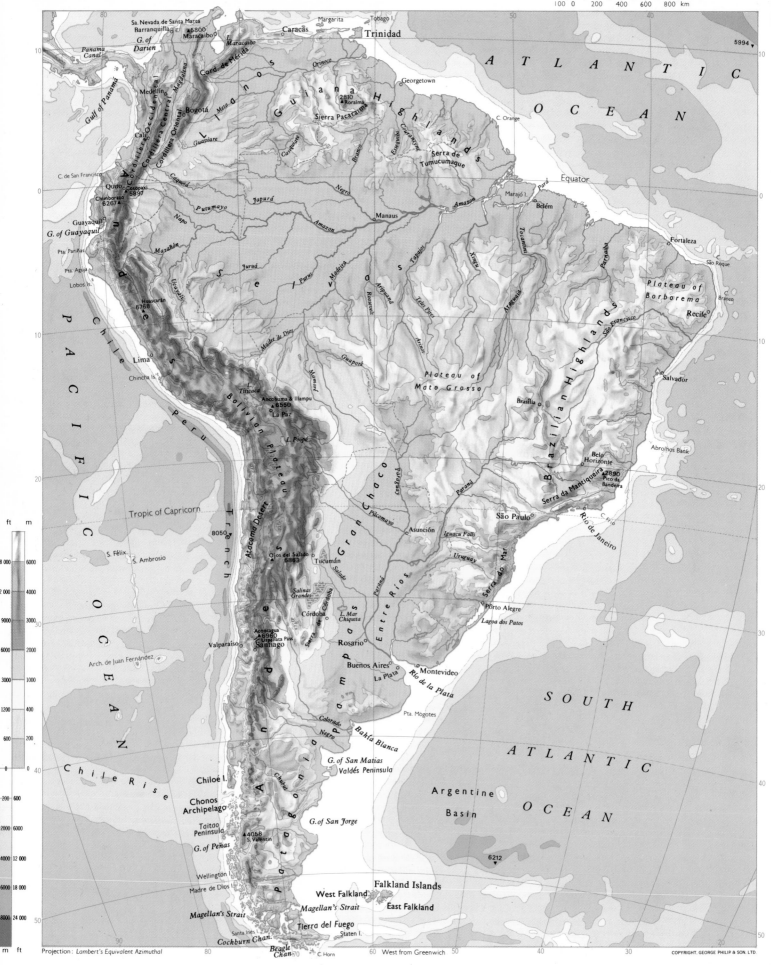

1:30 000 000

100   0   100 200 300 400 500 miles
100   0   200   400   600   800 km

ft   m

18 000   6000
12 000   4000
9000   3000
6000   2000
3000   1000
1200   400
600   200
0   0
200   600
2000   6000
4000   12 000
6000   18 000
8000   24 000

m   ft

ATLANTIC OCEAN

PACIFIC OCEAN

SOUTH ATLANTIC OCEAN

Panama Canal
Sa. Nevada de Santa Marta
Barranquilla
5800
Maracaibo
G. of Darien
L. Maracaibo
Cord. de Mérida
Caracas
Margarita
Tobago I.
Trinidad
5994
Medellín
Cali
Bogotá
Cordillera Occidental
Cordillera Central
Cordillera Oriental
Magdalena
Llanos
Orinoco
Georgetown
Guiana Highlands
Sierra Pacaraima
2810 Roraima
Serra de Tumucumaque
C. Orange
C. de San Francisco
Quito
Cotopaxi 5897
Chimborazo 6267
Guayaquil
G. of Guayaquil
Pta. Pariñas
Pta. Aguja
Lobos Is.
Guaviare
Caquetá
Putumayo
Napo
Marañón
Ucayali
Juruá
Purus
Japurá
Negro
Amazon
Madeira
Manaus
Equator
Marajó I.
Pará
Belém
Fortaleza
São Roque
C. Branco
Recife
Plateau of Borborema
Huascarán 6768
Madre de Dios
Roosevelt
Aripuanã
Tapajós
Xingu
Araguaia
Tocantins
São Francisco
Lima
Chincha Is.
Titicaca
Ancohuma & Illampu 6550
La Paz
L. Poopó
Bolivian Plateau
Mamoré
Guaporé
Beni
Plateau of Mato Grosso
Brasília
Belo Horizonte
Brazilian Highlands
Abrolhos Bank
Salvador
Tropic of Capricorn
Atacama Desert
8050
Ojos del Salado 6863
Tucumán
Salinas Grandes
Salado
Gran Chaco
Pilcomayo
Paraguay
Paraná
Asunción
Iguaçu Falls
São Paulo
Serra da Mantiqueira
2890 Pico da Bandeira
Serra do Mar
Rio de Janeiro
C. Frio
S. Félix
S. Ambrosio
Córdoba
Sierra de Córdoba
L. Mar Chiquita
Salado
Rosario
Entre Rios
Uruguay
Pôrto Alegre
Lagoa dos Patos
Aconcagua 6960
Uspallata Pass
Valparaíso
Santiago
Arch. de Juan Fernández
Andes
Pampas
Buenos Aires
La Plata
Río de la Plata
Montevideo
Pta. Mogotes
Colorado
Negro
Bahía Blanca
G. of San Matias
Valdés Peninsula
SOUTH ATLANTIC OCEAN
Argentine Basin
6212
Chiloé I.
Chonos Archipelago
Taitao Peninsula
G. of Peñas
Patagonia
Chubut
G. of San Jorge
4058 S. Valentin
Wellington I.
Madre de Dios I.
Magellan's Strait
Santa Inés I.
Cockburn Chan.
West Falkland
East Falkland
Falkland Islands
Tierra del Fuego
Staten I.
C. Horn
Beagle Chan.
Chile Rise
Peru Trench
Chile Trench

Projection: Lambert's Equivalent Azimuthal

West from Greenwich

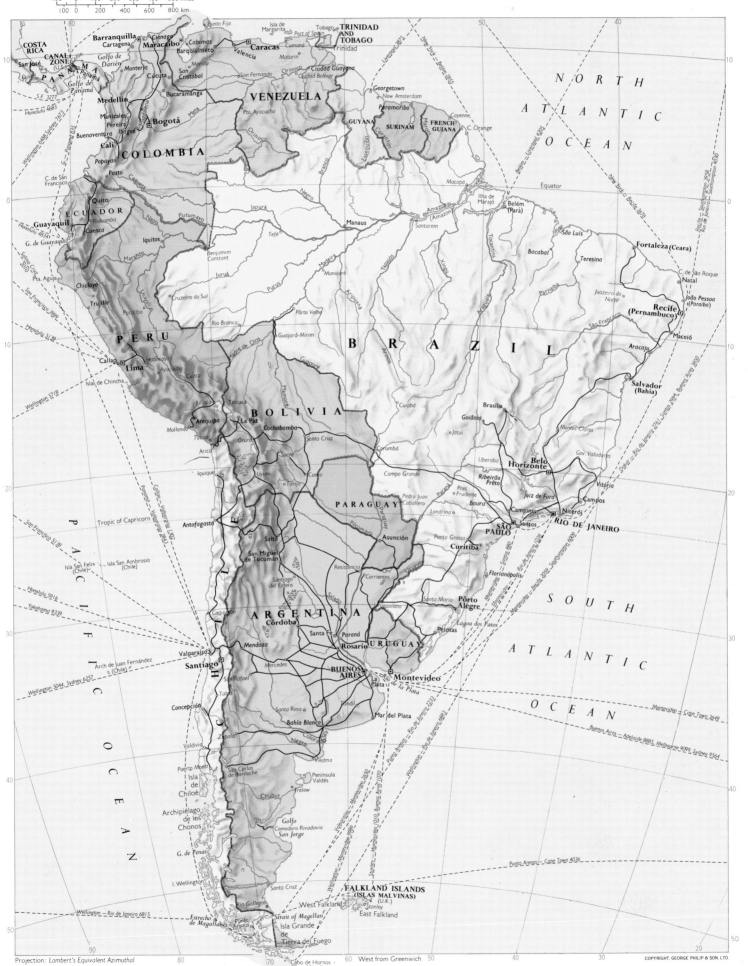

1:30 000 000

100 0 100 200 300 400 500 miles
100 0 200 400 600 800 km

Projection: Lambert's Equivalent Azimuthal

COPYRIGHT. GEORGE PHILIP & SON. LTD.

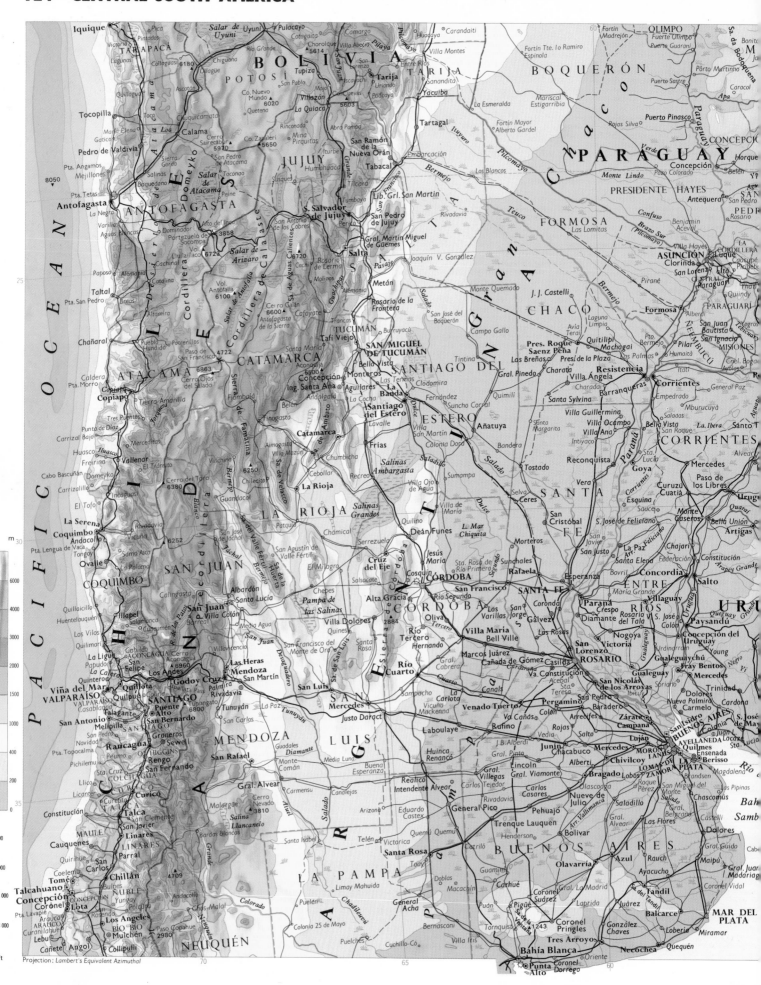

Projection: Lambert's Equivalent Azimuthal

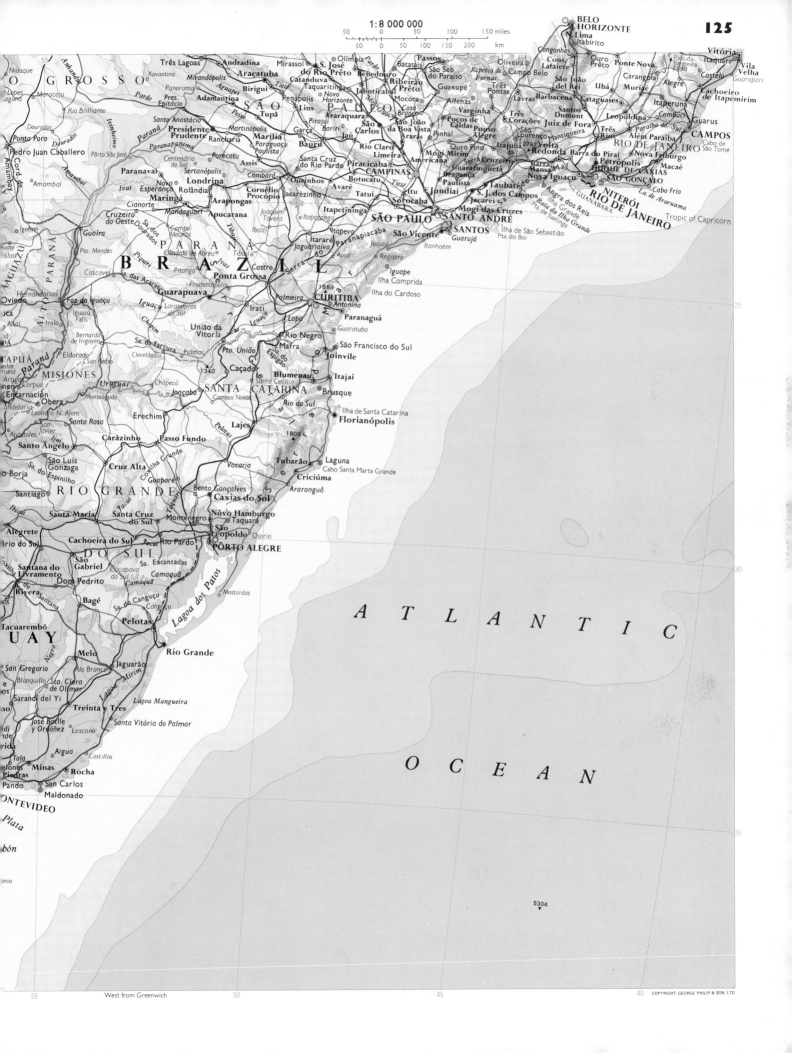

1:16 000 000

100   0   100   200   300   400   500 miles
100   0   100   200   300   400   500   600   700   800 km

A T L A N T I C

O C E A N

Equator

FR. GUIANA

Paramaribo
Nieuw Amsterdam
Totness
Albina St. Laurent
Kwakoegron Moengo Mana Iracoubo Sinnamary
Brokopondo St. Georges Cayenne
Kaw
Approuague
C. Orange
Oiapoque

RINAM
Serra Tumucumaque

AMAPÁ
Amapá
Araguari
Serra do Navio Pta. Grande
C. do Norte
Macapá
Ilha Caviana
Estuário do Rio Amazonas
Ilha Mexiana
C. Maguarinho

Mazagão
Afuá Chaves Souré Salinópolis
I. Grande Vigia Bragança
do Gurupá Curuçá
Ilha de Marajó
Viseu
Breves Muaná
Belém (Pará)
Abaetetuba Igarapé Açu
Cametá Acará Gururupu
Barcarena Turiaçu
Tucuruí Capim

Óbidos
Monte Alegre Prainha
Almeirim
Santarém Alenquer
Amazonas (Amazon) Pôrto de Móz
Aveiro Gurupá
Brasília Legal

P A R Á

Altamira

Itaituba

Marabá

Sa. dos Carajás

Imperatriz

São João do Araguaia
Tocantinópolis
Pôrto Franco

Carolina

Riachão

Balsas

B R A Z I L

Sa. do Cachimbo

Conceição do Araguaia
Araguacema

Sta. Isabel

Serra do Roncador

M A T O   G R O S S O

Planalto do
Mato Grosso

Diamantino

Randonópolis

Baliza

Aragarças
Araguaiana

G O I A S

Porto Nacional

Natividade
Peixe

Sa. Dourada

Campos Belos
São Domingos

Niquelândia
1678

Uruaçu
Aruanã

Posse

Formoso

Taguatinga
Barreiras

Sta. Maria da Vitória
São Francisco

DIST. FED.
Brasília
Corumbá

Anápolis
Luziânia
Vianópolis
Goiânia
Ipameri
Catalão

Araguari
Uberlândia
Ituiutaba
Prata
Araxá
Patrocínio

Uberaba
Frutal

MINAS GERAIS

M A R A N H Ã O
Barra do Corda
Grajaú
Colinas

Bacabal
Coroatá
Codó
Caxias
Teresina
Timon

P I A U I
Floriano
Oeiras
Amarante
Valença do Piauí
Novo Oque
Uruçuí
São João do Piauí
Paulistana
São Raimundo

Remanso
Casa Nova
Juàzeiro
Paulo Afonso
Petrolina

Caracol
São Dois Irmãos

Parnaguá
Sta. Filomena

Sa. da Estrondo

São Luís (Maranhão)
Rosário
Viana
Itapecuru-Mirim
Brejo
União

Parnaíba
Luís Correia
Piracuruca
Miguel Alves
Piripiri
Campo Maior
Batalha

Barreirinhas
Tutóia
Granja
Camocim

Fortaleza (Ceará)
Sobral
Maranguape
Ipu
Baturité
Aracati

Crateús
Quixadá
Limoeiro
Russas
Mossoró

Senador Pompeu
Iguatu
Orós
Caraúbas
RIO GRANDE
DO NORTE

C E A R Á
Cedro
Icó
Crato
Juàzeiro do Norte

Natal
C. de São Roque
Ceará Mirim
Nova Cruz

Sousa
Pombal
Patos
Campina Grande
Currais Novos
Caicó

PARAÍBA
João Pessoa (Paraíba)
Cabedelo

Arcoverde
Caruaru
PERNAMBUCO
RECIFE (Pernambuco)
C. de Santo Antão

Petrolândia
Garanhuns
Palmares
Rio Largo
Maceió
ALAGOAS
Penedo

Senhor do Bonfim
Campo Formoso

Juàzeiro
Xique-Xique
Barra

Jacobina
Serrinha
Feira de Santana

Santo Amaro
Salvador (Bahia)
Baía de Todos os Santos

B A H I A

Itaberaba
Mundo Novo
Alagoinhas
Esplanade

Bom Jesus da Lapa
1850
Itaeté
Maracás

Brumado
Caetité
Ituaçu
Jequié
Valença
Ubaitaba
Itacaré
Ilhéus
Itabuna
Vitória da Conquista

Caravelas
Banka
Abrolhos

Carinhanha
Januária
Monte Azul

Salinas
Jequitinhonha

Pedra Azul
Nanuque
Prado
Porto Seguro
Belmonte
Canavieiras

SERGIPE
Propriá
São Cristóvão
Estância
Aracajú

6059

Serra do Espinhaço

Montes Claros

Diamantina
Teófilo Otoni
Gov. Valadares
Conceição da Barra

Pirapora
Paracatú
Bocaiúva

Belo Horizonte
Caratinga
Aimorés
Mucuri

Patos de Minas
Ouro Prêto
Caratinga
Gov. Valadares

ESPÍRITO SANTO
Vitória

Araxá
Campo Grande
Água Clara
Três Lagoas
Andradina
Araçatuba

Ribeirão Prêto
São José do Rio Prêto

SÃO
PAULO
Marília
Bauru
Botucatu
Piracicaba
Campinas

Poços de Caldas
Juiz de Fora
Campos

Petrópolis
RIO DE JANEIRO
Niterói
GUANABARA

Fernando de Noronha
(Braz.)

Rocas

Trindade
(Braz.)

COPYRIGHT. GEORGE PHILIP & SON, LTD.

1:16 000 000

Projection: Sanson-Flamsteed's Sinusoidal

West from Greenwich

COPYRIGHT. GEORGE PHILIP & SON. LTD.

The number which precedes each entry in the index is the page of the atlas where that particular feature can be found. The geographical co-ordinates which follow the entry are primarily intended as a guide to locating the feature on the map and in some cases are only approximate.

Where the same name refers to places in different countries, these place-names are followed by the country name and are arranged according to the alphabetical order of the country. If the same name occurs a number of times within one country the names are followed by the name of the administrative subdivision in which they are found, and are arranged in the alphabetical order of the subdivision name.

If the same name occurs a number of times town names are given first followed by the names referring to other geographical features.

The symbol ■ indicates the name of a country and is always first in a list of identical place-names. The symbol ♦ indicates the name of an administrative subdivision of a country and these names are always last in a list of identical place-names.

Names beginning with M', Mc, M'c and Mac are all listed under Mac.

Former names of certain towns are referenced to the names in current use; Stalingrad=Volgograd. English conventional name forms for certain towns are referenced to the local spelling of that town name; Florence=Firenze.

The following is a list of abbreviations used in the index.

The Trucial States became fully independent in December 1971 and adopted the name—United Arab Emirates.
Papua and North East New Guinea both became independent in December 1973 and are now known together as Papua New Guinea.

Following the Local Government Acts, 1972, a number of the county boundaries and names in England and Wales, Scotland and Northern Ireland have changed. There is a list of the new county, region and district names on the last page of the Index.

Afghan. – Afghanistan
Afr. – Africa, African
Ala. – Alabama
Alas. – Alaska
Alb. – Albania
Alg. – Algeria
Alta. – Alberta
Amaz. – Amazonas
Amer. – America
And. P. – Andhra Pradesh
Ang. – Angola
Ant. – Antarctica
Arab. – Arabia
Arch. – Archipelago
Arg. – Argentina
Ariz. – Arizona
Ark. – Arkansas
A.S.S.R. – Autonomous Soviet Socialist Republic
Aust. – Austria
Austral. – Australia
B. – Bay, Bight, (Baie, Bahia, Baia)
B.C. – British Columbia
Bangla. – Bangladesh
Bav. – Bavaria (Bayern)
Beds. – Bedfordshire
Belg. – Belgium
Beng. – Bengal
Berks. – Berkshire
Bg. – Berg
Bk. – Bank
Bol. – Bolivia
Bots. – Botswana
Br., Brit. – British, Britain
Braz. – Brazil
Bucks. – Buckinghamshire
Bulg. – Bulgaria
C. – Cape (Cabo), Coast
Calif. – California
Cam. – Cameroon
Cambod. – Cambodia
Cambs. – Cambridgeshire & Isle of Ely
Can. – Canada, Canal
Can. Is. – Canary Islands
Cant. – Canton
Cap. – Capital
Cards. – Cardiganshire
Cas. – Castle
Cent. – Central
Cey. – Ceylon
Chan. – Channel
Ches. – Cheshire
Co. – County
Col. – Colombia, Columbia, Colony
Colo. – Colorado
Conn. – Connecticut

Cont. – Continent
C. Prov. – Cape Province
Cr. – Creek
C. Rica – Costa Rica
Cumb. – Cumberland
Cz. – Czechoslovakia
D.C. – District of Columbia
Del. – Delaware
Den. – Denmark
Dépt. – Département, Department
Des. – Desert
Dist. – District
Div. – Division
Dj. – Djebel
Dom. Rep. – Dominican Republic
Dun. – Dunbarton
E. – East
Ec. – Ecuador
Eg. – Egypt
Eng. – England
Equat. – Equatorial
Est. – Estuary
Eth. – Ethiopia
Eur. – Europe
Falk. Is. – Falkland Islands
Fd. – Fiord, Fjord
Fed. – Federal, Federation
Fin. – Finland
Fla. – Florida
For. – Forest
Fr. – France, French
Fr. Gui. – French Guiana
Fs. – Falls
F.T.A.I. – Fr. Terr. of the Affars and Issas
Ft. – Fort
G. – Gulf, Gebel
Ga. – Georgia
Gam. – Gambia
Ger. – Germany
Gl. – Glacier
Glos. – Gloucestershire
Gr. – Greece
Green. – Greenland
Grn. – Green
Grp. – Group
Gt. – Great
Guat. – Guatemala
Guin. – Guinea
Guy. – Guyana
Hants. – Hampshire
Hr., Harb. – Harbor, Harbour
Hd. – Head
Here. – Herefordshire
Herts. – Hertfordshire
Him. P. – Himachal Pradesh
Ho. – House
Hond. – Honduras

Hs. – Hills
Hts. – Heights
Hung. – Hungary
Hunt. – Huntingdon & Peterborough
I.(s) – Island(s) (Isle, Ile)
Ice. – Iceland
Ill. – Illinois
Ind. – Indiana, Indian
Indon. – Indonesia
I. of M. – Isle of Man
I. of W. – Isle of Wight
Ire. – Ireland
Isr. – Israel
Isth. – Isthmus
It. – Italy
J. – Jebel, Jabal
Jam. – Jamaica
Jap. – Japan
Jc., Junc. – Junction
Kans. – Kansas
Kg. (Malay) – Kampong (Village)
King. – Kingdom
Ky. – Kentucky
L. – Lake, Lough, Loch, Lago
La. – Louisiana
Lab. – Labrador
Lag. – Lagoon, Laguna, Lagôa
Lancs. – Lancashire
Ld. – Land
Leics. – Leicestershire
Les. – Lesotho
Lib. – Liberia
Lim. – Limerick
Lincs. – Lincolnshire
Lit. – Little
Lr. – Lower
Lt. Ho. – Lighthouse
Lux. – Luxembourg
Mad. – Madras
Mad. P. – Madhya Pradesh
Mal. – Malawi
Malag. – Malagasy Republic
Malay. – Malaysia
Man. – Manitoba
Mass. – Massachusetts
Maur. – Mauritania
Md. – Maryland
Me. – Maine
Medit. – Mediterranean
Mex. – Mexico
M. Grosso – Mato Grosso
Mich. (U.S.A.) – Michigan
Mich. (Mexico) – Michoacan
Mid. – Middle
Min. Ger. – Minas Gerais
Minn. – Minnesota
Miss. – Mississippi

Mo. – Missouri
Mon. – Monmouthshire
Mong. – Mongolia
Mont. – Montana
Mor. – Morocco
Mozam. – Mozambique
Mt. – Mountain, Mount
Mte. – Monte
Mth. – Mouth
Mtl. – Monti
Mtil (Rum.) – Muntil (Mts.)
Mts. – Mountains, Monts.
Mys. – Mysore
N. – North, Northern
Nat. – Natal, National
N.B. – New Brunswick
N.C. – North Carolina
N.D. – North Dakota
Neb. – Nebraska
Neth. – Netherlands
Nev. – Nevada
Newf. – Newfoundland
N. Guin. – New Guinea, Terr. of,
N.H. – New Hampshire
Nic. – Nicaragua
Nig. – Nigeria
N.J. – New Jersey
N. Mex. – New Mexico
Nor. – Norway
Northants. – Northamptonshire
Northumb. – Northumberland
Notts. – Nottinghamshire
N.S. – Nova Scotia
N.S.W. – New South Wales
N.Y. – New York
N.Z. – New Zealand
O. – Oasis, Ouadi
Oc. – Ocean
O.F.S. – Orange Free State
Okla. – Oklahoma
Ont. – Ontario
Oreg. – Oregon
Os. (Russ.) – Ostrov (Island)
Oz. (Russ.) – Ozero (Lake)
P. – Paso, Pass, Passo
Pa. – Pennsylvania
Pac. – Pacific
Pak. – Pakistan
Pan. – Panama
Par. – Paraguay
Pass. – Passage
P.E.I. – Prince Edward Island
Pen. – Peninsula
Phil. – Philippines
Pk. – Peak, Park
Pl. – Plain, Planina
Plat. – Plateau
Pol. – Poland

Port. – Portugal, Portuguese
Prét. – Préfecture
P. Rico – Puerto Rico
Prom. – Promontory
Prot. – Protectorate
Prov. – Province, Provincial
Pt. – Point, Port
Pta. – Punta (Point)
Pte. – Pointe (Point)
Pto. – Puerto, Puerto (Port)
Que. – Quebec
Queens. – Queensland
R. – River, Rio
Ra. – Range
Raj. – Rajasthan
Ras. – Ranges
Rd. – Road
Reg. – Region
Rep. – Republic
Res. – Reserve, Reservoir
Rf. – Reef
Rhod. – Rhodesia
R.I. – Rhode Island
Rks. – Rocks
Rosc. – Roscommon
R.S.F.S.R. – Russian Soviet Federal Socialist Republic
Rum. – Rumania
S. – Sea, South
Sa. – Sierra, Serra
Sab. – Sabah
Sal. – El Salvador
Salop. – Shropshire
Sar. – Sarawak
Sard. – Sardinia
Sask. – Saskatchewan
S. Afr. – Rep. of South Africa
S. Austral. – South Australia
S.C. – South Carolina
Scot. – Scotland
S.D. – South Dakota
Sd. – Sound
Sen. – Senegal
Sl. Arab. – Saudi Arabia
S. Leone – Sierra Leone
Sp., Span. – Spain, Spanish
S.S.R. – Soviet Socialist Republic
st. – State
S. – San
St. – Saint
Sta. – Santa
Ste. – Sainte
Sto. – Santo
Staffs. – Staffordshire
Stn. – Station
Str. – Strait
Sud. – Sudan

Sun. (Malay) – Sungel (River)
Sur. – Suriname(e)
Swazi. – Swaziland
Swed. – Sweden
Switz. – Switzerland
Tanz. – Tanzania
Tas. – Tasmania
Tenn. – Tennessee
Terr. – Territory
Tex. – Texas
Thai. – Thailand
Tipp. – Tipperary
tn. – Town
Trans. – Transvaal
Tr. States – Trucial States
Tun. – Tunisia
Tur. – Turkey
U.A.R. – United Arab Republic
Ugan. – Uganda
Ukr. – Ukraine
U.K. – United Kingdom of Great Britain. and Northern Ireland
Ut. P. – Uttar Pradesh
Urug. – Uruguay
U.S.A. – United States of America
U.S.S.R. – Union of Soviet Socialist Republics
Va. – Virginia
Val. – Valley
Vdkhr. (Russ.) – Vodokhranilishche (Reservoir)
Ven. – Venezuela
Vic. – Victoria
Viet. – Vietnam
Vil. – Village, Vilayet
Vol. – Volcano
Vt. – Vermont
W. – West, Wadi, Wady
War. – Warwickshire
Wash. – Washington
W. I. – West Indies
Wick. – Wicklow
Wilts. – Wiltshire
Wind. Is. – Windward Islands
Wis. – Wisconsin
Worcs. – Worcestershire
W. A. – Western Australia
W. Va. – West Virginia
Wyo. – Wyoming
Yorks. – Yorkshire
Y.-slav. – Yugoslavia
Zam. – Zambia

HHF

Aachen INDEX Aju

MAP
24 Aachen, Germany 50 47N 6 4E
7 Aadorf, Switz. 47 30N 8 55E
80 Aaiun, Span. Sahara 27 9N 13 12W
49 Aal, Denmark 55 39N 8 18E
87 Aâlâ en Nîl ♦ Sudan 8 50N 29 55E
25 Aalen, Germany 48 49N 10 6E
62 Aalma ech Chaab, Lebanon 33 7N 35 9E
16 Aalsmeer, Netherlands 52 17N 4 43E
49 Aalsö, Denmark 56 23N 10 52E
16 Aalst, Belgium 50 56N 4 2E
16 Aalten, Netherlands 51 56N 6 35E
25 Aarau, Switzerland 47 23N 8 4E
25 Aarburg, Switzerland 47 19N 7 54E
50 Aareavaara, Sweden 67 27N 23 29E
25 Aargau ♦, Switz. 47 26N 8 10E
16 Aarschot, Belgium 50 59N 4 49E
6 Aarwangen, Switz. 47 15N 7 46E
49 Aastrup, Denmark 55 34N 8 49E
90 Aba, Congo 3 58N 30 17E
85 Aba, Nigeria 5 10N 7 19E
87 Abâ, Jazîrat, Sudan 13 30N 32 31E
64 Abadan, Iran 30 22N 48 20E
87 Abade, Ethiopia 9 22N 38 3E
65 Abade, Iran 31 8N 52 40E
30 Abadin, Spain 43 21N 7 29W
82 Abadla, Algeria 31 2N 2 45W
127 Abaetetuba, Brazil 1 40S 51 15W
125 Abai, Paraguay 25 58S 55 54W
85 Abak, Nigeria 4 58N 7 50E
85 Abakaliki, Nigeria 6 22N 8 2E
59 Abakan, U.S.S.R. 53 40N 91 10E
86 Abal Nam, Si. Arabia 25 20N 38 37E
85 Abalemma, Niger 16 12N 7 50E
127 Aballetuba, Brazil 1 40S 51 15W
33 Abanilla, Spain 38 12N 1 3W
39 Abano Terme, Italy 45 22N 11 46E
33 Abarán, Spain 38 12N 1 23W
65 Abarqu, Iran 31 10N 53 20E
62 Abasan, Egypt 31 19N 34 21E
87 Abasberes, Ethiopia 11 33N 35 23E
74 Abashiri, Japan 44 0N 144 15E
98 Abau, Papua 10 1S 148 42E
27 Abaújszántó, Hungary 48 16N 21 12E
58 Abay, U.S.S.R. 49 38N 72 53E
87 Abaya L., Ethiopa 6 30N 37 50E
58 Abaza, U.S.S.R. 52 39N 90 6E
39 Abbadia San Salvatore, Italy 42 53N 11 40E
87 Abbay, R., (Nîl el Azraq), Ethiopia 10 17N 35 22E
114 Abbaye, Pt., U.S.A. 46 58N 88 4W
49 Abbetorp, Sweden 56 57N 16 8E
19 Abbeville, France 50 6N 1 49E
117 Abbeville, La., U.S.A. 30 0N 92 7W
115 Abbeville, S.C., U.S.A. 34 12N 82 21W
38 Abbiategrasso, Italy 45 23N 8 55E
99 Abbieglassie, Austral. 27 15S 147 28E
108 Abbotsford, B.C., Can. 49 0N 122 10W
113 Abbotsford, Que., Can. 45 25N 72 53W
116 Abbotsford, U.S.A. 44 55N 90 20W
66 Abbottabad, W. Pak. 34 10N 73 15E
63 'Abd al Kuri, Ind. Oc. 12 5N 52 20E
87 Abe, L., Ethiopia 11 8N 41 47E
81 Abéché, Chad. 13 50N 20 35E
32 Abejar, Spain 41 48N 2 47W
87 Abekr, Sudan 12 45N 28 50E
82 Abélessa, Algeria 22 58N 4 47E
87 Abelti, Ethiopia 8 10N 37 30E
84 Abengourou, Ivory C. 6 42N 3 27W
49 Abenra, Denmark 55 3N 9 25E
85 Abeokuta, Nigeria 7 3N 3 19E
90 Aber, Uganda 2 12N 32 25E
13 Aberayron, Wales 52 15N 4 16W
99 Abercorn, Australia 25 12S 151 5E
91 Abercorn = Mbala, Zambia 8 46S 31 17E
100 Abercrombie, R., Austral. 34 0S 149 23E
13 Aberdare, Wales 51 43N 3 27W
90 Aberdare Ra., Kenya 0 15S 36 50E
13 Aberdaron, Wales 52 48N 4 41W
100 Aberdeen, Australia 32 9S 150 56E
109 Aberdeen, Canada 52 20N 106 8W
92 Aberdeen, S. Africa 32 28S 24 2E
14 Aberdeen, Scot. 57 9N 2 6W
116 Aberdeen, S.D., U.S.A. 45 30N 98 30W
118 Aberdeen, Wash., U.S.A. 47 0N 123 58W
*14 Aberdeen ♦, Scotland 57 18N 2 30W
13 Aberdovey, Wales 52 33N 4 3W
14 Aberfeldy, Scot. 56 37N 3 50W
30 Abergaria-a-Velha, Port. 40 41N 8 32W
117 Abernathy, U.S.A. 33 49N 101 49W
13 Aberystwyth, Wales 52 25N 4 6W
86 Abha, Saudi Arabia 18 0N 42 34E
68 Abhayapuri, India 26 24N 90 38E
86 Abidiya, Sudan 18 18N 34 3E
84 Abidjan, Ivory Coast 5 26N 3 58W
116 Abilene, Kans., U.S.A. 39 0N 97 16W
117 Abilene, Texas, U.S.A. 32 22N 99 40W
13 Abingdon, England 51 40N 1 17W
116 Abingdon, Ill., U.S.A. 40 53N 90 23W
115 Abingdon, Va., U.S.A. 36 46N 81 56W
106 Abitibi L., Canada 48 40N 79 40W
87 Abiy Adi, Ethiopia 13 39N 39 3E
57 Abkhaz A.S.S.R. ♦, U.S.S.R. 43 0N 41 0E
59 Abkit, U.S.S.R. 64 10N 157 10E
86 Abnûb, Egypt 27 18N 31 4E
83 Abo, Massif d', Chad 21 41N 16 8E
85 Abocho, Nigeria 7 35N 6 56E
86 Abohar, India 30 10N 74 10E
84 Aboisso, Ivory Coast 5 30N 3 5W
85 Aboméy, Dahomey 7 10N 2 5E
21 Abondance, France 46 18N 6 42E
88 Abong Mbang, Cam. 4 0N 13 8E
85 Abonnema, Nigeria 4 41N 6 49E
27 Abony, Hungary 47 12N 20 3E
84 Aboso, Ghana 5 23N 1 57W
81 Abou Deïa, Chad 11 20N 19 20E

* Incorporated within the region of Grampian

MAP
14 Aboyne, Scotland 57 4N 2 48W
64 Abqaiq, Saudi Arabia 26 0N 49 45E
31 Abrantes, Portugal 39 24N 8 7W
30 Abraveses, Portugal 40 41N 7 55E
120 Abreojos, Pta., Mexico 26 50N 113 40W
19 Abreschviller, France 48 39N 7 6E
87 Abri, Esh Shimâliya, Sudan 20 50N 30 27E
87 Abri, Kordofân, Sudan 11 40N 30 21E
127 Abrolhos, Arquipélago dos, Brazil 18 0S 38 30W
46 Abrud, Rumania 46 19N 23 5E
39 Abruzzi ♦, Italy 42 15N 14 0E
118 Absaroka Ra., U.S.A. 44 40N 110 0W
64 Abu al Khasib, Iraq 30 25N 48 0E
64 Abu Ali, Si. Arab. 27 20N 49 27E
63 Abu Arish, Si. Arab. 16 53N 42 48E
86 Abû Ballas, Egypt 24 26N 27 36E
87 Abu Deleiq, Sudan 15 57N 33 48E
65 Abû Dhabi, Trucial States 24 28N 54 36E
62 Abû Dis, Jordan 31 47N 35 16E
86 Abu Dis, Sudan 19 12N 33 38E
87 Abu Dom, Sudan 16 18N 32 25E
87 Abû Gabra, Sudan 11 2N 26 50E
62 Abu Ghosh, Israel 31 48N 35 6E
87 Abû Gubeiha, Sudan 11 30N 31 15E
87 Abu Habl, W., Sudan 12 37N 31 0E
86 Abu Hamed, Sudan 19 32N 33 13E
86 Abu Haraz, Esh Shimâliya, Sudan 19 8N 32 18E
87 Abû Haraz, Nîl el Azraq, Sudan 14 35N 34 30E
87 Abû Higar, Sudan 12 50N 33 59E
64 Abu Kamal, Syria 34 30N 41 0E
64 Abu Markha, Si. Arab. 25 4N 38 22E
86 Abu Qîr, Egypt 31 18N 30 0E
86 Abu Qireiya, Egypt 24 5N 35 28E
86 Abu Qurqâs, Egypt 28 1N 30 44E
86 Abu Salama, Si. Arab. 27 10N 35 51E
86 Abû Simbel, Egypt 22 18N 31 40E
86 Abu Tig, Egypt 27 4N 31 15E
87 Abu Tiga, Sudan 12 47N 34 12E
87 Abû Zabad, Sudan 12 25N 29 10E
87 Abu Zagholi, Sudan 11 45N 34 29E
86 Abu Zenima, Egypt 29 0N 33 15E
85 Abuja, Nigeria 9 16N 7 2E
74 Abukumagawa, Japan 37 30N 140 30E
126 Abunã, Brazil 9 40S 65 20W
126 Abunã, R., Brazil 9 41S 65 20W
90 Aburo, Mt., Zaïre 2 4N 30 53E
101 Abut Hd., New Zealand 43 7S 170 15E
87 Abwong, Sudan 9 2N 32 14E
49 Aby, Sweden 58 40N 16 10E
84 Aby, Lagune, Ivory Coast 5 15N 3 14W
126 Acacías, Colombia 3 59N 73 46W
120 Acámbaro, Mexico 20 0N 100 40W
120 Acaponeta, Mexico 22 30N 105 20W
120 Acapulco de Juárez, Mexico 16 51N 99 56W
127 Acarai, Serra, Brazil 1 50N 57 50W
126 Acarigua, Venezuela 9 33N 69 12W
120 Acatlan, Mexico 18 10N 98 3W
120 Acayucán, Mexico 17 59N 94 58W
38 Acceglio, Italy 44 28N 6 59E
114 Accomac, U.S.A. 37 43N 75 40W
85 Accra, Ghana 5 35N 0 6W
12 Accrington, Eng. 53 46N 2 22W
124 Acebal, Argentina 33 20S 60 50W
41 Acerenza, Italy 40 50N 15 58E
41 Acerra, Italy 40 57N 14 22E
31 Aceuchal, Spain 38 39N 6 30W
126 Achaguas, Venezuela 7 46N 68 14W
67 Achak Gomba, China 33 30N 96 25E
68 Achalpur, India 21 22N 77 32E
26 Achenkirch, Austria 47 32N 11 45E
26 Achensee, Austria 47 26N 11 45E
68 Acher, India 23 10N 72 32E
25 Achern, Germany 48 37N 8 5E
15 Achill, Ireland 53 56N 9 55W
15 Achill Hd., Ireland 53 59N 10 15W
15 Achill I., Ireland 53 58N 10 5W
24 Achim, Germany 53 1N 9 2E
25 Achimota, Ghana 5 35N 0 15W
59 Achinsk, U.S.S.R. 56 20N 90 20E
87 Achol, Sudan 6 35N 31 32E
*90 Acholi ♦, Ugan. 3 5N 32 30E
41 Acireale, Italy 37 37N 15 9E
117 Ackerman, U.S.A. 33 20N 89 8W
121 Acklin's I., Bahamas 22 30N 74 0W
98 Acland Mt., Australia 24 50S 148 20E
108 Acme, Canada 51 33N 113 30W
124 Aconcagua, Arg. 32 50S 70 0W
124 Aconcagua, Cerro, Arg. 32 39S 70 0W
124 Aconcagua ♦, Chile 32 15S 70 30W
124 Aconquija, Mt., Argentina 27 0S 66 0W
6 Açores, Is. dos, N. Atlantic 38 44N 29 0W
39 Acquapendente, Italy 42 45N 11 50E
39 Acquasanta, Italy 42 46N 13 24E
41 Acquaviva delle Fonti, It. 40 53N 16 50E
40 Acqui, Italy 44 40N 8 28E
62 Acre = 'Akko, Israel 32 35N 35 4E
126 Acre, R., Brazil 10 45S 68 25W
126 Acre ♦, Brazil 9 1S 71 0W
41 Acri, Italy 39 29N 16 23E
27 Acs, Hungary 47 42N 18 0E
112 Actinolite, Canada 44 34N 77 20W
112 Acton, Canada 43 38N 80 3W
63 Ad Dam, Saudi Arabia 20 33N 44 45E
64 Ad Dammam, Si. Arab. 26 20N 50 5E
64 Ad Dar al Hamra, Saudi Arabia 27 20N 37 45E
65 Ad Dawhah, Qatar 25 15N 51 35E
64 Ad Dilam, Saudi Arabia 23 55N 47 10E
87 Ada, Ethiopia 8 48N 38 51E
85 Ada, Ghana 5 44N 0 40E

* Incorporated within the new Northern Province

MAP
116 Ada, Minn., U.S.A. 47 20N 96 30W
117 Ada, Okla., U.S.A. 34 50N 96 45W
42 Ada, Yugoslavia 45 49N 20 9E
4 Adair C., Canada 71 50N 71 0W
30 Adaja, R., Spain 41 15N 4 50W
63 Adale, Somali Rep. 2 58N 46 27E
48 Ådalslinden, Sweden 63 27N 16 55E
65 Adam, Oman 22 15N 57 28E
85 Adamaoua, Massif de l', Cameroon 7 20N 12 20E
85 Adamawa Highlands = Adamaoua, Cameroon 7 20N 12 20E
38 Adamello, Mt., Italy 46 10N 10 34E
87 Adami Tulu, Ethiopia 7 53N 38 41E
100 Adaminaby, Austral. 36 0S 148 45E
113 Adams, Mass., U.S.A. 42 38N 73 8W
113 Adams, N.Y., U.S.A. 43 50N 76 3W
116 Adams, Wis., U.S.A. 43 59N 89 50W
108 Adams L., Canada 51 20N 119 40W
118 Adams Mt., U.S.A. 46 10N 121 28W
70 Adam's Bridge, Sri Lanka 9 15N 79 40E
113 Adams Center, U.S.A. 43 51N 76 1W
70 Adam's Peak, Sri Lanka 6 55N 80 45E
31 Adamuz, Spain 38 02N 4 32W
64 Adana, Turkey 37 0N 35 16E
30 Adanero, Spain 40 56N 4 36W
64 Adapazari, Turkey 40 48N 30 25E
87 Adarama, Sudan 17 10N 34 52E
5 Adare C., Antarctica 71 0S 171 0E
99 Adavale, Austral. 25 52S 144 32E
87 Adayio, Ethiopia 14 29N 40 50E
38 Adda, R., Italy 45 25N 9 30E
87 Addis Ababa = Addis Abeba, Ethiopia 9 2N 38 42E
87 Addis Abeba, Ethiopia 9 2N 38 42E
87 Addis Alem, Ethiopia 9 0N 38 17E
112 Addison, N.Y., U.S.A. 42 9N 77 15W
113 Addison, Vt., U.S.A. 44 6N 73 18W
61 Addu Atoll, Ind. Oc. 0 30S 73 0E
85 Adebour, Niger 13 17N 11 50E
115 Adel, U.S.A. 31 10N 83 28W
99 Adelaide, Australia 34 55S 138 32E
5 Adelaide I., Antarc. 67 15S 68 30W
104 Adelaide Pen., Canada 67 60N 98 0W
5 Adélie, Terre, Antarctica 67 0S 140 0E
32 Ademuz, Spain 40 5N 1 13W
63 Aden, South Yemen 12 50N 45 0E
63 Aden, G. of, Asia 13 0N 50 0E
92 Adendorp, S. Africa 33 25S 24 30E
68 Adhoi, India 23 26N 70 32E
73 Adi, Indon. 4 15S 133 30E
87 Adi Daro, Ethiopia 14 20N 38 14E
87 Adi Keyih, Ethiopia 14 51N 39 22E
87 Adi Kwala, Ethiopia 14 38N 38 48E
87 Adi Ugri, Ethiopia 14 58N 38 48E
96 Adieu, C., Australia 32 0S 132 10E
87 Adigala, Ethiopia 10 24N 42 15E
39 Adige, R., Italy 45 9N 11 25E
87 Adigrat, Ethiopia 14 20N 39 26E
70 Adilabad, India 19 33N 78 35E
118 Adin, U.S.A. 41 10N 121 0W
65 Adin Khel, Afghanistan 32 45N 68 5E
70 Adirampattinam, India 10 28N 79 20E
113 Adirondack Mts., U.S.A. 44 0N 74 15W
87 Adis Dera, Ethiopia 10 12N 38 46E
85 Adjohon, Dahomey 6 41N 2 32E
46 Adjud, Rumania 46 07N 27 10E
90 Adjumani, Ugan. 3 20N 31 50E
107 Adlavik Is., Canada 55 2N 58 45W
57 Adler, U.S.S.R. 43 28N 39 52E
83 Admer, Algeria 20 21N 5 27E
83 Admer, Erg d', Algeria 24 0N 9 5E
5 Admiralty B., Falkland Is. Dependencies 62 0S 59 0W
96 Admiralty G., Austral. 14 20S 125 55E
98 Admiralty Is., Territory of New Guinea 2 5S 146 15E
118 Admiralty Inlet, U.S.A. 48 0N 122 40W
5 Admiralty Ra., Antarc. 72 0S 164 0E
85 Ado, Nigeria 6 36N 2 56E
85 Ado Ekiti, Nigeria 7 38N 5 12E
87 Adok, Sudan 8 10N 30 20E
87 Adola, Ethiopia 11 14N 41 44E
73 Adonara, Indonesia 8 15S 123 5E
70 Adoni, India 15 33N 77 18W
27 Adony, Hungary 47 06N 18 52E
20 Adour, R., France 43 32N 1 32W
69 Adra, India 23 30N 86 42E
33 Adra, Spain 36 43N 3 3W
63 Adraj, Saudi Arabia 20 1N 51 0E
41 Adrano, Italy 37 40N 14 49E
82 Adrar, Algeria 27 51N 0 11W
85 Adrar des Iforhas, Mali 19 40N 1 40E
81 Adré, Chad 13 40N 22 20E
83 Adri, Libya 27 32N 13 2E
39 Adria, Italy 45 4N 12 3E
114 Adrian, Mich., U.S.A. 41 55N 84 0W
117 Adrian, Tex., U.S.A. 35 19N 102 37W
34 Adriatic Sea, Europe 43 0N 16 0E
73 Adua, Indon. 1 45S 129 50E
90 Aduku, Uganda 2 03N 32 45E
70 Adur, India 9 8N 76 40E
87 Adwa, Ethiopia 14 15N 38 52E
86 Adwa, Saudi Arabia 27 15N 42 35E
57 Adzhar A.S.S.R. ♦, U.S.S.R. 42 0N 42 0E
84 Adzopé, Ivory Coast 6 7N 3 49W
49 Æbelö I., Denmark 55 39N 10 10E
49 Æbeltoft, Denmark 56 12N 10 41E
49 Æbeltoft Vig. B., Den. 56 9N 10 35E
35 Ægean Is., Greece 38 0N 25 0E
35 Ægean Sea, Europe 37 0N 25 0E
47 Ænes, Norway 60 5N 6 8E
41 Æolian Is. = Eólie, I., Italy 38 40N 15 7E
75 Aerhatai Shan, Mongolia 46 40N 92 45E
49 Æro, Denmark 54 53N 10 20E
49 Ærosköbing, Denmark 54 53N 10 20E
45 Aëtós, Greece 37 15N 21 50E

MAP
83 Afafi, Massif d', Niger 22 11N 14 48E
45 Afándou, Greece 36 18N 28 12E
82 Afarag, Erg, Algeria 23 50N 2 47E
87 Afdera, Mt., Ethiopia 13 16N 41 5E
82 Affreville = Khemis Miliania, Algeria 36 11N 2 14E
14 Affric, R., Scot. 57 15N 5 0W
65 Afghanistan ■, Asia 33 0N 65 0E
63 Afgoi, Somali Rep. 2 7N 44 59E
64 Afif, Saudi Arabia 23 53N 42 56E
85 Afikpo, Nigeria 5 53N 7 54E
82 Aflisses, O., Algeria 28 30N 0 50E
82 Aflou, Algeria 34 7N 2 3E
87 Afodo, Ethiopia 10 18N 34 49E
41 Afragola, Italy 40 54N 14 15E
78 Africa, Cont. 10 0N 20 0E
113 Afton, U.S.A. 42 14N 75 31W
82 Aftout, Algeria 26 50N 3 45W
127 Afuá, Brazil 0 15S 50 10W
62 Afula, Israel 32 37N 35 17E
64 Afyon Karahisar, Turkey 38 20N 30 15E
85 Agadès, Niger 16 58N 7 59E
82 Agadir, Morocco 30 28N 9 35W
82 Agadir Tissint, Morocco 29 57N 7 16W
74 Agano, R., Japan 37 50N 139 30E
59 Agapa, U.S.S.R. 71 27N 89 15E
68 Agar, India 23 40N 76 2E
87 Agaro, Ethiopia 7 50N 36 38E
67 Agartala, India 23 50N 91 23E
46 Agăș, Rumania 46 28N 26 15E
108 Agassiz, Canada 49 14N 121 52W
87 Agat, Ethiopia 15 38N 38 16E
85 Agbelouvé, Togo 6 35N 1 14E
84 Agboville, Ivory Coast 5 55N 4 15W
57 Agdam, U.S.S.R. 40 0N 46 58E
57 Agdash, U.S.S.R. 40 44N 47 22E
20 Agde, France 43 19N 3 28E
82 Agdz, Morocco 30 47N 6 30W
20 Agen, France 44 12N 0 38E
83 Ager Tay, Niger 20 0N 17 41E
49 Agersö, Denmark 55 13N 11 12E
49 Agger, Denmark 56 47N 8 13E
49 Aggersborg, Denmark 57 0N 9 16E
40 Aggius, Sardinia 40 56N 9 4E
66 Aghil Mts., China 36 0N 77 0E
66 Aghil Pass, China 36 15N 76 35E
59 Aginskoye, U.S.S.R. 51 6N 114 32E
41 Agira, Italy 37 40N 14 30E
82 Aglou, Morocco 29 50N 9 50W
20 Agly, R., France 42 46N 3 3E
84 Agnibilékrou, Ivory C. 7 10N 3 11W
46 Agnita, Rumania 45 59N 24 40E
41 Agnone, Italy 41 49N 14 20E
85 Agofie, Ghana 8 27N 0 15E
38 Agogna, R., Italy 45 8N 8 42E
85 Agogo, Ghana 6 50N 1 1W
87 Agogo, Sudan 7 50N 28 45E
18 Agon, France 49 2N 1 34W
48 Agon I., Sweden 61 34N 17 23E
39 Agordo, Italy 46 18N 12 2E
20 Agout, R., France 43 47N 1 41E
68 Agra, India 27 17N 77 58E
126 Agrado, Colombia 2 15N 75 46W
32 Agramunt, Spain 41 48N 1 6E
32 Agreda, Spain 41 51N 1 55W
49 Agri, Denmark 56 14N 10 32E
42 Agri, R., Italy 40 17N 16 15E
64 Ağri Daği, Turkey 39 50N 44 15E
40 Agrigento, Italy 37 19N 13 33E
45 Agrinion, Greece 38 37N 21 27E
41 Agrópoli, Italy 40 23N 14 59E
127 Agua Clara, Brazil 20 25S 52 45W
120 Agua Prieta, Mexico 31 20N 109 32W
126 Aguaclara, Colombia 4 45N 73 0W
126 Aguadas, Colombia 5 40N 75 38W
121 Aguadilla, Puerto Rico 18 27N 67 10W
107 Aguanish, Canada 50 14N 62 02W
126 Aguarico, R., Ecuador 0 0 77 30W
124 Aguas Blancas, Chile 24 15S 69 55W
120 Aguascalientes, Mexico 22 0N 102 12W
120 Aguascalientes ♦, Mexico 22 0N 102 20W
30 Agueda, Port. 40 34N 8 27W
30 Agueda, R., Spain 40 45N 6 37W
31 Aguedo, Spain 38 59N 4 52W
82 Aguelt el Kadra, Maur. 25 3N 7 6W
82 Agueni N'Ikko, Morocco 32 29N 5 47W
85 Aguié, Niger 13 31N 7 46E
30 Aguilafuente, Spain 41 13N 4 7W
31 Aguilar, Spain 37 31N 4 40W
30 Aguilar de Campóo, Sp. 42 47N 4 15W
33 Aguilas, Spain 37 23N 1 35W
126 Aguja, C. de la, Colombia 11 18N 74 12W
126 Aguja, Pta., Peru 6 0S 81 0W
87 Agulaa, Ethiopia 13 40N 39 40E
92 Agulhas, Kaap, S. Africa 34 52S 20 0E
72 Agung, Indonesia 8 20S 115 28E
62 Agur, Israel 31 42N 34 55E
90 Agur, Uganda 2 28N 32 55E
73 Agusan, R., Phil. 9 20N 125 50E
57 Agvali, U.S.S.R. 42 36N 46 8E
48 Agön, Sweden 61 33N 17 23E
83 Ahaggar, Algeria 23 0N 6 30E
85 Ahamansu, Ghana 7 38N 0 35E
92 Aha Mts., Botswana 19 45S 21 0E
64 Ahar, Iran 38 35N 47 0E
101 Ahaura, New Zealand 42 20S 171 32E
24 Ahaus, Germany 52 4N 7 1E
83 Ahelledjem, Algeria 26 37N 6 58E
94 Ahimanawa Ra., N.Z. 39 5S 176 30E
101 Ahipara B., N.Z. 35 5S 173 5E
24 Ahlen, Germany 51 45N 7 52E
68 Ahmadabad (Ahmedabad), India 23 0N 72 40E
70 Ahmadnagar (Ahmednagar), India 19 7N 74 46E
68 Ahmadpur, Pakistan 29 12N 71 10E
87 Ahmar Mts., Ethiopia 9 20N 41 15E
85 Ahoada, Nigeria 5 8N 6 36E

MAP
24 Ahr, R., Germany 50 25N 6 52W
24 Ahrensbok, Germany 54 0N 10 34E
24 Ahrweiler, Germany 50 31N 7 3E
64 Ahsā, Wahatā al, Saudi Arabia 25 50N 49 0E
120 Ahuachapán, Salvador 13 54N 89 52W
49 Ahus, Sweden 55 57N 14 22E
64 Ahvaz, Iran 31 20N 48 40E
51 Ahvenanmaa, Fin. 60 15N 20 0E
85 Ahzar, Mali 15 30N 3 20E
65 Aibaq, Afghanistan 36 15N 68 5E
25 Aichach, Germany 48 28N 11 9E
74 Aichi-ken ♦, Japan 35 0N 137 15E
41 Aidone, Italy 37 26N 14 26E
41 Aiello Calabro, Italy 39 6N 16 12E
25 Aigle, Switzerland 46 18N 6 58E
19 Aignay-le-Duc, France 47 40N 4 43E
20 Aigre, France 45 54N 0 1E
125 Aigua, Uruguay 34 13S 54 46W
20 Aigueperse, France 46 3N 3 13E
21 Aigues-Mortes, France 43 35N 4 12E
21 Aiguilles, France 44 47N 6 51E
20 Aiguillon, France 44 18N 0 21E
20 Aigurande, France 46 27N 1 49E
76 Aihun, China 49 55N 127 30E
126 Aija, Peru 9 50S 77 45W
67 Aijal, India 23 40N 92 44E
115 Aiken, U.S.A. 33 34N 81 50W
19 Aillant-sur-Tholon, France 47 52N 3 20E
107 Aillik, Canada 55 11N 59 18W
19 Ailly-sur-Noye, France 49 45N 2 20E
14 Ailsa Craig, I., Scot. 55 15N 5 7W
59 Aim, U.S.S.R. 59 0N 133 55E
73 Aimere, Indonesia 8 45S 121 3E
124 Aimogasta, Argentina 28 33S 66 50W
127 Aimorés, Brazil 19 30S 41 4W
127 Aimorés, Serra dos, Brazil 17 50S 40 30W
21 Ain, R., France 45 52N 5 11E
21 Ain ♦, France 46 5N 5 20E
65 Ain Banaiyah, Si. Arab. 23 0N 51 0E
83 Aïn-Beida, Algeria 35 50N 7 35E
82 Aïn ben Khellil, Algeria 33 15N 0 49W
82 Aïn Ben Tili, Maur 25 59N 9 27W
82 Aïn Benian, Algeria 36 48N 2 55E
86 Ain Dalla, Egypt 27 20N 27 23E
64 Ain Dar, Si. Arabia 25 55N 49 10E
83 Aïn el Hadjel, Algeria 35 45N 3 56E
86 Ain el Mafki, Egypt 27 30N 28 15E
86 Ain Girba, Egypt 29 20N 25 14E
82 Aïn M'lila, Algeria 36 2N 6 35E
86 Ain Qeiqab, Egypt 29 42N 24 55E
82 Aïn Rich, Algeria 34 38N 24 55E
82 Aïn-Sefra, Algeria 32 47N 0 37W
86 Ain Sheikh, Egypt 26 47N 27 45E
86 Ain Sukhna, Egypt 29 32N 32 20E
82 Aïn Tédelès, Algeria 36 0N 0 21E
82 Aïn-Témouchent, Alg. 35 16N 1 8W
82 Aïn Touta, Algeria 35 26N 5 54E
86 Ain Zeitun, Egypt 29 10N 25 48E
82 Aïn Zorah, Morocco 34 37N 3 32W
63 Ainabo, Somali Rep. 9 0N 46 25E
54 Ainazi, U.S.S.R. 57 50N 24 24E
81 Aine Galakka, Chad 18 10N 18 30E
45 Ainos Oros, Greece 38 10N 20 35E
116 Ainsworth, U.S.A. 42 33N 99 52W
59 Aion, U.S.S.R. 69 50N 169 0E
126 Aipe, Colombia 3 13N 75 15W
85 Aïr (Azbine), Niger 18 30N 8 0E
19 Airaines, France 49 58N 1 55E
14 Aird, The, C., Scot. 57 26N 4 30W
14 Airdrie, Scotland 55 53N 3 57W
19 Aire, Fr. 50 37N 2 22E
32 Aire, Isla del, Spain 39 48N 4 16E
12 Aire, R., Eng. 53 42N 1 30W
19 Aire, R., France 49 18N 5 0E
20 Aire-sur-l'Adour, France 43 42N 0 15W
18 Airvault, France 46 50N 0 8W
87 Aisaita, Ethiopia 11 33N 41 25E
19 Aisne, R., France 49 12N 4 47E
19 Aisne ♦, France 49 42N 3 40E
82 Aït Melloul, Morocco 30 25N 9 29W
33 Aitana, Sierra de, Spain 38 35N 0 24W
98 Aitape, Terr. of N. Guinea 3 0S 142 25E
116 Aitkin, U.S.A. 46 40N 93 40W
45 Aitolia Kai Akarnania ♦, Greece 38 45N 21 18E
45 Aitolikón, Greece 38 26N 21 21E
43 Aitoska Planina, Bulgaria 42 45N 27 30E
75 Aitush, China 39 54N 75 40E
46 Aiud, Rumania 46 19N 23 44E
21 Aix-en-Provence, Fr. 43 32N 5 27E
24 Aix-la-Chapelle = Aachen, Germany 50 47N 6 4E
21 Aix-les-Bains, France 45 41N 5 53E
20 Aix-les-Thermes, Fr. 42 43N 1 51E
20 Aix-sur-Vienne, France 45 48N 1 8E
45 Aiyina, Greece 37 45N 23 26E
44 Aiyinion, Greece 40 28N 22 28E
45 Aiyion, Greece 38 15N 22 5E
18 Aizenay, France 46 44N 1 38W
54 Aizpute, U.S.S.R. 56 43N 21 40E
21 Ajaccio, Corsica 41 55N 8 40E
21 Ajaccio, G. de, France 41 52N 8 40E
68 Ajanta Ra., India 20 28N 75 50E
112 Ajax, Canada 43 50N 79 1W
83 Ajdabiyah, Libya 30 54N 20 4E
83 Ajdîr, Ra's, Libya 33 4N 11 44E
39 Ajdoušcina, Yugoslavia 45 54N 13 54E
87 Ajibar, Ethiopia 10 35N 38 36E
62 'Ajlun, Jordan 32 18N 35 47E
65 Ajman, Trucial States 25 25N 55 30E
68 Ajmer, India 26 28N 74 37E
119 Ajo, U.S.A. 32 18N 112 54W
87 Ajok, Sudan 9 15N 28 28E
73 Aju, Kepulauan, Indonesia 0 35N 131 5E

MAP

84 Ajua, Ghana — 4 50N 1 55W
64 Ak Dağ, Turkey — 36 30N 30 0E
85 Akaba, Togo — 8 10N 1 2E
82 Akabli, Algeria — 26 49N 1 31E
87 Akaki Beseka, Ethiopia — 8 55N 38 45E
87 Akala, Sudan — 15 39N 36 13E
101 Akaroa, N.Z. — 43 49S 172 59E
95 Akaroa Harb., N.Z. — 43 54S 172 59E
86 Akasha, Sudan — 21 10N 30 32E
74 Akashi, Japan — 34 45N 135 0E
82 Akbou, Algeria — 36 31N 4 31E
85 Akegbe, Nigeria — 6 17N 7 28E
73 Akelamo, Indonesia — 1 35N 129 40E
47 Akershus Fylke ♦, Norway — 60 10N 11 15E
70 Akeru, R., India — 17 25N 80 0E
45 Akhaía ♦, Greece — 38 5N 21 45E
57 Akhalkalaki, U.S.S.R. — 41 27N 43 25E
57 Akhaltsikhe, U.S.S.R. — 41 40N 43 0E
45 Akharnai, Greece — 38 5N 23 44E
45 Akhelóös, R., Greece — 39 5N 21 25E
45 Akhendriá, Greece — 34 58N 25 16E
44 Akhéron, R., Greece — 39 31N 20 29E
64 Akhisar, Turkey — 38 56N 27 48E
45 Akhladhókambos, Gr. — 37 31N 22 35E
86 Akhmîm, Egypt — 26 31N 31 47E
43 Akhtopol, Bulgaria — 42 6N 27 56E
57 Akhtubinsk (Petropavlovskiy), U.S.S.R. — 48 27N 46 7E
57 Akhty, U.S.S.R. — 41 30N 47 45E
54 Akhtyrka, U.S.S.R. — 50 25N 35 0E
106 Akimiski I., Canada — 52 50N 81 30W
56 Akimovka, U.S.S.R. — 46 44N 35 0E
45 Akincilar, Turkey — 37 57N 27 25E
98 Akinum, Terr. of New Guinea — 6 15S 149 30E
49 Akirkeby, Denmark — 55 4N 14 55E
74 Akita, Japan — 39 45N 140 0E
74 Akita-ken ♦, Japan — 39 40N 140 30E
84 Akjoujt, Mauritania — 19 45N 14 15W
82 Akka, Morocco — 29 28N 8 9W
62 'Akko, Israel — 32 35N 35 4E
58 Akkol, U.S.S.R. — 43 36N 70 45E
45 Akköy, Turkey — 37 30N 27 18E
85 Aklampa, Dahomey — 8 15N 2 10E
104 Aklavik, Canada — 68 25N 135 0W
82 Aknoul, Morocco — 34 40N 3 55W
85 Ako, Nigeria — 10 19N 10 48E
87 Akobo, R., Ethiopia — 7 10N 34 25E
68 Akola, India — 20 42N 77 2E
85 Akonolinga, Cameroon — 3 50N 12 18E
87 Akordat, Ethiopia — 15 30N 37 40E
85 Akosombo Dam, Ghana — 6 20N 0 5E
68 Akot, India — 21 10N 77 10E
87 Akot, Sudan — 6 31N 30 9E
105 Akpatok I., Canada — 60 30N 68 0W
50 Akranes, Iceland — 64 19N 22 6W
47 Akrehamn, Norway — 59 15N 5 10E
45 Akreïjit, Mauritania — 18 19N 9 11W
45 Akritas Venétiko, Akra, Greece — 36 43N 21 54E
116 Akron, Colo., U.S.A. — 40 13N 103 15W
112 Akron, Ohio, U.S.A. — 41 7N 81 31W
44 Akrotiri, Akra, Greece — 40 26N 25 27W
66 Aksai Chih, Kashmir — 35 30N 79 50E
64 Aksaray, Turkey — 38 25N 34 2E
58 Aksarka, U.S.S.R. — 66 31N 67 50E
64 Aksehir, Turkey — 38 18N 31 30E
59 Aksenovo Zilovskoye, U.S.S.R. — 53 20N 117 40E
75 Aksu, China — 41 4N 80 5E
87 Aksum, Ethiopia — 14 5N 38 40E
58 Aktogay, U.S.S.R. — 46 57N 79 40E
53 Aktyubinsk, U.S.S.R. — 50 10N 57 3E
85 Aku, Nigeria — 6 40N 7 18E
85 Akure, Nigeria — 7 15N 5 5E
50 Akureyri, Iceland — 65 40N 18 6W
67 Akyab, Burma — 20 15N 92 45E
83 Al Abyār, Libya — 32 9N 20 29E
63 Al Ain, Saudi Arabia — 19 35N 54 40E
64 Al Amadiyah, Iraq — 37 5N 43 30E
64 Al Amarah, Iraq — 31 55N 47 15E
64 Al Aqabah, Jordan — 29 37N 35 0E
65 Al Ashkhara, Oman — 21 50N 59 30E
83 Al 'Azīzīyah, Libya — 32 30N 13 1E
64 Al Badi, Si. Arabia — 22 0N 46 35E
62 Al Barah, Jordan — 31 55N 35 12E
83 Al Barkāt, Libya — 24 56N 10 14E
64 Al Basrah, Iraq — 30 30N 47 55E
81 Al Baydā, Libya — 32 30N 21 40E
83 Al Bu'ayrāt, Libya — 31 24N 15 44E
64 Al Diwāniyah, Iraq — 32 15N 45 30E
64 Al Fallujah, Iraq — 33 20N 43 55E
64 Al Faw, Iraq — 30 0N 48 30E
64 Al Hadhtgam, Iraq — 34 0N 41 13E
64 Al Hamad, Si. Arabia — 31 30N 39 30E
64 Al Hamar, Si. Arabia — 22 23N 46 6E
64 Al Hariq, Saudi Arabia — 23 29N 46 27E
64 Al Hasakah, Syria — 36 35N 40 45E
63 Al Hauta, S. Yemen — 16 5N 48 20E
64 Al Hayy, Iraq — 32 5N 46 0E
64 Al Hillah, Iraq — 32 30N 44 25E
64 Al Hillah, Saudi Arabia — 23 35N 46 50E
64 Al Hilwah, Saudi Arabia — 23 24N 46 48E
64 Al Hina, Iraq — 32 30N 44 10E
64 Al Hindiya, Iraq — 32 30N 44 10E
82 Al Hoceima, Morocco — 35 15N 3 58W
83 Al Hufrah, Awbārī, Libya — 25 32N 14 1E
83 Al Hufrah, Misrātah, Libya — 29 5N 18 3E
64 Al Hufuf, Si. Arabia — 25 25N 49 45E
83 Al Husayyāt, Libya — 30 24N 20 37E
62 Al Husn, Jordan — 32 29N 35 6E
81 Al Irq, Libya — 27 21N 35E
63 Al Ittihad = Madinat al Shaab, S. Yemen — 12 50N 45 0E
64 Al Jahrah, Kuwait — 29 25N 47 40E

MAP

64 Jalamid, Si. Arabia — 31 20N 39 45E
81 Al Jarzirah, Libya — 26 10N 42 25E
81 Al Jawf, Libya — 24 10N 23 24E
63 Al Jazir, Oman — 18 30N 56 31E
64 Al Jubail, Si. Arabia — 27 0N 49 50E
63 Al Juwara, Oman — 19 0N 57 13E
65 Al Khābūrah, Oman — 23 57N 57 5E
62 Al Khalih, Jordan — 31 32N 35 6E
117 Al Khums (Homs), Libya — 32 40N 14 17E
64 Al Kut, Iraq — 32 30N 46 0E
64 Al Kuwayt, Kuwait — 29 20N 48 0E
64 Al Ladhiqiyah, Syria — 35 30N 35 45E
86 Al Lith, Saudi Arabia — 20 9N 40 15E
64 Al Madīnah, Saudi Arabia — 24 35N 39 52E
62 Al-Mafraq, Jordan — 32 17N 36 14E
64 Al Majma'ah, Saudi Arabia — 25 57N 45 22E
65 Al Manamah, Bahrain — 26 10N 50 30E
81 Al Marj, Libya — 32 25N 20 30E
63 Al Masirah, Oman — 20 25N 58 50E
64 Al Mawsil, Iraq — 36 15N 43 5E
64 Al Miqdaldiyah, Iraq — 34 0N 45 0E
64 Al Mubarraz, Saudi Arabia — 25 30N 49 40E
65 Al Muharraq, Bahrain — 26 15N 50 40E
64 Al Musayyib, Iraq — 32 40N 44 25E
64 Al Muwaylih, Saudi Arabia — 27 40N 35 30E
83 Al Qaddāhīyah, Libya — 31 15N 15 9E
83 Al Qamishli, Turkey — 37 10N 41 10E
83 Al Qaryah ash Sharqiyah, Libya
83 Al Qaṣabāt, Libya — 32 39N 14 1E
64 Al Qatif, Saudi Arabia — 26 35N 50 0E
64 Al Qatrun, Iraq — 24 56N 15 3E
64 Al Quaisumah, Si. Arabia — 28 10N 46 20E
62 Al Quds, Israel/Jordan — 31 47N 35 10E
86 Al Qunfidha, Si. Arabia — 19 3N 41 4E
65 Al Quraiyat, Oman — 23 17N 58 53E
64 Al Qurnah, Iraq — 31 1N 47 25E
64 Al 'Ula, Saudi Arabia — 26 35N 38 0E
83 Al Uqaylah, Libya — 30 12N 19 10E
64 Al Uqayr, Saudi Arabia — 25 40N 50 15E
64 Al 'Uwayqiyah, Si. Arabia — 30 30N 42 0E
64 Al 'Uyūn, Saudi Arabia — 26 30N 43 50E
86 Al Wajh, Si. Arabia — 26 10N 36 30E
65 Al Wakrah, Qatar — 25 10N 51 40E
64 Al Wariah, Si. Arabia — 27 50N 47 30E
83 Al Wātiyah, Libya — 32 28N 11 57E
38 Ala, Italy — 45 46N 11 0E
48 Ala, Sweden — 61 13N 17 9E
74 Ala Shan, China — 40 0N 104 0E
115 Alabama, R., U.S.A. — 31 30N 87 35W
115 Alabama ♦, U.S.A. — 31 0N 87 0W
45 Alaçati, Turkey — 38 16N 26 23E
30 Alaejos, Spain — 41 18N 5 13W
38 Alagna Valsésia, Italy — 45 51N 7 56E
127 Alagoa Grande, Brazil — 7 3S 35 35W
127 Alagoas ♦, Brazil — 9 0S 36 0W
127 Alagoinhas, Brazil — 12 0S 38 20W
32 Alagón, Spain — 41 46N 1 12W
30 Alagón, R., Spain — 39 50N 6 50W
72 Alahanpandjang, Indon. — 1 10S 100 45E
121 Alajuela, Costa Rica — 10 2N 84 8W
93 Alakamisy, Malag. — 21 19S 47 14E
52 Alakurtti, Finland — 67 0N 30 30E
86 Alam Ajaib, Egypt — 25 55N 27 14E
31 Alameda, Spain — 37 12N 4 39W
119 Alameda, N. Mex., U.S.A. — 35 10N 106 43W
118 Alameda, S.D., U.S.A. — 43 0N 112 30W
120 Alamitos, Sierra de los, Mexico — 26 30N 101 8W
119 Alamo, U.S.A. — 37 21N 115 10W
119 Alamogordo, U.S.A. — 32 59N 106 0W
120 Alamos, Mexico — 27 0N 109 0W
119 Alamosa, U.S.A. — 37 30N 106 0W
51 Aland, Finland — 60 15N 20 0E
70 Aland, India — 17 36N 76 35E
31 Alandroal, Portugal — 38 41N 7 24W
31 Alange, Presa de, Spain — 38 45N 6 18W
84 Alangouassou, Ivory C. — 7 30N 4 34W
31 Alanis, Spain — 38 3N 5 43W
64 Alanya, Turkey — 36 38N 32 0E
93 Alaotra, L., Malag. — 17 30S 48 30E
58 Alapayevsk, U.S.S.R. — 57 55N 62 0E
30 Alar del Rey, Spain — 42 38N 4 20W
32 Alaraz, Spain — 40 45N 5 17W
53 Alaşehir, Turkey — 38 23N 28 30E
76 Alashanchih, China — 38 58N 105 14E
104 Alaska ♦, U.S.A. — 65 0N 150 0W
104 Alaska, G. of, Pac. Oc. — 58 0N 145 0W
104 Alaska Pen., Alaska — 56 0N 160 0W
104 Alaska Range, Alaska — 62 50N 151 0W
38 Alássio, Italy — 44 1N 8 10E
40 Alatri, Italy — 41 44N 13 21E
54 Alatyr, U.S.S.R. — 54 45N 46 35E
54 Alatyr, R., U.S.S.R. — 54 45N 45 30E
126 Alausi, Ecuador — 2 0S 78 50W
118 Alava, C., U.S.A. — 48 10N 124 40W
32 Alava ♦, Spain — 42 48N 2 28W
41 Alaverdi, U.S.S.R. — 41 4N 44 37E
99 Alawoona, Australia — 34 45S 140 30E
32 Alayor, Spain — 39 57N 4 8E
57 Alazan, R., U.S.S.R. — 41 25N 46 35E
38 Alba, Italy — 44 41N 8 1E
46 Alba ♦, Rumania — 46 10N 23 30E
46 Alba-Iulia, Rumania — 46 8N 23 39E
46 Albac, Rumania — 46 28N 23 1E
33 Albacete ♦, Spain — 38 50N 2 0W
100 Albacutya L., Australia — 35 45S 141 58E
38 Albaida, Spain — 38 51N 0 31W
32 Albalate de las Nogueras, Spain — 40 22N 2 18W
32 Albalate del Arzobispo, Spain — 41 6N 0 31W

MAP

44 Albania ■, Europe — 41 0N 20 0E
40 Albano Laziale, Italy — 41 44N 12 40E
96 Albany, Australia — 35 1S 117 58E
115 Albany, Ga., U.S.A. — 31 40N 84 10W
114 Albany, Minn., U.S.A. — 45 37N 94 38W
113 Albany, N.Y., U.S.A. — 42 40N 73 47W
118 Albany, Oreg., U.S.A. — 44 41N 123 0W
117 Albany, Tex., U.S.A. — 32 45N 99 20W
106 Albany, R., Canada — 51 30N 87 0W
124 Albardón, Argentina — 31 20S 68 30W
32 Albarracin, Spain — 40 25N 1 26W
32 Albarracin, Sierra de, Spain — 40 30N 1 30W
98 Albatross B., Australia — 12 45S 141 30E
39 Albegna, R., Italy — 42 40N 11 28E
115 Albemarle, U.S.A. — 35 27N 80 15W
115 Albemarle Sd., U.S.A. — 36 0N 76 30W
38 Albenga, Italy — 44 3N 8 12E
30 Alberche, R., Spain — 40 10N 4 30W
124 Alberdi, Paraguay — 26 14S 58 20W
32 Alberes, Mts., Spain — 42 28N 2 56W
96 Albergra, R., Australia — 26 50S 133 40E
33 Alberique, Spain — 39 7N 0 31W
108 Alberni, Canada — 49 20N 124 50W
24 Albersdorf, Germany — 54 8N 9 19E
100 Albert, Australia — 32 45S 147 31E
45 Albert, Canada — 51 1N 64 38W
19 Albert, France — 50 0N 2 38E
104 Albert Canyon, Canada — 51 0N 121 55E
*90 Albert, L., Zaïre — 1 30N 31 0E
99 Albert L., S. Australia — 35 30S 139 10E
116 Albert L., U.S.A. — 42 40N 120 8W
116 Albert Lea, U.S.A. — 43 32N 93 20W
90 Albert Nile, R., Uganda — 3 16N 31 38E
108 Alberta ♦, Canada — 54 40N 115 0W
92 Albertinia, S. Africa — 34 11S 21 34E
42 Albertirsa, Hungary — 47 14N 19 37E
107 Alberton, Canada — 46 50N 64 0W
100 Alberton, Australia — 38 36S 146 37E
90 Albertville = Kalemie, Zaïre — 5 55S 29 9E
21 Albertville, France — 45 40N 6 22E
65 Albarchrye Reshteh-Ye Kūkhā-Ye, Iran — 36 0N 52 0E
20 Albi, France — 43 56N 2 9E
116 Albia, U.S.A. — 41 0N 92 50W
127 Albina, Surinam — 5 37N 54 15W
38 Albina, Pta., Angola — 15 52S 11 44E
38 Albino, Italy — 45 47N 9 48E
118 Albion, Idaho, U.S.A. — 42 21N 113 37W
114 Albion, Mich., U.S.A. — 42 15N 84 45W
116 Albion, Nebr., U.S.A. — 41 47N 98 0W
112 Albion, Pa., U.S.A. — 41 53N 80 21W
32 Albocácer, Spain — 40 21N 0 1E
48 Albök, Sweden — 56 57N 16 47E
49 Alborán, I., Spain — 35 57N 3 0W
49 Alborg, Denmark — 57 2N 9 54E
49 Alborg Bugt, Denmark — 56 50N 10 35E
33 Albox, Spain — 37 23N 2 8W
108 Albreda, Canada — 52 35N 119 10W
31 Albufeira, Portugal — 37 5N 8 15W
25 Albula, R., Switzerland — 46 28N 9 38E
33 Albuñol, Spain — 36 48N 3 11W
119 Albuquerque, U.S.A. — 35 5N 106 47W
41 Alburno, Mte., Italy — 40 32N 15 20E
31 Alburquerque, Spain — 39 15N 7 1W
100 Albury, Australia — 36 0S 146 50E
48 Alby, Sweden — 62 30N 15 28E
49 Albaek, Denmark — 57 36N 10 25E
49 Albaek Bugt, Denmark — 57 36N 10 40E
31 Alcácer do Sal, Portugal — 38 22N 8 33W
31 Alcáçovas, Portugal — 38 23N 8 9W
32 Alcalá de Chisvert, Sp. — 40 19N 0 13E
33 Alcalá de Guadaira, Sp. — 37 20N 5 50W
32 Alcalá de Henares, Sp. — 40 28N 3 22W
33 Alcalá de los Gazules, Spain — 36 29N 5 43W
31 Alcalá la Real, Spain — 37 27N 3 57W
40 Alcamo, Italy — 37 59N 12 55E
32 Alcanadre, Spain — 42 24N 2 7W
32 Alcanadre, R., Spain — 41 43N 0 12W
31 Alcanena, Portugal — 39 27N 8 40W
31 Alcanede, Portugal — 39 25N 8 49W
32 Alcañices, Spain — 41 41N 6 21W
32 Alcañiz, Spain — 41 2N 0 8W
127 Alcântara, Brazil — 2 20S 44 30W
31 Alcántara, Spain — 39 41N 6 57W
33 Alcantarilla, Spain — 37 59N 1 12W
33 Alcaracejos, Spain — 38 24N 4 58E
33 Alcaraz, Spain — 38 40N 2 29W
33 Alcaraz, Sierra de, Spain — 38 40N 2 20W
33 Alcaudete, Spain — 37 35N 4 5W
33 Alcázar de San Juan, Sp. — 39 24N 3 12W
33 Alcira, Spain — 39 9N 0 30W
33 Alcobaça, Portugal — 39 32N 9 0W
32 Alcobendas, Spain — 40 32N 3 38W
32 Alcolea del Pinar, Spain — 41 2N 2 28W
32 Alcora, Spain — 40 5N 0 14W
31 Alcoutim, Portugal — 37 25N 7 28W
118 Alcova, U.S.A. — 42 37N 106 52W
33 Alcoy, Spain — 38 43N 0 30W
32 Alcubierre, Sierra de, Sp. — 41 45N 0 22W
32 Alcublas, Spain — 39 48N 0 43W
32 Alcudia, Spain — 39 45N 3 14E
32 Alcudia, Bahía de, Spain — 39 45N 3 14E
33 Alcudia, Sierra de la, Sp. — 38 34N 4 30W
3 Aldabra Is., Br. Indian Oc. Terr. — 9 22S 46 28E
59 Aldan, U.S.S.R. — 58 40N 125 30E
59 Aldan, R., U.S.S.R. — 63 30N 135 10E
13 Aldeburgh, England — 52 9N 1 35E
31 Aldeia Nova, Portugal — 37 55N 7 24W
47 Alden, Norway — 61 19N 4 45E
118 Alder, U.S.A. — 45 27N 112 3W

MAP

18 Alderney, I., Chan. Is. — 49 42N 2 12W
13 Aldershot, England — 51 15N 0 43W
108 Aldersyde, Canada — 50 40N 113 53W
116 Aledo, U.S.A. — 41 10N 90 50W
87 Alefa, Ethiopia — 11 55N 36 55E
125 Alegre, Brazil — 20 50S 41 30W
125 Alegrete, Brazil — 29 40S 56 0W
58 Aleisk, U.S.S.R. — 52 40N 83 0E
95 Alejandro Selkirk, I., S. Pacific — 33 50S 80 15W
53 Aleksandriya, U.S.S.R. — 50 45N 26 22E
56 Aleksandriya, U.S.S.R. — 48 42N 33 3E
57 Aleksandriyskaya, U.S.S.R. — 43 59N 47 0E
55 Aleksandrov, U.S.S.R. — 56 23N 38 44E
57 Aleksandrov Gay., U.S.S.R. — 50 15N 48 35E
42 Aleksandrovac, Y.-slav — 44 28N 21 13E
56 Aleksandrovka, U.S.S.R. — 48 55N 32 20E
43 Aleksandrovo, Bulgaria — 43 14N 24 51E
59 Aleksandrovsk-Sakhalinskiy, U.S.S.R. — 50 50N 142 20E
59 Aleksandrovskiy Zavod, U.S.S.R. — 50 40N 117 50E
58 Aleksandrovskoye, U.S.S.R. — 60 0N 77 50E
28 Aleksandrów Kujawski, Poland — 52 53N 18 43E
28 Aleksandrów Łódzki, Poland — 51 49N 19 17E
55 Alekseyevka, U.S.S.R. — 50 43N 38 40E
55 Aleksin, U.S.S.R. — 54 31N 37 9E
42 Aleksinac, Yugoslavia — 43 31N 21 42E
124 Alemania, Argentina — 25 40S 65 30W
47 Alen, Norway — 62 49N 11 17E
18 Alençon, France — 48 27N 0 4E
110 Alenuihaha Chan., Hawaiian Is.
98 Alenquer, Brazil — 1 56S 54 46W
64 Aleppo, Syria — 36 10N 37 15E
108 Alert B., Canada — 50 30N 127 35W
20 Alès, France — 44 9N 4 5E
46 Aleşd, Rumania — 47 3N 22 22E
38 Alessándria, Italy — 44 54N 8 37E
49 Alestrup, Denmark — 56 42N 9 29E
34 Alesund, Norway — 62 28N 6 12E
87 Alet, Sudan — 8 14N 29 2E
20 Alet-les-Bains, France — 42 0N 2 14E
52 Aleutian Is., Pac. Oc. — 52 0N 175 0W
116 Alexander, U.S.A. — 47 51N 103 40W
104 Alexander Arch., Alaska — 57 0N 135 0W
86 Alexander, B., S. Africa — 28 36S 16 33E
5 Alexander I., Antarc. — 69 0N 70 0W
104 Alexandra, Australia — 37 8S 145 40E
101 Alexandra, N.Z. — 45 14S 169 25E
75 Alexandretta = Iskenderun, Turkey — 36 32N 36 10E
108 Alexandria, B.C., Can — 52 35N 122 20W
106 Alexandria, Ont., Can. — 45 19N 74 38W
86 Alexandria = El Iskandarîya, Egypt — 31 0N 30 0E
92 Alexandria, S. Africa — 33 38S 26 28E
114 Alexandria, Ind., U.S.A. — 40 18N 85 40W
117 Alexandria, La., U.S.A. — 31 20N 92 30W
116 Alexandria, Minn., U.S.A. — 45 50N 95 20W
116 Alexandria, S.D., U.S.A. — 43 40N 97 45W
116 Alexandria, Va., U.S.A. — 38 47N 77 1W
113 Alexandria Bay, U.S.A. — 44 20N 75 52W
99 Alexandrina L., Australia — 35 25S 139 10E
44 Alexandroúpolis, Gr. — 40 50N 25 54E
108 Alexis Creek, Canada — 52 10N 123 20W
32 Alfambra, Spain — 40 33N 1 5W
30 Alfândega da Fé, Port. — 41 20N 6 59W
32 Alfaro, Spain — 42 10N 1 50W
43 Alfatar, Bulgaria — 43 59N 27 13E
24 Alfeld, Germany — 52 0N 9 49E
125 Alfenas, Brazil — 21 40S 44 0W
39 Alfonsine, Italy — 44 30N 12 1E
113 Alfred, Me., U.S.A. — 43 28N 70 40W
112 Alfred, N.Y., U.S.A. — 42 15N 77 45W
12 Alfreton, England — 53 6N 1 22W
48 Alfta, Sweden — 61 21N 16 4E
50 Alftanes, Iceland — 64 29N 22 10W
112 Alganac, U.S.A. — 42 36N 82 34W
33 Algar, Spain — 36 40N 5 39W
47 Algård, Norway — 58 46N 5 53E
33 Algarinejo, Spain — 37 19N 4 9W
31 Algarve, Portugal — 37 15N 8 10W
33 Algeciras, Spain — 36 9N 5 28W
33 Algemesi, Spain — 39 11N 0 27W
82 Algeria ■, Africa — 35 0N 3 11E
40 Alghero, Italy — 40 33N 8 19E
82 Algiers = Alger, Algeria — 36 42N 3 8E
92 Algoabaai, S. Africa — 33 50S 25 45E
30 Algodonales, Spain — 36 54N 5 24W
30 Algodor, R., Spain — 39 51N 3 48W
114 Algoma, Mich., U.S.A. — 44 35N 87 27W
118 Algoma, Oreg., U.S.A. — 42 25N 121 54W
106 Algonquin Park, Can. — 45 50S 78 35W
116 Alhama de Almería, Sp. — 36 57N 2 34W
32 Alhama de Aragón, Sp. — 41 18N 1 54W
33 Alhama de Granada, Sp. — 37 0N 3 59W
33 Alhama de Murcia, Sp. — 37 51N 1 25W
33 Alhambra, Spain — 38 54N 3 4W
119 Alhambra, U.S.A. — 34 0N 118 10W
31 Alhandra, Spain
31 Alhaurín el Grande, Sp. — 36 39N 4 41W
82 Alhucemas, Morocco — 35 8N 3 58W
57 Ali Bayramly, U.S.S.R. — 39 43N 48 52E
64 Ali al Gharbi, Iraq — 32 30N 46 45E
87 Ali Sabieh, Fr. Terr. Afars & Issas — 11 10N 42 44E
40 Alia, Italy — 37 47N 13 39E
65 Aliabad, Iran — 28 10N 57 35E
32 Aliaga, Spain — 40 40N 0 42W

MAP

44 Aliakmon, R., Greece — 40 10N 22 0E
70 Alibag, India — 18 38N 72 56E
87 Alibo, Ethiopia — 9 52N 37 5E
42 Alibunar, Yugoslavia — 45 5N 20 57E
33 Alicante ♦, Spain — 38 23N 0 30W
33 Alicante, Spain — 38 30N 0 37W
32 Alice, S. Africa — 32 48S 26 55E
117 Alice, U.S.A. — 27 47N 98 1W
41 Alice, Punta dell', Italy — 39 23N 17 10E
41 Alice, R., Australia — 23 50S 145 0E
108 Alice Arm, Canada — 55 29N 129 23W
23 Alice Springs, Australia — 23 36S 133 53E
96 Aliceldale, S. Africa — 33 15S 26 4E
115 Aliceville, U.S.A. — 33 9N 88 10W
41 Alicudi, Italy — 38 33N 14 20E
49 Alida, Canada — 49 25N 101 55W
68 Aligarh, Raj., India — 25 55N 76 15E
68 Aligarh, Ut. P., India — 27 55N 78 10E
65 Aligudarz, Iran — 33 25N 49 45E
31 Alijó, Portugal — 41 16N 7 27W
41 Alimena, Italy — 37 42N 14 4E
45 Alimnía, Greece — 36 16N 27 43E
67 Aling Kangri, Range, China — 31 45N 84 45E
49 Alingaabro, Denmark — 56 56N 10 32E
48 Alingsås, Sweden — 57 56N 12 31E
69 Alipore, India — 22 31N 88 24E
68 Alipur, Pakistan — 29 25N 70 55E
69 Alipur Duar, India — 26 30N 89 35E
112 Aliquippa, U.S.A. — 40 38N 80 18W
30 Aliste, R., Spain — 41 48N 6 14W
45 Alivérion, Greece — 38 24N 24 2E
92 Aliwal North, S. Africa — 30 45S 26 45E
31 Aljezur, Portugal — 37 18N 8 49W
31 Aljustrel, Portugal — 37 55N 8 10W
85 Alkamari, Niger — 13 27N 13 10E
63 Alkhalaf, Oman — 20 30N 58 13E
16 Alkmaar, Netherlands — 52 37N 4 45E
119 All American Canal, U.S.A. — 32 45N 115 0W
85 Allada, Dahomey — 6 41N 2 9E
68 Allah Dad, Pakistan — 25 38N 67 34E
69 Allahabad, India — 25 25N 81 58E
59 Alakh Yun, U.S.S.R. — 60 50N 137 5E
82 Allal Razi, Morocco — 34 30N 6 39W
82 Allal Tazi, Morocco — 34 30N 6 39W
71 Allanmyo, Burma — 19 16N 95 17E
92 Allanridge, S. Africa — 27 45S 26 40E
100 Allansford, Australia — 38 26S 142 39E
106 Allanwater, Canada — 50 14N 90 10W
86 Allaqi, Wadi, Egypt — 22 15N 34 55E
107 Allard Lake, Canada — 50 40N 63 10W
30 Allariz, Spain — 42 11N 7 50W
20 Allassac, France — 45 15N 1 29E
114 Allegan, U.S.A. — 42 32N 85 52W
112 Allegany, U.S.A. — 41 30N 78 30W
114 Alleghany, U.S.A. — 38 0N 80 0W
112 Allegheny Res., U.S.A. — 41 58N 78 55W
112 Allegheny, R., U.S.A. — 41 14N 79 50W
15 Allen, Bog of, Ireland — 53 15N 7 0W
15 Allen, L., Ireland — 54 30N 8 5W
62 Allenby (Hussein) Bridge, Jordan — 31 53N 35 33E
120 Allende, Mexico — 28 20N 100 50W
113 Allentown, U.S.A. — 40 36N 75 30W
26 Allentsteig, Austria — 48 41N 15 20E
70 Alleppey, India — 9 30N 76 28E
49 Alleröd, Denmark — 55 54N 12 19E
21 Allevard, France — 45 24N 6 5E
116 Alliance, Nebr., U.S.A. — 42 10N 102 50W
112 Alliance, Ohio, U.S.A. — 40 53N 81 7W
19 Allier, R., France — 46 57N 3 4E
21 Allier ♦, France — 46 25N 3 0E
98 Alligator Creek, Mackay, Australia — 21 20S 149 12E
98 Alligator Creek, Townsville, Australia — 19 20S 146 55E
49 Allingåbro, Denmark — 56 28N 10 20E
50 Alliston, Canada — 44 15N 79 55W
14 Alloa, Scotland — 56 7N 3 49W
20 Allos, France — 44 15N 6 38E
107 Alma, Canada — 48 35N 71 40W
116 Alma, Kans., U.S.A. — 39 1N 96 22W
114 Alma, Mich., U.S.A. — 43 25N 84 40W
116 Alma, Nebr., U.S.A. — 40 10N 99 25W
114 Alma, Wis., U.S.A. — 44 19N 91 54W
58 Alma Ata, U.S.S.R. — 43 20N 76 50E
31 Almada, Portugal — 38 40N 9 9W
98 Almaden, Australia — 17 22S 144 40E
31 Almadén, Spain — 38 49N 4 52W
118 Almanor, L., U.S.A. — 40 15N 121 11W
33 Almansa, Spain — 38 51N 1 5W
30 Almanzor, Pico de, Spain — 40 15N 5 18W
33 Almanzora, R., Spain — 37 22N 2 21W
32 Almazán, Spain — 41 30N 2 30W
32 Almazora, Spain — 39 57N 0 3W
127 Almeirim, Brazil — 1 30S 52 0W
31 Almeirim, Portugal — 39 12N 8 37W
16 Almelo, Netherlands — 52 22N 6 42E
32 Almenar, Spain — 41 43N 2 12W
33 Almenara, Sierra de, Spain — 37 34N 1 32W
31 Almendralejo, Spain — 38 41N 6 26W
33 Almería, Spain — 36 52N 2 32W
33 Almería ♦, Spain — 37 20N 2 20W
33 Almería, G. de, Spain — 37 20N 2 20W
45 Almiropótamos, Greece — 38 16N 24 11E
45 Almirós, Greece — 39 11N 22 45E
31 Almodóvar, Portugal — 37 31N 8 2W

* Renamed L. Mobutu Sese Seko

Almodóvar INDEX Ankober

MAP
31 Almodóvar del Campo, Spain 38 43N 4 10W
31 Almogía, Spain 36 50N 4 32W
31 Almonaster la Real, Sp. 37 52N 6 48W
112 Almont, U.S.A. 42 53N 83 2W
113 Almonte, Canada 45 15N 76 15W
31 Almonte, R., Spain 39 41N 6 12W
69 Almora, India 29 38N 79 4E
33 Almoradi, Spain 38 7N 0 46W
30 Almorox, Spain 40 14N 4 24W
31 Almuñécar, Spain 36 43N 3 41W
49 Almvik, Sweden 57 49N 16 30E
82 Alnif, Morocco 31 10N 5 8W
85 Almoustarat, Mali 17 35N 0 8E
48 Alnön I., Sweden 62 26N 17 33E
12 Alnwick, England 55 25N 1 42W
90 Aloi, Uganda 2 16N 33 10E
109 Alonsa, Canada 50 50N 99 0W
73 Alor, I., Indonesia 8 15S 124 30E
71 Alor Setar, Malaysia 6 7N 100 22E
31 Alora, Spain 36 49N 4 46W
31 Alosno, Spain 37 33N 7 7W
82 Alougoum, Morocco 30 17N 6 56W
30 Alpedrinha, Portugal 40 6N 7 27W
114 Alpena, U.S.A. 45 6N 83 24W
21 Alpes-Maritimes ♦, France 43 55N 7 10E
21 Alpes-de-Haute-Provence ♦, Fr. 44 8N 6 10E
25 Alpes Valaisannes, Switzerland 46 4N 7 30E
98 Alpha, Australia 23 45S 46 30E
38 Alpi Apuan, Italy 44 7N 10 14E
19 Alpi Craie, Italy 45 40N 7 0E
25 Alpi Lepontine, Italy 46 22N 8 27E
38 Alpi Orobie, Italy 46 7N 10 0E
25 Alpi Retiche, Switzerland 46 45N 10 0E
31 Alpiarca, Portugal 39 15N 8 35W
119 Alpine, Ariz., U.S.A. 33 57N 109 4W
117 Alpine, Tex., U.S.A. 30 35N 103 35W
22 Alps, Europe 47 0N 8 0E
49 Alrö, Denmark 55 52N 10 5E
49 Als, Aalborg, Denmark 56 46N 10 18E
19 Alsace, France 48 15N 7 25E
32 Alsasua, Spain 42 54N 2 10W
49 Alseda, Sweden 57 27N 15 20E
48 Alsen, Sweden 63 23N 13 56E
24 Alsfeld, Germany 50 44N 9 19E
27 Alsónémedi, Hungary 47 34N 19 15E
50 Alsten, Norway 65 58N 12 40E
32 Alta, Sierra, Spain 40 31N 1 30W
124 Alta Gracia, Argentina 31 40S 64 30W
108 Alta Lake, Canada 50 10N 123 0W
50 Altaelva, Norway 69 46N 23 45E
126 Altagracia, Venezuela 10 45N 71 30W
75 Altai, China 48 6N 87 2E
75 Altai = Aerhatai Shan, Mongolia 46 40N 92 45E
115 Altamaha, R., U.S.A. 31 50N 82 0W
127 Altamira, Brazil 3 0S 52 50W
126 Altamira, Colombia 2 3N 75 47W
124 Altamira, Chile 25 47S 69 51W
30 Altamira, Cuevas de, Spain 43 20N 4 5W
113 Altamont, U.S.A. 42 43N 74 3W
41 Altamura, Italy 40 50N 16 33E
76 Altanbulag, Mongolia 50 16N 106 30E
120 Altar, Mexico 30 40N 111 50W
120 Altata, Mexico 24 30N 108 0W
114 Altavista, U.S.A. 37 9N 79 22W
25 Altdorf, Switzerland 46 52N 8 36E
33 Altea, Spain 38 38N 0 2W
24 Altenberg, Germany 50 46N 13 47E
24 Altenbruch, Germany 53 48N 8 44E
24 Altenburg, Germany 50 59N 12 28E
24 Altenkirchen, Germany 50 41N 7 38E
26 Altenmarkt, Austria 47 43N 14 39E
31 Alter do Chão, Portugal 39 12N 7 40W
19 Altkirch, France 47 37N 7 15E
38 Alto Adige = Trentino-Alto Adige, Italy 46 5N 11 0E
127 Alto Araguaia, Brazil 17 15S 53 20W
91 Alto Chindio, Mozam. 16 19S 35 25E
120 Alto Cuchumatanes, Guatemala 15 30N 91 10W
124 Alto del Inca, Chile 24 10S 68 10W
91 Alto Ligonha, Mozam. 15 30S 38 11E
91 Alto Molocue, Mozam 15 50S 37 35E
125 Alto Paraná, R., Brazil 25 0S 54 35W
125 Alto Uruguai, R., Brazil 24 0S 53 30W
112 Alton, Canada 43 54N 80 5W
116 Alton, U.S.A. 38 55N 90 5W
99 Alton Downs, Australia 26 12S 138 58E
100 Altona, Australia 37 50S 145 40E
24 Altona, Germany 53 32N 9 56E
113 Altoona, U.S.A. 40 32N 78 24W
38 Altopáscio, Italy 43 50N 10 40E
25 Altstätten, Switzerland 47 22N 9 33E
64 Altun Kopru, Iraq 35 46N 44 10E
118 Alturas, U.S.A. 41 36N 120 37W
117 Altus, U.S.A. 34 30N 99 25W
75 Altyn Tagh, China 39 0N 90 0E
57 Alucra, Turkey 40 22N 38 47E
54 Aluksône, U.S.S.R. 57 24N 27 3E
63 Alula, Somali Rep. 11 50N 50 45E
56 Alupka, U.S.S.R. 44 23N 34 2E
56 Alushta, U.S.S.R. 44 40N 34 25E
73 Alusi, Indonesia 7 35S 131 40E
32 Alustante, Spain 40 36N 1 40W
117 Alva, U.S.A. 36 50N 98 50W
30 Alvaiázere, Portugal 39 49N 8 23W
49 Alvangen, Sweden 58 0N 12 7E
120 Alvarado, Mexico 18 40N 95 50W
117 Alvarado, U.S.A. 32 25N 97 15W
49 Alvastra, Sweden 58 20N 14 44E
47 Alvdal, Norway 62 6N 10 37E
124 Alvear, Argentina 29 5S 57 40W
31 Alverca, Portugal 38 56N 9 1W
49 Alvesta, Sweden 56 54N 14 35E
48 Alvho, Sweden 61 30N 14 45E
100 Alvie, Austral. 38 15N 143 30E
117 Alvin, U.S.A. 29 23N 95 12W
112 Alvinston, Canada 42 50N 81 53W
31 Alvito, Portugal 38 15N 8 0W
48 Alvros, Sweden 62 3N 14 40E
49 Älvsborgs län ♦, Sweden 58 30N 12 30E
50 Alvsby, Sweden 65 42N 20 52E
49 Alvsered, Sweden 57 14N 12 51E
68 Alwar, India 27 38N 76 34E
70 Alwaye, India 10 8N 76 24E
97 Alyangula, Australia 13 55S 136 30E
59 Alyaskitovyy, U.S.S.R. 64 45N 141 30E
57 Alyata, U.S.S.R. 39 58N 49 25E
116 Alzada, U.S.A. 45 3N 104 22W
38 Alzano Lombardo, Italy 45 44N 9 43E
25 Alzey, France 49 48N 8 4E
81 Am-Dam, Chad 12 40N 20 35E
81 Am Djeress, Chad 16 15N 22 50E
81 Am Guereda, Chad 12 53N 21 14E
81 Am Timan, Chad 11 0N 20 10E
88 Am-Zoer, Chad 14 13N 21 23E
96 Amadeus, L., Australia 24 54S 131 0E
87 Amadi, Sudan 5 29N 30 25E
90 Amadi, Zaïre 3 40N 26 40E
64 Amadia, Iraq 37 6N 43 30E
105 Amadjuak, Canada 64 0N 72 50W
105 Amadjuak L., Canada 65 0N 71 0W
31 Amadora, Portugal 38 45N 9 13E
112 Amador, U.S.A. 43 12N 82 36E
126 Amaga, Colombia 6 3N 75 42W
74 Amagasaki, Japan 34 42N 135 20E
49 Amager, Denmark 55 37N 12 35E
85 Amagunze, Nigeria 6 20N 7 40W
73 Amahai, Indonesia 3 2S 128 15E
74 Amakusa-Shotō, Japan 32 15N 130 10E
48 Amål, Sweden 59 2N 12 40E
70 Amalapuram, India 16 35N 81 55E
126 Amalfi, Colombia 6 55N 75 4W
41 Amalfi, Italy 40 39N 14 34E
45 Amaliás, Greece 37 47N 21 22E
68 Amalner, India 21 5N 75 5E
77 Amami-guntō, Japan 28 0N 129 0E
39 Amandola, Italy 42 59N 13 21E
85 Amanfrom, Ghana 7 20N 0 25E
58 Amangeldy, U.S.S.R. 50 10N 65 10E
41 Amantea, Italy 39 8N 16 3E
127 Amapá, Brazil 2 5N 50 50W
127 Amapá ♦, Braz. 1 40N 52 0W
73 Amar, Indonesia 4 44S 131 40E
87 Amar Gedid, Sudan 14 27N 25 13E
64 Amara, Iraq 31 57N 47 12E
87 Amara, Sudan 10 25N 34 10E
127 Amarante, Brazil 6 14S 42 50W
30 Amarante, Portugal 41 16N 8 5W
109 Amaranth, Canada 50 36N 98 43W
68 Amaravati, India 20 55N 77 45E
70 Amaravati, R., India 10 50N 77 42E
31 Amareleja, Portugal 38 12N 7 13W
127 Amargosa, Brazil 13 2S 39 36W
117 Amarillo, U.S.A. 35 14N 101 46W
39 Amaro, Mte., Italy 42 5N 14 6E
69 Amarpur, Bihar, India 25 5N 87 0E
67 Amarpur, Tripura, India 23 30N 91 45E
64 Amasra, Turkey 41 45N 32 30E
85 Amassama, Nigeria 5 1N 6 2E
64 Amasya, Turkey 40 40N 35 50E
93 Amatikulu, S. Africa 29 3S 31 33E
120 Amatitlán, Guatemala 14 29N 90 38W
39 Amatrice, Italy 42 38N 13 16E
127 Amazon, R., S. America 2 0S 53 30W
126 Amazonas ♦, Brazil 4 20S 64 0W
126 Amazonas ♦, Colombia 1 0S 72 0W
126 Amazonas ♦, Ven. 3 30N 66 0W
127 Amazonas, R., S. America 2 0S 53 30W
70 Ambad, India 19 38N 75 50E
93 Ambahakily, Malag. 21 36S 43 41E
68 Ambala, India 30 23N 76 56E
70 Ambalangoda, Sri Lanka 6 15N 80 5E
70 Ambalapuzha, India 9 25N 76 25E
93 Ambalavao, Malagasy Rep. 21 50S 46 56E
88 Ambam, Cameroon 2 20N 11 15E
93 Ambanifilao, Malag. 12 48S 49 47E
93 Ambanja, Malagasy Rep. 13 40S 48 27E
93 Ambararata, Malag. 13 41S 48 27E
59 Ambarchik, U.S.S.R. 69 40N 162 20E
93 Ambarijeby, Malag. 14 56S 47 41E
70 Ambarnath, India 19 12N 73 22E
93 Ambaro, B. d', Malag. 13 23S 48 38E
70 Ambasamudram, India 8 43N 77 25E
126 Ambato, Ecuador 1 5S 78 42W
124 Ambato, Sierra de, Arg. 28 25N 66 10W
93 Ambato-Boeni, Malag. 16 28S 46 43E
93 Ambatolampy, Malag. 20 39S 47 35E
93 Ambatondrazaka, Malagasy Rep. 17 55S 48 28E
93 Ambatosoratra, Malag. 17 37S 48 31E
93 Ambenja, Malagasy Rep. 15 17S 46 58E
73 Ambeno, Timor (Port) 9 20S 124 30E
25 Amberg, Germany 49 25N 11 52E
120 Ambergris Cay, British Honduras 18 0N 88 0W
21 Ambérieu-en-Bugey, France 45 57N 5 20E
101 Amberley, N.Z. 43 9S 172 44E
20 Ambert, France 45 33N 3 44E
93 Ambevongo, Malagasy Rep. 15 25S 42 26E
93 Ambia, Malagasy Rep. 16 11S 45 33E
84 Ambidédi, Mali 14 35N 11 47W
69 Ambikapur, India 23 15N 83 15E
86 Ambikol, Sudan 21 20N 30 50E
93 Ambinanindrano, Malag. 20 5S 48 23E
49 Ambjörnarp, Sweden 57 25N 13 17E
12 Ambleside, Eng. 54 26N 2 58W
87 Ambo, Begemdir & Simen, Ethiopia 12 20N 37 30E
87 Ambo, Shewa, Ethiopia 0N 37 48E
126 Ambo, Peru 10 5S 76 10W
93 Ambodifototra, Malag. 16 59S 49 52E
93 Ambodilazana, Malag. 18 6S 49 10E
93 Ambohimahasoa, Malag. 21 7S 47 13E
93 Ambohimanga du Sud, Malag. 20 52S 47 36E
73 Ambon, Indonesia 3 35S 128 20E
93 Ambongao, Cones d', Malag. 17 0S 45 0E
90 Amboseli L., Kenya 2 40S 37 10E
93 Ambositra, Malagasy Rep. 20 31S 47 25E
119 Amboy, Calif., U.S.A. 34 33N 115 51W
113 Amboy, N.J., U.S.A. 40 31N 74 18W
93 Ambre, C. d', Malag. 11 57S 49 17E
112 Ambridge, U.S.A. 40 36N 80 15W
88 Ambriz, Angola 7 48S 13 8E
88 Ambrizete, Angola 7 10S 12 52E
70 Ambut, India 12 48N 78 43E
99 Amby, Australia 26 30S 148 11E
58 Amderma, U.S.S.R. 69 45N 61 30E
120 Ameca, Mexico 20 30N 104 0W
120 Ameca, R., Mexico 20 30N 104 0W
120 Amecameca, Mexico 19 10N 98 57W
16 Ameland, Netherlands 53 27N 5 45E
39 Amelia, Italy 42 34N 12 25E
20 Amélie-les-Bains-Palalda, France 42 29N 2 41E
59 Amen, U.S.S.R. 68 45N 180 0E
41 Amendolara, Italy 39 58N 16 34E
118 American Falls, U.S.A. 42 46N 112 56W
118 American Falls Res., U.S.A. 43 0N 112 50W
5 American Highland, Antarctica 73 0S 75 0E
101 American Samoa, Pacific Ocean 14 20S 170 40W
125 Americana, Brazil 22 45S 47 20W
115 Americus, U.S.A. 32 0N 84 10W
16 Amersfoort, Neth. 52 9N 5 23E
93 Amersfoort, S. Africa 26 59S 29 53E
116 Ames, U.S.A. 42 0N 93 40W
113 Amesbury, U.S.A. 42 50N 70 52W
109 Amesdale, Canada 50 2N 92 55W
106 Ameson, Canada 49 50N 84 35W
45 Amfiklia, Greece 38 38N 22 35E
45 Amfilokhia, Greece 38 52N 21 9E
44 Amfipolis, Greece 40 48N 23 52E
45 Amfissa, Greece 38 32N 22 22E
59 Amga, R., U.S.S.R. 61 0N 132 0E
59 Amgu, U.S.S.R. 45 45N 137 15E
67 Amherst, Burma 16 2N 97 20E
107 Amherst, Canada 45 48N 64 8W
113 Amherst, Mass., U.S.A. 42 21N 72 30W
112 Amherst, Ohio, U.S.A. 41 23N 82 15W
117 Amherst, Tex., U.S.A. 34 0N 102 24W
112 Amherst, I., Can. 44 8N 76 45W
39 Amiata Mte., Italy 42 54N 11 40E
19 Amiens, France 49 54N 2 16E
45 Amigdhalokefáli, Gr. 35 23N 23 30E
44 Amindaion, Greece 40 42N 21 42E
3 Amirante Is., Ind. Oc. 6 0S 53 0E
109 Amisk L., Canada 54 35N 102 15W
117 Amite, U.S.A. 30 47N 90 31W
47 Amli, Norway 58 45N 8 32E
12 Amlwch, Wales 53 24N 4 21W
87 Amm Adam, Sudan 16 20N 36 1E
62 Amman, Jordan 32 0N 35 52E
48 Ammerån, Sweden 63 9N 16 13E
25 Ammersee, Ger. 48 0N 11 7E
48 Ammerån, Sweden 63 9N 16 13E
62 Ammi'ad, Israel 32 55N 35 32E
64 Ammókhostos, Cyprus 35 8N 33 55E
75 Amne Machin Shan, China 34 25N 99 40E
19 Amnéville, France 49 16N 6 9E
32 Amorebieta, Spain 43 13N 2 44W
45 Amorgós, Greece 36 50N 25 57E
31 Amory, U.S.A. 33 59N 88 30W
106 Amos, Canada 48 35N 78 5W
47 Amot, Norway 59 35N 8 0E
47 Amotsdal, Norway 59 37N 8 26E
82 Amour, Djebel, Algeria 33 42N 1 37E
77 Amoy = Hsiamen, China 24 25N 118 4E
93 Ampanihy, Malagasy Rep. 24 40S 44 45E
93 Ampariby Est., Malag. 23 57S 47 20E
93 Ampasindava, B. d', Malag. 13 40S 48 15E
93 Ampasindava, Presqu'île d', Malag. 13 42S 47 55W
85 Amper, Nigeria 9 25N 9 40E
82 Ampère, Algeria 35 44N 5 27E
93 Ampombiantambo, Malag. 12 42S 48 57E
32 Amposta, Spain 40 43N 0 34E
93 Ampotaka, Malag. 25 3S 44 41E
93 Ampoza, Malagasy Rep. 22 20S 44 44E
62 Amqa, Israel 32 59N 35 10E
107 Amqui, Canada 48 28N 67 27W
68 Amraoti, India 20 55N 77 45E
68 Amreli, India 21 35N 71 17E
82 Amrenene el Kasba, Algeria 22 10N 0 30E
68 Amritsar, India 31 35N 74 57E
68 Amroha, India 28 53N 78 30E
24 Amrum, Germany 54 37N 8 21E
83 Amsel, Algeria 22 47N 5 29E
16 Amsterdam, Netherlands 52 23N 4 54E
113 Amsterdam, U.S.A. 42 58N 74 10W
3 Amsterdam, I., Ind. Oc. 37 30S 77 30E
26 Amstetten, Austria 48 7N 14 51E
58 Amu Darya, R., U.S.S.R. 37 50N 65 0E
126 Amuay, Venezuela 11 50N 70 10W
4 Amund Ringnes I., Can. 78 0N 97 0W
104 Amundsen Gulf, Canada 70 30N 123 0W
5 Amundsen Sea, Antarc. 72 0S 115 0W
48 Amungen, Sweden 61 10N 15 40E
72 Amuntai, Indonesia 2 28S 115 25E
59 Amur, R., U.S.S.R. 53 30N 122 30E
73 Amurang, Indonesia 1 5N 124 40E
101 Amuri Pass, N.Z. 42 31S 172 11E
32 Amurrio, Spain 43 3N 3 0W
59 Amurzet, U.S.S.R. 47 50N 131 5E
30 Amusco, Spain 42 10N 4 28W
45 Amvrakikós Kólpos, Greece 39 0N 27 55E
57 Amvrosiyvka, U.S.S.R. 47 43N 38 30E
82 Amzeglouf, Algeria 26 50N 0 1E
64 An Nafud, Arabia 28 15N 41 0E
64 An Najaf, Iraq 32 3N 44 15E
62 An-Nâqūrah, Lebanon 33 7N 35 8E
64 An Nasiriyah, Iraq 31 0N 46 15E
71 An Nhon (Binh Dinh), S. Vietnam 13 55N 109 7E
64 An Nu'ayriyah, Si. Arab. 27 30N 48 30E
83 An Nawfaliyah, Libya 30 54N 17 58E
15 An Uaimh, Ire. 53 39N 6 40W
100 Ana Branch, R., Australia 32 20S 143 0E
62 Anabta, Jordan 32 19N 35 7E
47 Ana-Sira, Norway 58 17N 6 25E
126 Anaco, Venezuela 9 27N 64 28W
118 Anaconda, U.S.A. 46 7N 113 0W
118 Anacortes, U.S.A. 48 30N 122 40W
117 Anadarko, U.S.A. 35 4N 98 15W
30 Anadia, Portugal 40 26N 8 27W
64 Anadolu, Turkey 38 0N 39 0E
59 Anadyr, U.S.S.R. 64 35N 177 20E
59 Anadyr, R., U.S.S.R. 66 50N 171 0E
59 Anadyrskiy Zaliv, U.S.S.R. 64 0N 180 0E
45 Anáfi, Greece 36 22N 25 48E
45 Anafópoulo, Greece 36 17N 25 50E
40 Anagni, Italy 41 44N 13 8E
108 Anahim Lake, Canada 52 28N 125 18W
120 Anáhuac, Mexico 27 14N 100 9W
64 Anah, Iraq 34 25N 42 0E
70 Anai Mudi, Mt., India 10 12N 77 20E
70 Anaimalai Hills, India 10 20N 76 40E
98 Anakie, Australia 23 32S 147 45E
57 Anaklia, U.S.S.R. 42 22N 41 35E
93 Analalava, Malagasy Rep. 14 35S 48 0E
93 Analapasy, Malagasy Rep. 25 11S 46 40E
85 Anam, Nigeria 6 19N 6 41E
68 Anambar, R., Pakistan 30 10N 68 50E
72 Anambas, Kepulauan, Indonesia 3 20N 106 30E
116 Anamoose, U.S.A. 47 55N 100 7W
116 Anamosa, U.S.A. 42 7N 91 28W
64 Anamur, Turkey 36 8N 32 58E
74 Anan, Japan 33 54N 134 40E
68 Anand, India 22 32N 72 59E
69 Anandpur, India 21 16N 86 13E
45 Anánes, Greece 36 33N 24 9E
70 Anantapur, India 14 39N 77 42E
66 Anantnag, Kashmir 33 45N 75 10E
56 Ananyev, U.S.S.R. 47 44N 29 57E
56 Anapa, U.S.S.R. 44 55N 37 25E
127 Anápolis, Brazil 16 15S 48 50W
65 Anar, Iran 30 55N 55 13E
65 Anarak, Iran 33 25N 53 40E
47 Ana-Sira, Norway 58 17N 6 22E
64 Anatolia = Anadolu, Turkey 38 0N 29 0E
118 Anatone, U.S.A. 46 9N 117 4W
124 Añatuya, Argentina 28 20S 62 50W
81 Anaye, Niger 19 15N 12 50E
18 Ancenis, France 47 21N 1 10W
104 Anchorage, Alaska 61 10N 149 50W
30 Ancião, Portugal 39 56N 8 27W
126 Ancohuma, Nevada, Bolivia 16 0S 68 50W
120 Ancon, Pan. Canal Zone 8 57N 79 33W
126 Ancón, Peru 11 50S 77 10W
39 Ancona, Italy 43 37N 13 30E
128 Ancud, Chile 42 0S 73 50W
128 Ancud, G. de, Chile 42 0S 73 0W
124 Andacolla, Argentina 37 10S 70 42W
124 Andacollo, Chile 30 15S 71 10W
124 Andalgalá, Argentina 27 40S 66 30W
47 Andalsnes, Norway 62 35N 7 43E
31 Andalucía, Spain 37 35N 5 0W
31 Andalucía, Reg., Spain 37 35N 5 0W
31 Andalusia = Andalucia, Spain 37 35N 5 0W
115 Andalusia, U.S.A. 31 51N 86 30W
71 Andaman Is., India 12 30N 92 30E
71 Andaman Sea, Ind. Oc. 13 0N 96 0E
71 Andaman Str., Andaman Islands, India 12 15N 92 20E
92 Andara, S.W. Africa 18 2S 21 9E
19 Andelot, France 46 51N 5 56E
16 Andenne, Belgium 50 30N 5 5E
85 Andéranboukane, Mali 15 26N 3 2E
25 Andermatt, Switzerland 46 38N 8 35E
24 Andernach, Germany 50 24N 7 25E
20 Andernos, France 44 44N 1 6W
49 Anderslöv, Sweden 55 26N 13 19E
100 Anderson, Australia 38 3S 145 25E
118 Anderson, Calif., U.S.A. 40 30N 122 19W
114 Anderson, Ind., U.S.A. 40 5N 85 40W
117 Anderson, Mo., U.S.A. 36 43N 94 29W
115 Anderson, S.C., U.S.A. 34 32N 82 40W
93 Anderson, Mt., S. Africa 25 5S 30 42E
104 Anderson, R., Canada 69 0N 127 0W
49 Anderstorp, Sweden 57 19N 13 39E
126 Andes, mts., S. America 20 0S 68 0W
50 Andfjorden, Norway 69 10N 16 20E
70 Andhra, L., India 18 30N 73 32E
70 Andhra Pradesh ♦, India 15 0N 80 0E
45 Andikithira, Greece 35 52N 23 15E
45 Andimilos, Greece 36 47N 24 12E
45 Andiparos, Greece 37 0N 25 3E
45 Andipaxoi, Greece 39 9N 20 13E
45 Andipsara, Greece 39 30N 25 29E
58 Andizhan, U.S.S.R. 41 10N 72 0E
65 Andkhui, Afghanistan 36 52N 65 8E
100 Ando, Austral. 36 43S 149 16E
93 Andoharaoro, Malag. 22 58S 43 45E
70 Andol, India 17 51N 78 4E
32 Andorra ■, Europe 42 30N 1 30E
32 Andorra La Vella, Andorra 42 31N 1 32E
13 Andover, Eng. 51 13N 1 29W
112 Andover, N.Y., U.S.A. 42 11N 77 48W
112 Andover, Ohio, U.S.A. 41 35N 80 35W
93 Andrahary, Mt., Malag. 13 37S 49 17E
32 Andraitx, Sp. 39 35N 2 25E
93 Andramasina, Malag. 19 11S 47 35E
93 Andrano-Velona, Malag. 18 10S 46 52E
93 Andranopasy, Malag. 21 17S 43 44E
104 Andreanof Is., Alaska 51 0N 178 0W
54 Andreapol, U.S.S.R. 56 40N 32 17E
28 Andrespol, Poland 51 45N 19 34E
115 Andrews, S.C., U.S.A. 33 29N 79 30W
117 Andrews, Tex., U.S.A. 32 18N 102 33W
41 Andria, Italy 41 13N 16 17E
41 Andrian, Italy 46 30N 11 13E
93 Andriba, Malagasy Rep. 17 30S 46 58E
42 Andrijevica, Y.-slav. 42 45N 19 48E
45 Andritsaina, Greece 37 29N 21 52E
93 Androka, Malagasy Rep. 24 58S 44 2E
121 Andros I., Bahama Is. 24 30N 78 0W
45 Andros, Greece 37 50N 24 50E
27 Andrychów, Poland 49 51N 19 18E
31 Andújar, Spain 38 3N 4 5W
88 Andulo, Angola 11 25S 16 45E
49 Aneby, Sweden 57 48N 14 49E
85 Anécho, Togo 6 12N 1 34E
121 Anegada I., Virgin Is. 18 45N 64 20W
82 Anergane, Morocco 31 4N 7 14W
32 Aneto, Pico de, Sp. 42 37N 0 40E
83 Anfeg, Algeria 22 29N 5 58E
71 Ang Thong, Thailand 14 35N 100 31E
59 Anga, U.S.S.R. 60 35N 132 0E
76 Angangki, China 47 9N 123 48E
59 Angara, R., U.S.S.R. 58 30N 97 0E
59 Angarsk, U.S.S.R. 52 30N 104 0E
99 Angaston, Australia 34 30S 139 8E
48 Ange, Sweden 62 31N 15 35E
48 Angebo, Sweden 61 58N 16 22E
120 Angel de la Guarda, I., Mexico 29 30N 113 30W
49 Ängelholm, Sweden 56 15N 12 58E
118 Angels Camp, U.S.A. 38 8N 120 30W
48 Angelsberg, Sweden 59 57N 15 58E
67 Angenong, China 31 57N 94 10E
87 Anger, R., Ethiopia 9 30N 36 35E
87 Angereb, Ethiopia 13 11N 37 7E
87 Angereb, R., Ethiopia 14 0N 36 0E
48 Angermanalven, Sweden 62 40N 18 0E
24 Angermünde, Germany 53 1N 14 0E
113 Angers, Canada 45 31N 75 30W
18 Angers, France 47 30N 0 35W
19 Angerville, France 48 19N 2 0E
50 Angesån, Sweden 66 50N 22 15E
39 Anghiari, Italy 43 32N 12 3E
109 Angikuni L., Canada 62 10N 99 40W
72 Angkor, Khmer Rep. 13 22N 103 50E
32 Anglès, Spain 41 57N 2 38E
12 Anglesey, I., Wales 53 17N 4 20W
•12 Anglesey ♦, Wales 53 17N 4 20W
20 Anglet, France 43 29N 1 31W
117 Angleton, U.S.A. 29 12N 95 23W
19 Anglure, France 48 35N 3 50E
4 Angmagssalik, Green. 65 40N 37 20W
90 Ango, Zaïre 4 10N 26 5E
91 Angoche, I., Mozam. 16 20S 39 50E
124 Angol, Chile 37 56S 72 45W
89 Angola ■, Africa 12 0S 18 0E
114 Angola, Ind., U.S.A. 41 40N 85 0W
112 Angola, N.Y., U.S.A. 42 38N 79 2W
98 Angoram, New Guinea 4 4S 144 4E
20 Angoulême, France 45 39N 0 10E
20 Angoumois, Fr. 45 30N 0 25E
58 Angran, U.S.S.R. 80 59N 69 3E
125 Angra dos Reis, Brazil 23 0S 44 10W
92 Angra-Juntas, S.W. Afr. 27 39S 15 31E
90 Angu, Zaïre 3 25N 24 28E
121 Anguilla, I., Leeward Is. 18 14N 63 5W
† 14 Angus ♦, Scot. 56 45N 2 55W
14 Angus, Braes of, Scotland 56 51N 3 0W
77 Anhwa, China 28 18N 111 25E
77 Ani, China 28 50N 115 29E
45 Anidhros, Greece 36 38N 25 43E
85 Anié, Togo 7 42N 1 8E
119 Animas, U.S.A. 31 58N 108 58W
119 Animas Pk., U.S.A. 31 33N 108 56W
49 Animskog, Sweden 58 53N 12 35E
71 Anin, Burma 15 36N 97 50E
93 Anivorano, Malag. 18 44S 48 58E
68 Anjangaon, India 21 10N 77 20E
68 Anjar, India 23 6N 70 10E
77 Anjen, China 26 42N 113 19E
73 Anjer-Lor, Indonesia 6 6S 105 56E
93 Anjiabé, Malag. 12 7S 49 20E
70 Anjidiv I., India 14 40N 74 10E
18 Anjou, France 47 20N 0 15W
93 Anjozorobe, Malagasy Rep. 18 22S 47 52E
76 Anju, Korea 39 40N 125 45E
85 Anka, Nigeria 12 13N 5 58E
77 Ankang, China 32 38N 109 5E
64 Ankara, Turkey 40 0N 32 54E
93 Ankaramena, Malag. 21 57S 46 39E
93 Ankazoabo, Malag. 22 18S 44 31E
93 Ankazobé, Malagasy Rep. 18 20S 47 10E
93 Ankazotokana, Malag. 21 20S 48 9E
75 Anki, China 25 1N 118 4E
77 Anking, China 30 34N 117 1E
93 Ankisabé, Malag. 19 17S 46 29E
68 Anklesvar, India 21 38N 73 3E
87 Ankober, Ethiopia 9 35N 39 40E

* Incorporated within the county of Gwynedd
† Incorporated within the region of Tayside

MAP
*86 Ankole, Ugan. 0 30s 30 30E
90 Ankoro, Zaïre 6 45s 26 55E
77 Anlu, China 31 12N 113 38E
48 Ann, Sweden 63 19N 12 34E
5 Ann C., Antarctica 66 30s 50 30E
113 Ann C., U.S.A. 42 39N 70 37w
48 Ann L., Sweden 63 15N 12 34E
114 Ann Arbor, U.S.A. 42 17N 83 45w
117 Anna, U.S.A. 37 28N 89 10w
55 Anna, U.S.S.R. 51 38N 40 23E
83 Annaba, Algeria 36 50N 7 46E
24 Annaberg, Germany 50 34N 12 58E
48 Annalee, R., Ireland 54 3N 7 15w
100 Annalera Telegraph 41 16s 143 59E
Office, Australia
71 Annam = Trung-Phon. 16 30N 107 30E
Vietnam
71 Annamitique, Chaine, S. 17 0N 106 0E
E. Asia
14 Annan, R., Scot. 55 7N 3 25w
107 Annapolis Royal, Can. 44 44N 65 32w
49 Anneberg, Halland, 57 32N 12 6E
Sweden
21 Annecy, France 45 55N 6 8E
21 Annecy, L. d', France 45 52N 6 10E
21 Annemasse, France 46 12N 6 16E
75 Anning, China 24 58N 102 30E
115 Anniston, U.S.A. 33 45N 85 50w
**78 Annobón, Sp. Guin. 1 35s 3 35E
21 Annonay, France 45 15N 4 40E
21 Annot, France 43 58N 6 38E
121 Annotto Bay, Jamaica 18 17N 77 3w
100 Annuello, Australia 34 53s 142 55E
49 Annville, U.S.A. 40 18N 76 32w
45 Ano Arkhánai, Greece 35 16N 25 11E
44 Ano Porróïa, Greece 41 17N 23 2E
45 Ano Viánnos, Greece 35 2N 25 21E
116 Anoka, U.S.A. 45 10N 93 26w
93 Anorotsangana, Malag. 13 56s 47 55E
77 Anping, Taiwan 23 0N 120 6E
79 Ansbach, Germany 49 17N 10 34E
87 Anseba, R., Ethiopia 16 15N 37 45E
126 Anserma, Colombia 5 13N 75 48w
76 Ashan, China 41 3N 122 58E
77 Ashun, China 26 2N 105 57E
76 Ansi, China 40 21N 96 10E
116 Ansley, U.S.A. 41 19N 99 24w
82 Ansó, Spain 42 51N 0 48w
117 Anson, U.S.A. 32 46N 99 54w
96 Anson Bay, Australia 13 20s 129 30E
85 Ansongo, Mali 15 25N 0 35E
113 Ansonia, U.S.A. 41 21N 73 6w
106 Ansonville, Canada 48 46N 80 43w
14 Anstruther, E. and W., 56 14N 2 40w
Scotland
73 Ansudu, Indonesia 2 11s 139 22E
76 Anta, China 46 18N 125 34E
126 Antabamba, Peru 14 40s 73 0w
64 Antakya, Turkey 36 14N 36 10E
93 Antalaha, Malagasy Rep. 14 57s 50 20E
64 Antalya, Turkey 36 52N 30 45E
64 Antalya Körfezi, Turkey 36 15N 31 30E
89 Antananarivo = 18 55s 47 35E
Tananarive, Malagasy Rep.
93 Antanimbaribé, Malag. 21 30s 44 48E
89 Antarctica, cont.
5 Antarctic Pen., Antarc. 67 0s 60 0w
30 Antela, Laguna de, 42 7N 7 41w
Spain
91 Antelope, Rhodesia 21 2s 28 31E
49 Anten, Sweden 58 5N 12 22E
124 Antequera, Paraguay 24 8s 57 7w
31 Antequera, Spain 37 5N 4 33w
119 Antero Mt., U.S.A. 38 45N 106 43w
44 Anthemoús, Greece 40 31N 23 15E
117 Anthony, Kans., U.S.A. 37 8N 98 2w
119 Anthony, N. Mex., 32 1N 106 37w
U.S.A.
82 Anti Atlas, Mts., Mor. 30 30N 6 30w
21 Antibes, France 43 34N 7 6E
21 Antibes, C. d', France 43 31N 7 7E
107 Anticosti I., Canada 49 20N 62 40w
18 Antifer, C. d', France 49 41N 0 10E
107 Antigo, U.S.A. 45 8N 89 5w
107 Antigonish, Canada 45 38N 61 58w
120 Antigua, Guatemala 14 34N 90 41w
121 Antigua, I., Leeward Is. 17 0N 61 50w
119 Antimony, U.S.A. 38 7N 112 0w
113 Antioch, U.S.A. 38 1N 121 45w
126 Antioquia, Colombia 6 40N 75 55w
126 Antioquia ◊, Colombia 7 0N 75 30w
116 Antler, U.S.A. 48 58N 101 18w
117 Antlers, U.S.A. 34 15N 95 35w
124 Antofagasta, Chile 23 50s 70 30w
124 Antofagasta ◊, Chile 24 0s 69 0w
124 Antofalla, Arg. 25 30s 68 5w
117 Anton, U.S.A. 33 49N 102 5w
119 Anton Chico, U.S.A. 35 12N 105 5w
93 Antongil, B. d', 15 30s 49 50E
Malagasy Rep.
93 Antonibe, Malag. 15 7s 47 24E
93 Antonibe, Presqu'ile d', 15 30s 49 50E
Malag.
125 Antonina, Brazil 25 26s 48 42w
†91 António Enes, Mozam. 16 8s 40 0E
117 Antonito, U.S.A. 37 4N 106 1w
57 Antonovo, U.S.S.R. 49 25N 51 42E
18 Antrain, France 48 28N 1 30w
15 Antrim, N. Ireland 54 43N 6 13w
15 Antrim, Mts. of, N. 54 57N 6 8w
Ireland
††15 Antrim ◊, U.K. 54 58N 6 20w
39 Antrodoco, Italy 42 25N 13 4E
55 Antropovo, U.S.S.R. 58 26N 42 51E
93 Antsalova, Malagasy 18 40s 44 37E
Rep.
93 Antsirabé, Malagasy 19 55s 47 2E
Rep.
93 Antsohihy, Malagasy 14 50s 47 50E
Rep.

MAP
76 Antung, China 40 10N 124 18E
113 Antwerp, U.S.A. 44 12N 75 36w
16 Antwerp = Antwerpen, 51 13N 4 25E
Belgium
16 Antwerpen, Belgium 51 13N 4 25E
16 Antwerpen ◊, Belg. 51 15N 4 40E
68 Anupgarh, India 29 10N 73 10E
70 Anuradhapura, Sri 8 22N 80 28E
Lanka
16 Anvers = Antwerp(en), 51 13N 4 25E
Belgium
5 Anvers I., Antarctica 64 30s 63 40w
96 Anxious B., Australia 33 24s 134 45E
84 Anyama, Ivory Coast 5 30N 4 3w
76 Anyang, China 36 7N 114 26E
77 Anyi, China 35 0N 111 44E
77 Anyuan, China 24 59N 115 31E
62 Anza, Jordan 32 22N 35 12E
58 Anzhero-Sudzhensk, 56 10N 83 40E
U.S.S.R.
40 Anzio, Italy 41 28N 12 37E
48 Anzoátegui ◊, Venezuela 9 0N 64 30w
32 Aoiz, Spain 42 46N 1 22w
74 Aomori, Japan 40 45N 140 45E
74 Aomori-ken ◊, Japan 40 45N 140 40E
28 Aonla, India 28 16N 79 11E
82 Aoreora, Morocco 28 51N 10 53w
38 Aosta, Italy 45 43N 7 20E
85 Aoudéras, Niger 17 45N 8 20E
82 Aouinet Torkoz, Mor. 28 31N 9 46w
82 Aoukar = Mali 23 50N 2 45w
84 Aouker, Mauritania 23 48N 4 0w
82 Aoulef el Arab, Algeria 26 55N 1 2E
82 Aoullouz, Morocco 30 44N 8 1w
119 Apache, Ariz., U.S.A. 31 46N 109 6w
126 Apaporis, R., Colombia 0 30s 70 30w
73 Aparri, Philippines 18 22N 121 38E
126 Aparurén, Venezuela 5 6N 62 8w
46 Apateu, Rumania 46 36N 21 47E
42 Apatin, Yugoslavia 45 40N 19 0E
120 Apatzingán, Mexico 19 0N 102 20w
16 Apeldoorn, Netherlands 52 13N 5 57E
24 Apen, Germany 53 12N 7 47E
73 Apenam, Indonesia 8 35s 116 13E
9 Apennines, Italy 44 20N 10 20E
126 Apía, Colombia 5 5N 75 58w
101 Apia, W. Samoa 13 50s 171 50w
126 Apiacás, Serra dos, 9 50s 57 0w
Brazil
14 Apiaí, Brazil 24 31s 48 50w
120 Apizaco, Mexico 19 26N 98 9w
85 Aplahové, Dahomey 6 56N 1 41E
94 Aplao, Peru 16 0s 72 40w
73 Apo, Mt., Philippines 6 53N 125 14E
24 Apolda, Germany 51 1N 11 30E
45 Apollonia, Greece 36 58N 24 43E
81 Apollonia, Libya 32 52N 21 59E
126 Apolo, Bolivia 14 30s 68 30w
116 Apostle Is., U.S.A. 47 0N 90 30w
125 Apóstoles, Argentina 28 0s 56 0w
56 Apostolovo, U.S.S.R. 47 39N 33 39E
126 Apoteri, Guyana 4 2N 58 32w
114 Appalachian Mts., 38 0N 80 0w
U.S.A.
115 Appalachicola, R., 30 0N 85 0w
U.S.A.
41 Appenninni, Italy 41 0N 15 0E
38 Appenninno Ligure, Italy 44 30N 9 0E
25 Appenzell-Ausser 47 23N 9 23E
Rhoden ◊, Switz.
25 Appenzell-Inner Rhoden 47 20N 9 25E
◊, Switz.
72 Appiano, Italy 46 27N 11 17E
113 Apple Hill, Canada 45 13N 74 46w
12 Appleby, England 54 35N 2 29w
115 Appleton, U.S.A. 44 17N 88 25w
127 Approuague, Fr. Guiana 4 20N 52 0w
55 Aprelevka, U.S.S.R. 55 33N 37 4E
40 Apricena, Italy 41 47N 15 25E
40 Aprigliano, Italy 39 17N 16 19E
40 Aprilia, Italy 41 38N 12 38E
57 Apsheronsk, U.S.S.R. 44 28N 39 42E
21 Apt, France 43 53N 5 24E
125 Apucarana, Brazil 23 55s 51 33w
126 Apure, R., Venezuela 8 0N 69 20w
126 Apure ◊, Venezuela 7 10N 68 50w
126 Apurímac, R., Peru 12 10s 73 30w
126 Apurito, R., Venezuela 7 50N 67 0w
46 Apuseni, Munţii, 46 30N 22 45E
Rumania
65 Aq Chah, Afghanistan 37 0N 66 5E
86 'Aqaba, Jordan 29 31N 35 0E
64 'Aqaba, Khalï jal, Red 28 15N 33 20E
Sea
86 Aqiq, Sudan 18 14N 38 12E
86 Aqiq, G. of, Sudan 18 20N 38 10E
86 Aqiq, Khalig, Sudan 18 20N 38 10E
64 'Aqra, Iraq 36 46N 43 45E
62 'Aqraba, Jordan 32 9N 35 20E
64 Aqsu, China 41 10N 80 15E
127 Aquidauana, Brazil 20 30s 55 50w
120 Aquiles Serdán, Mexico 28 37N 105 54w
62 Ar Ramadi, Iraq 33 25N 43 20E
62 Ar-Ramthã, Jordan 32 34N 36 0E
64 Ar Rass, Saudi Arabia 25 50N 43 40E
64 Ar Rifai, Saudi Arabia 31 50N 46 10E
64 Ar Riyãd, Si. Arabia 24 41N 46 42E
64 Ar Rub 'al Khãlī Si. 21 0N 51 0E
Arab.
64 Ar Rutbah, Iraq 33 0N 40 15E
86 Arab, Khalig el, Egypt 30 55N 29 0E
64 Arab, Shott al, Iraq 30 0N 48 31E
85 Araba, Nigeria 13 7N 5 0E
56 Arabatskaya Strelka, 45 40N 35 0E
U.S.S.R.

MAP
39 Arabba, Italy 46 30N 11 51E
126 Arabelo, Venezuela 4 55N 64 13w
60 Arabia, Asia 25 0N 45 0E
60 Arabian Sea, Ind. Oc. 16 0N 65 0E
127 Aracaju, Brazil 10 55s 37 4w
126 Aracataca, Colombia 10 38N 74 9w
127 Aracati, Brazil 4 30s 37 54w
125 Araçatuba, Brazil 21 10s 50 30w
31 Aracena, Spain 37 53N 6 38w
127 Aracruz, Brazil 19 49s 40 16w
127 Araçuai, Brazil 16 52s 42 4w
42 Arad, Rumania 46 10N 21 20E
81 Arada, Chad 15 0N 20 20E
42 Aradu Nou, Rumania 46 8N 21 20E
73 Arafura Sea, E. Indies 10 0s 135 0E
57 Aragats, U.S.S.R. 40 30N 44 15E
32 Aragón, Spain 41 25N 1 0w
32 Aragón, R., Spain 42 35N 0 50w
40 Aragona, Italy 37 24N 13 36E
126 Aragua, Venezuela 9 35N 64 0w
126 Aragua ◊, Venezuela 10 0N 67 10w
126 Aragua de Barcelona, 9 28N 64 49w
Ven.
8 Araguacema, Brazil 8 50s 49 20w
127 Araguaia, R., Brazil 7 0s 49 15w
127 Araguari, Brazil 18 38s 48 11w
127 Araguari, R., Brazil 1 0N 51 40w
82 Arak, Algeria 25 20N 3 45E
64 Arãk, Iran 34 0N 49 40E
67 Arakan Coast, Burma 19 0N 94 0E
67 Arakan Yoma, Burma 20 0N 94 40E
45 Arákhova, Greece 38 28N 22 35E
64 Araks, R. = Aras, 39 10N 47 10E
Rud-e, Iran
57 Araks, R., U.S.S.R. 39 40N 47 0E
58 Aral Sea, U.S.S.R. 44 30N 60 0E
58 Aralsk, U.S.S.R. 46 50N 61 20E
58 Aralskoye More, 44 30N 60 0E
U.S.S.R.
100 Araluen, Australia 35 36s 149 48E
46 Aramã, Mţii de, 47 10N 22 30E
Rumania
98 Aramac, Australia 22 58s 145 14E
69 Arambagh, India 22 53N 87 48E
15 Aran, I., Ireland 55 0N 8 30w
15 Aran Is., Ireland 53 5N 9 42w
32 Aranda de Duero, Spain 41 39N 3 42w
42 Arandelovac, Y.-slav. 44 18N 20 37E
32 Aranjuez, Spain 40 1N 3 40w
117 Aransas Pass, U.S.A. 28 0N 97 9w
71 Aranyaprathet, Thailand 13 41N 102 30E
126 Aranzazu, Colombia 5 16N 75 30w
84 Araouane, Mali 18 55N 3 30w
95 Arapawa I., N.Z. 41 13s 174 20E
64 Arapkir, Turkey 39 5N 38 30E
125 Arapongas, Brazil 23 29s 51 28w
94 Arapuni, N.Z. 38 3s 175 37E
125 Araranguá, Brazil 29 0s 49 30w
127 Araraquara, Brazil 21 50s 48 0w
126 Araraquara, Colombia 8 24s 72 17w
125 Araras, Brazil 5 15s 60 35w
125 Ararás, Serra dos, Brazil 25 0s 53 10w
100 Ararat, Australia 37 16s 143 0E
64 Ararat, Turkey 39 50N 44 15E
69 Araria, India 26 9N 87 33E
87 Araro, Ethiopia 4 41N 38 50E
47 Aras, Norway 59 42N 10 31E
64 Aras, Rud-e, Iran 39 10N 47 10E
126 Arauca, Colombia 7 0N 70 40w
126 Arauca, R., Venezuela 7 30N 69 0w
126 Arauca ◊, Colombia 6 40N 71 0w
124 Arauco, Chile 37 16s 73 25w
124 Arauco ◊, Chile 37 40s 73 25w
126 Arauquita, Colombia 7 2N 71 25w
126 Araure, Venezuela 9 34N 69 13w
87 Arawa, Ethiopia 9 57N 41 58E
127 Araxá, Brazil 19 35s 46 55w
126 Araya, Pen. de, 10 40N 64 0w
Venezuela
87 Arba, Ethiopia 9 0N 40 20E
90 Arba Jahan, Kenya 2 5N 39 2E
87 Arba Minch, Ethiopia 6 0N 37 30E
40 Arbatax, Italy 39 57N 9 42E
126 Arbeláez, Colombia 4 17N 74 26w
64 Arbïl, Iraq 36 15N 5E
49 Arboga, Sweden 59 24N 15 52E
19 Arbois, France 46 55N 5 46E
87 Arbore, Ethiopia 5 3N 36 50E
47 Arborea, Italy 39 46N 8 34E
109 Arborg, Canada 51 0N 97 20w
48 Arbrå, Sweden 61 28N 16 22E
14 Arbroath, Scot. 56 34N 2 35w
118 Arbuckle, U.S.A. 39 3N 122 2w
40 Arbus, Italy 39 30N 8 33E
56 Arbuzinka, U.S.S.R. 47 52N 31 25E
19 Arc, Fr. 47 28N 5 34E
20 Arcachon, France 44 40N 1 10w
20 Arcachon, Bassin d', Fr. 44 42N 1 10w
112 Arcade, U.S.A. 42 34N 78 25w
115 Arcadia, Fla., U.S.A. 27 20N 81 50w
117 Arcadia, La., U.S.A. 32 34N 92 53w
116 Arcadia, Nebr., U.S.A. 41 29N 99 4w
112 Arcadia, Pa., U.S.A. 40 46N 78 54w
116 Arcadia, Wis., U.S.A. 44 13N 91 29w
118 Arcata, U.S.A. 40 55N 124 4w
77 Arcen, Neth. 51 29N 6 11E
52 Arcevia, Italy 43 31N 12 58E
52 Archangel = 64 40N 41 0E
Arkhangelsk, U.S.S.R.
42 Archar, Bulgaria 43 50N 22 54E
113 Archbald, U.S.A. 41 30N 75 31w
31 Archena, Spain 38 9N 1 16w
98 Archer B., Australia 13 20s 141 30E
90 Archers Post, Kenya 0 35N 37 35E
31 Archidona, Spain 37 6N 4 22w
40 Arci, Monte, Sardinia 39 47N 8 44E
39 Arcidosso, Italy 42 51N 11 30E
82 Arcila = Asilah, 35 29N 6 0w
Morocco

MAP
19 Arcis-sur-Aube, France 48 32N 4 10E
38 Arco, Italy 45 55N 10 54E
118 Arco, U.S.A. 43 45N 113 16w
109 Arcola, Canada 49 40N 102 30w
31 Arcos de la Frontera, 36 44N 5 47w
Spain
70 Arcot, India 12 53N 79 20E
127 Arcoverde, Brazil 8 25s 37 4w
4 Arctic Ocean, Arctica 78 0N 160 0w
104 Arctic Red River, Can. 67 15N 134 0w
38 Arda, R., Italy 41 40N 25 0E
42 Arda, R., Bulgaria 41 40N 25 40E
64 Ardakan, Iran 30 20N 52 5E
55 Ardatov, U.S.S.R. 54 51N 46 15E
21 Ardèche ◊, France 44 42N 4 16E
15 Ardee, Ireland 53 51N 6 32w
16 Arden Stby., Denmark 56 46N 9 52E
16 Ardennes, Belgium 49 30N 5 10E
19 Ardennes ◊, France 49 35N 4 40E
19 Ardentes, France 46 45N 1 50E
65 Ardestan, Iran 33 20N 52 25E
14 Ardgour, Scotland 56 45N 5 25w
44 Ardhas, R., Greece 41 36N 26 25E
40 Ardhéa, Greece 40 58N 22 3E
31 Ardila, R., Spain 38 10N 7 20w
45 Ardino, Bulgaria 41 34N 25 9E
73 Ardjuno, Indonesia 7 49s 112 39E
100 Ardlethan, Australia 34 22s 146 53E
96 Ardmore, Australia 21 35s 139 20E
117 Ardmore, Okla., U.S.A. 34 10N 97 5w
112 Ardmore, Pa., U.S.A. 39 58N 75 18w
116 Ardmore, S.D., U.S.A. 43 0N 103 40w
15 Ardnacrusha, Ireland 52 43N 8 38w
14 Ardnamurchan Pt., 56 44N 6 14w
Scotland
100 Ardno, Australia 37 49s 141 3E
41 Ardore Marina, Italy 38 11N 16 10E
19 Ardres, France 50 50N 2 0E
14 Ardrossan, Scot. 55 39N 4 50w
70 Ardud, Rumania 47 37N 22 52E
49 Ards Pen., N. Ire. 54 30N 5 25w
46 Ardunac, Turkey 41 8N 42 5E
63 Are, Sweden 63 22N 13 15E
18 Areia Branca, Brazil 5 0s 37 0w
47 Aremark, Norway 59 15N 11 42E
30 Arenales, Cerro, Chile 47 5s 73 40w
30 Arenas, Spain 40 17N 5 6w
30 Arenas, Pta., Ven. 10 20N 62 39w
30 Arenas de San Pedro, 40 12N 5 5w
Spain
47 Arendal, Norway 58 28N 8 46E
24 Arendsee, Germany 52 52N 11 27E
32 Arenys de Mar, Spain 41 35N 2 33E
38 Arenzano, Italy 44 24N 8 40E
45 Areópolis, Greece 36 40N 22 22E
94 Arequipa, Peru 16 20s 71 30w
87 Arero, Ethiopia 4 41N 38 50E
20 Arès, France 44 47N 1 8w
30 Arévalo, Spain 41 3N 4 43w
39 Arezzo, Italy 43 28N 11 50E
32 Arga, R., Spain 42 18N 1 47w
44 Argalasti, Greece 39 13N 23 13E
39 Argamasilla de Alba, Sp. 39 8N 3 5w
20 Argana, Morocco 30 47N 9 26w
13 Arganil, Portugal 40 13N 8 3w
20 Argelès-Gazost, France 43 0N 0 6w
20 Argelès-sur-Mer, Fr. 42 34N 3 1E
19 Argent-sur-Sauldre, Fr. 47 33N 2 25E
108 Argenta, Canada 50 20N 116 55w
39 Argenta, Italy 44 37N 11 50E
18 Argentan, France 48 45N 0 1w
38 Argentario, Mte., Italy 42 23N 11 11E
21 Argentat, France 45 6N 1 56E
38 Argentera, Italy 44 23N 6 58E
19 Argenteuil, France 48 57N 2 14E
107 Argentia, Canada 47 18N 53 58w
40 Argentiera, C. dell', Italy 40 44N 8 8E
126 Argentina, Colombia 0 34N 74 17w
128 Argentina ◊, South 35 0s 66 0w
America
128 Argentino, L., Arg. 50 10s 73 0w
20 Argenton Château, 47 3N 0 18w
France
20 Argenton-sur-Creuse, 46 36N 1 30E
France
18 Argentré, France 48 5N 0 40w
46 Argeş, R., Rumania 44 30N 25 50E
46 Argeş ◊, Rumania 45 0N 24 45E
44 Argiras, R., Rumania 45 30N 24 45E
44 Argolikós Kólpos, 37 20N 22 52E
Greece
44 Argolis ◊, Greece 37 38N 22 50E
19 Argonne, France 49 0N 5 20E
44 Argos, Greece 37 40N 22 43E
44 Argos Orestikón, Gr. 40 27N 21 26E
44 Agostólion, Greece 38 12N 20 33E
32 Arguedas, Spain 42 11N 1 36w
119 Arguello, Pt., U.S.A. 34 34N 120 40w
59 Argun, R., U.S.S.R. 53 20N 121 28E
85 Argungu, Nigeria 12 40N 4 31E
116 Argyle, U.S.A. 48 23N 96 49w
*14 Argyll ◊, Scot. 56 18N 5 19w
56 Arhus, Denmark 56 8N 10 11E
74 Ariake-wan, Japan 31 30N 131 10E
92 Ariamsvlei, S.W. Africa 28 9s 19 51E
41 Ariano Irpino, It. 41 10N 15 4w
39 Ariano nel Polèsine, It. 44 56N 12 5E
85 Aribinda, Upper Volta 14 17N 0 52w
126 Arica, Chile 18 32s 70 20w
126 Arica, Colombia 2 0s 71 50w
96 Arid, C., Australia 34 1s 123 10E
20 Ariège, R., France 43 30N 1 50E
20 Ariège ◊, France 42 56N 1 30E
46 Aries, R., Rumania 46 24N 23 20E

MAP
42 Arilje, Y.-slav. 43 44N 20 7E
121 Arima, Trinidad 10 38N 61 17w
126 Arinos, R., Brazil 11 15s 57 0w
120 Ario de Rosales, Mex. 19 12N 101 42w
126 Aripuanã, Brazil 9 25s 60 30w
126 Aripuanã, R., Brazil 7 30s 60 0w
126 Ariquemes, Brazil 9 55s 63 6w
86 Arish, W. el, Egypt 30 25N 34 52E
15 Arismendi, Ven. 8 29N 68 22w
14 Arisaig, Scot. 56 50N 5 40w
87 Arissa, Ethiopia 11 10N 41 35E
108 Aristazabal, I., Canada 52 40N 129 10w
119 Arivaca, U.S.A. 31 37N 111 25w
93 Arivonimamo, Malag. 19 1s 47 11E
70 Ariyalur, India 11 8N 79 8E
32 Ariza, Spain 41 19N 2 3w
124 Airzaro, Salar de, Arg. 24 40s 67 50w
119 Arizona ◊, U.S.A. 34 20N 111 30w
124 Arizona, Argentina 35 45s 65 25w
120 Arizpe, Mexico 30 20N 110 11w
48 Arjang, Sweden 59 24N 12 9E
50 Arjeplog, Sweden 66 3N 18 2E
126 Arjona, Colombia 10 14N 75 22w
31 Arjona, Spain 37 56N 4 4w
59 Arka, U.S.S.R. 60 15N 142 0E
75 Arka Tag, China 36 30N 90 0E
55 Arkadak, U.S.S.R. 51 58N 43 19E
117 Arkadelphia, U.S.A. 34 5N 93 0w
14 Arkaig, L., Scot. 56 58N 5 10w
117 Arkansas, R., U.S.A. 35 20N 93 30w
117 Arkansas ◊, U.S.A. 35 0N 92 30w
117 Arkansas City, U.S.A. 37 4N 97 3w
44 Arkathos, R., Greece 39 20N 21 4E
44 Arkhángelos, Greece 36 13N 28 7E
52 Arkhangelsk, U.S.S.R. 64 40N 41 0E
87 Arkiko, Ethiopia 15 33N 39 30E
15 Arklow, Ireland 52 48N 6 10w
24 Arkoi, Greece 37 24N 26 44E
24 Arkona, Kap, Germany 54 41N 13 26E
70 Arkonam, India 13 7N 79 43E
49 Arkösund, Sweden 58 29N 16 56E
45 Arkhoúdhi, Greece 38 33N 20 43E
59 Arktichesky, Mys, 81 10N 95 0E
U.S.S.R.
20 Arlanc, France 45 25N 3 42E
30 Arlanza, R., Spain 42 6N 4 9w
30 Arlanzón, R., Spain 42 3N 3 40w
118 Arlee, U.S.A. 47 10N 114 4w
21 Arles, France 43 41N 4 40E
15 Armagh, N. Ire. 54 22N 6 40w
*15 Armagh ◊, N. Ire. 54 16N 6 35w
19 Armagnac, France 43 44N 0 10E
19 Armançon, R., France 47 51N 4 7E
57 Armavir, U.S.S.R. 45 2N 41 7E
126 Armenia, Colombia 4 35N 75 45w
57 Armenian S.S.R. ◊, 40 0N 41 0E
U.S.S.R.
46 Armeniş, Rumania 45 13N 22 17E
50 Armentières, France 50 40N 2 50E
126 Armero, Colombia 4 58N 74 54w
99 Armidale, Australia 30 36s 151 40E
116 Armour, U.S.A. 43 20N 98 25w
106 Armos, Canada 48 34N 86 3w
105 Armstead, U.S.A. 45 0N 112 56w
108 Armstrong, B.C., Can. 50 25N 119 10w
106 Armstrong, Ont., Can. 50 20N 89 0w
14 Armstrong, U.S.A. 26 59N 90 48w
70 Armur, India 18 48N 78 16E
44 Arnaia, Greece 40 30N 23 40E
18 Arnay-le-Duc, France 47 10N 4 27E
32 Arnedillo, Spain 42 12N 2 14w
32 Arnedo, Spain 42 12N 2 5w
47 Arnes, Norway 60 7N 11 28E
16 Arnhem, Netherlands 51 58N 5 55E
96 Arnhem B., Australia 12 20s 136 10E
96 Arnhem, C., Australia 12 18s 137 10E
96 Arnhem Ld., Australia 13 10s 135 0E
70 Arni, India 12 43N 79 19E
44 Arnissa, Greece 40 47N 21 49E
38 Arno, R., Italy 43 44N 10 20E
95 Arnold, N.Z. 42 29s 171 25E
116 Arnold, Nebr., U.S.A. 41 29N 100 10w
112 Arnold, Pa., U.S.A. 40 36N 79 44w
26 Arnoldstein, Austria 46 33N 13 43E
109 Arnot, Canada 55 46N 96 42w
106 Arnprior, Canada 45 23N 76 25w
24 Arnsberg, Germany 51 25N 8 10E
24 Arnstadt, Germany 50 50N 10 56E
126 Aroa, Venezuela 10 26N 68 54w
24 Arolsen, Germany 51 23N 9 1E
39 Aroma, Italy 45 45N 8 32E
30 Arosa, Ria de, Spain 42 28N 8 57w
20 Arpajon, Cantal, Fr. 44 54N 2 28E
20 Arpajon, Seine et Oise, 48 37N 2 12E
France
99 Arrabury, Australia 26 45s 141 0E
31 Arraias, Portugal 39 8N 7 59w
120 Arraiján, Panama 8 56N 79 36w
24 Arran, I., Scotland 55 34N 5 12w
108 Arrandale, Canada 54 57N 130 0w
15 Arras, France 50 17N 2 46E
20 Arreau, France 42 54N 0 22E

* Incorporated within the new Southern Province
* Renamed Pagalu

† Renamed Angoche
†† In April 1973 districts replaced counties in N. Ireland

* Incorporated within the region of Strathclyde

* In April 1973 districts replaced counties in N. Ireland

5

Arrecife INDEX Áyios

MAP
86 Arrecife, Canary Is. 28 59N 13 40W
124 Arrecifes, Argentina 34 06S 60 9W
18 Arrée, Mts. d', France 48 26N 3 55W
120 Arriaga, Mexico 21 55N 101 23W
49 Arrild, Denmark 55 8N 8 58E
18 Arromanches-les- Bains, France 49 20N 0 38W
31 Arronches, Portugal 39 8N 7 16W
18 Arrou, France 48 6N 1 8E
118 Arrow Rock Res., U.S.A. 43 45N 115 50W
108 Arrowhead, Canada 50 40N 117 55W
101 Arrowtown, N.Z. 44 57S 168 50E
31 Arroyo de la Luz, Spain 39 30N 6 38W
119 Arroyo Grande, U.S.A. 35 9N 120 32W
49 Års, Denmark 56 48N 9 30E
20 Ars, France 46 13N 1 30W
19 Ars-sur-Moselle, France 49 5N 6 4E
109 Arsenault L., Canada 55 5N 108 50W
76 Arshan, China 46 59N 120 0E
39 Arsiero, Italy 45 49N 11 22E
70 Arsikere, India 13 15N 76 15E
55 Arsk, U.S.S.R. 56 10N 49 50E
48 Arskogen, Sweden 62 8N 17 20E
45 Árta, Greece 39 8N 21 2E
32 Artá, Spain 39 40N 3 20E
44 Arta ♦, Greece 39 15N 21 5E
120 Arteaga, Mexico 18 50N 102 20W
30 Arteijo, Spain 43 19N 8 29W
57 Artem, Os., U.S.S.R. 40 28N 50 20E
84 Artémou, Mauritania 15 38N 12 16W
56 Artemovsk, U.S.S.R. 48 35N 37 55E
57 Artemovski, U.S.S.R. 54 45N 93 35E
19 Artenay, France 48 5N 1 50E
24 Artern, Germany 51 22N 11 18E
32 Artesa de Segre, Spain 41 54N 1 3E
92 Artesia, Botswana 24 2S 26 19E
117 Artesia, U.S.A. 32 55N 104 25W
117 Artesia Wells, U.S.A. 28 17N 99 18W
116 Artesian, U.S.A. 44 2N 97 54W
20 Arthez-de-Béarn, France 43 29N 0 38W
84 Arthington, Liberia 6 35N 10 45W
101 Arthur's Pass, N.Z. 42 54S 171 35E
124 Artigas, Uruguay 30 20S 56 30W
57 Artik, U.S.S.R. 40 38N 44 50E
19 Artois, France 50 20N 2 30E
45 Artotina, Greece 38 42N 22 2E
76 Arts Bogd Uul, mts., Mongolia 44 40N 102 20E
64 Artvin, Turkey 41 14N 41 44E
73 Aru, Kepulauan, Indonesia 6 0S 134 30E
90 Arua, Uganda 3 1N 30 58E
127 Aruanã, Brazil 15 0S 51 10W
121 Aruba I., Neth. W. Ind. 12 30N 70 0W
20 Arudy, France 43 7N 0 28W
100 Arumpo, Australia 33 48S 142 55E
69 Arun, R., Nepal 27 30N 87 15E
70 Aruppukottai, India 9 31N 78 8E
90 Arusha, Tanzania 3 20S 36 40E
90 Arusha ♦, Tanz. 4 0S 36 30E
90 Arusha Chini, Tanz. 3 32S 37 20E
87 Arusi ♦, Ethiopia 7 45N 39 00E
70 Aruvi, Aru, Sri Lanka 8 48N 79 53E
90 Aruwimi, R., Zaïre 1 30N 25 0E
118 Arvada, U.S.A. 44 43N 106 6W
70 Arvaklu, Sri Lanka 8 20N 79 58E
76 Arvayheer, Mongolia 46 15N 102 45E
21 Arve, R., France 46 11N 6 8E
68 Arvi, India 20 59N 78 16E
107 Arvida, Canada 48 16N 71 14W
50 Arvidsjaur, Sweden 65 35N 19 10E
48 Arvika, Sweden 59 40N 12 36E
44 Aryiaradhes, Greece 39 27N 19 58E
58 Arys, U.S.S.R. 42 20N 68 30E
40 Arzachena, Italy 41 5N 9 27E
55 Arzamas, U.S.S.R. 55 27N 43 55E
82 Arzew, Algeria 35 50N 0 23W
57 Arzgir, U.S.S.R. 45 18N 44 23E
39 Arzignano, Italy 45 30N 11 20E
26 Aš, Czechoslovakia 50 13N 12 12E
62 As Salt, Jordan 32 2N 35 43E
64 As Samawah, Iraq 31 15N 45 15E
62 As-Samū, Jordan 31 24N 35 4E
64 As Sulaimānīyah, Iraq 35 35N 45 29E
83 As Sultān, Libya 31 4N 17 8E
65 As Suwaih, Oman 22 10N 59 33E
64 As Suwayda, Syria 32 40N 36 30E
64 As Suwayrah, Iraq 32 55N 45 0E
92 Asab, S.W. Africa 25 30S 18 0E
85 Asaba, Nigeria 6 12N 6 38E
64 Asadabad, Iran 34 50N 48 10E
84 Asafo, Ghana 6 20N 2 40W
74 Asahigawa, Japan 43 45N 142 30E
87 Asale, L., Ethiopia 14 0N 40 20E
74 Asama, Japan 33 0N 140 0E
85 Asamankese, Ghana 5 50N 0 40W
84 Asankrangwa, Ghana 5 45N 2 30W
69 Asansol, India 23 40N 87 1E
48 Asarna, Sweden 62 40N 14 20E
87 Asbe Teferi, Ethiopia 9 4N 40 49E
92 Asbesberge, S. Africa 29 0S 23 0E
107 Asbestos, Canada 45 47N 71 58W
113 Asbury Park, U.S.A. 40 15N 74 1W
120 Ascensión, B. de la, Mex. 20 20N 87 20W
7 Ascension, I., Atlantic Oc. 8 0S 14 15W
25 Aschach, Germany 48 23N 14 0E
25 Aschaffenburg, Ger. 49 58N 9 8E
24 Aschendorf, Germany 53 2N 7 22E
24 Aschersleben, Germany 51 45N 11 28E
39 Asciano, Italy 43 14N 11 32E
39 Ascoli Piceno, Italy 42 51N 13 34E
41 Ascoli Satriano, Italy 41 11N 15 32E
126 Ascope, Peru 7 46S 79 8W
124 Ascotán, Chile 21 45S 68 17W
87 Aseb, Ethiopia 13 0N 42 40E
49 Aseda, Sweden 57 10N 15 20E
82 Asedjrad, Algeria 24 51N 1 29E
87 Aselle, Ethiopia 8 0N 39 0E
43 Asenovgrad, Bulgaria 42 1N 24 51E
47 Aseral, Norway 58 37N 7 25E
19 Asfeld, France 49 27N 4 5E
86 Asfûn el Matâ'na, Eg. 25 26N 32 30E
47 Asgardstrand, Norway 59 22N 10 27E
119 Ash Fork, U.S.A. 35 14N 112 32W
117 Ash Grove, U.S.A. 37 21N 93 36W
64 Ash Shām, Bādiyat, Asia 31 30N 40 0E
64 Ash Shāmīyah, Iraq 31 55N 44 35E
64 Ash Shatrah, Iraq 31 30N 46 10E
62 Ash Shuna, Jordan 32 32N 35 34E
86 Ashaira, Saudi Arabia 21 40N 40 40E
85 Ashanti, Ghana 7 30N 2 0W
115 Ashburn, U.S.A. 31 42N 83 40W
101 Ashburton, N.Z. 43 53S 171 48E
96 Ashburton, R., Australia 22 5S 115 0E
101 Ashburton, R., New Zealand 44 2S 171 50E
12 Ashby-de-la-Zouch, England 52 45N 1 29W
108 Ashcroft, Canada 50 40N 121 20W
62 Ashdod Yam, Israel 31 49N 34 35E
62 Ashdot Ya'aqov, Israel 32 39N 35 35E
115 Asheboro, U.S.A. 35 43N 79 46W
117 Asherton, U.S.A. 28 25N 99 43W
115 Asheville, U.S.A. 35 39N 82 30W
106 Asheweig, R., Canada 54 0N 88 0W
13 Ashford, England 51 8N 0 53E
99 Ashford, Australia 29 15S 151 3E
118 Ashford, U.S.A. 46 45N 122 2W
74 Ashikaga, Japan 36 28N 139 29E
74 Ashizuri-Zaki, Japan 32 35N 132 50E
58 Ashkhabad, U.S.S.R. 38 0N 57 50E
117 Ashland, Kans., U.S.A. 37 13N 99 43W
114 Ashland, Ky., U.S.A. 38 25N 82 40W
107 Ashland, Me., U.S.A. 46 34N 68 26W
118 Ashland, Mont., U.S.A. 45 41N 106 12W
116 Ashland, Nebr., U.S.A. 41 5N 96 27W
112 Ashland, Ohio, U.S.A. 40 52N 82 20W
118 Ashland, Oreg., U.S.A. 42 10N 122 38W
113 Ashland, Pa., U.S.A. 40 45N 76 22W
114 Ashland, Va., U.S.A. 37 46N 77 30W
116 Ashland, Wis., U.S.A. 46 40N 90 52W
116 Ashley, N.D., U.S.A. 46 3N 99 23W
113 Ashley, Pa., U.S.A. 41 12N 75 55W
108 Ashmont, Canada 54 7N 111 29W
96 Ashmore Reef, Australia 12 14S 123 05E
86 Ashmûn, Egypt 30 18N 30 55E
62 Ashquelon, Israel 31 42N 34 55E
112 Ashtabula, U.S.A. 41 52N 80 50W
70 Ashti, India 18 50N 75 15E
92 Ashton, S. Africa 33 50S 20 5E
118 Ashton, U.S.A. 44 6N 111 30W
12 Ashton-u.-Lyme, England 53 30N 2 8E
107 Ashuanipi, L., Canada 52 30N 66 10E
77 Ashun, China 25 10N 106 0E
60 Asia, cont. 45 0N 75 0E
73 Asia, Kepulauan, Indonesia 1 0N 131 13E
39 Asiago, Italy 45 52N 11 30E
82 Asilah, Morocco 35 29N 6 0W
40 Asinara, Italy 41 5N 8 15E
40 Asinara, G. dell', Italy 41 0N 8 30E
40 Asinara I., Italy 41 5N 8 15E
58 Asino, U.S.S.R. 57 0N 86 0E
63 Asir, Si. Arabia 18 40N 42 30E
63 Asir, Ras, Somali Rep. 11 55N 51 0E
70 Aska, India 19 37N 84 42E
47 Asker, Norway 59 50N 10 26E
49 Askersund, Sweden 58 53N 14 55E
47 Askim, Norway 59 35N 11 10E
49 Askloster, Sweden 57 13N 12 11E
86 Asl, Egypt 29 33N 32 44E
65 Asmar, Afghanistan 35 10N 71 27E
87 Asmera (Asmara), Ethiopia 15 19N 38 55E
49 Asnaes, Denmark 55 40N 11 0E
49 Asnen, Sweden 56 35N 15 45E
47 Asnes, Norway 60 37N 11 59E
82 Asni, Morocco 31 17N 7 58W
49 Asnaes, Denmark 55 49N 11 31E
49 Asnaes, Halvö, Denmark 55 40N 11 0E
74 Aso, Japan 33 0N 130 42E
90 Asoa, Zaïre 4 35N 25 48E
39 Asola, Italy 45 12N 10 25E
34 Asotin, U.S.A. 46 14N 117 2W
33 Aspe, Spain 38 20N 0 40W
119 Aspen, U.S.A. 39 12N 106 56W
117 Aspermont, U.S.A. 33 11N 100 15W
101 Aspiring, Mt., N.Z. 44 23S 168 46E
21 Aspres, France 44 32N 5 44E
68 Aspur, India 23 58N 74 7E
82 Assa, Morocco 28 35N 9 6W
84 Assaba, Massif de l', Mauritania 16 10N 11 45W
67 Assam ♦, India 25 45N 92 30E
85 Assamakka, Niger 19 21N 5 38E
16 Asse, Belgium 50 54N 4 6E
83 Assekrem, Algeria 23 16N 5 49E
40 Assémini, Italy 39 18N 9 0E
16 Assen, Netherlands 53 0N 6 35E
49 Assens, Odense, Den. 56 41N 10 3E
49 Assens, Randers, Den. 55 16N 9 55E
109 Assiniboia, Canada 49 40N 106 0W
109 Assiniboine, R., Canada 49 53N 97 8W
106 Assinica L., Canada 50 30N 75 20W
84 Assinie, Ivory Coast 5 9N 3 17W
125 Assis, Brazil 22 40S 50 20W
39 Assisi, Italy 43 4N 12 36E
45 Assos, Greece 38 22N 20 33E
58 Assynt, Scot. 58 25N 5 10W
14 Assynt, L., Scot. 58 25N 5 15W
45 Astakidha, Greece 35 53N 26 50E
20 Astaffort, France 44 4N 0 40E
53 Astara, U.S.S.R. 38 30N 48 50E
38 Asti, Italy 44 54N 8 11E
30 Astillero, Spain 43 24N 3 49W
45 Astipálaia, Greece 36 32N 26 22E
105 Aston C., Canada 70 10N 67 40W
30 Astorga, Spain 42 29N 6 8W
118 Astoria, U.S.A. 46 16N 123 50W
49 Astorp, Sweden 56 6N 12 55E
57 Astrakhan, U.S.S.R. 46 25N 48 5E
30 Astudillo, Spain 42 12N 4 22W
30 Asturias, Spain 43 15N 6 0W
124 Asunción, Paraguay 25 21S 57 30W
49 Asunden, Sweden 57 47N 13 18E
87 Asutri, Sudan 15 25N 35 45E
90 Aswa, R., Uganda 2 30N 33 5E
86 Aswad, Rasal, Si. Arab. 21 20N 39 0E
86 Aswân, Egypt 24 4N 32 57E
86 Aswân High Dam = Sadd el Aali, Egypt 24 5N 32 54E
86 Asyût, Egypt 27 11N 31 4E
86 Asyûti, Wadi, Egypt 27 18N 31 20E
27 Aszód, Hungary 47 39N 19 28E
64 At Tafilah, Jordan 30 45N 35 30E
86 At Ta'if, Saudi Arabia 21 5N 40 27E
124 Atacama, Arg. 25 40S 67 40W
124 Atacama ♦, Chile 27 30S 70 0W
128 Atacama, Desierto de, Chile 24 0S 69 20W
124 Atacama, Salar de, Chile 24 0S 68 20W
126 Ataco, Colombia 3 35N 75 23W
83 Atakor, Algeria 23 27N 5 31E
85 Atakpamé, Togoland 7 31N 1 13E
78 Atalaia, Brazil 9 25S 36 0W
45 Atalándi, Greece 38 39N 22 58E
126 Atalaya, Peru 10 45S 73 50W
74 Atami, Japan 35 0N 139 55E
80 Atar, Mauritania 20 30N 13 5W
59 Atara, U.S.S.R. 63 10N 129 10E
82 Ataram, Erg d', Algeria 23 57N 2 0E
31 Atarfe, Spain 37 13N 3 40W
119 Atascadero, U.S.A. 35 32N 120 44W
58 Atasu, U.S.S.R. 48 30N 71 0E
73 Atauro, Port. Timor 8 10S 125 30E
86 Atbara, Sudan 17 42N 33 59E
86 Atbara, R., Sudan 17 40N 33 56E
117 Atchafalaya B., U.S.A. 29 30N 91 20W
116 Atchison, U.S.A. 39 40N 95 0W
85 Atebubu, Ghana 7 47N 1 0W
32 Ateca, Spain 41 20N 1 49W
39 Aterno, R., Italy 42 18N 13 45E
38 Atesine, Alpi, Italy 46 55N 11 30E
39 Atessa, Italy 42 5N 14 27E
16 Ath, Belgium 50 38N 3 47E
64 Ath Thamami, Si. Arab. 27 45N 35 30E
108 Athabasca, Canada 54 45N 113 20W
109 Athabasca L., Canada 59 10N 109 30W
108 Athabasca, R., Canada 55 50N 112 40W
15 Athboy, Ireland 53 37N 6 55W
15 Athenry, Ireland 53 18N 8 45W
113 Athens, Canada 44 39N 75 55W
45 Athens = Athinai, Greece 37 58N 23 46E
115 Athens, Ala., U.S.A. 34 49N 86 58W
115 Athens, Ga., U.S.A. 33 56N 83 24W
113 Athens, N.Y., U.S.A. 42 15N 73 48W
114 Athens, Ohio, U.S.A. 39 52N 82 6W
113 Athens, Pa., U.S.A. 41 57N 76 36W
117 Athens, Tex., U.S.A. 32 11N 95 48W
112 Atherly, Canada 44 37N 79 20W
98 Atherton, Australia 17 17S 145 30E
85 Athiéme, Dahomey 6 37N 1 40E
45 Athinai, Greece 37 58N 23 46E
15 Athlone, Ireland 53 26N 7 57W
70 Athni, India 16 44N 75 6E
14 Atholl, Forest of, Scotland 56 51N 1 0W
107 Atholville, Canada 48 5N 67 5W
44 Athos, Mts., Greece 40 9N 24 22E
15 Athy, Ireland 53 0N 7 0W
87 Ati, Sudan 13 5N 29 2E
90 Atiak, Uganda 3 12N 32 2E
126 Atico, Peru 16 14S 73 40W
32 Atienza, Spain 41 12N 2 52W
106 Atikokan, Canada 48 40N 91 40W
107 Atikonak L., Canada 53 45N 64 30W
72 Atjeh ♦, Indon. 4 50N 96 0E
59 Atka, U.S.S.R. 60 50N 151 48E
55 Atkarsk, U.S.S.R. 51 55N 45 2E
116 Atkinson, U.S.A. 42 35N 98 59W
115 Atlanta, Ga., U.S.A. 33 50N 84 24W
117 Atlanta, Tex., U.S.A. 33 7N 94 8W
116 Atlantic, U.S.A. 41 25N 95 0W
114 Atlantic City, U.S.A. 39 25N 74 25W
6 Atlantic Ocean 0 0 20 0W
126 Atlántico ♦, Colombia 10 45N 75 0W
78 Atlas, Great, Mts., Afr. 33 0N 5 0W
104 Atlin, Canada 59 31N 133 41W
62 Atlit, Israel 32 42N 34 56E
47 Atlöy, Norway 61 21N 4 58E
70 Atmakur, India 14 37N 79 40E
115 Atmore, U.S.A. 31 2N 87 30W
108 Atnarko, Canada 52 25N 126 0W
117 Atoka, U.S.A. 34 22N 96 10W
45 Atokos, Greece 38 28N 20 49E
120 Atotonilco el Alto, Mexico 20 20N 98 40W
31 Atouguia, Portugal 39 20N 9 20W
49 Atrafors, Sweden 57 02N 12 40E
65 Atrak, R., Iran 37 50N 57 0E
49 Atran, Sweden 57 07N 12 55E
68 Atrauli, India 28 2N 78 20E
126 Atrato, R., Colombia 74 0N 77 0W
39 Atri, Italy 42 35N 14 0E
86 Atsbi, Ethiopia 13 52N 39 50E
115 Attalla, U.S.A. 34 2N 86 5W
106 Attawapiskat, Can. 53 0N 82 30W
106 Attawapiskat, L., Can. 52 20N 88 0W
106 Attawapiskat, R., Canada 53 0N 82 30W
24 Attendorn, Germany 51 8N 7 54E
26 Attersee, Austria 47 55N 13 31E
114 Attica, U.S.A. 40 20N 87 15W
19 Attichy, France 49 25N 3 3E
19 Attigny, France 49 28N 4 35E
107 Attikamagen L., Can. 54 54N 66 25W
45 Attiki ♦, Greece 38 10N 23 40E
62 Attil, Jordan 32 23N 35 4E
113 Attleboro, U.S.A. 41 56N 71 18W
66 Attock, Pakistan 33 52N 72 20E
71 Attopeu, Laos 14 56N 106 50E
70 Attur, India 11 35N 78 30E
75 Atunze = Tehtsin, China 28 45N 98 58E
49 Atvidaberg, Sweden 58 12N 16 0E
119 Atwater, U.S.A. 37 21N 120 37W
112 Atwood, Canada 43 42N 81 2W
116 Atwood, U.S.A. 39 52N 101 3W
114 Au Sable, R., U.S.A. 44 39N 84 10W
21 Aubagne, France 43 17N 5 37E
73 Aubarede Pt., Phil. 17 15N 122 20E
19 Aube ♦, France 48 15N 4 0E
21 Aubenas, France 44 37N 4 24E
19 Aubenton, France 49 50N 4 12E
19 Aubigny-sur-Nère, Fr. 47 30N 2 24E
20 Aubin, France 44 33N 2 15E
20 Aubrac, Mts. d', Fr. 44 38N 2 58E
115 Auburn, Ala., U.S.A. 32 37N 85 30W
118 Auburn, Calif., U.S.A. 38 50N 121 10W
114 Auburn, Ind., U.S.A. 41 20N 85 0W
116 Auburn, Nebr., U.S.A. 40 25N 95 50W
113 Auburn, N.Y., U.S.A. 42 57N 76 39W
115 Auburndale, U.S.A. 28 5N 81 45W
20 Aubusson, France 45 57N 2 11E
20 Auch, France 43 39N 0 36E
19 Auchel, France 50 30N 2 29E
85 Auchi, Nigeria 7 6N 6 13E
101 Auckland, N.Z. 36 52S 174 46E
101 Auckland ♦, N.Z. 37 0S 175 0E
101 Auckland Is., New Zealand 51 0S 166 0E
20 Aude, dépt., France 43 8N 2 28E
20 Aude, R., France 44 13N 3 15E
20 Aude ♦, France 43 8N 2 28E
106 Auden, Canada 50 17N 87 54W
18 Auderville, France 49 43N 1 57W
18 Audierne, France 48 1N 4 34W
19 Audincourt, France 47 30N 6 50E
87 Audo Ra., Ethiopia 6 20N 41 50E
116 Audubon, U.S.A. 41 43N 94 56W
24 Aue, Germany 50 34N 12 43E
24 Auerbach, Germany 50 30N 12 25E
18 Auffay, France 49 43N 1 07E
99 Augathella, Australia 26 2S 146 29E
92 Augrabies Falls, S. Afr. 28 35S 20 20E
25 Augsburg, Germany 48 22N 10 54E
41 Augusta, Italy 37 14N 15 12E
117 Augusta, Ark., U.S.A. 35 17N 91 25W
115 Augusta, Ga., U.S.A. 33 29N 81 59W
117 Augusta, Kans., U.S.A. 37 40N 97 0W
107 Augusta, Me., U.S.A. 44 20N 69 46E
118 Augusta, Mont., U.S.A. 47 30N 112 29W
116 Augusta, Wis., U.S.A. 44 41N 91 8W
49 Augustenborg, Den. 54 57N 9 53E
117 Augustine, U.S.A. 31 30N 94 37W
28 Augustów, Poland 53 51N 23 00E
96 Augustus, Mt., Australia 24 14S 116 48E
98 Augustus Downs, Australia 18 35S 139 55E
87 Aukan, Ethiopia 15 29N 40 50E
38 Aula, Italy 44 12N 9 57E
20 Aulnay, France 46 2N 0 22W
18 Aulne, R., France 48 17N 4 16W
116 Ault, U.S.A. 40 40N 104 42W
18 Ault-Onival, France 50 5N 1 29E
20 Aulus-les-Bains, Fr. 42 49N 1 19E
19 Aumale, France 49 46N 1 46E
20 Aumont-Aubrac, Fr. 44 43N 3 17E
85 Auna, Nigeria 10 9N 4 42E
70 Aundh, India 17 33N 74 23E
20 Aunis, France 46 0N 0 50W
73 Auponhia, Indonesia 1 58S 125 27E
21 Aups, France 43 37N 6 15E
47 Aurahorten, Mt., Nor. 59 15N 6 53E
69 Auraiya, India 26 28N 79 33E
69 Aurangabad, Bihar, India 24 45N 84 18E
70 Aurangabad, Maharashtra, India 19 50N 75 23E
18 Auray, France 47 40N 3 0W
83 Aures (Awras), Algeria 35 8N 6 30E
24 Aurich, Germany 53 28N 7 30E
47 Aurlandsvangen, Norway 60 55N 7 12E
20 Aurillac, France 44 55N 2 26E
39 Auronza, Italy 46 33N 12 27E
112 Aurora, Canada 44 0N 72 30E
92 Aurora, S. Africa 32 40S 18 29E
116 Aurora, Colo., U.S.A. 39 44N 104 55W
114 Aurora, Ill., U.S.A. 41 42N 88 20W
117 Aurora, Mo., U.S.A. 36 58N 93 42W
116 Aurora, Nebr., U.S.A. 40 55N 98 0W
112 Aurora, Ohio, U.S.A. 41 21N 81 20W
47 Aursskog, Norway 59 55N 11 26E
92 Aus, S.W. Africa 26 35S 16 12E
47 Austad, Norway 58 58N 7 37E
27 Austerlitz = Slavikov, Cz. 49 10N 16 52E
47 Austevoll, Norway 60 5N 5 13E
116 Austin, Minn., U.S.A. 43 37N 92 59W
118 Austin, Nev., U.S.A. 39 30N 117 1W
112 Austin, Pa., U.S.A. 41 40N 78 7W
117 Austin, Tex., U.S.A. 30 20N 97 45W
96 Austin, L., Australia 27 40S 118 0E
98 Austral Downs, Austral. 20 32S 137 33E
97 Australia ■, Oceania 23 0S 135 0E
100 Australian Alps, Australia 36 30S 148 8E
100 Australian Cap. Terr., Australia 35 15S 149 8E
5 Australian Dependency, Antarctica 73 0S 90 0E
26 Austria ■, Europe 47 0N 14 0E
50 Austvagöy, Norway 68 20N 14 40E
20 Auterive, France 43 21N 1 29E
19 Authie, R., France 50 22N 1 38E
120 Autlan, Mexico 19 40N 104 30W
19 Autun, France 46 58N 4 17E
20 Auvergne, France 45 20N 3 0E
19 Auxerre, France 47 48N 3 32E
19 Auxi-le-Château, Fr. 50 15N 2 8E
19 Auxonne, France 47 10N 5 20E
20 Auzances, France 46 2N 2 30E
47 Avaldsnes, Norway 59 21N 5 20E
19 Avallon, France 47 30N 3 53E
107 Avalon Pen., Canada 47 0N 53 20W
117 Avalon Res., U.S.A. 32 30N 104 30W
70 Avanigadda, India 16 0N 80 56E
125 Avaré, Brazil 23 4S 48 58W
44 Avas, Greece 40 57N 25 56E
64 Aveh, Iran 35 40N 49 15E
127 Aveiro, Brazil 3 10S 55 5W
30 Aveiro, Port. 40 37N 8 38W
30 Aveiro ♦, Portugal 40 40N 8 35W
124 Avellaneda, Argentina 34 50S 58 10W
41 Avellino, Italy 40 54N 14 46E
47 Averöya, Norway 63 0N 7 35E
41 Aversa, Italy 40 58N 14 11E
118 Avery, U.S.A. 47 22N 115 56W
126 Aves, Islas de, Venezuela 12 0N 67 40W
19 Avesnes-sur-Helpe, Fr. 50 8N 3 55E
48 Avesta, Sweden 60 9N 16 10E
20 Aveyron ♦, France 44 22N 2 45E
39 Avezzano, Italy 42 2N 13 24E
45 Avgó, Greece 35 33N 25 37E
124 Aviá Terai, Argentina 26 45S 60 50W
39 Aviano, Italy 46 3N 12 35E
41 Avigliano, Basilicata, Italy 40 44N 15 41E
38 Avigliano, Piemonte, Italy 45 7N 7 13E
21 Avignon, France 43 57N 4 50E
30 Avila, Spain 40 39N 4 43W
30 Avila ♦, Spain 40 30N 5 0W
30 Avila, Sierra de, Spain 40 40N 5 0W
30 Avilés, Spain 43 35N 5 57W
45 Avionárion, Greece 38 31N 24 8E
39 Avisio, R., Italy 46 14N 11 18E
31 Aviz, Portugal 39 4N 7 53W
19 Avize, France 48 59N 4 0E
100 Avoca, Australia 37 5S 143 20E
112 Avoca, U.S.A. 42 24N 77 25W
100 Avoca, R., Australia 35 50S 143 30E
15 Avoca, R., Ireland 52 48N 6 10W
108 Avola, Canada 51 45N 119 30W
41 Avola, Italy 36 56N 15 7E
112 Avon, N.Y., U.S.A. 43 0N 77 42W
116 Avon, S.D., U.S.A. 43 0N 98 3W
13 Avon, R., Hants., England 50 57N 1 45W
13 Avon, R., Worcs., England 52 8N 1 53W
98 Avon Downs, Australia 19 58S 137 25E
99 Avon Is., Pacific Ocean 19 37S 158 17E
112 Avon Lake, U.S.A. 41 28N 82 3W
91 Avondale, Rhodesia 17 43S 30 58E
109 Avonlea, Canada 50 0N 105 0W
113 Avonmore, Canada 45 11N 74 57W
13 Avonmouth, England 51 30N 2 42W
18 Avranches, France 48 40N 1 20W
46 Avrig, Rumania 45 43N 24 21E
20 Avrillé, Vendée, France 46 28N 1 28W
42 Avtovac, Y.-slav 43 9N 18 35E
87 Awag el Baqar, Sudan 10 10N 33 10E
65 Awali, Bahrain 26 0N 50 30E
70 Awarja, R., India 18 0N 76 15E
62 Awarta, Jordan 32 10N 35 17E
87 Awasa, L., Ethiopia 7 0N 38 30E
87 Awash, Ethiopia 9 1N 40 10E
87 Awash, R., Ethiopia 11 30N 42 0E
84 Awaso, Ghana 6 15N 2 22W
101 Awatere, R., N.Z. 41 55S 173 35E
83 Awbari, Libya 26 46N 12 57E
14 Awe, L., Scotland 56 15N 5 15W
87 Aweil, Sudan 8 42N 27 20E
85 Awgu, Nigeria 6 4N 7 24E
81 Awjilah, Libya 29 8N 21 7E
4 Axel Heiberg I., Can. 80 0N 90 0W
49 Axelfors, Sweden 57 26N 13 7E
85 Axim, Ghana 4 51N 2 15W
46 Axintele, Rumania 44 37N 26 47E
44 Axiós, R., Greece 40 57N 22 35E
48 Axmarsbruk, Sweden 61 3N 17 10E
13 Axminster, England 50 47N 3 1W
24 Axstedt, Germany 53 26N 8 43E
49 Axvall, Sweden 58 23N 13 34E
19 Ay, France 49 3N 4 0E
126 Ayabaca, Peru 4 40S 79 53W
74 Ayabe, Japan 35 20N 135 20E
124 Ayacucho, Argentina 37 5S 58 20W
126 Ayacucho, Peru 13 0S 74 0W
58 Ayaguz, U.S.S.R. 48 10N 80 0E
70 Ayakudi, India 10 57N 77 6E
31 Ayamonte, Spain 37 12N 7 24W
59 Ayan, U.S.S.R. 56 30N 138 16E
56 Ayancık, Turkey 41 57N 34 18E
126 Ayapel, Colombia 8 19N 75 9W
126 Ayapel, Sa. de, Colombia 7 45N 75 30W
56 Ayaş, Turkey 40 10N 32 14E
126 Ayaviri, Peru 14 50S 70 35W
45 Aydın, Turkey 37 52N 27 55E
85 Ayenngré, Togo 8 40N 1 1E
71 Ayeritam, Malaysia 5 24N 100 15E
113 Ayers Cliff, Canada 45 10N 72 3W
96 Ayers Rock, Australia 25 23S 131 5E
44 Ayia, Greece 39 43N 22 45E
45 Ayia Anna, Greece 38 52N 23 24E
45 Ayia Marina, Kasos, Gr. 35 27N 26 53E
45 Ayia Marina, Leros, Gr. 37 11N 26 48E
44 Ayia Paraskevi, Greece 39 14N 26 16E
45 Ayia Roumeli, Greece 35 14N 23 58E
45 Ayiássos, Greece 39 5N 26 23E
45 Ayios Andréas, Greece 37 21N 22 45E
44 Ayios Evstrátios, Gr. 39 34N 24 58E
45 Ayios Ioánnis, Akra, Greece 35 20N 25 40E

Áyios INDEX Bancroft

MAP
45 Ayios Kirkikos, Greece 37 34N 26 17E
44 Ayios Matthaíos, Greece 39 30N 19 47E
45 Ayios Miron, Greece 35 15N 25 1E
45 Ayios Nikólaos, Greece 35 11N 25 41E
45 Ayios Pétros, Greece 38 38N 20 33E
45 Ayios Yeóryios, Gr. 37 28N 23 57E
45 Aykathonisi, Greece 37 28N 27 0E
13 Aylesbury, Eng. 51 48N 0 49W
112 Aylmer, Canada 42 48N 80 59W
104 Aylmer L., Canada 64 0N 109 0W
64 Ayn Zalah, Iraq 36 45N 42 35E
83 Ayn Zaqqut, Libya 29 0N 19 30E
33 Ayna, Spain 38 34N 2 3W
124 Ayolas, Paraguay 27 10S 56 59W
87 Ayom, Sudan 7 49N 28 23E
59 Ayon, Ostrov, U.S.S.R. 69 50N 169 0E
33 Ayora, Spain 39 3N 1 3W
98 Ayr, Australia 19 35S 147 25E
14 Ayr, Scotland 55 28N 4 37W
14 Ayr, R., Scotland 55 29N 4 28W
* 14 Ayr ♦, Scotland 55 25N 4 25W
14 Ayre, Pt. of, Isle of Man 54 27N 4 21W
87 Aysha, Ethiopia 10 50N 42 23E
98 Ayton, Australia 15 45S 145 25E
43 Aytos, Bulgaria 42 47N 27 16E
43 Aytoska Planina, Bulgaria 42 45N 27 30E
120 Ayutla, Mexico 16 58N 99 17W
71 Ayutthaya = Phra Nakhon Si A., Thai. 14 25N 100 30E
44 Ayvacık, Turkey 39 36N 26 23E
64 Ayvalık, Turkey 39 20N 26 46E
62 Az Zahiriya, Jordan 31 25N 34 58E
64 Az Zahran, Si. Arabia 26 10N 50 7E
62 Az-Zarqā, Jordan 32 5N 36 4E
82 Az Zāwiyah, Libya 32 52N 12 56E
64 Az-Zilfī, Saudi Arabia 26 12N 44 52E
83 Az Zintān, Libya 31 59N 12 9E
64 Az Zubayr, Iraq 30 20N 47 50E
31 Azambuja, Portugal 39 4N 8 51W
69 Azamgarh, India 26 35N 83 13E
85 Azaouak, Vallée de l', Mali 15 50N 3 20E
64 Azārbāijān ♦, Iran 37 0N 44 30E
85 Azare, Nigeria 11 55N 10 10E
18 Azay-le-Rideau, France 47 16N 0 30E
82 Azazga, Algeria 36 48N 4 22E
82 Azeffoun, Algeria 36 51N 4 26E
82 Azemmour, Morocco 33 14N 9 20W
57 Azerbaijan S.S.R. ♦, U.S.S.R. 40 20N 48 0E
87 Azezo, Ethiopia 12 28N 37 15E
82 Azilal, Beni Mallal, Morocco 32 0N 6 30W
69 Azimganj, India 24 14N 84 16E
31 Aznalcóllar, Spain 37 32N 6 17W
126 Azogues, Ecuador 2 35S 78 0W
62 Azor, Israel 32 2N 34 48E
6 Azores, Is., Atlantic Oc. 38 44N 29 0W
57 Azov, U.S.S.R. 47 3N 39 25E
56 Azov Sea = Azovskoye More, U.S.S.R. 46 0N 36 30E
56 Azovskoye More, U.S.S.R. 46 0N 36 30E
58 Azovy, U.S.S.R. 64 55N 64 35E
32 Azpeitia, Spain 43 12N 2 19W
82 Azrou, Morocco 33 28N 5 19W
119 Aztec, U.S.A. 36 54N 108 0W
121 Azúa, Dom. Rep. 18 25N 70 44W
31 Azuaga, Spain 38 16N 5 39W
32 Azuara, Spain 41 15N 0 53W
32 Azuara, R., Spain 41 12N 0 55W
120 Azúcar, Presa del, Mexico 26 0N 99 5W
31 Azuer, R., Spain 38 50N 3 15W
121 Azuero, Pen. de, Panama 7 30N 80 30W
124 Azul, Argentina 36 42S 59 43W
83 Azzaba, Algeria 36 48N 7 6E
39 Azzano Decimo, Italy 45 53N 12 46E
44 B. Curri, Albania 42 22N 20 5E
71 Ba Don, N. Vietnam 17 45N 106 26E
71 Ba Ngoi = Cam Lam, S. Vietnam 5 0N 109 10E
73 Baa, Indonesia 10 50S 123 0E
30 Baamonde, Spain 43 7N 7 44W
16 Baarle Nassau, Belg. 51 27N 4 56E
16 Baarn, Netherlands 52 12N 5 17E
63 Bāb el Māndeb, Red Sea 12 35N 43 25E
43 Baba, Mt., Bulgaria 42 44N 23 59E
44 Baba Burun, Turkey 39 29N 26 2E
57 Baba dag, U.S.S.R. 41 0N 48 55E
46 Babadag, Rumania 44 53N 28 44E
43 Babaeski, Turkey 41 26N 27 06E
126 Babahoyo, Ecuador 1 40S 79 30W
85 Babana, Nigeria 10 31N 3 46E
83 Babar, Algeria 35 10N 7 6E
68 Babar, Pakistan 31 7N 69 32E
73 Babar, I., Indonesia 8 0S 129 30E
68 Babarkach, Pakistan 29 45N 68 0E
55 Babayevo, U.S.S.R. 59 24N 35 55E
118 Babb, U.S.A. 48 56N 113 27W
25 Babenhausen, Germany 49 57N 8 56E
27 Babia Gora, Europe 49 38N 19 38E
87 Babile, Ethiopia 9 16N 42 11E
98 Babinda, Australia 17 27S 146 0E
100 Babinda Hill, Australia 31 55S 146 28E
108 Babine L., Canada 54 40N 126 10W
73 Babo, Indonesia 2 30S 133 30E
27 Babocsa, Hungary 46 2N 17 21E
65 Babol, Iran 36 40N 52 50E
65 Babol Sar, Iran 36 45N 52 45E
90 Baboma, Zaïre 2 30N 28 10E
27 Baborówo Kietrz, Poland 50 7N 18 1E
88 Baboua, Cent. Afr. Rep. 5 49N 14 58E
42 Babuna, R., Y.-slav. 41 27N 21 38E
85 Babura, Nigeria 12 51N 8 59E

* *Incorporated within the region of Strathclyde*

55 Babushkin, U.S.S.R. 55 45N 37 40E
42 Babušnica, Y.-slav. 43 7N 22 27E
77 Babuyan Is., Philippines 19 10N 121 40E
64 Babylon, Iraq 32 40N 44 30E
113 Babylon, U.S.A. 40 42N 73 20W
42 Bač, Yugoslavia 45 29N 19 17E
71 Bac Kan, Vietnam 22 5N 105 50E
71 Bac Lieu = Vinh Loi, Vietnam 9 20N 104 45E
71 Bac Ninh, Vietnam 21 13N 106 4E
71 Bac-Phan, Vietnam 21 30N 105 0E
71 Bac Quang, Vietnam 22 30N 104 48E
127 Bacabal, Brazil 5 20S 56 45W
73 Bacarra, Philippines 18 15N 120 37E
46 Bacău, Rumania 46 35N 26 55E
46 Bacău ♦, Rumania 46 30N 26 45E
19 Baccarat, France 48 28N 6 42E
100 Bacchus Marsh, Austral. 37 28S 144 25E
46 Băceşti, Rumania 46 50N 27 11E
126 Bachaquero, Ven. 9 56N 71 8W
25 Bacharach, Germany 50 3N 7 46E
58 Bachclina, U.S.S.R. 57 45N 67 20E
87 Bachuma, Ethiopia 6 31N 36 1E
42 Bačina, Yugoslavia 43 42N 21 23E
104 Back, R., Canada 65 10N 104 0W
42 Bačka Palanka, Y.-slav. 45 17N 19 27E
42 Bačka Topola, Y.-slav. 45 96N 19 37E
49 Bäckefors, Sweden 58 48N 12 9E
42 Bački Petrovac, Y.-slav. 45 29N 19 32E
25 Backnang, Germany 48 57N 9 26E
99 Backstairs Passage, Australia 35 40S 138 5E
73 Bacolod, Philippines 10 40N 122 57E
18 Bacqueville, France 49 47N 1 0E
27 Bács-Kiskun ♦, Hung. 46 43N 19 30E
27 Bácsalmás, Hungary 46 8N 19 17E
73 Bacuit, Philippines 11 20N 119 20E
116 Bad, R., U.S.A. 44 10N 100 50W
26 Bad Assee, Austria 47 43N 13 45E
112 Bad Axe, U.S.A. 43 48N 82 59W
25 Bad Bergzabern, Germany 49 6N 8 0E
24 Bad Bramstedt, Ger. 53 56N 9 53E
24 Bad Doberan, Germany 54 6N 11 55E
24 Bad Driburg, Germany 51 44N 9 0E
25 Bad Ems, Germany 15 22N 7 44E
24 Bad Frankenhausen, Germany 51 21N 11 3E
26 Bad Freienwalde, Germany 52 46N 14 2E
24 Bad Godesberg, Ger. 50 41N 7 4E
24 Bad Hersfeld, Ger. 50 52N 9 42E
26 Bad Hofgastein, Aus. 47 17N 13 6E
25 Bad Homburg, Ger. 50 17N 8 33E
24 Bad Honnef, Ger. 50 39N 7 13E
26 Bad Ischl, Austria 47 44N 13 38E
25 Bad Kissingen, Ger. 50 11N 10 5E
25 Bad Kreuznach, Ger. 49 47N 7 47E
116 Bad Lands, U.S.A. 43 40N 102 10W
24 Bad Lauterberg, Ger. 51 38N 10 29E
26 Bad Leonfelden, Austria 48 31N 14 18E
24 Bad Lippspringe, Ger. 51 47N 8 46E
25 Bad Mergentheim, Ger. 49 29N 9 47E
24 Bad Münstereifel, Germany 50 33N 6 46E
25 Bad Nauheim, Germany 50 24N 8 45E
24 Bad Oeynhausen, Ger. 52 16N 8 45E
24 Bad Oldesloe, Germany 53 56N 10 17E
25 Bad Orb, Germany 50 16N 9 21E
24 Bad Pyrmont, Germany 51 59N 9 5E
24 Bad St. Peter, Switz. 54 23N 8 32E
24 Bad Salzuflen, Germany 52 8N 8 44E
24 Bad Segeberg, Germany 53 58N 10 16E
25 Bad Tölz, Germany 47 43N 11 34E
25 Bad Waldsee, Germany 47 56N 9 46E
24 Bad Wildungen, Ger. 51 7N 9 10E
25 Bad Wimpfen, Germany 49 12N 9 10E
25 Bad Windsheim, Germany 49 29N 10 25E
24 Bad Zwischenahn, Ger. 53 15N 8 0E
70 Badagara, India 11 35N 75 40E
85 Badagri, Nigeria 6 25N 2 55E
31 Badajoz, Spain 38 50N 6 59W
31 Badajoz ♦, Spain 38 40N 6 30W
65 Badakhshan ♦, Afghanistan 36 30N 71 0E
32 Badalona, Spain 41 26N 2 15E
65 Badalzai, Afghanistan 29 50N 65 35E
64 Badanah, Saudi Arabia 30 58N 41 30E
72 Badas, Brunei 4 33N 114 25E
72 Badas, Kepulauan, Indonesia 0 45N 107 5E
66 Baddo, R., Pakistan 28 15N 65 0E
73 Bade, Indonesia 7 10S 139 35E
27 Baden, Austria 48 1N 16 13E
112 Baden, Canada 43 14N 80 40W
25 Baden, Switzerland 47 28N 8 18E
25 Baden-Württemberg ♦, Germany 48 40N 9 0E
14 Badenoch, Scotland 57 0N 4 0W
87 Badeso, Ethiopia 9 58N 40 52E
26 Badgastein, Austria 47 7N 13 9E
107 Badger, Canada 49 0N 56 4W
68 Badin, Pakistan 24 38N 68 54E
39 Badia Polesina, Italy 45 6N 11 30E
68 Badnera, India 20 48N 77 44E
84 Badogo, Mali 11 2N 8 13W
69 Badrinath, India 30 45N 79 30E
63 Baduen, Somali Rep. 7 15N 47 40E
78 Badulla, Sri Lanka 7 1N 81 7E
49 Baekke, Denmark 55 35N 9 6E
31 Baena, Spain 37 37N 4 20W
126 Baetas, Brazil 6 5S 62 15W
126 Baeza, Ecuador 2 1S 79 57W
33 Baeza, Spain 37 57N 3 25W
65 Bafa, Iran 31 40N 55 25E
45 Bafa Gölü, Turkey 37 30N 27 29E
84 Bafatá, Port Guinea 12 8N 15 20E
4 Baffin Bay, Canada 72 0N 65 0W
105 Baffin I., Canada 68 0N 77 0W

MAP
85 Bafia, Cameroon 4 40N 11 10E
85 Bafilo, Togo 9 22N 1 22E
84 Bafing, R., Guinea 11 40N 10 45W
84 Bafoulabé, Mali 13 50N 10 55W
65 Bafq, Iran 31 40N 55 20E
56 Bafra, Turkey 41 34N 35 54E
65 Baft, Iran 29 15N 56 38E
85 Bafut, Cameroon 6 6N 10 2E
90 Bafwakwandji, Zaïre 1 12N 26 52E
90 Bafwasende, Zaïre 1 3N 27 5E
70 Bagalkot, India 16 10N 75 40E
90 Bagamoyo, Tanzania 6 28S 38 55E
90 Bagamoyo ♦, Tanzania 6 30S 38 50E
73 Baganga, Philippines 7 34N 126 33E
72 Bagan Siapiapi, Indon. 2 12N 100 50E
68 Bagasra, India 21 59N 71 77E
87 Bagawi, Sudan 12 20N 34 18E
59 Bagdarin, U.S.S.R. 54 26N 113 36E
125 Bagé, Brazil 31 20S 54 15W
118 Baggs, U.S.A. 41 8N 107 46W
64 Baghdād, Iraq 33 20N 44 30E
69 Bagherhat, Bangladesh 22 40N 89 47E
40 Bagheria, Italy 38 5N 13 30E
65 Baghin, Iran 30 12N 56 45E
65 Baghlan, Afghanistan 36 12N 69 0E
116 Bagley, U.S.A. 47 30N 95 22W
39 Bagnacavallo, Italy 44 25N 11 58E
41 Bagnara Cálabra, Italy 38 16N 15 49E
20 Bagnères-de-Bigorre, Fr. 43 5N 0 9E
20 Bagnères-de-Luchon, Fr. 42 47N 0 38E
38 Bagni di Lucca, Italy 44 1N 10 37E
39 Bagno di Romagna, It. 43 50N 11 59E
39 Bagnoli di Sopra, Italy 45 11N 11 53E
18 Bagnoles-de-l'Orne 48 32N 0 25W
39 Bagnolo Mella, Italy 45 27N 10 14E
20 Bagnols-les-Bains, Fr. 44 30N 3 40E
21 Bagnols-sur-Cèze, Fr. 44 10N 4 36E
39 Bagnorégio, Italy 42 38N 12 7E
38 Bagolino, Italy 45 49N 10 28E
107 Bagotville, Canada 48 22N 70 54W
75 Bagrash Kol, China 42 0N 87 0E
42 Bagrdan, Yugoslavia 44 5N 21 11E
73 Baguio, Philippines 16 26N 120 34E
32 Bahabón de Esgueva, Spain 41 52N 3 43W
68 Bahadurgarh, India 28 40N 76 57E
121 Bahama, Canal Viejo de, W. Indies 22 10N 77 30W
121 Bahamas ■, W. Indies 24 40N 74 0W
86 Bahariya, El Wâhât el, Egypt 28 0N 28 50E
71 Bahau, Malaysia 2 48N 102 26E
68 Bahawalnagar, Pakistan 30 0N 73 15E
68 Bahawalpur, Pakistan 29 37N 71 40E
68 Bahawalpur ♦, Pakistan 29 5N 71 3E
69 Baheri, India 28 45N 79 34E
87 Baheta, Ethiopia 13 27N 42 10E
90 Bahi, Tanzania 5 58S 35 21E
121 Bahía, Islas de la, Hond. 16 45N 86 15W
124 Bahía Blanca, Arg. 38 35S 62 13W
126 Bahía de Caráquez, Ec. 0 40S 80 27W
128 Bahía Laura, Argentina 48 10S 66 30W
126 Bahía Negra, Paraguay 20 5S 58 5W
90 Bahi Swamp, Tanz. 6 10S 35 0E
87 Bahir Dar, Ethiopia 11 33N 37 25E
82 Bahmer, Algeria 27 32N 0 10W
27 Bahōnye, Hungary 46 25N 17 28E
88 Bahr Aouk, Central African Rep. 9 20N 20 40E
87 Bahr Dar, Ethiopia 11 37N 37 10E
87 Bahr el Abiad, Sudan 9 30N 31 40E
87 Bahr el Arab, Sudan 9 50N 27 10E
87 Bahr el Azraq, Sudan 10 30N 35 0E
87 Bahr el Ghazâl, Sudan 9 0N 30 0E
87 Bahr el Ghazâl ♦, Sudan 7 0N 28 0E
87 Bahr el Jebel, Sudan 7 30N 30 30E
88 Bahr Salamat, Chad 10 0N 19 0E
86 Bahr Yûsef, Egypt 28 25N 30 35E
64 Bahra, Saudi Arabia 21 25N 39 32E
86 Bahra el Burullus, Eg. 31 28N 30 48E
86 Bahra el Manzala, Eg. 31 28N 32 01E
69 Bahraich, India 27 38N 81 50E
65 Bahrain ■, Persian Gulf 26 0N 50 35E
65 Bahramabad, Iran 30 28N 56 2E
65 Bahu Kalat, Iran 25 50N 61 20E
84 Bai, Mali 13 35N 3 28W
46 Baia-Mare, Rumania 47 40N 23 17E
31 Baia Setúbal, Portugal 38 23N 9 0W
46 Baia-Sprie, Rumania 47 41N 23 43W
81 Baïbokoum, Cameroon 7 40N 14 45E
46 Băicoi, Rumania 45 3N 25 52E
107 Baie Comeau, Canada 49 12N 68 10W
107 Baie de l'Abri, Canada 50 3N 67 0W
107 Baie de la Trinité, Can. 49 25N 67 20W
107 Baie Johan Beetz, Can. 50 18N 62 50W
107 Baie St. Paul, Canada 47 28N 70 32W
107 Baie Verte, Canada 49 55N 56 12W
20 Baignes, France 45 28N 0 25W
19 Baigneux-les-Juifs, Fr. 47 31N 4 39E
64 Ba'iji, Iraq 35 0N 43 30E
70 Bailadila, Mt., India 18 43N 81 15E
15 Baile Atha Cliath = Dublin, Ireland 53 20N 6 18W
87 Bailei, Ethiopia 6 44N 40 18E
31 Bailén, Spain 38 8N 3 48W
46 Băileşti, Rumania 44 01N 23 20E
70 Bailhongal, India 15 55N 74 53E
19 Bailleul, France 50 44N 2 41E
98 Baimuru, Papua 7 30S 144 49E
115 Bainbridge, Ga., U.S.A. 30 53N 84 34W
113 Bainbridge, N.Y., U.S.A. 42 17N 75 29W
18 Bain-de-Bretagne, Fr. 47 50N 1 40W
73 Baing, Indonesia 10 14S 120 34E
116 Bainville, U.S.A. 48 8N 104 10W
117 Baird, U.S.A. 32 25N 99 25W
104 Baird Mts., Alaska 67 10N 160 15W
100 Bairnsdale, Australia 37 43S 147 35E
85 Baissa, Nigeria 7 14N 10 38E
76 Baissoklyn, Mongolia 47 55N 102 20E

MAP
69 Baitadi, Nepal 29 35N 80 25E
86 Baiyuda, Sudan 17 35N 32 07E
27 Baja, Hungary 46 12N 18 59E
120 Baja, Pta., Mexico 29 50N 116 0W
86 Bajah, Wadi, Si. Arab. 23 14N 39 20E
68 Bajana, India 23 7N 71 49E
42 Bajanovac, Y.-slav. 42 28N 21 45E
99 Bajimba, Australia 29 22S 152 0E
42 Bajina Bašta, Y.-slav. 43 58N 19 35E
69 Bajitpur, Bangladesh 24 13N 91 0E
42 Bajmok, Y.-slav. 45 57N 19 24E
121 Bajo Boquete, Panama 8 49N 82 27W
85 Bajoga, Nigeria 10 57N 11 20E
98 Bajool, Australia 23 40S 150 35E
27 Bak, Hungary 46 43N 16 51E
81 Bakala, Cent. Afr. Rep. 6 15N 20 20E
39 Bakar, Yugoslavia 45 18N 14 32E
58 Bakchar, U.S.S.R. 57 1N 82 5E
72 Bake, Indonesia 3 05S 100 20E
84 Bakel, Senegal 14 56N 12 20W
119 Baker, Calif., U.S.A. 35 16N 116 2W
116 Baker, Mont., U.S.A. 46 22N 104 12W
118 Baker, Nev., U.S.A. 38 59N 114 7W
118 Baker, Oreg., U.S.A. 44 50N 117 55W
94 Baker Is., Pacific Oc. 0 10N 176 35E
104 Baker, L., Canada 64 0N 97 0W
104 Baker Lake, Can. 64 20N 96 10W
118 Baker Mt., U.S.A. 48 50N 121 49W
106 Baker's Dozen Is., Can. 57 30N 79 0W
119 Bakersfield, Calif., U.S.A. 35 25N 119 0W
113 Bakersfield, Vt., U.S.A. 44 46N 72 48W
56 Bakhchisaray, U.S.S.R. 44 40N 33 45E
54 Bakhmach, U.S.S.R. 51 10N 32 45E
64 Bakhtiari ♦, Iran 32 0N 49 0E
87 Bakia, Cent. Afr. Rep. 5 18N 25 45E
64 Bakinskikh Komissarov, U.S.S.R. 39 20N 49 15E
43 Bakırköy, Turkey 40 59N 28 53E
47 Bakke, Norway 58 25N 6 39E
27 Bakony, R., Hungary 47 35N 17 54E
27 Bakony Forest = Bakony Hegyseg, Hungary 47 10N 17 30E
27 Bakony Hegyseg, Hung. 47 10N 17 30E
85 Bakori, Nigeria 11 34N 7 25E
81 Bakouma, Cent. Afr. Rep. 5 40N 22 56E
26 Bakov, Czechoslovakia 50 27N 14 55E
57 Baku, U.S.S.R. 40 25N 49 45E
88 Bakwanga = Mbuji Mayi, Congo 6 9S 23 40E
112 Bala, Canada 45 2N 79 38W
62 Bal'a, Jordan 32 20N 35 6E
12 Bala, Wales, U.K. 52 54N 3 36W
12 Bala, L., Wales 52 53N 3 38W
72 Balabac I., Philippines 8 0N 117 0E
72 Balabac, Selat, E. Indies 7 53N 117 5E
64 Balabakk, Lebanon 34 0N 36 10E
72 Balabalangan, Kepulauan, Indonesia 2 20S 117 30E
46 Bălaciţa, Rumania 44 23N 23 05E
65 Balad Bani Bu 'Ali, Muscat & 'Oman 22 0N 59 20E
69 Balaghat, India 21 49N 80 12E
70 Balaghat Ra., India 18 50N 76 30E
32 Balaguer, Spain 41 50N 0 50E
55 Balakhna, U.S.S.R. 56 35N 43 32E
99 Balaklava, Australia 34 7S 138 22E
56 Balaklava, U.S.S.R. 44 30N 33 30E
56 Balakleya, U.S.S.R. 49 28N 36 55E
55 Balakovo, U.S.S.R. 52 4N 47 55E
55 Balanda, U.S.S.R. 51 30N 44 40E
69 Balangir, India 20 43N 83 35E
73 Balangnipa, Indonesia 5 15S 120 25E
68 Balapur, India 21 22N 76 45E
55 Balashikha, U.S.S.R. 55 49N 37 59E
55 Balashov, U.S.S.R. 51 30N 43 10E
68 Balasinor, India 22 57N 73 23E
69 Balasore, India 21 35N 87 3E
27 Balassagyarmat, Hung. 48 4N 19 15E
86 Balât, Egypt 25 36N 29 19E
27 Balaton, Hungary 46 50N 17 40E
27 Balatonfüred, Hungary 46 58N 17 54E
27 Balatonszentgyörgy, Hungary 46 41N 17 19E
33 Balazote, Spain 38 54N 2 09W
120 Balboa, Pan. Can. Zone 9 0N 79 30W
120 Balboa Hill, Panama Canal Zone 9 6N 79 44W
15 Balbriggan, Ireland 53 35N 6 10W
124 Balcarce, Argentina 38 0S 58 10W
109 Balcarres, Canada 50 50N 103 35W
43 Balchik, Bulgaria 43 28N 28 11E
101 Balclutha, N.Z. 46 15S 169 45E
117 Bald Knob, U.S.A. 35 20N 91 35W
114 Baldwin, Fla., U.S.A. 30 15N 82 10W
114 Baldwin, Mich., U.S.A. 43 54N 85 53W
113 Baldwinsville, U.S.A. 43 10N 76 19W
39 Bale, Yugoslavia 45 4N 13 46E
32 Baleares, Islas, Sp. 39 30N 3 0E
32 Baleares ♦, Spain 39 30N 3 0E
32 Balearic Is. = Baleares, Islas, Sp. 39 30N 3 0E
73 Balekambang, Indon. 7 13S 106 27E
73 Baler, Philippines 15 46N 121 34E
98 Balfe Creek, Australia 20 12S 145 57E
93 Balfour, S. Afr. 26 38S 28 35E
62 Balfouriyya, Israel 32 38N 35 18E
85 Bali, Cameroon 5 54N 10 0E
72 Bali, I., Indonesia 8 20S 115 0E
73 Bali, Selat, Indonesia 8 30S 114 35E
72 Bali ♦, Indonesia 8 20S 115 0E
27 Baligród, Poland 49 20N 22 17E
64 Balikesir, Turkey 39 35N 27 58E
73 Balimbing, Philippines 5 10N 120 3E
71 Baling, Malaya 5 41N 100 55E
42 Balinț, Rumania 45 48N 21 54E
77 Balintang Chan., Phil. 19 50N 122 0E
77 Balintang Is., Phil. 19 55N 122 0E
67 Balipara, India 26 50N 92 45E

MAP
113 Baliston Spa, U.S.A. 43 0N 73 52W
127 Baliza, Brazil 16 0S 52 20W
9 Balkan Pen., Europe 42 0N 22 0E
43 Balkan Mts. = Stara Planina, Europe 43 15N 23 0E
65 Balkh = Wazirabad, Afghanistan 36 44N 66 47E
58 Balkhash, U.S.S.R. 46 50N 74 50E
58 Balkhash, Ozero, U.S.S.R. 40 0N 74 50E
14 Ballachulish, Scot. 56 40N 5 10W
100 Ballan, Australia 38 50N 144 28E
100 Ballarat, Austral. 37 33S 143 50E
96 Ballard, L., Austral. 29 20S 120 10E
70 Ballarpur, India 19 50N 79 23E
14 Ballater, Scotland, U.K. 57 2N 3 2W
100 Balkdale, Australia 36 20N 146 33E
120 Ballenas, Canal de las, Mexico 29 10N 113 45W
5 Balleny Is., Antarctica 66 30S 163 0E
69 Ballia, India 25 46N 84 12E
99 Ballina, Australia 28 50S 153 31E
15 Ballina, Mayo, Ireland 54 7N 9 10W
15 Ballina, Tipp., Ireland 52 49N 8 27W
15 Ballinasloe, Ireland 53 20N 8 12W
49 Balling, Denmark 56 38N 8 51E
117 Ballinger, U.S.A. 31 45N 99 58W
15 Ballinrobe, Ireland 53 36N 9 13W
15 Ballinskelligs B., Ire. 51 46N 10 11W
53 Ballo Pt., Sierra Leone 8 55N 13 18W
15 Ballycastle, N. Ire. 55 12N 6 15W
15 Ballymena, N. Ire. 54 53N 6 18W
15 Ballymoney, N. Ire. 55 5N 6 30W
15 Ballyshannon, Ireland 54 30N 8 10W
128 Balmaceda, Chile 46 0S 71 50W
27 Balmazújváros, Hung. 47 37N 21 21E
100 Balmoral, Australia 37 15S 141 48E
14 Balmoral, Scotland 57 3N 3 13W
117 Balmorhea, U.S.A. 31 2N 103 41W
99 Balonne, R., Australia 28 47S 147 56E
89 Balovale, Zambia 13 30S 23 15E
100 Balpunga, Australia 33 46S 141 45E
69 Balrampur, India 27 30N 82 20E
100 Balranald, Australia 34 32S 143 34E
46 Bals, Rumania 44 22N 24 5E
112 Balsam L., Canada 44 35N 78 50W
120 Balsas, R., Mexico 18 30N 101 20W
48 Balsta, Sweden 59 35N 17 30E
46 Balta, Rumania 44 54N 22 38E
116 Balta, U.S.A. 48 12N 100 7W
56 Balta, U.S.S.R. 48 2N 29 45E
30 Baltanás, Spain 41 56N 4 15E
51 Baltic Sea, Europe 56 0N 20 0E
51 Baltiisk, U.S.S.R. 54 38N 19 55E
86 Baltim, Egypt 31 35N 31 10E
112 Baltimore, Canada 44 2N 78 10W
15 Baltimore, Ire. 52 29N 9 22W
114 Baltimore, U.S.A. 39 18N 76 37W
24 Baltrum, Germany 53 43N 7 25E
65 Baluchistan ♦, Pakistan 27 30N 65 0E
69 Balurghat, India 25 15N 88 44E
59 Balygychan, U.S.S.R. 63 56N 154 12E
65 Bam, Iran 29 7N 58 14E
67 Bam La, China 29 25N 98 35E
85 Bama, Nigeria 11 33N 13 33E
84 Bamako, Mali 12 34N 7 55W
100 Bamawn, Australia 35 17S 144 39E
85 Bamba, Mali 17 5N 1 0W
81 Bambari, Cent. Afr. Rep. 5 40N 20 35E
98 Bambaroo, Australia 18 57S 146 15E
25 Bamberg, Germany 49 54N 10 53E
115 Bamberg, U.S.A. 33 19N 81 1W
87 Bambesi, Ethiopia 9 45N 34 40E
84 Bambey, Senegal 14 42N 16 28W
90 Bambili, Zaïre 3 40N 26 0E
98 Bamboo, Australia 14 34S 143 20E
90 Bambouti, Cent. Afr. Rep. 5 25N 27 12E
85 Bamenda, Cameroon 5 57N 10 11E
108 Bamfield, Canada 48 45N 125 10W
66 Bamian ♦, Afghan. 35 0N 67 0E
85 Bamkin, Cameroon 6 3N 11 27E
65 Bampur, Iran 27 15N 60 21E
65 Bampur, R., Iran 27 20N 59 30E
71 Ban Ban, Laos 19 40N 103 34E
71 Ban Bua Chum, Thai. 15 11N 101 12E
71 Ban Bua Yai, Thailand 15 40N 102 25E
71 Ban Houei Sai, Laos 20 22N 100 32E
71 Ban Kantang, Thailand 7 25N 99 35E
71 Ban Khe Bo, Vietnam 19 10N 104 39E
71 Ban Khun Yuam, Thai 18 50N 97 53E
71 Ban Mae Sariang, Thai. 17 45N 97 59E
71 Ban Me Thuot, S. Vietnam 2 40N 108 10E
71 Ban Nong Ping, Thai 15 9N 100 11E
71 Ban Phai, Thailand 16 6N 102 40E
71 Ban Takua Pa, Thai. 8 55N 98 25E
71 Ban Thateng, Laos 15 25N 106 27E
65 Banadar Daryay Oman ♦, Iran 25 30N 56 0E
126 Banadia, Colombia 6 54N 71 49W
90 Banalia, Zaïre 1 32N 25 5E
71 Banam, Khmer Rep. 11 20N 105 17E
84 Banamba, Mali 13 29N 7 22W
*88 Banana, Zaïre 6 0S 12 20E
98 Banana, Australia 24 32S 150 12E
127 Bananal, I. do, Brazil 11 30S 50 30W
69 Banaras = Varanasi, India 25 22N 83 8E
68 Banas, R., Gujarat, India 24 25N 72 30E
69 Banas, R., Madhya Pradesh, India 24 15N 81 30E
86 Bânâs, Ras., Egypt 23 57N 35 50E
42 Banat ♦, Rumania 45 45N 21 15E
15 Banbridge, N. Ire. 54 21N 6 16W
13 Banbury, Eng. 52 4N 1 21W
14 Banchory, Scot. 57 3N 2 30W
106 Bancroft, Canada 45 10N 77 50W
91 Bancroft = Chililabombwe, Zambia 12 18S 27 43E

* *Renamed Muanda*

MAP

43 Band, Rumania 46 30N 24 25E
69 Banda, India 25 30N 80 26E
73 Banda, Kepulauan, 4 37S 129 50E
  Indonesia
120 Banda, Punta, Mexico 31 47N 116 50W
73 Banda, Sea, Indonesia 6 0S 130 0E
72 Banda Atjeh, Indonesia 5 35N 95 20E
99 Banda Banda, Mt., 31 12S 152 12E
  Australia
73 Banda Elat, Indonesia 5 40S 133 5E
74 Bandai, Japan 37 40N 140 15E
84 Bandama, R., Ivory 6 32N 5 30W
  Coast
68 Bandanwara, India 26 9N 74 38E
70 Bandar = 16 12N 81 12E
  Masulipatnam, India
65 Bandar 'Abbās, Iran 27 15N 56 15E
71 Bandar Maharani = 2 3N 102 34E
  Muar, Malaysia
71 Bandar Penggaram = 1 50N 102 56E
  Batu Pahat, Malaysia
65 Bandar-e Büshehr, Iran 28 55N 50 55E
65 Bandar-e Chârak, Iran 26 45N 54 20E
64 Bandar-e Deylam, Iran 30 5N 50 10E
65 Bandar-e Lengeh, Iran 26 35N 54 58E
64 Bandar-e Ma'shur, Iran 30 35N 49 10E
65 Bandar-e-Nakhilu, Iran 26 58N 53 30E
65 Bandar-e Rig, Iran 29 30N 50 45E
65 Bandar-e Shah, Iran 37 0N 54 10E
64 Bandar-e-Shahpur, Iran 30 30N 49 5E
64 Bandar-i-Pahlavi, Iran 37 30N 49 5E
91 Bandawe, Malawi 11 58S 34 5E
30 Bande, Spain 42 3N 7 58W
124 Bandera, Argentina 28 55S 62 20W
117 Banderas, U.S.A. 29 45N 99 3W
120 Banderas, Bahia de, 20 40N 105 30W
  Mexico
65 Bandi-i-Turkistan, Ra., 35 0N 64 0E
  Afghanistan
70 Bandia, R., India 19 30N 80 25E
84 Bandiagara, Mali 14 12N 3 29W
40 Bandirma, Turkey 40 20N 28 0E
73 Bandjar, Indonesia 7 24S 108 30E
72 Bandjarmasin, Indon. 3 20S 114 35E
73 Bandjarnegara, Indon. 7 24S 109 42E
15 Bandon, Ireland 51 44N 8 45W
91 Bandula, Mozambique 19 0S 33 7E
88 Bandundu, Zaïre 3 15S 17 22E
73 Bandung, Indonesia 6 36S 107 48E
46 Băneasa, Rumania 45 56N 27 55E
33 Bañeres, Spain 38 44N 0 38W
121 Banes, Cuba 21 0N 75 42W
108 Banff, Canada 51 20N 115 40W
57 Banff, Scotland 57 40N 2 32W
*14 Banff ♦, Scot. 57 23N 3 10W
84 Banfora, Upper Volta 10 40N 4 40W
71 Bang Hieng, Laos 16 24N 105 40E
71 Bang Lamung, Thailand 12 58N 101 0E
71 Bang Saphan, Thailand 11 14N 99 28E
91 Bangala Dam, Rhod. 21 7S 31 25E
70 Bangalore, India 12 59N 77 40E
99 Bangalow, Australia 28 41S 153 30E
85 Bangante, Cameroon 5 8N 10 32E
69 Bangaon, India 23 0N 88 47E
88 Bangassou, Central 4 55N 23 55E
  African Republic
73 Banggai, Indonesia 1 40S 123 30E
72 Banggi, P., Malaysia 7 50N 117 0E
83 Banghazi, Libya 32 11N 20 3E
73 Bangil, Indonesia 7 36S 112 50E
87 Bangjang, Sudan 11 23N 32 41E
73 Bangka, Pulau, Celebes, 1 50N 125 5E
  Indon.
72 Bangka, Pulau, 2 0S 105 50E
  Sumatera, Indon.
72 Bangka, Selat, Indonesia 3 30N 105 30E
72 Bangkalan, Indonesia 7 2S 112 46E
72 Bangkinang, Indonesia 0 18N 100 5E
72 Bangko, Indonesia 2 5S 102 9E
71 Bangkok = Krung 13 45N 100 35E
  Thep, Thailand
67 Bangladesh ■, South 24 0N 90 0E
  Asia
84 Bangolo, Ivory Coast 7 1N 7 29W
15 Bangor, N. Ireland 54 40N 5 40W
12 Bangor, Wales 53 13N 4 9W
107 Bangor, Me., U.S.A. 44 48N 68 42W
113 Bangor, Pa., U.S.A. 40 51N 75 13W
73 Bangued, Philippines 17 40N 120 37E
88 Bangui, Cent. Afr. Rep. 4 23N 18 35E
90 Banguru, Zaïre 0 30N 27 10E
91 Bangweulu, L. Zambia 11 0S 30 0E
91 Bangweulu Swamp, 11 20S 30 15E
  Zambia
85 Bani Bangou, Niger 15 3N 2 42E
121 Bani, Dom. Rep. 18 16N 70 22W
82 Bani, Djebel, Morocco 29 16N 8 0W
84 Bani, R., Mali 12 40N 6 30W
62 Bani Na'im, Jordan 31 31N 35 10E
62 Bani Suhaylah, Egypt 31 21N 34 19E
84 Bania, Ivory Coast 9 4N 3 6W
98 Baniara, Terr. of Papua 9 44S 149 54E
83 Baninah, Libya 32 0N 20 12E
64 Baniyas, Syria 35 10N 36 0E
42 Banja Luka, Y.-slav. 44 49N 17 26E
72 Banjak, Kepulauan, 2 10N 97 10E
  Indonesia
73 Banjumas, Indonesia 7 32S 109 18E
73 Banjuwangi, Indonesia 8 13S 114 21E
49 Bankeryd, Sweden 57 53N 14 6E
91 Banket, Rhodesia 17 27S 30 19E
85 Bankilaré, Niger 14 35N 0 44E
69 Bankipore, India 25 35N 85 10E
98 Banks I., Australia 10 10S 142 5E
108 Banks I., B.C. Canada 53 20N 130 0W
4 Banks I., N. W. Terr., 73 30N 120 0W
  Canada
101 Banks Peninsula, N.Z. 43 45S 173 15E
99 Banks Str., Australia 40 40S 148 10E
69 Bankura, India 23 11N 87 18E

42 Bankya, Bulgaria 42 43N 23 8E
15 Bann, N. Ire. 55 2N 6 35W
18 Bannalec, France 47 57N 3 42W
100 Bannerton, Australia 34 42S 142 47E
106 Banning, Canada 48 44N 91 56W
88 Banningville = 3 15S 17 22E
  Bandundu, Congo
112 Bannockburn, Canada 44 41N 77 31W
91 Bannockburn, Rhodesia 20 17S 29 48E
14 Bannockburn, Scotland 56 5N 3 55W
68 Bannu, Pakistan 33 0N 70 18E
32 Bañolas, Spain 42 16N 2 44E
21 Banon, France 44 2N 5 38E
31 Baños de la Encina, Sp. 38 10N 3 46W
30 Baños de Molgas, Spain 42 15N 7 40W
27 Bánovce, Cz. 48 44N 18 16E
27 Banská Bystrica, Cz. 48 46N 19 14E
27 Banská Stiavnica, Cz. 48 25N 18 55E
43 Bansko, Bulgaria 41 52N 23 28E
68 Banswara, India 23 32N 74 24E
85 Bantama, Ghana 7 48N 0 42W
85 Bante, Dahomey 8 25N 1 53E
73 Banten, Indonesia 6 5S 106 8E
15 Bantry, Ireland 51 40N 9 28W
15 Bantry, B., Ireland 51 35N 9 50W
73 Bantul, Indonesia 7 55S 110 19E
68 Bantva, India 21 29N 70 12E
70 Bantval, India 12 55N 75 0E
43 Banya, Bulgaria 42 33N 24 50E
18 Banyuls, France 42 29N 3 8E
68 Bap, India 27 23N 72 18E
70 Bapatla, India 15 55N 80 30E
18 Bapaume, France 50 7N 2 50E
62 Bâqa el Gharbiya, Israel 32 25N 35 2E
64 Baqûbah, Iraq 33 45N 44 50E
124 Baquedano, Chile 23 20S 69 52W
56 Bar, U.S.S.R. 49 4N 27 40E
42 Bar, Yugoslavia 42 8N 19 8E
107 Bar Harbor, U.S.A. 44 15N 68 20W
72 Barabai, Indonesia 2 32S 115 34E
58 Barabinsk, U.S.S.R. 55 20N 78 0E
116 Baraboo, U.S.A. 43 28N 89 46W
121 Baracoa, Cuba 20 20N 74 30W
124 Baradero, Argentina 33 52S 59 29W
116 Baraga, U.S.A. 46 49N 88 29W
121 Barahona, Dom. Rep. 18 13N 71 7W
32 Barahona, Spain 41 17N 2 39W
67 Barail Range, India 25 15N 93 20E
67 Barakhola, India 25 0N 92 45E
69 Barakot, India 21 33N 84 59E
99 Barakula, Australia 26 30S 150 33E
98 Baralaba, Australia 24 13S 149 50E
109 Baralzon, L., Canada 59 40N 97 45W
70 Baramati, India 18 11N 74 33E
69 Baramba, India 20 25N 85 23E
86 Barameiya, Sudan 18 32N 36 38E
66 Baramula, Kashmir 34 15N 74 20E
68 Baran, India 25 9N 76 40E
126 Baranoa, Colombia 10 48N 74 55W
104 Baranof I., U.S.A. 57 0N 135 10W
28 Baranya ♦, Hungary 46 0N 18 15E
54 Baranovichi, U.S.S.R. 53 10N 26 0E
28 Baranów Sandomierski, 50 29N 21 30E
  Pol.
126 Barão de Melgaço, 11 50S 60 45W
  Brazil
46 Baraolt, Rumania 46 5N 25 34E
73 Barapasi, Indonesia 2 15S 137 5E
69 Barasat, India 22 46N 88 31E
87 Barasoli, Ethiopia 13 38N 42 0W
73 Barat Daja, Kepulauan, 7 30S 128 0E
  Ind.
117 Barataria B., U.S.A. 29 15N 89 45W
68 Baraut, India 29 13N 77 7E
126 Baraya, Colombia 3 10N 75 4W
125 Barbacena, Brazil 21 15S 43 56W
126 Barbacoas, Colombia 1 45N 78 0W
126 Barbacoas, Ven. 9 29N 66 58W
121 Barbados ■, Wind. Is. 13 0N 59 30W
39 Barbastro, Yugoslavia 45 0N 14 4E
32 Barbastro, Spain 42 2N 0 5E
93 Barberton, S. Africa 25 42S 31 2E
112 Barberton, U.S.A. 41 0N 81 40E
69 Barbigha, India 25 21N 85 47E
115 Barbourville, U.S.A. 36 57N 83 52W
121 Barbuda I., Leeward Is. 17 30N 61 40W
30 Barca d'Alva, Portugal 41 0N 7 0W
98 Barcaldine, Australia 23 33S 145 13E
31 Barcarrota, Spain 38 31N 6 51W
81 Barce = Al Marj, Libya 32 25N 20 40E
32 Barcelona, Spain 41 21N 2 10E
126 Barcelona, Venezuela 10 10N 64 40W
32 Barcelona ♦, Spain 41 30N 2 0E
21 Barcelonette, France 44 23N 6 40E
126 Barcelos, Brazil 1 0S 63 0W
28 Barcin, Poland 52 52N 17 55E
98 Barcoo, R., Australia 24 33S 145 30E
27 Barcs, Hungary 45 58N 17 28E
28 Barczewo, Poland 53 50N 20 42E
57 Barda, U.S.S.R. 40 25N 47 10E
124 Bardas Blancas, Arg. 35 49S 69 45W
27 Bardejov, Cz. 49 18N 21 15E
63 Bardera, Somali Rep. 2 20N 42 27E
28 Bardo, Poland 50 31N 16 42E
38 Bardi, Italy 44 38N 9 43E
81 Bardiyah, Libya 31 45N 25 0E
68 Bardoli, India 21 12N 73 5E
12 Bardsey I., Wales 52 46N 4 47W
114 Bardstown, U.S.A. 37 50N 85 29W
69 Bareilly, India 28 22N 79 27E
18 Barentin, France 49 33N 0 58E
18 Barenton, France 48 38N 0 50W
4 Barents Sea, Arctic Oc. 73 0N 39 0E
87 Barentu, Ethiopia 15 2N 37 35E
18 Barfleur, France 49 40N 1 17W

38 Barga, Italy 44 5N 10 30E
63 Bargal, Somali Rep. 11 25N 51 0E
98 Bargara, Australia 24 50S 152 25E
38 Barge, Italy 44 43N 7 19E
87 Bargnop, Sudan 9 32N 28 25E
100 Bargo, Australia 34 18S 150 35E
24 Bargteheide, Germany 53 42N 10 13E
59 Barguzin, U.S.S.R. 53 37N 109 37E
69 Barh, India 25 29N 85 46E
69 Barhaj, India 26 18N 83 44E
100 Barham, Australia 35 40S 114 10E
72 Barhau, Indonesia 5 20S 102 10E
69 Barhi, India 24 15N 85 25E
68 Bari, India 26 39N 77 39E
41 Bari, Italy 41 6N 16 52E
68 Bari Doab, Pakistan 30 20N 73 0E
71 Baria = Phuoc Le, S. 10 39N 107 19E
  Vietnam
82 Barika, Algeria 35 23N 5 22E
126 Barinas, Venezuela 8 36N 70 15W
126 Barinas ♦, Venezuela 8 10N 69 50W
90 Baring C., Canada 70 0N 116 30W
90 Baringo, Kenya 0 47N 36 16E
90 Baringo ♦, Kenya 0 55N 36 0E
90 Baringo, L., Kenya 0 47N 36 16E
126 Barinitas, Venezuela 8 45N 70 25W
69 Baripada, India 21 57N 86 45E
86 Bâris, Egypt 24 42N 30 31E
72 Barisal, Bangladesh 22 50N 90 32E
72 Barisan, Bukit, Indonesia 3 30S 102 15E
72 Barito, R., Indonesia 2 50S 114 50E
21 Barjac, France 44 20N 4 22E
21 Barjols, France 43 34N 6 2E
83 Barjūji, W., Libya 25 26N 12 12E
65 Barkah, Muscat & Oman 23 40N 58 0E
106 Bark L., Ontario, 46 58N 82 25W
  Canada
112 Bark L., Ontario, 45 25N 77 40W
  Canada
86 Barka, Sudan 17 30N 37 34E
65 Barka, Oman 23 40N 58 0E
117 Barker, U.S.A. 43 20N 78 35W
108 Barkley Sound, Canada 48 50N 125 10W
93 Barkly Downs, Australia 20 30S 138 30E
93 Barkly East, S. Africa 30 58S 27 33E
92 Barkly West, S. Africa 28 5S 24 31E
93 Barkly Tableland, 19 50S 138 40E
  Australia
75 Barkol, China 43 37N 93 2E
86 Barkol, Wadi, Sudan 17 40N 32 0E
116 Barksdale, U.S.A. 29 47N 100 2W
19 Bar-le-Duc, France 48 47N 5 10E
28 Barlinek, Poland 53 0N 15 15E
96 Barlee Ra., W. Austral. 23 30S 116 0E
41 Barletta, Italy 41 20N 16 17E
55 Barysh, U.S.S.R. 49 2N 25 18E
49 Barlingbo, Sweden 57 5N 18 27E
100 Barlow L., Canada 61 50N 103 0W
100 Barmedman, Australia 34 9S 147 21E
68 Barmer, India 25 45N 71 20E
12 Barmouth, Wales 52 44N 4 3W
24 Barmstedt, Germany 53 47N 9 46E
68 Barnagar, India 23 7N 75 19E
12 Barnard Castle, England 54 33N 1 55W
58 Barnaul, U.S.S.R. 53 20N 83 40E
100 Barnes, Australia 36 2S 144 47W
115 Barnesville, U.S.A. 33 6N 84 9W
12 Barnet, England 51 37N 0 15W
113 Barneveld, U.S.A. 43 16N 75 14W
18 Barneville, France 49 23N 1 46W
99 Barney, Mt., Australia 28 13S 152 23E
99 Barngo, Australia 25 3S 147 20E
117 Barnhart, U.S.A. 31 10N 101 8W
12 Barnsley, Eng. 53 33N 1 29W
13 Barnstaple, Eng. 51 5N 4 3W
116 Barnsville, U.S.A. 46 43N 96 28W
13 Baro, Nigeria 8 35N 6 18E
87 Baro, R., Ethiopia 8 25N 33 40E
68 Baroda, Gujarat, India 22 20N 73 10E
68 Baroda, Mad. P., India 25 29N 76 35E
69 Barpali, India 21 11N 83 35E
69 Barpeta, India 26 20N 91 10E
83 Barqin, Libya 27 33N 13 34E
114 Barques, Pte. aux, 44 5N 82 55W
  U.S.A.
31 Barquinha, Portugal 39 28N 8 25W
126 Barquisimeto, 10 4N 69 19W
  Venezuela
19 Barr, France 48 25N 7 28E
127 Barra, Brazil 11 5S 43 10W
14 Barra, Scotland 57 0N 7 30W
84 Barra, Gambia 13 21N 16 36W
14 Barra Hd., Scot. 56 47N 7 40W
14 Barra, I., Scotland 57 0N 7 30W
14 Barra, Sd. of, Scot. 57 4N 7 25W
125 Barra do Corda, Brazil 5 30S 45 10W
125 Barra do Pirai, Brazil 22 30S 43 50W
93 Barra Falsa, Pta. da, 22 58S 35 37E
  Mozam.
125 Barra Mansa, Brazil 22 35S 44 12W
69 Barrackpur, India 22 44N 88 30E
41 Barrafranca, Italy 37 22N 14 10E
126 Barranca, Lima, Peru 10 45S 77 50W
126 Barranca, Loreto, Peru 4 50S 76 50W
126 Barrancabermeja, Col. 7 0N 73 50W
126 Barrancas, Colombia 10 57N 72 50W
126 Barrancas, Venezuela 8 55N 62 5W
31 Barrancos, Portugal 38 10N 6 58W
126 Barranqueras, Arg. 27 30S 59 0W
126 Barranquilla, Atlántico, 11 0N 74 50W
  Colombia
126 Barranquilla, Vaupés, 1 39N 72 19W
  Colombia
126 Barras, Colombia 1 45S 73 13W
113 Barre, U.S.A. 44 15N 72 30W
124 Barreal, Argentina 31 33S 69 28W
127 Barreiras, Brazil 12 8S 45 0W

127 Barreirinhas, Brazil 2 30S 42 50W
31 Barreiro, Portugal 38 40N 9 6W
127 Barreiros, Brazil 8 49S 35 12W
21 Barrême, France 43 57N 6 23E
73 Barren I., Andaman Is. 12 17N 95 50E
93 Barren Is., Malagasy 18 25S 43 40E
  Rep.
99 Barren Junc., Austral. 30 5S 149 0E
127 Barretos, Brazil 20 30S 48 35W
108 Barrhead, Canada 54 10N 114 30W
106 Barrie, Canada 44 25N 79 45W
98 Barrier Rf., Gt., Austral. 19 0S 149 0E
114 Barrington, Ill., U.S.A. 42 8N 88 5W
113 Barrington, R.I., U.S.A. 41 43N 71 20W
109 Barrington L., Canada 56 55N 100 15W
100 Barrington Tops., 32 6S 151 28E
  Australia
99 Barringun, Australia 29 1S 145 41E
12 Barrow, England 54 8N 3 15W
96 Barrow I., Austral. 20 45S 115 20E
104 Barrow, Alaska 71 16N 156 50W
104 Barrow, Pt., Alaska 71 22N 156 30W
96 Barrow Ra., Austral. 26 0S 127 40E
15 Barrow, R., Ireland 52 46N 7 0W
4 Barrow Strait, Canada 74 20N 95 0W
126 Barruecopardo, Spain 41 4N 6 40W
30 Barruelo, Spain 42 54N 4 17W
13 Barry, Wales 51 23N 3 19W
106 Barry's Bay, Canada 45 30N 77 40W
49 Barsø, Denmark 55 7N 9 33E
119 Barstow, Calif., U.S.A. 34 58N 117 2W
117 Barstow, Tex., U.S.A. 31 30N 103 25W
19 Bar-sur-Aube, France 48 14N 4 40E
19 Bar-sur-Seine, France 48 7N 4 20E
126 Bartica, Guyana 6 25N 58 40W
98 Bartle Frere, Mt., 17 27S 145 50E
  Austral.
117 Bartlesville, U.S.A. 36 50N 95 58W
117 Bartlett, U.S.A. 30 46N 97 30W
108 Bartlett, L., Canada 62 50N 118 20W
41 Bartolomeo in Galdo, 41 23N 15 2E
  Italy
91 Bartolomeu Dias, 21 10S 35 8E
  Mozambique
12 Barton-upon-Humber, 53 41N 0 27W
  England
28 Bartoszyce, Poland 54 15N 20 55E
115 Bartow, U.S.A. 27 53N 81 49W
126 Barú, I. de, Colombia 10 15N 75 35W
76 Baruun Urt, Mongolia 46 46N 113 15E
24 Baruth, Germany 52 3N 13 31E
54 Barvenkovo, U.S.S.R. 48 57N 37 0E
68 Barwani, India 22 2N 74 57E
99 Barwon, R., Australia 29 10S 148 47E
55 Barysh, U.S.S.R. 49 2N 25 18E
65 Basa'idu, Iran 26 35N 55 20E
88 Basankusa, Zaïre 1 5N 19 50E
46 Basarabi, Rumania 44 10N 28 26E
124 Bascuñán, Cabo, Chile 28 52S 71 35W
25 Basel (Basle), Switz. 47 35N 7 35E
25 Basel Landschaft ♦, 47 26N 7 45E
  Switz.
25 Basel-Stadt ♦, Switz. 47 35N 7 35E
116 Basento, R., Italy 40 35N 16 10E
77 Bashi Channel, Phil. 21 15N 122 0E
72 Bashkir A.S.S.R. ♦, 54 0N 57 0E
  U.S.S.R.
98 Basilaki, I., Terr. of 10 40S 150 53E
  Papua
73 Basilan, I., Philippines 6 35N 122 0E
73 Basilan, Selat, 13 10S 122 0E
  Philippines
13 Basildon, England 51 34N 0 29E
41 Basilicata ♦, Italy 40 30N 16 0E
118 Basin, U.S.A. 44 22N 108 2W
13 Basingstoke, Eng. 51 15N 1 5W
67 Basirhat, Bangladesh 22 40N 88 54E
106 Baskatong, Res., Can. 46 46N 75 50W
96 Baskerville C., Austral. 17 10S 122 15E
70 Basmat, India 19 15N 77 12E
70 Basoda, India 23 52N 77 54E
90 Basoka, Zaïre 1 16N 23 40E
88 Basongo, Zaïre 4 15S 20 20E
32 Basque Provinces = 42 50N 2 45W
  Vascongadas, Sp.
64 Basra = Al Basrah, Iraq 30 30N 47 50E
14 Bass Rock, Scot. 56 5N 2 40W
99 Bass Strait, Australia 40 0S 146 0E
39 Bassano, del Grappa, 45 45N 11 45E
  Italy
85 Bassari, Togo 9 19N 0 57E
84 Basse, Gambia 13 13N 14 15W
121 Basse-Terre, I., 16 0N 61 40W
  Guadeloupe
70 Bassein, India 19 26N 72 48E
67 Bassein Myit, Burma 16 45N 94 30E
20 Basses-Pyrénées ♦, 43 16N 0 0W
  France
121 Basseterre, St. 17 17N 62 43W
  Christopher
116 Bassett, Nebr., U.S.A. 42 37N 99 30W
115 Bassett, Va., U.S.A. 36 48N 79 59W
68 Bassi, India 30 44N 76 21E
19 Bassigny, France 48 0N 5 10E
24 Bassum, Germany 52 50N 8 42E
49 Båstad, Sweden 56 25N 12 51E
65 Bastak, Iran 27 15N 54 25E
70 Bastar, India 19 15N 81 40E
21 Bastia, Corsica 42 40N 9 30E
39 Bastia Umbra, Italy 43 4N 12 34E
77 Bastion, C. = Chinmu 18 10N 109 35E
  Chiao, China
16 Bastogne, Belgium 50 1N 5 43E
117 Bastrop, U.S.A. 30 5N 97 22W

92 Basuto, Botswana 19 50S 26 25E
93 Basutoland = Lesotho, 29 0S 28 0E
  Africa
32 Bat Yam, Israel 32 2N 34 44E
88 Bata, Equatorial Guinea 1 57N 9 50E
46 Bata, Rumania 46 1N 22 4E
73 Bataan, Philippines 14 40N 120 25E
73 Bataan Pen., Phil. 14 38N 120 30E
121 Batabanó, Cuba 22 40N 82 20W
121 Batabanó, G. de, Cuba 22 30N 82 30W
73 Batac, Philippines 18 3N 120 34E
59 Batagaya, U.S.S.R. 67 38N 134 38E
43 Batak, Bulgaria 41 57N 24 12E
31 Batalha, Portugal 39 40N 8 50W
90 Batama, Zaïre 0 58N 26 33E
59 Batamay, U.S.S.R. 63 30N 129 15E
77 Batan I., Philippines 20 58N 122 5E
77 Batan Is., Philippines 20 25N 121 59E
75 Batanes Is., Phil. 20 30N 122 0E
75 Batang = Paan, China 30 0N 99 3E
73 Batang, Indonesia 6 55S 109 40E
81 Batangafo, Central 7 25N 18 20E
  African Republic
73 Batangas, Philippines 13 35N 121 10E
73 Batanta, I., Indonesia 0 55N 130 40E
125 Batatais, Brazil 20 54S 47 37W
112 Batavia, U.S.A. 43 0N 78 10W
57 Bataysk, U.S.S.R. 47 3N 39 45E
96 Batchelor, Australia 13 4S 131 1E
100 Bateman's B., Australia 35 40S 150 12E
33 Batesburg, U.S.A. 33 54N 81 32W
117 Batesville, Ark., U.S.A. 35 48N 91 40W
117 Batesville, Miss., U.S.A. 34 17N 89 58W
117 Batesville, Tex., U.S.A. 28 59N 99 38W
54 Batetski, U.S.S.R. 58 47N 30 16E
13 Bath, England 51 22N 2 22W
107 Bath, Maine, U.S.A. 43 50N 69 49W
112 Bath, N.Y., U.S.A. 42 20N 77 17W
14 Bathgate, Scotland 55 54N 3 38W
100 Bathurst, Australia 33 25S 149 31E
107 Bathurst, Canada 47 37N 65 43W
* 84 Bathurst, Gambia 13 28N 16 40W
98 Bathurst B., Australia 14 16S 144 25E
104 Bathurst C., Canada 70 30N 128 30W
99 Bathurst Harb., Austral. 43 15S 146 10E
96 Bathurst I., Australia 11 30S 130 10E
104 Bathurst I., Canada 76 30N 130 10W
104 Bathurst Inlet, Canada 67 15N 108 30W
100 Bathurst L., Australia 35 3S 149 44E
84 Batie, Upper Volta 9 53N 2 53W
73 Batjan, Pulau, Indonesia 0 50S 130 27E
100 Batlow, Australia 35 31S 148 15E
112 Batman, Turkey 37 55N 41 5E
82 Batna, Algeria 35 34N 6 15E
91 Batoka, Zambia 16 45S 27 15E
117 Baton Rouge, U.S.A. 30 30N 91 5W
120 Batopilas, Mexico 27 48N 107 54E
88 Batouri, Cameroon 4 30N 14 25E
71 Battambang, Khmer 13 7N 103 12E
  Rep.
70 Batticaloa, Sri Lanka 7 43N 81 45E
41 Battipáglia, Italy 40 38N 15 0E
62 Battir, Israel 31 44N 35 8E
13 Battle, England 50 55N 0 30E
98 Battle Camp, Australia 15 24S 144 50E
114 Battle Creek, U.S.A. 42 20N 85 10W
107 Battle Harbour, Canada 52 13N 55 42W
116 Battle Lake, U.S.A. 46 20N 95 43W
118 Battle Mountain, U.S.A. 40 45N 117 0W
109 Battle R., Canada 52 30N 111 30W
109 Battlefields, Rhodesia 18 37S 29 47E
109 Battleford, Canada 52 45N 108 15W
27 Battonya, Hungary 46 16N 21 03E
72 Batu, Kepulauan, 0 30S 98 25E
  Indonesia
87 Batu, Mt., Ethiopia 6 55N 39 45E
71 Batu Gajah, Malaysia 4 28N 101 3E
71 Batu Pahat, Malaysia 1 50N 102 56E
72 Batuata, P., Indon. 6 30S 122 20E
73 Batulaki, Philippines 5 40N 125 30E
57 Batumi, U.S.S.R. 41 30N 41 30E
72 Baturadj, Indonesia 4 11S 104 15E
127 Baturité, Brazil 4 28S 38 45W
127 Baturité, Serra de, Brazil 4 25S 39 0W
73 Baubau, Indonesia 5 25S 123 50E
85 Bauchi, Nigeria 10 22N 9 48E
18 Baud, France 47 52N 3 1W
88 Baudouinville, U.S.A. 48 46N 44 35W
† 90 Baudouinville, Zaïre 7 0S 29 48E
20 Baugé, France 47 31N 0 8W
98 Bauhinia, Australia 24 45S 149 20E
47 Baume les Dames, Fr. 47 22N 6 22E
49 Baunei, Italy 40 2N 9 41E
127 Bauru, Brazil 22 10S 49 0W
127 Baús, Brazil 18 22S 52 47W
24 Bauska, U.S.S.R. 56 25N 25 15E
24 Bautzen, Germany 51 11N 14 25E
25 Bavaria = Bayern, 49 7N 11 30E
  Germany
48 Båven, Sweden 59 35N 17 30E
71 Bawdwin Mines, Burma 23 5N 97 50E
72 Bawean, Indonesia 5 46S 112 35E
85 Bawku, Ghana 11 3N 0 19W
71 Bawlake, Burma 19 0N 97 30E
115 Baxley, U.S.A. 31 43N 82 23W
117 Baxter Springs, U.S.A. 37 3N 94 45W
107 Bay Bulls, Canada 47 22N 52 50W
114 Bay City, Mich., U.S.A. 43 35N 83 51W
118 Bay City, Oreg., U.S.A. 45 45N 123 58W
117 Bay City, Tex., U.S.A. 28 59N 95 55W
73 Bay, Laguna de, Phil. 14 20N 121 11E
117 Bay St. Louis, U.S.A. 30 18N 89 22W
117 Bay Shore, U.S.A. 40 44N 73 15W
117 Bay Springs, U.S.A. 31 58N 89 18W
101 Bay View, New Zealand 39 25S 176 50E
90 Baya, Zaïre 11 53S 27 25E
121 Bayamo, Cuba 20 20N 76 40W
121 Bayamón, Puerto Rico 18 24N 66 10W
76 Bayan, Mongolia 47 20N 107 55E

* Incorporated within the region of Grampian

* Renamed Mobayi

* Renamed Banjul
† Renamed Moba

Bayan Agt INDEX Berga

MAP
76 Bayan Agt, Mongolia 48 32N 101 16E
75 Bayan Khara Shan, China 34 0N 98 0E
76 Bayan-Ovoo, Mongolia 47 55N 112 0E
76 Bayan-Uul, Mongolia 49 6N 112 12E
68 Bayana, India 26 55N 77 18E
58 Bayanaul, U.S.S.R. 50 45N 75 45E
76 Bayandalay, Mongolia 43 30N 103 29E
76 Bayandelger, Mongolia 47 45N 108 7E
88 Bayanga, Cen. Afr. 2 53N 16 19E
75 Bayanhongor, Mongolia 46 40N 100 20E
76 Bayantsogt, Mongolia 47 58N 105 1E
76 Bayanzürh, Mongolia 47 48N 107 15E
116 Bayard, U.S.A. 41 48N 103 17W
73 Baybay, Philippines 10 41N 124 48E
64 Bayburt, Turkey 40 15N 40 20E
25 Bayerischer Wald, Germany 49 0N 13 0E
25 Bayern ♦, Germany 49 7N 11 30E
18 Bayeux, France 49 17N 0 42W
123 Bayfield, Canada 43 34N 81 39W
116 Bayfield, U.S.A. 46 50N 90 48W
64 Bayir, Jordan 30 45N 36 55E
59 Baykal, Oz., U.S.S.R. 53 0N 108 0E
59 Baykit, U.S.S.R. 61 50N 95 50E
58 Baykonur, U.S.S.R. 47 48N 65 50E
92 Baynes Mts., S.W. Afr. 17 15S 13 0E
73 Bayombong, Phil. 16 30N 121 10E
19 Bayon, France 48 30N 6 20E
30 Bayona, Spain 42 6N 8 52W
18 Bayonne, Fr. 43 30N 1 28W
126 Bayovar, Peru 5 50S 81 0W
70 Baypore, R., India 11 10N 75 47E
58 Bayram-Ali, U.S.S.R. 37 37N 62 10E
25 Bayreuth, Germany 49 56N 11 35E
25 Bayrischzell, Germany 47 39N 12 1E
64 Bayrūt, Lebanon 33 53N 35 31E
62 Bayt Aula, Jordan 31 37N 35 2E
62 Bayt Fajjar, Jordan 31 38N 35 9E
62 Bayt Fūrīk, Jordan 32 11N 35 20E
62 Bayt Jala, Jordan 31 43N 35 11E
62 Bayt Lahm, Jordan 31 43N 35 12E
62 Bayt Rīma, Jordan 32 2N 35 6E
62 Bayt Sāhūr, Jordan 31 42N 35 13E
62 Bayt Ummar, Jordan 31 38N 35 7E
62 Bayta at Tahtā, Jordan 32 9N 35 18E
62 Baytin, Jordan 31 56N 35 14E
117 Baytown, U.S.A. 29 42N 94 57W
85 Bayzo, Niger 13 52N 4 35E
33 Baza, Spain 37 30N 2 47W
57 Bazar Dyuzi, U.S.S.R. 41 12N 48 10E
55 Bazarny Karabulak, U.S.S.R. 52 30N 46 20E
55 Bazarnyy Syzgan, U.S.S.R. 53 45N 46 40E
57 Bazartobe, U.S.S.R. 49 26N 51 45E
93 Bazaruto, I. do, Mozam. 21 40S 35 28E
20 Bazas, France 44 27N 0 13W
62 Bazuriye, Lebanon 33 15N 35 16E
116 Beach, U.S.A. 46 57N 104 0W
112 Beach City, U.S.A. 40 38N 81 35W
71 Beachburg, Canada 45 46N 76 50W
99 Beachport, Australia 37 29S 140 0E
13 Beachy Head, Eng. 50 44N 0 16E
107 Beacon, U.S.A. 41 32N 73 58W
99 Beaconsfield, Australia 41 6S 146 56E
128 Beagle, Canal, S. Amer. 55 0S 68 30W
93 Bealanana, Malag. 14 33N 48 44E
101 Bealey, New Zealand 43 2S 171 36E
112 Beamsville, Canada 43 12N 79 28W
4 Bear I. (Nor.), Arctic Oc. 74 30N 19 0E
15 Bear I., Ireland 51 38N 9 50W
112 Bear L., Canada 45 28N 79 34W
118 Bear L., U.S.A. 42 0N 111 20W
118 Bearcreek, U.S.A. 45 11N 109 6W
106 Beardmore, Canada 49 36N 87 59W
5 Beardmore Glacier, Antarctica 84 30S 170 0E
116 Beardstown, U.S.A. 40 0N 90 25W
15 Bearhaven, Ire. 51 40N 9 54W
20 Béarn ♦, France 43 28N 0 36W
106 Bearskin Lake, Canada 53 58N 91 2W
118 Bearpaw Mt., U.S.A. 48 15N 109 55W
33 Beas de Segura, Spain 38 15N 2 53W
32 Beasain, Spain 43 3N 2 11W
121 Beata, C., Dom. Rep. 17 40N 71 30W
91 Beatrice, Rhodesia 18 15S 30 55E
116 Beatrice, U.S.A. 40 20N 96 40W
99 Beatrice, C., Australia 14 10S 137 10E
108 Beatton River, Canada 57 26N 121 20W
119 Beatty, U.S.A. 36 58N 116 46W
21 Beaucaire, France 43 48N 4 39E
19 Beauce, Plaines de, France 48 10N 2 0E
107 Beauceville, Canada 46 13N 70 46W
99 Beaudesert, Australia 28 0S 152 48E
100 Beaufort, Australia 37 25S 143 25E
72 Beaufort, Sab. 5 30N 115 40E
115 Beaufort, N.C., U.S.A. 34 45N 76 40W
115 Beaufort, S.C., U.S.A. 32 25N 80 40W
4 Beaufort Sea, Arctic Oc. 70 30N 146 0W
92 Beaufort-West, S. Africa 32 18S 22 36E
19 Beaugency, France 47 47N 1 38E
106 Beauharnois, Canada 45 20N 73 20W
21 Beaujeu, France 46 10N 4 35E
21 Beaujolais, France 46 0N 4 25E
20 Beaulieu, Loiret, France 47 31N 2 49E
21 Beaulieu, Vendée, Fr. 46 41N 1 37W
108 Beaulieu, R., Canada 62 30N 113 0W
14 Beauly, Scotland 57 29N 4 27W
14 Beauly, R., Scot. 57 26N 4 35W
12 Beaumaris, Wales 53 16N 4 7W
20 Beaumont, France 44 45N 0 46E
117 Beaumont, U.S.A. 30 5N 94 8W
18 Beaumont-le-Roger, Fr. 49 4N 0 47E
19 Beaumont-sur-Oise, Fr. 49 9N 2 17E
19 Beaumetz-les-Loges, Fr. 50 15N 2 40E
19 Beaune, Côte-d'Or, Fr. 47 2N 4 50E
19 Beaune-la-Rolande, France 48 4N 2 25E
MAP
38 Beaurepaire, France 45 22N 5 1E
109 Beausejour, Canada 50 5N 96 35E
19 Beauvais, France 49 25N 2 8E
109 Beauval, Canada 55 9N 107 35W
20 Beauvoir, Deux Sèvres, France 46 12N 0 30W
18 Beauvoir, Vendée, Fr. 46 55N 2 1W
117 Beaver, Okla., U.S.A. 36 52N 100 31W
112 Beaver, Pa., U.S.A. 40 40N 80 18W
119 Beaver, Utah, U.S.A. 38 20N 112 45W
109 Beaver, R., Can. 54 20N 108 40W
116 Beaver City, U.S.A. 40 13N 99 50W
116 Beaver Dam, U.S.A. 43 28N 88 50W
112 Beaver Falls, U.S.A. 40 44N 80 20W
108 Beaver Lodge, Canada 55 11N 119 29W
109 Beaverhill L., Canada 54 5N 94 50W
112 Beaverton, Canada 44 26N 79 8W
68 Beawar, India 26 3N 74 18E
125 Bebedouro, Brazil 21 0S 48 25W
24 Bebra, Germany 50 59N 9 48E
93 Beboa, Malagasy Rep. 17 22S 44 33E
13 Beccles, England 52 27N 1 33E
68 Bečej, Yugoslavia 45 36N 20 3E
46 Beceni, Rumania 45 23N 26 48E
30 Becerreá, Spain 42 51N 7 10W
82 Béchar, Algeria 31 38N 2 18E
92 Bechuanaland = Botswana, Africa 23 0S 24 0E
26 Bechyně, Cz. 49 17N 14 29E
114 Beckley, U.S.A. 37 50N 81 8W
18 Bécon, France 47 30N 0 50W
27 Bečva, R., Cz. 49 31N 17 40E
33 Bédar, Spain 37 11N 1 59W
20 Bédarieux, France 43 37N 3 10E
21 Bédarrides, France 44 2N 4 54E
87 Bedele, Ethiopia 8 31N 35 44E
24 Bederkesa, Germany 53 37N 8 50E
13 Bedford, England 52 8N 0 29W
92 Bedford, S. Africa 32 40S 26 10E
114 Bedford, Ind., U.S.A. 38 50N 86 30W
116 Bedford, Iowa, U.S.A. 40 40N 94 41W
112 Bedford, Ohio, U.S.A. 41 23N 81 32W
112 Bedford, Pa., U.S.A. 40 1N 78 30W
114 Bedford, Va., U.S.A. 37 25N 79 30W
98 Bedford, C., Australia 15 14S 145 21E
13 Bedford ♦, England 52 4N 0 28W
28 Bedków, Poland 51 36N 19 44E
108 Bednesti, Canada 53 50N 123 10W
39 Bednja, R., Yugoslavia 46 12N 16 25E
55 Bednodemyanovsk, U.S.S.R. 53 55N 43 15E
98 Bedourie, Australia 24 13S 139 22E
28 Bedzin, Poland 50 19N 19 7E
100 Beech Forest, Australia 38 37S 143 37E
114 Beech Grove, U.S.A. 39 40N 86 2W
100 Beechworth, Australia 36 20S 146 55E
109 Beechy, Canada 50 53N 107 24W
24 Beelitz, Germany 52 14N 12 58E
100 Beemunnel, Australia 31 40S 147 51E
99 Beenleigh, Australia 27 45S 153 0E
62 Be'er Sheva', Israel 31 15N 34 48E
62 Be'er Sheva', N., Israel 31 12N 34 40E
62 Be'er Toviyyao, Israel 31 44N 34 42E
62 Be'eri, Israel 31 25N 34 30E
62 Be'erotayim, Israel 32 19N 34 59E
62 Beersheba = Be'er Sheva', Israel 31 15N 34 48E
24 Beeskow, Germany 52 9N 14 14E
12 Beeston, England 52 55N 1 11W
24 Beetzendorf, Germany 52 42N 11 6E
117 Beeville, U.S.A. 28 27N 97 44W
88 Befale, Zaïre 0 25N 20 45E
93 Befotaka, Diégo-Suarez, Malag. 14 30S 48 0E
93 Befotaka, Fianarantsoa, Malag. 23 49S 47 0E
100 Bega, Australia 36 48S 149 55E
46 Bega, Canalul, Rumania 45 37N 20 46E
18 Bégard, France 48 38N 3 18W
87 Begemdir & Simen ♦ Ethiopia 13 55N 37 30E
47 Begna, Norway 60 41N 9 42E
30 Begonte, Spain 43 10N 7 40W
69 Begu-Sarai, India 25 24N 86 9E
81 Béhagle = Lai, Chad 9 25N 16 30E
64 Behbehan, Iran 30 30N 50 15E
68 Behror, India 27 51N 76 20E
65 Behshahr, Iran 36 45N 53 35E
81 Beida (Al Bayda), Libya 32 30N 21 40E
16 Beilen, Netherlands 52 52N 6 27E
25 Beilngries, Ger. 49 1N 11 27E
100 Beilpajah, Australia 32 54S 143 52E
87 Beilul, Ethiopia 13 2N 42 20E
*91 Beira, Mozambique 19 50S 34 52E
64 Beirut = Bayrūt, Lebanon 33 53N 35 31E
62 Beisan (Beit Shean), Isr. 32 30N 35 30E
91 Beit Bridge, Zambia 14 58S 30 15E
62 Beit Hanum, Egypt 31 32N 34 32E
62 Beit Lahiya, Egypt 31 32N 34 30E
62 Beit 'Ur et Tahta, Jordan 31 54N 35 5E
62 Beit Yosef, Israel 32 34N 35 33E
91 Beitbridge, Rhodesia 22 12S 30 0E
62 Beituniya, Jordan 31 54N 35 10E
46 Beiuş, Rumania 46 40N 22 21E
31 Beja, Portugal 38 2N 7 53W
31 Beja ♦, Portugal 37 55N 7 55W
83 Béja, Tunisia 36 43N 9 12E
82 Bejaïa, Algeria 36 42N 5 2E
30 Béjar, Spain 40 23N 5 46W
65 Bejestan, Iran 34 30N 58 5E
73 Bekasi, Indonesia 6 20S 107 0E
27 Békés, Hungary 46 47N 21 9E
27 Békés ♦, Hungary 46 45N 21 0E
27 Békéscsaba, Hungary 46 40N 21 10E
93 Bekily, Malagasy Rep. 24 13S 45 19E
47 Bekkjarvik, Norway 60 1N 5 13E
87 Bekoji, Ethiopia 7 40N 38 20E
71 Bekok, Malaysia 2 20N 103 7E

* Renamed Sofala

MAP
93 Bekopaka, Malagasy Rep. 19 9S 44 45E
85 Bekwai, Ghana 6 30N 1 34W
69 Bela, India 25 50N 82 0E
66 Bela, Pakistan 26 12N 66 20E
42 Bela Crkva, Yugoslavia 44 55N 21 27E
42 Bela Palanka, Y.-slav. 43 13N 22 17E
124 Bela Vista, Brazil 17 0S 49 0W
93 Bela Vista, Mozam. 26 10S 32 44E
20 Bélâbre, France 46 34N 1 8E
87 Belaia, Mt., Ethiopia 11 25N 36 8E
31 Belalcázar, Spain 38 35N 5 10W
42 Belanovica, Y.-slav. 44 15N 20 23E
93 Belavenona, Malag. 24 50S 47 4E
72 Belawan, Indonesia 3 33N 98 32E
52 Belaya, R., U.S.S.R. 54 45N 56 0E
57 Belaya Glina, U.S.S.R. 46 5N 40 48E
57 Belaya Kalitva, U.S.S.R. 48 13N 40 50E
55 Belaya Kholunitsa, U.S.S.R. 58 55N 50 43E
54 Belaya Tserkov, U.S.S.R. 49 45N 30 10E
46 Belceşti, Rumania 47 19N 22 7E
28 Bełchatów, Poland 51 21N 19 22E
4 Belcher, C., U.S.A. 75 0N 160 0W
106 Belcher Is., Canada 56 20N 79 20W
32 Belchite, Spain 41 18N 0 43W
49 Beldringe, Denmark 55 28N 10 21E
52 Belebei, U.S.S.R. 54 85N 54 5E
127 Belém (Pará), Brazil 1 20S 48 30W
124 Belén, Argentina 27 40S 67 5W
126 Belén, Colombia 1 26N 75 56W
119 Belen, U.S.A. 34 40N 106 50W
43 Belene, Bulgaria 43 39N 25 10E
20 Bélesta, France 42 55N 1 56E
63 Belet Uen, Somali Rep. 4 30N 45 5E
55 Belev, U.S.S.R. 53 50N 36 5E
15 Belfast, N. Ire. 54 35N 5 56W
93 Belfast, S. Afr. 25 42S 30 2E
107 Belfast, Maine, U.S.A. 44 30N 69 0W
112 Belfast, N.Y., U.S.A. 42 21N 78 9W
15 Belfast, L., N. Ire. 54 40N 5 50W
107 Belfeoram, Canada 47 32N 55 30W
116 Belfield, U.S.A. 46 54N 103 11W
19 Belfort, France 47 38N 6 50E
19 Belfort ♦, France 47 38N 6 52E
118 Belfry, U.S.A. 45 10N 109 2W
70 Belgaum, India 15 55N 74 35E
38 Belgioioso, Italy 45 9N 9 21E
16 Belgium ■, Europe 51 30N 5 0E
98 Belgooly, Ireland 51 44N 8 30W
55 Belgorod, U.S.S.R. 50 35N 36 35E
56 Belgorod Dnestrovskiy, U.S.S.R. 46 11N 30 23E
118 Belgrade, U.S.A. 45 50N 111 10W
42 Belgrade = Beograd, Y.-slav. 44 50N 20 37E
115 Belhaven, U.S.A. 35 34N 76 35W
85 Beli, Nigeria 7 52N 10 58E
42 Beli Drim, R., Y.-slav. 42 25N 20 34E
42 Beli Manastir, Y.-slav. 45 45N 18 36E
42 Beli Timok, Y.-slav. 43 39N 22 14E
40 Belice, R., Italy 37 44N 12 58E
88 Belinga, Gabon 1 10N 13 2E
91 Belingwe, Rhodesia 20 29S 29 57E
91 Belingwe, N., mt., Rhod. 20 37S 29 55E
72 Belinju, Indonesia 1 35S 105 50E
55 Belinsky (Chembar), U.S.S.R. 53 0N 43 25E
72 Belitung, I., Indonesia 3 10S 107 50E
46 Beliu, Rumania 46 30N 22 0E
120 Belize, Br. Honduras 17 25N 88 0W
42 Beljanica, Y.-slav. 44 08N 21 43E
107 Bell, Canada 53 50N 53 10E
107 Bell I., Canada 50 46N 55 35W
99 Bell Bay, Australia 41 12S 146 50E
105 Bell Pen, Canada 64 0N 81 0W
124 Bell Ville, Argentina 32 40S 62 40W
108 Bella Bella, Canada 52 10N 128 10W
108 Bella Coola, Canada 52 25N 126 40W
124 Bella Unión, Uruguay 30 15S 57 10W
124 Bella Vista, Argentina 28 33S 59 0W
84 Bella Yella, Liberia 7 24N 10 9W
38 Bellágio, Italy 45 59N 9 15E
112 Bellaire, U.S.A. 40 1N 80 46W
100 Bellarwi, Australia 34 15S 147 14E
70 Bellary, India 15 10N 76 56E
99 Bellata, Australia 29 53S 149 46E
116 Belle Fourche, U.S.A. 44 43N 103 52W
116 Belle Fourche, R., U.S.A. 44 25N 105 0W
115 Belle Glade, U.S.A. 26 43N 80 38W
18 Belle Ile, France 47 20N 3 10W
107 Belle Isle, Canada 51 57N 55 25W
18 Belle-Isle-en-Terre, Fr. 48 33N 3 23W
107 Belle Isle, Str. of, Can. 51 30N 56 30W
116 Belle Plaine, Minn., U.S.A. 44 35N 93 48W
116 Belle Plaine, Iowa, U.S.A. 41 51N 92 18W
21 Belledonne, France 45 11N 6 0E
107 Belledune, Canada 47 55N 65 50W
114 Bellefontaine, U.S.A. 40 20N 83 45W
112 Bellefonte, U.S.A. 40 56N 77 45W
21 Bellegarde, Ain, Fr. 46 04N 3 49E
19 Bellegarde, Creuse, Fr. 45 59N 2 19E
19 Bellegarde, Loiret, Fr. 48 0N 2 26E
106 Belleville, Canada 44 15N 77 37W
21 Belleville, Rhône, Fr. 46 7N 4 45E
18 Belleville, Vendée, Fr. 46 48N 1 28W
116 Belleville, Ill., U.S.A. 38 30N 90 0W
116 Belleville, Kans., U.S.A. 39 51N 97 38W
113 Belleville, N.Y., U.S.A. 43 46N 76 10W
108 Bellevue, Canada 46 35N 84 10W
118 Bellevue, Idaho, U.S.A. 43 25N 144 23W
112 Bellevue, Ohio, U.S.A. 41 20N 82 48W
112 Bellevue, Pa., U.S.A. 40 29N 80 3W
21 Belley, France 45 46N 5 41E
105 Bellin (Payne Bay), Canada 60 0N 70 0W
99 Bellingen, Australia 30 25S 152 50E
MAP
118 Bellingham, U.S.A. 48 45N 122 27W
5 Bellingshausen Sea, Antarctica 66 0S 80 0W
25 Bellinzona, Switzerland 46 11N 9 1E
126 Bello, Colombia 6 20N 75 33W
99 Bellona Reefs, Pacific Ocean 21 26S 159 0E
113 Bellows Falls, U.S.A. 43 10N 72 30W
68 Bellpat, Pakistan 29 0N 68 5E
32 Bellpuig, Spain 41 37N 1 1E
39 Belluno, Italy 46 8N 12 6E
112 Bellville, Ohio, U.S.A. 40 38N 82 32W
117 Bellville, Tex., U.S.A. 29 58N 96 18W
112 Bellwood, U.S.A. 40 36N 78 21W
113 Belmar, U.S.A. 40 10N 74 2W
31 Bélmez, Spain 38 17N 5 17W
100 Belmont, Australia 33 4S 151 42E
112 Belmont, Canada 42 54N 81 7W
112 Belmont, U.S.A. 42 14N 78 3W
127 Belmonte, Brazil 16 0S 39 0W
30 Belmonte, Portugal 40 21N 7 20W
32 Belmonte, Spain 39 34N 2 43W
15 Belmullet, Ireland 54 13N 9 58W
127 Belo Horizonte, Brazil 19 55S 43 56W
59 Belogorsk, R.S.F.S.R., U.S.S.R. 51 0N 128 20E
56 Belogorsk, Ukraine, U.S.S.R. 45 3N 34 35E
43 Belogradets, Bulgaria 43 22N 27 18E
42 Belogradchik, Bulgaria 43 37N 22 40E
93 Beloha, Malagasy Rep. 25 10S 45 3E
116 Beloit, Kans., U.S.A. 39 32N 98 9W
116 Beloit, Wis., U.S.A. 42 35N 89 0W
55 Belokholunitskiy, U.S.S.R. 58 55N 50 43E
52 Belomorsk, U.S.S.R. 64 35N 34 30E
67 Belonia, India 23 15N 91 30E
54 Belopolye, U.S.S.R. 51 14N 34 20E
52 Beloretsk, U.S.S.R. 54 0N 58 0E
93 Belo-sur-Mer, Malagasy Rep. 19 42S 44 33E
93 Belo-sur-Tsiribihana, Malag. 19 40S 43 30E
58 Belovo, U.S.S.R. 54 30N 86 0E
104 Beloye More, U.S.S.R. 66 0N 38 0E
57 Beloye Ozero, U.S.S.R. 45 15N 46 50E
52 Beloye, Oz., U.S.S.R. 60 10N 37 35E
55 Belozersk, U.S.S.R. 60 0N 37 30E
41 Belpasso, Italy 37 37N 15 0E
40 Belsito, Italy 37 50N 13 47E
99 Beltana, Australia 30 48S 138 25E
127 Belterra, Brazil 2 45S 55 0W
39 Beltinci, Yugoslavia 46 37N 16 20E
115 Belton, S.C., U.S.A. 34 31N 82 39W
117 Belton, Tex., U.S.A. 31 4N 97 30W
56 Beltsy, U.S.S.R. 47 48N 28 0E
15 Belturbet, Ireland 54 6N 7 28W
58 Belukha, U.S.S.R. 49 50N 86 50E
72 Beluran, Sab. 5 48N 117 35E
27 Beluša, Czechoslovakia 49 5N 18 27E
42 Belušic, Yugoslavia 43 50N 21 10E
41 Belvedere Marittimo, It. 39 37N 15 52E
20 Belvès, France 44 46N 1 0E
116 Belvidere, Ill., U.S.A. 42 15N 88 55W
113 Belvidere, N.J., U.S.A. 40 48N 75 5W
31 Belvis de la Jara, Spain 39 45N 4 57W
98 Belyando, R., Australia 22 45S 146 37E
58 Belyy, Jar, U.S.S.R. 58 26N 84 30E
54 Belyy, U.S.S.R. 55 48N 32 51E
58 Belyy, Ostrov, U.S.S.R. 73 30N 71 0E
54 Belz, U.S.S.R. 50 23N 24 1E
24 Belzig, Germany 52 8N 12 36E
117 Belzoni, U.S.A. 33 12N 90 30W
93 Bemaraha, Plat. du, Malag. 20 0S 45 15E
93 Bemarivo, Tuléar, Malag. 21 45S 44 45E
93 Bemarivo, R., Malag. 21 45S 44 45E
93 Bemavo, Malagasy Rep. 21 33S 45 25E
85 Bembèrèke, Dahomey 10 11N 2 43E
91 Bembesi, Rhod. 20 0S 28 58E
91 Bembesi, R., Rhod. 20 0S 28 58E
31 Bembézar, R., Spain 38 0N 5 20W
116 Bemidji, U.S.A. 47 30N 94 50W
100 Ben Bullen, Australia 33 12S 150 2E
14 Ben Cruachan, Mt., Scot. 56 26N 5 8W
14 Ben Dearg, mt., Scotland 56 54N 3 49W
83 Ben Gardane, Tunisia 33 11N 11 11E
14 Ben Hope, mt., Scot. 58 24N 4 36W
14 Ben Lawers, mt., Scot. 56 33N 4 13W
99 Ben Lomond, mt., Australia 41 33S 147 40E
14 Ben Lomond, mt., Scot. 56 12N 4 39W
14 Ben Macdhui, Scot. 57 4N 3 40W
14 Ben More, Mull, Scot. 56 26N 6 2W
14 Ben More, Perth, Scot. 56 23N 4 31W
14 Ben More Assynt, Scotland 58 7N 4 51W
14 Ben Nevis, mt., Scot. 56 48N 5 0W
14 Ben Vorlich, mt., Dun., Scot. 56 17N 4 47W
14 Ben Vorlich, mt., Perth, Scot. 56 22N 4 15W
14 Ben Wyvis, mt., Scot. 57 40N 4 35W
85 Bena, Nigeria 11 20N 5 50E
88 Bena Dibele, Zaïre 4 4S 22 50E
31 Benagalbón, Spain 36 45N 4 15W
99 Benageria, Australia 31 35S 140 25E
82 Benahmed, Morocco 33 4N 7 9W
100 Benalla, Australia 36 30S 146 0E
100 Benambra, Mt., Austral. 36 31S 147 34E
31 Benameji, Spain 37 16N 4 33W
100 Benanee, Australia 34 26S 142 56E
69 Benares = Varanasi, India 25 22N 83 8E
31 Benavente, Portugal 38 59N 8 49W
30 Benavente, Spain 42 2N 5 43W
30 Benavides, Spain 42 30N 5 54W
117 Benavides, U.S.A. 27 35N 98 28W
MAP
14 Benbecula, I., Scot. 57 26N 7 20W
99 Benbonyathe Hill, Australia 30 25S 139 15E
96 Bencubbin, Austral. 30 45S 117 48E
118 Bend, U.S.A. 44 2N 121 15W
63 Bender Beila, Somali Rep. 9 30N 50 48E
63 Bender Cassim, Somali Rep. 11 12N 49 18E
56 Bendery, U.S.S.R. 46 50N 29 50E
100 Bendigo, Australia 36 40S 144 15E
84 Bénéna, Mali 13 9N 4 17W
93 Benei Beraq, Israel 32 5N 34 50E
26 Benešov, Cz. 49 46N 14 41E
19 Bénestroff, France 48 54N 6 45E
20 Benet, France 46 22N 0 35W
41 Benevento, Italy 41 7N 14 45E
19 Benfeld, France 48 22N 7 34E
91 Benga, Mozambique 16 11S 33 40E
41 Bengal, Bay of, Indian Oc. 15 0N 00 90E
73 Bengawan Solo, S. Indon. 7 5S 112 25E
83 Benghazi = Banghāzī, Libya 32 11N 20 3E
72 Bengkalis, Indonesia 1 30N 102 10E
72 Bengkulu, Indonesia 3 50S 102 12E
109 Bengough, Canada 49 25N 105 10W
39 Benguela, Angola 12 37S 13 25E
82 Benguerir, Morocco 32 16N 7 56W
93 Benguérua, I., Mozam. 21 58S 35 28E
86 Benha, Egypt 30 26N 31 8E
90 Beni, Zaïre 0 30N 29 27E
126 Beni, R., Bolivia 10 30S 96 0W
82 Beni Abbès, Algeria 30 5N 2 5W
82 Beni Haoua, Algeria 36 30N 1 30E
86 Beni Mazâr, Egypt 28 32N 30 44E
82 Beni Mellal, Morocco 32 21N 6 21W
82 Beni Ounif, Algeria 32 0N 1 10W
82 Beni Saf, Algeria 35 17N 1 22W
86 Beni Suêf, Egypt 29 5N 31 6E
32 Benicarló, Spain 40 23N 0 23E
33 Benidorm, Spain 38 33N 0 9W
33 Benidorm, Islote de, Sp. 38 31N 0 9W
85 Benin, Bight of, W. Africa 5 0N 3 0E
85 Benin City, Nigeria 6 20N 5 31E
33 Benisa, Spain 38 43N 0 03E
124 Benjamin Aceval, Paraguay 24 58S 57 34W
126 Benjamin Constant, Brazil 4 40S 70 15W
116 Benkelman, U.S.A. 40 7N 101 32W
98 Benlidi, Australia 23 34S 145 38E
104 Bennett, Canada 59 50N 135 0W
115 Bennettsville, U.S.A. 34 38N 79 39W
113 Bennington, U.S.A. 42 52N 73 12W
72 Benoa, Indonesia 8 50S 115 20E
18 Bénodet, France 47 53N 4 7W
93 Benoni, S. Afr. 26 11S 28 18E
82 Benoud, Algeria 32 20N 0 16E
25 Bensheim, Germany 49 40N 8 38E
119 Benson, U.S.A. 31 59N 110 19W
65 Bent, Iran 26 20N 59 25E
73 Benteng, Indonesia 6 10S 120 30E
98 Bentinck I., Australia 17 3S 139 35E
117 Benton, Ark., U.S.A. 34 30N 92 35W
116 Benton, Ill., U.S.A. 38 0N 88 55W
114 Benton Harbor, U.S.A. 42 10N 86 28W
71 Bentong, Malaysia 3 31N 101 55E
87 Bentiu, Sudan 9 10N 29 55E
87 Bentu Liben, Ethiopia 8 32N 38 21E
85 Benue Plateau ♦, Nigeria 8 0N 8 30E
85 Benue, R., Nigeria 7 50N 6 30E
73 Beo, Indonesia 4 25N 126 50E
42 Beograd, Y.-slav. 44 50N 20 37E
118 Beowawe, U.S.A. 40 45N 117 0W
74 Beppu, Japan 33 15N 131 30E
62 Ber Dagan, Israel 32 1N 34 49E
87 Berakit, Ethiopia 14 38N 39 29E
44 Berati, Albania 40 43N 19 59E
86 Berber, Sudan 18 0N 34 0E
63 Berbera, Somali Rep. 10 30N 45 2E
88 Berbérati, Central African Rep. 4 15N 15 40E
33 Berberia, Cabo, Spain 38 39N 1 24E
126 Berbice, R., Guyana 5 20N 58 10W
38 Berceto, Italy 44 30N 10 0E
25 Berchtesgaden, Ger. 47 37N 13 1E
19 Berck-sur-Mer, France 50 25N 1 36E
56 Berdichev, U.S.S.R. 49 57N 28 30E
58 Berdsk, U.S.S.R. 54 47N 83 2E
56 Berdyansk, U.S.S.R. 46 45N 36 50E
114 Berea, Kentucky, U.S.A. 37 35N 84 18W
112 Berea, Ohio, U.S.A. 41 21N 81 50W
73 Berebere, Indonesia 2 25N 128 45E
63 Bereda, Somali Rep. 11 45N 51 0E
84 Berekum, Ghana 7 29N 2 34W
86 Berenice, Egypt 24 2N 35 25E
109 Berens, R., Canada 51 50N 93 30W
109 Berens River, Canada 52 25N 97 0W
54 Berestechko, U.S.S.R. 50 22N 25 5E
46 Bereşti, Rumania 46 6N 27 50E
46 Beretău, R., Rumania 47 30N 22 7E
27 Berettyo, R., Hungary 47 32N 21 47E
27 Berettyóújfalu, Hung. 47 13N 21 33E
93 Berevo, Malagasy Rep. 19 44S 44 58E
93 Berevo-sur-Ranobe, Malagasy Rep. 17 14S 44 17E
54 Bereza, U.S.S.R. 52 31N 24 51E
54 Berezhany, U.S.S.R. 49 26N 24 58E
54 Berezina, R., U.S.S.R. 54 10N 28 10E
54 Berezna, U.S.S.R. 51 35N 30 46E
54 Berezniki, U.S.S.R. 59 25N 56 5E
56 Berezovka, U.S.S.R. 47 25N 30 55E
58 Berezovo, U.S.S.R. 64 0N 65 0E
47 Berg, Østfold, Norway 59 10N 11 18E
32 Berga, Spain 42 6N 1 48E
49 Berga, Kalmar, Sweden 57 14N 16 3E

Berga INDEX Bittou

MAP
49 Berga, Kronoberg, Swed. 56 55N 14 0E
64 Bergama, Turkey 39 8N 27 15E
38 Bèrgamo, Italy 45 42N 9 40E
30 Bergantiños, Spain 43 20N 8 40W
24 Bergedorf, Germany 53 28N 10 12E
24 Bergen, Germany 54 24N 13 26E
16 Bergen, Noord Holland, Netherlands 52 40N 4 42E
47 Bergen, Norway 60 23N 5 20E
112 Bergen, U.S.A. 43 5N 77 56W
16 Bergen-op-Zoom, Neth. 51 30N 4 18E
20 Bergerac, France 44 51N 0 30E
24 Bergheim, Germany 50 57N 6 38E
24 Bergisch-Gladbach, Ger. 50 59N 7 9E
49 Bergkvara, Sweden 56 23N 16 5E
48 Bergsjö, Sweden 61 59N 17 3E
82 Berguent, Morocco 34 1N 2 0W
19 Bergues, France 50 58N 2 24E
16 Bergum, Netherlands 53 13N 5 59E
48 Bergvik, Sweden 61 16N 16 50E
72 Berhala, Selat, Indonesia 1 0S 104 15E
69 Berhampore, India 24 2N 88 27E
70 Berhampur, India 19 15N 84 54E
46 Berheci, R., Rumania 46 7N 27 19E
104 Bering Str., U.S.A. 66 0N 170 0W
16 Beringen, Belgium 51 3N 5 14E
59 Beringovskiy, U.S.S.R. 63 3N 179 19E
56 Berislav, U.S.S.R. 46 50N 33 30E
124 Berisso, Argentina 34 40S 58 0W
33 Berja, Spain 36 50N 2 56W
47 Berkyk, Norway 62 50N 9 59E
82 Berkane, Morocco 34 52N 2 20W
118 Berkeley, U.S.A. 38 0N 122 20W
114 Berkley Springs, U.S.A. 39 38N 78 12W
5 Berkner I., Antarctica 79 30S 50 0W
43 Berkovitsa, Bulgaria 43 16N 23 8E
13 Berkshire ♦, England 51 30N 1 20W
13 Berkshire Downs, England 51 30N 1 18W
31 Berlanga, Spain 38 17N 5 50W
24 Berleburg, Germany 51 3N 8 22E
31 Berlenga, I., Portugal 39 24N 9 31W
24 Berlin, Germany 52 32N 13 24E
114 Berlin, Md., U.S.A. 38 19N 75 12W
113 Berlin, N.H., U.S.A. 44 29N 71 10W
24 Berlin, E. ♦, E. Germany 52 30N 13 30E
24 Berlin, W. ♦, W. Germany 52 30N 13 20E
31 Bermeja, Sierra, Spain 36 45N 5 11W
124 Bermejo, R., Formosa, Argentina 26 30S 58 50W
124 Bermejo, R., San Juan, Argentina 30 0S 68 0W
32 Bermeo, Spain 43 25N 2 47W
30 Bermillo de Sayago, Sp. 41 22N 6 8W
121 Bermuda, I., Atlantic Oc. 32 45N 65 0W
25 Bern (Berne), Switz. 46 57N 7 28E
25 Bern (Berne) ♦, Switz. 46 45N 7 40E
125 Bernardo de Irigoyen, Argentina 26 15S 53 40W
41 Bernalda, Italy 40 24N 16 44E
119 Bernalillo, U.S.A. 35 17N 106 37W
71 Bernam, R., Malaysia 3 45N 101 5E
124 Bernasconi, Argentina 37 55S 63 44W
25 Bernau, Germany 47 53N 12 20E
18 Bernay, France 49 5N 0 35E
25 Bernau, Germany 47 53N 12 20E
26 Berndorf, Austria 47 59N 16 1E
25 Berne = Bern, Switz. 46 57N 7 28E
25 Berner Alpen, Switzerland 46 27N 7 35E
25 Bernese Oberland = Oberland, Switz. 46 27N 7 35E
96 Bernier I., Austral. 24 50S 113 12E
25 Bernina, Pic, Switz. 46 20N 9 54E
85 Béroubouey, Dahomey 10 34N 2 46E
26 Beroun, Czechoslovakia 49 57N 14 5E
26 Berounka, R., Cz. 50 0N 13 47E
42 Berovo, Yugoslavia 41 42N 22 51E
100 Berowra, Australia 33 35S 151 12E
83 Berrahal, Algeria 36 54N 7 33E
21 Berre, France 43 28N 5 11E
21 Berre, Étang de, France 43 27N 5 5E
82 Berrechid, Morocco 33 18N 7 36W
99 Berri, Australia 34 14S 140 35E
100 Berrigan, Australia 35 38S 145 49E
82 Berrouaghia, Algeria 36 10N 2 53E
100 Berry, Australia 34 46S 150 43E
19 Berry, France 47 0N 2 0E
117 Berryville, U.S.A. 36 23N 93 35W
24 Bersenbrück, Germany 52 33N 7 56E
116 Berthaund, U.S.A. 40 21N 105 5W
116 Berthold, U.S.A. 48 19N 101 45W
19 Bertincourt, France 50 5N 2 58E
88 Bertoua, Cameroons 4 30N 13 45E
116 Bertrand, U.S.A. 40 35N 99 38W
62 Berur Hayil, Israel 31 34N 34 38E
100 Berwick, Australia 38 2S 145 23E
113 Berwick, U.S.A. 41 4N 76 17W
* 14 Berwick ♦, Scotland 55 46N 2 30W
12 Berwick-upon-Tweed, England 55 47N 2 0W
12 Berwyn Mts., Wales 52 54N 3 26W
42 Berzasca, Rumania 44 39N 21 58E
27 Berzence, Hungary 46 12N 17 11E
93 Besalampy, Malagasy Republic 16 43S 44 29E
19 Besançon, France 47 9N 6 0E
72 Besar, Indonesia 2 40S 116 0E
71 Beserah, Malaysia 3 50N 103 21E
54 Beshenkovichi, U.S.S.R. 55 2N 29 29E
42 Beška, Yugoslavia 45 8N 20 6E
57 Beslan, U.S.S.R. 43 22N 44 28E
42 Besna Kobila, Yugoslavia 42 31N 22 10E
45 Beşparmak Daği, Turkey 37 32N 27 30E
46 Bessarabiya, U.S.S.R. 46 20N 29 0E
56 Bessavabka, U.S.S.R. 46 21N 28 51E

* *Incorporated within the region of Borders*

21 Bessèges, France 44 18N 4 8E
116 Bessemer, U.S.A. 46 27N 90 0W
18 Bessin, France 49 21N 1 0W
18 Bessines-sur- Gartempe, France 46 6N 1 22E
62 Bet Alfa, Israel 32 31N 35 25E
62 Bet Guvrin, Israel 31 37N 34 54E
62 Bet Hashitta, Israel 32 31N 35 27E
62 Bet Ha'tmeq, Israel 32 58N 35 8E
62 Bet Qeshet, Israel 32 41N 35 21E
62 Bet She'an, Israel 32 30N 35 30E
62 Bet Yosef, Israel 32 34N 35 33E
82 Bet Tadjine, Djebel, Algeria 29 0N 3 30W
93 Betafo, Malagasy Rep. 19 50S 46 51E
30 Betanzos, Spain 43 15N 8 12W
88 Bétaré-Oya, Cameroon 5 40N 14 5E
32 Bétera, Spain 39 35N 0 28W
93 Bethal, S. Afr. 26 27S 29 28E
62 Bethany = Elizarilya, Jordan 31 47N 35 15E
92 Bethany, S. Afr. 29 34S 25 59E
116 Bethany, U.S.A. 40 18N 94 0W
113 Bethel, Conn., U.S.A. 41 22N 73 25W
112 Bethel, Pa., U.S.A. 40 20N 80 2W
113 Bethel, Vt., U.S.A. 43 50N 72 37W
62 Bethlehem = Bayt Lahm, Jordan 31 43N 35 12E
93 Bethlehem, S. Africa 28 14S 28 18E
113 Bethlehem, U.S.A. 40 39N 75 24W
92 Bethulie, S. Africa 30 30S 25 59E
19 Béthune, France 50 30N 2 38E
18 Béthune, R., France 49 56N 1 5E
126 Betijoque, Venezuela 9 23N 70 44W
93 Betioky, Malagasy Republic 23 48S 44 20E
19 Beton Bazoches, France 48 42N 3 15E
71 Betong, Thailand 5 45N 101 5E
99 Betoota, Australia 25 40S 140 42E
93 Betroka, Malagasy Republic 23 16S 46 0E
107 Betsiamites, Canada 48 56N 68 40W
93 Betsiboka, R., Malagasy Republic 17 0S 47 0E
92 Betsjoeanaland, S. Africa 26 30S 22 30E
69 Bettiah, India 26 48N 84 33E
38 Bèttola, Italy 44 46N 9 35E
68 Betul, India 21 48N 77 59E
72 Betung, Indonesia 2 0S 103 10E
46 Beuca, Rumania 44 14N 24 56E
21 Beuil, France 44 6N 7 0E
100 Beulah, Australia 35 58S 142 29E
109 Beulah, Canada 50 16N 101 02W
116 Beulah, U.S.A. 47 18N 101 47W
24 Bevensen, Germany 53 5N 10 34E
96 Beverley, Australia 32 9S 116 56E
12 Beverley, England 53 52N 0 26W
108 Beverly, Canada 53 36N 113 21W
113 Beverly, Mass., U.S.A. 42 32N 70 50W
118 Beverly, Wash., U.S.A. 46 55N 119 59W
119 Beverly Hills, U.S.A. 34 4N 118 29W
16 Beverwijk, Netherlands 52 28N 4 38E
25 Bex, Switzerland 46 15N 7 0E
84 Beyin, Ghana 5 1N 2 41W
43 Beykoz, Turkey 41 8N 29 07E
84 Beyla, Guinea 8 30N 8 38W
20 Beynat, France 45 8N 1 44E
58 Beyneu, U.S.S.R. 45 10N 55 3E
64 Beypazarı, Turkey 40 10N 31 48E
64 Beyşehir Gölü, Turkey 37 40N 31 45E
42 Bezdan, Yugoslavia 45 28N 18 57E
62 Bezet, Israel 33 4N 35 8E
54 Bezhitsa, U.S.S.R. 53 19N 34 17E
20 Béziers, France 43 20N 3 12E
70 Bezwada = Vijayawada, India 16 31N 80 39E
70 Bhadra, R., India 13 0N 76 0E
69 Bhadrakh, India 21 10N 86 30E
70 Bhadravati, India 13 49N 76 15E
69 Bhagalpur, India 25 10S 87 0E
70 Bhaisa, India 19 10N 77 58E
68 Bhakkar, Pakistan 31 40N 71 5E
69 Bhakra Dam, India 31 30N 76 45E
67 Bhamo, Burma 24 15N 97 15E
70 Bhamragarh, India 19 30N 80 40E
69 Bhandara, India 21 5N 79 42E
68 Bhanrer Ra., India 23 40N 79 45E
68 Bharatpur, India 27 15N 77 30E
70 Bhatghar L., India 73 48N 18 10E
68 Bhatinda, India 30 15N 74 57E
70 Bhatkal, India 14 2N 74 35E
69 Bhatpara, India 22 50N 88 25E
70 Bhattiprolu, India 16 7N 80 45E
68 Bhaun, Pakistan 32 55N 72 40E
68 Bhaunagar = Bhavnagar, India 21 45N 72 10E
70 Bhavani, India 11 27N 77 43E
70 Bhavani, R., India 11 30N 77 15E
68 Bhavnagar, India 21 45N 72 10E
70 Bhawanipatna, India 19 55N 83 30E
68 Bhera, Pakistan 32 29N 72 57E
68 Bhilsa = Vidisha, India 23 28N 77 53E
68 Bhilwara, India 25 25N 74 38E
70 Bhima, R., India 17 20N 76 30E
70 Bhimavaram, India 16 30N 81 30E
68 Bhind, India 26 30N 78 46E
70 Bhiwandi, India 19 15N 73 0E
68 Bhiwani, India 28 50N 76 9E
70 Bhiwndi, India 19 15N 73 0E
70 Bhongir, India 17 30N 78 56E
68 Bhopal, India 23 20N 77 53E
70 Bhor, India 18 12N 73 53E
69 Bhubaneswar, India 20 15N 85 50E
68 Bhuj, India 23 15N 69 49E
68 Bhusaval, India 21 15N 69 49E
69 Bhutan ■, Asia 27 25N 89 50E
* 85 Biafra, Bight of, Africa 3 30N 9 20E
73 Biak, Indonesia 1 0S 136 0E
28 Biata, Poland 50 24N 17 40E
27 Biała, R., Poland 49 46N 20 53E

* *Renamed Bight of Bonny*

28 Biała Piska, Poland 53 37N 22 5E
28 Biała Podlaska, Poland 52 4N 23 6E
28 Białograd, Poland 54 2N 15 58E
28 Biały Bor, Poland 53 53N 16 51E
28 Białystok, Poland 53 10N 23 10E
28 Białystok ♦, Poland 53 9N 23 10E
41 Biancavilla, Italy 37 39N 14 50E
91 Biano Plateau = Manika Plateau, Zaïre 9 55S 26 24E
73 Biaro, Indonesia 2 5N 125 26E
20 Biarritz, France 43 29N 1 33W
25 Biasca, Switzerland 46 22N 18 58E
86 Biba, Egypt 28 55N 31 0E
109 Bibby I., Canada 61 55N 93 0W
25 Biberach, Germany 48 5N 9 49E
30 Bibey, R., Spain 42 24N 7 13W
84 Bibiani, Ghana 6 30N 2 8W
70 Bibile, Sri Lanka 7 10N 81 25E
98 Biboohra, Australia 16 35S 145 27E
90 Bibungwa, Zaïre 2 40S 28 15E
107 Bic, Canada 48 20N 68 41W
44 Bicaj, Albania 42 0N 20 25E
46 Bicaz, Rumania 46 53N 26 5E
41 Biccari, Italy 41 23N 15 12E
87 Bichena, Ethiopia 10 28N 38 10E
114 Bicknell, Ind., U.S.A. 38 50N 87 20W
119 Bicknell, Utah, U.S.A. 38 16N 111 35W
46 Bicsad, Rumania 47 56N 23 28E
85 Bida, Nigeria 9 3N 5 58E
70 Bidar, India 17 55N 77 35E
107 Biddeford, U.S.A. 43 30N 70 28W
100 Biddon, Australia 31 30S 148 47E
62 Biddu, Jordan 31 50N 35 8E
87 Biddwara, Ethiopia 5 11N 38 34E
62 Biddya, Jordan 32 7N 35 4E
13 Bidford, England 52 9N 1 53W
71 Bidor, Malaysia 4 6N 101 15E
89 Bié Plateau, Angola 12 0S 16 0E
118 Bieber, U.S.A. 41 4N 121 6W
25 Biel (Bienne), Switzerland 47 8N 7 14E
28 Bielawa, Poland 50 43N 16 37E
27 Bielé Karpaty, Cz. 49 5N 18 0E
24 Bielefeld, Germany 52 2N 8 31E
25 Bielersee, Switzerland 47 6N 7 5E
38 Biella, Italy 45 33N 8 3E
28 Bielsk Podlaski, Poland 52 47N 23 12E
27 Bielsko-Biała, Poland 49 50N 19 8E
71 Biên Hoa, Vietnam 11 3N 106 53E
109 Bienfait, Canada 49 10N 102 50W
25 Bienne = Biel, Switz. 47 8N 7 14E
31 Bienvenida, Spain 38 18N 6 12W
106 Bienville, Lac, Canada 55 10N 73 15W
32 Biescas, Spain 42 37N 0 20W
92 Biesiesfontein, S. Africa 30 57S 17 58E
25 Bietigheim, Germany 48 57N 9 8E
41 Biferno, R., Italy 41 40N 14 38E
109 Big Beaver, Canada 49 10N 105 10W
106 Big Beaver House, Can. 52 59N 89 50W
118 Big Belt Mts., U.S.A. 46 50N 111 30W
93 Big Bend, Swaziland 26 50S 32 2E
117 Big Bend Nat. Park, U.S.A. 29 15N 103 15W
117 Big Black, R., U.S.A. 32 35N 90 30W
116 Big Blue, R., U.S.A. 40 20N 96 40W
115 Big Cypress Swamp, U.S.A. 26 12N 81 10W
104 Big Delta, U.S.A. 64 15N 145 0W
116 Big Falls, U.S.A. 48 11N 93 48W
118 Big Horn, U.S.A. 46 11N 107 25W
118 Big Horn Mts. = Bighorn Mts., U.S.A. 44 30N 107 30W
118 Big Horn, R., U.S.A. 45 30N 108 10W
117 Big Lake, U.S.A. 31 12N 101 25W
118 Big Moose, U.S.A. 43 49N 74 58W
116 Big Muddy, R., U.S.A. 48 25N 104 45W
119 Big Pine, U.S.A. 37 12N 118 23W
118 Big Piney, U.S.A. 42 32N 110 3W
109 Big Quill L., Canada 51 48N 105 40W
114 Big Rapids, U.S.A. 43 42N 85 27W
109 Big River, Canada 53 50N 107 0W
112 Big Run, U.S.A. 40 57N 78 55W
114 Big Sable Pt., U.S.A. 44 5N 86 30W
104 Big Salmon, Canada 61 50N 136 0W
117 Big Sandy, U.S.A. 48 12N 110 9W
116 Big Sandy Cr., U.S.A. 38 52N 103 11W
116 Big Sioux, R., U.S.A. 44 20N 96 53W
118 Big Snowy Mt., U.S.A. 46 50N 109 15W
117 Big Spring, U.S.A. 32 10N 101 25W
116 Big Springs, U.S.A. 41 4N 102 3W
116 Big Stone L., U.S.A. 44 25N 96 35W
116 Big Stone City, U.S.A. 45 20N 96 30W
115 Big Stone Gap, U.S.A. 36 52N 82 45W
106 Big Trout L., Canada 53 40N 90 0W
20 Biganos, France 44 39N 0 59W
118 Bigfork, U.S.A. 48 3N 144 2W
109 Biggar, Canada 52 10N 108 0W
99 Biggenden, Australia 25 31S 152 4E
118 Bighorn Mts., U.S.A. 44 30N 107 20W
84 Bignona, Senegal 12 52N 16 23W
20 Bigorre, France 43 5N 0 2E
118 Bigtimber, U.S.A. 45 53N 110 0W
90 Bigwa, Tanzania 7 10S 39 10E
39 Bihać, Yugoslavia 44 49N 15 57E
69 Bihar, India 25 5N 85 40E
69 Bihar ♦, India 25 0N 86 0E
90 Biharamulo, Tanzania 2 25S 31 25E
27 Biharkeresztes, Hung. 47 8N 21 44E
46 Bihor, Munţii, Rumania 46 29N 22 47E
46 Bihor ♦, Rumania 47 0N 22 10E
84 Bijagós, Arquipélago dos, Port. Guinea 11 15N 16 10W
68 Bijaipur, India 26 2N 77 36E
70 Bijapur, Mad. P., India 18 50N 80 50E
70 Bijapur, Mysore, India 16 50N 75 55E
64 Bijar, Iran 35 52N 47 35E
42 Bijeljina, Yugoslavia 44 46N 19 17E
68 Bijnor, India 29 27N 78 11E
68 Bikaner, India 28 2N 73 18E
69 Bikapur, India 26 30N 82 7E
59 Bikin, U.S.S.R. 46 50N 134 20E
94 Bikini, atoll, Pac. Oc. 12 0N 167 30E
88 Bikoro, Zaïre 0 48S 18 15E
85 Bikoué, Cameroon 5 55S 11 50E
68 Bilara, India 26 14N 73 53E
69 Bilaspur, Mad. P., India 22 2N 82 15E
68 Bilaspur, Punjab, India 31 19N 76 50E
71 Bilauk Taungdang, Thailand 13 30N 99 15E
32 Bilbao, Spain 43 16N 2 56W
46 Bilbor, Rumania 47 18N 25 30E
42 Bileca, Yugoslavia 42 53N 18 27E
64 Bilecik, Turkey 40 5N 30 5E
59 Bilibino, U.S.S.R. 68 3N 166 20E
91 Bilibiza, Mozam. 12 30S 40 20E
59 Bilir, U.S.S.R. 65 40N 131 20E
44 Bilishti, Albania 40 37N 20 59E
116 Bill, U.S.A. 43 18N 105 18W
85 Billa, Nigeria 8 55N 12 15E
100 Billabong Cr., Australia 35 12S 144 50E
100 Billimari, Australia 33 20S 148 37E
12 Billingham, Eng. 54 36N 1 18W
118 Billings, U.S.A. 45 43N 108 29W
48 Billingsfors, Sweden 58 59N 12 15E
20 Billom, France 45 43N 3 20E
81 Bilma, Nigeria 18 50N 13 30E
42 Bilo Gora, Y.-slav. 45 53N 17 15E
98 Biloela, Australia 24 33S 150 40E
117 Biloxi, U.S.A. 30 30N 89 0W
99 Bilpa Morea Claypan, Austral. 25 0S 140 0E
81 Biltine, Chad 14 40N 20 50E
98 Bilyana, Australia 18 5S 145 50E
73 Bima, Indonesia 8 22S 118 49E
86 Bimban, Egypt 24 24N 32 54E
85 Bimbila, Ghana 8 54N 0 5E
68 Bina-Etawah, India 24 13N 78 14E
42 Binačka Morava, R., Yugoslavia 42 30N 19 35E
73 Binaja, Indonesia 3 20S 129 25E
73 Binalbagan, Philippines 10 12N 122 50E
100 Binalong, Australia 34 40S 148 39E
72 Binatang, Malaysia 2 10N 111 40E
98 Binbee, Australia 20 15S 147 48E
16 Binche, Belgium 50 26N 4 10E
72 Bindjai, Indonesia 3 50N 98 30E
91 Bindura, Rhodesia 17 18S 31 18E
99 Bingara, N.S.W., Australia 29 40S 150 40E
99 Bingara, Queens., Australia 28 10S 144 37E
25 Bingen, Germany 49 57N 7 53E
84 Bingerville, Ivory Coast 5 18N 3 49W
107 Bingham, U.S.A. 45 5N 69 50W
118 Bingham Canyon, U.S.A. 40 31N 112 10W
113 Binghamton, U.S.A. 42 9N 75 54W
64 Bingöl, Turkey 39 20N 41 0E
71 Binh Dinh = An Nhon, Vietnam 13 55N 109 7E
71 Binh Son, Vietnam 15 20N 108 40E
100 Binnaway, Australia 31 28S 149 24E
73 Binongko, Indonesia 5 55S 123 55E
65 Bint, Iran 26 22N 59 25E
62 Bint Jaibail, Lebanon 33 8N 34 25E
72 Bintan, Indonesia 1 0N 104 0E
72 Bintuhan, Indonesia 4 50S 103 25E
72 Bintulu, Malaysia 3 10N 113 0E
62 Binyamina, Israel 32 32N 34 56E
87 Binza, Sudan 5 25N 28 40E
83 Binzert = Bizerte, Tunisia 37 15N 9 50E
124 Bio-Bio ♦, Chile 37 35S 72 0W
87 Bio Culma, Ethiopia 7 20N 42 15E
39 Biograd, Yugoslavia 43 56N 15 29E
42 Biokovo, Yugoslavia 43 23N 17 0E
82 Biougra, Morocco 30 15N 9 14W
62 Biq'at Bet Netofa, Israel 32 49N 35 22E
70 Bir, India 19 0N 75 54E
86 Bir Abu Hashim, Egypt 23 42N 34 6E
86 Bîr Abû M'nqar, Egypt 26 33N 27 33E
86 Bir Adal Deib, Sudan 22 35N 36 10E
83 Bir al Malfa, Libya 31 58N 15 18E
86 Bir 'Asal, Egypt 25 55N 34 20E
81 Bir Autrun, Sudan 18 15N 26 40E
83 Bir Dhu'fân, Libya 31 59N 14 32E
86 Bir Diqnash, Egypt 31 3N 25 23E
82 Bir el Abbes, Algeria 26 7N 6 9W
83 Bir-el-Ater, Algeria 34 46N 8 3E
86 Bîr el Basur, Egypt 29 51N 25 49E
86 Bîr el Gellaz, Egypt 30 50N 26 40E
86 Bîr el Shaqqa, Egypt 30 54N 25 1E
86 Bîr Fuad, Egypt 30 35N 26 28E
86 Bîr Haimur, Egypt 22 45N 33 40E
86 Bîr Kanayis, Egypt 24 59N 33 15E
86 Bîr Kerawein, Egypt 27 10N 28 25E
82 Bir Lemouissat, Maur 25 0N 10 32W
86 Bîr Maql, Egypt 23 7N 33 40E
86 Bîr Misaha, Egypt 22 13N 27 59E
83 Bir Mogreïn, (Fort Trinquet), Mauritania 25 10N 11 25W
86 Bîr Murr, Egypt 23 28N 30 10E
62 Bir Nabala, Jordan 31 52N 35 12E
86 Bîr Nakheila, Egypt 24 1N 30 50E
86 Bîr Qâtrani, Egypt 30 55N 26 10E
86 Bîr Ranga, Egypt 24 25N 35 15E
87 Bir Ras, F.T.A.I. 12 0N 44 0E
86 Bîr Sahara, Egypt 22 54N 28 40E
86 Bîr Seiyâla, Egypt 25 10N 34 50E
82 Bir Semguine, Morocco 30 1N 5 39W
86 Bîr Shalatein, Egypt 23 5N 35 25E
86 Bîr Shebb, Egypt 22 25N 29 40E
86 Bîr Shût, Egypt 23 50N 35 15E
86 Bîr Terfawi, Egypt 22 57N 28 55E
86 Bîr Umm Qubûr, Egypt 24 35N 34 2E
86 Bîr Ungât, Egypt 22 8N 33 48E
86 Bîr Za'farâna, Egypt 29 10N 32 40E
83 Bir Zāmus, Libya 24 16N 15 6E
86 Bîr Zeidûn, Egypt 25 45N 34 40E
62 Bir Zeit, Jordan 31 59N 35 11E
73 Bira, Indonesia 2 3S 132 2E
46 Bîra, Rumania 47 2N 27 3E
84 Biramfero, Guinea 11 40N 9 10W
81 Birao, Central African Republic 10 20N 22 40E
90 Birawa, Zaïre 2 20S 28 48E
46 Bîrca, Rumania 43 59N 23 36E
109 Birch Hills, Canada 53 10N 105 10W
108 Birch Mts., Canada 58 0N 113 0W
100 Birchip, Australia 35 52S 143 0E
46 Birchiş, Rumania 45 58N 22 0E
109 Bird, Canada 56 35N 94 5W
116 Bird City, U.S.A. 39 48N 101 33W
98 Bird I., Australia 22 10S 155 28E
92 Bird I., S. Afr. 32 3S 18 17E
99 Birdhip, Australia 35 52S 142 50E
99 Birdsville, Australia 25 51S 139 20E
96 Birdum, Australia 15 50S 133 0E
64 Birecik, Turkey 37 0N 38 0E
72 Bireuen, Indonesia 5 14N 96 39E
87 Birhan, Ethiopia 10 45N 37 55E
84 Birifo, Gambia 13 30N 14 0E
125 Birigui, Brazil 21 18S 50 16W
98 Birimgan, Australia 22 41S 147 25E
65 Birjand, Iran 32 57N 59 10E
86 Birk, Saudi Arabia 18 8N 41 30E
86 Birka, Si.-Arab. 22 11N 40 38E
12 Birkenhead, Eng. 53 24N 3 1W
86 Birket Qârûn, Egypt 29 30N 30 40E
26 Birkfeld, Austria 47 21N 15 45E
82 Birkhadem, Algeria 36 43N 3 3E
46 Bîrlad, Rumania 46 15N 27 38E
13 Birmingham, Eng. 52 30N 1 55W
115 Birmingham, U.S.A. 33 31N 86 50W
85 Birni Ngaouré, Niger 13 5N 2 51E
85 Birni Nkonni, Niger 13 55N 5 15E
85 Birnin Gwari, Nigeria 11 0N 6 45E
85 Birnin Kebbi, Nigeria 12 32N 4 12E
85 Birnin Kudu, Nigeria 11 30N 9 29E
59 Birobidzhan, U.S.S.R. 48 50N 132 50E
62 Birqin, Jordan 32 23N 35 15E
15 Birr, Ireland 53 7N 7 55W
100 Birregurra, Australia 38 19S 143 51E
68 Birsilpur, India 28 11N 72 58E
52 Birsk, U.S.S.R. 55 25N 55 30E
46 Birtin, Rumania 46 59N 22 31E
109 Birtle, Canada 50 30N 101 5W
56 Biryuchiy, Ostrov, U.S.S.R. 46 10N 35 0E
54 Birzai, U.S.S.R. 56 11N 24 45E
46 Bîrzava, Rumania 46 7N 21 59E
73 Bisa, Indonesia 1 10S 127 40E
41 Bisàccio, Italy 41 0N 15 20E
40 Bisacquino, Italy 37 42N 13 13E
69 Bisalpur, India 28 14N 79 48E
119 Bisbee, U.S.A. 31 30N 110 0W
34 Biscay, B. of, Atlantic Ocean 45 0N 2 0W
115 Biscayne B., U.S.A. 25 40N 80 12W
41 Biscéglie, Italy 41 14N 16 30E
26 Bischofshofen, Austria 47 26N 13 14E
24 Bischofswerda, Ger. 51 8N 14 11E
19 Bischwiller, France 48 41N 7 50E
5 Biscoe I., Antarctica 66 0S 67 0W
106 Biscotasing, Canada 47 19N 82 8W
126 Biscucuy, Venezuela 9 22N 69 59W
39 Biševo I., Yugoslavia 42 57N 16 3E
87 Bisha, Ethiopia 15 30N 37 31E
86 Bisha, Wadi, Si.-Arab. 20 30N 43 0E
119 Bishop, Calif., U.S.A. 37 20N 118 26W
117 Bishop, Tex., U.S.A. 27 35N 97 49W
12 Bishop Auckland, England 54 40N 1 40W
107 Bishop's Fall, Canada 49 2N 55 24W
13 Bishop's Stortford, England 51 52N 0 11E
90 Bisina, L., Uganda 1 38N 33 56E
41 Bisignano, Italy 30 30N 16 17E
82 Biskra, Algeria 34 50N 5 44E
28 Biskupiec, Poland 53 53N 20 58E
73 Bislig, Philippines 8 15N 126 27E
24 Bismark, Germany 52 39N 11 31E
116 Bismarck, U.S.A. 46 49N 100 49W
98 Bismarck Arch., Territory of New Guinea 3 30S 148 30E
98 Bismarck Sea, Territory of New Guinea 4 10S 146 50E
90 Biso, Uganda 1 44N 31 26E
116 Bison, U.S.A. 45 34N 102 28W
48 Bispgarden, Sweden 63 2N 16 40E
84 Bissau, Port Guinea 11 45N 15 45W
109 Bissett, Canada 46 14N 78 4W
84 Bissikrima, Guinea 10 50N 10 58W
46 Bistreţu, Rumania 43 54N 23 23E
39 Bistrica = Ilirska Bistrica, Y.-slav. 45 34N 14 14E
46 Bistriţa, Rumania 47 9N 24 35E
46 Bistriţa, R., Rumania 47 10N 24 30E
46 Bistriţa Năsăud ♦, Rumania 47 15N 24 30E
46 Bistriţei, Munţii, Rumania 47 15N 25 40E
69 Biswan, India 27 29N 81 2E
28 Bisztynek, Poland 54 8N 20 53E
88 Bitam, Gabon 2 5N 11 25E
19 Bitche, France 48 58N 7 25E
88 Bitkine, Chad 11 59N 18 13E
64 Bitlis, Turkey 38 20N 42 3E
42 Bitola (Bitolj), Y.-slav. 41 5N 21 21E
41 Bitonto, Italy 41 7N 16 40E
118 Bitter Creek, U.S.A. 41 39N 108 36W
86 Bitter L., Gt., Egypt 30 15N 32 40E
86 Bitter L. = Buheirat-Murrat el Kubra, Egypt 30 15N 32 40E
24 Bitterfeld, Germany 51 36N 12 20E
92 Bitterfontein, S. Africa 31 0S 18 32E
118 Bitteroot, R., U.S.A. 46 30N 114 20W
118 Bitterroot Range, U.S.A. 46 0N 114 20W
40 Bitti, Italy 40 29N 9 20E
85 Bittou, Upper Volta 11 17N 0 18W

MAP
108 Bitumount, Canada 57 26N 112 40W
85 Biu, Nigeria 10 40N 12 3E
46 Bivolari, Rumania 47 31N 27 27E
46 Bivolu, Rumania 47 16N 25 58E
74 Biwa-Ko, Japan 35 15N 135 45E
116 Biwabik, U.S.A. 47 33N 92 19W
58 Biysk, U.S.S.R. 52 40N 85 0E
117 Bizana, S. Afr. 30 50s 29 52E
83 Bizerte (Binzert), Tunisia 37 15N 9 50E
57 Bjandovan. Mys. 39 45N 49 28E
U.S.S.R.
49 Bjärka-Säby, Sweden 58 16N 15 44E
50 Bjarnanes, Iceland 64 20N 15 6W
42 Bjelasica. Y.-slav. 42 50N 19 40E
42 Bjelo Polje, Y.-slav. 43 1N 19 45E
42 Bjelovar, Yugoslavia 45 56N 16 49E
49 Bjerringbro, Denmark 56 23N 9 39E
48 Björbo, Sweden 60 27N 14 44E
48 Björkhamre, Sweden 61 24N 16 25E
49 Björkhult, Sweden 57 50N 15 40E
48 Björneborg, Sweden 59 14N 14 16E
49 Bjuv, Sweden 56 5N 12 55E
48 Björbo, Sweden 60 27N 14 44E
48 Björneborg, Sweden 59 14N 14 16E
42 Blace, Yugoslavia 43 18N 21 17E
28 Blachownia, Poland 50 45N 18 56E
108 Black Diamond, Can. 50 45N 114 22W
116 Black Hills, U.S.A. 44 0N 103 50W
109 Black L., Can. 59 20N 105 30W
114 Black L., U.S.A. 45 28N 84 15W
13 Black Mt. = Mynydd 51 45N 3 45W
Du. Wales
13 Black Mts., Wales 51 52N 3 50W
117 Black Mesa, Mt., U.S.A. 36 57N 102 55W
119 Black Range, Mts., 33 30N 107 55W
U.S.A.
112 Black R., Canada 44 50N 79 5W
117 Black, R., Ark., U.S.A. 36 15N 90 45W
113 Black, R., N.Y., U.S.A. 43 50N 75 30W
116 Black, R., Wis., U.S.A. 44 18N 90 52W
35 Black Sea. Europe 43 30N 35 0E
100 Black Sugarloaf, Mt., 31 18s 151 35E
Australia
84 Black Volta, R., Afr. 9 0N 2 40W
115 Black Warrior, R., 30 0N 87 45W
U.S.A.
98 Blackall, Australia 24 26s 145 27E
101 Blackball, N.Z. 42 22s 171 26E
98 Blackbull, Australia 18 0s 141 7E
12 Blackburn, Eng. 53 44N 2 30W
99 Blackbutt, Australia 26 51s 152 6E
116 Blackduck, U.S.A. 47 43N 94 32W
118 Blackfoot, U.S.A. 43 13N 112 12W
118 Blackfoot, R., U.S.A. 47 0N 113 35W
100 Blackheath, Australia 33 39s 150 17E
12 Blackpool, Eng. 53 48N 3 3W
98 Blackridge, Australia 22 35s 147 35E
112 Blackriver, U.S.A. 44 46N 83 17W
107 Blacks Harbour. Can. 45 3N 66 49W
114 Blacksburg, U.S.A. 37 17N 80 23W
15 Blacksod B. Ireland 54 6N 10 0W
114 Blackstone, U.S.A. 37 6N 78 0W
96 Blackstone Ra., Australia 26 00s 129 00E
100 Blacktown. Australia 33 48s 150 55E
107 Blackville, Canada 47 5N 65 58W
98 Blackwater, Australia 23 35s 149 0E
66 Blackwater, Canada 53 20N 123 0w
99 Blackwater Cr., Austral. 25 40s 145 0E
15 Blackwater, R., Cork, 52 5N 9 3W
Ire.
15 Blackwater, R., Meath, 53 46N 7 0W
Ireland
MAP
15 Blackwater, R., Northern 54 25N 7 0W
Ireland
117 Blackwell. U.S.A. 36 55N 97 20W
49 Bladinge, Sweden 56 52N 14 29E
42 Blagaj, Yugoslavia 43 16N 17 55E
20 Blagnac. France 43 38N 1 24E
108 Blagodarnoye, U.S.S.R. 45 7N 43 37E
42 Blagoevgrad (Gorna 42 2N 23 5E
Dzhumayo), Bulgaria
59 Blagoveshchensk. 50 20N 127 30E
U.S.S.R.
118 Blaine, U.S.A. 48 59N 122 43W
109 Blaine Lake, Canada 52 51N 106 52W
19 Blainville, France 48 33N 6 23E
116 Blair, U.S.A. 41 38N 96 10W
98 Blair Athol, Australia 22 42s 147 31E
14 Blair Atholl. Scot. 56 46N 3 50W
14 Blairgowrie. Scot. 56 36N 3 20W
108 Blairmore, Canada 49 40N 114 25W
112 Blairs Mills, U.S.A. 40 17N 77 45W
112 Blairsville, U.S.A. 40 27N 79 15W
46 Blaj. Rumania 46 10N 23 57E
116 Blake Pt., U.S.A. 48 12N 88 27W
115 Blakely, U.S.A. 31 22N 85 0W
19 Blâmont. France 48 35N 6 50E
80 Blanc, C., Mauritania 20 50N 17 0W
83 Blanc, C. Tunisia 37 15N 9 56E
21 Blanc. Mont. 45 48N 6 50E
France-Italy
107 Blanc Sablon, Canada 51 24N 57 8W
128 Blanca. Bahia, Argentina 39 10s 61 30W
117 Blanchard, U.S.A. 35 8N 97 40W
99 Blanche L., S. Austral.. 29 15s 139 40E
Australia
96 Blanche L., W. Austral., 22 25s 123 17E
Australia
92 Blanco. S. Africa 33 55s 22 23E
117 Blanco, U.S.A. 30 7N 98 30W
121 Blanco, C. Costa Rica 9 34N 85 8W
124 Blanco, C., Peru 4 10s 81 10W
33 Blanco, C., Spain 39 21N 2 51E
118 Blanco, C., U.S.A. 42 50N 124 40W
13 Blandford Forum. 50 52N 2 10W
England
119 Blanding, U.S.A. 37 35N 109 30W
32 Blanes. Spain 41 40N 2 48E
19 Blangy, France 49 14N 0 17E
26 Blanice. R.. Cz. 49 10N 14 5E

MAP
16 Blankenberge, Belgium 51 20N 3 9E
24 Blankenburg, Germany 51 46N 10 56E
20 Blanquefort, France 44 55N 0 38W
125 Blanquillo, Uruguay 32 53s 55 37W
27 Blansko, Cz. 49 22N 16 40E
91 Blantyre, Malawi 15 45s 35 0E
15 Blarney, Ireland 51 57N 8 35W
28 Błaski, Poland 51 38N 18 30E
43 Blatnuitsa (Duran-culak), 43 41N 28 32E
Bulg.
12 Blaydon, England 54 56N 1 47W
20 Blaye, France 45 8N 0 40W
20 Blaye-les-Mines, France 44 1N 2 8E
100 Blayney, Austral. 33 32s 149 14E
96 Blaze, Pt., Australia 12 56s 130 11E
27 Błazowa, Poland 49 53N 22 7E
24 Bleckede, Germany 53 18N 10 43E
39 Bled, Yugoslavia 46 27N 14 7E
58 Blednaya, Gora, 65 50N 65 30E
U.S.S.R.
26 Bleiburg, Austria 46 35N 14 49E
46 Blejești, Rumania 44 19N 25 27E
49 Blekinge län ♦, Swed. 56 20N 15 20E
112 Blenheim, Canada 42 21N 82 2W
101 Blenheim, New Zealand 41 38s 174 5E
82 Blidet Amor, Algeria 32 59N 5 58E
48 Blidö, Sweden 59 37N 18 53E
49 Blidsberg, Sweden 57 56N 13 30E
101 Bligh Sound, New 44 47s 167 32E
Zealand
106 Blind River, Canada 46 15N 83 0W
44 Blinishti, Albania 41 52N 19 58E
73 Blitar, Indonesia 8 5s 112 11E
113 Block I., U.S.A. 41 13N 71 35W
113 Block Island Sound, 41 17N 71 35W
U.S.A.
92 Bloemfontein, S. Africa 29 6s 26 14E
92 Bloemhof, S. Afr. 27 38s 25 32E
18 Blois, France 47 35N 1 20E
48 Blomskog, Sweden 59 16N 12 2E
15 Bloody Foreland, Ire. 55 10N 8 18W
116 Bloomer, U.S.A. 45 8N 91 30W
112 Bloomfield, Canada 43 59N 77 39W
116 Bloomfield, Iowa, U.S.A. 40 44N 92 26W
116 Bloomfield, Nebr., 42 38N 97 15W
U.S.A.
119 Bloomfield, N. Mexico, 36 46N 107 59W
98 Bloomfield R., Mission, 15 56s 145 22E
Austral.
113 Bloomington, Ill., U.S.A. 40 25N 89 0w
114 Bloomington, Ind., 39 10N 86 30w
U.S.A.
113 Bloomsburg, U.S.A. 41 0N 76 30W
73 Blora, Indonesia 6 57s 111 25E
112 Blossburg, U.S.A. 41 40N 77 4W
93 Blouberg, S. Afr. 23 8s 29 0E
115 Blountstown, U.S.A. 30 28N 85 5W
26 Bludenz, Austria 47 10N 9 50E
114 Blue I., U.S.A. 41 40N 87 40W
118 Blue Lake, U.S.A. 40 53N 124 0w
119 Blue Mesa Res., U.S.A. 38 30N 107 15W
121 Blue Mountain Peak, 18 0N 76 40W
Jamaica
100 Blue Mts., Australia 33 40s 150 0E
121 Blue Mts., Jamaica 18 0N 76 40W
118 Blue Mts., U.S.A. 45 15N 119 0w
97 Blue Mud B., Australia 13 30s 136 0E
87 Blue Nile = Nîl el 12 30N 34 30E
Azraq ♦, Sudan
87 Blue Nile = Nîl el 10 30N 35 0E
Azraq, Sudan
115 Blue Ridge, Mts., U.S.A. 37 18N 81 14W
121 Bluefields, Nicaragua 12 0N 83 50W
15 Bluestack, mt., Ire. 54 46N 8 5W
98 Bluff, Australia 23 40s 149 0E
101 Bluff, New Zealand 46 37s 168 20E
98 Bluff Downs, Australia 19 37s 145 30E
114 Bluffton, U.S.A. 40 43N 85 9w
125 Blumenau, Brazil 27 0s 49 0w
24 Blumenthal, Germany 53 5N 12 20E
116 Blunt, U.S.A. 44 32N 100 0w
118 Bly, U.S.A. 42 23N 121 0w
48 Blyberg, Sweden 61 9N 14 15E
112 Blyth, Canada 43 45N 81 25w
12 Blyth, England 55 8N 1 32w
119 Blythe, U.S.A. 33 40N 114 33w
112 Blytheswood, Canada 42 8N 82 37W
49 Blådinge, Sweden 56 52N 14 29E
47 Bo, Norway 59 25N 9 3E
84 Bo, Sierra Leone 7 55N 11 50W
71 Bo Duc, Vietnam 11 58N 106 50E
126 Boa Esperança, Braz. 3 21N 61 23W
126 Boa Vista, Brazil 2 48N 60 30W
121 Boaco, Nicaragua 12 29N 85 35W
30 Boal, Spain 43 25N 6 49W
100 Bobadah, Australia 32 19s 146 41E
98 Bobadah, Australia 19 46s 147 33E
70 Bobbili, India 18 35N 83 30E
38 Bóbbio, Italy 44 57N 9 22E
106 Bobcaygeon, Canada 44 33N 78 35W
25 Böbingen, Germany 48 15N 10 50E
84 Bobo-Dioulasso, Upper 11 8N 4 13W
Volta
43 Boboc, Rumania 45 13N 26 59E
28 Bobolice, Poland 53 58N 16 37E
43 Boboshevo, Bulgaria 42 9N 23 0E
42 Bobov Dol, Bulgaria 42 20N 23 0E
27 Bóbr, R., Poland 51 58N 15 15E
56 Bobrinets, U.S.S.R. 48 4N 32 5E
55 Bobrov, U.S.S.R. 51 5N 40 2E
54 Bobruysk, U.S.S.R. 53 20N 124 40w
100 Bobundara, Australia 36 32s 148 59E
126 Bobures, Venezuela 9 15N 71 11W
126 Boca de Uracoa, Ven. 9 8N 62 20W
126 Boca do Acre, Brazil 8 50s 66 27W
17 Bocage, France 49 0N 1 0W
127 Bocaiúva, Brazil 17 7s 43 49W

MAP
84 Bocanda, Ivory Coast 7 5N 4 31W
81 Bocaranga, Central 7 0N 15 35E
African Republic
126 Bocas del Dragon, Ven. 11 0N 61 50W
121 Bocas del Toro, Panama 9 15N 82 20w
26 Boceguillas, Spain 41 20N 3 39w
27 Bochnia, Poland 49 58N 20 27E
25 Bocholt, Germany 51 50N 6 35E
26 Bochov, Czechoslovakia 50 9N 13 3E
24 Bochum, Germany 51 28N 7 12E
24 Bockenem, Germany 52 1N 10 8E
127 Boçsa Montaná, Rum. 45 21N 21 47E
88 Boda, Central African 4 19N 17 26E
Republic
50 Boda, Kalmar, Sweden 57 15N 17 0E
49 Böda, Sweden 57 15N 17 3E
99 Bodalla, Australia 36 4s 150 4E
59 Bodaybo, U.S.S.R. 57 50N 114 0E
25 Bodensee, Germany 47 35N 9 25E
24 Bodenteich, Germany 52 49N 10 41E
70 Bodhan, India 18 40N 77 55E
70 Bodinayakkanur, India 10 2N 77 10E
85 Bodinga, Nigeria 12 58N 5 10E
73 Bodjonegoro, Indonesia 7 11s 111 54E
13 Bodmin, England 50 28N 4 44w
13 Bodmin Moor, England 50 33N 4 36w
27 Bodrog, R., Hungary 48 15N 21 35E
64 Bodrum, Turkey 37 5N 27 30E
27 Bódva, R., Hungary 48 19N 20 45E
92 Boegoebergdam, S. 29 7s 22 9E
Africa
21 Boën, France 45 44N 4 0E
88 Boende, Zaïre 0 24s 21 12E
117 Boerne, U.S.A. 29 48N 98 41W
84 Boffa, Guinea 10 16N 14 3W
48 Bofors, Sweden 59 19N 14 34E
71 Bogale, Burma 16 14N 95 26E
84 Bogalusa, U.S.A. 30 50N 89 55W
100 Bogan Gate, Australia 33 6s 147 49E
99 Bogan, R., Australia 32 23s 147 40E
98 Bogandyera Mt., 35 45s 148 0E
Australia
100 Bogantungan, Austral. 23 41s 147 17E
117 Bogata, U.S.A. 33 26N 95 10W
42 Bogatic, Yugoslavia 44 51N 19 30E
43 Bogdan, Mt., Bulgaria 42 37N 24 20E
99 Boggabilla, Australia 28 36s 150 24E
99 Boggabri, Australia 30 45s 150 0E
15 Boggeragh Mts., Ire. 52 2N 8 55W
82 Boghari = Ksar el 35 51N 2 52E
Boukhari, Algeria
13 Bognor Regis, Eng. 50 47N 0 40W
49 Bogø, Denmark 54 55N 12 2E
73 Bogo, Philippines 11 3N 124 0E
54 Bogoduchov, U.S.S.R. 50 9N 35 33E
100 Bogong, Mt., Australia 36 40s 147 15E
73 Bogor, Indonesia 6 36s 106 48E
85 Bogoro, Nigeria 9 37N 9 29E
55 Bogoroditsk, U.S.S.R. 53 47N 38 8E
54 Bogorodsk, U.S.S.R. 56 4N 43 30E
59 Bogorodskoye, U.S.S.R. 52 22N 140 30E
84 Bogoso, Ghana 5 38N 2 3w
126 Bogotá, Colombia 4 34N 74 0W
58 Bogotol, U.S.S.R. 56 15N 89 50E
69 Bogra, Bangladesh 24 26N 89 22E
59 Boguchany, U.S.S.R. 58 40N 97 30E
55 Boguchar, U.S.S.R. 49 55N 40 32E
84 Bogué, Mauritania 16 45N 14 10W
28 Boguszów Lubawka, 50 43N 15 56E
Poland
49 Bogø, Denmark 54 55N 12 2E
19 Bohain, France 49 59N 3 28E
25 Bohemian Forest = 49 30N 12 40E
Böhmerwald, Germany
39 Bohinjska Bistrica, 46 17N 14 1E
Yugoslavia
25 Böhmerwald, Germany 49 30N 12 40E
25 Bohmte, Germany 52 24N 8 20E
73 Boholl, I., Philippines 9 50N 124 10E
84 Bohotleh, Somali Rep. 8 20N 46 25E
85 Boi, Nigeria 9 35N 9 27E
125 Boi, Pta. de, Brazil 23 55s 45 15w
41 Boiano, Italy 41 28N 14 29E
107 Boiestown, Canada 46 27N 66 26W
98 Boigu I., Terr. of Papua 9 15s 143 30E
96 Boileau, C., Australia 17 40s 122 7E
43 Boinitsa, Bulgaria 43 58N 22 28E
118 Boise, U.S.A. 43 43N 116 9W
117 Boise City, U.S.A. 36 45N 102 30W
109 Boissevain, Canada 49 15N 100 0w
39 Boite, R., Italy 46 24N 12 13E
24 Boitzenburg, Germany 53 16N 13 36E
24 Boizenburg, Germany 53 22N 10 42E
80 Bojador C., Sp. Sahara 26 0N 14 30W
28 Bojanow, Poland 51 43N 16 42E
49 Böjden, Denmark 55 6N 10 7E
65 Bojnurd, Iran 37 30N 57 20E
85 Boju, Nigeria 7 22N 7 55E
42 Boka, Yugoslavia 45 22N 20 52E
42 Boka Kotorska, 42 23N 18 32E
Yugoslavia
84 Bokala, Ivory Coast 8 31N 4 33w
84 Boké, Guinea 10 56N 14 17W
85 Bokkos, Nigeria 9 17N 9 1E
47 Boknafjorden, Norway 59 14N 5 40E
84 Bokoro, Chad 12 25N 17 14E
88 Bokole, Zaïre 0 12s 21 8E
71 Bokpyin, Burma 11 18N 98 42E
54 Boksitogorsk, U.S.S.R. 59 32N 33 56E
88 Bokungu, Zaïre 0 35s 22 50E
88 Bol, Chad 13 30N 15 0E
39 Bol, Yugoslavia 43 18N 16 38E
73 Bolaang, Indonesia 0 58s 122 6E
100 Bolac, S. Australia 37 43s 142 57E

MAP
58 Bolchereche, U.S.S.R. 56 4N 74 45E
46 Boldești, Rumania 45 3N 26 2E
87 Bole, Ethiopia 6 36N 37 20E
54 Bolekhov, U.S.S.R. 49 0N 24 0E
46 Boleni, Rumania 45 48N 27 51E
28 Bolesławiec, Poland 51 17N 15 37E
85 Bolgatanga, Ghana 10 44N 0 53W
56 Bolgrad, U.S.S.R. 45 40N 28 32E
73 Bolinao C., Philippines 16 30N 119 55E
126 Bolivar, Antioquia, 5 50N 76 1w
Colombia
126 Bolivar, Cauca, 2 0N 77 0w
Colombia
117 Bolivar, Mo., U.S.A. 37 38N 93 22W
117 Bolivar, Tenn., U.S.A. 35 14N 89 0w
126 Bolívar ♦, Colombia 9 0N 74 40w
126 Bolivia ■. S. America 17 6s 64 0W
42 Boljevac, Yugoslavia 43 51N 21 58E
55 Bolkhov, U.S.S.R. 53 25N 36 0E
21 Bollène, France 44 18N 4 45E
48 Bollnäs, Sweden 61 21N 16 24E
48 Bollstabruk, Sweden 63 1N 17 40E
49 Bolmen, Sweden 56 55N 13 40E
88 Bolo Silase, Ethiopia 8 51N 39 27E
88 Bolobo, Zaïre 2 6s 16 20E
39 Bologna, Italy 44 30N 11 20E
19 Bologne, France 48 10N 5 8E
54 Bologoye, U.S.S.R. 57 55N 34 0E
54 Bolomba, Zaïre 0 35s 19 0E
73 Bolong, Philippines 6 6N 122 16E
71 Boloven, Cao Nguyen, 15 10N 106 30E
Laos
69 Bolpur, India 23 40N 87 45E
39 Bolsena, Italy 42 40N 11 58E
39 Bolsena, L. di, Italy 42 35N 11 55E
55 Bolshaya Glushitsa, 52 24N 50 16E
U.S.S.R.
56 Bolshaya Lepetrikha, 47 11N 33 57E
U.S.S.R.
57 Bolshaya Martynovka, 47 12N 41 46E
U.S.S.R.
59 Bolshevik, ostrov, 78 30N 102 0E
U.S.S.R.
52 Bolshezemelskaya 67 0N 56 0E
Tundra, U.S.S.R.
42 Bolshoi Kavkas, 42 50N 44 0E
U.S.S.R.
54 Bolshoi Tuters, O., 59 44N 26 57E
U.S.S.R.
58 Bolshoy Atlym, U.S.S.R. 62 25N 66 50E
56 Bolshoy Tokmak, 47 16N 35 42E
U.S.S.R.
54 Bol'soj T'uters, O., 59 44N 26 57E
U.S.S.R.
16 Bolsward, Netherlands 53 3N 5 32E
32 Boltaña, Spain 42 28N 0 4E
25 Boltigen, Switzerland 46 38N 7 24E
112 Bolton, Canada 43 54N 79 51w
12 Bolton, England 53 35N 2 26w
64 Bolu, Turkey 40 45N 31 35E
39 Bolzano (Bozen), Italy 46 30N 11 20E
127 Bom Despacho, Brazil 19 43s 45 15w
127 Bom Jesus da Lapa, 13 15s 43 25w
Brazil
88 Boma, Zaïre 5 50s 13 4E
100 Bomaderry, Australia 34 52s 150 37E
81 Bômba, Khalij, Libya 32 20N 23 15E
100 Bombala, Australia 36 56s 149 15E
31 Bombarral, Portugal 39 15N 9 9w
70 Bombay, India 18 55N 72 50E
90 Bomboma, Zaïre 2 25N 18 55E
90 Bombombwa, Zaïre 2 18N 19 3E
75 Bomda, China 29 59N 96 25E
100 Bomera, Australia 31 33s 149 49E
84 Bomi Hills, Liberia 7 1N 10 38E
90 Bomili, Zaïre 1 45N 27 5E
90 Bomokandi, R., Zaïre 3 10N 28 15E
88 Bomongo, Zaïre 1 27N 18 21E
88 Bomu, R., Cent. Afr. 4 40N 23 30E
Rep.
83 Bon C., Tunisia 37 1N 11 2E
2 Bonaduz, Switz. 46 49N 9 25E
121 Bonaire, I., Neth. W. 12 10N 68 15W
Ind.
100 Bonang, Australia 37 11s 148 41E
121 Bonanza, Nicaragua 13 54N 84 35W
97 Bonaparte Archipelago, 14 0s 124 30E
Austral.
30 Bonar, Spain 42 52N 5 19W
48 Bonäset, Sweden 63 16N 18 45E
107 Bonaventure, Canada 48 5N 65 32w
107 Bonavista, Canada 48 40N 53 5W
107 Bonavista, B., Canada 48 58N 53 2W
39 Bondeno, Italy 44 53N 11 22E
88 Bondo, Zaïre 3 55N 23 53E
84 Bondoukoro, Upper 9 51N 4 25w
Volta
84 Bondoukou, Ivory C. 8 2N 2 47w
84 Bondowoso, Indonesia 7 56s 113 49E
73 Bone, Teluk, Indon. 4 10s 120 50E
73 Bone Rate, I., Indon. 7 25s 121 5E
73 Bone Rate, Kepulauan, 6 30s 121 10E
Indon.
41 Bonefro, Italy 41 42N 14 55E
14 Bo'ness, Scotland 56 0N 3 38W
71 Bong Son = Hoai 14 28N 103 7E
Nhon, S. Vietnam
88 Bongandanga, Zaïre 1 24N 21 3E
87 Bonge, Ethiopia 6 5N 37 16E
84 Bongor, Chad 10 35N 15 20E
84 Bongouanou, Ivory 6 42N 4 15w
Coast
117 Bonham, U.S.A. 33 30N 96 10W
38 Bonifacio, Corsica 41 24N 9 10E
40 Bonifacio, Bouches de, 41 12N 9 15E
Corsica

MAP
94 Bonin Is., Pacific Ocean 27 0N 142 0E
24 Bonn, Germany 50 43N 7 6E
20 Bonnat, France 46 20N 1 53E
107 Bonne B., Canada 49 31N 58 0w
107 Bonne Espérance, I., 51 24N 57 40w
Canada
117 Bonne Terre, U.S.A. 37 55N 90 38W
118 Bonners Ferry, U.S.A. 48 38N 116 21W
18 Bonnétable, France 48 11N 0 25E
18 Bonneuil Matours, Fr. 46 41N 0 34E
21 Bonneville, France 46 5N 6 24E
100 Bonnie Doon, Australia 37 2s 145 53E
96 Bonnie Rock, Australia 30 29s 118 22E
19 Bonny, France 47 34N 2 50E
85 Bonny, Nigeria 4 25N 7 13E
85 Bonny, R., Nigeria 4 20N 7 14E
109 Bonnyville, Canada 54 20N 110 45W
23 Bonoi, Indonesia 1 45s 137 41E
40 Bonorva, Italy 40 25N 8 47E
72 Bontang, Indonesia 0 10N 117 30E
73 Bonthain, Indonesia 5 34s 119 56E
84 Bonthe, Sierra Leone 7 30N 12 33W
84 Bonyeri, Ghana 5 1N 2 46w
27 Bonyhád, Hungary 46 18N 18 32E
117 Booker, U.S.A. 36 29N 100 30w
100 Bool Lagoon, Australia 33 58s 144 53E
16 Boom, Belgium 51 6N 4 20E
99 Boonah, Australia 28 0s 152 35E
116 Boone, Iowa, U.S.A. 42 5N 93 46w
115 Boone, N.C., U.S.A. 36 14N 81 43w
117 Booneville, Ark., U.S.A. 35 10N 93 54w
115 Booneville, Miss., U.S.A. 34 39N 88 34w
98 Boongoondoo, Australia 22 55s 145 55E
114 Boonville, Ind., U.S.A. 38 3N 87 13w
116 Boonville, Mo., U.S.A. 38 57N 92 45w
113 Boonville, N.Y., U.S.A. 43 31N 75 20w
99 Booroondarra, Australia 30 22s 145 27E
99 Boorooddarra Downs, 31 10s 145 27E
Australia
100 Booroorban, Australia 34 53s 144 46E
100 Boorowa, Australia 34 28s 148 44E
100 Boort, Australia 36 7s 143 46E
105 Boothia, Gulf of, Can. 70 0N 90 0w
104 Boothia Pen., Canada 70 30N 95 0w
12 Bootle, England 53 28N 3 1w
88 Booué, Gabon 0 5s 11 55E
99 Bopeechee Station, 29 35s 137 30E
Australia
53 Bopo, Nigeria 7 33N 7 50E
24 Boppard, Germany 50 13N 7 36E
26 Bor, Czechoslovakia 49 41N 12 45E
87 Bôr, Sudan 6 10N 31 40E
49 Bor, Sweden 57 9N 14 10E
42 Bor, Yugoslavia 44 8N 22 7E
118 Borah, Mt., U.S.A. 44 19N 113 46w
63 Boram, Somali Rep. 9 55N 43 7E
87 Borang, Sudan 4 50N 30 59E
49 Boras, Sweden 57 43N 12 56E
65 Borazjan, Iran 29 22N 51 10E
31 Borba, Portugal 38 50N 7 26w
57 Borçka, Turkey 41 25N 40 41E
20 Bordeaux, France 44 50N 0 36w
107 Borden, Canada 46 18N 63 47w
4 Borden I., Canada 78 30N 111 0w
100 Bordertown, Austral. 36 14s 140 58E
38 Bordighera, Italy 43 47N 7 43E
82 Bordj bou Arridj, 36 4N 4 45E
Algeria
83 Bordj Djeneïne, Tunisia 31 47N 10 3E
83 Bordj el Hobra, Algeria 32 9N 4 51E
27 Bordj Fly Ste. Marie, 27 19N 2 32w
Algeria
83 Bordj-in-Eker, Algeria 24 9N 5 3E
82 Bordj Ménaïel, Algeria 36 46N 3 43E
33 Bordj Nili, Algeria 33 28N 3 2E
82 Bordj Zelfana, Algeria 32 27N 4 15E
28 Borek Wlkp., Poland 51 54N 17 1E
49 Borensberg, Sweden 58 34N 15 17E
16 Borger, Netherlands 52 54N 7 33E
117 Borger, U.S.A. 35 40N 101 20w
49 Borgarnes, Sweden 58 23N 14 41E
49 Borgholm, Sweden 56 52N 16 39E
41 Borgia, Italy 38 50N 16 30E
38 Borgo San Dalmazzo, It. 44 19N 7 29E
38 Borgo San Lorenzo, It. 43 57N 11 21E
38 Borgo Valsugano, Italy 46 11N 11 30E
39 Borgoricefegato, Italy 45 1N 13 14E
38 Borgomanero, Italy 45 41N 8 28E
38 Borgonovo Val Tidone, 45 1N 9 28E
Italy
38 Borgosésia, Italy 45 43N 8 9E
48 Borgvattnet, Sweden 63 26N 15 48E
47 Borhaug, Norway 58 6N 6 33E
55 Borisoglebsk, U.S.S.R. 51 27N 42 5E
54 Borisov, U.S.S.R. 54 17N 28 28E
55 Borisoglebskiy, U.S.S.R. 56 28N 43 59E
55 Borisovo-Sudskoye, 59 58N 35 57E
U.S.S.R.
126 Borispol, U.S.S.R. 50 21N 30 59E
126 Borja, Peru 4 20s 77 40w
32 Borja, Spain 41 48N 1 34w.
32 Borjas Blancas, Spain 41 31N 0 52E
24 Borken, Germany 51 3N 9 21E
81 Borkou, Chad 18 15N 18 50E
48 Borlänge, Sweden 60 29N 15 26E
5 Borley, C., Antarctica 66 15N 52 30E
48 Borlänge, Sweden 60 29N 15 26E
38 Bórmida, R., Italy 44 29N 8 30E
38 Bórmio, Italy 46 28N 10 22E
24 Borna, Germany 51 8N 12 31E
72 Borneo, I., E. Indies 1 0N 115 0E
49 Bornholm, I., Denmark 55 10N 15 0E
31 Bornholmsgattet, Europe 55 15N 14 20E
31 Bornos, Spain 36 48N 5 42w
85 Bornu Yassa, Nigeria 12 14N 12 25E
54 Borodino, U.S.S.R. 55 31N 35 40E
59 Borogontsy, U.S.S.R. 62 42N 131 8E
84 Boromo, Upper Volta 11 45N 2 58w
73 Borongan, Philippines 11 37N 125 26E

* *Renamed Ras Nouadhibou*

MAP

98 Bororen, Australia 24 13s 151 33E
87 Borotangba Mts., Central African Rep. 6 30N 25 0E
43 Borovan, Bulgaria 43 27N 23 45E
54 Borovichi, U.S.S.R. 58 25N 33 55E
55 Borovsk, U.S.S.R. 55 12N 36 24E
49 Borrby, Sweden 55 27N 14 10E
32 Borriol, Spain 40 4N 0 4W
97 Borroloola, Australia 16 4s 136 17E
46 Borsa, Rumania 47 41N 24 50E
68 Borsad, India 22 24N 72 56E
27 Borsod-Abaúj- Zemplén ♦, Hungary 48 20N 21 0E
20 Bort-les-Orgues, France 45 24N 2 29E
64 Borujerd, Iran 33 55N 48 50E
57 Borzhomi, U.S.S.R. 41 48N 43 28E
54 Borzna, U.S.S.R. 51 18N 32 26E
59 Borzya, U.S.S.R. 50 24N 116 31E
49 Borås, Sweden 57 43N 12 56E
40 Bosa, Italy 40 17N 8 32E
42 Bosanska Brod, Y.-slav. 45 10N 18 0E
39 Bos. Dubica, Y.-slav. 45 10N 16 50E
39 Bos. Grahovo, Y.-slav. 44 12N 16 26E
39 Bos. Kostajnica, Y.-slav. 45 11N 16 33E
39 Bos. Krupa, Y.-slav. 44 53N 16 10E
39 Bos. Petrovac, Y.-slav. 44 35N 16 21E
42 Bos. Samac, Y.-slav. 45 3N 18 29E
39 Bosanski Novi, Y.-slav. 45 2N 16 22E
41 Boscotrecase, Italy 40 46N 14 28E
92 Boshoek, S. Afr. 25 30s 27 9E
92 Boshof, S. Afr. 28 31s 25 13E
65 Boshruyeh, Iran 33 50N 57 30E
42 Bosilegrad, Yugoslavia 42 30N 22 27E
111 Boskovice, Cz. 49 29N 16 40E
42 Bosna, R., Yugoslavia 44 50N 18 10E
42 Bosna i Hercegovina ♦, Yugoslavia 44 0N 18 0E
39 Bosnia = Bosna, Yugoslavia 44 0N 18 0E
73 Bosnik, Indonesia 1 5s 136 10E
74 Bōsō-Hanto, Japan 35 20N 140 20E
88 Bosobolo, Zaïre 4 15N 19 50E
64 Bosporus = Karadeniz Boğazı, Turkey 41 10N 29 10E
81 Bossangoa, Central African Republic 6 35N 17 30E
50 Bossekop, Norway 69 57N 23 15E
81 Bossembélé, Central African Republic 5 25N 17 40E
117 Bossier City, U.S.A. 32 28N 93 38W
96 Bossut, C., Australia 18 42s 121 35E
12 Boston, England 52 59N 0 2W
113 Boston, U.S.A. 42 20N 71 0W
108 Boston Bar, Canada 49 52N 121 22W
42 Bosut, R., Yugoslavia 45 5N 19 2E
117 Boswell, Okla., U.S.A. 34 1N 95 30W
112 Boswell, Pa., U.S.A. 40 9N 79 2W
68 Botad, India 22 15N 71 40E
100 Botany B., Australia 34 2s 151 6E
43 Botevgrad, Bulgaria 42 55N 23 47E
92 Bothaville, S. Africa 27 23s 26 34E
50 Bothnia, G. of, Eur. 63 0N 21 0E
112 Bothwell, Canada 42 37N 81 54W
30 Boticas, Portugal 41 41N 7 40W
92 Botletle R., Botswana 20 10s 24 10E
46 Botoroaga, Rumania 44 8N 25 32E
84 Botro, Ivory Coast 7 51N 5 19W
46 Botoşani, Rumania 47 42N 26 41E
46 Botoşani ♦, Rumania 47 50N 26 50E
89 Botswana ■, Africa 22 0s 24 0E
116 Bottineau, U.S.A. 48 49N 100 25W
24 Bottrop, Germany 51 34N 6 59E
125 Botucatu, Brazil 22 55s 48 30W
107 Botwood, Canada 49 6N 55 23W
82 Bou Alam, Algeria 33 50N 1 26E
82 Bou Ali, Algeria 27 11N 0 4W
84 Bou Djébéha, Mali 18 25N 2 45W
82 Bou Garfa, Algeria 27 4N 7 59W
82 Bou Guema, Algeria 28 49N 0 19E
82 Bou Iblane, Djebel. Mor. 33 50N 4 0W
82 Bou Ismail, Algeria 36 38N 2 42E
82 Bou Izakarn, Morocco 29 12N 6 46W
82 Bou Kahil, Djebel, Alg. 34 22N 9 23E
83 Bou Saâda, Algeria 35 11N 4 9E
83 Bou Salem, Tunisia 36 45N 9 2E
84 Bouaké, Ivory Coast 7 40N 5 2W
88 Bouar, Central African Republic 6 0N 15 40E
82 Bouârfa, Morocco 32 32N 1 58E
81 Bouca, Central African Republic 6 45N 18 25E
20 Boucau, France 43 32N 1 29W
21 Bouches-du-Rhône ♦, France 43 37N 5 2E
82 Bouda, Algeria 27 50N 0 27W
82 Boudenib, Morocco 31 59N 3 31W
82 Boufarik, Algeria 36 34N 2 58E
96 Bougainville C., Australia 13 57s 126 4E
82 Bougaroun, C., Algeria 37 6N 6 30E
84 Bougouni, Mali 11 30N 7 20W
16 Bouillon, Belgium 49 44N 5 3E
82 Bouïra, Algeria 36 20N 3 59E
82 Boujad, Morocco 32 46N 6 24W
96 Boulder, Australia 30 55s 121 28E
116 Boulder, Colo., U.S.A. 40 3N 105 10W
118 Boulder, Mont., U.S.A. 46 14N 112 4W
119 Boulder City, U.S.A. 36 0N 114 58W
119 Boulder Dam = Hoover Dam, U.S.A. 36 0N 114 45W
106 Bouleau, Lac au, Can. 47 40N 77 35W
82 Boulhaut, Morocco 33 30N 7 1W
98 Boulia, Australia 22 52s 139 51E
19 Bouligny, France 49 17N 5 45E
18 Boulogne, R., France 46 50N 1 25W
20 Boulogne-sur-Gesse, Fr. 43 18N 0 38E
19 Boulogne-sur-Mer. Fr. 50 42N 1 36E
85 Boulsa, Upper Volta 12 39N 0 34W
85 Boultoum, Niger 14 45N 10 25E

MAP

82 Boumalne, Morocco 31 25N 6 0W
84 Bouna, Ivory Coast 9 10N 3 0W
84 Boundiali, Ivory Coast 9 30N 6 20W
118 Bountiful, U.S.A. 40 57N 111 58W
59 Bour Khaya, U.S.S.R. 71 50N 133 10E
20 Bourbon- l'Archambault, France 46 36N 3 4E
20 Bourbon-Lancy, France 46 37N 3 45E
20 Bourbonnais, Fr. 46 28N 3 0E
19 Bourbonne, France 47 59N 5 45E
85 Bourem, Mali 17 0N 0 24W
20 Bourg, France 45 3N 0 34W
21 Bourg-Argental, France 45 18N 4 32E
21 Bourg-St.-Andéol, Fr. 44 23N 4 39E
21 Bourg-St.-Maurice, Fr. 45 35N 6 46E
20 Bourganeuf, France 45 57N 1 45E
21 Bourg-de-Péage, France 45 2N 5 3E
21 Bourg-en-Bresse, France 46 13N 5 12E
113 Bourget, Canada 45 25N 75 9W
21 Bourget, L. du, France 45 44N 5 52E
18 Bourgneuf, France 47 2N 1 58W
21 Bourgneuf, B. de, Fr. 47 3N 2 10W
19 Bourgogne, Fr. 47 0N 4 30E
21 Bourgoin-Jallieu, France 45 36N 5 17E
99 Bourke, Australia 30 8s 145 55E
106 Bourlamaque, Canada 48 5N 77 56W
20 Bournemouth, England 50 43N 1 53W
20 Bourriot-Bergonce, Fr. 44 7N 0 14W
20 Boussac, France 46 22N 2 13E
20 Boussens, France 43 12N 0 58E
84 Boutilimit, Mauritania 17 45N 14 40W
7 Bouvet I., S. Atlantic Ocean 55 0s 3 30E
82 Bouznika, Morocco 33 46N 7 6W
19 Bouzonville, France 49 17N 6 32E
41 Bova Marina, Italy 37 59N 15 56E
41 Bovalino Marina, Italy 38 9N 16 10E
39 Bovec, Yugoslavia 46 20N 13 33E
16 Bovigny, Belgium 50 12N 5 55E
118 Bovill, U.S.A. 46 58N 116 27W
41 Bovino, Italy 41 15N 15 20E
108 Bow, R., Canada 51 10N 115 0W
116 Bow Island, Canada 49 50N 111 23W
112 Bowdle, U.S.A. 45 30N 100 2W
98 Bowen, Australia 20 0s 148 16E
100 Bowen Mts., Australia 37 0s 148 0E
117 Bowie, Ariz., U.S.A. 32 15N 109 30W
117 Bowie, Tex., U.S.A. 33 33N 97 50W
12 Bowland, Forest of, England 54 0N 2 30W
114 Bowling Green, Ky., U.S.A. 37 0N 86 25W
114 Bowling Green, Ohio, U.S.A. 41 22N 83 40W
98 Bowling Green, C., Australia 19 19s 147 25E
116 Bowman, U.S.A. 46 12N 103 21W
5 Bowman, I., Antarc. 65 0s 104 0E
99 Bowmans, Australia 34 8s 138 10E
106 Bowmanville, Canada 43 55N 78 40W
14 Bowmore, Scot. 55 45N 6 18W
108 Bowness, Canada 50 55N 114 25W
99 Bowral, Australia 34 26s 150 27E
100 Bowser, Australia 36 19s 146 23E
92 Bowwood, Zambia 17 5s 26 20E
118 Boxelder Creek, U.S.A. 47 20N 108 30W
49 Boxholm, Sweden 58 12N 15 3E
56 Boyabat, Turkey 41 28N 34 42E
126 Boyacá ♦, Colombia 5 30N 72 30W
113 Boyce, U.S.A. 31 25N 92 39W
106 Boyd L., Canada 61 30N 103 20W
15 Boyle, Ireland 53 58N 8 19W
114 Boyne City, U.S.A. 45 12N 84 55W
15 Boyne, R., Ireland 53 40N 6 34W
115 Boynton Beach, U.S.A. 26 31N 80 3W
45 Bozburun, Turkey 36 43N 28 8E
64 Bozcaada, Tur. 39 49N 26 3E
118 Bozeman, U.S.A. 45 40N 111 0W
28 Bozepole Wlk., Poland 54 33N 17 56E
42 Bozevac, Yugoslavia 44 32N 21 24E
20 Bozouls, France 44 28N 2 43E
81 Bozoum, Central African Republic 6 25N 16 35E
46 Bozovici, Rumania 44 56N 22 1E
38 Bra, Italy 44 41N 7 50E
16 Brabant ♦, Belg. 50 46N 4 30E
49 Brabrand, Denmark 56 9N 10 7E
39 Brac, Yugoslavia 43 20N 16 40E
12 Bracadale, L., Scot. 57 20N 6 30W
42 Bracciano, Italy 42 6N 12 10E
106 Bracebridge, Canada 45 5N 79 20W
83 Brach, Libya 27 31N 14 20E
20 Bracieux, France 47 30N 1 30E
48 Bräcke, Sweden 62 45N 15 26E
112 Brackenridge, U.S.A. 40 38N 79 44W
117 Brackettville, U.S.A. 29 21N 100 20W
16 Brad, Rumania 46 10N 22 50E
41 Brádano, R., Italy 40 41N 16 20E
112 Braddock, U.S.A. 40 24N 79 51W
112 Bradenton, U.S.A. 27 25N 82 35W
112 Bradford, Canada 44 8N 79 33W
12 Bradford, Eng. 53 47N 1 45W
112 Bradford, Pa., U.S.A. 41 58N 78 41W
113 Bradford, Vt., U.S.A. 43 59N 72 9W
46 Brădiceni, Rumania 45 3N 23 4E
117 Bradley, Ark., U.S.A. 33 7N 93 39W
112 Bradley, S.D., U.S.A. 45 10N 97 40W
91 Bradley Institute, Rhodesia 17 7s 31 25E
107 Bradore Bay, Canada 51 27N 57 18W
117 Brady, U.S.A. 31 8N 99 25W
49 Braedstrup, Denmark 55 58N 9 37E
13 Braemar, Scot. 57 2N 3 20W
99 Braemar, Queens., Australia 33 12s 139 35E
99 Braemar, S. Austral., Australia 33 12s 139 35E
113 Braeside, Canada 45 25N 76 24W
30 Braga, Portugal 41 35N 8 32W
30 Braga ♦, Portugal 41 30N 8 30W

MAP

124 Bragado, Argentina 35 2s 60 27W
127 Bragança, Brazil 1 0s 47 2W
30 Bragança, Portugal 41 48N 6 50W
30 Bragança ♦, Port. 41 30N 6 45W
125 Bragança Paulista, Braz. 22 55s 46 32W
69 Brahmanbaria, Bangladesh 23 50N 91 15E
69 Brahmani, R., India 21 0N 85 15E
67 Brahmaputra, R., India 26 30N 93 30E
12 Braich-y-pwll, Wales 52 47N 4 46W
100 Braidwood, Australia 35 27s 149 49E
46 Bráila, Rumania 45 19N 27 59E
46 Bráila ♦, Rumania 45 5N 27 30E
116 Brainerd, U.S.A. 46 20N 94 10W
13 Braintree, Eng. 51 53N 0 34E
113 Braintree, U.S.A. 42 11N 71 0W
24 Brak, R., S. Afr. 29 35s 23 10E
24 Brake, Germany 53 19N 8 30E
92 Brakne-Hoby, Sweden 56 12N 15 8E
92 Brakwater, S.W. Africa 22 28s 17 3E
24 Brålanda, Sweden 58 34N 12 21E
108 Bralorne, Canada 50 50N 123 15W
49 Bramminge, Denmark 55 28N 8 42E
13 Bramon, Sweden 62 14N 17 40E
106 Brampton, Canada 43 45N 79 45W
24 Bramsche, Germany 52 25N 7 58E
98 Bramwell, Australia 12 8s 142 37E
126 Branco, R., Brazil 1 30N 61 15W
49 Brande, Denmark 55 57N 9 8E
24 Brandenburg, Germany 52 24N 12 33E
92 Brandfort, S. Africa 28 40s 26 30E
109 Brandon, Canada 49 50N 100 0W
113 Brandon, U.S.A. 43 48N 73 4W
15 Brandon B., Ireland 52 17N 10 8W
15 Brandon, Mt., Ireland 52 15N 10 15W
124 Brandsen, Argentina 35 48s 58 15W
47 Brandval, Norway 60 19N 12 1E
92 Brandvlei, S. Africa 30 25s 20 30E
26 Brandýs, Czechoslovakia 50 10N 14 40E
113 Branford, U.S.A. 41 15N 72 48W
28 Braniewo, Poland 54 25N 19 50E
99 Bransby, Australia 28 10s 142 0E
5 Bransfield Str., Falkland Is. 63 0s 59 0W
117 Branson, Colo., U.S.A. 37 4N 103 53W
117 Branson, Mo., U.S.A. 36 40N 93 18W
106 Brantford, Canada 43 15N 80 15W
20 Brantôme, France 45 22N 0 39E
100 Branxholme, Australia 37 52s 141 49E
100 Branxton, Australia 32 38s 151 21E
38 Branzi, Italy 46 0N 9 46E
107 Bras d'or, L., Canada 46 3N 60 43W
126 Brasiléia, Brazil 10 9s 68 35W
127 Brasilia, Braz. 15 47s 47 55E
54 Braslav, U.S.S.R. 55 38N 27 0E
39 Braslovce, Yugoslavia 46 21N 15 3E
46 Braşov, Rumania 45 7N 25 39E
46 Braşov ♦, Rumania 45 45s 25 15E
85 Brass, Nigeria 4 35N 6 14E
85 Brass, R., Nigeria 4 15N 6 13E
16 Brasschaat, Belgium 51 19N 4 27E
72 Brassey, Barisan, Malaysia 5 0N 117 15E
115 Brasstown Bald, Mt., U.S.A. 34 54N 83 45W
25 Brateş, Rumania 46 55N 26 3E
27 Bratislava, Cz. 48 10N 17 7E
59 Bratsk, U.S.S.R. 56 10N 101 30E
113 Brattleboro, U.S.A. 42 53N 72 37W
47 Brattvaer, Norway 63 25N 7 48E
46 Braţul Chilia, R., Rum. 45 25N 29 20E
46 Braţul Stintu Gheorghe, R., Rumania 45 0N 29 20E
46 Braţul Sulina, R., Rum. 45 10N 29 20E
42 Bratunac, Yugoslavia 44 13N 19 21E
26 Braunau, Austria 48 15N 13 3E
24 Braunschweig, Ger. 52 17N 10 28E
63 Brava, Somali Rep. 1 20N 44 8E
120 Bravo del Norte, R., Mexico 30 30N 105 0W
119 Brawley, U.S.A. 32 58N 115 30W
19 Bray, France 49 15N 1 40E
19 Bray-sur-Seine, France 48 25N 3 14E
126 Brazil ■, S. Amer. 10 0s 50 0W
114 Brazil, U.S.A. 39 30N 87 8W
13 Brazilian Highlands, Brazil 18 0s 46 30W
124 Brazo Sur, R., Par.-Arg. 19 30s 64 35W
117 Brazos, R., U.S.A. 30 30N 96 20W
88 Brazzaville, Congo 4 9s 15 12E
42 Brčko, Yugoslavia 44 54N 18 46E
98 Breadalbane, Australia 23 48s 139 33E
14 Breadalbane, Scot. 56 30N 4 15W
101 Breaksea Sd., N.Z. 45 35s 166 35E
101 Bream Bay, N.Z. 35 56s 174 35E
101 Bream Head, N.Z. 35 51s 174 36E
124 Breas, Chile 25 29s 70 24W
73 Brebes, Indonesia 6 52s 109 3E
112 Brechin, Canada 44 33N 79 10W
14 Brechin, Scotland 56 44N 2 40W
118 Breckenridge, Colo., U.S.A. 39 30N 106 2W
116 Breckenridge, Minn., U.S.A. 46 20N 96 36W
117 Breckenridge, Tex., U.S.A. 32 48N 98 55W
13 Brecknock ♦, Wales 51 58N 3 25W
27 Breclav, Czechoslovakia 48 46N 16 53E
13 Brecon, Wales 51 57N 3 23W
13 Brecon Beacons, Wales 51 53N 3 27W
16 Breda, Netherlands 51 35N 4 45E
49 Bredaryd, Sweden 57 10N 13 45E
92 Bredasdorp, S. Africa 34 33s 20 2E
100 Bredbo, Australia 35 58s 149 10E
100 Breeza, Australia 31 16s 150 14E
42 Bregalnica, R., Y.-slav. 41 50N 22 20E
26 Bregenz, Austria 47 30N 9 45E

MAP

49 Bregning, Denmark 56 8N 8 30E
18 Bréhal, France 48 53N 1 30W
18 Bréhat I. de, France 48 51N 3 0W
21 Breil, France 43 56N 7 31E
25 Breisach, Germany 48 2N 7 37E
47 Brekke, Sogn og Fjordane, Norway 61 1N 5 26E
47 Bremangerlandet, Nor. 61 51N 5 0E
47 Bremangerpollen, Norway 61 51N 5 0E
24 Bremen, Germany 53 4N 8 47E
24 Bremen ♦, Germany 53 6N 8 46E
24 Bremerhaven, Germany 53 34N 8 35E
118 Bremerton, U.S.A. 47 30N 122 48W
24 Bremervörde, Germany 53 28N 9 10E
59 Bremnes, Norway 59 47N 5 8E
47 Bremsnes, Norway 63 6N 7 40E
31 Brenes, Spain 37 32N 5 54W
47 Brenner Pass, Alps 47 0N 11 30E
106 Brent, Canada 46 0N 78 30W
13 Brent, England 51 33N 0 18W
41 Bréscia, Italy 45 33N 10 13E
16 Breskens, Netherlands 51 23N 3 33E
28 Breslau = Wrocław., Pol. 51 5N 17 5E
19 Bresle, R., France 50 4N 1 21E
19 Bresles, France 49 25N 2 13E
25 Bressanone, Italy 46 43N 11 40E
14 Bressay I., Scot. 60 10N 1 5W
21 Bresse, Plaine de, France 46 20N 5 10E
18 Bressuire, France 46 51N 0 30W
18 Brest, France 48 24N 4 31W
54 Brest, U.S.S.R. 52 10N 23 40E
18 Bretagne, France 48 0N 3 0W
46 Bretcu, Rumania 46 7N 26 18E
48 Breteuil, Eur, France 48 50N 0 53E
19 Breteuil, Oise, France 49 38N 2 18E
117 Breton Sd., U.S.A. 29 40N 89 12W
101 Brett, C., New Zealand 35 10s 174 20E
25 Bretten, Germany 49 2N 8 43E
115 Brevard, U.S.A. 35 19N 82 42W
47 Brevik, Norway 59 4N 9 42E
99 Brewarrina, Australia 30 0s 146 51E
107 Brewer, U.S.A. 44 43N 68 50W
113 Brewster, N.Y., U.S.A. 41 23N 73 37W
118 Brewster, Wash., U.S.A. 48 10N 119 51W
4 Brewster, Kap, Greenland 70 7N 22 0W
115 Brewton, U.S.A. 31 9N 87 2W
93 Breyten, S. Afr. 26 16s 30 0E
55 Breytovo, U.S.S.R. 58 18N 37 50E
82 Brézina, Algeria 33 4N 1 14E
26 Breznice, Cz. 49 32N 13 57E
27 Brezno, Czechoslovakia 48 50N 19 40E
81 Bria, Central Africa 6 30N 21 58E
21 Briançon, France 44 54N 6 39E
18 Briare, France 47 38N 2 45E
100 Bribbaree, Australia 34 10s 147 51E
99 Bribie I., Australia 27 0s 152 58E
19 Bricon, France 48 5N 5 0E
19 Bricquebec, France 49 29N 1 39W
108 Bridge, R., Canada 50 50N 122 40W
113 Bridgehampton, U.S.A. 40 56N 72 19W
13 Bridgend, Wales 51 30N 3 35W
118 Bridgeport, Calif., U.S.A. 38 14N 119 15W
113 Bridgeport, Conn., U.S.A. 41 12N 73 12W
117 Bridgeport, Tex., U.S.A. 33 15N 97 45W
116 Bridger, U.S.A. 45 20N 108 58W
114 Bridgeton, U.S.A. 39 29N 75 10W
96 Bridgetown, Australia 33 58s 116 7E
121 Bridgetown, Barbados 13 0N 59 30W
107 Bridgetown, Canada 44 55N 65 12W
96 Bridgewater, Australia 33 58s 116 7E
100 Bridgewater, Australia 36 36s 143 59E
107 Bridgewater, Canada 44 25N 64 31W
113 Bridgewater, Mass., U.S.A. 41 59N 70 56W
116 Bridgewater, S.D., U.S.A. 43 34N 97 29W
13 Bridgnorth, Eng. 52 33N 2 25W
13 Bridgton, U.S.A. 44 5N 70 41W
13 Bridgwater, Eng. 51 7N 3 0W
13 Bridlington, Eng. 54 6N 0 11W
13 Bridport, Eng. 50 43N 2 45W
19 Brie, Plaine de, Fr. 48 35N 3 10E
18 Brie-Comte-Robert, Fr. 48 40N 2 35E
18 Briec, France 48 6N 4 0W
19 Brienne-le-Château, Fr. 48 24N 4 30E
19 Brienon, France 48 0N 3 30E
25 Brienz, Switzerland 46 46N 8 2E
25 Brienzersee, Switz. 46 44N 7 53E
19 Briey, France 49 14N 5 57E
25 Brig, Switzerland 46 18N 7 59E
13 Brigg, England 53 33N 0 30W
116 Briggsdale, U.S.A. 40 40N 104 20W
120 Brigham City, U.S.A. 41 30N 112 1W
100 Bright, Australia 36 42s 146 56E
99 Brighton, Australia 35 1s 138 30E
106 Brighton, Canada 44 3N 77 44W
13 Brighton, Eng. 50 50N 0 9W
116 Brighton, Colo., U.S.A. 39 59N 104 50W
113 Brighton, Pa., U.S.A. 40 42N 80 19W
64 Brighton, Mich., U.S.A. 42 33N 83 48W
18 Brignogan-Plage, Fr. 48 40N 4 20W
21 Brignoles, France 43 25N 6 5E
32 Brihuega, Spain 40 45N 2 52E
84 Brikama, Gambia 13 15N 16 45W
108 Brilliant, Canada 49 19N 117 55W
112 Brilliant, U.S.A. 40 15N 80 39W
24 Brilon, Germany 51 23N 8 32E
41 Bríndisi, Italy 40 39N 17 55E

MAP

100 Bringagee, Australia 34 28s 145 44E
117 Brinkley, U.S.A. 34 55N 91 15W
33 Brinkworth, Austral. 33 40s 138 20E
107 Brion I., Canada 47 46N 61 26W
18 Brionne, France 49 11N 0 43E
31 Brioude, France 45 18N 3 23E
18 Briouze, France 48 42N 0 23W
113 Bristol, Conn., U.S.A. 41 44N 72 37W
113 Bristol, Mass., U.S.A. 41 40N 71 15W
112 Bristol, Pa., U.S.A. 40 7N 74 52W
116 Bristol, S.D., U.S.A. 45 25N 97 43W
119 Bristol, I., U.S.A. 34 23N 116 0W
13 Bristol Channel, England 51 18N 3 30W
5 Bristol I., Falkland Is. 58 45s 28 0W
Dependencies
5 Br. Antarctic Territory, 66 0s 45 0W
Antarctica
108 Br. Columbia ♦, Can. 55 0N 125 15W
126 Br. Guiana = Guyana, 5 0N 59 0W
S. Am.
•120 British Honduras ■, 17 0N 88 30W
Central America
3 British Indian Ocean 5 0s 70 0E
Terr. ■, Ind.-Oc.
93 Brits, S. Africa 25 37s 27 48E
92 Britstown, S. Africa 30 37s 23 30E
37 Britt, Canada 45 46N 80 35W
18 Brittany = Bretagne, 48 0N 3 0W
France
49 Brittatorp, Sweden 57 3N 14 58E
116 Britton, U.S.A. 45 50N 97 47W
20 Brive-la-Gaillarde, 45 10N 1 32E
France
32 Briviesca, Spain 42 32N 3 19W
98 Brixton, Australia 23 32s 144 52E
27 Brno, Czechoslovakia 49 10N 16 35E
48 Bro, Värmland, Sweden 59 13N 13 2E
68 Broach, India 21 47N 73 0E
115 Broad B., Scot. 58 14N 6 16W
115 Broad R., U.S.A. 34 30N 81 26W
15 Broad Haven, Ireland 54 20N 9 55W
14 Broad Law, Mt., 55 30N 3 22W
Scotland
98 Broad Sd., Australia 22 0s 149 45E
100 Broadford, Australia 37 14s 145 4E
13 Broads, The, Eng. 52 30N 1 15E
98 Broadsound Ra., Australia 22 50s 149 30E
116 Broadus, U.S.A. 45 28N 105 27W
49 Broager, Denmark 54 53N 9 40E
49 Broaryd, Sweden 57 7N 13 15E
109 Brochet, Manitoba, Can. 57 55N 101 40W
106 Brochet, Québec, Can. 47 12N 72 42W
109 Brochet, L., Canada 58 50N 101 30W
24 Brocken, Germany 51 48N 10 40E
100 Brocklesby, Australia 35 48s 146 40E
112 Brockport, U.S.A. 43 12N 77 56W
113 Brockton, Mass., U.S.A. 42 8N 71 2W
113 Brockton, N.Y., U.S.A. 42 24N 79 27W
106 Brockville, Canada 44 37N 75 38W
116 Brockway, U.S.A. 47 18N 105 46W
112 Brockwayville, U.S.A. 41 14N 78 48W
71 Brocton, U.S.A. 42 25N 79 26W
42 Brodarevo, Yugoslavia 43 14N 19 44E
105 Brodeur Pen., Canada 72 0N 88 0W
14 Brodick, Scotland 55 34N 5 9W
28 Brodnica, Poland 53 15N 19 25E
54 Brody, U.S.S.R. 50 5N 25 10E
118 Brogan, U.S.A. 44 14N 117 32W
18 Broglie, France 49 0N 0 30E
28 Brok, Poland 52 43N 21 52E
100 Broken B., Australia 33 30s 151 15E
116 Broken Bow, Nebr., U.S.A. 41 25N 99 35W
117 Broken Bow, Okla., U.S.A. 34 2N 94 43W
100 Broken Hill, Australia 31 58s 141 29E
91 Broken Hill = Kabwe, Zambia 14 27s 28 28E
49 Brokind, Sweden 58 13N 15 42E
109 Bromhead, Canada 49 18N 103 40W
13 Bromley, Eng. 51 20N 0 5E
49 Bromölla, Sweden 56 5N 14 28E
49 Brønderslev, Denmark 57 16N 9 57E
84 Brong Ahafo, Ghana 7 50N 2 0E
93 Bronkhorstspruit, S. Africa 25 46s 28 45E
55 Bronnitsy, U.S.S.R. 55 27N 38 10E
54 Bronnitsy, U.S.S.R. 55 27N 38 10E
117 Bronte, U.S.A. 31 54N 100 18W
41 Bronte, Italy 37 48N 14 49E
116 Brookfield, U.S.A. 39 50N 92 50W
117 Brookhaven, U.S.A. 31 40N 90 25W
118 Brookings, Oreg., U.S.A. 42 4N 124 10W
116 Brookings, S.D., U.S.A. 44 20N 96 45W
98 Brooklands, Australia 18 5s 144 0E
112 Brooklin, Canada 43 55N 78 55W
113 Brooklyn, U.S.A. 40 45N 73 58W
108 Brookmere, Canada 49 52N 120 53W
104 Brooks Ra., Alaska 68 40N 147 0W
115 Brooksville, U.S.A. 28 32N 82 21W
96 Brookton, West. Australia 32 22s 116 57E
114 Brookville, Ind., U.S.A. 39 25N 85 0W
112 Brookville, Pa., U.S.A. 41 10N 79 6W
99 Brooloo, Australia 26 30s 152 36E
14 Broom, L., Scot. 57 55N 5 15W
96 Broome, Australia 18 0s 122 15E
14 Broons, France 48 20N 2 16W
14 Brora, R., Scot. 58 4N 4 19W
49 Brosarp, Sweden 55 44N 14 8E
15 Brosna, R., Ireland 53 8N 8 0W
46 Broşteni, Rumania 47 14N 25 43E
118 Brothers, U.S.A. 43 56N 120 39W
47 Bröttum, Norway 61 2N 10 38E

* Incorporated within the county of Powys

* Renamed Belize

MAP

98 Broughton, Australia 20 10s 146 20e
100 Broughton Is., Austral. 32 37s 152 20e
14 Broughty Ferry, Scotland 56 29n 2 50w
27 Broumov, Cz. 50 35n 16 20e
54 Brovary, U.S.S.R. 50 34n 30 48e
49 Brovst, Denmark 57 6n 9 31e
116 Browerville, U.S.A. 46 3n 94 50w
99 Brown Mt., Australia 32 30n 138 0e
13 Brown Willy, Mt., England 50 35n 4 34w
117 Brownfield, U.S.A. 33 10n 102 15w
118 Browning, U.S.A. 48 35n 113 10w
109 Brownlee, Canada 50 43n 105 59w
118 Brownsville, Oreg., U.S.A. 44 29n 123 0w
117 Brownsville, Tenn., U.S.A. 35 35n 89 15w
117 Brownsville, Tex., U.S.A. 25 56n 97 25w
117 Brownwood, U.S.A. 31 45n 99 0w
117 Brownwood, L., U.S.A. 31 51n 98 35w
31 Brozas, Spain 39 37n 6 47w
71 Bruas, Malaysia 4 31n 100 46e
19 Bruay-en-Artois, France 50 29n 2 33e
96 Bruce, Mt., Austral. 22 31s 118 6e
106 Bruce Mines, Canada 46 20n 83 45w
112 Bruce Pen., Canada 45 0n 81 15w
27 Bruchsal, Germany 49 1n 8 39e
27 Bruck, Niederösterreich, Austria 48 1n 16 47e
26 Bruck, Steiermark, Austria 47 24n 15 16e
25 Brückenau, Germany 50 17n 9 48e
13 Brue, R., England 51 10n 2 50w
26 Bruges = Brugge, Belgium 51 13n 3 13e
25 Brugg, Switzerland 47 29n 8 11e
26 Brugge, Belgium 51 13n 3 13e
24 Brühl, Germany 50 49n 6 51e
108 Brule, Canada 53 15n 117 58w
18 Brûlon, France 47 58n 0 15w
127 Brumado, Brazil 14 14s 41 40w
19 Brumath, France 48 43n 7 40e
47 Brumunddal, Norway 60 53n 10 56e
115 Brundidge, U.S.A. 42 57n 115 55w
118 Bruneau, U.S.A. 42 57n 115 55w
42 Bruneau, R., U.S.A. 42 45n 115 50w
*72 Brunei, Brunei 4 52n 115 0e
72 Brunei ■, Asia 4 50n 115 0e
48 Brunflo, Sweden 63 5n 14 50e
47 Brunkeberg, Norway 59 26n 8 28e
48 Brunna, Sweden 59 52n 17 25e
25 Brunnen, Switzerland 46 59n 8 37e
101 Brunner, New Zealand 42 27s 171 20e
101 Brunner, L., N.Z. 42 27s 171 20e
48 Brunnsvik, Sweden 60 12n 15 8e
109 Bruno, Canada 52 20n 105 30w
48 Brunsberg, Sweden 59 38n 12 52e
24 Brunsbüttelkoog, Ger. 53 52n 9 13e
24 Brunswick = Braunschweig, Germany 52 17n 10 28e
115 Brunswick, Ga., U.S.A. 31 10n 81 30w
107 Brunswick, Me., U.S.A. 43 53n 69 50w
114 Brunswick, Md., U.S.A. 39 20n 77 38w
116 Brunswick, Mo., U.S.A. 39 26n 93 10w
112 Brunswick, Ohio, U.S.A. 41 15n 81 50w
96 Brunswick B., Australia 15 15s 124 50e
128 Brunswick, Pen. de, Chile 53 30s 71 30w
27 Bruntál, Cz. 50 0n 17 27e
99 Bruny I., Australia 43 20s 147 15e
42 Brusartsi, Bulgaria 43 40n 23 5e
116 Brush, U.S.A. 40 17n 103 33w
113 Brushton, U.S.A. 44 50n 74 62w
25 Brusio, Switzerland 46 14n 10 8e
125 Brusque, Brazil 27 5s 49 0w
16 Brussel, Belgium 50 51n 4 21e
16 Brussels = Brussel, Belgium 50 51n 4 21e
112 Brussels, Canada 43 45n 81 25w
47 Bruvik, Norway 60 29n 5 40e
16 Bruxelles, Belgium 50 51n 4 21e
19 Bruyères, France 48 10n 6 40e
69 Bruzual, Venezuela 8 3n 69 19w
28 Brwinow, Poland 52 9n 20 40e
42 Bryagovo, Bulgaria 41 58n 25 8e
114 Bryan, Ohio, U.S.A. 41 30n 84 30w
117 Bryan, Texas, U.S.A. 30 40n 96 27w
54 Bryansk, U.S.S.R. 53 13n 34 25e
57 Bryanskoye, U.S.S.R. 44 9n 47 10e
32 Bryant, U.S.A. 44 39n 97 26w
28 Brydges, Canada 42 54n 81 28w
47 Bryggja, Norway 61 56n 5 27e
47 Bryne, Norway 58 44n 5 38e
49 Bryrup, Denmark 56 2n 9 30e
115 Bryson City, U.S.A. 35 28n 83 25w
42 Brza Palanka, Y.-slav. 44 28n 22 37e
42 Brzava, R., U.S.S.R. 45 21n 20 45e
28 Brzeg, Poland 52 36n 18 55e
28 Brzeg, Poland 50 52n 17 30e
28 Brzeg Dln., Poland 51 16n 16 41e
28 Brzesko, Poland 49 59n 20 34e
28 Brzeszcze, Poland 49 59n 19 10e
28 Brzeziny, Poland 51 49n 19 42e
27 Brzozów, Poland 49 41n 22 3e
49 Braedstrup, Denmark 55 58n 9 37e
49 Bräkne-Hoby, Sweden 56 14n 15 6e
49 Brönderslev, Denmark 57 16n 9 57e
49 Brösarp, Sweden 55 43n 14 6e
49 Bralanda, Sweden 58 34n 12 21e
83 Bu Athiah, Libya 30 1n 15 30e
84 Bu Craa, Spanish Sahara 37 21s 143 11e
100 Buangor Mt., Australia 37 21s 143 11e
73 Buapinang, Indonesia 4 40s 121 30e
73 Buayan, Philippines 6 3n 125 25e
84 Buba, Port. Guinea 11 40n 14 59w
90 Bubanza, Burundi 3 6s 29 23e
64 Bubiyan, Kuwait 29 30n 48 15e
126 Bucaramanga, Col. 7 0n 73 0w
39 Buccianico, Italy 42 20n 14 10e

46 Bucecea, Rumania 47 47n 26 28e
43 Bucha, R., Bulgaria 41 53n 24 26e
54 Buchach, U.S.S.R. 49 5n 25 25e
100 Buchan, Australia 37 20s 148 12e
14 Buchan, Scot. 57 32n 2 8w
14 Buchan Ness, Scotland 57 29n 1 48w
109 Buchanan, Canada 51 40n 102 45w
84 Buchanan, Liberia 5 57n 10 2w
96 Buchanan, L., Australia 25 30s 123 2e
117 Buchanan, L., U.S.A. 30 50n 98 25w
107 Buchans, Canada 49 0n 57 2w
46 Bucharest, Rumania 44 27n 26 10e
46 Bucharest = București, Rumania 44 27n 26 10e
24 Buchholz, Germany 53 19n 9 51e
25 Buchloe, Germany 48 3n 10 45e
24 Buckeburg, Germany 52 16n 9 2e
119 Buckeye, U.S.A. 33 28n 112 40w
114 Buckhannon, U.S.A. 39 2n 80 10w
14 Buckhaven, Scot. 56 10n 3 2w
14 Buckie, Scotland 57 40n 2 58w
106 Buckingham, Canada 45 37n 75 24w
13 Buckingham, Eng. 52 0n 0 59w
13 Buckingham ♦, England 51 50n 0 55w
96 Buckingham B., Australia 12 10s 135 40e
70 Buckingham Can., India 14 0n 80 5e
118 Buckley, U.S.A. 47 10n 122 2w
117 Bucklin, U.S.A. 37 37n 99 40w
19 Bucquoy, France 50 9n 2 43e
107 Buctouche, Canada 46 30n 64 45w
46 București, Rumania 44 27n 26 10e
114 Bucyrus, U.S.A. 40 48n 83 0w
17 Budacul, Munte, Rumania 47 5n 25 40e
27 Budafok, Hungary 47 26n 19 2e
67 Budalin, Burma 22 20n 95 10e
27 Budapest, Hungary 47 29n 19 5e
68 Budaun, India 28 5n 79 10e
5 Budd Coast, Antarctica 67 0s 112 0e
40 Buddusò, Italy 40 35n 9 18e
13 Bude, England 50 49n 4 33w
46 Budești, Rumania 44 13n 26 30e
69 Budge Budge, India 22 30n 88 25e
32 Budia, Spain 40 38n 2 46w
39 Büdrio, Italy 44 31n 11 31e
42 Budva, Yugoslavia 42 17n 18 50e
28 Budzyn, Poland 52 54n 16 59e
85 Buea, Cameroon 4 10n 9 9e
119 Buena Vista, Colo., U.S.A. 38 56n 106 6w
114 Buena Vista, Va., U.S.A. 37 47n 79 23w
119 Buena Vista L., U.S.A. 35 15n 119 21w
120 Buenaventura, Mex. 27 4n 101 32w
126 Buenaventura, B. de, Colombia 3 48n 77 17w
32 Buendia, Pantano de, Spain 40 25n 2 43w
124 Buenos Aires, Arg. 34 30s 58 20w
126 Buenos Aires, Colombia 1 36n 73 18w
128 Buenos Aires, Lago, Chile 46 35s 72 30w
124 Buenos Aires ♦, Argentina 36 30s 60 0w
126 Buesaco, Colombia 1 23n 77 9w
109 Buffalo, Canada 50 49n 110 42w
117 Buffalo, Mo., U.S.A. 37 40n 93 5w
112 Buffalo, N.Y., U.S.A. 42 55n 78 50w
117 Buffalo, Okla., U.S.A. 36 55n 99 42w
117 Buffalo, S.D., U.S.A. 45 39n 103 31w
118 Buffalo, Wyo., U.S.A. 44 25n 106 50w
108 Buffalo L., Canada 60 0n 115 30w
108 Buffalo Head Hills, Can. 58 0n 116 20w
109 Buffalo Narrows, Can. 55 52n 108 28w
93 Buffels, R., S. Africa 29 36s 17 15e
115 Buford, U.S.A. 34 5n 84 0w
23 Bug, R., Poland 51 20n 23 40e
56 Bug, R., U.S.S.R. 48 0n 31 0e
126 Buga, Colombia 4 0n 77 0w
90 Buganda ♦, Uganda 0 1n 31 30e
90 Buganga, Uganda 0 25n 32 0e
20 Bugeat, France 45 36n 1 55e
115 *Buggs I., L., U.S.A. 36 20n 78 30w
42 Bugojno, Yugoslavia 44 2n 17 25e
58 Bugrusian, U.S.S.R. 53 42n 52 15e
72 Bugsuk, I., Philippines 8 15n 117 15e
58 Bugulma, U.S.S.R. 54 38n 52 45e
85 Buguma, Nigeria 4 42n 6 55e
76 Buguun Shara, Mongolia 49 0n 104 0e
86 Buheirat-Murrat-el-Kubra, Egypt 30 15n 32 40e
46 Buhaești, Rumania 46 47n 27 32e
118 Buhl, Idaho, U.S.A. 42 35n 114 54w
116 Buhl, Minn., U.S.A. 47 30n 92 46w
46 Buhuși, Rumania 46 41n 26 45e
117 Buick, U.S.A. 37 8n 91 2w
13 Builth Wells, Wales 52 10n 3 26w
65 Buina Qara, Afghan. 36 20n 67 0e
55 Buinsk, U.S.S.R. 55 0n 48 18e
21 Buis-les-Baronnies, Fr. 44 17n 5 16e
30 Buitrago, Spain 41 0n 3 38w
32 Bujalance, Spain 37 54n 4 23w
30 Buján, Spain 42 45n 8 43w
32 Bujaraloz, Spain 41 29n 0 10w
39 Buje, Yugoslavia 45 24n 13 39e
65 Bujnurd, Iran 37 35n 57 15e
90 Bujumbura (Usumbura), Burundi 3 16s 29 18e
27 Bük, Hungary 47 22n 16 45e
28 Buk, Poland 52 21n 16 30e
59 Bukachacha, U.S.S.R. 52 55n 116 50e
91 Bukana, Zaïre 9 10s 25 50e
90 Bukandula, Uganda 0 13n 31 50e
90 Bukavu, Zaïre 2 20s 28 52e
64 Bukedi ♦, Ugan. 1 3n 33 55e
90 Bukene, Tanzania 4 15s 32 48e
58 Bukhara, U.S.S.R. 39 50n 64 10e
90 Bukima, Tanzania 1 50s 33 25e

71 Bukit Mertajam, Malay. 5 22n 100 28e
72 Bukittinggi, Indonesia 0 20s 100 20e
70 Bukkapatnam, India 14 14n 77 46e
90 Bukoba, Tanzania 1 20s 31 49e
90 Bukoba ♦, Tanzania 1 30s 32 0e
47 Bukowno, Poland 50 17n 19 35e
87 Bukrale, Ethiopia 4 32n 42 0e
85 Bukuru, Nigeria 9 42n 8 48e
90 Bukuya, Uganda 0 40n 31 52e
84 Bula, Port. Guinea 12 7n 15 43w
75 Bulak, China 45 2n 82 5e
73 Bulan, Philippines 12 40n 123 52e
68 Bulandshahr, India 28 28n 77 58e
67 Bulantai, China 36 33n 92 18e
86 Bûlâq, Egypt 25 10n 30 38e
91 Bulawayo, Rhodesia 20 7s 28 32e
68 Buldana, India 20 30n 76 18e
76 Bulgan, Mongolia 48 35n 103 34e
43 Bulgaria ■, Europe 42 35s 25 30e
90 Bulgroo, Australia 25 47s 143 58e
63 Bulhar, Somali Rep. 10 25n 44 30e
73 Buli, Teluk, Indonesia 1 5n 128 25e
72 Buliluyan, C., Phil. 8 20n 117 15e
87 Bulki, Ethiopia 6 11n 36 31e
59 Bulkur, U.S.S.R. 71 50n 126 30e
117 Bull Shoals L., U.S.A. 36 40n 93 5w
31 Bullaque, R., Spain 39 20n 4 13w
33 Bullas, Spain 38 2n 1 40w
25 Bulle, Switzerland 46 37n 7 3e
98 Bullfinch, Australia 30 58s 119 3e
100 Bulli, Australia 34 15s 150 57e
98 Bullock Creek, Austral. 17 40s 144 30e
91 Bulloo, R., Australia 27 0s 144 40e
99 Bulloo Downs, Austral. 28 28s 143 0e
101 Bulls, New Zealand 40 10s 175 24e
19 Bully-les-Mines, France 50 27n 2 44e
124 Bulnes, Chile 36 42s 72 19w
90 Bulo Burti, Somali Rep. 3 50n 45 33e
98 Bulolo, New Guinea 7 10s 146 40e
98 Buloo Downs, Australia 28 30s 144 10e
44 Bulqiza, Albania 41 27n 20 18e
68 Bulsar, India 20 40n 72 58e
73 Bultfontein, S. Africa 28 18s 26 10e
73 Bulu Karakelong, Indon. 4 35n 126 50e
73 Bulun, Philippines 9 0n 125 30e
59 Bulun, U.S.S.R. 70 37n 127 30e
75 Bulun Tokchai =
Puluntohai, China 47 2n 87 29e
88 Bumba, Zaïre 2 13n 22 30e
91 Bumbiri I., Tanz. 1 40s 31 55e
119 Bumble Bee, U.S.A. 34 8n 112 18w
85 Bumhum, Nigeria 14 10n 8 10e
67 Bumhpa Bum, Burma 26 40n 97 20e
73 Bumi, R., Rhodesia 17 30s 28 30e
98 Buna, Papua 8 31s 148 30e
64 Bunaiyin, Saudi Arabia 23 10n 51 8e
100 Bunaloo, Australia 35 47s 144 35e
90 Bunazi, Tanzania 1 3s 31 23e
96 Bunbury, Australia 33 20s 115 35e
99 Buncrana, Ireland 55 8n 7 28w
99 Bundaberg, Australia 24 54s 152 22e
68 Bundi, India 25 30n 75 35e
15 Bundoran, Ireland 54 24n 8 17w
72 Bundukia, Sudan 5 14n 30 55e
100 Bundure, Australia 35 15s 146 2e
90 Bungendore, Australia 35 14s 149 30e
74 Bungo-Suidō, Japan 33 0n 132 15e
72 Bunguran N. Is., Indon. 4 45n 108 0e
98 Bungwahl, Australia 32 25s 153 0e
88 Bunia, Zaïre 1 35n 30 20e
66 Bunji, Kashmir 35 45n 74 40e
72 Bunju, Indonesia 3 35n 117 50e
116 Bunkerville, U.S.A. 36 47n 114 6w
117 Bunkie, U.S.A. 31 1n 92 12w
115 Bunnell, U.S.A. 29 28n 81 12w
31 Buñol, Spain 39 25n 0 47w
72 Buntok, Indonesia 1 40s 114 58e
85 Bununu, Nigeria 9 51n 9 32e
85 Bununu Doss, Nigeria 10 6n 9 25e
*90 Bunyoro ♦, Ugan. 1 45n 31 30e
23 Buol, Indonesia 1 15n 121 32e
85 Buórkhaya, Mys, U.S.S.R. 71 50n 133 10e

25 Burgdorf, Switzerland 47 3n 7 37e
27 Burgenland ♦, Austria 47 20n 16 20e
92 Burgersdorp, S. Africa 31 0s 26 20e
107 Burgeo, Canada 47 37n 57 38w
40 Búrgio, Italy 37 37n 13 18e
116 Butler, Mo., U.S.A. 38 17n 94 18w
25 Burglengenfeld, Ger. 49 11n 12 2e
30 Burgo de Osma, Spain 41 35n 3 4w
30 Burgohondo, Spain 40 26n 4 47w
32 Burgos, Spain 42 21n 3 41w
32 Burgos ♦, Spain 42 21n 3 42w
24 Burgstädt, Germany 50 55n 12 49e
52 Burgsteinfurt, Ger. 52 9n 7 23e
49 Burgsvik, Sweden 57 3n 18 19e
31 Burguillos del Cerro, Sp. 38 23n 6 35w
19 Burgundy = Bourgogne, France 47 0n 4 30e
68 Burhanpur, India 21 18n 76 20e
18 Burhou Rocks, Channel Islands, U.K. 49 45n 2 1w
87 Buri Pen., Ethiopia 15 25n 39 55e
73 Burias I., Philippines 12 55n 123 5e
90 Burigi, L., Tanzania 2 2s 31 22e
107 Burin, Canada 47 1n 55 14w
62 Burin, Jordan 32 11n 35 15e
87 Buriram, Thailand 15 0n 103 0e
87 Burji, Ethiopia 5 29n 37 51e
117 Burkburnett, U.S.A. 34 7n 98 35w
54 Burke, U.S.A. 43 11n 115 56w
98 Burke, R., Australia 22 35n 140 5e
98 Burketown, Australia 17 45s 139 33e
106 Burk's Falls, Canada 45 37n 79 10w
118 Burley, U.S.A. 42 37n 113 55w
112 Burlington, Canada 43 25n 79 45w
116 Burlington, Colo., U.S.A. 39 21n 102 18w
116 Burlington, Iowa, U.S.A. 40 50n 91 5w
116 Burlington, Kans., U.S.A. 38 15n 95 47w
115 Burlington, N.C., U.S.A. 36 7n 79 27w
113 Burlington, N.J., U.S.A. 40 5n 74 50w
113 Burlington, Vt., U.S.A. 44 27n 73 14w
118 Burlington, Wash., U.S.A. 48 29n 122 19w
114 Burlington, Wis., U.S.A. 42 41n 88 18w
59 Burlyu-Tyube, U.S.S.R. 46 30n 79 10e
67 Burma ■, Asia 21 0n 96 30e
54 Burnet, U.S.A. 30 45n 98 11w
115 Burney, U.S.A. 40 56n 121 41w
112 Burnham, U.S.A. 40 37n 77 34w
99 Burnie, Australia 41 4s 145 56e
12 Burnley, England 53 47n 2 15w
116 Burns, Oreg., U.S.A. 43 40n 119 4w
116 Burns, Wyo., U.S.A. 41 13n 104 18w
108 Burns L., Canada 54 20n 125 45w
112 Burnt, R., Canada 44 40n 78 42w
108 Burntwood L., Canada 55 35n 99 40w
62 Burqa, Jordan 32 18n 35 11e
100 Burra, Australia 33 40s 138 55e
100 Burracoppin, Australia 31 16s 118 30e
100 Burragorang, L., Australia 33 52s 150 37e
100 Burrendong Res., Australia 32 45s 149 10e
100 Burrewarra Pt., Austral. 35 50s 150 15e
32 Burriana, Spain 39 50n 0 4w
100 Burrinjuck Res., Australia 34 50s 148 45e
120 Burro, Serranías del, Mexico 29 0n 102 0w
64 Bursa, Turkey 40 15n 29 5e
49 Burseryd, Sweden 57 12n 13 17e
98 Burta, Australia 30 31s 141 5e
106 Burton L., Canada 54 45n 78 20w
12 Burton-upon-Trent, England 52 48n 1 39w
100 Burtundy, Australia 33 45s 142 15e
73 Buru, I., Indonesia 3 30s 126 30e
84 Burufu, Ghana 10 25n 2 50w
65 Burujird, Iran 33 58n 48 41e
86 Burullus, Bahra el, Egypt 31 25n 31 0e
90 Burundi ■, Africa 3 15s 30 0e
72 Burung, Indonesia 0 21n 108 25e
90 Burungi, Burundi 3 57s 29 37e
85 Burutu, Nigeria 5 20n 5 29e
116 Burwell, U.S.A. 41 49n 99 8w
12 Bury, England 53 36n 2 19w
12 Bury St. Edmunds, England 52 15n 0 42e
59 Buryat A.S.S.R. ♦, U.S.S.R. 53 0n 110 0e
28 Burzenin, Poland 51 28n 18 47e
39 Busalla, Italy 44 34n 8 58e
91 Busango Swamp, Zam. 14 15s 25 45e
64 Busayyah, Iraq 30 0n 46 10e
108 Busby, Canada 53 55n 114 0w
44 Bushati, Albania 41 58n 19 34e
119 Bushell, Canada 59 35n 108 35w
90 Bushenyi, Ugan. 0 35s 30 10e
116 Bushman Land, S. Afr. 29 30s 19 30e
116 Bushnell, Ill., U.S.A. 40 32s 90 30w
116 Bushnell, Nebr., U.S.A. 41 18n 103 50w
65 Bushrulyeh, Iran 33 55n 57 25e
90 Busia ♦, Kenya 0 25n 34 6e
84 Busie, Ghana 10 29n 2 22w
88 Businga, Zaïre 3 16n 20 59e
90 Busitema, Uganda 0 35s 34 2e
91 Bussang, France 47 50n 6 50e
96 Busselton, Australia 33 42s 115 15e
16 Bussum, Netherlands 52 16n 5 10e
98 Bustard Hd., Australia 24 0s 151 48e
30 Busto, C., Spain 43 34n 6 28w
39 Busto Arsizio, Italy 45 40n 8 50e
88 Busu-Djanoa, Zaïre 1 50n 21 5e
88 Büsum, Germany 54 7n 8 50e
90 Buta, Zaïre 2 50n 24 53e
90 Butare, Rwanda 2 31s 29 52e

*14 Bute ♦, Scot. 55 40n 5 10w
90 Butemba, Uganda 1 9n 31 37e
90 Butembo, Zaïre 0 9n 29 18e
41 Butera, Italy 37 10n 14 10e
90 Butiaba, Uganda 1 50n 31 20e
116 Butler, Mo., U.S.A. 38 17n 94 18w
112 Butler, Pa., U.S.A. 40 52n 79 52w
118 Butte, Mont., U.S.A. 46 0n 112 31w
116 Butte, Nebr., U.S.A. 42 56n 98 54w
71 Butterworth, Malaysia 5 24n 100 23e
93 Butterworth, S. Africa 32 20s 28 11e
73 Butung, Indonesia 8 57n 125 33e
73 Butung, I., Indonesia 5 0s 122 45e
55 Buturlinovka, U.S.S.R. 50 50n 40 35e
24 Butzbach, Germany 50 24n 8 40e
69 Buxar, India 25 34n 83 58e
92 Buxton, S. Afr. 27 38s 24 42e
12 Buxton, Eng. 53 16n 1 54w
19 Buxy, France 46 44n 4 40e
59 Buyaga, U.S.S.R. 59 50n 127 0e
44 Buyak Kemikli Burun, Turkey 40 20n 26 15e
57 Buynaksk, U.S.S.R. 42 36n 47 42e
76 Buyr Nuur, Mongolia 47 50n 117 35e
45 Büyük Cekmece, Tur. 37 45n 27 40e
18 Büyük Cekmece, Tur. 41 2n 28 35e
18 Buzançais, France 46 54n 1 25e
46 Buzău, Rumania 45 10n 26 50e
46 Buzău, R., Rumania 45 10n 27 20e
46 Buzău ♦, Rumania 45 20n 26 30e
46 Buzău, Pasul, Rumania 45 35n 26 12e
81 Buzaymah, Libya 24 35n 22 0e
74 Buzen, Japan 33 35n 131 5e
39 Buzet, Yugoslavia 45 24n 13 58e
91 Buzi, R., Mozambique 19 52s 34 30e
42 Buziaş, Rumania 45 38n 21 36e
52 Buzuluk, U.S.S.R. 52 48n 52 12e
55 Buzuluk, R., U.S.S.R. 50 50n 52 12e
113 Buzzards Bay, U.S.A. 41 45n 70 38w
91 Bwana Mkubwe, Zaïre 13 8s 28 38e
43 Byala, Bulgaria 42 53n 27 55e
43 Byala, Bulgaria 43 28n 25 44e
43 Byala Slatina, Bulgaria 43 26n 23 55e
57 Byandovan, Mys, U.S.S.R. 39 45n 49 28e
28 Bychawa, Poland 51 1n 22 36e
28 Bydgoszcz, Poland 53 10n 18 0e
28 Bydgoszcz ♦, Pol. 53 16n 17 33e
54 Byelorussia = White Russia, U.S.S.R. 53 30n 27 0e
116 Byers, U.S.A. 39 46n 104 13w
116 Byesville, U.S.A. 39 56n 81 32w
47 Bygland, Norway 58 50n 7 48e
47 Byglandsfjord, Norway 58 40n 7 50e
47 Byglandsfjorden, Nor. 58 44n 7 50e
117 Byhalia, U.S.A. 34 53n 89 41w
54 Bykhov, U.S.S.R. 53 31n 30 14e
47 Bykle, Norway 59 20n 7 22e
54 Bykovo, U.S.S.R. 49 50n 45 25e
119 Bylas, U.S.A. 33 11n 110 9w
105 Bylot I., Canada 73 0n 78 0w
5 Byrd Land = Marie Byrd Land, Ant. 79 30s 125 0w
5 Byrd Sub-Glacial Basin, Antarctica 82 0s 120 0w
107 Byrock, Australia 30 40s 146 27e
99 Byron B., Canada 54 42n 57 40w
99 Byron Bay, Australia 28 30s 153 30e
59 Byrranga, Gory, U.S.S.R. 75 0n 100 0e
49 Byrum, Denmark 57 16n 11 0e
50 Byske, R., Sweden 65 20n 20 0e
28 Bystrzyca Ktodzka, Pol. 50 19n 16 39e
62 Bytom, Poland 50 25n 19 0e
28 Bytom, Poland 50 25n 19 0e
54 Bytów, Poland 54 10n 17 30e
62 Bytom Ordz., Poland 51 44n 18 55e
71 Ca Mau = Quan Long, Vietnam 9 7n 105 8e
71 Ca Mau, Mui = Bai Bung, S. Vietnam 8 35n 104 42e
124 Caacupé, Paraguay 25 23n 57 5w
127 Caatingas, Brazil 7 0s 52 30w
125 Caazapá, Paraguay 26 8s 56 19w
30 Caballeria, Cabo de, Sp. 40 5n 4 5e
30 Cabañaquinta, Spain 43 10n 5 38w
32 Cabanatuan, Phil. 15 30n 121 5e
32 Cabanes, Spain 40 9n 0 2e
107 Cabano, Canada 47 40n 68 56w
126 Cabedelo, Brazil 7 0s 34 50w
33 Cabeza de Buey, Spain 38 44n 3 12w
31 Cabeza del Buey, Spain 38 44n 5 13w
124 Cabildo, Chile 32 30s 71 5w
126 Cabimas, Venezuela 10 30n 71 25w
88 Cabinda, Angola 5 33s 12 11e
118 Cabinet Mts., U.S.A. 48 0n 115 30w
128 Cabo Blanco, Arg. 47 56s 65 47w
91 Cabo Delgado ♦, Mozambique 10 35s 40 35e
125 Cabo Frio, Brazil 22 51s 42 3w
126 Cabo Pantoja, Peru 1 0s 75 10w
6 Cabo York, Peninsula del, Australia 13 30s 142 70e
106 Cabonga Reservoir, Canada 47 35n 76 40w
117 Cabool, U.S.A. 37 10n 92 8w
99 Caboolture, Australia 27 5s 152 47e
120 Caborca (Heroica), Mex. 30 40n 112 10w
112 Cabot Hd., Canada 45 14n 81 18w

* Renamed Bandar Seri Begawan   * Incorporated within the new Eastern Province   ** Incorporated within the new Western Province   * Incorporated within the region of Strathclyde

13

MAP

113 Cabot. Mt. U.S.A. 44 30N 71 25w
107 Cabot Strait. Canada 47 15N 59 40w
31 Cabra. Spain 38 30N 4 28w
33 Cabra del Santo Cristo, Spain 37 42N 3 16w
100 Cabramurra, Australia 35 58s 148 25E
40 Cábras. Italy 39 57N 8 30E
33 Cabrera. I. Spain 39 6N 2 59E
30 Cabrera. Sierra. Spain 42 12N 6 40w
109 Cabri. Canada 50 35N 108 25w
33 Cabriel. R.. Spain 39 20N 1 20w
127 Cabuyaro. Colombia 8 30s 39 20w
126 Cabruta. Venezuela 7 50N 66 10w
73 Caburan. Philippines 6 3N 125 45E
126 Cabuyaro. Colombia 4 18N 72 49w
30 Cacabelos. Spain 42 36N 6 44w
42 Cacak. Yugoslavia 43 54N 20 20E
126 Cáceres. Brazil 16 5s 57 40w
126 Cáceres. Colombia 7 35N 75 20w
31 Cáceres. Spain 39 26N 6 23w
31 Cáceres ♦. Spain 39 45N 6 0w
106 Cache B.. Canada 26 80 1w
31 Cachepo. Portugal 37 20N 7 49w
84 Cacheu. Port. Guinea 12 14N 16 8w
124 Cachi. Argentina 25 5s 66 10w
126 Cáchira. Colombia 7 21N 73 17w
127 Cachimbo. Serra do, Brazil 9 30s 55 0w
127 Cachoeira. Brazil 12 30s 39 0w
125 Cachoeira do Sul, Brazil 30 3s 52 53w
125 Cachoeiro de Itapemirim, Brazil 20 51s 41 7w
31 Cachopo. Portugal 37 20N 7 49w
88 Cacolo. Angola 10 9s 19 21E
89 Caconda. Angola 13 48s 15 8E
99 Cadarga. Australia 26 8s 150 58E
27 Cadca, Czechoslovakia 49 26N 18 45E
117 Caddo, U.S.A. 34 8N 96 18w
12 Cader Idris. Wales 52 43N 3 56w
120 Cadereyta Jiménez, Mexico 25 40N 100 0w
32 Cadí. Sierra del. Spain 42 17N 1 42E
106 Cadillac. Canada 49 45N 108 0w
20 Cadillac. France 44 38N 0 20w
114 Cadillac. U.S.A. 44 16N 85 25w
73 Cadiz. Philippines 11 30N 123 15E
31 Cádiz. Spain 36 30N 6 20w
112 Cádiz. U.S.A. 40 13N 81 0w
31 Cádiz. G. de. Spain 36 35N 6 20w
31 Cádiz ♦. Spain 36 36N 5 45w
108 Cadomin. Canada 52 59N 117 28w
20 Cadours. France 43 44N 1 2E
18 Caen. France 49 10N 0 22w
12 Caernarfon. Wales 53 8N 4 17w
12 Caernarfon B.. Wales 53 4N 4 40w
12 Caernarfon ♦. Wales 53 8N 4 17w
• 12 Caernarvon = Wales 53 8N 4 17w
62 Caesarea = Qesari. Israel 32 30N 34 53E
127 Caeté. Brazil 20 0s 43 40w
13 Caetité. Brazil 13 50s 42 50w
124 Cafayate. Argentina 26 2s 66 0w
126 Cafifi. Colombia 5 13N 71 4w
92 Cafu. Angola 16 30s 15 8E
73 Cagayan. R.. Philippines 18 25N 121 42E
73 Cagayan de Oro. Phil. 8 30N 124 40E
39 Cagli. Italy 43 32N 12 38E
40 Cágliari. Italy 39 15N 9 6E
40 Cágliari, G. di. Italy 39 8N 9 10E
41 Cagnano Varano, Italy 41 49N 15 47E
21 Cagnes-sur-Mer. France 43 40N 7 9E
126 Cagua. Venezuela 10 11N 67 27w
121 Caguas. Puerto Rico 18 14N 66 4w
15 Caha Mts.. Ireland 51 45N 9 40w
15 Cahir. Ireland 52 23N 7 56w
15 Cahirciveen. Ireland 51 57N 10 13w
15 Cahore Pt.. Ireland 52 34N 6 11w
20 Cahors. France 44 27N 1 27E
126 Cahuapanas. Peru 5 15s 77 0w
91 Caianda. Angola 11 29s 23 31E
121 Caibarién. Cuba 22 30N 79 30w
126 Caicara. Venezuela 7 50N 66 10w
127 Caicó. Brazil 6 20s 37 0w
121 Caicos Is.. West Indies 21 40N 71 40w
121 Caicos Passage. W. Ind. 22 45N 72 45w
128 Caihaique. Chile 45 30s 71 45w
112 Cainsville. Canada 43 9N 80 15w
5 Caird Coast. Antarctica 75 0s 25 0w
14 Cairn Gorm. Scot. 57 7N 3 40w
14 Cairn Toul. Scot. 57 3N 3 44w
14 Cairngorm Mts., Scotland 57 6N 3 42w
98 Cairns. Australia 16 55s 145 51E
86 Cairo = El Qahira. Egypt 30 1N 31 14E
115 Cairo. Ga.. U.S.A. 30 52N 84 12w
117 Cairo. Missouri, U.S.A. 37 0N 89 10w
38 Cairo Montenotte, Italy 44 23N 8 16E
† 14 Caithness ♦. Scot. 58 25N 3 35w
14 Caithness, Ord of C., Scotland 58 35N 3 37w
89 Caiundo, Angola 15 50s 17 52E
126 Caiza, Bolivia 21 50s 63 50w
126 Cajamarca, Peru 7 5s 78 28w
20 Cajarc. France 44 29N 1 50E
127 Cajázeiras. Brazil 7 0s 38 30w
42 Cajetina. Yugoslavia 43 47N 19 42E
42 Cajniče. Yugoslavia 43 34N 19 5E
57 Cakirgöl. Turkey 40 33N 39 40E
31 Cala. Spain 37 59N 6 21w
31 Cala, R.. Spain 37 50N 6 8w
85 Calabar. Nigeria 4 57N 8 20E
126 Calabozo. Venezuela 9 0N 67 28w
41 Calábria ♦. Italy 39 4N 16 30E
31 Calaburras, Pta. de. Spain 36 30N 4 38w
32 Calaceite. Spain 41 1N 0 11E
46 Calafat. Rumania 43 58N 22 59E
128 Calafate. Argentina 50 25s 72 25w
32 Calahorra. Spain 42 18N 1 59w
19 Calais. France 50 57N 1 56E

MAP

107 Calais, U.S.A. 45 5N 67 20w
118 Calais, Pas de, France 50 57N 1 20E
124 Calalaste, Sierra de, Arg. 25 0s 67 0w
124 Calama, Brazil 8 0s 62 50w
124 Calama, Chile 22 30s 68 55w
126 Calamar, Bolivar, Colombia 10 15N 74 55w
126 Calamar, Vaupés, Col. 1 58N 72 32w
73 Calamian Group, Phil. 11 50N 119 55E
32 Calamocha, Spain 40 50N 1 17w
126 Calanaque, Brazil 0 5s 64 0w
31 Calañas, Spain 37 40N 6 53w
25 Calanda, Spain 40 56N 0 15w
40 Calangianus, Italy 40 56N 9 12E
73 Calapan, Philippines 13 25N 121 7E
46 Cǎlǎraşi, Rumania 44 14N 27 23E
33 Calasparra, Spain 38 14N 1 41w
41 Calatafimi, Italy 37 56N 12 50E
32 Calatayud, Spain 41 20N 1 40w
73 Calauag, Philippines 13 55N 122 15E
41 Calava, C., Italy 38 11N 14 55E
73 Calavite, Cape, Phil. 13 26N 120 10E
77 Calayan, I., Philippines 19 20N 121 30E
24 Calbe, Germany 51 57N 11 47E
126 Calca, Peru 13 10s 72 0w
38 Calci, Italy 43 44N 10 31E
69 Calcutta, India 22 36N 88 24E
39 Caldaro, Italy 46 23N 11 15E
126 Caldas ♦, Colombia 5 15N 75 30w
31 Caldas da Rainha, Port. 39 24N 9 8w
30 Caldas de Reyes, Spain 42 36N 8 39w
12 Calder, R., Eng. 53 44N 1 57w
124 Caldera, Chile 27 5s 70 55w
64 Caldiran, Turkey 39 7N 44 0E
118 Caldwell, Idaho, U.S.A. 43 45N 116 42w
117 Caldwell, Kans., U.S.A. 37 5N 97 37w
117 Caldwell, Texas, U.S.A. 30 30N 96 42w
92 Caledon, S. Africa 34 14s 19 26E
92 Caledon B., Australia 12 45s 137 0E
92 Caledon, R., S. Africa 30 0s 26 46E
112 Caledonia, Canada 43 7N 79 58w
112 Caledonia, U.S.A. 42 57N 77 54w
32 Calella, Spain 41 37N 2 40E
92 Calemba, Angola 16 0s 15 38E
119 Calexico, U.S.A. 32 40N 115 33w
12 Calf of Man, Isle of Man 54 4N 4 48w
108 Calgary, Canada 51 0N 114 10w
115 Calhoun, U.S.A. 34 30N 84 55w
73 Calicoan, I., Philippines 10 59N 125 50E
70 Calicut, (Kozhikode), India 11 15N 75 43E
119 Caliente, U.S.A. 37 43N 114 34w
116 California, Mo., U.S.A. 38 37N 92 30w
112 California, Pa., U.S.A. 40 4N 79 55w
118 California ♦, U.S.A. 37 25N 120 0w
120 California, Baja, T.N. ♦, Mexico 30 0N 115 0w
120 California, Baja, T.S. ♦, Mexico 25 50N 111 50w
120 California, Golfo de, Mexico 27 0N 111 0w
120 California, Lr. = California, Baja, Mex. 25 50N 111 50w
124 Calilegua, Argentina 23 45s 64 42w
46 Cǎlimani, Munţii, Rumania 47 12N 25 0E
46 Cǎlineşti, Rumania 45 21N 24 18E
124 Calingasta, Argentina 31 15s 69 30w
119 Calipatria, U.S.A. 33 8N 115 30w
118 Calistoga, U.S.A. 38 36N 122 32w
41 Calitri, Italy 40 54N 15 25E
18 Callac, France 48 25N 3 27w
63 Callafo, Ethiopia 6 48N 43 47E
15 Callan, Ireland 52 33N 7 25w
126 Callao, Peru 12 0s 77 0w
116 Callaway, U.S.A. 41 20N 99 56w
98 Callide, Australia 24 23s 150 33E
108 Calling L., Canada 55 20N 113 20w
98 Calliope, Australia 24 0s 151 16E
33 Callosa de Ensarriá., Sp. 38 40N 0 8w
33 Callosa de Segura, Spain 38 1N 0 53w
92 Calola, Angola 16 25s 17 48E
41 Calore, R., Italy 41 8N 14 45E
99 Caloundra, Australia 26 45s 153 10E
31 Calpe, Spain 38 39N 0 8E
40 Caltabellotta, Italy 37 36N 13 11E
41 Caltagirone, Italy 37 13N 14 30E
41 Caltanissetta, Italy 37 30N 14 3E
21 Caluire-et-Cuire, Fr. 45 49N 4 51E
88 Calulo, Angola 10 1s 14 56E
88 Calunda, Angola 9 0s 13 20E
38 Caluso, Italy 45 18N 7 52E
18 Calvados ♦, Fr. 49 5N 0 15w
117 Calvert, U.S.A. 30 59N 96 50w
114 Calvert I., Canada 51 30N 128 0w
92 Calvinia, S. Africa 31 28s 19 45E
31 Calzada Almuradiel, Sp. 38 32N 3 28w
31 Calzada de Calatrava, Spain 38 42N 3 46w
13 Cam, R., Eng. 52 13N 0 9E
71 Cam Lam, (Ba Ngoi), S. Vietnam 5 0N 109 10E
71 Cam Ranh, S. Vietnam 11 54N 109 12E
88 Camabatela, Angola 8 20s 15 26E
121 Camaguëy, Cuba 21 20N 78 0w
126 Camaguán, Venezuela 8 6N 67 36w
126 Camaná, Peru 16 30s 72 50w
126 Camaquã, R., Brazil 30 50s 52 50w
18 Camaret, France 48 16s 4 37w
126 Camargo, Bolivia 20 38s 65 15w
21 Camargue, Fr. 43 34N 4 34E
30 Camariñas, Spain 43 8N 9 12w
121 Camarón, C., Honduras 16 0N 85 0w
128 Camarones, Argentina 44 50s 65 40w
128 Camarones, Chile 19 0s 69 58w
118 Camas, U.S.A. 45 35N 122 24w
118 Camas Valley, U.S.A. 43 0N 123 46w

MAP

30 Cambados, Spain 42 31N 8 49w
100 Cambalong, Australia 37 35s 149 10E
125 Cambará, Brazil 23 2s 53 5w
68 Cambay, India 22 23N 72 33E
68 Cambay, G. of, India 20 45N 72 30E
126 Cambuya, R., Peru 1 10s 74 0w
33 Cambil, Spain 37 40N 3 33w
*71 Cambodia = Khmer Rep. ■, S. E. Asia 12 15N 105 0E
50 Camborne, Eng. 50 13N 5 18w
19 Cambrai, France 50 11N 3 14E
119 Cambria, U.S.A. 35 36N 121 6w
12 Cambrian Mts., Wales 52 10N 3 52w
13 Cambridge, Eng. 52 13N 0 8E
101 Cambridge, N.Z. 37 54s 175 29E
118 Cambridge, Idaho, U.S.A. 44 36N 116 52w
114 Cambridge, Md., U.S.A. 38 33N 76 2w
114 Cambridge, Mass., U.S.A. 42 20N 71 8w
116 Cambridge, Minn., U.S.A. 45 34N 93 15w
116 Cambridge, Nebr., U.S.A. 40 20N 100 12w
113 Cambridge, N.Y., U.S.A. 43 2N 73 22w
112 Cambridge, Ohio, U.S.A. 40 1N 81 22w
13 Cambridge & Isle of Ely ♦, Eng. 52 21N 0 5E
104 Cambridge Bay, Can. 69 10N 105 0w
96 Cambridge Gulf, Australia 14 45s 128 0E
112 Cambridge Springs, U.S.A. 41 47N 80 4w
32 Cambrils, Spain 41 8N 1 3E
100 Camden, Australia 34 5s 150 38E
117 Camden, Ala., U.S.A. 31 59N 87 15w
117 Camden, Ark., U.S.A. 33 30N 92 50w
114 Camden, Me., U.S.A. 44 14N 69 6w
114 Camden, N.J., U.S.A. 39 57N 75 1w
115 Camden, S.C., U.S.A. 34 17N 80 34w
18 Camembert, France 48 53N 0 10E
39 Camerino, Italy 43 10N 13 4E
119 Cameron, Ariz., U.S.A. 35 55N 111 31w
117 Cameron, La., U.S.A. 29 50N 93 18w
117 Cameron, Mo., U.S.A. 39 42N 94 0w
117 Cameron, Tex., U.S.A. 30 53N 97 0w
106 Cameron Falls, Canada 49 8N 88 20w
71 Cameron Highlands, Malaya 4 27N 101 22E
108 Cameron Hills, Canada 60 20N 118 0w
88 Cameroon ■, Africa 3 30N 12 30E
41 Camerota, Italy 40 2N 15 21E
85 Cameroun, Mt., Cam. 4 45N 8 55E
85 Cameroun, R., Cam. 4 0N 9 35E
127 Cametá, Brazil 2 0s 49 30w
77 Camiguin, I., Phil. 19 55N 122 0E
30 Caminha, Portugal 41 50N 8 50w
30 Camino, U.S.A. 38 47N 120 40w
99 Camira Creek, Australia 29 15s 153 10E
112 Camlachie, Canada 43 3N 82 9w
112 Cammal, U.S.A. 41 24N 77 28w
127 Camocim, Brazil 2 55s 40 50w
38 Camogli, Italy 44 21N 9 9E
124 Camopi, R., Fr. Guiana 3 12N 52 17w
116 Camp Crook, U.S.A. 45 36N 103 59w
117 Camp Wood, U.S.A. 29 47N 100 0w
124 Campagna, Italy 40 40N 15 5E
124 Campana, Argentine 34 10s 58 55w
128 Campana, I., Chile 48 20s 75 10w
31 Campanario, Spain 38 52N 5 36w
41 Campania ♦, Italy 40 50N 14 45E
109 Campbell L., Canada 63 15N 106 25w
100 Campbell Town, Australia 41 52s 147 30E
112 Campbellford, Canada 44 17N 77 50w
114 Campbellsville, U.S.A. 37 23N 85 12w
108 Campbellton, Alta., Can. 53 32N 113 15w
107 Campbellton, N.B., Can. 47 57N 66 43w
14 Campbeltown, Scotland 55 25s 5 36w
120 Campeche, Mexico 19 50N 90 32w
120 Campeche, Golfo de, Mexico 19 30N 93 0w
120 Campeche ♦, Mexico 19 50N 90 32w
100 Camperdown, Australia 38 4s 143 12E
41 Campi Salentina, Italy 40 22N 180 2E
40 Campidano, Italy 39 30N 8 40E
38 Campiglia Marittima, Italy 43 3N 10 37E
32 Campillo de Altobuey, Spain 39 36N 1 49w
31 Campillo de Llerena, Spain 38 30N 5 50w
31 Campillos, Spain 37 4N 4 51w
127 Campina Grande, Brazil 7 20s 35 47w
125 Campinas, Brazil 22 50s 47 0w
127 Campinho, Brazil 14 30s 39 10w
39 Campli, Italy 42 44N 13 40E
88 Campo, Cameroon 2 15N 9 58E
127 Campo Belo, Brazil 21 0s 45 30w
33 Campo de Criptana, Sp. 39 25N 3 7w
31 Campo de Gibraltar, Spain 36 15N 5 25w
127 Campo Formoso, Brazil 10 30s 40 20w
127 Campo Grande, Brazil 20 25s 54 40w
127 Campo Maior, Brazil 4 50s 42 12w
31 Campo Maior, Portugal 39 6N 7 7w
39 Campo Túres, Italy 46 53N 11 30E
126 Campoalegre, Colombia 2 41N 75 20w
41 Campobasso, Italy 41 34N 14 40E
40 Campobello di Licata, Italy 37 16N 13 55E
124 Campobello di Mazara, Italy 37 38N 12 45E
40 Campofelice, Italy 37 54N 13 53E
40 Camporeale, Italy 37 54N 13 3E
127 Campos Belos, Brazil 13 10s 46 45w

MAP

33 Campos del Puerto, Sp. 39 26N 3 1E
125 Campos Novos, Brazil 27 21s 51 20w
32 Camprodón, Spain 42 19N 2 23E
46 Câmpurile, Rumania 46 5N 26 49E
108 Camrose, Canada 53 0N 112 50w
99 Camurra, Australia 29 21s 149 52E
71 Can Tho, S. Vietnam 10 2N 105 46E
113 Canaan, U.S.A. 42 1N 73 20w
104 Canada ■, N. Amer. 60 0N 100 0w
49 Cañada de Gómez, Arg. 32 55s 61 30w
117 Canadian, U.S.A. 35 56N 100 25w
117 Canadian, R., U.S.A. 35 27N 95 3w
107 Canairiktok, R., Can. 54 30N 62 30w
44 Çanakkale, Turkey 40 8N 26 30E
44 Çanakkale Boǧazi, Turkey 40 0N 26 0E
108 Canal Flats, Canada 50 10N 115 55w
19 Canal de l'Est, France 48 45N 5 35E
20 Canal latéral à la Garonne, France 44 25N 0 15E
124 Canalejas, Argentina 35 15s 66 34w
124 Canals, Argentina 33 35s 62 40w
33 Canáls, Spain 38 58N 0 35w
112 Canandaigua, U.S.A. 42 55N 77 18w
120 Cananea, Mexico 31 0N 110 20w
80 Canarias, Islas, Atlantic Ocean 29 30N 17 0w
121 Canarreos, Arch. de los, Cuba 21 35N 81 40w
80 Canary Is.=Canarias, Islas, Atlantic Oc. 29 30N 17 0w
115 Canaveral, C. = Kennedy, C., U.S.A. 28 28N 80 31w
127 Canavieiras, Brazil 15 39s 39 0w
100 Canbelego, Australia 31 32s 146 18E
100 Canberra, Australia 35 15s 149 8E
118 Canby, Calif., U.S.A. 41 26N 120 58w
116 Canby, Minn., U.S.A. 44 44N 96 15w
118 Canby, Oregon, U.S.A. 45 24N 122 45w
18 Cancale, France 48 40N 1 50w
45 Candea = Iráklion, Greece 35 20N 25 12E
41 Candela, Italy 41 8N 15 31E
125 Candelaria, Argentina 27 29s 55 44w
30 Candelaria, Pta. de la, Spain 43 45N 8 0w
30 Candeleda, Spain 40 10N 5 14w
46 Cândeşti, Rumania 45 15N 26 42E
45 Candia = Iráklion, Greece 35 20N 25 12E
116 Cando, U.S.A. 48 30N 99 14w
45 Canea = Khaniá, Greece 35 30N 24 4E
38 Canelli, Italy 44 44N 8 18E
125 Canelones, Uruguay 34 32s 56 10w
20 Canet-Plage, France 42 41N 3 2E
124 Cañete, Chile 37 50s 73 10w
126 Cañete, Peru 13 0s 76 30w
31 Cañete de las Torres, Sp. 37 53N 4 19w
32 Canfranc, Spain 42 42N 0 31w
89 Cangamba, Angola 13 40s 19 54E
30 Cangas, Spain 43 23N 5 17w
30 Cangas de Narcea, Sp. 43 10N 6 32w
30 Cangas de Onis, Spain 43 21N 5 8w
127 Canguaretama, Brazil 6 20s 35 5w
125 Canguçu, Brazil 31 22s 52 43w
38 Cani, Is., Tunisia 36 21N 10 5E
40 Canicatti, Italy 37 21N 13 50E
41 Canicattini, Italy 37 1N 15 3E
108 Canim L., Canada 51 45N 120 50w
72 Canipaan, Philippines 8 33N 117 15E
112 Canisteo, U.S.A. 42 17N 77 37w
112 Canisteo, R., U.S.A. 42 15N 77 30w
30 Cañizal, Spain 41 20N 5 22w
33 Canjáyar, Spain 37 1N 2 44w
64 Cankiri, Turkey 40 40N 33 30E
90 Cankuzo, Burundi 3 10s 30 31E
73 Canlaon, Mt., Philippines 9 27N 118 25E
108 Canmore, Canada 51 7N 115 18w
14 Canna I., Scot. 57 3N 6 33w
70 Cannanore, India 11 53N 75 27E
21 Cannes, France 43 32N 7 0E
96 Canning Basin, Austral. 19 50s 124 0E
69 Canning Town, India 22 23N 88 40E
112 Cannington, Canada 44 20N 79 2w
12 Cannock, Eng. 52 42N 2 2w
116 Cannon Ball, R., U.S.A. 46 20N 101 20w
126 Caño Colorado, Colombia 2 18N 68 22w
116 Canon City, U.S.A. 39 30N 105 20w
100 Canonba, Australia 31 21s 147 22E
98 Canonba, Australia 23 7s 150 17E
109 Canora, Canada 51 40N 102 30w
41 Canosa di Púglia, Italy 41 13N 16 4E
100 Canowinda, Australia 33 35s 148 38E
107 Canso, Canada 45 20N 61 0w
30 Cantabria, Sierra de, Spain 42 40N 2 30w
30 Cantábrica, Cordillera, Spain 43 0N 5 10w
30 Cantabrian Mts. = Cantábrica, Spain 43 0N 5 10w
20 Cantal ♦, France 45 4N 2 45E
30 Cantanhede, Portugal 40 20N 8 36w
126 Cantaura, Venezuela 9 19N 64 21w
30 Cantavieja, Spain 40 40N 0 25w
42 Cantavir, Yugoslavia 45 55N 19 46E
13 Canterbury, Eng. 51 17N 1 5E
101 Canterbury ♦, N.Z. 43 45s 171 19E
101 Canterbury Bight, N.Z. 44 16s 171 55E
101 Canterbury Plains, N.Z. 43 55s 171 22E
31 Cantillana, Spain 37 36N 5 50w

MAP

77 Canton = Kwangchow, China 23 10N 113 10E
115 Canton, Ga., U.S.A. 34 13N 84 29w
113 Canton, Ill., U.S.A. 40 32N 90 0w
113 Canton, Mass., U.S.A. 42 8N 71 8w
117 Canton, Miss., U.S.A. 32 40N 90 1w
116 Canton, Mo., U.S.A. 40 10N 91 33w
113 Canton, N.Y., U.S.A. 44 32N 75 3w
112 Canton, Ohio, U.S.A. 40 47N 81 22w
117 Canton, Okla., U.S.A. 36 5N 98 36w
116 Canton, S.D., U.S.A. 43 20N 96 35w
94 Canton I., Pac. Oc. 2 30s 172 0w
112 Canton L., U.S.A. 36 12N 98 40w
38 Cantù, Italy 45 44N 9 8E
127 Canudos, Brazil 7 13N 58 5w
126 Canutama, Brazil 6 30s 64 20w
119 Canutillo, U.S.A. 31 58N 106 36w
117 Canyon, Texas, U.S.A. 35 0N 101 57w
118 Canyon, Wyo., U.S.A. 44 43N 110 36w
119 Canyonlands Nat. Park, U.S.A. 38 25N 109 30w
118 Canyonville, U.S.A. 42 55N 123 14w
38 Canzo, Italy 45 54N 9 18E
107 Cap Chat, Canada 49 6N 66 40w
20 Cap Ferret, France 43 38N 1 15w
121 Cap Haïtien, Haiti 19 40N 72 20w
41 Capa Stilo, Italy 38 25N 16 25E
41 Capáccio, Italy 40 26N 15 4E
88 Capaia, Angola 8 27s 20 13E
126 Capanaparo, R., Ven. 7 0N 67 30w
126 Caparo, R., Venezuela 7 30N 70 30w
126 Capatárida, Ven. 11 11N 70 37w
20 Capbreton, France 43 39N 1 26w
20 Capdenac, France 44 34N 2 5E
96 Cape Barren I., Austral. 40 25s 184 15E
107 Cape Breton I., Can. 46 0N 61 0w
85 Cape Coast, Ghana 5 5N 1 15w
114 Cape Charles, U.S.A. 37 15N 75 59w
114 Cape Cod B., U.S.A. 41 50N 70 18w
105 Cape Dorset, Canada 64 30N 77 0w
105 Cape Dyer, Canada 66 30N 61 0w
117 Cape Fear, R., U.S.A. 34 30N 78 25w
117 Cape Girardeau, U.S.A. 37 20N 89 30w
100 Cape Jervis, S. Austral. 35 40s 138 5E
114 Cape May, U.S.A. 39 1N 74 53w
106 Cape Montague, Can. 46 5N 62 25w
84 Cape Palmas, Liberia 4 25N 7 49w
96 Cape Preston, Australia 20 51s 116 12E
92 Cape Province, S. Afr. 32 0s 23 0E
92 Cape Town (Kaapstad), S. Africa 33 55s 18 22E
6 Cape Verde Is., Atlantic Ocean 17 10N 25 20w
113 Cape Vincent, U.S.A. 44 9N 76 21w
98 C. York Pen., Australia 13 30s 142 30E
127 Capela, Brazil 10 15s 37 0w
98 Capella, Australia 23 2s 148 1E
98 Capella, G., W. Irian 4 45s 140 50E
20 Capendu, France 43 11N 2 31E
62 Capernaum = Kefar Nahum, Israel 32 54N 35 32E
20 Capestang, France 43 20N 3 2E
127 Capim, R., Brazil 3 0s 48 0w
119 Capitan, U.S.A. 33 40N 105 41w
42 Capizzi, Italy 37 50N 14 26E
42 Capljina, Yugoslavia 43 35N 17 43E
42 Capo Vaticano, Italy 38 37N 15 50E
91 Capoche, R., Mozam. 15 0s 32 45E
38 Capraia, I., Italy 43 2N 9 50E
38 Caprarola, Italy 42 21N 12 11E
41 Caprera, I., Italy 41 12N 9 28E
41 Capri, I., Italy 40 34N 14 15E
98 Capricorn, C. Australia 23 30s 151 13E
41 Caprino Veronese, Italy 45 37N 10 47E
42 Caprivi Strip, S.W. Afr. 18 0s 23 0E
69 Captainganj, India 26 55N 83 45E
100 Captain's Flat, Austral. 35 35s 149 27E
20 Captieux, France 44 18N 0 16w
41 Cápua, Italy 41 7N 14 5E
126 Caquetá ♦, Colombia 1 0N 74 0w
126 Caquetá, R., Colombia 1 0N 76 20w
126 Cáqueza, Colombia 4 25N 73 57w
46 Caracal, Rumania 44 8N 24 22E
126 Caracaraí, Brazil 1 50N 61 8w
126 Caracas, Venezuela 10 30N 66 55w
127 Caracol, Piauí, Brazil 9 15s 43 45w
126 Caracol, Rondonia, Brazil 9 15s 64 20w
99 Caradoc, Australia 30 35s 143 5E
100 Caragabal, Australia 33 54s 147 50E
100 Caraghan Mt., Australia 31 20s 148 52E
127 Carajás, Serra dos, Brazil 6 0s 51 30w
126 Caramanta, Colombia 5 33N 75 38w
125 Carangola, Brazil 20 56s 42 5w
46 Caransebeş, Rumania 45 28N 22 18E
41 Carapelle, R., Italy 41 20N 15 35E
42 Caraş Severin, Rumania 45 10N 22 10E
46 Carașova, Rumania 45 11N 21 51E
121 Caratasca, Laguna, Honduras 15 30N 83 40w
20 Caratec, France 48 40N 3 55w
127 Caraúbas, Paraiba, Braz. 7 43s 36 31w
38 Caravaca, Spain 38 8N 1 52w
38 Caravággio, Italy 45 30N 9 39E
127 Caravelas, Brazil 17 45s 39 15w
126 Caraveli, Peru 15 45s 73 25w
126 Carázinho, Brazil 28 0s 52 50w
30 Carballino, Spain 42 26N 8 5w
30 Carballo, Spain 43 13N 8 41w
109 Carberry, Canada 49 50N 99 25w
30 Carbia, Spain 42 48N 8 14w
108 Carbon, Canada 51 30N 113 20w
40 Carbonara, C., Italy 39 8N 9 30E

MAP
118 Carbondale, Colo., U.S.A. 39 30N 107 10w
117 Carbondale, Ill., U.S.A. 37 45N 89 10w
117 Carbondale, Pa., U.S.A. 41 37N 75 30w
107 Carbonear, Canada 47 42N 53 13w
33 Carboneras, Spain 37 0N 1 53w
33 Carboneras de Guadazaón, Spain 39 54N 1 50w
40 Carbonia, Italy 39 10N 8 30E
31 Carcabuey, Spain 37 27N 4 17w
33 Carcagente, Spain 39 8N 0 28w
108 Carcajou, Canada 57 45N 117 0w
121 Carcasse, C., Haiti 18 30N 74 28w
33 Carcassonne, France 43 13N 2 20E
33 Carche, Spain 38 26N 1 9w
104 Carcross, Canada 60 13N 134 45w
70 Cardamom Hills, India 9 30N 77 15E
33 Cardanete, Spain 39 42N 1 41w
121 Cárdenas, Cuba 23 0N 81 30w
121 Cárdenas, San Luis Potosí, Mexico 22 0N 99 41w
120 Cárdenas, Tabasco, Mexico 17 59N 93 21w
32 Cardenete, Spain 39 46N 1 41w
13 Cardiff, Wales 51 28N 3 11w
13 Cardigan, Wales 52 6N 4 41w
13 Cardigan B., Wales 52 30N 4 30w
•13 Cardigan ♦, Wales 52 6N 4 41w
13 Cardillo Downs, Australia 26 39s 140 35E
113 Cardinal, Canada 44 48N 75 24w
108 Cardón, Venezuela 11 37N 70 14w
104 Cardona, Spain 41 56N 1 40E
124 Cardona, Uruguay 33 53s 57 18w
32 Cardoner, R., Spain 42 0N 1 33E
109 Cardross, Canada 49 50N 105 40w
108 Cardston, Canada 49 15N 113 20w
98 Cardwell, Australia 18 14s 146 2E
46 Carei, Rumania 47 40N 22 29E
18 Carentan, France 49 19N 1 15w
118 Carey, Idaho, U.S.A. 43 19N 113 58w
114 Carey, Ohio, U.S.A. 40 58N 83 22w
96 Carey, L., Australia 29 0s 122 15E
84 Careysburg, Liberia 6 34N 10 30w
3 Cargados Garajos, Is., Indian Ocean 17 0s 59 0E
21 Cargèse, Corsica 42 7N 8 35E
18 Carhaix-Plouguer, France 48 18N 3 36w
124 Carhué, Argentina 37 10s 62 50w
126 Cariaco, Venezuela 10 29N 63 33w
126 Caribaná, Pta., Colombia 8 37N 76 52w
121 Caribbean Sea, W. Ind. 15 0N 75 0w
108 Cariboo Mts., Canada 53 0N 121 0w
109 Caribou, Canada 53 15N 121 55w
107 Caribou, U.S.A. 46 55N 68 0w
106 Caribou I., Canada 47 23N 85 48w
107 Caribou L., Canada 52 40N 90 40w
108 Caribou Mts., Canada 58 50N 115 40w
19 Carignan, France 49 38N 5 10E
38 Carignano, Italy 44 55N 7 40E
32 Cariñena, Spain 41 20N 1 13w
127 Carinhanha, Brazil 14 15s 44 0w
40 Carini, Italy 38 9N 13 10E
40 Carinola, Italy 41 11N 13 58E
26 Carinthia ♦ = Kärnten, Austria 46 52N 13 30E
126 Caripito, Venezuela 10 8N 63 6w
126 Caritianas, Brazil 9 20s 63 0w
127 Carius, Brazil 6 5s 39 30w
41 Carlentini, Italy 37 15N 15 2E
106 Carleton Place, Canada 45 8N 76 11w
92 Carletonville, S. Africa 26 23s 27 22E
118 Carlin, U.S.A. 40 50N 116 5w
15 Carlingford L., Ireland 54 0N 6 5w
116 Carlinville, U.S.A. 39 20N 89 55w
12 Carlisle, Eng. 54 54N 2 55w
112 Carlisle, U.S.A. 40 12N 77 10w
20 Carlitte, Pic, France 42 35N 1 43E
40 Carloforte, Italy 39 10N 8 18E
124 Carlos Casares, Arg. 35 53s 61 20w
124 Carlos Tejedor, Arg. 35 25s 62 25w
15 Carlow, Ireland 52 50N 6 58w
15 Carlow ♦, Ireland 52 43N 6 50w
119 Carlsbad, Calif., U.S.A. 33 11N 117 25w
117 Carlsbad, N. Mex., U.S.A. 32 20N 104 7w
109 Carlyle, Canada 49 40N 102 20w
116 Carlyle, U.S.A. 38 38N 89 23w
38 Carmagnola, Italy 44 50N 7 42E
109 Carman, Canada 49 30N 98 0w
108 Carmangay, Canada 50 10N 113 10w
107 Carmanville, Canada 49 23N 54 19w
13 Carmarthen, Wales 51 52N 4 20w
13 Carmarthen B., Wales 51 40N 4 30w
•13 Carmarthen ♦, Wales 53 40N 4 18w
20 Carmaux, France 44 3N 2 10E
119 Carmel, Calif., U.S.A. 36 38N 121 55w
113 Carmel, N.Y., U.S.A. 41 25N 73 38w
62 Carmel Mt., Israel 32 45N 35 3E
124 Carmelo, Uruguay 34 0s 58 10w
126 Carmen, Colombia 9 43N 75 8w
124 Carmen, Paraguay 27 13s 56 12w
120 Carmen, I., Mexico 26 0N 111 20w
128 Carmen de Patagones, Argentina 40 50s 63 0w
30 Cármenes, Spain 42 58N 5 34w
124 Carmensa, Argentina 35 15s 67 40w
114 Carmi, U.S.A. 38 6N 88 10w
98 Carmila, Australia 21 53s 149 5E
31 Carmona, Spain 37 28N 5 42w
92 Carnarvon, Queensland, Australia 25 0N 147 45E
96 Carnarvon, W. Austral., Australia 24 51s 113 42E
99 Carnarvon Ra., Queensland, Austral. 25 15s 148 30E

MAP
96 Carnegie L., Austral. 26 5s 122 30E
20 Carnon, France 43 32N 3 59E
88 Carnot, Cen. Afr. 4 59N 15 56E
96 Carnot B., Australia 17 20s 121 30E
15 Carnsore Pt., Ireland 52 10N 6 20w
114 Caro, U.S.A. 43 29N 83 27w
127 Carolina, Brazil 7 10s 47 30w
93 Carolina, S. Afr. 26 5s 30 6E
95 Caroline I., Pac. Ocean 9 15s 150 3w
94 Caroline Is., Pac. Ocean 8 0N 150 0E
108 Caroline, Canada 51 20N 111 40w
109 Caron, Canada 50 30N 105 50w
126 Caroni, R., Venezuela 6 0N 62 40w
126 Caroona, Australia 31 28s 150 5E
126 Carora, Venezuela 10 11N 70 5w
25 Carouge, Switzerland 46 11N 6 8E
41 Carovigno, Italy 40 42N 17 40w
113 Carp, Canada 45 20N 76 5w
38 Carpenédolo, Italy 45 22N 10 25E
99 Carpentaria, G. of, Australia 14 0s 139 0E
98 Carpentaria Downs, Australia 18 44s 144 20E
21 Carpentras, France 44 3N 5 2E
38 Carpi, Italy 44 47N 10 52E
41 Carpino, Italy 41 50N 15 51E
119 Carpinteria, U.S.A. 34 25N 119 37w
30 Carpio, Spain 41 13N 5 7w
100 Carpolac, Austral. 36 43s 141 18E
126 Carraipia, Colombia 11 16N 72 22w
15 Carrantuohill, Mt., Ire. 52 0N 9 49w
32 Carrara, Italy 44 5N 10 7E
32 Carrascosa del Campo, Spain 40 2N 2 45w
100 Carrathool, Australia 34 22s 145 30E
99 Carraweena, Australia 29 10s 140 0E
15 Carrickfergus, Northern Ireland 54 43N 5 50w
15 Carrickmacross, Ire. 54 0N 6 43w
99 Carrieton, Australia 32 27s 138 27E
30 Carrington, U.S.A. 47 30N 99 7w
30 Carrión, R., Spain 42 42N 4 47w
30 Carrión de los Condes, Spain 42 20N 4 37w
126 Carrizal, Colombia 12 1N 72 11w
124 Carrizal Bajo, Chile 28 5s 71 20w
124 Carrizalillo, Chile 29 0s 71 30w
117 Carrizo Cr., U.S.A. 36 30N 103 40w
117 Carrizo Springs, U.S.A. 28 28N 99 50w
117 Carrizozo, U.S.A. 33 40N 105 57w
116 Carroll, U.S.A. 42 2N 94 55w
115 Carrollton, Ga., U.S.A. 33 36N 85 5w
116 Carrollton, Ill., U.S.A. 39 20N 90 25w
114 Carrollton, Ky., U.S.A. 38 40N 85 10w
116 Carrollton, Mo., U.S.A. 39 19N 93 30w
112 Carrollton, Ohio, U.S.A. 40 31N 81 9w
14 Carron L., Scot. 57 22s 5 35w
14 Carron R., Scot. 57 30N 5 30w
14 Carrouges, France 48 34N 0 10w
64 Çarşamba, Turkey 41 15N 36 45E
116 Carson, U.S.A. 46 27N 101 29w
118 Carson City, U.S.A. 39 12N 119 52w
118 Carson Sink, U.S.A. 39 50N 118 40w
114 Carsonville, U.S.A. 43 25N 82 39w
14 Carstairs, Scot. 55 42N 3 41w
126 Cartagena, Colombia 10 25N 75 33w
33 Cartagena, Spain 37 38N 0 59w
126 Cartago, Colombia 4 45N 75 55w
121 Cartago, Costa Rica 9 50N 84 0w
31 Cartaxo, Portugal 39 10N 8 47w
31 Cartaya, Spain 37 16N 7 9w
14 Carter Fell, Scot. 55 21N 2 27w
115 Cartersville, U.S.A. 34 11N 84 48w
101 Carterton, N.Z. 41 2s 175 31E
116 Carthage, Ark., U.S.A. 34 4N 92 32w
116 Carthage, Ill., U.S.A. 40 25N 91 10w
117 Carthage, Mo., U.S.A. 37 10N 94 20w
113 Carthage, N.Y., U.S.A. 43 59N 75 37w
116 Carthage, S.D., U.S.A. 44 14N 97 38w
117 Carthage, Texas, U.S.A. 32 8N 94 20w
96 Cartier I., Australia 12 31s 123 29E
127 Cartwright, Canada 53 41N 56 58w
127 Caruaru, Brazil 8 15s 35 55w
126 Carúpano, Venezuela 10 45N 63 15w
116 Caruthersville, U.S.A. 36 10N 89 40w
19 Carvarzere, Italy 45 8N 12 7E
19 Carvin, France 50 30N 2 57E
31 Carvoeiro, Cabo, Port. 39 21N 9 24w
127 Carvoeiro, Brazil 1 30s 61 59w
126 Casa Agapito, Colombia 2 3N 73 58w
31 Casa Branca, Portugal 38 29N 8 12w
119 Casa Grande, U.S.A. 32 53N 111 51w
127 Casa Nova, Brazil 9 10s 41 5w
124 Casablanca, Chile 33 20s 71 25w
82 Casablanca, Morocco 33 36N 7 36w
41 Casacalenda, Italy 41 45N 14 50E
39 Casalbordino, Italy 42 10N 14 34E
38 Casale Monferrato, Italy 45 8N 8 28E
38 Casalmaggiore, Italy 44 59N 10 25E
38 Casalpusterlengo, Italy 45 10N 9 40E
84 Casamance, R., Senegal 12 54N 15 0w
41 Casamássima, Italy 40 58N 16 55E
126 Casanare, R., Col. 6 30N 71 20w
41 Casarano, Italy 40 0N 18 10E
31 Casares, Spain 36 27N 5 16w
120 Casas Grandes, Mexico 30 22N 108 0w
33 Casas Ibáñez, Spain 39 17N 1 30w
33 Casasimarro, Spain 39 22N 2 3w
30 Casatejada, Spain 39 54N 5 40w
30 Casavieja, Spain 40 17N 4 46w
118 Cascade, Idaho, U.S.A. 44 30N 116 2w
118 Cascade, Mont., U.S.A. 47 16N 111 46w
118 Cascade Locks, U.S.A. 45 44N 121 5w
118 Cascade Ra., U.S.A. 44 0N 122 10w
31 Cascais, Portugal 38 41N 9 25w

MAP
38 Cascina, Italy 43 40N 10 32E
38 Caselle Tormese, Italy 45 12N 7 39E
41 Caserta, Italy 41 5N 14 20E
15 Cashel, Ireland 52 31N 7 53w
118 Cashmere, U.S.A. 47 31N 120 30w
126 Casigua, Venezuela 11 2N 71 1w
73 Casiguran, Philippines 16 15N 122 15E
124 Casilda, Argentina 33 10s 61 10w
46 Casimcea, Rumania 44 45N 28 23E
99 Casino, Austral. 28 52s 153 3E
126 Casiquiare, R., Ven. 2 45N 66 20w
126 Casma, Peru 9 30s 78 20w
39 Casola Valsenio, Italy 44 12N 11 40E
39 Càsoli, Italy 42 7N 14 18E
32 Caspe, Spain 41 14N 0 1w
118 Casper, U.S.A. 42 52N 106 27w
53 Caspian Sea, U.S.S.R. 43 0N 50 0E
18 Casquets, Channel Islands 49 46N 2 15w
114 Cass City, U.S.A. 43 34N 83 15w
116 Cass Lake, U.S.A. 47 23N 94 38w
32 Cassá de la Selva, Spain 41 53N 2 52E
41 Cassanoallonio, Italy 39 47N 16 20E
19 Cassel, France 50 48N 2 30E
113 Casselman, Canada 45 18N 75 21w
116 Casselton, U.S.A. 47 0N 97 15w
108 Cassiar, Canada 59 16N 129 40w
108 Cassiar Mts., Canada 59 30N 130 30w
100 Cassilis, Austral. 32 3s 149 58E
108 Cassils, Canada 50 29N 112 15w
89 Cassinga, Angola 15 5s 16 23E
43 Cassino, Italy 41 30N 13 50E
127 Cassiporé, C., Brazil 3 50N 51 5w
21 Cassis, France 43 14N 5 32E
117 Cassville, U.S.A. 36 45N 93 59w
38 Cástagneto Carducci, It. 43 9N 10 36E
126 Castanheiro, Brazil 0 17s 65 38w
38 Castéggio, Italy 45 1N 9 8E
32 Castejón de Monegros, Spain 41 37N 0 15w
41 Castel di Sangro, Italy 41 41N 14 5E
38 Castel San Giovanni, It. 43 4N 9 25E
39 Castel San Pietro, Italy 44 23N 11 30E
41 Castelbuono, Italy 37 56N 14 4E
40 Casteldelfino, Italy 44 35N 7 4E
38 Castelfiorentino, Italy 43 36N 10 58E
38 Castelfranco Emilia, It. 44 37N 11 2E
19 Castelfranco Veneto, It. 45 40N 11 56E
20 Casteljaloux, France 44 19N 0 6E
40 Castellabate, Italy 40 18N 14 55E
40 Castellammare, G. di, It. 38 5N 12 55E
40 Castellammare del Golfo, Italy 38 2N 12 53E
41 Castellammare di Stábia, Italy 40 47N 14 29E
38 Castellamonte, Italy 45 23N 7 42E
41 Castellana Grotte, Italy 40 53N 17 10E
21 Castellane, France 43 50N 6 31E
41 Castellaneta, Italy 40 40N 16 57E
33 Castellar de Santisteban, Spain 38 16N 3 8w
38 Castelleone, Italy 45 19N 9 47E
124 Castelli, Argentina 36 7s 57 47w
32 Castelló de Ampurias, Spain 42 15N 3 4E
32 Castellón ♦, Spain 40 15N 0 5w
32 Castellón de la Plana, Spain 39 58N 0 3w
40 Castellote, Spain 40 48N 0 15w
32 Castelltersol, Spain 41 45N 2 8E
41 Castelmáuro, Italy 41 50N 14 40E
20 Castelnau-de-Médoc, Fr. 45 2N 0 48w
20 Castelnaudary, France 43 20N 1 58E
38 Castelnovo ne' Monti, Italy 44 27N 10 26E
38 Castelnuovo di Val di Cécina, Italy 43 12N 10 54E
30 Castelo Branco, Port. 39 50N 7 31w
31 Castelo Branco ♦, Portugal 39 52N 7 45w
31 Castelo de Paiva, Port. 41 2N 8 16w
31 Castelo de Vide, Port. 39 25N 7 27w
20 Castelsarrasin, France 44 2N 1 7E
40 Casteltérmini, Italy 37 32N 13 38E
40 Castelvetrano, Italy 37 40N 12 46E
100 Casterton, Australia 37 30s 141 30E
20 Castets, France 43 52N 1 6w
39 Castiblanco, Spain 39 17N 5 5w
39 Castiglione del Lago, It. 43 7N 12 3E
38 Castiglione della Pescáia, Italy 42 46N 10 53E
38 Castiglione della Stiviere, Italy 45 23N 10 30E
38 Castiglione Fiorentino, Italy 43 20N 11 55E
31 Castilblanco, Spain 39 17N 5 5w
31 Castilla La Nueva, Spain 39 45N 3 20w
31 Castilla La Vieja, Spain 41 55N 4 0w
126 Castilletes, Venezuela 11 51N 71 19w
30 Castille = Castilla, Spain 40 0N 3 30w
20 Castillon-en-Couserans, France 42 56N 1 1E
20 Castillon-la-Bataille, France 44 51N 0 2w
20 Castillonnés, France 44 39N 0 37E
32 Castillos, Uruguay 34 12s 53 52w
118 Castle Dale, U.S.A. 39 11N 111 1w
14 Castle Douglas, Scotland 54 57N 3 57w
121 Castle Harbour, Bermuda 32 17N 64 44w
101 Castle Point, New Zealand 40 54N 176 15E
118 Castle Rock, Colo., U.S.A. 39 26N 104 50w
118 Castle Rock, Wash., U.S.A. 46 20N 122 58w
15 Castlebar, Ireland 53 52N 9 17w

MAP
15 Castleblayney, Ireland 54 7N 6 44w
108 Castlegar, Canada 49 20N 117 40w
118 Castlegate, U.S.A. 39 45N 110 57w
100 Castlemaine, Australia 37 2s 144 12E
15 Castlereagh, Ireland 53 47N 8 30w
96 Castlereagh B., Austral. 12 10s 135 10E
100 Castlereagh, R., Austral. 30 30s 148 14E
113 Castleton, U.S.A. 42 33N 73 44w
12 Castletown, Isle of Man 54 4N 4 40w
108 Castlevale, Australia 24 30s 146 48E
108 Castor, Canada 52 15N 111 50w
41 Castres, France 43 37N 2 13E
121 Castries, West Indies 14 0N 60 50w
33 Castril, Spain 37 48N 2 46w
127 Castro, Brazil 24 45s 50 0w
128 Castro, Chile 42 30s 73 50w
31 Castro Alves, Brazil 12 46s 39 26w
31 Castro del Río, Spain 37 41N 4 29w
31 Castro Marim, Portugal 37 13N 7 26w
30 Castro Urdiales, Spain 43 23N 3 19w
31 Castro Verde, Portugal 37 41N 8 4w
32 Castrojeriz, Spain 42 17N 4 9w
30 Castropol, Spain 43 32N 7 0w
41 Castrop-Rauxel, Ger. 51 34N 7 19E
41 Castrovillari, Italy 39 49N 16 11E
31 Castroville, U.S.A. 29 20N 98 53w
31 Castuera, Spain 38 43N 5 37w
121 Cat I., Bahamas 24 30N 75 30w
73 Cat I., Philippines 10 15N 123 48E
106 Cat L., Canada 51 40N 91 50w
7 Cata, Czechoslovakia 47 58N 18 38E
126 Catacaos, Peru 5 20s 80 45w
21 Cataguases, Brazil 21 23s 42 39w
117 Catahoula L., U.S.A. 31 30N 92 5w
126 Catalão, Brazil 18 10s 47 57w
64 Catalca, Turkey 41 9N 28 28E
32 Catalonia = Cataluña, Spain 41 40N 1 15E
32 Cataluña ♦, Spain 41 40N 1 15E
124 Catamarca, Argentina 28 30s 65 50w
124 Catamarca ♦, Arg. 28 30s 65 50w
73 Catanduanes Is., Phil. 13 50N 124 20E
126 Catanduva, Brazil 21 5s 48 58w
41 Catánia, Italy 37 31N 15 4E
41 Catánia, G. di, Italy 37 25N 15 8E
41 Catanzaro, Italy 38 54N 16 38E
73 Catarman, Philippines 12 28N 124 1E
96 Catastrophe C., Austral. 34 59s 136 0E
73 Cateel, Philippines 7 47N 126 24E
92 Cathcart, S. Africa 32 18s 27 10E
100 Cathkin, Australia 37 9s 145 6E
17 Catine, France 46 30N 0 15w
84 Catio, Port. Guinea 11 17N 15 15w
126 Catismiña, Venezuela 4 5N 63 52w
120 Cativa, Panama 9 21N 79 49w
114 Catlettsburg, U.S.A. 38 23N 82 38w
98 Cato I., Australia 23 15s 155 32E
21 Catoche, C., Mexico 21 40N 87 0w
100 Catrimani, Brazil 0 27N 61 41w
126 Catskill, U.S.A. 42 14N 73 52w
42 Catskill Mts., U.S.A. 42 15N 74 15w
112 Cattaraugus, U.S.A. 42 22N 78 52w
39 Cáttolica, Italy 43 58N 12 43E
40 Cattólica Eraclea, Italy 37 27N 13 24E
92 Catuala, Angola 16 25s 19 2E
91 Catur, Mozambique 13 45s 35 30E
126 Cauca ♦, Colombia 2 30N 76 50w
126 Cauca, R., Colombia 8 0N 75 12w
126 Caucasia, Colombia 8 0N 75 12w
57 Caucasus Mts. = Bolshoi Kavkas, U.S.S.R. 42 50N 44 0E
19 Caudebec-en-Caux, France 49 30N 0 42E
19 Caudry, France 50 7N 3 22E
18 Caulnes, France 48 18N 2 10w
41 Caulónia, Italy 38 23N 16 25E
88 Caungula, Angola 8 15s 18 50E
124 Cáuquenes, Chile 36 0s 72 30w
126 Caura, R., Venezuela 6 20N 64 30w
91 Cauresi, R., Mozam. 17 40s 33 10E
107 Causapscal, Canada 48 19N 67 12w
20 Caussade, France 44 10N 1 33E
20 Cauterets, France 42 52N 0 8w
18 Caux, France 49 38N 0 35E
21 Cavaillon, France 43 50N 5 2E
21 Cavalaire-sur-Mer, France 43 10N 6 33E
41 Cava dei Tirreni, Italy 40 42N 14 42E
39 Cavalese, Italy 46 17N 11 29E
84 Cavally, R., Liberia 5 0N 7 40w
15 Cavan, Ireland 54 0N 7 22w
15 Cavan ♦, Ireland 53 58N 7 10w
114 Cave City, U.S.A. 37 13N 85 57w
100 Cavendish, Australia 37 31s 142 2E
106 Cavers, Canada 48 55N 87 41w
127 Caviana, Ilha, Brazil 0.15N 50 0w
73 Cavite, Philippines 14 20N 120 55E
38 Cavour, Italy 44 47N 7 22E
42 Cavtat, Yugoslavia 42 35N 18 13E
100 Cawndilla, L., Austral. 32 30s 142 15E
69 Cawnpore = Kanpur, India 26 35N 80 20E
126 Caxias, Braz. 5 0s 43 27w
126 Caxias do Sul, Brazil 29 10s 51 10w
82 Caxine, C., Algeria 35 56N 0 27w
88 Caxito, Angola 8 30s 13 30E
127 Cayambe, Ecuador 0 3N 78 22w
115 Cayce, U.S.A. 33 59N 81 2w
127 Cayenne, Fr. Guiana 5 0N 52 18w
19 Cayeux-sur-Mer., France 50 10N 1 30E
20 Caylus, France 44 15N 1 47E
121 Cayman Is., W. Indies 19 40N 79 50w
120 Cayo, Brit. Honduras 17 10N 89 0w

MAP
121 Cayo Romano, I., Cuba 22 0N 73 30w
112 Cayuga, Canada 42 59N 79 50w
113 Cayuga, U.S.A. 42 54N 76 44w
113 Cayuga L., U.S.A. 42 45N 76 45w
31 Cazalla de la Sierra, Sp. 37 56N 5 45w
46 Căzăneşti, Rumania 44 36N 27 3E
20 Cazaux et de Sanguinet, Etang de, France 44 29N 1 10w
20 Cazères, France 43 13N 1 5E
39 Cazin, Yugoslavia 44 57N 15 57E
42 Cazma, Yugoslavia 45 45N 16 39E
89 Cazombo, Angola 12 0s 22 48E
33 Cazorla, Spain 37 55N 3 2w
126 Cazorla, Venezuela 8 1N 67 0w
33 Cazorla, Sierra de, Spain 38 5N 2 55w
30 Cea, R., Spain 42 40N 5 5w
16 Ceadâr Lunga, U.S.S.R. 46 2N 28 46E
43 Ceamurlia de Jos, Rumania 44 43N 28 47E
15 Ceanannus Mor, Ireland 53 42N 6 53w
127 Ceará ♦, Brazil 5 0s 40 0w
127 Ceará Mirim, Brazil 5 38s 35 25w
32 Cebollera, Sierra de, Spain 42 0N 2 30w
30 Cebreros, Spain 40 27N 4 28w
73 Cebú, Philippines 10 18N 123 54E
73 Cebú, I., Philippines 10 15N 123 40E
40 Ceccano, Italy 41 34N 13 18E
27 Cece, Hungary 46 46N 18 39E
84 Cechi, Ivory Coast 6 15N 4 25w
99 Cecil Plains, Australia 27 30s 151 11E
38 Cécina, Italy 43 19N 10 33E
38 Cécina, R., Italy 43 19N 10 40E
30 Ceclavín, Spain 39 50N 6 45w
109 Cedar L., Canada 53 10N 100 30w
116 Cedar, R., U.S.A. 41 50N 91 20w
119 Cedar City, U.S.A. 37 41N 113 3w
117 Cedar Creek Res., U.S.A. 32 15N 96 0w
116 Cedar Falls, U.S.A. 42 39N 92 29w
115 Cedar Key, U.S.A. 29 9N 83 5w
116 Cedar Rapids, U.S.A. 42 0N 91 38w
115 Cedartown, U.S.A. 34 1N 85 15w
108 Cedarvale, Canada 55 1N 128 22w
118 Cedarville, U.S.A. 41 37N 120 13w
30 Cedeira, Spain 43 39N 8 2w
120 Cedral, Mexico 23 50N 100 42w
40 Cedrino, R., Italy 40 8N 9 25E
17 Cedro, Brazil 6 34s 39 3w
120 Cedros, I. de, Mexico 28 10N 115 20w
96 Ceduna, Australia 32 7s 133 46E
108 Ceepeecee, Canada 49 52N 126 42w
15 Cedynia, Poland 52 53N 14 12E
41 Céfalù, Italy 38 3N 14 1E
30 Cega, R., Spain 41 17N 4 10w
27 Ceglèd, Hungary 47 11N 19 47E
41 Céglie Messápico, Italy 40 39N 17 31E
46 Cehu Silvaniei, Rum. 47 24N 23 9E
46 Ceica, Rumania 46 53N 22 10E
30 Ceira, R., Portugal 40 15N 7 55w
83 Cekhira, Tunisia 34 20N 10 5E
42 Celano, Italy 42 6N 13 30E
30 Celanova, Spain 42 9N 7 58w
73 Celebes I. = Sulawesi, Indonesia 2 0s 120 0E
73 Celebes Sea, Indonesia 3 0N 123 0E
87 Celga, Ethiopia 12 38N 37 3E
42 Celic, Yugoslavia 44 43N 18 47E
114 Celina, U.S.A. 40 32N 84 31w
42 Celje, Yugoslavia 46 16N 15 18E
27 Celldömölk, Hungary 47 16N 17 10E
24 Celle, Germany 52 37N 10 4E
30 Celorica da Beira, Port. 40 38N 7 24w
117 Cement, U.S.A. 34 56N 98 8w
18 Cenis, Col du Mt., France 45 15N 6 55E
38 Ceno, R., Italy 44 40N 9 52E
20 Cenon, France 44 50N 0 33w
41 Centallo, Italy 44 30N 7 35E
116 Center, N.D., U.S.A. 47 9N 101 17w
117 Center, Texas, U.S.A. 31 50N 94 10w
116 Centerfield, U.S.A. 39 9N 111 56w
115 Centerville, Ala., U.S.A. 32 55N 87 7w
116 Centerville, Iowa, U.S.A. 40 45N 92 57w
112 Centerville, Pa., U.S.A. 40 3N 79 59w
116 Centerville, S.D., U.S.A. 43 10N 96 58w
115 Centerville, Tenn., U.S.A. 35 46N 87 29w
117 Centerville, Tex., U.S.A. 31 15N 95 56w
39 Cento San Giovanni, It. 44 43N 11 16E
90 Central ♦, Kenya 0 30s 33 30E
90 Central ♦, Malawi 13 30s 33 30E
91 Central ♦, Zambia 14 25s 28 50E
88 Central African Republic ■, Africa 7 0N 20 0E
114 Central City, Ky., U.S.A. 37 20N 87 7w
116 Central City, Nebr., U.S.A. 41 8N 98 0w
90 Central I., L. Rudolf, Kenya 3 30N 36 0E
113 Central Islip, U.S.A. 40 49N 63 13w
66 Central Makran Range, Pakistan 26 30N 64 15E
106 Central Patricia, Can. 51 20N 90 10w
98 Central Ra., New Guinea 5 0s 143 0E
9 Central Russian Uplands, Europe 54 0N 36 0E
59 Central Siberian Plateau, U.S.S.R. 65 0N 105 0E
116 Centralia, Ill., U.S.A. 38 32N 89 5w
116 Centralia, Mo., U.S.A. 39 12N 92 8w
118 Centralia, Wash., U.S.A. 46 46N 122 59w
41 Centúripe, Italy 37 37N 14 41E

* Incorporated within the county of Dyfed

MAP
45 Cephalonia = Kefallinía, 38 28N 20 30E
   Greece
42 Cepin, Yugoslavia 45 32N 18 34E
40 Ceprano, Italy 41 33N 13 30E
46 Ceptura, Rumania 45 1N 26 21E
73 Ceram I. = Seram I., 3 10S 129 0E
   Indon.
73 Ceram Sea, Indonesia 2 30S 128 30E
20 Cerbère, France 42 26N 3 10E
21 Cerbicales, Iles, France 41 33N 9 22E
46 Cerbu, Rumania 44 46N 24 46E
31 Cercal, Portugal 37 48N 8 40w
41 Cercemaggiore, Italy 41 27N 14 43E
32 Cerdaña, Spain 42 22N 1 35E
30 Cerdedo, Spain 42 33N 8 23w
39 Cerea, Italy 45 12N 11 13E
124 Ceres, Argentina 29 55S 61 55w
38 Ceres, Italy 45 19N 7 22E
92 Ceres, S. Afr. 33 21S 19 18E
38 Ceres, Italy 45 19N 7 22E
20 Céret, France 42 30N 2 42E
126 Cerete, Colombia 8 53N 75 48w
45 Cerigo = Kithira, 36 9N 23 0E
   Greece
41 Cerignola, Italy 41 17N 15 53E
20 Cérilly, France 46 37N 2 50E
19 Cerisiers, France 48 8N 3 30E
18 Cerizay, France 46 50N 0 40w
39 Cerknica, Yugoslavia 45 48N 14 21E
42 Cermerno, Y.-slav. 43 35N 20 25E
46 Cerna, Rumania 44 4N 28 17E
46 Cerna, R., Rumania 44 45N 24 0E
46 Cernavodă, Rumania 44 22N 28 3E
19 Cernay, France 47 44N 7 10E
42 Cernik, Yugoslavia 45 17N 17 22E
120 Cerralvo, I., Mexico 24 20N 109 45E
41 Cerreto Sannita, Italy 41 17N 14 34E
120 Cerritos, Mexico 22 20N 100 20w
119 Cerro, U.S.A. 36 47N 105 36w
126 Cerro Bolivar, Ven. 7 35N 62 45w
38 Certaldo, Italy 43 32N 11 2E
41 Cervaro, R., Italy 41 21N 15 30E
32 Cerveza, Sp. 41 40N 1 16E
30 Cervera de Pisuerga, Sp. 42 51N 4 30w
32 Cervera del Rio Alhama, 42 2N 1 58w
   Spain
39 Cérvia, Italy 44 15N 12 20E
39 Cervignano del Friuli, 45 49N 13 20E
   Italy
41 Cervinara, Italy 41 2N 14 36E
21 Cervoine, France 42 20N 9 29E
30 Cervo, Spain 43 40N 7 24w
40 Cervo, Pto., Italy 41 7N 9 30E
126 César ♦, Colombia 9 0N 73 30w
41 Cesaro, Italy 37 50N 14 38E
39 Cesena, Italy 44 9N 12 14E
39 Cesenático, Italy 44 12N 12 22E
39 Cesanático, Italy 44 12N 12 22E
54 Cēsis, U.S.S.R. 57 17N 25 28E
26 Ceská Lipa, Cz. 50 43N 14 35E
26 Ceská Socialistická 49 30N 15 0E
   Republika ♦, Cz.
27 Ceská Trebová, Cz. 49 54N 16 27E
26 Ceské Budějovice, Cz. 48 55N 14 25E
26 Ceské Velenice, Cz. 48 45N 15 1E
26 Ceskézémê ♦, Cz. 50 0N 14 0E
26 Ceskomoravská 49 20N 15 45E
   Vrchovina, Cz.
26 Ceský Brod, Cz. 50 4N 14 52E
26 Çeský Krumlov, Cz. 48 43N 14 21E
27 Ceský Tĕšín, Cz. 49 45N 18 39E
45 Ceşme, Turkey 38 20N 26 23E
84 Cess, Liberia 5 30N 9 30w
100 Cessnock, Australia 33 0S 151 15E
84 Cestos, R., Liberia 5 30N 9 30w
46 Cetate, Rumania 44 7N 23 2E
39 Cetina, R., Y.-slavia 43 50N 16 30E
42 Cetinje, Yugoslavia 42 23N 18 59E
41 Cetraro, Italy 39 30N 15 56E
82 Ceuta, Morocco 35 52N 5 18w
38 Ceva, Italy 44 23N 8 0E
20 Cévennes, mts., France 44 10N 3 50E
70 Ceylon = Sri Lanka ■, 7 30N 80 50E
   Asia
19 Chabeuil, France 44 54N 5 1E
21 Chablais, France 46 20N 6 36E
19 Chablis, France 47 47N 3 48E
82 Chabounia, Algeria 35 30N 2 38E
124 Chacabuco, Argentina 34 40S 60 27w
126 Chachapoyas, Peru 6 15S 77 50w
71 Chachoengsao, Thailand 13 45N 101 12E
71 Chachro, Pakistan 25 5N 70 15E
124 Chaco ♦, Arg. 25 0S 61 0w
128 Chaco Austral, Arg. 27 30S 61 40w
124 Chaco Boreal, Par. 22 30S 60 10w
128 Chaco Central, Arg. 24 0S 61 0w
81 Chad ■, Africa 12 30N 17 15E
59 Chadan, U.S.S.R. 51 17N 91 35E
126 Chadiza, Zambia 14 10S 33 34E
116 Chadron, U.S.A. 42 50N 103 0w
56 Chadyr Lunga, U.S.S.R. 46 3N 28 51E
126 Chafurray, Colombia 3 10N 73 14w
65 Chagai, Afghan. 29 30N 63 0E
59 Chagda, U.S.S.R. 58 45N 130 38E
19 Chagny, France 46 57N 4 45E
54 Chagoda, U.S.S.R. 59 10N 35 25E
60 Chagos Arch., Br. Indian 6 0S 72 0E
   Ocean Terr.
120 Chágres, R., Panama 9 5N 79 40w
   Canal Zone
65 Chah Bahar, Iran 25 20N 60 40E
65 Chahar Buriak, Afghan. 30 15N 62 0E
65 Chahbar, Iran 25 20N 60 40E
71 Chai-nat, Thailand 15 5N 100 25E
71 Chaillé-les-Marais, Fr. 46 25N 1 2w
68 Chaj Doab, Pakistan 32 0N 73 0E
124 Chajari, Argentina 30 42S 58 0w
90 Chake Chake, Tanzania 5 15S 39 45E
65 Chakhansur, Afghan. 31 10N 62 0E
68 Chaklashi, India 22 40N 72 52E

MAP
107 Chakonipau, L., Canada 56 10N 67 45w
69 Chakradharpur, India 22 45N 85 40E
68 Chakwal, Pakistan 32 50N 72 45E
76 Chalainor, China 49 31N 117 30E
20 Chalais, France 45 16N 0 3E
70 Chalakudi, India 10 18N 76 20E
76 Chalantun = Putehachi, 48 4N 122 45E
   China
45 Chalcis = Khalkis, 38 27N 23 42E
   Greece
107 Chaleur, Baie de, Can. 47 55N 65 30w
19 Chalhuanca, Peru 14 15S 73 5w
19 Chalindrey, France 47 48N 5 26E
68 Chalisgaon, India 20 30N 75 10E
57 Chalkar, U.S.S.R. 50 35N 51 52E
57 Chalkar Oz., U.S.S.R. 50 40N 51 45E
101 Chalky Inlet, N.Z. 46 3S 166 31E
18 Challans, France 46 50N 1 52w
126 Challapata, Bolivia 19 0S 66 50w
19 Challerange, France 49 18N 4 46E
118 Challis, U.S.A. 44 32N 114 25w
69 Chalna, Bangladesh 22 36N 89 35E
18 Chalonnes, France 47 20N 0 45w
19 Chalon-sur-Saône, 46 48N 4 50E
   France
19 Châlons-sur-Marne, Fr. 48 58N 4 20E
20 Chálus, France 45 39N 0 58E
12 Cham, Germany 49 12N 12 40E
91 Chama, U.S.A. 36 37N 106 37w
68 Chaman, Pakistan 30 58N 66 25E
70 Chamarajanagar- 11 52N 76 52E
   Ramasamudram, India
32 Chamartín de la Rosa, 40 28N 3 40w
   Spain
68 Chamba, India 32 35N 76 10E
68 Chambal, R., India 26 0N 76 55E
116 Chamberlain, U.S.A. 43 50N 99 21w
119 Chambers, U.S.A. 35 13N 109 30w
114 Chambersburg, U.S.A. 39 53N 77 41w
21 Chambéry, France 45 34N 5 55E
91 Chambeshi, Zambia 12 39S 28 1E
113 Chambly, Canada 45 27N 73 17w
18 Chambois, France 48 48N 0 6E
107 Chambord, Canada 48 25N 72 6w
20 Chamboulive, France 45 26N 1 42E
98 Chambri L., New Guin. 4 15S 143 10E
75 Chamdo, China 31 21N 97 2E
124 Chamical, Argentina 30 22S 66 27w
21 Chamonix, France 45 55N 6 51E
68 Champa, India 22 2N 82 43E
108 Champagne, Canada 60 49N 136 30w
19 Champagne, Fr. 49 0N 4 40E
19 Champagnole, France 46 45N 5 55E
114 Champaign, U.S.A. 40 8N 88 14w
20 Champaubert, France 48 50N 3 45E
20 Champdeniers, France 46 29N 0 25w
20 Champeix, France 45 37N 3 8E
96 Champion B., Australia 28 44S 114 36E
19 Champlain, Canada 46 27N 72 24w
113 Champlain, L., U.S.A. 44 30N 73 20w
120 Champotón, Mexico 19 20N 90 50w
31 Chamusca, Portugal 39 21N 8 29w
6 Chanasma, India 23 44N 72 5E
31 Chanca, R., Portugal 37 49N 7 15w
70 Chanda, India 19 57N 79 25E
68 Chandausi, India 28 27N 78 49E
68 Chandeleur Is., U.S.A. 29 45N 88 53w
117 Chandeleur Sd., U.S.A. 29 58N 88 40w
68 Chandigarh, India 30 30N 76 58E
107 Chandler, Canada 48 18N 64 46w
119 Chandler, Ariz., U.S.A. 33 20N 111 56w
117 Chandler, Okla., U.S.A. 35 43N 97 20w
75 Chandmani, Mongolia 45 22N 98 2E
69 Chandpur, Bangladesh 23 8N 90 42E
68 Chandpur, India 29 8N 78 19E
68 Chandpur, India 26 59N 68 30E
70 Changanacheri, India 9 25N 76 31E
77 Changchow, Fukien, 24 32N 117 44E
   China
76 Changchow, Shantung, 36 55N 118 3E
   China
76 Changchun, China 43 58N 125 19E
76 Changhua, Taiwan, 24 2N 120 30E
76 Changkiakow, China 40 52N 114 45E
76 Changkiang (Shihlu), 19 25N 108 57E
   Hainan, China
77 Changkiang, Kwangsi- 21 7N 110 21E
   Chuang, China
76 Changkwansai Ling, 44 40N 129 0E
   China
77 Changlo, China 24 0N 115 33E
77 Changning, China 26 25N 112 15E
76 Changpai Shan, mts., 42 25N 129 0E
   China
76 Changping, China 40 15N 116 15E
77 Changpu, China 24 2N 117 31E
77 Changsha, China 28 5N 113 1E
77 Changshow, China 29 49N 107 10E
76 Changshu, China 31 33N 120 45E
77 Changtai, China 24 34N 117 50E
77 Changteh, China 29 12N 111 43E
77 Changting, China 25 52N 116 20E
76 Changwu, China 34 21N 122 45E
75 Changyeh, China 39 0N 100 59E
92 Changuna, Angola 16 0S 14 8E
77 Chankiang (Tsamkong), 21 7N 110 21E
   China
70 Channapatna, India 12 40N 77 15E
12 Channel Is., U.K. 49 30N 2 40w
114 Channing, Mich., U.S.A. 46 9N 88 1w
117 Channing, Tex., U.S.A. 35 45N 102 20w
31 Chantada, Spain 42 36N 7 46w
71 Chanthaburi, Thailand 12 38N 102 12E
19 Chantilly, France 49 12N 2 29E
18 Chantonnay, France 46 40N 1 3w

MAP
104 Chantrey Inlet, Canada 67 30N 96 0w
117 Chanute, U.S.A. 37 45N 85 25w
75 Chanyi, China 25 56N 104 1E
31 Chanza, R., Spain 37 49N 7 15w
71 Chao Phraya, Mae Nam, 15 0N 100 20E
   Thai.
77 Chaoan, China 23 41N 116 38E
77 Chaochow, China 23 45N 116 32E
77 Chaohwa, China 32 16N 105 41E
77 Chaoping, China 24 1N 110 59E
75 Chaotung, China 27 19N 103 42E
77 Chaoyang, Kwangtung, 23 10N 116 30E
   China
76 Chaoyang, Liaoning, 41 46N 120 16E
   China
58 Chap Kuduk, U.S.S.R. 48 45N 55 5E
91 Chapala, Mozam. 15 50S 37 35E
120 Chapala, Lago de, 20 10N 103 20w
   Mexico
57 Chapayevo, U.S.S.R. 50 25N 51 10E
55 Chapayevsk, U.S.S.R. 53 0N 49 40E
125 Chapecó, Brazil 27 14S 52 41w
115 Chapel Hill, U.S.A. 35 53N 79 3w
106 Chapleau, Canada 47 45N 83 30w
19 Chaplino, U.S.S.R. 48 8N 36 15E
55 Chaplygin, U.S.S.R. 53 15N 39 55E
69 Chapra, India 25 48N 84 50E
80 Char, Mauritania 21 40N 12 45w
59 Chara, U.S.S.R. 56 54N 118 12E
124 Charadai, Argentina 27 35S 60 0w
126 Charagua, Bolivia 19 45S 63 10w
65 Charak, Iran 26 46N 54 18E
126 Charalá, Colombia 6 17N 73 10w
126 Charaña, Bolivia 17 30S 69 35w
126 Charapita, Colombia 0 37S 74 21w
124 Charata, Argentina 27 13S 61 14w
120 Charcas, Mexico 23 10N 101 20w
75 Charchan, China 38 4N 85 16E
5 Charcot I., Antarctica 70 0S 75 0w
13 Chard, England 50 52N 2 59w
58 Chardara, U.S.S.R. 41 16N 67 59E
112 Chardon, U.S.A. 41 34N 81 17w
58 Chardzhou, U.S.S.R. 39 0N 63 20E
20 Charente, R., France 45 41N 0 30w
20 Charente ♦, France 45 50N 0 16w
20 Charente- Maritime ♦, 45 50N 0 35w
   France
57 Charentsavan, U.S.S.R. 40 35N 44 41E
65 Charikar, Afghanistan 35 0N 69 10E
116 Chariton R., U.S.A. 40 10N 92 45w
69 Charkhari, India 25 24N 79 45E
68 Charkhi Dadri, India 28 37N 76 17E
75 Charklikh, China 39 16N 88 17E
15 Charleroi, Belgium 50 24N 4 27E
112 Charlerol, U.S.A. 40 8N 79 54w
114 Charles, C., U.S.A. 37 10N 75 52w
116 Charles City, U.S.A. 43 2N 92 41w
109 Charles L., Canada 59 45N 110 40w
114 Charles Town, U.S.A. 39 20N 77 50w
117 Charleston, Miss., U.S.A. 34 2N 90 3w
117 Charleston, Mo., U.S.A. 36 52N 89 20w
115 Charleston, S.C., U.S.A. 32 47N 79 56w
115 Charleston, W. Va., 38 24N 81 36w
   U.S.A.
93 Charlestown, S. Africa 27 26S 29 53E
114 Charlestown, U.S.A. 38 29N 85 40w
88 Charlesville, Zaïre 5 27S 20 59E
15 Charleville = Rath 52 21N 8 40w
   Luire, Ireland
99 Charleville, Austral. 26 24S 146 15E
19 Charleville- Mézières, 49 44N 4 40E
   France
114 Charlevoix, U.S.A. 45 19N 85 14w
21 Charlieu, France 46 10N 4 10E
114 Charlotte, Mich., U.S.A. 84 48N 42 36w
115 Charlotte, N.C., U.S.A. 35 16N 80 46w
121 Charlotte Amalie, Virgin 18 22N 64 56w
   Is.
96 Charlotte Harb., U.S.A. 26 45N 82 10w
96 Charlotte Waters, 25 56N 134 54E
   Australia
48 Charlottenberg, Sweden 59 54N 12 17E
114 Charlottesville, U.S.A. 38 1N 78 30w
107 Charlottetown, Canada 46 19N 63 3w
100 Charlton, Australia 36 16S 143 24E
116 Charlton, U.S.A. 40 59N 93 20w
106 Charlton I., Canada 52 0N 79 20w
19 Charmes, France 48 22N 6 17E
107 Charny, Canada 46 43N 71 15w
21 Charolles, France 46 27N 4 16E
19 Charost, France 47 0N 2 7E
82 Charouine, Algeria 29 0N 0 15w
91 Charre, Mozambique 17 19S 35 10E
20 Charroux, France 46 9N 0 25E
98 Charters Towers, 20 5S 146 13E
   Australia
18 Chartres, France 48 29N 1 30E
124 Chascomús, Argentina 35 30S 58 0w
91 Chasefu, Zambia 11 55N 32 58E
20 Chasseneuil-sur- 45 52N 0 29E
   Bonnieure, France
68 Chata, India 27 42N 77 30E
43 Chatal Balkan = Udvoy 42 50N 26 50E
   Balkan, Bulgaria
19 Château-Chinon, France 47 4N 3 56E
18 Château-du-Loir, France 47 40N 0 25E
18 Château Gontier, France 47 50N 0 42w
19 Château-Landon, France 48 8N 2 40E
19 Château Porcien, France 49 31N 4 13E
19 Château-Renault, France 47 36N 0 56E
19 Château-Salins, France 48 50N 6 30E
20 Château-Thierry, France 49 3N 3 20E
18 Châteaubourg, France 48 7N 1 25w
18 Châteaubriant, France 47 43N 1 23w
18 Châteaudun, France 48 3N 1 20E
18 Châteaugiron, France 48 3N 1 30w
113 Châteauguay, Canada 45 24N 73 44w
18 Château-la-Vallière, Fr. 47 30N 0 20E

MAP
18 Châteaulin, France 48 11N 4 8w
18 Châteaumeillant, Fr. 46 35N 2 12E
18 Châteauneuf, France 48 35N 1 15E
18 Châteauneuf-du-Faou, 48 11N 3 50w
   France
19 Châteauneuf-sur- 45 36N 0 3w
   Charente, France
19 Châteauneuf-sur- Cher, 46 52N 2 18E
   France
19 Châteauneuf-sur- Loire, 47 52N 2 13E
   France
21 Châteaurenard, France 43 53N 4 51E
20 Châteauroux, France 46 50N 1 40E
20 Châtelaillon-Plage, 46 5N 1 5w
   France
20 Châtel-Guyon, France 45 55N 3 4E
18 Châtelaudren, France 48 33N 2 59w
18 Châtellerault, France 46 50N 0 30E
18 Châtelus-Malvaleix, Fr. 46 18N 2 1E
107 Chatham, N.B., Can. 47 2N 65 28w
106 Chatham, Ont., Can. 42 23N 82 15w
13 Chatham, Eng. 51 22N 0 32E
117 Chatham, La., U.S.A. 32 22N 92 26w
113 Chatham, N.Y., U.S.A. 42 21N 73 32w
109 Chatham Str., Alaska 57 0N 134 40w
117 Châtillon, Loiret, France 47 36N 2 44E
19 Châtillon, Marne, France 49 5N 3 43E
38 Châtillon, Italy 45 45N 7 40E
19 Châtillon-Coligny, Fr. 47 50N 2 51E
19 Châtillon-en-Bazois, Fr. 47 3N 3 39E
21 Châtillon-en-Diois, 44 41N 5 29E
   France
19 Châtillon-sur-Seine, 47 50N 4 33E
   France
18 Châtillon-sur-Sèvre, Fr. 46 56N 0 45w
69 Chatmohar, Bangladesh 24 15N 89 26E
69 Chatra, India 24 12N 84 56E
68 Chatrapur, India 19 22N 85 2E
113 Chats, L. des, Canada 45 30N 76 20w
112 Chatsworth, Canada 44 27N 80 54w
115 Chattahoochee, U.S.A. 30 43N 84 51w
115 Chattanooga, U.S.A. 35 2N 85 17w
55 Chaudes-Aigues, France 44 51N 3 1E
20 Chauffailles, France 46 13N 4 20E
67 Chauk, Burma 20 53N 94 49E
67 Chaukan La, Burma 27 0N 97 15E
19 Chaulnes, France 49 48N 2 47E
19 Chaumont, France 48 7N 5 8E
44 Chaumont, U.S.A. 44 4N 76 9w
19 Chaumont-en-Vexin, Fr. 49 16N 1 53E
18 Chaumont-sur-Loire, Fr. 47 29N 1 11E
20 Chaunay, France 46 13N 0 9E
19 Chauny, France 49 37N 3 12E
18 Chaussey, Is., France 48 52N 1 49w
19 Chaussin, France 46 59N 5 22E
112 Chautauqua, U.S.A. 42 17N 79 30w
109 Chauvin, Canada 52 45N 110 10w
127 Chaves, Brazil 0 15S 49 55w
31 Chaves, Portugal 41 45N 7 32w
89 Chavuma, Zambia 13 10S 22 55E
23 Chazelles-sur-Lyon, 45 39N 4 22E
   France
113 Chazy, U.S.A. 44 52N 73 28w
26 Cheb (Eger), 50 9N 12 20E
   Czechoslovakia
55 Cheboksary, U.S.S.R. 56 8N 47 30E
114 Cheboygan, U.S.A. 45 38N 84 29w
55 Chechaouen, U.S.S.R. 59 10N 38 45E
82 Chech, Erg, Sahara 25 0N 2 15w
82 Chechaouen, Morocco 35 9N 5 15w
77 Checheng, China 34 4N 115 33E
57 Checheno-Ingush, 43 30N 45 29E
   A.S.S.R. ♦, U.S.S.R.
28 Checiny, Poland 50 46N 20 37E
117 Checotah, U.S.A. 35 31N 95 30w
107 Chedabucto B., Canada 45 25N 61 0w
96 Cheepie, Australia 26 43S 144 59E
20 Chef-Boutonne, France 46 7N 0 4w
91 Chegdomyn, U.S.S.R. 51 7N 132 52E
80 Chegga, Mauritania 25 15N 5 40w
118 Chehalis, U.S.A. 46 44N 122 59w
77 Cheju, Korea 33 28N 126 30E
77 Cheju Do, Korea 33 29N 126 34E
77 Chekalin, U.S.S.R. 54 10N 36 10E
77 Chekiang ♦, China 29 30N 120 0E
58 Cheleken, U.S.S.R. 39 26N 53 7E
92 Chela, Sa. da, Angola 16 20S 13 20E
109 Chelan, Canada 52 38N 103 22E
118 Chelan, U.S.A. 47 49N 120 0w
128 Chelfórd, Argentina 39 0S 66 40w
82 Chélif, O., Algeria 36 0N 0 8E
58 Chelkar, U.S.S.R. 47 40N 59 32E
58 Chelkar Tengiz, 48 0N 62 30E
   Solonchak, U.S.S.R.
82 Chellala Dahrania, Alg. 33 2N 0 1E
19 Chelles, France 48 52N 2 33E
27 Chelmek, Poland 51 8N 23 30E
28 Chełmno, Poland 53 20N 18 30E
13 Chelmsford, Eng. 51 44N 0 29E
28 Chełmza, Poland 53 10N 18 39E
113 Chelsea, Canada 45 30N 75 49w
117 Chelsea, Okla., U.S.A. 36 35N 95 25w
113 Chelsea, Vermont, 43 59N 72 27w
   U.S.A.
100 Chelsea, Australia 38 5S 145 8E
13 Cheltenham, England 51 55N 2 5w
32 Chelva, Spain 39 45N 1 0w
58 Chelyabinsk, U.S.S.R. 55 10N 61 35E
59 Chelyuskin, C., U.S.S.R. 77 30N 103 0E
71 Chemor, Malaysia 4 44N 101 6E
76 Chemult, U.S.A. 43 14N 121 54w
77 Chen, Gora, U.S.S.R. 65 10N 141 20E
68 Chenab, R., Pakistan 30 40N 73 30E
82 Chenachane, O., Algeria 25 30N 3 30w
113 Chenango Forks, U.S.A. 42 15N 75 51w

MAP
87 Chencha, Ethiopia 6 15N 37 32E
118 Cheney, U.S.A. 47 38N 117 34w
77 Chenfeng, China 25 25N 105 51E
77 Chengan, China 28 30N 107 30E
77 Chengchow, China 34 47N 113 46E
77 Chengchu, China 27 25N 118 46E
77 Chenghsien, China 29 30N 120 40E
75 Chengkiang, China 24 58N 102 59E
77 Chengkung, China 27 8N 108 57E
77 Chengpu, China 26 12N 110 5E
77 Chengteh, China 41 0N 117 55E
75 Chengtu, China 30 45N 104 0E
77 Chenhsien, China 25 46N 112 59E
77 Chenki, China 28 1N 110 2E
77 Chenning, China 25 57N 105 51E
76 Chentung, China 46 2N 123 1E
77 Chenyuan, Kansi, China 35 59N 107 2E
77 Chenyuan, Kweichow, 27 0N 108 20E
   China
71 Cheo Reo = Hau Bon, 13 25N 108 28E
   S. Vietnam
71 Cheom Ksan, Khmer 14 25N 105 0E
   Rep.
43 Chepelare, Bulgaria 41 44N 24 40E
126 Chepén, Peru 7 10S 79 15w
124 Chepes, Argentina 31 20S 66 35w
120 Chepo, Panama 9 10N 79 6w
55 Cheptsa, R., U.S.S.R. 58 30N 51 0E
90 Cheptulil, Mt., Kenya 1 25N 35 35E
116 Chequamegon B., U.S.A. 46 40N 90 30w
91 Chequeche, Mozam. 14 13S 38 30E
19 Cher ♦, France 47 10N 2 30E
19 Cher, R., France 47 10N 2 10E
69 Cheran, India 25 45N 90 44E
38 Cherasco, Italy 44 39N 7 50E
54 Cherava, U.S.A. 34 42N 79 54w
18 Cherbourg, France 49 39N 1 40w
82 Cherchell, Algeria 36 35N 2 12E
54 Cherdakly, U.S.S.R. 54 25N 48 58E
55 Cherdyn, U.S.S.R. 60 20N 56 20E
59 Cheremkhovo, U.S.S.R. 53 32N 102 40E
55 Cherepanovo, U.S.S.R. 54 15N 83 30E
55 Cherepovets, U.S.S.R. 59 5N 37 55E
82 Chergui, Chott Ech, Alg. 34 10N 0 25E
81 Cheri, Niger 13 26N 11 21E
54 Cherikov, U.S.S.R. 53 32N 31 20E
57 Cherkessk, U.S.S.R. 44 25N 42 10E
58 Cherlak, U.S.S.R. 54 15N 74 55E
43 Cherni, Mt., Bulgaria 42 35N 23 28E
54 Chernigov, U.S.S.R. 51 28N 31 20E
54 Chernobyl, U.S.S.R. 51 13N 30 15E
56 Chernomorskoye, 45 31N 32 46E
   U.S.S.R.
54 Chernovskoye, U.S.S.R. 58 48N 47 20E
59 Chernoye, U.S.S.R. 70 30N 89 10E
54 Chernyakhovsk, U.S.S.R. 54 29N 21 48E
59 Chernyshevskiy, U.S.S.R. 62 40N 112 30E
57 Chernyshkovskiy, 48 30N 42 28E
   U.S.S.R.
116 Cherokee, Iowa, U.S.A. 42 40N 95 30w
117 Cherokee, Okla., U.S.A. 36 45N 98 25w
117 Cherokees, L. of the, 36 50N 95 12w
   U.S.A.
128 Cherquenco, Chile 38 35S 72 0w
67 Cherrapunji, India 25 17N 91 47E
118 Cherry Creek, Nev., 39 50N 114 58w
   U.S.A.
112 Cherry Creek, N.Y., 42 18N 79 6w
   U.S.A.
100 Cherrypool, Australia 37 7S 142 13E
117 Cherryvale, U.S.A. 37 20N 95 33w
59 Cherskiy, U.S.S.R. 68 45N 161 18E
59 Cherskogo Khrebet, 65 0N 143 0E
   U.S.S.R.
57 Chertkovo, U.S.S.R. 49 25N 40 19E
56 Cherven, U.S.S.R. 53 45N 28 13E
43 Cherven-Bryag, Bulg. 43 17N 24 7E
13 Cherwell, R., Eng. 51 56N 1 18w
114 Chesapeake, B., U.S.A. 38 0N 76 12w
52 Chesha B., U.S.S.R. 67 20N 47 0E
13 Cheshire ♦, England 53 14N 2 30w
112 Chesley, Canada 44 17N 81 7w
33 Cheste, Spain 39 30N 0 41w
13 Chester, Eng. 53 12N 2 53w
118 Chester, Calif., U.S.A. 40 22N 121 22w
118 Chester, Ill., U.S.A. 37 58N 89 50w
118 Chester, Mont., U.S.A. 48 31N 111 0w
114 Chester, N.Y., U.S.A. 41 22N 74 16w
114 Chester, Pa., U.S.A. 39 54N 75 20w
115 Chester, S.C., U.S.A. 34 44N 81 13w
104 Chesterfield, Canada 63 0N 91 0w
13 Chesterfield, Eng. 53 14N 1 26w
104 Chesterfield Inlet, 63 30N 91 0w
   Canada
97 Chesterfield, Îles, Pac. 19 52S 158 15E
   Oc.
91 Chesterfield, Malag. 16 20S 43 58E
113 Chesterville, Canada 45 7N 75 15w
83 Chetaibi, Algeria 37 1N 7 20E
107 Cheticamp, Canada 46 37N 60 59w
120 Chetumal, Mexico 18 30N 88 20w
120 Chetumal, Bahia de, 18 40N 88 10w
   Cent. Amer.
108 Chetwynd, Canada 55 45N 122 0w
20 Chevanceaux, France 45 18N 0 14w
12 Cheviot, The, England 55 28N 2 8w
12 Cheviot Hills, Eng. & 55 20N 2 30w
   Scot.
99 Cheviot Ra., Australia 25 20S 143 45E
87 Chew Bahir, Ethiopia 4 40N 30 50E
118 Chewelah, U.S.A. 48 25N 117 56w
117 Cheyenne, Okla., U.S.A. 35 45N 99 32w
116 Cheyenne, Wyo., U.S.A. 41 9N 104 49w
116 Cheyenne, R., U.S.A. 44 50N 101 0w
120 Cheyenne Wells, U.S.A. 38 51N 102 23w
68 Chhabra, India 24 40N 76 54E
68 Chhatarpur, India 24 23N 79 35E
72 Chhang, Khmer Rep. 12 15N 104 14E
69 Chhatak, Bangladesh 25 5N 91 37E

Chhatarpur INDEX Clewiston

MAP
69 Chhatarpur, India 24 55N 79 43E
68 Chhindwara, India 22 2N 78 59E
71 Chhlong, Kg., Khmer Rep. 12 11N 106 2E
71 Chi, Nam, Thailand 15 40N 104 20E
77 Chiai, Taiwan 23 29N 120 25E
71 Chiang Mai, Thailand 18 55N 98 55E
89 Chianje, Angola 15 35S 13 40E
120 Chiapas ♦, Mexico 17 0N 92 45W
41 Chiaramonte Gulfi, It. 37 1N 14 41E
39 Chiaravalle, Italy 38 41N 16 24E
41 Chiaravalle Centrale, It. 38 41N 16 25E
38 Chiari, Italy 45 31N 9 55E
38 Chiávari, Italy 44 20N 9 20E
38 Chiavenna, Italy 46 18N 9 23E
74 Chiba, Japan 35 30N 140 7E
74 Chiba-ken ♦, Japan 35 30N 140 20E
93 Chibabava, Mozambique 20 25S 33 35E
89 Chibemba, Angola 15 48S 14 8E
106 Chibougamau, Canada 49 56N 74 24W
106 Chibougamau L., Can. 49 50N 74 20W
106 Chibougamau, R., Can. 49 50N 75 40W
85 Chibuk, Nigeria 10 52N 12 50E
93 Chibuto, Mozambique 24 40S 33 33E
70 Chicacole = Strikakulam, India 18 14N 84 4E
114 Chicago, U.S.A. 41 45N 87 40W
114 Chicago Heights, U.S.A. 41 29N 87 37W
114 Chicago North, U.S.A. 42 20N 87 50W
104 Chichagof I., Alaska 58 0N 136 0W
82 Chichaoua, Morocco 31 32N 8 44W
13 Chichester, Eng. 50 50N 0 47W
74 Chichibu, Japan 36 5N 139 10E
76 Chichirin, China 50 35N 123 45E
126 Chichiriviche, Ven. 10 56N 68 16W
76 Chichow, China 38 30N 115 25E
117 Chickasha, U.S.A. 35 0N 98 0W
31 Chiclana de la Frontera, Spain 36 26N 6 9W
126 Chiclayo, Peru 6 42S 79 50W
118 Chico, U.S.A. 39 45N 121 54W
118 Chico, R., Chubut, Argentina 44 0S 67 0W
128 Chico, R., Santa Cruz, Argentina 49 30S 69 30W
119 Chicoma Pk., U.S.A. 36 8N 106 40W
93 Chicomo, Mozambique 24 31S 34 6E
113 Chicopee, U.S.A. 42 6N 72 37W
107 Chicoutimi, Canada 48 28N 71 5W
70 Chidambaram, India 11 20N 79 45E
93 Chidenguele, Mozam. 24 55S 34 2E
105 Chidley C., Canada 60 30N 64 15W
112 Chiefs Pt., Canada 44 42N 81 18W
25 Chiemsee, Germany 47 53N 12 27E
71 Chiengmai, Thailand 18 55N 98 55E
39 Chienti, R., Italy 43 15N 13 30E
38 Chieri, Italy 45 0N 7 50E
38 Chiese, R., Italy 45 45N 10 35E
39 Chieti, Italy 42 22N 14 10E
107 Chignecto B., Canada 45 33N 64 50W
126 Chigorodó, Colombia 7 41N 76 42W
124 Chiguana, Bolivia 21 0S 67 50W
76 Chihfeng, China 42 18N 118 57E
77 Chihing, China 25 2N 113 45E
77 Chihkiang, Hunan, China 27 21N 109 45E
77 Chihkiang, Hupei, China 30 25N 111 30E
77 Chihkin, China 26 30N 105 45E
76 Chihli, G. of (Po Hai), China 38 30N 119 0E
77 Chihsien (Weihwei), China 35 29N 114 1E
120 Chihuahua, Mexico 28 40N 106 3W
120 Chihuahua ♦, Mexico 28 40N 106 3W
58 Chiili, U.S.S.R. 44 10N 66 55E
91 Chikawawa, Malawi 16 2S 34 50E
70 Chik Ballapur, India 13 25N 77 45E
68 Chikhli, India 20 20N 76 18E
70 Chikmagalur, India 13 15N 75 45E
70 Chikodi, India 16 26N 74 38E
91 Chikonde, Zambia 12 16S 31 38E
91 Chilanga, Zambia 15 33S 28 16E
120 Chilapa, Mexico 17 40N 99 20W
66 Chilas, Kashmir 35 25N 74 5E
99 Childers, Australia 25 15S 152 17E
117 Childress, U.S.A. 34 30N 100 50W
128 Chile ■, S. Amer. 35 0S 71 15W
124 Chilecito, Argentina 29 0S 67 40W
126 Chilete, Peru 7 10S 78 50W
69 Chilka L., India 19 40N 85 25E
108 Chilko L., Canada 51 20N 124 10W
98 Chillagoe, Australia 17 14S 144 33E
124 Chillán, Chile 36 40S 72 10W
116 Chillicothe, Ill., U.S.A. 40 55N 89 32W
116 Chillicothe, Mo., U.S.A. 39 45N 93 30W
114 Chillicothe, Ohio, U.S.A. 39 53N 82 58W
100 Chillingollah, Australia 35 16S 143 3E
108 Chilliwack, Canada 49 10N 122 0W
68 Chilo, India 27 12N 73 32E
93 Chiloane, I., Mozam. 20 40S 34 55E
128 Chiloé, I. de, Chile 42 50S 73 45W
120 Chilpancingo, Mexico 17 30N 99 40W
100 Chiltern, Australia 36 10S 146 36E
13 Chiltern Hills, Eng. 51 44N 0 42W
114 Chilton, U.S.A. 44 1N 88 12W
88 Chiluage, Angola 9 15S 21 42E
91 Chilubula, Zambia 10 14S 30 51E
91 Chilumba, Malawi 10 28S 34 12E
77 Chilung, Taiwan 25 3N 121 45E
91 Chilwa, L. (Shirwa), Malawi 15 15S 35 40E
118 Chimacum, U.S.A. 48 1N 122 53W
75 Chimai, China 33 35N 102 10E
16 Chimay, Belgium 50 3N 4 20E
58 Chimbay, U.S.S.R. 42 57N 59 47E
126 Chimborazo, Ec. 1 20S 78 55W
126 Chimbote, Peru 9 0S 78 35W
126 Chimichaguá, Col. 9 15N 73 49W
46 Chimishliya, U.S.S.R. 46 34N 28 44E
58 Chimkent, U.S.S.R. 42 40N 69 25E
91 Chimpembe, Zambia 9 31S 29 33E
67 Chin, Burma 22 0N 93 0E
77 Chin Chai, China 31 58N 115 59E
75 China ■, Asia 30 0N 110 0E
120 China, Mexico 25 40N 99 20W
126 Chinacota, Colombia 7 37N 72 36W
121 Chinandega, Nicaragua 12 30N 87 0W
117 Chinati Pk., U.S.A. 30 0N 104 25W
126 Chincha Alta, Peru 13 20S 76 0W
99 Chinchilla, Australia 26 45S 150 38E
33 Chinchilla de Monte Aragón, Spain 38 53N 1 40W
32 Chinchón, Spain 40 9N 3 26W
76 Chinchow, China 41 10N 121 2E
114 Chincoteague, U.S.A. 37 58N 75 21W
91 Chinde, Mozambique 18 45S 36 30E
67 Chindwin, R., Burma 22 30N 95 0E
77 Ching Ho, R., China 34 20N 109 0E
91 Chinga, Mozambique 15 13S 38 35E
75 Chinghai ♦, China 36 0N 97 0E
70 Chingleput, India 12 42N 79 58E
91 Chingola, Zambia 12 31S 27 53E
91 Chingole, Malawi 13 4S 34 17E
89 Chinguar, Angola 12 18S 16 45E
80 Chinguetti, Mauritania 20 25N 12 15W
93 Chingune, Mozâmbique 20 33S 35 0E
76 Chinhae, S. Korea 35 9N 128 40E
93 Chinhanguanine, Mozam. 25 21S 32 30E
68 Chiniot, Pakistan 31 45N 73 0E
77 Chinkiang, China 32 2N 119 29E
119 Chinle, U.S.A. 36 14N 109 38W
77 Chinmu Chiao, China 18 10N 109 35E
70 Chinnamanur, India 9 50N 77 16E
76 Chinnampo, N. Korea 38 52N 125 28E
70 Chinnur, India 18 57N 79 43E
119 Chino Valley, U.S.A. 34 54N 112 28W
18 Chinon, France 47 10N 0 15E
109 Chinook, Canada 51 28N 110 59W
118 Chinook, U.S.A. 48 35N 109 19W
69 Chinsura, India 22 53N 88 27E
70 Chintamani, India 13 26N 78 3E
76 Chinwangtao, China 40 0N 119 31E
39 Chióggia, Italy 45 13N 12 15E
45 Chíos = Khíos, Greece 38 27N 26 9E
108 Chip Lake, Canada 53 35N 115 35W
91 Chipata (Ft. Jameson), Zambia 13 38S 32 28E
91 Chipinga, Rhodesia 20 13S 32 36E
31 Chipiona, Spain 36 44N 6 26W
115 Chipley, U.S.A. 30 45N 85 32W
70 Chiplun, India 17 31N 73 34E
107 Chipman, Canada 46 6N 65 53W
91 Chipoka, Malawi 13 57S 34 28E
42 Chiprovtsi, Bulgaria 43 24N 22 52E
112 Chippawa, Canada 43 5N 79 10W
13 Chippenham, Eng. 51 27N 2 7W
116 Chippewa, R., U.S.A. 44 45N 91 55W
116 Chippewa Falls, U.S.A. 44 55N 91 22W
126 Chiquian, Peru 10 10S 77 0W
120 Chiquimula, Guatemala 14 51N 89 37W
126 Chiquinquirá, Col. 5 37N 73 50W
57 Chir, R., U.S.S.R. 48 45N 42 10E
70 Chirala, India 15 50N 80 20E
91 Chiramba, Mozambique 16 55S 34 39E
65 Chiras, Afghanistan 35 14N 65 40E
68 Chirawa, India 28 14N 75 42E
70 Chirayinkil, India 8 41N 76 49E
58 Chirchik, U.S.S.R. 81 58N 69 15E
81 Chirfa, Niger 20 55N 12 14E
119 Chiricahua Pk., U.S.A. 31 53N 109 14W
121 Chiriquí, Golfo de, Panama 8 0N 82 10W
121 Chiriquí, Lago de, Pan. 9 10N 82 0W
121 Chiriquí, Vol., Panama 8 55N 82 35W
91 Chirivira Falls, Rhod. 21 10S 32 12E
46 Chirnogi, Rumania 44 7N 26 32E
91 Chiromo, Malawi 16 30S 35 7E
43 Chirpan, Bulgaria 42 10N 25 19E
91 Chisamba, Zambia 14 55S 28 20E
77 Chishan, Taiwan 22 44N 120 31E
91 Chisimba Falls, Zambia 10 12S 30 56E
42 Chisineu Cris, Rumania 46 32N 21 37E
38 Chisone, R., Italy 45 0N 7 5E
117 Chisos Mts., U.S.A. 29 20N 103 15W
68 Chistian Mandi, W. Pak. 29 50N 72 55E
55 Chistopol, U.S.S.R. 55 25N 50 38E
126 Chita, Colombia 6 11N 72 28W
59 Chita, U.S.S.R. 52 0N 113 25E
70 Chitapur, India 17 10N 76 50E
89 Chitembo, Angola 13 30S 16 50E
91 Chitipa, Malawi 9 41S 33 19E
89 Chitokoloki, Zambia 13 43S 23 4E
68 Chitorgarh, India 24 52N 74 43E
70 Chitrakot, India 19 20N 81 40E
66 Chitral, Pakistan 35 50N 71 56E
70 Chitravati, R., India 14 30N 78 0E
121 Chitré, Panama 7 59N 80 27W
67 Chittagong, Bangladesh 22 19N 91 55E
67 Chittagong ♦, Bangladesh 24 5N 91 25E
70 Chittoor, India 13 15N 79 5E
70 Chittur, India 10 40N 76 45E
87 Chitu, Ethiopia 8 38N 37 58E
39 Chiusi, Italy 43 1N 11 58E
33 Chiva, Spain 39 27N 0 41W
38 Chivasso, Italy 45 10N 7 52E
124 Chivilcoy, Argentina 35 0S 60 0W
91 Chiwanda, Tanzania 11 23S 34 55E
91 Chiwefwe, Zambia 13 37S 29 31E
91 Chizera, Zambia 13 10S 25 0E
52 Chkalov, U.S.S.R. 52 0N 55 5E
55 Chkolovsk, U.S.S.R. 56 50N 43 10E
26 Chlumec, Cz. 50 9N 15 29E
28 Chmielnik, Poland 50 37N 20 43E
76 Choahsien, China 37 48N 114 46E
90 Choba, Kenya 2 30N 38 5E
92 Chobe, R., Botswana 18 10S 24 10E
92 Chobe National Park, Botswana 21 30S 25 0E
85 Chobol, Nigeria 11 53N 13 1E
28 Chocianów, Poland 51 35N 15 33E
28 Chociwel, Poland 53 29N 15 21E
126 Chocó ♦, Colombia 6 0N 77 0W
126 Chocontá, Colombia 5 9N 73 41W
28 Chodaków, Poland 52 16N 20 18E
70 Chodavaram, India 17 40N 82 50E
28 Chodecz, Poland 52 56N 19 2E
28 Chodziez, Poland 52 58N 17 0E
128 Choele Choel, Arg. 39 11S 65 40W
19 Choisy-le-Roi, France 48 45N 2 24E
120 Choix, Mexico 26 40N 108 10W
28 Chojna, Poland 52 58N 14 25E
28 Chojnice, Poland 53 42N 17 40E
28 Chojnów, Poland 51 25N 15 58E
87 Choke Mts., Ethiopia 11 18N 37 15E
59 Chokurdakh, U.S.S.R. 70 38N 147 55E
18 Cholet, France 47 4N 0 52W
121 Choluteca, Honduras 13 20N 87 14W
91 Choma, Zambia 16 48S 26 59E
87 Chomen Swamp, Ethiopia 9 20N 37 10E
68 Chomu, India 27 15N 75 40E
26 Chomutov, Cz. 50 28N 13 23E
76 Chŏnan, S. Korea 36 48N 127 9E
71 Chonburi, Thailand 13 21N 101 1E
126 Chone, Ecuador 0 40S 80 0W
76 Chŏngjin, N. Korea 41 47N 129 50E
76 Chŏngju, S. Korea 36 39N 127 27E
76 Chŏnju, S. Korea 35 50N 127 4E
128 Chonos, Arch. de los, Chile 45 0S 75 0W
68 Chopda, India 21 20N 75 15E
12 Chopim, R., Brazil 25 35S 53 5W
83 Chormet el Melah, Libya 30 11N 16 29E
124 Chorolque, Cerro, Bolivia 20 59S 66 5W
28 Choroszcz, Poland 53 10N 22 59E
54 Chortkov, U.S.S.R. 49 2N 25 46E
69 Chorul Tso, China 32 30N 82 30E
76 Chŏrwŏn, S. Korea 38 15N 127 10E
28 Chorzele, Poland 53 15N 21 2E
28 Chorzów, Poland 50 18N 19 0E
124 Chos-Malal, Argentina 37 15S 70 5W
74 Choshi, Japan 35 45N 140 45E
28 Choszczno, Poland 53 7N 15 25E
118 Choteau, U.S.A. 47 50N 112 10W
68 Chotila, India 22 30N 71 15E
166 Choum, Mauritania 21 15N 16 45E
77 Chow Hu, China 31 35N 117 30E
119 Chowchilla, U.S.A. 37 11N 120 12W
76 Choybalsan, Mongolia 48 3N 114 28E
76 Choyr, Mongolia 46 24N 108 30E
13 Christchurch, Eng. 50 44N 1 47W
101 Christchurch, N.Z. 43 33S 172 47E
112 Christian, I., Canada 44 50N 80 39W
92 Christiana, S. Africa 27 52S 25 8E
49 Christiansfeld, Denmark 55 21N 9 29E
49 Christiansö, I., Den. 55 19N 15 12E
121 Christiansted, Virgin Is. 17 45N 64 42W
92 Christiana, S. Africa 27 52S 25 8E
95 Christmas I., Pac. Oc. 1 58N 157 27W
26 Chrudim, Cz. 49 58N 15 43E
27 Chrzanów, Poland 50 10N 19 21E
91 Chtimba, Malawi 10 35S 34 13E
58 Chu, U.S.S.R. 43 36N 73 42E
71 Chu, R., N. Vietnam 19 50N 105 20E
108 Chu Chua, Canada 51 30N 120 10W
77 Chu Kiang, China 22 15N 113 45E
77 Chuanchow, China 24 57N 118 31E
77 Chuanhsien, China 25 50N 111 12E
74 Chūbu, Japan 36 45N 137 0E
128 Chubut, R., Argentina 43 0S 70 0W
77 Chuchow (Lishui), China 28 30N 119 50E
77 Chuchow, China 27 56N 113 3E
54 Chudovo, U.S.S.R. 59 10N 31 30E
54 Chudskoye, Oz., U.S.S.R. 58 13N 27 30E
74 Chugoku, Japan 35 0N 133 0E
74 Chūgoku-Sanchi, Japan 35 0N 133 0E
56 Chuguyev, U.S.S.R. 49 55N 36 45E
116 Chugwater, U.S.A. 41 48N 104 47W
76 Chuho = Shangchih, China 45 10N 127 59E
76 Chuhsien, Chekiang, China 28 57N 118 58E
77 Chuhsien, Shantung, China 35 31N 118 45E
77 Chuhsien, Szechwan, China 30 51N 107 1E
71 Chukai, Malaysia 4 13N 103 25E
55 Chukhloma, U.S.S.R. 58 45N 42 40E
77 Chuki, Chekiang, China 29 30N 120 4E
77 Chuki, Hupei, China 32 26N 110 0E
59 Chukotskiy Khrebet, U.S.S.R. 68 0N 175 0E
59 Chukotskiy, Mys, U.S.S.R. 66 10N 169 3E
59 Chukotskoye More, U.S.S.R. 68 0N 175 0W
119 Chula Vista, U.S.A. 33 44N 117 8W
126 Chulucanas, Peru 5 0S 80 0W
77 Chumatien, China 33 0N 114 4E
124 Chumbicha, Argentina 29 0S 66 10W
43 Chumerna, Bulg. 42 45N 25 55E
59 Chumikan, U.S.S.R. 54 40N 135 10E
71 Chumphon, Thailand 10 35N 99 14E
91 Chumuare, Mozam. 14 31S 31 50E
76 Chunchŏn, S. Korea 37 58N 127 44E
91 Chunga, Zambia 15 0S 26 2E
77 Chungan, China 27 45N 118 0E
77 Chunghsien, China 30 17N 108 4E
77 Chungking, China 29 30N 106 30E
77 Chungsiang, China 31 14N 112 42E
67 Chungtien, China 27 51N 99 42E
68 Chunian, Pakistan 31 10N 74 0E
91 Chunya, Tanzania 8 30S 33 27E
90 Chunya ♦, Tanzania 7 48S 33 0E
126 Chuquibamba, Peru 15 47N 72 44W
124 Chuquicamata, Chile 22 15S 69 0W
124 Chuquisaca ♦, Bol. 23 30S 63 30W
25 Chur, Switzerland 46 52N 9 32E
67 Churachandpur, India 24 20N 93 40E
108 Church House, Canada 50 20N 125 10W
109 Churchill, Canada 58 45N 94 5W
109 Churchill L., Canada 56 0N 108 20W
108 Churchill Pk., Canada 58 10N 125 10W
107 Churchill Falls, Canada 53 32N 64 26W
109 Churchill, R., Man., Canada 57 5N 96 30W
107 Churchill, R., Newf., Canada 53 15N 63 0W
68 Churu, India 28 20N 75 0E
126 Churuguaro, Venezuela 10 49N 69 32W
77 Chusan, China 30 0N 122 20E
66 Chushul, Kashmir 33 40N 78 40E
77 Chusnan, China 32 14N 110 30E
52 Chusovoy, U.S.S.R. 58 15N 57 40E
77 Chuting, China 27 28N 113 1E
55 Chuvash A.S.S.R.♦, U.S.S.R. 55 30N 48 0E
76 Chwangho, China 39 41N 123 2E
42 Ciacovu, Rumania 45 35N 21 10E
114 Cicero, U.S.A. 41 48N 87 48W
32 Cidacos, R., Spain 42 15N 2 10W
56 Cide, Turkey 41 40N 32 50E
28 Ciechanów, Poland 52 52N 20 38E
28 Ciechocinek, Poland 52 53N 18 45E
121 Ciego de Avila, Cuba 21 50N 78 50W
126 Ciénaga, Colombia 11 1N 74 15W
126 Ciénaga de Oro, Col. 8 53N 75 37W
121 Cienfuegos, Cuba 22 10N 80 30W
28 Cieplice Slaskie Zdrój, Poland 50 50N 15 40E
20 Cierp, France 42 55N 0 40E
30 Cies, Islas, Spain 42 12N 8 55W
27 Cieszyn, Poland 49 45N 18 35E
33 Cieza, Spain 38 17N 1 23W
32 Cifuentes, Spain 40 47N 2 37W
71 Ciha Pa., N. Vietnam 22 20N 103 47E
31 Cijara, Pantano de, Spain 39 18N 4 52W
57 Cıldır, Turkey 41 10N 43 20E
64 Cilician Gates P., Tur. 37 20N 34 52E
64 Cilician Taurus, Tur. 36 40N 34 0E
46 Cilnicu, Rumania 44 54N 23 4E
117 Cimarron, Kans., U.S.A. 37 50N 100 20W
117 Cimarron, N. Mex., U.S.A. 36 30N 104 52W
117 Cimarron, R., U.S.A. 37 10N 102 10W
46 Cimpia Turzii, Rumania 46 34N 23 53E
46 Cimpina, Rumania 45 10N 25 45E
46 Cimpulung, Argeş, Rumania 45 17N 25 3E
46 Cimpulung, Suceava, Rumania 47 32N 25 30E
43 Cimpuri, Rumania 46 0N 26 50E
32 Cinca, R., Spain 42 20N 0 9E
42 Cincer, Y.-slav. 43 55N 17 5E
115 Cinch, R., U.S.A. 36 0N 84 15W
114 Cincinnati, U.S.A. 39 10N 84 26W
16 Ciney, Belgium 50 18N 5 5E
39 Cinigiano, Italy 42 53N 11 23E
39 Cinogli, Italy 43 23N 13 10E
21 Cinto, Mt., Corsica 42 24N 8 54E
46 Cioranii, Rumania 44 45N 26 25E
39 Ciovo, Yugoslavia 43 30N 16 17E
104 Circle, Alaska, U.S.A. 65 50N 144 10W
116 Circle, Montana, U.S.A. 47 26N 105 35W
114 Circleville, Ohio, U.S.A. 39 35N 82 57W
119 Circleville, Utah, U.S.A. 38 12N 112 24W
13 Cirencester, Eng. 51 43N 1 59W
46 Cireşu, Rumania 44 47N 22 31E
19 Cirey-sur-Vezouze, France 48 35N 6 57E
38 Ciriè, Italy 45 14N 7 35E
41 Cirò, Italy 39 23N 17 3E
117 Cisco, U.S.A. 32 25N 99 0W
46 Cislău, Rumania 45 14N 26 33E
27 Cisna, Poland 49 12N 22 20E
126 Cisneros, Colombia 6 33N 75 4W
46 Cisnădie, Rumania 45 42N 24 9E
40 Cisterna di Latina, It. 41 35N 12 50E
41 Cisternino, Italy 40 45N 17 26E
57 Citeli-Ckaro, U.S.S.R. 41 33N 46 0E
92 Citrusdal, S. Africa 32 35S 19 0E
39 Città della Pieve, Italy 42 57N 12 0E
39 Città di Castello, Italy 43 27N 12 14E
39 Città Sant' Angelo, It. 42 32N 14 5E
39 Cittadella, Italy 45 39N 11 48E
39 Cittaducale, Italy 42 24N 12 58E
41 Cittanova, Italy 38 22N 16 0E
46 Ciucaş, mt., Rumania 45 31N 25 56E
120 Ciudad Acuña, Mexico 29 20N 101 10W
120 Ciudad Altamirano, Mexico 18 20N 100 40W
126 Ciudad Bolivar, Ven. 8 5N 63 30W
120 Ciudad Camargo, Mex. 27 41N 105 10W
120 Ciudad Delicias = Delicias, Mexico 28 10N 105 30W
120 Ciudad de Valles, Mex. 22 0N 98 30W
120 Ciudad del Carmen, Mex. 18 20N 97 50W
120 Ciudad Guerrero, Mex. 28 33N 107 28W
120 Ciudad Juárez, Mexico 31 40N 106 28W
120 Ciudad Madero, Mexico 22 19N 97 50W
120 Ciudad Mante, Mexico 22 50N 99 0W
120 Ciudad Obregón, Mex. 27 28N 109 59W
126 Ciudad Piar, Venezuela 7 27N 63 19W
31 Ciudad Real, Spain 38 59N 3 55W
31 Ciudad Real ♦, Spain 38 50N 4 0W
30 Ciudad Rodrigo, Spain 40 35N 6 32W
121 Ciudad Trujillo = Sto. Domingo, Dom. Rep. 18 30N 70 0W
120 Ciudad Victoria, Mex. 23 41N 99 9W
32 Ciudadela, Spain 40 0N 3 50E
46 Ciulniţa, Rumania 44 26N 27 22E
56 Civa, B., Turkey 41 20N 36 40E
39 Cividale del Friuli, It. 46 6N 13 25E
39 Civita Castellana, Italy 42 18N 12 24E
39 Civitanova Marche, It. 43 18N 13 41E
39 Civitavécchia, Italy 42 6N 11 46E
39 Civitella del Tronto, It. 42 48N 13 40E
20 Civray, France 46 10N 0 17E
64 Civril, Turkey 38 20N 29 55E
40 Cixerri, R., Sardinia 39 45N 8 40E
64 Cizre, Turkey 37 19N 42 10E
*14 Clackmannan ♦, Scotland 56 10N 3 47W
13 Clacton-on-Sea, England 51 47N 1 10E
108 Claire L., Canada 58 30N 112 0W
117 Clairemont, U.S.A. 33 9N 100 44W
112 Clairton, U.S.A. 40 18N 79 54W
21 Clairvaux-les-Laes, France 46 35N 5 45E
19 Clamecy, France 47 28N 3 30E
115 Clanton, U.S.A. 32 48N 86 36W
92 Clanwilliam, S. Africa 32 11S 18 52E
15 Clara, Ireland 53 20N 7 38W
100 Clare, Australia 33 20S 143 50E
114 Clare, U.S.A. 43 47N 84 45W
15 Clare I., Ireland 53 48N 10 0W
15 Clare, R., Ireland 53 20N 9 0W
113 Claremont, U.S.A. 43 23N 72 20W
117 Claremore, U.S.A. 36 20N 95 20W
15 Claremorris, Ireland 53 45N 9 0W
5 Clarence I., Antarctica 61 30S 53 50W
128 Clarence, I., Chile 54 0S 72 0W
97 Clarence, R., Auatralia 29 25S 153 22E
101 Clarence R., N.Z. 42 17S 173 15E
109 Clarence Str., Alaska 55 40N 132 10W
96 Clarence Str., Australia 12 0S 131 0E
117 Clarendon, Ark., U.S.A. 34 41N 91 20W
117 Clarendon, Tex., U.S.A. 34 58N 100 54W
107 Clarenville, Canada 48 10N 54 1W
108 Claresholm, Canada 50 0N 113 45W
5 Clarie Coast, Antarctica 67 0S 135 0E
116 Clarinda, U.S.A. 40 45N 95 0W
116 Clarion, Ohio, U.S.A. 42 41N 93 46W
112 Clarion, Pa., U.S.A. 41 12N 79 22W
112 Clarion, R., U.S.A. 41 19N 79 10W
116 Clark, U.S.A. 44 55N 97 45W
112 Clark Pt., Canada 44 4N 81 45W
118 Clark Fork, U.S.A. 48 9N 116 9W
118 Clark Fork, R., U.S.A. 48 0N 115 40W
115 Clark Res., U.S.A. 33 45N 82 20W
119 Clarkdale, U.S.A. 34 53N 112 3W
98 Clarke Ra., Australia 20 45S 148 20E
107 Clarke City, Canada 50 12N 66 38W
100 Clarkefield, Australia 37 30S 44 40E
107 Clarkes Harbour, Can. 43 25N 65 38W
118 Clarks Fork, R., U.S.A. 45 0N 109 30W
113 Clarks Summit, U.S.A. 41 31N 75 44W
114 Clarksburg, U.S.A. 39 18N 80 21W
117 Clarksdale, U.S.A. 34 12N 90 33W
118 Clarkston, U.S.A. 46 28N 117 2W
117 Clarksville, Ark., U.S.A. 35 29N 93 27W
115 Clarksville, Tenn., U.S.A. 36 32N 87 20W
117 Clarksville, Tex., U.S.A. 33 37N 94 59W
118 Clatskanie, U.S.A. 46 9N 123 12W
117 Claude, U.S.A. 35 8N 101 22W
73 Claveria, Philippines 18 37N 121 15E
116 Clay Center, U.S.A. 39 27N 97 9W
119 Claypool, U.S.A. 33 27N 110 55W
112 Claysville, U.S.A. 40 5N 80 25W
118 Clayton, Idaho, U.S.A. 44 12N 114 31W
117 Clayton, N. Mex., U.S.A. 36 30N 103 10W
118 Cle Elum, U.S.A. 47 15N 120 57W
15 Clear C., Ireland 51 26N 9 30W
15 Clear I., Ireland 51 26N 9 30W
118 Clear Lake, Calif., U.S.A. 39 5N 122 54W
116 Clear Lake, S.D., U.S.A. 44 48N 96 41W
118 Clear Lake, Wash., U.S.A. 48 27N 122 15W
118 Clear Lake Res., U.S.A. 41 55N 121 10W
114 Clearfield, Pa., U.S.A. 41 0N 78 27W
118 Clearfield, Utah, U.S.A. 41 10N 112 0W
118 Clearmont, U.S.A. 44 43N 106 29W
108 Clearwater, Canada 51 38N 120 2W
115 Clearwater, U.S.A. 27 58N 82 45W
106 Clearwater L., Canada 56 10N 75 0W
118 Clearwater, Mts., U.S.A. 46 20N 115 30W
109 Clearwater, R., Canada 56 40N 109 30W
109 Clearwater Prov. Park, Canada 54 0N 101 0W
117 Cleburne, U.S.A. 32 18N 97 25W
12 Cleethorpes, Eng. 53 33N 0 2W
13 Cleeve Cloud, Eng. 51 56N 2 0W
13 Cleeve Hill, Eng. 51 54N 2 0W
21 Clelles, France 44 50N 5 38E
5 Clerks Rocks, Falkland Is. Dependencies 56 0S 36 30W
98 Clermont, Australia 22 46S 147 38E
19 Clermont, France 49 22N 2 24E
19 Clermont-en-Argonne, France 49 5N 5 4E
20 Clermont-Ferrand, Fr. 45 46N 3 4E
20 Clermont-l'Hérault, France 43 38N 3 26E
19 Clerval, France 47 25N 6 30E
19 Cléry-Saint-André, France 47 50N 1 46E
38 Cles, Italy 46 21N 11 4E
99 Cleveland, Australia 27 31S 153 3E
12 Cleveland, England 54 29N 1 0W
117 Cleveland, Miss., U.S.A. 33 43N 90 43W
112 Cleveland, Ohio, U.S.A. 41 28N 81 43W
117 Cleveland, Okla., U.S.A. 36 21N 96 33W
115 Cleveland, Tenn., U.S.A. 35 9N 84 52W
117 Cleveland, Tex., U.S.A. 30 18N 95 0W
98 Cleveland, C., Australia 19 11S 147 1E
99 Cleveland, Mt., Austral. 41 25S 145 23E
112 Cleveland Heights, U.S.A. 41 32N 81 30W
125 Clevelândia, Brazil 26 24S 52 23W
15 Clew Bay, Ireland 53 54N 9 50W
115 Clewiston, U.S.A. 26 44N 80 50W

* Incorporated within the region of Central

MAP

15 Clifden, Ireland 53 30N 10 2W
101 Clifden, New Zealand 46 1s 167 42E
119 Cliff, U.S.A. 33 0N 108 44W
99 Clifton, Australia 27 59s 151 53E
119 Clifton, Ariz., U.S.A. 33 8N 109 23W
117 Clifton, Tex., U.S.A. 31 46N 97 35W
114 Clifton Forge, U.S.A. 37 49N 79 51W
109 Climax, Canada 49 10N 108 20W
115 Clingmans Dome, U.S.A. 35 35N 83 30W
119 Clint, U.S.A. 31 37N 106 11W
108 Clinton, B.C., Canada 51 0N 121 40W
112 Clinton, Ont., Canada 43 38N 81 33W
101 Clinton, New Zealand 46 12s 169 23E
117 Clinton, Ark., U.S.A. 35 37N 92 30W
116 Clinton, Ill., U.S.A. 40 8N 89 0w
114 Clinton, Ind., U.S.A. 39 40N 87 22W
116 Clinton, Iowa, U.S.A. 41 50N 90 18W
113 Clinton, Mass., U.S.A. 42 26N 71 40W
116 Clinton, Mo., U.S.A. 38 20N 93 40W
113 Clinton, N.C., U.S.A. 35 5N 78 15W
117 Clinton, Okla., U.S.A. 35 30N 99 0w
115 Clinton, S.C., U.S.A. 34 30N 81 54W
115 Clinton, Tenn., U.S.A. 36 6N 84 10W
98 Clinton C., Australia 22 30s 150 45E
104 Clinton Colden L., Can. 64 0N 107 0w
116 Clintonville, U.S.A. 44 35N 88 46W
18 Clisson, France 47 5N 1 16w
96 Cloates, Pt., Australia 22 29s 113 37E
93 Clocolan, S. Afr. 28 55s 27 34E
124 Clodomira, Argentina 27 35s 64 14W
15 Clonakilty, Ireland 51 37N 8 53W
15 Clonakilty B., Ireland 51 33N 8 50W
98 Cloncurry, Australia 20 40s 140 28E
15 Clones, Ireland 54 10N 7 13W
15 Clonmel, Ireland 52 22N 7 42W
24 Cloppenburg, Germany 52 50N 8 3E
116 Cloquet, U.S.A. 46 40N 92 30W
124 Clorinda, Argentina 25 16s 57 45W
118 Cloud Peak, U.S.A. 44 30N 107 10W
119 Cloudcroft, U.S.A. 33 0N 105 48W
119 Cloverdale, U.S.A. 38 49N 123 0w
119 Clovis, Calif., U.S.A. 36 54N 119 45W
117 Clovis, N. Mex., U.S.A. 34 20N 103 10W
100 Club Terrace, Australia 37 30s 148 59E
46 Cluj, Rumania 46 47N 23 38E
46 Cluj ♦, Rumania 46 45N 23 30E
100 Clunes, Australia 37 20s 143 45E
21 Cluny, France 46 26N 4 38E
21 Cluses, France 46 5N 6 35E
38 Clusone, Italy 45 54N 9 58E
101 Clutha, R., N.Z. 45 39s 169 25E
12 Clwyd, R., Wales 53 12N 3 22W
99 Clyde, Australia 28 48s 143 40E
105 Clyde, Canada 70 30N 68 30W
101 Clyde, New Zealand 45 12s 169 20E
112 Clyde, U.S.A. 43 8N 76 52W
14 Clyde, Firth of, Scotland 55 20N 5 0w
14 Clyde, R., Scotland 55 46N 3 58W
14 Clydebank, Scot. 55 54N 4 25W
112 Clymer, U.S.A. 42 3N 79 39W
30 Côa, R., Portugal 40 45N 7 0w
119 Coachella, U.S.A. 33 44N 116 13W
107 Coachman's Cove, Can. 50 6N 56 20W
117 Coahoma, U.S.A. 32 17N 101 20W
120 Coahuila ♦, Mexico 27 0N 112 30W
91 Coalane, Mozambique 17 48s 37 2E
120 Coalcomán, Mexico 18 40N 103 10W
108 Coaldale, Canada 49 45N 112 35W
117 Coalgate, U.S.A. 34 35N 96 13W
119 Coalinga, U.S.A. 36 10N 120 21W
108 Coalspur, Canada 53 15N 117 0w
12 Coalville, Eng. 52 43N 1 21W
118 Coalville, U.S.A. 40 58N 111 24W
126 Coari, Brazil 4 8s 63 7w
90 Coast ♦, Kenya 2 40s 39 45E
*90 Coast ♦, Tanzania 7 0s 39 30E
108 Coast Mts., Canada 52 0N 126 0w
118 Coast Range, N. Amer. 40 0N 124 0w
96 Coastal Plains Basin, Australia 30 10s 115 30E
14 Coatbridge, Scot. 55 52N 4 2w
120 Coatepeque, Guatemala 14 46N 91 55W
114 Coatesville, U.S.A. 39 59N 75 30W
107 Coaticook, Canada 45 10N 71 46W
105 Coats I., Canada 62 30N 82 0w
5 Coats Land, Antarctica 77 0s 25 0w
120 Coatzacoalcos, Mexico 18 7N 94 35W
46 Cobadin, Rumania 44 5N 28 13E
106 Cobalt, Canada 47 25N 79 42W
120 Cobán, Guatemala 15 30N 90 21W
100 Cobar, Australia 31 27s 145 48E
100 Cobargo, Australia 36 20s 149 55E
100 Cobboras, Mt. Austral. 36 46s 148 10E
15 Cóbh, Ireland 51 50N 8 18W
99 Cobham, Australia 30 10s 142 0E
126 Cobija, Bolivia 11 0s 68 50W
113 Cobleskill, U.S.A. 42 40N 74 30W
112 Coboconk, Canada 44 40N 78 50W
106 Cobourg, Canada 44 0N 78 20W
118 Cobre, U.S.A. 41 6N 114 25W
25 Coburg, Germany 50 15N 10 58E
126 Coca, Ecuador 0 25s 77 5w
30 Coca, Spain 41 13N 4 32w
126 Coca, R., Ecuador 0 25s 77 5w
70 Cocanada = Kakinada, India 16 55N 82 20E
33 Cocentaina, Spain 38 45N 0 27W
126 Cochabamba, Bolivia 17 15s 66 20W
126 Coche, I., Venezuela 10 47N 63 56W
25 Cochem, Germany 50 8N 7 7E
91 Cochemane, Mozam. 17 0s 32 54E
125 Cochilha Grande de Albardão, Brazil 28 30s 51 30W
70 Cochin, India 9 55N 76 22E
71 Cochin China = Nam-Phan, South Vietnam 10 30N 106 0E
119 Cochise, U.S.A. 32 6N 109 58W
115 Cochran, U.S.A. 32 25N 83 23W
108 Cochrane, Alta., Can. 51 20N 114 30W
106 Cochrane, Ont., Canada 49 0N 81 0w

MAP

128 Cochrane, L., Chile 47 10s 72 0w
96 Cockatoo I., Australia 16 6s 123 37E
100 Cockburn, N.S.W., Australia 32 5s 141 2E
100 Cockburn, S.A., Australia 32 5s 141 0E
128 Cockburn, Canal, Chile 54 30s 72 0w
71 Coco Chan., Andaman 13 50N 93 25E
71 Coco Is., India 14 0N 93 12E
126 Coco, Pta., Colombia 2 58N 77 43W
121 Coco, R. (Wanks), Central America 14 10N 85 0w
120 Coco Solo, Panama Canal Zone 9 22N 79 53W
115 Cocoa, U.S.A. 28 22N 80 40W
88 Cocobeach, Gabon 0 59N 9 34E
84 Cocoli, R., Port. Guin. 12 0N 14 0w
82 Cocopara Ra., Austral. 34 0s 146 4E
46 Cocora, Rumania 44 45N 27 3E
3 Cocos (Keeling) Is., Indian Oc. 12 12s 96 54E
114 Cod, C., U.S.A. 42 8N 70 10W
126 Codajás, Brazil 3 40s 62 0w
126 Codera, C., Venezuela 10 35N 66 4W
109 Coderre, Canada 50 11N 106 31W
39 Codigoro, Italy 44 50N 12 5E
127 Codó, Brazil 4 30s 43 55W
38 Codogno, Italy 45 10N 9 42E
46 Codrăipo, Italy 45 57N 13 0E
46 Codru, Munţii, Rumania 46 30N 22 15E
118 Cody, U.S.A. 44 35N 109 0w
106 Coe Hill, Canada 44 53N 77 44W
126 Coelemu, Chile 36 30s 72 48W
98 Coen, Australia 13 52s 143 12E
24 Coesfeld, Germany 51 56N 7 10E
118 Coeur d'Alene, U.S.A. 47 45N 116 51W
16 Coevorden, Netherlands 52 40N 6 44E
117 Coffeyville, U.S.A. 37 0N 95 40W
96 Coffin B. Pen., Austral. 34 20s 135 10E
99 Coffs Harbour, Australia 30 16s 153 5E
33 Cofrentes, Spain 39 13N 1 5w
46 Cogealac, Rumania 44 36N 28 36E
40 Coghinas, R., Italy 40 55N 8 48E
20 Cognac, France 45 41N 0 20w
38 Cogne, Italy 45 37N 7 21E
32 Cogolludo, Spain 40 59N 3 10w
118 Cohagen, U.S.A. 47 2N 106 45W
113 Cohoes, U.S.A. 42 47N 73 42W
100 Cohuna, Australia 35 45s 144 15E
121 Coiba I., Panama 7 30N 81 40W
128 Coig, R., Argentina 51 0s 70 20W
30 Coimbra, Portugal 40 15N 8 27W
30 Coimbra ♦, Portugal 40 12N 8 25w
31 Coin, Spain 36 40N 4 48W
126 Cojedes ♦, Venezuela 9 20N 68 20W
126 Cojimies, Ecuador 0 20N 80 0w
46 Cojocna, Rumania 46 45N 23 50E
120 Cojutepeque, Salvador 13 41N 88 54W
42 Coka, Yugoslavia 45 57N 20 12E
118 Cokeville, U.S.A. 42 4N 111 0w
38 Col di Tenda, France 44 7N 7 36E
70 Colaba Pt., India 18 54N 72 47E
100 Colac, Australia 38 10s 143 30E
70 Colachel, India 8 10N 77 15E
31 Colares, Portugal 38 48N 9 30W
100 Colbinabbin, Australia 36 38s 144 48E
112 Colborne, Canada 44 1N 77 52W
116 Colby, U.S.A. 39 27N 101 2w
124 Colchagua ♦, Chile 34 30s 71 0w
13 Colchester, Eng. 51 54N 0 55E
14 Coldstream, Scot. 55 39N 2 14w
112 Coldwater, Canada 44 44N 79 40W
117 Coldwater, U.S.A. 37 18N 99 24W
114 Coldwater, U.S.A. 41 48N 86 30W
99 Colebrook, Australia 42 32s 147 20E
113 Colebrook, U.S.A. 44 54N 71 29W
108 Coleman, Canada 49 40N 114 30W
117 Coleman, U.S.A. 31 52N 99 30W
98 Coleman, R., Australia 15 6s 141 38E
64 Cölemerik, Turkey 37 35N 43 45E
93 Colenso, S. Afr. 28 44s 29 50E
15 Coleraine, Australia 37 36s 141 40E
101 Coleridge, L., N.Z. 43 17s 171 30E
70 Coleroon, R., India 11 25N 79 0E
93 Colesberg, S. Africa 30 45s 25 5E
118 Colfax, La., U.S.A. 31 35N 92 39W
118 Colfax, Wash., U.S.A. 46 57N 117 28W
128 Colhué Huapi, L., Arg. 45 30s 69 0w
38 Cólico, Italy 46 8N 9 22E
100 Colignan, Australia 34 35s 142 25E
92 Coligny, France 46 24N 5 21E
120 Colima, Mexico 19 10N 103 40W
120 Colima ♦, Mexico 19 10N 103 40W
124 Colina, Chile 33 13s 70 45W
84 Colina do Norte Port. Guinea 12 28N 15 0w
127 Colinas, Brazil 6 0s 44 10W
100 Colinton, Australia 35 50s 149 10E
14 Coll, I., Scot. 56 40N 6 35W
126 Collaguasi, Chile 21 5s 68 45W
32 Collarada, Peña, Spain 42 43N 0 29w
119 Collbran, U.S.A. 39 16N 107 58W
38 Colle Salvetti, Italy 43 34N 10 27E
41 Colle Sannita, Italy 41 22N 14 48E
91 Colleen Bawn, Rhod. 21 0s 29 12E
115 College Park, U.S.A. 33 42N 84 27W
107 Collette, Canada 46 40N 65 30W
100 Collie, Australia 33 22s 116 8E
96 Collier Bay, Austral. 16 0s 124 0E
38 Colline Metallifere, It. 43 10N 11 0E
98 Collingwood, Australia 22 20s 142 31E
112 Collingwood, Canada 44 29N 80 13W
101 Collingwood, N.Z. 40 25s 172 40E
98 Collingwood B., Papua 9 30s 149 30E
106 Collins, Canada 50 17N 89 27W
100 Collinsville, Australia 20 30s 147 56E
124 Collipulli, Chile 37 55s 72 30W

MAP

82 Collo, Algeria 36 58N 6 37E
21 Collonges, France 46 9N 5 52E
15 Collooney, Ireland 54 11N 8 28W
19 Colmar, France 48 5N 7 20E
21 Colmars, France 44 11N 6 39E
31 Colmenar, Spain 36 54N 4 20W
32 Colmenar de Oreja, Sp. 40 6N 3 25W
30 Colmenar Viejo, Spain 40 39N 3 47W
117 Colmor, U.S.A. 36 18N 104 36W
12 Colne, England 53 51N 2 11W
100 Colo, R., Australia 33 25s 150 52E
39 Cologna Véneta, Italy 45 19N 11 21E
82 Colomb-Béchar = Béchar, Algeria 31 38N 2 18E
19 Colombey-les-Belles, Fr. 48 32N 5 54E
19 Colombey-les-deux Eglises, France 48 20N 4 50E
126 Colombia, Colombia 3 24N 79 49W
126 Colombia ■, S. America 3 45N 73 0w
70 Colombo, Sri Lanka 6 56N 79 58E
119 Colombus, U.S.A. 31 54N 107 43W
116 Colome, U.S.A. 43 20N 99 44W
114 Colón, Argentina 32 12s 58 30W
121 Colón, Cuba 22 42N 80 54W
120 Colón, Panama Rep. 9 20N 80 0w
39 Colonella, Italy 42 52N 13 50E
125 Colonia del Sacramento, Uruguay 34 25s 57 50W
124 Colonia Dora, Arg. 28 34s 62 59W
128 Colonia Las Heras, Arg. 46 30s 69 0w
128 Colonia Sarmiento, Arg. 45 30s 68 15W
114 Colonial Hts., U.S.A. 37 20N 77 25W
42 Colonne, C., Italy 39 2N 17 11E
109 Colonsay, Canada 51 59N 105 52W
14 Colonsay, I., Scot. 56 4N 6 12W
124 Colorado ♦, U.S.A. 37 40N 106 0w
119 Colorado Aqueduct, U.S.A. 34 0N 115 20W
117 Colorado City, U.S.A. 32 25N 100 50W
119 Colorado Desert, U.S.A. 34 20N 116 0w
119 Colorado Plateau, U.S.A. 36 40N 110 30W
116 Colorado Springs, U.S.A. 38 55N 104 50W
38 Colorno, Italy 44 55N 10 21E
113 Colton, New York, U.S.A. 44 34N 74 58W
118 Columbia, Wash., U.S.A. 46 41N 117 6W
117 Columbia, La., U.S.A. 32 7N 92 5w
113 Columbia, Miss., U.S.A. 31 16N 89 50W
116 Columbia, Mo., U.S.A. 38 58N 92 20W
113 Columbia, Pa., U.S.A. 40 2N 76 30W
115 Columbia, S.C., U.S.A. 34 0N 81 0w
115 Columbia, Tenn., U.S.A. 35 40N 87 0w
114 Columbia, District of ♦, U.S.A. 38 55N 77 0w
108 Columbia, C., Canada 83 0N 70 0w
118 Columbia, Mt., Canada 52 0N 117 30W
118 Columbia, R., N. Amer. 45 49N 120 0w
118 Columbia City, U.S.A. 41 8N 85 30W
118 Columbia Falls, U.S.A. 48 25N 114 16W
116 Columbia Hts., U.S.A. 45 5N 93 10W
118 Columbia Plateau, U.S.A. 47 30N 118 30W
112 Columbiana, U.S.A. 40 53N 80 40W
32 Columbretes, Is., Spain 39 50N 0 50E
115 Columbus, Ga., U.S.A. 32 30N 84 58W
114 Columbus, Ind., U.S.A. 39 14N 85 55W
117 Columbus, Kans., U.S.A. 37 15N 94 30W
113 Columbus, Miss., U.S.A. 33 30N 88 26W
118 Columbus, Mont., U.S.A. 45 45N 109 14W
116 Columbus, Nebr., U.S.A. 41 30N 97 25W
114 Columbus, N.D., U.S.A. 48 52N 102 48W
114 Columbus, Ohio, U.S.A. 39 57N 83 1w
117 Columbus, Tex., U.S.A. 29 42N 96 33W
116 Columbus, Wis., U.S.A. 43 20N 89 2w
89 Columbus, Angola 12 7s 23 36E
30 Colunga, Spain 43 29N 5 16w
118 Colusa, U.S.A. 39 15N 122 1w
118 Colville, U.S.A. 48 33N 117 58W
104 Colville, C., N.Z. 36 29s 175 21E
104 Colville, R., Alaska 69 15s 152 0w
12 Colwyn Bay, Wales 53 17N 3 44W
39 Comácchio, Italy 44 41N 12 10E
124 Comallo, Argentina 41 0s 70 5w
46 Comana, Rumania 44 10N 26 10E
117 Comanche, Okla., U.S.A. 34 27N 97 58W
117 Comanche, Tex., U.S.A. 31 55N 98 35W
115 Comabahee, R., U.S.A. 32 45N 80 50W
19 Combeaufontaine, Fr. 47 38N 5 54E
112 Comber, Canada 42 15N 82 34W
16 Comblain, Belgium 50 29N 5 35E
19 Combles, France 50 0N 2 50E
19 Combourg, France 48 25N 1 46W
20 Combronde, France 45 58N 3 5E
15 Comeragh Mts., Ireland 52 17N 7 35W
98 Comet, Australia 23 36s 148 38E
70 Comilla, Bangladesh 23 22N 91 18E
40 Comino I., Sardinia 40 28N 9 47E
36 Comino I., Malta 36 0N 14 22E
41 Cómiso, Italy 36 57N 14 35E
120 Comitán, Mexico 16 18N 92 9w
19 Commentry, France 46 20N 2 46E
115 Commerce, Ga., U.S.A. 34 10N 83 25W
117 Commerce, Tex., U.S.A. 33 15N 95 50W
19 Commercy, France 48 40N 5 34E
105 Committee B., Canada 68 0N 87 0w
5 Commonwealth B., Ant. 67 0s 144 0E
65 Communism, Pk.= Pk.=Kommunizma, Pk., U.S.S.R.

MAP

38 Como, Italy 45 48N 9 5E
38 Como, L. di, Italy 46 5N 9 17E
128 Comodoro Rivadavia, Argentina 45 50s 67 40W
3 Comores, Arch. des, Ind. Oc. 10 0s 50 0E
70 Comorin, C., India 8 3N 77 40E
42 Comoriște, Rumania 45 10N 21 35E
19 Compiègne, France 49 24N 2 50E
38 Compiglia Maríttima, Italy 43 4N 10 37E
31 Comporta, Portugal 38 22N 8 46W
99 Compton Downs, Australia 30 28s 146 30E
71 Con Dao, S. Vietnam 8 45N 106 45E
84 Conakry, Guinea 9 29N 13 49W
99 Conara Junc., Austral. 41 48s 143 70E
120 Conatlán, Mexico 24 30N 104 42W
18 Concarneau, France 47 52N 3 56W
127 Conceição, Brazil 2 11N 60 58W
91 Conceição, Mozam. 18 47s 36 7E
127 Conceição da Barra, Brazil 18 35s 39 45W
127 Conceição do Araguaia, Brazil 8 0s 49 2W
126 Concepción, Argentina 27 20s 65 35W
126 Concepción, Bolivia 15 50s 61 40W
124 Concepción, Chile 36 50s 73 0w
126 Concepción, Colombia 0 5N 75 37W
124 Concepción, Paraguay 23 30s 57 20W
126 Concepción, Venezuela 10 48N 71 46W
110 Concepción, C., U.S.A. 34 30N 120 34W
126 Concepción, L., Bolivia 17 20s 61 10W
126 Concepción, Punta, Mexico 26 55N 111 50W
124 Concepción ♦, Chile 37 0s 72 30W
120 Concepción del Oro, Mexico 24 40N 101 30W
124 Concepción del Uruguay, Argentina 32 35s 58 20W
92 Conception B., South West Africa 23 55s 14 22E
121 Conception I., Bahamas 23 52N 75 9w
91 Concession, Rhodesia 17 27s 30 56E
107 Conche, Canada 50 48N 57 0w
119 Concho, U.S.A. 34 32N 109 43W
117 Concho, R., U.S.A. 31 30N 100 8W
120 Conchos, R., Mexico 29 20N 105 0w
124 Concon, Chile 32 56s 71 33W
113 Concord, N.H., U.S.A. 43 5N 71 30W
113 Concord, N.C., U.S.A. 35 28N 80 35W
124 Concórdia, Argentina 31 20s 58 2w
126 Concórdia, Brazil 4 36s 66 36W
126 Concórdia, Colombia 2 39N 72 47W
19 Concots, France 44 26N 1 40E
118 Concrete, U.S.A. 48 35N 121 49W
99 Condamine, R., Australia 26 55s 150 3E
19 Condat, France 45 21N 2 46E
19 Condé, France 50 26N 3 34E
18 Condé-sur-Noireau, Fr. 48 51N 0 33W
127 Condeúba, Brazil 15 0s 42 0w
100 Condobolin, Australia 33 4s 147 6E
20 Condom, France 43 57N 0 22E
38 Condove, Italy 45 8N 7 19E
39 Conegliano, Italy 45 53N 12 18E
33 Conejera, I., Spain 39 11N 2 58E
112 Conemaugh, R., U.S.A. 40 24N 79 0w
19 Conflans-en-Jarnisy, France 49 10N 5 52E
20 Confolens, France 46 2N 0 40E
124 Confuso, R., Paraguay 24 10s 59 0w
13 Congleton, Eng. 53 10N 2 12W
88 Congo, R., Africa 1 30N 28 0E
88 Congo, Democratic Rep. of = Zaïre ■, Afr. 3 0s 22 0E
88 Congo, Rep. of ■, Africa 1 0s 16 0E
119 Congress, U.S.A. 34 11N 112 56W
127 Congucu, Brazil 31 25s 52 30W
31 Conil, Spain 36 17N 6 10W
106 Coniston, Canada 46 32N 80 51W
70 Conjeeveram = Kancheepuram, India 12 52N 79 45E
100 Conjuboy, Australia 18 35s 144 45E
99 Conlea, Australia 30 7s 144 35E
15 Conn, L., Ireland 54 3N 9 15W
15 Connacht, Ire. 53 23N 8 40W
112 Conneaut, U.S.A. 41 55N 80 32W
113 Connecticut, R., U.S.A. 42 15N 72 30W
113 Connecticut ♦, U.S.A. 41 40N 72 40W
118 Connell, U.S.A. 46 45N 118 58W
15 Connemara, Ire. 53 29N 9 45W
114 Connersville, U.S.A. 39 40N 85 10W
99 Connors Ra., Australia 21 40s 149 10E
100 Conoble, Australia 32 55s 144 42E
118 Conrad, U.S.A. 48 11N 112 0w
117 Conroe, U.S.A. 30 15N 95 28W
125 Conselheiro Lafaiete, Brazil 20 40s 43 48W
113 Conshohocken, U.S.A. 40 5N 75 18W
25 Constance = Konstanz, Germany 47 39N 9 10E
25 Constance, L. = Bodensee, Germany 47 35N 9 25E
46 Constanţa, Rumania 44 14N 28 38E
46 Constanţa ♦, Rumania 44 15N 28 15E
31 Constantina, Spain 37 51N 5 40W
82 Constantine, Algeria 36 25N 6 42E
124 Constitución, Chile 35 20s 72 30W
124 Constitución, Uruguay 31 0s 58 10W

MAP

31 Consuegra, Spain 39 28N 3 43W
109 Consul, Canada 49 20N 109 30W
118 Contact, U.S.A. 41 50N 114 56W
69 Contai, India 21 54N 87 55E
126 Contamana, Peru 7 10s 74 55W
39 Contarina, Italy 45 2N 12 13E
127 Contas, R., Brazil 13 5s 41 53W
21 Contes, France 43 49N 7 19E
113 Contoocook, U.S.A. 43 13N 71 45W
93 Contra Costa, Mozambique 25 9s 33 30E
126 Contratación, Col. 6 18N 73 29W
19 Contres, France 47 24N 1 26E
19 Contrexéville, France 48 6N 5 53E
126 Convención, Col. 8 28N 73 21W
41 Conversano, Italy 40 57N 17 8E
98 Conway, Australia 20 22s 148 42E
99 Conway, Ark., U.S.A. 35 5N 92 30W
113 Conway, N.H., U.S.A. 43 58N 71 8W
115 Conway, S.C., U.S.A. 33 49N 79 2w
*12 Conway, Wales 53 17N 3 50W
*12 Conway, R., Wales 53 10N 3 50W
69 Cooch Behar, India 26 22N 89 29E
116 Cook, U.S.A. 47 49N 92 39W
128 Cook, Bahia, Chile 55 10s 70 0w
104 Cook Inlet, Alaska 59 0N 151 0w
95 Cook Is., Pac. Ocean 20 0s 160 0w
101 Cook, Mount, N.Z. 43 36s 170 9E
101 Cook Strait, N.Z. 41 15s 174 29E
115 Cookeville, U.S.A. 36 12N 85 30W
92 Cookhouse, S. Africa 32 44s 25 47E
113 Cookshire, Canada 45 26N 71 38W
15 Cookstown, N. Ire. 54 40N 6 43W
112 Cooksville, Canada 43 36N 79 35W
98 Cooktown, Australia 15 30s 145 16E
99 Coolabah, Australia 31 0s 146 15E
99 Cooladdi, Australia 26 37s 145 23E
100 Coolah, Austral. 31 48s 149 41E
100 Coolamon, Australia 34 46s 147 8E
99 Coolangatta, Australia 28 11s 153 29E
96 Coolgardie, Austral. 30 55s 121 8E
119 Coolidge, U.S.A. 33 1N 111 35W
119 Coolidge Dam, U.S.A. 33 10N 110 30W
100 Cooma, Austral. 36 12s 149 8E
99 Coonabarabran, Austral. 31 14s 149 18E
99 Coonamble, Australia 30 56s 148 27E
70 Coondapoor, India 13 42N 74 40E
99 Coongie, Australia 27 9s 140 8E
99 Coongoola, Australia 27 43s 145 51E
70 Coonoor, India 11 10N 76 45E
117 Cooper, U.S.A. 33 20N 95 40W
115 Cooper, R., U.S.A. 33 0N 79 55W
99 Cooper Cr., Australia 28 0s 139 0E
113 Cooperstown, New York, U.S.A. 42 42N 74 57W
116 Cooperstown, N.D., U.S.A. 47 30N 98 14W
98 Coorabulka, Australia 23 41s 140 20E
100 Cooranbong, Australia 33 2s 151 30E
99 Coorong, The, Austral. 35 50s 139 20E
99 Cooroy, Australia 26 22s 152 54E
118 Coos Bay, U.S.A. 43 26N 124 7w
98 Cootamundra, Australia 34 36s 148 1E
15 Cootehill, Ireland 54 5N 7 5W
99 Cooyar, Australia 26 59s 151 51E
99 Cooyeana, Australia 44 25s 138 50E
120 Copainalá, Mexico 17 8N 93 11w
116 Cope, U.S.A. 39 44N 102 50W
33 Cope, Cabo, Spain 37 26N 1 28W
49 Copenhagen = København, Denmark 55 41N 12 34E
41 Copertino, Italy 40 17N 18 2w
124 Copiapó, Chile 27 15s 70 20E
99 Copley, Australia 30 31s 138 25E
118 Copparo, Italy 44 52N 11 49E
104 Copper Center, Alaska 62 10N 145 25W
106 Copper Cliff, Canada 46 30N 81 4W
114 Copper Harbour, U.S.A. 47 31N 87 55W
108 Copper Mountain, Can. 49 20N 120 30W
91 Copper Queen, Rhod. 17 29s 29 18E
91 Copperbelt ♦, Zambia 13 15N 27 30E
104 Coppermine, Canada 68 0N 116 0w
104 Coppermine, R., Canada 66 30N 115 30W
21 Coquet, R., Eng. 55 18N 1 45W
88 Coquilhatville = Mbandaka, Congo 0 1N 18 18E
118 Coquille, U.S.A. 43 15N 124 6W
124 Coquimbo, Chile 30 0s 71 20W
128 Coquimbo ♦, Chile 31 0s 71 0w
46 Corabia, Rumania 43 48N 24 30E
126 Coracora, Peru 15 5s 73 45W
41 Coradi, Is., Italy 40 27N 17 10E
105 Coral Harbour, Canada 64 0N 83 0w
98 Coral Sea, Pacific Ocean 15 0s 150 0E
98 Coral Sea Basin, Pacific Ocean 13 0s 147 0E
98 Coral Sea Islands Terr., Aust. 20 0s 155 0E
104 Coral Rapids, Canada 50 20N 81 40W
100 Corangamite, L., Australia 38 0s 143 30E
112 Coraopolis, U.S.A. 40 30N 80 10W
41 Corato, Italy 41 12N 16 22E
19 Corbeil-Essonnes, Fr. 48 36N 2 26E
20 Corbie, France 49 54N 2 30E
20 Corbières, mts., France 42 55N 2 35E
19 Corbigny, France 47 16N 3 40E
114 Corbin, U.S.A. 37 0N 84 3w
31 Corbones, R., Spain 37 25N 5 35W
13 Corby, England 52 29N 0 41w
33 Corcoles, R., Spain 39 12N 2 40W
30 Corcubión, Spain 42 56N 9 12W
115 Cordele, U.S.A. 31 55N 83 49W
117 Cordell, U.S.A. 35 18N 99 0w
39 Cordenons, Italy 45 59N 12 42E
21 Cordes, France 44 5N 1 57E
124 Córdoba, Argentina 31 20s 64 10W
120 Córdoba, Durango = Tiahualilo, Mexico 26 20N 103 20W

MAP
120 Córdoba, Vera Cruz, 18 50N 97 0w
  Mexico
31 Córdoba, Spain 37 50N 4 50w
124 Córdoba ♦, Arg. 31 22s 64 15w
126 Córdoba ♦, Colombia 8 20N 75 40w
31 Córdoba, Spain 38 5N 5 0w
124 Córdoba, Sierra de, Arg. 31 10s 64 25w
73 Cordon, Philippines 16 42N 121 32E
115 Cordova, Ala., U.S.A. 33 45N 87 12w
104 Cordova, Alaska, U.S.A. 60 36N 145 45w
32 Corella, Spain 42 7N 1 48w
98 Corfield, Australia 21 40s 143 21E
44 Corfu = Kerkira, 39 38N 19 50E
  Greece
30 Corgo, Spain 42 56N 7 25w
40 Cori, Italy 41 39N 12 53E
30 Coria, Spain 39 43N 6 33w
100 Coricudgy, Mt., Austral. 32 51s 150 24E
41 Corigliano Cálabro, It. 39 36N 16 31E
99 Corinna, Australia 41 35s 145 10E
45 Corinth = Korinthos, 37 56N 22 55E
  Greece
115 Corinth, Miss., U.S.A. 34 54N 88 30w
113 Corinth, N.Y., U.S.A. 43 15N 73 50w
45 Corinth Canal, Greece 37 48N 23 0E
45 Corinth, G. of = 38 16N 22 30E
  Korinthiakós, Gr.
127 Corinto, Brazil 18 20s 44 30w
121 Corinto, Nicaragua 12 30N 87 10w
46 Corj ♦, Rumania 45 5N 23 25E
15 Cork, Ireland 51 54N 8 30w
15 Cork ♦, Ireland 51 50N 8 50w
15 Cork Harbour, Ireland 51 46N 8 16w
18 Corlay, France 48 18N 3 5w
40 Corleone, Italy 37 48N 13 16E
41 Corleto Perticara, Italy 40 23N 16 2E
43 Corlu, Turkey 41 11N 27 49E
39 Cormóns, Italy 45 58N 13 29E
109 Cormorant, Canada 54 5N 100 45w
121 Corn Is., Cent. Amer. 12 0N 83 0w
125 Cornélio Procópio, Braz. 23 7s 50 40w
116 Cornell, U.S.A. 45 10N 91 8w
107 Corner Brook, Canada 49 0N 58 0w
100 Corner Inlet, Australia 38 40s 146 30E
38 Corniglio, Italy 44 29N 10 5E
117 Corning, Ark., U.S.A. 36 27N 90 34w
118 Corning, Calif., U.S.A. 39 56N 122 9w
116 Corning, Iowa, U.S.A. 40 57N 94 40w
112 Corning, N.Y., U.S.A. 42 10N 77 3w
106 Cornwall, Canada 45 5N 74 45w
13 Cornwall ♦, Eng. 50 26N 4 40w
4 Cornwallis I., Canada 75 0N 95 0w
126 Coro, Venezuela 11 25N 69 41w
127 Coroatá, Brazil 4 20s 44 0w
126 Corocoro, Bolivia 17 15s 69 19w
126 Coroico, Bolivia 16 0s 67 50w
101 Coromandel, N.Z. 36 45s 175 31E
70 Coromandel Coast, India 12 30N 81 0E
109 Coromorant, L., Canada 54 20N 100 50w
119 Corona, Calif., U.S.A. 33 49N 117 36w
119 Corona, N. Mex., U.S.A. 34 15N 105 32w
119 Coronado, U.S.A. 32 45N 117 9w
121 Coronado, Bahía de, 9 0N 83 40w
  Costa Rica
104 Coronation Gulf, Can. 68 0N 114 0w
5 Coronation I., Antarc. 60 45s 46 0w
124 Coronda, Argentina 31 58s 60 56w
124 Coronel, Chile 37 0s 73 10w
128 Coronel Dorrego, Arg. 38 40s 61 10w
124 Coronel Oviedo, Par. 25 24s 56 30w
124 Coronel Pringles, Arg. 38 0s 61 30w
124 Coronel Suárez, Arg. 37 30s 62 0w
124 Coronel Vidal, Arg. 37 28s 57 45w
127 Coronie, Surinam 5 55N 56 25w
44 Corovoda, Albania 40 31N 20 14E
100 Corowa, Australia 35 58s 146 21E
120 Corozal, Brit. Hond. 18 30N 88 30w
126 Corozal, Colombia 9 19N 75 18w
120 Corozal, Pan. Can. Zone 8 59N 79 34w
21 Corps, France 44 50s 5 56E
125 Corpus, Argentina 27 10s 55 30w
117 Corpus Christi, U.S.A. 27 50N 97 28w
117 Corpus Christi L., 28 2N 97 54w
  U.S.A.
126 Corque, Bolivia 18 10s 67 50w
32 Corral de Almaguer, Sp. 39 45N 3 10w
38 Corrégio, Italy 44 46N 10 47E
93 Correntes, C. das, 24 6s 35 34E
  Mozambique
20 Corrèze ♦, France 45 20N 1 45E
15 Corrib, L., Ireland 53 25N 9 10w
124 Corrientes, Argentina 27 30s 58 45w
126 Corrientes, C., Colombia 5 30N 77 34w
121 Corrientes, C., Cuba 21 43N 84 30w
126 Corrientes, R. Colombia 3 15s 75 58w
124 Corrientes ♦, Argentina 28 0s 57 0w
117 Corrigan, U.S.A. 31 0N 94 48w
112 Corry, U.S.A. 41 55N 79 39w
100 Corryong, Australia 36 12s 147 53E
21 Corse, C., Corsica 43 1N 9 25E
21 Corse, I., Mediterranean 42 0N 9 0E
  Sea
• 21 Corse ♦, France 42 0N 9 0E
21 Corsica = Corse, 42 0N 9 0E
  Mediterranean Sea
117 Corsicana, U.S.A. 32 5N 96 30w
21 Corté, France 42 19N 9 11E
31 Corte do Pinto, Port. 37 42N 7 29w
31 Cortegana, Spain 37 52N 6 49w
119 Cortez, U.S.A. 37 24N 108 35w
39 Cortina d'Ampezzo, It. 46 32N 12 9E
113 Cortland, U.S.A. 42 35N 76 11w
39 Cortona, Italy 43 16N 12 0E
31 Coruche, Portugal 38 57N 8 30w
64 Çorum, Turkey 40 30N 35 5E
127 Corumbá, Goias, Brazil 16 0s 48 50w
126 Corumbá, Mato Grosso, 19 0s 57 30w
  Brazil
30 Coruña ♦, Spain 43 0N 8 37w
46 Corund, Rumania 46 30N 25 13E

MAP
30 Corunna = La Coruña, 43 20N 8 25w
  Spain
127 Coruripe, Brazil 10 5s 36 10w
31 Corvallis, U.S.A. 44 36N 123 15w
106 Corvette, L., Canada 53 25N 73 55w
116 Corydon, U.S.A. 40 42N 93 22w
120 Cosamaloapán, Mexico 18 23N 95 50w
41 Cosenza, Italy 39 17N 16 14E
46 Coşereni, Rumania 44 38N 26 35E
112 Coshocton, U.S.A. 40 17N 81 51w
20 Cosne-s.-Loire, France 47 24N 2 54E
30 Cospeito, Spain 43 12N 7 34w
124 Cosquín, Argentina 31 15s 64 30w
38 Cossato, Italy 45 34N 8 10E
18 Cossé-le-Vivien, France 47 57N 0 54w
32 Costa Blanca, Sp. 38 25N 0 10w
32 Costa Brava, Spain 41 30N 3 0E
32 Costa del Sol, Sp. 36 30N 4 30w
32 Costa Dorada, Spain 40 45N 1 15E
121 Costa Rica ■, Central 10 0N 84 0w
  America
40 Costa Smeralda, Sardinia 41 5N 9 35E
38 Costigliole d'Asti, Italy 44 48N 8 11E
119 Costilla, U.S.A. 37 0N 105 30w
46 Coştiui, Rumania 47 53N 24 2E
24 Coswig, Germany 51 52N 12 31E
73 Cotabato, Philippines 7 14N 124 15E
124 Cotagaita, Bolivia 20 45s 65 30w
21 Côte d'Azur, Fr. 43 25N 6 50E
21 Côte d'Or, Fr. 47 10N 4 50E
21 Côte d'Or ♦, France 47 30N 4 50E
116 Coteau des Prairies, 44 30N 97 0w
  U.S.A.
110 Coteau du Missouri, 47 0N 101 0w
  Plat. du, U.S.A.
113 Coteau Sta., Canada 45 17N 74 14w
18 Cotentin, France 49 30N 1 30w
19 Côtes de Meuse, France 49 15N 5 22E
18 Côtes-du-Nord ♦, 48 25N 2 40w
  France
32 Cotiella, Spain 42 31N 0 19E
42 Cotina, R., Yugoslavia 43 36N 19 9E
125 Cotonou, Dahomey 6 20N 2 25E
126 Cotopaxi, Vol., Ecuador 0 30s 78 30w
41 Cotronei, Italy 39 9N 16 27E
13 Cotswold Hills, England 51 42N 2 10w
118 Cottage Grove, U.S.A. 43 48N 123 2w
24 Cottbus, Germany 51 44N 14 20E
24 Cottbus ♦, E. Ger. 51 43N 13 30E
110 Cottonwood, Canada 53 5N 121 50E
20 Couches, Pte. de la, Fr. 45 42N 1 15w
119 Cottonwood, U.S.A. 34 48N 112 1w
20 Couches, France 46 53N 4 30E
31 Couço, Portugal 38 59N 8 17w
112 Coudersport, U.S.A. 41 45N 78 1w
18 Couëron, France 47 13N 1 44w
18 Coueson, R., France 48 20N 1 15w
20 Couhé-Vérac, France 46 18N 0 12E
20 Coulanges, Deux Sèvres, 46 58N 0 35w
  France
19 Coulanges, Yonne, Fr. 47 30N 3 30E
19 Coulee City, U.S.A. 47 44N 119 12w
5 Coulman I., Antarctica 73 35s 170 0E
20 Coulommiers, France 48 50N 3 3E
107 Coulonge, L., Canada 46 50N 77 20w
104 Council, U.S.A. 64 55N 163 45w
116 Council Bluffs, U.S.A. 41 20N 95 50w
116 Council Grove, U.S.A. 38 41N 96 30w
20 Courantyne, R., S. 5 0N 57 45w
  Amer.
20 Courçon, France 46 15N 0 50w
21 Cours, France 46 7N 4 19E
20 Coursan, France 43 14N 3 4E
18 Courseulles, France 49 20N 0 29w
117 Courshatta, U.S.A. 32 3N 93 20w
112 Courtenay, Canada 49 45N 125 0w
16 Courtrai = Kortrijk, 50 50N 3 17E
  Belgium
112 Courtright, Canada 42 48N 82 55w
18 Courville, France 48 28N 1 15E
18 Coutances, France 49 3N 1 28w
18 Couterne, France 48 30N 0 25w
18 Coutras, France 45 3N 0 8w
32 Covarrubias, Spain 42 4N 3 31w
46 Covasna, Rumania 45 50N 26 10E
46 Covasna ♦, Rumania 45 50N 26 0E
13 Coventry, Eng. 52 25N 1 31w
109 Coventry L., Canada 61 15N 106 15w
30 Covilhã, Portugal 40 17N 7 31w
114 Covington, Ga., U.S.A. 33 36N 83 50w
114 Covington, Ky., U.S.A. 39 5N 84 30w
117 Covington, Okla., U.S.A. 36 21N 97 36w
117 Covington, Tenn., U.S.A. 35 34N 89 39w
98 Cowal Cr. Settlement, 10 30s 142 16E
  Australia
100 Cowal L., Australia 33 40s 147 25E
52 Cowan, Canada 52 5N 100 45w
96 Cowan L., Australia 31 45s 121 45E
100 Cowangie, Australia 35 12s 141 26E
110 Cowansville, Canada 45 14N 72 46w
99 Cowarie, Australia 27 45s 138 15E
14 Cowdenbeath, Scot. 56 7N 3 20w
99 Cowell, Australia 33 38s 136 40E
13 Cowes, England 50 45N 1 18w
100 Cowra, Austral. 33 49s 148 42E
127 Coxim, Brazil 18 30s 54 55w
67 Cox's Bazar, Bangladesh 21 25N 92 3E
107 Cox's Cove, Canada 49 7N 58 5w
120 Coyuca de Benitez, Mex. 17 1N 100 8w
120 Coyuca de Catalán, 18 58N 100 41w
  Mex.
116 Cozad, U.S.A. 40 55N 99 57w
38 Cozie, Alpi, It./Fr. 44 50N 7 5E
120 Cozumel, Isla de, Mex. 20 30N 86 40w
100 Craboon, Australia 32 3s 149 30E
99 Cracow, Australia 25 14s 150 24E
92 Cradock, S. Afr. 32 8s 25 36E
118 Crafton, U.S.A. 40 25N 80 4w
118 Craig, U.S.A. 40 32N 107 44w
15 Craigavon = 54 27N 6 26w
  Portadown, N. Ire.

MAP
91 Craigmore, Rhodesia 20 28s 32 30E
25 Crailsheim, Germany 49 7N 10 5E
46 Craiova, Rumania 44 21N 23 48E
98 Cramsie, Australia 23 20s 144 15E
109 Cranberry Portage, Can. 54 36N 101 22w
99 Cranbrook, Australia 40 0s 148 5E
108 Cranbrook, Canada 49 30N 115 55w
113 Crandon, U.S.A. 45 32N 88 52w
118 Crane, Oregon, U.S.A. 43 21N 118 39w
117 Crane, Texas, U.S.A. 31 26N 102 27w
113 Cranston, U.S.A. 41 47N 71 27w
15 Craon; France 50 0N 0 58w
19 Craonne, France 49 27N 3 46E
118 Crater Lake, U.S.A. 42 55N 122 3w
127 Crateús, Brazil 5 10s 40 50w
41 Crati, R., Italy 39 41N 16 30E
127 Crato, Brazil 7 10s 39 25w
31 Crato, Portugal 39 16N 7 39w
21 Crau, France 43 32N 4 40E
116 Crawford, U.S.A. 42 40N 103 25w
114 Crawfordsville, U.S.A. 40 2N 86 51w
13 Crawley, England 51 7N 0 10w
118 Crazy Mts., U.S.A. 46 14N 110 30w
19 Crécy-en-Brie, France 48 50N 2 53E
19 Crécy-en-Ponthieu, Fr. 50 15N 1 53E
19 Crécy-sur-Serre, France 49 40N 3 32E
116 Crediton, Canada 43 19N 81 33w
14 Cree, R., Scotland 55 3N 4 35w
109 Cree L., Canada 57 30N 107 0w
119 Creede, U.S.A. 37 56N 106 59w
120 Creel, Mexico 27 45N 107 38w
116 Creighton, U.S.A. 42 30N 97 52w
19 Creil, France 49 15N 2 34E
38 Crema, Italy 45 21N 9 40E
38 Cremona, Italy 45 8N 10 2E
42 Crepaja, Yugoslavia 45 1N 20 38E
19 Crépy, France 49 37N 3 32E
19 Crépy-en-Valois, France 49 14N 2 54E
39 Cres, Yugoslavia 44 58N 14 25E
116 Cresbard, U.S.A. 45 13N 98 57w
117 Crescent, Okla., U.S.A. 35 58N 97 36w
118 Crescent, Oreg., U.S.A. 43 30N 121 37w
118 Crescent City, U.S.A. 41 45N 124 12w
38 Crescentino, Italy 45 11N 8 7E
39 Crespino, Italy 44 59N 11 51E
106 Cressman, Canada 47 40N 72 55w
100 Cressy, Australia 38 10s 143 38E
21 Crest, France 44 44N 5 2E
38 Crested Butte, U.S.A. 38 57N 107 0w
112 Crestline, U.S.A. 40 46N 82 45w
108 Creston, Canada 49 10N 116 40w
116 Creston, Iowa, U.S.A. 41 0N 94 20w
118 Creston, Wash., U.S.A. 47 47N 118 36w
118 Creston, Wyo., U.S.A. 41 46N 107 50w
115 Crestview, U.S.A. 30 45N 86 35w
100 Creswick, Australia 37 19s 143 50E
45 Crete = Kriti, Greece 35 15N 25 0E
45 Crete, Sea of, Greece 26 0N 25 0E
32 Creus, C., Spain 42 20N 3 19E
20 Creuse ♦, France 46 0N 2 0E
20 Creuse, R., France 47 0N 0 34E
21 Creuzburg, Germany 51 3N 10 15E
39 Crevalcore, Italy 44 41N 11 10E
33 Crèvecœur-le-Grand, Fr. 49 37N 2 5E
33 Crevillente, Spain 38 12N 0 48w
13 Crewe, England 53 6N 2 28w
100 Crib Point, Australia 38 15s 145 11E
14 Crieff, Scotland 56 22N 3 50w
39 Crikvenica, Yugoslavia 45 11N 14 40E
108 Crillon, Mt., Canada 58 39N 137 14w
56 Crimea = Krymskaya, 45 0N 34 0E
  U.S.S.R.
24 Crimmitschau, Germany 50 48N 12 23E
46 Cristeşti, Rumania 47 15N 26 33E
120 Cristóbal, Pan. Can. 9 10N 80 0w
  Zone
46 Crişul Alb, R., Rum 46 25N 21 40E
46 Crişul Negru, R., Rum 46 38N 22 26E
46 Crişul Repede, R., Rum. 47 20N 22 25E
24 Crivitz, Germany 53 35N 11 39E
42 Crna Gora ♦, Y.-slav. 42 40N 19 20E
42 Crna Trava, Yugoslavia 42 49N 22 19E
42 Crni Drim, R., Y.-slav. 41 17N 20 40E
42 Crni Timok, R., Y.-slav. 43 53N 22 0E
42 Crnoljeva Planina, 42 20N 21 0E
  Yugoslavia
39 Črnomelj, Yugoslavia 45 33N 15 10E
15 Croagh Patrick, mt., Ire. 53 46N 9 40w
39 Croatia = Hrvatska, 45 20N 16 0E
  Y.-slav.
117 Crocker, Barisan, Sabah 5 0N 116 30E
117 Crockett, U.S.A. 31 20N 95 30w
96 Crocodile Is., Australia 11 43s 135 8E
41 Crocq, France 45 52N 2 21E
18 Croisic, Pte. du., Fr. 47 19N 2 31w
112 Croker, C., Canada 44 57N 80 59w
96 Croker, I., Australia 11 12N 132 32E
109 Cromarty, Canada 58 5N 94 10w
14 Cromarty, Scot. 57 40N 4 2w
13 Cromer, England 52 56N 1 18E
101 Cromwell, N.Z. 45 3s 169 14E
19 Cronat, France 46 43N 3 40E
100 Cronulla, Australia 34 3s 151 8E
121 Crooked I., Bahamas 22 50N 74 10w
99 Crooked, R., Australia 44 30N 121 0w
116 Crookston, Minn., 47 50N 96 40w
  U.S.A.
116 Crookston, Nebr., U.S.A. 42 56N 100 45w
114 Crooksville, U.S.A. 39 45N 82 8w
98 Crookwell, Australia 34 28s 149 24E
116 Crosby, Minn., U.S.A. 46 28N 93 57w
112 Crosby, Pa., U.S.A. 41 45N 78 23w
117 Crosbyton, U.S.A. 33 37N 101 12w
85 Cross, R, Nigeria 4 46N 8 20E
115 Cross City, U.S.A. 29 35N 83 5w

MAP
12 Cross Fell, Eng. 54 44N 2 29w
117 Cross Plains, U.S.A. 32 8N 99 7w
104 Cross Sound, U.S.A. 58 20N 136 30w
117 Crossett, U.S.A. 33 10N 91 57w
15 Crosshaven, Ireland 51 48N 8 19w
113 Croton-on-Hudson, 41 19N 73 55w
  U.S.A.
41 Crotone, Italy 39 5N 17 6E
118 Crow Agency, U.S.A. 45 40N 107 30w
15 Crow Hd., Ireland 51 34N 10 9w
100 Crowdy Hd., Australia 31 48s 152 44E
117 Crowell, U.S.A. 33 59N 99 45w
100 Crowes, Australia 38 43s 143 24E
117 Crowley, U.S.A. 30 15N 92 20w
114 Crown Point, U.S.A. 41 24N 87 23w
99 Crow's Nest, Australia 27 14s 152 2E
108 Crowsnest P., Canada 49 40N 114 40w
98 Croydon, Australia 18 15s 142 14E
13 Croydon, Eng. 51 18N 0 5w
46 Crozet, Ile, Indian 46 27s 52 0E
  Ocean
18 Crozon, France 48 15N 4 3w
126 Cruces, Pta., Colombia 6 39N 77 32w
98 Crummer Peaks, 6 40s 144 0E
  Territory of Papua
19 Cruz, C., Cuba 19 50N 77 50w
124 Cruz del Eje, Argentina 30 45s 64 50w
126 Cruzeiro, Brazil 22 50s 45 0w
126 Cruzeiro do Sul, Brazil 7 35s 72 35w
28 Cryfow Sl., Poland 51 2N 15 24E
116 Crystal City, Mo., 38 15N 90 23w
  U.S.A.
117 Crystal City, Tex., 28 40N 99 50w
  U.S.A.
114 Crystal Falls, U.S.A. 46 9N 88 11w
28 Cryfow Sl., Poland 51 2N 15 24E
115 Crystal River, U.S.A. 28 54N 82 35w
117 Crystal Springs, U.S.A. 31 59N 90 25w
27 Csongrád, Hungary 46 43N 20 12E
27 Csongrád ♦, Hungary 46 32N 20 15E
27 Csorna, Hungary 47 38N 17 18E
27 Csurgo, Hungary 46 16N 17 9E
64 Ctesiphon, Iraq 33 9N 44 35E
71 Cu Lao Hon, S. 10 22N 109 12E
  Vietnam
91 Cuácua, R., Mozam. 18 0s 36 0E
92 Cuamato, Angola 17 2s 15 7E
92 Cuamba = Nova 14 45s 36 22E
  Preixo, Mozam.
92 Cuando, Angola 16 25s 22 2E
89 Cuando, R., Angola 14 0s 19 30E
92 Cuando Cubango ♦, 16 25s 20 0E
  Angola
92 Cuangar, Angola 17 2s 18 40E
88 Cuango, Angola 6 15s 16 35E
92 Cuango, Angola 17 2s 18 40E
121 Cuba ■, W. Indies 22 0N 79 0w
31 Cuba, Portugal 38 10N 7 54w
119 Cuba, N. Mex., U.S.A. 36 0N 107 0w
112 Cuba, N.Y., U.S.A. 42 12N 78 18w
92 Cubango, R., Africa 16 15s 17 30E
89 Cuchi, Angola 14 37s 17 10E
27 Cucurpe, Mexico 30 20N 110 43w
126 Cucurrupi, Colombia 4 23N 76 56w
126 Cucuta, Colombia 7 54N 72 31w
42 Cudahy, U.S.A. 42 54N 87 50w
46 Cudalbi, Rumania 45 46N 27 41E
70 Cuddalore, India 11 46N 79 45E
70 Cuddapah, India 14 30N 78 47E
100 Cudgewa, Australia 36 10s 147 42E
33 Cudillero, Spain 43 33N 6 9w
96 Cue, Australia 27 20s 117 55E
32 Cuéllar, Spain 41 23N 4 21E
126 Cuenca, Ecuador 2 50s 79 0w
32 Cuenca, Spain 40 5N 2 10w
32 Cuenca ♦, Spain 40 0N 2 0w
32 Cuenca, Serrania de, 39 55N 1 50w
  Spain
32 Cuerda del Pozo, 41 51N 2 44w
  Pantano de la, So.
120 Cuernavaca, Mexico 18 50N 99 20w
117 Cuero, U.S.A. 29 5N 97 17w
21 Cuers, France 43 14N 6 5E
117 Cuervo, U.S.A. 35 5N 104 25w
120 Cuevas de Altamira, 43 20N 4 5w
  Spain
33 Cuevas del Almanzora, 37 18N 1 58w
  Spain
126 Cuevo, Bolivia 20 25s 63 30w
46 Cugir, Rumania 45 48N 23 25E
87 Cugno, Ethiopia 6 14N 42 31E
126 Cuiabá, Colombia 0 10s 75 23w
127 Cuiabá, Brazil 15 30s 56 0w
126 Cuiabá, R., Brazil 16 50s 56 30w
120 Cuidad Bolivia, Ven. 8 21N 70 34w
73 Cuyo, Philippines 10 50N 121 5E
14 Cuillin Hills, Scot. 57 14N 6 15w
14 Cuillin Sd., Scot. 57 4N 6 20w
89 Cuima, Angola 13 0s 15 45E
92 Cuiseaux, France 46 30N 5 22E
92 Cuito, R., Angola 16 50s 19 30E
46 Cujmir, Rumania 44 13N 22 57E
20 Culan, France 46 34N 2 20E
116 Culbertson, U.S.A. 48 9N 104 30w
100 Culcairn, Australia 35 41s 147 3E
30 Culebra, Sierra de la, 41 55N 6 20w
  Sp.
100 Culgoa, Australia 35 44s 143 6E
120 Culiacán, Mexico 24 50N 107 40w
73 Culion, I., Philippine: 11 54N 120 1E
33 Cúllar de Baza, Spain 37 35N 2 34w
100 Cullulleraine, Australia 34 15s 141 20E
14 Cullen, Scotland 57 45N 2 50w
115 Cullman, U.S.A. 34 13N 86 50w
33 Cullera, Spain 39 9N 0 17w
14 Culloden Moor, Scotland 57 29N 4 7w
21 Culoz, France 45 47N 5 46E
114 Culpeper, U.S.A. 38 29N 77 59w
127 Culuene, R., Brazil 12 15s 53 10w
96 Culver, Pt., Australia 32 54s 124 43E
101 Culverden, N.Z. 42 47s 172 49E

MAP
45 Cumali, Turkey 36 42N 27 28E
126 Cumaná, Venezuela 10 30N 64 5w
108 Cumberland, B.C., Can. 49 40N 125 0w
113 Cumberland, Que., Can. 45 30N 75 24w
114 Cumberland, Md., 39 40N 78 43w
  U.S.A.
116 Cumberland, Wis., 45 32N 92 3w
  U.S.A.
115 Cumberland I., U.S.A. 30 52N 81 30w
98 Cumberland Is., 20 45s 149 25E
  Australia
115 Cumberland Pen., Can. 67 0N 65 0w
115 Cumberland Plat., 36 0N 84 30w
  U.S.A.
115 Cumberland, R., U.S.A. 36 15N 87 0w
105 Cumberland Sd., Can. 65 30N 66 0w
• 12 Cumberland ♦, England 54 44N 2 55w
29 Cumborah, Australia 29 40s 147 45E
31 Cumbres Mayores, Sp. 38 4N 6 39w
12 Cumbrian Mts., Eng. 54 30N 3 0w
70 Cumbum, India 15 40N 79 10E
24 Cummerower See, Ger. 53 47N 12 52E
100 Cumnock, Australia 32 59s 148 46E
126 Cumurxatiba, Brazil 17 6s 39 13w
127 Cuñaré, Colombia 0 49N 72 32w
126 Cundinamarca ♦, Col. 5 0N 74 0w
92 Cunene, R., Angola 17 0s 15 0E
38 Cúneo, Italy 44 23N 7 31E
33 Cunillera, I., Sp. 38 59N 1 13E
20 Cunlhat, France 45 38N 3 32E
99 Cunnamulla, Australia 28 2s 145 38E
38 Cuorgnè, Italy 45 23N 7 39E
109 Cupar, Canada 51 0N 104 10w
14 Cupar, Scotland 56 20N 3 0w
126 Cupica, Colombia 6 50N 77 30w
126 Cupica, Golfo de, 6 25N 77 30w
  Colombia
42 Ćuprija, Yugoslavia 34 57N 21 26E
121 Curaçao, I., Neth. W.I. 12 10N 69 0w
124 Curacautahue, Chile 37 29s 73 28w
126 Curaray, R., Peru 1 30s 75 30w
126 Curaçá, Venezuela 6 19N 62 51w
126 Curbarado, Colombia 7 3N 76 54w
124 Curepto, Chile 35 8s 72 1w
126 Curiapo, Venezuela 8 33N 61 5w
124 Curicó, Chile 34 55s 71 20w
124 Curicó ♦, Chile 34 50s 71 15w
126 Curiplaya, Colombia 0 16N 74 52w
125 Curitiba, Brazil 25 20s 49 10w
100 Curlwaa, Australia 34 2s 141 59E
92 Curoca Norte, Angola 16 5s 12 58E
92 Currabubula, Australia 31 16s 150 44E
99 Curracunya, Australia 28 29s 144 1E
124 Currais Novos, Brazil 6 13s 36 30w
127 Curralinho, Brazil 1 35s 49 30w
118 Currant, U.S.A. 38 51N 115 32w
99 Currawilla, Australia 25 10s 141 20E
117 Current, R., U.S.A. 37 15N 91 10w
114 Currie, U.S.A. 40 16N 114 45w
93 Currie, Mt., S. Africa 30 29s 29 21E
100 Currituck Sd., U.S.A. 36 20N 75 50w
100 Currockbilly Mt., 35 25s 150 0E
  Australia
127 Curupira, Serra, 1 25N 64 30w
  Ven.-Braz.
120 Curundu, Pan. Can. 8 59N 79 38w
  Zone
127 Cururupu, Brazil 1 50s 44 50w
124 Curuzú Cuatiá, Arg. 29 50s 58 5w
127 Curvelo, Brazil 18 45s 44 27w
100 Curyo, Australia 35 53s 142 54E
120 Cushiuriáchic, Mexico 28 10N 106 50w
83 Cussabat, Libya 32 39N 14 1E
20 Cusset, France 46 8N 3 28E
117 Custer, U.S.A. 43 45N 103 38w
118 Cut Bank, U.S.A. 48 40N 112 15w
117 Cuthbert, U.S.A. 31 47N 84 47w
41 Cutro, Italy 39 1N 16 58E
99 Cuttaburra R., Austral. 29 10s 145 0E
69 Cuttack, India 20 25N 85 57E
96 Cuvier, C., Australia 23 14s 113 22E
101 Cuvier I., N.Z. 36 27s 175 50E
24 Cuxhaven, Germany 53 51N 8 41E
126 Cuyabeno, Ecuador 0 16s 75 53w
112 Cuyahoga, R., U.S.A. 41 30N 81 35w
112 Cuyahoga Falls, U.S.A. 41 8N 81 30w
73 Cuyo, Philippines 10 50N 121 5E
127 Cuyuni, R., Guyana 7 0N 59 30w
126 Cuzco, Peru 13 32s 72 0w
126 Cuzco, Mt., Bolivia 20 0s 66 50w
47 Cvrsnica, Mt., Y.-slav. 43 36N 17 35E
90 Cyangugu, Rwanda 2 29s 28 54E
28 Cybinka, Poland 52 12N 14 46E
45 Cyclades = Kikladhes, 37 20N 24 30E
  Greece
99 Cygnet, Australia 43 8s 147 1E
114 Cynthiana, U.S.A. 38 23N 84 10w
109 Cypress Hills, Canada 49 40N 109 30w
64 Cyprus ■, E. Medit. Sea 35 0N 33 0E
81 Cyrenaica ♦, Libya 27 0N 20 0E
81 Cyrene, Libya 32 39N 21 18E
28 Czaplinek, Poland 53 34N 16 14E
81 Czarna, Poland 32 39N 21 18E
28 Czarna Białostocka, 53 27N 23 11E
  Poland
53 Czarna Woda, Poland 53 51N 18 7E
28 Czarne, Poland 53 42N 16 58E
28 Czarnków, Poland 52 55N 16 38E
27 Czechoslovakia ■, 49 0N 17 0E
  Europe
27 Czechowice-Dziedzice, 49 54N 18 59E
  Poland
28 Czeladź, Poland 50 16N 19 2E
28 Czersk, Poland 53 46N 17 58E
28 Czempiń, Poland 52 9N 16 33E

MAP
28 Czersk, Poland 53 46N 17 58E
28 Czerwieńsk, Poland 52 1N 15 13E
27 Czerwionka, Poland 50 7N 18 37E
28 Częstochowa, Poland 50 49N 19 7E
28 Człopa, Poland 53 6N 16 6E
28 Człuchów, Poland 53 41N 17 22E
71 Da. R., N. Vietnam 16 0N 107 0E
71 Da Lat, S. Vietnam 12 3N 108 32E
71 Da-Nang, S. Vietnam 16 10N 108 7E
86 Dab'a, Ras el, Egypt 31 3N 28 31E
85 Dabai, Nigeria 11 25N 5 15E
126 Dabajuro, Venezuela 11 2N 70 40w
84 Dabakala, Ivory Coast 8 15N 4 20w
84 Dabatou, Guinea 11 50N 9 20w
62 Dabburiya, Israel 32 42N 35 22E
92 Daberas. S.W. Afr. 25 27s 18 30E
68 Dabhoi, India 22 10N 73 20E
28 Dabie, Poland 53 27N 14 45E
84 Dabola, Guinea 10 50N 11 5w
84 Dabou, Ivory Coast 5 20N 4 23w
85 Daboya, Ghana 9 30N 1 20w
87 Dabra Berhan, Ethiopia 9 42N 39 15E
87 Dabra Sina, Ethiopia 9 51N 39 45E
87 Dabra Tabor, Ethiopia 11 50N 37 58E
87 Dabra Zabit, Ethiopia 11° 48N 38 30E
28 Dabrowa Gornicza, Pol. 50 15N 19 10E
27 Dabrowa Tarnówska, Poland 50 10N 21 0E
28 Dabrówno. Poland 53 27N 20 2E
87 Dabus. R., Ethiopia 10 12N 35 0E
69 Dacca, Bangladesh 23 43N 90 26E
25 Dachau. Germany 48 16N 11 27E
54 Daday. Turkey 41 28N 33 35E
126 Dadanawa. Guyana 3 0N 59 30w
87 Daddato. Fr. Terr. of the Afars & Issas 12 24N 42 45E
115 Dade City, U.S.A. 28 20N 82 12w
85 Dadiya, Nigeria 9 35N 11 24E
68 Dadra and Nagar Haveli ♦, India 20 5N 73 0E
68 Dadri = Charkhi Dadri, India 28 37N 76 17E
68 Dadu, Pakistan 26 45N 67 45E
46 Dăeni, Rumania 44 51N 28 10E
73 Daet. Philippines 14 2N 122 55E
87 Dagaio, Ethiopia 6 8N 40 40E
84 Dagana. Senegal 16 30N 15 20w
86 Dagash. Sudan 19 19N 33 25E
57 Dagestan. A.S.S.R. ♦, U.S.S.R. 42 30N 47 0E
86 Daghfeli, Sudan 19 18N 32 40E
87 Daghirie, Ethiopia 11 40N 41 50E
54 Dagö = Hiiumaa. U.S.S.R. 58 50N 22 45E
90 Dagoreti, Kenya 1 18s 36 4E
73 Dagupan. Philippines 16 3N 120 20E
112 Dagus Mines. U.S.A. 41 20N 78 36w
73 Dah. W. Irian 7 25s 139 5E
86 Dahab, Egypt 28 30N 34 31E
87 Dahlak Kebir, Eth. 15 50N 40 10E
24 Dahlenburg, Germany 53 11N 10 43E
115 Dahlonega. U.S.A. 34 35N 83 59w
24 Dahme, Germany 51 51N 13 25E
85 Daho. Nigeria 10 28N 11 18E
*85 Dahomey ■, W. Afr. 8 0N 2 0E
84 Dahra, Senegal 15 22N 15 30w
82 Dahra, Massif de. Alg. 36 7N 1 21E
31 Daimiel. Spain 39 5N 3 35w
15 Daingean. Ireland 53 18N 7 15w
18 Daintree. Australia 16 20s 145 20E
74 Daio-Misaki, Japan 34 15N 136 45E
76 Dairen = Lu-ta, China 39 0N 121 31E
86 Dairût, Egypt 27 34N 30 43E
69 Daitari, India 21 10N 85 46E
72 Dajarra. Australia 21 42s 139 30E
85 Dakar, Senegal 14 34N 17 29w
86 Dakhla, El Wâhât el-, Egypt 25 30N 28 50E
85 Dakingari, Nigeria 11 37N 4 1E
68 Dakor. India 22 45N 73 11E
85 Dakoro, Niger 14 31N 6 46E
116 Dakota City, U.S.A. 42 27N 96 28w
42 Dakovica, Y.-slav. 42 22N 20 26E
42 Dakovo. Y.-slav. 45 19N 18 24E
84 Dakra, Senegal 15 22N 15 30w
84 Dalaba, Guinea 10 42N 12 15w
48 Dalälven. L., Sweden 61 27N 17 15E
76 Dalandzadgad, Mong. 43 3N 104 30E
71 Dalat. Vietnam 12 3N 108 32E
68 Dalbandin. Pakistan 29 0N 4 23E
14 Dalbeattie. Scot. 54 55N 3 50w
49 Dalbosjön. L., Sweden 58 40N 12 45E
73 Dalby. Australia 27 10s 151 17E
49 Dalby. Sweden 55 42N 13 22E
48 Dalby. Sweden 60 37N 13 5E
47 Dale. Sogn og Fjordane, Norway 61 22N 5 23E
47 Dale, Sogn og Fjordane, Norway 61 27N 7 28E
47 Dalen. Norway 59 26N 8 0E
86 Dalga, Egypt 27 39N 30 41E
117 Dalhart. U.S.A. 36 0N 102 30w
121 Dalhousie. Canada 48 0N 66 26w
68 Dalhousie. India 32 38N 76 0E
126 Dalj. Yugoslavia 45 28N 18 58E
14 Dalkeith. Scot. 55 54N 3 5w
108 Dall I.. Alaska 54 59N 133 25w
99 Dallarnil. Australia 25 19s 152 2E
118 Dallas. Oregon, U.S.A. 45 0N 123 15w
117 Dallas. Texas, U.S.A. 32 50N 96 50w
87 Dallol. Ethiopia 14 14N 40 17E
42 Dalmacija, Yugoslavia 43 20N 17 0E
42 Dalmatia = Dalmacija, Y.-slav. 43 20N 17 0E
84 Daloa. Ivory Coast 7 0N 6 30w
98 Dalrymple. Mt., Australia 21 1s 148 39E
49 Dalsjöfors, Sweden 57 46N 18 5E
49 Dalskog. Sweden 58 44N 12 18E

106 Dalton, Canada 60 10N 137 0w
73 Dalton, Ga., U.S.A. 34 45N 85 0w
113 Dalton, Mass., U.S.A. 42 28N 73 11w
116 Dalton, Nebr., U.S.A. 41 27N 103 0w
69 Daltonganj, India 24 0N 84 4E
108 Dalton Post, Canada 66 42N 137 0w
77 Dalupuri, I., Philippines 19 2N 121 8E
50 Dalvik, Iceland 65 58N 18 32w
96 Daly, R., Australia 14 0s 131 12E
96 Daly Waters, Australia 16 15s 133 24E
127 Dam, Surinam 4 45N 55 0w
86 Dama, Wadi, Si. Arab. 27 12N 35 50E
68 Daman, India 20 25N 72 57E
73 Damar, I., Indonesia 7 15s 128 30E
86 Damanhûr, Egypt 31 0N 30 30E
92 Damaraland, South-West Africa 21 0s 17 0E
64 Damascus = Dimashq, Syria 33 30N 36 18E
85 Damaturu, Nigeria 11 45N 11 55E
65 Damävand, Qolleh-ye, Iran 35 45N 52 10E
88 Damba, Angola 6 44s 15 29E
87 Damba, Ethiopia 12 8N 38 47E
46 Dâmbovita, R., Rum. 44 40N 26 0E
46 Dâmbovnic, R., Rum. 44 28N 25 18E
65 Damghan, Iran 36 10N 54 17E
46 Dămienesti, Rumania 46 44N 27 1E
86 Damietta = Dumyât, Egypt 31 24N 31 48E
93 Damiya, Jordan 32 6N 35 34E
65 Damin, Iran 27 30N 60 40E
64 Damman, Saudi Arabia 26 25N 50 2E
19 Dammarie, France 48 20N 1 30E
19 Dammartin, France 49 3N 2 41E
24 Damme, Germany 52 32N 8 12E
69 Damodar, R., India 23 17N 87 35E
68 Damoh, India 23 50N 79 28E
96 Dampier, Australia 20 40s 116 30E
96 Dampier Arch., Australia 20 38s 116 32E
96 Dampier Downs, Australia 18 30s 123 15E
73 Dampier, Selat, Indonesia 0 40s 131 0E
98 Dampier Str., Territory of New Guinea 5 50s 148 0E
18 Damville, France 48 51N 1 5E
19 Damvillers, France 49 20N 5 21E
85 Dan Chadi, Nigeria 12 47N 5 17E
85 Dan Dume, Nigeria 11 28N 7 8E
85 Dan Gulbi, Nigeria 11 40N 6 15E
85 Dan Sadau, Nigeria 11 25N 6 26E
73 Dana, Indonesia 11 0s 122 52E
106 Dana, Lac, Canada 50 50N 76 50w
87 Danakil Depression, Ethiopia 12 45N 41 0E
73 Danao, Philippines 10 31N 124 1E
113 Danbury, U.S.A. 41 23N 73 29w
119 Danby, U.S.A. 34 17N 115 0w
69 Dandeldhura, Nepal 29 20N 80 35E
100 Dandenong, Australia 37 52s 145 12E
107 Danforth, U.S.A. 45 39N 67 57w
71 Dang Raek, Phanom, Thailand 14 40N 104 0E
95 Danger Is., Pac. Oc. 10 53s 165 49w
92 Danger Pt., S. Africa 34 40s 19 17E
85 Dangora, Nigeria 11 30N 8 7E
85 Dangla, Ethiopia 11 18N 36 56E
118 Daniel, U.S.A. 42 56N 110 2w
107 Daniel's Harbour, Can. 50 13N 57 35w
92 Danielskull, S. Africa 28 11s 23 33E
113 Danielson, U.S.A. 41 50N 71 52w
55 Danilov, U.S.A. 58 16N 40 13E
42 Danilovgrad, Y.-slav. 42 38N 19 9E
55 Danilovka, U.S.S.R. 50 25N 44 12E
90 Danissa, Kenya 3 15N 40 58E
85 Danja, Nigeria 11 29N 7 30E
85 Dankalwa, Nigeria 11 52N 12 12E
85 Dankama, Nigeria 13 20N 7 44E
55 Dankov, U.S.S.R. 53 20N 39 5E
121 Danli, Honduras 14 4N 86 35w
113 Dannemora, U.S.A. 44 41N 73 44w
24 Dannenberg, Germany 53 7N 11 4E
101 Dannevirke, N.Z. 40 12s 176 8E
93 Dannhauser, S. Africa 28 0s 30 3E
73 Dansalan, Philippines 8 2N 124 30E
112 Dansville, U.S.A. 42 32N 77 41w
69 Dantan, India 21 57N 87 20E
22 Danube, R., Europe 45 0N 29 20E
113 Danvers, U.S.A. 42 34N 70 55w
114 Danville, Ill., U.S.A. 40 10N 87 40w
114 Danville, Ky., U.S.A. 37 40N 84 45E
115 Danville, Va., U.S.A. 36 40N 79 20E
28 Danzig = Gdansk, Pol. 54 22N 18 40E
73 Dão, Philippines 10 30N 122 6E
30 Dão, R., Portugal 40 28N 8 0w
68 Daosa, India 26 52N 76 20E
83 Daoud = Aïn Beida, Algeria 35 50N 7 29E
18 Daoulas, France 48 22N 4 17w
85 Dapango, Togo 10 55N 0 16E
100 Dapto, Australia 34 30s 150 47E
64 Dar al Hamra, Si. Arab. 27 22N 37 43E
90 Dar es Salaam, Tanz. 6 50s 39 12E
62 Dar'a, Syria 32 36N 36 7E
65 Darab, Iran 28 50N 54 30E
46 Darabani, Rumania 48 10N 26 39E
83 Daraj, Libya 30 10N 10 28E
42 Daravica, Y.-slav. 42 32N 20 8E
86 Daraw, Egypt 24 22N 32 51E
85 Darazo, Nigeria 11 1N 10 24w
66 Darband, Pakistan 34 20N 72 50E
69 Darbhanga, India 26 15N 86 8E
118 Darby, U.S.A. 46 2N 114 7w
108 D'Arcy, Canada 50 35N 122 30w
42 Darda, Yugoslavia 45 40N 18 41E
64 Dardanelle, Tur. 40 0N 26 20E
117 Dardanelle, U.S.A. 35 12N 93 9w
100 Dareton, Australia 34 4s 142 3E
38 Darfo, Italy 45 43N 10 11E

81 Dârfûr ♦, Sudan 12 35N 25 0E
34 Dargai, West Pakistan 34 25N 71 45E
58 Dargan Ata, U.S.S.R. 40 40N 62 20E
101 Dargaville, N.Z. 35 57s 173 52E
100 Dargo, Australia 37 7s 147 15E
100 Dargo, R., Australia 37 7s 147 15E
76 Darhan, Mongolia 49 27N 105 57E
84 Darharala, Ivory Coast 8 23N 4 20w
87 Dari, Sudan 5 48N 30 26E
120 Darien, Pan. Can. Zone 9 7N 79 46w
126 Darién, G. del, Columbia 9 0N 77 0w
126 Darién, Serranía del, Col. 8 30N 77 30w
126 Darién, Serranía del., Panama 8 30N 78 0w
69 Darjeeling, India 27 3N 88 18E
107 Dark Cove, Canada 49 54N 54 5w
97 Darling Downs, Australia 28 30s 152 0E
96 Darling Ra., Austral. 32 30s 116 0E
99 Darling, R., Australia 31 0s 144 30E
12 Darlington, Eng. 54 33N 1 33w
115 Darlington, S.C., U.S.A. 34 18N 79 50w
116 Darlington, Wis., U.S.A. 42 43N 90 7w
100 Darlington Point, Australia 34 34s 147 0E
28 Darłowo, Poland 54 25N 16 25E
46 Dărmănești, Rumania 46 21N 26 33E
25 Darmstadt, Germany 49 51N 8 40E
93 Darnall, S. Africa 29 23s 31 18E
19 Darnétal, France 49 25N 1 10E
19 Darney, France 48 5N 6 0E
13 Dean, Forest of, England 51 50N 2 35w
100 Darnick, Australia 32 48s 143 38E
5 Darnley, C., Antarctica 68 0s 69 0E
32 Daroca, Spain 41 9N 1 25w
98 Darr, Australia 24 34s 144 52E
118 Darrington, U.S.A. 48 14N 121 37w
65 Darror, R., Somali Rep. 10 30N 50 0E
69 Darsana, Bangladesh 23 35N 88 48E
68 Darsi, India 15 46N 79 44E
24 Darsser Ort, Germany 44 27N 12 30E
13 Dart, R., Eng. 50 34N 3 56w
100 Dartmoor, Australia 37 56s 141 19E
13 Dartmoor, Eng. 50 36N 4 0w
107 Dartmouth, Canada 44 40N 63 30w
13 Dartmouth, Eng. 50 21N 3 35w
98 Dartmouth, Australia 23 30s 144 40E
32 Dartuch, C., Spain 39 55N 3 49E
85 Daru, Papua 8 53s 143 22E
84 Daru, Sierra Leone 8 0N 10 52w
73 Darvel Bay, Sabah 4 50N 118 20E
68 Darwha, India 20 15N 77 45E
96 Darwin, Australia 12 20s 130 50E
4 Darwin, Mt., Rhodesia 16 45s 31 33E
65 Daryacheh-ye-Sistan, Iran 31 0N 61 0E
68 Daryapur, India 20 55N 77 20E
87 Dase, Ethiopia 14 53N 37 15E
87 Dashato, Ethiopia 7 25N 42 40E
76 Dashinchilen, Mongolia 48 0N 105 59E
87 Dashkesan, U.S.S.R. 40 40N 46 0E
66 Dasht, R., Pakistan 25 40N 62 20E
65 Dasht-e Kavir, Iran 34 30N 55 0E
65 Dasht-e Lut, Iran 31 30N 58 0E
66 Dasht-i-Khash, Afghanistan 32 0N 62 0E
65 Dasht-i-Margo, Afghanistan 30 40N 62 30E
68 Daska, Pakistan 32 20N 74 20E
92 Dassa-Zoume, Dahomey 7 46N 2 14E
92 Dasseneiland, S. Africa 33 37s 18 3E
45 Datça, Turkey 36 46N 27 40E
68 Datia, India 25 39N 78 27E
69 Dattapur, India 20 45N 78 15E
69 Daudkandi, Bangladesh 23 40N 90 40E
54 Daugava, U.S.S.R. 57 0N 24 0E
54 Daugavpils, U.S.S.R. 55 53N 26 32E
65 Daulat Yar, Afghan. 34 30N 65 45E
70 Daulatabad, India 19 57N 75 15E
24 Daun, Germany 50 5N 6 53E
105 Dauphin, Canada 51 15N 100 5w
109 Dauphin I., U.S.A. 30 16N 88 10w
109 Dauphin L., Canada 51 20N 99 45w
21 Dauphiné, France 45 15N 5 25E
86 Dauqa, Saudi Arabia 19 30N 41 0E
85 Daura, Nig. 11 31N 11 24E
84 Davadi, Senegal 14 10N 16 3w
68 Davangere, India 14 25N 75 50E
73 Davao, Philippines 7 0N 125 40E
73 Davao, G. of, Phil. 6 30N 125 48E
65 Davar Panah, Iran 27 25N 62 15E
13 Dave, England, U.K. 52 55N 1 50w
116 Davenport, Iowa, U.S.A. 41 30N 90 40w
118 Davenport, Wash., U.S.A. 47 40N 118 5w
99 Davenport Ra., Australia 20 28s 134 0E
116 David City, U.S.A. 41 18N 97 10w
121 David, Panama 8 30N 82 30w
54 David Gorodok, U.S.S.R. 52 4N 27 8E
47 Davik, Norway 61 53N 5 33E
119 Davis Dam, U.S.A. 35 20N 114 35w
107 Davis Inlet, Canada 55 50N 60 45w
117 Davis, U.S.A. 30 42N 104 15w
105 Davis Str., N. America 65 0N 58 0w
25 Davos, Switzerland 46 48N 9 49E
87 Dawa, R., Ethiopia 5 0N 39 5E
85 Dawaki, Nigeria 9 25N 9 33E
85 Dawaki, Nigeria 12 5N 8 23E
96 Dawayima, Israel 24 40s 150 40E
98 Dawes Ra., Australia 24 40s 150 40E
98 Dawson, Ga., U.S.A. 31 45N 84 28w
116 Dawson, N.D., U.S.A. 46 56N 99 45w
41 Dawson, I., Chile 53 50s 70 50w
98 Dawson, I., Australia 23 38s 149 46E
108 Dawson Creek, Canada 55 45N 120 15w
91 Dawson's, Rhodesia 17 0s 30 57E

100 Daylesford, Australia 37 21s 144 9E
62 Dayr al-Ghusün, Jordan 32 21N 35 4E
64 Dayr az Zawr, Syria 35 20N 40 5E
108 Daysland, Canada 52 50N 112 20w
115 Dayton, Ohio, U.S.A. 39 45N 84 10w
112 Dayton, Pa., U.S.A. 40 54N 79 18w
118 Dayton, Wash., U.S.A. 46 20N 118 0w
29 Dayton, Tenn., U.S.A. 35 30N 85 1w
29 Daytona Beach, U.S.A. 29 14N 81 0w
92 De Aar, S. Afr. 30 39s 24 0E
115 De Funiak Springs, U.S.A. 30 42N 86 10w
96 De Grey, R., Australia 20 30s 120 0E
25 De Kalb, U.S.A. 41 55N 88 45w
115 De Land, U.S.A. 29 1N 81 19w
115 De Leon, U.S.A. 32 9N 98 35w
59 De Long, Ostrova, U.S.S.R. 76 40N 149 20E
112 De Pere, U.S.A. 44 28N 88 1w
117 De Queen, U.S.A. 34 3N 94 24w
112 De Quincy, U.S.A. 30 30N 93 27w
117 De Ridder, U.S.A. 30 48N 93 15w
116 De Smet, U.S.A. 44 25N 97 35w
114 De Tour Village, U.S.A. 45 49N 83 56w
117 De Witt, U.S.A. 34 19N 91 20w
64 Dead Sea = Miyet, Bahr el, Jordan/Israel 31 30N 35 30E
32 Deadwood, U.S.A. 44 25N 103 43w
96 Deakin, Australia 30 46s 129 0E
12 Deal, England 51 13N 1 25E
92 Dealesville, S. Africa 28 41s 25 44E
119 Dean Funes, Argentina 30 20s 64 20w
100 Dean Marsh, Australia 38 25s 143 52E
112 Dearborn, U.S.A. 42 18N 83 15w
126 Dease Arm, Canada 66 45N 120 6w
108 Dease L., Canada 58 40N 130 5w
119 Death Valley, U.S.A. 36 0N 116 40w
119 Death Valley Junc., U.S.A. 36 15N 116 30w
18 Deauville, France 49 23N 0 2E
85 Deba Habe, Nigeria 10 14N 11 20E
55 Debaltsevo, U.S.S.R. 48 22N 38 26E
42 Debar, Yugoslavia 41 21N 20 37E
87 Debba, Ethiopia 14 20N 41 18E
109 Debden, Canada 53 30N 106 50w
82 Debdou, Morocco 33 59N 3 0w
90 Debeeti, Botswana 23 45s 26 32E
87 Debra Birhan, Ethiopia 9 41N 39 31E
87 Debre Markos, Ethiopia 10 20N 37 40E
87 Debre May, Ethiopia 11 20N 37 25E
87 Debre Sina, Ethiopia 9 51N 39 50E
87 Debre Tabor, Ethiopia 11 50N 38 26E
27 Debrecen, Hungary 47 33N 21 42E
42 Dečani, Yugoslavia 42 30N 20 10E
115 Decatur, Ala., U.S.A. 34 35N 87 0w
114 Decatur, Ill., U.S.A. 39 50N 89 0w
114 Decatur, Ind., U.S.A. 40 52N 85 28w
117 Decatur, Texas, U.S.A. 33 15N 97 35w
20 Decazeville, France 44 34N 2 15E
70 Deccan, India 14 0N 77 0E
5 Deception I., Antarc. 63 0s 60 15w
26 Děčín, Czechoslovakia 50 47N 14 12E
19 Decize, France 46 50N 3 28E
112 Deckerville, U.S.A. 43 33N 82 46w
41 Decollatura, Italy 39 2N 16 21E
116 Decorah, U.S.A. 43 20N 91 50w
46 Deda, Rumania 46 56N 24 50E
113 Dedham, U.S.A. 42 14N 71 10w
55 Dedilovo, U.S.S.R. 53 59N 37 50E
84 Dédougou, Upper Volta 12 30N 3 35w
70 Deduru Oya, Ceylon 7 32N 81 45E
91 Dedza, Malawi 14 20s 34 20E
12 Dee, R., Scotland, U.K. 57 4N 3 7w
12 Dee, R., Wales, U.K. 53 15N 3 7w
99 Deepdale, Australia 26 22s 114 20E
99 Deepwater, Australia 29 25s 151 51E
107 Deer Lake, Newf., Canada 49 11N 57 27w
109 Deer Lake, Ontario, Canada 52 36N 94 20w
118 Deer Lodge, U.S.A. 46 25N 112 40w
118 Deer Park, U.S.A. 47 55N 117 21w
116 Deer River, U.S.A. 47 21N 93 44w
98 Deeral, Australia 17 20s 145 55E
92 Deerdepoort, S. Africa 24 37s 26 27E
68 Deesa, India 24 18N 72 10E
114 Defiance, U.S.A. 41 20N 84 20w
62 Deganya, Israel 32 43N 35 34E
30 Degebe, R., Portugal 38 21N 7 37w
87 Degeh-Bur, Ethiopia 8 11N 43 31E
85 Degema, Nigeria 4 50N 6 48E
49 Degerfors, Sweden 59 20N 14 28E
49 Degerö, Sweden 59 13N 18 3E
25 Deggendorf, Germany 48 49N 12 59E
65 Deh Bid, Iran 30 39N 53 11E
65 Deh Kheyr, Iran 28 45N 54 40E
83 Dehibat, Tunisia 32 0N 10 47E
70 Dehiwala, Sri Lanka 6 50N 79 51E
65 Dehkhvareqan, Iran 37 50N 45 55E
68 Dehra Dun, India 30 20N 78 4E
68 Dehri, India 24 50N 84 15E
16 Deinze, Belgium 50 59N 3 32E
46 Dej, Rumania 47 10N 23 52E
87 Deje, Sweden 59 35N 13 29E
90 Dekar, Botswana 18 30s 23 10E
87 Dekemhare, Ethiopia 15 6N 39 0E
88 Dekese, Zaïre 3 24s 21 24E

100 Del Norte, U.S.A. 37 47N 106 27w
85 Del Rey, Rio, Nigeria 4 30N 8 48E
117 Del Rio, U.S.A. 29 15N 100 50w
117 Delagua, U.S.A. 32 35N 104 40w
86 Delai, Sudan 17 21N 36 6E
119 Delano, U.S.A. 35 48N 119 13w
92 Delareyville, S. Africa 26 41s 25 26E
114 Delaware, U.S.A. 40 20N 83 0w
113 Delaware, R., U.S.A. 41 50N 75 15w
114 Delaware, U.S.A. 40 20N 83 0w
114 Delaware ♦, U.S.A. 39 0N 75 40w
42 Delčevo, Yugoslavia 41 58N 22 46E
100 Delegate, Australia 37 3s 149 0E
25 Delémont, Switzerland 47 22N 7 20E
16 Delft, Netherlands 52 1N 4 22E
70 Delft I., Sri Lanka 9 30N 79 40E
16 Delfzijl, Netherlands 53 20N 6 55E
91 Delgado, C., Mozam. 10 45s 40 40E
86 Delgo, Sudan 20 6N 30 40E
112 Delhi, Canada 42 54N 80 29w
68 Delhi, India 28 38N 77 17E
113 Delhi, U.S.A. 42 17N 74 56w
42 Deli Jovan, Y.-slav. 44 13N 22 18E
120 Delicias, Mexico 28 10N 105 30w
112 Dell City, U.S.A. 31 58N 105 19w
116 Dell Rapids, U.S.A. 43 53N 96 44w
19 Delle, France 47 30N 7 2E
82 Dellys, Algeria 36 50N 3 57E
113 Delmar, U.S.A. 42 37N 73 47w
24 Delmenhorst, Germany 53 3N 8 37E
127 Delmiro, Brazil 9 24s 38 6w
39 Delnice, Yugoslavia 45 23N 14 50E
99 Deloraine, Australia 41 30s 146 40E
109 Deloraine, Canada 49 15N 101 0w
107 Delorme, L., Canada 54 30N 69 30w
42 Delovo, Yugoslavia 44 55N 20 52E
114 Delphi, U.S.A. 40 37N 86 40w
114 Delphos, U.S.A. 40 51N 84 17w
92 Delportshoop, S. Africa 28 22s 24 20E
115 Delray Beach, U.S.A. 26 27N 80 4w
48 Delsbo, Sweden 61 48N 16 32E
119 Delta, Colo., U.S.A. 38 44N 108 5w
118 Delta, Utah, U.S.A. 39 21N 112 29w
126 Delta Amacuro ♦, Ven. 8 30N 61 30w
99 Delungra, Australia 29 40s 150 45E
16 Delvinákion, Greece 39 57N 20 32E
44 Delvina, Albania 39 59N 20 4E
73 Demak, Indonesia 6 50s 110 40E
126 Demanda, Sierra de la, Sp. 42 15N 3 0w
87 Dembécha, Ethiopia 10 32N 37 30E
87 Dembi, Ethiopia 8 5N 36 25E
90 Dembia, Zaïre 3 33N 25 48E
87 Dembidolo, Ethiopia 8 34N 34 50E
66 Demchok, China 32 40N 79 29E
16 Demer, R., Belgium 51 0N 5 8E
106 Demerais, L., Canada 47 35N 77 0w
126 Demerara, R., Guyana 7 0N 58 0w
54 Demidov, U.S.S.R. 55 10N 31 30E
119 Deming, U.S.A. 32 10N 107 50w
126 Demini, R., Brazil 0 46N 62 56w
24 Demmin, Germany 53 54N 13 2E
108 Demmit, Canada 55 20N 119 50w
82 Demnate, Morocco 31 44N 6 59w
38 Demonte, Italy 44 18N 7 18E
115 Demopolis, U.S.A. 32 30N 87 48w
73 Dempo, Mt., Indonesia 4 10s 103 15E
54 Demyansk, U.S.S.R. 57 30N 32 27E
16 Den Burg, Netherlands 53 3N 4 47E
16 Den Helder, Neth. 52 57N 4 45E
16 Den Oever, Netherlands 52 56N 5 2E
19 Denain, France 50 20N 3 22E
53 Denbigh, Wales 53 12N 3 26w
*12 Denbigh ♦, Wales 53 8N 3 30w
67 Denchin, China 31 35N 95 15E
72 Dendang, Indonesia 3 7s 107 56E
16 Dendermonde, Belgium 51 2N 4 5E
87 Deneba, Ethiopia 9 47N 39 10E
85 Dengi, Nigeria 9 25N 9 55E
24 Denham, Australia 25 56s 113 31E
98 Denham Ra., Australia 21 55s 147 46E
109 Denholm, Canada 52 40N 108 0w
33 Denia, Spain 38 49N 0 8E
100 Deniliquin, Australia 35 30s 144 58E
116 Denison, Iowa, U.S.A. 42 0N 95 18w
117 Denison, Texas, U.S.A. 33 50N 96 40w
99 Denison Range, Australia 28 30s 136 5E
64 Denizli, Turkey 37 42N 29 2E
87 Denkez Iyesus, Ethiopia 12 27N 37 43E
100 Denman, Australia 32 24s 150 42E
4 Denmark, Australia 34 59s 117 18E
6 Denmark Str., Atlantic 66 0N 30 0w
112 Dennison, U.S.A. 40 21N 81 21w
73 Denpasar, Indonesia 8 45s 115 5E
118 Denton, Mont., U.S.A. 47 25N 109 56w
117 Denton, Texas, U.S.A. 33 12N 97 10w
98 D'Entrecasteaux Is., Papua 9 0s 151 0E
98 D'Entrecasteaux Pt., Australia 34 50s 115 57E
85 Denu, Ghana 6 4N 1 8E
117 Denver, U.S.A. 39 45N 105 0w
117 Denver City, U.S.A. 32 58N 102 48w
68 Deoband, India 29 42N 77 43E
69 Deobhog, India 19 53N 82 44E
69 Deoghar, India 24 30N 86 59E
68 Deoli, India 25 50N 75 20E
69 Deoria, India 26 31N 83 48E
68 Desai, Mts., Kashmir 35 40N 75 0E
112 Depew, U.S.A. 42 55N 78 43w
112 Deposit, U.S.A. 42 5N 75 23w
112 Depot Harb., Canada 45 18N 80 5w

* Renamed Benin

* Incorporated within the county of Clwyd

MAP
59 Deputatskiy, U.S.S.R. 69 18N 139 54E
68 Dera Ghazi Khan, Pak. 30 5N 70 43E
68 Dera Ismail Khan, Pak. 31 50N 70 50E
90 Derati Wells, Kenya 3 52N 36 37E
50 Derbent, U.S.S.R. 42 5N 48 15E
96 Derby, Australia 17 18s 123 40E
12 Derby, England 52 55N 1 28W
113 Derby, Conn., U.S.A. 41 20N 75 5W
12 Derby N.Y., U.S.A. 42 40N 78 59W
12 Derby ♦, England 52 55N 1 28W
27 Derecske, Hungary 47 20N 21 33E
3 Derg, L. Ireland 53 0N 8 20W
15 Derg, R., N. Ire. 54 42N 7 38W
55 Dergachi, U.S.S.R. 50 3N 36 3E
67 Dergaon, India 26 45N 94 0E
100 Dergholm, Australia 37 24s 141 14E
43 Dermantsi, Bulgaria 43 8N 24 17E
81 Derna, Libya 32 40N 22 35E
117 Dernieres Isles, U.S.A. 29 0N 90 45W
100 Derrinallum, Australia 37 57s 143 15E
100 Derriwong, Australia 33 6s 147 21E
15 Derryveagh Mts., Ire. 55 0N 8 40W
86 Derudub, Sudan 17 31N 36 7E
18 Derval, France 47 40N 1 41W
45 Derveni, Greece 38 8N 22 25E
109 Derwent, Canada 53 41N 111 0W
12 Derwent, R., Cumb., Eng. 54 42N 3 22W
12 Derwent, R., Derby, Eng. 53 26N 1 44W
12 Derwent, R., Yorks., England 54 13N 0 35W
12 Derwentwater, L. England 53 34N 3 9W
116 Des Moines, Iowa, U.S.A. 41 35N 93 37W
117 Des Moines, N. Mex., U.S.A. 36 50N 103 51W
116 Des Moines, R., U.S.A. 41 15N 93 0W
124 Desaguadero, R., Arg. 33 28s 67 15W
126 Desaguadero, R., Bolivia 17 30s 68 0W
118 Deschutes, R., U.S.A. 45 30N 121 0W
87 Dese, Ethiopia 11 5N 39 40E
128 Deseado, R., Argentina 40 0s 69 0W
128 Desenzano del Gardo, It. 45 28N 10 32E
119 Desert Center, U.S.A. 33 45N 115 27W
54 Desna, R., U.S.S.R. 52 0N 33 15E
46 Desnátui, R., Rum. 44 15N 23 27E
128 Desolación, I., Chile 53 0s 74 0W
33 Despeñaperros, Paso, Spain 38 24N 3 30W
42 Despotovac, Y.-slav. 44 6N 21 30E
85 Dessa, Niger 14 44N 1 6E
24 Dessau, Germany 51 49N 12 15E
87 Dessye = Dese, Ethiopia 11 5N 39 40E
99 D'Estrees B., Austral. 35 48s 137 45E
68 Desuri, India 25 18N 73 35E
19 Desvrès, France 50 40N 1 48E
99 Detention River, Australia 40 55s 145 32E
42 Detinja, R., Y.-slav. 43 51N 19 45E
24 Detmold, Germany 51 55N 8 50E
114 Detour Pt., U.S.A. 45 37N 86 35W
112 Detroit, Mich., U.S.A. 42 20N 83 5W
117 Detroit, Tex., U.S.A. 33 40N 95 10W
116 Detroit Lakes, U.S.A. 46 50N 95 50W
91 Dett, Rhodesia 18 32s 26 57E
86 Dettifoss, Iceland 65 49N 16 24W
16 Deurne, Belgium 51 12N 4 24E
16 Deurne, Netherlands 51 27N 5 49E
24 Deutsche Bucht, Ger. 54 10N 7 51E
26 Deutschlandsberg, Aus. 46 49N 15 14E
18 Deux-Sèvres ♦, Fr. 46 35N 0 20W
46 Deva, Rumania 45 53N 22 55E
70 Devakottai, India 9 55N 78 45E
68 Devaprayag, India 30 13N 78 35E
27 Dévaványa, Hungary 47 2N 20 59E
56 Deveci Dagi, Turkey 40 0N 36 0E
27 Devecser, Hungary 47 6N 17 26E
16 Deventer, Netherlands 52 15N 6 10E
14 Deveron, R., Scot. 57 22N 3 0W
46 Devesel, Rumania 44 28N 22 41E
70 Devgad, I., India 14 48N 74 5E
116 Devils Lake, U.S.A. 48 5N 98 50W
70 Devils Pt., Sri Lanka 9 26N 80 6E
43 Devin, Bulgaria 41 44N 24 24E
12 Devizes, England 51 21N 2 0W
43 Devnya, Bulgaria 43 13N 27 33E
44 Devolli, R., Albania 40 57N 20 15E
108 Devon, Canada 53 24N 113 26W
4 Devon I., Canada 75 0N 86 0W
99 Devonport, Australia 41 12s 146 28E
101 Devonport, N.Z. 36 49s 174 49E
12 Devonport, Eng. 50 23N 4 11W
13 Devonshire ♦, Eng. 50 50N 3 40W
68 Dewas, India 22 59N 76 3E
92 Dewetsdorp, S. Africa 29 33s 26 39E
68 Dewgad Baria, India 22 40N 73 55E
12 Dewsbury, Eng. 53 42N 1 38W
117 Dexter, Mo., U.S.A. 36 50N 90 0W
117 Dexter, N. Mex., U.S.A. 33 15N 104 25W
65 Deyhuk, Iran 33 15N 104 25W
68 Deyyer, Iran 27 55N 51 55E
64 Dezfül, Iran 32 20N 48 30E
64 Dezh Shapur, Iran 35 30N 46 25E
64 Dezhneva, Mys, U.S.S.R. 66 10N 169 3E
64 Dhaba, Saudi Arabia 27 25N 35 40E
45 Dháfni, Greece 37 48N 22 1E
86 Dhahaban, Si.-Arab. 21 58N 39 3E
62 Dhahiriya = Qz Zahiriya, Jordan 31 25N 34 58E
64 Dhahran, Si.-Arabia 26 9N 50 10E
44 Dhamasi, Greece 39 43N 22 11E
59 Dhamtari, India 29 19N 78 33E
69 Dhamtari, India 20 42N 81 35E
70 Dhanaora, India 20 17N 80 20E
69 Dhanbad, India 23 50N 86 30E

69 Dhankuta, Nepal 26 55N 87 20E
69 Dhanora, India 20 20N 80 22E
68 Dhar, India 22 35N 75 26E
68 Dharampur, Mad. P., India 22 13N 75 18E
68 Dharampur, Maharashtra, India 20 32N 73 17E
70 Dharapuram, India 10 45N 77 34E
70 Dharmapuri, India 12 10N 78 10E
70 Dharmavaram, India 14 29N 77 44E
68 Dharmsala, (Dharamsala), India 32 16N 73 23E
70 Dharwar, India 15 29N 75 5E
69 Dhaulagiri Mt., Nepal 28 45N 83 45E
68 Dhebar, L., India 24 10N 74 0E
69 Dhenkanal, India 20 45N 85 35E
45 Dhenoúsa, Greece 37 8N 25 48E
45 Dhesfina, Greece 38 25N 22 31E
44 Dheskáti, Greece 39 55N 21 49E
45 Dhespotikó, Greece 36 57N 24 58E
44 Dhidhimótikhon, Greece 41 22N 26 29E
45 Dhikti, Mt., Greece 35 8N 25 29E
45 Dhilianáta, Greece 38 15N 20 34E
45 Dhílos, Greece 37 23N 25 15E
45 Dhimitsána, Greece 37 36N 22 3E
45 Dhírfis, Mt., Greece 38 40N 23 54E
45 Dhodhekánisos, Greece 36 35N 27 0E
45 Dhofar, Muscat & Oman 17 0N 54 10E
44 Dholiana, Greece 39 54N 20 32E
45 Dhokos, Greece 37 20N 23 20E
68 Dholka, India 22 44N 72 29E
44 Dhomokós, Greece 39 10N 22 18E
68 Dholpur, India 26 45N 77 59E
70 Dhond, India 18 26N 74 40E
68 Dhoraji, India 21 45N 70 37E
44 Dhoxathon, Greece 41 9N 24 16E
68 Dhragonisi, Greece 37 27N 25 29E
68 Dhrangadhra, India 22 59N 71 31E
45 Dhriopós, Greece 37 25N 24 35E
68 Dhrol, India 22 40N 70 25E
65 Dhubaibah, Trucial States 23 25N 54 35E
69 Dhubri, India 26 2N 90 2E
68 Dhulia, India 20 58N 74 50E
86 Dhurm, Saudi Arabia 20 18N 42 53E
69 Dia, I., Greece 35 26N 25 13E
45 Dia, I., Greece 35 26N 25 13E
127 Diaole, I. du., Fr. Gui. 5 15N 52 45W
120 Diablo Heights, Panama Canal Zone 8 58N 79 34W
84 Diafarabé, Mali 14 17N 4 57W
84 Diala, Mali 13 59N 10 0W
84 Dialakoro, Mali. 12 18N 7 54W
84 Diallassagou, Mali. 13 47N 3 41W
124 Diamante, Argentina 32 5s 60 40W
127 Diamantina, Brazil 18 5s 43 40W
98 Diamantina, R., Australia 14 30s 56 30W
69 Diamond Harbour, India 22 11N 88 14E
97 Diamond Is., Australia 17 25s 151 5E
118 Diamond Mts., U.S.A. 40 0N 115 58W
118 Diamondville, U.S.A. 41 51N 110 30W
38 Diano Marina, Italy 43 55N 8 3E
84 Dianra, Ivory Coast 8 45N 6 14W
85 Diapaga, Upper Volta 12 5N 1 46E
84 Diapangou, Upper Volta 12 5N 0 10E
84 Diariguila, Guinea 10 35N 10 2W
65 Dibai (Dubai), Trucial Oman 25 15N 55 20E
88 Dibaya, Zaïre 6 20s 22 0E
88 Dibaya Lubue, Zaïre 4 12s 19 54E
65 Dibba, Trucial 'Oman 25 45N 56 16E
87 Dibbi, Ethiopia 4 10N 41 52E
64 Dibega, Iraq 35 50N 43 46E
44 Dibër, Albania 41 38N 20 15E
92 Dibete, Botswana 23 45N 26 32E
87 Dibi, Ethiopia 4 10N 41 52E
67 Dibrugha, India 27 29N 94 58E
126 Dibulla, Colombia 11 17N 73 19W
116 Dickinson, U.S.A. 46 50N 102 40W
115 Dickson, U.S.A. 36 5N 87 22W
113 Dickson City, U.S.A. 41 29N 75 40W
39 Dicomano, Italy 43 53s 11 30E
87 Didesa, W., Ethiopia 9 40N 35 50E
84 Didiéni, Mali 14 5N 7 50W
108 Didsbury, Canada 51 35N 114 10W
18 Didwana, India 27 17N 74 25E
21 Die, France 44 47N 5 23E
84 Diébougou, Upper Volta 11 0N 3 15W
33 Diefenbaker Lake, Canada 51 0N 106 55W
3 Diego Garcia, I., Ind. Oc. 9 50s 75 0E
93 Diego Suarez, Malagasy Republic 12 25s 49 20E
16 Diekirch, Luxembourg 49 52N 6 10E
18 Diélette, France 49 33N 1 52W
84 Diéma, Mali 14 32N 9 3W
84 Dieméring, Senegal 12 29N 16 47W
71 Diêp Biên Phu, N. Vietnam 21 20N 103 0E
24 Diepholz, Germany 52 37N 8 22E
18 Dieppe, France 49 54N 1 4E
16 Dieren, Netherlands 52 3N 6 6E
117 Dierks, U.S.A. 34 9N 94 0W
21 Diest, Belgium 50 58N 5 4E
21 Dieulefit, France 44 32N 5 4E
21 Dieuze, France 48 50N 6 40E
88 Diffa, Niger 13 34N 12 33E
16 Differdange, Lux. 49 31N 5 54E
68 Dig, India 27 28N 77 20E
69 Digba, Zaïre 4 25N 25 48E
107 Digby, Canada 44 41N 65 50W
25 Digges, Canada 58 40N 94 0W
105 Digges Is., Canada 62 40N 77 50W
67 Dighinala, Bangladesh 23 15N 92 5E
116 Dighton, U.S.A. 38 30N 100 26W
21 Digne, France 44 5N 6 12E

20 Digoin, France 46 29N 3 58E
73 Digos, Philippines 6 45N 125 20E
50 Digranes, Iceland 66 4N 14 44E
70 Digras, India 20 6N 77 45E
64 Dijlah, R., India 27 30N 96 30E
64 Dijlah, Iraq 37 0N 42 30E
19 Dijon, France 47 20N 5 0E
87 Dikala, Sudan 4 45N 31 28E
87 Dikhal, F.T.A.I. 11 8N 42 20E
92 Dikomu di Kai, Mt., Bots. 24 51s 24 36E
58 Dikson, U.S.S.R. 73 40N 80 5E
87 Dikumbiya, Ethiopia 14 45N 37 30E
84 Dikwa, Cameroon 12 4N 13 30E
3 Dila, Ethiopia 6 14N 38 22E
64 Dilam, Saudi Arabia 23 55N 47 10E
73 Dili, Port. Timor 8 39s 125 34E
73 Dilizhan, U.S.S.R. 41 46N 44 57E
24 Dillenburg, Germany 50 44N 8 17E
117 Dilley, U.S.A. 28 40N 99 12W
87 Dilling, Sudan 12 3N 29 35E
25 Dillingen, Germany 49 22N 6 42E
109 Dillon, Canada 55 56N 108 54W
118 Dillon, Mont., U.S.A. 45 9N 112 36W
115 Dillon, S.C., U.S.A. 34 26N 79 20W
6 Dilolo, Zaïre 10 28s 22 18E
99 Dilston, Australia 41 22s 147 10E
87 Dima, Ethiopia 6 19N 36 15E
100 Dimbokro, Ivory Coast 6 45N 4 30W
46 Dimbovita ♦, Rumania 45 0N 25 30E
98 Dimbulah, Australia 17 2s 145 4E
59 Dimitriya Lapteva, Proliv, U.S.S.R. 73 0N 140 0E
43 Dimitrovgrad, Bulgaria 42 5N 25 35E
42 Dimitrovgrad, Y.-slav. 43 0N 22 48E
117 Dimmitt, U.S.A. 34 36N 102 16W
87 Dimo, Sudan 5 19N 29 10E
43 Dimovo, Rumania 43 43N 22 50E
73 Dinagat I., Philippines 10 10N 125 40E
69 Dinajpur, E. Pak. 25 33N 88 43E
18 Dinan, France 48 28N 2 2W
16 Dinant, Belgium 50 16N 4 55E
69 Dinapore, India 25 38N 85 5E
64 Dinar, Turkey 38 5N 30 15E
17 Dinard, France 48 38N 2 6W
9 Dinaric Alps, Europe 44 0N 17 30E
87 Dinder, Nahr ed, Sudan 12 32N 35 0E
70 Dindi, R., India 16 24N 78 15E
70 Dindigul, India 10 25N 78 0E
24 Dingelstädt, Germany 51 19N 10 19E
90 Dingila, Zaïre 3 37N 26 44E
113 Dingmans Ferry, U.S.A. 41 13N 74 55W
98 Dingo, Australia 23 45s 149 27E
25 Dingolfing, Germany 48 38N 12 30E
84 Dinguiraye, Guinea 11 30N 10 35W
14 Dingwall, Scot. 57 36N 4 26W
85 Dingyadi, Nigeria 13 0N 5 3E
92 Dinokwe (Palla Road), Botswana 23 29s 26 37E
118 Dinosaur National Monument, U.S.A. 40 30N 108 45W
119 Dinuba, U.S.A. 36 37N 119 22W
49 Dio, Sweden 56 37N 14 15E
27 Diosgyör, Hungary 48 7N 20 43E
46 Diosig, Rumania 47 18N 22 2E
85 Dioundiou, Niger 12 37N 3 33E
84 Diourbel, Senegal 14 39N 16 12W
68 Diplo, Pakistan 24 25N 69 35E
73 Dipolog, Philippines 8 36N 123 20E
46 Dir, Pakistan 35 18N 71 59E
87 Dire, Mali 16 20N 3 25W
87 Dire Dawa, Ethiopia 9 35N 41 45E
98 Direction, C., Australia 12 51s 143 32E
121 Diriamba, Nicaragua 11 51N 86 19W
96 Dirk Hartog I., Australia 25 58s 113 1E
99 Dirranbandi, Australia 28 33s 148 17E
87 Disa, Sudan 12 5N 34 15E
46 Disappointment, C., U.S.A. 46 20N 124 0W
96 Disappointment L., Australia 23 20s 122 40E
10 Disaster B., Australia 37 15s 150 0E
104 Discovery, Canada 63 0N 115 0W
99 Discovery B., Australia 38 10s 140 40E
25 Disentis, Switzerland 46 42N 8 50E
86 Dishna, Egypt 26 9N 32 32E
85 Disina, Nigeria 11 35N 9 50E
4 Disko, Greenland 69 45N 53 30W
4 Disko B., Greenland 69 10N 52 0W
4 Disko Bugt, Greenland 69 10N 52 0W
54 Disna, U.S.S.R. 55 32N 28 11E
54 Disna, R., U.S.S.R. 55 32N 27 21E
126 Distrito Federal ♦, Ven. 10 30N 66 55W
86 Disûq, Egypt 31 8N 30 35E
84 Ditinn, Guinea 10 53N 12 11W
68 Diu, I., India 20 45N 70 58E
106 Diver, Canada 46 44N 79 30W
18 Dives, France 49 18N 0 8W
18 Dives, R., France 49 18N 0 7W
70 Divi Pt., India 15 59N 81 9E
57 Divichi, U.S.S.R. 41 15N 48 57E
118 Divide, U.S.A. 45 48N 112 47W
57 Divnoye, U.S.S.R. 45 55N 43 21E
84 Divo, Ivory Coast 5 48N 5 15W
65 Diwai Kol, Afghanistan 34 20N 68 0E
118 Dixie, U.S.A. 45 37N 115 27W
116 Dixon, Ill., U.S.A. 41 50N 89 30W
118 Dixon, Mont., U.S.A. 47 19N 114 25W
119 Dixon, N. Mex., U.S.A. 36 15N 105 57W
109 Dixon Entrance, U.S.A. 54 30N 132 0W
56 Diyarbakir, Turkey 37 55N 40 18E
85 Djabotaoure, Togo 8 35N 0 57E
83 Djado, Niger 21 4N 12 14E
83 Djado, Plateau du, Niger 21 29N 12 21E
73 Djailolo, Indonesia 1 5N 127 35E
73 Djailolo, Selat, Indonesia 0 5N 129 5E
73 Djajapura, Indonesia 2 28N 140 38E

73 Djajawidjaja, Pengunungan, Indonesia 7 0s 139 0E
73 Djakarta, Indonesia 6 9s 106 49E
42 Djakovo, Yugoslavia 45 19N 18 24E
82 Djamâa, Algeria 33 32N 5 59E
83 Djamba, Angola 16 45s 13 58E
88 Djambala, Congo 2 20s 14 30E
72 Djambi = Telanaipura, Indonesia 1 38s 103 30E
72 Djambi ♦, Indonesia 1 30s 103 0E
85 Djang, Cameroon 5 30N 10 4E
72 Djangeru, Indonesia 2 30s 116 40E
72 Djangeru, Indonesia 2 30s 116 40E
73 Djapara, Indonesia 6 30s 110 40E
73 Djatibarang, Indonesia 6 28s 108 18E
73 Djatinegara, Indonesia 6 13s 106 52E
73 Djawa Barat ♦, Indonesia 6 40s 107 0E
73 Djawa Tengah ♦, Indonesia 7 0s 110 0E
73 Djawa Timur ♦, Indonesia 7 25s 113 0E
83 Djebiniana, Tunisia 35 1N 11 0E
82 Djelfa, Algeria 34 40N 3 15E
90 Djema, Cen. Afr. 6 9N 25 15E
83 Djemadja I., Indon. 3 5N 105 45E
73 Djember, Indonesia 8 11s 113 41E
83 Djeneïene, Tunisia 31 45N 10 9E
84 Djenné, Mali 14 0N 4 30W
83 Djenoun, Garet el, Alg. 25 4N 5 31E
83 Djerba, Tunisia 33 52N 10 51E
83 Djerba, Ile de, Tunisia 33 56N 11 0E
83 Djerid, Chott, Tun. 33 42N 8 30E
73 Djerik, Indonesia 4 3s 131 20E
87 Djibouti, Fr. Terr. of the Afars & Issas 11 30N 43 5E
82 Djidjelli, Algeria 36 52N 5 50E
71 Djirlange, S. Vietnam 11 44N 108 15E
82 Djofra, Libya 28 59N 15 47E
73 Djombang, Indonesia 7 32s 112 12E
85 Djorong, Indonesia 4 2s 114 55E
85 Djougou, Dahomey 9 40N 1 45E
88 Djoum, Cameroon 2 41N 12 35E
90 Djourab, Erg du, Chad 16 40N 18 50E
90 Djugu, Congo 1 55N 30 35E
50 Djúpivogur, Iceland 64 39N 14 17W
48 Djursholm, Sweden 59 25N 18 6E
49 Djursland, Den. 56 27N 10 45E
49 Djursland, Den. 56 27N 10 45E
59 Dmitriya Lapteva, Proliv, U.S.S.R. 73 0N 140 0E
55 Dmitrov, U.S.S.R. 56 25N 37 32E
54 Dmitrovsk Orlovskiy, U.S.S.R. 52 29N 35 10E
56 Dneiper, R. = Dnepr, U.S.S.R. 52 29N 35 10E
56 Dnepr, R., U.S.S.R. 50 0N 31 0E
56 Dneprodzerzhinsk, U.S.S.R. 48 32N 34 30E
59 Dneprodzerzhinskoye Vdkhr., U.S.S.R. 49 0N 34 0E
56 Dnepropetrovsk, U.S.S.R. 48 30N 35 0E
56 Dneprorudnoye, U.S.S.R. 47 21N 34 58E
56 Dnestr, R., U.S.S.R. 48 30N 26 30E
56 Dnestrovski = Belgorod, U.S.S.R. 50 35N 36 35E
56 Dniester = Dnestr, U.S.S.R. 48 30N 26 30E
54 Dno, U.S.S.R. 57 50N 29 58E
90 Doba, Chad. 8 40N 16 50E
90 Dobane, Cen. Afr. 6 20N 24 39E
98 Dobbiaco, Italy 46 44N 12 13E
98 Dobbyn, Australia 19 44s 139 59E
47 Dobczyce, Poland 49 52N 20 25E
24 Döbeln, Germany 51 7N 13 10E
73 Doberai, Djazirah, Indonesia 1 25s 133 0E
46 Dobiegniew, Poland 52 59N 15 45E
128 Doblas, Argentina 37 5s 64 0W
73 Dobo, Indonesia 5 45s 134 15E
42 Doboj, Yugoslavia 44 46N 18 6E
47 Dobra, Poland 53 34N 15 20E
46 Dobra, Rumania 45 52N 25 40E
28 Dobre Miasto, Poland 53 58N 20 26E
43 Dobrinishta, Bulgaria 41 49N 23 34E
26 Dobris, Czechoslovakia 49 46N 14 10E
46 Dobrodzien, Poland 50 45N 18 25E
46 Dobrogea, Rum. 44 30N 28 15E
46 Dobruja = Dobrogea, Rum. 44 30N 28 15E
54 Dobrush, U.S.S.R. 52 28N 30 35E
54 Dobrzyn n. Wisła, Poland 52 39N 19 22E
87 Dobtong, Sudan 6 25N 31 40E
48 Döda Fallet, Swed. 63 4N 16 35E
45 Dodecanese = Dhodhekanisos, Greece 36 35N 27 0E
116 Dodge Center, U.S.A. 44 1N 92 57W
116 Dodge City, U.S.A. 37 42N 100 0W
116 Dodgeville, U.S.A. 42 55N 90 8W
87 Dodo, Sudan 5 10N 29 57E
87 Dodola, Ethiopia 6 59N 39 15E
90 Dodoma, Tanzania 6 8s 35 45E
90 Dodoma ♦, Tanzania 6 0s 36 0E
109 Dodsland, Canada 51 50N 108 45W
117 Dodson, U.S.A. 48 23N 108 4W
16 Doetinchem, Neth. 51 59N 6 18E
46 Doftana, Rumania 45 11N 25 45E
108 Dog L., Canada 51 10N 98 40W
108 Dog, R., Canada 57 50N 94 40W
56 Doganbey, Turkey 37 40N 27 10E
38 Dogliani, Italy 44 35N 7 55E
85 Dögondoutchi, Niger 13 38N 4 2E
85 Dogoraoua, Niger 14 0N 5 31E

68 Dogran, Pakistan 31 48N 73 35E
68 Dóhad, India 22 50N 74 15E
67 Dohazari, Bangladesh 22 10N 92 5E
106 Doherty, Canada 47 4N 72 35W
106 Doherty, Canada 46 58N 79 44W
73 Doi, I., Indonesia 2 21N 127 49E
47 Doi Luang, Thailand 18 20N 101 30E
47 Dokka, Norway 60 49N 10 7E
47 Dokka, R., Norway 61 7N 10 0E
16 Dokkum, Netherlands 53 20N 5 59E
68 Dokri Mohenjodaro, Pakistan 27 25N 68 7E
18 Dol, France 48 34N 1 47W
73 Dolak, Pulau, Indonesia 8 0s 138 30E
116 Doland, U.S.A. 44 55N 98 5W
107 Dolbeau, Canada 48 55N 72 18W
21 Dôle, France 47 7N 5 31E
87 Doleib, W., Sudan 10 30N 33 15E
12 Dolgellau, Wales 52 44N 3 53W
54 Dolginovo, U.S.S.R. 54 39N 27 29E
40 Dolianova, Italy 39 23N 9 11E
56 Dolinskaya, U.S.S.R. 48 16N 32 36E
88 Dolisie, Congo 4 0s 13 10E
46 Dolj ♦, Yugoslavia 44 10N 23 30E
16 Dollart, Netherlands 53 20N 7 10E
43 Dolna Banya, Bulgaria 42 18N 23 44E
43 Dolni Dubnik, Bulgaria 43 24N 24 26E
39 Dolo, Italy 45 25N 12 4E
87 Dolo Bay, Ethiopia 4 11N 42 3E
39 Dolomites = Dolomiti, Italy 46 30N 11 40E
39 Dolomiti, Italy 46 30N 11 40E
124 Dolores, Argentina 36 20s 57 40W
119 Dolores, Colo., U.S.A. 37 30N 108 30W
117 Dolores, Tex., U.S.A. 27 40N 99 38W
124 Dolores, Uruguay 33 34s 58 15W
42 Dolovo, Yugoslavia 44 55N 20 52E
128 Dolphin C., Falkland Is. 51 10s 59 0W
104 Dolphin and Union Str., Canada 69 5N 114 45W
51 Dolsk, Poland 51 59N 17 3E
127 Dom Pedrito, Brazil 31 0s 54 40W
85 Doma, Nigeria 8 25N 8 18E
91 Domasi, Malawi 15 2s 35 10E
26 Domazlice, Cz. 49 28N 13 0E
58 Dombarovskiy, U.S.S.R. 51 0N 59 10E
47 Dombås, Norway 62 6N 9 4E
19 Dombasle, France 49 8N 5 0E
89 Dombe Grande, Angola 12 56s 13 8E
21 Dombes, France 46 3N 5 0E
27 Dombóvár, Hungary 46 21N 18 9E
27 Dombrád, Hungary 48 13N 21 54E
71 Domel, I = Letsok-aw-kyun, Burma 11 30N 98 25E
20 Domérat, France 46 21N 2 32E
124 Domeyko, Chile 29 0s 71 30W
18 Domfront, France 48 37N 0 40W
124 Dominador, Chile 24 21s 69 20W
121 Dominica I., Leeward Is. 15 20N 61 20W
121 Dominican Rep. ■, W. Ind. 19 0N 70 30W
24 Dömitz, Germany 53 9N 11 13E
20 Domme, France 44 48N 1 12E
49 Dommerby, Denmark 56 33N 9 5E
63 Domo, Ethiopia 7 50N 47 10E
38 Domodossóla, Italy 46 6N 8 19E
19 Dompaire, France 48 14N 6 14E
20 Dompierre, France 46 31N 3 41E
84 Dompin, Ghana 5 5N 2 5W
19 Domrémy, France 48 26N 5 40E
48 Domsjö, Sweden 63 16N 18 41E
45 Domvraina, Greece 38 15N 22 59E
39 Domzale, Yugoslavia 46 9N 14 35E
70 Don, R., India 16 40N 75 55W
12 Don R., England, U.K. 53 57N 1 0W
14 Don R., Scotland, U.K. 57 14N 2 15W
57 Don, R., U.S.S.R. 49 35N 41 40E
31 Don Benito, Spain 38 53N 5 51W
120 Don Martin, Presa de, Mexico 27 30N 100 50W
91 Dona Ana, Mozambique 17 25s 35 17E
15 Donaghadee, Northern Ireland 54 38N 5 32W
100 Donald, Australia 36 23s 143 0E
108 Donalda, Canada 52 35N 112 34W
117 Donaldsonville, U.S.A. 30 2N 91 50W
115 Donalsonville, U.S.A. 31 3N 84 52W
25 Donau, R., Austria 47 55N 17 20E
25 Donaueschingen, Ger. 47 57N 8 30E
26 Donawitz, Austria 47 22N 15 4E
12 Doncaster, Eng. 53 31N 1 9W
89 Dondo, Angola 9 45s 14 25E
91 Dondo, Mozambique 19 33s 34 46E
73 Dondo, Teluk, Indon. 0 29N 120 45E
70 Dondra Head, Sri Lanka 5 55N 80 40E
15 Donegal, Ireland 54 39N 8 8W
15 Donegal ♦, Ireland 54 53N 8 0W
15 Donegal B., Ireland 54 30N 8 35W
55 Donets, U.S.S.R. 48 50N 38 45E
56 Donetsk, U.S.S.R. 48 0N 37 45E
85 Dong, Nigeria 9 20N 12 15E
71 Dong Hene, Laos 16 44N 105 14E
71 Dong Hoi, Vietnam 17 18N 106 36E
85 Donga, Nigeria 7 45N 10 2E
99 Dongara, Australia 29 14s 114 57E
69 Dongargarh, India 21 10N 80 40E
86 Dongola, Sudan 19 9N 30 22E
88 Dongou, Congo 2 0N 18 5E
117 Doniphan, U.S.A. 36 40N 90 50W
39 Donja Stubica, Y.-slav. 45 59N 16 0E
42 Donji Dušnik, Y.-slav. 43 12N 22 5E
42 Donji Miholjac, Y.-slav. 45 48N 18 10E
42 Donji Milanovac, Yugoslavia 44 28N 22 6E
42 Donji Vakuf, Y.-slav. 44 8N 17 24E
117 Donna, U.S.A. 26 12N 98 2W
107 Donnaconna, Canada 46 41N 71 41W

MAP

101 Donnelly's Crossing, N.Z.   35 42s 173 38E
112 Donora, U.S.A.   40 11N 79 50w
55 Donskoy, U.S.S.R.   53 55N 38 15E
39 Donya Lendava, Y.-slav.   46 35N 16 25E
21 Donzère, France   44 28N 4 43E
19 Donzy, France   47 20N 3 6E
14 Doon, R., Scot.   55 26N 4 28w
62 Dor (Tantura), Israel   32 37N 34 55E
38 Dora Báltea, R., Italy   45 42N 7 25E
96 Dora, L., Australia   22 0s 123 0E
38 Dora Riparia, R., Italy   45 7N 7 24E
87 Dorading, Sudan   8 30N 33 5E
49 Dörby, Sweden   56 20N 16 12E
13 Dorchester, Dorset, England   50 42N 2 28w
105 Dorchester, C., Canada   65 40N 78 0w
20 Dordogne, R., France   45 0N 0 36w
20 Dordogne ♦, Fr.   45 5N 0 40E
16 Dordrecht, Netherlands   51 48N 4 39E
92 Dordrecht, S. Africa   31 20s 27 3E
109 Dore L., Canada   54 45N 107 20w
20 Dore, Mt., France   45 32N 2 50E
20 Dore, R., France   45 59N 3 28E
25 Doren, Germany   48 16N 12 10E
40 Dorgali, Italy   40 18N 9 35E
85 Dori, Upper Volta   14 3N 0 2w
92 Doring, R., S. Africa   32 30s 19 30E
106 Dorion, Canada   45 23N 74 3w
113 Dorion-Vaudreuil, Can.   45 25N 75 4w
84 Dormaa-Ahenkro, Ghana   7 15N 2 52w
87 Dormo, Ras, Ethiopia   13 14N 42 35E
39 Dornberg, Yugoslavia   45 45N 13 50E
26 Dornbirn, Austria   47 25N 9 45E
19 Dornes, France   46 48N 3 18E
14 Dornoch, Scot.   57 52N 4 0w
14 Dornoch Firth, Scotland   57 52N 4 0w
85 Doro, Mali   16 9N 0 51w
27 Dorog, Hungary   47 42N 18 45E
54 Dorogobuzh, U.S.S.R.   54 50N 33 10E
46 Dorohoi, Rumania   47 56N 26 30E
75 Döröö Nuur, Mongolia   48 0N 93 0E
96 Dorre I., Australia   25 13s 113 12E
99 Dorrigo, Australia   30 19s 152 38E
118 Dorris, U.S.A.   41 59N 121 58w
112 Dorset, Canada   45 14N 78 55w
112 Dorset, U.S.A.   41 41N 8 42w
13 Dorset ♦, Eng.   50 48N 2 25w
24 Dorsten, Germany   51 40N 6 55E
24 Dortmund, Germany   51 32N 7 28E
24 Dorum, Germany   53 40N 8 33E
90 Doruma, Congo   4 42N 27 33E
87 Dorya, W., Ethiopia   5 15N 41 30E
64 Dörtyol, Turkey   36 52N 36 12E
128 Dos Bahías, C., Arg.   44 58s 65 32w
119 Dos Cabezas, U.S.A.   32 1N 109 37w
31 Dos Hermanas, Spain   37 16N 5 55w
85 Dosara, Nigeria   12 20N 6 5E
70 Doshi, Afghanistan   35 35N 68 50E
85 Dosso, Niger   13 0N 3 13E
49 Döstrup, Denmark   56 41N 9 42E
108 Dot. Canada   50 12N 121 25w
115 Dothan, U.S.A.   31 10N 85 25w
18 Douai, France   50 21N 3 4E
85 Douala, Cameroon   4 0N 9 45E
18 Douarnenez, France   48 6N 4 21w
46 Douăzeci Si Trei August, Rum.   43 50N 28 40E
99 Double I., Pt., Austral.   25 55s 153 30E
26 Doubravka, R., Cz.   49 40N 15 30E
19 Doubs, R., France   46 53N 5 1E
19 Doubs ♦, France   47 10N 6 20E
96 Doubtful B., Austral.   34 15s 119 28E
101 Doubtful Sd., N.Z.   45 20s 166 49E
101 Doubtless B., N.Z.   34 55s 173 26E
106 Doucet, Canada   48 15N 76 35w
18 Doudeville, France   49 43N 0 47E
18 Doué, France   47 11N 0 20w
84 Douentza, Mali   14 58N 2 48w
92 Douglas, S. Afr.   29 4s 23 46E
12 Douglas, I. of Man   54 9N 4 29w
119 Douglas, Ariz., U.S.A.   31 21N 109 30w
115 Douglas, Ga., U.S.A.   31 32N 82 52w
116 Douglas, Wyo., U.S.A.   42 45N 105 20w
107 Douglastown, Canada   48 46N 64 24w
115 Douglasville, U.S.A.   33 46N 84 43w
82 Douirat, Morocco   33 2N 4 11w
45 Doukáton, Akra, Gr.   38 34N 20 30E
19 Doulevant, France   48 22N 4 53E
19 Doullens, France   50 10N 2 20E
88 Doumé, Cameroon   4 15N 13 25E
84 Douna, Mali   12 40N 6 0w
14 Dounreay, Scot.   58 40N 3 28w
128 Dourados, Brazil   22 9s 54 50w
19 Dourdan, France   48 30N 2 0E
30 Douro, R., Portugal   41 1N 8 16w
21 Douvaine, France   46 19N 6 16E
83 Douz, Tunisia   33 25N 9 0E
14 Dove, R., England   54 20N 1 0w
107 Dove Brook, Canada   53 40N 57 40w
119 Dove Creek, U.S.A.   37 53N 108 59w
13 Dover, England   51 7N 1 19E
114 Dover, Del., U.S.A.   39 10N 75 31w
113 Dover, N.H., U.S.A.   43 5N 70 51w
113 Dover, N.J., U.S.A.   40 53N 74 34w
112 Dover, Ohio, U.S.A.   40 32N 81 30w
96 Dover, Pt., Australia   32 32s 125 32E
8 Dover, Strait of, England, U.K.   51 0N 1 30E
107 Dover-Foxcroft, U.S.A.   45 14N 69 14w
113 Dover Plains, U.S.A.   41 43N 73 43w
13 Dovey, R., Wales   52 32N 4 0w
47 Dovrefjell, Nor.   62 15N 9 33E
47 Dovre, Norway   62 0N 9 7E
91 Dowa, Malawi   13 38s 33 58E
114 Dowagiac, U.S.A.   42 0N 86 8w
* 15 Down ♦, N. Ire.   54 20N 6 0w
118 Downey, U.S.A.   42 29N 112 3w
13 Downham Market, England   52 36N 0 22E

118 Downieville, U.S.A.   39 42N 120 56w
15 Downpatrick, Northern Ireland   54 20N 5 43w
15 Downpatrick Hd., Ire.   54 20N 9 21w
99 Downs Division, Australia   27 10s 150 44E
113 Doylestown, U.S.A.   40 21N 75 10w
67 Doyung, China   33 40N 99 25E
82 Dra, Cap, Morocco   28 58N 11 0w
82 Draa, O., Morocco   30 29N 6 1w
16 Drachten, Netherlands   53 7N 6 5E
46 Draganestiolt, Rumania   44 9N 24 32E
46 Draganesti- Vlasca, Rumania   44 5N 25 33E
42 Dragaš, Yugoslavia   42 5N 20 35E
46 Drăgăsani, Rumania   44 39N 24 17E
46 Draginac, Yugoslavia   44 30N 19 25E
46 Dragocvet, Yugoslavia   44 0N 21 15E
126 Dragon's Mouth, Ven.   11 0N 61 50w
32 Dragonera, I., Spain   39 35N 2 19E
42 Dragovistica (Berivol), Bulgaria   42 22N 22 39E
21 Draguignan, France   43 30N 6 27E
118 Drain, U.S.A.   43 45N 123 17w
116 Drake, U.S.A.   47 56N 100 31w
5 Drake Pass., S. Oc.   58 0s 68 0w
93 Drakensberg, S. Afr.   31 0s 25 0E
44 Dráma, Greece   41 9N 24 10E
44 Dráma ♦, Greece   41 10N 24 0E
47 Drammen, Norway   59 42N 10 12E
46 Drănceni, Rumania   46 49N 28 10E
50 Drangajökull, Iceland   66 9N 22 15w
47 Drangedal, Norway   59 6N 9 3E
46 Dranov, Ostrov, Rum.   44 55N 29 30E
42 Drava, R., Yugoslavia   45 50N 18 0w
19 Draveil, France   48 41N 2 25E
19 Dravograd, Yugoslavia   46 36N 15 5E
28 Drawa, R., Poland   53 6N 15 56E
28 Drawno, Poland   53 13N 15 46E
28 Drawsko Pom, Poland   53 35N 15 50E
108 Drayton Valley, Can.   53 25N 114 58w
49 Drejö, Denmark   54 58N 10 25E
42 Dren, Yugoslavia   43 8N 20 44E
112 Dresden, Canada   42 40N 82 15w
24 Dresden, Germany   51 2N 13 45E
24 Dresden ♦, E. Germany   51 12N 14 0E
18 Dreux, France   48 44N 1 23E
28 Drezdenko, Poland   52 50N 15 49E
12 Driffield, England   54 0N 0 25w
106 Driftwood, Canada   49 8N 81 23E
112 Driftwood, U.S.A.   41 22N 78 9w
118 Driggs, U.S.A.   43 50N 111 8w
42 Drina, R., Yugoslavia   44 30N 19 10E
46 Drincea, R., Rumania   44 20N 22 55E
42 Drini, R., Albania   42 20N 20 0E
42 Drin-i-zi, R., Albania   41 37N 20 28E
42 Drinjača, R., Y.-slav.   44 20N 19 0E
47 Driva, Norway   62 33N 9 38E
47 Driva, R., Norway   62 34N 9 33E
47 Drivstua, Norway   62 26N 9 37E
42 Drniš, Yugoslavia   43 51N 16 10E
28 Drobin, Poland   52 42N 19 58E
47 Drobbakk, Norway   59 39N 10 39E
15 Drogheda, Ireland   53 45N 6 20w
54 Drogichin, U.S.S.R.   52 15N 25 8E
54 Drogobych, U.S.S.R.   49 20N 23 30E
15 Droichead Nua, Ire.   53 11N 6 50w
13 Droitwich, Eng.   52 16N 2 10w
21 Drôme, R., France   44 46N 4 46E
21 Drôme ♦, France   44 38N 5 15E
100 Dromedary, C., Austral.   36 17s 150 10E
100 Dromore, Australia   32 25s 143 55E
38 Dronero, Italy   44 29N 7 22E
98 Dronfield, Australia   21 12s 140 3E
49 Dronninglund, Den.   57 10N 10 19E
26 Drosendorf, Austria   48 52N 15 37E
100 Drouin, Australia   38 10s 145 53E
43 Drouzhba, Bulgaria   43 22N 28 0E
112 Drumbo, Canada   43 16N 80 35w
108 Drumheller, Canada   51 25N 112 40w
118 Drummond, U.S.A.   46 46N 113 4w
98 Drummond Ra., Austral.   23 45s 147 10E
106 Drummondville, Can.   45 55N 72 25w
117 Drumright, U.S.A.   35 59N 96 38w
54 Druskininkaj, U.S.S.R.   54 3N 23 58E
54 Drut, R., U.S.S.R.   52 32N 30 0E
54 Druya, U.S.S.R.   55 45N 27 15E
59 Druzhina, U.S.S.R.   68 14N 145 18E
42 Drvar, Yugoslavia   44 21N 16 2E
39 Drvenik, Y.-slav.   43 27N 15 5E
43 Dryanovo, Bulgaria   42 59N 25 28E
109 Dryden, Canada   49 50N 92 50w
117 Dryden, U.S.A.   30 3N 102 6w
5 Drygalski I., Antarctica   66 0s 92 0E
100 Drysdale, Australia   38 11s 144 32E
96 Drysdale, R., Austral.   15 0s 126 52E
47 Drøbak, Norway   59 39N 10 39E
112 Du Bois, U.S.A.   41 8N 78 46w
117 Du Quoin, U.S.A.   38 0N 89 10w
113 Duanesburg, U.S.A.   42 45N 74 11w
98 Duaringa, Australia   23 42s 149 42E
72 Duba, Saudi Arabia   27 10N 35 40E
65 Dubai = Dubayy, Trucial Oman   24 10N 55 20E
65 Dubbayy, Trucial Oman   24 10N 55 20E
100 Dubbo, Austral.   32 11s 148 35E
90 Dubele, Zaïre   2 56N 29 35E
39 Dubica, Yugoslavia   45 11N 16 48E
112 Dublin, Canada   43 32N 81 18w
15 Dublin, Ireland   53 20N 6 18w
115 Dublin, U.S.A.   32 30N 83 0w
117 Dublin, Tex., U.S.A.   32 0N 98 20w
15 Dublin, B., Ire.   53 18N 6 5w
15 Dublin ♦, Ire.   53 24N 6 20w
54 Dubna, U.S.S.R.   50 25N 25 45E
54 Dubno, U.S.S.R.   50 25N 25 45E

118 Dubois, U.S.A.   44 7N 112 9w
56 Dubossary, U.S.S.R.   47 15N 29 10E
56 Dubossasy Vdkhr., U.S.S.R.   47 30N 29 0E
57 Dubovka, U.S.S.R.   49 5N 44 50E
57 Dubovskoye, U.S.S.R.   47 28N 42 40E
69 Dubrajpur, India   23 48N 87 25E
84 Dubrékah, Guinea   9 46N 13 31w
54 Dubrovitsa, U.S.S.R.   51 31N 26 35E
42 Dubrovnik, Yugoslavia   42 39N 18 6E
59 Dubrovskoye, U.S.S.R.   58 55N 111 0E
116 Dubuque, U.S.A.   42 30N 90 41w
98 Duchess, Australia   21 20s 139 50E
95 Ducie I., Pacific Ocean   24 47s 124 40w
109 Duck, Mt., Canada   51 27N 100 35w
109 Duck Lake, Canada   52 50N 106 0w
109 Duck Mt. Prov. Park, Canada   51 45N 101 0w
51 Duderstadt, Germany   51 30N 10 15E
59 Dudinka, U.S.S.R.   69 30N 86 0E
13 Dudley, England   52 30N 2 5w
70 Dudna, R., India   19 36N 76 20E
30 Dueñas, Spain   41 52N 4 33w
49 Dueodde, Denmark   54 59N 15 4E
30 Duero, R., Spain   41 37N 4 25w
39 Dugi, I., Y.-slav.   44 0N 15 0E
39 Dugo Selo, Yugoslavia   45 51N 16 18E
72 Duhak, Iran   33 20N 57 30E
98 Duifken Pt., Australia   12 33s 141 38E
24 Duisburg, Germany   51 27N 6 42E
126 Duitama, Colombia   5 50N 73 2w
92 Duiwelskloof, S. Africa   23 42s 30 10E
90 Dukana, Kenya   3 59N 37 20E
42 Dukati, Albania   40 16N 19 32E
109 Duke I., Alaska   54 50N 131 20w
65 Dukhan, Qatar   25 25N 50 50E
54 Dukhovshchina, U.S.S.R.   55 15N 32 27E
27 Dukla, Poland   49 30N 21 35E
85 Duku, North-Eastern, Nigeria   10 43N 10 43E
85 Duku, North-Western, Nigeria   11 11N 4 55E
73 Dulawan, Philippines   7 5N 124 20E
121 Dulce, Golfo, Costa Rica   8 40N 83 20w
124 Dulce, R., Argentina   29 30s 63 0w
43 Dŭlgopol, Bulgaria   43 3N 27 22E
68 Dullewala, Pakistan   31 50N 71 25E
24 Dülmen, Germany   51 49N 7 18E
43 Dulovo, Bulgaria   43 48N 27 9E
98 Dululu, Australia   23 48s 150 15E
116 Duluth, U.S.A.   46 48N 92 10w
70 Dum Dum, India   22 39N 88 26E
67 Dum Duma, India   27 40N 95 40E
73 Dumaguete, Philippines   9 17N 123 15E
73 Dumai, Indonesia   1 35N 101 20E
73 Dumaran I., Phil.   10 33N 119 50E
73 Dumaring, Indonesia   1 46N 118 10E
117 Dumas, Ark., U.S.A.   33 52N 91 30w
117 Dumas, Okla., U.S.A.   35 50N 101 58w
47 Dumba I., Norway   61 43N 4 50E
14 Dumbarton, Scot.   55 58N 4 35w
46 Dumbrăveni, Rumania   46 14N 24 34E
64 Dümet al Jandal, Si. Arabia   29 55N 39 40E
14 Dumfries, Scot.   55 4N 3 37w
*14 Dumfries ♦, Scot.   55 12N 3 30w
69 Dumka, India   24 0N 87 22E
106 Dumoine, L., Canada   46 55N 77 55w
100 Dumosa, Australia   35 52s 143 6E
69 Dumraon, India   25 33N 84 8E
86 Dumyât, Egypt   31 24N 31 48E
86 Dumyât, Masabb, Egypt   31 28N 32 0E
15 Dun Laoghaire (Dunleary), Ireland   53 17N 6 9w
19 Dun-sur-Auron, France   46 53N 2 33E
27 Duna, R., Hungary   45 51N 18 48E
27 Dunaföldvár, Hungary   46 50N 18 57E
27 Dunaj, R., Cz.   47 50N 18 52E
43 Dunaj, R., Bulgaria   43 57N 29 32E
27 Dunajec, R., Poland   50 12N 20 52E
27 Dunajska Streda, Cz.   48 0N 17 37E
46 Dunărea, R., Rumania   45 30N 29 40E
27 Dunaszekcsö, Hungary   46 6N 18 45E
27 Dunaújváros, Hungary   47 0N 18 57E
42 Dunav, R., Y.-slav.   45 0N 20 21E
46 Dunavtsi, Rumania   43 57N 22 53E
101 Dunback, New Zealand   45 23s 170 36E
98 Dunbar, Australia   16 0s 142 22E
*14 Dunbarton ♦, Scotland   56 4N 4 42w
14 Dunblane, Scot.   56 10N 3 58w
108 Duncan, Canada   48 45N 123 40w
119 Duncan, Ariz., U.S.A.   32 46N 109 6w
117 Duncan, Okla., U.S.A.   34 25N 98 0w
108 Duncan, L., Brit. Col., Canada   50 20N 117 0w
106 Duncan, L., Quebec, Canada   53 35N 77 55w
71 Duncan Pass., Ind. Oc.   11 0N 92 30E
14 Duncansby, Scot.   58 37N 3 3w
112 Dundalk, Canada   44 10N 80 24w
15 Dundalk, Ireland   53 55N 6 45w
15 Dundalk, B., Ireland   53 55N 6 15w
105 Dundas, Canada   43 17N 79 59w
109 Dundas I., Canada   54 30N 130 50w
96 Dundas, L., Australia   32 35s 121 50E
96 Dundas Str., Australia   11 15s 131 35E
14 Dundee, Scotland   56 29N 3 0w
99 Dundoo, Australia   27 40s 144 37E
15 Dundrum, N. Ire.   54 17N 5 50w
15 Dundrum B., Northern Ireland   54 12N 5 40w
68 Dundwára, India   27 48N 79 9E
101 Dunedin, New Zealand   45 50s 170 33E
115 Dunedin, U.S.A.   28 1N 82 45w
14 Dunfermline, Scot.   56 5N 3 28w

112 Dungannon, Canada   43 51N 81 35w
15 Dungannon, Northern Ireland   54 30N 6 47w
68 Dungarpur, India   23 52N 73 45E
15 Dungarvan, Ireland   52 6N 7 40w
15 Dungarvan Harb., Ire.   52 5N 7 35w
85 Dungas, Niger   13 4N 9 20E
67 Dungbura La, China   34 41N 93 18E
75 Dungbure Shan, Asia   35 0N 90 0E
13 Dungeness, England   50 54N 0 59E
92 Dungo, L. do, Angola   17 15s 19 0E
100 Dungog, Australia   32 22s 151 40E
86 Dungunab, Sudan   21 10N 37 9E
86 Dungunâb, Khalîg, Sudan   21 5N 37 12E
70 Dunhinda Falls, Sri Lanka   7 5N 81 6E
21 Dunières, France   45 13N 4 20E
98 Dunk I., Australia   17 59s 146 14E
100 Dunkeld, Australia   37 40s 142 22E
14 Dunkeld, Scot.   56 34N 3 36w
19 Dunkerque, France   51 2N 2 20E
13 Dunkery Beacon, England   51 15N 3 37w
16 Dunkirk = Dunkerque, France   51 2N 2 20E
112 Dunkirk, U.S.A.   42 30N 79 18w
87 Dunkuj, Sudan   11 15N 33 0E
87 Dunkur, Ethiopia   11 58N 35 58E
84 Dunkwa, Central, Ghana   6 0N 1 47w
85 Dunkwa, Central, Ghana   5 30N 1 0w
116 Dunlap, U.S.A.   41 50N 95 30w
20 Dun-le-Palestel, Fr.   46 18N 1 39E
15 Dunmanus B., Ireland   51 31N 9 50w
113 Dunmore, U.S.A.   41 27N 75 38w
115 Dunn, U.S.A.   35 18N 78 36w
15 Dunnellon, U.S.A.   29 4N 82 28w
14 Dunnet Hd., Scot.   58 38N 3 22w
116 Dunning, U.S.A.   41 52N 100 4w
112 Dunnville, Canada   42 57N 79 37w
100 Dunolly, Australia   36 46s 143 44E
14 Dunoon, Scot.   55 57N 4 56w
86 Dunqul, Egypt   23 40N 31 10E
116 Dunseith, U.S.A.   48 49N 100 2w
118 Dunsmuir, U.S.A.   41 0N 122 10w
13 Dunstable, Eng.   51 53N 0 31w
101 Dunstan Mts., N.Z.   44 53s 169 35E
108 Dunster, Canada   53 8N 119 50w
116 Dupree, U.S.A.   45 4N 101 35w
118 Dupuyer, U.S.A.   48 11N 112 31w
88 Duque de Bragança, Angola   8 50s 16 2E
127 Duque de Caxias, Brazil   22 45s 43 19w
112 Duquesne, U.S.A.   40 22N 79 55w
62 Dura, Jordan   31 31N 35 1E
96 Durack Ra., Australia   16 50s 127 40E
21 Durance, R., France   43 55N 4 45E
114 Durand, U.S.A.   42 54N 83 58w
120 Durango, Mexico   24 3N 104 39w
32 Durango, Spain   43 13N 2 40w
119 Durango, U.S.A.   37 10N 107 50w
120 Durango ♦, Mexico   25 0N 105 0w
117 Durant, U.S.A.   34 0N 96 25w
124 Durazno, Uruguay   33 25s 56 38w
44 Durazzo = Durrës, Albania   41 19N 19 28E
18 Durban, France   43 0N 2 49w
93 Durban, S. Afr.   29 49s 31 1E
31 Dúrcal, Spain   37 0N 3 34w
39 Durdevac, Yugoslavia   46 2N 17 3E
24 Düren, Germany   50 48N 6 30E
69 Durg, India   21 15N 81 22E
69 Durgapur, India   23 30N 87 9E
106 Durham, Canada   44 10N 80 48w
12 Durham, Eng.   54 47N 1 34w
115 Durham, U.S.A.   36 0N 78 55w
12 Durham ♦, England   54 42N 1 45w
99 Durham Downs, Australia   27 0s 141 49E
42 Durmitor Mt., Y.-slav.   43 18N 19 0E
96 Durrandella, Australia   24 3s 146 35E
44 Durrësi, Albania   41 19N 19 28E
99 Durrie, Australia   25 40s 140 15E
18 Durtal, France   47 40N 0 18w
90 Duru, Zaïre   4 20N 28 50E
49 Durup, Denmark   56 45N 8 57E
101 D'Urville Island, N.Z.   40 50s 173 55E
113 Duryea, U.S.A.   41 20N 75 45w
63 Dusa Mareb, Somali Rep.   6 0N 46 40E
86 Dûsh, Egypt   24 35N 30 41E
57 Dushak, U.S.S.R.   37 20N 60 10E
58 Dushanbe, U.S.S.R.   38 40N 68 50E
57 Dusheti, U.S.S.R.   42 0N 44 55E
101 Dusky Sd., N.Z.   45 47s 166 30E
24 Düsseldorf, Germany   51 15N 6 46E
28 Duszniki Zdrój, Poland   51 26N 16 22E
104 Dutch Harb., Alaska   53 54N 166 35w
92 Dutlhe, Botswana   23 58s 23 46E
85 Dutsan Wai, Nigeria   10 50N 9 10E
112 Dutton, Canada   42 40N 81 31w
48 Duved, Sweden   63 24N 12 55E
42 Duvno, Yugoslavia   43 42N 17 13E
64 Duwadami, Si. Arabia   24 35N 44 15E
65 Duzdab = Zahedan, Iran   29 30N 60 50E
43 Dve Mogili, Bulgaria   43 47N 25 55E
54 Dvina, Sev., U.S.S.R.   56 30N 24 0E
54 Dvina, Zap., U.S.S.R.   55 30N 28 0E
54 Dvinsk = Daugavpils, U.S.S.R.   55 33N 26 32E
52 Dvinskaya Guba, U.S.S.R.   65 0N 39 0E
39 Dvor, Yugoslavia   45 4N 16 22E
27 Dvorce, Czechoslovakia   49 50N 17 34E
26 Dvůr Králové, Cz.   50 27N 15 50E
68 Dwarka, India   22 18N 69 8E

112 Dwight, Canada   45 22N 79 0w
114 Dwight, U.S.A.   41 5N 88 25w
55 Dyakovskoya, U.S.S.R.   60 5N 41 12E
54 Dyatkovo, U.S.S.R.   53 48N 34 27E
98 Dyaul, I., New Guinea   3 0s 150 55E
105 Dyer, C., Canada   67 0N 61 0w
112 Dyer's B., Canada   45 9N 81 24w
117 Dyersburg, U.S.A.   36 2N 89 20w
27 Dyje, R., Czechoslovakia   48 50N 16 45E
98 Dyke Acland Bay, Papua   8 45s 148 45E
99 Dynevor Downs, Austral.   28 10s 144 20E
27 Dynów, Poland   49 50N 22 11E
47 Dypvag, Norway   79 40N 9 8E
50 Dyra Fd., Iceland   65 50N 23 30w
47 Dyrnes, Norway   63 25N 7 52E
49 Dysjön, Sweden   62 38N 15 31E
43 Dyulgeri, Bulgaria   42 18N 27 23E
57 Dzambeyty, U.S.S.R.   50 15N 52 30E
57 Dzaudzhikau = Ordzhonikidze, U.S.S.R.   43 0N 44 35E
56 Dzerzhinsk, U.S.S.R.   56 15N 43 15E
58 Dzhailma, U.S.S.R.   51 30N 61 50E
59 Dzhalinda, U.S.S.R.   53 40N 124 0E
58 Dzhambul, U.S.S.R.   43 10N 71 0E
56 Dzhankoi, U.S.S.R.   45 40N 34 30E
58 Dzhanybek, U.S.S.R.   49 25N 46 50E
58 Dzhardzhan, U.S.S.R.   68 10N 123 5E
59 Dzhelinde, U.S.S.R.   70 0N 114 20E
58 Dzherzhinsk, U.S.S.R.   53 48N 27 19E
59 Dzhetygara, U.S.S.R.   52 10N 61 0E
58 Dzhezkazgan, U.S.S.R.   47 10N 67 40E
58 Dzhizak, U.S.S.R.   40 20N 68 0E
59 Dzhugdzur, Khrebet, U.S.S.R.   57 30N 138 0E
58 Dzhungarskiye Vorota, U.S.S.R.   45 0N 82 0E
57 Dzhvari, U.S.S.R.   42 42N 42 4E
27 Działdowo, Poland   53 15N 20 15E
28 Działoszyce, Poland   50 22N 20 20E
28 Działoszyn, Poland   51 6N 18 50E
28 Dzierzgon, Poland   53 58N 19 20E
28 Dzierzoniow, Poland   50 45N 16 39E
83 Dzioua, Algeria   33 14N 5 14E
54 Dziwnów, Poland   54 2N 14 45E
75 Dzungaria, China   44 10N 88 0E
76 Dzuunbulag, Mongolia   46 58N 115 30E
76 Dzuunmod, Mongolia   47 45N 106 58E
24 Dömitz, Germany   53 9N 11 13E
47 Dönna, Norway   66 6N 12 30E

106 Eabamet, L., Canada   51 30N 88 0w
116 Eads, U.S.A.   38 30N 102 46w
118 Eagle, Alaska, U.S.A.   64 44N 141 29w
118 Eagle, Colo., U.S.A.   39 45N 106 55w
118 Eagle L., Calif., U.S.A.   40 35N 120 50w
116 Eagle L., Me., U.S.A.   46 23N 69 22w
116 Eagle Butt, U.S.A.   45 1N 101 12w
116 Eagle Grove, U.S.A.   42 37N 93 53w
117 Eagle Lake, U.S.A.   29 35N 96 21w
36 Eagle Nest, U.S.A.   36 33N 105 13w
117 Eagle Pass, U.S.A.   28 45N 100 35w
116 Eagle River, U.S.A.   45 55N 89 17w
100 Eaglehawk, Australia   36 43s 144 16E
99 Eaglehawk Neck, Australia   43 0s 147 58E
109 Earl Grey, Canada   50 57N 104 43w
117 Earle, U.S.A.   35 18N 90 26w
119 Earlimart, U.S.A.   35 57N 119 14w
14 Earlston, Scotland   55 39N 2 40w
14 Earn, L., Scot.   56 23N 4 14w
14 Earn, R., Scot.   56 20N 3 40w
101 Earnslaw, Mt., N.Z.   44 32s 168 27E
14 Earth, U.S.A.   34 18N 102 30w
115 Easley, U.S.A.   34 52N 82 35w
117 East, B., U.S.A.   29 2N 89 16w
101 East C., New Zealand   37 42s 178 35E
107 East P., Canada   46 39N 61 24w
107 East Angus, Canada   45 30N 71 40w
112 East Aurora, U.S.A.   42 46N 78 38w
112 East Bathurst, Canada   47 35N 65 40w
67 East Bengal, E. Pak.   23 0N 90 0E
112 East Brady, U.S.A.   40 59N 79 36w
114 East Chicago, U.S.A.   41 40N 87 30w
77 East China Sea, Asia   30 5s 126 0E
107 East Coulee, Canada   51 23N 112 27w
128 East Falkland, Falk. Is.   51 30s 58 30w
107 East Florenceville, Can.   46 26N 67 36w
116 East Grand Forks, Can., U.S.A.   47 55N 97 5w
113 East Greenwich, U.S.A.   41 39N 71 27w
113 East Hartford, U.S.A.   41 45N 72 39w
116 East Helena, U.S.A.   46 37N 111 58w
72 East Indies, Asia   0 0 120 0E
113 East Jordan, U.S.A.   45 10N 85 7w
112 East Lansing, U.S.A.   42 44N 84 37w
112 East Liverpool, U.S.A.   40 39N 80 35w
93 East London, S. Africa   33 0s 27 55E
*14 East Lothian ♦, Scotland   56 0N 2 40w
107 East Lynne, Australia   35 10s 150 16E
107 East Main (Eastmain), Canada   52 20N 78 30w
★90 East Mengo ♦, Uganda   1 0N 32 25E
113 East Orange, U.S.A.   40 45N 74 15w
67 East Pakistan = Bangladesh, Asia   24 0N 90 0E
114 East Palestine, U.S.A.   50 50N 80 32w
108 East Pine, Canada   55 48N 120 5w
116 East Point, U.S.A.   33 40N 84 28w
113 East Providence, U.S.A.   41 48N 71 22w
13 East Retford, Eng.   53 19N 0 55w
12 East Riding, England   53 55N 0 30w
116 East St. Louis, U.S.A.   38 36N 90 10w
24 East Schelde, R., Neth.   51 38N 3 40E
59 E. Siberian Sea, U.S.S.R.   73 0N 160 0E
113 East Stroudsburg, U.S.A.   41 1N 75 11w

* In April 1973 districts replaced counties in N. Ireland

♦ Incorporated within the region of Dumfries & Galloway
† Incorporated within the region of Strathclyde

♦ Incorporated within the region of Lothian

* Incorporated within the counties of Humberside and North Yorkshire
† Incorporated within the ★★ Incorporated within the new N. Buganda Province

MAP
114 East Tawas, U.S.A. 44 17N 83 31W
99 East Toorale, Australia 30 27s 145 28E
101 Eastbourne, N.Z. 41 19s 174 55E
13 Eastbourne, Eng. 50 46N 0 18E
109 Eastend, Canada 49 32N 108 50W
90 Eastern ♦, Kenya 0 0s 38 30E
70 Eastern Ghats, India 15 0N 80 0E
84 Eastern Province ♦, 8 15N 11 0w
  Sierra Leone
109 Easterville, Canada 53 8N 99 40W
113 Easthampton, U.S.A. 42 15N 72 41W
117 Eastland, U.S.A. 32 26N 98 45W
13 Eastleigh, Eng. 50 58N 1 21W
106 Eastmain (East Main), 52 20N 78 30W
  Canada
106 Eastmain, R., Canada 52 27N 72 26W
113 Eastman, Canada 45 18N 72 19W
115 Eastman, U.S.A. 32 13N 83 41W
114 Easton, Md., U.S.A. 38 47N 76 7W
113 Easton, Pa., U.S.A. 40 41N 75 15W
118 Easton, Wash., U.S.A. 47 14N 121 8W
107 Eastport, U.S.A. 44 57N 67 0W
106 Eastview, Canada 45 27N 75 40W
104 Eaton, U.S.A. 40 35N 104 42W
25 Eatonia, Canada 51 20N 109 25W
115 Eatonton, U.S.A. 33 22N 83 24W
115 Eau Claire, S.C., U.S.A. 34 5N 81 2W
116 Eau Claire, Wis., U.S.A. 44 46N 91 30W
20 Eauze, France 43 53N 0 7E
98 Ebagoola, Australia 14 15s 143 12E
85 Eban, Nigeria 9 40N 4 50E
13 Ebbw Vale, England 51 47N 3 12W
83 Ebeggui, Algeria 26 2N 6 0E
112 Ebensburg, U.S.A. 40 29N 78 43W
24 Ebensee, Austria 47 48N 13 46E
25 Eberbach, Germany 49 27N 8 59E
24 Eberswalde, Germany 52 49N 13 50E
25 Ebingen, Germany 48 13N 9 1E
41 Eboli, Italy 40 39N 15 2E
85 Ebolowa, Cameroon 2 55N 11 10E
92 Ebony, S.W. Africa 22 6s 15 15E
84 Ebrié, Lagune, Ivory C. 5 12N 4 40W
32 Ebro, R., Spain 41 49N 1 5W
30 Ebro, Pantano del, Spain 43 0N 3 58W
24 Ebstorf, Germany 53 1N 10 23E
44 Eceabat, Turkey 40 11N 26 21E
16 Eceuillé, France 47 10N 1 19E
82 Ech Chebbi, Algeria 26 41N 0 29E
59 Echaneni, S. Afr. 27 33s 32 6E
57 Echmiadzin, U.S.S.R. 40 12N 44 19E
106 Echo Bay, Canada 46 29N 84 4w
16 Echternach, Lux. 49 49N 6 3E
100 Echuca, Australia 36 3s 144 46E
31 Ecija, Spain 37 30N 5 10W
24 Eckernförde, Germany 54 26N 9 50E
112 Ecorse, U.S.A. 42 14N 83 10W
19 Ecos, France 49 9N 1 35E
16 Ecouché, France 48 42N 0 10W
126 Ecuador ■, S. Amer. 2 0s 78 0w
49 Ed, Sweden 58 55N 11 55E
86 Ed Dabbura, Sudan 17 40N 34 15E
86 Ed Damer, Sudan 17 27N 34 0E
86 Ed Debba, Sudan 18 0N 30 51E
78 Ed-Déffa, Egypt 30 40N 26 30E
87 Ed Deim, Sudan 10 10N 28 20E
87 Ed Dueim, Sudan 14 0N 32 10E
67 Ed Dzong, China 32 11N 90 12E
16 Edam, Netherlands 52 31N 5 3E
70 Edapally, India 11 19N 78 3E
14 Eday, I., Scotland 59 11N 2 47W
87 Edd, Ethiopia 14 0N 41 30E
14 Eddrachillis B., Scotland 58 16N 5 10W
13 Eddystone, Eng. 50 11N 4 16W
16 Ede, Netherlands 52 4N 5 40E
85 Ede, Nigeria 7 45N 4 29E
48 Ede, Sweden 62 10N 16 50E
85 Edea, Cameroon 3 51N 10 9E
109 Edehon L., Canada 60 25N 97 5W
83 Edekel, Adrar, Algeria 23 56N 6 47E
25 Edel Land, Australia 26 55s 114 0E
100 Eden, Austral. 37 3s 149 55E
112 Eden, N.Y., U.S.A. 42 39N 78 55W
117 Eden, Tex., U.S.A. 31 16N 99 50W
118 Eden, Wyo., U.S.A. 42 2N 109 27W
12 Eden, R., Eng. 54 32N 2 25W
92 Edenburg, S. Africa 29 43s 25 58E
15 Edenderry, Ireland 53 21N 7 3W
100 Edenhope, Australia 37 4s 141 19E
115 Edenton, U.S.A. 36 5N 76 36W
93 Edenville, S. Africa 27 37s 27 34E
99 Edeowie, Australia 31 26s 138 23E
116 Edgar, U.S.A. 40 25N 98 0W
113 Edgartown, U.S.A. 41 22N 70 28W
13 Edge Hill, Eng. 52 7N 1 28W
4 Edge I., Spitsbergen 77 45N 22 30E
115 Edgefield, U.S.A. 33 43N 81 59W
116 Edgeley, U.S.A. 46 27N 98 41W
116 Edgemont, U.S.A. 43 15N 103 53W
4 Edgeøya, Svalbard 77 45N 22 30E
112 Edgington, Canada 44 35N 79 46W
44 Edhessa, Greece 40 48N 22 5E
101 Edievale, N.Z. 45 49s 169 22E
84 Edina, Liberia 6 0N 10 19W
116 Edina, U.S.A. 40 6N 92 10W
117 Edinburg, U.S.A. 26 22N 98 10W
14 Edinburgh, Scot. 55 57N 3 12W
43 Edirne, Turkey 41 40N 26 45E
83 Edjeleh, Algeria 28 25N 9 40E
113 Edmeston, U.S.A. 42 42N 75 15W
117 Edmond, U.S.A. 35 37N 97 30W
118 Edmonds, U.S.A. 47 47N 122 11W
98 Edmonton, Australia 16 55s 145 45E
108 Edmonton, Canada 53 30N 113 30W
107 Edmundston, Canada 47 23N 68 20W
117 Edna, U.S.A. 29 0N 96 40W
108 Edna Bay, Alaska 55 55N 133 40W
38 Edolo, Italy 46 10N 10 21E
90 Edouard, L., Africa 0 25s 29 40E
64 Edremit, Turkey 39 40N 27 0E
48 Edsbyn, Sweden 61 23N 15 49E

5 Edsel Ford Ra., Antarc. 77 0s 143 0w
48 Edsele, Sweden 63 25N 16 32E
108 Edson, Canada 53 40N 116 28w
124 Eduardo Castex, Arg. 35 50s 64 25w
5 Edward VII Pen., 80 0s 160 0w
  Antarctica
* 90 Edward, L., Africa 0 25s 29 40E
100 Edward, R., Australia 35 15s 144 28E
117 Edwards Plat., U.S.A. 30 30N 101 5w
113 Edwardsville, U.S.A. 41 15N 75 56w
16 Eeklo, Belgium 51 11N 3 33E
92 Eersterivier, S. Africa 34 0s 18 45E
26 Eferding, Austria 48 18N 14 1E
83 Eferi, Algeria 24 30N 9 28E
114 Effingham, U.S.A. 39 8N 88 30w
85 Effiums, Nigeria 6 35N 8 0E
85 Efiduasi, Ghana 6 45N 1 25w
46 Eforie Sud, Rumania 44 1N 28 37E
32 Ega, R., Spain 42 32N 1 58w
40 Egadi, Isole, Italy 37 55N 12 10E
106 Eganville, Canada 45 32N 77 5w
116 Egeland, U.S.A. 48 42N 99 6w
27 Eger, Hungary 47 53N 20 27E
27 Eger, R., Hungary 47 43N 20 32E
96 Egerton, Mt., Austral. 24 42s 117 44E
109 Egg L., Canada 54 30N 73 0w
26 Eggenburg, Lr. Aus. 48 38N 15 50E
19 Egletons, France 45 24N 2 3E
101 Egmont, C., N.Z. 39 16s 173 45E
101 Egmont, Mt., N.Z. 39 17s 174 5E
87 Egogi Bad, Ethiopia 13 10N 41 60E
64 Eğridir Gölü, Turkey 37 53N 30 50E
49 Egtved, Denmark 55 38N 9 18E
126 Egua, Colombia 5 5N 68 0w
85 Egume, Nigeria 7 30N 7 14E
20 Eguzon, France 46 27N 1 33E
58 Egvekinot, U.S.S.R. 66 19N 179 10w
27 Egyek, Hungary 47 39N 20 52E
86 Egypt ■, Africa 28 0N 31 0E
85 Eha Amufu, Nigeria 6 30N 7 40E
74 Ehime-ken ♦, Japan 33 30N 132 40E
25 Ehingen, Germany 48 16N 9 43E
26 Ehrwald, Austria 47 24N 10 56E
25 Eibar, Spain 43 11N 2 28w
25 Eichstätt, Germany 48 53N 11 12E
47 Eidanger, Norway 59 7N 9 43E
47 Eide, Hordaland, 60 31N 6 44E
  Norway
24 Eider, R., Germany 54 15N 8 50E
47 Eidsberg, Norway 59 32N 11 16E
47 Eidsfoss, Norway 59 36N 10 2E
99 Eidsvold, Australia 25 25s 151 12E
47 Eidsvoll, Norway 60 19N 11 14E
25 Eifel, Germany 50 10N 6 45E
91 Eiffel Flats, Rhodesia 18 20s 30 0E
47 Eigersund, Norway 58 26N 6 1E
14 Eigg, I., Scot. 56 54N 6 10w
96 Eighty Mile Beach, 19 30s 120 40E
  Australia
63 Eil, Somali Rep. 8 0N 49 50E
14 Eil, L., Scotland 56 50N 5 15w
100 Eildon, L., Australia 37 10s 146 0E
24 Eilenburg, Germany 51 28N 12 38E
62 Ein Arik, Jordan 31 54N 35 8E
87 Ein el Luweiqa, Sudan 14 5N 33 50E
99 Einasleigh, Australia 18 32s 144 5E
98 Einasleigh, R., Austral. 17 33s 143 0E
24 Einbeck, Germany 51 48N 9 50E
16 Eindhoven, Netherlands 51 26N 5 30E
25 Einsiedeln, Switzerland 47 7N 8 46E
50 Eiríksjökull, Iceland 64 46N 20 24w
126 Eirunepé, Brazil 6 35s 70 0w
25 Eisenach, Germany 50 58N 10 18E
24 Eisenberg, Germany 50 59N 11 50E
26 Eisenerz, Austria 47 32N 15 54E
24 Eisenhüttenstadt, East 52 9N 14 41E
  Germany
26 Eisenkappel, Austria 46 29N 14 36E
27 Eisenstadt, Austria 47 51N 16 31E
16 Eiserfeld, Germany 50 50N 8 0E
25 Eisfeld, Germany 50 25N 10 54E
24 Eisleben, Germany 51 31N 11 31E
62 Eizariya (Bethany), 31 47N 35 15E
  Jordan
49 Ejby, Denmark 55 25N 9 56E
30 Eje, Sierra del, Spain 42 24N 6 54w
30 Ejea de los Caballeros, 42 7N 1 9w
  Spain
126 Ejido, Venezuela 8 33N 71 14w
85 Ejura, Ghana 7 25N 1 25E
116 Ekalaka, U.S.A. 45 55N 104 30E
49 Ekeryd, Sweden 57 37N 14 6E
85 Eket, Nigeria 4 38N 7 56w
101 Eketahuna, N.Z. 40 38s 175 43E
44 Ekhinos, Greece 41 16N 25 1w
58 Ekibastuz, U.S.S.R. 51 40N 75 22E
59 Ekimchan, U.S.S.R. 53 0N 133 0w
48 Ekoln, I., Sweden 59 45N 17 40E
49 Eksjö, Sweden 57 40N 14 58E
106 Ekwan, R., Canada 53 30N 84 0w
82 El Abiodh, Algeria 32 53N 0 31E
82 El Aïoun, Morocco 34 33N 2 30w
86 El 'Aiyat, Egypt 29 36N 31 15E
86 El Alamein, Egypt 30 48N 28 58E
31 El Arahal, Spain 37 15N 5 33w
86 El Araq, Egypt 28 40N 26 20E
82 El Aricha, Algeria 34 30N 1 26E
62 El Arīhā, Jordan 31 52N 35 27E
86 El 'Arîsh, Egypt 31 8N 33 50E
83 El Arrouch, Algeria 36 37N 6 53E
82 El Arnaud, Algeria 36 8N 5 30E
30 El Astillero, Spain 43 24N 3 49w
86 El Badâri, Egypt 27 4N 31 25E
86 El Bahrein, Egypt 28 30N 26 25E
86 El Ballâs, Egypt 26 2N 32 43E
86 El Balyana, Egypt 26 10N 32 3E
86 El Baqeir, Sudan 18 40N 33 40E

30 El Barco de Ávila, Sp. 40 21N 5 31w
30 El Barco de Valdeorras, 42 23N 7 0w
  Spain
126 El Baúl, Venezuela 8 57N 68 17w
86 El Bauga, Sudan 18 18N 33 52E
86 El Bawiti, Egypt 28 25N 28 45E
82 El Bayadh, Algeria 33 40N 1 1E
31 El Bierzo, Spain 42 45N 6 30w
82 El Biodh, Mauritania 26 0N 6 32w
126 El Banco, Colombia 10 28N 74 52w
33 El Bonillo, Spain 38 57N 2 35w
126 El Bordo, Colombia 2 6N 76 58w
32 El Bordo de Dueñas, Sp. 40 46N 1 39w
119 El Portal, U.S.A. 37 44N 119 49w
126 El Callao, Venezuela 7 25N 61 50w
32 El Camp, Spain 41 5N 1 10E
117 El Campo, U.S.A. 29 10N 96 20w
126 El Carmen, Venezuela 1 16N 66 52w
31 El Castillo, Spain 37 41N 6 19w
119 El Centro, U.S.A. 32 50N 115 40w
126 El Cerro, Bolivia 17 30s 61 40w
31 El Cerro, Spain 37 45N 6 57w
31 El Cocuy, Colombia 6 25N 72 27w
31 El Coronil, Spain 37 5N 5 38w
128 El Cuy, Argentina 39 55s 68 25w
120 El Cuyo, Mexico 21 30N 87 40w
86 El Dab'a, Egypt 31 0N 28 27E
86 El Deir, Egypt 25 25N 32 20E
63 El Dere, Somali Rep. 3 50N 47 8E
126 El Dificul, Colombia 9 51N 74 14w
120 El Dios, Mexico 20 40N 87 20w
126 El Diviso, Colombia 1 22N 78 14w
84 El Djouf, Mauritania 20 0N 11 30E
126 El Dorado, Colombia 1 11N 71 52w
117 El Dorado, Ark., U.S.A. 33 10N 92 40w
117 El Dorado, Kans., 37 55N 96 56w
  U.S.A.
117 El Dorado Springs, 37 54N 93 59w
  U.S.A.
82 El Eglab, Algeria 26 20N 4 30E
30 El Escorial, Spain 40 35N 4 7w
86 El Faiyûm, Egypt 29 19N 30 50E
86 El Fâsher, Sudan 13 33N 25 26E
86 El Fashn, Egypt 28 50N 30 54E
31 El Ferrol, Spain 43 29N 3 14w
87 El Fifi, Sudan 10 4N 25 0E
120 El Fuerte, Mexico 26 30N 108 40w
63 El Gal, Somali Rep. 10 58N 50 20E
87 El Gebir, Sudan 13 40N 29 40E
86 El Gedida, Egypt 25 40N 28 30E
81 El Geneina, Sudan 13 27N 22 45E
87 El Geteina, Sudan 14 50N 32 27E
87 El Gezira, Sudan 14 0N 33 0E
86 El Giza, Egypt 30 0N 31 10E
82 El Goléa, Algeria 30 30N 2 50E
82 El Guettar, Algeria 34 5N 4 38E
82 El Hadjire, Algeria 32 36N 5 30E
87 El Hagiz, Sudan 15 15N 35 50E
82 El Haql, Saudi Arabia 29 15N 34 59E
86 El Hajeb, Morocco 33 41N 5 23w
86 El Hammâm, Egypt 30 52N 29 25E
82 El Hank, Algeria 25 38N 5 29w
82 El Hank, Mauritania 24 37N 7 0w
87 El Hawata, Sudan 13 25N 34 42E
86 El Heiz, Egypt 27 50N 28 40E
86 El 'Idisât, Egypt 25 30N 32 35E
86 El Iskandariya, Egypt 31 0N 30 0E
82 El Jadida, Morocco 33 16N 9 31w
82 El Jorf Lasfar, C., Mor. 33 5N 8 54w
83 El Kab, Sudan 19 27N 32 46E
83 El Kala, Algeria 36 50N 8 30E
87 El Kamlin, Sudan 15 3N 33 11E
82 El Kantara, Algeria 35 14N 5 45E
83 El Kantara, Tunisia 33 45N 10 58E
83 El Karaba, Sudan 18 32N 33 41E
83 El Kef, Tunisia 36 12N 8 47E
82 El Kelâa des Srarhna, 32 4N 7 27w
  Morocco
86 El Khandaq, Sudan 18 30N 30 30E
86 El Khârga, Egypt 25 30N 30 33E
87 El Khartûm, Sudan 15 31N 32 35E
87 El Khartûm Bahrî, 15 40N 32 31E
  Sudan
83 El-Khroubs, Algeria 36 10N 6 55E
82 El Khureiba, Si. Arab. 28 3N 35 10E
82 El Kseur, Algeria 36 46N 4 49E
82 El Ksiba, Morocco 32 45N 6 1w
86 El Kuntilla, Egypt 30 1N 34 45E
64 El Ladhiqiya, Syria 35 20N 35 30E
86 El Laqeita, Egypt 25 50N 33 15E
87 El* Leiya, Sudan 16 15N 35 28E
86 El Mafâza, Sudan 13 38N 34 30E
86 El Maghra, Bir, Egypt 30 8N 28 54E
86 El Mahalla el Kubra, 31 0N 31 0E
  Egypt
86 El Mahârîq, Egypt 25 35N 30 35E
82 El Maiz, Algeria 28 19N 0 9w
86 El-Maks el-Bahari, Eg. 24 30N 30 40E
82 El Manshâh, Egypt 26 26N 31 50E
82 El Mansour, Algeria 27 47N 0 14w
82 El Mansûra, Egypt 31 0N 31 19E
126 El Mantico, Venezuela 7 27N 62 32w
86 El Manzala, Egypt 31 10N 31 50E
86 El Marâgha, Egypt 26 35N 31 10E
87 El Masid, Sudan 15 15N 33 0E
87 El Matariya, Egypt 31 15N 32 0E
83 El Meghaier, Algeria 33 55N 5 58E
126 El Mene, Venezuela 10 43N 71 1w
82 El Meraguen, Algeria 28 0N 0 7w
86 El Metemma, Sudan 16 50N 33 10E
126 El Miamo, Venezuela 7 39N 61 46w
82 El Milhas, Mauritania 25 57N 7 5w
86 El Milia, Algeria 36 59N 6 13E
86 El Minyâ, Egypt 28 7N 30 33E
32 El Molar, Spain 40 42N 3 45w
82 El Mreyye, Mauritania 18 0N 6 0w
87 El Obeid, Sudan 13 8N 30 10E
120 El Oro = Sta. María 25 50N 105 20w
  del Oro, Mexico

83 El Oued, Algeria 33 20N 6 58E
126 El Palmar, Venezuela 7 58N 61 53w
120 El Palmito, Presa, 25 40N 105 3w
  Mexico
32 El Panadés, Spain 41 10N 1 30E
30 El Pardo, Spain 40 31N 3 47w
119 El Paso, U.S.A. 31 50N 106 30w
31 El Pedroso, Spain 39 2N 2 45w
31 El Pedroso, Spain 37 51N 5 45w
126 El Pilar, Venezuela 10 32N 63 9w
32 El Pobo de Dueñas, Sp. 40 46N 1 39w
120 El Progreso, Honduras 15 26N 87 51w
33 El Provencio, Spain 39 23N 2 35w
121 El Pueblito, Mexico 29 3N 105 4w
86 El Qâhira, Egypt 30 1N 31 14E
86 El Qantara, Egypt 30 51N 32 20E
86 El Qasr, Egypt 25 44N 28 42E
87 El Qubba, Sudan 11 10N 27 5E
86 El Qurna, Egypt 25 45N 32 38E
86 El Quseima, Egypt 30 40N 34 15E
86 El Qusiya, Egypt 27 29N 30 44E
86 El Râshda, Egypt 25 36N 28 57E
87 El Rheauya, Mauritania 25 52N 6 30w
86 El Ribero, Spain 42 30N 8 30w
86 El Ridisiya, Egypt 24 56N 32 51E
31 El Ronquillo, Spain 37 44N 6 10w
31 El Rubio, Spain 37 22N 5 0w
86 El Saff, Egypt 29 34N 31 16E
126 El Salado, Colombia 8 56N 73 55w
31 El Sancejo, Spain 37 4N 5 6w
126 El Sauce, Nicaragua 13 0N 86 40w
86 El Shallal, Egypt 24 0N 32 53E
86 El Suweis, Egypt 29 58N 32 31E
108 El Templador, Ven. 8 59N 62 44w
86 El Thamad, Egypt 29 40N 34 28E
126 El Tigre, Venezuela 8 55N 64 15w
126 El Tocuyo, Venezuela 9 47N 69 48w
124 El Tofo, Chile 29 22s 71 18w
128 El Tûr, Egypt 28 14N 33 36E
128 El Turbio, Arg. 51 30s 72 40w
100 El Uqsur, Egypt 25 41N 32 38E
32 El Vado, Spain 41 2N 3 18w
126 El Valle, Colombia 6 5N 77 25w
41 El Vallès, Spain 41 35N 2 20E
126 El Vigia, Venezuela 8 38N 71 39w
86 El Waqf, Egypt 25 45N 32 15E
87 El Wâsta, Egypt 29 19N 31 12E
87 El Weguet, Ethiopia 5 28N 42 17E
87 Ela, Ethiopia 12 50N 42 20E
44 Elafónisos, Greece 36 29N 22 56E
100 Elaine, Australia 37 44s 144 2E
70 Elamanchili = 17 26N 82 50E
  Yellamanchilli, India
59 Elandsvlei, S. Africa 32 19s 19 31E
45 Elassa, Greece 35 18N 26 21E
44 Elassón, Greece 39 53N 22 12E
73 Elat, Indonesia 5 40s 133 5E
64 Elat, Israel 29 30N 34 56E
64 Elateia, Greece 38 37N 22 46E
64 Eláziğ, Turkey 38 37N 39 22E
85 Elmina, Ghana 5 5N 1 21w
115 Elba, Ala., U.S.A. 31 27N 86 4w
38 Elba, I., Italy 42 48N 10 15E
44 Elbasani, Albania 41 9N 20 9E
44 Elbasani-Berati, Albania 40 58N 20 0E
24 Elbe, R., Germany 53 15N 10 7E
118 Elberta, U.S.A. 44 35N 86 14w
115 Elberton, U.S.A. 34 7N 82 51w
18 Elbeuf, France 49 17N 1 2E
28 Elbląg (Elbing), Poland 54 10N 19 25E
57 Elbrus, U.S.S.R. 43 30N 42 30E
16 Elburg, Netherlands 52 26N 5 50E
Elburz Mts. = Alborz 36 0N 52 0E
  . . ., Iran
33 Elche, Spain 38 15N 0 42w
33 Elche de la Sierra, Sp. 38 27N 2 3w
96 Elcho I., Australia 11 55s 135 45E
33 Elda, Spain 38 29N 0 47w
70 Eldon, Iowa, U.S.A. 40 50N 92 12w
116 Eldon, Mo., U.S.A. 38 20N 92 40w
116 Eldora, U.S.A. 42 20N 93 5w
124 Eldorado, Argentina 26 28s 54 43w
70 Eldorado, Ont., Canada 44 40N 77 32w
109 Eldorado, Sask., Can. 59 35N 108 30w
120 Eldorado, Mexico 24 0N 107 30w
114 Eldorado, Ill., U.S.A. 37 50N 88 25w
117 Eldorado, Tex., U.S.A. 30 52N 100 35w
90 Eldoret, Kenya 0 30N 35 25E
112 Eldred, U.S.A. 41 57N 78 24w
117 Electra, U.S.A. 34 0N 99 0w
93 Elefantes, R., Mozam. 24 0s 32 50E
55 Elektrogorsk, U.S.S.R. 55 56N 38 50E
55 Elektrostal, U.S.S.R. 55 41N 38 32E
85 Elele, Nigeria 5 5N 6 50E
43 Elena, Bulgaria 42 55N 25 53E
119 Elephant Butte Res., 33 45N 107 30w
  U.S.A.
70 Elephant Pass, Sri 9 35N 80 25E
  Lanka
43 Eleshnitsa, Bulgaria 41 52N 23 36E
121 Eleuthera I., Bahamas 25 0N 76 20w
44 Elevsís, Greece 38 4N 23 26E
44 Elevtherouópolis, Greece 40 52N 24 20E
48 Elgáhogna, mt., Norway 62 7N 12 7E
90 Elgeyo-Marakwet ♦, 0 45N 35 30E
  Kenya
107 Elgin, N.B., Canada 45 48N 65 10w
113 Elgin, Ont., Canada 44 36N 76 13w
14 Elgin, Scotland 57 39N 3 20w
114 Elgin, Ill., U.S.A. 42 0N 88 20w
116 Elgin, Nebr., U.S.A. 41 58N 98 3w
119 Elgin, Nev., U.S.A. 37 27N 114 36w

116 Elgin N.D., U.S.A. 46 24N 101 46w
118 Elgin, Oreg., U.S.A. 45 37N 118 0w
117 Elgin, Texas, U.S.A. 30 21N 97 22w
90 Elgon, Mt., Africa 1 10N 34 30E
73 Eliase, Indonesia 8 10s 130 55E
117 Elida, U.S.A. 33 56N 103 41w
109 Elie, Canada 49 48N 97 52w
44 Elikón, Mt., Greece 38 18N 22 45E
90 Elin Pelin, Bulgaria 42 40N 23 38E
91 Elisabethville = 11 32s 27 38E
  Lubumbashi, Zaïre
57 Elista, U.S.S.R. 46 25N 44 17E
87 Elit, Ethiopia 15 10N 37 0E
99 Eliza, L., Australia 37 25s 140 0E
99 Elizabeth, Australia 34 45s 138 39E
113 Elizabeth, U.S.A. 40 37N 74 12w
115 Elizabeth City, U.S.A. 36 18N 76 16w
90 Elizabetha, Zaïre 1 3N 23 37E
115 Elizabethton, U.S.A. 36 20N 82 13w
86 Elizabethtown, Ky., 37 40N 85 54w
  U.S.A.
113 Elizabethtown, N.Y., 44 13N 73 36w
  U.S.A.
113 Elizabethtown, Pa., 40 8N 76 36w
  U.S.A.
32 Elizondo, Spain 43 12N 1 30w
117 Elk City, U.S.A. 35 25N 99 25w
106 Elk Lake, Canada 47 40N 80 25E
109 Elk Point, Canada 54 10N 110 55w
118 Elk River, Idaho, U.S.A. 46 50N 116 8w
116 Elk River, Minn., U.S.A. 45 19N 93 34w
114 Elkhart, Ind., U.S.A. 41 42N 85 55w
117 Elkhart, Kans., U.S.A. 37 3N 101 54w
31 Elkhorn, Canada 50 0N 101 11w
116 Elkhorn, U.S.A. 42 40N 88 15w
57 Elkhotovo, U.S.S.R. 43 19N 44 15E
43 Elkhovo, Bulgaria 42 10N 26 40E
112 Elkin, U.S.A. 36 17N 80 50w
114 Elkins, U.S.A. 38 53N 79 53w
108 Elko, Canada 49 20N 115 10w
118 Elko, U.S.A. 40 40N 115 50w
4 Ellef Ringnes I., Can. 78 30N 102 2w
117 Ellen, Mt., U.S.A. 38 4N 110 56w
116 Ellendale, U.S.A. 46 3N 98 30w
118 Ellensburg, U.S.A. 47 0N 120 30w
113 Ellenville, U.S.A. 41 42N 74 23w
100 Ellerslie, Australia 38 10s 142 44E
4 Ellesmere I., Canada 79 30N 80 0w
95 Ellesmere, L., N.Z. 43 46s 172 27E
74 Ellesworth Land, Ant. 74 0s 80 0w
* Ellice Is., Pacific Ocean 8 0s 176 0E
38 Ellinwood, U.S.A. 38 27N 98 37w
93 Elliot, S. Afr. 31 22s 27 48E
106 Elliot Lake, Canada 46 35N 82 35w
116 Ellis, U.S.A. 39 0N 99 39w
112 Elliston, Ont., Canada 43 38N 80 34w
107 Elmira, P.E.I., Canada 46 30N 61 59w
112 Elmira, U.S.A. 42 8N 76 49w
100 Elmore, Australia 36 30s 144 37E
24 Elmshorn, Germany 53 44N 9 40E
44 Elmvale, Canada 44 35N 79 54w
112 Elmwood, Canada 44 11N 81 3w
112 Elora, Canada 43 43N 80 26w
126 Elorza, Venezuela 7 3N 69 31w
119 Eloy, U.S.A. 32 46N 111 46w
19 Eloyes, France 48 6N 6 36E
99 Elphinstone, Australia 21 30s 148 17E
106 Elrose, Canada 51 20N 108 0w
49 Elsas, Canada 48 32N 82 55w
49 Elsinore = Helsingor, 56 2N 12 35E
  Denmark
119 Elsinore, Cal., U.S.A. 33 40N 117 15w
119 Elsinore, Utah, U.S.A. 38 40N 112 2w
24 Elspe, Germany 51 10N 8 1E
24 Elsterwerda, Germany 51 27N 13 32E
100 Eltham, Australia 37 43s 145 12E
101 Eltham, N.Z. 39 26s 174 19E
57 Elton, U.S.S.R. 49 5N 46 52E
70 Eluru = Ellore, India 16 48N 81 8E
31 Elvas, Portugal 38 50N 7 17w
17 Elven, France 47 44N 2 36w
47 Elverum, Norway 60 53N 11 34E
100 Elvire, Mt., Australia 29 14s 119 33E
38 Elvo, R., Italy 45 32N 8 14E
47 Elvran, Norway 63 24N 11 3E
114 Elwood, Ind., U.S.A. 40 20N 85 50w
116 Elwood, Nebr., U.S.A. 40 54N 99 51w
13 Ely, England, U.K. 52 24N 0 16E
116 Ely, Minn., U.S.A. 47 54N 91 52w
119 Ely, Nev., U.S.A. 39 10N 114 50w
62 Elyashiv, Israel 32 23N 34 55E
112 Elyria, U.S.A. 41 22N 82 8w
48 Emadalen, Sweden 61 20N 14 45E
54 Emaiygi, R., U.S.S.R. 58 30N 26 30E
58 Emba, U.S.S.R. 48 50N 58 8E
109 Embarcación, Arg. 23 10s 64 0w
109 Embarras Portage, Can. 58 27N 111 29w
45 Embona, Greece 36 13N 27 51E
21 Embrun, France 44 34N 6 30E
90 Embu, Kenya 0 32s 37 38E
90 Embu ♦, Kenya 0 30s 37 35E
24 Emden, Germany 53 22N 7 12E
62 'Emeq Yizre'el, Israel 32 35N 35 12E
98 Emerald, Australia 23 30s 148 11E
106 Emerson, Canada 49 0N 97 10w
119 Emery, U.S.A. 38 59N 111 17w
116 Emery Park, U.S.A. 32 10N 110 59w
81 Emi Koussi, Mt., Chad 20 0N 18 55E

* Renamed L. Idi Amin Dada

* Renamed Tuvalu

MAP

38 Emilia-Romagna ♦, Italy 44 33N 10 40E
38 Emillus, Mt., Italy 45 41N 7 23E
68 Eminabad, Pakistan 32 2N 74 8E
43 Emine, Nos, Bulgaria 42 40N 27 56E
112 Emlenton, U.S.A. 41 11N 79 41W
24 Emlichheim, Germany 52 37N 6 51E
49 Emmaboda, Sweden 56 37N 15 32E
25 Emme, R., Switzerland 47 0N 7 42E
16 Emmen, Netherlands 52 48N 6 57E
25 Emmendingen, Ger. 48 7N 7 51E
25 Emmental, Switz. 47 0N 7 35E
24 Emmerich, Germany 51 50N 6 12E
98 Emmet, Australia 24 45s 144 30E
116 Emmetsburg, U.S.A. 43 3N 94 40W
118 Emmett, U.S.A. 43 51N 116 33W
27 Emöd, Hungary 47 57N 20 47E
43 Emona, Bulgaria 42 43N 27 53E
120 Empalme, Mexico 28 1N 110 49W
93 Empangeni, S. Afr. 28 50s 31 52E
124 Empedrado, Argentina 28 0s 58 46W
38 Empoli, Italy 43 43N 10 57E
116 Emporia, Kans., U.S.A. 38 25N 96 16W
115 Emporia, Va., U.S.A. 36 41N 77 32W
112 Emporium, U.S.A. 41 30N 78 17W
109 Empress, Canada 51 0N 110 0W
24 Ems, R., Germany 52 37N 7 16E
112 Emsdale, Canada 45 30N 79 19W
24 Emsdetten, Germany 52 11N 7 31E
100 Emu, Australia 36 45s 145 29E
98 Emu Park, Australia 23 13s 150 50E
48 Emådalen, Sweden 61 20N 14 44E
62 En Gedi, Israel 31 28N 35 25E
62 En Harod, Israel 32 33N 35 22E
62 'En Kerem, Israel 31 47N 35 6E
87 En Nahud, Sudan 12 45N 28 25E
82 en Namous, O., Alg. 31 15N 0 10W
48 Enafors, Sweden 63 17N 12 20E
126 Enambú, Colombia 1 1N 70 17W
92 Enana, S. Africa 17 30s 16 23E
48 Enånger, Sweden 61 30N 17 9E
14 Enard B., Scot. 58 5N 5 20W
72 Encanto, Cape, Phil. 20 20N 121 40E
125 Encarnación, Paraguay 27 15s 56 0W
120 Encarnación de Diaz, Mexico 21 30N 102 20W
84 Enchi, Ghana 5 53N 2 48W
117 Encinal, U.S.A. 28 3N 99 25W
119 Encino, U.S.A. 34 46N 106 16W
71 Encounter B., Austral. 35 45s 138 45E
71 Endau, Malaysia 2 40N 103 38E
71 Endau, R., Malaysia 2 30N 103 30E
73 Ende, Indonesia 8 45s 121 30E
98 Endeavour Str., Austral. 10 45s 142 0E
49 Endelave, Denmark 55 46N 10 18E
95 Enderbury I., Pac. Oc. 3 8s 171 5W
108 Enderby, Canada 50 35N 119 10W
5 Enderby Land, Antarc. 66 0s 53 0E
24 Enderlin, U.S.A. 46 45N 97 41W
113 Endicott, N.Y., U.S.A. 42 6N 76 2W
118 Endicott, Wash., U.S.A. 47 0N 117 45W
27 Endröd, Hungary 46 55N 20 47E
44 Enebakk, Norway 59 46N 11 9E
44 Enez, Turkey 40 45N 26 5E
83 Enfida, Tunisia 36 6N 10 28E
13 Enfield, Eng. 51 39N 0 4W
121 Engaño, C., Dom. Rep. 18 30N 68 20W
73 Engaño, C., Philippines 18 35s 122 23E
62 Engedi, Israel 31 28N 35 25E
55 Engels, U.S.S.R. 51 28N 46 6E
47 Enger, Norway 60 35N 10 20E
72 Enggano, I., Indonesia 5 20s 102 40E
16 Enghien, Belgium 50 37N 4 2E
72 Engkilili, Sarawak 1 3N 111 42E
12 England ♦, U.K. 53 0N 2 0W
117 England, U.S.A. 34 30N 91 58W
107 Englee, Canada 50 45s 56 5W
100 Englefield, Austral. 37 20s 141 40E
116 Englewood, Colo., U.S.A. 39 40N 105 0W
117 Englewood, Kans., U.S.A. 37 7N 99 59W
109 English, R., Canada 50 30N 93 50W
106 English River, Canada 49 20N 91 0W
69 English Bazar, India 24 58N 88 21E
13 English Chan., Europe 50 0N 2 0W
97 English Company Is., Austral. 12 0s 137 0E
77 Engteng (Yungting), China 24 46N 116 45E
117 Enid, U.S.A. 36 26N 97 52W
44 Enipévs, R., Greece 39 22N 22 17E
95 Eniwetok, Pac. Oc. 11 30N 152 16E
91 Enkeldoorn, Rhodesia 19 2s 30 52E
48 Enköping, Sweden 59 37N 17 4E
41 Enna, Italy 37 34N 14 15E
109 Ennadai, Canada 61 0N 101 0W
109 Ennadai L., Canada 61 0N 101 0W
81 Ennedi, Chad 17 15N 22 0E
98 Enngonia, Australia 29 21s 145 50E
47 Enningdal, Norway 58 59N 11 33E
15 Ennis, Ireland 52 51N 8 59W
118 Ennis, Mont., U.S.A. 45 27N 111 48W
117 Ennis, Texas, U.S.A. 32 15N 96 40W
15 Enniscorthy, Ireland 52 30N 6 35W
15 Enniskillen, Northern Ireland 54 20N 7 40W
15 Ennistimon, Ireland 52 56N 9 18W
26 Enns, Austria 48 12N 14 28E
26 Enns, R., Austria 48 8N 14 27E
121 Enriquillo, L., Dom. Rep. 18 20N 72 5W
16 Enschede, Netherlands 52 13N 6 53E
124 Ensenada, Argentina 34 55s 57 55W
120 Ensenada, Mexico 31 50N 116 50W
77 Enshih, China 30 18N 109 27E
19 Ensisheim, France 47 50N 7 20E
90 Entebbe, Uganda 0 4N 32 28E
118 Enterprise, Oreg., U.S.A. 45 30N 117 11W
119 Enterprise, Utah, U.S.A. 37 37N 113 36W

MAP

108 Entrance, Canada 53 25N 117 50W
124 Entre Rios, Bolivia 21 30s 64 25W
91 Entre Ríos, Mozam. 14 57s 37 20E
124 Entre Ríos ♦, Arg. 30 30s 58 30W
96 Entrecasteaux, Pt. d', Australia 34 50s 115 56E
32 Entrepeñas, Pantano de, Spain 40 34N 2 42W
108 Entwistle, Canada 53 30N 115 0W
85 Enugu, Nigeria 6 30N 7 30E
85 Enugu Ezike, Nigeria 7 0N 7 29E
118 Enumclaw, U.S.A. 47 12N 122 0W
18 Envermeu, France 49 53N 1 15E
126 Envigado, Colombia 6 10N 75 35W
38 Enza, R., Italy 44 33N 10 22E
41 Eólie o Lipari, Is., Italy 38 30N 14 50E
98 Epa, Territory of Papua 8 28s 146 52E
44 Epanomí, Greece 40 25N 22 59E
16 Epe, Netherlands 52 21N 5 59E
85 Epe, Nigeria 6 36N 3 59E
19 Épernay, France 49 3N 3 56E
19 Épernon, France 48 35N 1 40E
64 Ephesus, Turkey 38 0N 27 30E
118 Ephraim, U.S.A. 39 30N 111 37W
118 Ephrata, U.S.A. 47 28N 119 32W
32 Epila, Spain 41 36N 1 17W
19 Épinac-les-Mines, Fr. 46 59N 4 31E
19 Épinal, France 48 19N 6 27E
46 Episcopia Bihorului, Rum. 47 12N 21 55E
45 Epitálion, Greece 37 37N 21 30E
13 Epping, Eng. 51 42N 0 8E
89 Epukiro, S.W. Africa 21 30s 19 0E
88 Equatorial Guinea ■, Africa 2 0s 78 0E
18 Equeurdreville-Hainneville, Fr. 49 40N 1 40W
87 Er Rahad, Sudan 12 45N 30 32E
87 Er Rif, Morocco 35 1N 4 1W
87 Er Roseires, Sudan 11 55N 34 30E
87 Er Rumman, Jordan 32 9N 35 48E
68 Erandol, India 20 56N 75 20E
67 Erâwadî Myit, R., Burma 19 30N 95 15E
38 Erba, Italy 45 49N 9 12E
87 Erba, Sudan 19 5N 36 40E
59 Ercha, U.S.S.R. 69 45N 147 20E
64 Erciyas Daği, Tur. 38 30N 35 30E
76 Erdene, Mongolia 44 30N 111 10E
76 Erdenedalay, Mongolia 46 3N 105 1E
25 Erding, Germany 48 18N 11 55E
125 Erechim, Brazil 27 35s 52 15W
64 Ereğli, Turkey 41 15N 31 30E
41 Erei, Monti, Italy 37 20N 14 20E
32 Eresma, R., Spain 41 13N 4 30W
45 Eressós, Greece 39 11N 25 57E
92 Erfenis Dam, S. Afr. 28 30s 26 50E
47 Erfjord, Norway 59 20N 6 14E
87 Erfoud, Morocco 31 30N 4 15W
24 Erfurt, Germany 50 58N 11 2E
24 Erfurt ♦, E. Ger. 51 10N 10 30E
64 Ergani, Turkey 38 26N 39 49E
43 Erğene, R., Turkey 41 20N 27 0E
57 Ergeni Vozyshennost, U.S.S.R. 47 0N 44 0E
76 Erhlien, China 43 42N 112 2E
76 Erhtao Kiang, China 42 40N 127 10E
30 Eria, R., Spain 42 10N 6 8W
87 Eriba, Sudan 16 40N 36 10E
14 Eribol, L., Scot. 58 28N 4 41W
40 Erice, Italy 38 4N 12 34E
112 Erie, U.S.A. 42 10N 80 7W
112 Erie, L., Can.-U.S.A. 42 30N 82 0W
112 Erie Beach, Canada 42 17N 82 1W
112 Erie Canal, U.S.A. 43 15N 78 0W
106 Erieau, Canada 42 16N 81 57W
63 Erigavo, Somali Rep. 10 35N 47 35E
44 Erikoúsa, Greece 39 55N 19 14E
109 Eriksdale, Canada 50 52N 98 7W
48 Erikslund, Sweden 62 31N 15 54E
45 Erimanthos, Gr. 37 57N 21 50E
74 Erimo-misaki, Japan 41 50N 143 15E
108 Erith, Canada 53 25N 116 46W
45 Erithraí, Greece 38 13N 23 20E
87 Eritrea ♦, Ethiopia 14 0N 41 0E
30 Erjas, R., Portugal 39 45N 6 52W
48 Erker, L., Sweden 59 51N 18 29E
25 Erlangen, Germany 49 35N 11 0E
16 Ermelo, Netherlands 52 35N 5 35E
93 Ermelo, S. Afr. 26 31s 29 59E
64 Ermenek, Turkey 36 44N 33 0E
45 Ermióni, Greece 37 23N 23 15E
45 Ermoúpolis = Síros, Greece 37 28N 24 57E

MAP

115 Erwin, U.S.A. 36 10N 82 28W
24 Erzgebirge, Germany 50 25N 13 0E
59 Erzin, U.S.S.R. 50 15N 95 10E
64 Erzincan, Turkey 39 46N 39 30E
64 Erzurum, Turkey 39 57N 41 15E
86 Es Sahrâ' Esh Sharqiya, Egypt 26 0N 33 30E
83 Es Sider, Libya 30 50N 18 21E
85 Es Souk, Mali 18 48N 1 2E
86 Es Sînâ', Egypt 29 0N 34 0E
87 Es Sûkî, Sudan 13 20N 34 58E
90 Esambo, Zaïre 3 48s 23 30E
74 Esan-misaki, Japan 41 40N 141 10E
49 Esbjerg, Denmark 55 29N 8 29E
119 Escalante, U.S.A. 37 47N 111 37W
119 Escalante, R., U.S.A. 37 45N 111 0W
120 Escalón, Mexico 26 40N 104 20W
30 Escalona, Spain 40 9N 4 29W
115 Escambia, R., U.S.A. 30 45N 87 15W
114 Escanaba, U.S.A. 45 44N 87 5W
16 Esch-sur-Alzette, Luxembourg 49 32N 6 0E
25 Eschallens, Switzerland 46 39N 6 38E
24 Eschede, Germany 52 44N 10 13E
24 Eschwege, Germany 51 10N 10 3E
24 Eschweiler, Germany 50 49N 6 14E
120 Escobal, Panama 9 6N 80 1W
119 Escondido, U.S.A. 33 9N 117 4W
120 Escuinapa, Mexico 22 50N 105 50W
120 Escuintla, Guatemala 14 20N 90 48W
107 Escuminac, Canada 48 0N 67 0W
126 Escutillas = Ceba, Colombia 6 33N 70 24W
85 Eséka, Cameroon 3 41N 10 44E
24 Esens, Germany 53 40N 7 35E
32 Esera, R., Spain 42 24N 0 22E
65 Esfahan ♦, Iran 33 0N 53 0E
30 Esgueva, R., Spain 41 46N 4 14W
64 Esh Sham = Dimashq, Syria 33 30N 36 18E
93 Eshowe, S. Afr. 28 50s 31 30E
62 Eshta'ol, Israel 31 47N 35 0E
84 Esiama, Ghana 4 48N 2 25W
38 Esino, R., Italy 43 28N 13 8E
12 Esk, R., England 54 27N 0 48W
14 Esk, R., Scotland 55 12N 3 10W
50 Eskifjördur, Iceland 65 3N 13 55W
49 Eskilstuna, Sweden 59 22N 16 32E
109 Eskimo Pt., Canada 61 10N 94 15W
64 Eskişehir, Turkey 39 50N 30 35E
32 Esla, Pantano del, Spain 41 40N 5 50W
32 Esla, R., Spain 41 45N 5 50W
49 Eslöv, Sweden 55 50N 13 20E
126 Esmeraldas, Ecuador 1 0N 79 40W
47 Espa, Norway 60 35N 11 15E
126 Espada, Pta., Colombia 12 5N 71 7W
20 Espalion, France 44 32N 2 47E
33 Espalmador, I., Spain 38 48N 1 26E
106 Espanola, Canada 46 15N 81 46W
32 Espardell, I. del, Sp. 38 47N 1 29E
32 Esparraguera, Spain 41 33N 1 52E
58 Espe, U.S.S.R. 44 0N 74 5E
31 Espejo, Spain 37 40N 4 34W
96 Esperance, Austral. 33 45s 121 55E
96 Esperance B., Austral. 33 48s 121 55E
124 Esperanza, Santa Fé, Argentina 31 29s 61 3W
20 Espéraza, France 42 56N 2 14E
47 Espevaer Lt. Ho., Nor. 59 35N 5 7E
31 Espichel, C., Portugal 38 22N 9 16W
31 Espiel, Spain 38 11N 5 1W
125 Espigão, Serra do, Brazil 26 35s 50 30W
126 Espinal, Colombia 4 9N 74 53W
30 Espinho, Portugal 41 1N 8 38W
125 Espinilho, Serra do, Brazil 28 30s 55 0W
126 Espino, Venezuela 8 34N 66 1W
30 Espinosa de los Monteros, Spain 43 5N 3 34W
120 Espíritu Santo, B. del, Mexico 19 15N 79 40W
120 Espiritu Santo, I., Mex. 24 30N 110 23W
32 Espluga de Francolí, Sp. 41 24N 1 7E
33 Espuña, Sierra de, Spain 37 51N 1 35W
91 Espungabera, Mozam. 20 29s 32 45E
124 Esquel, Argentina 42 40s 71 20W
104 Esquimalt, Canada 48 30N 123 23W
124 Esquina, Argentina 30 0s 59 30W
82 Essaouira (Mogador), Morocco 31 32N 9 42W
90 Essebie, Zaïre 2 58N 30 40E
16 Essen, Belgium 51 28N 4 28E
24 Essen, Germany 51 28N 6 59E
126 Essequibo, R., Guyana 5 45N 58 50W
116 Essex, Canada 42 9N 82 50W
113 Essex, U.S.A. 44 17N 73 21W
13 Essex ♦, England 51 48N 0 30E
24 Esslingen, Germany 48 43N 9 19E
19 Essonne ♦, France 48 30N 2 20E
48 Essvik, Sweden 62 18N 17 24E
32 Estadilla, Spain 42 4N 0 16E
128 Estados, I. de los, Arg. 54 40s 64 30W
32 Estagel, France 42 47N 2 40E
127 Estância, Brazil 11 16s 37 26W
30 Estarreja, Portugal 40 45N 8 35W
20 Estats, P. d', Sp.-Fr. 42 40N 1 40E
92 Estcourt, S. Afr. 28 58s 29 53E
39 Este, Italy 45 12N 11 40E
121 Esteli, Nicaragua 13 9N 86 22W
32 Estella, Spain 42 40N 2 0W
116 Estelline, S.D., U.S.A. 44 39N 96 52W
117 Estelline, Texas, U.S.A. 34 35N 100 27W
31 Estena, R., Spain 39 23N 4 44W
31 Estepa, Spain 37 17N 4 52W
31 Estepona, Spain 36 24N 5 7W
109 Esterhazy, Canada 50 37N 102 5W
19 Esternay, France 48 44N 3 33E
32 Esterri de Aneu, Spain 42 38N 1 1E

MAP

109 Estevan, Canada 49 10N 103 0W
116 Estherville, U.S.A. 43 25N 94 50W
19 Estissac, France 48 16N 3 48E
109 Eston, Canada 51 8N 108 40W
54 Estonian S.S.R. ♦, U.S.S.R. 48 30N 25 30E
31 Estoril, Portugal 38 42N 9 23W
30 Estrêla, Serra da, Port. 40 10N 7 45W
33 Estrella, Spain 38 25N 3 35W
31 Estremadura, Portugal 39 0N 9 0W
31 Estremoz, Portugal 38 51N 7 39W
127 Estrondo, Serra do, Brazil 7 20s 48 0W
27 Esztergom, Hungary 47 47N 18 44E
30 Et Tieta, Morocco 29 37N 9 15W
62 Et Turra, Jordan 32 39N 35 59E
68 Etah, India 27 35N 78 40E
19 Étain, France 49 13N 5 38E
107 Etamamu, Canada 50 18N 59 59W
19 Étampes, France 48 26N 2 10E
19 Étang, France 46 52N 4 10E
19 Étaples, France 50 30N 1 39E
68 Etawah, India 26 48N 79 6E
115 Etawah, R., U.S.A. 34 20N 84 15W
85 Eteh, Nigeria 7 2N 7 28E
85 Etelia, Mali 19 10N 0 55E
82 Etel, Oued el, Algeria 28 31N 3 37W
109 Ethelbert, Canada 51 32N 100 25W
78 Ethiopia ■, Africa 8 0N 40 0E
78 Ethiopian Highlands, Ethiopia 10 0N 37 0E
14 Etive, L., Scot. 56 30N 5 12W
41 Etna, Mt., Italy 37 45N 15 0E
47 Etne, Norway 59 40N 5 56E
92 Etosha Pan, S.W. Africa 18 40s 16 30E
92 Etoshapan, S.W. Africa 18 40s 16 30E
115 Etowah, U.S.A. 35 20N 84 30W
19 Étretat, France 49 42N 0 12E
44 Etropole, Bulgaria 43 50N 24 0E
16 Ettelbrück, Lux. 49 50N 6 5E
25 Ettlingen, Germany 48 58N 8 25E
14 Ettrick Water, Scotland 55 31N 2 55W
90 Etuku, Zaïre 3 42s 25 45E
120 Etzatlán, Mexico 20 48N 104 5W
18 Eu, France 50 3N 1 26E
100 Eubalong, Australia 33 10s 146 55E
100 Eubalong West, Austral. 33 7s 146 29E
45 Euboea = Évvoia, Greece 38 40N 23 40E
96 Eucla Basin, Australia 31 19s 126 9E
96 Eucla Motel, Australia 31 46s 128 50E
112 Euclid, U.S.A. 41 32N 81 31W
100 Eucumbene, L., Austral. 36 2s 148 40E
115 Eufaula, U.S.A. 31 55N 85 11W
117 Eufaula, L., U.S.A. 35 15N 95 28W
117 Eufawla, U.S.A. 35 20N 95 33W
118 Eugene, U.S.A. 44 0N 123 8W
120 Eugenia, Punta, Mexico 27 50N 115 5W
99 Eugowra, Australia 33 2s 148 24E
100 Eumungerie, Australia 31 56N 148 36E
100 Eunice, La., U.S.A. 30 35N 92 28W
117 Eunice, N. Mex., U.S.A. 32 30N 103 10W
16 Eupen, Belgium 50 37N 6 3E
64 Euphrates = Furat, Nahr al, Asia 33 30N 43 0E
18 Eure ♦, France 49 6N 1 0E
18 Eure-et-Loir ♦, Fr. 48 22N 1 30E
4 Eureka, Canada 80 0N 85 56W
117 Eureka, Calif., U.S.A. 40 50N 124 0W
117 Eureka, Kans., U.S.A. 37 50N 96 20W
118 Eureka, Mont., U.S.A. 48 53N 115 6W
118 Eureka, Nev., U.S.A. 39 32N 116 2W
116 Eureka, S.D., U.S.A. 45 49N 99 38W
119 Eureka, Utah, U.S.A. 40 0N 112 0W
100 Eurca, Australia 36 38s 145 35E
30 Europa, Picos de, Spain 43 10N 5 0W
31 Europa, Pta. de, Gibraltar 36 3N 5 21W
31 Europa Pt. = Europa, Pta. de, Gib. 36 3N 5 21W
16 Europoort, Netherlands 51 57N 4 10E
74 Euse, Japan 34 40N 135 37E
24 Euskirchen, Germany 50 40N 6 45E
24 Eutin, Germany 54 7N 10 38E
24 Eutingen, Germany 48 29N 8 45E
62 Eval, Mt., Jordan 32 15N 35 15E
47 Evanger, Norway 60 39N 6 7E
116 Evans, U.S.A. 40 25N 104 43W
106 Evans, L., Canada 50 50N 77 0W
113 Evans Mills, U.S.A. 44 6N 75 48W
116 Evans P., U.S.A. 41 0N 105 35W
118 Evanston, Ill., U.S.A. 42 0N 87 40W
116 Evanston, Wy., U.S.A. 41 10N 111 0W
114 Evansville, Ind., U.S.A. 38 0N 87 35W
114 Evansville, Wis., U.S.A. 42 47N 89 18W
20 Evato, Malagasy Rep. 20 37s 47 10E
20 Évaux-les-Bains, France 46 12N 2 29E
116 Eveleth, U.S.A. 47 35N 92 40W
62 Even Yahuda, Israel 32 16N 34 53E
59 Evensk, U.S.S.R. 61 57N 159 14E
47 Evenstad, Norway 61 25N 11 9E
96 Everard, L., Austral. 31 30s 135 0E
99 Everard Ras., Australia 27 5s 132 28E
69 Everest, Mt., Nepal 28 5N 86 58E
112 Everett, Pa., U.S.A. 40 2N 78 24W
118 Everett, Wash., U.S.A. 48 0N 122 10W
115 Everglades, U.S.A. 26 0N 80 30W
13 Evesham, Eng. 52 6N 1 57W
21 Evian-les-Bains, France 46 24N 6 35E
88 Evinayong, Equat. Guinea 1 50N 10 35E

MAP

45 Evinos, R., Greece 38 27N 21 40E
21 Evisa, Corsica 42 15N 8 48E
31 Evora, Port. 38 33N 7 57W
31 Évora ♦, Portugal 38 33N 7 50W
18 Évreux, France 49 0N 1 8E
18 Évron, France 48 23N 0 58W
44 Evros ♦, Greece 41 10N 26 0E
45 Évrótas, R., Greece 36 50N 22 40E
45 Evvoia ♦, Greece 38 40N 23 40E
116 Ewing, U.S.A. 42 18N 98 22W
88 Ewo, Congo 0 48s 14 45E
10 Exaltación, Bolivia 13 10s 65 20W
100 Excelsior, Australia 33 6s 149 59E
59 Excelsior, S. Africa 28 56s 27 6E
116 Excelsior Springs, U.S.A. 39 20N 94 10W
20 Excideuil, France 45 20N 1 4E
112 Exeter, Canada 43 20N 81 30W
13 Exeter, England 50 43N 3 31W
117 Exeter, Cal., U.S.A. 36 24N 119 8W
116 Exeter, Nebr., U.S.A. 40 43N 97 30W
113 Exeter, N.H., U.S.A. 43 0N 70 58W
13 Exmoor, Eng. 51 10N 3 55W
96 Exmouth, Australia 22 23s 114 7E
13 Exmouth, Eng. 50 37N 3 24W
96 Exmouth G., Australia 22 15s 114 15E
98 Expedition Range, Australia 24 30s 149 12E
31 Extremadura, Sp. 39 30N 6 5W
121 Exuma Sound, Bahamas 24 30N 76 20W
90 Eyasi, L., Tanzania 3 30s 35 0E
109 Eyeberry L., Canada 63 9N 104 40W
14 Eyemouth, Scot. 55 53s 2 5W
20 Eygurande, France 45 40N 2 26E
64 Eyisen, Turkey 41 0N 36 50E
50 Eyjafjörður, Iceland 66 15N 18 30W
20 Eymet, France 44 40N 0 25E
20 Eymoutiers, France 45 45N 1 45E
50 Eyrarbakki, Iceland 63 52N 21 9W
96 Eyre, Australia 32 15s 126 25E
98 Eyre Cr., Australia 26 40s 139 0E
99 Eyre L., (North), Australia 28 30s 137 20E
99 Eyre L., (South), Australia 29 18s 137 25E
101 Eyre Mts., New Zealand 45 25s 168 25E
96 Eyre Pen., Australia 33 30s 137 17E
86 Ez Zeidab, Sudan 17 25N 33 55E
82 Ez Zergoun, W., Alg. 32 45N 2 25E
32 Ezcaray, Spain 42 19N 3 0W
44 Ezine, Turkey 39 48N 26 12E
49 Fåborg, Denmark 55 6N 10 15E
119 Fabens, U.S.A. 31 30N 106 8W
38 Fabriano, Italy 43 20N 12 52E
19 Fabrizia, Italy 38 29N 16 19E
46 Făcăeni, Rumania 44 32N 27 53E
126 Facatativá, Colombia 4 49N 74 22W
20 Facture, France 44 39N 0 58W
81 Fada, Chad 17 13N 21 30E
85 Fada-n-Gourma, Upper Volta 12 10N 0 30E
27 Fadd, Hungary 46 28N 18 49E
54 Faddeyevski, Ostrov, U.S.S.R. 76 0N 150 0E
64 Fadhili, Saudi Arabia 26 55N 49 10E
86 Fadlab, Sudan 17 42N 34 2E
39 Faenza, Italy 44 17N 11 53E
85 Fafa, Mali 15 22N 0 48E
30 Fafe, Portugal 41 27N 8 11W
46 Făgăraş, Rumania 45 48N 24 58E
46 Făgăraş, Munţii, Rumania 45 40N 24 40E
49 Fågelsjö, Sweden 61 50N 14 35E
49 Fagerhult, Kalmar, Sweden 57 8N 15 40E
48 Fagersta, Sweden 60 1N 15 46E
46 Făget, Rumania 45 52N 22 10E
46 Făget, Munţii, Rumania 45 50N 22 9E
49 Fågelvik, Sweden 58 6N 13 6E
128 Fagnano, L., Argentina 54 30s 68 0W
41 Fagnano Castello, Italy 39 31N 16 4E
19 Fagnières, France 48 58N 4 20E
65 Fahraj, Iran 29 0N 59 0E
77 Fahsien, China 21 19N 110 33E
65 Fahûd, Oman 22 18N 56 28E
64 Faid, Saudi Arabia 27 1N 42 52E
98 Fair, C., Australia 12 24s 143 16E
15 Fair Hd., N. Ire. 55 14N 6 10W
119 Fairbank, U.S.A. 31 44N 110 12W
104 Fairbanks, Alaska 64 59N 147 40W
116 Fairbury, U.S.A. 40 5N 97 5W
117 Fairfax, U.S.A. 36 37N 96 45W
100 Fairfield, Australia 33 53s 150 57E
115 Fairfield, Ala., U.S.A. 33 30N 87 0W
117 Fairfield, Calif., U.S.A. 38 14N 122 1W
113 Fairfield, Conn., U.S.A. 41 8N 73 16W
118 Fairfield, Idaho, U.S.A. 43 27N 114 52W
114 Fairfield, Ill., U.S.A. 38 20N 88 20W
116 Fairfield, Iowa, U.S.A. 41 0N 91 58W
118 Fairfield, Mont., U.S.A. 47 40N 112 0W
117 Fairfield, Texas, U.S.A. 31 40N 96 0W
101 Fairlie, New Zealand 44 5s 170 49E
116 Fairmont, Minn., U.S.A. 43 39N 94 30W
114 Fairmont, W. Va., U.S.A. 39 29N 80 10W
108 Fairmont Hot Springs, Canada 50 20N 115 56W
116 Fairplay, U.S.A. 39 9N 107 0W
113 Fairport, N.Y., U.S.A. 43 8N 77 29W
112 Fairport, Ohio, U.S.A. 41 45N 81 17W
98 Fairview, Australia 15 31s 144 17E
108 Fairview, Canada 56 5N 118 25W
116 Fairview, N. Dak., U.S.A. 47 49N 104 7W
117 Fairview, Okla., U.S.A. 36 19N 98 30W
118 Fairview, Utah, U.S.A. 39 50N 111 0W

MAP
104 Fairweather, Mt., Alaska 58 55N 137 45W
116 Faith, U.S.A. 45 2N 102 4W
65 Faizabad, Afghanistan 37 7N 70 33E
69 Faizabad, India 26 45N 82 10E
68 Faizpur, India 21 14N 75 49E
121 Fajardo, P. Rico 18 20N 65 39W
73 Fakfak, Indonesia 3 0S 132 15E
127 Fakiya, Bulgaria 42 10N 27 4E
84 Fakobli, Ivory Coast 7 23N 7 23W
49 Fakse, Denmark 55 15N 12 8E
49 Fakse B., Denmark 55 11N 12 6E
49 Fakse Ladeplads, Den. 55 16N 12 9E
18 Falaise, France 48 54N 0 12W
44 Falakrón Oros, Greece 41 15N 23 58E
67 Falam, Burma 23 0N 93 45E
32 Falces, Spain 42 24N 1 48W
46 Fălciu, Rumania 46 17N 28 7E
82 Falcon, C., Algeria 35 50N 0 50W
126 Falcón ♦, Venezuela 11 0N 69 50W
117 Falcón Dam, U.S.A. 26 50N 99 20W
39 Falconara Marittima, It. 43 37N 13 23E
112 Falconer, U.S.A. 42 7N 79 13W
84 Faléa, Mali 12 16N 11 17W
56 Faleshty, U.S.S.R. 47 32N 27 44E
117 Falfurrias, U.S.A. 27 8N 98 8W
108 Falher, Canada 55 50N 117 15W
112 Falkenberg, Canada 45 9N 79 21W
49 Falkenberg, Germany 51 34N 13 13E
49 Falkenberg, Sweden 56 54N 12 30E
24 Falkensee, Germany 52 35N 13 6E
24 Falkenstein, Germany 50 27N 12 24E
14 Falkirk, Scot. 56 0N 3 47W
128 Falkland Is., S. Atlantic 51 30S 59 0W
5 Falkland Is. Dep., S. Oc. 57 0S 40 0W
128 Falkland Sd., Falk. Is. 52 0S 60 0W
45 Falkonéra, Greece 36 50N 23 52E
49 Falköping, Sweden 58 12N 13 33E
119 Fall Brook, U.S.A. 33 25N 117 12W
113 Fall River, U.S.A. 41 45N 71 5W
118 Fall River Mills, U.S.A. 41 1N 121 46W
42 Fallon, Mont., U.S.A. 46 52N 105 8W
118 Fallon, Nev., U.S.A. 39 31N 118 51W
116 Falls City, Nebr., U.S.A. 40 0N 95 40W
118 Falls City, Oreg., U.S.A. 44 54N 123 29W
112 Falls Creek, U.S.A. 41 8N 78 49W
85 Falmey, Niger 12 36N 2 51E
121 Falmouth, Jamaica 18 30N 77 40W
13 Falmouth, Eng. 50 9N 5 5W
114 Falmouth, U.S.A. 38 40N 84 20W
13 Falmouth B., Eng. 50 7N 5 3W
74 False B., S. Afr. 34 15S 18 40E
70 False Divi Pt., India 15 53N 80 50E
32 Falset, Spain 41 7N 0 50E
49 Falster, Denmark 54 45N 11 55E
49 Falsterbo, Sweden 55 23N 12 50E
49 Falsterbokanalen, Sweden 55 25N 12 56E
46 Fălticeni, Rumania 47 21N 26 20W
62 Faluja, Israel 31 48N 31 37E
48 Falun, Sweden 60 37N 15 37E
64 Famagusta = Ammókhostos, Greece 35 8N 33 55E
87 Famaka, Sudan 11 24N 34 52E
124 Famatina, Sierra, de, Argentina 29 5S 68 0W
93 Fampotabe, Malag. 15 56S 50 0E
44 Fan i Madh, R., Alb. 41 56N 20 16E
84 Fana, Mali 13 0N 6 56W
47 Fana, Norway 60 16N 5 20E
93 Fanambana, Malagasy Rep. 13 34S 50 0E
44 Fanárion, Greece 39 50N 21 47E
77 Fancheng, China 31 2N 118 13E
93 Fandriana, Malagasy Republic 20 14S 47 21E
14 Fannich, L., Scot. 57 40N 5 0W
98 Fanning, Australia 19 56S 146 30E
95 Fanning I., Pac. Oc. 3 51N 159 22W
108 Fanny Bay, Canada 49 27N 124 58W
39 Fano, Italy 43 50N 13 0E
49 Fanø, I., Denmark 55 25N 8 25E
108 Fanshaw, Alaska 57 11N 133 30W
49 Fanø, Denmark 55 25N 8 25E
64 Fao (Al Fāw), Iraq 30 0N 48 30E
65 Faqirwali, Pakistan 29 27N 73 0E
39 Fara in Sabina, Italy 42 13N 12 44E
4 Faraday Seamount Group, N. Atlantic Oc.
90 Faradje, Zaïre 3 50N 29 45E
93 Farafangana, Malagasy Republic 22 49S 47 50E
86 Farâfra, El Wâhât el-, Egypt 27 15N 28 20E
65 Farah, Afghanistan 32 20N 62 7E
93 Farahalana, Malag. 14 26S 50 10E
86 Faraid, Gebel, Egypt 23 33N 35 19E
84 Faramana, Upper Volta 11 56N 4 45W
84 Faranah, Guinea 10 3N 10 45W
63 Farasān, Jazā'ir, Red Sea 16 45N 41 55E
63 Farasan Kebir, Saudi Arabia 16 40N 42 0E
93 Faratsiho, Malag. 19 24S 46 57E
33 Fardes, R., Spain 37 25N 3 10W
13 Fareham, Eng. 50 52N 1 11W
4 Farewell C. = Farvel, K., Greenland 59 48N 43 55W
101 Farewell C., N.Z. 40 29S 172 43E
126 Farfán, Ecuador 0 16N 76 41W
116 Fargo, U.S.A. 47 0N 97 0W
62 Faria, R., Jordan 32 12N 35 27E
116 Faribault, U.S.A. 44 12N 93 20W
68 Faridkot, India 30 44N 74 45E
69 Faridpur, Bangladesh 23 36N 89 53E
69 Faridpur, India 18 14N 79 34E
48 Farila, Sweden 61 48N 15 50E
84 Farim, Port. Guinea 12 27N 15 17W
65 Fariman, Iran 35 40N 60 0E
99 Farina, South Australia 30 3S 138 15E

48 Faringe, Sweden 59 55N 18 7E
49 Färjestaden, Sweden 56 38N 16 25E
45 Farmakonisi, Greece 37 17N 27 8E
117 Farmerville, U.S.A. 32 48N 92 23W
113 Farmington, N.H., U.S.A. 43 25N 71 7W
119 Farmington, N. Mex., U.S.A. 36 45N 108 28W
118 Farmington, Utah, U.S.A. 41 0N 111 58W
119 Farmington, R., U.S.A. 42 0N 73 5W
114 Farmville, U.S.A. 37 19N 78 22W
13 Farnborough, Eng. 51 17N 0 46W
113 Farnham, Canada 45 20N 72 55W
124 Farnham, Mt., Canada 45 20N 72 55W
127 Faro, Brazil 2 0S 56 45W
31 Faro, Port. 37 2N 7 55W
31 Faro ♦, Portugal 37 12N 8 10W
8 Faroe Is., N. Atl. Oc. 62 0N 7 0W
99 Farquhar, C., Australia 23 38S 113 36E
65 Farrashband, Iran 28 57N 52 5E
112 Farrell, U.S.A. 41 13N 80 29W
99 Farrell Flat, Austral. 33 48S 138 48E
69 Farrukhabad, India 27 30N 79 32E
65 Fārs ♦, Iran 29 30N 55 0E
44 Fársala, Greece 39 17N 22 23E
49 Farsö, Denmark 56 48N 9 20E
49 Farstrup, Denmark 56 59N 9 28E
47 Farsund, Norway 58 5N 6 55E
49 Farsø, Denmark 56 46N 9 19E
125 Fartura, Serra da, Brazil 26 21S 52 52W
85 Faru, Nigeria 12 48N 6 12E
49 Farum, Denmark 55 49N 12 21E
65 Farur, Iran 26 20N 54 30E
4 Farvel, Kap, Greenland 59 48N 43 55W
117 Farwell, U.S.A. 34 25N 103 0W
65 Fasa, Iran 29 0N 53 32E
41 Fasano, Italy 40 50N 17 20E
87 Fashoda, Sudan 9 50N 32 2E
53 Faskari, Nigeria 11 42N 6 58E
15 Fastnet Rock, Ireland 51 22N 9 37W
54 Fastov, U.S.S.R. 50 7N 29 57E
69 Fatehgarh, India 27 25N 79 35E
69 Fatehpur, Raj., India 28 0N 75 4E
69 Fatehpur, Ut. P., India 27 8N 81 7E
77 Fati, China 23 10N 113 10E
84 Fatick, Senegal 14 19N 16 27W
31 Fátima, Portugal 39 37N 8 39W
77 Fatkeng, China 23 58N 113 29E
84 Fatoya, Guinea 11 37N 9 10W
77 Fatshan, China 23 10N 113 4E
19 Faucilles, Monts, France 48 5N 5 50E
116 Faulkton, U.S.A. 45 4N 99 8W
19 Fauquemont, France 49 3N 6 36E
19 Fauquemberques, Fr. 50 36N 2 5E
46 Făurei, Rumania 45 6N 27 19E
92 Fauresmith, S. Africa 29 44S 25 17E
47 Fauske, Norway 67 17N 15 25E
93 Faux-Cap, Malag. 25 33S 45 32E
41 Favara, Italy 37 19N 13 39E
40 Favignana, Italy 37 56N 12 18E
21 Favone, France 41 47N 9 26E
106 Favourable Lake, Can. 52 40N 93 0W
106 Fawn, R., Canada 52 40N 89 0W
50 Faxaflói, Iceland 64 29N 23 0W
48 Faxälven, Sweden 63 13N 17 13E
87 Faya = Largeau, Chad 17 58N 19 6E
21 Fayence, France 43 38N 6 42E
116 Fayette, Ala., U.S.A. 33 40N 87 50W
116 Fayette, Mo., U.S.A. 39 10N 92 40W
115 Fayetteville, Ark., U.S.A. 36 0N 94 5W
115 Fayetteville, N.C., U.S.A. 35 0N 78 58W
115 Fayetteville, Tenn., U.S.A. 35 0N 86 30W
32 Fayón, Spain 41 15N 0 20E
68 Fazilka, India 30 27N 74 2E
68 Fazilpur, Pakistan 29 18N 70 29E
80 F'Derik, Mauritania 22 40N 12 45W
15 Feale, R., Ireland 52 26N 9 28W
115 Fear, C., U.S.A. 33 45N 78 0W
118 Feather, R., U.S.A. 39 30N 121 20W
101 Featherston, N.Z. 41 6S 175 20E
91 Featherstone, Rhodesia 18 42S 30 55E
100 Feathertop, Mt., Australia 36 53S 147 1E
18 Fécamp, France 49 45N 0 22E
82 Fedala = Mohammedia, Morocco 33 44N 7 21W
124 Federación, Argentina 31 0S 57 55W
83 Fedjadj, Chott el, Tunisia 33 52N 9 14E
47 Fedje, Norway 60 47N 4 43E
56 Fedorovka, U.S.S.R. 47 4N 35 18E
24 Fehérgyarmat, Hungary 48 0N 22 30E
24 Fehmarn, Germany 54 26N 11 10E
24 Fehmarn Baelt, Den. 54 35N 11 20E
101 Feilding, New Zealand 40 13S 175 35E
27 Feira, Zambia 15 35S 30 16E
27 Fejér ♦, Hungary 47 9N 18 30E
49 Fejø, Denmark 54 55N 11 30E
33 Felanitx, Spain 39 27N 3 7E
26 Feldbach, Austria 46 57N 15 52E
24 Feldberg, Germany 53 20N 13 26E
25 Feldberg, mt., Germany 47 51N 7 58E
26 Feldkirch, Austria 47 15N 9 37E
26 Feldkirchen, Austria 46 44N 14 6E
120 Felipe Carrillo Puerto, Mexico 19 38N 88 3W
13 Felixstowe, Eng. 51 58N 1 22W
20 Felletin, France 45 53N 2 11E
87 Fellit, Ethiopia 16 40N 38 1E
39 Feltre, Italy 46 1N 11 55E
49 Femø, Denmark 54 58N 11 53E
47 Femunden, Norway 62 10N 11 53E
76 Fen Ho, R., China 35 25N 110 30E
106 Fenelon Falls, Canada 44 31N 78 43W
93 Fénérive, Malagasy Rep. 17 22S 49 25E

87 Fenerwa, Ethiopia 13 5N 39 3E
44 Fengári, Greece 40 25N 25 32E
76 Fengcheng, Heilungkiang, China 45 41N 128 54E
77 Fengcheng, Kiangsi, China 28 2N 115 46E
76 Fengcheng, Liaoning, China 40 28N 124 4E
76 Fengfeng, China 36 40N 114 24E
77 Fenghsien, China 33 56N 106 41E
77 Fenghwa, China 29 37N 121 29E
77 Fengkieh (Kweichow), China 31 0N 109 33E
77 Fenglo, China 31 30N 112 29E
77 Fengsiang, China 34 27N 107 30E
77 Fengsin, China 28 41N 115 11E
77 Fengtu, China 29 58N 107 59E
77 Fengy, China 23 48N 106 50E
77 Fengyuan, Taiwan 24 10N 120 45E
98 Feni Is., Terr. of New Guinea 4 5S 153 25E
116 Fennimore, U.S.A. 42 58N 90 41W
69 Fenny, Bengladesh 22 55N 91 32E
93 Fenoarivo, Malagasy Rep. 18 26S 46 34E
21 Feno, C. de, Corsica 41 58N 8 33E
13 Fens, The, Eng. 52 45N 0 2E
109 Fenton, Canada 53 0N 105 35W
114 Fenton, U.S.A. 42 47N 83 44W
77 Fenyang, China 37 19N 111 46E
56 Feodosiya, U.S.S.R. 45 2N 35 28E
83 Fer, C. de, Algeria 37 3N 7 10E
65 Ferdows, Iran 33 58N 58 2E
19 Fère-Champenoise, Fr. 48 45N 4 0E
19 Fère-en-Tardenois, Fr. 49 10N 3 30E
40 Ferentino, Italy 41 42N 13 14E
63 Ferfer, Somali Rep. 5 18N 45 20E
58 Fergana, U.S.S.R. 40 50N 71 50E
106 Fergus, Canada 43 43N 80 24W
116 Fergus Falls, U.S.A. 46 25N 96 0W
98 Fergusson I., Papua 9 30S 150 40E
83 Fériana, Tunisia 34 59N 8 33E
42 Feričanci, Yugoslavia 45 32N 18 0E
83 Ferkane, Algeria 34 37N 7 26E
84 Ferkéssédougou, Ivory Coast 9 35N 5 6W
106 Ferland, Canada 50 19N 88 27W
26 Ferliach, Austria 46 32N 14 18E
84 Ferlo, Vallée du, Senegal 15 15N 14 15W
• 15 Fermanagh ♦, N. Ireland
39 Fermo, Italy 43 10N 13 42E
30 Fermoselle, Spain 41 19N 6 27W
15 Fermoy, Ireland 52 4N 8 18W
31 Fernan Núñez, Spain 37 40N 4 44W
124 Fernández, Argentina 27 55S 63 50W
115 Fernandina, U.S.A. 30 40N 81 30W
127 Fernando de Noronha, I., Brazil 4 0S 33 10W
127 Fernando de Noronha ♦, Brazil 4 0S 33 10W
† 79 Fernando Póo, I., Africa 3 30N 8 40E
118 Ferndale, Calif., U.S.A. 40 37N 124 12W
118 Ferndale, Wash., U.S.A. 48 51N 122 41W
108 Fernie, Canada 49 30N 115 5W
98 Fernlees, Australia 23 55S 148 10E
118 Fernley, U.S.A. 39 42N 119 20W
68 Feroke, India 11 9N 75 46E
41 Ferrai, Greece 40 53N 26 10E
68 Ferozepore, India 30 55N 74 40E
41 Ferrandina, Italy 40 30N 16 28E
39 Ferrara, Italy 44 50N 11 36E
40 Ferrato, C., Sardinia 39 18N 9 39E
31 Ferreira do Alentejo, Portugal 38 4N 8 6W
126 Ferreñafe, Peru 6 35S 79 50W
21 Ferrette, France 47 30N 7 20E
117 Ferriday, U.S.A. 31 35N 91 33W
38 Ferriete, Italy 44 40N 9 30E
19 Ferrières, France 48 5N 2 48E
30 Ferrol, Spain 43 29N 8 15W
119 Ferron, U.S.A. 39 3N 111 3W
40 Fertília, Italy 40 37N 8 13E
116 Fertile, U.S.A. 47 31N 96 18W
27 Fertőszentmiklos, Hung. 47 35N 16 53E
82 Fès, Morocco 34 0N 5 0W
90 Feshi, Zaïre 6 0S 18 10E
116 Fessenden, U.S.A. 47 42N 99 44W
47 Fet, Norway 59 57N 11 12E
46 Feteşti, Rumania 44 22N 27 51E
46 Fethiye, Turkey 36 36N 29 6E
14 Fetlar, I., Scot. 60 36N 0 52W
21 Feurs, France 45 45N 4 13E
14 Ffestiniog, Wales 52 58N 3 56W
124 Fiambalá, Argentina 27 45S 67 37W
93 Fianarantsoa ♦, Malag. 19 30S 47 0E
81 Fianga, Cameroon 9 55N 15 9E
46 Fibiş, Rumania 45 57N 21 26E
107 Fichot, I., Canada 51 12N 55 40W
25 Fichtelgebirge, Ger. 50 10N 12 0E
92 Ficksburg, S. Africa 28 51S 27 53E
38 Fidenza, Italy 44 51N 10 3E
87 Fierenana, Ethiopia 18 29S 48 24E
44 Fiëri, Albania 40 43N 19 33E
14 Fife ♦, Scot. 56 13N 3 2W
14 Fife Ness, Scot. 56 17N 2 35W
87 Fifth Cataract, Sudan 18 15N 33 50E
20 Figeac, France 44 37N 2 2E
39 Figline Valdarno, Italy 43 37N 11 28E
87 Figtree, Rhodesia 20 22S 28 20E
30 Figueira da Foz, Port. 40 7N 8 54W
31 Figueira dos Vinhos, Portugal 39 55N 8 16W
32 Figueras, Spain 42 18N 2 58E
82 Figuig, Morocco 32 5N 1 11W
93 Fihaonana, Malag. 18 36S 47 12E
93 Fiherenana, R., Malag. 23 19S 43 37E
101 Fiji ■, Pacific Ocean 17 20S 179 0E
101 Fiji Is., Pacific Ocean 17 20S 179 0E

62 Fik, Syria 32 46N 35 41E
85 Fika, Nigeria 11 15N 11 13E
33 Filabres, Sierra de los, Spain 37 13N 2 20W
41 Filadélfia, Italy 38 47N 16 17E
27 Fil'akovo, Cz. 48 17N 19 50E
5 Filchner Ice Shelf, Antarctica 78 0S 60 0W
118 Filer, U.S.A. 42 30N 114 35W
12 Filey, England 54 13N 0 18W
46 Filiaşi, Rumania 44 32N 23 31E
44 Filiátes, Greece 39 38N 20 16E
45 Filiatrá, Greece 37 9N 21 35E
41 Filicudi, I., Italy 38 35N 14 33E
48 Filipstad, Sweden 59 43N 14 9E
25 Filisur, Switzerland 46 41N 9 40E
44 Filitouri, R., Greece 41 15N 25 40E
109 Fillmore, Canada 49 50N 103 25W
119 Fillmore, U.S.A. 34 23N 118 58W
39 Filottrano, Italy 43 28N 13 20E
56 Filyos, Turkey 41 34N 32 4E
64 Filyos çayi, Turkey 41 35N 32 10E
38 Finale Ligure, Italy 44 10N 8 21E
38 Finale nell' Emilia, It. 44 50N 11 18E
33 Fiñana, Spain 37 10N 2 50W
109 Finch, Canada 45 10N 75 5W
14 Findhorn, R., Scot. 57 30N 3 45W
114 Findlay, U.S.A. 41 0N 83 41W
109 Finger L., Canada 53 15N 93 35W
91 Fingoè, Mozambique 15 12S 31 50E
64 Finike, Turkey 36 21N 30 10E
18 Finistère ♦, France 48 20N 4 0W
30 Finisterre, Spain 42 54N 9 16W
30 Finisterre, C., Spain 42 50N 9 19W
52 Finland ■, Europe 70 0N 27 0E
52 Finland, G. of, Europe 60 0N 26 0E
100 Finley, Australia 35 38S 145 40E
116 Finley, U.S.A. 47 35N 97 50W
15 Finn, R., Ire. 54 50N 7 55W
50 Finnmark fylke ♦, Norway 69 30N 25 0E
98 Finschhafen, N.E. New Guinea 6 35S 147 48E
47 Finse, Norway 60 36N 7 30E
49 Finspång, Sweden 58 45N 15 43E
48 Finsta, Sweden 59 45N 18 34E
25 Finsteraarhorn, Switzerland 46 31N 8 10E
24 Finsterwalde, Germany 51 37N 13 42E
96 Finucane I., Australia 20 19S 118 30E
39 Fiora, R., Italy 42 25N 11 35E
38 Fiorenzuola d'Arda, It. 44 56N 9 54E
62 Fiq, Syria 32 46N 35 41E
84 Fire River, Canada 48 47N 83 36W
109 Firedrake L., Canada 61 25N 104 40W
39 Firenze, Italy 43 47N 11 15E
21 Firminy, France 45 23N 4 18E
65 Firoz Kohi, Afghanistan 34 45N 63 0E
68 Firozabad, India 27 10N 78 25E
86 First Cataract, Egypt 24 1N 32 51E
65 Firūzābād, Iran 28 52N 52 35E
65 Firuzkuh, Iran 35 50N 52 40E
74 Fish, R., S.W. Africa 27 40S 17 30E
100 Fish Creek, Australia 38 43S 146 7E
14 Fishguard, Wales 51 59N 4 59W
109 Fishing L., Canada 52 10N 95 30W
84 Fishtown, Liberia 4 24N 7 45E
47 Fiskum, Norway 59 42N 9 48E
19 Fismes, France 49 20N 3 40E
47 Fister, Norway 59 10N 6 5E
113 Fitchburg, U.S.A. 42 35N 71 47W
32 Fitero, Spain 42 4N 1 52W
47 Fitjar, Norway 59 55N 5 17E
81 Fitri, L., Chad 12 50N 17 28E
118 Fitzgerald, U.S.A. 31 45N 83 10W
106 Fitzpatrick, Canada 47 29N 72 46W
124 Fitz Roy, Argentina 47 0S 67 0W
98 Fitzroy, R., Queens., Austral. 23 10S 150 10E
96 Fitzroy, R., W.A., Austral. 17 30S 124 0E
96 Fitzroy Crossing, Australia 18 9S 125 38E
112 Fitzwilliam I., Canada 45 30N 81 45W
42 Fiume = Rijeka, Yugoslavia 45 20N 14 21E
39 Fiumefreddo Brúzio, It. 39 14N 16 4E
90 Fizi, Zaïre 4 17S 28 55E
47 Fjaera, Nor. 59 52N 6 22E
49 Fjellerup, Denmark 56 29N 10 34E
49 Fjerritslev, Denmark 57 5N 9 15E
82 Fkih ben Salah, Mor. 32 45N 6 45W
47 Fla, Buskerud, Norway 60 25N 9 28E
47 Flå, Sör Tröndelag, Nor. 63 13N 10 18E
116 Flagler, U.S.A. 39 20N 103 4W
119 Flagstaff, U.S.A. 35 10N 111 40W
108 Flagstone, Canada 49 4N 115 10W
106 Flaherty, I., Canada 56 15N 79 15W
118 Flambeau, R., U.S.A. 45 40N 90 50W
12 Flamborough Hd., England 54 8N 0 4W
118 Flaming Gorge Dam, U.S.A. 40 50N 109 25W
118 Flaming Gorge L., U.S.A. 41 15N 109 30W
116 Flandreau, U.S.A. 44 5N 96 38W

14 Flannan Is., Scot. 58 9N 7 52W
49 Flaren I., Sweden 57 2N 14 5E
50 Flåsjön, Sweden 64 5N 15 50E
117 Flat River, U.S.A. 37 50N 90 30W
50 Flatey, Barðastrandarsýsla, Iceland 66 10N 17 52W
50 Flatey, Suður-þingeyjarsýsla, Iceland 65 22N 22 56W
118 Flathead L., U.S.A. 47 50N 114 0W
98 Flattery, C., Australia 14 58S 145 21E
118 Flattery, C., U.S.A. 48 21N 124 31W
19 Flavy-le-Martel, Fr. 49 43N 3 12E
116 Flaxton, U.S.A. 48 52N 102 24W
12 Fleetwood, Eng. 53 55N 3 1W
47 Flekkefjord, Norway 58 18N 6 39E
47 Flemington, Norway 61 19N 11 28E
49 Flensborg Fjord, W. Germany 54 50N 9 40E
24 Flensburg, Germany 54 46N 9 28E
18 Flers, France 48 47N 0 33W
47 Flesberg, Norway 59 51N 9 28E
112 Flesherton, Canada 44 15N 80 34W
12 Fletton, Eng. 52 34N 0 13W
20 Fleurance, France 43 52N 0 40E
25 Fleurier, Switzerland 46 54N 6 35E
48 Flickerbäcken, Sweden 61 47N 12 34E
109 Flin Flon, Canada 54 50N 102 0W
114 Flint, U.S.A. 43 5N 83 40W
14 Flint, Wales 53 15N 3 7W
95 Flint, I., Pacific Ocean 11 26S 151 48W
115 Flint, R., U.S.A. 31 20N 84 10W
• 12 Flint ♦, Wales 53 15N 3 12W
100 Flinton, Australia 27 55S 149 32E
49 Fliseryd, Sweden 57 6N 16 15E
32 Flix, Spain 41 14N 0 32E
19 Flixecourt, France 50 0N 2 5E
48 Floda, Kopparbergs, Sweden 60 30N 14 53E
12 Flodden, England 55 37N 2 8W
116 Floodwood, U.S.A. 46 55N 92 55W
47 Flora, Norway 63 27N 11 22E
47 Flora, Sogn & Fjordane, Norway 61 35N 5 1E
114 Flora, U.S.A. 38 40N 88 30W
20 Florac, France 44 20N 3 37E
39 Florence = Firenze, Italy 43 47N 11 15E
115 Florence, Ala., U.S.A. 34 50N 87 50W
119 Florence, Ariz., U.S.A. 33 0N 111 25W
119 Florence, Colo., U.S.A. 38 26N 105 0W
118 Florence, Oreg., U.S.A. 44 0N 124 3W
115 Florence, S.C., U.S.A. 34 5N 79 50W
16 Florennes, Belgium 50 15N 4 35E
20 Florensac, France 43 23N 3 28E
16 Florenville, Belgium 49 40N 5 19E
121 Flores, Azores 39 13N 31 13W
120 Flores, Guatemala 16 59N 89 40W
108 Flores I., Canada 49 20N 126 10W
73 Flores, Indonesia 8 35S 121 0E
72 Flores Sea, Indonesia 6 30S 124 0E
117 Floresville, U.S.A. 29 10N 98 10W
127 Floriano, Brazil 6 50S 43 0W
125 Florianópolis, Brazil 27 30S 48 30W
121 Florida, Cuba 21 32N 78 14W
125 Florida, Uruguay 34 7S 56 10W
115 Florida ♦, U.S.A. 28 30N 82 0W
115 Florida, Straits of, U.S.A. 25 0N 80 0W
121 Florida Keys, U.S.A. 25 0N 80 40W
41 Florídia, Italy 37 6N 15 9E
27 Floridsdorf, Austria 48 15N 16 25E
44 Flórina, Greece 40 48N 21 26E
44 Flórina ♦, Greece 40 48N 21 40E
47 Florø, Norway 61 35N 5 1E
47 Flosta, Norway 58 32N 8 56E
48 Florringen, Sweden 61 50N 12 16E
113 Flower Sta., Canada 45 10N 76 42W
107 Flower's Cove, Canada 51 14N 56 46W
117 Floydada, U.S.A. 33 58N 101 18W
73 Fluk, Indonesia 1 42S 127 38E
32 Flumen, R., Spain 42 0N 0 25W
40 Flumendosa, R., Italy 39 30N 9 25E
41 Fluminimaggiore, Italy 39 25N 8 30E
16 Flushing = Vlissingen, Netherlands 51 26N 3 34E
32 Fluvià, R., Spain 42 12N 3 7E
98 Fly, R., Papua 7 50S 141 20E
47 Flå, Norway 63 12N 10 20E
12 Foam Lake, Canada 51 40N 103 15W
42 Foča, Yugoslavia 43 31N 18 47E
46 Focşani, Rumania 45 41N 27 15E
98 Fofo Fofo, T. of Papua 8 9S 147 6E
82 Foggaret el Arab, Alg. 27 13N 2 59E
82 Foggaret ez Zoua, Alg. 27 20N 3 0E
41 Fóggia, Italy 41 28N 15 31E
85 Foggo, Nigeria 11 21N 9 57E
38 Foglia, R., Italy 43 50N 12 32E
107 Fogo I., Canada 49 40N 54 5W
27 Fohnsdorf, Austria 47 12N 14 40E
24 Föhr, Germany 54 40N 8 30E
20 Foix, France 42 58N 1 38E
42 Fojnica, Yugoslavia 43 59N 17 51E
45 Fokis ♦, Greece 38 30N 22 15E
47 Fokstua, Norway 62 7N 9 18E
50 Folda, Nord-Tröndelag, Norway 64 41N 10 50E
50 Folda, Nordland, Norway 67 38N 14 50E
27 Földeák, Hungary 46 19N 20 30E
92 Foley, U.S.A. 30 25N 87 40W
106 Foleyet, Canada 48 15N 82 25W
47 Folgefonni, Norway 60 23N 6 34E
47 Folla, Norway 62 58N 12 40E

* In April 1973 districts replaced counties in N. Ireland
† Renamed Macias Nguema Biyoga
* Incorporated within the county of Clwyd

Folkestone INDEX Fullerton

MAP
13 Folkestone, Eng. 51 5N 1 11E
115 Folkston, U.S.A. 30 55N 82 0W
117 Follett, U.S.A. 36 30N 100 12W
38 Follónica, Italy 42 55N 10 45E
118 Folsom, U.S.A. 38 41N 121 7W
109 Fond du lac, Canada 59 20N 107 10W
116 Fond du lac, U.S.A. 43 46N 88 26W
109 Fond du Lac, R., Canada 58 55N 104 50W
113 Fonda, U.S.A. 42 57N 74 23W
82 Fondak, Morocco 35 34N 5 35W
40 Fondi, Italy 41 21N 13 25E
30 Fonfria, Spain 41 37N 6 9W
47 Fongen, Norway 63 11N 11 38E
40 Fonni, Italy 40 5N 9 16E
30 Fonsagrada, Spain 43 8N 7 4W
120 Fonseca, G. de, C. Amer. 13 10N 87 40W
19 Fontaine-Française, Fr. 47 32N 5 21E
19 Fontainebleau, France 48 24N 2 40E
126 Fonte Boa, Brazil 2 25S 66 0W
85 Fontem, Cameroon 5 32N 9 52E
20 Fontenay-le-Comte, Fr. 46 28N 0 48W
107 Fontenelle, Canada 48 54N 64 33W
50 Fontur, Iceland 66 23N 14 32W
27 Fonyód, Hungary 46 44N 17 33E
77 Foochow (Minhow), China 26 2N 119 25E
38 Foppiano, Italy 46 21N 8 24E
49 Föra, Sweden 57 2N 16 52E
19 Forbach, France 49 10N 6 52E
100 Forbes, Austral. 33 22S 148 0E
69 Forbesganj, India 26 17N 87 18E
85 Forcados, Nigeria 5 26N 5 26E
85 Forcados, R., Nigeria 5 25N 5 20E
32 Forcall, R., Spain 40 40N 0 12W
21 Forcalquier, France 43 58N 5 47E
25 Forchheim, Germany 49 42N 11 4E
96 Ford, C., Australia 13 31N 129 55E
112 Ford City, U.S.A. 40 47N 79 31W
47 Förde, Norway 61 28N 5 45E
20 Fordongianus, Italy 40 0N 8 50E
99 Fords Bridge, Australia 29 41S 145 29E
117 Fordyce, U.S.A. 33 50N 92 20W
84 Forécariah, Guinea 9 20N 13 10W
4 Forel, Mont., Greenland 66 52N 36 55W
108 Foremost, Canada 49 26N 112 41W
41 Forenza, Italy 40 50N 15 50E
112 Forest, Canada 43 9N 82 0W
117 Forest, U.S.A. 32 21N 89 27W
117 Forest City, Ark., U.S.A. 35 0N 90 50W
116 Forest City, Iowa, U.S.A. 43 12N 93 39W
115 Forest City, N.C., U.S.A. 35 23N 81 50W
113 Forest City, Pa., U.S.A. 41 39N 75 29W
118 Forest Grove, U.S.A. 45 31N 123 4W
108 Forest Lawn, Canada 51 4N 114 0W
108 Forestburg, Canada 52 35N 112 1W
107 Forestville, Canada 48 48N 69 20W
114 Forestville, U.S.A. 44 41N 87 29W
20 Forez, Mts. du, France 45 40N 3 50E
14 Forfar, Scotland 56 40N 2 53W
19 Forges-les-Eaux, France 49 37N 1 30E
106 Forget, Canada 49 40N 102 50W
118 Forks, U.S.A. 47 56N 124 40W
39 Forlì, Italy 44 14N 12 2E
116 Forman, U.S.A. 46 9N 97 43W
38 Formazza, Italy 46 23N 8 26E
12 Formby Pt., Eng. 53 33N 3 7W
33 Formentera, I., Spain 38 40N 1 30E
32 Formentor, C. de, Spain 39 58N 3 13E
40 Fórmia, Italy 41 15N 13 34E
38 Formigine, Italy 44 37N 10 51E
20 Formiguères, France 42 37N 2 5E
77 Formosa = Taiwan, Asia 23 30N 121 0E
124 Formosa, Argentina 26 15S 58 10W
124 Formosa ♦, Arg. 26 5S 58 10W
90 Formosa Bay, Kenya 2 40S 40 20E
77 Formosa Str., Asia 24 40N 120 0E
49 Fornaes, C., Denmark 56 27N 10 58E
32 Fornells, Spain 40 4N 4 4E
30 Fornos de Algodres, Portugal 40 38N 7 32W
38 Fornovo di Taro, Italy 44 42N 10 7E
14 Forres, Scotland 57 37N 3 38W
100 Forrest, Vic., Australia 38 22S 143 40E
96 Forrest, W.A., Australia 30 50S 128 2E
48 Fors, Jämtland, Sweden 63 0N 16 40E
48 Fors, Kopparberg, Swed. 60 14N 16 20E
48 Forsa, Sweden 61 44N 16 55E
47 Forsand, Norway 58 54N 6 5E
98 Forsayth, Australia 18 33S 143 34E
48 Forsbacka, Sweden 60 39N 16 54E
48 Forse, Sweden 63 8N 17 1E
49 Forserum, Sweden 57 42N 14 30E
49 Forshaga, Sweden 59 33N 13 29E
49 Forshem, Sweden 58 38N 13 30E
48 Forsmo, Sweden 63 16N 17 11E
24 Forst, Germany 51 43N 14 37E
100 Forster, Australia 32 12S 152 31E
115 Forsyth, Ga., U.S.A. 33 4N 83 55W
118 Forsyth, Mont., U.S.A. 46 14N 106 37W
106 Fort Albany, Canada 52 15N 81 35W
120 Fort Amador, Panama Canal Zone 8 56N 79 32W
119 Fort Apache, U.S.A. 33 50N 110 0W
*81 Fort Archambault, Chad 9 5N 18 23E
108 Fort Assiniboine, Can. 54 20N 114 45W
14 Fort Augustus, Scotland 57 9N 4 40W
108 Fort Babine, Canada 55 22N 126 37W
92 Fort Beaufort, S. Afr. 32 46S 26 40E
118 Fort Benton, U.S.A. 47 50N 110 40W
118 Fort Bragg, U.S.A. 39 28N 123 50W
118 Fort Bridger, U.S.A. 41 22N 110 20W
85 Fort Charlet = Djanet, Algeria 24 35N 9 32E
105 Fort Chimo, Canada 58 9N 68 12W
109 Fort Chipewyan, Can. 58 46N 111 9W

* *Renamed Sarh*

120 Fort Clayton, Panama Canal Zone 9 0N 79 35W
116 Fort Collins, U.S.A. 40 30N 105 4W
106 Fort Coulonge, Canada 45 50N 76 45W
81 Fort Crampel, Central African Republic 7 8N 19 18E
93 Fort-Dauphin, Malag. 25 2S 47 0E
120 Fort Davis, Panama Canal Zone 9 17N 79 56W
117 Fort Davis, U.S.A. 30 38N 103 53W
119 Fort Defiance, U.S.A. 35 47N 109 4W
121 Fort-de-France, Martinique 14 36N 61 2W
83 Fort de Polignac = Illizi, Algeria 26 31N 8 32E
88 Fort de Possel, Central African Republic 5 5N 19 10E
116 Fort Dodge, U.S.A. 42 29N 94 10W
113 Fort Edward, U.S.A. 43 16N 73 35W
83 Fort Flatters = Zaouiet El-Khala, Alg. 27 10N 6 40E
81 Fort Foureau, Cameroon 12 0N 14 55E
109 Fort Frances, Canada 48 35N 93 25W
104 Fort Franklin, Canada 65 30N 123 45W
119 Fort Garland, U.S.A. 37 28N 105 30W
107 Fort George, Canada 53 40N 79 0W
106 Fort George, R., Canada 53 50N 77 0W
104 Fort Good-Hope, Can. 66 14N 128 40W
80 Fort Gouraud = F'Dérik, Maur. 22 40N 12 45W
108 Fort Grahame, Canada 56 30N 124 35W
90 Fort Hall = Muranga, Kenya 1 0S 37 50E
119 Fort Hancock, U.S.A. 31 19N 105 56W
119 Fort Hauchuca, U.S.A. 31 32N 110 30W
67 Fort Hertz (Putao), Burma 27 28N 97 30E
106 Fort Hope, Canada 51 30N 88 10W
91 Fort Jameson = Chipata, Zambia 13 38S 32 38E
**91 Fort Johnston, Malawi 14 25S 35 16E
117 Fort Kent, U.S.A. 47 12N 68 30W
118 Fort Klamath, U.S.A. 42 45N 122 0W
82 Fort Lallemand, Algeria 31 13N 6 17E
†81 Fort-Lamy, Chad 12 4N 15 8E
83 Fort Lapperrine = Tamanrasset, Algeria 22 56N 5 30E
116 Fort Laramie, U.S.A. 42 15N 104 30W
115 Fort Lauderdale, U.S.A. 26 10N 80 5W
108 Fort Liard, Canada 60 20N 123 30W
121 Fort Liberté, Haiti 19 42N 71 51W
116 Fort Lupton, U.S.A. 40 8N 104 48W
108 Fort Mackay, Canada 57 12N 111 41W
107 Fort McKenzie, Canada 56 50N 69 0W
108 Fort Macleod, Canada 49 45N 113 30W
82 Fort MacMahon, Algeria 29 51N 1 45E
104 Fort McPherson, Canada 67 30N 134 55W
116 Fort Madison, U.S.A. 40 39N 91 20E
115 Fort Meade, U.S.A. 27 45N 81 45W
82 Fort Miribel, Algeria 29 31N 2 55E
116 Fort Morgan, U.S.A. 40 10N 103 50W
83 Fort Motylinski, Algeria 22 47N 5 59E
115 Fort Myers, U.S.A. 26 30N 82 0W
108 Fort Nelson, Canada 58 50N 122 30W
108 Fort Nelson, R., Canada 59 20N 123 30W
104 Fort Norman, Canada 64 57N 125 30W
83 Fort Pacot (Chirfa), Niger 20 55N 12 14E
115 Fort Payne, U.S.A. 34 25N 85 44W
118 Fort Peck, U.S.A. 47 1N 105 30W
118 Fort Peck Dam, U.S.A. 48 0N 106 20W
118 Fort Peck Res., U.S.A. 47 40N 107 0W
116 Fort Pierce, U.S.A. 27 29N 80 19W
116 Fort Pierre, U.S.A. 44 25N 100 25W
82 Fort Pierre Bordes, Algeria 20 0N 2 55E
113 Fort Plain, U.S.A. 42 56N 74 39W
90 Fort Portal, Uganda 0 40N 30 20E
108 Fort Providence, Can. 61 20N 117 30W
109 Fort Qu'Appelle, Can. 50 45N 103 50W
120 Fort Randolph, Panama Canal Zone 9 23N 79 53W
109 Fort Reliance, Canada 62 40N 109 0W
108 Fort Resolution, Can. 61 10N 114 40W
91 Fort Rixon, Rhodesia 20 2S 29 17E
91 Fort Rosebery = Mansa, Zambia 11 10S 28 50E
106 Fort Rupert (Rupert House), Canada 51 30N 78 40W
83 Fort Saint, Tunisia 30 13N 9 31E
108 Fort St. James, Canada 54 30N 124 10W
108 Fort St. John, Canada 56 15N 120 50W
68 Fort Sandeman, Pakistan 31 20N 69 25E
108 Ft. Saskatchewan, Can. 53 40N 113 15W
117 Fort Scott, U.S.A. 38 0N 94 40W
104 Fort Selkirk, Canada 62 43N 137 22W
106 Fort Severn, Canada 56 0N 87 40W
120 Fort Sherman, Panama Canal Zone 9 22N 79 56W
57 Fort Shevchenko, U.S.S.R. 44 30N 50 10W
81 Fort Sibut, Central African Republic 5 52N 19 10W
108 Fort Simpson, Canada 61 45N 121 30W
108 Fort Smith, Canada 60 1N 112 4W
117 Fort Smith, U.S.A. 35 25N 94 25W
119 Fort Stanton, U.S.A. 33 33N 105 36W
117 Fort Stockton, U.S.A. 30 48N 103 2W
117 Fort Sumner, U.S.A. 34 24N 104 8W
119 Fort Thomas, U.S.A. 33 2N 109 59W
80 Fort Trinquet = Bir Mogrein, Maur. 25 10N 11 25W
115 Fort Valley, U.S.A. 32 33N 83 52W
108 Fort Vermilion, Canada 58 30N 115 57W
91 Fort Victoria, Rhodesia 20 8S 30 55E
115 Ft. Walton Beach, U.S.A. 30 25N 86 40W
114 Fort Wayne, U.S.A. 41 5N 85 10W
106 Fort William = Thunder Bay, Canada 48 20N 89 10W

* *Renamed Kousseri*
** *Renamed Mangoche*
† *Renamed Ndjamena*

14 Fort William, Scot. 56 48N 5 8W
117 Fort Worth, U.S.A. 32 45N 97 25W
116 Fort Yates, U.S.A. 46 8N 100 38W
104 Fort Yukon, Alaska 66 35N 145 12W
127 Fortaleza, Brazil 3 35S 38 35W
126 Forte Coimbra, Brazil 19 55S 57 48W
89 Forte Rocadas, Angola 16 38S 15 22E
107 Forteau, Canada 51 28N 57 1W
96 Fortescue, Australia 21 4S 116 4E
96 Fortescue, R., Australia 21 20S 116 45E
14 Forth, Firth of, Scotland 56 5N 2 55W
14 Forth, R., Scot. 56 9N 4 18W
82 Forthassa Rharbia, Alg. 32 52N 1 11W
126 Fortin Corrales, Par. 22 21S 60 35W
126 Fortin Guachalla, Par. 22 22S 62 23W
126 Fortin Siracuas, Paraguay 21 3S 61 46W
124 Fortin Teniente Montania, Paraguay 22 1S 59 45W
39 Fortore, R., Italy 41 40N 15 0E
14 Fortrose, Scot. 57 35N 4 10W
33 Fortuna, Spain 38 11N 1 7W
118 Fortuna, Cal., U.S.A. 48 38N 124 8W
116 Fortuna, N.D., U.S.A. 48 55N 103 48W
107 Fortune Bay, Canada 47 30N 55 22W
104 Forty Mile, Canada 64 20N 140 30W
38 Fos, France 43 20N 4 57E
21 Fos, France 43 26N 4 57E
126 Fos do Jordão, Brazil 9 30S 72 14W
76 Foshan, China 48 32N 130 38E
39 Fossacesia, Italy 42 15N 14 30E
38 Fossano, Italy 44 39N 7 40E
118 Fossil, U.S.A. 45 0N 120 9W
98 Fossilbrook, Australia 17 47S 144 29E
39 Fossombrone, Italy 43 41N 12 49E
116 Fosston, U.S.A. 47 33N 95 39W
100 Foster, Australia 38 40S 146 15E
113 Foster, Canada 45 20N 72 30W
114 Fostoria, U.S.A. 41 8N 83 25W
18 Fougères, France 48 21N 1 14W
88 Fougamou, Gabon 1 38S 11 39E
70 Foul Pt., Sri Lanka 8 35N 81 25E
14 Foula, I., Scot. 60 10N 2 5W
93 Foulpointe, Malag. 17 41S 49 31E
82 Foum el Alba, Mali 20 45N 3 0W
82 Foum el Kreneg, Alg. 29 0N 0 58W
83 Foum Tatahouine, Tun. 32 57N 10 29E
82 Foum Zguid, Morocco 30 2N 6 59W
85 Foumban, Cameroon 5 45N 10 50E
84 Foundiougne, Senegal 14 5N 16 32W
116 Fountain, Colo., U.S.A. 38 42N 104 40W
118 Fountain, Utah, U.S.A. 39 41N 111 50W
19 Fourchambault, France 47 0N 3 3E
107 Fourchu, Canada 45 43N 60 17W
19 Fourmies, France 50 1N 4 2E
45 Fournás, Greece 39 3N 21 52E
45 Foúrnoi, Greece 37 36N 26 32E
19 Fours, France 46 50N 3 42E
84 Fouta Djalon, Guinea 11 20N 12 10W
121 Foux, Cap-à-, Haiti 19 43N 73 27W
101 Foveaux Str., N.Z. 46 42S 168 10E
119 Fowler, Calif., U.S.A. 36 41N 119 47W
116 Fowler, Colo., U.S.A. 38 10N 104 0W
117 Fowler, Kans., U.S.A. 37 28N 100 7W
96 Fowlers Bay, Austral. 32 0S 132 29E
117 Fowlerton, U.S.A. 28 26N 98 50W
77 Fowling, China 27 8N 117 12E
77 Fowling, China 29 39N 107 29E
109 Fox Valley, Canada 50 30N 109 25W
105 Foxe Basin, Canada 68 30N 77 0W
105 Foxe Channel, Canada 66 0N 80 0W
105 Foxe Pen., Canada 65 0N 76 0W
48 Foxen, L., Sweden 59 25N 11 55E
118 Foxpark, U.S.A. 41 4N 106 6W
101 Foxton, New Zealand 40 29S 175 18E
15 Foyle, Lough, Northern Ireland 55 6N 7 8W
30 Foz, Spain 43 33N 7 20W
92 Foz do Cunene, Angola 17 15S 11 55E
126 Foz do Gregório, Brazil 6 47S 71 0W
125 Foz do Iguaçu, Brazil 25 30S 54 30W
113 Frackville, U.S.A. 40 46N 76 15W
32 Fraga, Spain 41 32N 0 21E
113 Framlingham, U.S.A. 42 18N 71 26W
127 Franca, Brazil 20 25S 47 30W
39 Francavilla al Mare, It. 42 25N 14 16E
41 Francavilla Fontana, It. 40 32N 17 35E
17 France ■, Europe 47 0N 3 0E
108 Frances L., Canada 61 30N 129 20W
96 Frances Creek, Australia 13 40S 131 40E
88 Franche Comté ♦, France 46 30N 5 50E
107 Francis Harbour, Can. 52 34N 55 44W
82 Francis-Garnier, Algeria 36 30N 1 30E
120 Francisco I. Madero, Coahuila, Mexico 25 48N 103 18W
41 Francofonte, Italy 37 13N 14 50E
108 Francois L., Canada 54 0N 125 30W
16 Franeker, Netherlands 53 12N 5 33E
87 Frankado, Fr. Terr. of the Afars & Issas 12 30N 43 12E
24 Frankenberg, Germany 51 3N 8 47E
25 Frankenthal, Germany 49 32N 8 21E
114 Frankfort, Ind., U.S.A. 40 20N 86 33W
116 Frankfort, Kans., U.S.A. 39 42N 96 26W
114 Frankfort, Ky., U.S.A. 38 12N 85 44W
114 Frankfort, Mich., U.S.A. 44 38N 86 14W
24 Frankfurt ♦, E. Ger. 52 30N 14 0E
25 Frankfurt am Main, Germany 50 7N 8 40E
24 Frankfurt an der Oder, Germany 52 50N 14 31E
25 Fränkische Alb, Germany 49 20N 11 30E
25 Fränkische Saale, R., Ger. 50 7N 9 49E
25 Fränkische Schweiz, E. Ger. 49 45N 11 10E
115 Franklin, Ky., U.S.A. 36 40N 86 30W
117 Franklin, La., U.S.A. 29 45N 91 30W
113 Franklin, Mass., U.S.A. 42 4N 71 23W
116 Franklin, Nebr., U.S.A. 40 9N 98 55W
113 Franklin, N.H., U.S.A. 43 28N 71 39W
113 Franklin, N.J., U.S.A. 41 9N 74 38W
112 Franklin, Pa., U.S.A. 41 22N 79 45W
115 Franklin, Tenn., U.S.A. 35 54N 86 53W
115 Franklin, Va., U.S.A. 36 40N 76 58W
114 Franklin, W. Va., U.S.A. 38 38N 79 21W
5 Franklin I., Antarctica 76 10S 168 30E
118 Franklin, L., U.S.A. 40 20N 115 26W
104 Franklin Mts., Canada 66 0N 125 0W
104 Franklin Str., Canada 72 0N 96 0W
105 Franklin ♦, Canada 71 0N 99 0W
118 Franklin D. Roosevelt L., U.S.A. 48 30N 118 16W
117 Franklinton, U.S.A. 30 53N 90 10W
112 Franklinville, U.S.A. 42 21N 78 28W
118 Franks Peak, U.S.A. 43 50N 109 5W
100 Frankston, Australia 38 8S 145 8E
48 Fränsta, Sweden 62 30N 16 11E
58 Frantsa Iosifa, Zemlya, U.S.S.R. 76 0N 62 0E
106 Franz, Canada 48 25N 84 30W
4 Franz Josef Fd., Green 73 20N 22 0E
58 Franz Josef Land = Frantsa Iosifa, USSR 76 0N 62 0E
24 Franzburg, Germany 54 9N 12 52E
40 Frascati, Italy 41 48N 12 41E
99 Fraser I., Australia 25 15S 153 10E
108 Fraser L., Canada 54 0N 124 50W
99 Fraser (Great Sandy) I., Australia 25 15S 153 0E
108 Fraser, R., Canada 53 30N 120 40W
92 Fraserburg, S. Africa 31 55S 21 30E
14 Fraserburgh, Scot. 57 41N 2 0W
106 Fraserdale, Canada 49 55N 81 30W
44 Frashëri, Albania 40 23N 20 26E
19 Frasne, France 46 50N 6 10E
106 Frater, Canada 47 20N 84 25W
25 Frauenfeld, Switzerland 47 34N 8 54E
124 Fray Bentos, Uruguay 33 10S 58 15W
30 Frechilla, Spain 42 8N 4 50W
49 Fredericia, Denmark 55 34N 9 45E
114 Frederick, Md., U.S.A. 39 25N 77 23W
117 Frederick, Okla., U.S.A. 34 22N 99 0W
116 Frederick, S.D., U.S.A. 45 55N 98 29W
98 Frederick Reef, Australia 20 58S 154 23E
109 Frederick Sd., Alaska 57 10N 134 0W
117 Fredericksburg, Tex., U.S.A. 30 17N 98 55W
114 Fredericksburg, Va., U.S.A. 38 16N 77 29W
117 Frederickstown, U.S.A. 37 35N 90 15W
107 Fredericton, Canada 45 57N 66 40W
107 Fredericton Junc., Can. 45 41N 66 40W
48 Frederiksberg, Sweden 60 12N 14 25E
49 Frederiksborg Amt ♦, Den. 55 50N 12 10E
4 Frederikshåb, Green. 62 0N 49 30W
49 Frederikshavn, Den. 57 28N 10 31E
4 Frederikshåb, Green. 62 0N 49 50W
49 Frederikssund, Den. 55 50N 12 3E
121 Frederiksted, Virgin Is. 17 43N 64 53W
119 Fredonia, Ariz., U.S.A. 36 59N 112 36W
117 Fredonia, Kans., U.S.A. 37 34N 95 50W
112 Fredonia, N.Y., U.S.A. 42 26N 79 20W
47 Fredrikstad, Norway 59 13N 10 57E
113 Freehold, U.S.A. 40 15N 74 18W
113 Freeland, U.S.A. 41 3N 75 48W
96 Freeling, Mt., Australia 22 35S 133 06E
116 Freeman, U.S.A. 43 25N 97 20W
107 Freeport, Canada 44 15N 66 20W
116 Freeport, Ill., U.S.A. 42 18N 89 40W
117 Freeport, Tex., U.S.A. 28 55N 95 22W
84 Freetown, Sierra Leone 8 30N 13 10W
31 Fregenal de la Sierra, Spain 38 10N 6 39W
40 Fregene, Italy 41 50N 12 12E
18 Fréhel C., France 48 40N 2 20W
24 Freiberg, Germany 50 55N 13 20E
96 Freeling, Mt., Australia 22 35S 133 6E
25 Freibourg = Fribourg, Switz. 46 49N 7 9E
25 Freiburg, Baden, Ger. 48 0N 7 52E
24 Freiburg, Sachsen, Ger. 53 49N 9 17E
128 Freire, Chile 39 0S 72 50W
124 Freirina, Chile 28 30S 70 27W
25 Freising, Germany 48 24N 11 47E
26 Freistadt, Austria 48 30N 14 30E
24 Freital, Germany 51 0N 13 40E
21 Fréjus, France 43 25N 6 44E
96 Fremantle, Austral. 32 1S 115 47E
114 Fremont, Mich., U.S.A. 43 29N 85 59W
116 Fremont, Nebr., U.S.A. 41 30N 96 30W
114 Fremont, Ohio, U.S.A. 41 20N 83 5W
118 Fremont, L., U.S.A. 43 0N 109 50W
119 Fremont, R., U.S.A. 38 15N 110 20W
112 French Cr., U.S.A. 41 30N 80 2W
127 French Guiana ■, S. Amer. 4 0N 53 0W
100 French I., Australia 28 24S 145 25E
101 French Pass, N.Z. 40 55S 173 55E
87 French Terr. of the Afars & Issas ■, Afr. 11 30N 42 15E
118 Frenchglen, U.S.A. 42 56N 119 0W
109 Frenchman Butte, Can. 53 36N 109 36W
118 Frenchman, R., Canada 49 25N 108 20W
116 Frenchman Cr., U.S.A. 40 34N 101 35W
82 Frenda, Algeria 35 2N 1 1E
127 Fresco, R., Brazil 7 15S 51 30W
5 Freshfield, C., Antarc. 68 25S 151 10E
120 Fresnillo, Mexico 23 10N 103 0W
119 Fresno, U.S.A. 36 47N 119 50W
118 Fresno Res., U.S.A. 48 47N 110 0W
30 Fresno Alhandiga, Sp. 40 42N 5 37W
25 Freudenstadt, Germany 48 27N 8 25E
19 Frévent, France 50 15N 2 17E
99 Freycinet Pen., Austral. 42 10S 148 25E
84 Fria, Guinea 10 27N 13 32W
124 Frias, Argentina 28 40S 65 5W
25 Fribourg, Switzerland 46 49N 7 9E
25 Fribourg ♦, Switz. 45 40N 7 0E
49 Fridafors, Sweden 56 25N 14 39E
25 Friedberg, Bayern, Ger. 48 21N 10 59E
2 Friedberg, Hessen, Ger. 50 19N 8 45E
25 Friedland, Germany 53 40N 13 33E
25 Friedrichshafen, Ger. 47 39N 9 29E
24 Friedrichskoog, Ger. 54 1N 8 52E
24 Friedrichsort, Germany 54 24N 10 11E
24 Friedrichstadt, Germany 54 23N 9 6E
101 Friendly (Tonga) Is., Pacific Ocean 19 50S 174 30W
26 Friesach, Austria 46 57N 14 24E
24 Friesack, Germany 52 43N 12 35E
16 Friesland ♦, Neth. 53 5N 5 50E
24 Friesoythe, Germany 53 1N 7 51E
106 Frigate, L., Canada 53 15N 74 45W
120 Frijoles, Panama Canal Zone 9 11N 79 48W
49 Frillesås, Sweden 57 20N 12 12E
49 Frinnaryd, Sweden 57 55N 14 50E
92 Frio, C., S.W. Africa 18 0S 12 0E
117 Frio, R., U.S.A. 29 40N 99 40W
117 Friona, U.S.A. 34 40N 102 42W
49 Fristad, Sweden 57 50N 13 0E
117 Fritch, U.S.A. 35 40N 101 35W
49 Fritsla, Sweden 57 33N 12 47E
24 Fritzlar, Germany 51 8N 9 19E
39 Fruili-Venezia-Giulia ♦, Italy 46 0N 13 0E
105 Frobisher B., Canada 63 0N 67 0W
109 Frobisher, L., Canada 56 30N 108 0W
105 Frobisher Sd., Canada 62 30N 66 0W
116 Froid, U.S.A. 48 20N 104 29W
57 Frolovo, U.S.S.R. 49 45N 43 30E
118 Fromberg, U.S.A. 45 19N 108 58W
28 Frombork, Poland 54 21N 19 41E
13 Frome, England 51 16N 2 17W
99 Frome, L., Australia 30 45S 139 45E
99 Frome Downs, Austral. 31 12S 139 48W
18 Fromentine, France 46 53N 2 9W
30 Frómista, Spain 42 16N 4 25W
118 Front Range, U.S.A. 40 0N 105 10W
114 Front Royal, U.S.A. 38 55N 78 10W
31 Fronteira, Portugal 39 3N 7 39W
120 Frontera, Mexico 18 30N 92 40W
20 Frontignan, France 43 27N 3 45E
40 Frosinone, Italy 41 38N 13 20E
41 Frosolone, Italy 41 34N 14 27E
114 Frostburg, U.S.A. 39 43N 78 57W
50 Frostisen, Norway 68 14N 17 10E
19 Frouard, France 48 47N 6 8E
48 Frövi, Sweden 59 28N 15 24E
50 Fröya I., Norway 63 45N 8 45E
47 Froya, Norway 63 43N 8 40E
19 Fruges, France 50 30N 2 8E
46 Frumoasa, Rumania 46 28N 25 48E
58 Frunze, U.S.S.R. 42 40N 74 50E
42 Fruška Gora, Yugoslavia 45 7N 19 30E
127 Frutal, Brazil 20 0S 49 0W
25 Frutigen, Switzerland 46 35N 7 38E
27 Frýdek-Místek, Cz. 49 40N 18 20E
26 Frýdlant, Severočeský, Cz. 50 56N 15 9E
27 Frýdlant, Severomoravsky, Cz. 49 35N 18 20E
27 Fryvaldov = Jesenik, Cz. 50 0N 17 8E
25 Fränkische, Alb, Germany 49 23N 11 30E
25 Fränkische Saale, Germany 50 7N 9 49E
48 Fränsta, Sweden 62 30N 16 11E
48 Frövi, Sweden 59 28N 15 22E
47 Fröya, Sör-Tröndelag, Norway 63 43N 8 40E
45 Fthiótis ♦, Greece 38 50N 22 25E
48 Fu, Sweden 60 57N 14 44E
38 Fucécchio, Italy 43 44N 10 51E
76 Fuchin, China 47 10N 132 0E
77 Fuchow, Kiangsi, China 27 50N 116 14E
76 Fuchow, Liaoning, China 39 45N 121 45E
77 Fuchun K., China 30 1N 120 1E
77 Fuchung, China 24 25N 110 16E
20 Fucino, L., Italy 42 0N 13 30E
31 Fuencaliente, Spain 38 25N 4 18W
31 Fuengirola, Spain 36 32N 4 41W
33 Fuente-Alamo, Spain 38 44N 1 24W
31 Fuente de Cantos, Sp. 38 15N 6 18W
31 Fuente del Maestre, Sp. 38 31N 6 28W
31 Fuente el Fresno, Spain 39 14N 3 46W
31 Fuente Ovejuna, Spain 38 15N 5 25W
31 Fuentes de Andalucia, Spain 37 28N 5 20W
32 Fuentes de Ebro, Spain 41 31N 0 38W
31 Fuentes de León, Spain 38 5N 6 32W
30 Fuentes de Oñoro, Sp. 40 33N 6 52W
30 Fuentesaúco, Spain 41 15N 5 30W
120 Fuerte, R., Mexico 26 0N 109 0W
124 Fuerte Olimpo, Par. 21 0S 58 0W
80 Fuerteventura, I., Canary Is. 28 30N 14 0W
77 Fuga, I., Philippines 19 55N 121 10E
50 Fuglöysund, Norway 70 15N 20 20E
65 Fujaira, Trucial States 25 7N 56 18E
74 Fuji San, Japan 35 20N 138 40E
74 Fuji-no-miya, Japan 35 20N 138 40E
77 Fukien ♦, China 26 0N 117 30E
77 Fukow, China 34 11N 114 36E
74 Fukuchiyama, Japan 35 25N 135 9E
74 Fukui, Japan 36 0N 136 10E
74 Fukui-ken ♦, Japan 36 0N 136 12E
74 Fukuoka, Japan 33 30N 130 30E
74 Fukuoka-ken ♦, Japan 33 30N 131 0E
74 Fukushima-ken ♦, Japan 37 30N 140 15E
74 Fukuyama, Japan 34 35N 133 20E
24 Fulda, Germany 50 32N 9 41E
119 Fullerton, Calif., U.S.A. 33 52N 117 58W
116 Fullerton, Nebr., U.S.A. 41 25N 98 0W

MAP

27 Fülöpszállás, Hungary 46 49N 19 16E
116 Fulton, Mo., U.S.A. 38 50N 91 55w
113 Fulton, N.Y., U.S.A. 43 20N 76 22w
48 Fululälven, Sweden 61 18N 13 4E
48 Fulufjället, Sweden 61 32N 12 41E
27 Fülöpszállás, Hungary 46 49N 19 16E
19 Fumay, France 50 0N 4 40E
10 Fumbusi, Ghana 10 25N 1 20w
20 Fumel, France 44 30N 0 58E
74 Funabashi, Japan 35 45N 140 0E
94 Funafuti, I., Pac. Oc. 8 30s 179 0E
80 Funchal, Madeira 32 45N 16 55w
126 Fundación, Colombia 10 31N 74 11w
30 Fundão, Portugal 40 8N 7 30w
91 Fundu, Zambia 14 58s 30 14E
45 Fundy, B. of, Canada 45 0N 66 0w
126 Funes, Colombia 1 0N 77 28w
77 Fungchun, China 23 27N 111 30E
77 Funing, China 23 45N 105 30E
77 Funiu Shan, China 33 40N 112 30E
85 Funsi, Ghana 10 21N 1 54w
85 Funtua, Nigeria 11 30N 7 18E
49 Fur, Denmark 56 50N 9 0E
64 Furat, Nahr al, Asia 33 30N 43 0E
55 Furmanov, U.S.S.R. 57 25N 41 3E
55 Furmanovo, U.S.S.R. 49 42N 49 25E
99 Furneaux Group, Australia 40 10s 147 50E
12 Furness, England 54 14N 3 8w
25 Fürstenau, Germany 52 32N 7 40E
26 Fürstenfeld, Austria 47 3N 16 3E
25 Fürstenfeldbruck, Ger. 48 10N 11 15E
25 Fürstenwalde, Ger. 52 20N 14 3E
25 Fürth, Germany 49 29N 11 0E
25 Fürth i. Wald, Ger. 49 19N 12 51E
25 Furtwangen, Germany 48 3N 8 14E
48 Furudal, Sweden 61 10N 15 11E
48 Furusund, Sweden 59 40N 18 55E
105 Fury and Hecla Str., Canada 69 40N 81 0w
47 Fusa, Norway 60 12N 5 37E
84 Fusagasugá, Colombia 4 21N 74 22w
41 Fuscaldo, Italy 39 25N 16 1E
74 Fuse, Japan 34 40N 135 37E
44 Fushë Arrëzi, Albania 42 4N 20 2E
76 Fushun, China 42 0N 123 59E
76 Fusin, China 42 12N 121 33E
25 Füssen, Germany 47 12N 121 33E
77 Fusui, China 22 35N 107 58E
77 Futing, China 27 15N 120 10E
77 Futsing, China 25 46N 119 29E
85 Futuk, Nigeria 9 45N 10 56E
86 Fuwa, Egypt 31 12N 30 33E
77 Fuyang Ho, China 38 14N 116 5E
76 Fuyuan, China 48 9N 134 3E
47 Füzesgyarmat, Hung. 47 6N 21 14E
75 Fyekundo = Yushu, China 33 6N 96 48E
49 Fyn, Denmark 55 20N 10 30E
14 Fyne, L., Scot. 56 0N 5 20w
49 Fyns Amt ♦, Denmark 55 15N 10 30E
49 Fyresvatn, Denmark 54 59N 9 59E
47 Fyresvatn, Norway 59 6N 8 10E
85 Gaanda, Nigeria 10 10N 12 27E
87 Gaba, Ethiopia 6 20N 35 7E
56 Gaba Tula, Kenya 0 20N 38 35E
63 Gabah, C., Somali Rep. 8 0N 50 0w
85 Gabarin, Nigeria 11 8N 10 27E
88 Gabela, Angola 11 0s 14 37E
92 Gaberones = Gaborone, Botswana 24 37s 25 57E
85 Gabès, Tunisia 33 53N 10 2E
83 Gabès, Golfe de, Tunisia 34 0N 10 30E
86 Gabgaba, W., Egypt 22 10N 33 5E
82 Gabin, Poland 52 23N 19 41E
100 Gabo I., Australia 37 33s 149 57E
92 Gabon ■, Africa 0 10s 10 0E
92 Gaborone, Botswana 24 37s 25 57E
43 Gabriels, U.S.A. 44 26N 74 12w
43 Gabrovo, Bulgaria 42 52N 25 27E
18 Gacé, France 48 49N 0 20E
65 Gach Saran, Iran 30 15N 50 45E
42 Gacko, Yugoslavia 43 10N 18 33E
85 Gada, Nigeria 13 38N 5 36E
70 Gadag, India 15 30N 75 45E
87 Gadamai, Sudan 17 11N 36 10E
68 Gadap, Pakistan 25 5N 67 28E
68 Gadarwara, India 22 50N 78 50E
50 Gäddede, Sweden 64 30N 14 15E
24 Gadebusch, Germany 53 41N 11 6E
87 Gadein, Sudan 8 10N 28 45E
68 Gadhada, India 22 0N 71 35E
36 Gádor, Sierra de, Spain 36 57N 2 45w
115 Gadsden, Ala., U.S.A. 34 1N 86 0w
119 Gadsden, Ariz., U.S.A. 32 35N 114 47w
70 Gadwal, India 16 10N 77 50E
46 Găeşti, Rumania 44 48N 25 19E
40 Gaeta, Italy 41 12N 13 35E
41 Gaeta, G. di, Italy 41 0N 13 25E
115 Gaffney, U.S.A. 35 10N 81 31w
83 Gafsa, Tunisia 34 24N 8 51E
54 Gagarin (Gzhatsk), U.S.S.R. 55 30N 35 0E
107 Gagetown, Canada 45 46N 66 29w
55 Gagino, U.S.S.R. 55 15N 45 1E
41 Gagliano del Capo, It. 39 50N 18 23E
48 Gagnef, Sweden 60 36N 15 5E
84 Gagnoa, Ivory Coast 6 4N 5 55w
107 Gagnon, Canada 51 50N 68 5w
109 Gagnon, L., Canada 61 55N 110 40w
89 Gago Coutinho, Angola 14 18s 21 18E
92 Gagra, U.S.S.R. 43 12N 40 10E
20 Gah, France 43 12N 0 7E
69 Gahini, Rwanda 1 50s 30 30E
69 Gahmar, India 25 27N 83 55E
69 Gaibandha, Bangladesh 25 20N 89 36E
45 Gaïdhouronísi, Gr. 34 53N 25 41E
117 Gail, U.S.A. 32 48N 101 25w
18 Gail, R., Austria 46 37N 13 15E
20 Gaillac, Tarn, France 43 54N 1 54E

18 Gaillon, France 49 10N 1 20E
112 Gaines, U.S.A. 41 45N 77 35w
115 Gainesville, Fla., U.S.A. 29 38N 82 20w
115 Gainesville, Ga., U.S.A. 34 17N 83 47w
117 Gainesville, Mo., U.S.A. 36 35N 92 26w
117 Gainesville, Tex., U.S.A. 33 40N 97 10w
12 Gainsborough, England 53 23N 0 46w
14 Gairloch L., Scot. 57 43N 5 45w
42 Gaj, Yugoslavia 45 28N 17 3E
85 Gajale, Nigeria 11 25N 8 10E
85 Gajiram, Nigeria 12 29N 13 9E
70 Gal Oya Res., Sri Lanka 8 5N 80 55E
69 Galachipa, Bangladesh 22 8N 90 26E
85 Galadí, Nigeria 13 5N 6 20E
90 Galana, R., Kenya 3 0s 39 10E
89 Galangue, Angola 13 48s 16 3E
27 Galanta, Czechoslovakia 48 11N 17 45E
95 Galápagos, Is., Pac. Oc. 0 0 89 0w
71 Galas, R., Malaya 4 55N 101 57E
14 Galashiels, Scot. 55 37N 2 50w
45 Galatás, Greece 37 30N 23 26E
46 Galaţi, Rumania 45 27N 28 2E
46 Galaţi ♦, Rumania 45 45N 27 30E
41 Galatina, Italy 40 10N 18 10E
41 Galátone, Italy 40 8N 18 3E
115 Galax, U.S.A. 36 42N 80 57w
45 Galaxidhion, Greece 38 22N 22 23E
98 Galbraith, Australia 16 25s 141 30E
47 Galdhöpiggen, Nor 61 38N 8 18E
73 Galela, Indonesia 1 50N 127 55E
33 Galera, Spain 37 45N 2 33w
126 Galera, Pta. de la, Col. 10 48N 75 16w
116 Galesburg, U.S.A. 40 57N 90 23w
112 Galeton, U.S.A. 41 43N 77 40w
46 Galicea Mare, Rumania 44 4N 23 19E
55 Galich, R.S.F.S.R., U.S.S.R. 58 23N 42 18E
54 Galich, Uk., U.S.S.R. 49 10N 24 40E
43 Galiche, Bulgaria 43 34N 23 50E
30 Galicia, Spain 42 43N 8 0w
32 Galilee = Hagalil, Israel 32 53N 35 18E
112 Galion, U.S.A. 40 43N 82 48w
83 Galite, Is. de la, Tunisia 37 30N 8 59E
119 Galivro Mts., U.S.A. 32 40N 110 30w
38 Gallarate, Italy 45 40N 8 48E
115 Gallatin, U.S.A. 36 24N 86 27w
70 Galle, Sri Lanka 6 5N 80 10E
128 Gállego, R., Spain 42 23N 0 30w
128 Gallegos, R., Argentina 51 50s 71 0w
41 Galliate, Italy 45 27N 8 44E
126 Gallinas, Pta., Col. 12 28N 71 40w
41 Gallipoli, Italy 40 8N 18 0E
44 Gallipoli = Gelibolu, Turkey 40 28N 26 43E
114 Gallipolis, U.S.A. 38 50N 82 10w
112 Gallitzin, U.S.A. 40 28N 78 32w
50 Gallivare, Sweden 67 7N 20 32E
48 Gällö, Sweden 62 56N 15 15E
40 Gallo, C. di, Italy 38 13N 13 19E
32 Gallocanta, Laguna de, Spain 40 58N 1 30w
14 Galloway, Scotland 55 0N 4 25w
14 Galloway, Mull of, Scotland 54 38N 4 50w
119 Gallup, U.S.A. 35 30N 108 54w
32 Gallur, Spain 41 52N 1 19w
85 Galmi, Niger 13 58N 5 41E
62 Gal'on, Israel 31 38N 34 51E
100 Galong, Australia 34 37s 148 34E
106 Galt, Canada 43 21N 80 19w
48 Galtström, Sweden 62 10N 17 30E
26 Galtür, Austria 46 58N 10 11E
15 Galty Mts., Ireland 52 22N 8 10w
15 Galtymore, Mt., Ireland 52 22N 8 12w
73 Galumpang, Indonesia 2 32s 119 32E
116 Galva, U.S.A. 41 10N 90 0w
32 Galve de Sorbe, Spain 41 13N 3 10w
117 Galveston, U.S.A. 29 15N 94 48w
117 Galveston B., U.S.A. 29 30N 94 50w
124 Gálvez, Argentina 32 0s 61 20w
31 Gálvez, Spain 39 42N 4 16w
15 Galway, Ireland 53 16N 9 4w
15 Galway ♦, Ireland 53 16N 9 20w
15 Galway ♦, Ireland 53 10N 9 3w
43 Galyamo Konare, Bulg. 42 16N 24 33E
87 Gamare, L., Ethiopia 11 32N 41 40E
126 Gamarra, Colombia 8 20N 73 45w
85 Gamawa, Nigeria 12 10N 10 31E
85 Gambaga, Ghana 10 30N 0 28w
68 Gambat, Pakistan 27 17N 68 26E
87 Gambela, Ethiopia 8 14N 34 38E
85 Gambia, R., & ■ W. Africa 13 20N 15 45w
120 Gamboa, Panama Canal Zone 9 8N 79 42w
68 Gamboli, Pakistan 29 53N 68 24E
88 Gamboma, Congo (Fr.) 1 55s 15 52E
98 Gamboola, Australia 16 29s 143 43E
127 Gameleira, Brazil 7 50s 35 0w
119 Gamerco, U.S.A. 35 33N 108 56w
49 Gamleby, Sweden 57 54N 16 20E
127 Gammelgarn, Sweden 57 24N 18 49E
73 Gamsungi, Indonesia 0 20N 128 50E
61 Gan (Addu Atoll), Indian Ocean 0 10s 71 10E
62 Gan Shemu'el, Israel 32 28N 34 56E
62 Gan Yavne, Israel 31 48N 34 42E
119 Ganado, Ariz., U.S.A. 35 46N 109 41w
117 Ganado, Tex., U.S.A. 29 4N 96 31w
106 Gananoque, Canada 44 20N 76 10w
65 Ganaveh, Iran 29 35N 50 35E
68 Ganak, R., India 28 0N 67 32E
68 Gandava, Pakistan 28 32N 67 32E
107 Gander, Canada 48 58N 54 35w
107 Gander L., Canada 48 58N 54 45w
73 Ganderowe Falls, Rhod. 17 20s 29 10E
32 Gandesa, Spain 41 3N 0 26E
68 Gandhi Sagar, India 24 40N 75 40E
85 Gandi, Nigeria 12 55N 5 49E
33 Gandia, Spain 38 58N 0 9w
38 Gandino, Italy 45 50N 9 52E

85 Gandole, Nigeria 8 28N 11 35E
73 Ganedidalem = Gani, Indon. 0 48s 128 14E
86 Ganetti, Sudan 18 0N 31 10E
69 Ganga, R., India 25 0N 88 0E
69 Ganga, Mouths of the, India 21 30N 90 0E
68 Ganganagar, India 29 56N 73 56E
68 Gangapur, India 26 32N 76 37E
85 Gangara, Niger 14 35N 8 40E
70 Gangavati, India 15 30N 76 36E
67 Gangaw, Burma 22 5N 94 15E
20 Ganges, France 43 56N 3 42E
69 Ganges = Ganga, R., India 25 0N 88 0E
68 Gangoh, India 29 46N 77 18E
68 Gangtok, India 27 20N 88 40E
68 Ganj, India 27 45N 78 47E
20 Gannat, France 46 7N 3 11E
118 Gannett Pk., U.S.A. 43 15N 109 47w
116 Gannvalley, U.S.A. 44 3N 98 57w
27 Ganserdorf, Austria 48 20N 16 43E
84 Ganta (Gompa), Liberia 7 15N 8 59w
96 Gantheaume B., Australia 27 40s 114 10E
54 Gantsevichi, U.S.S.R. 52 42N 26 30E
57 Ganyushkino, U.S.S.R. 46 35N 49 20E
87 Ganzi, Sudan 4 30N 31 15E
85 Gao ♦, Mali 18 0N 1 0E
71 Gao Bang, N. Vietnam 22 37N 106 18E
84 Gaoua, Upper Volta 10 20N 3 8w
84 Gaoual, Guinea 11 45N 13 25w
82 Gaouz, Morocco 31 52N 4 20w
21 Gap, France 44 33N 6 5E
121 Garachiné, Panama 8 0N 78 12w
127 Garanhuns, Brazil 8 50s 36 30w
84 Garawe, Liberia 4 35N 8 0w
90 Garba Tula, Kenya 0 30N 38 32E
117 Garber, U.S.A. 36 30N 97 36w
118 Garberville, U.S.A. 40 11N 123 50w
46 Gârbovi, Rumania 44 47N 26 47E
21 Gard ♦, France 44 2N 4 10E
38 Garda, L. di, Italy 45 40N 10 40E
21 Gardanne, France 43 27N 5 27E
54 Gardelegen, Germany 52 32N 11 21E
117 Garden City, Kans., U.S.A. 38 0N 100 45w
117 Garden City, Tex., U.S.A. 31 52N 101 28w
65 Gardez, Afghanistan 33 31N 68 59E
45 Gardhíki, Greece 38 50N 21 55E
81 Gardinan, Chad 15 45N 19 40E
106 Gardiner, Canada 49 19N 81 2w
118 Gardiner, Mont., U.S.A. 45 3N 110 53w
117 Gardiner, New Mexico, U.S.A. 36 55N 104 29w
113 Gardiners I., U.S.A. 41 4N 72 5w
113 Gardner, U.S.A. 42 35N 72 0w
118 Gardnerville, U.S.A. 38 59N 119 47w
63 Gardo, Somali Rep. 9 18N 49 20E
42 Garešnica, Y.-slav. 45 36N 16 56E
38 Garéssio, Italy 44 12N 8 1E
118 Garfield, Utah, U.S.A. 40 45N 112 15w
118 Garfield, Wash., U.S.A. 47 3N 117 8w
45 Gargaliánoi, Greece 37 4N 21 38E
20 Gargans, Mt., France 45 37N 1 39E
106 Gargantua, C., Canada 47 35N 85 0w
85 Gargango, Mali 15 56N 0 13E
68 Garhshankar, India 31 13N 76 11E
108 Garibaldi, Canada 49 56N 123 15w
40 Garigliano, R., Italy 41 13N 13 44E
90 Garissa, Kenya 0 25s 39 40E
90 Garissa ♦, Kenya 0 20s 40 0E
85 Garkida, Nigeria 10 27N 12 36E
85 Garko, Nigeria 11 45N 8 53E
117 Garland, U.S.A. 41 47N 112 10w
38 Garlasco, Italy 45 11N 8 55E
58 Garm, U.S.S.R. 39 0N 70 20E
90 Garmo, Norway 61 51N 8 48E
65 Garmsar, Iran 35 20N 52 25E
116 Garner, U.S.A. 43 4N 93 37w
25 Garmisch- Partenkirchen, Germany 47 30N 11 5E
69 Garo Hills, India 25 30N 90 30E
63 Garoe, Somali Rep. 8 35N 48 40E
99 Garoke, Australia 36 45s 141 30E
32 Garona, R., Spain 42 55N 0 45E
20 Garonne, R., France 45 2N 0 36w
85 Garoua (Garwa), Cam. 9 19N 13 21E
24 Garrel, Germany 52 58N 7 59E
84 Garraway, Liberia 4 35N 8 0w
20 Garrigues, Fr. 43 40N 3 30E
118 Garrison, Mont., U.S.A. 46 37N 112 56w
116 Garrison, N.D., U.S.A. 47 39N 101 27w
117 Garrison, Tex., U.S.A. 31 50N 94 28w
116 Garrison Res., U.S.A. 47 30N 102 0w
31 Garrovillas, Spain 39 40N 6 33w
33 Garrucha, Spain 37 11N 1 49w
104 Garry L., Canada 65 40N 100 0w
14 Garry, R., Scot., U.K. 57 5N 4 52w
14 Garry, Glen, Scot. 57 3N 5 7w
106 Garson, Canada 50 5N 96 50w
20 Gartempe, R., France 46 47N 0 49E
87 Gartok, Sudan 5 31N 31 20E
75 Gartok, Tibet 31 59N 80 30E
20 Gartz, Germany 54 17N 13 21E
85 Garu, Ghana 10 55N 0 20w
85 Garua, Nigeria 9 19N 13 5E
92 Garub, S.W. Africa 26 37s 16 0E
127 Garupá, Brazil 1 25s 51 35w
73 Garut, Indonesia 7 14s 107 53E
31 Garvão, Portugal 37 42N 8 21w
101 Garvie Mts., N.Z. 45 27s 169 59E
69 Garwa, India 24 11N 83 47E
28 Garwolin, Poland 51 55N 21 38E
114 Gary, U.S.A. 41 35N 87 20w
126 Garzón, Colombia 2 10N 75 40w

58 Gasan Kuli, U.S.S.R. 37 40N 54 20E
20 Gascogne, France 43 45N 0 20E
20 Gascogne, G. de, France-Spain 44 0N 2 0w
20 Gascony = Gascogne, France 43 45N 0 20E
32 Gascueña, Spain 40 18N 2 31w
87 Gash, W., Ethiopia 15 0N 37 15E
85 Gashaka, Nigeria 7 20N 11 29E
75 Gashiun Nor, China 42 20N 100 40E
85 Gashua, Nigeria 12 54N 11 0E
98 Gasmata, Terr. of New Guinea 6 15s 150 30E
107 Gaspé, Canada 48 52N 64 30w
107 Gaspé, C., Canada 48 48N 64 7w
107 Gaspé Pass., Canada 49 10N 64 0w
107 Gaspé Pen., Canada 48 45N 65 40w
107 Gaspesian Prov. Park, Can. 49 0N 66 45w
114 Gassaway, U.S.A. 38 42N 80 43w
38 Gássino Torinese, Italy 45 8N 7 50E
85 Gassol, Nigeria 8 34N 10 25E
115 Gastonia, U.S.A. 35 17N 81 10w
45 Gastoúni, Greece 37 51N 21 15E
45 Gastoúri, Greece 39 34N 19 54E
128 Gastre, Argentina 42 10s 69 15w
33 Gata, C. de, Spain 36 41N 2 13w
30 Gata, Sierra de, Spain 40 20N 6 20w
42 Gátaia, Rumania 45 26N 21 30E
54 Gatchina, U.S.S.R. 59 35N 30 0E
12 Gateshead, Eng. 54 57N 1 37w
115 Gatesville, U.S.A. 31 29N 97 45w
91 Gaths, Rhodesia 26 2s 30 32E
19 Gatinais, France 48 5N 2 40E
106 Gatineau, Canada 45 28N 75 40w
106 Gatineau, R., Canada 46 20N 76 0w
38 Gattinara, Italy 45 37N 8 22E
120 Gatun, Pan. Can. Zone 9 16N 79 55w
120 Gatun Dam, Pan. Can. 9 16N 79 55w
120 Gatun, L., Panama 9 7N 79 56w
120 Gatun Locks, Pan. Can. 9 16N 79 55w
33 Gaucin, Spain 36 31N 5 19w
109 Gauer L., Canada 57 0N 97 30w
54 Gauhati, India 26 5N 91 55E
54 Gauja, R., U.S.S.R. 57 10N 24 45E
47 Gaula, R., Norway 62 57N 11 0E
43 Gaussberg, Mt., Antarc. 66 45s 89 0E
47 Gausta, Norway 59 50N 8 37E
32 Gavá, Spain 41 18N 2 0E
20 Gavarnie, France 42 44N 0 3w
25 Gavater, Iran 25 10N 61 23E
45 Gavdhopoúla, Greece 34 56N 24 0E
45 Gavdhos, Greece 34 50N 24 5E
31 Gavião, Portugal 39 28N 7 56w
48 Gävleborgs Län ♦, Sweden 61 20N 16 15E
38 Gavorrano, Italy 42 55N 10 55E
18 Gavray, France 49 55N 1 20w
55 Gavrilov Yam, U.S.S.R. 57 10N 39 37E
45 Gávrion, Greece 37 54N 24 44E
92 Gawachab, S.W. Afr. 27 4s 17 55E
68 Gawilgarh Hills, India 21 15N 76 45E
99 Gawler, Australia 34 30s 138 42E
96 Gawler Ranges, Australia 32 30s 135 45E
69 Gaya, India 24 47N 85 4E
85 Gaya, Niger 11 58N 3 28E
85 Gaya, Nigeria 11 57N 9 0E
84 Gayéri, Upper Volta 12 9N 0 11E
62 Gaza, Egypt 31 30N 34 28E
93 Gaza ♦, Mozambique 23 10s 32 45E
62 Gaza Strip, Egypt 31 29N 34 25E
85 Gazaoua, Niger 13 32N 7 55E
98 Gazelle Pen., New Guin. 4 30s 152 0E
92 Gazi, Zaïre 1 3N 24 30E
64 Gaziantep, Turkey 37 6N 37 23E
85 Gbanga, Liberia 7 19N 9 13w
85 Gbekebo, Nigeria 6 26N 4 48E
85 Gboko, Nigeria 7 17N 9 4E
85 Gbongan, Nigeria 7 28N 4 20E
28 Gdansk, Pol. 54 22N 18 40E
28 Gdansk ♦, Poland 54 10N 18 30E
28 Gdanska, Zatoka, Poland 54 30N 19 20E
54 Gdov, U.S.S.R. 58 40N 27 55E
28 Gdynia, Poland 54 35N 18 33E
73 Gebe, I., Indonesia 0 5N 129 25E
86 Gebeit Mine, Sudan 21 3N 36 29E
20 Gebze, Turkey 40 47N 29 25E
87 Gecoa, Ethiopia 7 30N 35 18E
87 Gedaref, Sudan 14 2N 35 28E
62 Gederra, Israel 31 49N 34 46E
87 Gedo, Ethiopia 9 2N 37 25E
20 Gèdre, France 42 47N 0 2E
49 Gedser, Denmark 54 35N 11 55E
49 Gedser Odde, C., Den. 54 30N 11 5E
100 Geelong, Australia 38 2s 144 20E
99 Geeraardsbergen, Belg. 50 45N 3 53E
24 Geesthacht, Germany 53 31N 8 51E
90 Geh, Iran 26 10N 60 0E
62 Geita, Israel 32 49N 35 30E
90 Geita ♦, Tanz. 2 50s 32 10E
87 Gel River, Sudan 7 5N 29 10E
87 Gel, R., Sudan 7 5N 29 10E
33 Gela, Golfo di, Italy 37 0N 14 8E
63 Geladi, Ethiopia 6 59N 46 30E
16 Gelderland ♦, Netherlands 52 5N 6 10E
24 Geldern, Germany 51 32N 6 18E
16 Geldrop, Netherlands 51 25N 5 32E

16 Geleen, Netherlands 50 57N 5 49E
84 Gelehun, Sierra Leone 8 10N 10 50w
56 Gelendzhik, U.S.S.R. 44 33N 38 17E
44 Gelibolu, Turkey 40 28N 26 43E
25 Gelnhausen, Germany 50 12N 9 12E
24 Gelsenkirchen, Ger. 51 30N 7 5E
24 Gelting, Germany 54 43N 9 53E
71 Gemas, Malaysia 2 37N 102 36E
16 Gembloux, Belgium 50 34N 4 43E
100 Gembrook, Australia 37 58s 145 37E
85 Gembu, Nigeria 8 58N 12 31E
88 Gemena, Zaïre 3 20N 19 40E
64 Gemerek, Turkey 39 15N 36 10E
92 Gemiston, S. Africa 26 15s 28 10E
64 Gemlik, Turkey 40 28N 29 13E
39 Gemona del Friuli, Italy 46 16N 13 7E
86 Gemsa, Egypt 27 39N 33 35E
87 Gemu-Gofa ♦, Ethiopia 5 40N 36 40E
25 Gemünden, Germany 50 3N 9 43E
87 Genale, Ethiopia 6 0N 39 30E
20 Gençay, France 46 23N 0 23E
16 Gendringen, Neth. 51 52N 6 21E
86 Geneina, Gebel, Egypt 29 2N 33 55E
124 General Acha, Arg. 37 20s 64 38w
124 Gen. Alvear, B. A., Arg. 36 0s 60 0w
124 Gen. Alvear, Mend., Arg. 35 0s 67 40w
124 General Artigas, Par. 26 52s 56 16w
124 General Belgrano, Arg. 36 0s 58 30w
124 General Cabrera, Arg. 32 53s 63 58w
124 General Guido, Arg. 36 40s 57 50w
124 Gen. Juan Madariaga, Argentina 37 0s 57 0w
124 General La Madrid, Arg. 37 30s 61 0w
73 General MacArthur, Phil. 11 18N 125 28E
124 General Martin Miguel de Güemes, Arg. 24 50s 65 0w
124 General Paz, Argentina 27 45s 57 36w
128 General Paz, L., Chile 44 0s 72 0w
124 General Pico, Argentina 35 45s 63 50w
124 General Pinedo, Arg. 27 15s 61 30w
124 General Pinto, Arg. 34 45s 61 50w
124 General Roca, Arg. 30 0s 67 40w
73 General Santos, Philippines 6 12N 125 14E
124 General Viamonte, Arg. 35 1s 61 3w
124 General Villegas, Arg. 35 0s 63 0w
118 Genesee, Idaho, U.S.A. 46 31N 116 59w
112 Genesee, Mich., U.S.A. 43 7N 83 38w
112 Genesee, Pa., U.S.A. 42 0N 77 54w
112 Genesee, R., U.S.A. 41 35N 78 0w
116 Geneseo, Ill., U.S.A. 41 25N 90 10w
117 Geneseo, Kans., U.S.A. 38 32N 98 8w
112 Geneseo, N.Y., U.S.A. 42 49N 77 49w
25 Geneva = Genève, Switz. 46 12N 6 9E
115 Geneva, Ala., U.S.A. 31 2N 85 52w
116 Geneva, Nebr., U.S.A. 40 35N 97 35w
112 Geneva, N.Y., U.S.A. 42 53N 77 0w
112 Geneva, Ohio, U.S.A. 41 49N 80 58w
114 Geneva, L., U.S.A. 42 38N 88 30w
25 Geneva, L. = Léman, L. 46 26N 6 30E
25 Genève, Switz. 46 12N 6 9E
25 Genève ♦, Switz. 46 10N 6 10E
25 Gengenbach, Germany 48 25N 8 0E
56 Genichesk, U.S.S.R. 46 12N 34 50E
31 Genil, R., Spain 37 12N 3 50w
25 Génissiat, Barrage de, France 46 1N 5 48E
16 Genk, Belgium 50 58N 5 32E
19 Genlis, France 47 15N 5 12E
16 Gennep, Netherlands 51 41N 5 59E
18 Gennes, France 47 20N 0 17w
38 Genoa = Génova, Italy 44 24N 8 57E
116 Genoa, Nebr., U.S.A. 41 31N 97 44w
113 Genoa, N.Y., U.S.A. 42 40N 76 32w
100 Genoa, Australia 37 28s 149 35E
100 Genoa, R., Australia 37 25s 149 30E
38 Génova, Italy 44 24N 8 56E
38 Génova, Golfo di, Italy 44 0N 9 0E
16 Gent, Belgium 51 2N 3 37E
73 Genteng, Indonesia 7 25s 106 23E
24 Genthin, Germany 52 24N 12 10E
98 Geographe B., Australia 33 30s 115 15E
96 Geographe Chan., Australia 24 30s 113 0E
57 Geokchay, U.S.S.R. 40 42N 47 43E
107 George, Canada 46 12N 62 32w
92 George, S. Afr. 33 58s 22 29E
100 George, L., New South Wales, Australia 35 10s 149 25E
90 George, L., Uganda 0 5N 30 10E
115 George, L., Fla., U.S.A. 29 15N 81 35w
113 George, L., N.Y., U.S.A. 43 30N 73 30w
105 George R. = Port Nouveau, Can. 58 30N 65 50w
101 George Sound, New Zealand 44 52s 167 25E
5 George V Coast, Antarc. 67 0s 148 0E
99 George Town, Australia 41 5s 148 55E
71 George Town = Pinang, Malaysia 5 25N 100 19E
71 George Town, W., Malaysia 5 25N 100 19E
117 George West, U.S.A. 28 18N 98 5w
98 Georgetown, Australia 18 17s 143 33E
106 Georgetown, Ont., Can. 43 40N 80 0w
107 Georgetown, P.E.I., Can. 46 13N 62 24w
84 Georgetown, Gambia 13 30N 14 47w
126 Georgetown, Guyana 6 50N 58 12w
119 Georgetown, Colo., U.S.A. 39 46N 105 49w
114 Georgetown, Ohio, U.S.A. 38 50N 83 50w
115 Georgetown, S.C., U.S.A. 33 22N 79 15w
117 Georgetown, Tex., U.S.A. 30 45N 98 10w

MAP

43 Georgi Dimitrov, Bulgaria 43 37N 23 4E
114 Georgia ♦, U.S.A. 32 0N 82 0w
106 Georgian B., Canada 45 15N 81 0w
57 Georgian S.S.R. ♦, U.S.S.R. 41 0N 45 0E
57 Georgievsk, U.S.S.R. 44 12N 43 28E
98 Georgina, R., Australia 20 15s 138 0E
55 Georgiu-Dezh, U.S.S.R. 51 3N 39 20E
24 Gera, Germany 50 53N 12 5E
24 Gera ♦, E. Ger. 50 45N 11 30E
125 Geral, Serra, Santa Catarina, Brazil 26 25s 50 0w
127 Geral de Goias, Serra, Brazil 12 0s 46 0w
118 Geraldine, U.S.A. 47 45N 110 18w
96 Geraldton, Australia 28 48s 114 32E
106 Geraldton, Canada 49 44N 86 59w
19 Gerardmer, France 48 3N 6 50E
104 Gerdine, Mt., Alaska 61 32N 152 30w
56 Gerede, Turkey 40 45N 32 10E
33 Gérgal, Spain 37 7N 2 31w
63 Geriban, Somali Rep. 7 10N 48 55E
71 Gerik, Malaysia 5 23N 101 0E
116 Gering, U.S.A. 41 51N 103 40w
62 Gerizim, Jordan 32 13N 35 15E
118 Gerlach, U.S.A. 40 43N 119 27w
27 Gerlachovka, Mt., Cz. 49 11N 20 7E
25 Gerlafingen, Switzerland 47 10N 7 34E
49 Gerlev, Denmark 56 36N 10 9E
63 Gerlogubi, Ethiopia 6 53N 45 3E
42 German Planina, Yugoslavia 42 33N 22 0E
108 Germansen Landing, Canada 55 43N 124 40w
24 Germany, East ■, Eur. 52 0N 12 0E
24 Germany, West ■, Eur. 52 0N 9 0E
25 Germersheim, Germany 49 13N 8 0E
25 Gernsheim, Germany 49 44N 8 29E
25 Gerolstein, Germany 50 12N 6 24E
32 Gerona, Spain 41 58N 2 46E
32 Gerona ♦, Spain 42 11N 2 30E
49 Gerrild, Denmark 56 30N 10 50E
20 Gers ♦, France 43 35N 0 38E
70 Gersoppa Falls, India 14 12N 74 46E
92 Gerufa, Botswana 19 8s 26 0E
64 Gerze, Turkey 41 45N 35 10E
24 Geseke, Germany 51 38N 8 29E
73 Geser, Indonesia 3 50N 130 35E
38 Gesso, R., Italy 44 21N 7 20E
30 Getafe, Spain 40 18N 3 44w
107 Gethsémani, Canada 50 17N 60 28w
114 Gettysburg, Pa., U.S.A. 39 47N 77 18w
116 Gettysburg, S.D., U.S.A. 45 3N 99 56w
5 Getz Ice Shelf, Antarc. 75 0s 130 0w
20 Gevaudan, Fr. 44 40N 3 40E
42 Gevgelija, Yugoslavia 41 9N 22 30E
31 Gévora, R., Spain 38 53N 6 57w
21 Gex, France 46 21N 6 3E
44 Geyikli, Turkey 39 50N 26 12E
118 Geyser, U.S.A. 47 17N 110 30w
50 Geysir, Iceland 64 19N 20 18w
56 Geyve, Turkey 40 32N 30 18E
69 Ghaghara, R., India 26 0N 84 20E
64 Ghail, Saudi Arabia 21 40N 46 20E
87 Ghalla, Wadi el, Sudan 12 0N 28 58E
85 Ghana ■, W. Africa 6 0N 1 0w
66 Ghandhi Dam, India 24 30N 75 35E
69 Ghansor, India 22 39N 80 1E
92 Ghanzi, Botswana 21 50s 21 45E
92 Ghanzi ♦, Botswana 21 50s 21 45E
86 Gharbiya, Es Sahrâ el, Egypt 27 40N 26 30E
86 Ghard Abù Muharik, Egypt 26 50N 30 0E
82 Ghardaïa, Algeria 32 31N 3 37E
82 Gharyân, Libya 32 10N 13 0E
86 Chârib, G., Egypt 28 6N 32 54E
83 Ghât, Libya 24 59N 10 19E
64 Ghat Ghat, Si. Arabia 20 6N 45 5E
69 Ghatal, India 22 40N 87 46E
69 Ghatampur, India 26 8N 80 13E
70 Ghatprabha, R. India 16 15N 75 20E
69 Ghazal, Bahr el, Chad 15 0N 17 0E
82 Ghazaouet, Algeria 35 8N 1 50w
69 Ghaziabad, India 28 42N 77 35E
69 Ghazipur, India 25 38N 83 35E
65 Ghazni, Afghanistan 33 30N 68 17E
66 Ghazni ♦, Afghan. 33 0N 68 0E
38 Ghedi, Italy 45 24N 10 16E
46 Ghelari, Rumania 45 42N 22 45E
63 Ghelinsor, Somali Rep. 6 35N 46 55E
16 Ghent (Gent), Belgium 51 4N 3 43E
16 Ghent = Gand, Belgium 51 4N 3 43E
46 Gheorghe Gheorghiu-Dej, Rumania 46 17N 26 47E
46 Gheorgheni, Rumania 46 43N 25 41E
44 Gherghani, Rumania 44 37N 25 37E
46 Gherla, Rumania 47 0N 23 57E
40 Ghilarza, Italy 40 8N 8 50E
21 Ghisonaccia, France 42 1N 9 26E
70 Ghod, R., India 18 40N 74 15E
66 Ghorat ♦, Afghan. 34 0N 64 20E
106 Ghost River, Canada 51 25N 83 20w
86 Ghot Ogrein, Egypt 31 10N 25 20E
68 Ghotaru, India 27 20N 70 1E
68 Ghotki, Pakistan 28 5N 69 18E
83 Ghudâmis, Libya 30 11N 9 29E
69 Ghugri, India 22 39N 80 41E
70 Ghugus, India 20 0N 79 0E
68 Ghulam Mohammad Barrage, W. Pak. 25 30N 67 0E
65 Ghurian, Afghanistan 34 17N 61 25E
71 Gia Lai = Pleiku, S. Vietnam 14 3N 108 0E
71 Gia Nghia, S. Vietnam 12 0N 107 42E
67 Giamda Dzong, China 30 3N 93 2E
38 Giannutri, I., Italy 42 16N 11 5E
26 Giant Mts. = Krkonose, Cz. 50 50N 16 10E

15 Giant's Causeway, Northern Ireland 55 15N 6 30w
81 Giarabub = Jaghbub, Libya 29 42N 24 38E
41 Giarre, Italy 37 44N 15 10E
38 Giaveno, Italy 45 3N 7 20E
121 Gibara, Cuba 21 0N 76 20w
116 Gibbon, U.S.A. 40 49N 98 45w
87 Gibe, R., Ethiopia 6 25N 36 10E
40 Gibellina, Italy 37 48N 13 0E
92 Gibeon, S.W. Africa 25 7s 17 45E
31 Gibraleón, Spain 37 23N 6 58w
31 Gibraltar, Europe 36 7N 5 22w
31 Gibraltar, Str. of, Mediterranean Sea 35 55N 5 40w
96 Gibson Des., Australia 24 0s 126 0E
108 Gibsons, Canada 49 24N 123 32w
4 Gida, G., U.S.S.R. 72 30N 77 0E
68 Giddalur, India 15 20N 78 57E
87 Gidde, Ethiopia 5 40N 37 25E
117 Giddings, U.S.A. 30 11N 96 58w
87 Gide, Ethiopia 9 52N 35 5E
19 Gien, France 47 40N 2 36E
24 Giessen, Germany 50 34N 8 40E
86 Gifatin, Geziret, Egypt 27 10N 33 50E
24 Gifhorn, Germany 52 29N 10 32E
74 Gifu, Japan 35 30N 136 45E
74 Gifu-ken ♦, Japan 36 0N 137 0E
57 Gigant, U.S.S.R. 46 28N 41 30E
120 Giganta, Sa. de la, Mex. 25 30N 111 30w
43 Gigen, Bulgaria 43 40N 24 28E
1 Gigha, I., Scot. 55 42N 5 45w
38 Giglio, I., Italy 42 20N 10 52E
20 Gignac, France 43 39N 3 32E
32 Giguela, R., Spain 39 47N 3 0w
30 Gijón, Spain 43 32N 5 42w
119 Gila Bend, U.S.A. 33 0N 112 46w
119 Gila Bend Mts., U.S.A. 33 15N 113 0w
119 Gila, R., U.S.A. 33 5N 108 40w
46 Gilau, Rumania 46 45N 23 23w
74 Gilau, Terr. of N. Guin. 5 38s 149 3E
85 Gilbedi, Nigeria 13 40N 5 45E
98 Gilbert, R., Australia 17 0s 142 0E
94 Gilbert and Ellice Is., Pacific Ocean 1 0s 176 0E
109 Gilbert Plains, Canada 51 9N 100 28w
98 Gilbert River Post Office, Australia 18 9s 142 50E
98 Gilberton, Australia 19 16s 143 35E
108 Gilford I., Canada 50 40N 126 30w
96 Gilgandra, Australia 31 38s 148 35E
90 Gilgil, Kenya 0 30s 36 20E
66 Gilgit, Kashmir 35 50N 74 15E
96 Giligulgul, Australia 26 26s 150 0E
92 Gilima, Zaïre 3 53N 28 15E
42 Giljeva Planina, Yugoslavia 43 9N 20 0E
109 Gillam, Canada 56 20N 94 40w
49 Gilleleje, Denmark 56 8N 12 19E
115 Gillette, U.S.A. 44 20N 105 38w
98 Gilliat, Australia 20 40s 141 28E
13 Gillingham, England 51 23N 0 34E
117 Gilmer, U.S.A. 32 44N 94 55w
100 Gilmore, Australia 35 14s 148 12E
108 Gilmour, Canada 44 48N 77 37w
46 Gilort, R., Rumania 44 38N 23 32E
87 Gilo, Ethiopia 7 35N 34 30E
119 Gilo, R., U.S.A. 33 5N 108 40w
19 Gilroy, U.S.A. 37 1N 121 37w
48 Gimåfors, Sweden 62 40N 16 25E
87 Gimbi, Ethiopia 9 3N 35 42E
38 Gimigliano, Italy 38 55N 16 32E
109 Gimli, Canada 50 40N 97 10w
48 Gimo, Sweden 60 11N 18 12E
21 Gimont, France 43 38N 0 52E
62 Gimzo, Israel 31 56N 34 56E
70 Gin Ganga, Sri Lanka 6 5N 80 7E
99 Gin Gin, Australia 25 0s 152 0E
86 Gināh, Egypt 25 21N 30 30E
70 Gindie, Australia 23 45s 148 10E
99 Gingin, Australia 31 22s 115 37E
99 Gingiova, Rumania 43 54s 23 50E
87 Ginir, Ethiopia 7 12N 40 40E
41 Ginosa, Italy 40 35N 16 45E
63 Giohar, Somali Rep. 2 20N 45 1E
41 Gioia, G. di, Italy 38 30N 15 50E
41 Gioia Táuro, Italy 38 26N 15 53E
41 Gioia del Colle, Italy 40 49N 16 55E
41 Gioiosa Jonica, Italy 38 20N 16 19E
45 Gióna, Óros, Greece 38 38N 22 14E
73 Giong, Teluk, Sabah 4 50N 118 20E
21 Giovi, P. dei, Italy 44 30N 8 55E
19 Giovinazzo, Italy 41 10N 16 40E
100 Gippsland, Australia 37 45s 147 1E
68 Gir Hills, India 21 0N 71 0E
68 Girab, India 26 2N 70 38E
27 Giraltovce, Cz. 49 7N 21 32E
117 Girard, Kans., U.S.A. 37 30N 94 50w
112 Girard, Ohio, U.S.A. 41 10N 80 42w
116 Girard, Pa., U.S.A. 42 1N 80 21w
126 Girardot, Colombia 4 18N 74 48w
41 Girbovu, Rumania 44 48N 23 21E
14 Girdle Ness, Scot. 57 9N 2 2w
64 Giresun, Turkey 40 45N 38 30E
86 Girga, Egypt 26 17N 31 55E
100 Girgarre, Austral. 36 18s 145 2E
65 Girishk, Afghanistan 31 47N 64 24E
85 Giro, Nigeria 11 7N 4 42E
20 Giromagny, France 47 44N 6 50E
20 Gironde, R., France 45 27N 0 53w
20 Gironde ♦, France 44 45N 0 30w
32 Gironella, Spain 42 2N 1 53E
98 Giru, Australia 19 30s 147 5E
14 Girvan, Scot. 55 15N 4 50w
101 Gisborne, New Zealand 38 39s 178 5E

90 Gisenyi, Rwanda 1 41s 29 30E
47 Giske, Norway 62 30N 6 3E
49 Gislaved, Sweden 57 19N 13 32E
19 Gisors, France 49 15N 1 40E
90 Gitega (Kitega), Burundi 3 26s 29 56E
41 Giugliano in Camp., Italy 40 55N 14 12E
39 Giulianova, Italy 42 45N 13 58E
43 Giurgeni, Rumania 44 46N 27 51E
43 Giurgiu, Rumania 43 52N 25 57E
62 Giv'at Brenner, Is. 31 52N 34 47E
49 Give, Denmark 55 51N 9 13E
19 Givet, France 50 8N 4 49E
21 Givors, France 45 35N 4 45E
19 Givry, France 46 41N 4 46E
86 Giza (El Giza), Egypt 30 1N 31 11E
59 Gizhiga, U.S.S.R. 62 0N 150 27E
61 Gizhiginskaya, Guba, U.S.S.R. 61 0N 158 0E
28 Gizycko, Poland 54 2N 21 48E
41 Gizzeria, Italy 38 57N 16 10E
44 Gjegjan, Albania 41 58N 20 3E
47 Gjerpen, Norway 59 15N 9 33E
47 Gjerstad, Norway 58 54N 9 0E
44 Gjiri-i-Vlorës, Alb. 40 29N 19 27E
44 Gjirokastra, Albania 40 7N 20 16E
104 Gjoa Haven, Canada 68 20N 96 0w
47 Gjovdal, Norway 58 52N 8 19E
47 Gjøvik, Norway 60 47N 10 43E
107 Glace Bay, Canada 46 11N 59 58w
108 Glacier B., Alaska 58 30N 136 10w
118 Glacier National Park, U.S.A. 48 40N 114 0w
118 Glacier Peak Mt., U.S.A. 48 3N 121 0w
117 Gladewater, U.S.A. 32 30N 94 58w
50 Gladhammar, Sweden 23 52s 151 16E
109 Gladstone, Canada 50 20N 99 0w
114 Gladstone, U.S.A. 45 52N 87 1w
114 Gladwin, U.S.A. 43 59N 84 29w
48 Glafsfjorden, Sweden 59 30N 12 45E
27 Głagów Małopolski, Poland 50 10N 21 56E
50 Gláma, Iceland 65 48N 23 0w
47 Gláma, R., Norway 60 30N 12 8E
42 Glamoč, Yugoslavia 44 3N 16 51E
13 Glamorgan ♦, Wales 51 37N 3 35w
73 Glan, Philippines 5 45N 125 20E
49 Glan, Sweden 58 37N 16 0E
25 Glarus, Switzerland 47 3N 9 4E
116 Glasco, Kans., U.S.A. 39 25N 97 50w
113 Glasco, N.Y., U.S.A. 42 3N 73 57w
14 Glasgow, Scot. 55 52N 4 14w
114 Glasgow, Ky., U.S.A. 37 2N 85 55w
118 Glasgow, Mont., U.S.A. 48 12N 106 35w
13 Glastonbury, Eng. 51 9N 2 42w
113 Glastonbury, U.S.A. 41 42N 72 36w
24 Glauchau, Germany 50 50N 12 33E
55 Glazov, U.S.S.R. 58 0N 52 30E
108 Gleichen, Canada 50 50N 113 0w
26 Gleisdorf, Austria 47 6N 15 44E
113 Glen, U.S.A. 44 7N 71 10w
119 Glen Canyon Dam, U.S.A. 37 0N 111 25w
119 Glen Canyon Nat. Recreation Area, U.S.A. 37 30N 111 0w
113 Glen Cove, U.S.A. 40 51N 73 37w
99 Glen Innes, Australia 29 40s 151 39E
113 Glen Lyon, U.S.A. 41 10N 76 7w
100 Glen Thompson, Australia 37 38s 142 35E
116 Glen Ullin, U.S.A. 46 48N 101 46w
99 Glenalbyn, Australia 36 30s 143 48E
18 Glénans, Is. de, France 47 42N 4 0w
101 Glenbrook, N. Zealand 33 46s 150 37E
99 Glencoe, Australia 37 43s 140 31E
112 Glencoe, Canada 42 45N 81 46w
93 Glencoe, S. Afr. 28 11s 30 11E
116 Glencoe, U.S.A. 44 45N 94 10w
106 Glendale, Canada 46 45N 84 2w
91 Glendale, Rhodesia 17 22s 31 5E
119 Glendale, Ariz., U.S.A. 33 40N 112 8w
119 Glendale, Calif., U.S.A. 34 7N 118 18w
118 Glendale, Oreg., U.S.A. 42 44N 123 29w
118 Glendive, U.S.A. 47 7N 104 40w
116 Glendo, U.S.A. 42 30N 105 0w
99 Glenelg, Australia 34 58s 138 30E
100 Glenelg, R., Australia 37 10s 141 30E
15 Glengariff, Ireland 51 45N 9 33w
117 Glenmora, U.S.A. 31 1N 92 34w
99 Glenmorgan, Australia 27 15s 149 30E
100 Glennie's Creek, Australia 32 30s 151 8E
118 Glenn's Ferry, U.S.A. 43 0N 115 15w
99 Glenorchy, Tas., Austral. 42 49s 147 18E
100 Glenorchy, Vic., Austral. 36 55s 142 41E
98 Glenore, Australia 17 50s 141 12E
98 Glenormiston, Austral. 22 55s 138 50E
99 Glenreagh, Australia 30 2s 153 1E
118 Glenrock, U.S.A. 42 53N 105 55w
96 Glenroy, Australia 17 16s 126 14E
113 Glens Falls, U.S.A. 43 20N 73 40w
15 Glenville, Ireland 54 48N 8 18w
114 Glenville, U.S.A. 38 56N 80 50w
108 Glenwood, Alta., Can. 49 21N 113 24w
107 Glenwood, Newf., Can. 49 0N 54 47w
116 Glenwood, Iowa, U.S.A. 41 7N 95 41w
116 Glenwood, Minn., U.S.A. 45 38N 95 21w
118 Glenwood Sprs., U.S.A. 39 39N 107 15w
50 Glettinganes, Iceland 65 30N 13 37w
39 Glina, Yugoslavia 45 20N 16 6E
28 Glinojeck, Poland 52 49N 20 21E
47 Glittertind, Nor. 61 40N 8 32E
28 Gliwice (Gleiwitz), Pol. 50 22N 18 41E
119 Globe, U.S.A. 33 25N 110 53w
46 Glodeanu-Silistea, Rumania 44 50N 26 48E
26 Glödnitz, Austria 46 53N 14 7E

46 Glodyany, U.S.S.R. 47 45N 27 31E
26 Gloggnitz, Austria 47 41N 15 56E
28 Głogow, Poland 51 37N 16 5E
28 Głogowek, Poland 50 21N 17 53E
12 Glossop, Eng. 53 27N 1 56w
100 Gloucester, Australia 32 0s 151 59E
13 Gloucester, Eng. 51 52N 2 15w
113 Gloucester, U.S.A. 42 38N 70 39w
96 Gloucester, I., Austral. 20 0s 148 30E
13 Gloucestershire ♦, Eng. 51 44N 2 10w
113 Gloversville, U.S.A. 43 5N 74 18w
107 Glovertown, Canada 48 40N 54 03w
28 Głowno, Poland 51 59N 19 42E
27 Głubczyce, Poland 50 13N 17 52E
57 Glubokiy, U.S.S.R. 48 35N 40 25E
54 Glubokoye, U.S.S.R. 55 10N 27 45E
28 Głuchołazy, Poland 50 19N 15 24E
24 Glücksburg, Germany 54 48N 9 34E
24 Glückstadt, Germany 53 46N 9 28E
54 Glukhov, U.S.S.R. 51 40N 33 50E
54 Glussk, U.S.S.R. 52 53N 28 41E
49 Glyngöre, Denmark 56 46N 8 52E
26 Glödnitz, Austria 46 53N 13 21E
26 Gmünd, Kärnten, Aust. 46 54N 13 31E
26 Gmünd, Niederösterreich, Aust. 48 45N 15 0E
26 Gmunden, Austria 47 55N 13 48E
48 Gnarp, Sweden 62 3N 17 16E
48 Gnesta, Sweden 59 3N 17 17E
28 Gniew, Poland 53 50N 18 50E
28 Gniewkowo, Poland 52 54N 18 25E
28 Gniezno, Poland 52 30N 17 35E
24 Gnoien, Germany 53 58N 12 41E
48 Gnopp, Sweden 8 47N 29 50E
49 Gnosjö, Sweden 57 22N 13 43E
96 Gnowangerup, Australia 33 58s 117 59E
71 Gô Cong, S. Vietnam 10 12N 107 0E
72 Goa, India 15 33N 73 59E
92 Goageb, S.W. Africa 26 49s 17 15E
100 Goalen Hd., Australia 36 33s 150 4E
69 Goalpara, India 26 10N 90 40E
69 Goalundo, Bangladesh 23 50N 89 47E
84 Goaso, Ghana 6 48N 2 30w
14 Goat Fell, Scotland 55 37N 5 11w
87 Goba, Ethiopia 7 1N 39 59E
92 Gobabis, S. W. Africa 22 16s 19 0E
66 Gobi, desert, Asia 44 0N 111 0E
68 Gobichettipalayam, India 11 31N 77 21E
87 Gobo, Sudan 5 40N 30 10E
24 Goch, Germany 51 40N 6 9E
107 Godavari Point, India 17 0N 82 20E
70 Godavari, R., India 19 5N 79 0E
69 Godbout, Canada 49 20N 67 38w
69 Godda, India 24 50N 87 20E
90 Goddua, Libya 26 26N 14 19E
42 Godech, Bulgaria 43 1N 23 4E
49 Godegård, Sweden 58 43N 15 8E
106 Goderich, Canada 43 45N 81 41w
18 Goderville, France 49 38N 0 22E
69 Godhavn, Greenland 69 15N 53 38w
68 Godhra, India 22 49N 73 40E
27 Gödöllő, Hungary 47 38N 19 25E
124 Godoy Cruz, Argentina 32 56s 68 52w
106 Gods L., Canada 54 40N 94 10w
106 Gods, R., Canada 55 30N 93 30w
69 Godthåb, Greenland 64 10N 51 46w
66 Godwin Austen (K2), Asia 36 0N 77 0E
92 Goeie Hoop, Kaap die, S. Africa 34 24s 18 30E
16 Goeland, L., Canada 50 50N 76 40w
16 Goeree, Netherlands 51 50N 4 0E
16 Goes, Netherlands 51 30N 3 55E
106 Gogama, Canada 47 35N 81 35w
96 Gogango, Australia 23 40s 150 2E
116 Gogebic, L., U.S.A. 46 30N 89 34w
68 Gogha, India 21 32N 72 9E
28 Gogolin, Poland 50 30N 18 0E
67 Gogra, R. = Ghaghara, India 26 0N 84 20E
87 Gogriâl, Sudan 8 30N 28 0E
127 Goiânia, Brazil 16 35s 49 20w
127 Goiás, Brazil 15 55s 50 10w
127 Goiás ♦, Brazil 12 10s 48 0w
30 Góis, Portugal 40 10N 8 6w
26 Goisern, Austria 47 38N 13 38E
87 Gojam ♦, Ethiopia 10 55s 36 30E
70 Gojeb, W., Ethiopia 7 12N 36 40E
69 Gokak, India 16 11N 74 52E
69 Gokarannath, India 27 57N 80 39E
68 Gokarn, India 14 33N 74 17E
49 Göl, Denmark 57 4N 9 42E
100 Gol Gol, Australia 34 12s 142 14E
69 Gola, India 28 3N 80 32E
69 Golakganj, India 26 8N 89 52E
92 Golaya Pristen, U.S.S.R. 46 29N 32 23E
4 Golchikha, U.S.S.R. 71 45N 84 0E
118 Golconda, U.S.A. 40 58N 117 32w
118 Gold Beach, U.S.A. 42 25N 124 25w
99 Gold Coast, Australia 28 0s 153 25E
85 Gold Coast, W. Afr. 4 0N 1 40w
118 Gold Hill, U.S.A. 42 28N 123 2w
108 Gold River, Canada 49 40N 126 10E
116 Golden, Canada 51 20N 117 0w
116 Golden, U.S.A. 39 42N 105 30w
101 Golden Bay, N.Z. 40 40s 172 50E
19 Golden Gate, U.S.A. 37 54N 122 30w
106 Golden Lake, Canada 45 34N 77 21w
109 Golden Prairie, Canada 50 13N 109 37w
70 Golden Rock, India 10 45N 78 48E
15 Golden Vale, Ireland 52 33N 8 17w
118 Goldendale, U.S.A. 45 53N 120 48w
108 Goldfield, U.S.A. 37 45N 117 13w
109 Goldpines, Canada 50 45N 93 05w
115 Goldsboro, U.S.A. 35 24N 77 59w

117 Goldsmith, U.S.A. 32 0N 102 40w
117 Goldthwaite, U.S.A. 31 25N 98 32w
31 Golegã, Portugal 39 24N 8 29w
28 Goleniów, Poland 53 35N 14 50E
121 Golfito, Costa Rica 8 41N 83 5w
41 Golfo degli Aranci, It. 41 0N 9 38E
42 Golija, Yugoslavia 43 22N 20 15E
42 Golija, Mts., Yugoslavia 43 15N 18 45E
28 Golina, Poland 52 15N 18 4E
75 Golmo, China 36 30N 95 10E
21 Golo, R., France 42 31N 9 32E
57 Golovanevsk, U.S.S.R. 48 25N 30 30E
56 Gölpazari, Turkey 40 17N 30 17E
14 Golspie, Scot. 57 58N 3 58w
28 Golub Dobrzyn, Poland 53 7N 19 2E
42 Golubac, Yugoslavia 44 38N 21 38E
43 Golyama Kamchiya, R., Bulgaria 43 2N 27 18E
90 Goma, Zaïre 1 37s 29 10E
87 Goma, Ethiopia 8 29N 36 53E
90 Goma, Rwanda 2 11s 29 18E
92 Gomare, Botswana 19 25s 22 8E
69 Gomati, R., India 26 30N 81 50E
90 Gombe, R., Tanzania 4 30s 32 50E
85 Gombi, Nigeria 10 12N 12 45E
54 Gomel, U.S.S.R. 52 28N 31 0E
80 Gomera, I., Canary Is. 28 10N 17 5w
120 Gómez Palacio, Mexico 25 40N 104 40w
24 Gommern, Germany 52 54N 11 47E
73 Gomogomo, Indonesia 6 25s 134 53E
65 Gonâbâd, Iran 34 15N 58 45E
121 Gonâve, G. de la, Haiti 19 29N 72 42w
121 Gonaïves, Haiti 19 20N 72 50w
27 Gönc, Hungary 48 28N 21 14E
65 Gonda, India 27 9N 81 58E
68 Gondal, India 21 58N 70 52E
87 Gonder, Ethiopia 12 23N 37 30E
69 Gondia, India 21 23N 80 10E
91 Gondola, Mozambique 19 4s 33 37E
30 Gondomar, Portugal 41 10N 8 35w
30 Gondomar, Spain 42 7N 8 45w
19 Gondrecourt-le-Château, Fr. 48 26N 5 30E
85 Gongola, R., Nigeria 10 30N 10 22E
28 Goniadz, Poland 53 30N 22 44E
85 Goniri, Nigeria 11 30N 12 15E
40 Gonnesa, Italy 39 17N 8 27E
58 Gonno-Altaysk, U.S.S.R. 51 50N 86 5E
44 Gonnos, Greece 39 52N 22 29E
40 Gonnosfanadiga, Italy 39 30N 8 39E
119 Gonzales, Calif., U.S.A. 36 35N 121 30w
117 Gonzales, Tex., U.S.A. 29 30N 97 30w
124 González Chaves, Arg. 38 02s 60 05w
100 Goobang Cr., Australia 33 20s 147 50E
92 Good Hope, C. = Goeie Hoop, S. Afr.
74 Gooderham, Canada 44 54N 78 21w
109 Goodeve, Canada 51 10N 103 10w
43 Goodland, U.S.A. 39 22N 101 44w
117 Goodnight, U.S.A. 36 1N 101 13w
109 Goodsoil, Canada 54 24N 109 12w
78 Goodsprings, U.S.A. 35 51N 115 30w
12 Goole, England 53 42N 0 52w
100 Goolgowi, Australia 33 58s 154 39E
99 Goolma, Australia 32 18s 149 10E
99 Goolwa, Australia 35 30s 138 47E
99 Goombalie, Australia 29 59s 145 26E
91 Goonda, Mozambique 19 48s 33 57E
100 Goondiwindi, Australia 28 30s 150 21E
100 Goonumbla, Australia 32 59s 148 11E
16 Goor, Netherlands 52 13N 6 33E
99 Gooray, Australia 28 25s 150 2E
107 Goose Bay, Canada 53 15N 60 20w
118 Goose L., U.S.A. 42 0N 120 30w
98 Goothinga, Australia 17 36s 140 50E
15 Gooty, India 15 7N 77 41E
69 Gopalganj, Bangladesh 1n 89 55E
69 Gopalganj, India 26 28N 84 30E
25 Göppingen, Germany 48 42N 9 40E
33 Gor, Spain 37 23N 2 58w
28 Góra, Poland 51 40N 16 31E
69 Gorakhpur, India 26 47N 83 32E
55 Gorbatov, U.S.S.R. 56 12N 43 2E
32 Gorbea, Peña, Spain 43 1N 2 50w
121 Gorda, Punta, Nicaragua 14 10N 83 10w
99 Gordon, S. Australia 32 7s 138 20E
116 Gordon, U.S.A. 42 49N 102 6w
96 Gordon Downs, Australia 18 48s 128 40E
93 Gordonia, S. Afr. 28 13s 21 10E
98 Gordonvale, Australia 17 5s 145 50E
81 Goré, Chad 7 59N 16 49E
87 Gore, Ethiopia 8 12N 35 32E
101 Gore, New Zealand 46 5s 168 58E
106 Gore B., Canada 45 57N 82 20w
15 Gorey, Ireland 52 41N 6 18w
65 Gorgan, Iran 36 55N 54 30E
1 Gorgona, I., Colombia 3 0N 78 10w
38 Gorgona I., Italy 43 27N 9 52E
87 Gorgora, Ethiopia 12 15N 37 17E
113 Gorham, U.S.A. 44 23N 71 10w
113 Gorham Mt., U.S.A. 43 42N 70 37w
55 Gorki = Gorkiy, U.S.S.R. 56 20N 44 0E
55 Gorkovskoye Vdkhr., U.S.S.R. 57 2N 43 4E

Divided into three new counties; West, Mid and South Glamorgan

MAP

49 Gorlev, Denmark 55 30N 11 15E
27 Gorlice, Poland 49 35N 21 11E
28 Görlitz, Germany 51 10N 14 59E
55 Gorlovka, U.S.S.R. 48 25N 37 58E
117 Gorman, U.S.A. 32 15N 98 43W
43 Gorna Oryakhovitsa, Bulgaria 43 7N 25 40E
39 Gorna Radgona, Y.-slav. 46 40N 16 2E
42 Gornja Tuzla, Y.-slav. 44 35N 18 46E
39 Gornji Grad, Y.-slav. 46 20N 14 52E
42 Gornji Milanovac, Y.-slav. 44 00N 20 29E
42 Gornji Vakuf, Y.-slav. 43 57N 17 34E
43 Gorno Ablanovo, Bulg. 43 37N 25 43E
58 Gorno Filinskoye, USSR 60 5N 70 0E
55 Gornyy, U.S.S.R. 51 50N 48 30E
56 Gorodenka, U.S.S.R. 48 41N 25 29E
55 Gorodets, U.S.S.R. 56 38N 43 28E
55 Gorodische, U.S.S.R. 53 13N 45 40E
54 Gorodnitsa, U.S.S.R. 50 46N 27 26E
54 Gorodnya, U.S.S.R. 51 55N 31 33E
54 Gorodok, Byelorussia, U.S.S.R. 55 30N 30 3E
54 Gorodok, Ukraine, U.S.S.R. 49 46N 23 32E
54 Gorodok, U.S.S.R. 55 30N 30 3E
98 Goroka, New Guinea 5 50S 145 30E
100 Goroke, Australia 36 43S 141 29E
54 Gorokhov, U.S.S.R. 50 15N 24 45E
55 Gorokhovets, U.S.S.R. 56 13N 42 39E
85 Gorom Gorom, Upper Volta 14 26N 0 14W
91 Goromonzi, Rhodesia 17 52S 31 22E
73 Gorong, Kepulauan, Indonesia 4 5S 131 15E
91 Gorongosa, Sa. da, Mozam. 18 27S 32 2E
93 Gorongose, R., Mozam. 20 40S 34 30E
73 Gorontalo, Indonesia 0 35N 123 13E
85 Goronyo, Nigeria 13 29N 5 39E
18 Gorron, France 48 25N 0 50W
15 Gort, Ireland 53 4N 8 50W
69 Gorumahisani, India 22 20N 86 24E
27 Gorzkowice, Poland 51 13N 19 36E
28 Gorzno, Poland 53 12N 19 38E
28 Gorzów Slaski, Poland 51 3N 18 22E
28 Gorzów Wielkopolski, Poland 52 43N 15 15E
100 Gosford, Australia 33 23N 151 18E
114 Goshen, Ind., U.S.A. 41 36N 85 46W
113 Goshen, N.Y., U.S.A. 41 23N 74 21W
92 Goshen, S. Africa 25 50S 25 0E
24 Goslar, Germany 51 55N 10 23E
39 Gospić, Yugoslavia 44 35N 15 23E
13 Gosport, Eng. 50 48N 1 8W
47 Gossa, I., Norway 62 52N 6 50E
42 Gostivar, Yugoslavia 41 48N 20 57E
28 Gostyn, Poland 51 50N 17 3E
28 Gostynin, Poland 52 26N 19 29E
49 Göta, Sweden 58 6N 12 10E
49 Göta Kanal, Sweden 58 35N 14 15E
49 Göta älv, Sweden 57 42N 11 54E
49 Göteborg, Sweden 57 43N 11 59E
49 Gotene, Sweden 58 33N 13 30E
24 Gotha, Germany 50 56N 10 42E
49 Gothenburg = Goteborg, Sweden 57 43N 11 59E
116 Gothenburg, U.S.A. 40 58N 100 8W
49 Gotland, Sweden 57 30N 18 30E
74 Gotō-rettō, Japan 32 55N 129 5E
43 Gotse Delchev (Nevrokop), Bulgaria 41 43N 23 46E
51 Gotska Sandö, nationalpark, Swed. 58 24N 19 15E
24 Göttingen, Germany 51 31N 9 55E
27 Gottwaldov (Zlin), Cz. 49 14N 17 40E
16 Gouda, Netherlands 52 1N 4 42E
84 Goudiry, Senegal 14 15N 12 45E
7 Gough I., S. Atl. Oc. 40 10S 9 45W
106 Gouin Res., Canada 48 35N 74 40W
84 Gouitafla, Ivory Coast 7 30N 5 53W
82 Goula Touila, Mali 21 50N 1 57E
100 Goulburn, Australia 32 22S 149 31E
96 Goulburn Is., Australia 11 40S 133 20E
100 Goulburn, R., Australia 36 30S 145 20E
84 Goulia, Ivory Coast 10 1N 7 11W
82 Goulimine, Morocco 28 50N 10 0W
82 Goulmima, Morocco 31 41N 4 57W
44 Gouménissa, Greece 40 56N 22 37E
83 Goumeur, Chad 20 40N 18 30E
88 Goundam, Mali 16 25N 3 45W
88 Gounou-Gaya, Chad 9 38N 15 31E
45 Goúra, Greece 37 56N 22 20E
82 Gourara, Algeria 29 0N 0 30E
82 Gouraya, Algeria 36 31N 1 56E
20 Gourdon, France 44 44N 1 23E
85 Gouré, Niger 14 0N 10 10E
92 Gourits, R., S. Africa 34 15S 21 45E
85 Gourma Rharous, Mali 16 55N 2 5W
81 Gouro, Chad 19 30N 19 30E
100 Gourock Ra., Australia 36 0S 149 25E
84 Goursi, Upper Volta 12 42N 2 37W
113 Gouverneur, U.S.A. 44 18N 75 30W
20 Gouzon, France 46 12N 2 14E
109 Govan, Canada 51 20N 105 0W
56 Goverla, U.S.S.R. 49 9N 24 30E
127 Governador Valadares, Brazil 18 15S 41 57W
112 Gowanda, U.S.A. 42 29N 78 58W
13 Gower, The, Wales 51 35N 4 10W
15 Gowna, L., Ireland 53 52N 7 35W
124 Goya, Argentina 29 10S 59 10W
99 Goyder's Lagoon, Australia 27 3S 139 58E
126 Goyllarisquizga, Peru 10 19S 76 31W
81 Goz Beida, Chad 12 20N 21 30E
87 Goz Regeb, Sudan 16 3N 35 33E
28 Goździca, Poland 51 28N 15 4E
36 Gozo (Ghaudex), Malta 36 0N 14 13E
92 Graaff-Reinet, S. Africa 32 13S 24 32E

49 Graasten, Denmark 54 57N 9 34E
24 Grabow, Germany 53 17N 11 31E
28 Grabów, Poland 51 31N 18 7E
39 Gračac, Yugoslavia 44 18N 15 57E
42 Gračanica, Yugoslavia 44 43N 18 18E
19 Graçay, France 47 10N 1 50E
118 Grace, U.S.A. 42 38N 111 46W
116 Graceville, U.S.A. 45 36N 96 23W
121 Gracias a Dios, C., Honduras 15 0N 83 20W
42 Gradačac, Yugoslavia 44 52N 18 26E
42 Gradeska Planina, Yugoslavia 41 30N 22 15E
43 Gradets, Bulgaria 42 46N 26 30E
42 Gradignan, France 44 47N 0 36W
43 Gradnitsa, Bulgaria 42 57N 24 58E
39 Grado, Italy 45 40N 13 20E
30 Grado, Spain 43 23N 6 4W
99 Gradule, Australia 28 32S 149 15E
117 Grady, U.S.A. 34 52N 103 15E
46 Graeca, Lacul, Rum. 44 5N 26 10E
98 Grafton, Australia 29 35S 152 0E
116 Grafton, U.S.A. 48 30N 97 25W
99 Grafton, C., Australia 16 51S 146 0E
41 Gragnano, Italy 40 42N 14 30E
100 Graham, Australia 34 2S 148 33E
106 Graham, Canada 49 20N 90 30W
115 Graham, N.C., U.S.A. 36 5N 79 22W
117 Graham, Tex., U.S.A. 33 7N 98 38W
108 Graham I., Canada 53 40N 132 30W
58 Graham Bell, Os., U.S.S.R. 80 5N 70 0E
5 Graham Land, Antarc. 65 0S 64 0W
119 Graham Mt., U.S.A. 32 46N 109 58W
109 Grahamdale, Canada 51 30N 98 34W
92 Grahamstown, S. Africa 33 19S 26 31E
42 Grahovo, Yugoslavia 42 40N 18 4E
83 Graïba, Tunisia 34 30N 10 13E
84 Grain Coast, W. Afr. 4 20N 10 0W
54 Graivoron, U.S.S.R. 50 29N 35 39E
127 Grajaú, Brazil 5 50S 46 30W
28 Grajewo, Poland 53 39N 22 30E
42 Gramada, Bulgaria 43 49N 22 39E
20 Gramat, France 44 48N 1 43E
41 Grammichele, Italy 37 12N 14 37E
100 Grampians, Mts., Australia 37 0S 142 20E
100 Grampian Highlands, Scotland 56 50N 4 0W
14 Gramsh, Albania 40 52N 20 12E
80 Gran Canaria, Can. Is. 27 55N 15 35W
76 Gran Chaco, S. Amer. 25 0S 61 0W
38 Gran Paradiso, It. 49 33N 7 17E
39 Gran Sasso d'Italia, Mt., It. 42 25N 13 30E
121 Granada, Nicaragua 11 58N 86 0W
33 Granada, Spain 37 10N 3 35W
116 Granada, U.S.A. 38 5N 102 13W
31 Granada ♦, Spain 37 5N 4 30W
15 Granard, Ireland 53 47N 7 30W
48 Granbo, Sweden 61 16N 16 33E
117 Granbury, U.S.A. 32 28N 97 48W
106 Granby, Canada 45 25N 72 45W
114 Grand I., U.S.A. 46 30N 86 40W
107 Grand L., N.B., Canada 45 57N 66 7W
107 Grand L., Newf., Can. 48 45N 57 45W
118 Grand L., U.S.A. 29 55N 92 45W
118 Grand, R., Mo., U.S.A. 39 45N 93 20W
118 Grand, R., S.D., U.S.A. 45 45N 101 30W
121 Grand Bahama I., Bahama Islands 26 40N 78 30W
107 Grand Bank, Canada 47 6N 55 48W
84 Grand Bassa, Liberia 6 0N 10 2W
84 Grand Bassam, Ivory C. 5 10N 3 49W
84 Grand Béréby, Ivory Coast 4 38N 6 55W
121 Grand-Bourg, Guadeloupe 15 53N 61 19W
75 Grand Canal = Yun Ho, China 35 0N 117 0E
119 Grand Canyon National Park, U.S.A. 36 15N 112 30W
121 Grand Cayman, I.W. 19 20N 81 20W
84 Grand Cess, Liberia 4 40N 8 12W
118 Grand Coulee, U.S.A. 47 48N 119 1W
118 Grand Coulee Dam, U.S.A. 48 0N 118 50W
82 Grand Erg Occidental, Alg. 30 20N 1 0E
82 Grand Erg Oriental, Alg. 30 0N 6 30E
107 Grand Falls, Can. 47 2N 67 46W
108 Grand Forks, Canada 49 0N 118 30W
116 Grand Forks, U.S.A. 48 0N 97 3W
114 Grand Haven, U.S.A. 43 3N 86 13W
116 Grand Island, U.S.A. 40 59N 98 25W
117 Grand Isle, U.S.A. 29 15N 89 58W
119 Grand Junction, U.S.A. 39 0N 108 30W
106 Grand Lac, Canada 47 35N 77 35W
84 Grand Lahou, Ivory Coast 5 10N 5 0W
118 Grand Lake, U.S.A. 40 20N 105 54W
18 Grand Lieu, Lac de, Fr. 47 6N 1 40W
107 Grand Manan I., Canada 44 45N 66 52W
114 Grand Marais, Canada 47 45N 90 25W
114 Grand Marais, U.S.A. 46 39N 85 59W
106 Grand Mère, Canada 46 36N 72 40W
85 Grand Popo, Togo 6 1N 1 44E
109 Grand Rapids, Canada 53 12N 99 19W
114 Grand Rapids, Mich., USA 42 57N 85 40W
116 Grand Rapids, Minn., USA 47 19N 93 29W
25 Grand St.-Bernard, Col. du, Switz. 45 53N 7 11E
118 Grand Teton, U.S.A. 43 45N 110 57W
118 Grand Valley, U.S.A. 39 30N 108 2W
109 Grand View, Canada 51 11N 100 51W
30 Grandas de Salime, Sp. 43 13N 6 53W
128 Grande, B., Argentina 50 30S 68 20W
126 Grande R., Bolivia 18 35S 63 0W

127 Grande, R., Baia, Brazil 11 30S 44 30W
127 Grande, R., Minas Gerais, Brazil 20 0S 50 0W
33 Grande, R., Spain 39 6N 0 48W
117 Grande, R., U.S.A. 29 20N 100 40W
107 Grande, Serra, Maranhao, Brazil 4 30S 41 20W
107 Grande Baie, Canada 48 19N 70 52W
108 Grande Cache, Canada 53 50N 119 27W
120 Grande de Santiago, R., Mexico 21 20N 105 50W
107 Grande-Entrée, Canada 47 30N 61 40W
108 Grande Prairie, Canada 55 15N 118 50W
107 Grande Rivière, Canada 48 26N 64 30W
107 Grande Vallée, Canada 49 14N 65 8W
107 Grandes Bergeronnes, Can. 48 16N 69 35W
117 Grandfalls, U.S.A. 31 21N 102 51W
31 Grândola, Portugal 38 12N 8 35W
19 Grandpré, France 49 20N 4 50E
118 Grandview, U.S.A. 46 13N 119 58W
19 Grandvilliers, France 49 40N 1 57E
124 Graneros, Chile 34 5S 70 45W
127 Granja, Brazil 3 17S 40 50W
30 Granja de Moreruela, Spain 41 48N 5 44W
31 Granja de Torrehermosa, Spain 38 19N 5 35W
49 Gränna, Sweden 58 1N 14 28E
32 Granollers, Spain 41 39N 2 18E
24 Gransee, Germany 53 0N 13 10E
106 Grant, Canada 50 6N 86 18W
116 Grant, U.S.A. 40 53N 101 42W
116 Grant City, U.S.A. 40 30N 94 25W
119 Grant Range Mts., USA 38 30N 115 30W
12 Grantham, Eng. 52 55N 0 39W
14 Grantown-on-Spey, Scotland 57 19N 3 36W
119 Grants, U.S.A. 35 14N 107 57W
118 Grant's Pass, U.S.A. 42 30N 123 22W
116 Grantsburg, U.S.A. 45 46N 92 44W
118 Grantsville, U.S.A. 40 35N 112 32W
18 Granville, France 48 50N 1 35W
114 Granville, N.Y., U.S.A. 43 24N 73 30W
116 Granville, N.D., U.S.A. 48 18N 100 48W
109 Granville L., Canada 56 0N 100 35W
33 Grao de Gandia, Spain 39 0N 0 27W
117 Grapeland, U.S.A. 31 30N 95 25W
104 Gras, L. de, Canada 65 0N 110 30W
93 Graskop, S. Afr. 24 56S 30 49E
48 Gräsmark, Sweden 59 58N 12 44E
48 Graso, Sweden 60 28N 18 35E
118 Grass Range, U.S.A. 47 0N 109 0W
109 Grass R. Prov. Park, Canada 54 35N 101 0W
118 Grass Valley, Calif., U.S.A. 39 18N 121 0W
118 Grass Valley, Oreg., U.S.A. 45 28N 120 48W
41 Grassano, Italy 40 38N 16 17E
21 Grasse, France 43 38N 6 56E
107 Grate's Cove, Canada 48 8N 53 0W
25 Graubünden (Grisons) ♦, Switzerland 46 45N 9 30E
20 Graulhet, France 43 45N 1 58E
32 Graus, Spain 42 11N 0 20E
20 Grave, Pte. de, France 45 34N 1 4W
109 Gravelbourg, Canada 49 50N 105 35W
19 Gravelines, France 51 0N 2 10E
112 Gravenhurst, Canada 44 52N 79 20W
48 Graversfors, Sweden 58 42N 16 8E
13 Gravesend, Eng. 51 25N 0 22E
99 Gravesend, Australia 29 35S 150 20E
41 Gravina di Púglia, Italy 40 48N 16 25E
21 Gravois, Pointe-à, Haiti 16 15N 73 45W
21 Gravone, R., Corsica 42 3N 8 50E
49 Grävsnäs, Sweden 58 5N 12 29E
19 Gray, France 47 27N 5 35E
114 Grayling, U.S.A. 44 40N 84 42W
118 Grays Harbor, U.S.A. 46 55N 124 8W
118 Grays L., U.S.A. 43 8N 111 30W
109 Grayson, Canada 50 45N 102 40W
54 Grayvoron, U.S.S.R. 50 29N 35 39W
26 Graz, Austria 47 4N 15 27E
31 Grazalema, Spain 36 46N 5 23W
42 Grdelica, Yugoslavia 42 55N 22 1E
121 Great Abaco I., Bahamas 26 15N 77 10W
96 Great Australian Bight, Australia 33 30S 130 0E
101 Great Barrier I., N.Z. 37 12S 175 25E
98 Gt. Barrier Rf., Austral. 19 0S 149 0E
113 Great Barrington, U.S.A. 42 11N 73 22W
110 Great Basin, U.S.A. 40 0N 116 30W
104 Great Bear L., Canada 65 30N 120 0W
104 Great Bear R., Canada 65 0N 124 0W
116 Great Bend, U.S.A. 38 25N 98 55W
92 Great Bentley, England 51 51N 1 5E
86 Great Bitter Lake, Eg. 30 15N 32 40E
15 Great Blasket, I., Ire. 52 5N 10 30W
8 Great Britain, Europe 54 0N 2 15W
92 Great Bushman Land, S. Afr. 29 20S 19 20E
108 Great Central, Canada 49 20N 125 10W
71 Great Coco I., Burma 14 0S 93 25E
98 Great Divide, Australia 23 0S 146 0E
121 Great Exuma I., Bahama Is. 23 30N 75 50W
118 Great Falls, U.S.A. 47 27N 111 12W

92 Great Fish R., S. Africa 31 30S 20 16E
92 Great Fish R., S. Africa 33 28S 27 5E
87 Great Hanish, Ethiopia 13 40N 43 0E
121 Great Inagua I., Bahamas 21 0N 73 20W
107 Great Jarvis, Canada 47 39N 57 12W
92 Great Karoo = Groot Karoo, S. Africa 32 30S 23 0E
99 Great Lake, Australia 41 50S 146 30E
109 Great Lakes, Canada 44 0N 82 0W
12 Great Orme's Head, Wales 53 20N 3 52W
12 Great Ouse, R., England 52 20N 0 8E
90 Great Ruaha, R., Tanz. 7 30S 35 0E
118 Great Salt Lake, U.S.A. 41 0N 112 30W
118 Great Salt Lake Desert, U.S.A. 40 20N 113 50W
117 Great Salt Plains Res., U.S.A. 36 40N 98 15W
96 Great Sandy Desert, Australia 21 0S 124 0E
99 Great Sandy I. = Fraser I., Austral. 25 15S 153 0E
84 Great Scarcies, R., Sierra Leone 9 30N 12 40W
108 Great Slave L., Canada 61 30N 114 20W
96 Gt. Victoria Des., Australia 29 30S 126 30E
76 Great Wall, China 38 30N 109 30E
92 Great Whale, R., Can. 55 20N 75 30W
121 Great Whernside, mt., England 54 9N 1 59W
92 Great Winterhoek, mt., S. Afr. 33 07S 19 10E
12 Great Yarmouth, England 52 40N 1 45E
121 Greater Antilles, W. Ind. 17 40N 74 0W
54 Grebenka, U.S.S.R. 50 9N 32 22E
48 Grebbestad, Sweden 58 42N 11 15E
40 Greco, Mt., Italy 41 48N 14 0E
36 Gredos, Sierra de, Spain 40 20N 5 0W
44 Greece ■, Europe 40 0N 23 0E
116 Greeley, Colo., U.S.A. 40 30N 104 40W
116 Greeley, Nebr., U.S.A. 41 36N 98 32W
100 Green C., Australia 37 13S 150 1E
115 Green Cove Springs, U.S.A. 29 59N 81 40W
114 Green Bay, U.S.A. 44 30N 88 0W
116 Green B., U.S.A. 45 0N 87 30W
101 Green I., New Zealand 45 54S 170 27E
98 Green I., New Guinea 4 30S 154 30E
119 Green R., Ky., U.S.A. 37 15N 86 30W
119 Green R., Utah, U.S.A. 39 0N 110 0W
118 Green R., Wyo., U.S.A. 41 44N 109 28W
116 Green R., Wyo., U.S.A. 43 2N 110 2W
112 Greenbush, Mich., U.S.A. 44 35N 83 19W
116 Greenbush, Minn., U.S.A. 48 46N 96 10W
114 Greencastle, Ind., U.S.A. 39 40N 86 48W
113 Greene, U.S.A. 42 20N 75 45W
114 Greenfield, Ind., U.S.A. 39 47N 85 51W
116 Greenfield, Iowa, U.S.A. 41 18N 94 28W
113 Greenfield, Mass., U.S.A. 42 38N 72 38W
117 Greenfield, Miss., U.S.A. 37 28N 93 50W
116 Greenfield Park, Can. 45 26N 73 28W
4 Greenland, N. Amer. 66 0N 45 0W
4 Greenland Sea, Arctic Ocean 73 0N 10 0W
15 Greenore, Ireland 54 2N 6 8W
15 Greenore Pt., Ireland 52 15N 6 20W
118 Greenport, U.S.A. 41 5N 72 23W
100 Greens Creek, Australia 36 57S 143 0E
115 Greensboro, Ga., U.S.A. 33 34N 83 12W
115 Greensboro, N.C., U.S.A. 36 7N 79 46W
114 Greensburg, Ind., U.S.A. 39 20N 85 30W
117 Greensburg, Kans., U.S.A. 37 38N 99 20W
112 Greensburg, Pa., U.S.A. 40 18N 79 31W
84 Greenville, Liberia 5 7N 9 6W
115 Greenville, Ala., U.S.A. 31 50N 86 37W
118 Greenville, Calif., U.S.A. 40 15N 121 0W
114 Greenville, Ill., U.S.A. 38 53N 89 22W
107 Greenville, Me., U.S.A. 45 30N 69 32W
114 Greenville, Mich., U.S.A. 43 12N 85 14W
115 Greenville, Miss., U.S.A. 33 25N 91 0W
115 Greenville, N.C., U.S.A. 35 37N 77 26W
115 Greenville, Ohio, U.S.A. 40 5N 84 38W
112 Greenville, Pa., U.S.A. 41 23N 80 22W
115 Greenville, S.C., U.S.A. 34 54N 82 24W
115 Greenville, Tenn., U.S.A. 36 13N 82 51W
117 Greenville, Tex., U.S.A. 33 5N 96 5W
13 Greenwich, Eng. 51 28N 0 0
113 Greenwich, N.Y., U.S.A. 43 2N 73 36W
114 Greenwich, Ohio, U.S.A. 41 1N 82 32W
108 Greenwood, Canada 49 10N 118 40W
117 Greenwood, Miss., U.S.A. 33 30N 90 4W
115 Greenwood, S.C., U.S.A. 34 13N 82 13W
114 Gregory, U.S.A. 43 14N 99 20W
98 Gregory, R., Australia 18 58S 139 0E
98 Gregory Downs, Austral. 18 35S 138 45E
99 Gregory Lake, Australia 20 10S 127 30E
98 Gregory Ra., Australia 19 0S 143 10E
24 Greiffenberg, Germany 53 6N 13 57E
24 Greifswald, Germany 54 6N 13 23E
24 Greifswalder Bodden, Germany 54 15N 13 40E
24 Greifswalder Oie, Ger. 54 15N 13 55E
26 Grein, Austria 48 14N 14 51E
26 Greiner Wald, Austria 48 30N 15 0E
24 Greiz, Germany 50 39N 12 12E
52 Gremikha, U.S.S.R. 67 50N 39 40E
49 Grenå, Denmark 56 25N 10 53E
117 Grenada, U.S.A. 33 45N 89 50W
121 Grenada I., West Indies 12 10N 61 40W

20 Grenade, France 43 47N 1 17E
121 Grenadines, West Indies 12 40N 61 20W
49 Grenen, Den. 57 44N 10 40E
100 Grenfell, Australia 33 52S 148 8E
109 Grenfell, Canada 50 30N 102 50W
21 Grenoble, France 45 12N 5 42E
116 Grenora, U.S.A. 48 38N 103 54W
100 Grenville, Australia 37 57S 143 40E
98 Grenville, C., Australia 12 0S 143 13E
49 Grenå, Denmark 56 25N 10 53E
21 Gréoux-les-Bains, Fr. 43 55N 5 52E
12 Gresham, U.S.A. 45 36N 122 31W
73 Gresik, Indonesia 9 13S 112 38E
38 Gressoney St. Jean, It. 45 49N 7 47E
117 Gretna, U.S.A. 30 0N 90 2W
14 Gretna Green, Scotland 55 0N 3 3W
24 Greven, Germany 52 7N 7 36E
44 Grevená, Greece 40 4N 21 25E
44 Grevená ♦, Greece 40 2N 21 25E
24 Grevenbroich, Germany 51 6N 6 32E
16 Grevenmacher, Lux. 49 41N 6 26E
24 Grevesmühlen, Ger. 53 51N 11 10E
49 Grevie, Sweden 56 22N 12 46E
99 Grey, C., Australia 13 0S 136 35E
99 Grey Range, Australia 27 0S 143 30E
101 Grey, R., N.Z. 42 17N 171 35E
107 Grey Res., Canada 48 20N 56 30W
118 Greybull, U.S.A. 44 30N 108 3W
101 Greymouth, N.Z. 42 29S 171 13E
101 Greytown, N.Z. 41 5S 175 29E
93 Greytown, S. Afr. 29 1S 30 36E
55 Gribanovskiy, U.S.S.R. 51 28N 41 50E
92 Griekwastad, S. Africa 28 49S 23 15E
115 Griffin, U.S.A. 33 17N 84 14W
100 Griffith, Australia 34 14S 145 46E
109 Griffith Mine, Canada 50 47N 93 25W
120 Grijalva, R., Mexico 16 20N 92 20W
48 Grillby, Sweden 59 38N 17 15E
76 Grim, C., Australia 40 45S 144 45E
54 Grimailov, U.S.S.R. 49 20N 26 5E
81 Grimari, Central African Republic 5 43N 20 0E
49 Grimeton, Sweden 57 6N 12 25E
24 Grimma, Germany 51 14N 12 44E
24 Grimmen, Germany 54 6N 13 2E
112 Grimsby, Canada 43 12N 79 33W
12 Grimsby, Eng. 53 35N 0 5W
50 Grimsey, Iceland 66 33N 18 0W
108 Grimshaw, Canada 56 10N 117 40W
47 Grimstad, Norway 58 22N 8 35E
25 Grindelwald, Switz. 46 38N 8 2E
49 Grindsted, Denmark 55 46N 8 55E
107 Grindstone Island, Can. 47 25N 62 0W
46 Grindu, Rumania 44 47N 26 47E
46 Grindușul, Mt., Rumania 46 40N 26 7E
116 Grinnell, U.S.A. 41 45N 92 50W
30 Griñón, Spain 40 13N 3 51W
47 Grip, Norway 63 16N 7 37E
93 Griqualand East, S. Afr. 30 30S 29 0E
92 Griqualand West, S. Afr. 28 40S 23 30E
107 Griquet, Canada 51 30N 55 35W
20 Grisolles, France 43 49N 1 19E
25 Grisons ♦, Switz. 46 40N 9 30E
48 Grisslehamn, Sweden 60 5N 18 49E
19 Griz Nez, France 50 50N 1 35E
39 Grmeč Planina, Y.-slav. 44 43N 16 16E
26 Gröbming, Austria 47 27N 13 54E
24 Grobina, Yugoslavia 44 40N 20 42E
28 Gródkow, Poland 50 43N 17 40E
54 Grodno, U.S.S.R. 53 42N 23 52E
117 Groesbeck, U.S.A. 31 32N 96 34W
18 Groix, France 47 38N 3 29W
18 Groix, I. de, France 47 38N 3 28W
28 Grójec, Poland 51 50N 20 58E
24 Gronau, Germany 52 13N 7 2E
50 Grong, Norway 64 25N 12 8E
16 Groningen, Netherlands 53 15N 6 35E
16 Groningen ♦, Neth. 53 16N 6 40E
49 Grönskåra, Sweden 57 5N 13 43E
117 Groom, U.S.A. 35 12N 100 59W
92 Groot, R., S. Africa 33 10S 23 35E
92 Groot Berg, R., S. Africa 32 50S 18 20E
92 Groot-Brakrivier, S. Afr. 34 2S 22 18E
92 Groot Karoo 32 35S 23 0E
*92 Groot Namakwaland 26 0S 18 0E
96 Groote Eylandt, Australia 14 0S 136 50E
92 Grootfontein, S.W. Africa 19 31S 18 6E
92 Grootlaagte, R., Afr. 21 10S 21 20E
33 Grosa, Punta, Spain 39 6N 1 36E
38 Grósio, Italy 46 18N 10 17E
21 Grosne, R., France 46 30N 4 40E
26 Gross-Enzersdorf, Austria 48 12N 16 34E
24 Gross Ottersleben, Ger. 52 5N 11 33E
127 Grossa, Pta., Brazil 1 20N 50 0W
24 Grossenbrode, Germany 54 21N 11 4E
41 Grosseto, Italy 42 45N 11 7E
24 Grossenhain, Germany 51 17N 13 32E
26 Grossgerungs, Austria 48 34N 14 57E
107 Grosswater B., Canada 54 20N 57 40W
113 Groton, U.S.A. 41 22N 75 5W
41 Grottaglie, Italy 40 32N 17 25E
41 Grottaminarda, Italy 41 5N 15 4E
18 Grouin, Pointe du, France 48 43N 1 51W
106 Groundhog, R., Canada 48 45N 82 20W
118 Grouse Creek, U.S.A. 41 51N 113 57W
112 Grove City, U.S.A. 41 10N 80 5W
48 Grovelsjön, Sweden 62 6N 12 16E

* Renamed Namaland

Groveton INDEX Hammam bou Hadjar

MAP
113 Groveton, N.H., U.S.A. 44 34N 71 30W
117 Groveton, Tex., U.S.A. 31 5N 95 4W
39 Groznjan, Yugoslavia 45 22N 13 43E
57 Groznyy, U.S.S.R. 43 20N 45 45E
42 Grubišno Polje, Y.-slav. 45 44N 17 12E
28 Grudusk, Poland 53 3N 20 38E
28 Grudziadz, Poland 53 30N 18 47E
20 Gruissan, France 43 8N 3 7E
41 Grumo Appula, Italy 41 2N 16 43E
48 Grums, Sweden 59 22N 13 5E
24 Grünberg, Germany 50 37N 8 55E
116 Grundy Center, U.S.A. 42 22N 92 45W
47 Grungedal, Norway 59 44N 7 43E
117 Gruver, U.S.A. 36 19N 101 20W
25 Gruyères, Switzerland 46 35N 7 4E
42 Gruza, Yugoslavia 43 54N 20 46E
55 Gryazi, U.S.S.R. 52 30N 39 58E
55 Gryazovets, U.S.S.R. 58 50N 40 20E
27 Grybów, Poland 49 36N 20 55E
48 Gryckbo, Sweden 60 40N 15 29E
28 Gryfice, Poland 53 55N 15 13E
28 Gryfino, Poland 53 16N 14 29E
49 Grytgöl, Sweden 58 49N 15 33E
48 Grythyttan, Sweden 59 41N 14 32E
5 Grytviken, S. Georgia 53 50S 37 10W
48 Grängesberg, Sweden 60 6N 15 1E
49 Gränna, Sweden 58 1N 14 28E
48 Gräsö, Sweden 60 21N 18 28E
49 Gronskara, Sweden 57 5N 15 43E
25 Gstaad, Switzerland 46 28N 7 18E
121 Guacanayabo, Golfo de, Cuba 20 40N 77 20W
126 Guacara, Venezuela 10 14N 67 53W
126 Guachiría, R., Col. 5 30N 71 30W
31 Guadajoz, R., Spain 37 50N 4 51W
120 Guadalajara, Mexico 20 40N 103 20W
32 Guadalajara, Spain 40 37N 3 12W
32 Guadalajara ♦, Sp. 40 47N 3 0W
31 Guadalcanal, Spain 38 5N 5 52W
33 Guadalén, R., Spain 38 30N 3 7W
124 Guadales, Argentina 34 30S 67 55W
31 Guadalete, R., Spain 36 45N 5 47W
31 Guadalhorce, R., Spain 36 50N 4 42W
33 Guadalimar, R., Spain 38 10N 2 53W
33 Guadalmena, R., Spain 38 31N 2 50W
33 Guadalmez, R., Spain 38 33N 4 42W
32 Guadalope, R., Spain 41 0N 0 13W
31 Guadalquivir, R., Spain 38 0N 4 0W
31 Guadalupe, Spain 39 27N 5 17W
119 Guadalupe, U.S.A. 34 59N 120 33W
119 Guadalupe Pk., U.S.A. 31 50N 105 30W
117 Guadalupe, R., U.S.A. 29 25N 97 30W
120 Guadalupe Bravos, Mex. 31 20N 106 10W
30 Guadarrama, Sierra de, Spain 41 0N 4 0W
121 Guadeloupe, I., Fr. W.I. 16 20N 61 40W
121 Guadeloupe Passage, Leeward Is. 16 50N 68 15W
31 Guadiamar, R., Spain 37 9N 6 20W
31 Guadiana, R., Portugal 37 45N 7 35W
33 Guadiana Menor, R., Sp. 37 45N 3 7W
31 Guadiaro, R., Spain 36 39N 5 17W
31 Guadiato, R., Spain 37 55N 4 53W
32 Guadiela, R., Spain 40 30N 2 23W
33 Guadix, Spain 37 18N 3 11W
128 Guafo, Boca del, Chile 43 35S 74 0W
126 Guaina, Venezuela 5 9N 63 36W
126 Guainia ♦, Col. 2 30N 69 00W
125 Guaira, Brazil 24 5S 54 10W
128 Guaitecas, Islas, Chile 44 0S 74 30W
126 Guajará-Mirim, Brazil 10 50S 65 20W
121 Guajira, Pen. de la, Colombia 12 0N 72 0W
39 Gualdo Tadino, Italy 43 14N 12 46E
124 Gualeguay, Argentina 33 10S 59 20W
124 Gualeguaychú, Arg. 33 3S 58 31W
94 Guam I., Pacific Ocean 13 27N 144 45E
126 Guama, Venezuela 10 16N 68 49W
126 Guamareyes, Colombia 0 30S 73 0W
124 Guamini, Argentina 37 1S 62 28W
126 Guampi, Sierra de, Ven. 6 0N 65 35W
120 Guamúchil, Mexico 25 25N 108 3W
121 Guanabacoa, Cuba 23 8N 82 18W
125 Guanabara ♦, Brazil 23 0S 43 25W
121 Guanacaste, Costa Rica 10 40N 85 30W
121 Guanacaste, Cordillera del, Costa Rica 10 40N 85 4W
120 Guanacevi, Mexico 25 40N 106 0W
121 Guanajay, Cuba 22 56N 82 42W
120 Guanajuato, Mexico 21 0N 101 20W
120 Guanajuato ♦, Mexico 20 40N 101 20W
126 Guanare, Venezuela 8 42N 69 12W
126 Guanare, R., Venezuela 8 50N 68 50W
124 Guandacol, Argentina 29 30S 68 40W
121 Guane, Cuba 22 10N 84 0W
126 Guanipa, R., Venezuela 9 20N 63 30W
126 Guanta, Venezuela 10 14N 64 36W
121 Guantánamo, Cuba 20 10N 75 20W
126 Guapí, Colombia 2 36N 77 54W
121 Guápiles, Costa Rica 10 10N 83 46W
126 Guaporé, Brazil 12 0S 64 0W
126 Guaporé, R., Brazil 13 0S 63 0W
126 Guaqui, Bolivia 16 41S 68 54W
32 Guara, Sierra de, Spain 42 19N 0 15W
127 Guarapuava, Brazil 25 20S 51 30W
125 Guaratinguetá, Brazil 22 49S 45 9W
125 Guaratuba, Brazil 25 53S 48 38W
30 Guarda, Port. 40 32N 7 20W
30 Guarda ♦, Port. 40 40N 7 20W
63 Guardafui, C. = Asir, Ras, Somali Rep. 11 55N 51 10E
33 Guardamar de Segura, Spain 38 5N 0 39W
41 Guardavalle, Italy 38 31N 16 30E
39 Guardiagrele, Italy 42 11N 14 11E
30 Guardo, Spain 42 47N 4 50W
31 Guareña, Spain 38 51N 6 6W
30 Guareña, R., Spain 41 25N 5 25W
126 Guárico ♦, Venezuela 8 40N 66 35W
125 Guarujá, Brazil 24 2S 46 25W
125 Guarus, Brazil 21 30S 41 20W
126 Guasdualito, Venezuela 7 15N 70 44W
126 Guasipati, Venezuela 7 28N 61 54W
38 Guastalla, Italy 44 55N 10 40E
120 Guatemala ■, Central America 15 40N 90 30W
126 Guatire, Venezuela 10 28N 66 32W
126 Guaviare, R., Colombia 3 30N 71 0W
125 Guaxupé, Brazil 21 10S 47 5W
126 Guayabal, Colombia 4 43N 71 37W
121 Guayama, Puerto Rico 17 59N 66 7W
126 Guayaquil, Ecuador 2 15S 79 52W
126 Guayaquil, Golfo de, Ecuador 3 10S 81 0W
124 Guaymallen, Argentina 32 50S 68 45W
120 Guaymas, Mexico 27 50N 111 0W
87 Guba, Ethiopia 4 52N 39 18E
91 Guba, Zaïre 10 38S 26 27E
39 Gúbbio, Italy 43 20N 12 34E
24 Gubin, Germany 51 58N 14 45E
85 Gubio, Nigeria 12 30N 12 42E
55 Gubkin, U.S.S.R. 51 17N 37 32E
42 Guča, Yugoslavia 43 46N 20 15E
71 Guchil, Malaysia 5 35N 102 10E
76 Guchin-Us, Mongolia 45 28N 102 10E
71 Gudalur, India 11 30N 76 29E
57 Gudata, U.S.S.R. 43 7N 40 32E
113 Guddy Barrage, W. Pak. 28 30N 69 50E
49 Gudenå, Denmark 56 27N 9 40E
57 Gudermes, U.S.S.R. 43 24N 46 20E
49 Gudhjem, Denmark 55 12N 14 58E
70 Gudivada, India 16 30N 81 15E
70 Gudiyatam, India 12 57N 78 55E
48 Gudmundra, Sweden 62 56N 17 47E
70 Gudur, India 14 12N 79 55E
19 Guebwiller, France 47 55N 7 12E
32 Guecho, Spain 43 21N 2 59W
84 Guéckédou, Guinea 8 40N 10 5W
83 Guelma, Algeria 36 25N 7 29E
106 Guelph, Canada 43 35N 80 20W
82 Guelt es Stel, Algeria 35 12N 3 1E
83 Guemar, Algeria 33 30N 6 57E
18 Guéméné-sur-Scorff, Fr. 48 4N 3 13W
124 Güemes, Argentina 24 50S 65 0W
85 Guéné, Dahomey 11 44N 3 16E
18 Guer, France 47 54N 2 8W
88 Guéréda, Chad 14 31N 22 5E
18 Guérande, France 47 20N 2 26W
82 Guercif, Morocco 34 14N 3 21W
20 Guéret, France 46 11N 1 51E
19 Guérigny, France 47 6N 3 10E
32 Guernica, Spain 43 19N 2 40W
116 Guernsey, U.S.A. 42 19N 104 45W
18 Guernsey I., Chan. Is. 49 30N 2 35W
82 Guerrara, Oasis, Algeria 32 51N 4 35E
82 Guerrara, Saoura, Algeria 28 5N 0 8W
120 Guerrero ♦, Mexico 17 30N 100 0W
82 Guerzim, Algeria 29 45N 1 47W
83 Guettara, Algeria 29 40N 8 3W
21 Gueugnon, France 46 36N 4 3E
117 Gueydan, U.S.A. 30 3N 92 30W
83 Guezendi = Ghesendor, Chad 21 14N 18 14E
39 Guglionesi, Italy 51 55N 14 54E
65 Guhra, Iran 27 36N 56 8E
126 Guiana Highlands, S. America 5 0N 60 0W
92 Guibes, S.W. Africa 26 41S 16 49E
85 Guider, Cameroon 9 55N 13 59E
85 Guidimouni, Niger 13 42N 9 31E
84 Guiglo, Ivory Coast 6 45N 7 30W
30 Guijo de Coria, Spain 40 6N 6 28W
13 Guildford, Eng. 51 14N 0 34W
107 Guilford, Me., U.S.A. 45 12N 69 25W
21 Guillaumes, France 44 5N 6 52E
21 Guillestre, France 44 39N 6 40E
18 Guilvinec, France 47 48N 4 17W
127 Guimarães, Brazil 2 9S 44 35W
30 Guimarães, Portugal 41 28N 8 24W
73 Guimaras I., Philippines 10 35N 122 37E
85 Guinea, Gulf of, W. Afr. 3 0N 2 30E
84 Guinea, Port. ■, W. Africa 12 0N 15 0W
84 Guinea ■, W. Africa 10 20N 10 0W
121 Güines, Cuba 22 50N 82 0W
18 Guingamp, France 48 34N 3 10W
18 Guipavas, France 48 26N 4 29W
32 Guipúzcoa ♦, Sp. 43 12N 2 15W
82 Guir, O., Algeria 39 29N 2 58W
·85 Guirgo, Upper Volta 11 54N 1 21W
126 Güiria, Venezuela 10 32N 62 18W
19 Guiscard, France 49 40N 3 0E
19 Guise, France 49 52N 3 35E
30 Guitiriz, Spain 43 11N 7 50W
73 Guivan, Philippines 11 5N 125 55E
20 Gujan-Mestras, France 44 38N 1 4W
68 Gujarat ♦, India 23 20N 71 0E
68 Gujranwala, Pakistan 32 10N 74 12E
68 Gujrat, Pakistan 32 40N 74 2E
71 Gukhothae, Thailand 17 2N 99 50E
57 Gukovo, U.S.S.R. 48 1N 39 58E
85 Gulak, Nigeria 10 50N 13 30E
100 Gular, Austral. 31 19N 148 27E
65 Gulbahar, Afghanistan 35 5N 69 10E
70 Gulbargâ, India 17 20N 76 50E
54 Gulbene, U.S.S.R. 57 8N 26 52E
49 Guldborg Sd., Denmark 54 39N 11 50E
70 Guledagud, India 16 3N 75 48E
96 Gulf Basin, Australia 15 20S 129 0E
117 Gulfport, U.S.A. 30 28N 89 3W
99 Gulgong, Australia 32 20S 149 30E
68 Gulistan, Pakistan 30 36N 66 35E
109 Gull Lake, Canada 50 10N 108 55W
49 Gullringen, Sweden 57 48N 15 44E
45 Güllük, Turkey 37 12N 27 36E
85 Gulma, Nigeria 12 40N 4 23E
87 Gulnam, Sudan 6 55N 29 30E
64 Gulpaigan, Iran 33 26N 50 20E
44 Gülpinar, Turkey 39 32N 26 10E
58 Gulshad, U.S.S.R. 46 45N 74 25E
47 Gulsvik, Norway 60 24N 9 38E
90 Gulu, Uganda 2 48N 32 17E
90 Gulwe, Tanzania 6 30S 36 25E
56 Gulyaypole, U.S.S.R. 47 45N 36 21E
100 Gum Lake, Australia 32 42S 143 9E
75 Guma, China 37 37N 78 18E
68 Gumal, R., Pakistan 32 5N 70 5E
68 Gumbaz, Pakistan 30 2N 69 0E
85 Gumel, Nigeria 12 39N 9 22E
32 Gumiel de Hizán, Spain 41 46N 3 41W
98 Gumlu, Australia 19 53S 147 41E
74 Gumma-ken ♦, Japan 36 30N 138 20E
24 Gummersbach, Ger. 51 2N 7 32E
85 Gummi, Nigeria 12 4N 5 9E
64 Gümüşane, Turkey 40 30N 39 30E
56 Gümüşhaciköy, Turkey 40 50N 35 18E
73 Gumzai, Indonesia 5 28S 134 42E
68 Guna, India 24 40N 77 19E
87 Guna Mt., Ethiopia 11 50N 37 40E
100 Gunbar, Australia 34 3S 145 24E
100 Gunbower, Australia 35 59S 144 24E
100 Gundagai, Australia 35 3S 148 6E
73 Gundih, Indonesia 7 10S 110 56E
70 Gundlakamma, R., India 15 30N 80 15E
100 Gunebang, Australia 33 5S 146 38E
100 Gungal, Australia 32 17S 150 32E
87 Gungi, Ethiopia 10 20N 38 3E
88 Gungu, Zaïre 5 43S 19 20E
99 Gunnedah, Australia 30 59S 150 15E
119 Gunnison, Colo., U.S.A. 38 32N 106 56W
118 Gunnison, Utah, U.S.A. 39 11N 111 48W
119 Gunnison, R., U.S.A. 38 50N 108 30W
70 Guntakal, India 15 11N 77 27E
115 Guntersville, U.S.A. 34 18N 86 16W
70 Guntur, India 16 23N 80 30E
71 Gunungsitoli, Indon. 1 15N 97 30E
73 Gunungapi, Indonesia 6 45S 126 30E
72 Gunungsugih, Indon. 4 58S 105 7E
70 Gunupur, India 19 5N 83 50E
109 Gunworth, Canada 51 20N 108 10W
25 Gunzenhausen, Ger. 49 6N 10 45E
66 Gupis, Kashmir 36 15N 73 20E
68 Gura, India 25 12N 71 39E
46 Gura Humorului, Rum. 47 35N 25 53E
46 Gura Teghii, Rumania 45 30N 26 25E
87 Gurage, mt., Ethiopia 8 20N 38 20E
64 Gurchan, Iran 34 55N 49 25E
68 Gurdaspur, India 32 5N 75 25E
117 Gurdon, U.S.A. 33 55N 93 10W
57 Gurdzhaani, U.S.S.R. 41 43N 45 52E
65 Gurgan, Iran 36 51N 54 25E
68 Gurgaon, India 28 33N 77 10E
46 Gurghiu, Munții, Rumania 46 41N 25 15E
38 Guria, Italy 44 30N 9 0E
26 Gurk, R., Austria 46 48N 14 20E
69 Gurkha, Nepal 28 5N 84 40E
69 Gurla Mandhata, Tibet 30 30N 81 10E
99 Gurley, Australia 29 45S 149 48E
98 Gurrumbah, Australia 17 30S 144 55E
71 Gurun, Malaysia 5 49N 100 27E
64 Gürün, Turkey 38 41N 37 22E
127 Gurupá, Brazil 1 20S 51 45W
127 Gurupá, I. Grande de, Brazil 1 0S 51 45W
127 Gurupi, R., Brazil 3 20S 47 20W
76 Gurvandzagal, Mong. 49 35N 115 2E
57 Guryev, U.S.S.R. 47 5N 52 0E
90 Gus, Kenya 3 2N 36 57E
85 Gusau, Nigeria 12 18N 6 31E
54 Gusev, U.S.S.R. 54 35N 22 20E
85 Gushiago, Ghana 9 55N 0 15W
42 Gusinje, Yugoslavia 42 35N 19 50E
76 Gusinoozersk, U.S.S.R. 51 16N 106 27E
55 Gus-Khrsutalnyy, USSR 55 42N 40 35E
40 Gúspini, Sardinia 39 32N 8 38E
48 Gusselby, Sweden 59 38N 15 14E
27 Güssing, Austria 47 3N 16 20E
39 Gustanj, Yugoslavia 46 36N 14 49E
119 Gustine, U.S.A. 37 21N 121 0W
24 Gustrow, Germany 53 47N 12 12E
49 Gusum, Sweden 58 16N 16 30E
24 Gütersloh, Germany 51 54N 8 25E
98 Guthalungra, Australia 19 52S 147 50E
100 Guthega Dam, Austral 36 20S 148 27E
117 Guthrie, U.S.A. 35 55N 97 30W
116 Guttenberg, U.S.A. 42 46N 91 10W
126 Guyana ■, S. Amer. 5 0N 59 0W
20 Guyenne, France 44 30N 0 40E
117 Guyman, U.S.A. 36 45N 101 30W
99 Guyra, Australia 30 15S 151 40E
67 Gwa, Burma 17 30N 94 40E
91 Gwaai, Rhodesia 19 15S 27 45E
99 Gwabegar, Australia 30 31S 149 0E
85 Gwadabawa, Nigeria 13 20N 5 15E
66 Gwādar, Pakistan 25 10N 62 18E
85 Gwagwada, Nigeria 10 15N 7 15E
68 Gwalior, India 26 12N 78 10E
85 Gwanara, Nigeria 18 55N 3 10E
91 Gwanda, Rhodesia 20 55S 29 0E
85 Gwandu, Nigeria 12 30N 4 41E
90 Gwane, Zaïre 4 45N 25 48E
85 Gwaram, Nigeria 11 15N 9 51E
85 Gwarzo, Nigeria 12 20N 8 55E
85 Gwasero, Nigeria 9 30N 8 30E
65 Gwatar, Iran 25 10N 61 22E
15 Gweebarra B., Ireland 54 52N 8 21W
15 Gweedore, Ireland 55 4N 8 15W
92 Gweta, Botswana 20 12S 25 17E
85 Gwi, Nigeria 9 0N 7 10E
114 Gwinn, U.S.A. 46 15N 87 29W
85 Gwio Kura, Nigeria 12 40N 11 2E
84 Gwolu, Ghana 10 58N 1 59W
85 Gwoza, Nigeria 11 12N 13 40E
99 Gwydir, R., Australia 29 30S 149 0E
69 Gya La, China 28 45N 84 45E
67 Gyangtse, China 28 50N 89 33E
58 Gydanskiy P-ov., U.S.S.R. 70 0N 78 0E
47 Gyland, Norway 58 24N 6 45E
99 Gympie, Australia 26 11S 152 38E
74 Gyoda, Japan 36 10N 139 30E
27 Gyoma, Hungary 46 56N 20 58E
27 Gyongyos, Hungary 47 48N 20 15E
27 Győr, Hungary 47 41N 17 40E
27 Győr-Sopron ♦, Hung. 47 40N 17 20E
109 Gypsumville, Canada 51 45N 98 40W
48 Gyttorp, Sweden 59 31N 14 58E
27 Gyula, Hungary 46 38N 21 17E
54 Gzhatsk = Gagarin, U.S.S.R. 55 30N 35 0E
71 Ha Nam = Phu-Ly, N. Vietnam 20 35N 105 50E
25 Haag, Germany 48 11N 12 12E
50 Haapamäki, Finalnd 62 18N 24 28E
54 Haapsalu, U.S.S.R. 58 56N 23 30E
49 Haarby, Denmark 55 13N 10 8E
16 Haarlem, Netherlands 52 23N 4 39E
101 Haast, R., New Zealand 43 58S 169 25E
66 Hab Nadi Chauki, Pak. 25 0N 66 50E
66 Hab, R., Pakistan 25 15N 67 8E
64 Haba, Saudi Arabia 27 10N 47 0E
90 Habaswein, Kenya 1 2N 39 30E
108 Habay, Canada 55 43N 124 40W
69 Habiganj, Bangladesh 24 24N 91 30E
49 Hablingbo, Sweden 57 12N 18 16E
49 Habo, Sweden 57 55N 14 6E
24 Hachenburg, Germany 50 40N 7 49E
74 Hachijō-jima, Jap. 33 20N 139 45E
74 Hachinohe, Japan 40 30N 141 29E
74 Hachiōji, Japan 35 30N 139 30E
99 Hack, Mt., Australia 30 45S 138 55E
108 Hackett, Canada 52 9N 112 28W
68 Hadali, West Pakistan 32 16N 72 11E
86 Hadarba, Ras, Egypt 22 4N 36 51E
65 Hadd, Ras al, Oman 22 35N 59 50E
14 Haddington, Scot. 55 57N 2 48W
85 Hadeija, Nigeria 12 30N 9 59E
85 Hadeija, R., Nigeria 12 20N 9 30W
62 Hadera, Israel 32 27N 34 55E
49 Haderslev, Denmark 55 15N 9 30E
49 Haderslev ♦, Den. 55 18N 9 15E
86 Hadhra, Saudi Arabia 20 10N 41 5E
63 Hadhramaut = Hadramawt, S. Yemen 15 30N 49 30E
83 Hadjeb el Aïoun, Tunisia 35 21N 9 32E
63 Hadramawt, Southern Yemen 15 30N 49 30E
12 Hadrians Wall, England 55 0N 2 30W
49 Hadsten, Denmark 56 19N 10 3E
49 Hadsund, Denmark 56 44N 10 8E
76 Haeju, North Korea 38 3N 125 45E
64 Hafar al Batin, Si. Arab. 28 25N 46 50E
68 Hafizabad, Pakistan 32 5N 73 40E
67 Haflong, India 25 10N 93 5E
50 Hafnarfjörður, Iceland 64 4N 21 57W
64 Haft-Gel, Iran 31 30N 49 32E
63 Hafun, Ras, Somali Rep. 10 29N 51 20E
63 Hafun, Somali Rep. 10 25N 51 16E
62 Hagalil, Israel 32 53N 35 18E
81 Hagar Banga, Sudan 10 40N 22 45E
70 Hagari, R., India 14 0N 76 45E
24 Hagen, Germany 51 21N 7 29E
24 Hagenow, Germany 53 25N 11 10E
117 Hagerman, U.S.A. 33 5N 104 22W
114 Hagerstown, U.S.A. 39 39N 77 46W
20 Hagetmau, France 43 39N 0 37W
48 Hagfors, Sweden 60 3N 13 45E
48 Häggenås, Sweden 63 24N 14 55E
50 Hagi, Iceland 65 28N 23 25W
74 Hagi, Japan 34 30N 131 30E
44 Hagion Evstratios, Greece 39 30N 25 0E
44 Hagion Oros, Greece 40 37N 24 6E
15 Hags Hd., Ireland 52 57N 9 30W
16 Hague, The = s'-Gravenhage, Neth. 52 7N 4 17E
19 Haguenau, France 48 49N 7 47E
76 Haicheng, China 40 56N 122 51E
62 Haifa, Israel 32 46N 35 0E
24 Haiger, Germany 50 44N 8 12E
77 Haihong, China 20 55N 110 3E
77 Haikow, China 20 0N 110 20E
64 Hā'il, Saudi Arabia 27 28N 42 2E
76 Hailar, China 49 12N 119 37E
76 Hailar Ho, China 49 30N 118 30E
118 Hailey, U.S.A. 43 30N 114 15W
106 Haileybury, Canada 47 30N 79 38W
76 Hailun, China 47 24N 127 0E
77 Haimen, China 31 48N 121 8E
77 Hainan, China 19 0N 110 0E
16 Hainaut ♦, Belgium 50 30N 4 0E
27 Hainburg, Austria 48 9N 16 56E
118 Haines, U.S.A. 44 51N 117 59W
115 Haines City, U.S.A. 28 6N 81 35W
26 Hainfeld, Austria 48 3N 15 48E
77 Haining, China 30 23N 120 30E
71 Haiphong, N. Vietnam 20 55N 105 42E
77 Haitan Tao, China 25 30N 119 45E
121 Haiti ■, Hispaniola 19 0N 72 30W
86 Haiya Junc., Sudan 18 20N 36 40E
77 Haiyen, China 30 28N 120 57E
73 Haja, Indonesia 3 19S 129 37E
27 Hajdú-Bihar ♦, Hung. 47 30N 21 30E
27 Hajdúböszörmény, Hungary 47 40N 21 30E
27 Hajdudurog, Hungary 47 48N 21 30E
27 Hajdúhadház, Hungary 47 40N 21 40E
27 Hajdúnánás, Hungary 47 50N 21 26E
27 Hajdúsámson, Hungary 47 37N 21 42E
27 Hajdúszoboszló, Hung. 47 27N 21 22E
66 Haji Langar, Kashmir 35 50N 79 20E
69 Hajipur, India 25 45N 85 20E
65 Hajr, Oman 24 0N 56 34E
91 Hakansson, Mts., Zaïre 8 40S 25 45E
49 Hakantorp, Sweden 58 18N 12 55E
74 Hakken-Zan, mt., Japan 34 11N 135 53E
74 Hakodate, Japan 41 45N 140 44E
64 Halab = Aleppo, Syria 36 10N 37 15E
64 Halabjah, Iraq 35 10N 45 58E
86 Halaib, Sudan 22 5N 36 30E
86 Halbe, Saudi Arabia 19 40N 42 15E
24 Halberstadt, Germany 51 53N 11 2E
101 Halcombe, N.Z. 40 8S 175 30E
73 Halcyon, Mt., Philippines 13 0N 121 30E
48 Halden, Norway 59 7N 11 23E
24 Haldensleben, Germany 52 17N 11 30E
67 Haldia, India 22 5N 88 3E
69 Haldwani, India 29 25N 79 30E
115 Haleyville, U.S.A. 34 15N 87 40W
84 Half Assini, Ghana 5 1N 2 50W
118 Halfway, U.S.A. 44 56N 117 8W
62 Halhul, Jordan 31 35N 35 7E
86 Hali, Saudi Arabia 18 40N 41 15E
106 Haliburton, Canada 45 3N 78 30W
27 Halicz, Cz. 49 5N 22 38E
98 Halifax, Australia 18 32S 146 22E
107 Halifax, Canada 44 38N 63 35W
12 Halifax, Eng. 53 43N 1 51W
98 Halifax B., Australia 18 50S 147 0E
92 Halifax I., S.W. Afr. 26 38S 15 4E
65 Halil, R., Iran 27 40N 58 30E
26 Hall, Austria 47 17N 11 30E
4 Hall Land, Greenland 81 20N 60 0W
49 Hallabro, Sweden 56 22N 15 5E
49 Halland, Sweden 56 55N 12 50E
49 Hallands län ♦, Sweden 56 50N 12 50E
49 Hallands Väderö, Swed. 56 27N 12 34E
49 Hallandsås, Sweden 56 22N 13 0E
16 Halle, Belgium 50 44N 4 13W
24 Halle, Sachsen-Anhalt, Ger. 51 29N 12 0E
24 Halle, Nordrhein-Westfalen, Ger. 52 4N 8 20E
24 Halle ♦, E. Ger. 51 28N 11 58E
49 Hallefors, Kalmar, Sweden 57 35N 15 45E
26 Hallein, Austria 47 40N 13 5E
49 Hällekis, Sweden 58 38N 13 27E
99 Hallett, Australia 33 25S 138 55E
117 Hallettsville, U.S.A. 29 28N 96 57W
49 Hallevadsholm, Sweden 58 37N 11 33E
70 Hallia, R., India 16 55N 79 10E
116 Halliday, U.S.A. 47 20N 102 25W
47 Hallingdalselv, R., Nor. 60 34N 9 12E
47 Hallingskeid, Norway 60 40N 7 17E
96 Hall's Creek, Australia 18 20S 128 0E
48 Hallsberg, Sweden 59 5N 15 7E
48 Hallstahammar, Swed. 59 38N 16 15E
26 Hallstatt, Austria 47 33N 13 38E
48 Hallstavik, Sweden 60 5N 18 37E
113 Hallstead, U.S.A. 41 56N 75 45W
73 Halmahera, I., Indon. 0 40N 128 0E
46 Halmeu, Rumania 47 57N 23 2E
49 Halmstad, Sweden 56 41N 12 52E
83 Halq el Oued, Tunisia 36 53N 10 10E
49 Hals, Denmark 56 59N 10 18E
47 Halsa, Möre og Romsdal, Norway 63 3N 8 14E
47 Halsafjorden, Norway 63 5N 8 10E
• 49 Hälsingborg, Sweden 56 3N 12 42E
116 Halstad, U.S.A. 47 21N 96 41W
47 Haltdalen, Norway 62 56N 11 8E
24 Haltern, Germany 51 44N 7 10E
92 Ham, France 49 44N 3 3E
64 Hamā, Syria 35 5N 36 40E
92 Hamab, S.W. Africa 28 7S 19 16E
87 Hamad, Sudan 15 20N 33 32E
74 Hamada, Japan 34 50N 132 10E
64 Hamadān, Iran 34 52N 48 32E
64 Hamadān ♦, Iran 35 0N 49 0E
86 Hamadh, Saudi Arabia 24 55N 39 3E
82 Hamadia, Algeria 35 28N 1 57E
84 Hamale, Ghana 10 56N 2 45W
74 Hamamatsu, Japan 34 45N 137 45E
47 Hamar, Norway 60 48N 11 7E
87 Hamar Koke, Ethiopia 5 15N 36 45E
50 Hamaröy, Norway 68 5N 15 38E
86 Hamâta, Gebel, Egypt 24 17N 35 0E
24 Hamburg, Germany 53 32N 9 59E
117 Hamburg, Ark., U.S.A. 33 15N 91 47W
116 Hamburg, Iowa, U.S.A. 40 37N 95 38W
112 Hamburg, N.Y., U.S.A. 42 44N 78 50W
113 Hamburg, Pa., U.S.A. 40 33N 76 0W
24 Hamburg ♦, Germany 53 30N 10 0E
51 Hämeenlinna, Finland 61 3N 24 26E
24 Hameln, Germany 52 7N 9 24E
113 Hamer, U.S.A. 42 38N 76 11W
96 Hamersley Ra., Australia 22 0S 117 45E
76 Hamhung, N. Korea 40 0N 127 30E
75 Hami, China 42 54N 93 28E
100 Hamilton, Australia 37 37S 142 0E
121 Hamilton, Bermuda 32 15N 64 45W
106 Hamilton, Canada 43 20N 79 50W
101 Hamilton, New Zealand 37 47S 175 19E
14 Hamilton, Scot. 55 47N 4 2W
14 Hamilton, Mo., U.S.A. 39 45N 93 59W
118 Hamilton, Mont., U.S.A. 46 20N 114 6W
113 Hamilton, N.Y., U.S.A. 42 49N 75 31W
114 Hamilton, Ohio, U.S.A. 39 20N 84 35W
117 Hamilton, Tex., U.S.A. 31 40N 98 5W
107 Hamilton Inlet, Canada 54 20N 57 30W
98 Hamilton, R., Queens., Australia 22 55S 140 25E
96 Hamilton, R., S. Austral., Australia 26 40S 134 20E
98 Hamilton Hotel, Australia 22 45S 140 40E
109 Hamiota, Canada 50 11N 100 38W
115 Hamlet, U.S.A. 34 56N 79 40W
99 Hamley Bridge, Australia 34 17S 138 35E
112 Hamlin, N.Y., U.S.A. 43 17N 77 55W
117 Hamlin, Tex., U.S.A. 32 58N 100 8W
24 Hamm, Germany 51 40N 7 58E
82 Hammam bou Hadjar, Alg. 35 23N 0 58W

* Renamed Helsingborg

Hammamet INDEX Herman

MAP
83 Hammamet, Tunisia 36 24N 10 38E
83 Hammamet, G. de, Tunisia 36 10N 10 48E
48 Hammarö, I., Sweden 59 20N 13 30E
48 Hammarstrand, Sweden 63 7N 16 20E
49 Hammel, Denmark 56 16N 9 52E
25 Hammelburg, Germany 50 7N 9 54E
114 Hammenton, U.S.A. 39 40N 74 47W
49 Hammeren, Den. 55 18N 14 47E
50 Hammerfest, Norway 70 39N 23 41E
113 Hammond, Can. 45 26N 75 15W
114 Hammond, Ind., U.S.A. 41 40N 87 30W
117 Hammond, La., U.S.A. 30 32N 90 30W
49 Hamneda, Sweden 56 41N 13 51E
101 Hampden, N.Z. 45 18S 170 50E
13 Hampshire ♦, England 51 3N 1 20W
13 Hampshire Downs, England 51 10N 1 10W
117 Hampton, Ark., U.S.A. 33 35N 92 29W
116 Hampton, Iowa, U.S.A. 42 42N 93 12W
113 Hampton, N.H., U.S.A. 42 56N 70 48W
115 Hampton, S.C., U.S.A. 32 52N 81 2W
114 Hampton, Va., U.S.A. 37 4N 76 18W
96 Hampton Harbour, Australia 20 30S 116 30E
96 Hampton Tableland, Australia 32 0N 127 0E
64 Hamra, Saudi Arabia 24 2N 38 55E
48 Hamrange, Sweden 60 59N 17 5E
87 Hamrat esh Sheykh, Sudan 14 45N 27 55E
47 Hamre, Norway 60 33N 5 20E
65 Hamun Helmand, Iran 31 15N 61 15E
66 Hamun-i-Mashkel, Pak. 28 30N 63 0E
66 Hamun-i-Lora, Pakistan 29 38N 64 58E
77 Han K., Hupei, China 31 40N 112 20E
77 Han K., Kwangtung, China 23 45N 116 35E
86 Hanak, Saudi Arabia 25 32N 37 0E
94 Hanang, mt., Tanz. 4 30S 35 25E
25 Hanau, Germany 50 8N 8 56E
76 Hancheng, China 35 14N 110 22E
77 Hanchow Wan, China 35 0N 119 0E
116 Hancock, Mich., U.S.A. 47 10N 88 35W
116 Hancock, Minn., U.S.A. 45 26N 95 46W
113 Hancock, Pa., U.S.A. 41 57N 75 19W
74 Handa, Japan 34 53N 137 0E
63 Handa, Somali Rep. 10 37N 51 2E
48 Handen, Sweden 59 12N 18 12E
90 Handeni ♦, Tanz. 5 30S 38 0E
111 Handlová, Cz. 48 45N 18 35E
76 Handshur, China 48 29N 118 2E
86 Handub, Sudan 19 15N 37 25E
62 Hanegev, Israel 30 50N 35 0E
108 Haney, Canada 49 12N 122 40W
119 Hanford, U.S.A. 36 25N 119 45W
75 Hangayn Nuruu, Mongolia 48 0N 99 0E
77 Hangchow, China 30 12N 120 1E
77 Hangchow Wan, China 30 30N 121 30E
77 Hangchwang, China 34 34N 117 27E
49 Hanger, Sweden 57 6N 13 58E
92 Hangklip, K., S. Africa 34 26S 18 48E
51 Hangö (Hanko), Finland 59 59N 22 57E
76 Hanh, Mongolia 51 32N 100 35E
63 Hanish J., Red Sea 13 45N 42 46E
62 Hanita, Israel 33 5N 35 10E
116 Hankinson, U.S.A. 46 9N 96 58W
51 Hanko = Hangö, Finland 59 59N 22 57E
77 Hankow, China 30 32N 114 20E
119 Hanksville, U.S.A. 38 19N 110 45W
76 Hanku, China 39 16N 117 50E
101 Hanmer, New Zealand 42 32S 172 50E
96 Hann, Mt., Australia 15 50S 125 50E
108 Hanna, Canada 51 40N 112 0W
116 Hannaford, U.S.A. 47 23N 98 18W
116 Hannah, U.S.A. 49 0N 98 56W
106 Hannah B., Canada 51 20N 80 0W
100 Hannahs Bridge, Australia 31 55S 149 41E
116 Hannibal, U.S.A. 39 42N 91 22W
86 Hannik, Sudan 18 12N 32 20E
24 Hannover, Germany 52 23N 9 43E
49 Hanö, I., Sweden 56 2N 14 50E
49 Hanöbukten, Sweden 55 35N 14 30E
71 Hanoi, N. Vietnam 21 5N 105 55E
112 Hanover, Canada 44 9N 81 2W
92 Hanover, S. Africa 31 4S 24 29E
113 Hanover, N.H., U.S.A. 43 43N 72 17W
112 Hanover, Ohio, U.S.A. 40 5N 82 17W
114 Hanover, Pa., U.S.A. 39 46N 76 59W
24 Hanover = Hannover, Germany 52 23N 9 43E
128 Hanover, I., Chile 51 0S 74 50W
49 Hansholm, Denmark 57 8N 8 38E
68 Hansi, India 29 10N 75 57E
48 Hansjö, Sweden 61 10N 14 40E
49 Hansted, Denmark 57 8N 8 36E
76 Hantan, China 36 42N 114 30E
76 Hanuy Gol, Mongolia 48 20N 101 30E
100 Hanwood, Australia 34 26S 146 3E
77 Hanyang, China 30 32N 114 10E
49 Hanö, Sweden 56 0N 14 50E
49 Hanöbukten, Sweden 55 50N 14 30E
50 Haparanda, Sweden 65 52N 24 8E
117 Happy, U.S.A. 34 47N 101 50W
118 Happy Camp, U.S.A. 41 52N 123 30W
107 Happy Valley, Canada 53 15N 60 20W
68 Hapur, India 28 45N 77 45E
64 Haql, Saudi Arabia 29 10N 35 0E
73 Har, Indonesia 5 16S 133 14E
76 Har-Ayrag, Mongolia 45 50N 109 16E
62 Har Tuv, Israel 31 46N 35 0E
75 Har Us Nuur, Mongolia 48 0N 92 0E
62 Har Yehuda, Israel 31 35N 34 57E
76 Hara Narinula, (Lang Shan), China 41 30N 107 0E
64 Harad, Saudi Arabia 24 15N 49 0E
63 Haradera, Somali Rep. 4 33N 47 38E
MAP
64 Haradh, Saudi Arabia 24 15N 49 0E
47 Haramsöya, Norway 62 39N 6 12E
64 Haran, Turkey 36 48N 39 0E
87 Harat, Ethiopia 16 5N 39 26E
81 Haraze, Chad 14 20N 19 12E
81 Haraze-Mangueigne, Cent. Afr. Rep. 7 22N 17 3E
76 Harbin, China 45 46N 126 51E
49 Harboör, Denmark 56 38N 8 10E
114 Harbor Beach, U.S.A. 43 50N 82 38W
114 Harbor Springs, U.S.A. 45 28N 85 0W
107 Harbour Breton, Can. 47 29N 55 50W
107 Harbour Deep, Canada 50 25N 56 30W
107 Harbour Grace, Canada 47 40N 53 22W
24 Harburg, Germany 53 27N 9 58E
98 Harcourt, Australia 24 17S 149 55E
68 Harda, India 22 27N 77 5E
47 Hardangerfjorden, Norway 60 15N 6 0E
47 Hardangerjökulen, Norway 60 30N 7 0E
47 Hardangervidda, Nor. 60 20N 7 20E
92 Hardap Dam, S.W. Afr. 24 32S 17 50E
16 Hardenberg, Neth. 52 34N 6 37E
118 Hardin, U.S.A. 45 50N 107 35W
93 Harding, S. Afr. 30 22S 29 55E
108 Hardisty, Canada 52 40N 111 25W
118 Hardman, U.S.A. 45 12N 119 49W
69 Hardoi, India 27 26N 80 15E
68 Hardwar, India 29 58N 78 16E
113 Hardwick, U.S.A. 44 30N 72 20W
117 Hardy, U.S.A. 36 20N 91 30W
128 Hardy, Pen., Chile 55 30S 68 20W
62 Hare Gilboa, Israel 32 31N 35 25E
62 Hare Meron, Israel 32 59N 35 24E
24 Haren, Germany 52 47N 7 18E
87 Harer, Ethiopia 9 20N 42 8E
87 Harer ♦, Ethiopia 7 12N 42 0E
87 Hareto, Ethiopia 9 23N 37 6E
18 Harfleur, France 49 30N 0 10E
63 Hargeisa, Somali Rep. 9 30N 44 2E
46 Hârghita Mţii, Rumania 46 25N 25 35E
46 Hârghita ♦, Rumania 46 30N 25 30E
48 Hargshamn, Sweden 60 12N 18 30E
65 Hari, R., Afghanistan 34 20N 64 30E
72 Hari, R., Indon. 1 10S 101 50E
82 Haricha, Hamada el, Mali 22 40N 3 15W
70 Harihar, India 14 32N 75 44E
34 Harim, J. al, Oman 26 0N 56 10E
69 Haringhata, R., Bangladesh 22 0N 89 58E
70 Haripad, India 9 14N 76 28E
65 Harirúd, Iran 35 0N 61 0E
86 Harkat, Saudi Arabia 20 25N 39 40E
116 Harlan, Iowa, U.S.A. 41 37N 95 20W
115 Harlan, Tenn., U.S.A. 36 58N 83 20W
12 Harlech, Wales 52 52N 4 7W
118 Harlem, U.S.A. 48 29N 108 39W
16 Harlingen, Netherlands 53 11N 5 25E
117 Harlingen, U.S.A. 26 30N 97 50W
118 Harlowton, U.S.A. 46 30N 109 54W
48 Harmånger, Sweden 61 55N 17 20E
87 Harmil, Ethiopia 16 30N 40 10E
118 Harney Basin, U.S.A. 43 30N 119 0W
118 Harney L., U.S.A. 43 0N 119 0W
116 Harney Pk., U.S.A. 43 52N 103 33W
48 Härnön, I., Sweden 62 38N 18 0E
25 Härnösand, Sweden 62 38N 18 5E
32 Haro, Spain 42 35N 2 55W
49 Håroy, Denmark 55 13N 10 8E
107 Harp L., Canada 55 10N 61 40W
70 Harpenhalli, India 14 47N 76 2E
84 Harper, Liberia 4 25N 7 43E
49 Harplinge, Sweden 56 45N 12 45E
64 Harput, Turkey 38 48N 39 15E
68 Harrand, Pakistan 29 28N 70 3E
64 Harrat al Kishb, Saudi Arabia 22 30N 40 15E
64 Harrat al Umuirid, South Arabia 26 50N 38 0E
86 Harrat Khaibar, Saudi Arabia 25 45N 40 0E
86 Harrat Nawāsīf, Saudi Arabia 21 30N 42 0E
106 Harricanaw, R., Canada 50 30N 79 10W
115 Harriman, U.S.A. 36 0N 84 35W
107 Harrington Harb., Can. 50 31N 59 30W
14 Harris, Scot. 57 50N 6 55W
96 Harris L., Australia 31 10S 135 10E
14 Harris, Sd. of, Scotland 57 44N 7 6W
117 Harrisburg, Ill., U.S.A. 37 42N 88 30W
116 Harrisburg, Nebr., U.S.A. 41 36N 103 46W
118 Harrisburg, Oreg., U.S.A. 44 25N 123 10W
112 Harrisburg, Pa., U.S.A. 40 18N 76 52W
93 Harrismith, S. Africa 28 15S 29 8E
117 Harrison, Ark., U.S.A. 36 10N 93 4W
118 Harrison, Idaho, U.S.A. 47 30N 116 51W
116 Harrison, Nebr., U.S.A. 42 42N 103 52W
104 Harrison B., Alaska 70 25N 151 0W
114 Harrisonburg, U.S.A. 38 28N 78 52W
116 Harrisonville, U.S.A. 38 45N 93 45W
106 Harriston, Canada 43 57N 80 53W
112 Harrisville, U.S.A. 44 40N 83 19W
12 Harrogate, Eng. 53 59N 1 32W
112 Harrow, Canada 42 2N 82 53W
13 Harrow, Eng. 51 35N 0 15W
24 Harsefeld, Germany 53 26N 9 31E
50 Harstad, Norway 68 48N 16 30E
114 Hart, U.S.A. 43 42N 86 21W
26 Hartberg, Austria 47 17N 15 58E
47 Harteigen, Mt., Norway 60 11N 7 5E
113 Hartford, Conn., U.S.A. 41 47N 72 41W
114 Hartford, Ky., U.S.A. 37 26N 86 50W
116 Hartford, S.D., U.S.A. 43 40N 96 58W
116 Hartford, Wis., U.S.A. 43 18N 88 25W
114 Hartford City, U.S.A. 40 22N 85 20W
107 Hartland, Canada 46 20N 67 32W
MAP
13 Hartland Pt., U.K. 51 2N 4 32W
12 Hartlepool, U.K. 54 42N 1 11W
91 Hartley, Rhodesia 18 10S 30 7E
108 Hartley Bay, Canada 46 4N 80 45W
92 Hartmannberge, S. Afr. 17 0S 13 0E
109 Hartney, Canada 49 30N 100 35W
115 Hartselle, U.S.A. 34 25N 86 55W
117 Hartshorne, U.S.A. 34 51N 95 30W
115 Hartsville, U.S.A. 34 23N 80 2W
115 Hartwell, U.S.A. 34 21N 82 52W
68 Harunabad, Pakistan 29 35N 73 2E
70 Harur, India 12 3N 78 29E
119 Harvard, Mt., U.S.A. 39 0N 106 5W
114 Harvey, Ill., U.S.A. 41 40N 87 40W
116 Harvey, N.D., U.S.A. 47 50N 99 58W
13 Harwich, Eng. 51 56N 1 18E
112 Harwood, Canada 44 7N 78 11W
68 Haryana ♦, India 29 0N 76 10E
24 Harz, Germany 51 40N 10 40E
24 Harzgerode, Germany 51 38N 11 8E
64 Hasa, Si. Arabia 26 0N 49 0E
87 Hasaheisa, Sudan 14 25N 33 20E
86 Hasani, Saudi Arabia 25 0N 37 8E
68 Hasanpur, India 28 51N 78 9E
24 Haselünne, Germany 52 40N 7 30E
62 Hasharon, Israel 32 12N 34 49E
62 Hashefela, Israel 31 30N 34 43E
48 Hasjö, Sweden 63 2N 16 20E
117 Haskell, Kans., U.S.A. 35 51N 95 40W
117 Haskell, Tex., U.S.A. 33 10N 99 45W
25 Haslach, Germany 48 16N 8 7E
49 Hasle, Denmark 55 11N 14 44E
49 Haslev, Denmark 55 18N 11 57E
20 Hasparren, France 43 24N 1 18W
64 Hassan, India 13 0N 76 5E
16 Hasselt, Belgium 50 56N 5 21E
82 Hassene, Ad., Algeria 21 0N 4 0E
25 Hassfurt, Germany 50 2N 10 30E
83 Hassi Berrekrem, Alg. 33 45N 5 16E
83 Hassi Daoula, Algeria 33 4N 5 38E
83 Hassi el Biod, Algeria 28 30N 6 0E
82 Hassi Inifel, Algeria 29 50N 3 41E
83 Hassi Marroket, Algeria 30 10N 3 0E
50 Hassi el Heïda, Algeria 29 34N 0 14W
82 Hassi Messaoud, Alg. 31 43N 6 8E
83 Hassi Rhénami, Alg. 31 57N 5 58E
124 Hassi Taguenza, Algeria 29 8N 0 23W
82 Hassi Zerzour, Morocco 30 51N 3 56W
49 Hässleby, Sweden 57 37N 15 30E
49 Hässleholmen, Sweden 56 9N 13 45E
112 Hastings, Canada 44 18N 77 56W
13 Hastings, Eng. 50 51N 0 36E
101 Hastings, New Zealand 39 39S 176 52E
114 Hastings, Mich., U.S.A. 42 40N 85 20E
116 Hastings, Minn., U.S.A. 44 41N 92 51W
116 Hastings, Nebr., U.S.A. 40 34N 98 22W
112 Hastings, Pa., U.S.A. 40 40N 78 45W
99 Hastings Ra., Australia 31 15S 152 14E
49 Hästveda, Sweden 56 16N 13 55E
71 Hat Nhao, Laos 14 46N 106 32E
119 Hatch, U.S.A. 32 45N 107 8W
96 Hatches Cr., Australia 20 56S 135 12E
46 Haţeg, Rumania 45 36N 22 55E
46 Haţeg, Mţii, Rumania 45 25N 23 0E
100 Hatfield Post Office, Australia 33 54N 143 49E
75 Hatgal, Mongolia 50 40N 100 0E
68 Hathras, India 27 36N 78 6E
126 Hato de Corozal, Col. 6 11N 71 45W
100 Hattah, Australia 34 48N 142 17E
115 Hatteras, C., U.S.A. 35 10N 75 30W
117 Hattiesburg, U.S.A. 31 20N 89 20W
109 Hatton, Canada 50 2N 109 50W
27 Hatvan, Hungary 47 40N 19 45E
71 Hau Bon (Cheo Reo), S. Vietnam 13 25N 108 28E
120 Hauchinango, Mexico 20 12N 97 45W
47 Haug, Norway 60 23N 10 26E
47 Haugastöl, Norway 60 30N 7 50E
47 Haugesund, Norway 59 23N 5 13E
47 Haukelisaeter, Norway 59 51N 7 9E
63 Haura, South Yemen 13 50N 47 35E
101 Hauraki Gulf, N.Z. 36 35S 175 5E
26 Hausruck, Austria 48 6N 13 30E
82 Haut Atlas, Morocco 32 0N 7 0W
19 Haut-Rhim ♦, France 48 0N 7 15E
90 Haut Zaïre ♦, Zaïre 2 20N 26 0E
64 Hauta Oasis, Si. Arab. 23 40N 47 0E
64 Hautah, Wahāt al, Si. Arab. 23 40N 47 0E
20 Haute-Garonne ♦, France 43 28N 1 30E
20 Haute-Loire ♦, Fr. 45 5N 3 50E
19 Haute-Marne ♦, Fr. 48 10N 5 20E
19 Haute-Saône ♦, Fr. 47 45N 6 10E
21 Haute-Savoie ♦, France 46 0N 6 20E
20 Haute-Vienne ♦, Fr. 45 50N 1 10E
107 Hauterive, Canada 49 10N 68 25W
21 Hautes-Alpes ♦, Fr. 44 42N 6 20E
20 Hautes-Pyrénées ♦, France 43 0N 0 10E
112 Hauteurs de Gâtine, France 46 35N 0 45W
21 Hauteville-Lompnes, France 45 59N 5 35E
19 Hautmont, France 50 15N 3 55E
19 Hauts-de-Seine ♦, France 48 52N 2 15E
121 Havana, Cuba 23 8N 82 22W
121 Havana = La Habana, Cuba 23 8N 82 22W
116 Havana, U.S.A. 40 19N 90 3W
46 Havarna, Rumania 48 4N 26 43E
119 Havasu, L., U.S.A. 34 37N 114 30W
49 Havdhem, Sweden 57 10N 18 20E
16 Havelange, Belgium 50 23N 5 15E
106 Havelock, N.B., Can. 46 2N 65 24W
107 Havelock, Ont., Canada 44 26N 77 53W
101 Havelock, New Zealand 41 17S 173 48E
71 Havelock I., Andaman I. 11 55N 93 2E
MAP
13 Haverfordwest, Wales 51 48N 4 59W
113 Haverhill, U.S.A. 42 50N 71 2W
70 Haveri, India 14 53N 75 24E
13 Havering, Eng. 51 33N 0 20E
113 Haverstraw, U.S.A. 41 12N 73 58W
49 Håverund, Sweden 58 50N 12 28E
46 Havirna, Rumania 48 4N 26 43E
19 Havlíčkuv Brod, Cz. 49 36N 15 33E
49 Havnby, Denmark 55 5N 8 34E
118 Havre, U.S.A. 48 40N 109 34W
107 Havre-Aubert, Canada 47 12N 62 0W
107 Havre St. Pierre, Can. 50 18N 63 33W
64 Havza, Turkey 41 0N 35 35E
115 Haw, R., U.S.A. 37 43N 80 52W
110 Hawaii ♦, U.S.A. 20 30N 157 0W
110 Hawaii I., Hawaii 20 0N 155 0W
110 Hawaiian Is., Pac. Oc. 20 30N 156 0W
109 Hawarden, Canada 51 25N 106 30W
116 Hawarden, U.S.A. 43 2N 96 28W
101 Hawea Lake, N.Z. 44 28S 169 19E
14 Hawick, Scotland 55 25N 2 48W
101 Hawke B., N.Z. 39 25S 177 20E
106 Hawke Junc., Canada 48 05N 84 35W
99 Hawker, Australia 31 59S 138 22E
101 Hawke's Bay ♦, N.Z. 39 45S 176 35E
107 Hawke's Harbour, Can. 53 2N 55 50W
106 Hawkesbury, Canada 45 35N 74 40W
112 Hawkestone, Canada 44 31N 79 27W
115 Hawkinsville, U.S.A. 32 17N 83 30W
99 Hawkwood, Australia 25 45S 150 50E
116 Hawley, U.S.A. 46 58N 98 20W
118 Hawthorne, U.S.A. 38 37N 118 47W
87 Hawzen, Ethiopia 13 58N 39 28E
116 Haxtun, U.S.A. 40 40N 102 39W
100 Hay, Australia 34 30S 144 51E
13 Hay, Wales 52 4N 3 9W
108 Hay Lakes, Canada 53 12N 113 2W
108 Hay River, Canada 60 50N 115 50W
116 Hay Springs, U.S.A. 42 40N 102 38W
19 Hayange, France 49 20N 6 2E
119 Hayden, Ariz., U.S.A. 33 2N 110 54W
118 Hayden, Wyo., U.S.A. 40 30N 107 22W
98 Haydon, Australia 18 0S 141 30E
116 Hayes, U.S.A. 44 22N 101 1W
109 Hayes, R., Canada 56 0N 93 20W
4 Hayes Pen., Greenland 75 30N 65 0W
64 Haymana, Turkey 39 30N 32 35E
117 Haynesville, U.S.A. 33 0N 93 7W
116 Hays, U.S.A. 38 55N 99 25W
116 Hayward, U.S.A. 46 2N 91 30W
13 Hayward's Heath, England 51 0N 0 5W
114 Hazard, U.S.A. 37 18N 83 10W
69 Hazaribagh, India 23 58N 85 26E
69 Hazaribagh Rd., India 24 12N 85 57E
19 Hazebrouck, France 50 42N 2 31E
115 Hazelhurst, U.S.A. 31 50N 82 35W
108 Hazelton, Canada 55 20N 127 42W
116 Hazelton, N.D., U.S.A. 46 30N 100 15W
113 Hazelton, Pa., U.S.A. 40 58N 76 0W
118 Hazen, Nev., U.S.A. 39 37N 119 2W
65 Hazrat Immam, Afghan. 37 15N 68 50E
96 Head of Bight, Australia 31 30S 131 25E
91 Headlands, Rhodesia 18 15S 32 2E
118 Healdsburg, U.S.A. 38 33N 122 51W
117 Healdton, U.S.A. 34 16N 97 31W
100 Healesville, Australia 37 35S 145 30E
12 Heanor, Eng. 53 1N 1 20W
3 Heard I., Southern Oc. 53 0S 74 0E
117 Hearne, U.S.A. 30 54N 96 35W
106 Hearst, Canada 49 40N 83 41W
116 Heart, R., U.S.A. 46 40N 101 30W
107 Heart's Content, Can. 47 54N 53 27W
107 Heath Pt., Canada 49 8N 61 40W
100 Heathcote, Australia 36 58S 144 43E
117 Heavener, U.S.A. 34 54N 94 36W
117 Hebbronville, U.S.A. 27 20N 98 40W
117 Heber Springs, U.S.A. 35 29N 91 39W
118 Hebgen, L., U.S.A. 44 50N 111 15W
105 Hebron, Canada 58 10N 62 50W
62 Hebron (Al Khalil), Jordan 31 32N 35 6E
116 Hebron, N.D., U.S.A. 46 56N 102 2W
48 Heby, Sweden 59 56N 16 53E
108 Hecate Str., Canada 53 10N 130 30W
25 Hechingen, Germany 48 20N 8 58E
116 Hecla, U.S.A. 45 56N 98 8W
109 Hecla I., Canada 51 10N 96 50W
47 Heddal, Norway 59 36N 9 20E
18 Hédé, France 48 18N 1 49W
48 Hede, Jämtland, Sweden 62 23N 13 30E
48 Hedemora, Sweden 60 18N 15 58E
117 Hedley, U.S.A. 34 53N 100 39W
47 Hedmark fylke ♦, Nor. 61 17N 11 40E
47 Hedrum, Norway 59 7N 10 5E
16 Heemstede, Netherlands 52 22N 4 37E
16 Heerde, Netherlands 52 24N 6 2E
16 Heerenveen, Neth. 52 57N 5 55E
16 Heerlen, Netherlands 50 55N 6 0E
27 Hegyalja, Mts., Hun. 48 25N 21 25E
24 Heide, Germany 54 10N 9 7E
25 Heidelberg, Germany 49 23N 8 41E
92 Heidelberg, C. Prov., S. Africa 34 6S 20 59E
93 Heidelberg, Trans., S. Africa 26 30S 28 23E
25 Heidenheim, Germany 48 40N 10 10E
93 Heilbron, S. Afr. 27 16S 27 59E
25 Heilbronn, Germany 49 8N 9 13E
26 Heiligenblut, Austria 47 2N 12 51E
24 Heiligenhafen, Germany 54 21N 10 58E
24 Heiligenstadt, Germany 51 22N 10 9E
76 Heilungkiang ♦, China 47 30N 129 0E
47 Heim, Norway 63 26N 9 5E
51 Heinola, Finland 61 13N 26 24E
109 Heinsburg, Canada 53 50N 110 30W
71 Heinze Is., Burma 14 25N 97 45E
47 Heistad, Norway 59 35N 9 40E
64 Hejaz = Hijāz, Si. Arab. 26 0N 37 30E
MAP
64 Hekimhan, Turkey 38 50N 38 0E
50 Hekla, Iceland 63 56N 19 35W
34 Hel, Poland 54 38N 18 50E
48 Helagsfjället, Swed. 62 54N 12 25E
31 Helechosa, Spain 39 22N 4 53W
117 Helena, Ark., U.S.A. 34 30N 90 35W
118 Helena, Mont., U.S.A. 46 40N 112 0W
100 Helensburgh, Australia 34 11S 151 1E
14 Helensburgh, Scot. 56 0N 4 44W
101 Helensville, N.Z. 36 41S 174 29E
62 Helets, Israel 31 36N 34 39E
49 Helgasjön, Sweden 57 0N 14 50E
50 Helgeland, Nor. 66 20N 13 30E
47 Helgeroa, Norway 59 0N 9 45E
24 Helgoland, I., Germany 54 10N 7 51E
48 Helgum, Sweden 63 25N 16 50E
24 Heligoland = Helgoland, Germany 54 10N 7 51E
86 Heliopolis, Egypt 30 6N 31 17E
93 Hell-Ville, Malag. 13 25S 48 16E
49 Hellebaek, Denmark 56 4N 12 32E
47 Helleland, Norway 58 33N 6 7E
16 Hellendoorn, Neth. 52 24N 6 27E
16 Hellevoetsluis, Neth. 51 50N 4 8E
5 Hellick Kenyon Plateau, Antarctica 82 0S 110 0W
33 Hellin, Spain 38 31N 1 40W
49 Hellum, Denmark 57 16N 10 10E
65 Helmand, R., Afghan. 31 0N 67 0E
16 Helmond, Netherlands 51 29N 5 41E
14 Helmsdale, Scot. 58 7N 3 40W
14 Helmsdale, R., Scot. 58 10N 3 50W
24 Helmstedt, Germany 52 16N 11 0E
49 Helnaes, Denmark 55 9N 10 0E
118 Helper, U.S.A. 39 44N 110 56W
49 Helsinge, Denmark 56 2N 12 12E
49 Helsingör, Denmark 56 2N 12 35E
51 Helsinki (Helsingfors), Finland 60 15N 25 3E
86 Helwân, Egypt 29 50N 31 20E
47 Hem, Norway 59 26N 10 0E
70 Hemavati, R., India 12 50N 67 0E
119 Hemet, U.S.A. 33 45N 116 59W
116 Hemingford, U.S.A. 42 21N 103 4W
117 Hemphill, U.S.A. 31 21N 93 49W
117 Hempstead, U.S.A. 30 5N 96 5W
49 Hemse, Sweden 57 15N 18 22E
48 Hemsö, I., Sweden 62 43N 18 5E
48 Hemsön, Sweden 62 42N 18 5E
32 Henares, R., Spain 40 55N 3 0W
20 Hendaye, France 43 23N 1 47W
124 Henderson, Argentina 36 18S 61 43W
114 Henderson, Ky., U.S.A. 37 50N 87 38W
119 Henderson, Nev., U.S.A. 36 2N 115 0W
115 Henderson, Pa., U.S.A. 35 25N 88 40W
117 Henderson, Tex., U.S.A. 32 5N 94 49W
115 Hendersonville, U.S.A. 35 21N 82 28W
99 Hendon, Australia 28 5S 151 50E
46 Hendorf, Rumania 46 4N 24 5E
16 Hengelo, Netherlands 52 15N 6 48E
77 Henghsien, China 22 36N 109 16E
76 Hengshan, China 27 10N 112 45E
77 Hengyang, China 26 57N 112 28E
••19 Hénin-Liétard, France 50 25N 2 58E
114 Henlopen C., U.S.A. 38 48N 75 5W
48 Hennan, L., Sweden 62 3N 15 55E
49 Henne, Denmark 55 44N 8 11E
18 Hennebont, France 47 49N 3 19W
92 Hennenman, S. Africa 27 59S 27 1E
117 Hennessy, U.S.A. 36 8N 97 53W
24 Hennigsdorf, Germany 52 38N 13 13E
109 Henribourg, Canada 53 25N 105 38W
19 Henrichemont, France 47 20N 2 21E
117 Henrietta, U.S.A. 33 50N 98 15W
106 Henrietta Maria C., Can. 55 10N 82 30W
116 Henry, U.S.A. 41 5N 89 20W
117 Henryetta, U.S.A. 35 2N 96 0W
112 Hensall, Canada 43 27N 81 32W
76 Hentiyn Nuruu, Mongolia 48 30N 108 30E
100 Henty, Australia 35 30N 147 0E
67 Henzada, Burma 17 38N 95 35E
118 Heppner, U.S.A. 45 27N 119 34W
112 Hepworth, Canada 44 40N 81 10W
47 Herad, Vest-Agder, Norway 58 8N 6 47E
50 Héra ðsflói, Iceland 65 42N 14 12W
50 Héradsvötn, Iceland 65 25N 19 5W
65 Herāt, Afghanistan 34 20N 62 7E
20 Hérault, R., France 43 20N 3 32E
20 Hérault ♦, France 43 34N 3 15E
109 Herbert, Canada 50 30N 107 10W
98 Herbert Downs, Australia 23 0S 139 11E
98 Herberton, Australia 17 28S 145 25E
18 Herbignac, France 47 27N 2 18W
24 Herborn, Germany 50 40N 8 19E
28 Herby, Poland 50 45N 18 50E
42 Hercegnovi, Y.-slav. 42 30N 18 33E
42 Hercegovina ♦, Yugoslavia 43 20N 18 0E
50 Her ðubrei , Iceland 65 11N 16 21W
47 Herdla, Norway 60 34N 4 56E
13 Hereford, Eng. 52 4N 2 42W
117 Hereford, U.S.A. 34 50N 102 28W
• 13 Hereford ♦, Eng. 52 4N 2 43W
47 Herefoss, Norway 58 32N 8 32E
16 Herentals, Belgium 51 12N 4 51E
49 Herfölge, Denmark 55 26N 12 9E
24 Herford, Germany 52 7N 8 40E
49 Herfölge, Denmark 55 26N 12 9E
19 Héricourt, France 47 32N 6 55E
116 Herington, U.S.A. 38 43N 97 0W
25 Herisau, Switzerland 47 22N 9 17E
20 Hérisson, France 46 32N 2 42E
113 Herkimer, U.S.A. 43 0N 74 59W
18 Herm I., Chan. Is. 49 30N 2 28W
† 26 Hermagor, Austria 46 38N 13 23E
116 Herman, U.S.A. 45 51N 96 8W

• Incorporated within the county of Hereford and Worcester
† Renamed Hermagor-Pressegger-See
•• Renamed Hénin-Beaumont

MAP
116 Hermann. U.S.A. 38 40N 91 25w
24 Hermannsburg, Ger. 52 49N 10 6E
92 Hermanus. S. Africa 34 27s 19 12E
20 Herment. France 45 45N 2 24E
100 Hermidale, Australia 31 30s 146 42E
118 Hermiston, U.S.A. 45 50N 119 16W
101 Hermitage. N.Z. 43 44s 170 5E
107 Hermitage B., Canada 47 33N 56 10W
128 Hermite. Is., Chile 55 50s 68 0W
120 Hermosillo. Mexico 29 10N 111 0w
27 Hernad, R., Hungary 48 20N 21 15E
125 Hernandarias. Paraguay 25 20s 54 40W
124 Hernando. Argentina 32 28s 64 50W
117 Hernando, U.S.A. 34 50N 89 59W
24 Herne. Germany 51 33N 7 12E
13 Herne Bay. Eng. 51 22N 1 8E
49 Herning. Denmark 56 8N 8 58E
120 Heroica Nogales. Mexico 31 14N 110 56w
106 Heron Bay, Canada 48 40N 85 25w
47 Heröy. Norway 62 18N 5 45E
116 Herreid. U.S.A. 45 53N 100 5w
31 Herrera. Spain 39 12N 5 3w
31 Herrera de Alcántar. Spain 39 39N 7 25W
30 Herrera de Pisuerga. Sp. 42 35N 4 20w
31 Herrera del Duque. Sp. 39 10N 5 3w
99 Herrick. Tasmania 41 5s 147 55E
117 Herrin. U.S.A. 37 50N 89 0w
49 Herrljunga, Sweden 58 5N 13 1E
25 Hersbruck, Germany 49 30N 11 25E
47 Hersvik. Norway 61 10N 4 53E
13 Hertford. Eng. 51 47N 0 4w
13 Hertford ♦. Eng. 51 51N 0 5w
16's Hertogenbosch. Neth. 51 42N 5 18E
92 Hertzogville, S. Africa 28 9s 25 30E
30 Hervás. Sapin 40 16N 5 52w
97 Hervey Bay, Australia 25 0s 153 0E
95 Hervey Is., Pac. O. 19 30s 159 0w
106 Hervey Junc., Canada 46 50N 72 29w
24 Herzberg. Cottbus, Ger. 51 40N 13 13E
24 Herzberg. Niedersachsen, Ger. 51 38N 10 20E
62 Herzliyya, Israel 32 10N 34 50E
26 Herzogenburg, Austria 48 17N 15 41E
19 Hesdin. France 50 21N 2 0E
24 Hesel. Germany 53 18N 7 36E
47 Heskestad. Norway 58 28N 6 22E
112 Hespeler. Canada 43 28N 80 19w
24 Hesse = Hessen. Germany 50 57N 9 20E
24 Hessen ♦, Germany 50 57N 9 20E
116 Hettinger. U.S.A. 46 8N 102 38W
24 Hettstedt. Germany 51 39N 11 30E
18 Heve. C. de la. France 49 30N 0 5E
27 Heves ♦. Hungary 47 50N 20 0E
62 Hevron, N., Isr.-Jord. 33 30s 34 52E
92 Hex River. S. Africa 33 30s 19 35E
21 Hexham, Eng. 54 58N 2 7w
100 Heyfield. Australia 37 59s 146 47E
12 Heysham. Eng. 54 5N 2 53w
100 Heywood, Australia 38 8s 141 37E
116 Hiawatha, Kans., U.S.A. 39 55N 95 33w
118 Hiawatha, Utah, U.S.A. 39 37N 111 1w
116 Hibbing. U.S.A. 47 30N 93 0w
117 Hickman. U.S.A. 36 35N 89 8w
115 Hickory. U.S.A. 35 46N 81 17w
113 Hicksville. U.S.A. 40 46N 73 30w
46 Hida-Gawa. Rumania 46 26N 27 59E
74 Hida-Sammyaku, Japan 36 30N 137 40E
120 Hidalgo ♦, Mexico 20 30N 99 10w
120 Hidalgo del Parral. Mex. 26 10N 104 50w
24 Hiddensee. Germany 54 30N 13 6E
26 Hieflau. Austria 47 36N 14 46E
32 Hiendelaencina. Spain 41 5N 3 0w
80 Hierro I. Can. I. 27 57N 17 56E
77 Hifung. China 22 59N 115 17E
117 Higgins, U.S.A. 36 9N 100 1w
115 Higgs I. L, U.S.A. 36 2N 78 30w
107 High L. Canada 56 40N 61 10w
82 High Atlas = Haut Atlas. N. Afr. 32 30N 5 0w
117 High Island, U.S.A. 29 32N 94 22w
115 High Point. U.S.A. 35 57N 79 58w
108 High Prairie, Canada 55 30N 116 30w
108 High River. Canada 50 30N 113 50w
115 High Springs. U.S.A. 29 50N 82 40w
93 High Veld = Hoëveld, S. Africa 26 30s 30 0E
13 High Wycombe. England 51 37N 0 45w
98 Highbank, New Zealand 47 34s 171 45E
114 Highland Pk., Ill., U.S.A. 42 10N 87 50w
112 Highland Pk., Mich., U.S.A.
116 Highmore, U.S.A. 44 35N 99 26w
119 Higley, U.S.A. 33 27N 111 46w
126 Higuerote, Venezuela 7 24N 61 3w
54 Hiiumaa, U.S.S.R. 58 50N 22 45E
32 Hijar. Spain 41 10N 0 27w
64 Hijaz. Saudi Arabia 26 0N 37 30E
99 Hiko. U.S.A. 37 30N 115 13w
74 Hikone. Japan 35 15N 136 10E
101 Hikurangi, New Zealand 37 54s 178 5E
101 Hikurangi. Mt., N.Z. 37 55s 178 4E
25 Hildburghausen. Ger. 50 24N 10 43E
24 Hildesheim. Germany 52 9N 9 55E
118 Hill City. Idaho, U.S.A. 43 20N 115 2w
116 Hill City. Kans., U.S.A. 39 25N 99 51w
116 Hill City. Minn.. U.S.A. 46 57N 93 35w
116 Hill City. S. Dak., U.S.A. 43 58N 103 35w
109 Hill Island L. Canada 60 30N 109 50w
64 Hilla. Iraq 32 30N 44 27E
64 Hilla. Saudi Arabia 23 35N 46 50E
49 Hillared. Sweden 57 37N 13 10E
49 Hilleröd. Denmark 55 56N 12 19E
49 Hillerstorp, Sweden 57 20N 13 52E
49 Hilleröd. Denmark 55 56N 12 19E
13 Hillingdon. Eng. 51 33N 0 29w
114 Hillman. U.S.A. 45 5N 83 52w

MAP
109 Hillmond, Canada 53 26N 109 41w
116 Hillsboro, Kans., U.S.A. 38 28N 97 10w
119 Hillsboro, N. Mex., U.S.A. 33 0N 107 35w
116 Hillsboro, N.D., U.S.A. 47 23N 97 9w
113 Hillsboro, N.H., U.S.A. 43 8N 71 56w
119 Hillsboro, N. Mex., U.S.A. 33 0N 107 35w
118 Hillsboro, Oreg., U.S.A. 45 31N 123 0w
117 Hillsboro, Tex., U.S.A. 32 0N 97 10w
114 Hillsdale, Mich., U.S.A. 41 55N 84 40w
113 Hillsdale, N.Y., U.S.A. 42 11N 73 30w
106 Hillsport, Canada 49 27N 85 34w
100 Hillston, Australia 33 30s 145 31E
110 Hilo, Hawaii 19 44N 155 5w
73 Hilonghilong, mt., Phil. 9 10N 125 45E
112 Hilton, U.S.A. 43 16N 77 48w
16 Hilversum, Netherlands 52 14N 5 10E
68 Himachal Pradesh ♦, India 31 30N 77 0E
67 Himalaya, Asia 29 0N 84 0E
44 Himara, Albania 40 8N 19 43E
74 Himeji, Japan 34 50N 134 40E
74 Himi, Japan 36 50N 137 0E
49 Himmerland, Den. 56 45N 9 30E
64 Hims = Homs, Syria 34 40N 36 45E
72 Hinako, Kepulauan, Indonesia 0 50N 97 20E
98 Hinchinbrook I., Australia 18 20s 146 15E
13 Hinckley, Eng. 52 33N 1 21w
118 Hinckley, U.S.A. 39 18N 112 41w
49 Hindås, Sweden 57 42N 12 29E
68 Hindaun, India 26 44N 77 5E
90 Hinde Rapids (Hells Gate), Congo 5 25s 27 3E
100 Hindmarsh L., Austral. 35 50s 141 55E
69 Hindol, India 20 40N 85 10E
49 Hindsholm, Den. 55 30N 10 40E
70 Hindupur, India 13 49N 77 32E
49 Hindås, Sweden 57 42N 12 27E
108 Hines Creek, Canada 56 20N 118 40w
77 Hingan, China 25 39N 110 43E
68 Hinganghat, India 20 30N 78 59E
77 Hingham, U.S.A. 48 40N 110 29w
77 Hingi, China 25 4N 105 2E
77 Hingkwo, China 26 15N 115 13E
77 Hingning, China 24 2N 115 55E
66 Hingol, R., Pakistan 25 30N 65 30E
70 Hingoli, India 19 41N 77 15E
70 Hinlopen Strait, Spitsbergen 79 30N 19 0E
4 Hinlopenstretet, Svalbard 79 35N 18 40E
77 Hinna, Nigeria 10 25N 11 28E
50 Hinnöy, Norway 68 40N 16 28E
74 Hi-no-misaki, Japan 35 28N 132 45E
31 Hinojosa del Duque, Spain 38 30N 5 17w
118 Hinsdale, U.S.A. 48 26N 107 2w
25 Hinterrhein, R., Switz. 46 40N 9 25w
109 Hinton, Canada 53 26N 117 28w
114 Hinton, U.S.A. 37 40N 80 51w
16 Hippolytushoef, Neth. 52 54N 4 58E
69 Hirakud, India 21 32N 83 51E
74 Hirakud Dam, India 21 32N 83 45E
74 Hiratsuka, Japan 35 40N 139 36E
83 Hirhafok, Algeria 23 49N 5 45E
74 Hirlau, Rumania 47 23N 27 0E
74 Hirosaki, Japan 40 34N 140 28E
74 Hiroshima, Japan 34 30N 132 30E
74 Hiroshima-ken ♦, Japan 34 50N 133 0E
74 Hirsoholmene, den. 57 30N 10 36E
19 Hirson, France 49 55N 4 4E
46 Hirsova, Rumania 44 40N 27 59E
49 Hirtshals, Denmark 57 36N 9 57E
47 Hisoy, Norway 58 26N 8 44E
68 Hissar, India 29 12N 75 45E
74 Hitachi, Japan 36 40N 140 35E
13 Hitchin, Eng. 51 57N 0 16w
74 Hitoyoshi, Japan 32 13N 130 45E
47 Hitra, Norway 63 30N 8 45E
24 Hitzacker, Germany 53 9N 11 1E
77 Hiungyao, China 40 10N 122 9E
109 Hjalmar L., Canada 61 35N 109 15w
48 Hjälmare Kanal, Swed. 59 20N 15 59E
48 Hjälmaren, Sweden 59 18N 15 40E
47 Hjartdal, Norway 59 37N 8 41E
49 Hjärtsäter, Sweden 58 35N 12 3E
47 Hjerkinn, Norway 62 13N 9 33E
49 Hjerpsted, Denmark 55 2N 8 39E
49 Hjo, Sweden 58 22N 14 17E
49 Hjorted, Sweden 57 37N 16 19E
49 Hjortkvarn, Sweden 58 54N 15 26E
48 Hjälmare kanal, Sweden 59 24N 15 56E
48 Hjälmaren, Sweden 59 15N 15 45E
49 Hjörring, Denmark 57 28N 10 0E
26 Hlinsko, Czechoslovakia 49 45N 15 54E
85 Hlohovec, Czechoslovakia 48 26N 17 49E
85 Ho, Ghana 6 37N 0 27E
71 Hoa Binh, Vietnam 20 50N 105 12E
71 Hoa Da (Phan Ri), S. Vietnam 11 16N 108 40E
108 Hoadley, Canada 52 45N 114 30w
71 Hoai Nhon (Bon Son), S. Vietnam 14 28N 103 37E
105 Hoare B., Canada 65 30N 62 30w
99 Hobart, Tasmania 42 50s 147 21E
117 Hobart, U.S.A. 35 0N 99 5w
116 Hobbs, U.S.A. 32 40N 103 3w
49 Hobjaerg, Denmark 56 19N 9 32E
126 Hobo, Colombia 2 35s 75 30w
16 Hoboken, Belgium 51 11N 4 21E
113 Hoboken, U.S.A. 40 45N 74 4w
49 Hobro, Denmark 56 39N 9 46E
49 Hoburg C., Sweden 56 54N 18 8E
49 Hoburgen, Sweden 56 55N 18 7E

MAP
117 Hochatown, U.S.A. 34 11N 94 39w
77 Hochih, China 24 43N 107 43E
25 Höchst, Germany 50 6N 8 33E
25 Hochwan, China 30 0N 106 15E
25 Hockenheim, Germany 49 18N 8 33E
63 Hodeïda, Yemen 14 50N 43 0E
109 Hodgson, Canada 51 20N 97 40w
27 Hódmezövásárhely, Hungary 46 28N 20 22E
82 Hodna, Chott el, Algeria 35 30N 5 0E
27 Hodonin, Cz. 48 50N 17 0E
18 Hoëdic, I., France 47 21N 2 52w
16 Hoek van Holland, Netherlands 52 0N 4 7E
93 Hoëveld, South Africa 26 30s 30 0E
77 Hofei, China 31 52N 117 15E
77 Hofeng, China 29 55N 110 5E
24 Hofgeismar, Germany 51 29N 9 23E
48 Hofors, Sweden 60 35N 16 15E
50 Hofsjökull, Iceland 64 49N 18 48w
50 Hofsós, Iceland 65 53N 19 26w
74 Hofu, Japan 34 0N 130 30E
64 Hofuf, Saudi Arabia 25 20N 49 40E
47 Hög-Gia, Mt., Norway 62 23N 10 7E
49 Höganäs, Sweden 56 13N 12 34E
115 Hogansville, U.S.A. 33 14N 84 50w
49 Hogeland, U.S.A. 48 50N 108 29w
48 Högen, Sweden 61 47N 14 11E
49 Högfors, Orebro, Swed. 59 58N 15 3E
48 Högfors, Västmanlands, Sweden 60 2N 16 3E
83 Hoggar = Ahaggar, Algeria 23 0N 6 30E
49 Högsäter, Sweden 58 38N 12 5E
49 Högsby, Sweden 57 10N 16 1E
48 Högsjö, Sweden 59 4N 15 44E
25 Hohe Rhön, Ger. 50 24N 9 58E
26 Hohe Tauern, Austria 47 11N 12 46E
27 Hohenau, Austria 48 36N 16 55E
24 Hohenems, Austria 47 22N 9 42E
24 Hohenstein Ernstthal, Germany 50 48N 12 43E
115 Hohenwald, U.S.A. 35 35N 87 30w
24 Hohenwestedt, Ger. 54 6N 9 40E
85 Hohoe, Ghana 7 8N 0 32E
77 Höhpi, China 35 59N 114 13E
72 Hôi An, S. Vietnam 15 30N 108 19E
71 Hoi Xuan, N. Vietnam 20 25N 105 9E
77 Hoima, Uganda 1 25N 31 20E
77 Hoiping, China 22 30N 112 12E
49 Hoisington, U.S.A. 38 33N 98 50w
49 Höjer, Denmark 54 58N 8 42E
76 Hokang, China 47 36N 130 28E
49 Hokensås, Sweden 58 0N 14 5E
49 Hökerum, Sweden 57 51N 13 16E
101 Hokianga Harbour, N.Z. 35 31s 173 22E
101 Hokitika, New Zealand 42 42s 171 0E
74 Hokkaidō ♦, Japan 43 30N 143 0E
47 Hokksund, Norway 59 44N 9 59E
71 Hokow, China 22 39N 103 57E
87 Hol-Hol, Fr. Terr. of the Afars £ Issas 11 20N 42 50E
77 Holan Shan, China 38 40N 105 50E
49 Holbaek, Denmark 55 43N 11 43E
100 Holbrook, Australia 35 42s 147 18E
119 Holbrook, U.S.A. 35 0N 110 0w
49 Holbaek, Denmark 55 43N 11 43E
108 Holden, Canada 53 13N 112 11w
118 Holden Fillmore, U.S.A. 39 0N 112 26w
117 Holdenville, U.S.A. 35 5N 96 25w
53 Holderness, Eng. 53 45N 0 5w
109 Holdrege, U.S.A. 40 25N 99 30w
47 Hole, Norway 60 6N 10 12E
70 Hole-Narsipur, India 12 48N 76 16E
27 Holešov, Czechoslovakia 49 20N 17 35E
121 Holguin, Cuba 20 50N 76 20w
27 Holíč, Czechoslovakia 48 49N 17 10E
87 Holla, Mt., Ethiopia 7 5N 36 35E
26 Hollabrunn, Austria 48 34N 16 5E
92 Hollams Bird I., South-West Africa 24 40s 14 30E
12 Holland, England 52 50N 0 10w
114 Holland, U.S.A. 42 47N 86 0w
112 Holland Landing, Can. 44 7N 79 30w
73 Hollandia = Djajapura, Indonesia 2 28s 140 38E
92 Hollams Bird I., South-West Africa 24 40s 14 30E
47 Höllen, Norway 58 6N 7 49E
113 Hollidaysburg, U.S.A. 40 26N 78 25w
117 Hollis, U.S.A. 34 45N 99 55w
119 Hollister, Calif., U.S.A. 37 55N 121 30w
118 Hollister, Idaho, U.S.A. 42 21N 114 34w
117 Holly, U.S.A. 38 7N 102 7w
115 Holly Hill, U.S.A. 29 15N 81 3w
117 Holly Springs, U.S.A. 34 45N 89 25w
119 Hollywood, Calif., U.S.A. 34 7N 118 25w
115 Hollywood, Fla., U.S.A. 26 0N 80 9w
48 Holm, Sweden 62 40N 16 40E
108 Holman Island, Canada 71 0N 118 0w
50 Hólmavik, Iceland 65 42N 21 40w
47 Holmedal, Fjordane, Norway 61 22N 5 11E
47 Holmedal, Hordaland, Norway 59 46N 5 50E
48 Holmegil, Norway 59 10N 11 44E
47 Holmestrand, Norway 59 31N 10 14E
47 Holmsbu, Norway 59 32N 10 27E
48 Holmsjön, Sweden 62 26N 16 0E
49 Holmsland Klit, Den. 56 0N 8 5E
50 Holmsund, Sweden 63 41N 20 20E

MAP
34 Hölö, Sweden 59 3N 17 36E
46 Holod, Rumania 46 49N 22 8E
62 Holon, Israel 32 2N 34 47E
98 Holroyd, R., Australia 14 0s 141 0E
47 Holsen, Norway 61 25N 6 8E
49 Holstebro, Denmark 56 22N 8 37E
50 Holt, Iceland 63 33N 19 48w
49 Holte, Denmark 55 50N 12 29E
107 Holton Harbour, Can. 54 31N 57 12w
119 Holtville, U.S.A. 32 50N 115 27w
24 Holzminden, Germany 51 49N 9 31E
90 Homa Bay, Kenya 0 36s 34 22E
90 Homa Bay ♦, Kenya 0 50s 34 30E
67 Homalin, Burma 24 55N 95 0E
24 Homberg, Hessen, Ger. 51 2N 9 20E
85 Hombori, Mali 15 20N 1 38w
25 Homburg, Ger. 49 19N 7 21E
105 Home B., Canada 68 40N 67 0w
98 Home Hill, Australia 19 43s 147 25E
118 Homedale, U.S.A. 43 42N 116 59w
104 Homer, Alaska, U.S.A. 59 40N 151 35w
117 Homer, La., U.S.A. 32 50N 93 4w
98 Homestead, Australia 20 20s 145 40E
115 Homestead, Fla., U.S.A. 25 29N 80 27w
112 Homestead, Idaho, U.S.A. 45 3N 116 58w
117 Homewood, U.S.A. 36 26N 96 24w
70 Homnabad, India 17 45N 77 45E
93 Homoine, Mozambique 23 55s 35 8E
46 Homorod, Rumania 46 5s 25 15E
83 Homs (Al Khums), Libya 32 40N 14 17E
64 Homs (Hims), Syria 34 40N 36 45E
71 Hon Chong, S. Vietnam 10 16N 104 38E
25 Honan ♦, China 33 15N 113 15E
126 Honda, Colombia 5 12N 74 45w
117 Hondo, U.S.A. 29 22N 99 6w
121 Honduras ■, Central America 14 40N 86 30w
120 Honduras, Golfo de, Central America 16 50N 87 0w
47 Hönefoss, Norway 60 10N 10 12E
113 Honesdale, U.S.A. 41 34N 75 17w
118 Honey, L., U.S.A. 40 13N 120 14w
19 Honfleur, France 49 25N 0 13E
49 Höng, Denmark 55 30N 11 14E
71 Höng, N. Vietnam 22 0N 104 0E
71 Hongha, R., N. Vietnam 22 0N 104 0E
77 Hong Kong ■, China 22 11N 114 14E
77 Honghai, B., China 22 45N 115 15E
86 Honkorâb, Ras, Egypt 24 35N 35 10E
110 Honolulu, Hawaii 21 19N 157 52w
74 Honshu, Japan 36 0N 138 0E
32 Hontoria del Pinar, Sp. 41 50N 3 10w
118 Hood Mt.,U.S.A. 45 15N 122 0w
118 Hood, Pt., Australia 34 19s 119 03E
118 Hood River, U.S.A. 45 45N 121 37w
118 Hoodsport, U.S.A. 47 30N 123 7w
24 Hooge, Germany 54 31N 8 36E
16 Hoogeveen, Neth. 52 44N 6 30E
16 Hoogezand, Neth. 53 11N 6 45E
69 Hooghly, R., India 21 59N 88 10E
16 Hook Hd., Ireland 52 8N 6 57w
98 Hook I., Australia 20 4s 149 0E
16 Hook of Holland=Hoek v. Holland, Neth. 52 0N 4 7E
117 Hooker, U.S.A. 36 55N 101 10w
113 Hoopeston, U.S.A. 40 30N 87 40w
92 Hoopstad, S. Africa 27 50s 25 55E
16 Hoorn, Netherlands 52 38N 5 4E
113 Hoosick Falls, U.S.A. 42 54N 73 21w
119 Hoover Dam, U.S.A. 36 0N 114 45w
57 Hopá, Turkey 41 28N 41 30E
116 Hope, Ark., U.S.A. 33 40N 93 30w
116 Hope, N.D., U.S.A. 47 21N 97 42w
5 Hope Bay, Ant. 65 0s 59 0w
104 Hope Pt., Alaska 68 20N 166 50w
115 Hope Town, Bahama Is. 26 30N 76 30w
107 Hopedale, Canada 55 27N 60 22w
92 Hopefield, S. Africa 33 3s 18 22E
120 Hopelchén, Mexico 19 46N 89 50w
47 Hopen, Möre og Romsdal, Norway 63 27N 8 2E
100 Hopetoun, Vic., Australia 35 48s 142 35E
96 Hopetoun, W. Austral., Australia 33 54s 120 6E
92 Hopetown, S. Africa 29 34s 24 3E
77 Hoping, China 24 31N 115 2E
100 Hopkins, R., Australia 37 55s 142 40E
100 Hopkinsville, U.S.A. 36 52N 87 26w
118 Hopland, U.S.A. 39 0N 123 0w
77 Hopo, China 23 12N 109 6E
49 Hoptrup, Denmark 55 11N 9 28E
46 Horazdovice, Cz. 49 19N 13 42E
49 Hörby, Sweden 55 50N 13 44E
47 Hordaland fylke ♦, Nor. 60 25N 6 15E

MAP
65 Hormuz, I., Iran 27 8N 56 28E
65 Hormuz Str., Persian G. 26 30N 56 30E
26 Horn, Austria 48 39N 15 40E
50 Horn, Isafjarðarsýsla, Iceland 66 28N 22 28w
50 Horn, Suður-Múlasýsla, Iceland 65 10N 13 31w
128 Horn, Cape = Hornos, C. de, Chile 55 50s 67 30w
15 Horn Head, Ireland 55 13N 8 0w
108 Horn Mts., Canada • 62 0N 119 0w
50 Horna Fd., Iceland 64 18N 15 15w
50 Hornachuelos, Spain 37 50N 5 14w
50 Hornavan, Sweden 66 15N 17 30E
49 Hornbaek, Frederiksborg, Denmark 56 5N 12 26E
31 Hornbeck, U.S.A. 31 22N 93 20w
118 Hornbrook, U.S.A. 41 58N 122 37w
24 Hornburg, Germany 52 2N 10 36E
49 Hornbaek, Frederiksborg, Denmark 56 6N 12 27E
49 Hornbaek, Viborg, Denmark 56 28N 9 58E
13 Horncastle, Eng. 53 13N 0 8w
48 Horndal, Sweden 60 18N 16 23E
106 Horne Payne, Canada 49 14N 84 48w
13 Hornell, U.S.A. 42 23N 77 41w
47 Hornindal, Norway 61 58N 6 30E
47 Hornnes, Norway 58 34N 7 45E
128 Hornos, Cabo de, Chile 55 50s 67 30E
19 Hornoy, France 49 50N 1 54E
63 Hornsberg, Jamtland, Sweden 63 14N 14 40E
48 Hornsberg, Kronobergs, Sweden 56 37N 13 47E
100 Hornsby, Australia 33 42s 151 2E
12 Hornsea, England 53 55N 0 10w
49 Hornslandet Pen., Swed. 61 35N 17 37E
49 Hornslet, Denmark 56 18N 10 19E
74 Horoshiri Dake, Japan 42 40N 142 40E
26 Horovice, Cz. 49 48N 13 53E
49 Horqueta, Paraguay 23 15s 56 55w
49 Horred, Sweden 57 22N 12 28E
118 Horse Cr., U.S.A. 41 33N 104 45w
107 Horse Is., Canada 50 15N 55 50w
100 Horse Lake, Australia 32 4s 142 5E
49 Horsens, Denmark 55 52N 9 51E
49 Horsens Fjord, Denmark 55 50N 10 0E
119 Horseshoe Dam, U.S.A. 33 45N 111 35w
13 Horsham, Eng. 51 4N 0 20w
26 Horsovsky Tyn, Cz. 49 31N 12 58E
47 Horten, Norway 59 25N 10 32E
27 Hortobágy, R., Hung. 47 30N 21 6E
116 Horton, U.S.A. 39 42N 95 30w
49 Hörviken, Sweden 56 2N 14 44E
106 Horwood, L., Canada 48 01N 82 55w
87 Hosaina, Ethiopia 7 30N 37 47E
70 Hosdurga, India 13 40N 76 17E
72 Hose, Pegunungan, Malaysia 2 5N 114 6E
68 Hoshangabad, India 22 45N 77 45E
68 Hoshiarpur, India 31 30N 75 58E
116 Hosmer, U.S.A. 45 36N 99 29w
70 Hospet, India 15 15N 76 20E
32 Hospitalet de Llobregat, Spain 41 21N 2 6E
128 Hoste, I., Chile 55 0s 69 0w
20 Hostens, France 44 30N 0 40w
71 Hot, Thailand 18 8N 98 29E
117 Hot Creek Ra., U.S.A. 39 0N 116 0w
117 Hot Springs, Ark. USA. 34 0N 93 0w
116 Hot Springs, S. Dak., U.S.A. 43 25N 103 30w
92 Hotazel, S. Africa 27 17s 23 00E
116 Hotchkiss, U.S.A. 38 55N 107 47w
75 Hotien (Khotan), China 37 6N 79 59E
50 Hoting, Sweden 64 8N 16 15E
44 Hotolishti, Albania 41 10N 20 25E
92 Hottentotsbaai, S. W. Africa 26 8s 14 59E
18 Houat, I., France 47 24N 2 58w
119 Houck, U.S.A. 35 15N 109 15w
19 Houdan, France 48 48N 1 35E
16 Houffalize, Belgium 50 8N 5 48E
117 Houghton, U.S.A. 47 9N 88 39w
114 Houghton L., U.S.A. 44 20N 84 40w
12 Houghton-le-Spring, England
101 Houhora, N.Z. 34 49s 173 9E
107 Houlton, U.S.A. 46 5N 68 0w
117 Houma, U.S.A. 29 35N 90 50w
83 Houmt Souk = Djerba, Tunisia 33 53N 10 37E
84 Houndé, Upper Volta 11 34N 3 31w
108 Houston, Canada 54 25N 126 30w
117 Houston, Mo., U.S.A. 37 20N 92 0w
117 Houston, Tex., U.S.A. 29 50N 95 20w
96 Houtman Abrolhos, Australia 28 43s 113 48E
49 Hova, Sweden 58 53N 14 14E
47 Hövag, Norway 58 10N 8 15E
75 Hovd (Jargalant), Mongolia 48 2N 91 37E
47 Hovden, Aust-Agder, Norway 59 33N 7 22E
13 Hove, England 50 50N 0 10w
49 Hovmantorp, Sweden 56 47N 15 7E
76 Hövsgöl Nuur, Mongolia 51 0N 100 30E
48 Hovsta, Sweden 59 22N 15 15E
87 Howar, W., (Shau) Sud. 17 0N 25 30E
87 Howar, W., Ethiopia 25 16s 152 32E
116 Howard, Kans., U.S.A. 37 30N 96 16w
114 Howard, Penn., U.S.A. 41 0N 77 40w
116 Howard, S.D., U.S.A. 44 2N 97 30w
118 Howe, U.S.A. 43 48N 113 0w
98 Howe, C., Australia 37 30s 150 0E
114 Howell, U.S.A. 42 38N 84 0w
113 Howick, Canada 45 10N 73 53w

MAP

93 Howick, S. Afr. 29 28S 30 14E
98 Howick Group, Austral. 14 20S 145 30E
107 Howley, Canada 49 12N 57 2W
69 Howrah, India 22 37N 88 27E
15 Howth Hd., Ireland 53 21N 6 0W
24 Höxter, Germany 51 45N 9 26E
14 Hoy I., Scot. 58 50N 3 15W
24 Hoya, Germany 52 47N 9 10E
47 Höyanger, Norway 61 25N 6 50E
47 Höydalsmo, Norway 59 30N 8 15E
24 Hoyerswerda, Germany 51 26N 14 14E
47 Höyland, Norway 58 50N 5 43E
30 Hoyos, Spain 40 9N 6 45W
67 Hpungan Pass, Burma 27 30N 96 55E
26 Hradec Králové, Cz. 50 15N 15 50E
27 Hrádek, Czechoslovakia 48 46N 16 16E
27 Hranice, Czechoslovakia 49 34N 17 45E
27 Hron., R. 48 0N 18 4E
   Czechoslovakia
28 Hrubieszów, Poland 50 49N 23 51E
27 Hrubý Nízký Jesenik, 50 7N 17 10E
   Cz.
39 Hrvatska, Yugoslavia 45 20N 16 0E
21 Hsaichwan Shan, China 21 34N 112 30E
77 Hsaio Shan, China 34 0N 111 30E
67 Hsenwi, Burma 23 22N 97 55E
77 Hsiamen, China 24 30N 118 7E
77 Hsinchow, China 19 37N 109 17E
77 Hsinchu, Taiwan 24 48N 120 55E
77 Hsinhsing, China 22 45N 112 11E
77 Hsiuning, China 29 51N 118 15E
71 Hua Hin, Thailand 12 18N 99 51E
124 Huachipato, Chile 36 45S 73 09W
126 Huacho, Peru 11 10S 77 35W
126 Huachón, Peru 10 35S 76 0W
126 Huacrachuco, Peru 8 35S 76 50W
77 Huain, China 36 26N 119 12E
120 Huajuapan, Mexico 17 50N 98 0W
124 Hualien, Taiwan 24 0N 121 30E
126 Huallaga, R., Peru 7 30S 76 10W
119 Hualpai Pk., U.S.A. 35 8N 113 58W
126 Huancabamba, Peru 5 10S 79 15W
126 Huancané, Peru 15 10S 69 50W
126 Huancapi, Peru 13 25S 74 0W
126 Huancavelica, Peru 12 50S 75 5W
126 Huancayo, Peru 12 5S 75 0W
77 Huanglui, China 18 30N 108 46E
77 Huangnipo, China 27 40N 105 10E
126 Huánuco, Peru 9 55S 76 15W
126 Huaraz, Peru 9 30S 77 32W
126 Huarmey, Peru 10 5S 78 0W
126 Huascarán, Peru 9 0S 77 30W
124 Huasco, Chile 28 24S 71 15W
120 Huatabampo, Mexico 26 50N 109 50W
120 Huautla, Mexico 18 20N 96 50W
126 Huayllay, Peru 11 03S 76 21W
120 Huaynamota, Mexico 21 56N 104 30W
117 Hubbard, U.S.A. 31 50N 96 50W
70 Hubli, India 15 22N 75 15E
77 Huchow, China 30 57N 120 1E
120 Huchuetenango, Guat. 15 25N 91 30W
24 Hückelhoven-Ratheim, 51 6N 6 3E
   Ger.
12 Huddersfield, Eng. 53 38N 1 49W
86 Hudi, Sudan 17 43N 34 28E
48 Hudiksvall, Sweden 61 43N 17 10E
109 Hudson, Canada 50 6N 92 09W
113 Hudson, Mass., U.S.A. 42 23N 71 35W
114 Hudson, Mich., U.S.A. 41 50N 84 20W
113 Hudson, N.Y., U.S.A. 42 15N 73 46W
116 Hudson, Wis., U.S.A. 44 57N 92 45W
118 Hudson, Wyo., U.S.A. 42 54N 108 37W
105 Hudson Bay, Canada 60 0N 86 0W
109 Hudson Bay, Can. 52 51N 102 23W
113 Hudson Falls, U.S.A. 43 18N 73 34W
108 Hudson Hope, Canada 56 0N 121 54W
113 Hudson, R., U.S.A. 41 35N 74 0W
104 Hudson Str., Canada 62 0N 70 0W
71 Hué, S. Vietnam 16 30N 107 35E
30 Huebra, R., Spain 40 54N 6 28E
46 Huedin, Rumania 46 52N 23 2E
18 Huelgoat, France 48 22N 3 46W
33 Huelma, Spain 37 39N 3 28W
31 Huelva, Spain 37 18N 6 57W
31 Huelva, R., Spain 37 45N 6 15W
31 Huelva ♦, Spain 37 40N 7 0W
124 Huentelauquén, Chile 31 38S 71 33W
33 Huércal Overa, Spain 37 23N 1 57W
124 Huerta, Sa. de la, Arg. 31 10S 67 30W
33 Huertas, C. de las, 38 21N 0 24W
   Spain
32 Huerva, R., Spain 41 13N 1 15W
32 Huesca, Spain 42 8N 0 25W
33 Huesca ♦, Spain 42 20N 0 1E
33 Huéscar, Spain 37 44N 2 35W
120 Huétamo, Mexico 18 36N 100 54W
32 Huete, Spain 40 10N 2 43W
96 Hugh, R., Australia 24 40S 134 0E
98 Hughenden, Australia 20 52S 144 10E
104 Hughes, Alaska 66 0N 154 20W
116 Hugo, Colo., U.S.A. 39 12N 103 27W
117 Hugo, Okla., U.S.A. 34 0N 95 30W
117 Hugoton, U.S.A. 37 18N 101 22W
76 Huhehot, China 40 52N 111 36E
120 Huichapán, Mexico 20 24N 99 40W
92 Huila, Angola 15 30S 15 0E
126 Huila ♦, Colombia 2 30N 75 45W
126 Huila, Nevado del, 3 0N 76 0W
   Colombia
77 Huiling Shan, China 21 35N 111 57E
76 Huinan, China 42 40N 126 0E
124 Huinca Renancó, Arg. 34 51S 64 22W
64 Huiya, Saudi Arabia 24 40N 49 15E
67 Hukawng Valley, Burma 26 30N 96 30E
77 Hukow, China 29 38N 116 15E
87 Hukuma, Sudan 14 55N 36 2E
92 Hukuntsi, Botswana 23 58S 21 45E
87 Hula, Ethiopia 6 33N 38 30E
64 Hulaifa, Saudi Arabia 25 58N 41 0E
76 Hulan, China 46 0N 126 44E

62 Húlda, Israel 31 50N 34 51E
76 Hulin, China 45 45N 133 0E
106 Hull, Canada 45 20N 75 40W
12 Hull, England 53 45N 0 20W
12 Hull, R., Eng. 53 55N 0 23W
16 Hulst, Netherlands 51 17N 4 2E
49 Hultsfred, Sweden 57 30N 15 52E
76 Huma, China 51 44N 126 42E
124 Humahuaca, Argentina 23 10S 65 25W
126 Humaitá, Brazil 7 35S 62 40W
124 Humaita, Paraguay 27 2S 58 31W
92 Humansdorp, S. Africa 34 2S 24 46E
12 Humber, R., Eng. 53 42N 0 20W
112 Humberstone, Canada 42 53N 79 16W
117 Humble, U.S.A. 29 59N 95 10W
109 Humboldt, Canada 52 15N 105 9W
116 Humboldt, Iowa, U.S.A. 42 42N 94 15W
115 Humboldt, Tenn., U.S.A. 35 50N 88 55W
118 Humboldt, R., U.S.A. 40 55N 116 0W
4 Humboldt Gletscher, 79 30N 62 0W
   Greenland
100 Hume, L., Australia 36 0S 147 0E
27 Humenné, Cz. 48 55N 21 50E
119 Humphreys Pk., U.S.A. 35 24N 111 38W
26 Humpolec, Cz. 49 31N 15 20E
100 Humula, Australia 35 30S 147 46E
83 Hūn, Libya 29 2N 16 0E
50 Huna Flói, Iceland 65 50N 20 50W
77 Hunan ♦, China 27 30N 111 30E
76 Hunchun, China 42 49N 130 31E
49 Hundested, Denmark 55 58N 11 52E
48 Hundshögen, mt., Swed. 62 57N 13 46E
46 Hunedoara, Rumania 45 40N 22 50E
46 Hunedoara ♦, Rum. 45 45N 22 54E
24 Hünfeld, Germany 50 40N 9 47E
77 Hung Ho, R., China 32 25N 115 35E
27 Hungary ■, Europe 47 20N 19 20E
9 Hungary, Plain of, Eur. 47 0N 20 0E
99 Hungerford, Australia 28 58S 144 24E
77 Hunghai Wan, China 22 45N 115 15E
77 Hungho (Sinti), China 29 49N 113 30E
77 Hungkiang, China 27 0N 109 49E
76 Hungnam, Korea 39 55N 127 45E
77 Hungshui Ho, China 24 20N 107 10E
77 Hungtze Hu, China 33 20N 118 35E
84 Huni Valley, Ghana 5 33N 1 56W
92 Hunsberge, S.W. Africa 27 58S 17 5E
25 Hunsrück, mts., Ger. 50 0N 7 30E
12 Hunstanton, U.K. 52 57N 0 30E
70 Hunsur, India 12 16N 76 16E
24 Hunte, R., Germany 52 47N 8 28E
116 Hunter, N.D., U.S.A. 47 12N 97 17W
113 Hunter, N.Y., U.S.A. 42 13N 74 13W
108 Hunter I., Canada 51 55N 128 0W
99 Hunter I., Australia 40 30S 144 46E
100 Hunter, R., Australia 32 25S 150 50E
100 Hunter R., Australia 32 45S 150 50E
91 Hunters Road, Rhodesia 19 9S 29 49E
99 Hunterton, Australia 26 12S 148 30E
101 Hunterville, N.Z. 39 56S 175 35E
114 Huntingburg, U.S.A. 38 20N 86 58W
106 Huntingdon, Canada 45 10N 74 10W
13 Huntingdon, Eng. 52 20N 0 11W
113 Huntingdon, N.Y., 40 52N 73 25W
   U.S.A.
112 Huntingdon, Pa., U.S.A. 40 28N 78 1W
107 Huntingdon I., Canada 53 48N 56 45W
•13 Huntingdon & 52 23N 0 10W
   Peterborough ♦, Eng.
118 Huntington, Id., USA 44 12N 117 21W
114 Huntington, Ind., U.S.A. 40 52N 85 30W
118 Huntington, Ut., USA 39 24N 111 1W
114 Huntington, W. Va., 38 20N 82 30W
   U.S.A.
119 Huntington Beach, 34 40N 118 0W
   U.S.A.
119 Huntington Park, U.S.A. 34 58N 118 15W
101 Huntly, New Zealand 37 34S 175 11E
14 Huntly, Scot. 57 27N 2 48W
106 Huntsville, Canada 45 20N 79 14W
115 Huntsville, Ala., U.S.A. 34 45N 86 35W
117 Huntsville, Tex., U.S.A. 30 50N 95 35W
91 Hunyani, R., Rhodesia 18 0S 31 0E
91 Hunyani Dams. Rhod. 18 0S 31 10E
98 Huon Gulf, N.E.N. 7 0S 147 30E
   Guin.
99 Huonville, Australia 43 0S 147 5E
77 Hupei ♦, China 31 5N 113 5E
27 Hurbanovo, Cz. 47 51N 18 11E
112 Hurd C., Canada 45 15N 81 40W
46 Hurezani, Rumania 44 49N 23 40E
86 Hurghada, Egypt 27 15N 33 50E
119 Hurley, N. Mex., U.S.A. 32 45N 108 7W
116 Hurley, Wis., U.S.A. 46 26N 90 10W
112 Huron, Ohio, U.S.A. 41 22N 82 34W
116 Huron, S.D., U.S.A. 44 30N 98 20W
112 Huron, L., Can.-U.S.A. 45 0N 83 0W
119 Hurricane, U.S.A. 37 10N 113 12W
87 Hurso, Ethiopia 9 35N 41 33E
100 Hurstbridge, Australia 37 40S 145 10E
47 Hurum, Buskerud, Nor. 59 36N 10 23E
47 Hurum, Oppland, Nor. 61 9N 8 46E
99 Hurunui, R., N.Z. 42 48S 172 25E
49 Hurup, Den. 56 46N 8 25E
49 Husaby, Sweden 58 35N 13 25E
50 Húsavik, Iceland 66 3N 17 21W
46 Husi, Rumania 46 41N 28 7E
49 Huskvarna, Sweden 57 47N 14 15E
62 Husn, Jordan 32 29N 35 52E
47 Husöy, Norway 61 3N 4 44E
47 Husøy, Sogn og 61 3N 4 44E
   Fjordane, Norway
76 Hutag, Mongolia 49 25N 102 34E
117 Hutchinson, Kans., USA 38 3N 97 59W
117 Hutchinson, Minn, USA 44 50N 94 22W

76 Huto Ho, China 38 30N 113 45E
16 Huttenberg, Austria 46 56N 14 33E
16 Hüttental, Germany 50 53N 8 1E
117 Huttig, U.S.A. 33 5N 92 10W
62 Huwarā, Jordan 32 9N 35 15E
87 Huwun, Ethiopia 4 23N 40 6E
16 Huy, Belgium 50 31N 5 15E
59 Hvalør, Norway 59 4N 11 1E
50 Hvammsfjörður, Iceland 65 4N 22 5W
50 Hvammur, Dalasýsla, 65 13N 21 49W
   Iceland
39 Hvar, Yugoslavia 43 10N 16 45E
39 Hvarski Kanal, Y.-slav. 43 15N 16 35E
50 Hvítá, Arnessýsla, 64 0N 20 58W
   Iceland
50 Hvítá, Mýrasýsla, 64 40N 21 5W
   Iceland
50 Hvítárvatn, Iceland 63 37N 19 50W
47 Hvitsten, Norway 59 35N 10 42E
76 Hwachwan, China 47 1N 130 50E
77 Hwaian, China 32 20N 114 30E
77 Hwaiyang, China 33 50N 115 2E
76 Hwang-ho R., China 40 50N 107 30E
77 Hwangan, China 31 30N 114 40E
77 Hwangshih, China 30 27N 115 0E
77 Hwangyen, China 28 34N 121 12E
77 Hwanjen, China 41 24N 125 26E
76 Hwaten, China 43 0N 126 52E
76 Hweian, China 25 2N 118 56E
77 Hweichang, China 25 33N 115 41E
76 Hweilai, China 23 0N 116 15E
76 Hweimin, China 37 36N 117 30E
75 Hweiteh, China 26 32N 103 6E
77 Hwokiu, China 32 23N 116 16E
76 Hyannis, U.S.A. 42 3N 101 45W
114 Hyattsville, U.S.A. 38 59N 76 55W
48 Hybo, Sweden 61 49N 16 15E
70 Hyderabad, India 17 10N 78 29E
68 Hyderabad, Pakistan 25 23N 68 36E
68 Hyderabad ♦, Pak. 25 3N 68 24E
21 Hyères, France 43 8N 6 9E
21 Hyères, Is. d', France 43 0N 6 28E
76 Hyesan, N. Korea 41 20N 128 10E
108 Hyland, R., Canada 60 30N 128 20W
47 Hyland Post, Canada 57 40N 128 10W
47 Hylestad, Norway 59 6N 7 29E
49 Hyllested, Denmark 56 17N 10 46E
49 Hyltebruk, Sweden 56 59N 13 15E
99 Hyndman Pk., U.S.A. 44 4N 114 0W
117 Hyrum, U.S.A. 41 35N 111 56W
118 Hysham, U.S.A. 46 21N 107 11W
13 Hythe, Eng. 51 4N 1 5E

51 4N 1 5E
50 Hyvinkää, Finland 60 38N 24 50E
82 I-n-Tabedog, Mali 19 54N 1 3E
82 Iabès, Erg., Algeria 27 30N 2 2W
126 Iaco, R., Brazil 10 25S 70 30W
93 Iakora, Malagasy Rep. 23 6S 46 40E
46 Ialomita ♦, Rumania 44 30N 27 30E
46 Ianca, Rumania 45 6N 27 29E
46 Iara, Rumania 46 31N 23 35E
47 Iaşi (Jassy), Rumania 47 10N 27 40E
46 Iaşi ♦, Rumania 47 20N 27 0E
105 Iaucdjovac, (Port 58 25N 78 15W
   Harrison), Canada
126 Iaurête, Colombia 0 30N 69 5W
73 Iba, Philippines 15 22N 120 0E
85 Ibadan, Nigeria 7 22N 3 58E
126 Ibagué, Colombia 4 27N 73 14W
39 Iballja, Albania 42 12N 20 0E
46 Ibăneşti, Rumania 46 45N 24 50E
85 Ibar, R., Yugoslavia 43 15N 20 40E
74 Ibaraki-ken ♦, Japan 36 10N 140 10E
126 Ibarra, Ecuador 0 21N 78 7W
87 Ibba, Sudan 4 49N 29 2E
87 Ibba, Bahr el, Sudan 5 30N 28 55E
24 Ibbenbüren, Germany 52 16N 7 41E
90 Ibembo, Zaïre 2 35N 23 35E
8 Iberian Peninsula, Eur. 40 0N 5 0W
106 Iberville, Canada 5 19N 73 17W
106 Iberville, Lac d', Can. 55 40N 73 30W
85 Ibi, Nigeria 8 15N 9 50E
127 Ibia, Brazil 19 30S 46 30W
127 Ibiracu, Brazil 19 50S 40 30W
33 Ibiza, I., Spain 39 0N 1 30E
73 Ibo, Mozambique 12.22S 40 32E
73 Ibonma, Indonesia 3 22S 133 31E
127 Ibotirama, Brazil 12 13S 43 12W
44 Ibriktepe, Turkey 41 2N 26 33E
86 Ibshawâi, Egypt 29 21N 30 40E
73 Ibu, Indonesia 1 35N 127 25E
24 Iburg, Germany 52 10N 8 3E
91 Ibwe Munyama, Zambia 16 5S 28 31E
126 Icá, Peru 14 0S 75 30W
126 Ica, R., Brazil 2 55S 69 0W
126 Icabarú, Venezuela 4 20N 61 45W
126 Içana, Brazil 0 21N 67 19W
50 Iceland, I. ◊, Atlantic 65 0N 19 0W
   Oc.
59 Icha, U.S.S.R. 55 30N 156 0E
77 Ichang, China 30 48N 111 29E
70 Ichchapuram, India 19 10N 84 40E
74 Ichiharan, Japan 35 45N 139 42E
74 Ichihara, Japan 35 28N 140 5E
126 Ichilo, R., Bolivia 16 30S 64 45W
74 Ichinomiya, Japan 35 20N 136 50E
82 Icht, Morocco 29 6N 8 54W
77 Ichun, Kiangsi, China 27 51N 114 12E
76 Ichun, Shensi, China 35 24N 109 9E
76 Ichun, China 30 30N 112 29E
4 Icy C., Alaska 70 25N 162 0W
104 Icy Str., Alaska 58 20N 135 30W
116 Ida Grove, U.S.A. 42 20N 95 25W
13 Ilfracombe, Eng. 51 13N 4 8W
87 Idaga Hamus, Ethiopia 14 13N 39 35E
85 Idah, Nigeria 6 10N 6 40E
118 Idaho ♦, U.S.A. 44 10N 114 0W
118 Idaho City, U.S.A. 43 50N 115 52W
118 Idaho Falls, U.S.A. 43 30N 112 10W

118 Idaho Springs, U.S.A. 39 49N 105 30W
30 Idanha-a-Nova, Port. 39 50N 7 15W
75 Idar-Oberstein, Ger. 49 43N 7 19E
85 Idanre, Nigeria 7 8N 5 5E
81 Idd el Ghanam, Sudan 11 30N 24 25E
83 Iddan, Somali Rep. 6 10N 49 5E
83 Idehan, Libya 27 10N 11 30E
83 Idehan Marzūq, Libya 24 50N 13 51E
70 Idar, India 23 50N 73 0E
83 Idelès, Algeria 23 58N 5 53E
86 Idfû, Egypt 25 0N 32 49E
45 Idhi Oros, Crete 35 15N 24 45E
45 Idhra, Greece 37 20N 23 28E
72 Idi, Indonesia 4 55N 97 45E
88 Idiofa, Zaïre 4 55S 19 42E
48 Idkerberget, Sweden 60 22N 15 15E
62 Idna, Jordan 31 34N 34 58E
39 Idrija, Yugoslavia 46 0N 14 5E
54 Iditsa, U.S.S.R. 56 25N 28 57E
25 Idstein, Germany 50 13N 8 17E
85 Idua, Somali Rep. 7 47N 49 45E
85 Ife, Nigeria 7 30N 4 31E
85 Iférouâne, Niger 19 5N 8 35E
82 Ifni, Morocco 29 25N 10 10W
85 Ifon, Nigeria 6 58N 5 40E
90 Iganga, Uganda 0 30N 33 28E
127 Igarapava, Brazil 20 3S 47 47W
127 Igarapé Açu, Brazil 1 4S 47 33W
59 Igarka, U.S.S.R. 67 30N 87 20E
70 Igatpuri, India 19 40N 73 35E
85 Igbetti, Nigeria 8 44N 4 8E
85 Igbo-Ora, Nigeria 7 10N 3 15E
85 Igboho, Nigeria 8 40N 3 50E
48 Iggesund, Sweden 61 39N 17 10E
82 Igherm, Morocco 30 7N 8 18W
82 Ighil, Djebel, Morocco 31 37N 6 31W
82 Ighil Izane, Algeria 35 44N 0 31E
40 Iglene, Algeria 22 57N 4 58E
40 Iglésias, Italy 39 19N 8 27E
82 Igli, Algeria 30 25N 2 12W
105 Igloolik Island, Canada 69 20N 81 30W
82 Igma, Algeria 29 6N 6 11W
86 Igma, Gebel el, Egypt 28 55N 34 0E
106 Ignace, Canada 49 30N 91 40W
55 Igoshevo, U.S.S.R. 59 25N 42 35E
44 Igoumenitsa, Greece 39 32N 20 18E
125 Iguaçu, Cat. del, Brazil 25 41N 54 26W
125 Iguaçu Falls, Brazil 25 41N 54 26W
125 Iguaçu, R., Brazil 25 30S 53 10W
32 Igualada, Spain 41 37N 1 37E
125 Iguape, R., Brazil 24 40S 48 0W
127 Iguatu, Brazil 6 20S 39 18W
85 Iguéla, Gabon 2 0S 9 16E
85 Igumale, Nigeria 6 47N 7 55E
85 Ihiala, Nigeria 5 40N 6 55E
93 Ihosy, Malagasy Rep. 22 24S 46 8E
93 Ihotry, L., Malag. 21 56S 43 41E
74 Iida, Japan 35 35N 138 0E
50 Iisalmi, Finland 63 32N 27 10E
74 Iizuka, Japan 33 38N 130 42E
85 Ijebu-Igbo, Nigeria 6 56N 4 1E
85 Ijebu-Ode, Nigeria 6 47N 3 52E
16 IJmuiden, Netherlands 52 28N 4 35E
16 IJsselmeer, Netherlands 52 45N 5 20E
17 Ikamatua, New Zealand 42 15S 171 41E
85 Ikare, Nigeria 7 18N 5 40E
45 Ikaria, I., Greece 37 35N 26 10E
49 Ikast, Denmark 56 8N 9 10E
85 Ikeja, Nigeria 6 28N 3 45E
88 Ikela, Zaïre 1 0S 23 35E
85 Ikerre, Nigeria 7 25N 5 19E
43 Ikhtiman, Bulgaria 42 27N 23 48E
74 Iki, Japan 33 45N 129 42E
90 Ikimba L., Tanzania 1 30S 31 20E
85 Ikire, Nigeria 7 10N 4 15E
85 Ikirun, Nigeria 7 54N 4 40E
85 Ikole, Nigeria 7 40N 5 37E
85 Ikom, Nigeria 6 0N 8 42E
93 Ikopa, R., Malagasy 17 45S 46 40E
   Rep.
85 Ikot Ekpene, Nigeria 5 12N 7 40E
90 Ikungu, Tanzania 1 33S 33 42E
85 Ila, Nigeria 8 0N 4 5E
69 Ilam, Nepal 26 58N 87 58E
76 Ilan, China 46 14N 129 33E
59 Ilanskiy, U.S.S.R. 56 14N 96 3E
16 Ilaomita, R., Rumania 44 47N 27 0E
85 Ilaro Agege, Nigeria 9 34N 78 3E
70 Ilayangudi, India 9 34N 78 37E
98 Ilbilbie, Australia 21 45S 149 20E
109 Ile à la Crosse, L', Can. 55 30N 108 0W
18 Ile Bouchard, L', France 47 7N 0 26E
19 Ile de France ♦, Fr. 49 0N 2 20E
88 Ilebo, Zaïre 4 17S 20 47E
52 Ilek, R., U.S.S.R. 51 30N 53 10E
85 Ilero, Nigeria 8 0N 3 20E
85 Ilesha, West-Central, 7 37N 4 40E
   Nigeria
85 Ilesha, Western, Nigeria 8 57N 3 28E
109 Ilford, Canada 56 4N 95 40W
98 Ilfracombe, Australia 23 30S 144 30E
13 Ilfracombe, Eng. 51 13N 4 8W
31 Ilha Berlenga, Portugal 39 25N 9 30W
30 Ilhavo, Portugal 40 33N 8 43E
127 Ilheus, Brazil 14 49S 39 2W
46 Ilia, Rumania 45 57N 22 40E
45 Ilia ♦, Greece 37 45N 21 35E
58 Ilich, U.S.S.R. 41 0N 68 10E

124 Ilico, Chile 34 50s 72 20W
116 Iliff, U.S.A. 40 50N 103 3W
45 Iliki, Greece 38 24N 23 15E
44 Iliodhrómia, Greece 39 12N 23 50E
113 Ilion, U.S.A. 43 0N 75 3W
•58 Iliysk, U.S.S.R. 44 10N 77 20E
70 Ilkal, India 15 57N 76 8E
52 Ilkeston, Eng. 52 59N 1 19W
76 Ilkhuri Shan, China 51 30N 124 0E
12 Ilkley, England 53 56N 1 49W
73 Ilana B., Philippines 7 35N 123 45E
124 Illapel, Chile 32 0S 71 10W
62 'Illar, Jordan 32 23N 35 7E
20 Ille, France 42 40N 2 37E
20 Ille-et-Vilaine ♦, Fr. 48 10N 1 30W
25 Iller, R., Germany 47 53N 10 10E
30 Illescas, Spain 40 8N 3 51W
63 Illig, Somali Rep. 7 47N 49 45E
126 Illimani, Mte., Bolivia 16 30S 67 50W
111 Illinois, R., U.S.A. 40 10N 90 20W
111 Illinois ■, U.S.A. 40 15N 89 30W
31 Illora, Spain 37 17N 3 53W
54 Ilmen, oz., U.S.S.R. 5 15N 31 10E
24 Ilmenau, Germany 50 41N 10 55E
126 Ilo, France 17 40N 71 20W
73 Ilobu, Nigeria 7 45N 4 25E
73 Iloilo, Philippines 10 45N 122 33E
42 Ilok, Yugoslavia 45 15N 19 20E
85 Ilora, Nigeria 7 45N 3 50E
85 Ilorin, Nigeria 8 30N 4 35E
50 Ilovatka, U.S.S.R. 50 30N 46 50E
57 Ilovlya, U.S.S.R. 49 15N 44 2E
57 Ilovlya, R., U.S.S.R. 49 38N 44 20E
28 Iłowa, Poland 51 30N 15 10E
54 Ilukste, U.S.S.R. 55 55N 26 20E
46 Ilwa Micǎ, Rumania 47 17N 24 40E
73 Ilwaki, Indonesia 7 55S 126 30E
56 Ilyichevsk, U.S.S.R. 46 10N 30 35E
74 Imabari, Japan 34 4N 133 0E
82 Imadahane, Morocco 32 8N 7 0W
23 Imaloto, R., Malag. 23 10S 45 15E
**59 Iman, U.S.S.R. 45 50N 133 40E
87 Imi (Hinna), Ethiopia 6 35N 42 30E
82 Imi n'Tanoute, Morocco 31 13N 8 51E
76 Imienpo, China 45 0N 128 16E
57 Imishly, U.S.S.R. 39 49N 48 4E
82 Imiter, Morocco 29 43N 8 10W
118 Imlay, U.S.A. 40 45N 118 9W
112 Imlay City, U.S.A. 43 0N 83 2W
13 Immingham, Eng. 53 37N 0 12W
115 Immokalee, U.S.A. 26 25N 81 20W
39 Imola, Italy 44 20N 11 42E
42 Imotski, Yugoslavia 43 27N 17 21E
127 Imperatriz, Maranhão, 5 30S 47 29W
   Brazil
38 Impéria, Italy 43 52N 8 0E
109 Imperial, Canada 51 21N 105 28W
119 Imperial, Calif., U.S.A. 32 52N 115 34W
116 Imperial, Nebr., U.S.A. 40 38N 101 39W
119 Imperial Dam, U.S.A. 32 50N 114 30W
88 Impfondo, Congo 1 40N 18 0E
69 Imphal, India 24 15N 94 0E
19 Imphy, France 46 56N 3 15E
†44 Imroz, Turkey 40 10N 26 0E
16 Imst, Austria 47 15N 10 44E
73 Imuruan B., Philippines 10 40N 119 10E
62 'Imwas, Jordan 31 51N 34 59E
83 I-n-Azaoua, Niger 20 45N 7 31E
82 In Belbel, Algeria 27 55N 1 12E
85 In Delimane, Mali 15 52N 1 31E
82 I-n-Echaïe, Mali 20 10N 2 5W
85 In-Gall, Mali 16 51N 7 1E
82 In Rhar, Algeria 27 10N 1 59E
82 In Salah, Algeria 27 10N 2 32E
85 In Tallak, Mali 16 19N 3 15E
74 Ina, Japan 35 50N 138 0E
101 Inangahua Junc., N.Z. 41 52S 171 59E
73 Inanwatan, Indonesia 2 10S 132 5E
126 Iñapari, Peru 11 0S 69 40W
50 Inari, Finland 68 54N 27 5E
74 Inawashiro-Ko, Japan 37 28N 140 2E
32 Inca, Spain 39 43N 2 54E
124 Incaguasi, Chile 29 12S 71 5W
87 Inchini, Ethiopia 8 55N 37 37E
76 Inchon, S. Korea 37 32N 126 45E
30 Incio, Spain 42 39N 7 21W
93 Incomáti, R., Mozam. 25 15s 32 35E
20 Incudine, Mte. l', Fr. 41 50N 9 12E
87 Inda Silase, Ethiopia 14 10N 38 15E
87 Indalsälven, Swed. 62 36N 17 30E
87 Indbir, Ethiopia 8 7N 37 52E
119 Independence, Calif., 36 51N 118 7W
   U.S.A.
116 Independence, Iowa, 42 27N 91 52W
   U.S.A.
117 Independence, Kans., 37 10N 95 50W
   U.S.A.
116 Independence, Mo., 39 3N 94 25W
   U.S.A.
118 Independence, Oreg., 44 53N 123 6W
   U.S.A.
4 Independence Fjord, 82 10N 29 0W
   Green.
118 Independence Mts., USA 41 30N 116 2W
46 Independența, Rum. 45 25N 27 42E

* Incorporated within the
  county of Cambridge

* Renamed Kapchagai
† Renamed Gökçeada
** Renamed Dalnerechensk

Inderborskly INDEX Jandaq

MAP
57 Inderborskly, U.S.S.R. 48 30N 51 42E
61 India ■, Asia 20 0N 80 0E
119 India, U.S.A. 33 46N 116 15W
108 Indian Cabin, Canada 59 50N 117 12W
109 Indian Head, Canada 50 30N 103 35W
107 Indian House L., Can. 56 30N 64 30W
3 Indian Ocean 5 0S 75 0E
112 Indiana, U.S.A. 40 38N 79 9W
114 Indiana ♦, U.S.A. 40 0N 86 0W
114 Indianapolis, U.S.A. 39 42N 86 10W
116 Indianola, Iowa, U.S.A. 41 20N 93 38W
117 Indianola, Miss., U.S.A. 33 27N 90 40W
52 Indiga, U.S.S.R. 67 50N 48 50E
59 Indigirka, R., U.S.S.R. 69 0N 147 0E
42 Indija, Yugoslavia 45 6N 20 7E
72 Indonesia ■, Asia 5 0S 115 0E
68 Indore, India 22 42N 75 53E
73 Indramaju, Indonesia 6 21S 108 20E
73 Indramaju, Tg., Indonesia 6 20S 108 20E
70 Indravati, R., India 19 0N 81 15E
18 Indre, R., France 47 2N 1 8E
19 Indre ♦, France 47 12N 1 39E
18 Indre-et-Loire ♦, France 47 12N 0 40E
47 Indre Söndeled, Norway 58 46N 9 5E
68 Indus, R., Pakistan 28 40N 70 10E
64 Inebolu, Turkey 41 55N 33 40E
42 Ineu, Rumania 46 26N 21 51E
92 Infante, Kaap, S. Afr. 34 27S 20 51E
33 Infantes, Spain 38 43N 3 1W
30 Infiesto, Spain 43 21N 5 21W
85 In-Gall, Mali 16 51N 7 1E
100 Ingebyra, Australia 36 39S 148 31E
88 Ingende, Zaïre 0 12S 18 57E
124 Ingenio Santa Ana, Arg. 27 25S 65 40W
112 Ingersoll, Canada 43 4N 80 55W
49 Ingesvang, Denmark 56 10N 9 20E
98 Ingham, Australia 18 43S 146 10E
12 Ingleborough, mt., England 54 11N 2 23W
100 Inglega, Australia 31 20S 147 50E
100 Inglewood, Australia 36 29S 143 53E
99 Inglewood, Australia 28 25S 151 8E
101 Inglewood, New Zealand 39 9S 174 14E
119 Inglewood, U.S.A. 33 58N 118 27W
50 Ingólfshöfði, Iceland 63 48N 16 39W
52 Ingolstadt, Germany 48 45N 11 26W
118 Ingomar, U.S.A. 46 43N 107 37E
107 Ingonish, Canada 46 42N 60 18E
84 Ingore, Port. Guinea 12 24N 15 48W
56 Ingul, R., U.S.S.R 47 30N 32 15E
56 Ingulec, U.S.S.R. 47 42N 33 4E
56 Ingulets, R., U.S.S.R. 47 20N 33 20E
57 Inguri, R., U.S.S.R. 42 58N 42 17E
93 Inhaca, I., Mozambique 26 1S 32 57E
93 Inhafenga, Mozambique 20 36S 33 47E
93 Inhambane ♦, Mozambique 22 30S 34 20E
91 Inhaminga, Mozam. 18 26S 35 0E
93 Inharrime, Mozambique 24 30S 35 0E
93 Inharrime, R., Mozambique 24 30S 35 0E
91 Inhassoro, Mozambique 21 50S 35 15E
33 Iniesta, Spain 39 27N 1 45W
77 Ining, Kwangsi-Chuang, China 25 8N 109 57E
75 Ining (Kuldja), Sinkiang-Uigur, China 43 57N 81 20E
126 Inirida, R., Colombia 3 0N 68 40W
15 Inishbofin I., Ireland 53 35N 10 12W
15 Inishowen, Pen., Ire. 55 14N 7 15W
99 Injune, Australia 25 46S 148 32E
2 Inklin, Can. 58 50N 132 30W
108 Inklin, R., Can. 58 50N 132 20W
118 Inkom, U.S.A. 42 51N 112 7W
13 Inkpen Beacon, Eng. 51 22N 1 28W
67 Inle Aing, Burma 20 30N 96 58E
25 Inn, R., Austria 47 15N 10 55E
99 Innamincka, Australia 27 44S 140 46E
14 Inner Hebrides, Is., U.K. 58 0N 7 0W
14 Inner Sound, Skye, Scotland 57 30N 5 55W
76 Inner Mongolia ♦, China 44 50N 117 40E
112 Innerkip, Canada 43 12N 80 41W
106 Innetalling I., Canada 55 50N 79 5W
98 Innisfail, Australia 17 33S 146 5E
108 Innisfail, Canada 52 0N 114 0W
26 Innsbruck, Austria 47 16N 11 23E
126 Inosu, Colombia 12 22N 71 38W
28 Inowrocław, Poland 52 50N 18 20E
126 Inquisive, Bolivia 16 50S 66 45W
67 Insein, Burma 16 46N 96 18E
46 Insurăţei, Rumania 44 50N 27 40E
124 Intendente Alvear, Arg. 35 12S 63 32W
116 Interior, U.S.A. 43 46N 101 59W
25 Interlaken, Switzerland 46 41N 7 50E
116 International Falls, U.S.A. 48 30N 93 25W
71 Interview I., India 12 55N 92 42E
71 Inthanon, Mt., Thailand 18 35N 98 29E
124 Intiyaco, Argentina 28 50S 60 0W
128 Inútil, B., Chile 53 30S 70 15W
14 Inverbervie, Scot. 56 50N 2 17W
101 Invercargill, N.Z. 46 24S 168 24E
99 Inverell, Australia 29 48S 151 36E
14 Invergordon, Scot. 57 41N 4 10W
108 Invermere, Canada 50 51N 116 9W
107 Inverness, Canada 46 15N 61 19W
14 Inverness, Scotland 57 29N 4 12W
115 Inverness, U.S.A. 28 50N 82 20W
*14 Inverness ♦, Scotland 57 6N 4 40W
14 Inverurie, Scot. 57 15N 2 21W
96 Investigator Group, Australia 34 45S 134 20E
99 Investigator Str., Australia 35 30S 137 0E
112 Invona, U.S.A. 40 46N 78 35W
91 Inyanga, Rhodesia 18 12S 32 40E
91 Inyangahi, mt., Rhod. 18 20S 32 20E

MAP
91 Inyantue, Rhodesia 18 30S 26 40E
91 Inyazura, Rhodesia 18 40S 31 40E
119 Inyo Range, U.S.A. 37 0N 118 0W
119 Inyokern, U.S.A. 35 37N 117 54W
55 Inza, U.S.S.R. 53 55N 46 25E
55 Inzhavino, U.S.S.R. 52 22N 42 23E
44 Ioánnina (Janinà) ♦, Gr. 39 39N 20 57E
117 Iola, U.S.A. 38 0N 95 20W
46 Ion Corvin, Rumania 44 7N 27 50E
14 Iona I., Scot. 56 20N 6 25W
54 Ionava, U.S.S.R. 55 8N 24 12E
118 Ione, Calif., U.S.A. 38 20N 121 0W
118 Ione, Wash., U.S.A. 48 44N 117 29W
114 Ionia, U.S.A. 42 59N 85 7W
35 Ionian Sea, Europe 37 30N 17 30E
45 Iónioi Nisoi, Greece 38 40N 20 8E
54 Ioniškis, U.S.S.R. 56 13N 23 35E
57 Iori, R., U.S.S.R. 41 12N 46 10E
45 Ios, I., Greece 36 41N 25 20E
116 Iowa ♦, U.S.A. 42 18N 93 30W
116 Iowa City, U.S.A. 41 40N 91 35W
116 Iowa Falls, U.S.A. 42 30N 93 15W
90 Ipala, Tanzania 4 30S 33 5E
127 Ipameri, Brazil 17 44S 48 9W
45 Ipáti, Greece 38 52N 22 14E
57 Ipatovo, U.S.S.R. 45 45N 42 50E
27 Ipel, R., Europe 48 10N 19 35E
126 Ipiales, Colombia 0 50N 77 37W
75 Ipin, China 28 48N 104 33E
44 Ipiros ♦, Greece 39 30N 20 30E
126 Ipixuna, Brazil 7 0S 71 30W
71 Ipoh, Malaysia 4 26N 101 4E
81 Ippy, Cent. Afr. Rep. 6 5N 21 58E
44 Ipsala, Turkey 40 55N 26 23E
44 Ipsárion Oros, Gr. 40 40N 24 40E
99 Ipswich, Australia 27 38S 152 37E
13 Ipswich, Eng. 52 4N 1 9E
113 Ipswich, N.H., U.S.A. 42 40N 70 50W
116 Ipswich, S.D., U.S.A. 45 28N 99 20W
127 Ipu, Brazil 4 23S 40 44W
72 Ipuh, Indonesia 2 58S 101 8E
54 Iput, R., U.S.S.R. 53 0N 32 10E
126 Iquique, Chile 20 19S 70 5W
126 Iquitos, Peru 3 45S 73 10W
127 Iracoubo, French Guiana 5 30N 53 10W
45 Iráklia, I., Greece 36 50N 25 28E
45 Iráklion, Greece 35 20N 25 12E
45 Iráklion ♦, Greece 35 10N 25 10E
125 Irala, Paraguay 25 55S 54 35W
90 Iramba ♦, Tanzania 4 30S 34 30E
65 Iran ■, Asia 33 0N 53 0E
72 Iran, Pegunungan, Malaysia 2 20N 114 50E
70 Iranamadu Tank, Sri Lanka 9 23N 80 29E
65 Iranshahr, Iran 27 75N 60 40E
126 Irapa, Venezuela 10 34N 62 35W
120 Irapuato, Mexico 20 40N 101 40W
64 Iraq ■, Asia 33 0N 44 0E
82 Irarrar, W., Mali 20 10N 1 30E
125 Irati, Brazil 25 25S 50 38W
62 Irbid, Jordan 32 35N 35 48E
88 Irebu, Zaïre 0 40S 17 55E
32 Iregua, R., Spain 42 22N 2 24E
15 Ireland's Eye, Ireland 53 25N 6 4W
85 Irele, Nigeria 7 40N 5 40E
76 Irentala Steppe, China 43 45N 112 15E
59 Iret, U.S.S.R. 60 10N 154 5E
55 Irgiz, Bol., U.S.S.R. 52 10N 49 10E
83 Irharharene, Algeria 27 37N 7 30E
83 Irharhar, O., Algeria 27 30N 6 0E
*73 Irian Barat ♦, Indonesia 4 0S 137 0E
88 Iriba, Chad 15 7N 22 15E
84 Irié, Guinea 8 15N 9 10W
90 Iringa, Tanzania 7 48S 35 43E
90 Iringa ♦, Tanz. 7 48S 35 43E
91 Iringa ♦, Tanz. 9 0S 35 0E
70 Irinjalakuda, India 10 21N 76 14E
77 Iriomote, Japan 24 25N 123 58E
15 Irish Republic ■, Europe 53 0N 8 0E
59 Irkutsk, U.S.S.R. 52 10N 104 20E
64 Irmak, Turkey 39 58N 33 25E
18 Iroise, France 48 15N 4 45W
99 Iron Baron, Australia 33 3S 137 11E
46 Iron Gate = Porţile de Fier, Rum. 44 42N 22 30E
99 Iron Knob, Australia 32 46S 137 8E
114 Iron Mountain, U.S.A. 45 49N 88 4W
114 Iron River, U.S.A. 46 6N 88 40W
13 Ironbridge, Eng. 52 38N 2 29W
112 Irondale, Canada 44 51N 78 30W
92 Ironhurst, Australia 18 0S 143 35E
92 Ironstone Kopje, Mt., Botswana 25 17S 24 5E
117 Ironton, Mo., U.S.A. 37 40N 90 40W
114 Ironton, Ohio, U.S.A. 38 35N 82 40W
114 Ironwood, U.S.A. 46 30N 90 10W
106 Iroquois Falls, Canada 48 40N 80 40W
54 Irpen, U.S.S.R. 50 30N 30 8E
67 Irrawaddy = Erawadi Myit, Burma 19 30N 95 15E
76 Irshih, China 47 8N 119 57E
41 Irsina, Italy 40 45N 16 15E
58 Irtysh, R., U.S.S.R. 53 36N 75 30E
90 Irumu, Zaïre 1 32N 29 53E
32 Irún, Spain 43 20N 1 52W
32 Irurzun, Spain 42 55N 1 50W
14 Irvine, Scotland 55 37N 4 40W
114 Irvine, U.S.A. 37 42N 83 58W
14 Irvine, R., Scotland 55 35N 4 40W
15 Irvinstown, N. Ire. 54 28N 7 38W
100 Irymple, Australia 34 14S 142 8E
85 Isa, Nigeria 13 14N 6 24E
98 Isaac. R., Australia 21 30S 148 30E
116 Isabel, U.S.A. 45 27N 101 22W
121 Isabela, Cord., Nic. 13 30N 85 25W
50 Ísafjarðardjúp, Iceland 66 10N 23 0W
50 Ísafjörður, Iceland 66 5N 23 9W
68 Isagarh, India 24 48N 77 51E

MAP
90 Isaka, Tanzania 3 56S 32 59E
88 Isangi, Zaïre 0 52N 24 10E
39 Isarco, R., Italy 46 40N 11 35E
45 Isari, Greece 37 22N 22 0E
19 Isbergues, France 50 36N 2 24E
46 Isbiceni, Rumania 43 45N 24 40E
40 Ischia, I., Italy 40 45N 13 51E
126 Iscuandé, Colombia 2 28N 77 59W
49 Isefjord, Denmark 55 53N 11 50E
38 Iseo, Italy 45 40N 10 3E
90 Iseramagazi, Tanz. 4 37S 32 10E
20 Isère, R., France 45 15N 5 30E
21 Isère ♦, France 45 15N 5 40E
24 Iserlohn, Germany 51 22N 7 40E
41 Isérnia, Italy 41 35N 14 12E
74 Ise-Wan, Japan 34 45N 136 45E
85 Iseyin, Nigeria 8 0N 3 36E
63 Isha Baidoa, Somali Rep. 3 8N 43 30E
76 Ishan, China 24 30N 108 41E
85 Ishara, Nigeria 6 40N 3 40E
77 Ishigaki, Japan 24 26N 124 10E
74 Ishikari-Wan, Japan 43 20N 141 20E
74 Ishikawa-ken ♦, Japan 36 30N 136 30E
58 Ishim, U.S.S.R. 56 10N 69 18E
58 Ishim, R., U.S.S.R. 57 45N 71 10E
74 Ishinomaki, Japan 38 32N 141 20E
65 Ishkashim, Afghanistan 36 30N 71 40E
66 Ishkuman, Kashmir 36 40N 73 50E
44 Ishmi, Albania 41 33N 19 34E
114 Ishpeming, U.S.A. 46 30N 87 40W
85 Ishua, Nigeria 7 15N 5 50E
56 Işik, Turkey 40 40N 32 35E
58 Isil Kul, U.S.S.R. 54 55N 71 16E
20 Isili, Italy 39 45N 9 6E
90 Isiolo, Kenya 0 24N 37 33E
93 Isipingo, S. Afr. 30 00S 30 57E
93 Isipingo Beach, S. Afr. 30 00S 30 57E
90 Isiro, Zaïre 2 53N 27 58E
98 Isisford, Australia 24 15S 144 21E
64 Iskenderun, Turkey 36 32N 36 10E
56 Iskilip, Turkey 40 50N 34 20E
43 Iskyr, R., Bulgaria 43 35N 24 20E
14 Isla, R., Scotland 56 44N 3 20W
31 Isla Cristina, Spain 37 13N 7 17W
66 Islamabad, Pakistan 33 40N 73 0E
68 Islamkot, Pakistan 24 42N 70 13E
70 Islampur, India 17 2N 72 9E
106 Island Falls, Canada 49 35N 81 20W
107 Island Falls, U.S.A. 46 0N 68 25W
109 Island L., Canada 53 40N 94 30W
113 Island Pond, U.S.A. 44 50N 71 50W
107 Islands, B. of, Canada 49 11N 58 15W
101 Islands, B. of, N.Z. 35 20S 174 20E
14 Islay, I., Scotland 55 46N 6 10W
14 Islay Sound, Scotland 55 45N 6 5W
107 Isle aux Morts, Canada 47 35N 59 0W
116 Isle Royale, U.S.A. 48 0N 88 50W
119 Isleta, U.S.A. 34 58N 106 46W
56 Ismail, U.S.S.R. 45 22N 28 46E
86 Ismâ'iliya, Egypt 30 37N 32 18E
116 Ismay, U.S.A. 46 33N 104 44W
86 Isna, Egypt 25 17N 32 30E
40 Isola del Liri, Italy 41 39N 13 32E
38 Isola della Scala, Italy 45 16N 11 0E
41 Isola di Capo Rizzuto, Italy 38 56N 17 5E
64 Isparta, Turkey 37 47N 30 30E
43 Isperikh, Bulgaria 43 43N 26 50E
41 Ispica, Sicily, Italy 36 47N 14 53E
57 Ispir, Turkey 40 40N 40 50E
62 Israel ■, Asia 32 0N 34 50E
84 Issia, Ivory Coast 6 33N 6 33W
20 Issoire, France 45 32N 3 15E
19 Issoudun, France 46 57N 2 0E
19 Is-sur-Tille, France 47 30N 5 10E
58 Issyk-Kul, U.S.S.R. 42 30N 77 30E
64 Istanbul, Turkey 41 0N 29 0E
45 Istiaia, Greece 38 57N 23 10E
126 Istmina, Colombia 5 10N 76 39W
42 Istok, Yugoslavia 42 45N 20 24E
115 Istokpoga, L., U.S.A. 27 22N 81 14W
55 Istra, U.S.S.R. 55 55N 36 50E
39 Istra, Yugoslavia 45 10N 14 0E
43 Istranca Dağlari, Turkey 41 48N 27 30E
21 Istres, France 43 31N 4 59E
127 Itabaiana, Paraíba, Brazil 7 18S 35 19W
127 Itaberaba, Brazil 12 32S 40 18W
127 Itabira, Brazil 19 37S 43 13W
127 Itabuna, Brazil 14 48S 39 16W
127 Itaete, Brazil 13 0S 41 5W
127 Itaituba, Brazil 4 10S 55 50W
125 Itajai, Brazil 27 0S 48 45W
125 Itajubá, Brazil 22 24S 45 30W
91 Itaka, Tanzania 8 50S 32 49E
36 Italy ■, Europe 42 0N 13 0E
127 Itambe, mt., Brazil 18 30S 43 45W
93 Itampolo, Malag. 24 41S 43 57E
85 Itanhaém, Brazil 24 9S 46 47W
127 Itapecuru, R., Brazil 3 20S 44 15W
127 Itaperuna, Brazil 21 10S 42 0W
125 Itapetininga, Brazil 23 36S 48 7W
125 Itapeva, Brazil 23 59S 48 59W
127 Itapicuru, R., Bahia, Brazil 10 50S 38 40W
127 Itapicuru, R., Maranhão, Brazil 5 40S 44 30W
125 Itapuá ♦, Paraguay 26 40S 55 40W
125 Itaquari, Brazil 20 12S 40 25W
126 Itaquatiana, Brazil 2 58S 58 30W
124 Itaqui, Brazil 29 0S 56 30W
125 Itararé, Brazil 24 6S 49 23W
68 Itarsi, India 22 36N 77 51E
126 Itatuba, Brazil 5 40S 63 20W
77 Itbayat I., Philippines 20 45N 121 50E
13 Itchen, R., Eng. 50 57N 1 20W
45 Itéa, Greece 38 25N 22 25E
45 Ithaca = Itháki, Greece 38 25N 20 43E
113 Ithaca, U.S.A. 42 25N 76 30W
45 Itháki, Greece 38 25N 20 43E

MAP
45 Itháki, I., Greece 38 25N 20 40E
74 Ito, Japan 34 58N 139 5E
77 Itoman, Okinawa 26 7N 127 40E
126 Itonamas, R., Bolivia 13 0S 64 25W
86 Itsa, Egypt 29 15N 30 40E
40 Ittiri, Italy 40 38N 8 32E
125 Itu, Brazil 23 10S 47 15W
85 Itu, Nigeria 5 10N 7 58E
127 Ituaçu, Brazil 13 50S 41 18W
126 Ituango, Colombia 7 4N 75 45W
127 Ituiutaba, Brazil 19 0S 49 25W
127 Itumbiara, Brazil 18 20S 49 10W
91 Itunge Port, Tanz. 9 40S 33 55E
124 Iturbe, Argentina 23 0S 65 25W
90 Ituri, R., Zaïre 1 45N 26 45E
59 Iturup, Ostrov, U.S.S.R. 45 0N 148 0E
124 Ituyuro, R., Argentina 22 40S 63 50W
24 Itzehoe, Germany 53 56N 9 31E
50 Ivalo, Finland 68 38N 27 35E
50 Ivalojoki, Finland 68 30N 27 0E
44 Ivanaj, Albania 42 17N 19 25E
100 Ivanhoe, Australia 32 56S 144 20E
109 Ivanhoe L., Canada 60 25N 106 30W
39 Ivanió Grad, Yugoslavia 45 41N 16 25E
42 Ivanjica, Yugoslavia 43 35N 20 12E
39 Ivanjscie, Y.-slav. 46 12N 16 13E
55 Ivankovskoye Vdkhr., U.S.S.R. 56 48N 36 55E
54 Ivano-Frankovsk, (Stanislav), U.S.S.R. 49 0N 24 40E
55 Ivanovo, R.S.F.S.R., U.S.S.R. 57 5N 41 0E
54 Ivanovo, White Russia, U.S.S.R. 52 7N 25 29E
93 Ivato, Malagasy Rep. 20 37S 47 10E
43 Ivaylovgrad, Bulgaria 41 32N 26 8E
125 Ivinheima, R., Brazil 21 48S 54 15W
33 Iviza = Ibiza, Spain 39 0N 1 30E
93 Ivohibe, Malagasy Rep. 22 31S 46 57E
84 Ivory Coast ■, Afr. 7 30N 5 0E
49 Ivösjön, Sweden 56 8N 14 25E
38 Ivrea, Italy 45 30N 7 52E
105 Ivugivik, (N.D. d'Ivugivic), Canada 62 18N 77 50W
72 Iwahig, Philippines 8 35N 117 32E
74 Iwakuni, Japan 34 15N 132 8E
74 Iwata, Japan 34 49N 137 59E
74 Iwate-ken ♦, Japan 39 30N 141 30E
85 Iwo, Nigeria 7 39N 4 9E
27 Iwonicz-Zdroj, Poland 49 37N 21 47E
126 Ixiamas, Bolivia 13 50S 68 5W
93 Ixopo, South Africa 30 11S 30 5E
120 Ixtepec, Mexico 16 40N 95 10W
120 Ixtlán de Juárez, Mexico 17 23N 96 28W
120 Ixtlán del Río, Mexico 21 5N 104 28W
77 Iyang, China 28 40N 112 20E
120 Izabal, L., Guatemala 15 30N 89 10W
120 Izamal, Mexico 20 56N 89 1W
28 Izbica Kujawski, Poland 52 25N 18 30E
57 Izberbash, U.S.S.R. 42 35N 47 45E
16 Izegem, Belgium 50 55N 3 12E
43 Izgrev, Bulgaria 43 36N 26 58E
52 Izhevsk, U.S.S.R. 56 50N 53 0E
56 Izmail, U.S.S.R. 45 22N 28 46E
53 Izmir (Smyrna), Turkey 38 25N 27 8E
64 Izmit, Turkey 40 45N 29 50E
31 Iznajar, Spain 37 15N 4 19W
33 Iznalloz, Spain 37 24N 3 30W
39 Izola, Yugoslavia 45 32N 13 39E
74 Izumisano, Japan 34 40N 135 43E
74 Izumo, Japan 35 20N 132 55E
54 Izyaslav, U.S.S.R. 50 5N 25 50E
56 Izyum, U.S.S.R. 49 12N 37 28E
87 Jaba, Ethiopia 6 20N 35 7E
62 Jaba', Jordan 32 20N 35 13E
62 Jabaliya, Egypt 31 32N 34 27E
33 Jabalón, R., Spain 38 45N 3 35W
69 Jabalpur, India 23 9N 79 58E
64 Jablah, Syria 35 20N 36 0E
39 Jablanac, Yugoslavia 44 42N 14 56E
26 Jablonec, Cz. 50 43N 15 10E
27 Jablonica, Cz. 48 37N 17 26E
28 Jablonowo, Poland 53 23N 19 10E
125 Jaboticabal, Brazil 21 15S 48 17W
42 Jabukovac, Yugoslavia 44 22N 22 21E
126 Jaburu, Brazil 4 0S 66 25W
32 Jaca, Spain 42 35N 0 33W
125 Jacarei, Brazil 23 20S 46 0W
125 Jacarèzinho, Brazil 23 5S 50 0W
124 Jáchal, Argentina 30 5S 69 0W
26 Jáchymov, Cz. 50 22N 12 55E
107 Jack Lane B., Canada 55 45N 60 35W
106 Jackfish, Canada 48 45N 87 0W
107 Jackman, U.S.A. 45 40N 70 17W
117 Jacksboro, U.S.A. 33 14N 98 15W
99 Jackson, Australia 26 40S 149 30E
115 Jackson, Ala., U.S.A. 31 32N 87 53W
117 Jackson, Calif., U.S.A. 37 25N 89 42W
118 Jackson, Ill., U.S.A. 38 25N 120 47W
114 Jackson, Ky., U.S.A. 37 35N 83 22W
114 Jackson, Mich., U.S.A. 42 18N 84 25W
116 Jackson, Minn., U.S.A. 43 35N 95 30W
117 Jackson, Miss., U.S.A. 32 20N 90 10W
114 Jackson, Ohio, U.S.A. 39 0N 82 40W
115 Jackson, Tenn., U.S.A. 35 40N 88 50W
118 Jackson, Wyo., U.S.A. 43 30N 110 49W
108 Jackson Bay, Can. 50 32N 125 57W
101 Jackson Bay, N.Z. 43 58S 168 42E
118 Jackson, L., U.S.A. 43 55N 110 40W
101 Jacksons, New Zealand 42 46N 171 32E
115 Jacksonville, Ala., U.S.A. 33 49N 85 45W
115 Jacksonville, Fla., U.S.A. 30 15N 81 38W
116 Jacksonville, Ill., U.S.A. 39 42N 90 15W
115 Jacksonville, N.C., U.S.A. 34 50N 77 29W
118 Jacksonville, Oreg., U.S.A. 42 13N 122 56W
117 Jacksonville, Tex., U.S.A. 31 58N 95 12W

MAP
115 Jacksonville Beach, U.S.A. 30 19N 81 26W
121 Jacmel, Haiti 18 20N 72 40W
119 Jacob Lake, U.S.A. 36 45N 112 12W
68 Jacobabad, Pakistan 28 20N 68 29E
46 Jacobeni, Rumania 47 25N 25 20E
127 Jacobina, Brazil 11 11S 40 30W
62 Jacob's Well, Jordan 32 13N 35 13E
107 Jacques Cartier, Mt., Canada 48 57N 66 0W
107 Jacques Cartier Pass, Canada 49 50N 62 30W
84 Jacqueville, Ivory Coast 5 12N 4 25W
127 Jacuipe, R., Brazil 12 30S 39 5W
24 Jade, Germany 53 22N 8 14E
24 Jadebusen, B., Ger. 53 30N 8 15E
91 Jadotville = Likasi, Zaïre 10 55S 26 48E
42 Jadovnik, Y.-slav. 43 20N 19 45E
32 Jadraque, Spain 40 55N 2 55W
83 Jâdû, Libya 32 0N 12 0E
126 Jaén, Peru 5 25S 78 40W
31 Jaén, Spain 37 44N 3 43W
31 Jaén ♦, Spain 37 50N 3 30W
82 Jafène, Sahara 20 35N 5 30W
62 Jaffa = Tel Aviv-Yafo, Israel 32 4N 34 48E
99 Jaffa C., Australia 36 49S 139 38E
70 Jaffna, Sri Lanka 9 45N 80 2E
68 Jagadhri, India 30 10N 77 20E
69 Jagadishpur, India 25 30N 84 21E
70 Jagdalpur, India 19 3N 82 6E
92 Jagersfontein, S. Afr. 29 44S 25 27E
81 Jaghbub, Libya 29 42N 24 38E
25 Jagst, R., Germany 49 13N 10 0E
70 Jagtial, India 18 50N 79 0E
125 Jaguariaiva, Brazil 24 10S 49 50W
127 Jaguaribe, R., Brazil 6 0S 38 35W
121 Jaguey, Cuba 22 35N 81 7W
100 Jagungal, Mount, Australia 36 12S 148 28W
70 Jagtial, India 18 50N 79 0E
68 Jahangirabad, India 28 19N 78 4E
64 Jahrom, Iran 28 30N 53 31E
69 Jainti, India 26 45N 89 40E
68 Jaipur, India 26 54N 72 52E
65 Jajarm, Iran 37 5N 56 20E
42 Jajce, Yugoslavia 44 19N 17 17E
85 Jajere, Nigeria 11 58N 10 25E
69 Jajpur, India 20 53N 86 22E
50 Jakobstad (Pietarsaari), Finland 63 40N 22 43E
42 Jakupica, Y.-slav. 41 45N 21 22E
117 Jal, U.S.A. 32 8N 103 8W
65 Jalas, Iran 27 30N 62 40E
65 Jalalabad, Afghanistan 34 30N 70 29E
69 Jalalabad, India 26 41N 79 42E
68 Jalalpur Jattan, Pakistan 32 38N 74 19E
120 Jalapa, Guatemala 14 45N 89 59W
120 Jalapa, Mexico 19 30N 96 50W
64 Jalas, Jabal al, Saudi Arabia 27 30N 36 30E
69 Jalaun, India 26 8N 79 25E
69 Jaleswar, Nepal 26 38N 85 48E
68 Jalgaon, Mad. P., India 21 2N 76 31E
68 Jalgaon, Maharashtra, India 21 0N 75 42E
85 Jalingo, Nigeria 8 55N 11 25E
120 Jalisco ♦, Mexico 20 0N 104 0W
30 Jallas, R., Spain 42 57N 9 0W
100 Jallumba, Austral. 36 55N 141 57E
70 Jalna, India 19 48N 75 57E
32 Jalón, R., Spain 41 20N 1 40W
120 Jalpa, Mexico 21 38N 102 58W
69 Jalpaiguri, India 26 32N 88 46E
65 Jalq, Iran 27 35N 62 33E
94 Jaluit I., Pacific Ocean 6 0N 169 30E
85 Jamaari, Nigeria 11 44N 9 53E
121 Jamaica, I. ■, W. Indies 18 10N 77 30W
69 Jamalpur, Bangladesh 24 52N 90 2E
69 Jamalpur, India 25 18N 86 28E
69 Jamalpurganj, India 23 2N 88 1E
127 Jamanxim, R., Brazil 6 30S 55 50W
73 Jambe, Indonesia 1 15S 132 10E
68 Jambusar, India 22 3N 72 51E
73 Jamdena, I., Indonesia 7 45S 131 20E
106 James B., Canada 53 30N 80 30W
116 James, R., U.S.A. 44 50N 98 0W
96 James Ras., Australia 24 10N 132 0E
5 James Ross I., Br. Antarctic Terr. 66 58S 50 49W
92 Jamestown, S. Africa 31 6S 26 45E
99 Jamestown, Australia 33 10S 138 32E
114 Jamestown, Ky., U.S.A. 37 0N 85 5W
116 Jamestown, N.D., USA 47 0N 98 30W
112 Jamestown, N.Y., USA 42 5N 79 18W
112 Jamestown, Penn., U.S.A. 41 22N 80 27W
115 Jamestown, Tenn., U.S.A. 36 25N 85 0W
70 Jamkhandi, India 16 30N 75 15E
62 Jamma'in, Jordan 32 8N 35 12E
70 Jammalamadugu, India 14 51N 78 25E
49 Jammerbugt, Den. 57 15N 9 20E
68 Jammu, Jammu & Kashmir 32 46N 75 57E
66 Jammu & Kashmir ♦, India 34 25N 77 0W
68 Jamnagar, India 22 30N 70 0E
68 Jamner, India 20 45N 75 45E
68 Jampur, Pakistan 29 39N 70 32E
66 Jamrud, Pakistan 33 59N 71 24E
69 Jamshedpur, India 22 44N 86 20E
69 Jamtara, India 23 59N 86 41E
48 Jämtlands län ♦, Swed. 62 40N 13 50E
92 Jan Kemp, S. Africa 27 55S 24 51E
4 Jan Mayen Is., Arctic Ocean 71 0N 11 0W
66 Jand, Pakistan 33 30N 72 0E
64 Jandaq, Iran 34 3N 54 22E

* *Incorporated with the region of Highland*

* *Renamed Irian Jaya*

Jandola INDEX Kakinada

MAP
68 Jandola, Pakistan 32 20N 70 9E
99 Jandowae, Australia 26 45S 151 7E
31 Jándula, R., Spain 38 25N 3 55W
116 Janesville, U.S.A. 42 39N 89 1W
85 Janga, Ghana 10 5N 1 0W
70 Jangaon, India 17 44N 79 5E
65 Jani Khel, Afghanistan 32 45N 68 25E
42 Janja, Yugoslavia 44 40N 19 17E
42 Janjevo, Yugoslavia 42 35N 21 19E
42 Janjina, Yugoslavia 42 58N 17 25E
27 Jánoshalma, Hungary 46 18N 19 21E
27 Jánosháza, Hungary 47 8N 17 12E
28 Janów, Poland 50 43N 22 30E
28 Janów Lubelski, Poland 52 11N 23 11E
28 Janowiec Wlkp., Poland 52 45N 17 30E
127 Januária, Brazil 15 25S 44 25W
19 Janville, France 48 10N 1 50E
18 Janzé, France 47 55N 1 28W
76 Jaoho, China 47 12N 134 15E
68 Jaora, India 23 40N 75 10E
74 Japan ■, Asia 36 0N 136 0E
73 Japen, I., Indonesia 1 50S 136 0E
73 Japen, Selat, Indonesia 1 20S 136 10E
73 Japero, Indonesia 4 59S 137 11E
126 Jaque, Panama 7 27N 78 15W
31 Jaraicejo, Spain 39 40N 5 49E
30 Jaraiz, Spain 40 4N 5 45W
119 Jarales, U.S.A. 34 44N 106 51W
32 Jarama, R., Spain 40 50N 3 20W
30 Jarandilla, Spain 40 8N 5 39W
68 Jaranwala, Pakistan 31 15N 73 20E
62 Jarash, Jordan 32 17N 35 54E
48 Järbo, Sweden 60 42N 16 38E
118 Jarbridge, U.S.A. 41 56N 115 27W
33 Jardin, R., Spain 38 50N 2 10W
121 Jardines de la Reina, Is., Cuba 20 50N 78 50W
75 Jargalant (Kobdo), Mongolia 48 0N 91 43E
76 Jargalant, Mongolia 47 2N 115 1E
19 Jargeau, France 47 50N 2 7E
24 Jarmen, Germany 53 56N 13 20E
48 Järna, Kopp., Sweden 60 33N 14 26E
48 Järna, Stockholm, Sweden 59 7N 17 35E
20 Jarnac, France 45 40N 0 11W
19 Jarny, France 49 9N 5 53E
28 Jarocin, Poland 51 59N 17 29E
26 Jaroměr, Cz. 50 22N 15 52E
27 Jarosław, Poland 50 2N 22 42E
49 Järpas, Sweden 58 23N 12 57E
48 Järpen, Sweden 63 20N 13 40E
87 Jarso, Ethiopia 5 15N 37 30E
48 Järved, Sweden 63 16N 18 43E
112 Jarvis, Canada 42 56N 80 6W
95 Jarvis I., Pacific Ocean 0 15S 159 55W
27 Jarvornik, Cz. 50 23N 17 2E
69 Jarwa, India 27 45N 82 30E
42 Jasa Tomió, Y.-slav. 45 26N 20 50E
28 Jasien, Poland 51 46N 15 0E
71 Jasin, Malaysia 2 20N 102 26E
65 Jāsk, Iran 25 38N 57 45E
27 Jasło, Poland 49 45N 21 30E
108 Jasper, Alb., Canada 52 55N 118 0W
113 Jasper, Ont., Canada 44 52N 75 57W
115 Jasper, Ala., U.S.A. 33 48N 87 16W
70 Jasper, Ark., U.S.A. 36 0N 93 10W
115 Jasper, Fla., U.S.A. 30 31N 82 58W
117 Jasper, La., U.S.A. 30 59N 93 58W
116 Jasper, S.D., U.S.A. 43 52N 96 22W
108 Jasper Place, Canada 53 33N 113 25W
39 Jastrebarsko, Y.-slavia 45 41N 15 39E
28 Jastrowie, Poland 53 26N 16 49E
27 Jastrzebie Zdroj, Poland 49 57N 18 35E
27 Jászapáti, Hungary 47 32N 20 10E
27 Jászárokszállas, Hung. 47 39N 20 1E
27 Jászberény, Hungary 47 30N 19 55E
27 Jászkiser, Hungary 47 27N 20 20E
27 Jászladány, Hungary 47 23N 20 18E
127 Jataí, Brazil 17 50S 51 45W
68 Jati, Pakistan 24 27N 68 19E
33 Játiva, Spain 39 0N 0 32W
127 Jatobal, Brazil 4 35S 49 33W
62 Jatt, Israel 32 24N 35 2E
125 Jaú, Brazil 22 10S 48 30W
63 Jau al Milah, Yemen 15 5N 45 40E
126 Jauja, Peru 11 45S 75 30W
54 Jaunelgava, U.S.S.R. 56 35N 25 0E
69 Jaunpur, India 25 46N 82 44E
72 Java Sea, Indonesia 4 35S 107 15E
73 Java = Djawa, Indonesia 7 0S 110 0E
70 Javadi Hills, India 12 40N 78 40E
33 Jávea, Spain 38 48N 0 10E
75 Javhlant = Ulyasutay, Mongolia 47 42N 13 10E
70 Javla, India 17 18N 75 9E
18 Javron, France 48 25N 0 25W
28 Jawor, Poland 51 4N 16 11E
27 Jaworzno, Poland 50 13N 19 22E
117 Jay, U.S.A. 33 17N 94 46W
109 Jaydot, Canada 49 15N 110 15W
117 Jayton, U.S.A. 33 17N 100 35W
119 Jean, U.S.A. 35 47N 115 20W
104 Jean Marie River, Canada 62 0N 121 0W
117 Jeanerette, U.S.A. 29 52N 91 38W
112 Jeannette, U.S.A. 40 20N 79 36W
121 Jean-Rabel, Haiti 20 0N 73 30W
82 Jebba, Morocco 35 11N 4 43W
85 Jebba, Nigeria 9 9N 4 48E
42 Jebel, Rumania 40 35N 21 15E
87 Jebel Aulia, Sudan 15 10N 32 31E
87 Jebel Qerri, Sudan 16 16N 32 50E
14 Jedburgh, Scot. 55 28N 2 33W
27 Jedlicze, Poland 49 43N 21 40E
28 Jedlnia-Letnisko, Poland 51 25N 21 19E
28 Jedrzejów, Poland 50 35N 20 15E
24 Jeetze, R., Germany 52 58N 11 6E
116 Jefferson, Iowa, U.S.A. 42 3N 94 25W
112 Jefferson, Ohio, U.S.A. 41 40N 80 46W
117 Jefferson, Tex., U.S.A. 32 45N 94 23W
116 Jefferson, Wis., U.S.A. 43 0N 88 49W
118 Jefferson, Mt., Calif., U.S.A. 38 51N 117 0W
118 Jefferson, Mt., Oreg., U.S.A. 44 45N 121 50W
115 Jefferson City, U.S.A. 36 8N 83 30W
114 Jeffersonville, U.S.A. 38 20N 85 42W
85 Jega, Nigeria 12 15N 4 23E
54 Jekabpils, U.S.S.R. 56 29N 25 57E
28 Jelenia Góra, Poland 50 50N 15 45E
54 Jelgava, U.S.S.R. 56 41N 22 49E
42 Jelica, Y.-slavia 43 50N 20 17E
87 Jelli, Sudan 5 25N 31 45E
106 Jellicoe, Canada 49 40N 87 30W
27 Jelšava, Czechoslovakia 48 37N 20 15E
72 Jembongan, I., Malaysia 6 45N 117 20E
16 Jemeppe, Belgium 50 37N 5 30E
83 Jemmapes = Azzaba, Algeria 36 48N 7 6E
26 Jemnice, Cz. 49 1N 15 34E
24 Jena, Germany 50 56N 11 33E
117 Jena, U.S.A. 31 41N 92 7W
83 Jendouba, Tunisia 36 29N 8 47E
77 Jenhwai, China 28 5N 106 10E
87 Jenia, Ethiopia 4 10N 37 25E
62 Jenin, Jordan 32 28N 35 18E
114 Jenkins, U.S.A. 37 13N 82 41W
117 Jennings, U.S.A. 30 10N 92 45W
49 Jenny, Sweden 57 47N 16 35E
100 Jeparit, Australia 36 8S 142 1E
127 Jequié, Brazil 13 51S 40 5W
127 Jequitinhonho, Brazil 16 30S 41 0W
127 Jequitinhonho, Rio, Brazil 15 51S 38 53W
82 Jerada, Morocco 34 40N 2 10W
71 Jerantut, Malay. 3 56N 102 22E
121 Jérémie, Haiti 18 40N 74 10W
120 Jerez, Punta, Mexico 22 58N 97 40W
120 Jerez de García Salinas, Mexico 22 39N 103 0W
31 Jerez de la Frontera, Sp. 36 41N 6 7W
31 Jerez de los Caballeros, Spain 38 20N 6 45W
98 Jericho, Australia 23 38S 146 6E
62 Jericho = El Arīhā, Jordan 31 52N 35 27E
24 Jerichow, Germany 52 30N 12 2E
100 Jerilderie, Australia 35 20S 145 41E
113 Jermyn, U.S.A. 41 31N 75 31W
119 Jerome, U.S.A. 34 50N 112 0W
18 Jersey I., Chan. Is. 49 13N 2 7W
113 Jersey City, U.S.A. 40 41N 74 8W
112 Jersey Shore, U.S.A. 41 17N 77 18W
116 Jerseyville, U.S.A. 39 5N 90 20W
62 Jerusalem, Israel and Jordan 31 47N 35 10E
100 Jervis B., Austral. Comm. Terr. 35 8S 150 46E
39 Jesenice, Cz. 50 6N 13 28E
27 Jesenik (Frývaldov), Cz. 50 15N 17 11E
27 Jesenik, Cz. 50 0N 17 8E
27 Jesenske, Cz. 48 20N 20 10E
72 Jesselton = Kota Kinabalu, Malaysia 6 0N 116 12E
24 Jessnitz, Germany 51 42N 12 19E
69 Jessore, Bangladesh 23 10N 89 10E
115 Jesup, U.S.A. 31 30N 82 0W
124 Jesús María, Argentina 30 59S 64 5W
117 Jetmore, U.S.A. 38 10N 99 57W
68 Jetpur, India 21 45N 70 10E
47 Jevnaker, Norway 60 15N 10 26E
112 Jewett, Ohio, U.S.A. 40 22N 81 2W
117 Jewett, Tex., U.S.A. 31 20N 96 8W
113 Jewett City, U.S.A. 41 36N 72 0W
70 Jeypore, India 18 50N 82 38E
28 Jeziorany, Poland 53 58N 20 46E
68 Jhajjar, India 28 37N 76 14E
66 Jhal Jhao, Pakistan 26 20N 65 35E
68 Jhalawar, India 24 35N 76 10E
68 Jhang Maghiana, Pakistan 31 15N 72 15E
68 Jhansi, India 25 30N 78 36E
69 Jharia, India 23 45N 86 18E
69 Jharsugra, India 21 52N 84 6E
68 Jhelum, Pakistan 33 0N 73 45E
68 Jhelum, R., Pakistan 31 50N 72 10E
68 Jhunjhunu, India 28 10N 75 20E
69 Jiangshan, China 28 45N 118 37E
87 Jibalan Nubah, Sudan 12 0N 31 0E
85 Jibiya, Nigeria 13 5N 7 12E
46 Jibou, Rumania 47 15N 23 17E
26 Jičín, Czechoslovakia 50 25N 15 20E
67 Jida, India 29 2N 94 58E
63 Jiddah, Saudi Arabia 21 29N 39 16E
62 Jifna, Jordan 31 58N 35 13E
26 Jihlava, Czechoslovakia 49 28N 15 35E
26 Jihočeský ♦, Cz. 49 8N 14 35E
27 Jihomoravský ♦, Cz. 49 5N 16 30E
63 Jijiga, Ethiopia 9 20N 42 50E
33 Jijona, Spain 38 34N 0 30W
85 Jikamshi, Nigeria 12 12N 7 45E
32 Jiloca, R., Spain 41 0N 1 20W
26 Jilové, Czechoslovakia 49 52N 14 29E
87 Jima, Ethiopia 7 40N 36 55E
42 Jimbolia, Rumania 45 47N 20 57E
31 Jimena de la Frontera, Spain 36 27N 5 24W
120 Jiménez, Mexico 27 10N 105 0W
68 Jind, India 29 19N 76 16E
100 Jindabyne, Australia 36 25S 148 35E
26 Jindrichuv Hradeç, Cz. 49 10N 15 2E
90 Jinja, Uganda 0 25N 33 12E
84 Jinjini, Ghana 7 20N 3 42W
65 Jinnah Barrage, Pakistan 32 58N 71 33E
121 Jinotega, Nicaragua 13 6N 85 59W
121 Jinotepe, Nicaragua 11 50N 86 10W
76 Jinné, China 51 32N 121 25E
126 Jiparaná (Machado), R., Brazil 8 45S 62 20W
126 Jipijapa, Ecuador 1 0S 80 40W
120 Jiquilpán, Mexico 19 57N 102 42W
64 Jisresh Shughur, Syria 35 49N 36 18E
71 Jitra, Malaysia 6 16N 100 25E
46 Jiu, R., Rumania 44 50N 23 20E
26 Jizera, R., Cz. 50 21N 14 48E
86 Jizl Wadi, Saudi Arabia 26 30N 38 0E
125 Joaçaba, Brazil 27 5S 51 31W
89 João de Almeida, Angola 15 10S 13 50E
127 João Pessoa, Brazil 7 10S 34 52W
124 Joaquín V. González, Argentina 25 10S 64 0W
124 Joatinga, Pta., Brazil 23 20S 44 30W
18 Jobourg, Nez de, Fr. 49 41N 1 57W
33 Jódar, Spain 37 50N 3 21W
68 Jodhpur, India 26 23N 73 2E
19 Joeuf, France 49 12N 6 1E
107 Joggins, Canada 45 42N 64 27W
73 Jogjakarta, Indonesia 7 49S 110 22E
93 Johannesburg, S. Afr. 26 10S 28 8E
48 Johannisnäs, Sweden 62 45N 16 15E
49 Johansfors, Halland, Sweden 56 50N 12 58E
49 Johansfors, Kronoberg, Sweden 56 42N 15 32E
118 John Days, R., U.S.A. 45 0N 120 0W
14 John o' Groats, Scotland 58 39N 3 3W
117 Johnson, U.S.A. 37 35N 101 48W
113 Johnson Cy., N.Y., U.S.A. 42 9N 67 0W
115 Johnson Cy., Tenn., U.S.A. 36 18N 82 21W
117 Johnson Cy., Tex., U.S.A. 30 15N 98 24W
112 Johnsonburg, U.S.A. 41 30N 78 40W
108 Johnsons Crossing, Can. 60 33N 133 27W
*91 Johnston Falls, Zambia 10 31S 28 45E
95 Johnston I., Pac. Oc. 17 10N 169 8E
113 Johnstown, N.Y., U.S.A. 43 1N 74 20W
112 Johnstown, Pa., U.S.A. 40 19N 78 53W
71 Johor, S., Malaysia 1 45N 103 47E
71 Johor ♦, Malaysia 2 5N 103 20E
19 Joigny, France 48 0N 3 20E
125 Joinvile, Brazil 26 15S 48 55W
19 Joinville, France 48 27N 5 10E
5 Joinville I., Antarctica 63 15N 55 30W
50 Jokkmokk, Sweden 66 35N 19 50E
114 Joliet, U.S.A. 41 30N 88 0W
106 Joliette, Canada 46 3N 73 24W
73 Jolo I., Philippines 6 0N 121 0E
73 Jome, I., Indonesia 1 16S 127 30E
49 Jönaker, Sweden 58 44N 16 43E
106 Jones C., Canada 54 33N 79 35W
4 Jones Sd., Canada 76 0N 85 0W
117 Jonesboro, Ark., U.S.A. 35 50N 90 45W
117 Jonesboro, Ill., U.S.A. 37 26N 89 18W
117 Jonesboro, La., U.S.A. 32 15N 92 41W
107 Jonesport, U.S.A. 44 32N 67 38W
49 Jönköping, Sweden 57 45N 14 10E
107 Jonquière, Canada 48 27N 71 14W
49 Jonsberg, Sweden 58 30N 16 48E
49 Jonsered, Sweden 57 45N 12 10E
20 Jonzac, France 45 27N 0 28W
117 Joplin, U.S.A. 37 0N 94 25W
73 Jordan, Philippines 10 41N 122 38E
118 Jordan, U.S.A. 47 25N 106 58W
64 Jordan ■, Asia 31 0N 36 0E
62 Jordan, R., Jordan-Israel 32 10N 35 32E
118 Jordan Valley, U.S.A. 43 0N 117 2W
27 Jordanów, Poland 49 41N 19 49E
67 Jorhat, India 26 45N 94 20E
50 Jörn, Sweden 65 5N 20 12E
47 Jörpeland, Norway 59 3N 6 1E
85 Jos, Nigeria 9 53N 8 51E
42 Jošanička Banja, Y.-slav. 43 24N 20 47E
125 José Batlle y Ordóñez, Uruguay 33 20S 55 10W
28 Josefow, Poland 52 10N 21 11E
46 Joseni, Rumania 47 42N 25 29E
118 Joseph, U.S.A. 45 27N 117 13W
107 Joseph, Lac, Canada 52 40N 65 40W
112 Joseph L., Canada 45 15N 79 50W
96 Joseph Bonaparte G., Australia 14 0S 29 0E
119 Joseph City, U.S.A. 35 0N 110 16W
18 Josselin, France 47 57N 2 33W
47 Jostedal, Norway 61 35N 7 15E
47 Jostedalsbre, Mt., Nor. 61 45N 7 0E
47 Jotunheimen, Nor. 61 35N 8 25E
64 Jounieh, Lebanon 33 59N 35 30E
117 Jourdanton, U.S.A. 28 54N 98 32W
108 Joussard, Canada 55 22N 115 50W
121 Jovellanos, Cuba 22 40N 81 10W
21 Joyeuse, France 44 29N 4 16E
93 Jozini Dam, S. Africa 27 27S 32 7E
120 Juan Aldama, Mex. 24 20N 103 23W
119 Juan Bautista, U.S.A. 36 55N 121 33W
118 Juan de Fuca Str., U.S.A. 48 15N 124 0W
93 Juan de Nova, I., Mozam. Chan. 17 3S 42 45E
95 Juan Fernández, Arch. de, Pacific Ocean 33 50S 80 0W
124 Juan L. Lacaze, Uruguay 34 26S 57 25W
124 Juárez, Argentina 37 40S 59 43W
120 Juárez, Sierra de, Mexico 32 0N 116 0W
127 Juàzeiro, Brazil 9 30S 40 30W
127 Juàzeiro do Norte, Braz. 7 10S 39 18W
87 Jûbâ, Sudan 4 57N 31 35E
63 Juba, R., Africa 1 30N 42 35E
64 Jubaila, Saudi Arabia 24 55N 46 25E
86 Jûbâl, Madiq, Egypt 27 30N 34 0E
69 Jubbulpore = Jabalpur, India 23 9N 79 58E
24 Jübeck, Germany 54 31N 9 24E
57 Jubga, U.S.S.R. 44 19N 38 48E
80 Juby, C., Morocco 28 0N 12 59W
32 Júcar, R., Spain 40 8N 2 13W
120 Juchitán, Mexico 16 27N 95 5W
62 Judaea = Yehuda, Israel 31 35N 34 57E
26 Judenburg, Austria 47 12N 14 38E
113 Judith Pt., U.S.A. 41 20N 71 30W
118 Judith, R., U.S.A. 47 30N 109 30W
118 Judith Gap, U.S.A. 46 48N 109 46W
77 Juian, China 27 45N 120 38E
121 Juigalpa, Nicaragua 12 6N 85 26W
20 Juillac, France 45 20N 1 19E
24 Juist, I., Germany 53 40N 7 0E
127 Juiz de Fora, Brazil 21 43S 43 19W
124 Jujuy, Argentina 24 10S 65 25W
124 Jujuy ♦, Arg. 23 20S 65 40W
77 Jukao, China 32 24N 120 35E
116 Julesberg, U.S.A. 41 0N 102 20W
126 Juli, Peru 16 10S 69 25W
98 Julia Creek, Australia 20 40S 141 55E
126 Juliaca, Peru 15 25S 70 10W
119 Julian, U.S.A. 33 4N 116 38W
39 Julian Alps = Julijske Alpe, Y.-slav. 46 15N 14 1E
4 Julianehåb, Greenland 60 43N 46 0W
24 Jülich, Germany 50 55N 6 20E
38 Julijske Alpe, Y.-slav. 46 15N 14 1E
68 Jullundur, India 31 20N 75 40E
91 Jumbo, Rhodesia 17 30S 30 58E
121 Jumento Cays, W. Ind. 23 40N 75 40E
16 Jumet, Belgium 50 27N 4 25E
33 Jumilla, Spain 38 28N 1 19W
69 Jumla, Nepal 29 15N 82 13E
68 Jumna, R. = Yamuna, India 27 0N 78 30E
68 Junagadh, India 21 30N 70 30E
117 Junction, Tex., U.S.A. 30 29N 99 48W
119 Junction, Utah, U.S.A. 38 10N 112 15W
96 Junction B., Australia 11 52S 133 55E
116 Junction City, Kans., U.S.A. 39 4N 96 55W
118 Junction City, Oreg., U.S.A. 44 20N 123 12W
98 Jundah, Australia 24 46S 143 2E
125 Jundiaí, Brazil 23 10S 47 0W
104 Juneau, Alaska 58 26N 134 30W
25 Jungfrau, Switz. 46 32N 7 58E
68 Jungshahi, Pakistan 24 52N 67 44E
112 Juniata, R., U.S.A. 40 30N 77 40W
124 Junín, Argentina 34 33S 60 57W
128 Junin de los Andes, Arg. 39 45S 71 0W
76 Junkuren, R., Mongolia 47 40N 113 0E
70 Junnar, India 19 12N 73 58E
118 Juntura, U.S.A. 43 44N 119 4W
87 Jur, Nahr el, Sudan 8 45N 29 0E
14 Jura, I., Scot. 56 0N 5 50W
19 Jura, Fr.-Switz. 46 35N 6 5E
19 Jura ♦, France 46 47N 5 45E
14 Jura, Sd. of, Scot. 55 57N 5 45W
126 Jurado, Colombia 7 7N 77 46W
96 Jurien B., Australia 30 17S 115 0E
46 Jurilovca, Rumania 44 46N 28 52W
65 Jurm, Afghanistan 36 50N 70 45E
126 Juruá, R., Brazil 5 20S 67 40W
126 Juruena, Brazil 13 0S 58 10W
126 Juruena, R., Brazil 10 30S 58 20W
127 Juruti, Brazil 2 9S 56 4W
19 Jussey, France 47 50N 5 55E
124 Justo Daract, Argentina 33 52S 65 12W
24 Jüterbog, Germany 51 59N 13 6E
121 Juticalpa, Honduras 14 40N 85 50W
8 Jutland, Europe 56 0N 8 0E
18 Juvigny, France 48 43N 0 30W
19 Juvisy, France 48 43N 2 23E
65 Juwain, Afghanistan 31 45N 61 30E
19 Juzennecourt, France 48 10N 5 0E
67 Jye-kundo, China 33 0N 96 50E
50 Jylhama, Finland 64 34N 26 40E
49 Jylland, Den. 56 15N 9 20E
49 Jylland (Jutland), Den. 56 25N 9 30E
66 K2, Mt., Kashmir 36 0N 77 0E
92 Kaap die Goeie Hoop, S. Africa 34 24S 18 30E
92 Kaap Plato, S. Afr. 28 30S 24 0E
92 Kaapkruis, S. W. Afr. 21 43S 14 0E
73 Kabaena, I., Indonesia 5 15S 122 0E
84 Kabala, Sierra Leone 9 38N 11 37W
90 Kabale, Uganda 1 15S 30 0E
90 Kabalo, Zaïre 6 0S 27 0E
90 Kabambare, Zaïre 4 41S 27 39E
72 Kabandjahe, Indonesia 8 2N 98 27E
91 Kabango, Zaïre 8 35S 28 30E
84 Kabara, Mali 16 40N 2 50W
56 Kabardinka, U.S.S.R. 44 40N 37 57E
57 Kabardino-Balkar, A.S.S.R. ♦, U.S.S.R. 43 30N 43 30E
73 Kabasalan, Philippines 7 47N 122 44E
85 Kabba, Nigeria 7 57N 6 3E
85 Kabi, Niger 13 30N 12 35E
90 Kabinda, Zaïre 6 23S 24 28E
86 Kabna, Sudan 19 6N 32 40E
91 Kabompo, Zambia 13 30S 24 14E
91 Kabompo, R., Zambia 13 50S 24 10E
91 Kabondo, Zaïre 8 58S 25 40E
90 Kabongo, Zaïre 7 22S 25 33E
85 Kabou, Togo 9 28N 0 55E
83 Kaboudia, Rass, Tunisia 35 13N 11 10E
98 Kabra, Australia 23 25S 150 25E
65 Kabud Gonbad, Iran 37 5N 59 45E
85 Kabuiri, Nigeria 11 30N 13 30E
65 Kabul, Afghanistan 34 28N 69 18E
66 Kabul ♦, Afghan. 34 0N 68 30E
90 Kabunga, Zaïre 1 38S 28 3E
73 Kaburuang, Indonesia 3 50N 126 30E
87 Kabushiya, Sudan 16 54N 33 41E
72 Kabuwe, Indonesia 5 25S 102 14E
91 Kabwe (Broken Hill), Zambia 14 30S 28 29E
42 Kačanik, Yugoslavia 42 13N 21 12E
54 Kachanovo, U.S.S.R. 57 25N 27 38E
91 Kachebera, Zambia 13 56S 32 50E
67 Kachin ♦, Burma 26 0N 97 0E
90 Kachira, Lake, Uganda 0 40S 31 0E
58 Kachiry, U.S.S.R. 53 10N 75 50E
87 Kachisi, Ethiopia 9 40N 37 57E
57 Kackar, Turkey 40 45N 41 30E
71 Kadan Kyun, I., Burma 12 30N 98 20E
27 Kadarkút, Hungary 46 13N 17 39E
70 Kadayanallur, India 9 3N 77 22E
85 Kaddi, Nigeria 13 40N 5 40E
57 Kade, Ghana 6 7N 0 56W
68 Kadi, India 23 18N 72 23E
99 Kadina, Australia 34 0S 137 43E
70 Kadiri, India 14 12N 78 13E
57 Kadiyevka, U.S.S.R. 48 35N 38 30E
116 Kadoka, U.S.A. 43 50N 101 31W
55 Kadom, U.S.S.R. 54 37N 42 24E
85 Kaduna, Nigeria 10 30N 7 21E
85 Kaduna, R., Nigeria 10 5N 8 10E
84 Kadyoha, Ivory Coast 8 58N 5 53W
85 Kaelé, Cameroon 10 7N 14 15E
76 Kaesŏng, N. Korea 37 58N 126 35E
64 Kaf, Saudi Arabia 31 25N 37 20E
88 Kafakumba, Zaïre 9 38S 23 46E
53 Kafan, U.S.S.R. 39 18N 46 15E
85 Kafanchan, Nigeria 9 40N 8 20E
85 Kafareti, Nigeria 10 25N 11 12E
84 Kaffrine, Senegal 14 8N 15 36W
81 Kafia Kingi, Sudan 9 20N 24 25E
91 Kafinda, Zambia 12 32S 30 20E
45 Kafiréys, Akra, Gr. 38 9N 24 8E
65 Kafiristan, Afghan. 35 0N 70 30E
46 Kafr Ana, Israel 32 2N 34 48E
62 Kafr 'Ein, Jordan 32 3N 35 7E
86 Kafr el Dauwâr, Egypt 31 8N 30 8E
62 Kafr Kama, Israel 32 44N 35 26E
62 Kafr Kannâ, Israel 32 45N 35 20E
62 Kafr Malik, Jordan 32 0N 35 18E
62 Kafr Mandâ, Israel 32 49N 35 15E
62 Kafr Quaddum, Jordan 32 14N 35 7E
62 Kafr Ra'i, Jordan 32 23N 35 9E
62 Kafr Sir, Lebanon 33 19N 35 23E
62 Kafr Yasif, Israel 32 58N 35 10E
91 Kafue, Zambia 15 46S 28 9E
91 Kafue Flats, Zambia 15 32S 27 0E
91 Kafue Gorge, Zambia 16 0S 28 0E
91 Kafue Hook, Zam. 14 58S 26 0E
91 Kafue Nat. Park, Zambia 15 30S 25 40E
91 Kafulwe, Zambia 9 0S 29 1E
58 Kagan, U.S.S.R. 39 50N 64 45E
74 Kagawa-ken ♦, Japan 34 15N 134 0E
90 Kagera R., Tanzania 1 15S 31 20E
74 Kagoshima, Japan 31 36N 130 40E
74 Kagoshima-ken ♦, Japan 30 0N 130 0E
74 Kagoshima-wan, Japan 31 0N 130 40E
56 Kagul, U.S.S.R. 45 50N 28 15E
72 Kahajan, R., Indonesia 2 10S 114 0E
90 Kahama, Tanzania 4 8S 32 30E
90 Kahama ♦, Tanz. 3 40S 32 0E
90 Kahe, Tanzania 3 30S 37 25E
88 Kahemba, Zaïre 7 18S 18 55E
65 Kahnuj, Iran 27 55N 57 40E
116 Kahoka, U.S.A. 40 25N 91 42W
110 Kahoolawe, I., Hawaii 20 33N 156 35W
73 Kai, Kepulauan, Indonesia 5 55S 132 45W
92 Kai Kai, Botswana 19 52S 21 15E
85 Kaiama, Nigeria 9 36N 4 1E
101 Kaiapoi, N.Z. 42 24S 172 40E
77 Kaifeng, China 34 49N 114 30E
77 Kaihwa, China 29 0N 118 21E
92 Kaiingveld, S. Afr. 30 0S 22 0E
101 Kaikohe, N.Z. 35 25S 173 49E
101 Kaikoura, N.Z. 42 25S 173 43E
101 Kaikoura Pen., N.Z. 42 25S 173 43E
101 Kaikoura Ra., N.Z. 41 59S 173 41E
84 Kailahun, Sierra Leone 8 18N 10 39W
73 Kaimana, New Guinea 3 30S 133 45E
101 Kaimanawa Mts., N.Z. 39 15S 175 56E
69 Kaimganj, India 27 33N 79 24E
69 Kaimur Hill, India 24 30N 82 0E
98 Kainantu, New Guinea 6 15S 145 55E
101 Kaingaroa Forest, N.Z. 38 30S 176 30E
85 Kainji Res., Nigeria 10 1N 4 40E
101 Kaipara Harb., N.Z. 36 25S 174 14E
107 Kaipokok B., Canada 55 10N 59 20W
68 Kairana, India 29 33N 77 15E
98 Kairiru, I., Terr. of, New Guinea 3 20S 143 20E
73 Kaironi, Indonesia 0 47S 133 40E
83 Kairouan, Tunisia 35 45N 10 5E
98 Kairuku, Terr. of Papua 8 57S 146 35E
25 Kaiserslautern, Ger. 49 30N 7 43E
101 Kaitaia, New Zealand 35 8S 173 17E
101 Kaitangata, N.Z. 46 17S 169 51E
68 Kaithal, India 29 48N 76 26E
76 Kaitung, China 44 58N 123 2E
76 Kaiyüan, China 42 40N 124 30E
50 Kajaani, Finland 64 17N 27 46E
98 Kajabbi, Australia 20 0S 140 1E
72 Kajani, R., Indonesia 2 40N 116 40E
71 Kajang, Malaysia 2 59N 101 48E
73 Kajeli, Indonesia 3 20S 127 10E
90 Kajiado, Kenya 1 53S 36 48E
87 Kajo Kaji, Sudan 3 58N 31 40E
73 Kajoa, I., Indonesia 0 1N 127 28E
72 Kajuagung, Indonesia 3 28S 104 46E
50 Kajaani, Finland 64 15N 27 43E
106 Kakabeka Falls, Can. 48 24N 89 37W
90 Kakamega, Kenya 0 20N 34 46E
90 Kakamega ♦, Kenya 0 20N 34 46E
42 Kakanj, Yugoslavia 44 9N 18 7E
101 Kakanui Mts., N.Z. 45 10S 170 30E
74 Kakegawa, Japan 34 45N 138 1E
57 Kakhib, U.S.S.R. 42 28N 46 34E
56 Kakhovskoye Vdkhr., U.S.S.R. 47 5N 34 16E
89 Kakia, Botswana 24 48S 23 22E
70 Kakinada (Cocanada), India 16 50N 82 11E

* Renamed Mambilima Falls

MAP

85 Kala, Cameroon 12 2N 14 40E
70 Kala Oya., Sri Lanka 8 15N 80 0E
83 Kalaa-Kebira, Tunisia 35 59N 10 32E
68 Kalabagh, Pakistan 33 0N 71 28E
44 Kalabáka, Greece 39 42N 21 39E
89 Kalabo, Zambia 14 58s 22 33E
55 Kalach, U.S.S.R. 50 22N 41 0E
67 Kaladan, R., Burma 21 30N 92 45E
112 Kaladar, Canada 44 37N 77 5w
92 Kalahari, Des., Africa 24 0s 22 0E
92 Kalahari Gemsbok Nat. 26 0s 20 30E
  Pk., S. Afr.
70 Kalahasti, India 13 45N 79 44E
44 Kalaja e Turrës, Albania 41 10N 19 28E
93 Kalakamati, Bots. 20 40s 27 25E
59 Kalakan, U.S.S.R. 55 15N 116 45E
90 Kalama, Zaïre 2 52s 28 35E
118 Kalama, U.S.A. 46 0N 122 55w
44 Kalamariá, Greece 40 33N 22 55E
45 Kalamata, Greece 37 3N 22 10E
114 Kalamazoo, U.S.A. 42 20N 85 35w
114 Kalamazoo, R., U.S.A. 42 40N 86 0w
70 Kalamb, India 18 3N 74 48E
91 Kalambo Falls, Tanz. 8 37s 31 35E
45 Kálamos, Greece 38 37N 20 59E
45 Kálamos, I., Greece 38 37N 20 55E
45 Kalamoti, Greece 38 15N 26 4E
73 Kalao, I., Indonesia 7 21s 121 0E
73 Kalaotoa, I., Indonesia 7 20s 121 50E
48 Kälarne, Sweden 62 59N 16 8E
27 Kalárovo, Cz. 47 54N 18 0E
71 Kalasin, Thailand 16 26N 103 30E
66 Kalat, Pakistan 29 8N 66 31E
65 Kalat-i-Ghilzai, Afghan 32 15N 66 58E
45 Kálathos (Calato), 36 9N 28 8E
  Greece
57 Kalaus, R., U.S.S.R. 45 40N 43 30E
45 Kalávrita, Greece 38 3N 22 8E
84 Kalba, Ghana 9 30N 2 42w
47 Kaldhovd, Norway 60 5N 8 0E
56 Kalecik, Turkey 40 4N 33 26E
67 Kalegauk Kyun, Burma 15 33N 97 35E
90 Kalehe, Zaïre 2 6s 28 50E
90 Kalema, Tanzania 1 12s 31 55E
28 Kalety, Poland 50 35N 18 52E
67 Kalewa, Burma 23 15N 94 20E
90 Kálfafellssta ur, Iceland 64 11N 15 53w
96 Kalgoorlie, Australia 30 40s 121 22E
43 Kaliakra, Nos, Bulgaria 43 21N 28 30E
72 Kalianda, Indonesia 5 50s 105 45E
73 Kalibo, Philippines 11 43N 122 22E
90 Kalima, Zaïre 2 33s 26 32E
72 Kalimantan Barat ♦, 0 0 110 30E
  Indonesia
72 Kalimantan Selatan ♦, 2 30s 115 30E
  Indonesia
72 Kalimantan Tengah ♦, 2 0s 113 30E
  Indonesia
72 Kalimantan Timor ♦, 1 30N 116 30E
  Indonesia
45 Kálimnos, I., Greece 37 0N 27 0E
69 Kalimpong, India 27 4N 88 35E
70 Kalinadi, R., India 14 50N 74 20E
55 Kalinin, U.S.S.R. 56 55N 35 55E
54 Kaliningrad, U.S.S.R. 54 42N 20 32E
57 Kalinino, U.S.S.R. 45 12N 38 59E
54 Kalinkovichi, U.S.S.R. 52 12N 29 20E
43 Kalinovik, Yugoslavia 43 31N 18 29E
43 Kalipetrovo (Starčevo), 44 5N 27 14E
  Bulg.
90 Kaliro, Uganda 0 56N 33 30E
44 Kallirrákhi, Greece 40 40N 24 35E
118 Kalispell, U.S.A. 48 10N 114 22w
28 Kalisz, Poland 51 45N 18 8E
28 Kalisz Pom, Poland 53 17N 15 55E
90 Kaliua, Tanzania 5 5s 31 48E
70 Kaliveli Tank, India 12 5N 79 50E
50 Kalix R., Sweden 67 0N 22 0E
68 Kalka, India 30 56N 76 57E
114 Kalkaska, U.S.A. 0 44N 85 9w
92 Kalkfeld, S.W. Afr. 20 57s 16 14E
92 Kalkfontein, Botswana 22 4s 20 57E
92 Kalkfontein Dam, South 29 30s 24 15E
  Africa
92 Kalkrand, S.W. Africa 24 1s 17 35E
48 Kall L., Sweden 63 35N 13 10E
70 Kallakurichi, India 11 44N 79 1E
49 Källandsö, Sweden 58 40N 13 5E
49 Källby, Sweden 58 30N 13 8E
60 Kallia, Jordan 31 46N 35 30E
70 Kallidaikurichi, India 8 38N 77 31E
49 Kallinge, Sweden 56 15N 15 18E
45 Kallithéa, Greece 37 5s 23 41E
44 Kallmeti, Albania 41 51N 19 41E
45 Kallonís Kólpos, Greece 39 26N 26 10E
44 Kalltorp, Sweden 58 23N 13 20E
85 Kalmalo, Nigeria 13 40N 5 20E
49 Kalmar, Kalmar, Sweden 56 40N 16 20E
49 Kalmar län ♦, Swed. 57 25N 16 15E
49 Kalmar sund, Sweden 56 40N 16 25E
57 Kalmyk A.S.S.R. ♦, 46 5N 46 1E
  U.S.S.R.
57 Kalmykovo, U.S.S.R. 49 0N 51 35E
54 Kalna, India 23 13N 88 25E
98 Kalo, Terr. of Papua 10 0s 147 42E
27 Kalocsa, Hungary 46 32N 19 0E
43 Kalofer, Bulgaria 42 37N 24 59E
68 Kalol, Gujarat, India 23 15N 72 33E
68 Kalol, Gujarat, India 22 37N 73 31E
91 Kalola, Zaïre 10 0s 28 0E
91 Kalolimnos, Greece 37 4N 27 8E
91 Kalomo, Zambia 17 0s 26 30E
45 Kalonerón, Greece 37 20N 21 38E
69 Kalpi, India 26 8N 79 47E
70 Kalrayan Hills, India 11 45N 78 40E
70 Kalsubai, Mt., India 17 35N 73 45E
85 Kaltungo, Nigeria 9 48N 11 19E
68 Kalu, Pakistan 25 5N 67 39E
55 Kaluga, U.S.S.R. 54 35N 36 10E
91 Kalulushi, Zambia 12 50s 28 3E

49 Kalundborg, Denmark 55 41N 11 5E
54 Kalush, U.S.S.R. 49 3N 24 12E
28 Kałuszyn, Poland 52 13N 21 52E
70 Kalutara, Sri Lanka 6 35N 80 0E
27 Kalwaria, Poland 49 53N 19 41E
68 Kalyan, India 20 30N 74 3E
68 Kalyani, India 17 53N 76 59E
55 Kalyazin, U.S.S.R. 57 15N 37 45E
71 Kam Keut, Laos 18 20N 104 48E
92 Kama, Zaïre 3 30s 27 5E
52 Kama, R., U.S.S.R. 60 0N 53 0E
70 Kamachumu, Tanz. 1 37s 31 37E
74 Kamaishi, Japan 39 20N 142 0E
68 Kamalia, Pakistan 30 44N 72 42E
90 Kamango, Zaïre 0 40N 29 52E
91 Kamapanda, Zambia 12 5s 24 0E
63 Kamaran, Red Sea 15 28N 42 35E
91 Kamativi, Rhodesia 18 15s 0 27E
85 Kamba, Nigeria 11 50N 3 45E
70 Kambam, India 9 45N 77 16E
68 Kambar, Pakistan 27 37N 68 1E
84 Kambia, Sierra Leone 9 3N 12 53w
91 Kambolé, Zambia 8 47s 30 48E
90 Kambove, Zaïre 10 51s 26 33E
59 Kamchatka, P-ov., 57 0N 160 0E
  U.S.S.R.
98 Kamde, Indonesia 8 0s 140 58E
42 Kamenica, Yugoslavia 44 25N 19 40E
26 Kamenice, Cz. 49 18N 15 2E
39 Kamenjak, Rt., 44 47N 13 55E
  Yugoslavia
52 Kamenka, R.S.F.S.R., 65 58N 44 0E
  U.S.S.R.
55 Kamenka, R.S.F.S.R., 50 47N 39 20E
  U.S.S.R.
54 Kamenka Bugskaya, 50 8N 24 16E
  U.S.S.R.
56 Kamenka Dneprovskaya, 47 29N 34 14E
  U.S.S.R.
58 Kamensk, U.S.S.R. 56 25N 62 45E
57 Kamensk Shakhtinskiy, 48 23N 40 20E
  U.S.S.R.
55 Kamenskiy, U.S.S.R. 50 48N 45 25E
58 Kamenskoye, U.S.S.R. 62 45N 165 30E
43 Kamenyak, Bulgaria 43 24N 26 57E
26 Kamenz, Germany 51 17N 14 7E
44 Kami, Albania 42 17N 20 18E
118 Kamiah, U.S.A. 46 12N 116 2w
28 Kamien Krajenskie, 53 32N 17 32E
  Poland
28 Kamien Pomorski, 53 57N 14 43E
  Poland
28 Kamiensk, Poland 51 12N 19 29E
45 Kamilonísion, Greece 35 50N 26 15E
109 Kamilukuak, L., Can. 62 40N 100 0w
91 Kamina, Zaïre 8 45s 25 0E
109 Kaminak L., Canada 62 0N 95 0w
90 Kamituga Mungombe, 3 2s 28 10E
  Zaïre
108 Kamloops, Canada 50 40N 120 20w
68 Kamoke, Pakistan 32 4N 74 4E
88 Kamono, Congo (Fr.) 3 10s 13 20E
26 Kamp, R., Austria 48 35N 15 26E
72 Kampa, Indonesia 1 42s 105 24E
90 Kampala, Uganda 0 20N 32 30E
71 Kampar, W. Malaysia 4 18N 101 9E
72 Kampar, S., Indonesia 0 30N 102 0E
16 Kampen, Netherlands 52 33N 5 53E
91 Kampolombo, L., Zam. 11 30s 29 35E
71 Kampong Sedili Besar, 1 57N 104 8E
  Malaysia
71 Kampot, Khmer Rep. 10 36N 104 10E
90 Kamptee, India 21 9N 79 19E
84 Kampti, Upper Volta 10 7N 3 25w
73 Kamrau, Teluk, 3 30s 133 45E
  Indonesia
109 Kamsack, Canada 51 35N 101 50w
55 Kamskoye Ustye, 55 10N 49 20E
  U.S.S.R.
52 Kamskoye Vdkhr., 58 0N 56 0E
  U.S.S.R.
55 Kamyshin, U.S.S.R. 50 10N 45 30E
57 Kamyzyak, U.S.S.R. 46 4N 48 10E
106 Kanaaupscow, Canada 54 0N 76 40w
119 Kanab, U.S.A. 37 3N 112 29w
119 Kanab Creek, U.S.A. 37 0N 112 40w
74 Kanagawa-ken ♦, Japan 35 20N 139 20E
72 Kanakapura, India 12 33N 77 28E
44 Kanália, Greece 39 30N 22 53E
119 Kanarraville, U.S.A. 37 34N 113 12w
114 Kanawha, R., U.S.A. 39 40N 82 0w
86 Kanayis, Ras el, Egypt 31 30N 28 5E
74 Kanazawa, Japan 36 30N 136 38E
71 Kanchanaburi, Thailand 14 8N 99 31E
69 Kanchenjunga, Mt., Nep. 27 50N 88 10E
70 Kanchipuram 12 52N 79 45E
  (Conjeeveram), India
77 Kanchow, China 25 58N 114 55E
76 Kanchuan, China 36 29N 109 24E
28 Kanczuga, Poland 49 58N 22 25E
88 Kanda Kanda, Zaïre 6 52s 23 48E
*53 Kandagach, U.S.S.R. 49 20N 57 15E
21 Kandahar, Afghanistan 31 32N 65 43E
52 Kandalakshkiyzaliv, 66 0N 35 0E
  U.S.S.R.
72 Kandangan, Indonesia 2 50s 115 20E
73 Kandanghaur, Indonesia 6 21s 108 6E
68 Kandhkot, Pakistan 28 16N 69 8E
85 Kandi, Dahomey 11 7N 2 55E

69 Kandi, India 23 58N 88 5E
91 Kandinduna, Zam. 13 58s 24 19E
64 Kandira, Turkey 41 5N 30 10E
68 Kandla, India 23 0N 70 10E
100 Kandos, Australia 32 45s 149 58E
66 Kandrach, Pakistan 25 30N 65 30E
69 Kandukur, India 15 12N 79 57E
70 Kandy, Sri Lanka 7 18N 80 43E
112 Kane, U.S.A. 41 39N 78 53w
4 Kane Bassin, Greenland 79 30N 68 0w
84 Kanel, Senegal 13 18N 14 35w
77 Kanen, China 18 46N 108 33E
57 Kanevskaya, U.S.S.R. 46 3N 39 3E
39 Kanfanar, Yugoslavia 45 7N 13 50E
65 Kang, Afghanistan 30 55N 61 55E
84 Kangaba, Mali 11 56N 8 25w
71 Kangar, Malaysia 6 27N 100 12E
99 Kangaroo I., Austral. 35 45s 137 0E
98 Kangaroo Mts., Austral. 23 25s 142 0E
100 Kangaroo Flat, Austral. 36 45s 144 20E
65 Kangavar, Iran 34 40N 48 0E
72 Kangean, Kepulauan, 6 55s 115 23E
  Indonesia
4 Kangerdlugsuaé, 68 10N 32 20w
  Greenland
76 Kangnŭng, S. Korea 37 45N 128 59E
88 Kango, Gabon 0 11N 10 5E
77 Kangshan, Taiwan 22 43N 120 14E
69 Kangtissu Shan, Tibet 31 0N 82 0E
67 Kangto, Mt., India 27 50N 92 35E
70 Kanhangad, India 12 21N 74 58E
70 Kanheri, India 19 13N 72 50E
67 Kani, China 29 25N 95 25E
84 Kani, Ivory Coast 8 29N 6 36w
90 Kaniama, Zaïre 7 30s 24 12E
107 Kaniapiskau L., Can. 53 52N 69 20w
107 Kaniapiskau, R., Can. 55 15N 68 40E
52 Kanin, P-ov., U.S.S.R. 68 0N 45 0E
68 Kanin Nos, Mys, 68 45N 43 20E
  U.S.S.R.
44 Kanina, Albania 40 23N 19 30E
100 Kaniva, Australia 36 22s 141 18E
42 Kanjiza, Yugoslavia 46 3N 20 4E
114 Kankakee, U.S.A. 41 6N 87 50w
114 Kankakee, R., U.S.A. 41 13N 87 0w
84 Kankan, Guinea 10 3N 9 15w
59 Kankunskiy, U.S.S.R. 57 37N 126 8E
115 Kannapolis, U.S.A. 35 32N 80 37w
69 Kannauj, India 27 3N 79 26E
85 Kano, Nigeria 12 2N 8 30E
84 Kanoroba, Ivory Coast 9 7N 6 8w
72 Kanowit, Malaysia 2 14N 112 20E
96 Kanowna, Australia 30 32s 121 31E
74 Kanoya, Japan 31 25N 130 50E
74 Kantó-sammyaku, mts., 36 0N 138 30E
  Japan
67 Kanpetlet, Burma 21 10N 93 59E
69 Kanpur, India 26 35N 80 20E
116 Kansas, R., U.S.A. 39 15N 96 20w
116 Kansas ♦, U.S.A. 38 40N 98 0w
116 Kansas City, Kans., 39 0N 94 40w
  U.S.A.
116 Kansas City, Mo., 39 3N 94 30w
  U.S.A.
91 Kansenia, Zaïre 10 20s 26 0E
59 Kansk, U.S.S.R. 56 20N 95 37E
76 Kansu ♦, China 35 30N 104 30E
85 Kantché, Niger 13 31N 8 30E
77 Kantemirovka, U.S.S.R. 49 43N 39 55E
75 Kantse, China 31 30N 100 29E
15 Kanturk, Ire. 52 10N 8 55w
74 Kanuma, Japan 36 44N 139 42E
92 Kanus, S.W. Africa 27 50s 18 39E
92 Kanye, Botswana 25 0s 25 28E
92 Kanyu, China 34 56N 119 8E
92 Kanyu, Botswana 20 7s 24 37E
90 Kanzi, Ras, Tanzania 7 1s 39 33E
77 Kaoan, China 28 20N 115 17E
77 Kaohsiung, Taiwan 22 35N 120 16E
92 Kaokoveld, S. Afr. 19 0s 13 0E
84 Kaolack, Senegal 14 5N 16 8w
76 Kaolemi, China 24 11N 119 45E
77 Kaoyu Hu, China 32 50N 119 10E
68 Kapadvanj, India 23 5N 73 0E
88 Kapanga, Zaïre 8 30s 22 40E
55 Kapanovka, U.S.S.R. 47 28N 46 50E
91 Kapata, Zambia 14 16s 26 15E
45 Kapello, Akra, Gr. 36 9N 23 3E
91 Kapema, Zaïre 10 45s 28 22E
26 Kapfenberg, Austria 47 26N 15 18E
91 Kapiri Mposhi, Zam. 13 59s 28 43E
106 Kapiskau, Canada 52 50N 82 1w
106 Kapiskau, R., Canada 52 20N 83 40w
72 Kapit, Malaysia 2 0N 113 5E
101 Kapiti I., N.Z. 40 50s 174 56E
42 Kaplice, Czechoslovakia 48 42N 14 30E
87 Kapoeta, Sudan 4 50N 33 35E
27 Kápolnásnyék, Hung. 47 16N 18 41E
25 Kaposvár, Hungary 46 30N 18 0E
73 Kapotjol, Indonesia 2 0s 130 9E
24 Kappeln, Germany 54 37N 9 56E
92 Kapps, S.W. Africa 22 32s 17 18E
39 Kaprije, Y.-slavia 43 42N 15 43E
54 Kapsukas, U.S.S.R. 54 33N 23 19E
73 Kapuas, R., Indonesia 1 30N 113 30E
72 Kapuas Hulu, 1 30N 113 30E
  Pegunungan, Malaysia
91 Kapulo, Zambia 10 30s 32 55E
99 Kapunda, Australia 34 20s 138 56E
101 Kapuni, New Zealand 39 29s 174 8E
68 Kapurthala, India 31 23N 75 25E
106 Kapuskasing, Canada 49 25N 82 30w
106 Kapuskasing, R., Can. 49 50N 82 50w
57 Kapustin Yar, U.S.S.R. 48 37N 45 40E
99 Kaputar, Mt., Austral. 30 15s 150 10E
90 Kaputir, Kenya 2 5N 35 28E
27 Kapuvár, Hungary 47 36N 17 1E

45 Kara, Turkey 38 29N 26 19E
58 Kara, U.S.S.R. 69 10N 65 25E
45 Kara, I., Turkey 36 58N 27 30E
58 Kara Bogaz Gol, Zaliv, 41 0N 53 30E
  U.S.S.R.
45 Kara Burun, Turkey 38 41N 26 28E
58 Kara Kalpak A.S.S.R. 43 0N 60 0E
  ♦, U.S.S.R.
75 Kara Nor, China 38 45N 98 0E
58 Kara Sea, U.S.S.R. 75 0N 70 0E
86 Kara, Wadi, Si. Arab. 20 40N 42 0E
56 Karabük, Turkey 41 10N 32 30E
44 Karaburuni, Albania 40 25N 19 20E
58 Karabutak, U.S.S.R. 50 0N 60 45E
54 Karachala, U.S.S.R. 39 45N 48 53E
54 Karachayevsk, U.S.S.R. 43 50N 42 0E
70 Karad, India 17 15N 74 10E
64 Karadeniz Boğazı, 41 10N 29 5E
  Turkey
64 Karadeniz Dağlari, 41 30N 35 0E
  Turkey
85 Karaga, Ghana 9 58N 0 28w
58 Karagajly, U.S.S.R. 49 26N 76 0E
58 Karaganda, U.S.S.R. 49 50N 73 0E
59 Karaginskiy, Ostrov, 58 45N 164 0E
  U.S.S.R.
90 Karagwe ♦, Tanz. 1 15s 30 45E
70 Karaikal, India 10 59N 79 50E
70 Karaikkudi, India 10 0N 78 45E
65 Karaitivu I., Sri Lanka 9 45N 79 52E
65 Karaj, Iran 35 4N 51 0E
44 Karajë, Albania 41 11N 19 33E
65 Karak, Jordan 31 14N 35 40E
58 Karakas, U.S.S.R. 48 20N 83 30E
73 Karakitang, Indon. 3 14N 125 28E
92 Karakobis, Bots. 22 3s 20 37E
66 Karakoram, Kashmir 35 20N 76 0E
66 Karakoram Pass, 35 20N 78 0E
  Kashmir
76 Karakorum, Mongolia 47 30N 102 20E
59 Karakum, Peski, 39 30N 60 0E
  U.S.S.R.
59 Karakun, U.S.S.R. 57 5N 115 50E
45 Karamai, China 45 57N 84 30E
64 Karaman, Turkey 37 14N 33 13E
73 Karamea, Indonesia 3 53s 116 6E
101 Karamea Bight, N.Z. 41 22s 171 40E
90 Karamoja ♦, Uganda 3 0N 34 15E
73 Karamsad, India 22 35N 72 50E
73 Karanganjar, Indonesia 7 38s 109 37E
70 Karanja, India 20 29N 77 31E
56 Karaşar, Turkey 40 21N 31 55E
92 Karasburg, S.W. Africa 28 0s 18 44E
58 Karasino, U.S.S.R. 66 50N 86 50E
58 Karasuk ♦, Kenya 2 12N 35 15E
58 Karatau, U.S.S.R. 43 10N 70 28E
64 Karatiya, Israel 31 39N 34 43E
74 Karatsu, Japan 33 30N 130 0E
68 Karauli, India 26 30N 77 4E
91 Karawa, Zaïre 10 20s 26 0E
59 Karawanken, Eur. 46 30N 14 40E
58 Karazhal, U.S.S.R. 48 2N 70 49E
64 Karbala, Iraq 32 47N 44 3E
27 Kárböle, Sweden 61 59N 15 22E
27 Karcag, Hungary 47 19N 21 1E
49 Karda, Sweden 57 10N 13 49E
45 Kardhámila, Greece 38 35N 26 5E
44 Kardhitsa, Greece 39 23N 21 54E
44 Kárdhitsa ♦, Greece 39 15N 21 50E
54 Kärdla, U.S.S.R. 58 50N 22 40E
92 Kareeberg, S. Afr. 30 50s 22 0E
86 Karelia, Sudan 18 30N 31 49E
59 Karelian A.S.S.R. ♦, 65 30N 32 30E
  U.S.S.R.
90 Karema, Tanzania 6 49s 30 24E
71 Karen, Andaman Is. 12 49N 92 53E
99 Karfad, Arnud, Iran 37 55N 49 0E
99 Kargasok, U.S.S.R. 59 3N 80 53E
58 Kargat, U.S.S.R. 55 10N 80 15E
66 Kargil, Kashmir 34 32N 76 12E
58 Kargi, Turkey 41 11N 34 30E
66 Kargil, Kashmir 23 32N 76 12E
28 Kargowa, Poland 52 5N 15 51E
85 Karguéri, Niger 13 36N 10 30E
45 Kariai, Greece 40 14N 24 19E
91 Kariba, Rhodesia 16 28s 28 36E
91 Kariba Gorge, Zambia 16 30s 28 35E
91 Kariba L., Rhodesia 16 40s 28 25E
92 Karibib, S.W. Africa 21 0s 15 56E
70 Karikal, India 10 59N 79 50E
70 Karikkale, Turkey 39 55N 33 30E
72 Karimata, Kepulauan, 1 40s 109 0E
  Indon.
70 Karimata, Selat, Indon. 2 0s 108 20E
70 Karimnagar, India 18 26N 79 10E
70 Karimundjawa, 5 50s 110 30E
  Kepulauan, Indon.
63 Karin, Somali Rep. 10 50N 45 52E
45 Káristos, Greece 38 1N 24 29E
74 Kariya, Japan 34 58N 137 1E
70 Karkal, India 13 15N 74 56E
56 Karkinitskiy Zaliv, 45 36N 32 35E
  U.S.S.R.
62 Karkur, Israel 32 29N 34 57E
86 Karkur Tohl, Egypt 22 5N 25 5E
24 Karl-Marx-Stadt, Ger. 50 50N 12 55E
24 Karl-Marx-Stadt ♦, 50 45N 13 0E
  Germany
44 Karla, L. = Voiviis, 39 35N 22 45E
  Limni, Greece
28 Karlino, Poland 54 3N 15 53E

39 Karlobag, Y.-slavia 44 32N 15 5E
39 Karlovac, Y.-slavia 45 31N 15 36E
56 Karlovka, U.S.S.R. 49 29N 35 8E
26 Karlovy Vary, Cz. 50 13N 12 51E
58 Karlsborg, Ostergötland, 58 33N 14 33E
  Sweden
49 Karlshamn, Sweden 56 10N 14 51E
48 Karlskoga, Sweden 59 22N 14 33E
49 Karlskrona, Sweden 56 10N 15 35E
25 Karlsruhe, Germany 49 3N 8 23E
116 Karlstad, U.S.A. 48 38N 96 30w
47 Karmøy, Norway 59 15N 5 15E
29 Karnal, India 29 42N 77 2E
69 Karnali, R., Nepal 29 0N 82 0E
71 Karnaphuli Res., 22 40N 92 20E
  Bangladesh
117 Karnes City, U.S.A. 28 53N 97 53w
84 Karni, Ghana 10 45N 2 40w
26 Karnische Alpen, Europe 46 36N 13 0E
43 Karnobat, Bulgaria 42 40N 27 0E
26 Kärnten ♦, Austria 46 52N 13 30E
84 Karo, Upper Volta 12 16N 2 22w
91 Karoi, Rhodesia 16 48s 29 45E
91 Karonga, Malawi 9 57s 33 55E
99 Karoonda, Australia 35 1s 139 59E
45 Karos, Is., Greece 36 54N 25 40E
45 Karousádhes, Greece 39 47N 19 45E
49 Karpalund, Sweden 56 4N 14 5E
45 Kárpathos, I., Greece 35 37N 27 10E
45 Kárpathos, Stenón 36 0N 27 30E
  Greece
52 Karpogory, U.S.S.R. 63 59N 44 27E
49 Karrebaek, Denmark 55 12N 11 39E
64 Kars, Turkey 40 40N 43 5E
58 Karsakpay, U.S.S.R. 47 55N 66 40E
58 Karsha, U.S.S.R. 49 45N 51 35E
58 Karshi, U.S.S.R. 39 0N 65 55E
44 Kartál Oros, Gr. 41 15N 25 13E
58 Kartaly, U.S.S.R. 53 10N 60 50E
68 Karttzuza, Poland 31 27N 75 32E
112 Karthaus, U.S.A. 41 8N 78 9w
28 Kartuzy, Poland 54 22N 18 10E
73 Karufa, Indonesia 3 50s 133 20E
90 Karumba, Australia 17 31s 140 50E
90 Karumo, Tanzania 2 25s 32 50E
90 Karumwa, Tanzania 3 12s 32 38E
90 Karungu, Kenya 0 50s 34 10E
49 Karup, Denmark 56 19N 9 10E
70 Karur, India 10 59N 78 2E
27 Karviná, Cz. 49 53N 18 25E
91 Karwi, India 25 12N 80 57E
71 Kas Kong, Khmer Rep. 11 27N 102 12E
91 Kasache, Malawi 13 25s 34 20E
91 Kasai ♦, Zaïre 8 20s 22 0E
90 Kasai Oriental ♦, Zaïre 5 0s 24 30E
91 Kasai Occidental ♦, 6 30s 22 30E
  Zaïre
91 Kasaji, Zaïre 10 25s 23 27E
91 Kasama, Zambia 10 16s 31 9E
92 Kasane, S.W. Afr. 17 34s 24 50E
91 Kasanga, Tanzania 8 30s 31 10E
88 Kasangulu, Zaïre 4 15s 15 15E
90 Kasba L., Canada 60 20N 102 10w
82 Kasba Tadla, Morocco 32 36N 6 17w
109 Kasba L., Canada 60 20N 102 10w
65 Kaschmar, Iran 35 16N 58 26E
49 Kaseberga, Sweden 55 24N 14 8E
91 Kasempa, Zambia 13 30s 25 44E
91 Kasenga, Zaïre 10 20s 28 45E
90 Kasese, Uganda 0 13N 30 3E
91 Kasewa, Zambia 14 28s 28 53E
106 Kashabowie, Canada 48 40N 90 26w
65 Kashan, Iran 34 5N 51 30E
75 Kashgar, China 39 46N 75 52E
91 Kashimbo, Zaïre 11 12s 26 19E
55 Kashin, U.S.S.R. 57 20N 37 36E
77 Kashing, China 30 45N 120 41E
70 Kashipur, Orissa, India 19 16N 83 3E
68 Kashipur, Ut. P., India 29 15N 79 0E
55 Kashira, U.S.S.R. 54 45N 38 10E
74 Kashiwazaki, Japan 37 22N 138 33E
68 Kashmor, Pakistan 28 28N 69 32E
75 Kashpirovka, U.S.S.R. 53 0N 48 30E
67 Kashum Tso, Tibet 34 45N 86 0E
55 Kasimov, U.S.S.R. 54 55N 41 20E
90 Kasinge, Zaïre 6 15s 26 58E
116 Kaskaskia, R., U.S.A. 38 40N 89 12w
50 Kaskinen (Kaskö), 62 22N 21 15E
  Finland
50 Kaskö (Kaskinen), 62 22N 21 15E
  Finland
108 Kaslo, Canada 49 55N 117 0w
91 Kasongo, Zaïre 4 30s 26 33E
88 Kasongo Lunda, Zaïre 6 35s 17 0E
45 Kásos, I., Greece 35 20N 26 55E
45 Kásos, Stenón, Greece 35 30N 26 30E
57 Kaspi, U.S.S.R. 41 54N 44 17E
43 Kaspichan, Bulgaria 43 18N 27 11E
57 Kaspiyskiy, U.S.S.R. 45 22N 47 23E
57 Kaspiysk, U.S.S.R. 42 45N 47 40E
87 Kassab ed Doleib, Sud. 13 30N 33 35E
86 Kassala, Egypt 15 23N 36 26E
87 Kassala, Sudan 15 23N 36 26E
87 Kassala ♦, Sudan 15 20N 36 26E
44 Kassandra, Greece 40 0N 23 30E
25 Kassel, Germany 51 19N 9 32E
86 Kassinger, Sudan 18 46N 31 51E
54 Kassiopi, Gr. 39 48N 19 55E
73 Kasua, Indonesia 6 58s 139 21E
64 Kastamonu, Turkey 41 25N 33 43E
39 Kastav, Y.-slavia 45 22N 14 20E
45 Kastélli, Greece 35 29N 23 38E
45 Kastéllou, Akra, Gr. 35 12N 25 20E
49 Kastlösa, Sweden 56 26N 16 25E

* Renamed Oktabrsk

Kastóri INDEX Kiangpen

MAP
45 Kastóri, Greece 37 10N 22 17E
44 Kastoria, Greece 40 30N 21 19E
44 Kastoria ♦, Greece 40 30N 21 15E
44 Kastorias, Greece 40 30N 21 20E
55 Kastornoye, U.S.S.R. 51 55N 38 2E
45 Kastó, I., Greece 38 35N 20 55E
44 Kástron, Greece 39 53N 25 8E
45 Kastrosikiá, Greece 39 6N 20 36E
90 Kasulu, Tanz. 4 37S 30 5E
90 Kasulu ♦, Tanz. 4 37S 30 5E
57 Kasumkent, U.S.S.R. 41 47N 48 15E
91 Kasungu, Malawi 13 0S 33 29E
68 Kasur, Pakistan 31 5N 74 25E
59 Kata, U.S.S.R. 58 46N 102 40E
91 Kataba, Zambia 16 10S 25 10E
90 Katako Kombe, Zaïre 3 25S 24 20E
45 Katákolon, Greece 37 38N 21 19E
90 Katale, Tanzania 4 52S 31 7E
73 Kataloka, Indonesia 3 54S 131 27E
87 Katama, Ethiopia 9 35N 38 36E
100 Katamatite, Australia 36 6S 145 41E
90 Katanda, Zaïre 0 55S 29 21E
*90 Katanga ♦, Zaïre 8 0S 25 0E
66 Katanghan ♦, Afghan. 36 0N 69 0E
59 Katangli, U.S.S.R. 51 42N 143 14E
87 Katanich, Sudan 6 0N 33 40E
96 Katanning, Australia 33 40S 117 33E
45 Katastári, Greece 37 50N 20 45E
90 Katavi Swamps, Tanz. 6 50S 31 10E
44 Katerini, Greece 40 18N 22 37E
67 Katha, Burma 24 10N 96 30E
86 Katherina, Gebel, Egypt 28 30N 33 57E
96 Katherine, Australia 14 27S 132 20E
84 Kati, Mali 12 41N 8 4W
72 Katiet, Indonesia 2 21S 99 44E
69 Katihar, India 25 34N 87 36E
92 Katima Mulilo Rapids, Zambia 17 28S 24 13E
91 Katimbira, Malawi 12 40S 34 0E
84 Katiola, Ivory Coast 8 10N 5 10W
92 Katkopberg, S. Afr. 30 0S 20 0E
42 Katlanovo, Y.-slavia 41 52N 21 40E
104 Katmai, vol., Alaska 58 20N 154 59W
69 Katmandu, Nepal 27 45N 85 12E
45 Kato Akhaïa, Greece 38 8N 21 33E
44 Kato Stazros, Greece 40 39N 23 43E
68 Katol, India 21 17N 78 38E
90 Katonga, R., Uganda 0 15N 31 50E
100 Katoomba, Australia 33 30S 150 0E
28 Katowice, Poland 50 17N 19 5E
27 Katowice ♦, Poland 50 30N 19 0E
14 Katrine L., Scot. 56 15N 4 30W
48 Katrineholm, Sweden 59 9N 16 12E
93 Katsepe, Malagasy Rep. 15 45S 46 15E
85 Katsina, Nigeria 7 10N 9 20E
85 Katsina Ala, R., Nigeria 6 52N 9 40E
74 Katsuura, Japan 35 15N 140 20E
65 Kattawaz, Afghanistan 32 48N 68 23E
49 Kattegat, Denmark 57 0N 11 20E
90 Katumba, Zaïre 7 40S 25 17E
90 Katungu, Kenya 2 55S 40 3E
69 Katwa, India 23 30N 89 25E
16 Katwijk-aan-Zee, Neth. 52 12N 4 24E
28 Katy, Poland 51 2N 16 45E
71 Kau Tao, Thailand 10 6N 99 48E
110 Kauai, I., Hawaii 19 30N 155 30W
110 Kauai Chan., Hawaii 21 45N 158 50W
62 Kaufakha, Israel 31 29N 34 40E
25 Kaufbeuren, Germany 47 42N 10 37E
117 Kaufman, U.S.A. 32 35N 96 20W
110 Kauhajoki, Finland 62 25N 22 10E
114 Kaukauna, U.S.A. 44 20N 88 13W
92 Kaukauveld, S. Afr. 20 0S 20 15E
50 Kauliranta, Finland 66 27N 23 41E
54 Kaunas, U.S.S.R. 54 54N 23 54E
85 Kaura Namoda, Nigeria 12 37N 6 33E
50 Kautokeino, Norway 69 0N 23 4E
59 Kavacha, U.S.S.R. 60 16N 169 51E
42 Kavadarci, Y.-slavia 41 26N 22 3E
70 Kavali, India 14 55N 80 1E
44 Kavalla, Greece 40 57N 24 28E
44 Kaválla Kólpos, Gr. 40 50N 24 25E
44 Kaválla ♦, Greece 41 05N 24 30E
126 Kavanayén, Ven. 5 38N 61 48W
43 Kavarna, Bulgaria 43 26N 28 22E
98 Kavieng, New Guinea 2 30S 150 48E
†90 Kavirondo Gulf, Kenya 0 20S 34 15E
57 Kavkaz, Bolshoi, U.S.S.R. 42 50N 44 0E
45 Kavousi, Greece 35 7N 25 51E
127 Kaw = Caux, Fr. Guiana 4 30N 52 15W
87 Kawa, Sudan 13 42N 32 34E
112 Kawagama L., Canada 45 18N 78 45W
74 Kawago, Japan 36 0N 139 30E
74 Kawaguchi, Japan 35 52N 138 45E
91 Kawama, Zaïre 9 30S 28 30E
91 Kawambwa, Zambia 9 48S 29 3E
74 Kawana, Japan 35 5N 135 27E
69 Kawardha, India 22 0N 81 17E
74 Kawasaki, Japan 35 35N 138 42E
106 Kawene, Canada 48 45N 91 15W
101 Kawerau, New Zealand 38 7S 176 42E
101 Kawhia Harbour, N.Z. 38 5S 174 51E
67 Kawnro, China 22 48N 99 8E
71 Kawthaung, Burma 10 5N 98 36E
71 Kawthoolei ♦, Burma 18 0N 97 30E
85 Kaya, Upper Volta 13 25N 1 10W
67 Kayah ♦, Burma 19 15N 97 15E
70 Kayangulam, India 9 10N 76 33E
118 Kaycee, U.S.A. 43 45N 106 46W
119 Kayenta, U.S.A. 36 46N 110 15W
84 Kayes, Mali 14 25N 11 30W
84 Kayima, Sierra Leone 8 54N 11 15W
91 Kayomba, Zambia 13 11S 24 2E
85 Kayoro, Ghana 11 0N 1 28W
99 Kayrunnera, Australia 30 40S 142 30E
57 Kaysatskoye, U.S.S.R. 49 47N 46 49E
64 Kayseri, Turkey 38 45N 35 30E
118 Kaysville, U.S.A. 41 2N 111 58W

* Renamed Shaba
† Renamed Winam Gulf

MAP
59 Kazachye, U.S.S.R. 70 52N 135 58E
59 Kazachinskoye, U.S.S.R. 56 16N 107 36E
58 Kazakhstan ♦, U.S.S.R. 49 0N 50 0E
55 Kazan, U.S.S.R. 55 48N 49 3E
43 Kazanluk, Bulgaria 42 38N 25 35E
57 Kazanskaya, U.S.S.R. 49 50N 40 30E
56 Kazatin, U.S.S.R. 49 45N 28 50E
65 Kazerun, Iran 29 38N 51 40E
57 Kazi Magomed, USSR 40 3N 49 0E
28 Kazimierza Wielki, Poland 50 15N 20 30E
27 Kazincbarcika, Hungary 48 17N 20 36E
57 Kaztalovka, U.S.S.R. 49 47N 48 43E
88 Kazumba, Zaïre 6 25S 22 5E
64 Kazvin, Iran 36 15N 50 0E
58 Kazym, R., U.S.S.R. 63 40N 68 30E
28 Kcynia, Poland 53 0N 17 30E
84 Ké, Mali 13 58N 5 18W
45 Kéa, Greece 37 35N 24 22E
45 Kéa, I., Greece 37 30N 24 22E
119 Keams Canyon, U.S.A. 35 53N 110 9W
116 Kearney, U.S.A. 40 45N 99 3W
64 Keban, Turkey 38 50N 38 50E
87 Kebele, Ethiopia 12 52N 40 40E
84 Kebi, Ivory Coast 9 18N 6 37W
83 Kebili, Tunisia 33 47N 9 0E
81 Kebkabiya, Sudan 13 50N 24 0E
63 Kebri, Dehar, Ethiopia 6 45N 44 17E
73 Kebumen, Indonesia 7 42S 109 40E
27 Kecel, Hungary 46 31N 19 16E
27 Kecskemét, Hungary 46 57N 19 35E
87 Kedada, Ethiopia 5 30N 35 58E
71 Kedah ♦, Malaysia 5 50N 100 40E
54 Kedainiai, U.S.S.R. 55 15N 23 57E
107 Kedgwick, Canada 47 40N 67 20W
92 Kedia Hill, Botswana 21 28S 24 37E
73 Kediri, Indonesia 7 51S 112 1E
84 Kédougou, Senegal 12 35N 12 10W
28 Kedzierzyn, Poland 50 20N 18 12E
108 Keefers, Canada 50 0N 121 40W
77 Keelung = Chilung, Taiwan 25 3N 121 45E
113 Keene, U.S.A. 42 57N 72 17W
15 Keeper, Mt., Ireland 52 46N 8 17W
98 Keer-Weer, C., Australia 14 0S 141 32E
113 Keeseville, U.S.A. 44 29N 73 30W
92 Keetmanshoop, S.W. Africa 26 35S 18 8E
109 Keewatin, terr., Can. 63 20N 94 40W
116 Keewatin, U.S.A. 47 23N 93 0W
109 Keewatin ♦, Canada 63 20N 94 40W
87 Kefa ♦, Ethiopia 6 55N 36 30E
45 Kefallinia, I., Greece 38 28N 20 30E
73 Kefamenanu, Indonesia 9 28S 124 38E
62 Kefar Ata, Israel 32 48N 35 7E
62 Kefar Etsyon, Jordan 31 39N 35 7E
62 Kefar Hasidim, Israel 32 47N 35 5E
62 Kefar Hittim B., Israel 32 48N 35 27E
62 Kefar Sava, Israel 32 11N 34 54E
62 Kefar Szold, Israel 33 11N 35 34E
62 Kefar Vitkin, Israel 32 22N 34 53E
62 Kefar Yehezqel, Israel 32 34N 35 22E
62 Kefar Yona, Israel 32 20N 34 54E
62 Kefar Zekharya, Israel 31 43N 34 57E
85 Keffi, Nigeria 8 55N 7 43E
50 Keflavik, Iceland 64 2N 22 35W
108 Keg River, Canada 57 45N 117 50W
70 Kegalla, Sri Lanka 7 15N 80 21E
107 Kegashka, Canada 50 14N 61 18W
25 Kehl, Germany 48 34N 7 50E
12 Keighley, Eng. 53 52N 1 54W
92 Keimoes, S. Africa 28 41S 21 0E
85 Keïta, Niger 14 46N 5 56E
99 Keith, Australia 36 0S 140 20E
14 Keith, Scotland 57 33N 2 58W
104 Keith Arm, Canada 65 30N 122 0W
68 Kekri, India 26 0N 75 10E
59 Kël, U.S.S.R. 69 30N 124 10E
87 Kelamet, Ethiopia 16 0N 38 20E
71 Kelang, Malaysia 3 2N 101 26E
70 Kelani Ganga, R., Sri Lanka 6 58N 79 50E
71 Kelantan, R., Malaysia 5 35N 102 8E
71 Kelantan ♦, W. Malay. 5 10N 102 0E
44 Këlcyra, Albania 40 22N 20 12E
25 Kelheim, Germany 48 58N 11 57E
83 Kelibia, Tunisia 36 50N 11 3E
88 Kellé, Congo 0 8S 14 38E
85 Kellé, Niger 14 18N 10 10E
118 Keller, U.S.A. 48 2N 118 44W
96 Kellerberrin, Australia 31 36S 117 38E
4 Kellett C., Canada 72 0N 125 40W
112 Kelleys I., U.S.A. 41 35N 82 42W
118 Kellogg, U.S.A. 47 30N 116 5W
50 Kelloselkä, Finland 66 56N 28 53E
15 Kells = Ceanannas Mor, Ireland 53 42N 6 53W
54 Kelmentsy, U.S.S.R. 48 30N 26 50E
88 Kélo, Chad 9 10N 15 45E
108 Kelowna, Canada 49 50N 119 25W
108 Kelsey Bay, Canada 50 25N 126 0W
101 Kelso, New Zealand 45 54S 169 15E
14 Kelso, Scotland 55 36N 2 27W
118 Kelso, U.S.A. 46 10N 122 57W
71 Keluang, Malaysia 2 3N 103 18E
109 Kelvington, Canada 52 20N 103 30W
84 Ke-Macina, Mali 14 5N 5 20W
52 Kem, U.S.S.R. 65 0N 34 38E
52 Kem, R., U.S.S.R. 64 45N 32 20E
82 Kem-Kem, Morocco 30 40N 4 30W
73 Kema, Indonesia 1 22N 125 8E
64 Kemah, Turkey 39 32N 39 5E
108 Kemano, Canada 53 35N 128 0W
87 Kembolcha, Ethiopia 11 29N 39 42E
56 Kemenets-Podolskiy, U.S.S.R. 48 40N 26 30E
58 Kemerovo, U.S.S.R. 55 20N 85 50E
50 Kemi älv = Kemijoki, Finland 65 47N 24 32E
50 Kemijoki, Finland 65 47N 24 32E

MAP
50 Kemijärvi, Finland 66 43N 27 22E
118 Kemmerer, U.S.A. 41 52N 110 30W
5 Kemp Coast, Antarc. 69 0S 55 0E
117 Kemp L., U.S.A. 33 45N 99 15W
99 Kempsey, Australia 31 1S 152 50E
106 Kempt, L., Canada 47 25N 74 30W
25 Kempten, Germany 47 42N 10 18E
106 Kemptville, Can. 45 0N 75 38W
14 Ken L., Scot. 55 0N 4 0W
82 Kenadsa, Algeria 31 48N 2 26W
73 Kendal, Indonesia 6 56S 110 14E
12 Kendal, Eng. 54 19N 2 44W
100 Kendall, Australia 31 35S 152 44E
114 Kendallville, U.S.A. 41 25N 85 15W
73 Kendari, Indonesia 3 50S 122 30E
72 Kendawangan, Indon. 2 32S 110 17E
85 Kende, Nigeria 11 30N 4 12E
69 Kendrapara, India 20 35N 86 30E
118 Kendrick, U.S.A. 46 43N 116 41W
84 Kenema, Sierra Leone 7 50N 11 14W
88 Kenge, Zaïre 4 50S 16 55E
90 Kengeja, Tanzania 5 26S 39 45E
71 Keng Tawng, Burma 20 46N 98 20E
67 Keng Tung, Burma 21 0N 99 30E
92 Kenhardt, S. Africa 29 19S 21 12E
76 Kenho, China 50 43N 121 30E
84 Keniéba, Mali 11 16N 8 26W
84 Kéninkoumou, Maur. 15 17N 12 18W
82 Kénitra (Port Lyautey), Morocco 34 15N 6 40W
15 Kenmare, Ire. 51 52N 9 35W
116 Kenmare, U.S.A. 48 40N 102 4W
15 Kenmare, R., Ire. 51 40N 10 0W
100 Kenmore, Australia 34 44S 149 45E
98 Kenn Reef, Australia 21 12S 155 46E
112 Kennaway, Canada 45 9N 78 11W
116 Kennebec, U.S.A. 43 56N 99 54W
91 Kennedy, Rhodesia 18 52S 27 10E
115 Kennedy, C., U.S.A. 28 28N 80 31W
67 Kennedy Taungdeik, Burma 23 35N 94 4E
13 Kennet, R., Eng. 51 24N 1 7W
117 Kennett, U.S.A. 36 7N 90 0W
118 Kennewick, U.S.A. 46 11N 119 2W
14 Keno Hill, Canada 63 57N 135 25W
106 Kenogami, R., Canada 50 20N 85 20W
109 Kenora, Canada 49 50N 94 35W
114 Kenosha, U.S.A. 42 33N 87 48W
107 Kensington, Canada 46 28N 63 34W
116 Kensington, U.S.A. 39 48N 99 2W
98 Kensington Downs, Australia 22 31S 144 19E
112 Kent, Ohio, U.S.A. 41 8N 81 20W
118 Kent, Oreg., U.S.A. 45 11N 120 45W
117 Kent, Tex., U.S.A. 31 5N 104 12W
13 Kent ♦, Eng. 51 12N 0 40E
104 Kent Pen., Canada 68 30N 107 0W
58 Kentau, U.S.S.R. 43 32N 68 36E
114 Kentland, U.S.A. 40 45N 87 25W
114 Kenton, U.S.A. 40 40N 83 35W
114 Kentucky Dam, U.S.A. 37 2N 88 15W
115 Kentucky L., U.S.A. 36 0N 88 0W
114 Kentucky, R., U.S.A. 38 30N 85 0W
114 Kentucky ♦, U.S.A. 37 20N 85 0W
107 Kentville, Canada 45 6N 64 29W
117 Kentwood, U.S.A. 31 0N 90 30W
90 Kenya ■, Africa 2 20N 38 0E
90 Kenya, Mt., Kenya 0 10S 37 18E
116 Keokuk, U.S.A. 40 25N 91 30W
44 Kep-i-Gjuhëzës, Alb. 40 28N 19 15E
44 Kep-i-Palit, Albania 41 25N 19 21E
44 Kep-i-Rodonit, Albania 41 32N 19 30E
73 Kepi, Indonesia 6 32S 139 19E
28 Kepice, Poland 54 16N 16 51E
28 Kepno, Poland 51 18N 17 58E
98 Keppel B., Australia 23 21S 150 55E
64 Kepsut, Turkey 39 40N 28 15E
73 Kepulauan, R., Indon. 5 30S 139 0E
72 Kepulauan Sunda, Ketjil Barat ♦, Indon. 8 50S 117 30E
73 Kepulauan Sunda, Ketjil Timor ♦, Indon. 9 30S 122 0E
70 Kerala ♦, India 11 0N 76 15E
100 Kerang, Australia 35 40S 143 55E
45 Keratéa, Greece 37 48N 23 58E
65 Keray, Iran 26 15N 57 30E
56 Kerch, U.S.S.R. 45 20N 36 20E
56 Kerchinskiy Proliv, U.S.S.R. 45 10N 36 30E
85 Kerchoual, Mali 17 20N 0 20E
62 Kerem Maharal, Israel 32 39N 34 59E
98 Kerema, Papua 7 50S 145 50E
87 Keren, Ethiopia 15 45N 38 28E
84 Kerewan, Gambia 13 35N 16 10W
3 Kerguelen Is., Ind. Oc. 48 30S 69 40E
45 Keri, Greece 37 40N 20 49E
87 Keri Kera, Sudan 12 21N 32 37E
90 Kericho, Kenya 0 22S 35 15E
90 Kericho ♦, Kenya 0 30S 35 15E
72 Kerintji, Indon. 2 5S 101 0E
83 Kerkenna, Iles, Tunisia 34 48N 11 1E
44 Kérkira, Greece 39 38N 19 50E
16 Kerkrade, Netherlands 50 53N 6 4E
86 Kerma, Sudan 19 33N 30 32E
94 Kermadec Is., Pacific Ocean 31 8S 175 16W
65 Kermān, Iran 30 15N 57 1E
65 Kermān ♦, Iran 30 0N 57 0E
64 Kermanshah, Iran 34 23N 47 0E
64 Kermanshah ♦, Iran 34 0N 46 30E
45 Kerme Körfezi, Turkey 36 55N 27 50E
43 Kermen, Bulgaria 42 30N 26 16E
117 Kermit, U.S.A. 31 56N 103 3W
119 Kern, R., U.S.A. 35 40N 118 45W
109 Kerrobert, Canada 52 0N 109 11W
117 Kerrville, U.S.A. 30 1N 99 8W
15 Kerry ♦, Ireland 52 7N 9 35W
15 Kerry Hd., Ireland 52 26N 9 56W
87 Kersa, Ethiopia 9 28N 41 48E
48 Kerstinbo, Sweden 60 16N 16 58E

MAP
49 Kerteminde, Denmark 55 28N 10 39E
73 Kertosono, Indonesia 7 38S 112 9E
87 Keru, Ethiopia 15 40N 37 5E
76 Kerulen, Mongolia 48 0N 114 0E
82 Kerzaz, Algeria 29 29N 1 25W
106 Kesagami L., Can. 50 23N 80 15W
106 Kesagami, R., Can. 50 50N 80 0W
44 Kesan, Turkey 40 49N 26 38E
93 Kestell, S. Afr. 28 17S 28 42E
52 Kestenga, U.S.S.R. 66 0N 31 50E
12 Kesteven, Eng. 53 2N 0 25W
12 Keswick, Eng. 54 35N 3 9W
27 Keszthely, Hungary 46 50N 17 15E
85 Keta, Ghana 5 49N 1 0E
72 Ketapang, Indonesia 1 55S 110 0E
104 Ketchikan, Alaska 55 25N 131 40W
118 Ketchum, U.S.A. 43 50N 114 27W
85 Kete Krachi, Ghana 7 55N 0 1W
86 Ketef, Khalig Umm el, Egypt 23 40N 35 35E
68 Keti Bandar, Pakistan 24 8N 67 27E
68 Ketri, India 28 1N 75 50E
28 Ketrzyn, Poland 54 7N 21 22E
13 Kettering, Eng. 52 24N 0 44W
118 Kettle Falls, U.S.A. 48 41N 118 2W
27 Kety, Poland 49 51N 19 16E
118 Kevin, U.S.A. 48 51N 112 0W
116 Kewane, U.S.A. 41 18N 89 55W
114 Kewaunee, U.S.A. 44 27N 87 30W
114 Keweenaw B., U.S.A. 47 0N 88 0W
114 Keweenaw Pen., U.S.A. 47 30N 88 0W
114 Keweenaw Pt., U.S.A. 47 26N 87 40W
106 Key Harbour, Canada 45 50N 80 45W
121 Key West, U.S.A. 24 40N 82 0W
91 Keynshamburg, Rhod. 19 15S 29 40E
113 Keyport, U.S.A. 40 26N 74 12W
114 Keyser, U.S.A. 39 26N 79 0W
116 Keystone, S.D., U.S.A. 43 54N 103 27W
114 Keystone, W. Va., U.S.A. 37 30N 81 30W
59 Kezhma, U.S.S.R. 59 15N 100 57E
27 Kezmarok, Cz. 49 10N 20 28E
58 Khabarovo, U.S.S.R. 69 30N 60 30E
59 Khabarovsk, U.S.S.R. 48 20N 135 0E
57 Khachmas, U.S.S.R. 41 31N 48 42E
68 Khachraud, India 23 25N 75 20E
87 Khadari, W. el, Sud. 10 35N 26 16E
68 Khadro, Pakistan 26 11N 68 50E
57 Khadyzhensk, U.S.S.R. 44 26N 39 32E
69 Khagaria, India 25 18N 86 32E
64 Khaibar, Saudi Arabia 25 38N 39 28E
86 Khaibor, Si. Arab. 25 49N 39 16E
68 Khair, India 27 57N 77 46E
69 Khairabad, India 27 33N 80 47E
69 Khairagarh, India 21 27N 81 2E
68 Khairpur, Bahawalpur, Pakistan 29 34N 72 17E
68 Khairpur, Hyderabad, Pakistan 27 32N 68 49E
68 Khairpur ♦, Pak. 23 30N 69 8E
89 Khakhea, Botswana 24 48S 23 22E
82 Khalfallah, Saïda, Algeria 34 33N 0 16E
65 Khalij-e-Fars ♦, Iran 28 20N 51 45E
69 Khalilabad, India 26 48N 83 5E
44 Khálki, Greece 39 36N 22 30E
45 Khálki, I., Greece 36 15N 27 35E
44 Khalkidhikí ♦, Gr. 40 25N 23 20E
45 Khalkis, Greece 38 27N 23 42E
58 Khalmer-Sede = Tazovskiy, U.S.S.R. 67 30N 78 30E
58 Khalmer Yu, U.S.S.R. 67 58N 65 1E
55 Khalturin, U.S.S.R. 58 40N 48 50E
69 Khamaria, India 23 10N 80 52E
92 Khama's Country, Bots. 21 45S 26 30E
67 Khamba Dzong, Tibet 28 25N 88 30W
68 Khambhalia, India 22 14N 69 41E
68 Khamgaon, India 20 42N 76 37E
70 Khammam, India 17 11N 80 6E
75 Khan Tengri, China 42 25N 80 10E
62 Khan Yunus, Egypt 31 21N 34 18E
65 Khanabad, Afghanistan 36 45N 69 5E
64 Khanaqin, Iraq 34 23N 45 25E
45 Khandrá, Greece 35 3N 26 8E
68 Khandwa, India 21 49N 76 22E
59 Khandyga, U.S.S.R. 62 30N 134 50E
68 Khanewal, Pakistan 30 20N 71 55E
83 Khanga Sidi Nadji, Alg. 34 50N 6 50E
45 Khaniá, Greece 35 30N 24 4E
45 Khaniá ♦, Greece 35 0N 24 0E
45 Khanion Kólpos, Gr. 35 33N 23 55E
58 Khanka, Oz., U.S.S.R. 45 0N 132 30E
68 Khanna, India 30 42N 76 16E
68 Khanpur, Pakistan 28 42N 70 35E
58 Khanty-Mansiysk, U.S.S.R. 61 0N 69 0E
69 Kharagpur, India 22 20N 87 25E
86 Kharaij, Saudi Arabia 21 25N 41 0E
68 Kharan Kalat, Pakistan 28 34N 65 21E
65 Kharanaq, Iran 32 20N 54 45E
70 Kharda, India 18 40N 75 40E
64 Kharfa, Saudi Arabia 22 0N 46 35E
64 Kharg, Jazireh, Iran 29 15N 50 28E
86 Khârga, El Wâhât el, Egypt 25 0N 30 0E
86 Kharit, Wadi el, Eg. 24 5N 34 10E
68 Khargone, India 21 45N 75 40E
56 Kharkov, U.S.S.R. 49 58N 36 20E
43 Kharmanli, Bulgaria 41 55N 25 55E
55 Kharovsk, U.S.S.R. 59 56N 40 13E
64 Kharsaniya, Si. Arabia 27 10N 49 10E
87 Khartoum = El Khartûm, Sudan 15 31N 32 35E
87 Khartoum ♦, Sudan 16 0N 33 0E
65 Khasab, Oman 26 14N 56 15E
57 Khasavyurt, U.S.S.R. 43 30N 46 40E
92 Khasebake, Botswana 20 42S 24 29E
65 Khash, Iran 28 15N 61 5E
87 Khashm el Girba, Sudan 14 59N 35 58E
69 Khasi Hills, India 25 30N 91 30E

MAP
43 Khaskovo, Bulgaria 41 56N 25 30E
59 Khatanga, U.S.S.R. 72 0N 102 20E
4 Khatanga, Zaliv, U.S.S.R. 66 0N 112 0E
68 Khatauli, India 29 17N 77 43E
59 Khatyrka, U.S.S.R. 62 3N 175 15E
64 Khavar ♦, Iran 37 20N 46 0E
86 Khawa, Saudi Arabia 29 45N 40 25E
87 Khazzân Jabal el Awliyâ, Sudan 15 24N 32 20E
70 Khed, Maharashtra, India 18 51N 73 56E
70 Khed, Maharashtra, India 17 43N 73 27E
68 Khekra, India 28 52N 77 20E
82 Khemis Miliana, Algeria 36 11N 2 14E
82 Khemisset, Morocco 33 50N 6 1W
71 Khemmarat, Thailand 16 10N 105 15E
83 Khenchela, Algeria 35 28N 7 11E
82 Khenifra, Morocco 32 58N 5 46W
83 Kherrata, Algeria 36 27N 5 13E
72 Khenmarak Phouminville, Khmer Rep. 11 40N 102 58E
56 Kherson, U.S.S.R. 46 35N 32 35E
45 Khersónisos Akrotíri, Gr. 35 30N 24 10E
67 Khetinsiring, China 32 54N 92 50E
45 Khiliomódhion, Greece 37 48N 22 51E
59 Khilok, U.S.S.R. 51 30N 110 45E
55 Khimki, U.S.S.R. 55 50N 37 20E
45 Khíos, Greece 38 27N 26 9E
37 Khíos, I., Greece 38 20N 26 0E
43 Khisar-Momina Banya, Bulgaria 42 30N 24 44E
54 Khiuma = Hiiumaa, U.S.S.R. 58 50N 22 45E
58 Khiva, U.S.S.R. 41 30N 60 18E
64 Khiyav, Iran 38 30N 47 45E
82 Khlaouia, Mauritania 25 50N 6 32W
71 Khlong, R., Thailand 15 30N 98 50E
56 Khmelnitsky, U.S.S.R. 49 23N 27 0E
†71 Khmer Republic ■, S. E. Asia 12 15N 105 0E
64 Khoi, Iran 38 40N 45 0E
66 Khojak P., Afghan. 30 55N 66 30E
55 Khokholskiy, U.S.S.R. 51 35N 38 50E
54 Kholm, U.S.S.R. 57 10N 31 15E
59 Kholmsk, U.S.S.R. 35 5N 139 48E
92 Khomas Hochland, S.W. Afr. 22 40S 16 0E
64 Khomayn, Iran 33 40N 50 7E
92 Khomo, Botswana 21 7S 24 35E
71 Khon Kaen, Thailand 16 30N 102 47E
71 Khong, Khmer Rep. 13 55N 105 56E
71 Khong, R., Laos 15 0N 106 50E
71 Khong, R., Thailand 17 45N 104 20E
71 Khonh Hung (Soc Trang), South Vietnam 9 37N 105 50E
59 Khonu, U.S.S.R. 66 30N 143 25E
55 Khoper, R., U.S.S.R. 52 0N 43 20E
87 Khor el 'Atash, Sudan 13 20N 34 15E
45 Khóra, Greece 37 3N 21 42E
45 Khóra Sfákion, Greece 35 15N 24 9E
65 Khorasan ♦, Iran 34 0N 58 0E
71 Khorat Plat., Thailand 15 30N 102 50E
71 Khorat, Cao Nguyen, Thailand 15 30N 102 50E
71 Khorat = Nakhon Ratchasima, Thailand 14 59N 102 12E
82 Khorb el Ethel, Algeria 28 44N 6 11W
58 Khorog, U.S.S.R. 37 40N 71 55E
56 Khorol, U.S.S.R. 49 48N 33 15E
64 Khorramabad, Iran 33 30N 48 25E
64 Khorramshahr, Iran 30 29N 48 15E
75 Khotan = Hotien, China 37 6N 79 59E
56 Khotin, U.S.S.R. 48 31N 26 27E
82 Khouribga, Morocco 32 58N 6 50W
67 Khowai, India 24 5N 91 40E
54 Khoyniki, U.S.S.R. 51 54N 29 55E
57 Khrami, R., U.S.S.R. 41 30N 44 30E
55 Khrenovoye, U.S.S.R. 51 4N 40 6E
45 Khristianá, I., Greece 36 14N 25 13E
45 Khtapodhiá, I., Greece 37 24N 25 34E
64 Khufaifiya, Si. Arabia 24 50N 44 35E
71 Khu Khan, Thailand 15 7N 104 15E
69 Khulna, Bangladesh 22 45N 89 34E
57 Khulo, U.S.S.R. 41 33N 42 19E
57 Khunzakh, U.S.S.R. 42 35N 46 42E
65 Khur, Iran 32 55N 58 18E
68 Khurai, India 24 3N 78 23E
64 Khurais, Saudi Arabia 24 55N 48 5E
68 Khurja, India 28 15N 77 58E
64 Khurma, Saudi Arabia 21 58N 42 3E
63 Khūryān Mūryān, Jazā 'ir, Arabia 17 30N 55 58E
68 Khushab, Pakistan 32 20N 72 20E
66 Khuzdar, Pakistan 27 52N 66 30E
64 Khuzestan ♦, Iran 31 0N 50 0E
55 Khvalynsk, U.S.S.R. 52 30N 48 2E
55 Khvatovka, U.S.S.R. 52 24N 46 32E
65 Khvor, Iran 33 45N 55 0E
65 Khvormuj, Iran 28 40N 51 30E
64 Khvoy, Iran 38 35N 45 0E
54 Khvoynaya, U.S.S.R. 58 49N 34 28E
65 Khwaja Muhammad, Afghanistan 36 0N 70 0E
65 Khyber Pass, Afghan. 34 10N 71 8E
91 Kiabukwa, Zaïre 8 40S 24 48E
70 Kiadho, R., India 19 50N 76 55E
100 Kiama, Australia 34 40S 150 50E
73 Kiamba, Philippines 6 0N 124 40E
90 Kiambi, Zaïre 7 15S 28 0E
90 Kiambu, Kenya 1 8S 36 50E
76 Kiamusze, China 46 45N 130 30E
77 Kian, China 27 1N 114 58E
100 Kiandra, Australia 35 53S 148 31E
77 Kianghwa, China 25 26N 111 29E
77 Kiangling, China 30 28N 113 16E
77 Kiangpen, China 29 40N 106 30E

† Renamed Cambodia

MAP

77 Kiangshan, China 28 51N 118 38E
77 Kiangsi ♦, China 27 20N 115 40E
77 Kiangsu ♦, China 33 0N 119 50E
77 Kiangyin, China 31 51N 120 0E
77 Kiangyu, China 31 41N 104 26E
93 Kianja, Malagasy Rep. 20 18s 47 8E
76 Kiaochow Wan., China 36 10N 120 15E
76 Kiaohsien, China 36 20N 120 0E
90 Kibanga Port, Uganda 0 10s 32 58E
88 Kibangou, Congo 3 18s 12 22E
90 Kibara, Tanzania 2 8s 33 30E
90 Kibara, Mts., Zaïre 8 25s 27 10E
90 Kibombo, Zaïre 3 57s 25 53E
90 Kibondo, Tanzania 3 35s 30 45E
90 Kibondo ♦, Tanz. 4 0s 30 55E
90 Kibumbu, Burundi 3 32s 29 45E
90 Kibungu, Rwanda 2 10s 30 32E
90 Kibuye, Burundi 3 39s 29 59E
90 Kibuye, Rwanda 2 3s 29 21E
90 Kibwesa, Tanzania 6 30s 29 58E
49 Kibaek, Denmark 56 2N 8 51E
42 Kičevo, Yugoslavia 41 34N 20 59E
59 Kichiga, U.S.S.R. 59 50N 163 5E
77 Kichow, China 30 0N 115 30E
100 Kickabil, Australia 31 50s 148 30E
108 Kicking Horse Pass, 51 27N 116 25w
 Canada
85 Kidal, Mali 17 50N 1 22E
13 Kidderminster, England 52 24N 2 13w
90 Kidete, Tanzania 6 40s 30 40E
90 Kidete, Tanzania 6 25s 37 17E
84 Kidira, Senegal 14 28N 12 13w
101 Kidnappers, C., New 39 38s 117 5E
 Zealand
98 Kidston, Australia 18 52s 144 8E
90 Kidugalle, Tanzania 6 49s 38 15E
24 Kiel, Germany 54 16N 10 8E
24 Kiel Canal = 54 15N 9 40E
 Nord-Ostee-Kanal, Germany
28 Kielce, Poland 50 58N 20 42E
28 Kielce ♦, Poland 51' 0N 20 40E
24 Kieler Bucht, Germany 54 30N 10 30E
67 Kienchwan, China 26 30N 99 45E
91 Kienge, Zaïre 10 30s 27 30E
77 Kienhinghsien, China 26 50N 116 50E
77 Kienko, China 31 50N 105 30E
77 Kienning, China 27 4N 118 21E
77 Kienow, China 27 0N 118 10E
75 Kienshui, China 23 57N 102 45E
77 Kiensi, China 26 58N 106 0E
77 Kienteh, China 29 30N 119 28E
77 Kienyang, Fukien, China 27 30N 118 0E
77 Kienyang, Hunan, China 27 10N 109 50E
85 Kiessé, Niger 13 29N 4 1E
54 Kiev = Kiyev, U.S.S.R. 50 30N 30 28E
84 Kiffa, Mauritania 16 50N 11 15w
45 Kifisiá, Greece 38 4N 23 49E
45 Kifissós ♦, Greece 38 30N 23 0E
64 Kifri, Iraq 34 45N 45 0E
90 Kigali, Rwanda 1 5s 30 4E
90 Kigarama, Tanzania 1 1s 31 50E
* 90 Kigezi ♦, Uganda 0 45s 29 50E
90 Kigoma ♦, Tanz. 4 50s 30 30E
90 Kigoma-Ujiji, Tanz. 5 30s 30 0E
90 Kigomasha, Ras, Tanz. 4 58s 38 58E
99 Kihee, Australia 27 30s 142 25E
74 Kii-Suido, Japan 33 40N 135 0E
77 Kikiang, China 28 58N 106 44E
42 Kikinda, Yugoslavia 45 50N 20 30E
45 Kikládhes, Is., Greece 37 20N 24 30E
45 Kikládhes ♦, Greece 37 0N 25 0E
98 Kikori, Papua 7 13s 144 15E
98 Kikori, R., Papua 7 5s 144 0E
90 Kikwit, Zaïre 5 5s 18 45E
48 Kil, Sweden 59 30N 13 20E
48 Kilafors, Sweden 61 14N 16 36E
70 Kilakarai, India 9 12N 78 47E
110 Kilauea Crater, Hawaii 19 24N 155 17w
90 Kilcoy, Australia 26 59s 152 30E
15 Kildare, Ireland 53 10N 6 50w
15 Kildare ♦, Ireland 53 10N 6 50w
90 Kilembe, Uganda 0 15N 30 3E
117 Kilgore, U.S.A. 32 22N 94 40w
66 Kilian Qurghan, China 36 52N 78 3E
90 Kilifi, Kenya 3 40s 39 48E
90 Kilifi ♦, Kenya 3 30s 39 40E
90 Kilimanjaro, Mt., Tanz. 3 7s 37 20E
90 Kilimanjaro ♦, Tanz. 4 50s 37 40E
90 Kilindini, Kenya 4 4s 39 40E
64 Kilis, Turkey 36 50N 37 10E
56 Kiliya, U.S.S.R. 45 28N 29 16E
15 Kilkee, Ireland 52 41N 9 40w
15 Kilkenny, Ireland 52 40N 7 17w
15 Kilkenny ♦, Ireland 52 35N 7 15w
15 Kilkieran B., Ireland 53 18N 9 45w
44 Kilkis, Greece 40 58N 22 57E
44 Kilkis ♦, Greece 41 5N 22 50E
15 Killala, Ireland 54 13N 9 12w
15 Killala B., Ireland 54 20N 9 12w
15 Killaloe, Ireland 52 48N 8 28w
112 Killaloe Sta., Canada 45 34N 77 25w
99 Killarney, Australia 28 19s 152 14E
106 Killarney, Man., Can. 49 10N 99 40w
109 Killarney, Ont., Can. 45 55N 81 30w
15 Killarney, Ireland 52 2N 9 30w
15 Killarney, L's. of, Ire. 52 0N 9 30w
15 Killary Harb., Ireland 53 38N 9 52w
112 Killbuck, U.S.A. 40 29N 81 58w
109 Killdeer, Canada 49 6N 106 22w
116 Killdeer, U.S.A. 47 26N 102 48w
117 Killeen, U.S.A. 31 7N 97 45w
14 Killiecrankie P., 56 44N 3 46w
 Scotland
47 Killingdal, Norway 62 47N 11 26E
45 Killini, Greece 37 55N 21 8E
45 Killíni, Mts., Greece 37 54N 22 25E
15 Killybegs, Ireland 54 38N 8 26w
100 Kilmany, Austral. 38 8s 146 55E
14 Kilmarnock, Scot. 55 36N 4 30w
55 Kilmez, R., U.S.S.R. 56 58N 51 0E

91 Kilondo, Tanzania 9 45s 34 20E
90 Kilosa, Tanzania 6 48s 37 0E
15 Kilrush, Ireland 52 39N 9 30w
48 Kilsmo, Sweden 59 6N 15 35E
91 Kilwa ♦, Tanzania 9 0s 39 0E
91 Kilwa Kisiwani, Tanz. 8 58s 39 32E
91 Kilwa Kivinje, Tanz. 8 45s 39 25E
91 Kilwa Masoko, Tanz. 8 55s 39 30E
117 Kim, U.S.A. 37 18N 103 20w
90 Kimamba, Tanzania 6 45s 37 10E
96 Kimba, Australia 33 8s 136 23E
116 Kimball, Nebr., U.S.A. 41 17N 103 20w
116 Kimball, S.D., U.S.A. 43 47N 98 57w
98 Kimbe, Terr. of New 5 3s 150 45E
 Guinea
96 Kimberley, Australia 16 20s 127 0E
108 Kimberley, Canada 49 40N 116 10w
92 Kimberley, S. Africa 28 43s 24 46E
118 Kimberly, U.S.A. 42 33N 114 25w
45 Kimi, Greece 38 38N 24 6E
45 Kimolos, Greece 36 48N 24 37E
45 Kimolos, I., Greece 36 48N 24 35E
55 Kimovsk, U.S.S.R. 54 0N 38 29E
84 Kimparana, Mali 12 48N 5 0w
55 Kimry, U.S.S.R. 56 55N 37 15E
108 Kimsquit, Canada 52 45N 127 5w
49 Kimstad, Sweden 58 35N 15 58E
72 Kinabalu, mt., Sabah, E. 6 0N 116 0E
 Malaysia
45 Kinaros, I., Greece 36 59N 26 15E
109 Kincaid, Canada 49 40N 107 0w
106 Kincardine, Canada 44 10N 81 40w
* 14 Kincardine ♦, Scot. 56 56N 2 28w
109 Kindersley, Canada 51 30N 109 10w
84 Kindia, Guinea 10 0N 12 52w
90 Kindu, Zaïre 2 55s 25 50E
55 Kinel, U.S.S.R. 53 15N 50 40E
55 Kineshma, U.S.S.R. 57 30N 42 5E
90 Kinesi, Tanzania 1 25s 33 50E
119 King City, U.S.A. 36 11N 121 8w
4 King Frederik VI Land, 63 0N 43 0w
 Greenland
. 4 King Frederik VIII 77 30N 20 0w
 Land, Greenland
128 King George B., Falk. 51 30s 60 30w
 Is.
5 King George I., 60 0N 60 0w
 Antarctica
105 King George Is., Can. 53 40N 80 30w
96 King George Sd., 35 5s 118 0E
 Australia
71 King I. = Kadah Kyun, 12 30N 98 20E
 Burma
99 King I., Australia 39 40s 144 0E
96 King Leopold Ranges, 17 20s 124 20E
 Australia
96 King Sd., Australia 16 50s 123 20E
104 King William I., Can. 69 0N 98 0w
92 King William's Town, S. 32 51s 27 22E
 Africa
99 Kingaroy, Tanzania 26 32s 151 51E
117 Kingfisher, U.S.A. 35 50N 97 55w
54 Kingisepp, U.S.S.R. 59 25N 28 40E
54 Kingisepp (Kuressaare), 58 15N 22 15E
 U.S.S.R.
74 Kingko, China 23 4N 100 30E
119 Kingman, Ariz., U.S.A. 35 12N 114 2w
117 Kingman, Kans., U.S.A. 37 41N 96 9w
77 Kingmen, China 31 10N 112 15E
77 Kingning, China 27 55N 119 30E
4 Kings B., Spitzbergen 78 0N 15 0E
119 Kings, R., U.S.A. 36 57N 119 0w
119 Kings Canyon National 37 0N 118 45w
 Park, U.S.A.
12 King's Lynn, England 52 45N 0 25E
119 Kings Mt., U.S.A. 35 13N 81 20w
118 King's Peak, U.S.A. 40 46N 110 27w
115 Kingsport, U.S.A. 36 33N 82 36w
119 Kingsburg, U.S.A. 36 35N 119 36w
99 Kingscote, Australia 35 33s 137 31E
15 Kingscourt, Ireland 53 55N 6 48w
116 Kingsley, U.S.A. 42 37N 95 58w
116 Kingsley Dam, U.S.A. 41 20N 101 40w
106 Kingston, Canada 44 20N 76 30w
121 Kingston, Jamaica 18 0N 76 50w
101 Kingston, N.Z. 45 20s 168 43E
113 Kingston, N.Y., U.S.A. 41 55N 74 0w
113 Kingston, Pa., U.S.A. 41 19N 75 58w
113 Kingston, R.I., U.S.A. 41 29N 71 30w
99 Kingston South East, 36 51s 139 55E
 Australia
121 Kingstown, St. Vincent 13 10N 61 10w
115 Kingstree, U.S.A. 33 40N 79 48w
106 Kingsville, Canada 42 2N 82 45w
117 Kingsville, U.S.A. 27 30N 97 53w
77 Kingtehchen (Fowliang), 29 8N 117 21E
 China
67 Kingtung, China 24 30N 100 50E
14 Kingussie, Scot. 57 5N 4 2w
76 Kinhsien, China 36 6N 107 49E
77 Kinhwa, China 29 5N 119 32E
88 Kinkala, Congo 4 18s 14 49E
101 Kinleith, New Zealand 38 20s 175 56E
101 Kinloch, New Zealand 44 51s 168 20E
77 Kinmen (Quemoy) Is., 24 25N 118 24E
 china
112 Kinmount, Canada 44 48N 78 40w
47 Kinn, Norway 61 34N 4 45E
49 Kinna, Sweden 57 32N 12 42E
14 Kinnaird's Hd., Scotland 57 40N 2 0w
62 Kinneret, Israel 32 44N 35 34E
62 Kinneret, Yam, Israel 32 45N 35 35E
49 Kinnekulle, Sweden 58 38N 13 22E
14 Kinross, Scotland 56 13N 3 25w
† 14 Kinross ♦, Scotland 56 13N 3 25w
15 Kinsale, Ire. 51 42N 8 31w

15 Kinsale Harbour, Ire. 51 40N 8 30w
15 Kinsale Old Hd., Ire. 51 37N 8 32w
47 Kinsarvik, Norway 60 22N 6 43E
75 Kinsha (Yangtze), China 32 30N 98 30E
88 Kinshasa, Zaïre 4 20s 15 15E
117 Kinsley, U.S.A. 37 57N 99 30w
115 Kinston, U.S.A. 35 18N 77 35w
85 Kintampo, Ghana 8 5s 1 41w
72 Kintap, Indonesia 3 51s 115 13E
14 Kintyre, pen., Scot. 55 30s 5 35w
14 Kintyre, Mull of, 55 17N 5 4w
 Scotland
108 Kinuso, Canada 55 25N 115 25w
91 Kinyangiri, Tanzania 4 35s 34 37E
112 Kinzua, U.S.A. 41 52N 78 58w
112 Kinzua Dam, U.S.A. 41 53N 79 0w
45 Kióni, Greece 38 27N 20 41E
106 Kiosk, Canada 46 6N 78 53w
117 Kiowa, Kans., U.S.A. 37 3N 98 30w
117 Kiowa, Okla., U.S.A. 34 45N 95 50w
90 Kipanga, Tanzania 6 15s 35 20E
45 Kiparissia, Greece 37 15N 21 40E
45 Kiparissiakós Kólpos, 37 25N 21 25E
 Greece
106 Kipawa Res. Prov. Park, 47 0N 78 30w
91 Kipengere Ra., Tanz. 9 12s 34 15E
90 Kipili, Tanzania 7 28s 30 32E
90 Kipini, Kenya 2 30s 40 32E
15 Kippure, Mt., Ireland 53 11N 6 23w
91 Kipushi, Zaïre 11 48s 27 12E
88 Kir, Zaïre 1 29s 19 25E
75 Kitai, China 44 0N 89 27E
74 Kitaibaraki, Japan 36 50N 140 45E
74 Kitakami-Gawa, Japan 39 30N 141 15E
74 Kitakyūshū, Japan 33 50N 130 50E
90 Kitale, Kenya 1 0N 35 12E
90 Kitangiri, L., Tanzania 4 5s 34 20E
91 Kitaya, Tanzania 10 38s 40 8E
106 Kitchener, Canada 43 30N 80 30w
106 Kitchigami, R., Canada 50 35N 78 5w
90 Kitega = Citega, 3 30s 29 58E
 Burundi
90 Kitgum Matidi, Uganda 3 17N 32 52E
90 Kithira, Greece 36 9N 23 0E
45 Kithira, I., Greece 36 15s 23 0E
45 Kithnos, Greece 37 26N 24 27E
45 Kithnos, I., Greece 37 25N 24 25E
108 Kitimat, Canada 53 55N 129 0w
87 Kitiyab, Sudan 17 13N 33 35E
44 Kitros, Greece 40 22N 22 34E
112 Kittanning, U.S.A. 40 49N 79 30w
113 Kittatinny Mts., U.S.A. 41 0N 75 0w
113 Kittery, U.S.A. 43 7N 70 42w
90 Kitui, Kenya 1 17s 38 0E
90 Kitui ♦, Kenya 1 30s 38 25E
77 Kityang, China 23 30N 116 29E
77 Kiukiang, China 29 37N 116 2E
77 Kiungchow, China 19 57N 110 17E
77 Kiungchow Haihsia, 20 40N 110 0E
 China
68 Kivarli, India 24 33N 72 46E
90 Kivu, L., Zaïre 1 48s 29 0E
90 Kivu ♦, Zaïre 3 10s 27 0E
77 Kiyuanshan, China 28 6N 117 46E
77 Kiyang, China 26 36N 111 42E
54 Kiyev, U.S.S.R. 50 30N 30 28E
54 Kiyevskoye Vdkhr., 51 0N 30 0E
 U.S.S.R.
55 Kizel, U.S.S.R. 59 0N 57 0E
90 Kiziguru, Rwanda 1 46s 30 23E
57 Kızılcahaman, Turkey 40 30N 32 30E
64 Kızılırmak, Turkey 39 15N 36 0E
58 Kizil Kiya, U.S.S.R. 40 20N 72 35E
90 Kizimkazi, Tanzania 6 28s 39 30E
57 Kizlyar, U.S.S.R. 43 51N 46 40E
58 Kizyl-Arvat, U.S.S.R. 38 58N 56 15E
49 Kjellerup, Denmark 56 11N 9 29E
72 Klabat, Teluk, Indonesia 1 30s 105 40E
42 Kladanj, Yugoslavia 44 14N 18 42E
42 Kladnica, Yugoslavia 43 23N 20 2E
26 Kladno, Czechoslovakia 50 10N 14 7E
42 Kladovo, Yugoslavia 44 36N 22 33E
26 Klagenfurt, Austria 46 38N 14 20E
54 Klaipeda, U.S.S.R. 55 43N 21 10E
49 Klagerup, Sweden 55 36N 13 17E
49 Klagstorp, Sweden 55 22N 13 23E
49 Klakring, Denmark 55 42N 9 59E
118 Klamath Falls, U.S.A. 42 20N 121 50w
118 Klamath Mts., U.S.A. 41 20N 123 0w
118 Klamath, R., U.S.A. 41 40N 123 30w
71 Klang = Kelang, Mal. 3 1N 101 33E
39 Klanjec, Yugoslavia 46 3N 15 45E
49 Klarälven, Sweden 60 32N 13 15E
73 Klaten, Indonesia 7 43s 110 36E
26 Klatovy, Cz. 49 23N 13 18E
108 Klawak, Alaska 55 50N 133 0w
92 Klawer, S. Afr. 31 44s 18 36E
28 Kłecko, Poland 52 38N 17 25E
108 Kleena Kleene, Can. 52 0N 124 50w
118 Klein, U.S.A. 46 26N 108 31w
92 Klein-Karas, S.W. Afr. 27 33s 18 7E
92 Klein Karoo, S. Africa 33 45s 21 30E
39 Klekovača, mt., Y.-slav. 44 25N 16 32E
108 Klemtu, Canada 52 35N 128 55w
26 Klenovec, Cz. 49 30N 19 54E
42 Klenovec, Yugoslavia 31 32N 20 49E
47 Klepp, Norway 59 48N 5 36E
92 Klerksdorp, S. Africa 26 51s 26 38E
54 Kletnya, U.S.S.R. 53 30N 33 2E
54 Kletsk, U.S.S.R. 53 5N 26 45E
54 Kletskiy, U.S.S.R. 49 20N 43 0E
24 Kleve, Germany 51 46N 6 10E
118 Klickitat, U.S.A. 45 50N 121 10w

54 Kisi, China 45 21N 131 0E
90 Kisii, Kenya 0 40s 34 45E
90 Kisii ♦, Kenya 0 40s 34 45E
57 Kısır, Dağ, Turkey 41 0N 43 5E
90 Kisizi, Uganda 1 0s 29 58E
104 Kiska I., Alaska 52 0N 177 30E
27 Kiskomárom = 46 33N 17 10E
 Zalakomár, Hung.
27 Kiskőrös, Hungary 46 37N 19 20E
27 Kiskundorozsma, Hung. 46 16N 20 5E
27 Kiskunfélégyháza, 46 42N 19 53E
 Hungary
27 Kiskunhalas, Hungary 46 28N 19 37E
27 Kiskunmajsa, Hungary 46 30N 19 48E
79 Kismayu, Somali Rep. 0 20s 42 30E
74 Kisogawa, Japan 35 20N 137 0E
90 Kisoro, Uganda 1 17s 29 48E
27 Kispest, Hungary 47 27N 19 9E
84 Kissidougou, Guinea 9 5N 10 0w
115 Kissimmee, U.S.A. 28 18N 81 22w
115 Kissimmee, R., U.S.A. 27 20N 81 0w
39 Kistanje, Yugoslavia 43 58N 15 55E
27 Kisterenye, Hungary 48 3N 19 50E
27 Kisújszállás, Hungary 47 12N 20 50E
90 Kisumu, Kenya 0 3s 34 45E
27 Kisvárda, Hungary 48 14N 22 4E
90 Kiswani, Tanzania 4 5s 37 57E
91 Kiswere, Tanz. 9 27s 39 30E
116 Kit Carson, U.S.A. 38 48N 102 45w
12 Knaresborough, England 54 1N 1 29w
43 Knezha, Bulgaria 43 30N 23 56E
42 Knic, Yugoslavia 43 53N 20 45E
13 Knighton, Wales 52 21N 3 2w
118 Knight's Landing, USA 38 50N 121 49w
39 Knin, Yugoslavia 44 1N 16 17E
26 Knittelfeld, Austria 47 13N 14 51E
42 Knjazevac, Yugoslavia 43 35N 22 18E
96 Knob, C., Australia 34 32s 119 16E
16 Knockmealdown Mts., 52 16N 8 0w
 Ireland
16 Knokke, Belgium 51 20N 3 17E
100 Knowsley, Australia 36 50s 144 35E
114 Knox, U.S.A. 41 18N 86 36w
117 Knox City, U.S.A. 33 26N 99 38w
5 Knox Coast, Antarctica 66 30s 108 0E
116 Knoxville, Iowa, U.S.A. 41 20N 93 5w
115 Knoxville, Pa., U.S.A. 41 57N 77 26w
115 Knoxville, Tenn., U.S.A. 35 58N 83 57w
27 Knurów, Poland 50 13N 18 38E
47 Knutshø, Norway 62 18N 9 41E
92 Knysna, S. Afr. 34 2s 23 2E
28 Knyszyn, Poland 53 20N 22 56E
71 Ko Chang, Thailand 12 0N 102 20E
71 Ko Kut, Thailand 11 40N 102 32E
71 Ko Phangan, Thai. 9 45N 100 10E
71 Ko Phra Thong, Thai. 9 6N 98 15E
71 Ko Samui, Thailand 9 30N 100 0E
105 Koartac (Notre Dame de 61 5N 69 36E
 Koartac), Canada
73 Koba, Aru, Indon. 6 37s 134 37E
72 Koba, Bangka, Indon. 2 26s 106 14E
39 Kobarid, Yugoslavia 46 15N 13 30E
74 Kobayashi, Japan 31 56N 130 59E
74 Kōbe, Japan 34 45N 135 10E
56 Kobelyaki, U.S.S.R. 49 11N 34 9E
49 København, Denmark 55 41N 12 34E
24 Koblenz, Germany 50 21N 7 36E
87 Kobo, Ethiopia 12 2N 39 56E
54 Kobrin, U.S.S.R. 52 15N 24 22E
73 Kobroor, Kepulauan, 6 10s 134 30E
 Indonesia
57 Kobuleti, U.S.S.R. 41 55N 41 45E
54 Kobylin, Poland 51 43N 17 12E
28 Kobyłka, Poland 52 21N 21 10E
55 Kobylkino, U.S.S.R. 54 8N 43 46E
54 Kobylnik, U.S.S.R. 54 58N 26 39E
42 Kočarli, Turkey 37 45N 27 43E
42 Kočevje, Yugoslavia 44 28N 19 50E
125 Kočevje, Yugoslavia 45 39N 14 50E
69 Kochas, India 25 15N 83 56E
74 Kōchi, Japan 33 30N 133 35E
74 Kōchi-ken ♦, Japan 33 40N 133 30E
70 Kodaikanal, India 10 13N 77 32E
70 Koddiyar Bay, Sri Lanka 8 33N 81 15E
104 Kodiak I., U.S.A. 57 30N 152 45w
71 Kodiang, Malaysia 6 21N 100 18E
68 Kodinar, India 20 46N 70 46E
74 Kodori, R., U.S.S.R. 43 0N 41 40E
89 Koes, S.W. Africa 26 0s 19 15E
100 Koetong, Australia 36 10s 147 30E
26 Köflach, Austria 47 4N 15 4E
85 Koforidua, Ghana 6 3N 0 17w
74 Kōfu, Japan 35 40N 138 30E
99 Kogan, Australia 27 2s 150 40E
85 Kogin Baba, Nigeria 7 55N 11 35E
57 Kogizman, Turkey 40 5N 43 10E
20 Kogon, Guinea 11 20N 14 32w
65 Koh-i-Bab, mts., 34 30N 67 0E
 Afghanistan
66 Kohat, Pakistan 33 40N 71 29E
67 Kohima, India 25 35N 94 10E
5 Kohler Ra., Antarctica 77 0N 110 0w
54 Kohtla-Järve, U.S.S.R. 59 20N 27 20E
73 Kojabuti, Indonesia 2 36s 140 37E
26 Kojetin, Czechoslovakia 49 21N 17 20E
86 Koka, Sudan 20 5N 30 35E
58 Kokand, U.S.S.R. 40 0N 71 10E
73 Kokas, Indonesia 2 42s 132 26E
26 Kokava, Czechoslovakia 48 35N 19 50E
58 Kokchetav, U.S.S.R. 53 0N 69 10E
51 Kokemäenjoki = Kumo 61 32N 21 44E
 älv, Finland
55 Kokhma, U.S.S.R. 56 55N 41 18E
75 Kokiu, China 23 0N 103 0E
50 Kokkola (Gamlakarleby), 63 50N 23 8E
 Finland
85 Koko, Mid-Western, 6 5N 5 28E
 Nigeria
85 Koko, North-Western, 11 28N 4 29E
 Nigeria

* Incorporated within the
new Southern Province

* Incorporated within the
region of Grampian
† Incorporated within the
region of Tayside

MAP

71 Koko Kyunzu, Burma 14 10N 93 25E
67 Koko Shili, China 35 20N 91 0E
98 Kokoda, Papua 9 0s 148 0E
84 Kokolopozo, Ivory Coast 5 8N 6 5w
70 Kokomo, U.S.A. 40 30N 86 6w
75 Koko-Nor, China 37 10N 100 0E
98 Kokopo, New Guinea 4 23s 152 15E
85 Kokoro, Niger 14 12N 0 55E
105 Koksoak, R., Canada 54 5N 64 10w
59 Kokuora, U.S.S.R. 71 35N 144 50E
68 Kola, U.S.S.R. 68 45N 33 8E
73 Kola, I., Indonesia 5 35s 134 30E
52 Kola Pen. = Kolskiy P-ov., U.S.S.R. 67 30N 38 0E
73 Kolagede, Indonesia 7 54s 110 26E
84 Kolahun, Liberia 8 15N 10 4w
73 Kolaka, Indonesia 4 3s 121 46E
70 Kolar, India 13 12N 78 15E
70 Kolar Gold Fields, India 12 58N 78 16E
43 Kolarovgrad, Bulgaria 43 27N 26 42E
27 Kolarovo, Cz. 47 56N 18 0E
42 Kolašin, Yugoslavia 42 50N 19 31E
49 Kolby, Denmark 55 49N 10 33E
49 Kolby Kas, Denmark 55 48N 10 32E
55 Kolchugino, U.S.S.R. 56 17N 39 22E
84 Kolda, Senegal 12 55N 14 50w
4 Koldewey I., Greenland 77 0N 18 0w
49 Kolding, Denmark 55 30N 9 29E
82 Koléa, Algeria 36 38N 2 46E
73 Kolepom, I. = Dolak, I., Indon. 8 0s 138 30E
48 Kölfors, Sweden 62 9N 16 30E
52 Kolguyev, Ostrov, U.S.S.R. 69 20N 48 30E
70 Kolhapur, India 16 43N 74 15E
84 Kolia, Ivory Coast 9 46N 6 28w
26 Kolin, Czechoslovakia 50 2N 15 9E
49 Kolind, Denmark 56 21N 10 34E
24 Kolleda, Germany 51 11N 11 14E
70 Kollegal, India 12 9N 77 9E
70 Kolleru L., India 16 40N 81 10E
92 Kolmanskop, S.W. Afr. 26 45s 15 14E
24 Köln, Ger. 50 56N 9 58E
28 Kolno, Poland 53 25N 21 25E
28 Koło, Poland 52 14N 18 40E
28 Kołobrzeg, Poland 54 10N 15 35E
55 Kologriv, U.S.S.R. 58 48N 44 25E
84 Kolokani, Mali 13 35N 7 45w
55 Kolomna, U.S.S.R. 55 8N 38 45E
56 Kolomyya, U.S.S.R. 48 31N 25 2E
73 Kolondale, Indonesia 2 3s 121 25E
84 Kolondiéba, Mali 11 5s 6 54w
68 Kolosib, India 24 15N 92 45E
58 Kolpashevo, U.S.S.R. 58 20N 83 5E
54 Kolpino, U.S.S.R. 59 44N 30 39E
55 Kolpny, U.S.S.R. 52 12N 37 10E
52 Kolskiy Poluostrov, U.S.S.R. 67 30N 38 0E
52 Kolskiy Zaliv, U.S.S.R. 69 23N 34 0E
42 Kolubara, R., Y.-slav. 44 35N 20 15E
28 Kolumna, Poland 51 36N 19 14E
28 Koluszki, Poland 51 45N 19 46E
55 Kolyberovo, U.S.S.R. 55 15N 38 40E
59 Kolyma, R., U.S.S.R. 64 40N 153 0E
59 Kolymskoye, Okhotsko, U.S.S.R. 63 0N 157 0E
86 Kóm Ombo, Egypt 24 25N 32 52E
59 Komandorskiye Ostrava, U.S.S.R. 55 0N 167 0E
27 Komárno, Cz. 47 49N 18 5E
27 Komárom, Hungary 47 43N 18 7E
27 Komárom ♦, Hungary 47 35N 18 20E
54 Komarovo, U.S.S.R. 58 38N 33 40E
85 Kombissiri, Upper Volta 12 4N 1 20w
84 Kombori, Upper Volta 13 26N 3 56w
45 Komboti, Greece 39 6N 21 5E
84 Komen, Yugoslavia 45 49N 13 45E
85 Komenda, Ghana 5 4N 1 28w
52 Komi, A.S.S.R. ♦, U.S.S.R. 64 0N 55 0E
39 Kominža, Yugoslavia 38 3N 16 11E
27 Komló, Hungary 46 15N 18 16E
71 Kommamur Canal, India 16 0N 80 25E
57 Kommunarsk, U.S.S.R. 48 30N 38 45E
65 Kommunizma, U.S.S.R. 38 40N 72 20E
47 Komnes, Norway 59 30N 9 55E
73 Komodo, Indonesia 8 37s 119 20E
84 Komoé, Ivory Coast 5 12N 3 44w
73 Komoran, Pulau, Indon. 8 18s 138 45E
28 Komorze, Poland 62 8N 17 38E
44 Komotini, Greece 41 9N 25 26E
71 Kompong Cham, Khmer Rep. 11 54N 105 30E
71 Kompong Chhnang, Khmer Rep. 12 20N 104 35E
71 Kompong Som, Khmer Rep. 11 3N 103 41E
71 Kompong Speu, Khmer Rep. 11 26N 104 32E
71 Kompong Thom, Khmer Rep. 12 35N 104 51E
56 Komrat, U.S.S.R. 46 18N 28 40E
92 Komsberge, S. Afr. 32 40s 20 45E
59 Komsomoleto, Ostrov, U.S.S.R. 80 30N 95 0E
59 Komsomolsk, U.S.S.R. 50 30N 137 0E
55 Komsomolskiy, U.S.S.R. 53 30N 49 40E
85 Kona, Niger 13 33N 8 3E
85 Kona, Nigeria 8 58N 11 15E
67 Konam Dzong, China 29 5N 93 0E
117 Konawa, U.S.A. 34 59N 96 46w
70 Kondagaon, India 19 35N 81 35E
90 Konde, Tanzania 4 57s 39 45E
44 Kondiá, Greece 39 52N 25 10E
90 Kondoa, Tanz. 4 55s 35 50E
85 Konduga, Nigeria 11 35N 13 26E
84 Kong, Ivory Coast 8 54N 4 36w

71 Kong Koh, Cambodia 11 20N 103 0E
4 Kong Christian IX.s Land, Greenland 68 0N 36 0w
4 Kong Christian X.s Land, Greenland 74 0N 29 0w
4 Kong Frederik VI.s Kyst, Greenland 63 0N 43 0w
4 Kong Frederik VIII.s Land, Greenland 78 30N 26 0w
4 Kong Oscar Fjord, Greenland 72 20N 24 0w
49 Konga, Sweden 56 30N 15 6E
49 Kongea, Denmark 55 24N 8 39E
67 Konglu, Burma 27 13N 97 57E
77 Kongmoon, China 22 35N 113 1E
90 Kongolo, Zaïre 5 22s 27 0E
85 Kongoussi, Upper Volta 13 19N 1 32w
47 Kongsberg, Norway 59 39N 9 39E
47 Kongsvinger, Norway 60 12N 12 2E
47 Kongsvoll, Norway 62 20N 9 36E
91 Koni, Zaïre 10 40s 27 11E
91 Koni, Mts., Zaïre 10 36s 27 0E
28 Koniecpol, Poland 50 46N 19 40E
54 Königsberg = Kaliningrad, U.S.S.R. 54 42N 20 32E
24 Königslutter, Germany 52 14N 10 50E
24 Königswusterhausen, Germany 52 19N 13 38E
28 Konin, Poland 52 12N 18 15E
44 Konispol, Albania 39 42N 20 10E
44 Kónitsa, Greece 40 5N 20 48E
39 Konjice, Yugoslavia 43 42N 18 0E
85 Konkoure, R., Guinea 10 30N 13 40w
24 Könnern, Germany 51 40N 11 45E
70 Konnur, India 16 14N 74 49E
84 Kono, S. Leone 8 30N 11 5w
85 Konoðlu, Ghana 40 35N 31 50E
85 Konongo, Ghana 6 40N 1 15w
54 Konosha, U.S.S.R. 61 0N 40 5E
54 Konotop, U.S.S.R. 51 12N 33 7E
56 Konskaya, R., U.S.S.R. 47 30N 35 0E
28 Konskie, Poland 51 15N 20 23E
47 Konsmo, Norway 58 16N 7 23E
55 Konstantinovka, U.S.S.R. 48 32N 37 39E
55 Konstantinovski, R.S.F.S.R., U.S.S.R. 57 45N 39 35E
57 Konstantinovski, R.S.F.S.R., U.S.S.R. 47 33N 41 10E
28 Konstantynów Łódzki, Poland 51 45N 19 20E
23 Konstanz, Germany 47 39N 9 10E
85 Kontagora, Nigeria 10 23N 5 27E
71 Kontum, S. Vietnam 14 24N 108 0E
64 Konya, Turkey 37 52N 32 35E
25 Konz Karthaus, Ger. 49 41N 6 36E
4 Koog, Netherlands 52 27N 4 49E
96 Koolan I., Australia 16 0s 123 45E
100 Kooloonong, Austral. 34 48s 143 10E
100 Koondrook, Austral. 35 33s 144 8E
100 Koorakee, Australia 34 2s 143 10E
100 Koorawatha, Australia 34 2s 148 33E
118 Kooskia, U.S.A. 46 9N 115 59w
109 Koostatak, Canada 51 26N 97 26w
118 Kooteaai, R., U.S.A. 48 30N 115 30w
111 Kootenay L., Canada 49 30N 117 0w
100 Koo-wee-rup, Australia 38 13s 145 28E
27 Kopaonik, mts., Y.-slav. 43 10N 21 0E
70 Kopargaon, India 19 51N 74 28E
4 Kópavogur, Iceland 64 6N 21 55w
39 Koper, Yugoslavia 45 31N 13 44E
47 Kopervik, Norway 59 17N 5 17E
58 Kopeysk, U.S.S.R. 55 5N 61 31E
48 Köping, Sweden 59 31N 16 3E
39 Kopiste, Yugoslavia 42 48N 16 42E
44 Kopliku, Albania 42 15N 19 25E
49 Köpmanholmen, Sweden 63 10N 18 35E
49 Köpmannebro, Sweden 58 45N 12 30E
70 Koppal, India 15 23N 76 5E
47 Koppang, Norway 61 34N 11 3E
39 Koppera, Norway 63 24N 11 52E
39 Koppera, Norway 63 24N 11 50E
85 Koppom, Sweden 59 43N 12 10E
43 Koprivlen, Bulgaria 41 36N 23 53E
39 Koprivnica, Yugoslavia 46 12N 16 45E
43 Koprivshtitsa, Bulgaria 42 40N 24 19E
54 Kopychintsy, U.S.S.R. 49 7N 25 58E
45 Korakiána, Greece 39 42N 19 45E
42 Korab, mt., Yugoslavia 41 44N 20 40E
70 Koraput, India 18 50N 82 40E
69 Korba, India 22 20N 82 45E
24 Korbach, Germany 51 17N 8 50E
44 Korça, Albania 40 37N 20 50E
44 Korca ♦, Albania 40 40N 20 50E
39 Korcula, Y.-slav. 42 57N 17 8E
39 Korcula, I., Y.-slav. 42 57N 17 0E
39 Korčulanski Kanal, Yugoslavia 43 3N 16 40E
64 Kordestān ♦, Iran 36 0N 47 0E
87 Kordofān ♦, Sudan 13 0N 29 0E
70 Koregaon, India 17 40N 74 10E
54 Korenevo, U.S.S.R. 51 7N 34 55E
57 Korenovsk, U.S.S.R. 45 12N 39 22E
55 Korets, U.S.S.R. 50 40N 27 5E
86 Korgus, Sudan 19 16N 33 48E
84 Korhogo, Ivory Coast 9 29N 5 28w
84 Koribundu, Sierra Leone 7 41N 11 46w
99 Koridina, Australia 29 42s 143 25E
73 Korim, Indonesia 0 58s 136 10E
45 Korinthia ♦, Greece 37 50N 22 35E
45 Korinthiakós Kólpos, Greece 38 16N 22 30E
45 Kórinthos, Greece 37 56N 22 55E
84 Koriénmale, Mali 12 10N 2 0w
74 Kōriyama, Japan 37 10N 140 18E
75 Korla, China 41 45N 86 4E
27 Körmend, Hungary 47 5N 16 35E
39 Kornat, I., Yugoslavia 43 50N 15 20E
47 Korneshty, U.S.S.R. 47 21N 28 1E
27 Korneuburg, Austria 48 20N 16 20E

49 Korning, Denmark 56 30N 9 44E
47 Kornsjö, Norway 58 57N 11 39E
47 Kornstad, Norway 62 59N 7 27E
84 Koro, Ivory Coast 8 32N 7 30w
84 Koro, Mali 14 1N 2 58w
101 Koro, I., Fiji 17 19s 179 23E
55 Korocha, U.S.S.R. 50 55N 37 30E
100 Koroit, Australia 38 18s 142 24E
45 Koróni, Greece 36 48N 21 57E
44 Korónia, Limni, Greece 40 47N 23 37E
45 Koronis, Greece 37 12N 25 35E
28 Koronowo, Poland 53 19N 17 55E
73 Koror, Palaru Is. 7 20N 134 28E
27 Kőrös, R., Hungary 46 45N 20 20E
27 Korostarcsa, Hungary 46 53N 21 3E
54 Korostem, U.S.S.R. 50 57N 28 25E
93 Korraraika, B. de, Malag. 17 45s 43 57E
59 Korsakov, U.S.S.R. 46 36N 142 42E
47 Korshavn, Norway 58 2N 7 0E
59 Korshunovo, U.S.S.R. 58 37N 110 10E
49 Korsør, Denmark 55 20N 11 9E
28 Korsze, Poland 54 11N 21 9E
86 Korti, Sudan 18 0N 31 40E
16 Kortrijk, Belgium 50 50N 3 17E
100 Korumburra, Australia 38 26s 145 50E
55 Kovrov, U.S.S.R. 56 25N 41 25E
68 Korwai, India 24 7N 78 5E
59 Koryakskiy Khrebet, U.S.S.R. 61 0N 171 0E
45 Kos, Greece 36 50N 27 19E
45 Kos, I., Greece 36 50N 27 15E
87 Kosa, Ethiopia 7 5N 36 50E
55 Kosaya Gora, U.S.S.R. 54 10N 37 30E
53 Koschagy, U.S.S.R. 46 40N 54 0E
28 Kościan, Poland 52 5N 16 40E
28 Kościerzyna, Poland 54 8N 17 59E
117 Kosciusko, U.S.A. 33 3N 89 34w
100 Kosciusko, Mt., Austral. 36 27s 148 16E
27 Kösély, R., Hungary 47 25N 21 30E
70 Kosgi, India 16 58N 77 43E
86 Kosha, Sudan 20 50N 30 30E
68 Kosi, India 27 48N 77 29E
54 Košice, Czechoslovakia 48 42N 21 15E
93 Kosi-meer, S. Africa 27 0s 32 50E
42 Kosjeric, Yugoslavia 44 0N 19 55E
52 Koslan, U.S.S.R. 63 28N 48 52E
76 Kosŏnf, N. Korea 38 40N 128 22E
42 Kosovo-Metohija = Metahiska, Y.-slav. 42 30N 21 0E
42 Kosovska-Mitrovica, Yugoslavia 42 54N 20 52E
84 Kosso, Ivory Coast 5 3N 5 47w
39 Kostajnica, Yugoslavia 45 17N 16 30E
39 Kostanjevica, Y.-slav. 45 51N 15 27E
39 Kostelec, Cz. 50 14N 16 35E
43 Kostenets, Bulgaria 42 15N 23 52E
87 Kósti, Sudan 13 8N 32 43E
42 Kostolac, Yugoslavia 44 43N 21 15E
55 Kostroma, U.S.S.R. 57 50N 41 58E
55 Kostromskoye Vdkhr., U.S.S.R. 57 52N 40 49E
28 Kostrzyn, Poland 52 24N 17 14E
55 Kostyukovichi, U.S.S.R. 53 10N 32 4E
28 Koszalin, Poland 54 12N 16 8E
28 Koszalin ♦, Poland 54 10N 16 10E
27 Kőszeg, Hungary 47 23N 16 33E
68 Kot Adu, Pakistan 30 30N 71 0E
68 Kot Moman, Pakistan 32 13N 73 0E
70 Kota, India 25 14N 75 49E
71 Kota Baharu, Malaysia 6 7N 102 14E
72 Kota Kinabalu, Malaysia 6 0N 116 4E
71 Kota-Kota = Khota Kota, Malawi 12 55s 34 15E
71 Kota Tinggi, Malaysia 1 44N 103 53E
72 Kotaagung, Indonesia 5 38s 104 29E
72 Kotabaru, Indonesia 3 20s 116 20E
72 Kotabumi, Indonesia 4 49s 104 46E
73 Kotamobagu, Indonesia 0 57N 124 31E
72 Kotawaringin, Indon. 2 28s 111 27E
43 Kotel, Bulgaria 42 56N 26 30E
70 Kotelnich, U.S.S.R. 58 20N 48 10E
57 Kotelnikovo, U.S.S.R. 47 45N 43 15E
59 Kotelnyy, Ostrov, U.S.S.R. 75 10N 139 0E
70 Kothagudam, India 17 30N 80 40E
70 Kothapet, India 19 21N 79 28E
24 Köthen, Germany 51 44N 11 59E
68 Kothi, India 24 45N 80 40E
68 Kotiro, Pakistan 26 17N 67 13E
51 Kotka, Finland 60 30N 26 28E
68 Kotlas, U.S.S.R. 61 15N 47 0E
43 Kotlenska Planina, Bulgaria 42 56N 26 30E
66 Kotli, Kashmir 33 30N 73 55E
85 Kotonkoro, Nigeria 11 3N 5 58E
42 Kotor, Yugoslavia 42 25N 18 47E
39 Kotor Varoš, Y.-slav. 44 38N 17 22E
39 Kotoriba, Yugoslavia 46 37N 16 48E
57 Kotovsk, U.S.S.R. 47 55N 29 35E
68 Kotputli, India 27 43N 76 12E
68 Kotri, Pakistan 25 22N 68 22E
45 Kótronas, Greece 36 38N 22 29E
*26 Kötschach, Austria 46 41N 13 1E
70 Kottayam, India 9 35N 76 33E
70 Kottur, India 10 34N 76 56E
104 Kotuy, R., U.S.S.R. 70 30N 103 0E
104 Kotzebue, Alaska 66 50N 162 40w
57 Kouango, Cent. Afr. Rep. 5 0N 20 10E
84 Koudougou, Upper Volta 12 10N 2 20w
45 Koufonisia, I., Greece 36 57N 25 35E
92 Kougaberge, S. Africa 33 48s 24 20E
84 Kouibli, Ivory Coast 7 15N 7 14w
88 Kouilou, R., Congo 4 10s 12 5E

88 Kouki, Cent. Afr. Rep. 7 22N 17 3E
88 Koula Moutou, Gabon 1 15s 12 25E
84 Koulikoro, Mali 12 40N 7 50w
84 Koumankoun, Mali 11 58N 6 6w
84 Koumbia, Guinea 11 54N 13 40w
84 Koumbia, Upper Volta 11 10N 3 50w
84 Koumboum, Guinea 10 25N 13 0w
84 Koumpenntoum, Senegal 13 59N 14 34w
81 Koumra, Chad 8 50N 17 35E
84 Koundara, Guinea 12 29N 13 18w
58 Koumradskiy, U.S.S.R. 47 20N 75 0E
117 Kountze, U.S.A. 30 20N 94 22w
85 Koupéla, Upper Volta 12 11N 0 21E
83 Kourizo, Passe de, Chad 22 28N 15 27E
84 Kouroussa, Guinea 10 45N 9 45w
84 Koussané, Mali 14 53N 11 14w
84 Koutiala, Mali 12 25N 5 35E
84 Kouto, Ivory Coast 9 53N 6 25w
85 Kouvé, Togo 6 25N 0 59E
42 Kovačica, Yugoslavia 45 5N 20 38E
55 Kovel, U.S.S.R. 51 10N 25 0E
105 Kovik, Canada 61 40N 77 40w
70 Kovilpatti, India 9 10N 77 50E
55 Kovrov, U.S.S.R. 56 25N 41 25E
41 Kovin, Yugoslavia 44 44N 20 59E
70 Kovur, Andhra Pradesh, India 17 3N 81 39E
70 Kovur, Andhra Pradesh, India 14 30N 80 1E
28 Kowal, Poland 52 32N 19 7E
28 Kowalewo Pomorskie, Pol. 53 10N 18 52E
106 Kowkash, Canada 50 20N 87 20w
77 Kowloon, Hong Kong 22 20N 114 15E
71 Koyan, Pegunungan, Malaysia 3 15N 114 30E
70 Koyiu, China 23 2N 112 28E
104 Koyukuk, R., Alaska 65 45N 156 30w
56 Koyulhisar, Turkey 40 20N 37 52E
74 Koza, Okinawa 26 20N 127 47E
64 Kozan, Turkey 37 35N 35 50E
45 Kozáni, Greece 40 19N 21 47E
45 Kozáni ♦, Greece 40 18N 21 45E
39 Kozara, Mts., Y.-slav. 45 0N 17 0E
42 Kozarac, Yugoslavia 44 58N 16 48E
54 Kozelsk, U.S.S.R. 54 2N 35 38E
28 Koziegłowy, Poland 50 37N 19 8E
39 Kozje, Yugoslavia 46 5N 15 35E
28 Kozle, Poland 50 20N 18 8E
43 Kozlodui, Bulgaria 43 45N 23 42E
43 Kozlovets, Bulgaria 43 30N 25 20E
28 Kozmin, Poland 51 48N 17 27E
28 Kozuchów, Poland 51 45N 15 31E
85 Kpabia, Ghana 9 10N 0 20w
85 Kpandae, Ghana 8 30N 0 2w
85 Kpandu, Ghana 7 2N 0 18E
85 Kpessi, Togo 8 4N 1 16E
71 Kra, Kho Khot, Thailand 10 15N 99 30E
71 Kra Buri, Thailand 10 22N 98 46E
71 Kra, Isthmus of = Kra, Kho Khot, Thai. 10 15N 99 30E
73 Kragan, Indonesia 6 43s 111 38E
47 Kragerö, Norway 58 52N 9 25E
42 Kragujevac, Y.-slavia 44 2N 20 56E
28 Krajenka, Poland 53 18N 16 59E
72 Krakatau = Rakata, Pulau, Indonesia 6 10s 105 20E
27 Kraków, Pol. 50 4N 19 57E
73 Kraksaan, Indonesia 7 43s 113 23E
49 Kraksmala, Sweden 57 4N 15 0E
47 Kråkstad, Norway 59 40N 10 50E
26 Kralovice, Cz. 49 59N 13 29E
26 Kralovský Chlmec, Cz. 48 27N 22 0E
26 Kralupy, Czechoslovakia 50 13N 14 20E
42 Kraljevo, Yugoslavia 43 44N 20 41E
119 Kramer, U.S.A. 35 0N 117 38w
84 Kramfors, Sweden 62 55N 17 48E
82 Kramis, C., Algeria 36 26N 0 45E
44 Krangede, Sweden 63 9N 16 10E
44 Kraniá, Greece 39 53N 21 18E
45 Kranídhion, Greece 37 20N 23 10E
39 Kranj, Yugoslavia 46 16N 14 22E
39 Kranjska Gora, Y.-slav. 46 29N 13 48E
92 Kranzberg, S.W. Afr. 21 59s 15 37E
39 Krapina, Yugoslavia 46 10N 15 52E
39 Krapina, R., Yugoslavia 46 0N 15 55E
28 Krapkowice, Poland 50 47N 17 56E
55 Krasavino, U.S.S.R. 60 58N 46 29E
54 Kráslava, Czechoslovakia 55 27N 27 12E
55 Kraslice, Czechoslovakia 50 19N 12 31E
55 Krasnaya Gorbatka, U.S.S.R. 55 52N 41 45E
55 Krasnaya Polyana, U.S.S.R. 43 40N 40 25E
28 Kraśnik, Poland 50 55N 22 5E
28 Kraśnik Fabryczny, Pol. 50 58N 22 11E
56 Krasnoarmeisk, U.S.S.R. 48 18N 37 11E
57 Krasnoarmeysk, R.S.F.S.R., U.S.S.R. 48 30N 44 25E
57 Krasnoarmeysk, R.S.F.S.R., U.S.S.R. 50 32N 45 50E
57 Krasnodonetskaya, U.S.S.R. 48 5N 40 50E
55 Krasnodarskiy, U.S.S.R. 56 10N 48 22E
56 Krasnog Dardeiskoye, 45 32N 34 16E
49 Krasnograd, U.S.S.R. 49 27N 35 27E
57 Krasnogvardeyskoye, 45 52N 41 33E
52 Krasnokamsk, U.S.S.R. 58 0N 56 0E

54 Krasnokutsk, U.S.S.R. 50 10N 34 50E
56 Krasnoperekopsk, U.S.S.R. 46 0N 33 54E
58 Krasnoselkupsk, U.S.S.R. 65 20N 82 10E
55 Krasnoslobodsk, Mordovian ASSR, U.S.S.R. 54 30N 43 45E
57 Krasnoslobodsk, R.S.F.S.R., U.S.S.R. 48 42N 44 33E
55 Krasnoturinsk, U.S.S.R. 59 39N 60 1E
52 Krasnoufimsk, U.S.S.R. 56 30N 57 37E
55 Krasnovodsk, U.S.S.R. 40 0N 52 52E
59 Krasnoyarsk, U.S.S.R. 56 8N 93 0E
54 Krasnoye, Kal., U.S.S.R. 46 43N 48 23E
55 Krasnoye, R.S.F.S.R., U.S.S.R. 59 15N 47 40E
54 Krasnoye, Ukr., U.S.S.R. 49 56N 24 42E
55 Krasnozavodsk, U.S.S.R. 56 38N 38 16E
56 Krasny Liman, U.S.S.R. 48 58N 37 50E
57 Krasny Sulin, U.S.S.R. 47 52N 40 1E
54 Krasnystaw, Poland 50 57N 23 5E
54 Krasnyy, U.S.S.R. 49 56N 24 42E
55 Krasnyy Kholm, U.S.S.R. 58 10N 37 10E
54 Krasnyy Kut, U.S.S.R. 50 50N 47 0E
54 Krasnyy Luch, U.S.S.R. 48 13N 39 0E
57 Krasnyy Yar, Kal., U.S.S.R. 46 43N 48 23E
55 Krasnyy Yar, R.S.F.S.R., U.S.S.R. 50 42N 44 45E
55 Krasnyy Yar, R.S.F.S.R., U.S.S.R. 53 30N 50 30E
56 Krasnyyoskolskoye, Vdkhr., U.S.S.R. 49 30N 37 30E
27 Krasznua, R., Hungary 48 0N 22 20E
71 Kratie, Khmer Rep. 12 32N 106 10E
24 Kratovo, Yugoslavia 42 6N 22 10E
71 Kravanh, Phnom, Khmer Rep. 12 15N 103 5E
71 Krawang, Indonesia 6 19N 107 18E
24 Krefeld, Germany 51 20N 6 22E
44 Kremastón, Limni, Greece 38 52N 21 30E
56 Kremenchug, U.S.S.R. 49 5N 33 25E
56 Kremenchugskeye Vdkhr., U.S.S.R. 49 20N 32 30E
42 Kremenets, U.S.S.R. 50 8N 25 43E
42 Kremenica, Yugoslavia 40 55N 21 25E
55 Kremennaya, U.S.S.R. 49 1N 38 10E
43 Kremikovtsi, Bulgaria 42 46N 23 28E
24 Kremmen, Germany 52 45N 13 1E
118 Kremmling, U.S.A. 40 10N 106 30w
26 Kremnica, Cz. 48 45N 18 50E
26 Krems, Austria 48 25N 15 36E
26 Kremsmünster, Austria 48 3N 14 8E
82 Krettamia, Algeria 28 47N 3 27w
54 Krettsy, U.S.S.R. 58 15N 32 30E
85 Kribi, Cameroon 2 57N 9 56E
43 Krichem, Bulgaria 46 16N 24 28E
54 Krichev, U.S.S.R. 53 45N 31 50E
43 Krichim, Bulgaria 42 8N 24 32E
71 Krim, Kho Khot, Thailand 10 15N 99 30E
39 Krim, mt., Y.-slavia 45 53N 14 30E
38 Krionéri, Greece 38 20N 21 35E
70 Krishna, R., India 16 30N 77 0E
69 Krishnanagar, India 23 24N 88 33E
70 Krishnagiri, India 12 32N 78 16E
69 Krishnaraja Sagara, India 12 20N 76 30E
49 Kristianopel, Sweden 56 12N 16 0E
47 Kristiansand, Norway 58 9N 8 1E
49 Kristianstad, Sweden 56 2N 14 9E
47 Kristiansund, Norway 63 7N 7 45E
50 Kristiinankaupunki, Fin. 62 16N 21 21E
49 Kristinehamn, Sweden 59 18N 14 13E
51 Kristinestad, Finland 62 16N 21 21E
45 Kriti, I., Greece 35 15N 25 0E
42 Kritsá, Greece 35 10N 25 41E
42 Kriva, R., Y.-slavia 42 12N 22 18E
42 Kriva Palanka, Y.-slav. 42 11N 22 19E
42 Krivaja, R., Yugoslavia 45 16N 18 22E
42 Krivelj, Yugoslavia 44 8N 22 5E
57 Krivoy Rog, U.S.S.R. 47 51N 33 20E
39 Krizevci, Yugoslavia 46 5N 16 32E
39 Krk, Yugoslavia 45 8N 14 40E
39 Krk, I., Yugoslavia 45 5N 14 30E
39 Krka, R., Yugoslavia 45 50N 15 30E
26 Krkonoše, Cz. 50 50N 15 35E
27 Krnov, Czechoslovakia 50 5N 17 40E
28 Krobia, Poland 51 47N 16 59E
26 Kročehlavy, Cz. 50 8N 14 10E
71 Kroeng Krai, Thailand 14 55N 98 30E
45 Krokeaí, Greece 36 53N 22 32E
47 Kroken, Telemark, Norway 58 57N 9 8E
48 Kroken, Sweden 59 2N 11 23E
48 Krokom, Sweden 63 20N 14 30E
54 Krolevets, U.S.S.R. 51 35N 33 20E
26 Kromeriz, Cz. 49 18N 17 21E
26 Krompachy, Cz. 48 54N 20 52E
54 Kromy, U.S.S.R. 52 45N 35 48E
49 Kronobergs län ♦, Swed. 56 45N 14 30E
5 Kronprins Harald Kyst, Antarctica 70 0s 35 1E
5 Kronprins Olav Kyst, Antarctica 69 0s 42 0E
Kronprinsesse Märtha Kyst, Antarctica 73 30s 10 0w
24 Kronshtadt, U.S.S.R. 60 5N 29 35E
24 Kröpelin, Germany 54 4N 11 48E
58 Kropotkin, U.S.S.R. 58 50N 115 10E
24 Kropp, Germany 54 24N 9 32E
28 Krościenko, Poland 49 29N 20 25E
28 Krośniewice, Poland 52 15N 19 11E
27 Krosno, Poland 49 35N 21 56E
28 Krosno Odrz, Poland 52 3N 15 7E
28 Krotoszyn, Poland 51 42N 17 23E
44 Krraba, Albania 41 13N 20 0E
39 Krško, Y.-slavia 45 57N 15 30E

* Renamed Kötschach-Mauthern

MAP

42 Krstača. mt., Y.-slavia 42 57N 20 8E
93 Kruger Nat. Pk., S. Afr. 24 0s 31 40E
93 Krugersdorp, S. Africa 26 5s 27 46E
72 Krui, Indonesia 5 10s 104 0E
92 Kruidfontein, S. Africa 32 48s 21 59E
92 Kruis, Kaap, S.W. Africa 21 55s 13 57E
44 Kruja, Albania 41 32N 19 46E
54 Krulevshchina, U.S.S.R. 55 5N 27 45E
44 Kruma, Albania 42 37N 20 28E
43 Krumovgrad, Bulgaria 41 29N 25 38E
71 Krung Thep, Thailand 13 45N 100 35E
42 Krupanj, Yugoslavia 44 25N 19 22E
27 Krupina, Cz. 48 22N 19 5E
27 Krupinica, R., Cz. 48 15N 19 5E
42 Kruševac, Yugoslavia 43 35N 21 28E
42 Krušovo, Yugoslavia 41 23N 21 19E
28 Kruszwica, Poland 52 40N 18 20E
108 Kruzof I., Alaska 57 10N 135 40w
48 Krylbo, Sweden 60 7N 16 15E
56 Krymsk Abinsk, U.S.S.R. 44 50N 38 0E
56 Krymskaya, U.S.S.R. 45 0N 34 0E
27 Krynica, Poland 49 25N 20 57E
28 Krynica Morska, Poland 54 23N 19 28E
27 Krynki, Poland 53 17N 23 43E
46 Kryulyany, U.S.S.R. 47 12N 29 9E
27 Krzepice, Poland 50 58N 18 50E
28 Krzeszowice, Poland 50 8N 19 37E
28 Krzywin, Poland 51 58N 16 50E
28 Krzyz, Poland 52 52N 16 0E
24 Krőpelin, Germany 54 4N 11 48E
47 Krakstad, Norway 59 39N 10 55E
48 Krångede, Sweden 63 9N 16 6E
82 Ksabi, Algeria 29 8N 0 58w
82 Ksabi, Morocco 32 51N 4 13w
82 Ksar Chellala, Algeria 35 13N 2 19E
82 Ksar el Boukhari, Algeria 35 51N 2 52E
82 Ksar el Kebir, Morocco 35 0N 6 0w
82 Ksar es Souk, Morocco 31 58N 4 20w
83 Ksar Rhilane, Tunisia 33 0N 9 39E
82 Ksiba, Morocco 32 46N 6 0w
82 Ksour, Mts. des, Algeria 32 45N 0 30w
55 Kstova, U.S.S.R. 56 12N 44 13E
72 Kuala, Indonesia 2 46N 105 47E
71 Kuala Belait, Brunei 4 45N 114 25E
71 Kuala Dungun, Malay. 4 46N 103 25E
71 Kuala Kangsar, Malay. 4 49N 100 57E
71 Kuala Kerai, Malay. 5 32N 102 12E
71 Kuala Kubu Bahru, Malaysia 3 35N 101 3E
71 Kuala Lipis, Malaysia 4 22N 102 5E
71 Kuala Lumpur, Malay. 3 9N 101 41E
71 Kuala Pilah, Malaysia 2 45N 102 14E
71 Kuala Sedili, Malaysia 1 57N 104 8E
71 Kuala Selangor, Malay. 3 20N 101 15E
72 Kualakapuas, Indonesia 2 55s 114 20E
72 Kualakurun, Indonesia 1 10s 113 50E
72 Kualapembuang, Indon. 3 14s 112 38E
73 Kuandang, Indonesia 0 56N 123 1E
73 Kuantan, Malaysia 3 49N 103 20E
87 Kuara, Ethiopia 12 25N 39 30E
57 Kuba, U.S.S.R. 41 21N 48 32E
66 Kubak, Iran 27 10N 63 10E
56 Kuban, R., U.S.S.R. 45 5N 38 0E
55 Kubenskoye, Oz., U.S.S.R. 59 40N 39 25E
57 Kuberle, U.S.S.R. 47 0N 42 20E
43 Kubrat, Bulgaria 43 49N 26 31E
42 Kučevo, Yugoslavia 44 30N 21 40E
75 Kucha, China 41 50N 82 30E
70 Kuchaman, India 27 13N 74 47E
25 Kuchenspitze, Aust. 47 3N 10 14E
72 Kuching, Malaysia 1 33N 110 25E
44 Kuçove = Qytet Stalin, Albania 40 47N 19 57E
44 Küçükkuyu, Turkey 39 35N 26 27E
70 Kudaldur, R., India 18 20N 78 40E
72 Kudat, Malay. 6 55N 116 55E
100 Kudgee, Australia 32 43s 141 38E
70 Kudremukh, Mt., India 13 15N 75 20E
73 Kudus, Indonesia 6 48s 110 51E
81 Kufra, El Wâhât el, Libya 24 17N 23 15E
62 Kufrinja, Jordan 32 20N 35 41E
26 Kufstein, Austria 47 35N 12 11E
106 Kugong, I., Canada 56 25N 80 0w
65 Kuhak, Iran 27 12N 63 10E
65 Küh-e-Alijuq, Iran 31 30N 51 41E
65 Küh-e-Hazaran, Iran 29 35N 57 20E
65 Küh-e-Jebel Barez, Iran 29 0N 58 0E
65 Küh-e-Sorkh, Iran 35 30N 58 45E
65 Küh-e-Taftan, Iran 28 40N 61 0E
65 Kühha-ye-Bashakerd, Iran 26 45N 59 0E
65 Kühha-ye Sabalân, Iran 38 15N 47 45E
26 Kuhnsdorf, Austria 46 37N 14 38E
65 Kuhpayeh, Iran 32 44N 52 20E
89 Kuiseb, R., S.W. Africa 23 40s 15 30E
108 Kuiu I., Alaska 56 40N 134 15w
42 Kukavica, mt., Y.-slav. 42 48N 21 57E
85 Kukawa, Nigeria 12 58N 13 27E
44 Kukési, Albania 42 5N 20 20E
44 Kukési *, Albania 42 25N 20 15E
87 Kukko, Ethiopia 8 26N 41 35E
55 Kukmar, U.S.S.R. 56 15N 50 45E
55 Kukvidze, U.S.S.R. 50 40N 43 15E
42 Kula, Bulgaria 43 52N 22 36E
42 Kula, Yugoslavia 45 37N 19 32E
71 Kulai, Malaysia 1 44N 103 35E
90 Kulal, Mt., Kenya 2 42N 36 57E
57 Kulaly, O., U.S.S.R. 45 0N 50 0E
70 Kulasekharapattanam, India 8 20N 78 0E
54 Kuldiga, U.S.S.R. 56 58N 21 59E
75 Kuldja = Ining, China 44 0N 81 0E
87 Kuldu, Sudan 12 50N 28 30E
55 Kulebaki, U.S.S.R. 55 22N 42 25E
39 Kulen Vakuf, Yugoslavia 44 35N 16 2E

57 Kuli, U.S.S.R. 42 2N 46 12E
116 Kulm, U.S.A. 46 22N 98 58w
58 Kulsary, U.S.S.R. 46 59N 54 1E
57 Kultay, U.S.S.R. 45 5N 51 40E
69 Kulti, India 23 43N 86 50E
98 Kulumadau, Papua 9 15s 152 50E
58 Kulunda, U.S.S.R. 52 45N 79 15E
100 Kulwin, Australia 35 0s 142 42E
58 Kulyab, U.S.S.R. 37 55N 69 50E
75 Kum Darya, China 41 0N 89 0E
58 Kum Tekei, U.S.S.R. 43 10N 79 30E
57 Kuma, R., U.S.S.R. 44 55N 45 57E
85 Kumaganum, Nigeria 13 8N 10 38E
72 Kumai, Indonesia 2 52s 111 45E
74 Kumamoto, Japan 32 45N 130 45E
74 Kumamoto-ken ◆, Japan 32 30N 130 40E
74 Kumanovo, Japan 42 9N 21 42E
42 Kumanovo, Yugoslavia 42 9N 21 42E
101 Kumara, New Zealand 42 37s 171 12E
84 Kumasi, Ghana 6 41N 1 38w
85 Kumba, Cameroon 4 36N 9 24E
70 Kumbakonam, India 10 58N 79 25E
99 Kumbarilla, Australia 27 15s 150 55E
85 Kumbo, Cameroon 6 15N 10 36E
70 Kumbukkan Oya, Sri Lanka 6 35N 81 40E
77 Kume-guntō, Japan 26 8N 126 45E
55 Kumeny, U.S.S.R. 58 10N 49 47E
90 Kumi, Uganda 1 30N 33 58E
44 Kumkale, Turkey 40 30N 26 13E
48 Kumla, Örebro, Sweden 59 8N 15 10E
85 Kumo, Nigeria 10 1N 11 12E
70 Kumta, India 14 29N 74 32E
57 Kumtorkala, U.S.S.R. 43 2N 46 50E
57 Kumylzhenskaya, U.S.S.R. 49 51N 42 38E
27 Kunágota, Hungary 46 26N 21 3E
100 Kunama, Australia 35 35s 148 4E
75 Kunashir, Ostrov, U.S.S.R. 44 0N 146 0E
68 Kunch, India 26 0N 79 10E
54 Kunda, U.S.S.R. 59 30N 26 34E
98 Kundiawa, New Guinea 6 00s 145 00E
68 Kundla, India 21 21N 71 25E
65 Kunduz, Afghanistan 36 50N 68 50E
72 Kunene, R., S.W. Afr. 17 15s 13 40E
99 Kungala, Australia 29 58s 153 7E
49 Kungälv, Sweden 57 54N 12 0E
71 Kungan, China 30 0N 112 2E
76 Kungchuling, China 43 31N 124 58E
77 Kungho, China 36 28N 100 45E
76 Kungrad, U.S.S.R. 43 6N 58 54E
49 Kungsbacka, Sweden 57 30N 12 5E
52 Kungur, U.S.S.R. 57 20N 56 40E
98 Kungurri, Australia 21 3s 148 46E
77 Kungyifow, China 22 24N 112 41E
49 Kungälv, Sweden 57 53N 11 59E
72 Kunhegyes, Hungary 47 22N 20 36E
77 Kunhsien, China 32 30N 111 17E
72 Kuningan, Indonesia 6 59s 108 29E
75 Kunlun Shan, Asia 36 0N 86 30E
72 Kunmadaras, Hungary 47 28N 20 45E
75 Kunming, China 25 11N 102 37E
70 Kunnamkulam, India 10 38N 76 7E
76 Kunsan, S. Korea 35 59N 126 45E
77 Kunshan, China 31 16N 121 0E
27 Kunszentmárton, Hung. 46 50N 20 20E
27 Kunszentmiklós, Hung. 15 40s 128 39E
96 Kununurra, Australia 15 40s 128 39E
98 Kunwararo, Australia 22 55s 150 7E
50 Kuopio, Fin. 62 53N 27 35E
50 Kuopion Lääni ◆, Finland 63 25N 27 10E

64 Kurtalon, Turkey 37 55N 41 40E
87 Kuru (Chel) Bahr el, Sudan 8 10N 26 50E
92 Kuruman, S. Africa 27 28s 23 28E
74 Kurume, Japan 33 15N 130 30E
70 Kurunegala, Sri Lanka 7 30N 80 18E
59 Kurya, U.S.S.R. 61 15N 108 10E
45 Kuşadası, Turkey 37 52N 27 15E
45 Kuşadası Körfezı, Turkey 37 56N 27 0E
77 Kusagaki, Ryukyu Is. 30 54N 129 28E
108 Kusawa L., Canada 60 25N 136 20w
25 Kusel, Germany 49 31N 7 25E
76 Kushan, China 39 58N 123 30E
57 Kushchevskaya, U.S.S.R. 46 33N 39 35E
77 Kushin, China 32 12N 115 43E
74 Kushirogawa, Japan 43 0N 144 30E
65 Kushk, Afghanistan 34 55N 62 30E
58 Kushka, U.S.S.R. 35 20N 62 18E
69 Kushtia, Bangladesh 23 55N 89 5E
77 Kushum, R., U.S.S.R. 50 40N 50 20E
104 Kuskokwim Bay, Alaska 59 50N 162 56w
104 Kuskokwim, R., Alaska 61 48N 157 0w
87 Kussa, Ethiopia 4 9N 38 58E
58 Kustanai, U.S.S.R. 53 20N 63 45E
26 Kutá Horą, Cz. 49 57N 15 16E
57 Kutaisi, U.S.S.R. 42 19N 42 40E
72 Kutaradja = Banda Atjeh, Indonesia 5 35N 95 20E
72 Kutatjane, Indonesia 3 45N 97 50E
68 Kutch, G. of, India 22 50N 69 15E
68 Kutch, Rann of, India 24 0N 70 0E
39 Kutina, Yugoslavia 45 29N 16 48E
68 Kutiyana, India 21 36N 70 2E
42 Kutjevo, Yugoslavia 45 23N 17 55E
57 Kutkashen, U.S.S.R. 40 58N 47 47E
26 Kutá Horą, Cz. 49 57N 15 16E
28 Kutno, Poland 52 15N 19 23E
98 Kuttabul, Australia 21 5s 148 48E
87 Kutum, Sudan 14 20N 24 10E
27 Kúty, Czechoslovakia 48 40N 17 3E
54 Kuvshinovo, U.S.S.R. 57 34N 34 11E
64 Kuwait = Al Kuwayt, Kuwait 29 30N 47 30E
64 Kuwait ■, Arabia 29 30N 47 30E
76 Kuyang, China 41 8N 110 1E
55 Kuybyshev, R.S.F.S.R., U.S.S.R. 53 10N 50 15E
55 Kuybyshev, R.S.F.S.R., U.S.S.R. 55 27N 78 19E
55 Kuybyshevo, U.S.S.R. 47 25N 36 40E
55 Kuybyshevskoye Vdkhr., U.S.S.R. 55 2N 49 30E
52 Kuyto, Oz., U.S.S.R. 64 40N 31 0E
77 Kuyung, China 32 0N 119 8E
70 Kuzhithura, India 8 18N 77 11E
42 Kuzmin, Yugoslavia 45 2N 19 25E
55 Kuznetsk, U.S.S.R. 53 12N 46 40E
52 Kuzomen, U.S.S.R. 66 22N 36 50E
50 Kvaenangen, Norway 69 55N 21 15E
47 Kvam, Oppland, Norway 61 40N 9 42E
50 Kvarken, Finland 63 30N 21 0E
39 Kvarner, Yugoslavia 44 50N 14 10E
39 Kvarneric, Yugoslavia 44 43N 14 37E
48 Kvarnsveden, Sweden 60 32N 15 25E
47 Kväs, Norway 58 16N 7 14E
49 Kvillsfors, Sweden 57 24N 15 29E
47 Kvina, R., Norway 58 43N 6 52E
47 Kvinesdal, Norway 58 18N 6 59E
47 Kviteseid, Norway 59 24N 8 29E
47 Kväs, Norway 58 16N 7 14E
92 Kwakhanai, Botswana 21 39s 21 16E
127 Kwakoegron, Surinam 5 25N 55 25w
90 Kwale ◆, Kenya 4 15s 39 10E
85 Kwale, Nigeria 6 18N 5 28E
88 Kwamouth, Zaïre 3 9s 16 20E
92 Kwando, R., Angola & Zam. 16 48s 22 45E
77 Kwangan, China 30 35N 106 40E
77 Kwangchow, China 23 10N 113 10E
77 Kwangchow Wan, China 21 0N 110 0E
76 Kwangju, S. Korea 35 9N 126 55E
75 Kwangnan, China 24 10N 105 0E
77 Kwangshui, China 31 45N 114 0E
77 Kwangsi-Chuang ◆, China 23 30N 108 55E
77 Kwangtseh, China 27 30N 117 25E
77 Kwangtsi, China 30 2N 115 46E
77 Kwangtung, China 23 35N 114 0E
77 Kwangyuan, China 32 30N 105 49E
77 Kwanhsien, China 30 59N 103 40E
92 Kwaraga, Botswana 20 26s 24 32E
73 Kwatisore, Indonesia 3 7s 139 59E
77 Kweichih, China 30 40N 117 30E
77 Kweichow = Fengkieh, China 31 0N 109 33E
77 Kweichow ◆, China 27 0N 107 0E
77 Kweihsien, China 22 59N 109 44E
77 Kweihwa = Mingki, China 26 10N 117 14E
77 Kweiki, China 28 10N 117 17E
77 Kweilin, China 25 16N 110 15E
77 Kweiping, China 23 10N 110 0E
77 Kweiyang, Hunan, China 26 0N 113 35E
77 Kweiyang, Kweichow, China 26 30N 106 13E
28 Kwidzyn, Poland 54 5N 18 58E
96 Kwinana, Australia 32 15s 115 47E
90 Kwitaba, Burundi 3 56s 29 39E
77 Kwo Ho, China 33 20N 116 50E
77 Kwohwa, China 23 10N 107 0E
81 Kyabe, Chad 9 30N 19 0E

100 Kyabram, Australia 36 19s 145 4E
71 Kyaikto, Burma 17 20N 97 3E
59 Kyakhta, U.S.S.R. 50 30N 106 25E
67 Kyangin, Burma 18 20N 95 20E
67 Kyargas Nuur, Mongolia 49 0N 93 0E
67 Kyaring Tso, Tibet 31 5N 88 25E
67 Kyaukpadaung, Burma 20 52N 95 8E
67 Kyaukpyu, Burma 19 28N 93 30E
67 Kyaukse, Burma 21 36N 96 10E
90 Kyegegwa, Uganda 0 30N 31 0E
90 Kyeikdon, Burma 16 3N 98 25E
90 Kyenjojo, Uganda 0 40N 30 37E
91 Kyle Dam, Rhodesia 20 15s 31 0E
14 Kyle of Lochalsh, Scotland 57 17N 5 43w
100 Kyneton, Australia 37 10s 144 29E
74 Kyō-ga-Saki, Japan 35 45N 135 15E
90 Kyoga, L., Uganda 1 35N 33 0E
99 Kyogle, Australia 28 40s 153 0E
76 Kyongju, S. Korea 35 50N 129 13E
67 Kyongpyaw, Burma 17 12N 95 10E
74 Kyōto, Japan 35 0N 135 45E
74 Kyōto-fu ◆, Japan 35 15N 135 30E
64 Kyrenia, Cyprus 35 20N 33 20E
48 Kyrkebyn, Sweden 59 15N 13 3E
47 Kyrping, Norway 59 45s 6 5E
59 Kystatyam, U.S.S.R. 67 20N 123 10E
59 Kytalktakh, U.S.S.R. 65 30N 123 40E
76 Kyulyunken, U.S.S.R. 64 10N 137 5E
67 Kyunhla, Burma 23 25N 95 15E
108 Kyuquot, Canada 50 3N 127 25E
57 Kyuquot Sd., Canada 50 0N 127 25w
74 Kyushu, I., Japan 32 30N 131 0E
74 Kyūshū-Sanchi, Japan 32 45N 131 40E
42 Kyustendil, Bulgaria 42 25N 22 41E
57 Kyusyur, U.S.S.R. 70 39N 127 15E
100 Kywong, Australia 34 58s 146 44E
58 Kyzyl, U.S.S.R. 51 50N 94 30E
58 Kyzyl Kum, U.S.S.R. 42 0N 65 0E
58 Kyzyl Kum, Peski, U.S.S.R. 42 0N 65 0E
59 Kyzyl Rabot, U.S.S.R. 37 45N 74 55E
58 Kzyl-Orda, U.S.S.R. 44 50N 65 10E

19 La Albuera, Spain 38 45N 6 49w
32 La Alcarria, Spain 40 31N 2 45w
31 La Algaba, Spain 37 27N 6 1w
32 La Almarcha, Spain 39 41N 2 24w
32 La Almunia de Doña Godina, Spain 41 29N 1 23w
126 La Asunción, Ven. 11 2N 63 53w
124 La Banda, Argentina 27 45s 64 10w
31 La Bañeza, Spain 42 17N 5 43w
120 La Barca, Mexico 20 20N 102 40w
18 La Barge, U.S.A. 41 12N 110 4w
20 La Bassée, France 50 31N 2 49E
20 La Bastide, France 44 35N 3 55E
20 La Baule, France 47 18N 2 3w
115 La Belle, U.S.A. 26 45N 81 22w
32 La Bisbal, Spain 41 58N 3 2E
126 La Blanquilla, Ven. 11 51N 64 37w
120 La Boca, Pan. Can. Zone 9 0N 79 30w
19 La Bresse, France 48 0N 6 53E
31 La Bureba, Spain 42 36N 3 24w
124 La Calera, Chile 32 50s 71 10w
31 La Campiña, Spain 37 45N 4 45w
31 La Cañiza, Spain 42 13N 8 16w
20 La Capelle, France 49 59N 3 50E
124 La Carlota, Argentina 33 30s 63 20w
31 La Carolina, Spain 38 17N 3 38w
20 La Cavalerie, France 44 0N 3 10E
121 La Ceiba, Honduras 15 40N 86 50w
20 La Chaise Dieu, France 45 20N 3 40E
18 La Chaize-le-Vicomté, France 46 40N 1 18w
19 La Chapelle-d'Angillon, France 47 21N 2 25E
18 La Chapelle Glain, Fr. 47 38N 1 11w
19 La Charité, France 47 10N 3 0E
19 La Chartre, France 47 42N 0 34E
18 La Châtaignerie, France 46 38N 0 45w
19 La Châtre, France 46 35N 1 59E
25 La Chaux de Fonds, Switzerland 47 7N 6 50E
120 La Chorrera, Panama 8 50N 79 50w
21 La Ciotat, France 43 12N 5 36E
19 La Clayette, France 46 17N 4 19E
124 La Cocha, Argentina 27 50s 65 40w
* 85 La Concepción, Eq. Guinea 3 28N 84 0E
120 La Concordia, Mexico 16 8N 92 38w
118 La Conner, U.S.A. 48 22N 122 27w
30 La Coruña, Spain 43 20N 8 25w
30 La Coruña, Spain 43 10N 8 30w
30 La Corunne = La Coruña, Spain 43 20N 8 25w
21 La Côte-St. André, Fr. 45 24N 5 15E
20 La Courtine, France 45 43N 2 16E
20 La Crèche, France 46 23N 0 19w
108 La Crete, Canada 58 10N 116 29w
116 La Crosse, Kans., U.S.A. 38 33N 99 20w
116 La Crosse, Wis., U.S.A. 43 48N 91 13w
120 La Cruz, Colombia 1 35N 76 58w
120 La Cruz, Mexico 23 55N 106 54w
126 La Dorada, Colombia 5 30N 74 40w
124 La Esmeralda, Paraguay 22 16s 62 33w
124 La Esperanza, Jujuy, Arg. 24 9s 64 52w
126 La Esperanza, Bolivia 14 20s 62 0w
126 La Esperanza, Cuba 22 46s 83 44w
113 La Fargeville, U.S.A. 44 12N 75 58w
116 La Fayette, U.S.A. 32 15s 115 47E
19 La Fère, France 49 40N 3 20E
19 La Ferté, France 48 57N 3 6E
19 La Ferté Bernard, Fr. 48 10N 0 40E
18 La Ferté-Mace, France 48 35N 0 21w

19 La Ferté-St. Aubin, Fr. 47 42N 1 57E
18 La Ferté-Vidame, Fr. 48 37N 0 53E
18 La Flèche, France 47 42N 0 5w
115 La Folette, U.S.A. 36 23N 84 9w
30 La Fregeneda, Spain 40 58N 6 54w
126 La Fria, Venezuela 8 13N 72 15w
30 La Fuente de San Esteban, Spain 40 49N 6 15w
33 La Gineta, Spain 39 8N 2 1w
126 La Gloria, Colombia 8 37N 73 48w
126 La Gran Sabana, Ven. 5 30N 61 30w
21 La Grand 'Combe, France 44 13N 4 2E
21 La Grand Motte, France 48 35N 1 4E
118 La Grande, U.S.A. 45 15N 118 0w
96 La Grange, Australia 18 45s 121 43E
115 La Grange, Ga., U.S.A. 33 4N 85 0w
114 La Grange, Ky., U.S.A. 38 20N 85 20w
117 La Grange, Tex., U.S.A. 29 54N 96 52w
126 La Grita, Venezuela 8 8N 71 59w
126 La Guaira, Venezuela 10 36N 66 56w
126 La Guajira ◆, Col. 11 30N 72 30w
30 La Guardia, Spain 41 56N 8 52w
31 La Gudiña, Spain 42 4N 7 8w
18 La Guerche, France 47 1N 1 16w
19 La Guerche-sur-l'Aubois, France 46 58N 2 56E
121 La Habana, Cuba 23 8N 82 22w
116 La Harpe, U.S.A. 40 30N 91 0w
18 La Haye Descartes, Fr. 46 58N 0 42E
18 La Haye-du-Puits, Fr. 49 17N 1 33w
30 La Horra, Spain 41 44N 3 53w
126 La Isla, Colombia 6 51N 76 56w
114 La Jara, U.S.A. 37 16N 106 0w
32 La Junquera, Spain 42 25N 2 53E
117 La Junta, U.S.A. 38 0N 103 30w
124 La Ligua, Chile 32 30s 71 16w
32 La Linea de la Concepción, Sp. 36 15N 5 23w
109 La Loche L., Canada 56 40N 109 30w
21 La Londe, France 43 8N 6 14E
30 La Lora, Spain 42 45N 4 0w
16 La Louvière, Belgium 50 27N 4 10E
19 La Machine, France 46 54N 3 27E
40 La Maddalena, Italy 41 13N 9 25E
107 La Malbaie, Canada 47 40N 70 10w
33 La Mancha, dist., Spain 39 10N 2 54w
30 La Mariña, Spain 43 30N 7 40w
104 La Martre, L., Can. 63 0N 118 0w
104 La Martre, R., Canada 63 0N 118 0w
126 La Mesa, Colombia 4 38N 74 28w
119 La Mesa, Calif., U.S.A. 32 48N 117 5w
119 La Mesa, N. Mex., U.S.A. 32 6N 106 48w
32 La Mola, Punta de, Sp. 39 53N 4 19E
18 La Mothe Archard, Fr. 46 37N 1 39w
21 La Motte, France 44 20N 6 3E
21 La Motte-Chalançon, Fr. 44 30N 5 21E
116 La Moure, U.S.A. 46 27N 98 17w
32 La Muela, Spain 41 36N 1 7w
21 La Mure, France 44 55N 5 48E
33 La Nao, Cabo de, Spain 38 44N 0 14E
124 La Negra, Chile 23 46s 70 18w
20 La Pacaudière, France 46 10N 3 50E
121 La Palma, Panama 8 15N 78 0w
37 La Palma, Spain 37 21N 6 38w
124 La Paloma, Chile 30 35s 71 0w
20 La Pampa ◆, Arg. 38 0s 66 0w
126 La Paragua, Venezuela 6 50N 63 20w
124 La Paz, Entre Rios, Arg. 30 50s 59 45w
124 La Paz, San Luis, Arg. 33 30s 67 20w
120 La Paz, Honduras 14 20N 87 47w
120 La Paz, Mexico 24 10N 110 20w
120 La Paz, Bide, Mexico 24 20N 110 40w
126 La Pedrera, Colombia 1 18s 69 43w
60 La Perouse Str., Japan 45 40N 142 0E
120 La Piedad, Mexico 20 20N 102 1w
118 La Pine, U.S.A. 43 53N 121 30w
116 La Plant, U.S.A. 45 11N 100 40w
124 La Plata, Argentina 35 0s 57 55w
124 La Plata, Rio de, S. Amer. 35 0s 56 40w
32 La Pobla de Lillet, Sp. 42 16N 1 59E
31 La Pola de Gordón, Sp. 42 51N 5 41w
114 La Porte, U.S.A. 41 40N 86 40w
31 La Puebla, Spain 39 50N 4 25w
31 La Puebla de los Infantes, Spain 37 47N 5 24w
30 La Puebla de Montalbán, Spain 39 52N 4 22w
33 La Puerta, Spain 38 22N 2 45w
124 La Quiaca, Argentina 22 5s 65 35w
33 La Rambla, Spain 37 37N 4 45w
106 La Reine, Canada 48 50N 79 30w
20 La Réole, France 44 35N 0 1w
124 La Rioja, Argentina 29 20s 67 0w
32 La Rioja, Spain 42 20N 2 20w
124 La Rioja ◆, Arg. 29 30s 67 0w
30 La Robla, Spain 42 50N 5 41w
20 La Roche, France 46 4N 6 19E
18 La Roche Bernard, Fr. 47 31N 2 18w
20 La Roche-Canillac, Fr. 45 12N 1 57E
20 La Roche-sur-Yon, Fr. 46 40N 1 25w
20 La Rochefoucauld, Fr. 45 44N 0 24E
20 La Rochelle, France 46 10N 1 9w
33 La Roda, Spain 39 13N 2 15w
124 La Romana, Dom. Rep. 18 27N 68 57w
109 La Ronge, Canada 55 5N 105 20w
109 La Ronge L., Canada 55 10N 105 0w
33 La Sagra, Mt., Spain 37 57N 2 35w
126 La Salina, Venezuela 10 21N 71 27w
116 La Salle, U.S.A. 41 20N 89 5w
30 La Sanabria, Spain 42 0N 6 30w
106 La Sarre, Canada 48 45N 79 15w
107 La Scie, Canada 49 58N 55 36w
19 La Selva, Spain 42 0N 2 45E
124 La Serena, Chile 29 55s 71 10w
31 La Serena, Spain 38 45N 5 40w

* Renamed Ri-Aba

MAP

21 La Seyne-sur-Mer, Fr. 43 7N 5 52E
41 La Sila, Mts., Italy 39 15N 16 35E
83 La Skhirra = Cekhira. 34 20N 10 5E
   Tunisia
33 La Solana, Spain 38 59N 3 14w
20 La Souterraine, France 46 15N 1 30E
38 La Spézia. Italy 44 8N 9 50E
18 La Suze. France 47 54N 0 2E
126 La Tagua, Colombia 0 3N 74 40w
20 La Teste. France 44 34N 1 9w
21 La Tour-du-Pin. France 45 34N 5 27E
20 La Tranche. France 46 20N 1 26w
20 La Tremblade, France 45 46N 1 8w
106 La Tuque, Canada 47 30N 72 50w
128 La Unión. Colombia 40 10s 73 0w
126 La Unión, Colombia 1 35N 77 5w
120 La Unión, Salvador 13 20N 87 50w
33 La Unión. Spain 37 38N 0 53w
126 La Unión. Venezuela 7 28N 67 53w
20 La Urbana, Venezuela 7 8N 66 56w
126 La Valdivia. Chile 34 43s 72 5w
30 La Vecilla, Spain 42 51N 5 27w
121 La Vega. Dom. Rep. 19 20N 70 30w
126 La Venturosa. Col. 6 8N 68 48w
126 La Victoria, Venezuela 10 14N 67 20w
21 La Voulte, France 44 49N 4 48E
31 La Zarza. Spain 37 42N 6 51w
27 Laa, Austria 48 43N 16 23E
24 Laage. Germany 53 55N 12 21E
100 Laanecoorie Res., 36 52s 143 50E
   Australia
24 Laasphe. Germany 50 56N 8 23E
57 Laba. R., U.S.S.R. 45 0N 40 30E
73 Labala. Indonesia 8 35s 123 32E
20 Labastide, France 43 28N 2 39E
20 Labastide-Murat, Fr. 44 39N 1 33E
85 Labbézenga, Mali 15 2N 0 48E
83 Labdah = Leptis 32 40N 14 12E
   Magna, Libya
84 Labé. Guinea 11 24N 12 16w
26 Labe. R., Czechoslovakia 50 3N 15 20E
27 Laberec. R., Cz. 21 57N 49 7E
108 Laberge. L., Canada 61 15N 135 0w
39 Labin. Yugoslavia 45 5N 14 8E
57 Labinsk. U.S.S.R. 44 40N 40 48w
71 Labis. Malaysia 2 22N 103 2E
52 Labiszyn. Poland 52 57N 17 54E
73 Laboa. Indonesia 8 6s 122 50E
24 Laboe. Germany 54 25N 10 13E
20 Labouheyre. France 44 13N 0 55w
124 Laboulaye. Argentina 34 10s 63 30w
105 Labrador. Canada 53 20N 61 0w
107 Labrador City, Canada 52 42N 67 0w
126 Labranzagrande. Col. 5 33N 72 34w
126 Lábrea, Brazil 7 15s 64 51w
20 Labrède. France 44 41N 0 32w
72 Labuan. I. Malaysia 5 15N 115 38w
73 Labuha. Indonesia 0 30s 127 30E
73 Labuhan. Indonesia 6 26s 105 50E
73 Labuhanbadjo. Indon. 8 28s 120 1E
72 Labuk. Telok, Malaysia 6 10N 117 50E
52 Labytnangi, U.S.S.R. 66 29N 66 40E
107 Lac Bouchette, Canada 48 16N 72 11w
116 Lac du Flambeau. 46 1N 89 51w
   U.S.A.
107 Lac Edouard. Canada 47 40N 72 16w
108 Lac la Biche, Canada 54 45N 111 50w
109 Lac Seul, Canada 50 28N 92 0w
20 Lacanau, Etang de. Fr. 44 58N 1 7w
20 Lacanau Médoc. France 44 59N 1 5w
31 Lacara. R., Spain 39 7N 6 25w
20 Lacaune. Mts. de. Fr. 43 43N 2 50E
20 Lacaune. France 43 43N 2 40E
60 Laccadive Is.. Ind. Oc. 10 0N 72 30E
96 Lacepede Is.. W. 16 55s 122 0E
   Austral.
91 Lacerdónia. Mozam. 18 3s 35 35E
106 Lachine. Canada 45 30N 73 40w
100 Lachlan. R.. Australia 34 0s 144 45E
68 Lachmangarh. India 27 50N 75 4E
24 Lachute. Canada 45 39N 74 21E
112 Lackawanna. U.S.A. 42 49N 78 50w
113 Lacolle. Canada 45 5N 73 22w
108 Lacombe. Canada 52 30N 113 50w
113 Lacona. U.S.A. 43 37N 76 5w
40 Laconi. Italy 39 54N 9 4E
113 Laconia. U.S.A. 43 32N 71 30w
20 Lacq. France 43 25N 0 35w
116 Lacrosse. U.S.A. 46 51N 117 58w
66 Ladakh Ra.. Kashmir 34 0N 78 0E
52 Ladek Zdrój. Poland 50 21N 16 51E
45 Ladhon. R., Greece 37 40N 21 50E
56 Ládik. Turkey 40 57N 35 58E
92 Ladismith. S. Africa 33 28s 21 15E
65 Ládiz. Iran 28 55N 61 15E
68 Ladnun. India 27 38N 74 25E
52 Ladoga. L. = 61 15N 30 30E
   Ladozhskoye Oz.. U.S.S.R.
19 Ladon. France 48 0N 2 30E
91 Lady Babbie. Rhodesia 18 30s 29 20E
106 Lady Beatrix L.. Can. 52 50N 76 50w
92 Lady Grey. S. Africa 30 43s 27 13E
92 Ladybrand. S. Africa 29 9s 27 29E
108 Ladysmith. Canada 49 0N 124 0w
93 Ladysmith. S. Afr. 28 32s 29 46E
116 Ladysmith. U.S.A. 45 27N 91 4w
98 Lae. Terr. of N. Guin. 6 48s 146 53E
49 Laesø. Denmark 57 15N 10 53E
49 Laesø Rende. Den. 57 15N 10 50E
116 Lafayette. Colo.. U.S.A. 40 0N 105 2w
115 Lafayette. Ga.. U.S.A. 34 44N 85 15w
117 Lafayette. La.. U.S.A. 30 18N 92 0w
115 Lafayette. Tenn.. U.S.A. 36 35N 86 8w
106 Laferte. Canada 48 37N 78 48w
85 Lafia. Nigeria 8 30N 8 34E
85 Lafiagi. Nigeria 8 52N 5 20E
109 Laflèche. Canada 49 45N 106 40w
87 Lafon. Sudan 5 5s 32 29E
106 Laforest. Canada 47 4N 81 12w
48 Laforsen. Sweden 61 56N 15 3E

MAP

49 Lagan, Sweden 56 32N 12 58E
15 Lagan. R.. N. Ire. 54 35N 5 55w
50 Lagarfljót, Iceland 65 40N 14 18w
125 Lagarto, Serra do, Brazil 23 0s 57 15w
24 Lage. Germany 52 0N 8 47E
30 Lage, Spain 43 13N 9 0w
47 Lägen. Norway 61 29N 10 2E
24 Lägerdorf, Germany 53 53N 9 35E
82 Laghouat, Algeria 33 50N 2 59E
57 Lagich. U.S.S.R. 40 50N 48 20E
21 Lagnieu. France 45 55N 5 20E
19 Lagny. France 48 52N 2 40E
31 Lago. Italy 39 9N 16 8E
30 Lagôa, Portugal 37 8N 8 27w
30 Lagoaça, Portugal 41 11N 6 44w
57 Lagodekhi. U.S.S.R. 41 50N 46 22E
41 Lagonegro, Italy 40 8N 15 45E
73 Lagonoy Gulf, Phil. 13 50N 123 50E
85 Lagos. Nigeria 6 25N 3 27E
30 Lagos, Portugal 37 5N 8 41w
120 Lagos de Moreno. Mex. 21 21N 101 55w
32 Laguardia, Spain 42 33N 2 35w
20 Laguépie, France 44 8N 1 57E
125 Laguna, Brazil 28 30s 48 50w
124 Laguna, U.S.A. 35 3N 107 28w
30 Laguna Antela, Spain 47 7N 7 40w
119 Laguna Beach, U.S.A. 33 31N 117 52w
119 Laguna Dam, U.S.A. 32 55N 114 30w
31 Laguna dela Janda, 36 15N 5 45w
   Spain
124 Laguna Limpia, Arg. 26 32s 59 45w
124 Laguna Madre, U.S.A. 27 0N 97 20w
124 Laguna Olmos, Arg. 33 25s 63 19w
39 Laguna Veneta, Italy 45 23N 12 25E
126 Lagunas, Chile 21 0s 69 45w
126 Lagunas, Peru 5 10s 75 35w
126 Lagunillas, Venezuela 10 8N 71 16w
76 Laha, China 48 9N 124 30E
73 Lahad Datu, Malaysia 5 0N 118 30E
69 Laharpur, India 27 43N 80 56E
72 Lahat, Indonesia 3 45s 103 30E
73 Lahewa, Indonesia 1 22N 97 12E
65 Lahijan, Iran 37 10N 50 6E
24 Lahn, R., Germany 50 52N 8 35E
49 Laholm, Sweden 56 30N 13 2E
49 Laholmsbukten, Sweden 56 30N 12 45E
118 Lahontan Res., U.S.A. 39 28N 118 58w
68 Lahore, Pakistan 31 32N 74 22E
68 Lahore ♦, Pakistan 31 55N 74 5E
25 Lahr, Germany 48 20N 7 52E
51 Lahti, Finland 60 58N 25 40E
81 Lai (Béhagle), Chad 9 25N 16 30E
76 Lai Chau, N. Vietnam 22 5N 103 3E
76 Laichow Wan, China 37 30N 119 30E
99 Laidley, Australia 27 39s 152 20E
76 Laifeng, China 29 30N 109 30E
18 Laigle, France 48 46N 0 38E
19 Laignes, France 47 50N 4 20E
20 L'Aiguillon, France 46 20N 1 16w
90 Laikipia ♦, Kenya 0 30N 36 30E
64 Laila, Saudi Arabia 22 10N 46 40E
126 Laillahue, Chile 17 0s 69 30w
73 Laingsburg, S. Africa 33 9s 20 52E
72 Laipin, China 23 45N 109 10E
14 Lairg, Scotland 58 1N 4 24w
72 Lais, Indonesia 3 35s 102 0E
76 Laiyang, China 37 0N 120 42E
125 Lajes, Sta. Catarina, 27 48s 50 20w
   Brazil
42 Lajkovac, Yugoslavia 44 27N 20 14E
27 Lajosmizse, Hungary 47 3N 19 32E
69 Laka Chih, Tibet 30 40N 81 10E
68 Lakaband, Pakistan 31 2N 69 15E
73 Lakar, Indonesia 8 15s 128 17E
116 Lake Andes, U.S.A. 43 10N 98 32w
117 Lake Anse, U.S.A. 46 42N 88 25w
117 Lake Arthur, U.S.A. 30 8N 92 40w
100 Lake Boga, Australia 35 26s 143 38E
100 Lake Cargelligo, 33 15s 146 22E
   Australia
117 Lake Charles, U.S.A. 31 10N 93 10w
119 Lake City, Colo. U.S.A. 38 3N 107 27w
115 Lake City, Fla., U.S.A. 30 10N 82 40w
116 Lake City, Iowa, U.S.A. 42 12N 94 42w
114 Lake City, Mich., U.S.A. 44 20N 85 10w
116 Lake City, Minn., 44 28N 92 21w
   U.S.A.
112 Lake City, Pa., U.S.A. 42 2N 80 20w
115 Lake City, S.C., U.S.A. 33 51N 79 44w
115 Lake George, U.S.A. 43 25N 73 30w
105 Lake Harbour, Canada 62 30N 69 50w
119 Lake Havasu City, 34 25N 114 20w
   U.S.A.
108 Lake Louise, Canada 51 30N 116 10w
119 Lake Mead Nat. Rec. 36 20N 114 30w
   Area, U.S.A.
116 Lake Mills, U.S.A. 43 23N 93 33w
98 Lake Nash, Australia 20 57s 138 0E
111 Lake of the Woods, 49 0N 95 0w
   Can.
117 Lake Providence, U.S.A. 32 49N 91 12w
106 Lake River, Canada 54 30N 82 30w
106 Lake Superior Prov. 47 45N 85 0w
   Park, Can.
106 Lake Traverse, Canada 45 56N 78 4w
106 Lake Tyers, Australia 37 52s 148 5E
100 Lake Victoria Res., 34 0s 141 11E
   Australia
117 Lake Village, U.S.A. 33 20N 91 19w
115 Lake Wales, U.S.A. 27 55N 81 32w
115 Lake Worth, U.S.A. 26 36N 80 3w
106 Lakefield, Canada 44 25N 78 16w
119 Lakeside, Ariz., U.S.A. 34 12N 109 59w
116 Lakeside, Nebr., U.S.A. 42 5N 102 24w
114 Lakeview, N.Y., U.S.A. 42 43N 78 57w
118 Lakeview, Oreg., U.S.A. 42 15N 120 22w

MAP

113 Lakewood, N.J., U.S.A. 40 5N 74 13w
112 Lakewood, Ohio, U.S.A. 41 28N 81 50w
45 Lakhaniá, Gr. 35 58N 27 54E
45 Lákhi, Greece 35 24N 23 27E
69 Lakhimpur, India 27 14N 94 7E
23 Lakhpat, India 23 48N 68 47E
117 Lakin, U.S.A. 37 58N 101 18w
66 Lakki, Pakistan 32 38N 70 50E
45 Lakonía ♦, Greece 36 55N 22 30E
45 Lakonikós Kólpos, 36 40N 22 40E
   Greece
73 Lakor, I., Indonesia 8 15s 128 17E
84 Lakota, Ivory Coast 5 50N 5 30w
116 Lakota, U.S.A. 48 0N 98 22w
50 Lakselfjorden, Norway 70 45N 26 50E
50 Lakselv, Norway 70 2N 24 56E
50 Lakselvbukt, Norway 69 26N 19 40E
69 Lakshmi Kantapur, India 22 5N 88 20E
68 Lala Ghat, India 24 30N 92 40E
68 Lala Musa, Pakistan 32 40N 73 57E
90 Lalago, Tanzania 3 28s 33 58E
91 Lalapanzi, Rhodesia 19 20s 30 15E
100 Lalbert, Australia 35 38s 143 20E
69 Lalganj, India 25 52N 85 13E
87 Lalibala, Ethiopia 12 8N 39 10E
30 Lalín, Spain 42 40N 8 5w
20 Lalinde, France 44 50N 0 44E
†68 Lalitpur, India 24 42N 78 28E
67 Lalitapur, India 26 36N 85 32E
85 Lama Kara, Togo 9 30N 1 15E
71 Lamaing, Burma 15 25N 97 53E
116 Lamar, Colo., U.S.A. 38 9N 102 35w
117 Lamar, Mo., U.S.A. 37 30N 94 20w
126 Lamas, Peru 6 28s 76 31w
21 Lamastre, France 44 59N 4 35E
76 Lamatientze, China 46 6N 124 44E
26 Lambach, Austria 48 6N 13 51E
88 Lambaréné, Gabon 0 20s 10 12E
15 Lambay I., Ireland 53 30N 6 0w
126 Lambayeque ♦, Peru 6 45s 80 0w
116 Lambert, U.S.A. 47 44N 104 39w
14 Lambert Land, Green. 79 12N 20 30w
25 Lambesc, France 43 39N 5 16E
71 Lamh Kyun, (Sullivan 10 50N 98 20E
   I.), Burma
45 Lámbia, Greece 37 52N 21 53E
38 Lambro, R., Italy 45 18N 9 2E
85 Lame, Nigeria 10 27N 9 12E
118 Lame Deer, U.S.A. 45 45N 106 40w
30 Lamego, Portugal 41 5N 7 52w
107 Lameque, Canada 47 45N 64 38w
99 Lameroo, Australia 35 19s 140 33E
114 Lamesa, U.S.A. 32 45N 101 57w
45 Lamia, Greece 38 55N 22 41E
73 Lamitan, Philippines 6 40N 122 10E
14 Lammermuir Hills, 55 50N 2 40w
   Scotland
118 Lamoille, U.S.A. 40 47N 115 31w
73 Lamon Bay, Phil. 14 30N 122 20E
108 Lamont, Canada 53 40N 112 50w
126 Lampa, Peru 15 10s 70 30w
71 Lampang, Thailand 18 40N 98 53E
117 Lampasas, U.S.A. 31 5N 98 10w
120 Lampazos de Naranjo, 27 2N 100 32w
   Mexico
36 Lampedusa, I., Medit. 35 36N 12 40E
13 Lampeter, U.K. 52 6N 4 6w
83 Lampione, I., Medit. 35 33N 12 20E
109 Lampman, Canada 49 25N 102 50w
26 Lamprechtshausen, 48 0N 13 0E
   Austria
72 Lampung, Indonesia 1 48s 115 0E
90 Lamu, Kenya 2 10s 40 55E
119 Lamy, U.S.A. 35 30N 105 58w
61 Lan Tsan Kiang 34 27N 79 32E
   (Mekong), Asia
66 Lanak La, Kashmir 34 27N 79 32E
73 Lanao, L., Philippines 7 52N 124 15E
73 Lanark, Canada 44 59N 76 21w
14 Lanark, Scot. 55 40N 3 48w
*14 Lanark ♦, Scot. 55 37N 3 50w
14 Lancashire ♦, Eng. 53 40N 2 30w
107 Lancaster, N.B., Can. 45 17N 66 10w
113 Lancaster, Ont., Can. 45 10N 74 30w
12 Lancaster, Eng. 54 3N 2 48w
119 Lancaster, Calif., U.S.A. 34 47N 118 8w
113 Lancaster, Ky., U.S.A. 37 40N 84 40w
113 Lancaster, N.H., U.S.A. 44 27N 71 33w
112 Lancaster, N.Y., U.S.A. 42 53N 78 43w
113 Lancaster, Pa., U.S.A. 40 4N 76 19w
115 Lancaster, S.C., U.S.A. 34 45N 80 47w
116 Lancaster, Wis., U.S.A. 42 48N 90 43w
106 Lancaster Sd., Canada 74 0N 84 0w
100 Lancefield, Australia 37 18s 144 45E
76 Lanchow, China 36 4N 103 44E
39 Lanciano, Italy 42 15N 14 22E
27 Łancut, Poland 50 10N 22 20E
88 Lándana, Angola 5 11s 12 5E
25 Landau, Germany 49 12N 8 7E
26 Landeck, Austria 47 9N 10 34E
118 Lander, U.S.A. 42 50N 108 49w
18 Landerneau, France 48 28N 4 17w
49 Landeryd, Sweden 57 7N 13 15E
20 Landes ♦, France 43 57N 0 48w
32 Landete, Spain 39 56N 1 25w
66 Landi Kotal, Pakistan 34 7N 71 6E
49 Landivisiau, France 48 31N 4 6w
25 Landquart, Switzerland 46 58N 9 32E
19 Landrecies, France 50 7N 3 40E
13 Land's End, Eng. 50 4N 5 43w
49 Landsbro, Sweden 57 24N 14 56E
24 Landshut, W. Ger. 48 31N 12 10E
49 Landskrona, Sweden 56 53N 12 50E
49 Landvetter, Sweden 57 41N 12 17E
49 Lane, Sweden 58 25N 12 3E

MAP

113 Lanesboro, U.S.A. 41 57N 75 34w
115 Lanett, U.S.A. 33 0N 85 15w
72 Lang Suan, Thailand 9 57N 99 4E
56 Langaa, Den. 56 23N 9 51E
44 Lángadhás, Greece 40 46N 23 2E
37 Langádhia, Greece 37 43N 22 1E
48 Langan, Sweden 63 20N 14 30E
69 Langchen Khambah 31 25N 80 0E
   (Sutlej), Tibet
77 Langchung (Paoning), 31 30N 106 0E
   China
116 Langdon, U.S.A. 48 47N 98 24w
20 Langeac, France 45 7N 3 29E
86 Langeb, R., Sudan 17 28N 36 50E
92 Langeberge, C. Province, 33 55s 21 20E
   S. Africa
92 Langeberge, C. Province, 28 15s 22 33E
   S. Africa
49 Langeland, Denmark 54 56N 10 48E
54 Langelands Baelt, Den. 54 55N 10 56E
25 Langen, Germany 53 36N 8 36E
24 Langeness, Germany 54 34N 8 35E
25 Langenlois, Austria 48 29N 15 40E
26 Langensalza, Germany 51 6N 10 40E
24 Langeoog, Germany 53 44N 7 33E
49 Langeskov, Denmark 55 22N 10 35E
47 Langesund, Norway 59 0N 9 45E
76 Langfeng, China 48 4N 121 10E
49 Langhem, Sweden 57 36N 13 14E
38 Langhirano, Italy 44 39N 10 16E
57 Langholm, Scot. 55 9N 2 59w
50 Langjökull, Iceland 64 39N 20 12w
71 Langkawi I., Malaysia 6 20N 99 45E
72 Langkon, Malaysia 6 30N 116 40E
106 Langlade, Canada 48 14N 76 10w
118 Langlois, U.S.A. 42 54N 124 26w
25 Langnau, Switzerland 46 56N 7 47E
20 Langogne, France 44 43N 3 50E
20 Langon, France 44 33N 0 16w
50 Langöya, Norway 68 45N 15 10E
19 Langres, France 47 52N 5 20E
19 Langres, Plateau de, Fr. 47 45N 5 20E
72 Langsa, Indonesia 4 30N 97 57E
71 Langson, N. Vietnam 21 52N 106 42E
117 Langtry, U.S.A. 29 50N 101 33w
20 Languedoc ♦, Fr. 43 58N 3 22E
50 Langöykra, Norway 68 44N 14 45E
48 Lanna, Sweden 59 16N 14 56E
18 Lannemezan, France 43 8N 0 23E
98 Lannercost, Australia 18 35s 146 0E
18 Lannilis, France 48 35N 4 32w
18 Lannion, France 48 46N 3 29w
117 L'Annonciation, Can. 46 25N 74 55w
113 Lansdale, U.S.A. 40 14N 75 18w
100 Lansdowne, Australia 31 48s 152 30E
113 Lansdowne, Canada 44 25N 76 1w
106 Lansdowne House, Can. 52 5N 88 0w
107 L'Anse au Loup, Canada 51 32N 56 50w
108 Lansford, U.S.A. 40 48N 75 55w
114 Lansing, U.S.A. 42 47N 84 32w
21 Lanslebourg-Mont- 45 17N 6 52E
   Cenis, Fr.
67 Lantsien, China 32 4N 96 6E
73 Lantuna, Indonesia 8 19s 124 8E
124 Lanus, Argentina 34 44s 58 27w
40 Lanusei, Italy 39 53N 9 31E
80 Lanzarote, I., Islas 29 0N 13 40w
   Canarias
38 Lanzo Torinese, Italy 45 16N 7 29E
73 Lao, R., Italy 39 45N 15 45E
73 Laoag, Philippines 18 7N 120 34E
73 Laoang, Philippines 12 32N 125 8E
99 Laoha Ho, China 43 24N 120 39E
15 Laois ♦, Ireland 53 0N 7 20w
19 Laon, France 49 33N 3 35E
114 Laona, U.S.A. 45 32N 88 41w
71 Laos ■, Asia 17 45N 105 0E
125 Lapa, Brazil 25 46s 49 44w
42 Lapalisse, France 46 15N 3 44E
73 Laparan Cap, I., Phil. 6 0N 120 0E
114 Lapeer, U.S.A. 43 3N 83 20w
113 Laporte, U.S.A. 41 27N 76 30w
42 Lapovo, Yugoslavia 44 10N 21 2E
68 Lappland, Europe 68 7N 24 0E
113 Laprairie, Canada 45 25N 73 30w
124 Laprida, Argentina 37 34s 60 45w
59 Laptev Sea, U.S.S.R. 76 0N 125 0E
117 Lapush, U.S.A. 47 56N 124 33w
46 Lápusu, R., Rumania 47 25N 23 4E
82 L'Arba, Algeria 36 40N 3 9E
65 Lar, Iran 27 40N 54 14E
126 Lara ♦, Venezuela 10 10N 69 50w
84 Larabanga, Ghana 9 16N 1 56w
30 Laracha, Spain 43 15N 8 35w
82 Larache, Morocco 35 10N 6 5w
21 Laragne-Montéglin, 44 18N 5 49E
   France
116 Laramie, U.S.A. 41 15N 105 29w
116 Laramie Mts., U.S.A. 42 0N 105 30w
125 Laranjeiras do Sul, Braz. 25 23s 52 23w
73 Larantuka, Indonesia 8 5s 122 55E
73 Larap, Philippines 14 18N 122 39E
73 Larat, I., Tanimbar Is., 7 0s 132 0E
   Indonesia
19 L'Arbresle, France 45 50N 4 26E
49 Lärbro, Sweden 57 47N 18 50E
105 Larch, R., Canada 57 30N 71 0w
50 Lardal, Norway 59 25N 9 4E
91 Larde, Mozambique 16 28s 39 43E
106 Larder Lake, Canada 48 5N 79 40w
45 Lárdhos, Ákra, Greece 36 4N 28 10E
32 Laredo, Spain 43 26N 3 28w
117 Laredo, U.S.A. 27 34N 99 29w
81 Largeau (Faya), Chad 17 58N 19 6E

MAP

21 Largentière, France 44 34N 4 18E
14 Largs, Scotland 55 48N 4 51w
38 Lari, Italy 43 34N 10 35E
73 Lariang, Indonesia 1 35s 119 25E
116 Larimore, U.S.A. 47 55N 97 35w
41 Larino, Italy 41 48N 14 54E
44 Lárisa, Greece 39 38N 22 28E
45 Lárisa ♦, Greece 39 39N 22 24E
68 Larkana, Pakistan 27 32N 68 2E
64 Lárnax, Cyprus 35 0N 33 35E
15 Larne, N. Ireland 54 52N 5 50w
116 Larned, U.S.A. 38 15N 99 10w
20 Laroquebrou, France 44 58N 2 12E
96 Larrimah, Australia 15 35s 133 12E
5 Larsen Ice Shelf, Antarc. 67 0s 62 0w
85 Larteh, Ghana 5 50N 0 5w
90 Laru, Zaïre 2 54N 24 25E
47 Larvik, Norway 59 4N 10 0E
58 Laryak, U.S.S.R. 61 15N 80 0E
20 Larzac, Causse du, 44 0N 3 17E
   France
117 Las Animas, U.S.A. 38 8N 103 18w
63 Las Anod, Somali Rep. 8 26N 47 19E
33 Las Blancos, Spain 37 38N 0 49w
126 Las Bonitas, Venezuela 7 50N 65 40w
31 Las Brenãs, Arg. 27 5s 61 7w
31 Las Cabezas de San 37 0N 5 58w
   Juan, Spain
120 Las Cascadas, Panama 9 5N 79 41w
   Canal Zone
119 Las Cruces, U.S.A. 32 25N 106 50w
120 Las Delicias, Panama 9 27N 79 35w
124 Las Flores, Argentina 36 0s 59 0w
33 Las Huertas, Cabo de, 38 22N 0 24w
   Spain
63 Las Khoreh, Somali 11 4N 48 20E
   Rep.
128 Las Lajas, Argentina 38 30s 70 25w
126 Las Lajitas, Venezuela 5 55s 69 39w
126 Las Lomitas, Arg. 24 35s 60 50w
31 Las Marismas, Spain 37 5N 6 20w
126 Las Mercedes, Venezuela 9 7N 66 24w
31 Las Navas de la 37 56N 5 30w
   Concepción, Spain
31 Las Navas de Tolosa, 38 18N 3 38w
   Spain
124 Las Palmas, Argentina 27 8s 58 45w
80 Las Palmas, Can. Is. 28 10N 15 28w
80 Las Palmas ♦, Spain 28 10N 15 28w
128 Las Plumas, Argentina 43 40s 67 15w
124 Las Rosas, Argentina 32 30s 61 40w
121 Las Tablas, Panama 7 49N 80 14w
120 Las Tres Marias, Is., 20 12N 106 30w
   Mexico
124 Las Varillas, Argentina 32 0s 62 50w
119 Las Vegas, Nev., U.S.A. 36 10N 115 5w
119 Las Vegas, N.M., U.S.A. 35 50N 105 10w
125 Lascano, Uruguay 33 35s 54 18w
20 Lascaux, France 45 3N 1 10E
113 Lashburn, Canada 53 10N 109 40w
67 Lashio, Burma 23 0N 98 0E
68 Lashkar, India 26 10N 78 10E
45 Lasithi ♦, Greece 35 5N 25 50E
27 Lask, Poland 51 34N 19 8E
39 Laško, Yugoslavia 46 10N 15 16E
18 Lassay, France 48 27N 0 30w
118 Lassen, Pk., U.S.A. 40 20N 121 0w
88 Lastoursville, Gabon 0 55s 12 38E
39 Lastovo, Y.-slavia 42 46N 16 55E
39 Lastovo, I., Y.-slav. 42 46N 16 55E
39 Lastovski Kanal, Y.-slav. 42 50N 17 0E
126 Latacunga, Ecuador 0 50s 78 35w
64 Latakia = Al Ladhiqiya, 35 30N 35 45E
   Syria
106 Latchford, Canada 47 20N 79 50w
41 Laterza, Italy 40 38N 16 47E
24 Lathen, Germany 52 51N 7 21E
40 Latiano, Italy 40 33N 17 43E
40 Latina, Italy 41 26N 12 53E
39 Latisana, Italy 45 47N 13 1E
39 Latium = Lazio, Italy 42 10N 12 30E
27 Latorica, R., Cz. 48 31N 22 0E
99 Latrobe, Tas., Austral. 41 14s 146 30E
100 Latrobe, Vic., Australia 38 8s 146 44E
112 Latrobe, U.S.A. 40 19N 79 21w
41 Latrónico, Italy 40 5N 16 0E
31 Latrun, Jordan 31 50N 34 58E
70 Latur, India 18 25N 76 40E
101 Lau (Eastern) Group, 17 0s 178 30w
   Fiji Is.
24 Lauchhammer, Germany 51 35N 13 40E
47 Lauenal, Norway 58 15N 7 30E
24 Lauenburg, Germany 53 23N 10 33E
50 Laugarbakki, Iceland 65 20N 20 55w
32 Laujar, Spain 37 0N 2 54w
99 Launceston, Australia 41 24s 147 8E
13 Launceston, Eng. 50 38N 4 21w
15 Laune, R., Ireland 52 5N 9 40w
71 Laungbon Bok, Burma 13 50N 97 54E
25 Laupheim, Germany 48 13N 9 53E
99 Launa, Australia 23 52s 144 32E
14 Laurana di Borrello, It. 38 28N 16 5E
117 Laurel, Miss., U.S.A. 31 50N 89 0w
118 Laurel, Mont., U.S.A. 45 46N 108 49w
14 Laurencekirk, Scot. 56 50N 2 30w
115 Laurens, U.S.A. 34 32N 82 2w
107 Laurentian Plat., Can. 51 30N 65 0w
41 Lauria, Italy 40 3N 15 50E
5 Laurie I., Antarctica 60 0s 46 0w
106 Laurie L., Canada 56 35N 101 50w
113 Laurinburg, U.S.A. 34 50N 79 25w
114 Laurium, U.S.A. 47 31N 88 36w
25 Lausanne, Switzerland 46 32N 6 38E
72 Laut, I., Indonesia 3 40s 116 10E
72 Laut, Kepulauan, 4 45N 108 0E
   Indonesia

* Incorporated within the
   region of Strathclyde
† Renamed Patan

* Incorporated within the
   new Northern Province

41

MAP
72 Laut Ketjil, Kepulauan, 4 45s 115 40E
  Indonesia
24 Lauterbach, Germany 50 39N 9 23E
25 Lauterecken, Germany 49 38N 7 35E
101 Lautoka, Fiji Is. 17 37s 177 27E
107 Lauzon, Canada 46 48N 71 4w
118 Lava Hot Springs, 42 38N 112 1w
  U.S.A.
30 Lavadores, Spain 42 14N 8 41w
38 Lavagna, Italy 44 18N 9 22E
18 Laval, France 48 4N 0 48w
124 Lavalle, Argentina 32 45s 68 30w
44 Lávara, Greece 41 19N 26 22E
20 Lavardac, France 44 12N 0 20E
21 Lavaur, France 43 42N 1 49E
20 Lavaveix, France 46 5N 2 8E
20 Lavelanet, France 42 57N 1 51E
41 Lavello, Italy 41 4N 15 47E
106 Laverendrye Prov. Park, 46 15N 17 15w
  Canada
117 Laverne, U.S.A. 36 43N 99 58w
96 Laverton, Australia 28 44s 122 29E
62 Lavi, Israel 32 47N 35 25E
47 Lavik, Norway 61 6N 5 25E
45 Lávkos, Greece 39 9N 23 14E
30 Lavos, Portugal 40 6N 8 49w
31 Lavre, Portugal 38 46N 8 22w
59 Lavrentiya, U.S.S.R. 65 35N 171 0w
45 Lávrion, Greece 37 40N 24 4E
93 Lavumisa, Swaziland 27 20s 31 55E
72 Lawas, Malaysia 4 55N 115 40E
73 Lawele, Indonesia 5 16s 123 3E
98 Lawn Hill, Australia 18 36s 138 33E
67 Lawng Pit, Burma 25 46N 98 35E
84 Lawra, Ghana 10 39N 2 51w
101 Lawrence, New Zealand 45 55s 169 41E
116 Lawrence, Kans., U.S.A. 39 0N 95 10w
113 Lawrence, Mass., U.S.A. 42 40N 71 9w
114 Lawrenceburg, Indiana, 39 5N 84 50w
  U.S.A.
115 Lawrenceburg, Tenn., 35 12N 87 19w
  U.S.A.
115 Lawrenceville, U.S.A. 33 55N 83 59w
117 Lawton, U.S.A. 34 33N 98 25w
73 Lawu Mt., Indonesia 7 40s 111 13E
48 Laxa, Sweden 59 0N 14 37E
14 Laxford, L., Scot. 58 25N 5 10w
70 Laxmeshwar, India 15 9N 75 28E
118 Laytonville, U.S.A. 39 44N 123 29w
42 Lazarevac, Yugoslavia 44 23N 20 17E
39 Lazio ♦, It. 42 0N 12 30E
28 Łazy, Poland 50 27N 19 24E
20 Le Bacarès, France 43 47N 3 3E
21 Le Beausset, France 43 10N 5 46E
20 Le Blanc, France 46 37N 1 3E
20 Le Bleymard, France 44 30N 3 42E
20 Le Bourgneuf, France 48 10N 0 59w
20 Le Bouscat, France 44 53N 0 32w
107 Le Bouthillier, Canada 47 47N 64 55w
20 Le Bugue, France 44 55N 0 56E
20 Le Canourgue, France 44 26N 3 13E
19 Le Cateau, France 50 6N 3 30E
21 Le Chámbon, France 45 35N 4 26E
21 Le Chambon-
  Feugerolles, France 45 24N 4 18E
20 Le Château, France 45 52N 1 12w
20 Le Châtelet, Cher, Fr. 46 40N 2 20E
19 Le Châtelet, Seine et 48 30N 2 47E
  Marne, France
19 Le Chesne, France 49 30N 4 45E
21 Le Cheylard, France 44 55N 4 25E
18 Le Conquet, France 48 21N 4 46w
18 Le Creusot, France 46 50N 4 24E
18 Le Croisic, France 47 18N 2 30w
20 Le Donjon, France 46 22N 3 48E
20 Le Dorat, France 46 14N 1 5E
121 Le François, Martinique 14 38N 60 57w
18 Le Grand Fougeray, Fr. 47 44N 1 43w
18 Le Grand Pressigny, Fr. 46 55N 0 48E
18 Le Havre, France 49 30N 0 5E
21 Le Lavandou, France 43 8N 6 22E
25 Le Léman, Switzerland 46 30N 6 30E
18 Le Lion d'Angers, France 47 38N 0 42w
25 Le Locle, Switzerland 47 3N 6 44E
17 Le Louroux Béconnais, 47 30N 0 55w
  France
21 Le Luc, France 43 23N 6 21E
40 Le Madonie, Mts., Italy 37 50N 13 50E
18 Le Mans, France 48 0N 0 10E
91 Le Marinel, Congo 10 25s 25 17E
116 Le Mars, U.S.A. 43 0N 96 0w
107 Le Mayne, L., Canada 57 5N 68 30w
18 Le Merlerault, France 48 41N 0 16E
20 Le Monastier, France 44 57N 4 0E
21 Le Monétier-les-Bains, 44 58N 6 30E
  France
20 Le Mont-Dore, France 45 35N 2 50E
121 Le Moule, Guadeloupe 16 20N 61 22w
18 Le Muy, France 43 28N 6 34E
18 Le Palais, France 47 21N 3 10w
20 Le Perthus, France 42 30N 2 53E
18 Le Petit-Quevilly, Fr. 49 26N 1 0E
20 Le Puy, France 45 3N 3 52E
117 Le Roy, U.S.A. 38 8N 95 35w
20 Le Rozier, France 44 13N 3 12E
116 Le Sueur, U.S.A. 44 35N 93 52w
20 Le Teich, France 44 38N 0 59w
21 Le Teil, France 44 33N 4 41E
18 Le Teilleul, France 48 31N 0 52w
19 Le Thillot, France 47 52N 6 55E
18 Le Touquet, France 50 3N 1 36E
18 Le Tréport, France 50 3N 1 20E
18 Le Valdahon, France 47 8N 6 20E
20 Le Verdon, France 45 32N 1 5w
20 Le Vigan, France 44 0N 3 36E
13 Lea, R., Eng. 51 40N 0 3w
116 Lead, U.S.A. 44 20N 103 40w
109 Leader, Canada 50 50N 109 30w
14 Leadhills, Scot. 55 25N 3 47w
100 Leadville, Australia 32 1N 149 38E

MAP
119 Leadville, U.S.A. 39 17N 106 23w
105 Leaf, R., Canada 58 15N 71 0w
117 Leaf, R., U.S.A. 31 45N 89 20w
117 Leakey, U.S.A. 29 45N 99 45w
115 Leaksville, U.S.A. 36 30N 79 49w
89 Lealui, Zambia 15 10s 23 2E
106 Leamington, Canada 42 10N 82 30w
94 Leamington, New 37 55s 175 29E
  Zealand
13 Leamington, Eng. 52 18N 1 32w
118 Leamington, U.S.A. 39 37N 112 17w
125 Leandro Norte Alem, 27 34s 55 15w
  Arg.
46 Leaoto, Mt., Rumania 45 20N 25 20E
96 Learmonth, Australia 22 40s 114 10E
109 Leask, Canada 53 5N 106 45w
116 Leavenworth, Mo., USA 39 25N 95 0w
118 Leavenworth, Wash., 47 44N 120 37w
  U.S.A.
28 Łeba, Poland 54 45N 17 32E
73 Lebak, Philippines 6 32N 124 5E
42 Lebane, Yugoslavia 42 56N 21 44E
64 Lebanon ■, Asia 34 0N 36 0E
114 Lebanon, Ind., U.S.A. 40 3N 86 55w
116 Lebanon, Kans., U.S.A. 39 50N 98 35w
114 Lebanon, Ky., U.S.A. 37 35N 85 15w
116 Lebanon, Mo., U.S.A. 37 40N 92 40w
113 Lebanon, N.H., U.S.A. 43 38N 72 15w
114 Lebanon, Oreg., U.S.A. 44 31N 122 57w
113 Lebanon, Pa., U.S.A. 40 20N 76 28w
115 Lebanon, Tenn., U.S.A. 36 15N 86 20w
119 Lebec, U.S.A. 34 36N 118 59w
54 Lebedin, U.S.S.R. 50 35N 34 30E
55 Lebedyan, U.S.S.R. 53 0N 39 10E
93 Lebomboberge, S. Afr. 24 30s 32 0E
28 Łebork, Poland 54 33N 17 46E
31 Lebrija, Spain 36 53N 6 5w
124 Lebú, Chile 37 40s 73 47w
41 Lecce, Italy 40 20N 18 10E
38 Lecco, Italy 45 50N 9 27E
38 Lecco, L. di., Italy 45 51N 9 22E
32 Lécera, Spain 41 13N 0 43w
26 Lech, Austria 47 13N 10 9E
26 Lech, R., Germany 47 19N 10 7E
26 Lechtaler Alpen, Aust. 47 15N 10 30E
20 Lectoure, France 43 56N 0 38E
28 Łęczyca, Poland 52 5N 19 45E
26 Ledbury, Eng. 52 3N 2 25w
26 Ledec, Czechoslovakia 49 41N 15 18E
36 Ledesma, Spain 41 6N 5 59w
108 Leduc, Canada 53 20N 113 30w
28 Ledyczek, Poland 53 33N 16 59E
113 Lee, Mass., U.S.A. 42 17N 73 18w
118 Lee, Nev., U.S.A. 40 35N 115 36w
15 Lee, R., Ireland 51 51N 9 2w
116 Leech L., U.S.A. 47 15N 94 23w
117 Leedey, U.S.A. 35 53N 99 24w
12 Leeds, Eng. 53 48N 1 34w
115 Leeds, U.S.A. 33 32N 86 30w
12 Leek, England 53 7N 2 2w
24 Leer, Germany 53 13N 7 29E
115 Leesburg, U.S.A. 28 47N 81 52w
117 Leesville, U.S.A. 31 12N 93 15w
100 Leeton, Australia 34 23s 146 23E
112 Leetonia, U.S.A. 40 53N 80 45w
16 Leeuwarden, Neth. 53 15N 5 48E
96 Leeuwin, C., Australia 34 20s 115 9E
121 Leeward Is., W. Indies 16 30N 63 30w
117 Lefors, U.S.A. 35 30N 100 50w
96 Lefroy, L., Australia 31 21s 121 40E
108 Legal, Canada 53 55N 113 45w
73 Legazpi, Philippines 13 10N 123 45E
38 Leghorn = Livorno, 43 32N 10 18E
  Italy
91 Legion, Rhodesia 21 25s 28 30E
28 Legionowo, Poland 52 25N 20 50E
39 Legnago, Italy 45 10N 11 19E
38 Legnano, Italy 45 35s 8 55E
28 Legnica, Poland 51 12N 16 10E
42 Legrad, Yugoslavia 46 17N 16 51E
99 Legume, Australia 28 20s 152 12E
66 Leh, India 34 15N 77 35E
118 Lehi, U.S.A. 40 20N 112 0w
113 Lehighton, U.S.A. 40 50N 75 44w
46 Lehliu, Rumania 44 29N 26 20E
24 Lehrte, Germany 52 22N 9 58E
92 Lehututu, Botswana 23 54s 21 55E
68 Leiah, Pakistan 30 58N 70 58E
26 Leibnitz, Austria 46 47N 15 34E
12 Leicester ♦, England 52 39N 1 9w
13 Leicester ♦, England 52 40N 1 10w
98 Leichhardt Ra., Austral. 20 46s 147 40E
98 Leichhardt, R., Australia 17 50s 139 49E
72 Leichow = Haihang, 20 55N 110 3E
  China
72 Leichow Pantao, China 20 30N 110 0E
16 Leiden, Netherlands 52 9N 4 30E
16 Leie, R., Belgium 51 2N 3 45E
100 Leigh, R., Australia 37 50s 144 0E
99 Leigh Creek, Australia 30 28s 138 24E
15 Leinster, Mt., Ireland 52 38N 6 47w
24 Leipzig, Germany 51 20N 12 23E
24 Leipzig ♦, E. Ger. 51 20N 12 30E
31 Leiria, Portugal 39 46N 8 53w
31 Leiria ♦, Portugal 39 46N 8 53w
77 Leishan, China 25 55N 108 15E
14 Leith, Scotland 55 59N 3 10w
14 Leith Hill, Eng. 51 10N 0 23w
27 Leitha, R., Aust.-Hung. 47 57N 17 5E
15 Leitrim, Ireland 54 0N 8 5w
15 Leitrim ♦, Ire. 54 8N 8 0w
77 Leiyang, China 26 74N 112 50E
44 Lekáni, Greece 41 10N 24 35E
44 Lekhainá, Greece 37 57N 21 16E
35 Leknice, Poland 51 34N 14 45E
73 Leksula, Indonesia 3 46s 126 31E
117 Leland, U.S.A. 33 25N 90 35w
128 Leleque, Argentina 42 15s 71 0w
16 Lelystad, Netherlands 52 30N 5 25E

MAP
85 Lema, Nigeria 12 58N 4 13E
87 Lemagrut, bg., Ethiopia 3 9s 35 22E
25 Léman, Lac, Switzerland 46 26N 6 30E
90 Lemera, Zaïre 3 0s 28 55E
73 Lemery, Philippines 13 58N 120 56E
64 Lemesòs, Cyprus 34 42N 33 1E
24 Lemgo, Germany 52 2N 8 52E
118 Lemhi Ra., U.S.A. 44 30N 113 30w
116 Lemmon, U.S.A. 45 59N 102 10w
119 Lemoore, U.S.A. 36 23N 119 54w
45 Lempdes, France 45 22N 3 17E
49 Lemvig, Denmark 56 33N 8 20E
59 Lena, R., U.S.S.R. 64 30N 127 0E
18 Lencloître, France 46 50N 0 20E
39 Lendinara, Italy 45 4N 11 37E
24 Lengerich, Germany 52 12N 7 50E
71 Lenggong, Malaysia 5 17N 100 57E
71 Lengyeltóti, Hungary 46 40N 17 40E
49 Lenhovda, Sweden 57 0N 15 16E
87 Lenia, Ethiopia 4 10N 37 25E
57 Lenin, U.S.S.R. 48 20N 40 56E
58 Leninabad, U.S.S.R. 40 10N 69 40E
57 Leninakan, U.S.S.R. 41 0N 42 50E
54 Leningrad, U.S.S.R. 59 55N 30 20E
58 Leninogorsk, U.S.S.R. 50 20N 83 30E
58 Leninsk, U.S.S.R. 56 38N 46 10E
58 Leninsk-Kuznetskiy, 55 10N 86 10E
  U.S.S.R.
55 Leninskaya, U.S.S.R. 56 7N 44 29E
55 Leninskoye, R.S.F.S.R., 58 23N 47 3E
  U.S.S.R.
59 Leninskoye, R.S.F.S.R., 47 56N 132 38E
  U.S.S.R.
25 Lenk, Switzerland 46 27N 7 28E
58 Lenkoran, U.S.S.R. 39 45N 48 50E
67 Lenmalu, Indonesia 1 58s 130 0E
113 Lennoxville, Canada 45 23N 71 53w
38 Leno, Italy 45 24N 10 14E
115 Lenoir, U.S.A. 35 55N 81 36w
115 Lenoir City, U.S.A. 35 40N 84 20w
113 Lenox, U.S.A. 39 39N 100 1w
19 Lens, France 50 26N 2 50E
59 Lensk (Mukhtuya), 60 48N 114 55E
  U.S.S.R.
56 Lentini, Italy 45 3N 34 1E
41 Lentini, Italy 37 18N 15 0E
24 Lenzen, Germany 53 6N 11 26E
84 Léo, Upper Volta 11 3s 2 2w
26 Leoben, Austria 47 22N 15 5E
116 Leola, U.S.A. 45 47N 98 58w
13 Leominster, Eng. 52 15N 2 43w
116 Leominster, U.S.A. 42 32N 71 45w
120 León, Mexico 21 7N 101 30w
121 León, Nicaragua 12 20N 86 51w
30 León, Spain 42 38N 5 34w
30 León ♦, Spain 42 40N 5 55w
30 León, Montañas de, 42 30N 6 18w
  Spain
96 Leonara, Australia 28 47s 121 15E
114 Leonardtown, U.S.A. 38 19N 76 39w
41 Leonforte, Italy 37 39N 14 22E
100 Leongatha, Australia 38 30s 145 58E
45 Leonidhion, Greece 37 9N 22 52E
88 Léopold II, Lac, Zaïre 2 0s 18 0E
16 Leopoldina, Brazil 21 28s 42 40w
16 Leopoldsburg, Belgium 51 7N 5 13E
88 Léopoldville = 4 20s 15 15E
  Kinshasa, Zaïre
73 Leoti, Indonesia 38 31N 101 19w
109 Leoville, Canada 53 39N 107 33w
92 Lépa, L. do, Angola 17 0s 19 0E
31 Lepe, Spain 37 15N 7 12w
54 Lepel, U.S.S.R. 54 50N 28 40E
59 Lepikha, U.S.S.R. 64 45N 125 55E
92 Lépo, L. do, Angola 17 0s 19 0E
38 Lepontine Alps, Italy 46 22N 8 27E
71 Lepsény, Hungary 47 0N 18 15E
83 Leptis Magna, Libya 32 40N 14 12E
32 Lequeitio, Spain 43 20N 2 32w
48 Lerbäck, Sweden 58 56N 15 2E
40 Lercara Friddi, It. 37 42N 13 36E
85 Léré, Chad 9 39N 14 13E
93 Leribe, Lesotho 28 51s 28 3E
38 Lérici, Italy 44 4N 9 48E
32 Lérida, Spain 41 37N 0 39E
32 Lérida ♦, Spain 42 6N 1 0E
30 Lerma, Spain 42 0N 3 45w
45 Léros, I., Greece 37 10N 26 50E
19 Lérouville, France 48 50N 5 30E
14 Lerwick, Scotland 60 10N 1 10w
46 Les, Rumania 46 58N 21 50E
18 Les Abrets, France 45 32N 5 35E
18 Les Andelys, France 49 15N 1 25E
18 Les Baux, France 43 45N 4 51E
121 Les Cayes, Haiti 18 15N 73 46w
21 Les Echelles, France 45 27N 5 45E
18 Les Essarts, France 46 47N 1 12w
107 Les Etroits, Canada 47 24N 68 54w
18 Les Herbiers, France 46 52N 1 0w
20 Les Landes, Fr. 44 20N 1 0w
18 Les Ponts-de-Cé, France 47 25N 0 30w
18 Les Sables-D'Olonne, Fr. 46 30N 1 45w
21 Les Saintes Maries, Fr. 43 26N 4 9E
21 Les Vans, France 44 26N 4 9E
45 Lesbos, I. = Lésvos, 39 0N 26 20E
  Greece
39 Lésina, L. di, Italy 41 45N 15 25E
47 Lesja, Norway 62 12N 8 34E
47 Lesjaverk, Norway 62 12N 8 34E
5 Leskov, I., Falkland Is. 56 0s 28 0w
  Dependencies
44 Leskovic, Albania 40 10N 20 34E
42 Leskovika, Y.-slavia 43 0N 21 58E
117 Leslie, U.S.A. 35 50N 92 35w
28 Lesna, Poland 51 0N 15 15E
16 Lesneven, France 48 35N 4 20w

MAP
44 Lesniča, Yugoslavia 44 39N 19 20E
*52 Lesnoi, U.S.S.R. 66 50N 34 20E
54 Lesnoye, U.S.S.R. 58 15N 35 31E
93 Lesotho ■, Africa 29 40s 28 0E
59 Lesozavodsk, U.S.S.R. 45 30N 133 20E
20 Lesparre-Médoc, France 45 18N 0 57w
18 Lessay, France 49 14N 1 30w
16 Lesse, R., Belgium 50 15N 4 54E
121 Lesser Antilles, W. Ind. 12 30N 61 0w
108 Lesser Slave L., Can. 55 30N 115 10w
16 Lessines, Belgium 50 42N 3 50E
109 Lestock, Canada 51 25N 104 0w
92 Letlhakane, Botswana 17 58s 25 12E
45 Lésvos, I., Greece 39 0N 26 20E
28 Leszno, Poland 51 50N 16 30E
13 Letchworth, Eng. 51 58N 0 13w
46 Letea, Ostrov, Rum. 45 18N 29 20E
100 Lethbridge, Australia 37 58s 144 6E
108 Lethbridge, Canada 49 45N 112 45w
73 Leti, Indonesia 8 10s 127 40E
73 Leti, Kepulauan, 8 10s 128 0E
  Indonesia
92 Letiahau, R., Botswana 21 40s 23 30E
126 Leticia, Colombia 4 0s 70 0w
67 Letpadan, Burma 17 45N 96 0E
67 Letpan, Burma 19 28N 93 52E
71 Letsôk-aw-Kyun (Domel 11 30N 98 25E
  I.), Burma
100 Lette, Austral. 34 3s 143 4E
15 Letterkenny, Ireland 54 57N 7 42w
20 Leucate, France 42 56N 3 3E
25 Leuk, Switzerland 46 19N 7 37E
72 Leuser, G., Indonesia 4 0N 96 51E
16 Leutkirch, Germany 47 49N 10 1E
16 Leuven (Louvain), Belg. 50 52N 4 42E
16 Leuze, Hainaut, Belg. 50 36N 3 37E
16 Leuze, Namur, Belg. 50 33N 4 54E
55 Lev Tolstoy, U.S.S.R. 53 13N 39 29E
45 Levádhia, Greece 38 27N 22 54E
118 Levan, U.S.A. 39 37N 111 32w
44 Levan-Samari, Albania 40 40N 19 28E
50 Levanger, Norway 63 45N 11 19E
43 Levani, Bulgaria 43 8N 24 42E
38 Levanto, Italy 44 10N 9 37E
40 Levanzo, I., Italy 38 0N 12 19E
117 Levelland, U.S.A. 33 38N 102 17w
14 Leven, Scotland 56 12N 3 0w
93 Leven, Banc du, Malag. 12 30s 47 45E
14 Leven, L., Scot. 56 12N 3 22w
21 Levens, France 43 50N 7 12E
96 Leveque C., Australia 16 20s 123 0E
41 Leverano, Italy 40 16N 18 0E
24 Leverkusen, Germany 51 2N 6 59E
19 Levet, France 46 56N 2 22E
27 Levice, Czechoslovakia 48 13N 18 35E
5 Levick, Mt., Antarctica 75 0s 164 0E
39 Levico, Italy 46 0N 11 18E
19 Levier, France 46 58N 6 8E
101 Levin, New Zealand 40 37s 175 18E
107 Lévis, Canada 46 48N 71 9w
45 Levitha, I., Greece 37 0N 26 28E
113 Levittown, U.S.A. 40 10N 74 51w
43 Levka, Bulgaria 41 52N 26 15E
45 Lévka, Mt., Gr. 35 18N 24 3E
45 Levkás, Greece 38 48N 20 43E
45 Levkás, I., Greece 38 40N 20 43E
64 Levkôsia, Cyprus 35 10N 33 25E
27 Levoča, Czechoslovakia 48 59N 20 35E
19 Levroux, France 47 0N 1 38E
43 Levski, Bulgaria 43 21N 25 10E
43 Levskigrad, Bulgaria 42 38N 24 47E
116 Lewellen, U.S.A. 41 22N 102 5w
13 Lewes, England 50 53N 0 2E
114 Lewes, U.S.A. 38 45N 75 8w
104 Lewes, L., Canada 60 30N 134 20w
28 Lewin Brzeski, Poland 50 45N 17 37E
14 Lewis, Butt of, Scotland 58 30N 6 12w
14 Lewis, I., Scot. 58 10N 6 40w
118 Lewis, R., U.S.A. 46 0N 113 15w
112 Lewisburg, Pa., U.S.A. 50 57N 76 57w
115 Lewisburg, Tenn., USA 35 29N 86 46w
107 Lewisporte, Canada 49 15N 55 3w
118 Lewiston, Idaho, U.S.A. 46 58N 117 0w
118 Lewiston, Utah, U.S.A. 42 0N 111 56w
118 Lewistown, Mont., USA 47 0N 109 25w
112 Lewistown, Pa., U.S.A. 40 37N 77 33w
114 Lexington, Ill., U.S.A. 40 37N 88 47w
114 Lexington, Ky., U.S.A. 38 6N 84 30w
115 Lexington, Miss., U.S.A. 33 8N 90 2w
116 Lexington, Mo., U.S.A. 39 7N 93 55w
115 Lexington, N.C., U.S.A. 35 50N 80 13w
116 Lexington, Nebr., U.S.A. 40 48N 99 45w
115 Lexington, Ohio, U.S.A. 40 39N 82 35w
114 Lexington, Oreg., 45 29N 119 46w
  U.S.A.
115 Lexington, Tenn., USA 35 38N 88 25w
20 Lezay, France 46 17N 0 0E
44 Lezha, Albania 41 47N 19 42E
20 Lézignan-Corbières, Fr. 43 13N 2 43E
20 Lezoux, France 45 49N 3 21E
54 Lgov, U.S.S.R. 51 42N 35 10E
67 Lhariguo, China 30 39N 83 4E
75 Lhasa, China 29 50N 91 3E
75 Lhatse Dzong, China 29 10N 87 45E
72 Lhokseumawe, Indon. 5 20N 97 10E
19 L'Hospitalet, France 44 23N 1 23E
67 Lhuntse Dzong, China 27 39N 91 10E
50 Li, Finland 65 20N 25 20E
45 Liádhoi, I., Greece 36 50N 26 11E
72 Liang Liang, Philippines 5 58N 121 30E
72 Liangpran, Gunong, 1 0N 114 23E
  Indon.
76 Liao Ho, R., China 41 0N 121 55E
76 Liaochung, China 41 35N 122 45E
76 Liaoning ♦, China 41 40N 122 30E

MAP
76 Liaotung, China 40 10N 123 0E
76 Liaotung Wan, China 40 0N 120 45E
76 Liaoyang, China 41 15N 123 10E
76 Liaoyuan, China 42 55N 125 10E
44 Liapádhes, Greece 39 42N 19 40E
108 Liard, R., Canada 61 20N 122 30w
54 Libau = Liepaja, 56 30N 21 0E
  U.S.S.R.
118 Libby, U.S.A. 48 20N 115 10w
88 Libenge, Zaïre 3 40N 18 55E
117 Liberal, Kans., U.S.A. 37 4N 101 0w
117 Liberal, Mo., U.S.A. 37 35N 94 30w
26 Liberec, Czechoslovakia 50 47N 15 7E
121 Liberia, Costa Rica 10 40N 85 30w
84 Liberia ■, West Africa 6 30N 9 30w
126 Libertad, Venezuela 8 20N 69 37w
116 Liberty, Mo., U.S.A. 39 15N 94 24w
113 Liberty, N.Y., U.S.A. 41 48N 74 45w
117 Liberty, Tex., U.S.A. 30 5N 94 50w
27 Libiaz, Poland 50 7N 19 21E
78 Libïya, Sahrâ', N. Africa 27 35N 25 0E
44 Libohava, Albania 40 3N 20 10E
20 Libourne, France 44 55N 0 14w
16 Libramont, Belgium 49 55N 5 23E
44 Librazhdi, Albania 41 12N 20 22E
88 Libreville, Gabon 0 25N 9 26E
81 Libya ■, N. Africa 28 30N 17 30E
86 Libyan Plateau = 30 40N 26 30E
  Ed-Déffa, Egypt
124 Licantén, Chile 34 55s 72 0w
38 Licata, Italy 37 6N 13 55E
13 Lichfield, Eng. 52 40N 1 50w
92 Lichtenburg, S. Africa 26 8s 26 8E
25 Lichtenfels, Germany 50 7N 11 4E
41 Licosa, Punta, Italy 40 15N 14 53E
119 Lida, U.S.A. 37 30N 117 30w
54 Lida, U.S.S.R. 53 53N 25 15E
49 Lidhult, Sweden 56 50N 13 27E
49 Lidingö, Sweden 59 22N 18 8E
48 Lidköping, Sweden 58 31N 13 14E
85 Lido, Niger 12 54N -3 44E
28 Lido di Óstia, Italy 41 44N 12 14E
28 Lidzbark, Poland 53 15N 194 9E
54 Lidzbark Warminski, 54 7N 20 34E
  Poland
24 Liebenwalde, Germany 52 51N 13 23E
24 Lieberose, Germany 51 59N 14 18E
42 Liebling, Rumania 45 36N 21 20E
25 Liechtenstein ■, Europe 47 8N 9 35E
16 Liège, Belgium 50 38N 5 35E
16 Liège ♦, Belgium 50 32N 5 35E
28 Liegnitz = Legnica, 51 12N 16 10E
  Poland
90 Lienart, Zaïre 3 3N 25 31E
90 Lienartville, Zaïre 3 3N 25 31E
77 Lienhua, China 26 58N 113 59E
77 Lienyang, China 26 11N 119 30E
26 Lienz, Austria 46 50N 12 46E
54 Liepaja, U.S.S.R. 56 30N 21 0E
16 Lier, Belgium 51 7N 4 34E
76 Lieshankwan, China 40 56N 124 51E
46 Liesta, Rumania 45 38N 27 34E
19 Lieuvin, France 50 24N 2 47E
106 Lievre, R., Canada 45 40N 75 40w
26 Liezen, Austria 47 34N 14 15E
15 Liffey, R., Ireland 53 21N 6 20w
15 Lifford, Ireland 54 50N 7 30w
18 Liffré, Fr. 48 12N 1 30w
47 Lifjell, Norway 59 27N 8 45E
99 Lightning Ridge, 29 22s 148 0E
  Australia
16 Lier, Belgium 51 7N 4 34E
39 Lignano, Italy 45 42N 13 8E
19 Ligny-er-Barrois, Fr. 48 36N 5 20E
19 Ligny-le-Châtel, France 47 54N 3 45E
20 Ligueglione, France 37 37N 23 2E
38 Liguria ♦, Italy 44 30N 9 0E
38 Ligurian Sea, Italy 43 20N 9 0E
98 Lihir Group, Terr. of 3 0s 152 35E
  New Guin.
110 Lihue, Hawaii 21 59N 159 24w
67 Lihwa, China 30 4N 100 18E
91 Likasi, Zaïre 10 55s 26 48E
91 Likati, Zaïre 3 20N 24 0E
54 Likhoslavl, U.S.S.R. 57 12N 35 30E
57 Likhovski, U.S.S.R. 48 10N 40 10E
75 Likiang, China 26 50N 100 15E
91 Likoma I., Malawi 12 3s 34 45E
91 Likumburu, Tanzania 9 43s 35 8E
77 Liling, China 27 47N 113 30E
19 Lille, France 50 38N 3 3E
49 Lille Baelt, Denmark 55 30N 9 45E
18 Lillebonne, France 49 30N 0 32E
47 Lillehammer, Norway 61 8N 10 30E
19 Lillers, France 50 35N 2 28E
47 Lillesand, Norway 58 15N 8 23E
47 Lillestrøm, Norway 59 58N 11 5E
32 Lillo, Spain 39 45N 3 20w
91 Lilongwe, Malawi 14 0s 33 48E
73 Liloy, Philippines 8 4N 122 39E
100 Lilydale, Australia 37 45s 145 29E
126 Lima, Indonesia 3 37s 128 4E
73 Lima, Indonesia 3 37s 128 4E
126 Lima, Peru 12 0s 77 0w
48 Lima, Sweden 60 55N 13 20E
118 Lima, Mont., U.S.A. 44 41N 112 38w
114 Lima, Ohio, U.S.A. 40 42N 84 5w
30 Lima, R., Portugal 41 50N 8 18w
113 Limages, Canada 45 20N 75 16w
85 Liman Katagum, Nigeria 10 9N 9 49E
27 Limanowa, Poland 49 42N 20 22E
64 Limassol = Lemesós, 34 42N 33 1E
  Cyprus
124 Limay, R., Argentina 39 40s 69 45w
124 Limay Mahuida, Arg. 37 10s 66 45w
72 Limbang, Brunei 4 42N 115 6E
38 Limbara Monti, Italy 40 50N 9 8E
68 Limbdi, India 22 34N 71 51E
16 Limbourg ♦, Belg. 51 2N 5 25E

* Renamed L. Mai-Ndombe   * Renamed Umba

Limbri INDEX Los Muertos, Punta de

MAP
99 Limbri, Australia 31 3S 151 5E
25 Limburg, Germany 50 22N 8 4E
16 Limburg ♦, Neth. 51 20N 5 55E
48 Limedsforsen, Sweden 60 52N 13 25E
125 Limeira, Brazil 22 35S 47 28W
44 Limenária, Greece 40 38N 24 32E
15 Limerick, Ireland 52 40N 8 38W
15 Limerick ♦, Ireland 52 30N 8 50W
112 Limestone, U.S.A. 42 2N 78 39W
49 Limfjorden, Denmark 56 55N 9 0E
30 Limia, R., Spain 41 55N 8 8W
77 Limko, China 20 57N 109 43E
49 Limmared, Sweden 57 34N 13 20E
96 Limmen Bight, Australia 14 40S 135 35E
45 Limni, Greece 38 43N 23 18E
44 Limni Voiviïs, Gr. 39 35N 22 45E
44 Limnos, I., Greece 39 50N 25 5E
127 Limoeiro do Norte, Brazil 5 5S 38 0W
20 Limoges, France 45 50N 1 15E
121 Limón, Costa Rica 10 0N 83 2W
120 Limon, Panama 9 20N 79 45W
116 Limon, U.S.A. 39 18N 103 38W
120 Limon B., Pan. Can. Zone 9 22N 79 56W
38 Limone, Italy 44 12N 7 32E
20 Limousin, France 46 0N 1 0E
20 Limousin, Plateau de, Fr. 46 0N 1 0E
20 Limoux, France 43 4N 2 12E
93 Limpopo, R., Mozam 23 15S 32 5E
90 Limuru, Kenya 1 2S 36 35E
24 Lin, Albania 41 4N 20 38E
124 Linares, Chile 35 50S 71 40W
126 Linares, Colombia 1 23N 77 31W
120 Linares, Mexico 24 50N 99 40W
33 Linares, Spain 38 10N 3 40W
124 Linares ♦, Chile 36 0S 71 0W
40 Linas Mte., Italy 39 25N 8 38E
124 Lincoln, Argentina 34 55N 61 30W
101 Lincoln, New Zealand 43 38S 172 30E
12 Lincoln, Eng. 53 14N 0 32W
116 Lincoln, Ill., U.S.A. 40 10N 89 20W
116 Lincoln, Kans., U.S.A. 39 6N 98 9W
107 Lincoln, Maine, U.S.A. 45 27N 68 29W
116 Lincoln, Nebr., U.S.A. 40 50N 96 42W
119 Lincoln, N. Mex., U.S.A. 33 30N 105 26W
12 Lincoln ♦, England 53 14N 0 32W
4 Lincoln Sea, Arc. Oc. 84 0N 55 0W
12 Lincoln Wolds, England 53 20N 0 5W
115 Lincolnton, U.S.A. 35 30N 81 15W
98 Lind, Australia 18 58S 144 30E
118 Lind, U.S.A. 47 0N 118 33W
47 Lindås, Norway 60 44N 5 10E
49 Lindås, Sweden 56 38N 15 35E
25 Lindau, Ger. 47 33N 9 41E
117 Linden, U.S.A. 33 0N 94 20W
49 Linderöd, Sweden 55 56N 13 47E
49 Linderödsåsen, Sweden 55 53N 13 53E
48 Lindesberg, Sweden 59 36N 15 15E
47 Lindesnes, Norway 57 58N 7 3E
91 Lindi, Tanzania 9 58S 39 38E
90 Lindi, R., Zaïre 1 25N 25 50E
91 Lindi ♦, Tanzania 9 58S 39 38E
30 Lindoso, Portugal 41 52N 8 11W
24 Lindow, Germany 52 58N 12 58E
106 Lindsay, Canada 44 22N 78 43W
119 Lindsay, Calif., U.S.A. 36 14N 119 6W
117 Lindsay, Okla., U.S.A. 34 51N 97 37W
116 Lindsborg, U.S.A. 38 35N 97 40W
47 Lindås, Norway 60 44N 5 9E
49 Lindås, Sweden 56 38N 15 35E
76 Linfen, China 36 0N 111 30E
67 Lingakok, China 29 55N 87 38E
73 Lingayer, Philippines 16 1N 120 14E
73 Lingayer G., Phil. 16 10N 120 15E
24 Lingen, Germany 52 32N 7 21E
72 Lingga, Kepulauan, Indon. 0 10S 104 30E
48 Linghed, Sweden 60 48N 15 55E
116 Lingle, U.S.A. 42 10N 104 18W
77 Lingling, China 26 15N 111 40E
77 Linglo, China 24 20N 105 25E
77 Lingshar, China 22 28N 109 17E
77 Lingshih, China 36 55N 11 45E
77 Lingshui, China 18 27N 110 0E
84 Linguère, Senegal 15 25N 15 5W
71 Linh Cam, Vietnam 18 31N 105 31E
77 Linhai, China 28 50N 121 8E
77 Lini, China 35 5N 118 20E
44 Link, Albania 41 4N 20 38E
77 Linkao, China 19 56N 109 42E
76 Linkian, China 41 57N 126 59E
49 Linköping, Sweden 58 28N 15 36E
76 Linkow, China 45 16N 130 18E
49 Linköping, Sweden 58 24N 15 38E
14 Linlithgow, Scot. 55 58N 3 38W
118 Linn, Mt., U.S.A. 40 0N 123 0W
13 Linney Head, Wales 51 37N 5 4W
14 Linnhe, L., Scot. 56 36N 5 25W
83 Linosa, Medit. Sea 35 51N 12 50E
77 Linping, China 24 25N 114 32E
125 Lins, Brazil 21 40S 49 44W
75 Lintan, China 34 37N 103 40E
76 Lintao, China 35 16N 103 38E
25 Linth, R., Switzerland 46 54N 9 0E
25 Linthal, Switzerland 46 54N 9 0E
107 Linton, Canada 47 15N 72 16W
114 Linton, Ind., U.S.A. 39 0N 87 10W
116 Linton, N. Dak., U.S.A. 46 21N 100 12W
99 Linville, Australia 26 50S 152 11E
112 Linwood, Canada 43 35N 80 43W
77 Linwu, China 25 25N 112 10E
20 Linxe, France 43 56N 1 13W
92 Linyanti, R., Africa 18 10S 24 10E
26 Linz, Austria 48 18N 14 18E
24 Linz, Germany 50 33N 7 18E
20 Lion, G. du, France 43 0N 4 0W
41 Lioni, Italy 40 52N 15 10E
91 Lion's Den, Rhodesia 17 15S 30 5E
112 Lion's Head, Canada 44 58N 81 15W
54 Liozno, U.S.S.R. 55 0N 30 50E
91 Lipali, Mozambique 15 50S 35 50E
41 Lipari, Italy 38 26N 14 58E
41 Lipari, Is., Italy 38 40N 15 0E
55 Lipetsk, U.S.S.R. 52 45N 39 35E
28 Lipiany, Poland 53 2N 14 58E
77 Liping, China 26 12N 109 0E
42 Lipijan, Yugoslavia 42 31N 21 7E
56 Lipkany, U.S.S.R. 48 14N 26 25E
27 Lipnik, Czechoslovakia 49 32N 17 36E
28 Lipno, Poland 52 49N 19 15E
77 Lipo, China 25 33N 107 45E
42 Lipova, Rumania 46 8N 21 42E
56 Lipovets, U.S.S.R. 49 12N 29 1E
24 Lippstadt, Germany 51 40N 8 19E
28 Lipsco, Poland 51 10N 21 36E
117 Lipscomb, U.S.A. 36 16N 110 18W
28 Lipsko, Poland 51 9N 21 40E
45 Lipsói, I., Greece 37 19N 26 50E
27 Liptovsky Svaty Milkulaš, Cz. 49 6N 19 35E
100 Liptrap C., Australia 38 50S 145 55E
90 Lira, Uganda 2 17N 32 57E
40 Liri, R., Italy 41 25N 13 45E
32 Liria, Spain 39 37N 0 35W
88 Lisala, Zaïre 2 12N 21 38E
31 Lisboa, Portugal 38 42N 9 10W
31 Lisboa ♦, Portugal 39 0N 9 12W
31 Lisbon = Lisboa, Portugal 38 42N 9 10W
113 Lisbon, N.H., U.S.A. 44 13N 71 52W
116 Lisbon, N. Dak., U.S.A. 46 30N 97 46W
112 Lisbon, Ohio, U.S.A. 40 45N 80 42W
15 Lisburn, N. Ire. 54 30N 6 9W
104 Lisburn, C., Alaska 68 50N 166 0W
15 Liscannor, Ireland 52 57N 9 24W
15 Liscannor, B., Ireland 52 57N 9 24W
40 Liscia, R., Sardinia 41 5N 9 17E
107 Liscomb, Canada 45 2N 62 0W
77 Lishui, China 28 29N 119 54E
94 Lisianski I., Pac. Oc. 25 30N 174 0W
18 Lisieux, France 49 10N 0 12E
57 Lisichansk, U.S.S.R. 48 55N 38 30E
21 L'Isle, Tarn, France 43 52N 1 49E
21 L'Isle, Vaucluse, France 43 55N 5 3E
19 L'Isle Adam, France 49 6N 2 5E
20 L'Isle-Jourdain, Fr. 43 37N 1 5E
19 L'Isle-sur-le Doubs, Fr. 47 28N 6 33E
107 L'Islet, Canada 47 4N 70 23W
15 Lismore, Ireland 52 8N 7 58W
99 Lismore, Australia 28 44S 153 21E
24 List, Germany 55 1N 8 26E
47 Lista, Norway 58 7N 6 39E
5 Lister, Mt., Antarctica 78 0S 162 0E
99 Liston, Australia 28 35S 152 0E
106 Listowel, Canada 44 44N 80 58W
15 Listowel, Ireland 52 27N 9 30W
99 Listowel Dns., Australia 25 10S 145 12E
20 Lit-et-Mixe, France 44 2N 1 15W
77 Litang, China 23 6N 109 2E
73 Litang, Malaysia 5 27N 118 31E
113 Litchfield, Conn., U.S.A. 41 44N 73 12W
124 Litchfield, Ill., U.S.A. 39 10N 89 40W
116 Litchfield, Minn., U.S.A. 45 5N 95 0W
46 Liteni, Rumania 47 32N 26 32E
100 Lithgow, Australia 33 25S 150 8E
45 Lithinon, Akra, Greece 34 55N 24 44E
54 Lithuania S.S.R. ♦, U.S.S.R. 55 30N 24 0E
39 Litija, Yugoslavia 46 3N 14 50E
44 Litókhoron, Greece 40 8N 22 34E
26 Litomĕrice, Cz. 50 33N 14 10E
27 Litomysi, Cz. 49 52N 16 20E
26 Litschau, Austria 48 58N 15 4E
115 Little Abaco I., W. Ind. 26 50N 77 30W
63 Little Aden, S. Arabia 12 41N 45 6E
5 Little America, Antarc. 79 0N 160 0W
71 Little Andaman I., India 10 40N 92 15E
101 Little Barrier I., N.Z. 36 12S 175 8E
48 Little Belt, Denmark 55 8N 9 55E
118 Little Belt Mts., U.S.A. 46 50N 111 0W
116 Little Blue, R., U.S.A. 40 18N 97 45W
92 Little Bushman Land, S. Africa 29 10S 18 10E
71 Little Coco I., Andaman Islands 14 0N 93 15E
119 Little Colorado, R., U.S.A. 36 0N 111 31W
106 Little Current, Canada 45 55N 82 0W
106 Little Current, R., Can. 50 40N 86 0W
116 Little Falls, Minn., U.S.A. 45 58N 94 19W
113 Little Falls, N.Y., U.S.A. 43 3N 74 50W
109 Lit. Grand Rapids, Can. 52 0N 95 29W
118 Lit. Humbaldt, R., U.S.A. 41 20N 117 27W
121 Lit. Inagua I., Bahamas 21 40N 73 50W
119 Little Lake, U.S.A. 35 58N 117 58W
106 Little Longlac, Canada 49 42N 86 58W
116 Little Marais, U.S.A. 47 24N 91 8W
107 Little Mecatiná I., Can. 50 30N 59 25W
14 Little Minch, Scotland 57 35N 6 45W
• 107 Lit. Miquelon I., N. Amer. 46 45N 56 25W
116 Lit. Missouri R., U.S.A. 46 40N 103 50W
92 Little Namaqualand, S. Africa 29 0S 17 9E
13 Little Ouse, R., Eng. 52 25N 0 50E
68 Little Rann of Kutch, India 23 25N 71 25E
117 Little Red, R., U.S.A. 35 40N 92 15W
101 Little River, N.Z. 43 45S 172 49E
117 Little Rock, U.S.A. 34 41N 92 10W
90 Little Ruaha, R., Tanz. 7 50S 35 30E
114 Little Sable Pt., U.S.A. 43 40N 86 32W
89 Little Scarcies, R., Sierra Leone 9 30N 12 25W
108 Little Smoky River, Canada 54 40N 117 20W
118 Little Snake, R., U.S.A. 40 45N 108 15W
112 Little Valley, U.S.A. 42 15N 78 48W
114 Little Wabash, R., U.S.A. 38 40N 88 20W
106 Little Whale, R., Can. 55 50N 75 0W
117 Littlefield, U.S.A. 33 57N 102 17W
116 Littlefork, U.S.A. 48 24N 93 35W
13 Littlehampton, England 50 48N 0 32W
113 Littleton, U.S.A. 44 19N 71 47W
77 Liuan, China 31 49N 116 29E
77 Liucheng, China 24 5N 109 3E
77 Liuchow, China 24 10N 109 10E
91 Liuli, Tanzania 11 3S 34 38E
77 Liupa, China 33 40N 107 0E
76 Liupan Shan, China 35 40N 106 10E
89 Liuwa Plain, Zambia 14 20S 22 30E
46 Livada, Rumania 47 52N 23 5E
44 Livadherón, Greece 40 2N 21 57E
18 Livarot, France 49 0N 0 9E
115 Live Oak, U.S.A. 30 17N 83 0W
117 Livermore, Mt., U.S.A. 30 45N 104 8W
100 Liverpool, Australia 33 55S 150 52E
107 Liverpool, Can. 44 5N 64 41W
12 Liverpool, Eng. 53 25N 3 0W
99 Liverpool Plains, Australia 31 15S 150 0E
100 Liverpool Ra., Australia 31 42S 150 10E
120 Livingston, Guatemala 15 50N 88 50W
21 Livingston, Scot., U.K. 55 52N 3 33W
118 Livingston, U.S.A. 45 40N 110 40W
117 Livingstone, U.S.A. 30 44N 94 54W
5 Livingstone I., Antarc. 63 0S 60 15W
91 Livingstone (Maramba), Zambia 17 46S 25 52E
91 Livingstone Memorial, Zambia 12 20S 30 18E
91 Livingstone Mts., Tanz. 9 40S 34 20E
91 Livingstonia, Malawi 10 38S 34 5E
42 Livno, Yugoslavia 43 50N 17 0E
55 Livny, U.S.S.R. 52 30N 37 30E
38 Livorno, Italy 43 32N 10 18E
125 Livramento, Brazil 30 55S 55 30W
21 Livron-sur-Drôme, France 44 46N 4 51E
91 Liwale, Tanzania 9 48S 37 58E
91 Liwale Chini, Tanz. 9 40S 38 0E
45 Lixoúrion, Greece 38 14N 20 24E
13 Lizard Pt., Eng. 49 57N 5 11W
41 Lizzano, Italy 40 23N 17 25E
42 Ljig, Yugoslavia 44 13N 20 18E
42 Ljubija, Yugoslavia 44 55N 16 35E
42 Ljubinje, Yugoslavia 42 58N 18 5E
39 Ljubljana, Yugoslavia 46 4N 14 33E
39 Ljubno, Yugoslavia 46 25N 14 46E
42 Ljuboten, mt., Yugoslavia 42 12N 21 8E
42 Ljubovija, Yugoslavia 44 11N 19 22E
42 Ljubuški, Yugoslavia 43 12N 17 34E
49 Ljung, Sweden 58 1N 13 3E
48 Ljungan, Sweden 62 18N 17 23E
48 Ljungaverk, Sweden 62 30N 16 5E
49 Ljungby, Sweden 56 49N 13 55E
48 Ljusdal, Sweden 61 46N 16 3E
48 Ljusnan, Sweden 61 12N 17 8E
48 Ljusne, Sweden 61 13N 17 7E
39 Ljutomer, Yugoslavia 46 31N 16 11E
32 Llagostera, Spain 41 50N 2 54E
124 Llancanelo, Salina, Arg. 35 40S 69 8W
13 Llandovery, Wales 51 59N 3 49W
13 Llandrindod Wells, Wales 52 15N 3 23W
12 Llandudno, Wales 53 19N 3 51W
13 Llanelli, Wales 51 41N 4 11W
30 Llanes, Spain 43 25N 4 50W
12 Llangollen, Wales 52 58N 3 10W
13 Llanidloes, Wales 52 28N 3 31W
117 Llano R., U.S.A. 30 50N 99 0W
110 Llano Estacado, U.S.A. 34 0N 103 0W
126 Llanos, S. America 3 25N 71 35W
76 Llaoyang, China 41 14N 123 6E
31 Llerena, Spain 38 17N 6 0W
124 Llico, Chile 34 46S 72 5W
32 Llobregat, Spain 41 19N 2 9E
32 Lloret de Mar, Spain 41 41N 2 53E
69 Lloyd Barrage, Pakistan 27 46N 68 50E
98 Lloyd B., Australia 12 45S 143 27E
109 Lloydminster, Canada 53 20N 110 0W
33 Lluchmayor, Spain 39 29N 2 53E
124 Llullaillaco, volcán, Arg./Chile 24 30S 68 30W
77 Lo Ho, Honan, China 34 15N 111 10E
119 Loa, U.S.A. 38 18N 111 46W
124 Loa, R., Chile 21 30S 70 0W
38 Loano, Italy 44 8N 8 14E
24 Löbau, Germany 51 5N 14 42E
92 Lobaye, R., Central African Republic 4 30N 17 0E
24 Lobenstein, Germany 50 25N 11 39E
124 Loberia, Argentina 38 10S 58 40W
28 Łobez, Poland 53 38N 15 39E
89 Lobito, Angola 12 18S 13 35E
31 Lobón, Canal de, Spain 38 50N 6 55W
124 Lobos, Argentina 35 2S 59 0W
122 Lobos, Is., Peru 6 35S 80 45W
107 Lobstick L., Canada 54 0N 65 12W
28 Łobzenica, Poland 53 18N 17 15E
71 Loc Binh, Vietnam 21 46N 106 54E
71 Loc Ninh, Vietnam 11 50N 106 34E
25 Locarno, Switzerland 46 10N 8 47E
14 Lochaber, Scotland 56 55N 5 0W
16 Lochem, Netherlands 52 9N 6 26E
18 Loches, France 47 7N 1 0E
14 Lochgelly, Scot. 56 7N 3 18W
14 Lochgilphead, Scot. 56 2N 5 37W
98 Lochnagar, Australia 24 34S 144 52E
14 Lochnagar, Mt., Scot. 56 57N 3 14W
28 Łochow, Poland 52 33N 21 42E
14 Lochy, R., Scot. 56 52N 5 3W
112 Lock Haven, U.S.A. 41 7N 77 31W
107 Lockeport, Canada 43 47N 65 4W
14 Lockerbie, Scot. 55 7N 3 21W
100 Lockhart, Australia 35 14S 146 40E
117 Lockhart, U.S.A. 29 55N 97 40W
112 Lockport, U.S.A. 43 12N 78 42W
18 Locminé, France 47 54N 2 51W
41 Locri, Italy 38 14N 16 14E
18 Locronan, France 48 7N 4 15W
18 Loctudy, France 47 50N 4 12W
62 Lod, Israel 31 57N 34 54E
47 Lodalskåpa, Nor. 61 47N 7 13E
20 Lodève, France 43 44N 3 19E
118 Lodge Grass, U.S.A. 45 21N 107 27W
116 Lodgepole, U.S.A. 41 12N 102 40W
116 Lodgepole Cr., U.S.A. 41 20N 104 30W
68 Lodhran, Pakistan 29 32N 71 30E
38 Lodi, Italy 45 19N 9 30E
118 Lodi, U.S.A. 38 12N 121 16W
73 Lodji, Indonesia 1 38S 127 28E
32 Lodosa, Spain 42 25N 2 4W
49 Lodose, Sweden 58 5N 12 10E
90 Lodwar, Kenya 3 10N 35 40E
28 Łódz, Poland 51 45N 19 27E
28 Łódz ♦, Poland 51 45N 19 27E
71 Loei, Thailand 17 29N 101 35E
90 Loengo, Zaïre 4 48S 26 30E
26 Lofer, Austria 47 35N 12 41E
50 Lofoten, Norway 68 10N 13 0E
48 Lofsen, Sweden 62 7N 13 57E
49 Loftahammar, Sweden 57 54N 16 41E
48 Loftsdalen, Sweden 62 10N 13 20E
85 Loga, Niger 13 37N 3 14E
116 Logan, Kans., U.S.A. 39 23N 99 35W
114 Logan, Ohio, U.S.A. 39 25N 82 22E
118 Logan, Utah, U.S.A. 41 45N 111 50W
114 Logansport, U.S.A. 31 58N 93 58W
87 Logo, Sudan 5 20N 30 18E
87 Logo Dergo, Sudan 6 10N 29 18E
32 Logroño, Spain 42 28N 2 32W
32 Logroño ♦, Spain 42 28N 2 27W
31 Logrosán, Spain 39 20N 5 32W
49 Lögstör, Denmark 56 58N 9 14E
69 Lohardaga, India 23 27N 84 45E
63 Loheia, Yemen 15 45N 42 40E
51 Lohja, Finland 60 12N 24 5E
25 Lohr, Germany 50 0N 9 35E
67 Loikaw, Burma 19 40N 97 17E
51 Loimaa, Finland 60 50N 23 5E
19 Loir-et-Cher ♦, Fr. 47 40N 1 20E
18 Loire, R., France 47 16N 2 10W
21 Loire ♦, France 45 40N 4 5E
18 Loire-Atlantique ♦, France 47 25N 1 40W
19 Loiret ♦, France 47 58N 2 10E
24 Loitz, Germany 53 58N 13 8E
126 Loja, Ecuador 3 59S 79 16W
31 Loja, Spain 37 10N 4 10W
87 Loka, Sudan 4 13N 31 0E
77 Lokchong, China 25 15N 113 0E
47 Löken, Norway 59 50N 11 25E
92 Lokerane, Botswana 24 54S 24 42E
54 Lokhvitsa, U.S.S.R. 50 25N 33 18E
90 Lokichokio, Kenya 4 19N 34 13E
50 Lokka, Finland 67 49N 27 45E
49 Lökken, Denmark 57 22N 9 41E
47 Lökken, Norway 63 8N 9 45E
55 Loknya, U.S.S.R. 56 49N 30 4E
88 Lokobo, Sudan 4 20N 30 30E
85 Lokoja, Nigeria 7 47N 6 45E
77 Loktung, China 18 41N 109 5E
87 Lokuti, Sudan 4 21N 33 15E
77 Lokwei, China 19 12N 110 30E
87 Lol, Sudan 5 28N 29 36E
87 Lol, R., Sudan 9 0N 28 10E
84 Lola, Guinea 7 52N 8 29W
87 Lolibai, Gebel, Sudan 3 50N 33 50E
87 Lolimi, Sudan 4 35N 34 0E
49 Lolland, Denmark 54 45N 11 30E
24 Lollar, Germany 50 39N 8 43E
118 Lolo, U.S.A. 46 50N 114 8W
85 Lolodorf, Cameroon 3 16N 10 49E
90 Lolungchung, China 30 43N 96 7E
43 Lom, Bulgaria 43 48N 23 20E
42 Lom, R., Bulgaria 43 45N 23 7E
118 Loma, U.S.A. 47 59N 110 29W
90 Lomami, R., Zaïre 1 0S 24 40E
124 Lomas de Zomora, Arg. 34 45S 58 25W
118 Lombard, U.S.A. 46 7N 111 28W
38 Lombardia ♦, Italy 45 35N 9 45E
38 Lombard = Lombardia, Italy 45 35N 9 45E
20 Lombez, France 3 29N 0 55E
73 Lomblen, I., Indonesia 8 30S 123 32E
72 Lombok, I., Indonesia 8 35S 116 20E
85 Lomé, Togoland 6 9N 1 20E
88 Lomela, R., Zaïre 1 30S 22 50E
38 Lomello, Italy 45 11N 8 46E
117 Lometa, U.S.A. 31 15N 98 25W
88 Lomie, Cameroon 3 13N 13 38E
87 Loming, Sudan 4 27N 33 40W
49 Lomma, Sweden 55 43N 13 6E
108 Lomond, Canada 50 24N 112 36W
14 Lomond, L., Scot. 56 8N 4 38W
99 Lomond, mt., Australia 30 0S 151 45E
73 Lompobatang, mt., Indon. 5 24S 119 56E
119 Lompoc, U.S.A. 34 41N 120 32W
47 Lomsegga, Norway 61 49N 8 21E
28 Łomża, Poland 53 10N 22 2E
70 Lonavla, India 18 46N 73 29E
128 Loncoche, Chile 39 20S 72 50W
70 Londa, India 15 30N 74 30E
90 Londiani, Kenya 0 10S 35 33E
18 Londinières, France 49 50N 1 25E
106 London, Canada 43 0N 81 15W
13 London, England 51 30N 0 5W
114 London, Ky., U.S.A. 37 11N 84 5W
114 London, Ohio, U.S.A. 39 54N 83 28W
13 London ♦, England 51 30N 0 5W
15 Londonderry, N. Ireland 55 0N 7 20W
96 Londonderry, C., Australia 13 50S 127 15E
128 Londonderry, I., Chile 55 0S 71 0W
• 15 Londonderry ♦, N. Ire. 55 0N 7 20W
125 Londrina, Brazil 23 0S 51 10W
119 Lone Pine, U.S.A. 36 35N 118 2W
119 Long Beach, Calif., U.S.A. 33 46N 118 12W
113 Long Beach, N.Y., U.S.A. 40 35N 73 40W
118 Long Beach, Wash., U.S.A. 46 20N 124 1W
113 Long Branch, U.S.A. 40 19N 74 0W
12 Long Eaton, Eng. 52 54N 1 16W
98 Long I., Australia 22 8S 149 53E
121 Long I., Bahamas 23 20N 75 10W
106 Long I., Canada 44 23N 66 19W
98 Long I., New Guinea 5 25S 147 0E
113 Long I., U.S.A. 40 50N 73 20W
113 Long I. Sd., U.S.A. 41 10N 73 0W
106 Long L., Canada 49 30N 86 50W
113 Long L., U.S.A. 43 57N 74 25W
116 Long Pine, U.S.A. 43 33N 99 50W
98 Long Pocket, Australia 18 30S 146 0E
112 Long Pt., Canada 42 35N 80 10W
112 Long Pt. Bay, Canada 42 40N 80 20W
107 Long Ra., Canada 49 30N 57 30W
4 Long Str., U.S.S.R. 70 0N 175 0E
71 Long Xuyen, S. Vietnam 10 19N 105 28E
45 Longá, Greece 36 53N 21 55E
39 Longarone, Italy 46 15N 12 18E
67 Longdam, China 28 12N 98 16E
19 Longeau, France 47 47N 5 20E
5 Longford, Australia 41 32S 147 3E
15 Longford, Ireland 53 43N 7 50W
15 Longford ♦, Ireland 53 42N 7 45W
90 Longido, Tanzania 2 43S 36 35E
72 Longiram, Indonesia 0 5S 115 45E
106 Longlac, Canada 49 45N 86 25W
67 Longling, China 24 42N 98 58E
116 Longmont, U.S.A. 40 10N 105 4W
72 Longnawan, Indonesia 21 50N 114 55E
41 Longobucco, Italy 39 27N 16 37E
81 Longone, R., Cameroon 10 0N 15 40E
98 Longreach, Australia 23 28S 144 14E
118 Long's Peak, U.S.A. 40 20N 105 50W
98 Longton, Australia 21 0S 145 55E
12 Longtown, England 55 1N 2 59W
18 Longué, France 47 22N 0 8W
18 Longueau, France 49 52N 2 22E
113 Longueuil, Canada 45 32N 73 28W
19 Longuyon, France 49 27N 5 35E
108 Longview, Canada 50 32N 114 10W
117 Longview, Tex., U.S.A. 32 30N 94 45W
118 Longview, Wash., U.S.A. 46 9N 122 58W
19 Longwy, France 49 30N 5 45E
39 Lonigo, Italy 45 23N 11 22E
24 Löningen, Germany 54 43N 7 44E
39 Lonja, R., Yugoslavia 45 30N 16 40E
69 Lonkor Tso, China 32 40N 83 15E
117 Lonoke, U.S.A. 34 48N 91 57W
20 Lonouaille, France 46 30N 1 35E
19 Lons-le-Saunier, France 46 40N 5 31E
50 Lönsdal, Norway 66 46N 15 26E
49 Lönstrup, Denmark 57 29N 9 47E
73 Looc, Philippines 12 20N 112 5E
106 Lookout, C., Canada 55 20N 84 30W
115 Lookout, C., U.S.A. 34 30N 76 30W
90 Loolmalasin, mt., Tanz. 3 0S 35 53E
109 Loomis, Canada 49 15N 108 45W
109 Loon L., Canada 44 50N 77 15W
15 Loop Hd., Ireland 52 34N 9 55W
75 Lop Nor, China 40 20N 90 10E
42 Lopare, Yugoslavia 44 39N 18 46E
57 Lopatin, U.S.S.R. 43 50N 47 35E
59 Lopatina, G., U.S.S.R. 50 0N 143 30E
87 Lopaye, Sudan 6 37N 33 40E
76 Lopei, China 47 40N 131 12E
31 Lopera, Spain 37 56N 4 14W
88 Lopez C., Gabon 0 47S 8 40E
87 Lopodi, Sudan 5 5N 33 15E
50 Lopphavet, Norway 70 27N 21 15E
31 Lora del Rio, Spain 37 39N 5 33W
65 Lora Rud, Afghanistan 32 0N 67 15E
112 Lorain, U.S.A. 41 20N 82 5W
68 Loralai, Pakistan 30 29N 68 30E
33 Lorca, Spain 37 41N 1 42W
94 Lord Howe I., Pac. Oc. 31 33S 159 6E
119 Lordsburg, U.S.A. 32 15N 108 45W
98 Lorengau, New Guinea 2 10S 147 23E
127 Loreto, Brazil 7 5S 45 30W
39 Loreto, Italy 43 26N 13 36E
39 Loreto Aprutina, Italy 42 24N 13 59E
21 Lorgues, France 43 28N 6 22E
126 Lorica, Colombia 9 14N 75 49W
18 Lorient, France 47 45N 3 23W
100 Lorne, Australia 38 33S 143 59E
14 Lorne, Scot. 56 26N 5 10W
14 Lorne, Firth of, Scotland 56 20N 5 40W
25 Lörrach, Germany 47 36N 7 38E
19 Lorraine, France 49 0N 6 0E
106 Lorrainville, Canada 47 21N 79 23W
84 Los, Iles de, Guinea 9 30N 13 50W
119 Los Alamos, U.S.A. 35 57N 106 17W
124 Los Andes, Chile 32 50S 70 40W
124 Los Angeles, Chile 37 28S 72 23W
119 Los Angeles, U.S.A. 34 0N 118 10W
119 Los Angeles Aqueduct, U.S.A. 35 0N 118 20W
31 Los Barrios, Spain 36 11N 5 30W
124 Los Blancos, Argentina 23 45S 62 30W
33 Los Blancos, Spain 37 38N 0 49W
126 Los Gatos, U.S.A. 37 15N 121 59W
120 Los Lamentos, Mexico 30 36N 105 50W
119 Los Lunas, U.S.A. 34 55N 106 47W
120 Los Mochis, Mexico 25 45N 109 5W
32 Los Monegros, Spain 41 29N 0 3W
33 Los Muertos, Punta de, Spain 36 57N 1 54W

• In April 1973 districts replaced counties in N. Ireland

MAP

31 Los Palacios y Villafranca, Spain 37 10N 5 55W
121 Los Roques, Is., Venezuela 11 50N 66 45W
31 Los Santos de Maimona, Spain 38 37N 6 22W
126 Los Testigos, Is., Ven. 11 23N 63 6W
124 Los Vilos, Chile 32 0s 71 30W
31 Los Yébenes, Spain 39 36N 3 55W
77 Loshing, China 24 45N 108 58E
59 Loshkalakh, U.S.S.R. 62 45N 147 20E
39 Lošinj, I., Yugoslavia 54 45N 14 45E
14 Lossiemouth, Scot. 57 43N 3 17W
98 Losuia, Terr. of Papua 8 25s 146 3E
20 Lot, R., France 44 40N 1 40E
20 Lot ♦, France 44 39N 1 40E
124 Lota, Chile 37 5s 73 10W
20 Lot-et-Garonne ♦, France 44 22N 0 30E
47 Löten, Norway 60 51N 11 21E
19 Lothiers, France 46 42N 1 33E
88 Loting, China 22 50N 111 25E
25 Lötschberg, Switz. 46 26N 7 53E
25 Lötschbergtunnel, Switzerland 46 26N 7 43E
48 Lottefors, Sweden 61 25N 16 24E
18 Loudéac, France 48 11N 2 47W
115 Loudon, U.S.A. 35 41N 84 22W
112 Loudonville, U.S.A. 40 40N 82 15W
18 Loudun, France 47 0N 0 5E
18 Loue, R., France 47 4N 6 10E
12 Loughborough, Eng. 52 46N 1 11W
15 Loughrea, Ire. 53 11N 8 33W
21 Louhans, France 46 38N 5 12E
82 Louis Gentil, Morocco 32 16N 8 31W
114 Louisa, U.S.A. 38 5N 82 40W
107 Louisbourg, Canada 45 55N 60 0W
108 Louise I., Canada 52 55N 131 40W
106 Louiseville, Canada 46 20N 73 0W
98 Louisiade Arch., Papua 10 50s 152 30E
116 Louisiana, U.S.A. 39 25N 91 0W
117 Louisiana ♦, U.S.A. 30 50N 92 0W
114 Louisville, Ky., U.S.A. 38 15N 85 45W
117 Louisville, Miss., U.S.A. 33 7N 89 3W
20 Loulay, France 46 3N 0 30W
31 Loulé, Portugal 37 9N 8 0W
109 Lount L., Canada 50 10N 94 20W
26 Louny, Czechoslovakia 50 20N 13 48E
116 Loup City, U.S.A. 41 19N 98 57W
20 Lourdes, France 43 6N 0 3W
*93 Lourenço-Marques, Mozambique 25 58s 32 32E
†93 Lourenço-Marques, B. de, Mozambique 25 50s 32 45E
*93 Lourenço-Marques ♦, Mozam. 26 30s 32 45E
31 Loures, Portugal 38 50N 9 9W
31 Lourinha, Portugal 39 14N 9 17W
30 Lousã, Portugal 40 7N 8 14W
99 Louth, Australia 30 30s 145 8E
15 Louth, Ireland 53 47N 6 33W
12 Louth, England 53 23N 0 0
15 Louth ♦, Ireland 53 55N 6 30W
45 Loutrá Aidhipsoú, Gr. 38 54N 23 2E
45 Loutráki, Greece 38 0N 22 57E
18 Louviers, France 49 12N 1 10E
54 Lovat, R., U.S.S.R. 56 30N 31 20E
116 Loveland, U.S.A. 40 27N 105 4W
118 Lovell, U.S.A. 44 51N 108 20W
118 Lovelock, U.S.A. 40 17N 118 25W
38 Lóvere, Italy 45 50N 10 4E
117 Loving, U.S.A. 32 17N 104 4W
117 Lovington, U.S.A. 33 0N 103 20W
30 Lovios, Spain 41 55N 8 4W
51 Lovisa (Loviisa), Finland 60 28N 26 12E
26 Lovosice, Cz. 50 30N 14 2E
39 Lovran, Yugoslavia 45 18N 14 15E
42 Lovrin, Rumania 45 58N 20 48E
48 Lövstabukten, Sweden 60 35N 17 45E
99 Low Rocky Pt., Australia 42 59s 145 30E
90 Lowa, R., Zaïre 1 15s 27 40E
113 Lowell, U.S.A. 42 38N 71 19W
118 Lower L., U.S.A. 41 17N 120 3W
108 Lower Arrow L., Can. 49 40N 118 5W
26 Lower Austria = Niederösterreich, Aust.
101 Lower Group, Cook Is. 20 0s 160 0W
101 Lower Hutt, N.Z. 41 10s 174 55E
118 Lower Lake, U.S.A. 38 56N 122 36W
107 Lower Neguac, Canada 47 20N 65 10W
107 Lower Sackville, Canada 45 45N 63 43W
24 Lower Saxony = Niedersachsen, Ger.
106 Lower Seal, L., Canada 56 30N 74 23W
98 Lower Woolgar, Australia 19 47s 143 27E
13 Lowestoft, Eng. 52 29N 1 44E
28 Łowicz, Poland 52 6N 19 55E
113 Lowville, U.S.A. 43 48N 75 30W
77 Loyang, China 34 40N 112 28E
54 Loyev, U.S.S.R. 57 7N 30 40E
90 Loyoro, Uganda 3 22N 34 14E
77 Loyüan, China 26 25N 119 33E
77 Loyung, China 24 25N 109 25E
39 Lož, Yugoslavia 45 43N 14 14E
20 Lozère ♦, France 44 35N 3 30E
42 Loznica, Yugoslavia 44 32N 19 14E
52 Lozovaya, U.S.S.R. 49 0N 36 27E
121 Luabo, Mozambique 18 30s 36 10E
90 Luacano, Angola 11 15s 21 37E
39 Lož, Yugoslavia 45 43N 14 14E
90 Lualaba, R., Zaïre 5 45s 26 50E
91 Luampa, Zambia 14 34s 24 20E
73 Luan, Philippines 6 10N 124 25E
71 Luan Chau, N. Vietnam 21 38N 103 24E
88 Luanda, Angola 8 58s 13 9E
72 Luang Prabang, Laos 19 45N 102 10E
91 Luangwa Val., Zambia 13 30s 31 30E
91 Luanshya, Zambia 13 3s 28 28E

91 Luapula, R., Zaïre-Zambia 12 0s 28 50E
91 Luapula ♦, Zambia 11 0s 29 0E
30 Luarca, Spain 43 32N 6 32W
28 Lubaczów, Poland 10 50s 23 36E
88 Lubalo, Angola 9 10s 19 15E
28 Luban, Poland 51 5N 15 15E
54 Lubānas Ezers, U.S.S.R. 56 45N 27 0E
73 Lubang Is., Philippines 13 50N 120 12E
28 Lubartów, Poland 51 28N 22 42E
28 Lubawa, Poland 53 30N 19 48E
62 Lubban, Jordan 32 9N 35 14E
24 Lübben, Germany 51 56N 13 54E
24 Lübbenau, Germany 51 49N 13 59E
117 Lubbock, U.S.A. 33 40N 102 0W
24 Lübeck, Germany 53 52N 10 41E
24 Lübecker Bucht, Ger. 54 3N 11 0E
90 Lubefu, Zaïre 4 47s 24 27E
90 Lubefu, R., Zaïre 4 47s 24 27E
28 Lubien Kujawski, Poland 52 23N 19 9E
28 Lubin, Poland 51 24N 16 11E
28 Lublin, Poland 51 12N 22 38E
28 Lublin ♦, Poland 51 5N 22 30E
28 Lubliniec, Poland 50 43N 18 45E
54 Lubny, U.S.S.R. 50 3N 32 58E
72 Lubok Antu, Malaysia 1 3N 111 50E
28 Lubon, Poland 52 21N 16 51E
90 Lubongola, Zaïre 2 35s 27 50E
28 Lubotin, Cz. 49 17N 20 53E
28 Lubraniec, Poland 52 33N 18 50E
28 Lubsko, Poland 51 45N 14 57E
24 Lübtheen, Germany 53 18N 11 4E
73 Lubuagan, Philippines 17 21N 121 10E
91 Lubudi, R., Zaïre 9 30s 25 0E
72 Lubuhanbilik, Indonesia 2 33N 100 14E
72 Lubuk Linggau, Indon. 3 15s 102 55E
72 Lubuk Sikaping, Indon. 0 10N 100 15E
90 Lubumbashi, Zaïre 11 32s 27 28E
90 Lubunda, Zaïre 5 12s 26 41E
91 Lubungu, Zambia 14 35s 26 24E
90 Lubutu, Zaïre 0 45s 26 30E
21 Luc-en-Diois, France 44 36N 5 28E
112 Lucan, Canada 43 11N 81 25W
41 Lucania ♦, Italy 40 30N 16 0E
104 Lucania, Mt., Alaska 60 48N 141 25W
38 Lucca, Italy 43 50N 10 30E
14 Luce Bay, Scot. 54 45N 4 48W
115 Lucedale, U.S.A. 30 55N 88 34W
73 Lucena, Philippines 13 56N 121 37E
31 Lucena, Spain 37 27N 4 31W
32 Lucena del Cid, Spain 40 9N 0 17W
27 Lučenec, Cz. 48 18N 19 42E
41 Lucera, Italy 41 30N 15 20E
25 Lucerne = Luzern, Switz.
33 Luchena, R., Spain 37 50N 2 0W
91 Lucheringo, R., Mozam. 12 0s 36 5E
77 Luchow, China 28 57N 105 26E
24 Lüchow, Germany 52 58N 11 8E
89 Lucira, Angola 14 0s 12 35E
24 Luckau, Germany 51 50N 13 43E
24 Luckenwalde, Germany 52 5N 13 11E
69 Lucknow, India 26 50N 81 0E
43 Luçon, France 46 28N 1 10W
43 Luda Kamchiya, R., Bulgaria 42 50N 27 0E
39 Ludbreg, Yugoslavia 46 15N 16 38E
24 Lüdenscheid, Germany 51 13N 7 37E
92 Lüderitz, S.W. Africa 26 41s 15 8E
68 Ludhiana, India 30 57N 75 56E
24 Lüdinghausen, Ger. 51 46N 7 28E
114 Ludington, U.S.A. 43 58N 86 27W
13 Ludlow, Eng. 52 23N 2 42W
119 Ludlow, Calif., U.S.A. 34 43N 116 10W
113 Ludlow, Vt., U.S.A. 43 25N 72 40W
46 Ludus, Rumania 46 29N 24 5E
48 Ludvika, Sweden 60 8N 15 14E
25 Ludwigsburg, Germany 48 53N 9 11E
25 Ludwigshafen, Germany 49 27N 8 27E
24 Ludwigslust, Germany 53 19N 11 28E
54 Ludza, U.S.S.R. 56 32N 27 43E
88 Luebo, Zaïre 5 21s 21 17E
91 Lueki, Zaïre 3 20s 25 48E
91 Luena, Zaïre 9 28s 25 43E
91 Luena, Zambia 10 40s 30 25E
126 Luepa, Venezuela 5 43N 61 31W
117 Lufkin, U.S.A. 31 25N 94 40W
91 Lufupa, Zaïre 10 32s 24 50W
54 Luga, U.S.S.R. 58 40N 29 55E
54 Luga, R., U.S.S.R. 59 5N 28 30E
25 Lugano, Switzerland 46 0N 8 57E
25 Lugano, L. di, Switz. 46 0N 9 0E
57 Lugansk = Voroshilovgrad, U.S.S.R.
91 Lugela, Mozambique 16 25s 36 43E
91 Lugenda, R., Mozam. 12 35s 36 50E
63 Lugh Ganana, Somali Rep. 3 48N 42 40E
15 Lugnaquilla, Mt., Ire. 52 48N 6 28W
48 Lugnvik, Sweden 62 56N 17 55E
39 Lugo, Italy 44 25N 11 53E
30 Lugo, Spain 43 0N 7 35W
30 Lugo ♦, Spain 43 0N 7 30W
46 Lugoj, Rumania 45 42N 21 57E
30 Lugones, Spain 43 26N 5 50W
58 Lugovoy, U.S.S.R. 43 0N 72 20E
24 Luhe, R., Germany 53 7N 10 0E
89 Luiana, R., Angola 17 25s 23 30E
77 Luichow = Haihong, China
77 Luichow Pantao, China 20 30N 110 0E
127 Luis Correia, Brazil 3 0s 41 35W
88 Luisa, Zaïre 7 40s 22 30E
90 Luizi, Zaïre 6 0s 27 25E
124 Luján, Argentina 34 45s 59 5W
77 Lukang, Taiwan 24 0N 120 19E

88 Lukenie, R., Zaïre 3 0s 18 50E
69 Lukhisaral, India 27 11N 86 5E
43 Lŭki, Bulgaria 41 28N 23 43E
77 Luki, China 28 10N 109 58E
91 Lukolela, Zaïre 1 10s 17 12E
91 Lukosi, Rhodesia 18 30s 26 30E
89 Lukula, Zaïre 43 13N 24 11E
55 Lukoyanov, U.S.S.R. 55 2N 44 20E
89 Lukulu, Zambia 14 35s 23 25E
90 Lukutu, R., Zambia 0 30N 25 31E
90 Lula, Zaïre 0 30N 25 10E
50 Lule, R., Sweden 66 20N 20 50E
50 Luleå, Sweden 65 35N 22 10E
43 Lüleburgaz, Turkey 41 23N 27 28E
117 Luling, U.S.A. 29 45N 97 40W
88 Lulonga, R., Zaïre 1 0N 19 0E
88 Lulua, R., Zaïre 6 30s 22 50E
88 Luluabourg = Kananga, Zaïre 5 55s 22 18E
73 Lumadjang, Indonesia 8 8s 113 16E
89 Lumai, Angola 13 20s 21 25E
117 Lumberton, Miss., USA 31 4N 89 28W
119 Lumberton, N. Mex., U.S.A. 36 58N 106 57W
115 Lumberton, N.C., U.S.A. 34 37N 78 59W
90 Lumbres, France 50 40N 2 5E
90 Lumbwa, Kenya 0 12s 35 28E
108 Lumby, Canada 50 10N 118 50W
76 Lumeyen, Sudan 5 5s 33 28E
101 Lumsden, New Zealand 45 44s 168 27E
72 Lumut, Malaysia 4 13N 100 37E
72 Lumut, Tg., Indon. 3 50s 105 58E
68 Lun, Mongolia 47 55N 105 1E
68 Lunavada, India 23 8N 73 37E
46 Lunca, Rumania 47 22N 25 1E
47 Lund, Norway 68 42N 18 9E
49 Lund, Sweden 55 41N 13 12E
118 Lund, U.S.A. 38 53N 115 0W
47 Lunde, Norway 59 17N 9 5E
49 Lunderskov, Denmark 55 29N 9 19E
91 Lundi, R., Rhodesia 21 15s 31 25E
13 Lundy, I., Eng. 51 10N 4 41W
12 Lune, R., Eng. 54 0N 2 51W
24 Lüneburg, Germany 53 15N 10 23E
24 Lüneburg Heath = Lüneburger Heide, Ger.
24 Lüneburger Heide, Germany 53 0N 10 0E
21 Lunel, France 43 39N 4 9E
24 Lünen, Germany 51 36N 7 31E
107 Lunenburg, Canada 44 22N 64 18W
19 Lunéville, France 48 36N 6 30E
91 Lunga, R., Zambia 13 0s 26 33E
77 Lungan, China 23 10N 107 42E
77 Lungchuan, China 24 1N 116 8E
50 Lungholt, Iceland 63 35N 18 10E
84 Lungi Airport, S. Leone 8 40N 16 47E
77 Lungkiang, China 47 22N 123 4E
67 Lunglegh, India 22 55N 92 45E
77 Lungmoon, China 23 50N 114 18E
77 Lungshan, China 29 26N 109 31E
77 Lungsheng, China 25 58N 110 0E
76 Lungsi, China 35 0N 104 35E
77 Lungtsin, China 22 20N 106 52E
77 Lungyan, China 25 6N 117 2E
68 Luni, India 26 0N 73 6E
68 Luni, R., India 25 40N 72 20E
54 Luninets, U.S.S.R. 52 15N 27 0E
55 Lunino, U.S.S.R. 53 35N 45 6E
47 Lunner, Norway 60 19N 10 35E
91 Lunsemfwa Falls, Zam. 14 30s 29 6E
91 Lunsemfwa, R., Zambia 14 50s 30 10E
90 Luofu, Zaïre 0 1s 29 15E
88 Luozi, Zaïre 4 54s 14 0E
46 Lupeni, Rumania 45 21N 23 13E
27 Łupków, Poland 49 15N 22 4E
72 Lupundu, Zambia 14 18s 26 45E
124 Luque, Paraguay 25 19s 57 25W
32 Luque, Spain 37 35N 4 16W
114 Luray, U.S.A. 38 39N 78 26W
19 Lure, France 47 40N 6 30E
91 Luremo, Angola 8 30s 17 50E
15 Lurgan, N. Ire. 54 28N 6 20W
124 Luro, R., Mozambique 13 0s 38 40E
64 Luristan, Iran 33 20N 47 0E
91 Lusambo, Zaïre 4 58s 23 28E
44 Lushnja, Albania 40 55s 19 41E
90 Lushoto, Tanz. 4 47s 38 20E
90 Lushoto ♦, Tanz. 4 45s 38 20E
76 Lushun, China 38 51N 121 20E
124 Lusignan, France 46 26N 0 8E
20 Lusigny-sur-Barse, Fr. 48 16N 4 15E
116 Lusk, U.S.A. 42 47N 104 27W
20 Lussac-les-Châteaux, France 46 24N 0 43E
76 Lu-ta, China 39 0N 121 31E
13 Luton, England 51 53N 0 24W
72 Lutong, Malaysia 4 30N 114 0E
54 Lutsk, U.S.S.R. 50 50N 25 15E
116 Luverne, U.S.A. 43 35N 96 12W
91 Luvua, Zaïre 8 48s 25 17E
90 Luwegu, R., Tanzania 9 30s 36 20E
73 Luwuk, Indonesia 10 0s 122 40E
16 Luxembourg, Luxem. 49 37N 6 9E
16 Luxembourg ■, Europe 49 58N 5 30E
16 Luxembourg ♦, Belg. 49 58N 5 30E
19 Luxeuil-les-Bains, F. 47 49N 6 24E
86 Luxor = El Uqsr, Egypt 25 41N 32 38E
20 Luz, France 42 53N 0 1E
25 Luzern, Switz. 47 3N 8 18E
25 Luzern ♦, Switz. 47 2N 7 55E
3 Luziânia, Brazil 16 20s 48 0W
22 Luzické Hory, Cz. 50 40N 14 50E
73 Luzon, I., Phil. 16 0N 121 0E
20 Luzy, France 46 47N 3 58E
41 Luzzi, Italy 39 28N 16 17E

54 Lvov, U.S.S.R. 49 40N 24 0E
28 Lwówek, Poznan, Poland 52 28N 16 10E
28 Lwówek, Wroclaw, Poland 51 7N 15 38E
54 Lyakhovichi, U.S.S.R. 53 2N 26 32E
59 Lyakhovskiye, Ostrova, U.S.S.R. 73 40N 141 0E
57 Lyaki, U.S.S.R. 40 34N 47 22E
68 Lyallpur, Pakistan 31 30N 73 5E
43 Lyaskovets, Bulgaria 43 6N 25 44E
24 Lychen, Germany 53 13N 13 20E
49 Lyckeby, Sweden 56 12N 15 37E
50 Lycksele, Sweden 64 38N 18 40E
62 Lydda = Lod, Israel 31 57N 34 54E
93 Lydenburg, S. Africa 25 10s 30 29E
101 Lyell, New Zealand 41 48s 172 4E
101 Lyell Range, N.Z. 41 38s 172 20E
49 Lygnern, Sweden 57 30N 12 15E
47 Lykling, Norway 59 42N 5 12E
118 Lyman, U.S.A. 41 24N 110 15W
13 Lyme Regis, Eng. 50 44N 2 57W
13 Lymington, Eng. 50 46N 1 32W
113 Lyn, Canada 44 36N 75 47W
114 Lynchburg, U.S.A. 37 23N 79 10W
112 Lynden, Canada 43 14N 80 10W
118 Lynden, U.S.A. 48 56N 122 32W
100 Lyndhurst, N.S.W., Australia 33 41s 149 2E
98 Lyndhurst, Queens., Australia 18 56s 144 30E
99 Lyndhurst, S. Australia 30 15s 138 18E
112 Lyndonville, N.Y., U.S.A. 43 19N 78 25W
113 Lyndonville, Vt., U.S.A. 44 32N 72 1W
47 Lyngdal, Agder, Nor. 58 8N 7 7E
47 Lyngdal, Buskerud, Nor. 59 54N 9 32E
113 Lynn, U.S.A. 42 28N 70 57W
109 Lynn Canal, Alas. 58 50N 135 20W
106 Lynn L., Canada 56 30N 101 40W
13 Lynton, Eng. 51 14N 3 50W
54 Lyntupy, U.S.S.R. 55 4N 26 23E
109 Lynx L., Canada 62 30N 106 25W
13 Lyonnais, Fr. 45 45N 4 15E
21 Lyon, France 45 46N 4 50E
21 Lyons = Lyon, France 45 46N 4 50E
116 Lyons, Colo., U.S.A. 40 17N 105 15W
115 Lyons, Ga., U.S.A. 32 10N 82 15W
116 Lyons, Kans., U.S.A. 38 24N 98 13W
96 Lyons, R., Australia 24 0s 116 0E
112 Lyons, N.Y., U.S.A. 43 3N 77 0W
43 Lyubimets, Bulgaria 41 50N 26 5E
55 Lyubomi, U.S.S.R. 51 10N 24 2E
55 Lyubotin, U.S.S.R. 50 0N 36 4E
54 Lyubytino, U.S.S.R. 58 50N 33 16E
54 Lyudinovo, U.S.S.R. 53 52N 34 28E
43 Lyuta, Bulgaria 41 53N 23 22E
75 Ma (Hwang Ho), China 34 30N 99 0E
62 Ma'ad, Jordan 32 37N 35 36E
91 Maamba, Zambia 22 43s 26 18E
64 Ma'an, Jordan 30 12N 35 44E
16 Maanshan, China 31 40N 118 30E
16 Maas, R., Belgium 51 48N 4 55E
16 Maaseik, Belgium 51 8N 5 40E
72 Maasin, Philippines 10 5N 124 55E
16 Maassluis, Neth. 51 56N 4 16E
16 Maastricht, Netherlands 50 50N 5 40E
81 Maatin-es-Sarra, Libya 21 45N 22 0E
90 Mabenge, Zaïre 4 15s 24 12E
12 Mablethorpe, Eng. 53 21N 0 14E
82 Mabrouk, Mali 19 29N 1 15W
91 Mabton, U.S.A. 46 13N 120 1W
124 Macachin, Argentina 37 10s 63 43W
113 McAdoo, U.S.A. 40 54N 76 0W
125 Macaé, Brazil 22 20s 41 43W
126 Macaguane, Colombia 6 35N 71 41W
117 McAlester, U.S.A. 34 57N 95 40W
31 Macao = Macau, China 22 16N 113 35E
127 Macapá, Brazil 0 5N 51 10W
126 Macarena, Serrania de la, Col. 2 45N 73 55W
96 McArthur, R., Australia 16 45s 136 0E
77 Macau ■, China 22 16N 113 35E
127 Macau, Brazil 5 0s 36 40W
108 McBride, Canada 53 20N 120 10W
118 McCamey, U.S.A. 31 8N 102 15W
118 McCammon, U.S.A. 42 41N 111 58W
12 Macclesfield, Eng. 53 16N 2 9W
108 McClintock, Canada 57 45N 94 15W
104 McClintock Chan., Can. 71 0N 103 0W
118 McCloud, U.S.A. 41 14N 122 5W
104 M'Clure Str., Canada 75 0N 119 0W
117 McClusky, U.S.A. 47 30N 100 31W
117 McComb, U.S.A. 31 13N 90 30W
108 McConnell Creek, Can. 56 53N 126 30W
108 McCook, U.S.A. 40 15N 100 35W
118 McDame, Canada 59 44N 129 29W
118 McDermitt, U.S.A. 42 0N 117 45W
3 McDonald I., Indian Ocean 54 0s 73 0E
96 Macdonnell Ranges, Australia 23 40s 133 0E
104 Macdougall L., Canada 66 20N 98 30W
106 MacDowell L., Canada 52 15N 92 45W

14 Macduff, Scot. 57 40N 2 30W
106 Mace, Canada 48 55N 80 0W
32 Maceda, Spain 42 16N 7 39W
30 Macedo de Cavaleiros, Portugal 41 31N 6 57W
42 Macedonia = Makedonija, Y.-slav. 41 53N 21 40E
44 Macedonia = Makhedonia, Greece 40 39N 22 0E
127 Maceió, Brazil 9 40s 35 41W
31 Macenta, Portugal 39 41N 8 55W
84 Macenta, Guinea 8 35N 9 20W
39 Macerata, Italy 43 19N 13 28E
77 McGehee, U.S.A. 33 40N 91 25W
118 McGill, U.S.A. 39 27N 114 50W
15 Macgillycuddy's Reeks, mts., Ireland 52 2N 9 45W
109 Macgregor, Canada 49 57N 98 48W
116 McGregor, Iowa, U.S.A. 42 58N 91 15W
116 McGregor, Minn., U.S.A. 46 37N 93 17W
116 McGregor Ra., Australia 27 0s 142 45E
68 Mach, Pakistan 29 50N 67 20E
126 Machachi, Ecuador 0 30s 78 15W
126 Machado, R. = Jiparana, Brazil 8 45s 62 20W
124 Machagai, Argentina 26 56s 60 2W
90 Machakos, Kenya 1 30s 37 15E
90 Machakos ♦, Kenya 1 30s 37 15E
126 Machala, Ecuador 3 10s 79 50W
91 Machanga, Mozambique 20 59s 35 0E
87 Machar Marshes, Sudan 9 28N 33 21E
91 Machava, Mozambique 25 54s 32 28E
91 Machece, Mozambique 19 15s 35 32E
18 Machecoul, France 47 0N 1 49W
77 Macheng, China 31 0N 114 40E
59 Machevna, U.S.S.R. 61 20N 172 20E
31 Machezo, mt., Spain 39 21N 4 20W
107 Machias, U.S.A. 44 40N 67 34W
126 Machichaco, Cabo, Sp. 43 28N 2 47W
126 Machiques, Venezuela 10 4N 72 34W
126 Machupicchu, Peru 13 8s 72 30W
13 Machynlleth, Wales 52 36N 3 51W
98 McIlwraith Ra., Australia 13 50s 143 20E
46 Măcin, Rumania 45 16N 28 8E
82 Macina, Mali 14 40N 4 50W
84 Macina, Canal de, Mali 13 50N 5 40W
13 McIntosh, U.S.A. 45 57N 101 20W
99 Macintyre, R., Australia 28 50s 151 0E
30 Macizo Galaico, Spain 42 30N 7 30W
98 Mackay, Australia 21 36s 148 39E
118 Mackay, U.S.A. 43 58N 113 37W
96 Mackay, L., Australia 22 40s 128 35E
112 McKees Rock, U.S.A. 40 27N 80 3W
113 McKeesport, U.S.A. 40 21N 79 50W
108 Mackenzie, Canada 55 20N 123 05W
113 McKenzie, U.S.A. 36 10N 88 31W
104 Mackenzie, R., Canada 69 10N 134 20W
105 Mackenzie, Terr., Can. 61 30N 144 30W
44 Mackenzie ♦, Australia 44 2N 122 30W
*126 Mackenzie City, Guy. 6 0N 58 10W
114 Mackinaw City, U.S.A. 45 45N 84 41W
104 McKinley, Mt., Alaska 63 10N 151 0W
4 McKinley Sea, Arc. Oc. 84 0N 10 0W
117 McKinney, U.S.A. 33 10N 96 40W
90 Mackinnon Road, Kenya 3 40s 39 1E
119 McKittrick, U.S.A. 35 18N 119 39W
48 Mackmyra, Sweden 60 40N 17 3E
96 Macksville, Australia 30 40s 152 56E
116 McLaughlin, U.S.A. 45 50N 100 50W
99 Maclean, Australia 29 26s 153 16E
116 McLeansboro, U.S.A. 38 5N 88 30W
92 Maclear, South Africa 31 2s 28 23E
108 McLennan, Canada 55 42N 116 50W
108 MacLeod, B., Canada 62 45N 110 0W
96 McLeod L., Australia 24 9s 113 47E
108 MacLeod Lake, Canada 54 58N 123 0W
118 McLoughlin, Mt., U.S.A. 42 30N 122 30W
108 McLure, Canada 51 0N 120 20W
112 McMechen, U.S.A. 39 57N 80 44W
117 McMillan, U.S.A. 32 40N 104 20W
118 McMinnville, Oreg., U.S.A. 45 16N 123 11W
115 McMinnville, Tenn., U.S.A. 35 43N 85 45W
109 McMorran, Canada 51 19N 108 42W
5 McMurdo Sd., Antarc. 77 0s 170 0E
108 McMurray, Canada - 56 45N 111 27W
119 McNary, U.S.A. 34 4N 109 53W
93 Macodoene, Mozambique 23 32s 35 5E
40 Macomer, Sardinia 40 16N 8 48E
21 Mâcon, France 46 19N 4 50E
115 Macon, Ga., U.S.A. 32 50N 83 37W
117 Macon, Miss., U.S.A. 33 7N 88 31W
116 Macon, Mo., U.S.A. 39 40N 92 26W
91 Macossa, Mozambique 17 55s 33 56E
91 Macovane, Mozambique 21 30s 35 0E
116 McPherson, U.S.A. 38 25N 97 40W
99 Macquarie Harb., Australia 42 18s 145 25E
99 Macquarie, R., Australia 30 5s 147 31E
5 MacRobertson Coast, Antarctica 68 30s 63 0E
15 Macroom, Ireland 51 54N 8 57W
126 Mac Tier, Canada 45 9N 79 46W
126 Macu, Brazil 0 25N 69 15W
38 Macugnaga, Italy 45 57N 7 58E
126 Macuiro, Mozambique 19 15s 35 5E
91 Macuiza, Mozambique 18 7s 34 29E
126 Macujer, Columbia 0 24N 73 10W
91 Macuse, Mozambique 17 45s 37 17E
91 Macusse, Angola 17 48s 20 23E
120 Mácuzari, Presa, Mexico 27 10N 109 10W
86 Madā 'in Sālih, Saudi Arabia 26 51N 37 58E

MAP
85 Madagali, Nigeria 10 56N 13 33E
93 Madagascar, I., Africa 20 0s 47 0E
84 Madam, Ivory Coast 7 58N 3 32W
107 Madame I., Canada 45 30N 60 58W
70 Madanapalle, India 13 33N 78 34E
98 Madang, N.E. New 5 0s 145 46E
  Guin.
85 Madaoua, Niger 14 5N 6 27E
85 Madara, Nigeria 11 45N 10 35E
69 Madaripur, Bangladesh 23 2N 90 15E
67 Madauk, Burma 17 56N 96 52E
112 Madawaska, Canada 45 30N 77 55W
112 Madawaska, R., Canada 45 20N 77 30W
67 Madaya, Burma 22 20N 96 10E
87 Madbar, Sudan 6 17N 30 45E
40 Maddalena, I., Italy 41 15N 9 23E
41 Maddaloni, Italy 41 4N 14 23E
120 Madden Dam, Panama 9 13N 79 37W
  Canal Zone
120 Madden Lake, Panama 9 20N 79 37W
  Canal Zone
87 Madebele, Ethiopia 12 30N 41 10E
80 Madeira, Is., Atlan. Oc. 32 50N 17 0W
126 Madeira, R., Brazil 5 30s 61 20W
91 Madenda, Malawi 13 42s 35 1W
119 Madera, U.S.A. 37 0N 120 1W
73 Madha, India 18 0N 75 55E
69 Madhubani, India 26 21N 86 7E
90 Madhupur, India 24 18N 86 37E
68 Madhya Pradesh ♦, 21 50N 81 0E
  India
*90 Madi ♦, Uganda 3 0N 32 0E
90 Madi Opei, Uganda 3 47N 33 5E
117 Madill, U.S.A. 34 5N 96 49W
88 Madimba, Zaïre 5 0s 15 0E
91 Madimba, Mozambique 4 58s 15 6E
63 Madinat al Shaab, S. 12 50N 45 0E
  Yemen
88 Madingou, Congo 4 10s 13 33E
93 Madirovalo, Malag. 16 26s 46 32E
115 Madison, Fla., U.S.A. 30 29N 83 26W
114 Madison, Ind., U.S.A. 38 42N 85 20W
116 Madison, Nebr., U.S.A. 41 53N 97 25W
116 Madison, Ohio, U.S.A. 41 45N 81 4W
116 Madison, S.D., U.S.A. 44 0N 97 8W
116 Madison, Wis., U.S.A. 43 5N 89 25W
118 Madison, R., U.S.A. 45 0N 111 48W
118 Madison City, U.S.A. 43 5N 93 10W
118 Madison Junc., U.S.A. 44 42N 110 56W
114 Madisonville, U.S.A. 37 42N 87 30W
92 Madista, Botswana 21 15s 25 6E
73 Madiun, Indonesia 7 38s 111 32E
73 Madjalengka, Indonesia 6 55s 108 14E
73 Madjene, Indonesia 3 27s 118 57E
87 Madol, Sudan 9 3N 27 45E
54 Madona, U.S.S.R. 56 53N 26 5E
64 Madraqa, Saudi Arabia 21 57N 40 0E
70 Madras, India 13 8N 80 19E
70 Madras = Tamil Nadu 11 0N 77 0E
  ♦, India
118 Madras, U.S.A. 44 40N 121 10W
117 Madre L., U.S.A. 26 30N 90 20W
120 Madre, Laguna, Mexico 25 0N 97 30W
120 Madre, Sierra. Mexico 16 0N 93 0W
73 Madre, Sierra. Phil. 17 0N 122 0E
128 Madre de Dios, I., Chile 50 20N 75 10W
126 Madre de Dios, R., Bol. 11 30s 67 0W
120 Madre del Sur, Sierra, 17 30N 100 0W
  Mexico
120 Madre Occidental, 27 0N 107 0W
  Sierra, Mexico
120 Madre Oriental, Sierra, 25 0N 100 0W
  Mexico
68 Madri, India 24 16N 73 32E
30 Madrid, Spain 40 25N 3 45W
30 Madrid ♦, Spain 40 30N 3 45W
31 Madridejos, Spain 39 28N 3 33W
30 Madrigal de las Altas 41 5N 5 0W
  Torres. Sp.
31 Madrona, Sierra, Spain 38 27N 4 16W
31 Madroñera, Spain 39 26N 5 42W
87 Madu, Sudan 14 37N 26 4E
73 Madura, I., Indonesia 7 0s 113 20E
73 Madura, Selat, Indonesia 7 30s 113 20E
70 Madurai, India 9 55N 78 10E
70 Madurantakam, India 12 30N 79 50E
70 Maduru Oya, Sri Lanka 7 40N 81 7E
57 Madzhalis, U.S.S.R. 42 9N 47 47E
71 Mae Hong Son, Thai. 19 16N 98 1E
71 Mae Sot, Thailand 16 43N 98 34E
32 Maella, Spain 41 8N 0 7E
46 Mäeruş, Rumania 45 53N 25 31E
13 Maesteg, Wales 51 36N 3 40W
121 Maestra, Sierra, Cuba 20 15N 77 0W
32 Maestrazgo, Mts. del, 40 30N 0 25W
  Spain
25 Mafan, Libya 25 56N 14 56E
109 Mafeking, Canada 52 40N 101 10W
92 Mafeking, S. Africa 25 50s 25 38E
84 Mafèrè, Ivory Coast 5 30N 3 2W
100 Mafeteng, Lesotho 29 51s 27 15E
100 Maffra, Australia 37 53s 146 58E
90 Mafia I., Tanzania 7 45s 39 50E
125 Mafra, Brazil 26 10N 50 0W
31 Mafra, Portugal 38 55N 9 20W
127 Mafrense, Brazil 8 10s 41 10W
51 Mafungabusi Plateau, 18 30s 29 8E
  Rhodesia
54 Magadan, U.S.S.R. 59 30N 151 0E
90 Magadi, Kenya 1 54s 36 19E
90 Magadi, L., Kenya 1 54s 36 19E
93 Magaliesburg, S. Africa 26 1s 27 32E
128 Magallanes, Estrecho de, 52 30s 75 0W
  Chile
126 Magangue, Colombia 9 14N 74 45W
85 Magaria, Niger 13 4N 9 5W
84 Magburaka, Sierra Leone 8 47N 12 0W
62 Magdal, Israel 32 51N 35 30E
107 Magdalen Is., Canada 47 30N 61 40W

124 Magdalena, Argentina 35 5s 57 30W
126 Magdalena, Bolivia 13 13s 63 57W
120 Magdalena, Mexico 30 50N 112 0W
119 Magdalena, U.S.A. 34 10N 107 20W
126 Magdalena, B., Mexico 24 30N 112 10W
126 Magdalena ♦, Col. 10 0N 74 0W
120 Magdalena, I., Mexico 24 40N 112 15W
120 Magdalena, Llano de la, 25 0N 111 30W
  Mexico
72 Magdalena, mt., 4 25N 117 55E
  Malaysia
126 Magdalena, R., Col. 8 30N 74 0W
120 Magdalena, R., Mex. 30 50N 112 0W
24 Magdeburg, Germany 52 8N 11 36E
24 Magdeburg ♦, E. 52 20N 11 40E
  Germany
62 Magdiel, Israel 32 10N 34 54E
87 Magdub, Sudan 13 42N 25 5E
117 Magee, U.S.A. 31 53N 89 45W
15 Magee, I., N.Ire. U.K. 54 48N 5 44W
73 Magelang, Indonesia 7 29s 110 13E
128 Magellan's 52 30s 75 0W
  Str = Magallanes, Est de, Chile
38 Magenta, Italy 45 28N 8 53E
38 Maggia, R., Switzerland 46 18N 8 36E
38 Maggiorasca, Mt., Italy 44 33N 9 29E
38 Maggiore, L., Italy 46 0N 8 35E
84 Maghama, Mauritania 15 32N 12 57W
62 Maghar, Israel 32 54N 35 24E
82 Maghnia, Algeria 34 50N 1 43W
39 Magione, Italy 43 10N 12 12E
42 Maglaj, Yugoslavia 44 33N 18 7E
39 Magliano in Toscana, It. 42 36N 11 18E
41 Màglie, Italy 40 8N 18 17E
86 Magna, Saudi Arabia 28 25N 34 46E
20 Magnac-Laval, France 46 13N 1 11E
4 Magnetic Pole, 75 0N 101 0W
  1965(North), Canada
5 Magnetic Pole, 1965, 66 30s 139 30E
  (South), Antarctica
45 Magnisía ♦, Greece 39 24N 22 46E
52 Magnitogorsk, U.S.S.R. 53 20N 59 0E
117 Magnolia, Ark., U.S.A. 33 18N 93 12W
117 Magnolia, Miss., U.S.A. 31 8N 90 28W
47 Magnor, Norway 59 56N 12 15E
19 Magny-en-Vexin, France 49 9N 1 47E
91 Màgoé, Mozambique 15 45s 31 42E
102 Magog, Canada 45 18N 72 9W
91 Magoro, Uganda 1 45N 34 12E
91 Magoye, Zambia 16 1s 27 30E
91 Magpie L., Canada 51 0N 64 40W
108 Magrath, Canada 49 25N 112 50W
33 Magro, R., Spain 39 20N 0 45W
87 Magrur, W., Sudan 16 5N 26 30E
126 Maguarinho, C., Brazil 0 15s 48 30W
109 Maguse L., Canada 61 35N 95 20W
109 Maguse, R., Canada 61 20N 94 25W
67 Magwe, Burma 20 10N 95 0E
64 Mahabad, Iran 36 50N 45 45E
69 Mahabarat Lekh, Nepal 28 30N 82 0E
93 Mahabo, Malag. 20 23s 44 40E
70 Mahad, India 18 6N 73 29E
68 Mahadeo Hills, India 22 20N 78 30E
70 Mahadeopur, India 18 48N 80 0E
70 Mahagi, Zaïre 2 20N 31 0E
93 Mahajamba, B. de la, 15 24s 47 5E
  Malag.
93 Mahajamba, R., Malag. 17 0s 47 30E
68 Mahajan, India 28 48N 73 56E
93 Mahajilo, R., Malag. 19 30s 46 0E
72 Mahakam, R., Indonesia 1 0N 114 40E
92 Mahalapye, Botswana 23 1s 26 51E
86 Mahalla el Kubra, Egypt 31 10N 31 0E
64 Mahallat, Iran 33 55N 50 30E
69 Mahanadi R., India 20 33N 85 0E
93 Mahanoro, Malagasy 19 54s 48 48E
  Republic
113 Mahanoy City, U.S.A. 40 48N 76 10W
70 Maharashtra ♦, India 19 30N 75 30E
83 Maharès, Tunisia 34 32N 10 29E
90 Mahari Mts., Tanzania 6 20s 30 0E
93 Mahasolo, Malag. 19 7s 46 22E
70 Mahaweli Ganga, Sri 8 0N 81 10E
  Lanka
70 Mahboobabad, India 17 42N 80 2E
70 Mahbubnagar, India 16 45N 77 59E
64 Mahd Dhahab, Si. Arab. 25 55N 45 30E
83 Mahdia, Tunisia 35 28N 11 0E
70 Mahé, India 11 42N 75 34E
70 Mahendra Giri, mt., 8 20N 77 30E
  India
91 Mahenge, Tanzania 8 45s 36 35E
101 Mahia Pen., N.Z. 39 9s 177 55E
87 Mahmiya, Sudan 17 5N 33 56E
46 Mahmudia, Rumania 45 5N 29 5E
116 Mahnomen, U.S.A. 47 22N 95 57W
85 Mahoba, India 25 15N 79 55E
32 Mahón, Spain 39 50N 4 18E
68 Mahuta, Nigeria 11 32N 4 58E
68 Mahuva, India 25 7N 71 46E
18 Maïche, France 47 16N 6 48E
127 Maicuru, R., Brazil 1 0s 54 30W
41 Màida, Italy 38 51N 16 21E
13 Maidenhead, Eng. 51 31N 0 42W
87 Maidi, Yemen 16 20N 42 45E
109 Maidstone, Canada 53 5N 109 20W
13 Maidstone, Eng. 51 16N 0 31E
85 Maiduguri, Nigeria 12 0N 13 20E
19 Maignelay, France 49 32N 2 30E
93 Maingualida, Sierra, Ven. 5 30N 65 10W
69 Maijdi, Bangladesh 22 48N 91 10E
69 Maikala Ra., India 22 0N 81 0E
18 Mailly-le-Camp, France 48 41N 4 9E
68 Mailsi, Pakistan 29 48N 72 15E
65 Maimana, Afghanistan 35 53N 64 38E
24 Main, R., Germany 50 13N 11 0E
15 Main, R., N. Ire. 54 49N 6 20W

99 Main Barrier Ra., 31 10s 141 20E
  Australia
112 Main Channel, Canada 45 22N 81 45W
98 Main Coast Ra., 16 22s 145 10E
  Australia
25 Mainburg, Germany 48 37N 11 49E
71 Maindargi, India 17 33N 74 21E
18 Maine, France 48 0N 0 0E
107 Maine ♦, U.S.A. 45 20N 69 0W
18 Maine-et-Loire ♦, 47 31N 0 30W
  France
85 Maïne-Soroa, Niger 13 13N 12 2E
73 Maingkwan, Burma 26 15N 96 45E
73 Mainit, L., Philippines 9 31N 125 30E
14 Mainland, I., Orkneys, 59 0N 3 10W
  Scot.
14 Mainland, I., Shetlands, 60 15N 1 22W
  Scotland
68 Mainpuri, India 27 18N 79 4E
19 Maintenon, France 48 35N 1 35E
93 Maintirano, Malagasy 18 3s 44 1E
  Republic
25 Mainz, Germany 50 0N 8 17E
124 Maipú, Argentina 37 0s 58 0W
126 Maipures, Colombia 5 11N 67 49W
126 Maiquetia, Venezuela 10 36N 66 57W
38 Maira, R., Italy 44 29N 7 15E
67 Mairabari, India 26 30N 92 30E
121 Maisi, C., Cuba 20 10N 74 10W
19 Maisse, France 48 24N 2 21E
100 Maitland, N.S.W., 32 44s 151 36E
  Australia
99 Maitland, S. Australia, 34 23s 137 40E
  Australia
112 Maitland, R., Canada 43 45N 81 33W
85 Maiyema, Nigeria 12 5N 4 25E
74 Maizuru, Japan 35 25N 135 22E
126 Majagual, Colombia 8 33N 74 38W
62 Majd el Kurum, Israel 32 56N 35 15E
44 Maj'-el-Cikës, Albania 40 14N 19 33E
42 Majevica Planina, 44 45N 18 50E
  Yugoslavia
87 Maji, Ethiopia 6 20N 35 30E
64 Majma'a, Saudi Arabia 25 57N 45 22E
32 Majorca, I. = Mallorca, 39 30N 3 0E
  I., Spain
73 Maju, I., Indonesia 1 30N 126 30E
94 Makale, Ethiopia 13 40N 39 26E
91 Makamba, Burundi 4 8s 29 49E
106 Makanaks, Canada 48 45N 79 0W
88 Makari, Cameroon 12 35N 14 28E
92 Makarikari = 20 40s 25 45E
  Makgadikgadi, Bots.
59 Makarovo, U.S.S.R. 57 40N 107 45E
42 Makarska, Yugoslavia 43 20N 17 2E
55 Makaryev, U.S.S.R. 57 52N 43 50E
*73 Makasar, Indonesia 5 10s 119 20E
73 Makasar, Selat, 1 0s 118 20E
  Indonesia
58 Makat, U.S.S.R. 47 39N 53 19E
93 Makaw, Zaïre 3 29s 18 22E
44 Makedhonía ♦, Greece 40 39N 22 0E
42 Makedonija ♦, Y.-slavia 41 53N 21 40E
84 Makeni, Sierra Leone 8 55N 12 5W
56 Makeyevka, U.S.S.R. 48 0N 38 0E
92 Makgadikgadi, Botswana 20 40s 25 45E
92 Makgadikari Salt Pans, 20 40s 25 45E
  Botswana
73 Makgobistad, S. Africa 25 45s 25 12E
57 Makhachkala, U.S.S.R. 43 0N 47 15E
57 Makharadze, U.S.S.R. 41 55s 42 2E
43 Makhlata, Bulgaria 43 26N 24 17E
73 Makian, I., Indonesia 0 12N 127 20E
94 Makin, I., Pacific Ocean 3 30N 174 0E
58 Makinsk, U.S.S.R. 52 37N 70 26E
86 Makkah, Saudi Arabia 21 30N 39 54E
107 Makkovik, Canada 55 0N 59 10W
59 Maklakovo, U.S.S.R. 58 16N 92 29E
27 Makó, Hungary 46 14N 20 33E
88 Makokou, Gabon 0 40N 12 50E
90 Makongo, Zaïre 3 15N 26 17E
88 Makoua, Congo 0 5s 15 50E
27 Maków Podhal., Poland 49 43N 19 45E
45 Makrá, I., Greece 36 15N 25 54E
65 Makran, Iran & Pakistan 26 13N 61 30E
65 Makran Coast Range, 25 40N 4 0E
  Pakistan
68 Makrana, India 27 2N 74 46E
45 Mákri, Greece 40 52N 25 40E
58 Maksimkin Yar, 58 58N 86 50E
  U.S.S.R.
83 Maktar, Tunisia 35 48N 9 1E
64 Maku, Iran 39 15N 44 31E
92 Makumbe, Botswana 20 15s 24 26E
94 Makumbi, Zaïre 5 50s 20 43E
92 Makumbako, Botswana 22 30s 20 7E
74 Makurazaki, Japan 31 15N 130 20E
92 Makwassie, S. Africa 27 17s 26 0E
44 Mal i Gribës, Albania 40 17N 19 45E
44 Mal i Nemërçkës, Alb. 40 20N 20 11E
44 Mal i Tomorit, Albania 40 42N 20 11E
15 Mal B., Ireland 52 50N 9 30W
39 Mala Kapela, Y.-slavia 44 45N 15 30E
43 Malabang, Philippines 7 36N 124 3E
70 Malabar Coast, India 11 0N 75 0E
71 Malacca = Melaka, 2 15N 102 15E
  Malaysia
73 Malacca, Str. of, Indon. 3 0N 101 0E
27 Malacky, Cz. 48 27N 17 0E
118 Malad City, U.S.A. 42 10N 112 20W
33 Maladetta, Mt., Europe 42 40N 0 30E
87 Maladaburi, Ethiopia 10 37N 40 30E
126 Málaga, Colombia 6 42N 72 44W
31 Málaga, Spain 36 43N 4 23W

31 Málaga, Spain 36 38N 4 58W
117 Malaga, U.S.A. 32 12N 104 2W
90 Malagarasi, Tanzania 5 5s 30 50E
90 Malagarasi, R., Tanz. 3 50s 30 0E
93 Malagasy Rep. ■, Africa 19 0s 46 0E
31 Malagón, Spain 39 11N 3 52W
31 Malagón, R., Spain 37 40N 7 20W
93 Malaimbandy, Malag. 20 20s 45 36E
87 Malakâl, Sudan 9 33N 31 50E
66 Malakand, Pakistan 34 40N 71 55E
117 Malakoff, U.S.A. 32 10N 95 55W
108 Malakwa, Canada 50 55N 118 50W
59 Malamyzh, U.S.S.R. 50 0N 136 50E
73 Malang, Indonesia 7 59s 112 35E
88 Malanje, Angola 9 30s 16 17E
48 Mälaren, Sweden 59 30N 17 10E
124 Malargüe, Argentina 35 40s 69 30W
106 Malartic, Canada 48 9N 78 9W
64 Malatya, Turkey 38 25N 38 20E
59 Malawi ■, Africa 11 48N 7 39E
91 Malawi, L. (Lago 12 30s 34 30E
  Niassa), Africa
71 Malaya ♦, S.E. Asia 4 0N 102 0E
56 Malaya Belózerka, 47 12N 34 56E
  U.S.S.R.
54 Malaya Vishera, USSR 58 55N 32 25E
73 Malaybalay, Philippines 8 5N 125 15E
64 Malayer, Iran 28 22N 56 38E
72 Malaysia ■, S.E. Asia 5 0N 110 0E
64 Malazgirt, Turkey 39 10N 42 33E
98 Malbon, Australia 21 5s 140 17E
28 Malbork, Poland 54 3N 19 10E
87 Malca Dube, Ethiopia 6 40N 41 52E
24 Malchin, Germany 53 43N 12 44E
24 Malchow, Germany 53 29N 12 25E
28 Malcolm, Australia 28 51s 121 25E
16 Maldegem, Belgium 51 14N 16 29E
117 Malden, Mass., U.S.A. 42 26N 71 5W
117 Malden, Mo., U.S.A. 36 35N 90 0W
75 Maldive Is. ■, Indian 2 0N 73 0E
  Oc.
100 Maldon, Australia 37 0s 144 6E
125 Maldonado, Uruguay 35 0s 55 0W
120 Maldonado, Punta, Mex. 16 19N 98 35W
38 Malé, Italy 46 20N 10 55E
27 Malé Karpaty, Cz. 48 30N 17 20E
45 Maléa, Akra, Greece 36 28N 23 7E
68 Malegaon, India 20 30N 74 30E
91 Malei, Mozambique 17 12s 36 58E
87 Malek, Sudan 6 2N 31 38E
91 Malela, Zaïre 4 22s 26 8E
91 Malenge, Zambia 12 40s 26 42E
49 Mälerås, Sweden 56 54N 15 34E
106 Malerkotla, India 30 32N 75 58E
45 Males, Greece 35 6N 25 35E
91 Malesherbes, France 48 15N 2 24E
42 Maleske Planina, 41 38N 23 7E
  Y.-slav.-Bulg.
18 Malestroit, France 47 49N 2 25W
41 Malfa, Italy 38 35N 14 50E
57 Malgobek, U.S.S.R. 43 30N 44 52E
50 Malgomai L., Sweden 64 40N 16 30E
32 Malgrat, Spain 41 39N 2 46E
118 Malheur L., U.S.A. 43 19N 118 42W
118 Malheur, R., U.S.A. 43 55N 117 55W
84 Mali, Guinea 12 10N 12 20W
85 Mali ■, Africa 15 0N 10 0E
71 Mali Kanal, Y.-slavia 45 36N 19 24E
67 Mali, R., Burma 26 20N 97 40E
44 Mal-i-Gjalicës së Lumës, 42 2N 20 25E
  Alb.
39 Mali Kvarner, 44 50N 14 10E
  Yugoslavia
71 Mali Kyun, I., Burma 13 0N 98 20E
62 Malih, Nahr al, Jordan 32 20N 35 29E
73 Malik, Indonesia 0 39s 123 16E
73 Malili, Indonesia 2 42s 121 23E
90 Malimba, Mts., Zaïre 7 30s 29 30E
54 Malin, U.S.S.R. 50 46N 29 15E
72 Malinau, Indonesia 3 35N 116 30E
90 Malindi, Kenya 3 12s 40 5E
73 Maling, Mt., Indonesia 1 0N 121 0E
73 Malingping, Indonesia 6 45s 106 2E
91 Malinyi, Tanzania 8 56s 36 0E
44 Maliqi, Albania 40 40N 20 48E
43 Malita, Philippines 6 19N 125 39E
70 Malkapur, Maharashtra, 20 53N 76 17E
  India
70 Malkapur, Maharashtra, 16 57N 74 0W
  India
28 Małkinia Grn., Poland 52 42N 21 58E
43 Malko Turnovo, Bulg. 41 59N 27 31E
100 Mallacoota, Australia 37 40s 149 40E
100 Mallacoota Inlet, 37 40s 149 40E
  Australia
62 Mallaha, Israel 33 6N 35 35E
14 Mallaig, Scotland 57 0N 5 50W
69 Mallawan, India 27 4N 80 12E
86 Mallawi, Egypt 30 30N 30 44E
100 Mallee, Australia 35 10s 142 20E
21 Mallemort, France 43 44N 5 11E
45 Mállia, Greece 35 17N 25 27E
48 Mälles Venosta, Italy 46 42N 10 32E
45 Mallorca, I., Spain 39 30N 3 0E
113 Mallorytown, Canada 44 29N 75 53W
15 Mallow, Ireland 52 8N 8 40W
50 Malmbäck, Sweden 57 34N 14 28E
50 Malmberget, Sweden 67 11N 20 40E
16 Malmédy, Belgium 50 25N 6 2E
92 Malmesbury, S. Africa 33 28s 18 41E
49 Malmö, Sweden 55 36N 12 59E
49 Malmöhus län ♦, 55 45N 13 30E
  Sweden
55 Malmyzh, U.S.S.R. 56 35N 50 30E
49 Malmöhus län ♦, 55 45N 13 30E
  Sweden
46 Malnaş, Rumania 46 2N 25 49E

43 Malo Konare, Bulgaria 42 12N 24 24E
55 Maloarkhangelsk, 52 28N 36 30E
  U.S.S.R.
73 Malolos, Philippines 14 50N 21 2E
91 Malombe L., Malawi 14 40s 35 15E
43 Malomir, Bulgaria 42 16N 26 30E
117 Malone, U.S.A. 44 50N 74 19W
43 Malorad, Bulgaria 43 28N 23 41E
54 Malorita, U.S.S.R. 51 41N 24 3E
55 Maloyaroslovets, USSR 55 2N 36 20E
52 Malozemelskaya Tundra, 67 0N 50 0E
  U.S.S.R.
31 Malpartida, Spain 39 26N 6 30W
126 Malpelo I., Colombia 4 3N 80 35W
30 Malpica, Spain 43 19N 8 50W
70 Malprabha, R., India 15 40N 74 50E
118 Malta, Idaho, U.S.A. 42 15N 113 50W
118 Malta, Mont., U.S.A. 48 20N 107 55W
36 Malta ■, Europe 35 50N 14 30E
40 Malta Channel, Medit. 36 40N 14 0E
43 Malton, Canada 43 41N 79 38W
12 Malton, England 54 9N 0 48W
73 Maluku, Kepulauan, 3 0s 128 0E
  Indonesia
73 Maluku ♦, Indonesia 3 0s 128 0E
85 Malumfashi, Nigeria 11 48N 7 39E
48 Malung, Sweden 60 42s 13 44E
70 Malvalli, India 12 28N 77 8E
70 Malvan, India 16 2N 73 30E
13 Malvern, Eng. 52 7N 2 19W
117 Malvern, Ark., U.S.A. 34 22N 92 50W
112 Malvern, Ohio, U.S.A. 40 31N 31 12W
13 Malvern Hills, Eng. 52 0N 2 19W
93 Malvérnia, Mozambique 22 6s 31 42E
47 Malvik, Norway 63 25N 10 40E
126 Malvinas Is = Falkland 51 30s 59 0W
  Is., S. Atl. Oc.
90 Malya, Tanzania 3 5s 33 38E
59 Mama, U.S.S.R. 58 18N 112 54E
55 Mamadysh, U.S.S.R. 55 44N 51 23E
46 Mamaia, Rumania 44 18N 28 37E
127 Mamanguape, Brazil 6 50s 35 4w
73 Mamasa, Indonesia 2 55s 119 20E
90 Mambasa, Zaïre 1 22N 29 3E
73 Mamberamo, R., Indon. 2 0s 137 50E
91 Mambirima, Zaïre 11 25s 27 33E
90 Mambo, Tanzania 4 52s 38 22E
90 Mambrui, Kenya 3 5s 40 5E
85 Mamfe, Cameroon 5 50N 9 15E
106 Mammamattawa, Canada 50 25N 84 23W
41 Màmmola, Italy 38 23N 16 13E
119 Mammoth, U.S.A. 32 46N 110 43W
77 Mamoi, China 26 0N 119 25E
127 Mamoré, R., Bolivia 9 55s 65 20W
84 Mamou, Guinea 10 15N 12 0W
84 Mampatá, Port. Guinea 11 54N 14 53W
72 Mampawah, Indonesia 0 30N 109 5E
85 Mampong, Ghana 7 6N 1 26W
73 Mamudju, Indonesia 2 50s 118 50E
84 Man, Ivory Coast 7 30N 7 40W
12 Man, I. of, U.K. 54 15N 4 30W
70 Man, R., India 17 20N 75 0E
67 Man Na, Burma 23 27N 97 19E
127 Mana, Fr. Guina 5 45s 53 55W
72 Mana, Indonesia 4 25s 102 55E
87 Mana, R., Ethiopia 6 20N 40 41E
47 Måna, R., Norway 59 55N 8 50E
126 Manacacias, R., Col. 4 23N 72 4W
126 Manacapuru, Brazil 3 10s 60 50W
32 Manacor, Spain 39 32N 3 12E
73 Manado, Indonesia 1 40N 124 45E
121 Managua, Nicaragua 12 0N 86 20W
121 Managua, L., Nicaragua 12 20N 86 30W
94 Manaia, New Zealand 39 33s 174 8E
93 Manakana, Malagasy 13 43s 50 4E
  Rep.
93 Manakara, Malagasy 22 8s 48 1E
  Republic
98 Manam I., Terr. of New 4 5s 145 5E
  Guinea
93 Manamah, Bahrain I. 26 11N 50 35E
93 Manambaho, R., Malag. 17 35s 44 45E
93 Manambato, Malagasy 13 43s 49 7E
  Rep.
93 Manambolo, R., Malag. 19 20s 45 0E
93 Manambolosy, Malag. 16 2s 49 40E
93 Mananara, Malagasy 16 10s 49 30E
  Republic
93 Mananara, R., Malag. 23 25s 48 10E
93 Mananjary, Malagasy 21 13s 48 20E
  Republic
93 Manankoliva, Malag. 24 17s 47 19E
101 Manapouri, N.Z. 45 34s 167 39E
101 Manapouri, L., N.Z. 45 32s 167 32E
70 Manar, R., India 18 50N 77 20E
75 Manasalowo Chih, 30 45N 81 20E
  China
65 Manasir, Si. Arabia 24 30N 51 10E
69 Manaslu, Mt., Nepal 28 33N 84 33E
113 Manasquan, U.S.A. 40 7N 74 3W
75 Manass, China 44 20N 86 21E
119 Manassa, U.S.A. 37 12N 105 58W
67 Manaung Kyun, Burma 18 45N 93 40E
126 Manaus, Brazil 3 0s 60 0W
73 Manay, Philippines 7 17N 126 33E
114 Mancelona, U.S.A. 44 54N 85 5W
31 Mancha Real, Spain 37 48N 3 39W
18 Manche ♦, France 49 10N 1 20W
12 Manchester, Eng. 53 30N 2 15W
113 Manchester, Conn., 41 47N 72 30W
  U.S.A.
115 Manchester, Ga., U.S.A. 32 53N 84 32W
116 Manchester, Iowa, 42 28N 91 27W
  U.S.A.
114 Manchester, Ky., U.S.A. 37 10N 83 45W
113 Manchester, N.H., USA 42 58N 71 29W
112 Manchester, N.Y., USA 42 56N 77 16W
113 Manchester Depot, 43 10N 73 5W
  U.S.A.

* Incorporated within
the new Nile district

* Renamed Ujung Pandang

Manchouli INDEX Maruggio

MAP
76 Manchouli, China 49 46N 117 24E
59 Manchuria = Tung-pei, China 44 0N 126 0E
39 Manciano, Italy 42 35N 11 30E
87 Mancifa, Ethiopia 6 53N 41 50E
65 Mand, R., Iran 28 20N 52 30E
91 Manda, Chunya, Tanzania 6 51S 32 29E
91 Manda, Jombe, Tanzania 10 30S 34 40E
125 Mandaguari, Brazil 23 32S 51 42W
47 Mandal, Norway 58 2N 7 25E
76 Mandal Gobi, Mongolia 45 47N 106 15E
73 Mandala, Pontjak, Indon. 4 30S 141 0E
67 Mandalay = Mandale, Burma 22 0N 96 10E
67 Mandale, Burma 22 0N 96 10E
76 Mandalgovi, Mongolia 45 40N 106 22E
64 Mandali, Iraq 33 52N 45 28E
45 Mandalya Körfezi, Turkey 37 15N 27 20E
116 Mandan, U.S.A. 46 50N 101 0W
70 Mandapeta, India 16 47N 81 56E
73 Mandar, Teluk, Indonesia 3 35S 119 4E
40 Mandas, Italy 39 40N 9 8E
68 Mandasor (Mandsaur), India 24 3N 75 8E
72 Mandawai (Katingan), R., Indon. 1 30S 113 0E
38 Mandelieu-la- Napoule, France 43 34N 6 57E
90 Mandera, Kenya 3 55N 41 42E
90 Mandera ♦, Kenya 3 30N 41 0E
68 Mandi, India 31 39N 76 58E
91 Mandi, Zambia 14 30S 23 45E
73 Mandioli, Indonesia 0 40S 127 20E
69 Mandla, India 22 39N 80 30E
49 Mandö, Denmark 55 18N 8 33E
93 Mandoto, Malagasy Rep. 19 34S 46 17E
45 Mandoúdhion, Greece 38 48N 23 29E
45 Mandráki, Greece 36 36N 27 11E
93 Mandrase, R., Malag. 25 10S 46 30E
93 Mandritsara, Malagasy Republic 15 50S 48 49E
68 Mandsaur (Mandasor), India 24 3N 75 8E
41 Mandúria, Italy 40 25N 17 38E
68 Mandvi, India 22 51N 69 22E
70 Mandya, India 12 30N 77 0E
68 Mandzai, Pakistan 30 55N 67 6E
85 Mané, Upper Volta 12 59N 1 21W
70 Maner, R., India 18 30N 79 40E
98 Maneroo, Australia 23 40S 143 52E
86 Manfalût, Egypt 27 20N 30 52E
100 Manfred, Australia 33 19S 143 45E
41 Manfredónia, Italy 41 40N 15 55E
41 Manfredónia, G. di, Italy 41 30N 16 10E
85 Manga, Upper Volta 11 40N 1 4W
101 Mangaia, I., Cook Is. 21 55S 157 55W
70 Mangalagiri, India 16 26N 80 36E
46 Mangalia, Rumania 43 50N 28 35E
70 Mangalore, India 12 55N 74 47E
30 Manganeses, Spain 41 45N 5 43W
70 Mangaon, India 18 15N 73 20E
47 Manger, Norway 60 38N 5 3W
72 Manggar, Indonesia 2 50S 108 10E
73 Manggawitu, Indonesia 4 8S 133 32E
69 Mangla Dam, Pak. 33 32N 73 50E
68 Manglaur, India 29 44N 77 49E
93 Mangoky, R., Malag. 21 55S 44 40E
73 Mangole I., Indonesia 1 50S 125 55E
90 Mangombe, Zaïre 1 20S 26 48E
101 Mangonui, N.Z. 35 1S 173 32E
100 Mangoplah, Australia 33 25S 147 17E
30 Mangualde, Portugal 40 38N 7 48W
81 Mangueigne, Chad 10 40N 21 5E
125 Mangueira, Lagoa da, Braz. 33 0S 52 50W
83 Manguéni, Hamada, Chad 22 47N 12 56E
117 Mangum, U.S.A. 34 50N 99 30W
75 Mangyai, China 38 6N 91 37E
57 Mangyshlak P-ov., U.S.S.R. 43 40N 52 30E
116 Manhattan, Kans., U.S.A. 39 10N 96 40W
118 Manhattan, Nev., U.S.A. 38 40N 117 3W
93 Manhiça, Mozambique 25 23S 32 49E
127 Manhuaçu, Brazil 20 15S 42 2W
67 Mani, China 34 52N 87 11E
126 Mani, Colombia 4 49N 72 17W
93 Mania, R., Malag. 19 55S 46 10E
39 Maniago, Italy 46 11N 12 40E
91 Manica, Mozambique 18 58S 32 59E
93 Manica e Sofala ♦, Mozambique 19 10S 33 45E
91 Manicaland ♦, Rhodesia 19 0S 32 30E
126 Manicoré, Brazil 6 0S 61 10W
107 Manicouagan L., Can. 51 25N 68 15W
107 Manicouagan, R., Can. 50 30N 68 30W
64 Manifah, Si. Arabia 27 30N 49 0E
91 Manika, Plat. de, Zaïre 10 0S 25 5E
73 Manila, Philippines 14 40N 121 3E
118 Manila, U.S.A. 41 0N 109 44W
73 Manila B., Philippines 14 0N 120 0E
100 Manildra, Australia 33 11S 148 41E
99 Manilla, Australia 30 45S 150 43E
84 Manimpé, Mali 14 11N 5 28W
93 Maningory, Malag. 17 9S 49 30E
93 Manipur, R., Burma 23 45N 94 20E
67 Manipur ♦, India 24 30N 94 0E
64 Manisa, Turkey 38 38N 27 30E
114 Manistee, U.S.A. 44 15N 86 20W
114 Manistee, R., U.S.A. 44 20N 85 50W
114 Manistique, U.S.A. 45 59N 86 18W
109 Manitoba ♦, Can. 55 30N 97 0W
109 Manitoba, L., Canada 50 40N 98 30W
109 Manitou, Canada 49 20N 98 40W
114 Manitou Is., U.S.A. 45 8N 86 0W
109 Manitou L., Ont., Can. 49 15N 93 0W
MAP
107 Manitou L., Que., Can. 50 55N 65 17W
106 Manitoulin I., Canada 45 40N 82 30W
106 Manitowaning, Canada 45 46N 81 49W
114 Manitowoc, U.S.A. 44 8N 87 40W
126 Manizales, Colombia 5 5N 75 32W
93 Manja, Malagasy Rep. 21 26S 44 20E
93 Manjakandriana, Malag. 18 55S 47 47E
70 Manjeri, India 11 7N 76 11E
68 Manjhand, Pakistan 25 50N 68 10E
64 Manjil, Iran 36 46N 49 30E
96 Manjimup, Australia 34 15S 116 6E
70 Manjra, R., India 18 20N 77 20E
93 Mankaiana, Swaziland 26 38S 31 6E
116 Mankato, Kans., U.S.A. 39 49N 98 11W
116 Mankato, Minn., U.S.A. 44 8N 93 59W
93 Mankayane, Swaz. 26 38N 31 6E
84 Mankono, Ivory Coast 8 10N 6 10W
109 Mankota, Canada 49 25N 107 5W
32 Manlleu, Spain 42 2N 2 17E
100 Manly, Australia 33 48S 151 14E
68 Manmad, India 20 18N 74 28E
70 Mannar, Sri Lanka 9 1N 79 54E
70 Mannar, G. of, Asia 8 30N 79 0E
70 Mannar I., Sri Lanka 9 5N 79 45E
70 Mannargudi, India 10 45N 79 32E
25 Mannheim, Germany 49 28N 8 29E
108 Manning, Canada 56 53N 117 39W
115 Manning, U.S.A. 33 40N 80 9W
114 Mannington, U.S.A. 39 35N 80 25W
40 Mannu, C., Sardinia 40 2N 8 24E
40 Mannu, R., Italy 39 35N 8 56E
99 Mannum, Australia 34 57S 139 12E
84 Mano, Sierra Leone 8 3N 12 12W
73 Manokwari, Indonesia 0 54N 134 0E
45 Manolás, Greece 38 4N 21 21E
93 Manombo, Malag. 22 57S 43 28E
21 Manosque, France 43 49N 5 47E
107 Manouane L., Canada 50 45N 70 45W
32 Manresa, Spain 41 48N 1 50E
68 Mansa, Gujarat, India 23 27N 72 45E
68 Mansa, Punjab, India 30 0N 75 27E
91 Mansa, Zambia 11 13S 28 55E
105 Mansel I., Canada 62 0N 80 0W
100 Mansfield, Australia 37 0S 146 0E
12 Mansfield, Eng. 53 8N 1 12W
117 Mansfield, La., U.S.A. 32 2N 93 40W
113 Mansfield, Mass., U.S.A. 42 2N 71 12W
114 Mansfield, Ohio, U.S.A. 40 45N 82 30W
112 Mansfield, Pa., U.S.A. 41 48N 77 4W
118 Mansfield, Wash., U.S.A. 47 51N 119 44W
30 Mansilla de las Mulas, Spain 42 30N 5 25W
20 Mansle, France 45 52N 0 9E
127 Manso, R., Brazil 14 0S 52 0W
84 Mansôa, Port. Guinea 12 0N 15 20W
108 Manson Cr., Canada 55 37N 124 25W
82 Mansoura Djebel, Algeria 36 1N 4 31E
126 Manta, Ecuador 1 0S 80 40W
72 Mantalingajan, Mt., Philippines 8 55N 117 45E
90 Mantare, Tanzania 2 42S 33 13E
119 Manteca, U.S.A. 37 50N 121 12W
126 Mantecal, Venezuela 7 34N 69 17W
67 Mantekomu Hu, China 34 40N 89 0E
115 Manteo, U.S.A. 35 55N 75 41W
19 Mantes-la-Jolie, France 49 0N 1 41E
18 Manthelan, France 47 9N 0 47E
118 Manti, U.S.A. 39 23N 111 32W
125 Mantiqueira, Serra da, Brazil 22 0S 44 0W
114 Manton, U.S.A. 44 23N 85 25W
49 Mantorp, Sweden 58 21N 15 20E
38 Mántova, Italy 45 10N 10 47E
50 Mänttä, Finland 62 0N 24 40E
38 Mantua = Mántova, It. 45 10N 10 47E
112 Mantua, U.S.A. 41 15N 81 14W
55 Manturova, U.S.S.R. 58 10N 44 30E
25 Mäntyharju, Finland 61 24N 26 58E
126 Manu, Peru 12 10S 71 0W
101 Manua Is., American Samoa 14 13S 169 35W
73 Manucan, Philippines 8 14N 123 3E
73 Manui I., Indonesia 3 35S 123 5E
99 Manumbar, Australia 26 25S 152 10E
98 Manus I., Terr. of New Guinea 2 10S 147 0E
70 Manvi, India 15 57N 76 59E
116 Manville, U.S.A. 42 48N 104 36W
70 Manwath, India 19 19N 76 32E
117 Many, U.S.A. 31 36N 93 28W
98 Many Peaks, Australia 24 32S 151 25E
92 Manyane, Botswana 23 21S 21 42E
90 Manyara L., Tanzania 3 40S 35 50E
57 Manych, R., U.S.S.R. 47 0N 41 15E
57 Manych-Gudilo, Oz., U.S.S.R. 46 24N 42 38E
90 Manyonga, R., Tanzania 4 5S 34 0E
90 Manyoni, Tanzania 5 45S 34 55E
90 Manyoni ♦, Tanz. 6 30S 34 30E
68 Manzai, Pakistan 32 20N 70 15E
86 Manzala, Bahra el, Egypt 31 10N 31 56E
33 Manzanares, Spain 39 0N 3 22W
30 Manzaneda, Cabeza de, Spain 42 12N 7 15W
121 Manzanillo, Cuba 20 20N 77 10W
120 Manzanillo, Mexico 19 0N 104 20W
121 Manzanillo, Pta., Pan. 9 30N 79 40W
119 Manzano Mts., U.S.A. 34 30N 106 45W
93 Manzini, Swaziland 26 30S 31 25E
81 Mao, Chad 14 4N 15 19E
72 Maoke, Pengunungan, Indonesia 3 40S 137 30E
73 Mapia, Kepulauan, Indonesia 0 50N 134 20E
120 Mapimi, Mexico 25 50N 103 31W
90 Mapinga, Tanzania 6 40S 39 12E
93 Mapinhane, Mozam. 22 20S 35 0E
118 Mapleton, U.S.A. 44 4N 123 58W
MAP
116 Maplewood, U.S.A. 38 33N 90 18W
98 Maprik, N.E. N. Guin. 3 40S 143 5E
70 Mapuca, India 15 36N 73 46E
126 Mapuera, R., Brazil 0 30S 58 25W
64 Maqna, Saudi Arabia 28 25N 34 50E
88 Maquela do Zombo, Ang. 6 0S 15 15E
128 Maquinchao, Arg. 41 15S 68 50W
116 Maquoketa, U.S.A. 42 4N 90 40W
124 Mar Chiquita, L., Arg. 30 40S 62 50W
124 Mar del Plata, Arg. 38 0S 57 30W
33 Mar Menor, L., Spain 37 40N 0 45W
125 Mar, Serra do, Brazil 25 30S 49 0W
90 Mara, Tanz. 1 30S 34 32E
90 Mara ♦, Tanz. 1 30S 34 32E
90 Mara ♦, Tanz. 1 45S 34 20E
126 Maraã, Brazil 1 43S 65 25W
127 Marabá, Brazil 5 20S 49 5W
127 Maracá, I. de, Braz. 2 10N 50 30W
126 Maracaibo, Venezuela 10 40N 71 37W
126 Maracaibo, Lago de, Venezuela 9 40N 71 30W
125 Maracaju, Brazil 21 38S 55 9W
126 Maracay, Venezuela 10 15N 67 36W
83 Marādah, Libya 29 4N 19 4E
85 Maradi, Niger 13 35N 8 10E
85 Maradun, Nigeria 12 35N 6 18E
64 Maragheh, Iran 37 30N 46 12E
127 Marajó, Ilha de, Brazil 1 0S 49 30W
96 Maralinga, Australia 29 10S 131 15E
99 Marampa, Sierra Leone 8 45N 10 28W
46 Maramureș ♦, Rum. 47 45N 24 0E
119 Marana, U.S.A. 32 30N 111 9W
32 Maranchón, Spain 41 6N 2 15W
64 Marand, Iran 38 30N 45 45E
91 Marandellas, Rhodesia 18 5S 31 42E
127 Maranguape, Brazil 3 55S 38 50W
127 Maranhao ♦, Brazil 5 0S 46 0W
39 Marano, L. di, Italy 45 42N 13 13E
99 Maranoa R., Australia 27 10S 148 5E
126 Marañón, R., Peru 4 50S 75 35W
64 Maras, Turkey 37 37N 36 53E
46 Marașești, Rumania 45 52N 27 5E
41 Maratea, Italy 39 59N 15 43E
31 Marateca, Portugal 38 34N 8 40W
45 Marathókambos, Gr. 37 43N 26 42E
98 Marathon, Australia 20 51S 143 32E
106 Marathon, Canada 48 44N 86 23W
45 Marathón, Greece 38 11N 23 58E
113 Marathon, N.Y., U.S.A. 42 25N 76 3W
117 Marathon, Tex., U.S.A. 30 15N 103 15W
73 Maratua, I., Indonesia 2 10N 118 35E
63 Marbar, Oman 17 0N 54 45E
31 Marbella, Spain 36 30N 4 57W
96 Marble Bar, Australia 21 9S 119 44E
117 Marble Falls, U.S.A. 30 30N 98 15W
113 Marblehead, U.S.A. 42 29N 70 51W
24 Marburg, Germany 50 49N 8 44E
48 Marby, Sweden 63 7N 14 18E
27 Marcal, R., Hungary 47 21N 17 15E
27 Marcali, Hungary 46 35N 17 25E
38 Marcaria, Italy 45 7N 10 34E
13 March, England 57 33N 0 5E
82 Marchand = Rommani, Morocco 33 20N 6 40W
20 Marché, France 46 0N 1 20E
39 Marche ♦, Italy 43 22N 13 10E
16 Marche-en-Famenne, Belgium 50 14N 5 19E
31 Marchena, Spain 37 18N 5 23W
39 Marches = Marche, Italy 43 22N 13 10E
38 Marciana Marina, Italy 42 44N 10 12E
41 Marcianise, Italy 41 3N 14 16E
21 Marcigny, France 46 17N 4 2E
20 Marcillac-Vallon, Fr. 44 29N 2 27E
20 Marcillat, France 46 12N 2 38E
19 Marck, France 50 57N 1 57E
19 Marckolsheim, France 48 10N 7 30E
124 Marcos Juárez, Arg. 32 42S 62 5W
94 Marcus I., Pac. Oc. 24 0N 153 45E
113 Marcy Mt., U.S.A. 44 7N 73 55W
64 Mardin, Turkey 37 20N 40 36E
14 Maree L., Scot. 57 40N 5 30W
98 Mareeba, Australia 16 59S 145 28E
42 Marek, Bulg. 42 27N 23 9E
73 Marek, Indonesia 4 41S 120 24E
38 Maremma, Italy 42 45N 11 15E
84 Maréna, Mali 14 0N 7 30W
39 Marenberg, Yugoslavia 46 38N 15 13E
116 Marengo, U.S.A. 41 42N 92 5W
20 Marennes, France 45 49N 1 5W
90 Marenyi, Kenya 4 22S 39 8E
93 Marerano, Malagasy Rep. 21 23S 44 52E
40 Marettimo, I., Italy 37 58N 12 5E
20 Mareuil-sur-Lay, France 46 32N 1 14W
117 Marfa, U.S.A. 30 15N 104 0W
87 Margable, Ethiopia 12 54N 42 38E
56 Marganets, U.S.S.R. 47 40N 34 40E
70 Margao, India 14 12N 73 58E
107 Margaree Harbour, Can. 46 26N 61 8W
96 Margaret, R., Australia 18 0S 126 30E
108 Margaret Bay, Canada 51 20N 127 20W
120 Margarita, Panama Canal Zone 9 20N 79 55W
126 Margarita, Isla de, Ven. 11 0N 64 0W
44 Margarition, Greece 39 22N 20 26E
93 Margate, S. Afr. 30 50S 30 20E
13 Margate, England 51 23N 1 24E
58 Margelan, U.S.S.R. 40 30N 71 45E
20 Margeride, Mts. de la, France 44 43N 3 38E
41 Margherita di Savola, It. 41 25N 16 5E
46 Marghita, Rumania 47 22N 22 22E
28 Margonin, Poland 52 58N 17 5E
31 Marguerira, Portugal 38 41N 9 9W
108 Marguerite, Canada 52 30N 122 15W
82 Marhoum, Algeria 34 27N 0 11W
55 Mari, A.S.S.R. ♦, U.S.S.R. 56 30N 48 0E
MAP
99 Maria I., Australia 42 35S 148 0E
124 Maria Elena, Chile 22 18S 69 40W
124 Maria Grande, Arg. 31 45S 59 55W
101 Maria van Diemen, C., New Zealand 34 29S 172 40E
49 Mariager, Denmark 56 40N 10 0E
49 Mariager Fjord, Denmark 56 42N 10 19E
90 Mariakani, Kenya 3 50S 39 27E
94 Mariana Is., Pac. Oc. 17 0N 145 0E
94 Mariana Trench, Pacific Ocean 13 0N 145 0W
121 Marianao, Cuba 23 8N 82 24W
117 Marianna, Ark., U.S.A. 34 48N 90 48W
115 Marianna, Fla., U.S.A. 30 45N 85 15W
49 Mariannelund, Sweden 57 37N 15 35E
26 Mariánské Lázně, Cz. 49 57N 12 41E
118 Marias, R., U.S.A. 48 26N 111 40W
121 Mariato, Punta, Pan. 7 12N 80 52W
26 Mariazell, Austria 47 47N 15 19E
63 Marib, Yemen 15 25N 45 20E
49 Maribo, Denmark 54 48N 11 30E
39 Maribor, Yugoslavia 46 36N 15 40E
92 Marico, R., Bots./S. Afr. 24 25S 26 30E
119 Maricopa, Ariz., U.S.A. 33 5N 112 2W
119 Maricopa, Calif., U.S.A. 35 7N 119 27W
87 Maridi, Sudan 5 10N 29 25E
87 Maridi, W., Sudan 5 25N 29 21E
121 Marie Galante, I., W. Ind. 15 56N 61 16W
105 Mariecourt, Canada 61 30N 72 0W
48 Mariefred, Sweden 59 15N 17 12E
51 Mariehamn (Maarianhamina), Finland 60 5N 19 57E
16 Marienbourg, Belgium 50 6N 4 31E
24 Marienberg, Germany 50 40N 13 10E
16 Marienberg, Neth. 52 30N 6 35E
98 Marienberg, Terr. of New Guinea 3 54S 144 10E
92 Mariental, S.W. Africa 24 36S 18 0E
112 Marienville, U.S.A. 41 27N 79 8W
49 Mariestad, Sweden 58 43N 13 50E
115 Marietta, Ga., U.S.A. 34 0N 84 30W
114 Marietta, Ohio, U.S.A. 39 27N 81 27W
113 Marieville, Canada 45 24N 73 11W
21 Marignane, France 43 25N 5 13E
58 Mariinsk, U.S.S.R. 56 10N 87 20E
55 Mariinskiy Posad, U.S.S.R. 59 9N 47 20E
125 Marilia, Brazil 22 0S 50 0W
30 Marin, Spain 42 23N 8 42W
125 Marina di Ciro, Italy 39 22N 17 8E
99 Marina Plains, Australia 14 37S 143 57E
73 Marinduque, I., Phil. 13 25N 122 0E
114 Marine City, U.S.A. 42 45N 82 29W
40 Marineo, Italy 37 57N 13 23E
119 Marinette, Ariz., U.S.A. 33 41N 112 16W
114 Marinette, Wis., U.S.A. 45 4N 87 40W
125 Maringá, Brazil 23 35S 51 50W
31 Marinha Grande, Port. 39 45N 8 56W
115 Marion, Ala., U.S.A. 32 33N 87 20W
117 Marion, Ill., U.S.A. 37 45N 88 55W
114 Marion, Ind., U.S.A. 40 35N 85 40W
116 Marion, Iowa, U.S.A. 42 2N 91 36W
116 Marion, Kans., U.S.A. 38 25N 97 2W
114 Marion, Mich., U.S.A. 44 7N 85 8W
115 Marion, N.C., U.S.A. 35 42N 82 0W
114 Marion, Ohio, U.S.A. 40 38N 83 8W
115 Marion, S.C., U.S.A. 34 11N 79 22W
115 Marion, Va., U.S.A. 36 51N 81 29W
115 Marion, L., U.S.A. 33 30N 80 15W
98 Marion Reef, Australia 19 10S 152 17E
126 Maripa, Venezuela 7 26N 65 9W
119 Mariposa, U.S.A. 37 31N 119 59W
124 Mariscal Estigarribia, Paraguay 22 3S 60 40W
21 Maritime Alps, France 44 10N 7 10E
38 Maritime Alps = Alpes Maritimes, Fr.-It. 44 10N 7 10E
43 Maritsa, Bulgaria 42 1N 25 50E
45 Maritsá, Greece 36 22N 28 10E
43 Maritsa, R., Bulgaria 42 15N 24 0E
54 Mariyampole = Kapsukas, U.S.S.R. 54 33N 23 19E
65 Marjan, Afghanistan 32 5N 68 20E
86 Marka, Saudi Arabia 18 14N 41 19E
70 Markapur, India 15 44N 79 19E
49 Markaryd, Sweden 56 28N 13 35E
112 Markdale, Canada 44 19N 80 38W
117 Marked Tree, U.S.A. 35 35N 90 24W
24 Markelsdorfer Huk, Ger. 54 33N 11 0E
16 Marken, Netherlands 52 26N 5 12E
12 Market Drayton, England 52 55N 2 30W
13 Market Harborough, England 52 29N 0 55W
112 Markham, Canada 43 54N 79 16W
4 Markham I., Greenland 84 0N 0 45W
109 Markham L., Canada 62 30N 102 35W
5 Markham Mts., Antarc. 83 0S 164 0E
28 Marki, Poland 52 20N 21 2E
45 Markoupoulon, Greece 37 53N 23 57E
42 Markovac, Yugoslavia 44 14N 21 7E
59 Markovo, U.S.S.R. 64 40N 170 25E
85 Markoye, Upper Volta 14 39N 0 2E
55 Marks, U.S.S.R. 51 45N 46 50E
117 Marksville, U.S.A. 31 10N 92 2W
25 Markt Schwaben, Ger. 48 14N 11 49E
25 Marktredwitz, Germany 50 1N 12 2E
108 Marlboro, Canada 53 30N 116 50W
113 Marlboro, U.S.A. 42 19N 71 33W
98 Marlborough, Australia 22 46S 149 52E
101 Marlborough ♦, N.Z. 41 45S 173 33E
13 Marlborough Downs, England 51 25N 1 55W
19 Marle, France 49 43N 3 47E
117 Marlin, U.S.A. 31 25N 96 50W
100 Marlo, Australia 37 40S 148 34E
24 Marlow, Germany 54 8N 12 34E
117 Marlow, U.S.A. 34 40N 97 58W
MAP
70 Marmagao, India 15 25N 73 56E
20 Marmande, France 44 30N 0 10E
56 Marmara, I., Turkey 40 35N 27 38E
64 Marmara Denizi, Turkey 40 45N 28 15E
64 Marmaris, Turkey 36 50N 28 14E
116 Marmarth, U.S.A. 46 21N 103 52W
106 Marmion L., Canada 48 55N 91 30W
39 Marmolada, Mte., Italy 46 25N 11 55E
31 Marmolejo, Spain 38 3N 4 13W
106 Marmora, Canada 44 28N 77 41W
19 Marnay, France 47 20N 5 48E
24 Marne, Germany 53 57N 9 1E
19 Marne, R., France 48 53N 4 25E
19 Marne ♦, France 49 0N 4 10E
126 Marnoo, Australia 36 40S 142 54E
98 Maro, Chad 8 30N 19 0E
126 Maroa, Venezuela 2 43N 67 33W
93 Maroala, Malagasy Rep. 15 23S 47 59E
93 Maroantsetra, Malagasy Republic 15 26S 49 44E
93 Maromandia, Malagasy Rep. 14 13S 48 5E
127 Maroni, R., Fr. Guiana 4 0N 52 0W
44 Marónia, Greece 40 53N 25 24E
99 Maroochydore, Australia 26 35S 153 10W
100 Maroona, Australia 37 27S 142 54E
27 Maros, R., Hungary 46 25N 20 20E
93 Marosakoa, Malag. 15 26S 46 38E
39 Marostica, Italy 45 44N 11 40E
85 Maroua, Cameroon 10 40N 14 20E
126 Marova, Brazil 1 8N 62 35W
93 Marovoay, Malagasy Republic 16 6S 46 39E
92 Marquard, S. Africa 28 40S 27 28E
114 Marquette, U.S.A. 46 30N 87 21W
19 Marquise, France 50 50N 1 40E
99 Marra, Australia 31 12S 144 10E
87 Marra, Gebet, Sudan 7 20N 27 35E
39 Marradi, Italy 44 5N 11 37E
82 Marrakech, Morocco 31 40N 8 0W
100 Marrar, Austral. 34 50S 147 23E
64 Marrat, Si-Arabia 25 0N 45 35E
99 Marree, Australia 29 39S 138 1E
93 Marrimane, Mozam. 22 58S 33 34E
30 Marroqui, Punta, Spain 36 0N 5 37W
91 Marrubane, Mozam. 18 0S 37 0E
91 Marrupa, Mozambique 13 8S 37 30E
81 Marsa Susa (Apollonia), Libya 32 52N 21 59E
90 Marsabit, Kenya 2 18N 38 0E
90 Marsabit ♦, Kenya 2 45N 37 45E
40 Marsala, Italy 37 48N 12 25E
46 Mârsani, Rumania 44 1N 23 59E
36 Marsaxlokk (Medport), Malta 35 47N 14 32E
39 Marsciano, Italy 42 54N 12 20E
100 Marsden, Australia 33 47S 147 32E
20 Marseillan, France 43 23N 3 31E
21 Marseille, France 43 18N 5 23E
117 Marsh I., U.S.A. 29 35N 91 50W
84 Marshall, Liberia 6 8N 10 22W
117 Marshall, Ark., U.S.A. 35 58N 92 40W
114 Marshall, Mich., U.S.A. 42 17N 84 59W
116 Marshall, Minn., U.S.A. 44 25N 95 45W
116 Marshall, Mo., U.S.A. 39 8N 93 15W
117 Marshall, Tex., U.S.A. 32 29N 94 20W
94 Marshall Is., Pac. Oc. 9 0N 171 0E
116 Marshalltown, U.S.A. 42 0N 93 0W
116 Marshfield, Mo., U.S.A. 37 20N 92 58W
116 Marshfield, Wis., U.S.A. 44 42N 90 10W
41 Mársico, Italy 40 26N 15 43E
48 Märsta, Sweden 59 37N 17 52E
49 Marstal, Denmark 54 51N 10 30E
49 Marstrand, Sweden 57 53N 11 35E
117 Mart, U.S.A. 31 34N 96 51W
39 Marta, R., Italy 42 18N 11 47E
67 Martaban, Burma 16 30N 97 35E
67 Martaban, G. of = Moktama Kwe, Burma 15 40N 96 30E
41 Martano, Italy 40 14N 18 18E
72 Martapura, Indonesia 3 22S 114 56E
85 Marte, Nigeria 12 23N 13 46E
49 Martebo, Sweden 57 45N 18 30E
16 Martelange, Belgium 49 49N 5 43E
33 Martés, Sierra, Spain 39 20N 1 0W
113 Martha's Vineyard, U.S.A. 41 25N 70 35W
18 Martigné Ferchaud, France 47 50N 1 20W
25 Martigny, Switzerland 46 6N 7 3E
21 Martigues, France 43 24N 5 4E
82 Martil, Morocco 35 36N 5 15W
27 Martin, Cz. 49 6N 18 48E
126 Martin, S.D., U.S.A. 43 11N 101 45W
117 Martin, Tenn., U.S.A. 36 23N 88 51W
115 Martin, L., U.S.A. 32 45N 85 50W
31 Martin, R., Spain 41 2N 0 43W
41 Martina Franca, Italy 40 42N 17 20E
101 Martinborough, N.Z. 41 14S 175 29E
121 Martinique, I., W.I. 14 40N 61 0W
121 Martinique Passage, W.I. 15 15N 61 0W
45 Martinon, Greece 38 35N 23 15E
125 Martinópolis, Brazil 22 11S 51 12W
113 Martins Ferry, U.S.A. 40 5N 80 46W
26 Martinsberg, Austria 48 22N 15 9E
112 Martinsburg, Pa., U.S.A. 40 18N 78 21W
114 Martinsburg, W. Va., U.S.A. 39 30N 77 57W
114 Martinsville, Ind., U.S.A. 39 29N 86 23W
115 Martinsville, Va., U.S.A. 36 41N 79 52W
101 Marton, New Zealand 40 4S 175 23E
32 Martorell, Spain 41 28N 1 56E
31 Martos, Spain 37 44N 3 58W
57 Martuni, U.S.S.R. 40 9N 45 10E
85 Maru, Nigeria 12 22N 6 22E
72 Marudi, Malaysia 4 10N 114 25E
65 Maruf, Afghanistan 31 30N 67 0E
74 Marugame, Japan 34 15N 133 55E
41 Maruggio, Italy 40 20N 17 33E

Marulan INDEX Melton Mowbray

MAP
100 Marulan, Australia 34 43S 150 3E
92 Marunga, Angola 17 20S 20 2E
90 Marungu, Mts., Zaïre 7 30S 30 0E
20 Marvejols, France 44 33N 3 19E
119 Marvine Mt., U.S.A. 38 44N 111 40W
68 Marwar, India 25 43N 73 45E
58 Mary, U.S.S.R. 37 40N 61 50E
99 Mary R., Australia 26 10S 152 28E
105 Mary River, Canada 70 30N 78 0W
98 Mary Kathleen, Australia 20 35S 139 48E
99 Maryborough, Queens., Australia 25 31S 152 37E
100 Maryborough, Vic., Australia 37 0S 143 44E
15 Maryborough = Port Laoise, Ireland 53 2N 7 20W
55 Maryets, U.S.S.R. 56 17N 49 47E
109 Maryfield, Canada 49 50N 101 35W
114 Maryland ♦, U.S.A. 39 10N 76 40W
91 Maryland Jc., Rhodesia 12 45S 30 31E
12 Maryport, England 54 43N 3 30W
107 Mary's Harbour, Can. 52 18N 55 51W
107 Marystown, Canada 47 10N 55 10W
119 Marysvale, U.S.A. 38 25N 112 17W
108 Marysville, Canada 49 35N 116 0W
118 Marysville, Calif., U.S.A. 39 14N 121 40W
116 Marysville, Kans., U.S.A. 39 50N 96 38W
112 Marysville, Mich., U.S.A. 42 55N 82 29W
114 Marysville, Ohio, U.S.A. 40 15N 83 20W
99 Maryvale, Australia 28 4S 152 12E
115 Maryville, U.S.A. 35 50N 84 0W
83 Marzuq, Libya 25 53N 14 10E
126 Marzo, Punta, Colombia 6 50N 77 42W
62 Masada = Mesada, Israel 31 20N 35 19E
91 Masafa, Zambia 13 50S 27 30E
90 Masai Steppe, Tanzania 4 30S 36 30E
90 Masaka, Uganda 0 21S 31 45E
*90 Masaka ♦, Uganda 0 15S 31 30E
85 Masakali, Nigeria 13 2N 12 32E
72 Masalima, Kepulauan, Indonesia 4 55S 116 50E
73 Masamba, Indonesia 2 30S 120 15E
76 Masan, S. Korea 35 15N 128 30E
33 Masanasa, Spain 39 25N 0 25W
65 Masandam, Ras, Trucial Oman 26 30N 56 30E
91 Masasi, Tanzania 10 45S 38 52E
91 Masasi ♦, Tanzania 10 45S 38 50E
121 Masaya, Nicaragua 12 0N 86 7W
85 Masba, Nigeria 10 35N 13 1E
82 Mascara, Algeria 35 26N 0 6E
120 Mascota, Mexico 20 30N 104 50W
73 Masela, Indonesia 8 9S 129 51E
121 Maseme, Botswana 18 46S 25 3E
92 Maseru, Lesotho 29 18S 27 30E
91 Mashaba, Rhodesia 20 2S 30 29E
64 Mashabih, Saudi Arabia 25 35N 36 30E
65 Mashhad, Iran 36 20N 59 35E
85 Mashi, Nigeria 13 0N 7 54E
74 Mashike, Japan 43 31N 141 30E
66 Mashki Chah, Pakistan 29 5N 62 30E
106 Mashkode, Canada 47 2N 84 7W
91 Mashonaland, North, ♦, Rhodesia 16 30S 30 0E
91 Mashonaland, South, ♦, Rhodesia 18 0S 31 30E
57 Mashtagi, U.S.S.R. 40 35N 50 0E
50 Masi, Norway 69 26N 23 50E
88 Masi-Manimba, Zaïre 4 40S 18 5E
90 Masindi, Uganda 1 40N 31 43E
90 Masindi Port, Uganda 1 43N 32 2E
63 Masirah, Muscat & Oman 20 25N 58 50E
126 Masisea, Peru 8 35S 74 15W
90 Masisi, Zaïre 1 23S 28 49E
64 Masjed Solyman, Iran 31 55N 49 25E
15 Mask, L., Ireland 53 36N 9 24W
70 Maski, India 15 56N 76 46E
43 Maslen Nos, Bulg. 42 18N 27 48E
39 Maslinica, Yugoslavia 43 24N 16 13E
32 Masnou, Spain 41 28N 2 20E
93 Masoala, C., Malag. 15 59S 50 13E
93 Masoarivo, Malag. 19 3S 44 19E
93 Masomeloka, Malag. 20 17S 48 37E
116 Mason, S.D., U.S.A. 45 12N 103 27W
117 Mason, Tex., U.S.A. 30 45N 99 15W
118 Mason City, U.S.A. 48 0N 119 0W
65 Masqat, Oman 23 37N 58 36E
38 Massa, Italy 44 2N 10 7E
82 Massa, O., Morocco 30 0N 9 30W
38 Massa Marittima, Italy 43 3N 10 52E
114 Massachusetts B., U.S.A. 42 30N 70 0W
113 Massachusetts ♦, U.S.A. 42 25N 72 0W
62 Massade, Syria 33 12N 35 45E
41 Massafra, Italy 40 35N 17 8E
88 Massaguet, Chad 12 28N 15 26E
81 Massakory, Chad 13 0N 15 49E
93 Massangena, Mozam. 21 34S 33 0E
38 Massarosa, Italy 43 53N 10 17E
20 Massat, France 42 53N 1 21E
87 Massawa = Mitsiwa, Ethiopia 15 35N 39 25E
113 Massena, U.S.A. 44 52N 74 55W
81 Massenya, Chad 11 30N 16 25E
108 Masset, Canada 54 0N 132 0W
20 Massiac, France 45 15N 3 11E
20 Massif Central, Fr. 45 30N 2 21E
112 Massillon, U.S.A. 40 47N 81 30W
93 Massingir, Mozam. 23 46S 32 4E
98 Massman, Australia 16 25S 145 25E
113 Masson, Canada 45 31N 75 26W
5 Masson I., Antarctica 66 10S 93 20E
86 Mastaba, Saudi Arabia 20 52N 39 30E
10 Mastani = Momchilgrad, Bulgaria 41 33N 25 23E
101 Masterton, New Zealand 40 56S 175 39E
MAP
44 Mástikho, Akra, Gr. 38 10N 26 2E
66 Mastuj, Pakistan 36 20N 72 36E
38 Mastung, Pakistan 29 50N 66 42E
86 Mastura, Saudi Arabia 23 7N 38 52E
74 Masuda, Japan 34 45N 132 0E
70 Masulipatam, India 16 12N 81 12E
90 Maswa ♦, Tanzania 3 10S 34 15E
44 Mat, R., Albania 41 40N 20 0E
91 Matabeleland ♦, Rhodesia 20 0S 28 0E
73 Mataboor, Indonesia 1 41S 138 3E
31 Matachel, R., Spain 38 32N 6 0W
106 Matachewan, Canada 47 50N 80 55W
76 Matad, Mongolia 47 11N 115 27E
88 Matadi, Zaïre 5 52S 13 31E
109 Matador, Canada 50 49N 107 56W
121 Matagalpa, Nicaragua 13 10N 85 40W
106 Matagami, Canada 49 45N 77 34W
106 Matagami, L., Canada 49 50N 77 40W
117 Matagorda, U.S.A. 28 43N 96 0W
117 Matagorda, B., U.S.A. 28 30N 96 15W
117 Matagorda I., U.S.A. 28 10N 96 40W
72 Matak, I., Indonesia 3 18N 106 16E
100 Matakana, I., N.Z. 37 32S 176 5E
70 Matake, Sri Lanka 7 30N 80 44E
84 Matam, Senegal 15 34N 13 17W
85 Matameye, Niger 13 26N 8 28E
120 Matamoros, Coahuila, Mexico 25 45N 103 1W
120 Matamoros, Puebla, Mexico 18 2N 98 17W
120 Matamoros, Tamaulipas, Mexico 25 50N 97 30W
73 Matana, D., Indonesia 2 30S 121 25E
91 Matandu, R., Tanzania 8 35S 39 40E
107 Matane, Canada 48 50N 67 33W
85 Matankari, Niger 13 46N 4 1E
104 Matanuska, Alaska 61 38N 149 0W
126 Matanzá, Colombia 7 22N 73 2W
121 Matanzas, Cuba 23 0N 81 40W
45 Matapá, Akra, Greece 36 22N 22 27E
107 Matapedia, Canada 48 0N 66 59W
70 Matara, Sri Lanka 5 58N 80 30E
72 Mataram, Indonesia 8 41S 116 10E
126 Matarani, Peru 16 50S 72 10W
96 Mataranka, Australia 14 55S 133 4E
32 Mataró, Spain 41 32N 2 29E
32 Matarraña, R., Spain 40 55N 0 8E
42 Mataruška Bania, Yugoslavia 43 40N 20 45E
93 Matatiele, S. Africa 30 20S 28 49E
101 Mataura, New Zealand 46 11S 168 51E
120 Matehuala, Mexico 23 40N 100 50W
91 Mateke Hills, Rhodesia 21 48S 31 0E
39 Matélica, Italy 43 15N 13 0E
41 Matera, Italy 40 40N 16 37E
27 Mátészalka, Hungary 47 58N 22 20E
91 Matetsi, Rhodesia 18 12S 26 0E
83 Mateur, Tunisia 37 0N 9 48E
57 Mateyev, U.S.S.R. 47 35N 38 47E
48 Matfors, Sweden 62 21N 17 2E
20 Matha, France 45 52N 0 20W
109 Matheson I., Canada 51 45N 96 56W
117 Mathis, U.S.A. 28 4N 97 48W
100 Mathoura, Australia 35 50S 144 55E
68 Mathura, India 27 30N 77 48E
73 Mati, Philippines 6 55N 126 15E
44 Mati, R., Albania 41 40N 20 0E
120 Matias Romero, Mexico 16 53N 95 2W
91 Matibane, Mozambique 14 49S 40 45E
12 Matlock, Eng. 53 8N 1 32W
83 Matmata, Tunisia 33 30N 9 59E
87 Matna, Sudan 13 49N 35 10E
127 Mato Grosso ♦, Brazil 14 0S 55 0W
126 Mato Grosso, Planalto do, Brazil 15 0S 54 0W
58 Matochkin Shar, U.S.S.R. 73 10N 56 40E
91 Matopo Hills, Rhod. 20 36S 28 20E
91 Matopos, Rhodesia 20 20S 28 29E
30 Matosinhos, Portugal 41 11N 8 42W
21 Matour, France 46 19N 4 29E
65 Matrah, Oman 23 37N 58 30E
86 Matrûh, Egypt 31 19N 27 9E
67 Matsang Tsangpo (Brahmaputra), R., China 29 25N 88 0E
85 Matsena, Nigeria 13 5N 10 5E
57 Matsesta, U.S.S.R. 43 34N 39 44E
74 Matsue, Japan 35 25N 133 10E
74 Matsumoto, Japan 36 15N 138 0E
74 Matsusaka, Japan 34 35N 136 25E
74 Matsuyama, Japan 33 45N 132 45E
70 Mattancheri, India 9 50N 76 15E
106 Mattawa, Canada 46 20N 78 45W
107 Mattawamkeag, U.S.A. 45 30N 68 30W
25 Matterhorn, mt., Switz. 45 58N 7 39E
27 Mattersburg, Austria 47 44N 16 24E
126 Matthew's Ridge, Guyana 7 37N 60 10W
106 Mattice, Canada 49 40N 83 20W
113 Mattituck, U.S.A. 40 58N 72 32W
48 Mattmar, Sweden 63 18N 13 54E
114 Mattoon, U.S.A. 39 30N 88 20W
72 Matua, Indonesia 2 58S 110 52E
93 Matuba, Mozambique 24 28S 32 49E
126 Matucana, Peru 11 55S 76 15W
65 Matun, Afghanistan 33 22N 69 58E
126 Maturín, Venezuela 9 45N 63 11W
93 Mau-e-ele, Mozambique 24 18S 34 2E
90 Mau Escarpment, Ken. 0 40S 36 0E
68 Mau-Ranipur, India 25 16N 79 8E
106 Mauagami, R., Canada 49 30N 82 0W
19 Maubeuge, France 50 17N 3 57E
20 Maubourguet, France 43 29N 0 1E
89 Mauch Berg. S. Afr. 25 13S 30 30E
100 Maude, Australia 34 29S 144 18E
5 Maudheim, Antarctica 71 5S 11 0W
67 Maudin Sun, Burma 16 0N 94 30E
126 Maués, Brazil 3 20S 57 45W
110 Maui I., Hawaii 20 45N 156 20E
MAP
101 Mauke, I., Cook Is. 20 09S 157 20W
124 Maule ♦, Chile 36 5S 72 30W
20 Mauleon, France 43 14N 0 54W
114 Maumee, U.S.A. 41 35N 83 40W
114 Maumee, R., U.S.A. 41 35N 83 40W
73 Maumere, Indonesia 8 38S 122 13E
92 Maun, Botswana 20 0S 23 26E
110 Mauna Kea, Mt., Hawaii 19 50N 155 28W
110 Mauna Loa, Mt., Hawaii 19 50N 155 28W
69 Maunath Bhanjan, India 25 56N 83 33E
71 Maungmagan, Is., £ 14 0S 97 48E
118 Maupin, U.S.A. 45 12N 121 9W
18 Maure-de-Bretagne, Fr. 47 53N 2 0W
117 Maurepas L., U.S.A. 30 18N 90 35W
21 Maures, mts., France 43 15N 6 15E
20 Mauriac, France 45 13N 2 19E
96 Maurice L., Australia 29 30S 131 0E
21 Maurienne, Fr. 45 15N 6 20E
80 Mauritania ■, Afr. 20 50N 10 0W
3 Mauritius ■, Indian Ocean 20 0S 57 0E
18 Mauron, France 48 9N 2 18W
20 Maurs, France 44 43N 2 12E
116 Mauston, U.S.A. 43 48N 90 5W
26 Mauterndorf, Austria 47 9N 13 40E
20 Mauvezin, France 43 44N 0 53E
20 Mauzé-sur,le, Mignon, France 46 12N 0 41W
70 Mavelikara, India 9 14N 76 32E
89 Mavinga, Angola 15 50S 20 10E
68 Mavli, India 24 45N 73 55E
62 Mavqui'im, Israel 31 38N 34 32E
44 Mavrova, Albania 40 26N 19 32E
91 Mavuradonha Mts., Rhod. 16 30S 31 30E
90 Mawa, Zaïre 2 45N 26 33E
68 Mawana, India 29 6N 77 58E
68 Mawand, Pakistan 29 33N 68 38E
109 Mawer, Canada 50 46N 106 22W
67 Mawk Mai, Burma 20 14N 97 50E
5 Mawson Base, Antarc. 67 30S 65 0E
116 Max, U.S.A. 47 50N 101 20W
120 Maxcanú, Mexico 20 40N 90 10W
93 Maxixe, Mozambique 23 54S 35 17E
113 Maxville, Canada 45 18N 74 50W
94 Maxwelltown, N.Z. 39 51S 174 49E
98 Maxwelton, Australia 15 45S 142 30E
98 May Downs, Australia 22 25S 148 35E
87 May Nefalis, Ethiopia 15 0N 38 12E
121 May Pen, Jamaica 17 58N 77 15W
32 Maya, Spain 43 12N 1 29W
87 Maya Gudo, Mt., Ethiopia 7 30N 37 8E
120 Maya Mts., Brit. Hond. 16 30N 89 0W
59 Maya, R., U.S.S.R. 58 20N 135 0E
121 Mayaguana Island, Bahamas 21 30N 72 44W
121 Mayagüez, Puerto Rico 18 12N 67 9W
85 Mayahi, Niger 13 58N 7 40E
32 Mayals, Spain 41 22N 0 30E
121 Mayarf, Cuba 20 40N 75 39W
70 Mayavaram = Mayuram, India 11 3N 79 42E
118 Maybell, U.S.A. 40 30N 108 4W
87 Maychew, Ethiopia 12 50N 39 42E
99 Maydena, Austra.l. 42 40S 146 30E
44 Maydos, Turkey 40 13N 26 20E
74 Mayebashi, Japan 36 30N 139 0E
25 Mayen, Germany 50 18N 7 10E
18 Mayenne, France 48 20N 0 38W
18 Mayenne ♦, Fr. 48 10N 0 40W
119 Mayer, U.S.A. 34 28N 112 17W
108 Mayerthorpe, Canada 53 57N 115 15W
115 Mayfield, U.S.A. 36 45N 88 40W
119 Mayhill, U.S.A. 32 58N 105 30W
57 Maykop, U.S.S.R. 44 35N 40 25E
106 Maynooth, Canada 45 14N 77 56W
15 Maynooth, Ireland 53 22N 6 38W
99 Mayo ♦, Ireland 53 47N 9 7W
92 Mayoba, Botswana 22 45S 26 20E
73 Mayon, Mt., Philippines 13 15N 123 42E
101 Mayor I., N.Z. 37 16S 176 17E
30 Mayorga, Spain 42 10N 5 16W
57 Mayskiy, U.S.S.R. 43 47N 43 59E
114 Maysville, U.S.A. 38 43N 84 16W
70 Mayuram, India 11 3N 79 42E
112 Mayville, N.Y., U.S.A. 42 14N 79 31W
116 Mayville, N.D., U.S.A. 47 30N 97 23W
59 Mayya, U.S.S.R. 61 44N 130 18E
91 Mazabuka, Zambia 15 52S 27 44E
82 Mazagán = El Jadida, Morocco 33 11N 8 17W
127 Mazagão, Brazil 0 20S 51 50W
108 Mazama, Canada 49 43N 120 8W
20 Mazamet, France 43 30N 2 20E
126 Mazán, Peru 3 15S 73 0W
65 Mazanideran ♦, Iran 36 15S 73 0W
82 Mazar, O., Algeria 32 0N 1 38E
40 Mazara del Vallo, Italy 37 40N 12 34E
65 Mazar-i-Sharif, Afghan. 36 41N 67 0E
128 Mazarredo, Argentina 47 10S 66 50W
33 Mazarrón, Spain 37 38N 1 19W
33 Mazarrón, Golfo de, Sp. 37 27N 1 19W
126 Mazaruni, R., Guyana 6 15N 60 0W
120 Mazatenango, Guatemala 14 35N 91 30W
120 Mazatlán, Mexico 23 10N 106 30W
54 Mazeikiai, U.S.S.R. 56 20N 22 20E
65 Māzhān, Iran 32 30N 59 0E
54 Mazheikyai, U.S.S.R. 56 20N 22 20E
65 Mazinan, Iran 36 25N 56 48E
91 Mazoe, Rhodesia 17 28S 30 58E
91 Mazoi, Mozambique 16 42S 33 7E
87 Mazrub, Sudan 14 0N 29 20E
28 Mazurski, Pojezierze, Poland 53 50N 21 0E
41 Mazzarino, Italy 37 19N 14 12E
84 Mbaba, Senegal 14 59N 16 44W
93 Mbabane, Swaziland 26 18S 31 6E
84 Mbagne, Mauritania 16 6N 14 47W
MAP
84 Mbahiakro, Ivory Coast 7 33N 4 19W
88 M'Baiki, Cent. Afr. Rep. 3 53N 18 1E
91 Mbala, Zambia 8 46S 31 17E
90 Mbale, Uganda 1 8N 34 12E
85 M'Balmayo, Cameroon 3 33N 11 33E
91 Mbamba Bay, Tanz. 11 13S 34 49E
88 Mbandaka, Zaïre 0 1S 18 18E
85 Mbanga, Cameroon 4 30N 9 33E
90 Mbarara, Uganda 0 35S 30 25E
84 Mbatto, Ivory Coast 6 28N 4 22W
91 Mbenkuru, R., Tanz. 9 25S 39 50E
85 Mberubu, Nigeria 6 10N 7 38E
91 Mbesuma, Zambia 10 0S 32 2E
91 Mbeya, Tanzania 8 54S 33 29E
90 Mbeya ♦, Tanzania 8 15S 33 30E
87 Mbia, Sudan 6 15N 29 18E
91 Mbimbi, Zambia 13 25S 23 2E
91 Mbinga, Tanz. 10 50S 35 0E
91 Mbinga ♦, Tanz. 10 50S 35 0E
87 Mbiti, Sudan 5 42N 28 3E
87 Mboki, Cen. Afr. 5 19N 25 58E
84 Mboro, Senegal 15 9N 16 54W
84 Mboune, Senegal 14 42N 13 34W
84 Mbour, Senegal 14 22N 16 54W
91 Mbout, Mauritania 16 1N 12 38W
41 Mbozi, Tanzania 9 0S 32 58E
90 Mbulu ♦, Tanz. 3 52S 35 33E
90 Mbuji-Mayi, Zaïre 6 9S 23 40E
92 Mbumbi, S.W. Afr. 18 26S 19 59E
124 Mburucuyá, Argentina 28 1S 58 14W
82 Mcherrah, Algeria 27 0N 4 30W
91 Mchinja, Tanzania 9 44S 39 45E
91 Mchinji, Malawi 13 47S 32 58E
82 M'chounech, Algeria 34 57N 6 1E
82 Mdennah, Maur. 24 37N 6 0W
36 Mdina, Malta 35 51N 14 25E
119 Mead L., U.S.A. 36 10N 114 10W
106 Meade, Canada 49 26N 83 51W
117 Meade, U.S.A. 37 18N 100 25W
109 Meadow Lake, Canada 54 10N 108 10W
109 Meadow Lake, Prov. Park, Canada 54 25N 109 0W
112 Meadville, U.S.A. 41 39N 80 9W
112 Meaford, Canada 44 40N 80 36W
30 Mealhada, Portugal 40 22N 8 27W
107 Mealy Mts., Canada 53 30N 59 0W
64 Meander, R. = Menderes, Büyük, Turkey 37 45N 27 40E
108 Meander River, Canada 59 3N 117 30W
93 Meankany, Malag. 25 13S 44 26E
118 Meare's, C., U.S.A. 45 37N 124 0W
15 Meath ♦, Ireland 53 32N 6 40W
109 Meath Park, Canada 53 27N 105 22W
20 Meaulne, France 46 36N 2 28E
19 Meaux, France 48 58N 2 50E
93 Meave, Mozambique 21 4S 34 47E
91 Mecanhelas, Mozam. 15 12S 35 54E
86 Mecca = Makkah, Saudi Arabia 21 30N 39 54E
119 Mecca, U.S.A. 33 37N 116 3W
112 Mechanicsburg, U.S.A. 40 12N 77 0W
113 Mechanicville, U.S.A. 42 54N 73 41W
87 Mechara, Ethiopia 8 36N 40 20E
82 Méchéria, Algeria 33 35N 0 18W
24 Mechernich, Germany 50 35N 6 39E
57 Mechetinskaya, U.S.S.R. 46 45N 40 32E
44 Mecidiye, Turkey 40 38N 26 32E
56 Mecitözü, Turkey 40 32N 35 25E
24 Mecklenburg B., Ger. 54 20N 11 40E
91 Meconta, Mozambique 14 59S 39 50E
30 Meda, Portugal 40 57N 7 18W
96 Meda, R., Australia 17 20S 124 30E
82 Medaguine, Algeria 33 41N 3 26E
70 Medak, India 18 1N 78 15E
72 Medan, Indonesia 3 40N 98 38E
128 Medanosa, Pta., Arg. 48 0S 66 0W
70 Medawachchiya, Sri Lanka 8 30N 80 30E
82 Meddouza, Cap, Morocco 32 33N 9 9W
82 Médéa, Algeria 36 12N 2 50E
42 Mededa, Yugoslavia 43 44N 19 15E
126 Medellín, Colombia 6 15N 75 35W
16 Medemblik, Netherlands 52 46N 5 8E
87 Meder, Ethiopia 14 42N 40 44E
118 Medford, Oreg., U.S.A. 42 20N 122 52W
116 Medford, Wis., U.S.A. 45 9N 90 21W
46 Medgidia, Rumania 44 15N 28 19E
87 Medi, Sudan 5 4N 30 42E
124 Media Agua, Argentina 31 58S 68 25W
124 Media Luna, Argentina 34 45S 66 44W
46 Medias, Rumania 46 9N 24 22E
118 Medical Lake, U.S.A. 47 41N 117 42W
39 Medicina, Italy 44 29N 11 38E
118 Medicine Bow, U.S.A. 41 56N 106 11W
109 Medicine Hat, Canada 50 0N 110 45W
116 Medicine Lake, U.S.A. 48 30N 104 30W
117 Medicine Lodge, U.S.A. 37 20N 98 37W
126 Medina, Colombia 4 30N 73 21W
64 Medina = Al Madīnah, Saudi Arabia 24 35N 39 52E
112 Medina, N.Y., U.S.A. 43 15N 78 27W
116 Medina N.D., U.S.A. 46 57N 99 20W
112 Medina, Ohio, U.S.A. 41 9N 81 50W
117 Medina L., U.S.A. 29 35N 98 58W
117 Medina, R., U.S.A. 29 10N 97 20W
30 Medina de Rioseco, Sp. 41 53N 5 3W
30 Medina del Campo, Spain 41 18N 4 55W
31 Medina-Sidonia, Spain 36 28N 5 57W
32 Medinaceli, Spain 41 12N 2 30W
34 Mediterranean Sea, Europe 35 0N 15 0E
83 Medjerda, O., Tunisia 36 35N 8 30E
43 Medkovets, Bulgaria 43 37N 23 10E
20 Médoc, France 45 10N 0 56W
109 Medstead, Canada 53 19N 108 5W
39 Medulin, Yugoslavia 44 49N 13 55E
42 Medveda, Yugoslavia 42 50N 21 32E
55 Medveditsa, R., U.S.S.R. 50 30N 44 0E
55 Medvedok, U.S.S.R. 57 20N 50 1E
59 Medvezhi, Ostrava, U.S.S.R. 71 0N 161 0E
MAP
52 Medvezhyegorsk, U.S.S.R. 63 0N 34 25E
13 Medway, R., Eng. 51 12N 0 23E
55 Medyn, U.S.S.R. 54 59N 35 56E
27 Medzev, Czechoslovakia 48 43N 20 55E
27 Medzilaborce, Cz. 49 17N 21 52E
96 Meekatharra, Australia 26 32S 118 29E
118 Meeker, U.S.A. 40 1N 107 58E
107 Meelpaeg L., Canada 48 18N 56 35W
24 Meerane, Germany 50 51N 12 30E
68 Meerut, India 29 1N 77 50E
118 Meeteetsa, U.S.A. 44 10N 108 56W
82 Meftah Sidi Boubekeur, Algeria 35 1N 0 30E
87 Mega, Ethiopia 3 57N 38 30E
45 Megálo Khorio, Greece 36 27N 27 24E
45 Megálo Petali, I., Gr. 38 0N 24 15E
45 Megalópolis, Greece 37 25N 22 7E
45 Meganisi, I., Greece 38 39N 20 48E
107 Mégantic, Canada 45 36N 70 56W
45 Mégara, Greece 37 58N 23 22E
82 Megarine, Alg. 33 14N 6 2E
67 Meghalaya ♦, India 25 40N 89 55E
45 Megdhova, R., Greece 39 10N 21 45E
21 Mégève, France 45 51N 6 37E
67 Meghalayap, Pakistan 25 40N 89 55E
87 Meghezez, Mt., Ethiopia 9 18N 39 26E
69 Meghna, R., Bangladesh 23 45N 90 40E
62 Megiddo, Israel 32 36N 35 11E
46 Mehadia, Rumania 44 56N 22 23E
82 Mehaïguene, O., Algeria 32 20N 2 45E
46 Mehedinti ♦, Rumania 44 40N 22 45E
86 Meheisa, Sudan 19 38N 32 57E
69 Mehndawal, India 26 58N 83 5E
68 Mehsana, India 23 39N 72 26E
19 Mehun-sur-Yèvre, Fr. 47 10N 2 13E
76 Meihokow, China 42 37N 125 46E
77 Meihsien, China 24 20N 116 0E
67 Meiktila, Burma 21 0N 96 0E
24 Meiningen, Germany 50 32N 10 25E
30 Meira, Sierra de, Spain 43 15N 7 15W
25 Meiringen, Switzerland 46 43N 8 12E
24 Meissen, Germany 51 10N 13 29E
77 Meit'an, China 27 45N 107 28E
62 Meithalun, Jordan 32 21N 35 16E
88 Meiganga, Cameroon 6 20N 14 10E
20 Méjean, France 44 15N 3 30E
124 Mejillones, Chile 23 10S 70 30W
88 Mekambo, Gabon 1 2N 14 5E
87 Mekdela, Ethiopia 11 24N 39 10E
85 Mekkaw, Nigeria 7 26N 2 55E
71 Meklong = Samut Songkhram, Thailand 13 24N 100 1E
82 Meknès, Morocco 33 57N 5 33W
71 Mekong, R., Asia 18 0N 104 15E
73 Mekongga, Indon. 3 50S 121 30E
70 Melagiri Hills, India 12 20N 77 30E
82 Melah, Sebkhet el, Alg. 29 20N 1 30W
71 Melaka, Malaysia 2 15N 102 15E
71 Melaka ♦, Malaysia 2 20N 102 15E
72 Melalap, Malaysia 5 10N 116 5E
45 Melambes, Greece 35 8N 24 40E
94 Melanesia, Pacific Ocean 4 0S 155 0E
70 Melapalaiyam, India 8 39N 77 44E
50 Melbo, Norway 68 31N 14 50E
100 Melbourne, Australia 37 40S 145 0E
115 Melbourne, U.S.A. 28 13N 80 14W
38 Melcésine, Italy 45 46N 10 48E
120 Melchor Múzquiz, Mexico 27 50N 101 40W
120 Melchor Ocampo (San Pedro Ocampo), Mex. 24 52N 101 40W
39 Meldola, Italy 44 7N 12 3E
24 Meldorf, Germany 54 5N 9 5E
38 Melegnano, Italy 45 21N 9 20E
•55 Melekess, U.S.S.R. 54 25N 49 33E
42 Melenci, Yugoslavia 45 32N 20 20E
55 Melenki, U.S.S.R. 55 20N 41 37E
81 Melfi, Chad. 11 0N 17 59E
41 Melfi, Italy 41 0N 15 40E
109 Melfort, Canada 52 50N 105 40W
91 Melfort, Rhodesia 18 0S 31 25E
30 Melgaço, Portugal 42 7N 8 15W
30 Melgar de Fernamental, Spain 42 27N 4 17W
47 Melhus, Norway 63 17N 10 18E
45 Meligalá, Greece 37 15N 21 59E
82 Melilla, Morocco 35 21N 2 57W
18 Melilot, Israel 31 22N 34 37E
124 Melipilla, Chile 33 42S 71 15W
45 Mélissa Oros, Gr. 37 32N 26 4E
109 Melita, Canada 49 15N 101 5W
41 Mélito di Porto Salvo, It. 37 55N 15 47E
56 Melitopol, U.S.S.R. 46 50N 35 22E
26 Melk, Austria 48 13N 15 20E
48 Mellan-Fryken, Swed. 59 45N 13 10E
50 Mellansel, Sweden 63 25N 18 17E
20 Melle, France 46 14N 0 10W
24 Melle, Germany 52 12N 8 20E
83 Mellègue, O., Tunisia 36 32N 8 51E
116 Mellen, U.S.A. 46 19N 90 36W
49 Mellerud, Sweden 58 41N 12 28E
116 Mellette, U.S.A. 45 11N 98 29W
30 Mellid, Spain 42 55N 8 1W
98 Mellish Reef, Australia 17 25S 155 50E
87 Mellit, Sudan 14 15N 25 40E
43 Melnik, Bulgaria 40 58N 23 25E
26 Mělník, Czechoslovakia 50 22N 14 23E
125 Melo, Uruguay 32 20S 54 10W
73 Melolo, Indonesia 9 53S 120 40E
57 Melovoye, U.S.S.R. 49 25N 40 5E
82 Melrhir, Chott, Algeria 34 25N 6 24E
100 Melrose, N.S.W., Australia 32 42S 147 1E
14 Melrose, Scot. 55 35N 2 44W
117 Melrose, U.S.A. 34 27N 103 33W
118 Melstone, U.S.A. 46 45N 108 0W
24 Melsungen, Germany 51 8N 9 34E
12 Melton Mowbray, England 52 46N 0 52W

* *Incorporated within the new S. Buganda Province*

• *Renamed Dimitrovgrad*

Melunga INDEX Minto Lake

MAP
92 Melunga, Angola 17 15S 16 22E
19 Melun, France 48 32N 2 39E
92 Melunga, Angola 17 15S 16 22E
70 Melur, India 10 2N 78 23E
87 Melut, Sudan 10 30N 32 20E
109 Melville, Canada 51 0N 102 50W
97 Melville B., Australia 12 0S 136 45E
96 Melville I., Australia 11 30S 131 0E
4 Melville I., Canada 75 30N 111 0W
107 Melville, L., Canada 53 45N 59 40W
105 Melville Pen., Canada 68 0N 84 0W
27 Mélykút, Hungary 46 11N 19 25E
44 Memaliaj, Albania 40 25N 19 58E
91 Memba, Mozambique 14 11S 40 30E
73 Memboro, Indonesia 9 30S 119 30E
33 Membrilla, Spain 38 59N 3 21W
93 Memel, S. Africa 27 38S 29 36E
54 Memel = Klaipeda, U.S.S.R. 55 43N 21 10E
25 Memmingen, Germany 47 59N 10 12E
117 Memphis, Tenn., U.S.A. 35 7N 90 0W
117 Memphis, Tex., U.S.A. 34 45N 100 30W
113 Memphremagog L., U.S.A. 45 8N 72 17W
117 Mena, U.S.A. 34 40N 94 15W
12 Menai Strait, Wales 53 7N 4 20W
85 Ménaka, Niger 15 59N 2 18E
93 Menarandra, R., Malag. 25 0S 44 50E
117 Menard, U.S.A. 30 57N 99 58W
114 Menasha, U.S.A. 44 13N 88 27W
72 Menate, Indonesia 0 12S 112 47E
72 Mendawai, R., Indonesia 1 30S 113 0E
20 Mende, France 44 31N 3 30E
87 Mendebo Mts., Ethiopia 7 0N 39 22E
64 Menderes, R., Turkey 37 25N 28 45E
87 Mendi, Ethiopia 9 47N 35 4E
98 Mendi, Papua 6 10S 143 40E
13 Mendip Hills, Eng. 51 17N 2 40W
118 Mendocino, U.S.A. 39 26N 123 50W
69 Mendong Gompa, China 31 16N 85 11E
100 Mendooran, Australia 32 0S 149 22E
119 Mendota, Calif., U.S.A. 36 46N 120 24W
116 Mendota, Ill., U.S.A. 41 35N 89 5W
124 Mendoza, Argentina 32 50S 68 52W
124 Mendoza ♦, Arg. 33 0S 69 0W
72 Mendung, Indonesia 0 38N 103 8E
126 Mene Grande, Venezuela 9 49N 70 56W
16 Menen, Belgium 50 47N 3 7E
83 Ménerville, Algeria 36 45N 3 30E
40 Menfi, Italy 37 36N 12 57E
71 Meng Wang, China 22 18N 100 31E
39 Mengeš, Yugoslavia 46 24N 14 35E
72 Menggala, Indonesia 4 20S 105 15E
31 Mengíbar, Spain 37 58N 3 48W
71 Mengla, China 21 25N 101 30E
82 Mengoub, Algeria 29 49N 5 26W
67 Meng-pan, China 23 5N 100 19E
77 Mengshan, China 24 2N 110 32E
71 Meng-so, China 22 33N 99 31E
75 Mengtsz, China 23 20N 103 20E
67 Meng-wang, China 22 17N 100 32E
107 Menihek L., Canada 54 0N 67 0W
16 Menin, Belgium 50 47N 3 7E
100 Menindee, Australia 32 20N 142 25E
100 Menindee, L., Australia 32 20N 142 25E
67 Menkúng, China 28 38N 98 24E
114 Menominee, U.S.A. 45 9N 87 39W
114 Menominee, R., U.S.A. 45 30N 87 50W
116 Menomonie, U.S.A. 44 50N 91 54W
33 Menor, Mar, Spain 37 43N 0 48W
32 Menorca, I., Spain 40 0N 4 0E
72 Mentawai, Kepulauan, Indonesia 2 0S 99 0E
21 Menton, France 43 50N 7 29E
112 Mentor, U.S.A. 41 40N 81 21W
83 Menzel-Bourguiba, Tunisia 39 9N 9 49E
83 Menzel Chaker, Tunisia 35 0N 10 26E
96 Menzies, Australia 29 40S 120 58E
62 Me'ona (Tarshiha), Isr. 33 1N 35 15E
91 Mepaco, Mozambique 15 57S 30 48E
16 Meppel, Netherlands 52 42N 6 12E
24 Meppen, Germany 52 41N 7 20E
32 Mequinenza, Spain 41 22N 0 17E
117 Mer Rouge, U.S.A. 32 47N 91 48W
45 Merabéllou, Kólpos, Gr. 35 10N 25 50E
72 Merah, Indonesia 0 53N 116 54E
73 Merak, Indonesia 5 55S 106 1E
39 Merano (Meran), Italy 46 40N 11 10E
38 Merate, Italy 45 42N 9 23E
73 Merauke, Indonesia 8 29S 140 24E
73 Merbabu, Mt., Indonesia 7 30S 110 40E
100 Merbein, Australia 34 10S 142 2E
63 Merca, Somali Rep. 1 48N 44 50E
32 Mercadal, Spain 39 59N 4 5E
70 Mercara, India 12 30N 75 45E
39 Mercato Saraceno, Italy 43 57N 12 11E
119 Merced, U.S.A. 37 25N 120 30W
124 Mercedes, Buenos Aires, Argentina 34 40S 59 30W
124 Mercedes, Corrientes, Argentina 29 10S 58 5W
124 Mercedes, San Luis, Argentina 33 5S 65 21W
124 Mercedes, Uruguay 33 12S 58 0W
124 Merceditas, Chile 28 20S 70 35W
101 Mercer, New Zealand 37 16S 175 5E
112 Mercer, U.S.A. 41 14N 80 13W
105 Mercy C., Canada 65 0N 62 30W
18 Merdrignac, France 48 11N 2 27W
128 Meredith C., Falk. Is. 52 15S 60 40W
117 Meredith, L., U.S.A. 35 30N 101 35W
56 Merefa, U.S.S.R. 49 56N 36 2W
46 Merei, Rumania 45 7N 26 43E
19 Méréville, France 48 20N 2 5E
87 Merewa, Ethiopia 7 40N 36 54E
57 Mergenevskiy, U.S.S.R. 49 59N 51 15E
71 Mergui, Burma 12 30N 98 35E
71 Mergui Arch. = Myeik Kyunzu, Burma 11 30N 97 30E

MAP
120 Mérida, Mexico 20 50N 89 40W
31 Mérida, Spain 38 55N 6 25W
126 Mérida, Venezuela 8 36N 71 8W
126 Mérida, Cord. de, Venezuela 9 0N 71 0W
126 Mérida ♦, Venezuela 8 30N 71 10W
13 Meriden, England 52 27N 1 36W
113 Meriden, U.S.A. 41 33N 72 47W
118 Meridian, Idaho, U.S.A. 43 41N 116 25W
115 Meridian, Miss., U.S.A. 32 20N 88 42W
117 Meridian, Tex., U.S.A. 31 55N 97 37W
100 Merimula, Australia 36 54S 149 54E
25 Mering, Germany 48 15N 11 0E
100 Meringur, Australia 34 20S 141 19E
100 Merino, Australia 37 44S 141 35E
*12 Merioneth ♦, Wales 52 49N 3 55W
127 Merirumã, Brazil 1 15N 54 50W
117 Merkel, U.S.A. 32 30N 100 0W
16 Merksem, Belgium 51 16N 4 25E
19 Merlebach, France 49 5N 6 52E
49 Mern, Denmark 55 3N 12 3E
86 Merowe, Sudan 18 29N 31 46E
96 Merredin, Australia 31 28S 118 18E
14 Merrick, Mt., Scot. 55 8N 4 30W
113 Merrickville, Canada 44 54N 75 51W
118 Merrill, Oregon, U.S.A. 42 2N 121 37W
116 Merrill, Wis., U.S.A. 45 11N 89 41W
112 Merriton, Canada 43 12N 79 13W
108 Merritt, Canada 50 10N 120 45W
100 Merriwa, Australia 32 6S 150 22E
100 Merriwagga, Australia 33 47S 145 43E
106 Merry I., Canada 55 57N 77 40W
100 Merrygoen, Australia 31 51S 149 12E
117 Merryville, U.S.A. 30 47N 93 31W
87 Mersa Fatma, Ethiopia 14 57N 40 17E
16 Mersch, Luxembourg 49 44N 6 7E
24 Merseburg, Germany 51 20N 12 0E
12 Mersey, R., Eng. 53 20N 2 56W
64 Mersin, Turkey 36 51N 34 36E
71 Mersing, Malaysia 2 25N 103 50E
68 Merta, India 26 39N 74 4E
13 Merthyr Tydfil, Wales 51 45N 3 23W
100 Mertoa, Australia 36 33S 142 29E
31 Mértola, Portugal 37 40N 7 40E
117 Mertzon, U.S.A. 31 17N 100 48W
19 Méru, France 49 13N 2 8E
90 Meru, Kenya 0 3N 37 40E
90 Meru ♦, Kenya 0 3N 37 46E
90 Meru, mt., Tanzania 3 15S 36 46E
19 Merville, France 50 38N 2 38E
19 Méry, France 48 30N 3 52E
56 Merzifon, Turkey 41 53N 35 32E
25 Merzig, Germany 49 26N 6 37E
83 Merzouga, Erg Tin, Alg. 24 0N 11 4E
119 Mesa, U.S.A. 33 20N 111 56W
83 Mesach Mellet, Libya 24 30N 11 30E
62 Mesada, Israel 31 20N 35 19E
41 Mesagne, Italy 40 34N 17 48E
45 Mesaras, Kólpos, Greece 35 6N 24 47E
24 Meschede, Germany 51 20N 8 17E
87 Mesfinto, Ethiopia 13 30N 37 22E
106 Mesgouez, L., Canada 51 20N 75 0W
54 Meshchovsk, U.S.S.R. 54 22N 35 17E
65 Meshed = Mashhad, Iran 36 20N 59 35E
113 Meshoppen, U.S.A. 41 36N 76 3W
114 Mesick, U.S.A. 44 24N 85 42W
119 Mesilla, U.S.A. 32 20N 107 0W
18 Meslay-du-Maine, Fr. 47 58N 0 33W
25 Mesocco, Switzerland 46 23N 9 12E
45 Mesolóngion, Greece 38 27N 21 28E
64 Mesopotamia, reg., Asia 33 30N 44 0E
41 Mesoraca, Italy 39 5N 16 47E
45 Mésou Volimais, Greece 37 53N 27 35E
18 Messac, France 47 49N 1 50W
82 Messad, Algeria 34 8N 3 30E
85 Messaména, Cameroon 3 48N 12 49E
20 Messeix, France 45 37N 2 33E
41 Messina, Italy 38 10N 15 32E
93 Messina, S. Afr. 22 20S 30 12E
41 Messina, Str. di, Italy 38 5N 15 35E
45 Messini, Greece 37 4N 22 1E
45 Messinia ♦, Greece 37 10N 22 0E
45 Messiniakós, Kólpos, Greece 36 45N 22 5E
45 Mestá, Akra, Greece 38 16N 25 53E
43 Mesta, R., Bulgaria 41 30N 24 0E
31 Mestanza, Spain 38 35N 4 4W
26 Město Tepla, Cz. 49 59N 12 52E
39 Mestre, Italy 45 30N 12 14E
26 Městys Zelezná Ruda, Czechoslovakia 49 8N 13 15E
126 Meta ♦, Colombia 3 30N 73 0W
126 Meta, R., Ven.-Col. 6 20N 68 5W
106 Metagama, Canada 47 0N 81 55W
118 Metaline Falls, U.S.A. 48 54N 117 28W
124 Metán, Argentina 25 30S 65 0W
39 Metauro, R., Italy 43 45N 12 59E
108 Metchosin, Canada 48 15N 123 37W
87 Metehara, Ethiopia 8 58N 39 57E
87 Metema, Ethiopia 12 56N 36 13E
91 Metengobalame, Mozam. 14 49S 34 30E
45 Méthana, Greece 37 35N 23 23E
45 Methóni, Greece 36 49N 21 42E
113 Methuen, U.S.A. 42 43N 71 10W
101 Methven, N.Z. 43 38S 171 40E
43 Metkovets, Bulg. 43 37N 23 10E
42 Metkovic, Yugoslavia 43 6N 17 39E
83 Metlaoui, Tunisia 34 24N 8 24E
39 Metlika, Yugoslavia 45 40N 15 20E
99 Metowra, Australia 25 3S 146 15E
117 Metropolis, U.S.A. 37 10N 88 47W
44 Métsovon, Greece 39 48N 21 12E
70 Mettuppalaiyam, India 11 18N 76 59E
70 Mettur, India 11 48N 77 47E
69 Mettur Dam, India 11 45N 77 45E
62 Metulla, Israel 33 17N 35 34E
19 Metz, France 49 8N 6 10E
72 Meulaboh, Indonesia 4 11N 96 3E
19 Meulan, France 49 0N 1 52E

MAP
19 Meung-sur-Loire, France 47 50N 1 40E
72 Meureudu, Indonesia 5 19N 96 10E
19 Meurthe, R., France 48 47N 6 9E
19 Meurthe-et-Moselle ♦, France 48 52N 6 0E
16 Meuse, R., Europe 50 45N 5 41E
19 Meuse ♦, France 49 8N 5 25E
24 Meuselwitz, Germany 51 3N 12 18E
117 Mexia, U.S.A. 31 38N 96 32W
127 Mexiana, I., Brazil 0 0N 49 30W
120 Mexicali, Mexico 32 40N 115 30W
120 Mexico ■, America 20 0N 100 0W
120 México, Mexico 19 20N 99 10W
113 Mexico, Me., U.S.A. 44 35N 70 30W
116 Mexico, Mo., U.S.A. 39 10N 91 55W
120 México ♦, Mexico 19 20N 99 10W
127 Mexico, G. of, America 25 0N 90 0W
64 Meyadin, Syria 35 0N 40 30E
24 Meyenburg, Germany 53 19N 12 15E
20 Meymac, France 45 32N 2 10E
21 Meyrargues, France 43 38N 5 32E
20 Meyrueis, France 44 12N 3 27E
20 Meyssac, France 45 3N 1 40E
43 Mezdra, Bulgaria 43 12N 23 35E
20 Mèze, France 43 27N 3 36E
52 Mezen, U.S.S.R. 65 50N 44 20E
54 Mezha, R., U.S.S.R. 55 50N 31 45E
18 Mezidon, France 49 5N 0 1W
19 Mézières, Fr. 49 45N 4 42E
21 Mézilhac, France 44 49N 4 21E
20 Mézin, France 44 4N 0 16E
27 Mezöberény, Hungary 46 49N 21 3E
27 Mezöfalva, Hungary 46 55N 18 49E
27 Mezöhegyes, Hungary 46 19N 20 49E
27 Mezokövácsháza, Hung. 46 25N 20 57E
27 Mezökövesd, Hungary 47 49N 20 35E
20 Mézos, France 44 5N 1 10W
27 Mezötúr, Hungary 47 0N 20 41E
38 Mezzolombardo, Italy 46 13N 11 5E
91 Mgeta, Tanzania 8 22S 38 6E
54 Mglin, U.S.S.R. 53 2N 32 50E
91 Mhlaba Hills, Rhodesia 18 30S 30 30E
68 Mhow, India 22 33N 75 50E
120 Miahuatlán, Mexico 16 21N 96 36W
31 Miajadas, Spain 39 9N 5 54W
68 Mialar, India 26 15N 70 20E
98 Miallo, Australia 16 28S 145 22E
119 Miami, Ariz., U.S.A. 33 25N 111 0W
115 Miami, Fla., U.S.A. 25 52N 80 15W
117 Miami, Tex., U.S.A. 35 44N 100 38W
114 Miami, R., U.S.A. 39 20N 84 40W
115 Miami Beach, U.S.A. 25 49N 80 6W
114 Miamisburg, U.S.A. 39 40N 84 11W
64 Miandowāb, Iran 37 0N 46 5E
64 Mianeh, Iran 37 30N 47 40E
68 Mianwali, Pakistan 32 38N 71 28E
76 Miao Tao, China 38 10N 120 50E
77 Miaoli, Taiwan 24 33N 120 42E
93 Miarinarivo, Malagasy Republic 18 57S 46 55E
58 Miass, U.S.S.R. 54 59N 60 6E
28 Miasteczko Kraj, Poland 53 7N 17 1E
28 Miastko, Poland 54 0N 16 58E
108 Mica Res., Canada 51 55N 118 00W
46 Micăsasa, Rumania 46 7N 24 7E
25 Michelstadt, Germany 49 40N 9 0E
114 Michigan, L., U.S.A. 44 0N 87 0W
111 Michigan ♦, U.S.A. 44 40N 85 40W
114 Michigan City, U.S.A. 41 42N 86 56W
76 Michih, China 37 58N 110 0E
107 Michikamau L., Canada 54 0N 64 0W
106 Michipicoten Harb., Can. 47 55N 84 55W
106 Michipicoten I., Canada 47 40N 85 50W
120 Michoacan ♦, Mexico 19 0N 102 0W
43 Michurin, Bulgaria 42 9N 27 51E
55 Michurinsk, U.S.S.R. 52 58N 40 27E
98 Miclere, Australia 20 30S 147 30E
94 Micronesia, Pacific Ocean 17 0N 160 0E
72 Midai, I., Indonesia 3 0N 107 42E
109 Midale, Canada 49 25N 103 20W
118 Midas, U.S.A. 41 14N 116 56W
48 Middagsfjället, Sweden 63 27N 12 19E
16 Middelburg, Neth. 51 30N 3 36E
93 Middelburg, C. Prov., S. Africa 31 30S 25 0E
93 Middelburg, Trans., S. Africa 25 49N 29 28E
49 Middelfart, Denmark 55 30N 9 43E
118 Middle Alkali L., U.S.A. 41 30N 120 3W
71 Middle Andaman I., India 12 30N 92 30E
107 Middle Brook, Canada 48 40N 54 20W
113 Middleboro, U.S.A. 41 56N 70 52W
113 Middleburg, N.Y., U.S.A. 42 36N 74 19W
112 Middleburg, Pa., U.S.A. 40 46N 77 5W
113 Middlebury, U.S.A. 44 0N 73 9W
114 Middleport, U.S.A. 39 0N 82 5W
12 Middlesbrough, Eng. 54 35N 1 14W
113 Middlesex, U.S.A. 40 36N 74 30W
107 Middleton, Canada 44 57N 65 4W
113 Middletown, Conn., U.S.A. 41 37N 72 40W
114 Middletown, Del., U.S.A. 39 30N 84 21W
113 Middletown, N.Y., U.S.A. 41 28N 74 28W
113 Middletown, Pa., U.S.A. 40 12N 76 44W
92 Middelveld, S. Afr. 29 45S 22 30E
82 Midelt, Morocco 32 46N 4 44W
94 Midhurst, New Zealand 39 17S 174 18E
20 Midi, Canal du, France 43 45N 1 21E
32 Midi d'Ossau, Spain 42 50N 0 25W
106 Midland, Canada 44 45N 79 50W
114 Midland, Mich., U.S.A. 43 37N 84 17W
112 Midland, Pa., U.S.A. 40 39N 80 27W
117 Midland, Tex., U.S.A. 32 0N 102 3W
91 Midlands ♦, Rhod. 19 40S 29 0E

MAP
96 Midland Junc., Australia 31 50S 115 58E
15 Midleton, Ireland 51 52N 8 12W
98 Midlothian, Australia 17 10S 141 12E
117 Midlothian, U.S.A. 32 30N 97 0W
*14 Midlothian ♦, Scotland 55 45N 3 15W
69 Midnapore, India 22 25N 87 21E
93 Midongy, Massif de, Malag. 23 30S 47 0E
93 Midongy du Sud, Malag. 23 35S 47 1E
49 Midskog, Sweden 58 56N 14 5E
118 Midvale, U.S.A. 40 39N 111 58W
94 Midway Is., Pac. Oc. 28 13N 177 22W
118 Midwest, U.S.A. 43 27N 106 11W
42 Midzor, Bulgaria 43 24N 22 40E
28 Miechów, Poland 50 21N 20 5E
28 Miedzyborz, Poland 51 39N 17 24E
28 Miedzychód, Poland 52 35N 15 53E
28 Miedzylesie, Poland 50 41N 16 40E
28 Miedzyrzec Podlaski, Poland 51 58N 22 45E
28 Miedzyrzecz, Poland 52 26N 15 35E
28 Miedzyzdroje, Poland 53 56N 14 26E
28 Miejska Górka, Poland 51 39N 16 58E
74 Mie-ken ♦, Japan 34 30N 136 10E
20 Miélan, France 43 27N 0 19E
98 Mielelek, New Guinea 6 1S 148 58E
77 Mienchih, China 34 47N 111 49E
92 Mienga, Angola 17 12S 19 48E
77 Mienhsien, China 33 11N 106 35E
77 Mienyang, Hupei, China 30 10N 113 20E
77 Mienyang, Szechwan, China 31 18N 104 26E
46 Miercurea Ciuc, Rum. 46 21N 25 48E
69 Mieres, Spain 43 18N 5 48W
28 Mieroszów, Poland 50 40N 16 10E
87 Mieso, Ethiopia 9 15N 40 43E
28 Mieszkowice, Poland 52 47N 14 30E
112 Mifflintown, U.S.A. 40 34N 77 24W
62 Migdal, Israel 32 51N 35 30E
62 Migdal Afea, Israel 32 5N 34 58E
39 Migliarino, Italy 44 54N 11 56E
74 Mihara, Japan 34 24N 133 5E
19 Migennes, France 47 58N 3 31E
120 Miguel Alemán, Presa, Mexico 18 15N 96 40W
32 Mijares, R., Spain 40 15N 0 50W
31 Mijas, Spain 36 36N 4 40W
85 Mijilu, Nigeria 10 22N 13 19E
90 Mikese, Tanzania 6 48S 37 55E
57 Mikha Tskhakaya, U.S.S.R. 42 15N 42 7E
55 Mikhailov, U.S.S.R. 54 20N 39 0E
43 Mikhailovgrad, Bulgaria 43 27N 23 16E
56 Mikhailovka, Ukraine, U.S.S.R. 47 16N 35 27E
57 Mikhaylovka, Azerbaijan, U.S.S.R. 41 31N 48 52E
55 Mikhaylovka, R.S.F.S.R., U.S.S.R. 50 3N 43 5E
55 Mikhnevo, U.S.S.R. 55 4N 37 59E
45 Mikinai, Greece 37 43N 22 46E
91 Mikindani, Tanzania 10 15S 40 2E
51 Mikkeli, Finland 61 43N 27 25E
50 Mikkelin Lääni ♦, Finland 61 56N 28 0E
87 Mikniya, Sudan 17 0N 33 45E
28 Mikołajki, Poland 53 49N 21 37E
27 Mikołów, Poland 50 10N 18 50E
45 Míkonos, I., Greece 37 30N 25 25E
44 Mikrón Dhérion, Gr. 41 19N 26 6E
27 Mikulov, Cz. 48 48N 16 39E
90 Mikumi, Tanz. 7 26S 37 9E
52 Mikun, U.S.S.R. 62 20N 50 0E
74 Mikura Shima, Japan 33 40N 139 40E
82 Mila, Algeria 36 27N 6 16E
116 Milaca, U.S.A. 45 45N 93 40W
126 Milagro, Ecuador 2 0S 79 30W
38 Milan = Milano, Italy 45 28N 9 10E
116 Milan, Mo., U.S.A. 40 10N 93 5W
115 Milan, Tenn., U.S.A. 35 55N 88 45W
99 Milang, Australia 32 20S 138 55E
91 Milange, Mozambique 16 3S 35 45E
38 Milano, Italy 45 28N 9 10E
64 Milas, Turkey 37 20N 27 50E
41 Milazzo, Italy 38 13N 15 13E
116 Milbank, U.S.A. 45 17N 96 38W
109 Milden, Canada 51 29N 107 32W
112 Mildmay, Canada 44 3N 81 9W
100 Mildura, Australia 34 8S 142 7E
44 Miléai, Greece 39 20N 23 9E
99 Miles, Australia 26 37S 150 10E
117 Miles, U.S.A. 31 39N 100 11W
116 Miles City, U.S.A. 46 30N 105 50W
41 Mileto, Italy 38 37N 16 3E
41 Miletto, Mte., Italy 41 26N 14 23E
26 Milevsko, Cz. 49 27N 14 21E
113 Milford, Conn., U.S.A. 41 13N 73 4W
114 Milford, Del., U.S.A. 38 52N 75 27W
113 Milford, Mass., U.S.A. 42 8N 71 30W
113 Milford, Pa., U.S.A. 41 20N 74 47W
119 Milford, Utah, U.S.A. 38 20N 113 0W
13 Milford Haven, Wales 51 43N 5 2W
13 Milford Haven, B., Wales 51 40N 5 10W
101 Milford Sd., N.Z. 44 34S 167 47E
81 Milh, Ras el, Libya 32 0N 24 55E
82 Miliana, Ain Salah, Algeria 27 20N 2 32E
82 Miliana, Médéa, Algeria 36 12N 2 15E
28 Milicz, Poland 51 31N 17 19E
41 Militello, Italy 37 16N 14 46E
118 Milk, R., U.S.A. 48 40N 107 15W
108 Milk River, Canada 49 10N 111 30W
5 Mill, I., Antarctica 66 0S 101 30E
118 Mill City, U.S.A. 44 45N 122 28W
98 Millaa Millaa, Austral. 17 30S 145 32E
20 Millau, France 44 8N 3 4E
112 Millbridge, Canada 44 43N 77 35W
112 Millbrook, Canada 44 10N 78 23W
116 Mille Lacs, L., U.S.A. 46 10N 93 30W

MAP
106 Mille Lacs, L. des, Can 48 45N 90 35W
115 Milledgeville, U.S.A. 33 7N 83 15W
115 Millen, U.S.A. 32 50N 81 57W
116 Miller, U.S.A. 44 35N 98 59W
57 Millerovo, U.S.S.R. 48 57N 40 28E
112 Millersburg, Ohio, U.S.A. 40 32N 81 52W
112 Millersburg, Pa., U.S.A. 40 32N 76 58W
113 Millerton, U.S.A. 41 57N 73 32W
107 Millertown Junc., Can. 48 49N 56 28W
20 Millevaches, Plat. de, Fr. 45 45N 2 0E
99 Millicent, Australia 37 34S 140 21E
107 Millinocket, U.S.A. 45 45N 68 45W
99 Millmerran, Australia 27 53S 151 16E
108 Mills L., Canada 61 30N 118 20W
112 Millsboro, U.S.A. 40 0N 80 0W
100 Millthorpe, Australia 33 27S 148 14E
114 Millville, U.S.A. 39 22N 74 0W
117 Millwood Res., U.S.A. 33 45N 94 0W
19 Milly, France 48 24N 2 20E
39 Milna, Yugoslavia 43 20N 16 28E
105 Milne Inlet, Canada 72 30N 80 0W
116 Milnor, U.S.A. 46 19N 97 29W
45 Mílos, Greece 36 44N 24 25E
45 Mílos, I., Greece 36 44N 24 25E
42 Miloševo, Yugoslavia 45 42N 20 20E
28 Miłosław, Poland 52 12N 17 32E
25 Miltenberg, Germany 49 41N 9 13E
100 Milton, N.S.W., Australia 35 20S 150 27E
101 Milton, New Zealand 46 7S 169 59E
115 Milton, Fla., U.S.A. 30 38N 87 0W
112 Milton, Pa., U.S.A. 41 0N 76 53W
118 Milton-Freewater, U.S.A. 45 57N 118 24W
112 Milton West, Canada 43 33N 79 53W
15 Miltown Malbay, Ire. 52 51N 9 25W
112 Milverton, Canada 43 35N 80 43W
114 Milwaukee, U.S.A. 43 9N 87 58W
118 Milwaukie, U.S.A. 45 33N 122 39W
84 Mim, Ghana 6 57N 2 33W
20 Mimizan, France 44 12N 1 13W
26 Mimon, Czechoslovakia 50 38N 14 43E
77 Min K., China 26 0N 119 20E
124 Mina Pirquitas, Arg. 22 40S 66 40W
64 Mina Saud, Saudi Arabia 28 45N 48 20E
64 Mīnā'al Ahmadī, Kuwait 29 5N 48 10E
65 Mīnāb, Iran 27 10N 57 1E
109 Minaki, Canada 50 0N 94 40W
74 Minamata, Japan 32 10N 130 30E
107 Minas Basin, Canada 45 20N 64 12W
31 Minas de Rio Tinto, Sp. 37 42N 6 22W
31 Minas de San Quintín, Spain 38 49N 4 23W
127 Minas Gerais ♦, Brazil 18 50S 46 0W
120 Minas, Sierra de las, Guatemala 15 9N 89 31W
120 Minatitlán, Mexico 17 58N 94 35W
67 Minbu, Burma 20 10N 95 0E
100 Mincha, Australia 36 1S 144 6E
38 Mincio, R., Italy 45 8N 10 55E
73 Mindanao, I., Phil. 8 0N 125 0E
73 Mindanao Sea, Phil. 9 0N 124 0E
73 Mindanao Trench, Pac. Oc. 8 0N 128 0E
25 Mindelheim, Germany 48 4N 10 30E
112 Minden, Canada 44 56N 78 44W
24 Minden, Germany 52 18N 8 54E
117 Minden, U.S.A. 32 40N 93 20W
73 Mindiptana, Indonesia 5 45S 140 22E
73 Mindoro, I., Philippines 13 0N 121 0E
73 Mindoro Strait, Phil. 12 30N 120 30E
88 Mindouli, Congo 4 12S 14 28E
13 Minehead, Eng. 51 12N 3 29W
113 Mineola, U.S.A. 40 43N 95 30W
117 Mineral Wells, U.S.A. 32 50N 98 5W
57 Mineralnyye Vody, U.S.S.R. 44 18N 43 15E
113 Minersville, Pa., U.S.A. 40 40N 76 17W
119 Minersville, Utah, U.S.A. 38 14N 112 58W
112 Minerva, U.S.A. 40 43N 81 8W
41 Minervino Murge, Italy 41 6N 16 4E
115 Minette, U.S.A. 30 54N 87 43W
113 Minetto, U.S.A. 43 24N 76 28W
107 Mingan, Canada 50 20N 64 0W
76 Mingan = Pangkiang, China 43 4N 112 30E
57 Mingechaur, U.S.S.R. 40 52N 47 0E
57 Mingechaurskoye Vdkhr., U.S.S.R. 40 56N 47 20E
98 Mingela, Australia 19 42S 146 42E
67 Mingin, Burma 22 50N 94 30E
77 Mingki (Kweihwa), China 26 10N 117 14E
32 Minglanilla, Spain 39 34N 1 38W
77 Minhow = Foochow, China 26 2N 119 12E
42 Minicevo, Yugoslavia 43 42N 22 18E
118 Minidoka, U.S.A. 42 47N 113 34W
96 Minigwal L., Australia 29 31S 123 14E
77 Minkiang, China 32 30N 114 10E
85 Minna, Nigeria 9 37N 6 30E
116 Minneapolis, Kans., U.S.A. 39 11N 97 40W
116 Minneapolis, Minn., U.S.A. 44 58N 93 20W
116 Minnesota ♦, U.S.A. 46 40N 94 0W
47 Minnesund, Norway 60 23N 11 14E
30 Miño, R., Spain 41 58N 8 40W
32 Minorca = Menorca, Spain 40 0N 4 0E
116 Minot, U.S.A. 48 10N 101 15W
18 Minquiers, Les, Chan. Is. 48 58N 2 8W
24 Minsen, Germany 53 43N 7 58E
96 Minsk, U.S.S.R. 53 52N 27 30E
28 Minsk Mazowiecki, Pol. 52 10N 21 33E
66 Mintaka Pass, Kashmir 37 0N 74 58E
106 Minto L., Canada 48 0N 84 45W

* Incorporated within the county of Gwynedd

* Incorporated within the regions of Lothian and Borders

Mintsing INDEX Montelíbano

MAP
77 Mintsing, China 26 8N 118 57E
118 Minturn, U.S.A. 39 45N 106 25W
40 Minturno, Italy 41 15N 13 43E
86 Minûf, Egypt 30 26N 30 52E
59 Minusinsk, U.S.S.R. 53 50N 91 20E
67 Minutang, India 28 15N 96 30E
88 Minvoul, Gabon 2 9N 12 8E
75 Minya Konka, mt., China 29 36N 101 50E
100 Minyip, Australia 36 29S 142 36E
42 Mionica, Yugoslavia 44 14N 20 6E
73 Mios Num, I., Indon. 1 30S 135 10E
107 Miquelon, St. Pierre et, ♦, N. Amer. 47 8N 56 24W
57 Mir-Bashir, U.S.S.R. 40 11N 46 58E
39 Mira, Italy 45 26N 12 9E
30 Mira, Portugal 40 26N 8 44W
31 Mira, R., Portugal 37 30N 8 30W
41 Mirabella Eclano, Italy 41 3N 14 59E
120 Miraflores Locks, Panama Canal Zone 8 59N 79 36W
70 Miraj, India 16 50N 74 45E
124 Miramar, Argentina 38 15S 57 50W
93 Miramar, Mozambique 23 50S 35 35E
21 Miramas, France 43 33N 4 59E
20 Mirambeau, France 45 23N 0 35W
107 Miramichi B., Canada 47 15N 65 0W
20 Miramont-de-Guyenne, France 44 37N 0 21E
127 Miranda, Brazil 20 10S 56 15W
126 Miranda ♦, Venezuela 10 15N 66 25W
32 Miranda de Ebro, Spain 42 41N 2 57W
30 Miranda do Corvo, Spain 40 6N 8 20W
30 Miranda do Douro, Port. 41 30N 6 16W
30 Miranda do Ebro, Spain 41 30N 6 16W
117 Miranda City, U.S.A. 27 28N 98 59W
38 Mirandola, Italy 44 53N 11 2E
125 Mirandópolis, Brazil 21 9S 51 6W
91 Mirango, Malawi 13 32S 34 58E
98 Mirani, Australia 21 12S 148 59E
39 Mirano, Italy 45 29N 12 6E
29 Miraporvos, I., Bahama Is. 22 9N 74 30W
125 Mirassol, Brazil 20 46S 49 28W
100 Mirboo, Australia 38 15S 146 7E
86 Mirear, I., Egypt 23 15N 35 41E
19 Mirebeau, Côte d'Or, Fr. 47 25N 5 20E
18 Mirebeau, Vienne, Fr. 46 49N 0 10E
19 Mirecourt, France 48 20N 6 10E
65 Mirfa, Trucial Oman 24 0N 53 24E
54 Mirgorod, U.S.S.R. 49 58N 33 50E
72 Miri, Malaysia 4 18N 114 0E
98 Miriam Vale, Australia 24 20S 151 39E
125 Mirim, Brazil 32 40S 52 58W
125 Mirim, Lagoa, Brazil/Urug. 32 45S 52 50W
126 Mirimire, Venezuela 11 10N 68 43W
5 Mirny, Antarctica 66 0S 95 0E
59 Mirnyy, U.S.S.R. 62 33N 113 53E
100 Mirool, Australia 34 24S 147 5E
28 Mirosławiec, Poland 53 20N 16 5E
68 Mirpur Bibiwari, Pak. 28 33N 67 44E
68 Mirpur Khas, Pakistan 25 30N 69 0E
68 Mirpur Sakro, Pakistan 24 33N 67 41E
108 Mirror, Canada 52 30N 113 0W
28 Mirsk, Poland 50 58N 15 23E
76 Miryang, S. Korea 35 34N 128 42E
57 Mirzaani, U.S.S.R. 41 24N 46 5E
69 Mirzapur, India 25 10N 82 45E
107 Miscou I., Canada 47 57N 64 31W
64 Mish'ab, Ra'as al, Saudi Arabia 28 15N 48 43E
76 Mishan, China 45 31N 132 2E
114 Mishawaka, U.S.A. 41 40N 86 8W
86 Mishbih, Gebel, Egypt 22 48N 34 38E
74 Mishima, Japan 35 10N 138 52E
62 Mishmar Aiyalon, Isr. 31 52N 34 57E
62 Mishmar Ha' Emeq, Israel 32 37N 35 7E
62 Mishmar Ha Negev, Israel 31 32N 34 48E
62 Mishmar Ha Yarden, Israel 33 0N 35 56E
40 Misilmeri, Italy 38 2N 13 25E
98 Misima I., Papua 10 40S 152 50E
125 Misiones ♦, Arg. 27 0S 55 0W
124 Misiones ♦, Paraguay 27 0S 56 0W
65 Miskin, Oman 23 44N 56 52E
121 Miskitos, Cayos, Nicaragua 14 26N 82 50W
27 Miskolc, Hungary 48 7N 20 50E
90 Misoke, Zaïre 0 42S 28 2E
73 Misoöl, I., Indonesia 2 0S 130 0E
83 Misrâtah, Libya 32 18N 15 3E
106 Missanabie, Canada 48 20N 84 6W
82 Misserghin, Algeria 35 44N 0 49W
106 Missinaibi L., Canada 48 14N 83 15W
106 Missinaibi, R., Canada 50 30N 82 40W
116 Mission, S.D., U.S.A. 43 21N 100 36W
117 Mission, Tex., U.S.A. 26 15N 98 30W
108 Mission City, Canada 49 10N 122 15W
106 Missisa L., Canada 52 20N 85 7W
113 Mississippi L., Canada 45 5N 76 12W
117 Mississippi, R., U.S.A. 35 30N 90 0W
117 Mississippi Sd., U.S.A. 30 25N 89 0W
73 Mississippi ♦, U.S.A. 33 0N 90 0W
11 Mississippi ♦, U.S.A. 33 0N 90 0W
118 Missoula, U.S.A. 47 0N 114 0W
116 Missouri, R., U.S.A. 40 20N 95 40W
118 Missouri, Little, R., U.S.A. 46 0N 111 35W
116 Missouri ♦, U.S.A. 38 25N 92 30W
109 Mistake B., Canada 62 8N 93 0W
106 Mistassini L., Canada 51 0N 73 40W
107 Mistastin L., Canada 55 58N 63 40W
27 Mistelbach, Austria 48 34N 16 34E
41 Misterbianco, Italy 37 32N 15 0E
41 Mistretta, Italy 37 56N 14 20E
MAP
86 Mît Ghamr, Egypt 30 42N 31 12E
87 Mitatib, Sudan 15 59N 36 12E
99 Mitchell, Australia 26 29S 147 58E
112 Mitchell, Canada 43 29N 81 21W
114 Mitchell, Ind., U.S.A. 38 42N 86 25W
116 Mitchell, Nebr., U.S.A. 41 58N 103 45W
118 Mitchell, Oreg., U.S.A. 44 31N 120 8W
116 Mitchell, S.D., U.S.A. 43 40N 98 0W
115 Mitchell, Mt., U.S.A. 35 40N 82 20W
98 Mitchell, R., Australia 37 20S 147 0E
15 Mitchelstown, Ireland 52 16N 8 18W
68 Mitha Tiwana, Pakistan 32 13N 72 6E
44 Mithimna, Greece 39 20N 26 12E
100 Mitiamo, Australia 36 19S 144 14E
101 Mitiaro, I., Cook Is. 19 49S 157 43W
45 Mitilini, Greece 39 6N 26 35E
44 Mitilini = Lesvos, Greece 39 0N 26 20E
45 Mitilinoi, Greece 37 42N 26 56E
74 Mito, Japan 36 20N 140 30E
94 Mitre Pk., N.Z. 44 35S 167 45E
93 Mitsinjo, Malagasy Republic 16 1S 45 52E
87 Mitsiwa, Ethiopia 15 35N 39 25E
87 Mitsiwa Channel, Ethiopia 15 30N 40 0E
100 Mitta Mitta, Australia 36 45S 147 36E
100 Mitta Mitta, R., Australia 36 45S 147 36E
100 Mittagong, Australia 34 28S 150 29E
24 Mittelland Kanal, Ger. 52 23N 7 45E
24 Mittenwalde, Germany 52 16N 13 33E
24 Mittweida, Germany 50 59N 13 0E
100 Mittyack, Australia 35 8S 142 36E
126 Mitú, Colombia 1 8N 70 3W
126 Mituas, Colombia 3 52N 68 49W
90 Mitumba, Tanzania 7 8S 31 2E
90 Mitumba, Chaîne des, Zaïre 10 0S 26 20E
91 Mitwaba, Zaïre 8 2N 27 17E
90 Mityana, Uganda 0 23N 32 2E
88 Mitzick, Gabon 0 45N 11 40E
57 Mius, R., U.S.S.R. 47 30N 39 0E
74 Miyagi-Ken ♦, Japan 38 15N 140 45E
86 Miyâh, W. el, Egypt 25 10N 33 30E
74 Miyake-Jima, Japan 34 0N 139 30E
74 Miyako, Japan 39 40N 141 75E
77 Miyako-rettō, Japan 24 47N 125 20E
74 Miyakonojo, Japan 31 32N 131 5E
74 Miyazaki, Japan 31 56N 131 30E
74 Miyazaki-ken ♦, Japan 32 0N 131 30E
74 Miyazu, Japan 35 35N 135 10E
64 Miyet, Bahr el, Jordan-Israel 31 30N 35 30E
76 Miyun, China 40 25N 116 50E
73 Mizamis = Ozamiz, Philippines 8 15N 123 50E
83 Mizdah, Libya 31 30N 13 0E
15 Mizen Hd., Cork, Ire. 51 27N 9 50W
15 Mizen Hd., Wick., Ire. 52 52N 6 4W
46 Mizil, Rumania 44 59N 26 29E
49 Mjöbäck, Sweden 57 28N 12 53E
49 Mjölby, Sweden 58 20N 15 10E
47 Mjömna, Norway 60 55N 4 55E
49 Mjörn, Sweden 57 55N 12 25E
47 Mjösa, R., Sweden 60 40N 11 0E
90 Mkata, Tanzania 5 45S 38 20E
90 Mkokotoni, Tanz. 5 55S 39 15E
90 Mkomazi, Tanzania 4 40S 38 7E
91 Mkulwe, Tanzania 8 37S 32 20E
90 Mkumbi, Ras, Tanzania 7 38S 39 55E
91 Mkushi, Zambia 14 25S 29 15E
91 Mkushi River, Zambia 13 40S 29 30E
93 Mkuze, R., S. Afr. 27 45S 32 30E
90 Mkwaya, Tanzania 6 17S 35 40E
26 Mladá Boleslav, Cz. 50 27N 14 53E
42 Mladenovac, Y.-slav. 44 28N 20 44E
90 Mlala Hills, Tanzania 6 50S 31 40E
91 Mlange, Malawi 16 2S 35 33E
42 Mlava, R., Yugoslavia 44 35N 21 18E
28 Mława, Poland 53 9N 20 25E
39 Mlinište, Yugoslavia 44 15N 16 50E
42 Mljet, I., Yugoslavia 42 43N 17 30E
28 Młynary, Poland 54 12N 19 46E
85 Mme, Cameroon 6 18N 10 14E
47 Mo, Hordaland, Norway 60 49N 5 48E
50 Mo, Nordland, Norway 66 19N 14 9E
47 Mo, Telemark, Norway 59 28N 7 50E
48 Mo, Gävleborg, Sweden 61 19N 16 47E
73 Moa, I., Indonesia 8 0S 128 0E
84 Moa, R., Sierra Leone 7 0N 11 40W
119 Moab, U.S.A. 38 40N 109 35W
88 Moabi, Gabon 2 24S 10 59E
101 Moala, I., Fiji 18 36S 179 53E
99 Moalla Park, Australia 29 42S 143 3E
100 Moama, Australia 36 3S 144 45E
100 Moamba, Mozambique 25 34S 32 16E
30 Moaña, Spain 42 18N 8 43W
88 Moanda, Gabon 1 28S 13 21E
119 Moapa, U.S.A. 36 45N 114 43W
88 Mobaye, Cent. Afr. Rep. 4 25N 21 5E
116 Moberley, U.S.A. 39 25N 92 25W
106 Mobert, Canada 48 41N 85 40W
115 Mobile, U.S.A. 30 41N 88 3W
115 Mobile B., U.S.A. 30 30N 88 0W
115 Mobile, Pt., U.S.A. 30 15N 88 0W
49 Möborg, Denmark 56 24N 8 21E
116 Mobridge, U.S.A. 45 40N 100 28W
91 Mocabe Kasari, Zaïre 9 58S 26 12E
91 Moçambique, Mozam. 15 3S 40 42E
91 Moçambique ♦, Mozam. 14 45S 38 30E
92 Moçâmedes ♦, Ang. 16 35S 12 30E
92 Mochiara Grove, Bots. 20 43S 21 50E
92 Mochudi, Botswana 24 27S 26 7E
91 Mocimboa da Praia, Mozam. 11 25S 40 20E
46 Mociu, Rumania 46 46N 24 3E
49 Möckeln, Sweden 56 40N 14 15E
118 Moclips, U.S.A. 47 29N 124 10W
126 Mocoa, Colombia 1 15N 76 45W
MAP
125 Mococa, Brazil 21 28S 47 0W
120 Mocorito, Mexico 25 20N 108 0W
89 Mocuba, Mozambique 16 54S 37 25E
21 Modane, France 45 12N 6 40E
68 Modasa, India 23 30N 73 21E
92 Modder, R., S. Africa 28 50S 24 50E
92 Modderrivier, S. Africa 29 2S 24 38E
38 Módena, Italy 44 39N 10 55E
119 Modena, U.S.A. 37 55N 113 56W
119 Modesto, U.S.A. 37 43N 121 0W
41 Módica, Italy 36 52N 14 45E
39 Modigliana, Italy 44 9N 11 48E
73 Modjokerto, Indonesia 7 29S 112 25E
28 Modlin, Poland 52 24N 20 41E
26 Mödling, Austria 48 5N 16 17E
87 Modo, Sudan 5 31N 30 33E
27 Modra, Czechoslovakia 48 19N 17 20E
42 Modriča, Yugoslavia 44 57N 18 17E
100 Moe, Australia 38 12S 146 19E
91 Moebase, Mozambique 17 3S 38 41E
71 Moei, R., Thailand 17 25N 98 10E
18 Moëlan-s-Mer, France 47 49N 3 38W
127 Moengo, Surinam 5 45N 54 20W
14 Moffat, Scot. 55 20N 3 27W
68 Moga, India 30 48N 75 8E
63 Mogadiscio = Mogadishu, Somali Rep. 2 2N 45 25E
63 Mogadishu, Somali Rep. 2 2N 45 25E
82 Mogador = Essaouira, Morocco 31 32N 9 42W
30 Mogadouro, Portugal 41 22N 6 47W
74 Mogami-gawa, R., Japan 38 45N 140 0E
67 Mogaung, Burma 25 20N 97 0E
49 Mögeltønder, Denmark 54 57N 8 48E
33 Mogente, Spain 38 52N 0 45W
87 Mogho, Ethiopia 4 54N 40 16E
125 Mogi das Cruzes, Brazil 23 45S 46 20W
125 Mogi-Guaçu, R., Brazil 20 53S 48 10W
125 Mogi Mirim, Brazil 22 20S 47 0W
28 Mogielnica, Poland 51 42N 20 41E
54 Mogilev, U.S.S.R. 53 55N 30 18E
56 Mogilev Podolskiy, U.S.S.R. 48 20N 27 40E
100 Mogilla, Australia 36 41S 149 38E
28 Mogilno, Poland 52 39N 17 55E
89 Mogincual, Mozambique 15 35S 40 25E
39 Mogliano Veneto, Italy 45 33N 12 15E
59 Mogocha, U.S.S.R. 53 40N 119 50E
73 Mogoi, Indonesia 1 55S 133 10E
67 Mogôk, Burma 23 0N 96 40E
119 Mogollon, U.S.A. 33 25N 108 55W
119 Mogollon Mesa, U.S.A. 43 40N 111 0W
31 Moguer, Spain 37 15N 6 52W
27 Mohács, Hungary 45 58N 18 41E
116 Mohall, U.S.A. 48 46N 101 30W
65 Mohammadabad, Iran 37 30N 59 5E
82 Mohammedia, Morocco 33 44N 7 21W
119 Mohave Desert, U.S.A. 35 0N 117 30W
119 Mohawk, U.S.A. 32 45N 113 50W
49 Moheda, Sweden 57 1N 14 35E
89 Mohembo, Botswana 18 15S 21 43E
24 Möhne, R., Germany 51 29N 8 10E
76 Moho, China 53 15N 122 27E
49 Moholm, Sweden 58 37N 14 5E
19 Mohon, France 48 2N 2 31W
90 Mohoro, Tanzania 8 6S 39 8E
87 Moia, Sudan 5 3N 28 2E
70 Moinabad, India 17 44N 77 16E
46 Moineşti, Rumania 46 28N 26 21E
58 Mointy, U.S.S.R. 47 40N 73 45E
45 Moirais, Greece 35 4N 24 56E
21 Moirans, France 45 20N 5 33E
21 Moirans-en-Montagne, France 46 26N 5 43E
54 Moisäkula, U.S.S.R. 58 3N 24 38E
107 Moisie, Canada 50 7N 66 1W
20 Moissac, France 44 7N 1 5E
31 Moita, Portugal 38 38N 8 58W
126 Moitaco, Venezuela 8 1N 64 21W
33 Mojácar, Spain 37 6N 1 55W
30 Mojados, Spain 41 26N 4 40W
119 Mojave, U.S.A. 35 8N 118 8W
119 Mojave Desert, U.S.A. 35 0N 117 30W
87 Mojjio, Ethiopia 8 35N 39 5E
124 Mojo, Bolivia 21 48S 65 33W
87 Mojo, Ethiopia 8 35N 39 5E
72 Mojo, I., Indonesia 8 10S 117 40E
101 Mokai, New Zealand 38 32S 175 56E
91 Mokambo, Zaïre 12 25S 28 20E
69 Mokameh, India 25 24N 85 55E
101 Mokau, New Zealand 38 42S 174 39E
63 Mokha, Yemen 13 18N 43 15E
45 Mokhós, Greece 35 16N 25 27E
90 Mokhotlong, Les. 29 22S 29 2E
83 Moknine, Tunisia 35 35N 10 58E
67 Mokokchung, India 26 15N 94 30E
77 Mokpo, S. Korea 34 50N 126 30E
42 Mokra Gora, Yugoslavia 42 50N 20 30E
43 Mokren, Bulgaria 42 45N 26 39E
39 Mokronog, Yugoslavia 45 57N 15 9E
55 Moksha, R., U.S.S.R. 54 45N 43 40E
55 Mokshan, U.S.S.R. 52 25N 44 35E
84 Mokta Spera, Mauritania 16 38N 9 6W
67 Moktama Kwe, Burma 15 40N 96 30E
16 Mol, Belgium 51 11N 5 5E
32 Mola, C. de la, Spain 39 53N 4 20E
41 Mola di Bari, Italy 41 3N 17 5E
47 Moland, Norway 59 11N 8 6E
45 Moláoi, Greece 36 49N 22 56E
39 Molat, I., Yugoslavia 44 15N 14 50E
58 Molchanovo, U.S.S.R. 57 40N 83 50E
12 Mold, Wales 53 10N 3 10W
27 Moldava nad Bodvou, Czechoslovakia 48 38N 21 0E
46 Moldavia = Moldova, Rumania 46 30N 27 0E
56 Moldavian S.S.R.♦, U.S.S.R. 47 0N 28 0E
47 Molde, Norway 62 45N 7 9E
46 Moldova, Rumania 46 30N 27 0E
MAP
42 Moldova Nouă, Rum. 44 45N 21 41E
43 Moldoveanu, mt., Rumania 45 36N 24 45E
41 Molfetta, Italy 41 12N 16 35E
32 Molina de Aragón, Sp. 40 46N 1 52W
14 Moline, U.S.A. 41 30N 90 30W
39 Molinella, Italy 44 38N 11 40E
124 Molinos, Argentina 25 28S 66 15W
90 Moliro, Zaïre 8 12S 30 30E
39 Molise ♦, Italy 41 45N 14 30E
41 Moliterno, Italy 40 14N 15 50E
49 Mölle, Sweden 56 17N 12 31E
30 Molledo, Spain 43 8N 4 6W
126 Mollendo, Peru 17 0S 72 0W
32 Mollerusa, Spain 41 37N 0 54E
31 Mollina, Spain 37 8N 4 38W
24 Mölln, Germany 53 37N 10 41E
49 Mollösund, Sweden 58 4N 11 30E
49 Mölltorp, Sweden 58 30N 14 26E
49 Mölndal, Sweden 57 40N 12 3E
56 Molochansk, U.S.S.R. 47 15N 35 23E
56 Molochnaya, R., U.S.S.R. 47 0N 35 30E
54 Molodechno, U.S.S.R. 54 20N 26 50E
110 Molokai, I., U.S.A. 21 8N 157 0W
55 Moloma, R., U.S.S.R. 59 0N 48 15E
89 Molopo, R., Botswana 25 40S 24 30E
45 Mólos, Greece 38 47N 22 37E
59 Molotov, Mys, U.S.S.R. 81 10N 95 0E
88 Moloundou, Cam. 2 8N 15 15E
19 Molsheim, France 48 33N 7 29E
92 Molteno, S. Afr. 31 22S 26 22E
73 Molu, I., Indonesia 6 45S 131 40E
73 Molucca Sea, Indonesia 4 0S 124 0E
73 Moluccas = Maluku, Is., Indonesia 1 0S 127 0E
92 Molusi, Botswana 20 21S 24 29E
54 Molvotitsy, U.S.S.R. 57 21N 32 24E
90 Moma, Zaïre 1 35S 23 52E
91 Moma, Mozambique 16 47S 39 4E
92 Momanga, S.W. Africa 18 7S 21 41E
90 Mombasa, Kenya 4 2S 39 43E
30 Mombuey, Spain 42 3N 6 20W
43 Momchilgrad, Bulgaria 41 33N 25 23E
90 Momi, Zaïre 1 42S 27 0E
126 Mompós, Colombia 9 14N 74 26W
49 Mön, Denmark 54 57N 12 15E
67 Mon, R., Burma 20 25N 94 30E
121 Mona, I., Puerto Rico 18 5N 67 54W
121 Mona Passage, W. Ind. 18 0N 67 40W
31 Mona, Punta, Spain 36 43N 3 45W
14 Monach Is., Scot. 57 32N 7 40W
20 Monaco ■, Europe 43 46N 7 23E
14 Monadhliath Mts., Scotland 57 10N 4 4W
126 Monagas ♦, Venezuela 9 20N 63 0W
15 Monaghan, Ireland 54 15N 6 58W
15 Monaghan ♦, Ireland 54 10N 7 0W
117 Monahans, U.S.A. 31 35N 102 50W
91 Monapo, Mozambique 14 50S 40 12E
108 Monarch Mt., Canada 51 55N 125 57W
100 Monaro Ra., Australia 36 20S 149 0E
83 Monastir, Tunisia 35 50N 10 49E
54 Monastyriska, U.S.S.R. 49 8N 25 14E
32 Moncada, Spain 39 30N 0 24W
38 Moncalieri, Italy 45 0N 7 40E
38 Moncalvo, Italy 45 3N 8 15E
30 Monção, Portugal 42 4N 8 27W
31 Moncarapacho, Port. 37 5N 7 46W
32 Moncayo, Mt., Spain 41 48N 1 50W
24 Mönchen-Gladbach, Ger. 51 12N 6 23E
31 Monchique, Portugal 37 19N 8 38W
120 Monclova, Mexico 26 50N 101 30W
18 Moncontour, France 48 22N 2 38W
18 Moncoutant, France 46 43N 0 36W
107 Moncton, Canada 46 7N 64 51W
30 Mondego, Cabo, Port. 40 11N 8 54W
30 Mondego, R., Portugal 40 28N 8 0W
73 Mondeodo, Indonesia 3 21S 122 9E
39 Mondolfo, Italy 43 45N 13 8E
30 Mondoñedo, Spain 43 25N 7 23E
38 Mondovi, Italy 44 23N 7 56E
116 Mondovi, U.S.A. 44 37N 91 40W
21 Mondragon, France 44 13N 4 44E
40 Mondragone, Italy 41 8N 13 52E
45 Monemvasia, Greece 36 41N 23 3E
112 Monessen, U.S.A. 40 9N 79 50W
31 Monesterio, Spain 38 6N 6 15W
21 Monestier-de- Clermont, France 44 55N 5 38E
106 Monet, Canada 48 10N 75 40W
117 Monett, U.S.A. 36 55N 93 56W
39 Monfalcone, Italy 45 49N 13 32E
20 Monflanquin, France 44 32N 0 47E
31 Monforte, Portugal 39 6N 7 25W
30 Monforte de Lemos, Spain 42 31N 7 33W
71 Mong Cai, N. Vietnam 21 27N 107 54E
67 Möng Hsu, Burma 21 54N 98 30E
67 Möng Kung, Burma 21 35N 97 35E
71 Mong Lang, Burma 20 29N 97 52E
67 Möng Nai, Burma 20 32N 97 55E
67 Möng Pai, Burma 19 40N 97 15E
67 Möng Pawk, Burma 22 4N 99 16E
67 Mong Ton, Burma 20 25N 98 45E
67 Mong Wa, Burma 21 26N 100 27E
67 Mong Yai, Burma 22 28N 98 3E
87 Mongalla, Sudan 5 8N 31 55E
90 Moliro, Zaïre 8 12S 30 30E
96 Monger L., Australia 29 0S 117 15E
69 Monghyr, India 25 23N 86 30E
69 Mongla, Pakistan 22 8N 89 35E
81 Mongo, Chad 12 14N 18 43E
75 Mongolia ■, Asia 47 0N 103 0E
76 Mongolia, Inner, ♦, China 44 15N 117 0E
85 Mongonu, Nigeria 12 40N 13 32E
88 Mongororo, Chad 12 22N 22 26E
88 Mongoumba, Cen. Afr. 3 33N 18 40E
71 Mongpang, China 23 5N 100 25E
89 Mongu, Zambia 15 16S 23 12E
MAP
82 Môngua, Angola 16 43S 15 20E
21 Monistral-St.-Loire, France 45 17N 4 11E
20 Monistrol-sur-Loire, Fr. 45 17N 4 11E
109 Monk, Canada 47 7N 69 59W
91 Monkey Bay, Malawi 14 7S 35 1E
28 Mońki, Poland 53 23N 22 48E
98 Monkira, Australia 24 46S 140 30E
88 Monkoto, Zaïre 1 38S 20 35E
13 Monmouth 51 48N 2 43W
116 Monmouth, U.S.A. 40 50N 90 40W
•13 Monmouth ♦, Wales 51 34N 3 5W
119 Mono, L., U.S.A. 38 0N 119 0W
121 Mono, Punta del, Nic. 12 0N 83 30W
112 Monongahela, U.S.A. 40 12N 79 56W
41 Monópoli, Italy 40 57N 17 18E
27 Monor, Hungary 47 21N 19 27E
33 Monóvar, Spain 38 28N 0 53W
95 Monowai, N.Z. 45 53S 167 25E
95 Monowai, L., N.Z. 45 53S 167 25E
32 Monreal del Campo, Sp. 40 47N 1 20W
40 Monreale, Italy 38 6N 13 16E
117 Monroe, La., U.S.A. 32 32N 92 4W
114 Monroe, Mich., U.S.A. 41 55N 83 26W
113 Monroe, N.Y., U.S.A. 41 19N 74 11W
115 Monroe, N.C., U.S.A. 35 2N 80 37W
119 Monroe, Utah, U.S.A. 38 45N 111 39W
116 Monroe, Wis., U.S.A. 42 38N 89 40W
116 Monroe City, U.S.A. 39 40N 91 40W
115 Monroeville, U.S.A. 31 33N 87 15W
84 Monrovia, Liberia 6 18N 10 47W
119 Monrovia, U.S.A. 34 7N 118 1W
16 Mons, Belgium 50 27N 3 58E
49 Möns Klint, Den. 54 57N 12 33E
31 Monsaraz, Portugal 38 28N 7 22W
73 Monse, Indonesia 4 0S 123 10E
20 Monségur, France 44 38N 0 4E
39 Monsélice, Italy 43 13N 11 45E
20 Mont-de-Marsin 43 54N 0 31W
19 Mont d'Or, Tunnel, Fr. 46 45N 6 18E
107 Mont Joli, Canada 48 37N 68 10W
106 Mont Laurier, Canada 46 35N 75 30W
107 Mont Luis, France 42 31N 2 6E
18 Mont St. Michel, France 48 40N 1 30W
106 Mont Tremblant Prov. Park, Canada 46 30N 74 30W
24 Montabaur, Germany 50 26N 7 49E
39 Montagnana, Italy 45 13N 11 29E
92 Montagu, S. Africa 33 45S 20 8E
120 Montagu, I., Falk. Is. Dependencies 58 30S 26 15W
118 Montague, Calif., U.S.A. 41 47N 122 30W
113 Montague, Mass., U.S.A. 42 31N 72 33W
100 Montague I., Australia 36 16S 150 13E
120 Montague, I., Mexico 31 40N 144 46W
18 Montaigu, France 46 59N 1 18W
32 Montalbán, Spain 40 50N 0 45W
41 Montalbano di Elicona, Italy 38 1N 15 0E
41 Montalbano Iónico, It. 40 17N 16 33E
32 Montalbo, Spain 39 53N 2 42W
39 Montalcino, Italy 43 4N 11 30E
30 Montalegre, Portugal 41 49N 7 47W
39 Montalto di Castro, Italy 42 20N 11 36E
41 Montalto Uffugo, Italy 39 25N 16 9E
30 Montamarta, Spain 41 39N 5 49W
126 Montana ♦, Peru 6 0S 73 0W
110 Montana ♦, U.S.A. 47 0N 110 0W
30 Montañas de León, Sp. 42 30N 6 20W
31 Montánchez, Spain 39 15N 6 8W
126 Montañita, Colombia 1 30N 75 28W
19 Montargis, France 48 0N 2 43E
20 Montauban, France 44 0N 1 21E
113 Montauk, U.S.A. 41 3N 71 57W
93 Mont-aux-Sources, S. Africa 28 44S 28 52E
19 Montbard, France 47 38N 4 20E
19 Montbéliard, France 47 31N 6 48E
32 Montblanch, Spain 41 23N 1 4E
21 Montbrison, France 45 36N 4 3E
20 Montcalm, Pic de, Fr. 42 40N 1 25E
19 Montceau-les-Mines, Fr. 46 40N 4 23E
38 Montchanin, Fr. 46 47N 4 30E
113 Montclair, U.S.A. 40 53N 74 49W
19 Montcornet, France 49 40N 4 0E
20 Montcuq, France 44 21N 1 13E
20 Mont-de-Marsin, Fr. 43 54N 0 31W
19 Montdidier, France 49 38N 2 35E
127 Monte Alegre, Brazil 2 0S 54 0W
96 Monte Bello Is., W. Australia 20 30S 115 45E
21 Monte Carlo, Monaco 43 46N 7 23E
124 Monte Caseros, Arg. 30 10S 57 50W
124 Monte Comán, Arg. 34 40S 68 0W
8 Monte Libano, Col. 8 5N 75 29W
124 Monte Quemado, Arg. 25 53S 62 41W
30 Monte Redondo, Port. 39 53N 8 50W
40 Monte San Guiliano, It. 38 3N 12 33E
39 Monte San Savino, It. 43 20N 11 42E
41 Monte Sant' Angelo, It. 41 42N 15 59E
41 Monte Santo, C. di, It. 40 5N 9 42E
119 Monte Visto, U.S.A. 37 40N 106 8W
125 Monteagudo, Argentina 27 14S 54 8W
33 Montealegre, Spain 38 48N 1 17W
106 Montebello, Canada 45 40N 74 55W
39 Montebelluna, Italy 45 47N 12 3E
18 Montebourg, France 49 30N 1 20W
39 Montecastrilli, Italy 42 40N 12 30E
38 Montecatini Terme, It. 43 55N 10 48E
126 Montecristi, Ecuador 1 0S 80 40W
38 Montecristo, I., Italy 42 20N 10 20E
39 Montefalco, Italy 42 53N 12 38E
39 Montefiascone, Italy 42 31N 12 2E
31 Montefrio, Spain 37 20N 3 39W
38 Montéglin, France 44 13N 5 50E
121 Montego B., Jamaica 18 30N 78 0W
39 Montegranaro, Italy 43 13N 13 38E
33 Montejicar, Spain 37 33N 3 30W
67 Montekomu Hu, China 34 40N 89 0E
126 Montelibano, Colombia 8 5N 75 29W

* Renamed Gwent

Montélimar INDEX Mpraeso

MAP
21 Montélimar, France 44 33N 4 45E
41 Montella, Italy 40 50N 15 0E
31 Montellano, Spain 36 59N 5 36W
116 Montello, U.S.A. 43 49N 89 21W
38 Montelupo Florentino, Italy 43 44N 11 2E
31 Montemór-o-Novo, Port. 38 40N 8 12W
30 Montemór-o-Velho, Portugal 40 11N 8 40W
120 Montemorelos, Mexico 25 11N 99 42W
20 Montendre, France 45 16N 0 26W
125 Montenegro, Brazil 29 39S 51 29W
42 Montenegro ♦, Y.-slav. 42 40N 19 20E
39 Montenero di Bisaccia, Italy 42 0N 14 47E
91 Montepuez, Mozam. 13 8S 38 59E
91 Montepuez, R., Mozam. 12 40S 40 15E
39 Montepulciano, Italy 43 5N 11 46E
39 Montereale, Italy 42 31N 13 13E
19 Montereau, France 48 22N 2 57E
119 Monterey, U.S.A. 36 35N 121 57W
126 Montería, Colombia 8 46N 75 53W
124 Monteros, Argentina 27 11S 65 30W
39 Monterotondo, Italy 42 3N 12 36E
120 Monterrey, Mexico 25 40N 100 30W
127 Montes Claros, Brazil 16 30S 43 50W
31 Montes de Toledo, Sp. 39 35N 4 30W
118 Montesano, U.S.A. 47 0N 123 39W
41 Montesárchio, Italy 41 5N 14 37E
41 Montescaglioso, Italy 40 34N 16 40E
39 Montesilvano, Italy 42 30N 14 8E
39 Montevarchi, Italy 43 30N 11 32E
88 Monteverde, Angola 8 45S 16 45E
125 Montevideo, Uruguay 34 50S 56 11W
116 Montezuma, U.S.A. 41 32N 92 35W
21 Montfaucon, Haute-Loire, France 45 11N 4 20E
19 Montfaucon, Meuse, Fr. 49 16N 5 8E
19 Montfort-l'Amaury, Fr. 48 47N 1 49E
18 Montfort-sur-Meu, Fr. 48 8N 1 58W
21 Montgenèvre, France 44 56N 6 42E
68 Montgomery, Wales 52 34N 3 9W
115 Montgomery, Ala., U.S.A. 32 20N 86 20W
114 Montgomery, W. Va., U.S.A. 38 9N 81 21W
68 Montgomery = Sahiwal, Pakistan 30 45N 73 8E
• 13 Montgomery ♦, Wales 52 34N 3 9W
20 Montguyon, France 45 12N 0 12W
25 Monthey, Switzerland 46 15N 6 56E
40 Monti del Gennargentu, Sardinia 40 0N 9 15E
41 Monti Iblei, Italy 37 15N 14 45E
41 Monti Nébrodi, It. 37 48N 14 20E
41 Monti Peloritani, It. 38 2N 15 15E
38 Monticelli d'Ongina, It. 45 3N 9 56E
117 Monticello, Ark., U.S.A. 33 40N 91 48W
115 Monticello, Fla., U.S.A. 30 35N 83 50W
114 Monticello, Ind., U.S.A. 40 40N 86 45W
116 Monticello, Iowa, U.S.A. 42 18N 91 18W
115 Monticello, Ky., U.S.A. 36 52N 84 50W
116 Monticello, Minn., U.S.A. 45 17N 93 52W
117 Monticello, Miss., U.S.A. 31 35N 90 8W
113 Monticello, N.Y., U.S.A. 41 37N 74 42W
119 Monticello, Utah, U.S.A. 37 55N 109 27W
38 Montichiari, Italy 45 28N 10 29E
19 Montieri, France 48 30N 4 45E
20 Montignac, France 45 4N 1 10E
19 Montigny-les- Metz, Fr. 49 7N 6 10E
19 Montigny-sur- Aube, Fr. 47 57N 4 45E
31 Montijo, Spain 38 52N 6 39W
31 Montijo, Presa de, Sp. 38 55N 6 26W
31 Montilla, Spain 37 36N 4 40W
116 Montivideo, U.S.A. 44 55N 95 40W
19 Montlhéry, France 48 39N 2 15E
20 Montluçon, France 46 22N 2 36E
107 Montmagny, Canada 46 58N 70 34W
27 Montmarault, France 46 11N 2 54E
20 Montmartre, Canada 50 20N 103 15W
19 Montmédy, France 49 30N 5 20E
21 Montmélian, France 45 30N 6 4E
19 Montmirail, France 48 51N 3 30E
20 Montmoreau-St.-Cybard, France 45 23N 0 8E
107 Montmorency, Canada 46 53N 71 11W
20 Montmorillon, France 46 26N 0 50E
19 Montmort, France 48 55N 3 49E
98 Monto, Australia 24 52S 151 12E
39 Montório al Vomano, It. 42 35N 13 38E
31 Montoro, Spain 38 1N 4 27W
112 Montour Falls, U.S.A. 42 20N 76 51W
118 Montpelier, Idaho, U.S.A. 42 15N 111 29W
114 Montpelier, Ohio, U.S.A. 41 34N 84 40W
113 Montpelier, Vt., U.S.A. 44 15N 72 38W
20 Montpellier, France 43 37N 3 52E
20 Montpezat-de-Quercy, France 44 15N 1 30E
20 Montpon-Ménestrol, France 45 2N 0 11E
106 Montréal, Canada 45 31N 73 34W
20 Montréal, France 43 13N 2 8E
109 Montréal L., Canada 54 20N 105 45W
20 Montredon- Labessonnié, France 43 45N 2 18E
20 Montréjeau, France 43 6N 0 35E
18 Montrésor, France 47 10N 1 10E
19 Montreuil, France 50 27N 1 45E
18 Montreuil-Bellay, Fr. 47 8N 0 9W
25 Montreux, Switzerland 46 26N 6 55E
18 Montrésor, France 47 10N 1 10E
18 Montrevault, France 47 17N 1 2W
21 Montrevel-en-Bresse, France 46 21N 5 8E
18 Montrichard, France 47 20N 1 10E
14 Montrose, Scot. 56 43N 2 28W
119 Montrose, Col., U.S.A. 38 30N 107 52W
113 Montrose, Pa., U.S.A. 41 50N 75 55W
MAP
107 Monts, Pte des, Canada 49 27N 67 12W
20 Montsalvy, France 44 41N 2 30E
32 Montsant, Sierra de, Spain 41 17N 0 1E
19 Montsauche, France 47 13N 4 0E
32 Montsech, Sierra del, Spain 42 0N 0 45E
32 Montseny, Spain 42 29N 1 2E
121 Montserrat, I., W.I. 16 40N 62 10W
32 Montserrat, mt., Spain 41 36N 1 49E
30 Montuenga, Spain 41 3N 4 38W
32 Montuiri, Spain 39 34N 2 59E
88 Monveda, Zaïre 2 52N 21 30E
67 Mônywa, Burma 22 7N 95 11E
38 Monza, Italy 45 35N 9 15E
91 Monze, Zambia 16 17S 27 29E
66 Monze, C., Pakistan 24 47N 66 37E
32 Monzón, Spain 41 52N 0 10E
99 Moolawatana, Australia 29 55S 139 45E
106 Moonbeam, Canada 49 20N 82 10W
100 Moondarra, Australia 38 2S 146 30E
99 Moonie, Australia 27 37S 150 17E
99 Moonie, R., Australia 29 0S 148 30E
99 Moonta, Australia 34 6S 137 32E
99 Mooraberree, Australia 25 13S 140 54E
116 Moorcroft, U.S.A. 44 17N 104 58W
96 Moore, L., Australia 29 30S 117 30E
114 Moorefield, U.S.A. 39 5N 78 59W
113 Moores Res., U.S.A. 44 45N 71 50W
115 Mooresville, U.S.A. 35 36N 80 45W
14 Moorfoot Hills, Scotland 55 44N 3 8W
116 Moorhead, U.S.A. 47 0N 97 0W
100 Moorland, Australia 31 46S 152 38E
100 Mooroopna, Australia 36 25S 145 22E
92 Moorreesburg, S. Africa 33 6S 18 38E
25 Moosburg, Germany 48 28N 11 57E
106 Moose, R., Canada 51 20N 81 15W
106 Moose Factory, Canada 52 20N 80 40W
109 Moose Jaw, Canada 50 30N 105 30W
109 Moose Lake, U.S.A. 46 27N 92 48W
106 Moose River, Can. 51 10N 81 47W
107 Moosehead L., U.S.A. 45 40N 69 40W
109 Moosomin, Canada 50 9N 101 40W
106 Moosonee, Canada 51 25N 80 51W
113 Moosup, U.S.A. 41 44N 71 52W
92 Mopipi, Botswana 21 6S 24 55E
87 Mopoi, Central Africa 5 6N 26 54E
99 Moppin, Australia 29 12S 146 45E
84 Mopti, Mali 14 30N 4 0W
87 Moqatta, Sudan 14 38N 35 50E
126 Moquegua, Peru 17 15S 70 46W
27 Mór, Hungary 47 25N 18 12E
31 Móra, Portugal 38 55N 8 10W
48 Mora, Sweden 61 2N 14 38E
116 Mora, Minn., U.S.A. 45 52N 93 19W
119 Mora, N. Mex., U.S.A. 35 58N 105 21W
32 Mora de Ebro, Spain 41 6N 0 38E
32 Mora la Nueva, Spain 41 7N 0 39E
32 Mora de Rubielos, Spain 40 15N 0 45W
42 Morača, R., Y.-slavia 42 40N 19 20E
68 Moradabad, India 28 50N 78 50E
89 Morafenobe, Malagasy Rep. 17 50S 44 53E
28 Morag, Poland 53 55N 19 56E
33 Moral de Calatrava, Sp. 38 51N 3 33W
30 Moraleja, Spain 40 6N 6 43W
126 Morales, Colombia 2 45N 76 38W
117 Moran, Kans., U.S.A. 37 53N 94 35W
118 Moran, Wyo., U.S.A. 43 53N 110 37W
41 Morano Cálabro, Italy 39 51N 16 8E
121 Morant Pt., Jamaica 17 55N 76 12W
14 Morar L., Scot. 56 57N 5 40W
33 Moratalla, Spain 38 14N 1 49W
70 Moratuwa, Sri Lanka 6 45N 79 55E
27 Morava, R., Cz. 49 50N 16 50E
27 Moravia = Země, Cz. 49 7N 15 57E
116 Moravia, U.S.A. 40 50N 92 50W
26 Moravian Hts. = Ceskemoravská V., Cz. 49 30N 15 40E
42 Moravica, R., Y.-slavia 43 40N 20 8E
27 Moravice, R., Cz. 49 50N 17 43E
42 Moravita, Rumania 45 17N 21 14E
27 Moravská Ostrava, Cz. 49 50N 18 20E
27 Moravska Trebová, Cz. 49 45N 16 40E
26 Moravské Budějovice, Czechoslovakia 49 4N 15 49E
126 Morawhanna, Guyana 8 30N 59 40W
• 14 Moray ♦, Scot. 57 32N 3 25W
14 Moray Firth, Scot. 57 50N 3 30W
25 Morbach, Germany 49 48N 7 7E
38 Morbegno, Italy 46 8N 9 34E
18 Morbihan ♦, Fr. 47 55N 3 0W
20 Morcenx, France 44 0N 0 55W
18 Mordelles, France 48 5N 1 52W
109 Morden, Canada 49 15N 98 10W
100 Mordialloc, Australia 38 1S 145 6E
55 Mordovian S.S.R.♦, U.S.S.R. 54 20N 44 30E
55 Mordovo, U.S.S.R. 52 13N 40 50E
14 Mordvinske A S S R, U.S.S.R. 54 20N 44 30E
14 More L., Scot. 58 18N 4 52W
47 Möre og Romsdal ♦, Norway 63 0N 9 0E
45 Morea, Greece 37 45N 22 10E
116 Moreau, R., U.S.A. 45 15N 102 45W
12 Morecambe, Eng. 54 5N 2 52W
12 Morecambe B., Eng. 54 7N 3 0W
99 Moree, Australia 29 28S 149 48E
114 Morehead, U.S.A. 38 12N 83 22W
115 Morehead City, U.S.A. 34 46N 76 44W
126 Moreira, Brazil 0 34S 63 26W
126 Morelia, Mexico 19 40N 101 11W
98 Morella, Australia 23 0S 143 47E
32 Morella, Spain 40 35N 0 2E
120 Morelos ♦, Mexico 18 40N 99 10W
31 Morena, Sierra, Spain 38 20N 4 0W
119 Morenci, U.S.A. 33 7N 109 20W
46 Moreni, Rumania 44 59N 25 36E
115 Mores, I., Bahama Is. 26 15N 77 35W
MAP
108 Moresby I., Canada 52 30N 131 40W
21 Morestel, France 45 40N 5 28E
19 Moret, France 48 22N 2 48E
99 Moreton, I., Australia 27 10S 153 10E
98 Moreton Telegraph Office, Australia 12 22S 142 30E
19 Moreuil, France 49 46N 2 30E
21 Morez, France 46 31N 6 2E
99 Morgan, Australia 34 0S 139 35E
118 Morgan, U.S.A. 41 3N 111 44W
117 Morgan City, U.S.A. 29 40N 91 15W
114 Morganfield, U.S.A. 37 40N 87 55W
115 Morganton, U.S.A. 35 46N 81 48W
114 Morgantown, U.S.A. 39 39N 75 58W
99 Morganville, Australia 25 10S 152 0E
18 Morgat, France 48 15N 4 32E
93 Morgenzon, S. Africa 26 45S 29 36E
25 Morges, Switzerland 46 31N 6 29E
19 Morhange, France 48 55N 6 38E
38 Mori, Italy 45 51N 10 59E
119 Moriarty, U.S.A. 35 3N 106 2W
108 Morice L., Canada 53 50N 127 40W
126 Morichal, Colombia 2 10N 70 34W
126 Morichal Largo, R., Ven. 8 55N 63 0W
85 Moriki, Nigeria 12 52N 6 30E
108 Morinville, Canada 53 49N 113 41W
74 Morioka, Japan 39 45N 141 8E
14 Moriston, Glen, Scot. 57 10N 5 0W
14 Moriston, R., Scot. 57 10N 5 0W
100 Morkalla, Australia 34 18S 141 4E
20 Morlaàs, France 43 21N 0 18W
18 Morlaix, France 48 36N 3 52W
41 Mormanno, Italy 39 53N 15 59E
19 Mormant, France 48 37N 2 52E
99 Morney, Australia 25 22S 141 23E
100 Mornington, Australia 38 15S 145 5E
98 Mornington I., Australia 16 30S 139 30E
128 Mornington, I., Chile 49 50S 75 30W
45 Mórnos, R., Greece 38 30N 22 0E
87 Moro, Sudan 10 50N 30 9E
73 Moro G., Philippines 6 30N 123 0E
98 Morobe, Terr. of New Guinea 7 49S 147 38E
82 Morocco ■, N. Afr. 32 0N 5 50W
126 Morococha, Peru 11 40S 76 5W
90 Morogoro, Tanzania 6 50S 37 40E
120 Moroleón, Mexico 20 8N 101 32W
93 Morombé, Malagasy Rep. 21 45S 43 22E
124 Moron, Argentina 34 39S 58 37W
121 Morón, Cuba 22 0N 78 30W
32 Morón de Almazán, Sp. 41 29N 2 27W
31 Morón de la Frontera, Spain 37 6N 5 28W
93 Morondava, Malagasy Rep. 20 17S 44 17E
84 Morondo, Ivory Coast 8 57N 6 47W
84 Moronou, Ivory Coast 6 16N 4 59W
73 Morotai, I., Indonesia 2 10N 128 30E
90 Moroto Summit, Mt., Kenya 2 30N 34 43E
43 Morozov (Bratan), mt., Bulgaria 42 30N 25 10E
57 Morozovsk, U.S.S.R. 48 25N 41 50E
100 Morpeth, Australia 32 44S 151 39E
12 Morpeth, Eng. 55 11N 1 41W
117 Morrilton, U.S.A. 35 10N 92 45W
127 Morrinhos, Minas Gerais, Braz. 17 45S 49 10W
101 Morrinsville, N.Z. 37 40S 175 32E
109 Morris, Canada 49 25N 97 30W
115 Morris, Ill., U.S.A. 41 20N 88 20W
116 Morris, Minn., U.S.A. 45 33N 95 56W
106 Morrisburg, Canada 44 55N 75 7W
116 Morrison, U.S.A. 41 47N 90 0W
119 Morristown, Ariz., U.S.A. 33 54N 112 45W
113 Morristown, N.J., U.S.A. 40 48N 74 30W
116 Morristown, S.D., U.S.A. 45 57N 101 44W
115 Morristown, Tenn., U.S.A. 36 18N 83 20W
124 Morro, Pta., Chile 27 6S 71 0W
119 Morro Bay, U.S.A. 35 27N 120 54W
121 Morrosquillo, Golfo de, Colombia 9 35N 75 40W
49 Morrum, Sweden 56 12N 14 45E
49 Mors, Denmark 56 50N 8 45E
55 Morshank, U.S.S.R. 53 28N 41 50E
48 Mörsil, Sweden 63 19N 13 40E
20 Mortagne, Charente Maritime, France 45 28N 0 49W
18 Mortagne, Orne, France 48 30N 0 32E
18 Mortagne, Vendée, Fr. 46 59N 0 57W
19 Mortagne, R., France 48 30N 6 30E
18 Mortain, France 48 40N 0 57W
38 Mortara, Italy 45 15N 8 43E
19 Morteau, France 47 3N 6 35E
124 Morteros, Argentina 30 50S 62 0W
100 Mortlake, Australia 38 5S 142 50E
117 Morton, Tex., U.S.A. 33 39N 102 49W
118 Morton, Wash., U.S.A. 46 42N 122 11W
100 Morundah, Australia 34 57S 146 19E
100 Moruya, Australia 35 58S 150 3E
19 Morvan, Mts. du, Fr. 47 5N 4 0E
99 Morven, Australia 26 22S 147 5E
14 Morvern, Scot. 56 38N 5 44W
68 Morvi, India 22 25N 72 5E
28 Moryń, Poland 52 51N 14 22E
54 Mosalsk, U.S.S.R. 54 30N 34 55E
25 Mosbach, Germany 49 21N 9 9E
39 Mošćenice, Y.-slavia 45 17N 14 16E
39 Mosciano Sant' Angelo, Italy 42 42N 13 52E
118 Moscow, U.S.A. 46 45N 116 59W
55 Moscow = Moskva, U.S.S.R. 55 45N 37 35E
25 Mosel, R., Germany 49 48N 6 45E
16 Moselle, R., Lux. 49 42N 6 45E
19 Moselle ♦, France 48 59N 6 33E
MAP
118 Moses Lake, U.S.A. 47 16N 119 17W
101 Mosgiel, N.Z. 45 53S 170 21E
90 Moshi, Tanzania 3 22S 37 18E
90 Moshi ♦, Tanzania 3 22S 37 18E
92 Moshupa, Botswana 24 46S 25 29E
28 Mósina, Poland 52 15N 16 50E
50 Mosjöen, Norway 65 51N 13 12E
50 Moskenesöya, Norway 67 58N 13 0E
50 Moskenstraumen, Nor. 67 47N 13 0E
55 Moskva, U.S.S.R. 55 45N 37 35E
55 Moskva, R., U.S.S.R. 55 5N 38 51E
39 Moslavačka Gora, Yugoslavia 45 40N 16 37E
92 Mosomane (Artesia), Botswana 24 2S 26 19E
27 Mosonmagyaróvár, Hungary 47 52N 17 18E
• 27 Mosonszentjános, Hung. 47 47N 17 11E
42 Mošorin, Yugoslavia 45 19N 20 4E
56 Mospina, U.S.S.R. 47 52N 38 6E
126 Mosquera, Colombia 2 35N 78 30W
117 Mosquero, U.S.A. 35 48N 103 57W
32 Mosqueruela, Spain 40 21N 0 27W
121 Mosquitos, Golfo de los, Pan. 9 15N 81 10W
47 Moss, Norway 59 27N 10 40E
100 Moss Vale, Australia 34 32S 150 25E
88 Mossaka, Congo 1 15S 16 45E
89 Mossâmedes, Angola 15 7S 12 11E
109 Mossbank, Canada 50 0N 106 0W
101 Mossburn, N.Z. 45 41S 168 15E
92 Mosselbaai, S. Africa 34 11S 22 8E
88 Mossendjo, Congo 2 55S 12 42E
100 Mossgiel, Australi 33 15S 144 30E
98 Mossman, Australia 16 21S 145 15E
127 Mossoró, Brazil 5 10S 37 15W
91 Mossuril, Mozambique 14 58S 40 42E
26 Most, Czechoslovakia 50 31N 13 38E
42 Mostar, Yugoslavia 43 22N 17 50E
125 Mostardas, Brazil 31 2S 50 51W
83 Mostefa, Rass, Tunisia 36 55N 11 3E
47 Mosteröy, Norway 59 5N 5 37E
54 Mostiska, U.S.S.R. 49 48N 23 4E
54 Mosty, U.S.S.R. 53 27N 24 38E
64 Mosul = Al Mawsil, Iraq 36 20N 43 5E
77 Mosun, China 23 35N 109 30E
47 Mosvatn, L., Norway 59 52N 8 5E
32 Mota del Cuervo, Spain 39 30N 2 52W
30 Mota del Marqués, Sp. 41 38N 5 11W
49 Motala, Sweden 58 32N 15 1E
14 Motherwell, Scot. 55 48N 4 0W
69 Motihari, India 26 37N 85 1E
32 Motilla del Palancar, Spain 39 34N 1 55W
39 Motnik, Yugoslavia 46 14N 14 54E
126 Motocurunya, Ven. 4 24N 64 5W
120 Motozintea de Mendoza, Mexico 15 21N 92 14W
39 Motovun, Yugoslavia 45 20N 13 50E
33 Motril, Spain 36 44N 3 37W
46 Motru, R., Rumania 44 44N 22 59E
116 Mott, U.S.A. 46 25N 102 14W
41 Mottola, Italy 40 38N 17 0E
101 Motueka, N.Z. 41 7S 173 1E
120 Motul, Mexico 21 0N 89 20W
44 Moúdhros, Greece 39 50N 25 18E
84 Moudjéria, Mauritania 17 50N 12 15W
25 Moudon, Switzerland 46 40N 6 49E
88 Mouila, Gabon 1 50S 11 0E
100 Moulamein, Australia 35 3S 144 1E
100 Moulamein Cr., Australia 35 6S 144 3E
20 Moulins, France 46 35N 3 19E
67 Moulmein = Maulamyaing, Burma 16 30N 97 40E
82 Moulouya, O., Morocco 35 8N 2 22W
117 Moulton, U.S.A. 29 35N 97 8W
115 Moultrie, U.S.A. 31 11N 83 47W
115 Moultrie, L., U.S.A. 33 25N 80 10W
116 Mound City, Mo., U.S.A. 40 2N 95 25W
116 Mound City, S.D., U.S.A. 45 46N 100 3W
45 Moúnda, Akra, Greece 38 5N 27 45E
81 Moundou, Chad 8 40N 16 10E
112 Moundsville, U.S.A. 39 53N 80 43W
115 Mount Airy, U.S.A. 36 31N 80 37W
112 Mount Albert, Canada 44 10N 79 20W
118 Mount Angel, U.S.A. 45 4N 122 46W
96 Mount Barker, W.A., Australia 34 38S 117 40E
98 Mount Buckley, Australia 20 6S 148 0E
114 Mount Carmel, Ill., U.S.A. 38 20N 87 48W
113 Mount Carmel, Pa., U.S.A. 40 46N 76 25W
112 Mount Clemens, U.S.A. 42 35N 82 50W
98 Mount Coolon, Austral. 21 25S 147 25E
107 Mount Desert I., U.S.A. 44 25N 68 25W
115 Mount Dora, U.S.A. 28 49N 81 32W
98 Mount Douglas, Austral. 21 35S 146 50E
96 Mount Enid, Australia 21 42S 116 26E
100 Mount Evelyn, Austral. 37 45S 145 29W
106 Mount Forest, Canada 43 59N 80 43W
98 Mount Fox, Australia 18 45S 145 45E
93 Mount Frere, S. Africa 30 51S 29 0E
99 Mount Gambier, Australia 37 38S 140 44E
98 Mount Garnet, Austral. 17 37S 145 6E
114 Mount Hope, U.S.A. 37 52N 81 9W
116 Mount Horeb, U.S.A. 43 0N 89 42W
100 Mount Hotham, Austral. 37 2S 146 52E
98 Mount Isa, Australia 20 42S 139 26E
113 Mount Joy, U.S.A. 40 6N 76 30W
66 Mount Lavinia, Sri Lanka 6 50N 79 50E
99 Mount Lofty Ranges, Australia 35 0S 138 0E
MAP
96 Mount Magnet, Australia 28 2S 117 47E
101 Mount Maunganui, N.Z. 37 40S 176 14E
98 Mount Molloy, Austral. 16 32S 145 20E
98 Mount Morgan, Australia 23 40S 150 25E
112 Mount Morris, Mich., USA 43 8N 83 42W
112 Mount Morris, N.Y., USA 42 43N 77 50W
98 Mount Mulligan, Australia 16 45S 144 47E
96 Mount Nicholas, Australia 22 54S 120 27E
98 Mount Oxide, Australia 19 30S 139 29E
99 Mount Perry, Australia 25 13S 151 42E
116 Mount Pleasant, Iowa, USA 41 0N 91 35W
114 Mount Pleasant, Mich., USA 43 38N 84 46W
112 Mount Pleasant, Pa., USA 40 9N 79 31W
115 Mount Pleasant, S.C., USA 32 45N 79 48W
115 Mount Pleasant, Tenn., USA 35 31N 87 11W
117 Mount Pleasant, Tex., USA 33 5N 95 0W
118 Mount Pleasant, Ut., USA 39 40N 111 29W
113 Mount Pocono, U.S.A. 41 8N 75 21W
118 Mount Rainier Nat. Park., U.S.A. 46 50N 121 20W
108 Mount Robson, Canada 52 56N 119 15W
118 Mount Shasta, U.S.A. 41 20N 122 18W
100 Mount Singleton, Australia 32 30S 151 3E
116 Mount Sterling, Ill., U.S.A. 40 0N 90 40W
116 Mount Sterling, Ky., U.S.A. 38 0N 84 0W
98 Mount Surprise, Australia 18 10S 144 17E
96 Mount Tom Price, Australia 22 50S 117 40E
112 Mount Union, U.S.A. 40 22N 77 51W
116 Mount Vernon, Ind., U.S.A. 38 17N 88 57W
113 Mount Vernon, N.Y., USA 40 57N 73 49W
114 Mount Vernon, Ohio, USA 40 20N 82 30W
118 Mount Vernon, Wash., USA 48 27N 122 18W
96 Mount Whaleback, Australia 24 38S 113 33E
118 Mountain City, Nev., U.S.A. 41 54N 116 0W
115 Mountain City, Tenn., U.S.A. 36 30N 81 50W
117 Mountain Grove, U.S.A. 37 5N 92 20W
117 Mountain Home, Ark., U.S.A. 36 20N 92 25W
118 Mountain Home, Idaho, U.S.A. 43 11N 115 45W
116 Mountain Iron, U.S.A. 47 30N 92 87W
108 Mountain Park., Canada 52 50N 117 15W
117 Mountain View, Ark., U.S.A. 35 52N 92 10W
119 Mountain View, Calif., U.S.A. 37 26N 122 5W
119 Mountainair, U.S.A. 34 35N 106 15W
15 Mountmellick, Ireland 53 7N 7 20W
15 Mountnorris, N. Ireland 54 15N 6 29W
126 Moura, Brazil 1 25S 61 45W
31 Moura, Portugal 38 7N 7 30W
98 Moura, Australia 24 35S 149 58E
31 Mourão, Portugal 38 22N 7 22W
81 Mourdi, Depression du, Chad 18 10N 23 0E
84 Mourdiah, Mali 14 35N 7 25W
20 Mourenx, France 43 23N 0 36W
85 Mouri, Ghana 5 6N 1 14W
98 Mourilyan, Australia 17 35S 146 10E
19 Mourmelon-le-Grand, Fr. 49 8N 4 22E
15 Mourne Mts., N. Ire. 54 10N 6 0W
15 Mourne, R., N. Ireland 54 45N 7 25W
83 Mourzouq, Libya 25 53N 14 10W
16 Mouscron, Belgium 50 45N 3 12E
81 Moussoro, Chad 13 50N 16 35E
19 Mouthe, France 46 44N 6 12E
25 Moutier, Switzerland 47 16N 7 21E
21 Moutiers, France 45 29N 6 31E
73 Moutong, Indonesia 0 28N 121 13E
19 Mouy, France 49 18N 2 20E
82 Mouydir, Algeria 25 20N 4 15E
44 Mouzáki, Greece 39 25N 21 37E
15 Moville, Ireland 55 11N 7 3W
77 Mowming, China 21 50N 110 32E
15 Moy, R., Ireland 54 5N 8 50W
87 Moyale, Ethiopia 3 34N 39 4E
90 Moyale, Kenya 3 30N 39 0E
84 Moyamba, Sierra Leone 8 15N 12 30W
108 Moyie, Canada 49 17N 115 50W
126 Moyobamba, Peru 6 0S 77 0W
62 Moza, Israel 31 48N 35 8E
93 Mozambique ■, Africa 19 0S 35 0E
89 Mozambique = Moçambique, Mozambique 15 3S 40 42E
93 Mozambique Chan. Africa 20 0S 39 0E
57 Mozdok, U.S.S.R. 43 45N 44 48E
55 Mozhaisk, U.S.S.R. 55 30N 36 2E
39 Mozirje, Yugoslavia 46 22N 14 58E
90 Mozua, Zaïre 3 57N 24 2E
54 Mozyr, U.S.S.R. 52 0N 29 15E
90 Mpanda, Tanzania 6 23S 31 40E
90 Mpanda ♦, Tanzania 6 23S 31 40E
84 Mpésoba, Mali 12 31N 5 39W
91 Mpika, Zambia 11 51S 31 25E
85 Mpraeso, Ghana 6 50N 0 50W

Incorporated within the county of Powys

Incorporated within the regions of Grampian and Highland

Renamed Jánossomorja

Mpulungy INDEX Nambucca Heads

MAP
91 Mpulungy, Zambia 8 51S 31 5E
28 Mragowo, Poland 53 57N 21 18E
42 Mramor, Yugoslavia 43 20N 21 45E
82 Mrhaïer, Algeria 33 55N 5 58E
82 Mrimina, Morocco 29 50N 7 9W
42 Mrkonjić Grad, Y.-slav. 44 26N 17 4E
39 Mrkopalj, Yugoslavia 45 21N 14 52E
28 Mrocza, Poland 53 16N 17 35E
83 Msa, Oueden, Alg. 32 35N 5 20E
83 Msaken, Tunisia 35 49N 10 33E
91 M'Salu, R., Mozam. 12 25S 39 15E
91 Msambansovu, mt., Rhodesia 15 50S 30 3E
82 M'sila, Algeria 35 46N 4 30E
54 Msta, R., U.S.S.R. 58 30N 33 30E
54 Mstislavl, U.S.S.R. 54 0N 31 50E
27 Mszana Dolna, Poland 49 41N 20 5E
28 Mszczonów, Poland 51 58N 20 33E
91 Mtama, Tanzania 10 17S 39 21E
91 Mtilikwe, R., Rhodesia 21 0S 31 12E
55 Mtsensk, U.S.S.R. 53 25N 36 30E
57 Mtskheta, U.S.S.R. 41 52N 44 45E
91 Mtwara ♦, Tanzania 9 40S 38 30E
91 Mtwara-Mikindani, Tanzania 10 20S 40 20E
71 Mu, R., Burma 23 0N 95 20E
127 Muaná, Brazil 1 25S 49 15W
71 Muang Chiang Rai, Thailand 19 52N 99 50E
71 Muang Kalasin, Thai. 16 26N 103 30E
71 Muang Lampang, Thai. 18 16N 99 32E
71 Muang Lamphun, Thai. 18 40N 98 53E
71 Muang Nan, Thailand 18 52N 100 42E
71 Muang Phetchabun, Thai. 16 23N 101 12E
71 Muang Phichit, Thai. 16 29N 100 21E
71 Muang Ubon, Thai. 15 15N 104 50E
71 Muang Yasothon, Thai. 15 50N 104 10E
71 Muar = Bandar Maharani, Malaysia 2 3N 102 34E
71 Muar, R., Malaysia 2 15N 102 48E
72 Muarabungo, Indonesia 1 40S 101 10E
72 Muaradjuloi, Indonesia 0 12S 114 3E
72 Muaraenim, Indonesia 3 40S 103 50E
72 Muarakaman, Indon. 0 2S 116 45E
72 Muaratebo, Indonesia 1 30S 102 26E
72 Muaratembesi, Indon. 1 42S 103 2E
72 Muaratewe, Indonesia 0 50S 115 0E
64 Mubairik, Saudi Arabia 23 22N 39 8E
69 Mubarakpur, India 26 12N 83 24E
90 Mubende, Uganda 0 33N 31 22E
90 Mubende ♦, Ugan. 0 55N 31 0E
126 Mucajaí, Serra do, Braz. 2 23N 61 10W
24 Mücheln, Germany 51 18N 11 49E
91 Muchinga Mts., Zambia 11 30S 31 30E
55 Muchkapskiy, U.S.S.R. 51 52N 42 28E
14 Muck, I., Scot. 56 50N 6 15W
99 Muckadilla, Australia 26 32S 148 36E
93 Mucubela, Mozambique 16 53S 37 49E
127 Mucugê, Brazil 13 5S 37 49E
127 Mucuri, Brazil 18 0S 40 0W
118 Mud L., U.S.A. 40 15N 120 15W
64 Mudanya, Turkey 40 25N 28 50E
119 Muddy, R., U.S.A. 38 30N 110 55W
100 Mudgee, Australia 32 32S 149 31E
64 Mudhnib, Saudi Arabia 25 50N 44 18E
91 Muecate, Mozambique 14 55S 39 34E
91 Muêda, Mozambique 11 36S 39 28E
91 Mufulira, Zambia 12 32S 28 15E
90 Mufumbiro Range, Ugan. 1 25S 29 30E
30 Mugardos, Spain 43 27N 8 15W
31 Muge, Portugal 39 3N 8 40W
31 Muge, R., Portugal 39 15N 8 18W
39 Múggia, Italy 45 36N 13 47E
30 Mugia, Spain 43 3N 9 17W
90 Mugila, Mts., Zaïre 7 0S 28 50E
64 Muğla, Turkey 37 15N 28 28E
43 Müglizh, Bulgaria 42 37N 25 32E
69 Mugu, Nepal 29 45N 82 30E
86 Muhammad Qol, Sudan 20 53N 37 9E
86 Muhammad Râs, Egypt 27 50N 34 0E
69 Muhammadabad, India 26 4N 83 25E
62 Muharraqa = Sa'ad, Israel 31 28N 34 33E
90 Muhesi, R., Tanzania 6 40S 35 5E
25 Mühldorf, Germany 48 14N 12 23E
24 Mühlhausen, Germany 51 12N 10 29E
5 Mühlig-Hofmann-fjella, Antarctica 72 30S 5 0E
90 Muhutwe, Tanzania 1 35S 31 45E
71 Mui Bai Bung, S. Vietnam 8 35N 104 42E
71 Mui Ron, N. Vietnam 18 7N 106 27E
15 Muine Bheag, Ireland 52 42N 6 59W
30 Muiños, Spain 41 58N 7 59W
87 Muja, Ethiopia 12 2N 39 30E
62 Mujeidil, Israel 32 41N 35 14E
54 Mukachevo, U.S.S.R. 48 27N 22 45E
72 Mukah, Malaysia 2 55N 112 5E
63 Mukalla, South Yemen 14 33N 49 2E
86 Mukawwa, Geziret, Egypt 23 55N 35 53E
76 Mukden = Shenyang, China 41 35N 123 30E
63 Mukeiras, Yemen 13 59N 45 52E
63 Mukha, Yemen 13 18N 43 15E
55 Mukhtolovo, U.S.S.R. 55 29N 43 15E
91 Mukombwe, Zambia 15 48S 26 32E
72 Mukomuko, Indonesia 2 20S 101 10E
90 Mukomwenze, Zaïre 6 49S 27 15E
68 Muktsar, India 30 30N 74 30E
65 Mukur, Afghanistan 32 50N 67 50E
91 Mukwela, Zambia 17 0S 26 40E
33 Mula, Spain 38 3N 1 33W
70 Mula, R., India 19 16N 74 20E
73 Mulanay, Philippines 13 30N 122 30E
90 Mulange, Zaïre 3 40S 27 10E
121 Mulatas, Arch. de las, Panama 6 51N 78 31W

MAP
124 Mulchén, Chile 37 45S 72 20W
24 Mulde, R., Germany 50 55N 12 42E
116 Mule Creek, U.S.A. 43 19N 104 8W
90 Muleba, Tanzania 1 50S 31 37E
117 Muleshoe, U.S.A. 34 17N 102 42W
107 Mulgrave, Canada 45 38N 61 31W
98 Mulgrave I., Australia 10 5S 142 0E
33 Mulhacén, Spain 37 4N 3 20W
24 Mülheim, Germany 51 26N 6 53W
19 Mulhouse, France 47 40N 7 20E
67 Muli, China 28 21N 100 40E
14 Mull I., Scotland 56 27N 6 0W
14 Mull, Sound of, Scotland 56 30N 5 50W
70 Mullaittivu, Sri Lanka 9 15N 80 55E
116 Mullen, U.S.A. 42 5N 101 0W
100 Mullengudgery, Australia 31 43S 147 29E
114 Mullens, U.S.A. 37 34N 81 22W
72 Muller, Pegunungan, Indon. 0 30N 113 30E
98 Muller Ra., N.E. New Guinea 5 30S 143 0E
15 Mullet Pen., Ireland 54 10N 10 2W
96 Mullewa, Australia 28 29S 115 30E
24 Mullheim, Germany 47 48N 7 37E
117 Mullin, U.S.A. 31 33N 98 38W
15 Mullingar, Ireland 53 31N 7 20W
115 Mullins, U.S.A. 34 12N 79 15W
100 Mullion Creek, Australia 33 9S 148 7E
49 Mullsjö, Sweden 57 56N 13 55E
99 Mullumbimby, Australia 28 30S 153 30E
91 Mulobezi, Zambia 16 45S 25 7E
92 Mulonga Plain, Botswana 23 12S 23 30E
70 Mulshi L., India 18 30N 73 20E
68 Multai, India 21 39N 78 15E
68 Multan, Pakistan 30 15N 71 30E
68 Multan ♦, Pakistan 30 29N 72 29E
48 Multrå, Sweden 63 10N 17 24E
91 Mulumbe, Mts. Zaïre 8 40S 27 30E
91 Mulungushi Dam, Zam. 14 48S 28 48E
117 Mulvane, U.S.A. 37 30N 97 15W
86 Mulwad, Sudan 18 45N 30 39E
100 Mulwala, Australia 35 59S 146 0E
57 Mumra, U.S.S.R. 45 45N 47 41E
71 Mun, Nam, Thailand 15 17N 103 0E
73 Muna, I., Indonesia 5 0S 122 30E
25 Münchberg, Germany 50 11N 11 48E
24 Müncheberg, Germany 52 30N 14 9E
25 München, Germany 48 8N 11 33E
108 Muncho Lake, Canada 58 44N 125 50W
114 Muncie, U.S.A. 40 10N 85 20W
70 Mundakayam, India 9 30N 76 32E
108 Mundare, Canada 53 35N 112 30W
117 Munday, U.S.A. 33 26N 99 39W
24 Münden, Germany 51 25N 9 42E
33 Mundo, R., Spain 38 30N 2 15W
127 Mundo Novo, Brazil 11 50S 40 29W
68 Mundra, India 22 54N 69 26E
33 Munera, Spain 39 2N 2 29W
70 Muneru, R., India 16 45N 80 3E
98 Mungana, Australia 17 8S 144 27E
68 Mungaoli, India 24 24N 78 7E
41 Mungari, Mozambique 17 12S 33 42E
99 Mungindi, Australia 28 58S 149 1E
25 Munich = München, Germany 48 8N 11 35E
114 Munising, U.S.A. 46 25N 86 39W
89 Munhango, Angola 12 10S 18 38E
96 Munjiye, Saudi Arabia 18 47N 41 20W
49 Munka-Ljungby, Swed. 56 16N 12 58E
49 Munkedal, Sweden 58 28N 11 40E
48 Munkfors, Sweden 59 50N 13 30E
128 Muñoz Gamero, Pen., Chile 52 30S 73 5E
99 Munro, Australia 25 30S 142 45E
109 Munroe L., Canada 59 0N 98 40W
19 Munster, France 48 2N 7 8E
24 Münster, Niedersachsen, Germany 52 59N 10 5E
24 Münster, Nordrhein-Westfalen, Germany 51 58N 7 37E
15 Munster ♦, Ire. 52 20N 8 40W
46 Muntelui Mare, Rumania 46 30N 23 12E
72 Muntok, Indonesia 2 5S 105 10E
58 Munyak, U.S.S.R. 43 35N 59 30E
71 Muon Pak Beng, Laos 19 51N 101 4E
71 Muong La, Laos 20 52N 102 5E
71 Muong Ngoi, Laos 20 41N 102 39E
71 Muong Sing, Laos 21 12N 101 12E
71 Muong Soui, Laos 19 32N 102 47E
50 Muonio, Finland 67 57N 23 40E
50 Muonio, Sweden 67 57N 23 40E
50 Muonio älv, Sweden 67 48N 23 25E
89 Mupa, Angola 16 5S 15 50E
65 Muqab, Trucial Oman 23 0N 53 0E
87 Muqaddam, Wadi, Sud. 17 0N 32 0E
26 Mur, R., Austria 47 7N 13 55E
18 Mur-de-Bretagne, Fr. 48 12N 3 0W
39 Mura, R., Yugoslavia 46 37N 16 9E
128 Murallón, Cuerro, Chile 49 55S 73 30W
90 Muranda, Rwanda 1 52S 29 20E
90 Muranga (Ft. Hall), Kenya 0 45S 37 9E
55 Murashi, U.S.S.R. 59 30N 49 0E
20 Murat, France 45 7N 2 53E
26 Murau, Austria 47 6N 14 10E
40 Muravera, Italy 39 25N 9 35E
30 Murça, Portugal 41 24N 7 28W
100 Murchison, Australia 36 39S 145 14E
96 Murchison, R., Australia 27 30S 115 0E
• 90 Murchison Falls, Uganda 2 15N 31 38E
91 Murchison Rapids, Malawi 15 55S 34 35E
33 Murcia, Spain 38 2N 1 10W
33 Murcia ♦, Spain 37 50N 1 30W
116 Murdo, U.S.A. 43 56N 100 43W
46 Mureş ♦, Rumania 46 45N 24 40E
46 Mureşul, Rumania 46 0N 22 0E
20 Muret, France 43 30N 1 20E

MAP
115 Murfreesboro, U.S.A. 35 50N 86 21W
58 Murgab, U.S.S.R. 38 10N 73 59E
46 Murgeni, Rumania 46 12N 28 1E
99 Murgon, Australia 26 15S 151 54E
125 Muriaé, Brazil 21 8S 42 23W
30 Murias de Paredes, Spain 45 52N 6 19W
91 Muriel Mine, Rhodesia 17 14S 30 40E
73 Muris, Indonesia 2 23S 140 5E
24 Murits see, Germany 53 25N 12 40E
73 Murjo Mt., Indonesia 6 36S 110 53E
90 Murka, Kenya 3 27S 38 0E
52 Murmansk, U.S.S.R. 68 57N 33 10E
25 Murnau, Germany 47 40N 11 11E
21 Muro, Corsica 42 34N 8 54E
32 Muro, Spain 39 45N 3 3E
21 Muro, C. di, Corsica 41 44N 8 37E
41 Muro Lucano, Italy 40 45N 15 30E
55 Murom, U.S.S.R. 55 35N 42 3E
74 Muroran, Japan 42 25N 141 0E
30 Muros, Spain 42 45N 9 5W
30 Muros y de Noya, Ria de, Spain 42 45N 9 0W
74 Muroto-Misaki, Japan 33 15N 134 10E
118 Murphy, U.S.A. 43 11N 116 33W
117 Murphysboro, U.S.A. 37 50N 89 20W
86 Murrat, Sudan 18 51N 29 33E
115 Murray, Ky., U.S.A. 36 40N 88 20W
118 Murray, Utah, U.S.A. 40 41N 111 58W
99 Murray Br., Australia 35 6S 139 14E
107 Murray Harb., Canada 46 0N 62 28W
115 Murray, L., U.S.A. 34 8N 81 30W
99 Murray, R., Australia 35 50S 147 40E
92 Murraysburg, S. Africa 31 58S 23 47E
100 Murrayville, Australia 35 20S 140 16E
66 Murree, Pakistan 33 56N 73 28E
100 Murringo, Australia 34 16S 148 32E
99 Murrumbidgee, R., Australia 34 30S 145 30E
100 Murrumburrah, Australia 34 30S 148 15E
100 Murrurundi, Australia 31 42S 150 51E
86 Murshid, Sudan 21 40N 31 10E
69 Murshidabad, India 24 11N 88 19E
39 Murska Sobota, Y.-slavia 46 39N 16 12E
68 Murtazapur, India 20 40N 77 25E
100 Murtoa, Australia 36 29S 142 29E
30 Murtosa, Portugal 40 44N 8 40W
87 Muru, Sudan 6 36N 29 16E
90 Murungu, Tanzania 4 12S 31 10E
69 Murwara, India 23 46N 80 28E
99 Murwillumbah, Australia 28 18S 153 27E
26 Mürz, R., Austria 47 30N 15 25E
26 Mürzzuschlag, Austria 47 36N 15 41E
64 Mus, Turkey 38 45N 41 30E
86 Musa, Gebel (Sinai), Egypt 28 32N 33 59E
66 Musa Qala (Musa Kala), Afghanistan 32 20N 64 50E
68 Musaffargarh, Pakistan 30 10N 71 10E
86 Musairik, Wadi, Saudi Arabia 19 30N 43 10E
68 Musakhel, Pakistan 30 29N 69 52E
72 Musala, I., Indonesia 1 41N 98 28E
43 Musalla, mt., Bulgaria 42 13N 23 37E
76 Musan, N. Korea 42 12N 129 12E
91 Musangu, Zaïre 10 28S 23 55E
90 Musasa, Tanzania 3 25S 31 30E
65 Muscat = Masqat, Oman 23 37N 58 36E
63 Muscat & Oman ■, Arabia 23 0N 58 0E
116 Muscatine, U.S.A. 41 25N 91 5W
30 Musel, Spain 43 34N 5 42W
91 Musetula, Zambia 14 28S 24 1E
96 Musgrave Ras., Austral. 26 0S 132 0E
88 Mushie, Zaïre 2 56S 17 4E
85 Mushin, Nigeria 6 32N 3 21E
70 Musi, R., India 17 10N 79 25E
72 Musi, R., Indonesia 2 55S 103 40E
114 Muskegon, U.S.A. 43 15N 86 17W
114 Muskegon, R., U.S.A. 43 25N 86 0W
114 Muskegon Hts., U.S.A. 43 12N 86 17W
117 Muskogee, U.S.A. 35 50N 95 25W
86 Musmar, Sudan 18 6N 35 40E
91 Musofu, Zambia 13 30S 29 0E
90 Musoma, Tanzania 1 30S 33 48E
90 Musoma ♦, Tanz. 1 50S 34 30E
107 Musquaro, L., Canada 50 42N 61 15W
107 Musquodoboit Harbour, Canada 44 50N 63 9W
14 Musselburgh, Scot. 55 57N 3 3W
118 Musselshell, R., U.S.A. 46 30N 108 15W
20 Mussidan, France 45 2N 0 22E
40 Mussomeli, Italy 37 35N 13 43E
68 Mussoorie, India 30 27N 78 6E
92 Mussuco, Angola 17 2S 19 3E
64 Mustafa Kemalpasa, Turkey 40 3N 28 25E
64 Mustajidda, S. Arabia 26 30N 41 50E
69 Mustang, Nepal 29 10N 83 55E
83 Mustapha, C., Tunisia 36 55N 11 3E
128 Musters, L., Argentina 45 20S 69 25W
100 Muswellbrook, Australia 32 16S 150 56E
27 Muszyna, Poland 49 22N 20 55E
86 Mût, Egypt 25 28N 28 58E
64 Mut, Turkey 36 40N 33 28E
76 Mutan Kiang, China 46 18N 129 31E
93 Mutanda, Mozambique 21 0S 33 34E
91 Mutanda, Zambia 12 15S 26 13E
76 Mutankiang, China 44 35N 129 30E
126 Mutis, Colombia 1 4N 77 25W
91 Mutshatsha, Zaïre 10 35S 24 20E
98 Muttaburra, Australia 22 38S 144 29E
107 Mutton Bay, Canada 50 50N 59 2W
91 Mutuáli, Mozambique 14 55S 37 0E
70 Muvatupusha, India 9 53N 76 35E
64 Muwaih, Saudi Arabia 22 35N 41 32E
88 Muxima, Angola 9 25S 13 52E
59 Muya, U.S.S.R. 56 27N 115 39E
90 Muyaga, Burundi 3 14S 30 33E

MAP
66 Muzaffarabad, Kashmir 34 25N 73 30E
68 Muzaffargarth, Pakistan 30 5N 71 14E
68 Muzaffarnagar, India 29 26N 77 40E
69 Muzaffarpur, India 26 7N 85 32E
62 Muzeiri'a, Israel 32 3N 34 53E
58 Muzhi, U.S.S.R. 65 25N 64 40E
18 Muzillac, France 47 35N 2 30W
126 Muzo, Colombia 5 32N 74 6W
108 Muzon C., Alaska 54 40N 132 40W
75 Muztagh P., China 36 30N 87 22E
87 Mvôlô, Sudan 6 10N 29 53E
90 Mwadui, Tanzania 3 35S 33 40E
91 Mwandi Mission, Zam. 17 30S 24 51E
90 Mwango, Zaïre 6 48S 24 12E
90 Mwanza, Malawi 16 58S 24 28E
90 Mwanza, Tanzania 2 30S 32 58E
90 Mwanza, Katanga, Zaïre 7 55S 26 43E
91 Mwanza, Kwango, Zaïre 5 29S 17 43E
90 Mwanza ♦, Tanzania 2 30S 32 30E
90 Mwaya, Tanzania 9 32S 33 55E
15 Mweelrea, Mt., Ireland 53 37N 9 48W
88 Mweka, Zaïre 4 50S 21 40E
90 Mwenga, Zaïre 3 1S 28 21E
91 Mwepo, Zaïre 11 50S 26 10E
91 Mweru, L., Zambia 9 0S 29 0E
91 Mweza Range, Rhod. 21 0S 30 0E
91 Mwimbi, Tanzania 8 38S 31 39E
91 Mwinilunga, Zambia 11 43S 24 25E
91 Mwinilunga, Mt., Zambia 11 43S 24 25E
71 My Tho, S. Vietnam 10 29N 106 23E
82 Mya, O., Algeria 30 46N 4 44E
88 Myadhi, Gabon 1 16N 13 10E
100 Myall L., Australia 32 30S 152 25E
100 Myall, R., Australia 32 30S 152 25E
67 Myanaung, Burma 18 25N 95 10E
67 Myaungmya, Burma 16 30N 95 0E
113 Myerstown, U.S.A. 40 22N 76 18W
71 Myingyan, Burma 21 30N 95 30E
67 Myitkyina, Burma 25 30N 97 26E
27 Myjava, Czechoslovakia 48 41N 17 37E
69 Mymensingh = Nasirabad, E. Pak. 24 42N 90 30E
116 Myndmere, U.S.A. 46 23N 97 7W
71 Myogi, Burma 21 24N 96 28E
47 Myrdal, Norway 60 43N 7 10E
50 Mýrdalsjökull, Iceland 63 40N 19 6W
115 Myrtle Beach, U.S.A. 33 43N 78 50W
118 Myrtle Creek, U.S.A. 43 0N 123 19W
118 Myrtle Point, U.S.A. 43 0N 124 4W
100 Myrtleford, Australia 36 34S 146 44E
47 Mysen, Norway 59 33N 11 20E
27 Myslenice, Poland 49 51N 19 57E
28 Myslibórz, Poland 52 55N 14 50E
27 Mysłowice, Poland 50 15N 19 12E
70 Mysore, India 12 17N 76 41E
• 70 Mysore ♦, India 13 15N 77 0E
113 Mystic, U.S.A. 41 21N 71 58W
28 Myszkow, Poland 50 45N 19 22E
55 Mystishchi, U.S.S.R. 57 50N 37 50E
118 Myton, U.S.A. 40 10N 110 2W
50 Mývatn, Iceland 65 36N 17 0W
26 Mže, R., Czechoslovakia 49 47N 12 50E
91 Mzimba, Malawi 11 48S 33 33E
91 Mzuzu, Malawi 11 30S 33 55E
87 Na'am, Sudan 9 42N 28 27E
62 Na'an, Israel 31 53N 34 52E
51 Naantali, Finland 60 29N 22 2E
15 Naas, Ireland 53 12N 6 40W
92 Nababeep, S. Africa 29 36S 17 46E
69 Nabadwip, India 23 34N 88 20E
73 Nabas, Philippines 11 47N 122 6E
83 Nabeul, Tunisia 36 30N 10 51E
68 Nabha, India 30 26N 76 14E
62 Nabi Rubin, Israel 31 56N 34 44E
73 Nabire, Indonesia 3 15S 136 27E
68 Nabisar, Pakistan 25 8N 69 40E
90 Nabiswera, Uganda 1 27N 32 15E
93 Naboomspruit, S. Africa 24 32S 28 40E
86 Nabq, Egypt 28 5N 29 23E
62 Nābulus, Jordan 32 14N 35 15E
91 Nabúri, Mozambique 16 53S 38 59E
91 Nacala-Velha, Mozambique 14 32S 40 34E
91 Nacaroa, Mozambique 14 22S 39 56E
118 Naches, U.S.A. 46 48N 120 49W
77 Nachi, China 28 50N 105 25E
91 Nachingwea, Tanzania 10 49S 38 49E
91 Nachingwea ♦, Tanz. 9 20S 38 0E
68 Nachna, India 27 34N 71 41E
27 Náchod, Czechoslovakia 50 25N 16 8E
48 Nacka, Sweden 59 17N 18 12E
99 Nackara, S. Australia 32 48S 139 12E
119 Naco, U.S.A. 31 24N 109 58W
117 Nacogdoches, U.S.A. 31 33N 95 30W
120 Nacozari, Mexico 30 30N 109 50W
86 Nadi, Sudan 18 40N 33 41E
68 Nadiad, India 22 41N 72 56E
42 Nădlac, Rumania 46 10N 20 50E
82 Nador, Morocco 35 14N 2 58W
65 Nadushan, Iran 32 2N 53 35E
54 Nadvornaya, U.S.S.R. 48 40N 24 35E
58 Nadym, U.S.S.R. 63 35N 72 42E
58 Nadym, R., U.S.S.R. 65 30N 73 0E
47 Naerbö, Norway 58 40N 5 39E
49 Naestved, Denmark 55 13N 11 44E
85 Nafada, Nigeria 11 8N 11 20E
64 Naft Shāh, Iran 34 0N 45 30E
64 Nafūd ad Dahy, Saudi Arabia 22 0N 45 0E
83 Nafūsah, Jabal, Libya 32 12N 12 30E
86 Nag 'Hammâdi, Egypt 26 2N 32 18E
77 Naga, Ryukyu Is. 26 34N 127 43E
73 Naga, Philippines 13 38N 123 15E
82 Naga, Kreb en, Sahara 24 12N 6 0W
106 Nagagami, R., Canada 49 40N 84 40W
68 Nagar Parkar, Pakistan 24 28N 70 46E
67 Nagaland ♦, India 26 0N 94 30E

MAP
100 Nagambie, Australia 36 47S 145 10E
74 Nagano, Japan 36 40N 138 10E
74 Nagano-ken ♦, Japan 36 15N 138 0E
70 Nagappattinam, India 10 46N 79 51E
70 Nagari Hills, India 15 30N 79 45E
70 Nagarjuna Sagar, India 16 35N 79 17E
74 Nagasaki, Japan 32 47N 129 50E
74 Nagasaki-ken ♦, Japan 32 50N 129 40E
74 Nagashima, Japan 34 15N 136 15E
68 Nagaur, India 27 15N 73 45E
69 Nagbhir, India 20 34N 79 42E
67 Nagchu Dzong, China 31 22N 91 54E
70 Nagercoil, India 8 12N 77 33E
68 Nagina, India 29 30N 78 30E
65 Nagineh, Iran 34 20N 57 15E
77 Nago, Okinawa 26 36N 128 0E
25 Nagold, Ger. 48 38N 8 40E
98 Nagoorin, Australia 24 17S 151 15E
55 Nagorsk, U.S.S.R. 59 18N 50 48E
90 Nagorum, Kenya 4 1N 34 33E
74 Nagoya, Japan 35 10N 136 50E
68 Nagpur, India 21 8N 79 10E
67 Nagrong, Tibet 32 46N 84 16E
27 Nagyatád, Hungary 46 14N 17 22E
27 Nagyecsed, Hungary 47 53N 22 24E
27 Nagykanizsa, Hungary 46 28N 17 0E
27 Nagykörös, Hungary 46 55N 19 48E
27 Nagyléta, Hungary 47 23N 21 55E
77 Naha, Okinawa 26 12N 127 40E
62 Nahalal, Israel 32 41N 35 12E
108 Nahanni Butte, Canada 61 5N 123 30W
62 Naharayim, Israel 32 28N 35 33E
62 Nahariyya, Israel 33 1N 35 5E
64 Nahavand, Iran 34 10N 48 30E
25 Nahe, R., Germany 49 48N 7 33E
62 Nahf, Israel 32 56N 35 18E
86 Nahîya, Wadi, Egypt 27 37N 32 0E
86 Nahud, Saudi Arabia 18 12N 41 40E
46 Naiapu, Rumania 44 12N 25 47E
109 Naicam, Canada 52 30N 104 30W
63 Na'i Fah, Saudi Arabia 19 59N 50 46E
25 Naila, Germany 50 19N 11 43E
107 Nain, Canada 56 34N 61 40W
65 Na'in, Iran 32 54N 53 0E
69 Naini Tal, India 29 23N 79 30E
18 Naintré, France 46 46N 0 29E
73 Naira, I., Indonesia 4 28S 130 0E
14 Nairn, Scotland 57 35N 3 54W
• 14 Nairn ♦, Scot. 57 28N 3 52W
90 Nairobi, Kenya 1 17S 36 48E
52 Naistenyarvi, U.S.S.R. 62 25N 32 27E
90 Naivasha, Kenya 0 40S 36 30E
90 Naivasha ♦, Kenya 0 40S 36 30E
90 Naivasha L., Kenya 0 48S 36 20E
20 Najac, France 44 14N 1 58E
65 Najafābad, Iran 32 40N 51 15E
64 Najd, Saudi Arabia 26 30N 42 0E
32 Nájera, Spain 42 26N 2 44W
32 Najerilla, R., Spain 42 15N 2 45W
68 Najibabad, India 29 40N 78 20E
90 Nakalagba, Zaïre 2 50N 27 58E
74 Nakamura, Japan 33 0N 133 0E
74 Nakano Shima, Jap. 29 50N 130 0E
87 Nakfa, Ethiopia 16 40N 38 25E
53 Nakhichevan, A.S.S.R. ♦, U.S.S.R. 39 14N 45 30E
86 Nakhl, Egypt 29 55N 33 43E
64 Nakhl Mubarak, Saudi Arabia 24 10N 38 10E
59 Nakhodka, U.S.S.R. 43 10N 132 45E
71 Nakhon Phanom, Thai. 17 23N 104 43E
71 Nakhon Ratchasima (Khorat), Thailand 14 59N 102 12E
71 Nakhon Sawan, Thai. 15 35N 100 10E
71 Nakhon Si Thammarat, Thailand 8 29N 100 0E
71 Nakhon Sawan, Thai. 15 35N 100 10E
106 Nakina, Canada 50 10N 86 40W
28 Nakło n. Noteoja, Poland 53 9N 17 38E
68 Nakodar, India 31 8N 75 31E
91 Nakomis, U.S.A. 39 19N 89 19W
49 Nakskov, Denmark 54 50N 11 8E
48 Näkten, Sweden 62 48N 14 38E
76 Naktong-gang, S. Korea 35 7N 128 57E
68 Nakur, India 30 2N 77 32E
90 Nakuru, Kenya 0 15S 35 5E
90 Nakuru ♦, Kenya 0 15S 35 5E
90 Nakuru, L., Kenya 0 23S 36 5E
108 Nakusp, Canada 50 20N 117 45W
66 Nal, R., Pakistan 27 0N 65 50E
76 Nalayh, Mongolia 47 43N 107 22E
57 Nalchik, U.S.S.R. 43 30N 43 33E
48 Nälden, Sweden 63 21N 14 14E
48 Näldsjön, Sweden 63 25N 14 15E
85 Nalerigu, Ghana 10 35N 0 25W
70 Nalgonda, India 17 6N 79 15E
69 Nalharti, India 24 17N 87 52E
70 Nallamala Hills, India 15 30N 78 50E
30 Nalon, R., Spain 43 35N 6 10W
83 Nālūt, Libya 31 54N 11 0E
71 Nam Dinh, N. Vietnam 20 25N 106 5E
71 Nam Phong, Thailand 16 42N 102 52E
71 Nam-Phun, South Vietnam 10 30N 106 0E
71 Nam Tha, Laos 20 58N 101 30E
75 Nam Tso, China 30 40N 90 30E
77 Nama, China 23 45N 108 1E
70 Namakkal, India 11 13N 78 13E
77 Naman, China 25 0N 118 30E
58 Namangan, U.S.S.R. 41 30N 71 30E
91 Namapa, Mozambique 13 43S 39 50E
92 Namaqualand, S. Africa 30 0S 18 0E
90 Namasagali, Uganda 1 2N 33 0E
98 Namatanai, Terr. of New Guinea 4 35S 152 30E
84 Nambala, Mali 14 1N 5 58W
73 Namber, Indonesia 1 2S 134 57E
99 Nambour, Australia 26 38S 152 49E
99 Nambucca Heads, Australia 30 40S 152 48E

* *Renamed Kabarega Falls*

* *Renamed Karnataka*

* *Incorporated within the region of Highland*

MAP

75 Namcha Barwa, China 29 30N 95 10E
69 Namche Bazar, Nepal 27 51N 86 47E
91 Namecund, Mozambique 14 54s 37 37E
72 Nameh, Indonesia 2 34N 116 51E
91 Nameponda, Mozam. 15 50s 39 50E
27 Náměšt nad Oslavou, Czechoslovakia 49 12N 16 10E
27 Námestovo, Cz. 49 24N 19 25E
91 Nametil, Mozambique 15 40s 39 15E
92 Namib Des. = Namib-Woestyn, S.W. Africa 22 30s 15 0w
92 Namib-Woestyn, S.W. Africa 22 30s 15 0w
92 Namibia = South West Africa 22 0s 18 9E
69 Namja Pass, Nepal 30 0N 82 25E
73 Namlea, Indonesia 3 10s 127 5E
117 Namoa tao, China 23 30N 117 0E
99 Namoi, R., Australia 30 16s 149 15E
82 Namous, O., Algeria 30 44N 0 18w
118 Nampa, U.S.A. 43 40N 116 40w
91 Nampula, Mozambique 15 6s 39 7E
73 Namrole, Indonesia 3 46s 126 46E
50 Namsen, Norway 64 27N 11 42E
67 Namtu, Burma 23 5N 97 28E
91 Namtumbo, Tanz. 10 30s 36 4E
108 Namu, Canada 51 45N 127 50w
16 Namur, Belgium 50 27N 4 52E
16 Namur ♦, Belgium 50 17N 5 0E
92 Namutoni, S.W. Africa 18 49s 16 55E
91 Namwala, Zambia 15 44s 26 30E
28 Namysłów, Poland 51 6N 17 42E
77 Namyung, China 25 15N 114 5E
75 Nan shan, China 38 0N 98 0E
46 Nana, Rumania 44 17N 26 34E
83 Nana, W., Libya 30 0N 15 24E
74 Nanaimo, Canada 49 10N 124 0w
99 Nanango, Australia 26 40s 152 0E
74 Nanao, Japan 37 0N 137 0E
77 Nanchang, Hupei, China 31 50N 111 50E
77 Nanchang, Kiangsi, China 28 34N 115 48E
77 Nancheng, Kiangsi, China 27 30N 116 28E
77 Nancheng = Hanchung, China 33 10N 107 2E
77 Nanchung, China 30 47N 105 59E
77 Nanchwan, China 29 10N 107 15E
19 Nancy, France 48 42N 6 12E
69 Nanda Devi, Mt., India 30 30N 80 30E
70 Nander, India 19 10N 77 20E
101 Nandi, Fiji Is. 17 25s 176 50E
90 Nandi ♦, Kenya 0 15N 35 0E
90 Nandikotkur, India 15 52N 78 18E
68 Nandura, India 20 52N 76 25E
68 Nandurbar, India 21 20N 74 15E
68 Nandyal, India 15 30N 78 30E
85 Nanga Eboko, Cameroon 4 41N 12 22E
66 Nanga Parbat, mt., Kashmir 35 10N 74 35E
91 Nangade, Mozambique 11 5s 39 36E
72 Nangapinoh, Indonesia 0 20s 111 14E
72 Nangatajap, Indonesia 1 32s 110 34E
90 Nangeya Mts., Uganda 3 30N 33 30E
77 Nangfeng, China 27 10N 116 20E
19 Nangis, France 48 33N 3 0E
85 Nangodi, Ghana 10 58N 0 42w
84 Nangola, Mali 12 41N 6 35w
66 Nangrahar ♦, Afghan. 34 20N 70 0E
68 Nanjangud, India 12 6N 76 43E
91 Nanjeko, Zambia 5 31s 23 30E
91 Nanjirinji, Tanz. 9 41s 39 5E
68 Nankana Sahib, Pakistan 31 27N 73 38E
77 Nankang, China 25 42N 114 35E
77 Nankiang, China 32 20N 106 50E
77 Nanking, China 32 10N 118 50E
96 Nanninne, Australia 26 51s 118 18E
77 Nanning, China 22 51N 108 18E
69 Nanpara, India 27 52N 81 33E
77 Nanping, Fukien, China 26 45N 118 5E
77 Nanping, Szechwan, China 33 20N 103 56E
77 Nanpu, China 31 17N 105 59E
91 Nanripe, Mozambique 13 52s 38 52E
74 Nansei-Shotō, Japan 29 0N 129 0E
4 Nansen Sd., Canada 81 0N 91 0w
90 Nansio, Tanzania 2 3s 33 4E
20 Nant, France 44 1N 3 18E
77 Nantan, China 25 0N 107 35E
59 Nantay, U.S.S.R. 62 43N 129 37E
18 Nantes, France 47 12N 1 33w
19 Nanteuil-le-Haudouin, France 49 9N 2 48E
20 Nantiat, France 46 1N 1 11E
113 Nanticoke, U.S.A. 41 12N 76 1w
108 Nanton, Canada 50 20N 113 50w
77 Nantou, Taiwan 23 57N 120 35E
21 Nantua, France 46 10N 5 35E
111 Nantucket I., U.S.A. 41 16N 70 3w
77 Nantung, China 32 0N 120 50E
77 Nanyang, China 33 2N 112 35E
90 Nanyuki, Kenya 0 2N 37 4E
33 Nao, C. de la, Spain 38 44N 0 14E
107 Naococane L., Canada 52 50N 70 45w
74 Naoetsu, Japan 37 12N 138 10E
69 Naogaon, Bangladesh 24 52N 88 52E
44 Naoúsa, Greece 40 42N 22 9E
73 Napabalana, Indonesia 4 42s 127 43E
106 Napanee, Canada 44 15N 77 0w
113 Napanoch, U.S.A. 41 44N 74 2w
84 Napiéolédougou, Ivory Coast 9 18N 5 35w
101 Napier, New Zealand 39 30s 176 56E
94 Napier, S. Afr. 34 33s 19 54E
41 Naples = Napoli, Italy 40 50N 14 5E
115 Naples, Fla., U.S.A. 26 10N 81 45w
113 Naples, N.Y., U.S.A. 42 35N 77 25w
41 Naples, Gulf of, Italy 40 40N 14 10E
126 Napo, R., Peru 3 5s 73 0w

MAP

126 Napo ♦, Ecuador 0 30s 77 0w
116 Napoleon, N. Dak., U.S.A. 46 32N 99 49w
114 Napoleon, Ohio, U.S.A. 41 24N 84 7w
41 Nápoli, Italy 40 50N 14 5E
41 Nápoli, G. di, Italy 40 40N 14 10E
90 Napopo, Zaïre 4 15N 28 0E
99 Nappa Merrie, Australia 27 7N 141 7E
64 Naqâda, Egypt 25 53N 32 42E
84 Nara, Mali 15 25N 7 20w
74 Nara, Japan 34 40N 135 49E
68 Nara, Canal, Pakistan 26 0N 69 20E
66 Nara Visa, U.S.A. 35 39N 103 10w
99 Naracoorte, Austral. 36 50s 140 44E
100 Naradhan, Australia 33 34s 146 17E
74 Nara-ken ♦, Japan 34 30N 136 0E
70 Narasapur, India 16 26N 81 50E
70 Narasaropet, India 16 14N 80 4E
71 Narathiwat, Thailand 6 40N 101 55E
69 Narayanganj, Bangladesh 23 31N 90 33E
70 Narayanpet, India 16 45N 77 30E
20 Narbonne, France 43 11N 3 0E
54 Narcea, R., Spain 43 15N 6 30w
41 Nardó, Italy 40 10N 18 0E
66 Nari, R., Pakistan 29 10N 67 50E
65 Narin, Afghanistan 36 5N 69 0E
14 Narinda, B. de, Malag. 14 55s 47 30E
126 Narino ♦, Colombia 1 30N 78 0w
68 Narnaula, R., India 22 40N 77 30E
68 Narnaul, India 28 5N 76 11E
39 Narni, Italy 42 30N 12 30E
84 Naro, Ghana 10 22N 2 27w
40 Naro, Italy 37 18N 13 48E
55 Naro Fominsk, U.S.S.R. 55 23N 36 32E
55 Narodnaya, G., U.S.S.R. 65 5N 60 0E
90 Narok, Kenya 1 20s 33 30E
90 Narok ♦, Kenya 1 20s 33 30E
30 Narón, Spain 43 32N 8 9w
100 Narooma, Australia 36 14s 150 4E
68 Narowal, Pakistan 32 6N 74 52E
99 Narrabri, Australia 30 19s 149 46E
99 Narran, R., Australia 29 20s 147 30E
100 Narrandera, Australia 34 42s 146 31E
100 Narriah, Australia 33 56s 146 43E
96 Narrogin, Australia 32 58s 117 14E
100 Narromine, Australia 32 12s 148 12E
70 Narsampet, India 17 57N 79 58E
69 Narsinghpur, India 22 54N 79 14E
68 Narsari, India 20 57N 72 59E
66 Nawa Kot, Pakistan 28 21N 71 24E
54 Narva, U.S.S.R. 59 10N 28 5E
54 Narva, R., U.S.S.R. 59 10N 27 50E
50 Narvik, Norway 68 28N 17 26E
54 Narvskoye Vdkhr., U.S.S.R. 59 10N 28 5E
68 Narwana, India 29 39N 76 6E
52 Naryan-Mar, U.S.S.R. 68 0N 53 0E
99 Naryilco, Australia 28 37s 141 53E
58 Narym, U.S.S.R. 59 0N 81 58E
58 Narymskoye, U.S.S.R. 49 10N 84 15E
58 Naryn, U.S.S.R. 41 30N 76 10E
50 Nasa, Norway 66 29N 15 23E
85 Nasarawa, Nigeria 8 32N 7 41E
46 Năsăud, Rumania 47 19N 24 29E
7 Naseby, Eng., U.K. 52 24N 0 59w
101 Naseby, New Zealand 45 1s 170 10E
64 Naser, Buheirat en, Egypt 23 0N 32 30E
116 Nashua, Iowa, U.S.A. 42 55N 92 34w
118 Nashua, Mont., U.S.A. 48 10N 106 25w
111 Nashua, N.H., U.S.A. 42 50N 71 25w
117 Nashville, Ark., U.S.A. 33 56N 93 50w
115 Nashville, Ga., U.S.A. 31 13N 83 15w
115 Nashville, Tenn., U.S.A. 36 12N 86 46w
42 Našice, Yugoslavia 45 32N 18 4E
28 Nasielsk, Poland 52 35N 20 50E
68 Nasik, India 20 2N 73 50E
69 Nasirabad, Bangladesh 24 42N 90 30E
68 Nasirabad, India 26 15N 74 45E
68 Nasirabad, Pakistan 28 25N 68 25E
41 Naso, Italy 38 8N 14 46E
65 Nasratabad, Iran 29 55N 59 53E
121 Nassau, Bahamas 25 0N 77 30w
113 Nassau, U.S.A. 42 30N 73 34w
128 Nassau, Bahía, Chile 55 20s 68 0w
86 Nasser City = Kôm Ombo, Egypt 24 25N 32 52E
86 Nasser, L., = Naser, Buheirat en, Eg. 23 0N 32 30E
84 Nassian, Ivory Coast 7 58N 2 57w
49 Nässjö, Sweden 57 38N 14 45E
106 Nastopoka Is., Canada 57 0N 77 0w
48 Näsum, Sweden 56 10N 14 29E
48 Näsviken, Sweden 61 46N 16 52E
77 Nata, China 19 37N 109 17E
64 Nata, Saudi Arabia 27 15N 48 35E
92 Nata, Botswana 20 7s 26 4E
126 Natagaima, Colombia 3 37N 75 6w
127 Natal, Brazil 5 47s 35 13w
72 Natal, Indonesia 0 35N 99 0E
93 Natal ♦, S. Africa 28 30s 30 30E
42 Natalinci, Yugoslavia 44 15N 20 49E
65 Natanz, Iran 33 30N 51 55E
127 Natashquan, Canada 50 14N 61 46w
107 Natashquan Pt., Can. 50 8N 61 40w
107 Natashquan, R., Canada 51 48N 62 0w
117 Natchez, U.S.A. 31 35N 91 25w
117 Natchitoches, U.S.A. 31 47N 93 4w
99 Nathalia, Australia 36 1s 145 7E
68 Nathdwara, India 24 55N 73 50E
113 Natick, U.S.A. 42 16N 71 19w
65 Natih, Muscat & Oman 22 25N 56 30E
100 Natimuk, Australia 36 35s 141 59E
119 National City, U.S.A. 32 45N 117 7w
109 National Mills, Canada 52 52N 101 40w
85 Natitingou, Dahomey 10 20N 1 26E
116 Natoma, U.S.A. 39 14N 99 0w
90 Natron L., Tanzania 2 20s 36 0E
86 Natrûn, W. el, Egypt 30 25N 30 0E
72 Natuna Besar, Kepulauan, Indonesia 4 0N 108 0E

MAP

72 Natuna Selatan, Kepulauan, Indonesia 3 0N 109 55E
113 Natural Bridge, U.S.A. 44 5N 75 30w
99 Naturaliste C., Tas., Australia 40 50s 148 15E
96 Naturaliste, C., W. Australia, Australia 33 32s 115 0E
96 Naturaliste Channel, Australia 25 20s 113 0E
20 Naucelle, France 44 13N 2 20E
26 Nauders, Austria 46 54N 10 30E
24 Nauen, Germany 52 36N 12 52E
113 Naugatuck, U.S.A. 41 28N 73 4w
54 Naujoji Vilnia, U.S.S.R. 54 48N 25 27E
24 Naumburg, Germany 51 10N 11 48E
92 Nau-Nau, Botswana 18 57s 21 4E
101 Nauru I., Pacific Ocean 0 25N 166 0E
126 Nauta, Peru 4 20s 73 35w
120 Nautla, Mexico 20 20N 96 50w
30 Nava del Rey, Spain 41 22N 5 6w
30 Navacerrada, Puerto de, Spain 40 47N 4 0w
30 Navahermosa, Spain 39 41N 4 28w
30 Navalcarnero, Spain 40 17N 4 5w
30 Navalmoral de la Mata, Spain 39 52N 5 16w
31 Navalvillar de Pela, Sp. 39 9N 5 24w
15 Navan = An Uaimh 53 39N 6 40w
128 Navarino, I., Chile 55 0s 67 30w
32 Navarra ♦, Spain 42 40N 1 40w
20 Navarre, France 43 15N 1 20E
112 Navarre, U.S.A. 40 43N 81 31w
20 Navarreux, France 43 20N 0 47w
117 Navasota, U.S.A. 30 20N 96 5w
121 Navassa I., W.I. 18 30N 75 0w
38 Nave, Italy 45 35N 10 17E
14 Naver, R., Scot. 58 34N 4 10w
30 Navia, Spain 43 24N 6 42w
30 Navia, R., Spain 43 15N 6 50w
30 Navia de Suarna, Spain 42 58N 6 59w
124 Navidad, Chile 33 57s 71 50w
54 Navlya, U.S.S.R. 52 53N 34 15E
58 Navoi, U.S.S.R. 40 9N 65 22E
120 Navojoa, Mexico 27 0N 109 30w
54 Navolok, U.S.S.R. 62 33N 39 57E
45 Návpaktos, Greece 38 23N 21 42E
45 Návplion, Greece 37 33N 22 50E
68 Navsari, India 20 57N 72 59E
66 Nawa Kot, Pakistan 28 21N 71 24E
69 Nawabganj, Bareilly, U.P., India 28 32N 79 40E
69 Nawabganj, Bara Banki, U.P., India 26 56N 81 14E
69 Nawabganj, Bangladesh 24 35N 81 14E
68 Nawabshah, Pakistan 26 15N 68 25E
69 Nawada, India 24 50N 85 25E
69 Nawakot, Nepal 28 0N 85 10E
68 Nawalgarh, India 27 50N 75 15E
69 Nawapara, India 20 52N 82 33E
86 Nawi, Sudan 18 32N 13 50E
45 Náxos, Greece 37 8N 25 25E
45 Náxos, I., Greece 37 5N 25 30E
20 Nay, France 43 10N 0 18w
65 Nay Band, Iran 27 20N 52 40E
126 Naya, Colombia 3 13N 77 22w
126 Naya, R., Colombia 3 13N 77 22w
59 Nayakhan, U.S.S.R. 62 10N 159 0E
120 Nayarit ♦, Mexico 22 0N 105 0w
84 Nayé, Senegal 14 28N 12 43w
127 Nazaré, Brazil 13 0s 39 0w
31 Nazaré, Portugal 39 36N 9 4w
127 Nazaré da Mata, Brazil 7 44s 35 14w
62 Nazareth, Israel 32 42N 35 17E
120 Nazas, Mexico 25 10N 104 0w
120 Nazas, R., Mexico 25 20N 104 4w
13 Naze, The, Eng. 51 43N 1 19E
87 Nazeret, Ethiopia 8 45N 39 15E
67 Nazir Hat, Bangladesh 22 35N 91 55E
108 Nazko, Canada 52 50N 123 25w
93 Nchacoongo, Mozam. 24 20s 35 9E
91 Nchanga, Zambia 12 30s 27 49E
91 Ncheu, Malawi 14 50s 34 37E
84 Nchira, Ghana 12 54N 2 0w
90 Ndala, Tanzania 4 45s 33 23E
85 Ndali, Dahomey 9 50N 2 46E
90 Ndareda, Tanzania 4 12s 35 30E
81 Délé, Cent. Afr. Rep. 8 25N 20 36E
88 Ndendé, Gabon 2 29s 10 46E
84 N' Dioum, Senegal 16 31N 14 39w
88 Ndjolé, Gabon 0 10s 10 45E
91 Ndola, Zambia 13 0s 28 34E
90 Ndoto Mts., Kenya 2 0N 37 0E
84 Ndrhamcha, Sebkra de, Mauritania 18 30N 15 55w
90 Nduguti, Tanzania 4 18s 34 41E
50 Nea, Norway 63 15N 11 0E
45 Néa Epidhavros, Greece 37 40N 23 7E
44 Néa Filippiás, Greece 39 12N 20 53E
44 Néa Kallikrátia, Greece 40 21N 23 1E
44 Néa Vissi, Greece 41 34N 26 33E
15 Neagh, Lough, Northern Ireland 54 35N 6 25w
118 Neah Bay, U.S.A. 48 19N 124 29w
96 Neales, R., Australia 28 0s 136 0E
91 Neamarrói, Mozam. 15 58s 36 50E
46 Neamţ ♦, Rumania 47 0N 26 20E
45 Neápolis, Kozan, Greece 40 20N 21 24E
45 Neápolis, Kriti, Greece 35 15N 25 36E
45 Neápolis, Lakonía, Gr. 36 27N 23 8E
104 Near Is., Alaska 53 0N 172 0E
13 Neath, Wales 51 39N 3 49w
109 Nebbou, Upper Volta 11 9N 1 51w
55 Nebolchy, U.S.S.R. 59 12N 32 58E
116 Nebraska ♦, U.S.A. 41 30N 100 0w
116 Nebraska City, U.S.A. 40 40N 95 52w
108 Nechako, R., Canada 53 30N 125 0w
117 Neches, R., U.S.A. 31 80N 94 20w
25 Neckar, R., Germany 48 43N 9 1E

MAP

124 Necochea, Argentina 38 30s 58 50w
39 Nedelišče, Yugoslavia 46 23N 16 22E
47 Nederlandsöy I., Nor. 62 20N 5 35E
37 Nédha, R., Greece 37 25N 21 45E
82 Nedroma, Algeria 35 1N 1 45w
119 Needles, U.S.A. 34 50N 114 35w
124 Neembucú ♦, Paraguay 27 0s 58 0w
68 Neemuch (Nimach), India 24 30N 74 50E
114 Neenah, U.S.A. 44 10N 88 30w
109 Neepawa, Canada 50 20N 99 30w
83 Nefta, Tunisia 33 53N 7 58E
83 Neftah Sidi Boubekeur, Algeria 35 1N 0 4E
57 Neftegorsk, U.S.S.R. 44 25N 39 45E
53 Neftyannye Kamni, U.S.S.R. 40 20N 50 55E
70 Negapatam = Nagappattinam, India 10 46N 79 38E
114 Negaunee, U.S.A. 46 30N 87 36w
62 Negba, Israel 31 40N 34 41E
87 Negele, Ethiopia 5 20N 39 30E
71 Negeri Sembilan ♦, Malaysia 2 50N 102 10E
62 Negev = Hanegev, Israel 30 50N 35 0E
46 Negolu, Rumania 45 48N 24 32E
70 Negombo, Sri Lanka 7 12N 79 50E
42 Negotin, Makedonija, Yugoslavia 41 29N 22 9E
42 Negotin, Srbija, Y.-slav. 44 16N 22 37E
30 Negra, Peña, Spain 42 11N 6 30w
73 Negra Pt., Philippines 18 40N 120 50E
30 Negreira, Spain 42 54N 8 45w
46 Negreşti, Rumania 46 50N 27 30E
82 Négrine, Algeria 34 30N 7 30E
82 Negro, C., Morocco 35 40N 5 11w
128 Negro, R., Argentina 40 0s 64 0w
126 Negro, R., Brazil 0 25s 64 0w
125 Negro, R., Uruguay 32 30s 55 30w
73 Negros, I., Philppines 10 0N 123 0E
46 Negru Vodă, Rumania 43 47N 28 21E
65 Nehbandan, Iran 31 35N 60 5E
24 Neheim, Germany 51 27N 7 58E
46 Nehoiaşu, Rumania 45 24N 26 20E
109 Neidpath, Canada 50 12N 107 20w
118 Neihart, U.S.A. 47 0N 110 52w
77 Neikiang, China 29 35N 105 10E
100 Neilrex, Australia 31 38s 149 25E
118 Neilton, U.S.A. 47 24N 123 59w
30 Neira de Justá, Spain 42 53N 7 14w
24 Neisse, R., Pol.-Ger. 51 0N 15 0E
126 Neiva, Colombia 2 56N 75 18w
87 Nejo, Ethiopia 9 30N 35 28E
87 Nekemte, Ethiopia 9 4N 36 30E
86 Nékhebt, Egypt 25 10N 33 0E
49 Neksö, Denmark 55 4N 15 8E
30 Nelas, Portugal 40 32N 7 52w
47 Nelaug, Norway 58 39N 8 40E
98 Nelia, Austral. 20 39s 142 12E
55 Nelidovo, U.S.S.R. 56 13N 32 49E
116 Neligh, U.S.A. 42 11N 98 2w
57 Nelkan, U.S.S.R. 57 50N 136 15E
70 Nellikuppam, India 11 46N 79 43E
70 Nellore, India 14 27N 79 59E
57 Nelma, U.S.S.R. 47 30N 139 0E
100 Nelson, Australia 38 3s 141 2E
12 Nelson, England 53 50N 2 14w
101 Nelson, New Zealand 41 18s 173 16E
119 Nelson, Ariz., U.S.A. 35 35N 113 24w
119 Nelson, Nev., U.S.A. 35 46N 114 55w
128 Nelson, C., Austral. 38 14s 141 33E
128 Nelson, Estrecho, Chile 52 50s 123 25w
109 Nelson, R., Canada 55 30N 96 50w
101 Nelson ♦, N.Z. 42 11s 172 15E
100 Nelson Bay, Australia 32 43s 152 9E
108 Nelson Forks, Canada 59 30N 124 0w
109 Nelson House, Canada 55 50N 99 0w
93 Nelspruit, S. Afr. 25 29s 30 59E
84 Néma, Mauritania 16 40N 7 15w
84 Neman (Nemunas), R., U.S.S.R. 53 30N 25 10E
45 Neméa, Greece 37 49N 22 40E
106 Nemegos, Canada 47 40N 83 15w
46 Nemira, Mt., Rumania 46 17N 26 19E
106 Nemiscam, Canada 49 30N 111 15w
19 Nemours, France 48 16N 2 40E
54 Nemunas, R., U.S.S.R. 55 25N 21 10E
74 Nemuro, Japan 43 20N 145 35E
74 Nemuro-Kaikyō, Japan 43 30N 145 30E
59 Nemuy, U.S.S.R. 55 40N 135 55E
15 Nenagh, Ireland 52 52N 8 11w
7 Nene, R., England 52 38N 0 7E
91 Neno, Malawi 15 25s 34 40E
73 Nenusa, Kepulauan, Indonesia 4 45N 127 1E
117 Neodesha, U.S.A. 37 30N 95 37w
44 Néon Petritsi, Greece 41 16N 23 15E
117 Neosho, U.S.A. 36 56N 94 28w
117 Neosho, R., U.S.A. 35 59N 95 10w
69 Nepal ■, Asia 28 0N 84 30E
69 Nepalganj, Nepal 28 0N 81 40E
118 Nephi, U.S.A. 39 43N 111 52w
15 Nephin, Mt., Ireland 54 1N 9 21w
26 Nepomuk, Cz. 49 29N 13 35E
117 Neptune City, U.S.A. 40 13N 74 4w
42 Néra, R., Rumania 44 52N 21 45E
20 Nerac, France 44 19N 0 20E
59 Nerchinsk, U.S.S.R. 52 0N 116 39E
59 Nerchinskiy Zavod, U.S.S.R. 51 10N 119 30E
46 Nereju, Rumania 45 43N 26 43E
55 Nerekhta, U.S.S.R. 57 26N 40 38E

MAP

107 Neret L., Canada 54 40N 71 0w
42 Neretva, R., Yugoslavia 43 30N 17 50E
43 Neretvanski, Yugoslavia 43 7N 17 10E
55 Neri, R., U.S.S.R. 55 21N 23 1E
33 Nerja, Spain 36 43N 3 55w
33 Nerpio, Spain 38 11N 2 16w
37 Nerva, Spain 37 42N 6 30w
50 Nes, Iceland 65 53N 17 24w
62 Nes Ziyyona, Israel 31 56N 34 48w
47 Nesbyen, Norway 60 34N 9 6E
42 Nesebyr, Bulgaria 42 41N 27 46E
47 Nesflaten, Norway 59 38N 6 48E
50 Neskaupstaðu ur, Iceland 65 9N 13 42w
47 Nesland, Norway 59 31N 7 59E
47 Neslandsvatn, Norway 58 57N 9 10E
19 Nesle, France 49 45N 2 53E
47 Nesodden, Norway 59 48N 10 40E
14 Ness, Loch, Scot. 57 15N 4 30w
50 Nesseby, Norway 70 9N 28 51E
44 Nestórion Oros, Gr. 40 24N 20 55E
44 Néstos, R., Greece 41 20N 24 35E
47 Nesttun, Norway 60 19N 5 21E
54 Nesvizh, U.S.S.R. 53 14N 26 38E
62 Netanya, Israel 32 20N 34 51E
16 Nethe, R., Belgium 51 2N 4 55E
100 Netherby, Austral. 36 8s 141 40E
16 Netherlands ■, Eur. 52 0N 5 30E
127 Netherlands Guiana = Surinam, S. Amer. 4 0N 56 0w
41 Neto, R., Italy 39 10N 16 58E
19 Nettancourt, France 48 51N 4 57E
105 Nettilling L., Canada 66 30N 71 0w
40 Nettuno, Italy 41 29N 12 40E
120 Netzahualcoyotl, Presa, Mexico 17 10N 93 30w
25 Neu-Isenburg, Germany 50 3N 8 42E
24 Neu Ulm, Germany 48 23N 10 2E
24 Neubrandenburg, E. Ger. 53 33N 13 17E
24 Neubrandenburg Burg ♦, E. Germany 53 30N 13 20E
24 Neubukow, Germany 54 1N 11 40E
25 Neuburg, Germany 48 43N 11 11E
25 Neuchâtel, Switz. 47 0N 6 55E
25 Neuchâtel ♦, Switzerland 47 0N 6 55E
25 Neuchâtel, Lac de, Switz. 46 53N 6 50E
26 Neudau, Austria 47 11N 16 4E
24 Neuenhaus, Germany 52 30N 6 55E
19 Neuf-Brisach, France 48 0N 7 30E
16 Neufchâteau, Belgium 49 50N 5 25E
19 Neufchâteau, France 48 21N 5 40E
19 Neufchâtel, France 49 43N 1 30E
19 Neufchâtel-sur-Aisne, France 49 26N 4 0E
24 Neuhaus, Ger. 53 16N 10 54E
19 Neuilly-St. Front, Fr. 49 10N 3 15E
25 Neukalen, Germany 53 49N 12 48E
25 Neumarkt, Germany 49 16N 11 28E
24 Neumünster, Germany 54 4N 9 58E
19 Neung-sur-Beuvron, France 47 30N 1 50E
26 Neunkirchen, Austria 47 43N 16 4E
25 Neunkirchen, Germany 49 23N 7 6E
128 Neuquén, Argentina 38 0s 68 0E
124 Neuquén ♦, Argentina 38 0s 69 50w
24 Neuruppin, Germany 52 56N 12 48E
115 Neuse, R., U.S.A. 35 5N 77 40w
27 Neusiedl, Austria 47 57N 16 50E
27 Neusiedler See, Aust. 47 50N 16 47E
24 Neuss, Germany 51 12N 6 39E
25 Neussargues, France 45 9N 2 59E
25 Neustadt, Bay., Ger. 49 42N 12 10E
25 Neustadt, Bay., Ger. 48 48N 11 47E
25 Neustadt, Bay., Ger. 49 34N 10 37E
25 Neustadt, Bay., Ger. 50 23N 11 0E
24 Neustadt, Gera, Germany 50 45N 11 43E
24 Neustadt, Hessen, Ger. 50 51N 9 9E
24 Neustadt, Niedersachsen, Ger. 52 30N 9 30E

MAP

24 Neustadt, Potsdam, Ger. 52 50N 12 27E
25 Neustadt, Rhld.-Pfz., Ger. 49 21N 8 10E
24 Neustadt, S.-Holst., Ger. 54 6N 10 49E
24 Neustrelitz, Germany 53 22N 13 4E
20 Neuvic, France 45 23N 2 16E
19 Neuville, France 45 52N 4 51E
19 Neuville-aux-Bois, Fr. 48 4N 2 3E
20 Neuvy-St.-Sépulchure, France 46 35N 1 48E
19 Neuvy-sur-Barangeon, France 47 20N 2 15E
24 Neuwerk, I., Germany 53 55N 8 30E
50 Neuwied, Germany 50 26N 7 29E
52 Neva, R., U.S.S.R. 59 50N 30 30E
118 Nevada, U.S.A. 37 20N 94 40w
118 Nevada, Sierra, Spain 37 3N 3 15w
118 Nevada, Sierra, U.S.A. 39 0N 120 30w
119 Nevada ♦, U.S.A. 39 20N 117 0w
126 Nevada de Sta. Marta, Sa., Colombia 10 55N 73 50w
124 Nevado, Cerro, Argentina 35 30s 68 20w
120 Nevado de Colima, Mt., Mexico 19 35N 103 45w
62 Nevallat, Israel 31 59N 34 57E
59 Nevanka, U.S.S.R. 56 45N 98 55E
70 Nevasa, India 19 34N 75 0E
55 Nevel, U.S.S.R. 56 0N 29 55E
19 Nevers, France 47 0N 3 9E
100 Neville, Australia 33 50s 147 44E
109 Neville, Canada 49 58N 107 39w
121 Nevis I., Leeward Is. 17 0N 62 30w
47 Nevlunghavn, Norway 58 58N 9 53E
43 Nevrokop, Bulgaria 41 43N 23 46E

MAP
64 Nevşehir, Turkey 38 33N 34 40E
85 New Adawso, Ghana 6 50N 0 37E
114 New Albany, Ind., 38 20N 85 50W
 U.S.A.
117 New Albany, Miss., 34 30N 89 0W
 U.S.A.
113 New Albany, Pa., 41 35N 76 28W
 U.S.A.
126 New Amsterdam, Guy. 6 15N 57 30W
113 New Bedford, U.S.A. 41 40N 70 52W
115 New Bern, U.S.A. 35 8N 77 3W
113 New Bethlehem, U.S.A. 41 0N 79 22W
112 New Bloomfield, U.S.A. 40 24N 77 12W
117 New Boston, U.S.A. 33 27N 94 21W
117 New Braunfels, U.S.A. 29 43N 98 9W
101 New Brighton, N.Z. 43 29S 172 43E
113 New Britain, U.S.A. 41 41N 72 47W
98 New Britain I., Territory 6 0S 151 0E
 of New Guinea
113 New Brunswick, U.S.A. 40 30N 74 28W
107 New Brunswick ♦, 46 50N 66 30W
 Canada
85 New Bussa, Nigeria 9 53N 4 31E
5 New Byrd, Antarctica 80 0S 120 0W
94 New Caledonia, I., Pac. 21 0S 165 0E
 Oc.
31 New Castile = Castilla 39 45N 3 20W
 La Neuva, Spain
114 New Castle, Ind., U.S.A. 39 55N 85 23W
112 New Castle, Pa., U.S.A. 41 0N 80 20W
113 New City, U.S.A. 41 8N 74 0W
120 New Cristóbal, Panama 9 25N 79 40W
 Canal Zone
112 New Cumberland, 40 30N 80 36W
 U.S.A.
68 New Delhi, India 28 37N 77 13E
108 New Denver, Canada 50 0N 117 25W
116 New England, U.S.A. 46 36N 102 47W
99 New England Ra., 29 30S 152 0E
 Australia
13 New Forest, Eng. 50 53N 1 40W
107 New Glasgow, Canada 45 35N 62 36W
94 New Guinea, I. 4 0S 136 0E
 Australia
•98 N. Guin., Terr. of, 4 0S 146 0E
 Austral. Trust Terr.
117 New Hamburg, Canada 43 24N 80 43W
113 New Hampshire ♦, 43 40N 71 40W
 U.S.A.
116 New Hampton, U.S.A. 43 2N 92 20W
93 New Hanover, S. Africa 29 22S 30 31E
98 New Hanover I., New 2 30S 150 15E
 Guinea
113 New Haven, Conn., 41 20N 72 54W
 U.S.A.
112 New Haven, Mich., 42 44N 82 46W
 U.S.A.
108 New Hazelton, Canada 55 20N 127 30W
94 New Hebrides, Is., Pac. 15 0S 168 0E
 Oc.
117 New Iberia, U.S.A. 30 2N 91 54W
98 New Ireland, I., Terr. of 3 0S 151 0E
 New Guinea
113 New Jersey ♦, U.S.A. 39 50N 74 10W
112 New Kensington, U.S.A. 40 36N 79 43W
114 New Lexington, U.S.A. 39 40N 82 15W
106 New Liskeard, Canada 47 31N 79 41W
113 New London, Conn., 41 23N 72 8W
 U.S.A.
116 New London, Minn., 45 17N 94 55W
 U.S.A.
112 New London, Ohio, 41 4N 82 25W
 U.S.A.
116 New London, Wis., 44 23N 88 43W
 U.S.A.
117 New Madrid, U.S.A. 36 40N 89 30W
113 New Market, U.S.A. 43 4N 70 57W
118 New Meadows, U.S.A. 45 0N 116 10W
110 New Mexico ♦, U.S.A. 34 30N 106 0W
113 New Milford, Conn., 41 35N 73 25W
 U.S.A.
113 New Milford, Pa., 41 50N 75 45W
 U.S.A.
99 New Norfolk, Australia 42 46S 147 2E
117 New Orleans, U.S.A. 30 0N 90 5W
112 New Philadelphia, 40 29N 81 25W
 U.S.A.
101 New Plymouth, N.Z. 39 4S 174 5E
121 New Providence I., 25 0N 77 30W
 Bahamas
13 New Radnor, Wales 52 15N 3 10W
116 New Richmond, U.S.A. 45 6N 92 34W
117 New Roads, U.S.A. 30 43N 91 30W
113 New Rochelle, U.S.A. 40 55N 73 46W
116 New Rockford, U.S.A. 47 44N 99 7W
15 New Ross, Ireland 52 24N 6 58W
116 New Salem, U.S.A. 46 51N 101 25W
115 New Smyrna Beach, 29 0N 80 50W
 U.S.A.
99 New South Wales ♦, 33 0S 146 0E
 Australia
85 New Tamale, Ghana 9 10N 1 10W
116 New Ulm, U.S.A. 44 15N 94 30W
107 New Waterford, Canada 46 13N 60 4W
108 New Westminster, Can. 49 10N 122 52W
114 New York, U.S.A. 42 40N 76 0W
113 New York City, U.S.A. 40 45N 74 0W
94 New Zealand ■, 40 0S 176 0W
 Oceania
91 Newala, Tanzania 10 58S 39 10E
91 Newala ♦, Tanz. 10 46S 39 20E
13 Newark, England 53 6N 0 48W
114 Newark, Del., U.S.A. 39 42N 75 45W
113 Newark, N.J., U.S.A. 40 41N 74 12W
112 Newark, N.Y., U.S.A. 43 2N 77 10W
112 Newark, Ohio, U.S.A. 40 5N 82 30W
115 Newberg, U.S.A. 45 22N 123 0W
114 Newberry, U.S.A. 46 20N 85 32W
108 Newbrook, Canada 54 24N 112 57W
113 Newburgh, U.S.A. 41 30N 74 1W

13 Newbury, England 51 24N 1 19W
113 Newbury, U.S.A. 44 7N 72 6W
113 Newburyport, U.S.A. 42 48N 70 50W
100 Newcastle, Australia 32 52S 151 49E
107 Newcastle, N.B., Can. 47 1N 65 38W
112 Newcastle, Ont., Can. 43 54N 78 34W
15 Newcastle, Limerick, Ire. 52 27N 9 3W
15 Newcastle, Wicklow, 53 5N 6 4W
 Ireland
15 Newcastle, N. Ire. 54 13N 5 54W
113 Newcastle, Me., U.S.A. 43 4N 70 41W
98 Newcastle, Wyo., U.S.A. 43 50N 104 12W
98 Newcastle B., Australia 10 45S 142 30E
13 Newcastle Emlyn, Wales 52 2N 4 29W
98 Newcastle Range, 19 0S 143 30E
 Australia
12 Newcastle-under- Lyme, 53 2N 2 15W
 England
12 Newcastle-upon- Tyne, 54 59N 1 37W
 England
96 Newcastle Waters, 17 30S 133 28E
 Australia
112 Newdegate, Austral. 33 17N 118 58E
62 Newe Etan, Israel 32 30N 35 32E
62 Newe Sha'anan, Israel 32 47N 34 59E
62 Newe Zohar, Israel 31 9N 35 21E
116 Newell, U.S.A. 44 48N 103 25W
107 Newfoundland, I., Can. 48 30N 56 0W
107 Newfoundland ♦, 48 28N 56 0W
 Canada
13 Newham, England 51 31N 0 2E
13 Newhaven, Eng. 50 47N 0 4E
117 Newkirk, U.S.A. 36 52N 97 3W
96 Newman, Mt., Australia 23 20S 119 34E
112 Newmarket, Canada 44 5N 79 30W
15 Newmarket, Eng., U.K. 52 15N 0 23E
15 Newmarket, Ireland 52 13N 9 0W
113 Newmarket, U.S.A. 43 4N 70 57W
115 Newnan, U.S.A. 33 22N 84 48W
100 Newnes, Austral. 33 15S 150 10E
100 Newport, Australia 33 40S 151 20E
13 Newport, Essex, Eng. 51 58N 0 13E
13 Newport, I. of W., 50 42N 1 18W
 England
13 Newport, Mon., Wales 51 35N 3 0W
117 Newport, Ark., U.S.A. 35 38N 91 15W
114 Newport, Ky., U.S.A. 39 5N 84 23W
113 Newport, N.H., U.S.A. 43 23N 72 8W
118 Newport, Oreg., U.S.A. 44 41N 124 2W
112 Newport, Pa., U.S.A. 40 28N 77 8W
113 Newport, R.I., U.S.A. 41 13N 71 19W
115 Newport, Tenn., U.S.A. 35 59N 83 12W
113 Newport, Vt., U.S.A. 44 57N 72 17W
118 Newport, Wash., U.S.A. 48 11N 117 2W
119 Newport Beach, U.S.A. 33 40N 117 58W
114 Newport News, U.S.A. 37 2N 76 54W
13 Newquay, Eng. 50 24N 5 6W
15 Newry, N. Ire. 54 10N 6 20W
116 Newton, Iowa, U.S.A. 41 40N 93 3W
117 Newton, Kans., U.S.A. 38 2N 97 30W
114 Newton, Mass., U.S.A. 42 21N 71 10W
117 Newton, Miss., U.S.A. 38 2N 97 25W
113 Newton, N.J., U.S.A. 41 3N 74 46W
115 Newton, N.C., U.S.A. 35 42N 81 10W
117 Newton, Texas, U.S.A. 30 54N 93 42W
13 Newton Abbot, England 50 32N 3 37W
99 Newton Boyd, Australia 29 45S 152 0E
14 Newton Stewart, 54 57N 4 30W
 Scotland
100 Newtown, Australia 37 38S 143 40E
13 Newtown, Wales 52 31N 3 19W
15 Newtownards, N. Ire. 54 37N 5 40W
112 Newville, U.S.A. 40 10N 77 24W
24 Nexon, France 45 41N 1 10E
55 Neya, U.S.S.R. 58 21N 43 49E
65 Neyrîz, Iran 29 15N 54 55E
65 Neyshâbûr, Iran 36 10N 58 20E
70 Neyyattinkara, India 8 26N 77 5E
55 Nezhin, U.S.S.R. 51 5N 31 55E
118 Nezperce, U.S.A. 46 13N 116 15W
72 Ngabang, Indonesia 0 30N 109 55E
85 Ngambé, Cameroon 5 48N 11 29E
92 Ngami Depression, 20 30S 22 46E
 Botswana
91 Ngamo, Rhodesia 19 3S 27 25E
73 Ngandjuk, Indonesia 7 32S 111 55E
88 Ngaoundéré, Cameroon 7 15N 13 35E
101 Ngapara, N.Z. 44 57S 170 46E
90 Ngara, Tanzania 2 29S 30 40E
90 Ngara ♦, Tanzania 2 29S 30 40E
101 Ngau, I., Fiji 18 2S 179 18E
73 Ngawi, Indonesia 7 24S 111 26E
85 Ngetera, Nigeria 12 56N 10 29E
71 Ngha Lo, N. Vietnam 21 33N 104 28E
91 Ngoma, Malawi 13 8S 33 45E
91 Ngomahura, Rhodesia 20 33S 30 57E
91 Ngomba, Tanzania 8 20S 32 53E
84 Ngop, Sudan 6 17N 30 9E
84 Ngoring Nor, China 34 50N 98 0E
84 Ngorkou, Mali 15 40N 3 41W
90 Ngorongoro, Tanz. 3 11S 35 32E
90 Ngozi, Burundi 2 54S 29 50E
90 Ngudu, Tanzania 2 58S 33 25E
81 N'Guigrai, Niger 14 20N 13 20E
90 Ngunga, Tanzania 3 37S 33 37E
85 Ngungu, Sudan 8 22N 27 50E
85 Ngurru, Nigeria 12 56N 10 29E
90 Nguru Mts., Tanzania 6 0S 37 30E
93 Ngwenya, Swaziland 26 5S 31 7E
71 Nha Trang, S. Vietnam 12 16N 109 10E
93 Nhacoongo, Mozam. 24 18S 35 14E
93 Nhangulazi, Lago, 24 0S 34 30E
 Mozam.
93 Nhanvoo, L., Mozam. 22 0S 35 7E
100 Nhill, Australia 36 18S 141 40E
97 Nhulunbuy, Australia 12 25S 136 55E
84 Niafounké, Mali 16 0N 4 5W
114 Niagara, U.S.A. 45 45N 88 0W
106 Niagara Falls, N. Amer. 43 5N 79 5W

106 Niagara Falls, Can. 43 7N 79 5W
112 Niagara Falls, U.S.A. 43 5N 79 0W
112 Niagara-on-the-Lake, 43 15N 79 4W
 Canada
72 Niah, Malaysia 3 58S 113 46E
85 Niamey, Niger 13 27N 2 6E
84 Nianforando, Guinea 9 37N 10 36W
48 Nianfors, Sweden 61 36N 16 46E
90 Niangara, Zaïre 3 50N 27 50E
72 Nias, I., Indonesia 1 0N 97 40E
91 Niassa ♦, Mozam. 13 30S 36 0E
91 Niassa, Lago, Mozam. 12 30S 34 30E
38 Nibbiano, Italy 44 54N 9 20E
49 Nibe, Denmark 56 59N 9 38E
71 Nibong Tebal, Malaysia 5 10N 100 29E
121 Nicaragua ■, Central 11 40N 85 30W
 America
121 Nicaragua, Lago de, 12 50N 85 30W
 Nicaragua
41 Nicastro, Italy 39 0N 16 18E
29 Nice, France 43 42N 7 14E
115 Niceville, U.S.A. 30 30N 86 30W
74 Nichinan, Japan 31 28N 131 26E
121 Nicholas, Chan., W. Ind. 23 30N 80 30W
74 Nicholasville, U.S.A. 37 54N 84 31W
113 Nichols, U.S.A. 42 1N 76 22W
106 Nicholson, Canada 47 58N 83 47W
113 Nicholson, U.S.A. 41 37N 75 47W
60 Nicobar Is., Indian 9 0N 93 0E
 Ocean
108 Nicola, Canada 50 8N 120 40W
126 Nicolci, Colombia 8 26N 76 48W
106 Nicolet, Canada 46 17N 72 35W
60 Nicosia = Levkôsia, 35 10N 33 25E
 Cyprus
41 Nicosia, Italy 37 45N 14 22E
41 Nicótera, Italy 38 33N 15 57E
121 Nicoya, Golfo de, Costa 10 0N 85 0W
 Rica
121 Nicoya, Pen. de, Costa 9 45N 85 40W
 Rica
12 Nidd, R., England 54 1N 1 32W
24 Nidda, Germany 50 24N 9 2E
25 Nidda, R., Germany 50 25N 9 2E
24 Nidzica, Poland 53 25N 20 28E
24 Niebüll, Germany 54 47N 8 49E
24 Niederaula, Germany 50 48N 9 37E
19 Niederbronn, France 48 57N 7 39E
66 Niedere Tauern, Austria 47 18N 14 0E
24 Niedermarsberg, Ger. 51 30N 8 45E
26 Niederösterreich ◇, 48 25N 15 40E
 Austria
24 Niedersachsen ◇, 52 45N 9 0E
 Germany
31 Nisa, Portugal 39 30N 7 41W
28 Nisa, R., Poland 51 20N 15 0E
62 Nisab, South Yemen 14 25N 46 29E
43 Nisava, R., Yugoslavia 43 20N 22 10E
41 Niscemi, Italy 37 8N 14 21E
74 Nishinomiya, Japan 34 45N 135 20E
28 Nisiros, I., Greece 36 35N 27 12E
28 Nisko, Poland 50 35N 22 7E
49 Nisporeny, U.S.S.R. 47 4N 28 10E
98 Nissan I., Terr. of New 4 30S 154 10E
 Guinea
49 Nissan, Sweden 56 40N 12 51E
47 Nissedal, Norway 59 10N 8 30E
47 Nisser, Norway 59 7N 8 28E
49 Nissum Fjord, Denmark 56 20N 8 11E
85 Nitchequon, Canada 53 10N 70 58W
125 Niterói, Brazil 22 52S 43 0W
14 Nith, R., Scot. 55 20N 3 5W
27 Nitra, Czechoslovakia 48 19N 18 4E
27 Nitra, R., Cz. 48 30N 18 7E
47 Nittedal, Norway 60 1N 10 57E
101 Niuafo'ou, I., Tonga 15 30S 175 58W
101 Niue I. (Savage I.), Pac. 19 2S 169 54W
 Oc.
72 Niut, Mt., Indonesia 0 55N 109 30E
16 Nivelles, Belgium 50 35N 4 20E
19 Nivernais, Fr. 47 0N 3 40E
118 Nixon, Nev., U.S.A. 39 54N 119 22W
117 Nixon, Tex., U.S.A. 29 17N 97 45W
70 Nizam Sagar, India 18 10N 77 58E
70 Nizamabad, India 18 45N 78 7E
70 Nizamghat, India 28 20N 95 45E
59 Nizhanaya Tunguska, 64 20N 93 0E
 U.S.S.R.
59 Nizhneangarsk, U.S.S.R. 56 0N 109 30E
59 Nizhne Kolymsk, U.S.S.R. 68 40N 160 55E
58 Nizhne-Vartovskoye, 60 56N 76 38E
 U.S.S.R.
56 Nizhneserskiy, U.S.S.R. 45 27N 34 38E
59 Nizhneudinsk, U.S.S.R. 55 0N 99 20E
57 Nizhniy Baskunchak, 48 16N 46 52E
 U.S.S.R.
55 Nizhniy Novgorod = 56 20N 44 0E
 Gorkiy, U.S.S.R.
55 Nizhniy Lomov, 53 34N 43 38E
 U.S.S.R.
58 Nizhniy Tagil, U.S.S.R. 57 45N 60 0E
27 Nizké Tatry, Cz. 48 55N 20 0E
38 Nizza Monferrato, Italy 44 46N 8 22E
91 Njakwa, Malawi 11 1S 33 56E
91 Njinjo, Tanzania 8 48S 38 44E
91 Njombe, R., Tanzania 7 15S 34 20E
91 Njombe, Tanzania 9 20S 34 49E
85 Nkambe, Cameroon 6 35N 10 40E
91 Nkana, Zambia 13 0S 28 8E
85 Nkawkaw, Ghana 6 36N 0 49W
91 Nkhota Kota, Malawi 12 56S 34 15E
91 Nkongsamba, Cam. 4 55N 9 55E
91 Nkunka, Zambia 14 57S 25 58E

68 Nimach, India 24 30N 74 50E
68 Nimar, India 21 49N 76 22E
68 Nimba, Mt., Liberia 7 39N 8 30W
21 Nîmes, France 43 50N 4 23E
84 Nimfaion, Akra, Gr. 40 5N 24 20E
96 Nimingarra, Australia 20 31S 119 55E
100 Nimmitabel, Australia 36 29S 149 15E
59 Nimneryskiy, U.S.S.R. 58 0N 125 10E
87 Nimule, Sudan 3 32N 32 3E
39 Nin, Yugoslavia 44 16N 15 12E
108 Ninemile, Alaska 56 0N 130 7W
91 Ninety Mile Beach, New 34 45S 173 0E
 Zealand
100 Ninety Mile Beach, The, 38 30S 147 10E
 Austral.
76 Nineveh, Iraq 36 25N 43 10E
76 Ningan, China 44 16N 129 30E
77 Ninghwa, China 32 58N 119 59E
77 Ningming, China 22 10N 107 59E
77 Ningpo, China 29 50N 121 30E
77 Ningshan, China 33 11N 108 45E
77 Ningsia Hui ♦, China 37 45N 106 0E
77 Ningteh, China 26 45N 120 0E
67 Ningtsin, Tibet, China 29 44N 98 28E
77 Ningtu, China 26 30N 115 58E
77 Ningwu, China 39 2N 112 15E
71 Ninh Binh, N. Vietnam 20 15N 105 55E
77 Ninkiang, China 32 50N 106 20E
16 Ninove, Belgium 50 51N 4 2E
126 Nioaque, Brazil 21 5S 55 50W
116 Niobrara, U.S.A. 42 48N 97 59W
116 Niobrara, R., U.S.A. 42 30N 103 0W
88 Nioki, Zaïre 2 47S 17 40E
84 Niono, Mali 14 15N 6 0W
84 Nioro du Rip, Senegal 13 40N 15 50W
84 Nioro du Sahel, Mali 15 30N 9 30W
20 Niort, France 46 19N 0 29W
85 Niou, Upper Volta 12 42N 2 1W
98 Nipani, Austral. 24 45S 150 0E
70 Nipani, India 16 20N 74 25E
109 Nipawin, Canada 53 20N 104 0W
106 Nipigon, Canada 49 0N 88 17W
106 Nipigon, L., Can. 49 40N 88 30W
106 Nipissing L., Canada 46 20N 79 40W
119 Nipomo, U.S.A. 35 4N 120 29W
70 Nira, R., India 18 5N 74 25E
62 Nirim, Israel 31 14N 34 21E
70 Nirmal, India 19 3N 78 20E
69 Nirmali, India 26 20N 86 35E
43 Niš, Yugoslavia 43 19N 21 58E
29 Nisa, R., Poland 51 20N 15 0E

32 Noblejas, Spain 39 58N 3 26W
114 Noblesville, U.S.A. 40 1N 85 59W
38 Noce, R., Italy 46 22N 11 3E
41 Nocera Inferiore, Italy 40 45N 14 37E
41 Nocera Terinese, Italy 39 2N 16 9E
39 Nocera Umbra, Italy 43 8N 12 47E
41 Noci, Italy 40 47N 17 7E
99 Nockatunga, Australia 27 46S 142 36E
117 Nocona, U.S.A. 33 48N 97 45W
46 Nocrich, Rumania 45 55N 24 26E
59 Noda, U.S.S.R. 47 30N 142 5E
117 Noel, U.S.A. 36 36N 94 29W
120 Nogales, Mex. 31 36N 94 29W
119 Nogales, U.S.A. 31 33N 115 50W
74 Nogata, Japan 33 48N 130 54E
19 Nogent-en-Bassigny, Fr. 48 0N 5 20E
18 Nogent-le-Rotrou, Fr. 48 20N 0 50E
18 Nogent-sur-Seine, Fr. 48 30N 3 30E
55 Noginsk, Moskva, 55 50N 38 25E
 U.S.S.R.
59 Noginsk, Sib., U.S.S.R. 64 30N 90 50E
98 Nogoa, R., Australia 23 30S 148 20E
124 Nogoyá, Argentina 32 24S 59 48W
27 Nógrád ♦, Hungary 48 0N 19 30E
30 Nogueira de Ramuin, 42 21N 7 43W
 Spain
32 Noguera Pallaresa, R., 42 15N 1 0E
 Spain
32 Noguera Ribagorzana, 42 15N 0 45E
 R., Spain
68 Nohar, India 29 11N 74 49E
71 Noi, R., Thailand 14 50N 100 15E
18 Noire, Mts., France 48 11N 3 40W
20 Noirétable, France 45 48N 3 46E
18 Noirmoutier, France 47 0N 2 15W
18 Noirmoutier, I. de, Fr. 46 58N 2 10W
92 Nojane, Botswana 23 15S 20 14E
66 Nok Kundi, Pakistan 28 50N 62 45E
92 Nokaneng, Botswana 19 47S 22 17E
51 Nokhtuysk, U.S.S.R. 60 0N 117 45E
51 Nokia, Finland 61 30N 23 30E
109 Nokomis, Canada 51 35N 105 0W
88 Nokou, Chad 14 35N 14 47E
49 Nol, Sweden 57 56N 12 5E
88 Nola, Cent. Afr. Rep. 3 35N 16 10E
41 Nola, Italy 40 54N 14 29E
19 Nolay, France 46 58N 4 35E
48 Nolby, Sweden 62 17N 17 26E
38 Noli, C. di, Italy 44 12N 8 26E
55 Nolinsk, U.S.S.R. 57 28N 49 57E
92 Nmoa Omuramba, R., 19 6S 20 30E
 SW. Afr.
100 Nombinnie, Australia 32 56S 145 53E
104 Nome, Alaska 64 30N 165 30W
18 Nonancourt, France 48 47N 1 11E
18 Nonant-le-Pin, France 48 42N 0 12E
98 Nonda, Australia 20 40S 142 28E
71 Nong Khae, Thailand 14 29N 100 53E
71 Nong Khai, Thailand 17 50N 102 46E
87 Nono, Ethiopia 8 31N 37 28E
120 Nonoava, Mexico 27 22N 106 38W
45 Nonólithos, Greece 36 8N 27 46E
20 Nontron, France 45 31N 0 40E
100 Noojee, Australia 37 57S 146 1E
116 Noonan, U.S.A. 48 51N 103 1W
99 Noondoo, Australia 28 35S 148 30E
16 Noord Beveland, Neth. 51 45S 3 50E
16 Noord Brabant ♦, Neth. 51 40N 5 0E
16 Noord Holland ♦, Neth. 52 30N 4 45E
16 Noordoostpolder, Neth. 52 45N 5 45E
108 Nootka I., Canada 49 40N 126 50W
88 Noqui, Angola 5 55S 13 30E
48 Nora, Sweden 59 32N 15 2E
87 Nora, Ethiopia 16 6N 40 4E
100 Norah Head, Australia 33 15S 151 35E
106 Noranda, Canada 48 20N 79 0W
48 Norberg, Sweden 60 4N 15 56E
50 Norbottens län ♦, Swed. 66 58N 20 0E
39 Norcia, Italy 42 50N 13 5E
19 Nord ♦, France 50 15N 3 30E
24 Nord-Ostee Kanal, 54 5N 9 15E
 Germany
24 Nord-Süd Kanal, 53 0N 10 32E
 Germany
50 Nord-Trondelag Fylke 64 20N 12 0E
 ♦, Norway
47 Nordagutu, Norway 59 25N 9 20E
47 Nordaustlandet, Svalbard 79 55N 23 0E
49 Nordborg, Denmark 55 5N 9 50E
49 Nordby, Fanö, Den. 55 27N 8 24E
49 Nordby, Samsö, Den. 55 58N 10 32E
47 Norddal, Norway 62 15N 7 14E
49 Norddalsfjord kpl., 61 39N 5 23E
 Norway
24 Norddeich, Germany 53 29N 7 10E
108 Nordegg, Canada 52 29N 116 5W
24 Norden, Germany 53 35N 7 12E
24 Nordenham, Germany 53 29N 8 28E
47 Norderhov, Norway 60 7N 10 17E
24 Norderney, Germany 53 42N 7 9E
24 Norderney, I., Germany 53 42N 7 15E
49 Nordfjord, Sogn og 61 55N 5 30E
 Fjordane, Norway
49 Nordjyllands Amt ♦, 57 0N 10 0E
 Denmark
24 Nordhausen, Germany 51 29N 10 47E
24 Nordhorn, Germany 52-27N 7 4E
50 Nordkapp, Norway 71 10N 25 44E
4 Nordkapp, Svalbard 80 31N 20 0E
50 Nordland Fylke ♦, 65 40N 13 0E
 Norway
25 Nördlingen, Germany 48 50N 10 30E
24 Nordrhein-Westfalen ♦, 51 45N 7 30E
 Germany
24 Nordstrand, I., Germany 54 30N 8 55E
59 Nordvik, U.S.S.R. 73 40N 110 57E
47 Nore, Norway 60 10N 9 0E
47 Norefjell, Norway 60 16N 9 29E
47 Noresund, Norway 60 11N 9 37E

MAP
12 Norfolk ♦, Eng. 52 39N 1 0E
116 Norfolk, Nebr., U.S.A. 42 3N 97 25W
113 Norfolk, N.Y., U.S.A. 44 47N 75 1W
114 Norfolk, Va., U.S.A. 36 52N 76 15W
94 Norfolk I., Pacific 28 58s 168 3E
Ocean
117 Norfork Res., U.S.A. 36 25N 92 0W
59 Norilsk, U.S.S.R. 69 20N 88 0E
99 Norley, Australia 27 45s 143 48E
116 Normal, U.S.A. 40 30N 89 0W
117 Norman, U.S.A. 35 12N 97 30W
98 Norman, R., Australia 19 15s 142 10E
104 Norman Wells, Canada 65 40N 126 45W
98 Normanby I., Papua 9 55s 151 0E
14 Normanby, R., Australia 14 23s 144 10E
18 Normandie, France 48 45N 0 10E
18 Normandie, Collines de, 48 55N 0 45W
France
106 Normandin, Canada 48 49N 72 31W
18 Normandy = 48 45N 0 10E
Normandie, France
98 Normanton, Australia 17 40s 141 10E
128 Norquinco, Argentina 41 51s 70 55W
49 Norrahammar, Sweden 57 43N 14 7E
49 Nörre Aby, Denmark 55 27N 9 52E
49 Nörre Nebel, Denmark 55 47N 8 17E
49 Nörresundby, Denmark 57 5N 9 52E
118 Norris, U.S.A. 45 40N 111 48W
113 Norristown, U.S.A. 40 9N 75 15W
49 Norrköping, Sweden 58 37N 16 11E
48 Norrtälje, Sweden 59 46N 18 42E
96 Norseman, Australia 32 8s 121 43E
49 Norsholm, Sweden 58 31N 15 59E
50 Norsjö, Sweden 64 53N 19 30E
59 Norsk, U.S.S.R. 52 30N 130 0E
126 Norte de Santander ♦, 8 0N 73 0w
Col.
5 North C., Antarctica 71 0N 166 0E
107 North C., Canada 47 2N 60 20W
101 North C., New Zealand 34 23s 173 4E
4 North C., Spitsbergen 80 40N 20 0E
90 North I., Kenya 4 5N 36 5E
94 North I., New Zealand 38 0s 175 0E
113 North Adams, U.S.A. 42 42N 73 6W
71 North Andaman I., 13 15N 92 40E
India
6 North Atlantic Ocean 30 0N 50 0W
109 North Battleford, Can. 52 50N 108 10W
106 North Bay, Can. 46 20N 79 30W
106 North Belcher Is., Can. 56 30N 79 0W
108 North Bend, Canada 49 50N 121 35W
118 North Bend, Oreg., 43 28N 124 7w
U.S.A.
112 North Bend, Pa., U.S.A. 41 20N 77 42W
112 North Berwick, Scotland 56 4N 2 44W
113 North Berwick, U.S.A. 43 18N 70 43W
117 North Canadian, R., 36 48N 103 0W
U.S.A.
106 North Caribou L., Can. 52 50N 90 50W
115 North Carolina ♦, 35 30N 80 0w
U.S.A.
14 North Channel, Br. Is. 55 0N 5 30W
106 North Channel, North 46 0N 83 0w
America
114 North Chicago, U.S.A. 42 19N 87 50W
116 North Dakota ♦, U.S.A. 47 30N 100 0W
13 North Downs, England 51 17N 0 30W
112 North East, U.S.A. 42 17N 79 50W
67 North East Frontier 28 0N 95 0E
Agency ♦, India
4 N.E. Land, Spitsbergen 80 0N 24 0E
†98 N.E. New Guinea, Terr. 5 30s 144 30E
of ♦, N. Guin.
90 North Eastern ♦, Kenya 1.30N 40 0E
14 North Esk, R., Scotland 56 54N 2 45W
9 North European Plain, £ 55 0N 25 0E
13 N. Foreland, Pt., 51 22N 1 28E
England
24 N. Frisian 54 50N 8 20E
Is. = Nordfr'sche Inseln, Ger
90 North Horr, Kenya 3 20N 37 8E
108 North Kamloops, Can. 50 40N 120 25W
112 North Kingsville, U.S.A. 41 53N 80 42W
109 North Knife L., Canada 58 0N 97 0W
69 North Koel, R., India 23 50N 84 5E
76 North Korea ■, Asia 40 0N 127 0E
67 N. Lakhimpur, India 27 15N 94 10E
119 N. Las Vegas, U.S.A. 36 15N 115 6w
90 North Mara ♦, Tanzania 1 20s 34 20E
14 North Minch, Scot. 58 5N 5 55W
57 North Ossetian A.S.S.R. 43 30N 44 30E
♦, U.S.S.R.
119 North Palisade, U.S.A. 37 6N 118 32W
116 North Platte, U.S.A. 41 10N 100 50W
118 North Platte, R., U.S.A. 42 50N 106 50W
107 North Pt., Canada 47 5N 65 0w
4 North Pole, Arctic Reg. 90 0N 0 0E
118 North Powder, U.S.A. 45 2N 117 59W
* 12 North Riding ♦, Eng. 54 22N 1 30W
14 North Ronaldsay, I., 59 20N 2 30W
Scotland
8 North Sea, N. W. 56 0N 4 0E
Europe
45 North Sporades = 39 0N 24 10E
Voriai Sporádhes
99 North Stradbroke I., 27 30s 153 34E
Australia
107 North Sydney, Canada 46 12N 60 21W
56 N. Taranaki Bt., N.Z. 38 45s 174 20E
112 N. Tonawanda, U.S.A. 43 0N 78 50W
113 North Troy, U.S.A. 44 59N 72 24W
119 N. Truchas Pk., U.S.A. 36 0N 105 30w
106 North Twin I., Canada 53 20N 80 0W
14 North Tyne, R., Scot. 55 12N 2 30w
14 North Uist I., Scotland 57 40N 7 15W
108 North Vancouver, Can. 49 25N 123 20W
108 North Vermilion, Can. 58 25N 116 0w
114 North Vernon, U.S.A. 39 0N 85 35W
71 North Vietnam ■, Asia 22 0N 105 0E
100 North Village, Bermuda 32 15N 64 45W

12 North Walsham, 52 49N 1 22E
England
96 N.W.Basin, Austral. 25 45s 115 0E
96 North West C., 21 45s 114 9E
Australia
14 North West Highlands, 57 35N 5 2w
Scot.
121 N.W. Providence Chan., 26 0N 78 0w
W. Indies
107 North West River, Can. 53 30N 60 10W
104 Northwest Terr., Can. 65 0N 100 0w
91 North Western ♦, Zam. 13 30s 25 30E
12 North York Moors, 54 25N 0 50W
England
12 Northallerton, Eng. 54 20N 1 26w
96 Northam, Australia 31 35s 116 42w
91 Northam, S. Africa 24 55s 27 15E
96 Northampton, Australia 28 21s 114 33E
13 Northampton, England 52 14N 0 54w
113 Northampton, Mass., 42 22N 72 39W
U.S.A.
113 Northampton, Pa., 40 38N 75 24w
U.S.A.
96 Northampton, Australia 28 21s 114 33E
13 Northampton ♦, 52 16N 0 55W
England
98 Northampton Downs, 24 35s 145 48E
Austral.
113 Northbridge, U.S.A. 42 12N 71 40w
121 Northeast Providence 26 0N 76 0w
Channel, W. Indies
24 Northeim, Germany 51 42N 10 0E
91 Northern ♦, Malawi 11 0s 34 0E
87 Northern ♦, Sudan 19 0N 31 0E
91 Northern ♦, Zam. 10 30s 31 0E
70 Northern Circars, India 17 30N 82 30E
101 Northern Group, Cook 10 00s 160 00w
Is.
15 Northern Ireland ♦, 54 45N 7 0w
U.K.
106 Northern Lights L., Can. 49 15N 90 45w
84 Northern Province ♦, 9 0s 1J 30w
Sierra Leone
96 Northern Territory ♦, 16 0s 133 0E
Australia
116 Northfield, U.S.A. 44 37N 93 10w
115 Northport, Ala., U.S.A. 33 15N 87 35w
112 Northport, Mich., U.S.A. 45 8N 85 39W
118 Northport, Wash., 48 57N 117 56w
U.S.A.
12 Northumberland ♦, 55 12N 2 0W
England
98 Northumberland Is., 21 45s 150 20E
Austral.
107 Northumberland Str., 46 20N 64 0w
Canada
13 Northwich, Eng. 53 16N 2 30w
116 Northwood, Iowa, 43 27N 93 12w
U.S.A.
116 Northwood, N.D., 47 44N 97 30w
U.S.A.
91 Norton, Rhodesia 17 52s 30 40E
116 Norton, U.S.A. 39 50N 100 0w
104 Norton Sd., Alaska 64 0N 165 0w
24 Nortorf, Germany 54 14N 10 47E
113 Norwalk, Conn., U.S.A. 41 9N 73 25w
113 Norwalk, Ohio, U.S.A. 41 13N 82 38W
50 Norway ■, Eur. 67 0N 11 0E
114 Norway, U.S.A. 45 46N 87 57w
109 Norway House, Canada 53 55N 98 50W
5 Norwegian Dependency, 66 0N 15 0E
Antarctica
6 Norwegian Sea, North 66 0N 1 0E
Atlantic Ocean
112 Norwich, Canada 43 1N 80 39w
13 Norwich, England 52 38N 1 17E
113 Norwich, Conn., U.S.A. 41 33N 72 5w
113 Norwich, N.Y., U.S.A. 42 32N 75 30w
112 Norwich, Canada 44 25N 77 59w
113 Norwood, U.S.A. 42 10N 71 10w
56 Noshiro, R., Japan 40 15N 140 15E
58 Nosok, U.S.S.R. 70 10N 82 20E
58 Nosovka, U.S.S.R. 50 50N 31 30E
65 Nosratābād, Iran 29 55N 60 0E
14 Noss Hd., Scot. 58 29N 3 4w
49 Nossebro, Sweden 58 12N 12 43E
92 Nossob, S.W. Africa 22 15s 17 48E
92 Nossob, R., Africa 25 15s 20 30E
109 Notigi Dam, Canada 56 35N 99 0w
108 Notikewin, Canada 56 55N 117 50w
45 Notios Evvoïkós Kólpos, 38 20N 24 0E
Greece
77 Notituchow, China 24 25N 107 20E
41 Noto, Italy 36 52N 15 4E
41 Noto, G. di, Italy 36 50N 15 10E
47 Notodden, Norway 59 35N 9 17E
56 Noto-Hanto, Japan 37 0N 137 0E
107 Notre Dame, Canada 46 18N 64 46w
107 Notre Dame B., Canada 49 45N 55 30w
105 Notre Dame de Koartac, 60 55N 69 40w
Canada
105 Notre Dame d'Ivugivic, 62 20N 78 0w
Canada
107 Notre-Dame, R., Canada 50 50N 78 20w
47 Nötterøy, Norway 59 14N 10 24E
12 Nottingham, England 52 57N 1 10w
13 Nottingham ♦, England 53 10N 1 0w
114 Nottoway, R., U.S.A. 37 0N 77 45w
21 Notwani, R., Botswana 24 14s 26 20E
80 Nouadhibou, Mauritania 21 0N 17 0w
84 Nouakchott, Mauritania 20 10N 57 0w
94 Nouméa, New Caledonia 22 17s 166 30E
92 Noupoort, S. Africa 31 10s 24 57E
106 Nouveau Comptoir 53 2N 78 55w
(Paint Hills), Canada
94 Nouvelle Calédonie, 21 0s 165 0E
Pacific Ocean
19 Nouzonville, France 49 48N 4 44E
57 Novaleksandrovskaya, 45 29N 41 17E
U.S.S.R.

55 Nova-Annenskiy, 50 32N 42 39E
U.S.S.R.
27 Nová Bana, Cz. 48 28N 18 39E
26 Nova Bystrice, Cz. 49 2N 15 8E
88 Nova Chaves, Angola 10 50s 21 15E
127 Nova Cruz, Brazil 6 28s 35 25w
125 Nova Esperança, Brazil 23 8s 52 13w
127 Nova Friburgo, Brazil 22 10s 42 30w
88 Nova Gaia, Angola 10 10s 17 35E
42 Nova Gradiška, Y.-slav. 45 17N 17 28E
125 Nova Iguaçu, Brazil 22 45s 43 28w
127 Nova Iorque, Brazil 7 0s 44 5w
84 Nova Lamego, 12 19N 14 11w
Portuguese Guinea
127 Nova Lima, Brazil 19 59s 43 51w
89 Nova Lisboa, Angola 12 42s 15 54E
91 Nova Lusitânia, Mozam. 19 50s 34 34E
93 Nova Mambone, 21 0s 35 3E
Mozambique
39 Novo Mesto, Y.-slavia 45 47N 15 12E
26 Nova Paka, Cz. 50 29N 15 30E
73 Nova Sagres = Tutuaia, 8 25s 127 15E
Port. Timor
107 Nova Scotia ♦, Canada 45 10N 63 0w
93 Nova Sofala, Mozam. 20 7s 34 48E
42 Nova Varoš, Y.-slavia 43 29N 19 48E
127 Nova Venécia, Brazil 18 45s 40 24w
43 Nova Zagora, Bulgaria 42 32N 25 59E
46 Novaci, Rumania 45 10N 23 42E
42 Novaci, Yugoslavia 41 5N 21 29E
127 Novalorque, Brazil 6 48s 44 0w
38 Novara, Italy 45 27N 8 36E
56 Novaya Kakhovka, 46 42N 33 27E
U.S.S.R.
52 Novaya Ladoga, 60 7N 32 16E
U.S.S.R.
58 Novaya Lyalya, U.S.S.R. 58 50N 60 35E
59 Novaya Sibir, O., 75 10N 150 0E
U.S.S.R.
58 Novaya Zemlya, 75 0N 56 0E
U.S.S.R.
27 Nové Mésto, Cz. 49 33N 16 7E
33 Novelda, Spain 38 24N 0 45W
38 Novellara, Italy 44 50N 10 43E
39 Noventa Vicentina, It. 45 18N 11 30E
54 Novgorod, U.S.S.R. 58 30N 31 25E
54 Novgorod Severskiy, 52 2N 33 10E
U.S.S.R.
54 Novgorod Volynski, 50 38N 27 47E
U.S.S.R.
42 Novi Bečej, Y.-slavia 45 36N 20 10E
42 Novi Grad, Y.-slavia 45 19N 13 33E
42 Novi Knezeva, Y.-slav. 46 4N 20 8E
43 Novi Krichim, Bulgaria 42 22N 24 31E
38 Novi Ligure, Italy 44 45N 8 47E
43 Novi-Pazar, Bulgaria 43 25N 27 15E
42 Novi Pazar, Yugoslavia 43 12N 20 28E
42 Novi Sad, Yugoslavia 45 18N 19 52E
39 Novi Vinodolski, 45 10N 14 48E
Y.-slavia
39 Novigrad, Yugoslavia 44 10N 15 32E
54 Novoataysk, U.S.S.R. 53 30N 84 0E
91 Novo Freixo, 14 49s 36 30E
Mozambique
125 Nôvo Hamburgo, Braz. 29 37s 51 7w
88 Nova Redondo, Angola 11 10s 13 48E
42 Novo Selo, Bulgaria 44 11N 22 47E
55 Novo-Zavidovskiy, 56 32N 36 29E
U.S.S.R.
56 Novoazovsk, U.S.S.R. 47 15N 38 4E
54 Novobelitsa, U.S.S.R. 52 27N 31 2E
57 Novobogatinskoye, 47 26N 51 17E
U.S.S.R.
57 Novocherkassk, U.S.S.R. 47 27N 40 5E
54 Novodevichye, U.S.S.R. 53 37N 48 58E
54 Novograd Volynskiy, 50 40N 27 35E
U.S.S.R.
54 Novogrudok, U.S.S.R. 53 40N 25 50E
56 Novokayakent, U.S.S.R. 42 45N 48 41E
54 Novokazalinsk, U.S.S.R. 45 48N 62 6E
56 Novokhopersk, U.S.S.R. 51 5N 41 50E
56 Novokuznetsk, U.S.S.R. 54 0N 87 10E
56 Novomirgorod, U.S.S.R. 48 57N 31 33E
54 Novomoskovsk, 54 5N 38 15E
R.S.F.S.R., U.S.S.R.
56 Novomoskovsk, 48 33N 35 17E
Ukrainian S.S.R., U.S.S.R.
54 Novopolotsk, U.S.S.R. 55 38N 28 37E
57 Novorossiysk, U.S.S.R. 44 43N 37 52E
54 Novorzhev, U.S.S.R. 57 3N 29 25E
54 Novoselitsa, U.S.S.R. 48 14N 26 15E
57 Novoshakhtinsk, 47 39N 39 58E
U.S.S.R.
56 Novosibirsk, U.S.S.R. 55 0N 83 5E
59 Novosibirskiye Ostrava, 75 0N 140 0E
U.S.S.R.
54 Novosil, U.S.S.R. 52 58N 36 58E
54 Novosokolniki, U.S.S.R. 56 33N 28 42E
54 Novotroitsk, U.S.S.R. 51 10N 58 15E
54 Novotulskiy, U.S.S.R. 54 10N 37 36E
56 Novoukrainka, U.S.S.R. 46 25N 31 30E
54 Novouzensk, U.S.S.R. 50 32N 48 17E
54 Novovolynsk, U.S.S.R. 50 45N 24 4E
54 Novovyatsk, U.S.S.R. 58 24N 49 45E
42 Novska, Yugoslavia 45 19N 17 0E
56 Novy Bug, U.S.S.R. 47 34N 32 29E
26 Novy Bydzov, Cz. 50 14N 15 29E
27 Novy Jicin, Cz. 49 15N 18 0E
28 Novy Dwór, Poland 52 26N 20 44E
58 Novyy Oskol, U.S.S.R. 50 44N 37 55E
58 Novyy Port, U.S.S.R. 67 40N 72 30E
46 Novyye Aneny, U.S.S.R. 46 51N 29 13E
65 Now Shahr, Iran 36 40N 51 30E
28 Nowa Deba, Poland 50 26N 21 41E
28 Nowa Skalmierzyce, 51 43N 18 0E
Poland
100 Nowa Nowa, Australia 37 44s 148 3E
28 Nowa Sól, Poland 51 48N 15 44E
28 Nowe, Poland 53 41N 18 44E

28 Mowe Miasteczko, 51 42N 15 42E
Poland
28 Nowe Miasto, Łódz, 52 38N 20 34E
Pol.
28 Nowe Miasto, 53 27N 19 33E
Lubowskie, Poland
28 Nowe Warpno, Poland 53 42N 14 18E
31 Nowendoc, Australia 31 32s 151 44E
67 Nowgong, India 26 20N 92 50E
28 Nowingi, Australia 34 33s 142 15E
28 Nowogard, Poland 53 41N 15 10E
28 Nowogród, Poland 53 14N 21 53E
100 Nowra, Australia 34 53s 150 35E
66 Nowshera, Pakistan 34 0N 71 55E
28 Nowy Dwór, Białystok, 53 40N 23 0E
Poland
28 Nowy Dwór, Warszawa, 52 27N 20 44E
Poland
28 Nowy Korczyn, Poland 50 19N 20 48E
27 Nowy Sacz, Poland 49 40N 20 41E
28 Nowy Staw, Poland 54 13N 19 2E
28 Nowy Targ, Poland 49 30N 20 2E
28 Nowy Tomyśl, Poland 52 19N 16 10E
113 Noxen, U.S.A. 41 25N 76 4E
118 Noxon, U.S.A. 48 0N 115 54w
30 Noya, Spain 42 48N 8 53w
19 Noyant, France 47 30N 0 6E
19 Noyers, France 47 40N 4 0E
108 Noyes, I., Alaska 55 30N 133 40w
19 Noyon, France 49 34N 3 0E
82 Nriquinha, Angola 16 0s 21 25E
82 Nsa, O. en, Algeria 32 23N 5 20E
85 Nsanje, Malawi 16 55s 35 12E
85 Nsawam, Ghana 5 50N 0 24w
85 Nsukka, Nigeria 7 0N 7 50E
91 Nuanetsi, R., Rhodesia 21 10s 31 20E
84 Nuatja, Togo 7 0N 1 10E
87 Nuba Mts. = Nubâh, 12 0N 31 0E
Jibâlan, Sudan
87 Nubâh, Jibâlan, Sudan 12 0N 31 0E
86 Nûbiya, Es Sahrâ En, 21 30N 33 30E
Sudan
124 Nuble ♦, Chile 37 0s 72 0w
73 Nuboai, Indonesia 2 10s 136 30E
126 Nudo Ausangate, Mt., 13 45s 71 10w
Peru
126 Nudo de Vilcanota, Peru 14 30s 70 0w
63 Nudushan, Iran 32 2s 53 20E
117 Nueces, R., U.S.A. 28 18N 98 39w
109 Nueltin L., Canada 60 0N 100 0w
126 Nueva Antioquia, Col. 6 5N 69 26w
126 Nueva Esparta ♦, Ven. 11 0N 64 0w
128 Nueva Gerona, Cuba 21 53N 82 49w
128 Nueva Imperial, Chile 38 45s 72 58w
120 Nueva Palmira, Urug. 33 52s 58 20w
120 Nueva Rosita, Mexico 28 0N 101 20w
120 Nueva San Salvador, 13 40N 89 25w
Salvador
124 Nuéve de Julio, Arg. 35 30s 61 0w
128 Nuevitas, Cuba 21 30N 77 20w
128 Nuevo, Golfo, Argentina 43 0s 64 30w
120 Nuevo Laredo, Mexico 27 30N 99 40w
120 Nuevo León ♦, Mex. 25 0N 100 0w
126 Nuevo Rocafuerte, 0 55s 76 50w
Ecuador
101 Nugget Pt., N.Z. 46 27s 169 50E
21 Nugrus Gebel, Egypt 24 58N 39 34E
101 Nuhaka, New Zealand 39 3s 177 45E
3 Nuhurowa, I., Indon. 5 30s 132 45E
107 Numaksaluk, I., Canada 55 40N 60 12w
13 Nuneaton, England 52 32N 1 29w
91 Nungo, Mozambique 13 23s 37 43E
90 Nungwe, Tanzania 2 48s 32 2E
104 Nunivak I., Alaska 60 0N 166 0w
66 Nunkun, Mt., Kashmir 33 57N 76 8E
16 Nunspeet, Netherlands 52 21N 5 45E
40 Nuoro, Italy 40 20N 9 20E
21 Nuquay, Jabal, Libya 23 11N 19 30E
126 Nuqui, Colombia 5 42N 77 17w
100 Nurcoung, Australia 36 45s 141 42E
40 Nure, R., Italy 44 40N 9 32E
25 Nuremburg = Nürnberg, 49 26N 11 5E
Germany
99 Nuriootpa, Australia 34 27s 139 0E
54 Nurlat, U.S.S.R. 54 29N 50 45E
25 Nürnberg, Germany 49 26N 11 5E
91 Nurri, Sardinia 39 43N 9 13E
70 Nurzvid, India 16 47N 80 53E
73 Nusa Barung, Indonesia 8 22s 113 20E
73 Nusa Kambangan, 7 47s 109 0E
Indonesia
72 Nusa Tenggara ♦, 7 30s 117 0E
Indon.
72 Nusa Tenggara Barat, 8 50s 117 30E
Indon.
73 Nusa Tenggara Timur, 9 30s 122 0E
Indon
66 Nushki, Pakistan 29 35N 65 65E
105 Nutak, Canada 57 30N 61 59w
86 Nuwaiba, Egypt 28 58N 34 40E
84 Nuwakot, Nepal 28 10N 83 55E
70 Nuwara Eliya, Sri 6 58N 80 55E
Lanka

92 Nuwefontein, S.W. Afr. 28 1s 19 6E
92 Nuweveldberge, S. 32 10s 21 45E
Africa
96 Nuyts, Pt., Australia 35 4s 116 38E
84 Nyaake (Webo), Liberia 4 52N 7 37E
96 Nyabing, Australia 33 30s 118 7E
113 Nyack, U.S.A. 41 5N 73 57w
48 Nyadal, Sweden 62 48N 17 59E
58 Nyagyn, U.S.S.R. 62 8N 63 36E
100 Nyah, Australia 35 12s 143 21E
100 Nyah West, Australia 35 11s 143 21E
90 Nyahanga, Tanz. 2 20s 33 37E
90 Nyahururu, Tanzania 5 25s 33 23E
90 Nyakanazi, Tanzania 3 2s 31 10E
90 Nyakasu, Burundi 3 58s 30 6E
85 Nyakrom, Ghana 5 40N 0 50w
87 Nyâlâ, Sudan 12 2N 24 58E
91 Nyamandhlovu, Rhod. 19 55s 28 16E
90 Nyambiti, Tanzania 2 48s 33 27E
90 Nyamwaga, Tanz. 1 27s 34 33E
90 Nyandekwa, Tanz. 3 57s 32 32E
92 Nyangana, S.W. Africa 18 0s 20 40E
91 Nyangue, Tanz. 2 30s 33 12E
91 Nyangwena, Zambia 15 18s 28 45E
91 Nyanji, Zambia 14 25s 31 46E
85 Nyankpala, Ghana 9 21N 0 58W
90 Nyanza, Burundi 4 21s 29 36E
90 Nyanza, Rwanda 2 20s 29 42E
90 Nyanza ♦, Kenya 0 10s 34 15E
91 Nyasa = L. = Malawi, 12 0s 34 30E
L., E. Africa
71 Nyaunglebin, Burma 17 52N 96 42E
91 Nyazwidzi, R., Rhod. 19 35s 32 0E
49 Nyborg, Denmark 55 18N 10 47E
58 Nyboro, Sweden 56 44N 15 55E
58 Nyda, U.S.S.R. 66 40N 73 10E
67 Nyenchen Tanglha Shan, 30 30N 95 0E
China
90 Nyeri, Kenya 0 23s 36 56E
90 Nyeri ♦, Kenya 0 25s 36 55E
87 Nyerol, Sudan 8 41N 32 1E
87 Nyiel, Sudan 6 9N 31 4E
91 Nyika Plat., Malawi 10 30s 36 0E
91 Nyilumba, Tanz. 10 30s 40 22E
84 Nyinahin, Ghana 6 43N 2 3w
27 Nyirbátor, Hungary 47 49N 22 9E
27 Nyiregyháza, Hungary 48 0N 21 47E
49 Nykarleby 63 32N 22 31E
(Uusikaarlepyy), Finland
49 Nyköbing, Falster, 54 56N 11 52E
Denmark
49 Nyköbing, Mors, 56 48N 8 51E
Denmark
49 Nyköbing, Sjaelland, 55 55N 11 40E
Denmark
49 Nyköbing, Tisted, Den. 56 49N 8 50E
48 Nykroppa, Sweden 59 37N 14 18E
48 Nykvarn, Sweden 59 11N 17 25E
48 Nyland, Sweden 63 1N 17 45E
49 Nylstroom, S. Africa 24 42s 28 22E
100 Nymagee, Australia 32 7s 146 20E
49 Nymburk, Cz. 50 10N 15 1E
48 Nynäshamn, Sweden 58 54N 17 57E
100 Nyngan, Australia 31 30s 147 8E
25 Nyon, Switzerland 46 23N 6 14E
21 Nyons, France 44 22N 5 10E
100 Nyora, Australia 38 20s 145 41E
47 Nyord, Denmark 55 4N 12 13E
28 Nysa, Poland 50 40N 17 22E
24 Nysa, R., Pol.-Ger. 51 0N 15 0E
118 Nyssa, U.S.A. 43 56N 117 2w
49 Nysted, Denmark 54 40N 11 44E
90 Nyunzu, Zaïre 5 57s 27 58E
59 Nyurba, U.S.S.R. 63 17N 118 20E
90 Nzega, Tanzania 4 10s 33 12E
90 Nzega ♦, Tanz. 4 10s 33 10E
84 N'Zérékore, Guinea 7 49N 8 48w
91 Nzilo, Chutes de, Zaïre 10 18s 25 27E
90 Nzubuka, Tanzania 4 45s 32 50E
74 O-shima, Japan 34 45N 139 25E
116 Oacoma, U.S.A. 43 50N 99 26w
116 Oahe, U.S.A. 44 33N 100 29w
116 Oahe Dam, U.S.A. 44 28N 100 25w
116 Oahe Res, U.S.A. 45 30N 100 25w
100 Oahu, I., Hawaii 21 30N 158 0w
118 Oak Creek, U.S.A. 40 15N 106 50w
118 Oak Harb., U.S.A. 48 20N 122 38w
109 Oak Lake, Canada 49 45N 100 45w
114 Oak Park, U.S.A. 41 55N 87 45w
115 Oak Ridge, U.S.A. 36 1N 84 5w
99 Oakbank, Australia 33 0s 140 20E
119 Oakdale, Calif., U.S.A. 37 49N 120 56w
117 Oakdale, La., U.S.A. 30 50N 92 38w
12 Oakengates, Eng. 52 42N 2 29w
116 Oakes, U.S.A. 46 14N 98 4w
118 Oakesdale, U.S.A. 47 11N 117 9w
99 Oakey, Austral. 27 25s 151 43E
12 Oakham, Eng. 52 40N 0 43w
114 Oakhill, U.S.A. 38 0N 81 7w
114 Oakland, U.S.A. 37 50N 122 18w
114 Oakland City, U.S.A. 38 20N 87 20w
100 Oaklands, Australia 35 34s 146 10E
100 Oakleigh, Austral. 37 54s 145 6E
116 Oakley, U.S.A. 42 14N 113 55w
118 Oakridge, U.S.A. 43 51N 122 31w
116 Oakwood, U.S.A. 31 35N 95 47w
46 Oancea, Rumania 45 4N 28 7E
5 Oates Coast, Antarctica 69 0s 160 0E
12 Oatman, U.S.A. 35 1N 114 19w
120 Oaxaca, Mexico 17 2N 96 40w
120 Oaxaca ♦, Mexico 17 0N 97 0w
106 Oba, Canada 49 4N 84 7w
85 Obala, Cameroon 4 9N 11 32E
101 Oban, New Zealand 46 55s 168 10E
14 Oban, Scotland 56 25N 5 30w
106 Obatogamau L., Can. 49 34N 74 26w
63 Obbia, Somali Rep. 5 25N 48 30E

*Incorporated within the county of North Yorkshire
† Incorporated in Papua New Guinea

MAP

108 Obed, Canada 53 30N 117 10W
65 Obeh, Afghanistan 34 28N 63 10E
125 Obera, Argentina 27 21s 55 2W
25 Oberengadin, Switz. 46 35N 9 55E
25 Oberammergau, Ger. 47 35N 11 3E
26 Oberdrauburg, Austria 46 44N 12 58E
24 Oberhausen, Germany 51 28N 6 50E
116 Oberlin, Kans., U.S.A. 39 52N 100 31W
117 Oberlin. La., U.S.A. 30 42N 92 42W
112 Oberlin, Ohio, U.S.A. 41 15N 82 10W
19 Obernai, France 48 28N 7 30E
25 Oberndorf, Germany 48 17N 8 35E
100 Oberon, Austral. 33 45s 149 52E
26 Oberösterreich ♦, Austria 48 10N 14 0E
25 Oberpfalzer Wald, Germany 49 30N 12 25E
25 Oberstdorf, Germany 47 25N 10 16E
73 Obi, Kepulauan, Indonesia 1 30s 127 30E
85 Obiaruku, Nigeria 5 51N 6 9E
127 Obidos, Brazil 1 50s 55 30W
31 Obidos, Portugal 39 19N 9 10W
74 Obihiro, Japan 42 55N 143 10E
72 Obilnoye, U.S.S.R. 47 32N 44 30E
24 Obisfelde, Germany 52 27N 10 57E
126 Obispos, Venezuela 8 36N 70 5W
20 Objat, France 45 16N 1 24E
59 Obluchye, U.S.S.R. 49 10N 130 50E
55 Obninsk, U.S.S.R. 55 8N 36 13E
87 Obo, Cent. Afr. Rep. 5 20N 26 32E
87 Obo, Ethiopia 3 34N 38 52E
90 Oboa, Mt., Uganda 1 45N 34 45E
87 Obock, F.T.A. & I. 12 0N 43 20E
28 Oborniki, Poland 52 39N 16 59E
28 Oborniki Sl. Poland 51 17N 16 53E
87 Obot, Ethiopia 4 32N 37 13E
85 Obout, Cameroon 3 28N 11 47E
55 Oboyan, U.S.S.R. 51 20N 36 28E
52 Obozerskaya, U.S.S.R. 63 20N 40 15E
42 Obrenovac, Yugoslavia 44 40N 20 11E
39 Obrovac, Yugoslavia 44 11N 15 41E
59 Obshchi Syrt, U.S.S.R. 52 0N 53 0E
58 Obskaya Guba, U.S.S.R. 70 0N 73 0E
85 Obuasi, Ghana 6 17N 1 40W
85 Obubra, Nigeria 6 8N 8 20E
43 Obzor, Bulgaria 42 50N 27 52E
115 Ocala, U.S.A. 29 11N 82 5W
120 Ocampo, Mexico 28 9N 108 8W
32 Ocaña, Spain 39 55N 3 30W
116 Ocanomowoc, U.S.A. 43 7N 88 30W
117 Ocate, U.S.A. 36 12N 104 59W
126 Occidental, Cordillera, Col. 5 0N 76 0W
114 Ocean City, U.S.A. 39 18N 74 34W
108 Ocean Falls, Canada 52 25N 127 40W
94 Ocean I., Pacific Ocean 0 45s 169 50E
118 Ocean Park, U.S.A. 46 30N 124 2W
118 Oceanlake, U.S.A. 45 0N 124 0W
113 Oceanport, U.S.A. 40 20N 74 3W
119 Oceanside, U.S.A. 33 13N 117 26W
32 Ochagavia, Spain 42 55N 1 5W
56 Ochakov, U.S.S.R. 46 35N 31 30E
57 Ochamchire, U.S.S.R. 42 46N 41 32E
14 Ochil Hills, Scot. 56 14N 3 40W
25 Ochsenfurt, Germany 49 38N 10 3E
115 Ocilla, U.S.A. 31 35N 83 12W
48 Ockelbo, Sweden 60 54N 16 45E
115 Ocmulgee, R., U.S.A. 32 0N 83 19W
46 Ocna Mure Sului, Rum. 46 23N 23 49E
46 Ocna-Sibiului, Rum. 45 52N 24 2E
46 Ocnele Mari, Rumania 45 8N 24 18E
115 Oconee, R., U.S.A. 32 30N 82 55W
114 Oconto, U.S.A. 44 52N 87 53W
114 Oconto Falls, U.S.A. 44 52N 88 10W
121 Ocotal, Nicaragua 13 41N 86 41W
120 Ocotlán, Mexico 20 21N 102 42W
30 Ocreza, R., Portugal 39 50N 7 35W
27 Ocsa, Hungary 47 17N 19 15E
119 Octave, U.S.A. 34 10N 112 43W
18 Octeville, France 49 38N 1 40W
59 Octyabrskoy Revolyutsii, Os., U.S.S.R. 79 30N 97 0E
126 Ocumare del Tuy, Venez. 10 7N 66 46W
72 Ocussi, Port Timor 9 20s 124 30E
85 Oda, Ghana 5 50N 1 5W
50 Óðáðahraun, Ice. 65 5N 17 0W
49 Odákra, Sweden 56 9N 12 45E
92 Odanakumadona, Bots. 20 55s 24 46E
74 Odawara, Japan 35 20N 139 6E
47 Odda, Norway 60 3N 6 35E
49 Odder, Denmark 55 58N 10 10E
87 Odobobo, Ethiopia 12 11N 42 6E
63 Oddur, Somali Rep. 4 0N 43 35E
49 Odeborg, Sweden 58 33N 12 0E
31 Odenira, Portugal 37 35N 8 40W
64 Odemiş, Turkey 38 15N 28 0E
49 Odense, Denmark 55 22N 10 23E
24 Odenwald, Germany 49 18N 9 0E
24 Oder, R., Germany 53 0N 14 12E
39 Oderzo, Italy 45 47N 12 29E
113 Odessa, Canada 44 16N 76 42W
117 Odessa, Tex., U.S.A. 31 51N 102 23W
118 Odessa, Wash., U.S.A. 47 20N 118 35W
56 Odessa, U.S.S.R. 46 30N 30 45E
31 Odiel, R., Spain 37 30N 6 55W
84 Odienné, Ivory Coast 9 30N 7 34W
85 Odoben, Ghana 5 38N 0 56E
46 Odobeşti, Rumania 45 43N 27 4E
28 Odolanów, Poland 51 34N 17 40E
117 O'Donnell, U.S.A. 33 0N 101 48W
46 Odorhei, Rumania 46 21N 25 21E
55 Odoyevo, U.S.S.R. 53 56N 36 42E
27 Odra, R., Cz. 49 43N 17 47E
28 Odra, R., Poland 52 40N 14 28E
30 Odra, R., Spain 42 30N 4 15W
42 Odzaci, Yugoslavia 45 30N 19 17E
42 Odzak, Yugoslavia 45 3N 18 18E

127 Oeiras, Brazil 7 0s 42 8W
31 Oeiras, Portugal 38 41N 9 18W
116 Oelrichs, U.S.A. 43 11N 103 14W
24 Oelsnitz, Germany 50 24N 12 11E
116 Oelwein, U.S.A. 42 39N 91 55W
41 Ofanto, R., Italy 41 8N 15 50E
25 Offenbach, Germany 50 6N 8 46E
48 Offerdal, Sweden 63 28N 14 0E
39 Offida, Italy 42 56N 13 40E
18 Offranville, France 49 52N 1 0E
45 Ofidhousa, I., Greece 36 33N 26 8E
47 Ofotfjorden, Norway 68 27N 16 40E
106 Ogahalla, Canada 50 6N 85 51W
74 Ogaki, Japan 35 25N 136 35E
116 Ogallala, U.S.A. 41 12N 101 40W
85 Ogbomosho, Nigeria 8 1N 3 29E
116 Ogden, Iowa, U.S.A. 42 3N 94 0W
118 Ogden, Utah, U.S.A. 41 13N 112 1W
118 Ogdensburg, U.S.A. 44 40N 75 27W
115 Ogeechee, R., U.S.A. 32 30N 81 32W
38 Oglio, R., Italy 45 15N 10 15E
98 Ogmore, Australia 22 37s 149 35E
47 Ogna, Norway 58 31N 5 48E
59 Ognon, R., France 47 43N 6 32E
85 Ogoja, Nigeria 6 38N 8 39E
85 Ogoki, Canada 51 35N 86 0W
106 Ogoki Res., Canada 50 45N 88 15W
85 Ogooué, R., Gabon 1 0s 10 0E
43 Ogosta, R., Bulgaria 43 35N 23 35E
42 Ograzden, Y.-slav. 41 30N 22 50E
86 Ogrein, Sudan 17 55N 34 50E
39 Ogulin, Yugoslavia 45 16N 15 16E
85 Oguta, Nigeria 5 44N 6 44E
85 Ogwashi-Uku, Nigeria 6 15N 6 30E
85 Ogwe, Nigeria 5 0N 7 14E
101 Ohai, New Zealand 44 55s 168 0E
101 Ohakune, New Zealand 39 24s 175 24E
101 Ohau, L., New Zealand 44 15s 169 53E
16 Ohey, Belgium 50 26N 5 8E
16 O'Higgins ♦, Chile 34 15s 71 1W
114 Ohio, R., U.S.A. 38 0N 86 0W
24 Ohre, R., Czechoslovakia 50 10N 12 30E
42 Ohrid, Yugoslavia 41 8N 20 52E
42 Ohridsko, Jezero, Y.-slav. 41 8N 20 52E
93 Ohrigstad, S. Africa 24 41s 30 36E
25 Ohringen, Germany 49 11N 9 31E
112 Oil City, U.S.A. 41 26N 79 40W
45 Oinousa, I., Greece 38 33N 26 14E
19 Oise ♦, France 49 28N 2 30E
74 Oita, Japan 33 15N 131 36E
74 Oita-ken ♦, Japan 33 0N 131 30E
119 Ojai, U.S.A. 34 28N 119 16W
120 Ojocaliente, Mexico 30 25N 106 30W
124 Ojos del Salado, Arg. 27 0s 68 40W
55 Oka, R., U.S.S.R. 54 50N 38 0E
92 Okahandja, S.W. Africa 22 0s 16 59E
108 Okanagan L., Canada 50 0N 119 30W
118 Okanogan, U.S.A. 48 24N 119 24W
118 Okanogan, R., U.S.A. 48 40N 119 24W
27 Okány, Hungary 46 52N 21 21E
101 Okarito, New Zealand 43 15s 170 9E
92 Okavango, R., Angola 17 40s 19 30E
92 Okavango Swamp, Bots. 19 30s 23 0E
74 Okaya, Japan 36 0N 138 10E
74 Okayama, Japan 34 40N 133 54E
74 Okayama-ken ♦, Japan 34 36N 137 0E
85 Oke-Iho, Nigeria 8 1N 3 18E
115 Okeechobee, U.S.A. 27 16N 80 46W
115 Okeechobee L., U.S.A. 27 0N 80 50W
115 Okefenokee Swamp, U.S.A. 30 50N 82 15W
13 Okehampton, Eng. 50 44N 4 1W
85 Okene, Nigeria 7 32N 6 11E
24 Oker, R., Germany 52 7N 10 34E
59 Okha, U.S.S.R. 53 40N 143 0E
45 Okhi Oros, Greece 38 5N 24 25E
59 Okhotsk, U.S.S.R. 59 20N 143 10E
59 Okhotsk, Sea of Asia 55 0N 145 0E
59 Okhotskiy Perevoz, U.S.S.R. 61 52N 135 35E
59 Okhotsko Kolymskoy, U.S.S.R. 63 0N 157 0E
74 Oki-Shotô, Japan 36 15N 133 15E
92 Okiep, S. Africa 29 39s 17 53E
85 Okigwi, Nigeria 5 52N 7 20E
85 Okija, Nigeria 5 54N 6 55E
77 Okinawa, Japan 26 40N 128 0E
77 Okinawa-guntô, Ryûkyû Is. 26 0N 127 30E
77 Oki no Erabu, Ryûkyû Is. 27 15N 128 45E
85 Okitipupa, Nigeria 6 31N 4 50E
117 Oklahoma ♦, U.S.A. 35 20N 97 30W
117 Oklahoma City, U.S.A. 35 25N 97 30W
117 Okmulgee, U.S.A. 35 38N 96 0W
56 Oknitsa, U.S.S.R. 48 25N 27 20E
90 Okolo, Uganda 2 37N 31 8E
92 Okondeka, S.W. Afr. 21 38s 15 37E
28 Okonek, Poland 53 32N 16 51E
49 Oksby, Denmark 55 33N 8 8E
58 Oktyabrskoye, U.S.S.R. 62 28N 66 3E
54 Okulovka, U.S.S.R. 58 19N 33 28E
74 Okushiri-Tô, Japan 42 15N 139 30E
85 Okuta, Nigeria 9 14N 3 12E
85 Okwa, R., Botswana 22 25s 22 30E
85 Okwoga, Nigeria 7 3N 7 42E
117 Ola, U.S.A. 35 2N 93 10W
50 Olafsvik, Iceland 64 53N 23 43W

119 Olancha, U.S.A. 36 15N 118 1W
121 Olanchito, Honduras 15 30N 86 30W
49 Oland, Sweden 56 45N 16 50E
20 Olargues, France 43 34N 2 53E
124 Olascoaga, Argentina 35 15s 60 39W
116 Olathe, U.S.A. 38 50N 94 50W
124 Olavarría, Argentina 36 55s 60 20W
28 Olawa, Poland 50 57N 17 20E
40 Olbia, Sardinia 40 55N 9 30E
40 Olbia, G. di, Sardinia 40 55N 9 35E
121 Old Bahama Chan., W.I. 22 10N 77 30W
30 Old Castile = Castilla la Vieja, Spain 41 55N 4 0W
98 Old Cork, Australia 22 57s 142 0E
86 Old Dongola, Sudan 18 11N 30 44E
106 Old Factory, Canada 52 36N 78 43W
73 Ombai, Selat, Indon. 8 30s 124 50E
91 Old Forge, N.Y., U.S.A. 43 43N 74 58W
113 Old Forge, Pa., U.S.A. 41 20N 75 46W
91 Old Serenje, Zambia 13 7s 30 45E
90 Old Shinyanga, Tanz. 3 33s 33 27E
113 Old Speck, Mt., U.S.A. 44 33N 70 57W
107 Old Town, U.S.A. 45 0N 68 50W
109 Old Wives L., Canada 50 5N 105 55W
15 Oldcastle, Ire. 53 46N 7 10W
90 Oldeani, Tanzania 3 22s 35 35E
24 Oldenburg, Niedersachsen, Germany 53 10N 8 10E
24 Oldenburg, S.-Holst. Germany 54 16N 10 53E
16 Oldenzaal, Netherlands 52 19N 6 53E
12 Oldham, Eng. 53 33N 2 8W
108 Olds, Canada 51 50N 114 10W
112 Olean, U.S.A. 42 8N 78 25W
38 Oléggio, Italy 45 36N 8 38E
30 Oleiros, Portugal 39 56N 7 56W
59 Olekma, R., U.S.S.R. 58 0N 121 30E
59 Olekminsk, U.S.S.R. 60 40N 120 30E
59 Olenek, U.S.S.R. 68 20N 112 30E
59 Olenek, R., U.S.S.R. 71 0N 123 50E
54 Olenino, U.S.S.R. 56 15N 33 20E
18 Oléron, I. d', France 45 55N 1 15W
28 Oleśnica, Poland 51 13N 17 22E
28 Olesno, Poland 50 51N 18 26E
54 Olevsk, U.S.S.R. 51 18N 27 39E
96 Olga, Mt., Australia 25 20s 130 40E
59 Olga, U.S.S.R. 43 50N 135 0E
4 Olgastretet, Svalbard 78 35N 25 0E
49 Ølgod, Denmark 55 50N 8 37E
31 Olhão, Portugal 37 3N 7 48W
44 Olib, Yugoslavia 44 23N 14 44E
40 Olio, I., Yugoslavia 44 23N 14 44E
40 Oliena, Italy 40 18N 9 22E
32 Oliete, Spain 41 1N 0 41W
92 Olifantshoek, S. Africa 27 57s 22 42E
45 Olimbos, Greece 35 44N 27 11E
44 Olimbos, Oros, Greece 40 6N 22 23E
125 Olimpia, Brazil 20 44s 48 54W
124 Olimpo ♦, Paraguay 20 30s 58 45W
92 Oliphant, R., S.W. Africa 23 15s 18 15E
32 Olite, Spain 42 29N 1 40W
124 Oliva, Argentina 32 0s 63 38W
33 Oliva, Spain 38 58N 0 15W
30 Oliva, Punta del, Spain 43 37N 5 28W
30 Oliva de la Frontera, Sp. 38 17N 6 54W
127 Oliveira, Minas Gerais, Brazil 20 50s 44 50W
30 Oliveira de Azemeis, Portugal 40 49N 8 29W
91 Olivença, Mozambique 11 47s 35 13E
31 Olivenza, Spain 38 41N 7 9W
108 Oliver, Canada 49 20N 119 30W
57 Olkhovka, U.S.S.R. 49 48N 44 32E
28 Olkusz, Poland 50 18N 19 33E
124 Ollagüe, Chile 21 15s 68 10W
30 Olmedo, Spain 41 20N 4 43W
114 Olney, England 52 9N 0 42W
114 Olney, Ill., U.S.A. 38 40N 88 0W
117 Olney, Tex., U.S.A. 33 25N 98 45W
49 Olofström, Sweden 56 17N 14 32E
85 Oloma, Cameroon 3 29N 11 19E
27 Olomouc, Czechoslovakia 49 38N 17 12E
52 Olonets, U.S.S.R. 61 0N 33 0E
73 Olongapo, Philippines 14 50N 120 18E
20 Oloron-Ste.-Marie, France 43 11N 0 38W
32 Olot, Spain 42 11N 2 30E
42 Olovo, Yugoslavia 44 8N 18 35E
59 Olovyannaya, U.S.S.R. 50 50N 115 10E
24 Olpe, Germany 51 2N 7 50E
56 Olshanka, U.S.S.R. 48 16N 30 58E
28 Olsztyn, Poland 53 48N 20 29E
28 Olsztyn ♦, Poland 53 50N 20 27E
28 Olsztynek, Poland 53 34N 20 19E
46 Olt, R., Rumania 44 20N 24 40E
46 Olt ♦, Rumania 44 20N 24 30E
25 Olten, Switzerland 47 21N 7 53E
46 Oltenita, Rumania 44 7N 26 42E
117 Olton, U.S.A. 34 16N 102 7W
64 Oltu, Turkey 40 35N 41 50E
32 Oluego, Spain 41 47N 2 0W
31 Olvera, Spain 36 55N 5 18W
45 Olympia, Greece 37 39N 21 39E
118 Olympia, U.S.A. 47 0N 122 58W
118 Olympic Mts., U.S.A. 48 0N 124 0W
118 Olympic Nat. Park, U.S.A. 47 35N 123 30W
44 Olympus, Mt. = Olimbos, Oros, Greece 40 6N 22 23E
118 Olympus, Mt., U.S.A. 47 52N 123 40W
113 Olyphant, U.S.A. 41 27N 75 36W
87 Om Hajer, Ethiopia 14 20N 36 41E
74 Omachi, Japan 36 30N 137 50E
12 Omagh, N. Ire. 54 36N 7 20W
116 Omaha, U.S.A. 41 15N 96 0W
118 Omak, U.S.A. 48 24N 119 24W
63 Oman ■, Arabia 23 0N 58 0E
65 Oman, G. of, S.W. Asia 24 30N 58 30E

92 Omaruru, S.W. Africa 21 26s 16 0E
92 Omaruru, R., S.W. Afr. 21 44s 14 30E
126 Omate, Peru 16 45s 71 0W
73 Ombai, Selat, Indon. 8 30s 124 50E
47 Ombo, Norway 59 18N 6 0E
92 Ombombo, S. Africa 18 43s 13 57E
88 Omboue, Gabon 1 35s 9 15E
38 Ombrone, R., Italy 42 48N 11 15E
83 Omchi, Chad 21 2N 17 53E
92 Omdraai, Botswana 20 5s 21 56E
85 Omdurman, Sudan 15 40N 32 28E
38 Omegna, Italy 45 52N 8 23E
90 Omeonga, Zaïre 3 40s 24 22E
121 Ometepe, Isla de, Nicaragua 11 32N 85 35W
120 Ometepec, Mexico 16 39N 98 23W
62 Omez, Israel 32 22N 35 0E
39 Omiš, Yugoslavia 43 28N 16 40E
39 Omisalj, Yugoslavia 45 13N 14 32E
74 Omitara, S.W. Afr. 22 16s 18 2E
49 Omme, Denmark 55 56N 8 32E
43 Omortag, Bulgaria 43 8N 26 26E
39 Omura, Japan 33 8N 130 0E
43 Omuta, Bulgaria 43 8N 26 26E
74 Omuta, Japan 33 0N 130 26E
55 Omutninsk, U.S.S.R. 58 45s 52 4E
32 Oña, Spain 42 43N 3 25W
74 Onaga, Japan 39 32N 96 12W
116 Onalaska, U.S.A. 43 53N 91 14W
116 Onamia, U.S.A. 46 4N 93 38W
114 Onancock, U.S.A. 37 42N 75 49W
73 Onang, Indonesia 3 2s 118 55E
106 Onaping L., Canada 47 3N 81 30W
47 Onarheim, Norway 59 57N 5 35E
32 Oñate, Spain 43 3N 2 25W
120 Onavas, Mexico 28 28N 109 30W
116 Onawa, U.S.A. 42 2N 96 2W
114 Onaway, U.S.A. 45 21N 84 11W
46 Oncesti, Rumania 43 56N 25 52E
92 Oncocua, Angola 16 30s 13 40E
32 Onda, Spain 39 55N 0 17W
92 Ondangua, S. Africa 17 57s 16 4E
76 Ondorhaan, Mongolia 47 22N 110 31E
32 Ondárroa, Spain 43 19N 2 25W
27 Ondava, R., Cz. 48 50N 21 40E
85 Ondo, Nigeria 7 4N 4 47E
92 Ondombo, S.W. Afr. 21 3s 16 5E
52 Onega, C. of = Onezhskaya G., U.S.S.R. 64 30N 37 0E
52 Onega, L. = Onezhskoye Oz., U.S.S.R. 62 0N 35 30E
101 Onehunga, N.Z. 36 55s 174 30E
113 Oneida, U.S.A. 43 5N 75 40W
113 Oneida L., U.S.A. 43 12N 76 0W
116 O'Neill, U.S.A. 42 30N 98 38W
59 Onekotan, Ostrov, U.S.S.R. 49 25N 154 45E
90 Onema, Zaïre 4 35s 24 30E
115 Oneonta, Ala., U.S.A. 33 58N 86 29W
113 Oneonta, N.Y., U.S.A. 42 26N 75 5W
100 One Tree, Australia 34 13s 144 42E
52 Onezhskaya Guba, U.S.S.R. 64 30N 37 0E
52 Onezhskoye Ozero, U.S.S.R. 62 0N 35 30E
101 Onga, New Zealand 38 42s 175 19E
76 Ongiyn Gol, Mongolia 45 56N 103 0E
90 Ongoka, Zaïre 1 20s 26 0E
70 Ongole, India 15 33N 80 2E
57 Oni, U.S.S.R. 42 33N 43 26E
116 Onida, U.S.A. 44 42N 100 5W
93 Onilahy, R., Malagasy Rep. 23 30s 44 0E
85 Onitsha, Nigeria 6 6N 6 42E
74 Onoda, Japan 34 2N 131 10E
30 Ons, Islas de, Spain 42 23N 8 55W
49 Onsala, Sweden 57 26N 12 0E
96 Onslow, Australia 21 40s 115 0E
115 Onslow B., U.S.A. 34 10N 77 0W
16 Onstwedde, Netherlands 53 2N 7 4E
74 Ontake-san, Japan 35 50N 137 15E
32 Ontaneda, Spain 43 12N 3 57W
119 Ontario, Calif., U.S.A. 34 2N 117 40W
118 Ontario, Oreg., U.S.A. 44 1N 117 1W
106 Ontario ♦, Canada 52 0N 88 10W
112 Ontario, L., Can.-U.S.A. 43 40N 78 0W
33 Onteniente, Spain 38 50N 0 35W
116 Ontonagon, U.S.A. 46 58N 89 12W
33 Ontur, Spain 38 38N 1 29W
96 Oodnadatta, Austral. 27 33s 135 30E
118 Ooglaamie, Alaska 72 1N 157 0W
96 Ooldea, Australia 30 27s 131 50E
98 Oorindi, Australia 20 40s 141 1E
16 Oostende, Belgium 51 15N 2 50E
16 Oosterhout, Neth. 51 38N 4 51E
70 Ootacamund, India 11 30N 76 44E
92 Ootsi, Botswana 25 2s 25 45E
43 Opaka, Bulgaria 43 28N 26 10E
90 Opala, Zaïre 0 35s 24 15E
88 Opala, Zaïre 1 11s 24 45E
59 Opanake, Sri Lanka 6 35N 80 40E
43 Opan, Bulgaria 42 13N 25 41E
52 Opanica, Poland 52 18N 16 24E
106 Opasatika, Canada 49 30N 82 50W
109 Opasquia, Canada 53 16N 93 34W
39 Opatija, Yugoslavia 45 21N 14 17E
28 Opatow, Poland 50 50N 21 27E
27 Opava, Czechoslovakia 49 57N 17 58E
117 Opelousas, U.S.A. 30 35N 92 7W
106 Opemisca L., Canada 50 0N 75 0W
118 Opheim, U.S.A. 48 52N 106 30W
96 Ophthalmia Ra., Australia 23 15s 119 30E
85 Opi, Nigeria 6 36N 7 28E

106 Opinaca L., Canada 52 32N 76 31W
106 Opinaca, R., Canada 52 40N 77 0W
107 Opiskotish, L., Canada 53 0N 67 51W
85 Opobo, Nigeria 4 35N 7 34E
54 Opochka, U.S.S.R. 56 42N 28 45E
28 Opoczno, Poland 51 22N 20 18E
28 Opole, Poland 50 42N 17 58E
28 Opole ♦, Poland 50 40N 17 56E
30 Oporto = Porto, Port. 41 8N 8 40W
101 Opotiki, New Zealand 38 1s 177 19E
115 Opp, U.S.A. 31 19N 86 13W
47 Oppegård, Norway 59 48N 10 48E
25 Oppenheim, Germany 49 50N 8 22E
41 Oppido Mamertina, It. 38 16N 15 59E
47 Oppland fylke ♦, Norway 61 15N 9 30E
47 Oppstad, Norway 60 17N 11 40E
47 Opua, New Zealand 35 19s 174 9E
101 Opunake, New Zealand 39 26s 173 52E
62 Opuzen, Yugoslavia 43 1N 17 34E
117 Oracle, U.S.A. 32 45N 110 46W
46 Oradea, Rumania 47 2N 21 58E
42 Orahovac, Yugoslavia 42 24N 20 40E
42 Orahovica, Yugoslavia 45 35N 17 52E
69 Orai, India 25 58N 79 30E
21 Oraison, France 43 55N 5 55E
75 Oran, Algeria 35 37N 0 39W
100 Orange, Australia 33 15s 149 7E
21 Orange, France 44 8N 4 47E
113 Orange, Mass., U.S.A. 42 35N 72 15W
117 Orange, Tex., U.S.A. 30 0N 93 40W
114 Orange, Va., U.S.A. 38 17N 78 5W
127 Orange, C., Brazil 4 20N 51 30W
92 Orange, R. = Oranje, R., S. Africa 28 30s 18 0E
92 Orange Free State ♦, South Africa 28 30s 27 0E
115 Orangeburg, U.S.A. 33 27N 80 53W
93 Orange Grove, U.S.A. 27 57N 97 57W
106 Orangeville, Canada 43 55N 80 5W
24 Oranienburg, Germany 52 45N 13 15E
92 Oranje, R. S. Africa 28 30s 18 0E
92 Oranje Vrystaat ♦, S. Africa 28 30s 27 0E
92 Oranjemund (Orange Mouth), S.W. Afr. 28 32s 16 29E
24 Orapa, Botswana 24 13s 25 25E
73 Oras, Philippines 12 9N 125 22E
46 Oraşul Stalin = Braşov, Rumania 45 7N 25 39E
46 Orăştie, Rumania 45 50N 23 10E
27 Orava, R., Cz. 49 24N 19 20E
46 Oravita, Rumania 45 6N 21 43E
20 Orb, R., France 43 28N 3 5E
38 Orba, R., Italy 44 45N 8 40E
49 Ørbaek, Denmark 55 17N 10 39E
25 Orbe, Switzerland 46 43N 6 32E
18 Orbec, France 49 1N 0 23E
39 Orbetello, Italy 42 26N 11 11E
30 Orbigo, R., Spain 42 40N 5 45W
100 Orbost, Australia 37 40s 148 29E
49 Ørbyhus, Sweden 60 15N 17 43E
33 Orce, Spain 37 44N 2 28W
19 Orchies, France 50 28N 3 14E
121 Orchila, Isla, Venezuela 11 48N 66 10W
14 Orchy, Bridge of, Scotland, U.K. 56 30N 4 46W
14 Orchy, Glen, Scotland 56 27N 4 52W
38 Orco, R., Italy 45 20N 7 45E
96 Ord, Mt., Australia 17 20s 125 34E
96 Ord, R., Australia 16 20s 128 37E
30 Ordenes, Spain 43 5N 8 29W
119 Orderville, U.S.A. 37 18N 112 43W
76 Ordos, China 39 25N 108 45E
64 Ordu, Turkey 40 55N 37 53E
32 Orduña, Spain 42 58N 2 58W
113 Orduña, Mte., Spain 38 15N 103 42W
57 Ordzhonikidze, U.S.S.R. 43 0N 44 35E
57 Ordzhonikidze, U.S.S.R. 47 32N 34 3E
90 Ore, Zaïre 3 17N 29 30E
48 Ore, Sweden 61 8N 15 10E
25 Ore Mts. = Erzgebirge, Ger.-Cz. 50 25N 13 0E
42 Orebic, Yugoslavia 43 0N 17 11E
48 Orebro, Sweden 59 20N 15 18E
48 Orebro län ♦, Swed. 59 27N 15 0E
116 Oregon, U.S.A. 42 1N 89 20W
118 Oregon ♦, U.S.A. 44 0N 120 0W
118 Oregon City, U.S.A. 45 28N 122 35W
48 Oregrundsgrepen, Sweden 60 25N 18 15E
56 Orekhov, U.S.S.R. 47 30N 35 32E
55 Orekhovo-Zuyevo, U.S.S.R. 55 50N 38 55E
55 Orel, U.S.S.R. 52 57N 36 3E
31 Orellana, Canal de, Spain 39 2N 6 0W
31 Orellana, Pantano de, Spain 39 5N 5 10W
31 Orellana la Vieja, Sp. 39 1N 5 32W
118 Orem, U.S.A. 40 27N 111 45W
64 Oren, Turkey 37 3N 27 57E
30 Orense, Spain 42 19N 7 55W
30 Orense ♦, Spain 42 15N 7 30W
101 Orepuki, New Zealand 46 19s 167 46E
49 Öresund, Den./Swed. 55 45N 12 45E
13 Orford Ness, Eng. 52 6N 1 31E
31 Orgaz, Spain 39 39N 3 53W
56 Orgeyev, U.S.S.R. 47 9N 29 10E

MAP

21 Orgon, France 43 47N 5 3E
75 Orhon Gol, Mongolia 49 30N 106 0E
41 Oria, Italy 40 30N 17 38E
99 Orient, Australia 28 7s 143 3E
106 Orient Bay, Canada 49 20N 88 10w
90 Oriental ♦, Zaïre 2 20N 26 0E
50 Oriental, Cord., Col. 5 0N 74 0w
124 Oriente, Argentina 38 44s 60 37w
19 Origny, France 49 50N 3 30E
33 Orihuela, Spain 38 7N 0 55w
32 Orihuela del Tremedal, Spain 40 33N 1 39w
44 Oriku, Albania 40 20N 19 30E
112 Orilla, Canada 44 40N 79 24w
121 Orinoco, Delta del, Ven. 8 30N 61 0w
126 Orinoco, R., Venezuela 5 45N 67 40w
109 Orion, Canada 49 28N 110 49w
67 Orissa ♦, India 21 0N 85 0E
40 Oristano, Italy 39 54N 8 35E
40 Oristano, Golfo di, Italy 39 50N 8 22E
120 Orizaba, Mexico 18 50N 97 10w
43 Orizare, Bulgaria 42 44N 27 39E
47 Orje, Norway 59 28N 11 36E
42 Orjen, mt., Yugoslavia 42 35N 18 34E
33 Orjiva, Spain 36 53N 3 24w
47 Orkanger, Norway 63 18N 9 52E
49 Orkelljunga, Sweden 56 17N 13 17E
49 Orken, L., Sweden 57 11N 15 0E
92 Orkény, S. Africa 26 42s 26 40E
27 Orkery, Hungary 47 9N 19 26E
47 Orkla, Norway 63 18N 9 51E
14 Orkney ♦, Scot. 59 0N 3 0w
14 Orkney Is., Scot. 59 0N 3 0w
118 Orland, U.S.A. 39 46N 120 10w
115 Orlando, U.S.A. 28 30N 81 25w
41 Orlando, C.d', Italy 38 10N 14 43E
19 Orléanais, Fr. 48 0N 2 0E
19 Orléans, France 47 54N 1 52E
113 Orleans, U.S.A. 44 49N 72 10w
114 Orleans, I. d', Canada 46 54N 70 58w
26 Orlice, R., Cz. 50 5N 16 10E
27 Orlické Hory, Cz. 50 15N 16 30E
27 Orlov, Czechoslovakia 49 17N 20 51E
55 Orlov Gay, U.S.S.R. 51 4N 48 19E
42 Orlovat, Yugoslavia 45 14N 20 33E
66 Ormara, Pakistan 25 16N 64 33E
38 Ormea, Italy 44 9N 7 54E
46 Ormilia, Greece 40 16N 23 33E
73 Ormoc, Philippines 11 0N 124 37E
76 Ormond, New Zealand 38 33s 177 56E
115 Ormond, U.S.A. 29 13N 81 5w
39 Ormož, Yugoslavia 46 25N 16 10E
113 Ormstown, Canada 45 9N 74 0w
19 Ornans, France 47 7N 6 10E
18 Orne ♦, France 48 40N 0 0E
28 Orneta, Poland 54 8N 20 9E
49 Ornhöj, Denmark 56 12N 8 34E
48 Ornö, Sweden 59 4N 18 24E
48 Ornsköldvik, Sweden 63 17N 18 40E
120 Oro, R., Mexico 26 8N 105 58w
126 Orocué, Colombia 4 48N 71 20w
85 Orodo, Nigeria 5 34N 7 4E
119 Orogrande, U.S.A. 32 20N 106 4w
30 Orol, Spain 43 34N 7 39w
107 Oromocto, Canada 45 54N 66 37w
62 Oron, Israel 30 55N 35 1E
85 Oron, Nigeria 4 48N 8 14E
59 Oron, R., U.S.S.R. 69 21N 95 43E
112 Orono, Canada 44 0N 78 35w
30 Oropesa, Spain 39 57N 5 10w
73 Oroquieta, Philippines 8 32N 123 44E
127 Orós, Brazil 6 15s 38 55w
40 Orosei, G. di, Italy 40 15N 9 40E
27 Oroshaza, Hungary 46 32N 20 42E
59 Orotukan, U.S.S.R. 62 16N 151 42E
118 Oroville, Calif., U.S.A. 39 40N 121 30w
118 Oroville, Wash., U.S.A. 48 58N 119 30w
49 Orrefors, Sweden 56 50N 15 45E
112 Orrville, U.S.A. 40 50N 81 46w
48 Orsa, Sweden 61 7N 14 37E
41 Orsara di Puglia, Italy 41 17N 15 16E
48 Orsasjön, Sweden 61 7N 14 37E
54 Orsha, U.S.S.R. 54 30N 30 25E
52 Orsk, U.S.S.R. 51 20N 58 34E
49 Orslev, Soro, Denmark 55 22N 11 56E
39 Orsogna, Italy 42 13N 14 17E
46 Orşova, Rumania 44 41N 22 25E
49 Orsted, Denmark 56 31N 10 21E
38 Orta, L. d', Italy 45 48N 8 21E
41 Orta Nova, Italy 41 20N 15 40E
39 Orte, Italy 42 28N 12 23E
30 Ortegal, C., Spain 43 43N 7 52w
20 Orthez, France 43 29N 0 48w
30 Ortigueira, Spain 43 40N 7 50w
38 Ortles, mt., Italy 46 31N 10 33E
126 Ortón, R., Bolivia 10 50s 67 0w
39 Ortona, Italy 42 21N 14 24E
40 Orune, Sardinia 40 25N 9 20E
126 Oruro, Bolivia 18 0s 67 19w
48 Orust, Sweden 58 10N 11 40E
18 Orvault, France 47 17N 1 38E
51 Orvieto, Italy 42 43N 12 8E
112 Orwell, U.S.A. 41 32N 80 52w
13 Orwell, R., Eng. 52 2N 1 12E
42 Oryakhovo, Bulgaria 43 40N 23 57E
38 Orzinuovi, Italy 45 24N 9 55E
28 Orzysz, Poland 53 50N 21 58E
49 Os, Hordaland, Norway 60 9N 5 30E
52a Os, U.S.S.R. 57 9N 55 57E
121 Osa, Pen. de, Costa Rica 8 0N 84 0w
116 Osage, Iowa, U.S.A. 43 15N 92 50w
116 Osage, Wyo., U.S.A. 43 59N 104 25w
116 Osage, R., U.S.A. 38 15N 92 30w
116 Osage City, U.S.A. 38 43N 95 51w
74 Osaka, Japan 34 40N 135 30E
74 Osaka-fu ♦, Japan 34 40N 135 30E
39 Osar, Yugoslavia 44 43N 14 27E
116 Osawatomie, U.S.A. 38 30N 94 55w
116 Osborne, U.S.A. 39 30N 98 45w

MAP

49 Osby, Sweden 56 23N 13 59E
117 Osceola, Ark., U.S.A. 35 40N 90 0w
116 Osceola, Iowa, U.S.A. 41 0N 93 20w
24 Oschatz, Germany 51 17N 13 8E
24 Oschersleben, Germany 52 2N 11 13E
40 Oschiri, Italy 40 43N 9 7E
.42 Osečina, Yugoslavia 44 23N 19 34E
55 Osëry, U.S.S.R. 54 52N 38 28E
106 Oshawa, Canada 43 50N 78 45w
92 Oshikango, Angola 17 9s 16 10E
114 Oshkosh, Nebr., U.S.A. 41 27N 102 20w
114 Oshkosh, Wis., U.S.A. 44 3N 88 35w
54 Oshmyany, U.S.S.R. 54 26N 25 58E
85 Oshogbo, Nigeria 7 48N 4 37E
88 Oshwe, Zaïre 3 25s 19 28E
64 Osica de Jos, Rumania 44 14N 24 20E
28 Osieczna, Poland 51 55N 16 40E
42 Osijek, Yugoslavia 45 34N 18 41E
40 Osilo, Italy 40 45N 8 41E
39 Osimo, Italy 43 40N 13 30E
54 Osinniki, U.S.S.R. 53 58N 87 58E
54 Osintorf, U.S.S.R. 54 34N 30 31E
54 Osipovichi, U.S.S.R. 53 25N 28 33E
116 Oskaloosa, U.S.A. 41 18N 92 40w
49 Oskarshamn, Sweden 57 15N 16 27E
106 Oskelaneo, Canada 48 5N 75 15w
55 Oskol, R., U.S.S.R. 50 20N 38 0E
47 Oslo, Norway 59 53N 10 52E
47 Oslo, Norway 59 55N 10 45E
73 Oslob, Philippines 9 31N 123 26E
47 Oslofjord, Norway 58 30N 10 0E
70 Osmanabad, India 18 5N 76 10E
56 Osmancik, Turkey 40 45N 34 47E
56 Osmaniye, Turkey 37 5N 36 10E
48 Osmo, Sweden 58 58N 17 55E
24 Osnabrück, Germany 52 16N 8 2E
28 Ośno Lubuskie, Poland 52 28N 14 51E
27 Osobláha, Cz. 50 17N 17 44E
98 Osorno, S.W. Africa 22 3s 16 59E
125 Osorio, Brazil 29 53s 50 17w
128 Osorno, Chile 40 25s 73 0w
30 Osorno, Spain 42 24N 4 22w
128 Osorno, Vol., Chile 41 0N 72 30w
108 Osoyoos, Canada 49 0N 119 30w
98 Osprey Reef, Australia 13 52s 146 36E
16 Oss, Netherlands 51 46N 5 32E
99 Ossa, Mt., Austral. 41 80s 146 0E
46 Ossa, Oros, Greece 39 47N 22 42E
33 Ossa de Montiel, Spain 38 58N 2 45w
116 Ossabaw I., U.S.A. 31 45N 81 8w
113 Ossining, U.S.A. 41 9N 73 50w
113 Ossipee, U.S.A. 43 41N 71 9w
107 Ossokmanuan L., Can. 53 25N 65 0w
59 Ossora, U.S.S.R. 59 20N 163 13E
54 Ostashkov, U.S.S.R. 57 4N 33 2E
24 Oste, R., Germany 53 30N 9 12E
16 Ostend = Oostende, Belg. 51 15N 2 50E
54 Oster, U.S.S.R. 50 57N 30 46E
24 Osterburg, Germany 52 47N 11 44E
48 Osterby, Sweden 60 13N 17 55E
49 Osterbymo, Sweden 57 49N 15 15E
48 Osterdalälven, Sweden 61 30N 13 45E
24 Osterholz-Scharmbeck, Germany 53 14N 8 48E
49 Osterild, Denmark 57 3N 8 50E
48 Osterkorsberga, Sweden 57 17N 15 5E
48 Ostersund, Sweden 63 10N 14 38E
49 Osterøya, Norway 60 32N 5 30E
47 Østfold fylke ♦, Nor. 59 25N 11 25E
24 Ostfriesische Inseln, Germany 53 45N 7 15E
40 Ostia Lido (Lido di Roma), Italy 41 43N 12 17E
39 Ostiglia, Italy 45 4N 11 9E
27 Ostrava, Czechoslovakia 49 51N 18 18E
28 Ostrgrog, Poland 52 37N 16 33E
27 Ostróda, Poland 53 42N 19 58E
55 Ostrogozhsk, U.S.S.R. 50 55N 39 7E
28 Ostroleka, Poland 53 4N 21 38E
43 Ostrov, Bulgaria 43 40N 24 9E
46 Ostrov, Rumania 44 6N 27 24E
54 Ostrov, U.S.S.R. 57 25N 28 20E
28 Ostrów Lubelski, Poland 51 36N 17 44E
28 Ostrów Mazowiecka, Pol. 52 50N 21 51E
28 Ostrowiec, Poland 50 55N 21 22E
42 Ostrozac, Yugoslavia 43 43N 17 49E
28 Ostrzeszów, Poland 51 25N 17 52E
24 Ostseebad-Kühlungsborn, Ger. 54 10N 11 40E
47 Ostsinni, Norway 60 53N 10 3E
41 Ostuni, Italy 40 44N 17 34E
43 Osum, R., Bulgaria 43 35N 25 0E
44 Osumi, R., Albania 40 40N 20 10E
74 Osumi-Kaikyō, Japan 30 55N 131 0E
74 Osumi-Shotō, Japan 30 30N 130 45E
31 Osuna, Spain 37 14N 5 8w
113 Oswego, U.S.A. 43 29N 76 30w
12 Oswestry, Eng. 52 52N 3 3w
28 Oświęcim, Poland 50 2N 19 11E
101 Otago, New Zealand 45 20s 169 20E
101 Otago Harb., N.Z. 45 47s 170 42E
74 Otake, Japan 34 27N 132 25E
101 Otaki, New Zealand 40 45s 175 10E
26 Otava, R., Cz. 49 16N 13 32E
126 Otavalo, Ecuador 0 20N 78 20w
92 Otavi, S.W. Africa 19 40s 17 24E
92 Otchinjau, Angola 16 30s 13 56E
42 Otelec, Rumania 45 36N 20 50E
92 Otchinjau, Angola 16 30s 13 56E
30 Otero de Rey, Spain 43 6N 7 36w
118 Othello, U.S.A. 46 53N 119 8w
46 Othonoi, I., Greece 39 52N 19 22E
45 Othris, Mt., Gr. 39 4N 22 42E
101 Otira Gorge, N.Z. 42 53s 171 33E
116 Otis, U.S.A. 40 12N 102 58w
92 Otjiwarongo, S.W. Afr. 20 30s 16 33E

MAP

28 Otmuchow, Poland 50 28N 17 10E
39 Otočac, Yugoslavia 44 53N 15 12E
101 Otorohanga, N.Z. 38 12s 175 14E
47 Otra, Norway 58 8N 8 1E
41 Otranto, Italy 40 9N 18 28E
41 Otranto, C.d', Italy 40 7N 18 30E
41 Otranto, Str. of, Adriatic Sea 40 15N 18 40E
47 Otrøy, Norway 62 43N 6 50E
74 Otsu, Japan 42 35N 143 40E
47 Otta, Norway 61 46N 9 32E
70 Ottapalam, India 10 46N 76 23E
106 Ottawa, Canada 45 27N 75 42w
114 Ottawa, Ill., U.S.A. 41 20N 88 55w
116 Ottawa, Kans., U.S.A. 38 40N 95 10w
105 Ottawa Is., Canada 59 50N 80 0w
106 Ottawa, R., Canada 47 45N 78 35w
85 Ottélé, Cameroon 3 38N 11 19E
85 Ottéré, Gabon 1 42N 11 43E
109 Otter Rapids, Canada 55 42N 104 46w
24 Otterndorf, Germany 53 47N 8 52E
47 Otterøy, I., Norway 62 45N 6 50E
49 Ottersheim, Austria 48 21N 14 12E
49 Otterup, Denmark 55 30N 10 22E
112 Otterville, Canada 42 57N 80 36w
91 Otto Beit Bridge, Rhod. 15 59s 28 56E
92 Ottosdal, S. Afr. 26 46s 25 59E
92 Ottoshoop, S. Africa 25 45s 26 58E
48 Ottsjö, Sweden 63 13N 13 2E
116 Ottumwa, U.S.A. 41 0N 92 25w
85 Otu, Nigeria 8 14N 3 22E
85 Otukpa (Al Owuho), Nig. 7 9N 7 41E
85 Oturkpo, Nigeria 7 10N 8 15E
128 Otway, Bahia, Chile 53 30s 74 0w
100 Otway, C., Australia 38 52s 143 31E
28 Otwock, Poland 52 5N 21 20E
26 Ötz, Austria 47 13N 10 53E
26 Ötz, R., Austria 47 14N 10 50E
26 Ötztaler Alpen, Austria 46 58N 11 0E
88 Ouanda Djallé, Cen. Afr. Rep. 8 55N 22 53E
88 Ouango, Cent. Afr. Rep. 4 19N 22 30E
82 Ouargla, Algeria 31 59N 5 25E
82 Ouarkziz, Djebel, Alg. 28 50N 8 0w
82 Ouarzazate, Morocco 30 55N 6 55w
85 Ouatagouna, Mali 15 11N 0 43E
88 Oubangi, R., Zaïre 1 0N 17 50E
82 Oubarakai, O., Algeria 27 20N 9 0E
19 Ouche, R., France 47 11N 5 10E
16 Ouddorp, Netherlands 51 50N 3 57E
16 Oude Rijn, R., Neth. 52 12N 4 24E
16 Oudenaarde, Belgium 50 50N 3 37E
18 Oudon, France 47 22N 1 19w
18 Oudon, R., France 47 47N 1 2w
92 Oudtshoorn, S. Africa 33 35s 22 14E
82 Oued Sbita, Algeria 25 50N 5 2w
84 Ouellé, Ivory Coast 7 26N 4 1w
84 Ouessa, Upper Volta 11 4N 2 47w
18 Ouessant, Ile d', France 48 28N 5 6w
88 Ouesso, Congo 1 37N 16 5E
82 Ouezzane, Morocco 34 51N 5 42w
85 Ouidah, Dahomey 6 25N 2 0E
106 Ouimet, Canada 48 43N 88 35w
18 Ouistreham, France 49 17N 0 18w
82 Ouj, R., Algeria 6 15N 29 45E
80 Oujeft, Mauritania 20 2N 13 0w
82 Oulad Naïl, Mts. des, Algeria 34 30N 3 30E
50 Oulainen, Finland 64 17N 24 47E
82 Ouled Djellal, Algeria 34 28N 5 2E
82 Oulmès, Morocco 33 17N 6 0w
50 Oulu, Finland 65 1N 25 29E
50 Oulujoki, Finland 64 45N 26 30E
50 Oulujärvi, Finland 64 25N 27 0E
50 Oulun Lääni ♦, Finland 64 36N 27 20E
38 Oulx, Italy 45 2N 6 49E
83 Oum-el-Bouaghi, Algeria 35 55N 7 6E
82 Oum el Ksi, Algeria 29 4N 6 59w
84 Oumé, Ivory Coast 5 21N 5 27w
82 Oum-er-Rbia, Morocco 32 30N 6 30w
82 Oum-er-Rbia, O., Morocco 32 30N 6 30w
83 Ounane, Dj., Algeria 25 4N 7 10E
50 Ounasjoki, Finland 66 31N 25 44E
81 Ounianga Kébir, Chad 19 4N 20 29E
85 Ounlivou, Togo 7 20N 1 34E
16 Our, R., Luxembourg 49 55N 6 5E
82 Oureg, Oued el, Algeria 32 34N 2 10E
127 Ouricuri, Brazil 7 53s 40 5w
125 Ourinhos, Brazil 23 0s 49 54w
81 Ourini, Chad 16 7N 22 25E
31 Ourique, Portugal 37 38N 8 16w
125 Ouro Fino, Brazil 22 16s 46 25w
125 Ouro Prêto, Brazil 20 20s 43 30w
84 Ouro Sogui, Senegal 15 36N 13 19w
85 Ourthe, R., Belgium 50 29N 5 35E
74 Ou-Sammyaku, Japan 39 20N 140 35E
12 Ouse, R., Sussex, England 50 58N 0 3E
13 Ouse, R., Yorks., England 54 3N 0 7E
12 Ouse, Great, R., England 52 12N 0 7E

MAP

20 Oust, France 42 52N 1 13E
18 Oust, R., France 48 8N 2 49w
14 Outardes, R., Canada 50 0N 69 4w
14 Outer Hebrides, Is., Scotland 57 30N 7 40w
107 Outer I., Canada 51 10N 58 35w
30 Outes, Spain 42 52N 8 55w
92 Outjo, S.W. Africa 20 5s 16 7E
109 Outlook, Canada 51 30N 107 0w
19 Outlook, U.S.A. 48 53N 104 46w
19 Outreau, France 50 40N 1 36E
100 Ouyen, Australia 35 1s 142 22E
24 Ovada, Italy 44 39N 8 40E
114 Ovalau, I., Fiji 17 40s 178 48E
124 Ovalle, Chile 30 33s 71 18w
*92 Ovamboland, South West Africa 17 20s 16 30E
30 Ovar, Portugal 40 51N 8 40E
88 Ovem, Gabon 1 42N 11 43E
16 Over Flakkee, I., Neth. 51 45N 4 5E
126 Ovejas, Colombia 9 32N 75 14w
16 Overijssel ♦, Neth. 52 25N 6 35E
16 Overkalix, Sweden 66 19N 22 50E
16 Overpelt, Belgium 51 12N 5 20E
49 Overum, Sweden 58 0N 16 20E
116 Ovid, U.S.A. 41 0N 102 17w
30 Oviedo, Spain 43 25N 5 50w
30 Oviedo ♦, Spain 43 20N 6 0w
48 Oviken, Sweden 63 0N 14 23E
48 Oviksfjällen, Swed. 63 0N 13 49E
85 Qvoro, Nigeria 5 26N 7 16E
54 Ovruch, U.S.S.R. 51 25N 28 45E
49 Ovtrup, Denmark 55 43N 8 21E
101 Owaka, New Zealand 46 27s 169 40E
74 Owase, Japan 34 7N 136 5E
113 Owatonna, U.S.A. 44 3N 93 17w
113 Owego, U.S.A. 42 6N 76 17w
91 Owen Falls, Uganda 0 30N 33 5E
112 Owen Sound, Canada 44 35N 80 55w
98 Owen Stanley Range, Territory of Papua 8 30s 147 0E
88 Owendo, Gabon 0 17N 9 30E
114 Owensboro, U.S.A. 37 40N 87 5w
101 Owens, R., Austral. 36 30s 146 30E
85 Owerri, Nigeria 5 29N 7 0E
85 Owo, Nigeria 7 18N 5 30E
118 Owosso, U.S.A. 43 0N 84 10w
118 Owyhee, U.S.A. 42 0N 116 3w
118 Owyhee Res., U.S.A. 43 30N 117 30w
118 Owyhee, R., U.S.A. 43 10N 117 37w
15 Ox Mts., Ireland 54 6N 9 0w
48 Oxberg, Sweden 61 7N 14 11E
16 Oxford, Eng. 51 45N 1 15w
117 Oxford, Miss., U.S.A. 34 22N 89 30w
114 Oxford, N.C., U.S.A. 36 19N 78 36w
112 Oxford, Ohio, U.S.A. 39 30N 84 40w
13 Oxford ♦, England 51 45N 1 15w
109 Oxford L., Canada 54 50N 96 0w
45 Oxilithos, Greece 38 35s 24 7E
100 Oxley, Australia 34 12s 144 6E
100 Oxleys Pk., Australia 31 51s 50 22E
110 Oxnard, U.S.A. 34 10N 119 14w
72 Oya, Malaysia 2 55N 111 55E
59 Oyeren, Norway 59 50N 11 15E
14 Oykel, R., Scot. 58 2N 4 52w
59 Oymyakon, U.S.S.R. 63 25N 143 10E
85 Oyo, Nigeria 7 46N 3 56E
21 Oyonnax, France 46 16N 5 40E
99 Oyster B., Austral. 42 15s 148 5E
113 Oyster B., U.S.A. 40 52N 73 32w
47 Øystese, Norway 60 22N 6 9E
74 Ozaka, Japan 34 40N 135 30E
73 Ozamis (Mizamis), Phil. 8 15N 123 50E
117 Ozark, Ala., U.S.A. 31 29N 85 39w
117 Ozark, Ark., U.S.A. 35 30N 93 50w
117 Ozark, Mo., U.S.A. 37 0N 93 15w
117 Ozark Plateau, U.S.A. 37 20N 91 40w
116 Ozarks, L. of, U.S.A. 38 10N 93 0w
27 Ozd, Hungary 48 14N 20 15E
59 Ozernhisk, U.S.S.R. 53 40N 27 7E
40 Ozieri, Italy 40 35N 9 0E
28 Ozimek, Poland 50 41N 18 11E
117 Ozona, U.S.A. 30 43N 101 11w
28 Ozorków, Poland 51 57N 19 16E
120 Ozuluama, Mexico 21 40N 97 50w
20 Ozun, Rumania 45 47N 25 50E
84 Pa, Upper Volta 11 33N 3 19w
71 Pa Sak, R., Thailand 15 30N 101 0E
77 Pa-an, Burma 16 45N 97 40E
75 Paan (Batang), China 30 0N 99 3E
22 Paar, R., Germany 48 42N 11 27E
92 Paarl, S. Africa 33 45s 18 56E
66 Pab Hills, Pakistan 26 30N 66 45E
69 Pabianice, Poland 51 40N 19 20E
69 Pabna, Bangladesh 24 1N 89 18E
106 Pabo, Uganda 2 56N 32 3E
54 Pabrade, U.S.S.R. 55 0N 25 56E
126 Pacasmayo, Peru 7 20s 79 35w
40 Paceco, Italy 37 59N 12 32E
41 Pachino, Italy 36 43N 15 4E
126 Pacho, Colombia 5 8N 74 10w
120 Pachuca, Mexico 20 10N 98 40w
75 Pachung, China 31 30N 106 40E
99 Pacis, Australia 42 25s 146 42E
26 Pacov, Czechoslovakia 49 27N 15 0E
27 Pacsa, Hungary 46 44N 17 2E
18 Pacy, France 49 1N 1 23E
28 Paczków, Poland 50 28N 17 0E

MAP

73 Padaido, Kepulauan, Indonesia 1 5s 138 0E
73 Padalarang, Indonesia 7 50s 107 30E
72 Padang, Indonesia 1 0s 100 20E
72 Padang, I., Indonesia 1 0s 100 10E
72 Padang Pandjang, Indonesia 0 30s 100 20E
72 Padangsidimpuan, Indonesia 1 30N 99 15E
49 Padborg, Denmark 54 49N 9 21E
124 Paddock, S. Afr. 30 45s 30 16E
109 Paddockwood, Canada 53 30N 105 30w
24 Paderborn, Germany 51 42N 8 44E
46 Padesul, Rumania 45 40N 22 22E
46 Padina, Rumania 44 50N 27 8E
109 Padlei, Canada 62 10N 97 5w
105 Padloping Island, Canada 67 0N 63 0w
70 Padmanabhapuram, India 8 16N 77 17E
39 Pádova, Italy 45 24N 11 52E
70 Padra, India 22 15N 73 7E
117 Padre I., U.S.A. 27 0N 97 20w
70 Padrauna, India 26 54N 83 41E
30 Padrón, Spain 42 41N 8 39w
99 Padstow, Eng. 50 33N 4 57w
39 Padua = Pádova, Italy 45 24N 11 52E
114 Paducah, Ky., U.S.A. 37 0N 88 40w
117 Paducah, Tex., U.S.A. 34 3N 100 16w
31 Padul, Spain 37 1N 3 38w
41 Padula, Italy 40 20N 15 40E
70 Padwa, India 18 27N 82 37E
101 Paeroa, New Zealand 37 23s 175 41E
38 Paesana, Italy 44 40N 7 18E
126 Páez, Colombia 2 40N 75 59w
39 Pag, Yugoslavia 44 27N 15 5E
39 Pag, I., Yugoslavia 44 50N 15 0E
85 Paga, Ghana 11 1N 1 8w
72 Pagai Selatan, I., Indonesia 3 0s 100 15E
72 Pagai Utara, I., Indonesia 2 35s 100 0E
73 Pagain, I., Indonesia 3 0s 100 15E
73 Pagadian, Philippines 7 55N 123 30E
44 Pagaralam, Indonesia 4 0s 103 17E
44 Pagastikós Kólpos, Greece 39 15N 23 12E
72 Pagatan, Indonesia 3 33s 115 59E
116 Page, U.S.A. 47 11N 97 37w
87 Pagnau, Ethiopia 8 15N 34 7E
21 Pagny-sur-Moselle, Fr. 48 59N 6 2E
101 Pago Pago, Amer. Samoa 14 16s 170 43w
119 Pagosa Springs, U.S.A. 37 16N 107 4w

MAP

106 Pagwa River, Canada 50 2N 85 14w
110 Pahala, Hawaii 20 25N 156 0w
71 Pahang ♦, Malaysia 3 30N 103 9E
71 Pahang, R., Malaysia 3 40N 102 20E
101 Pahiatua, N.Z. 40 27s 175 50E
115 Pahokee, U.S.A. 26 50N 80 30w
119 Pahrump, U.S.A. 36 15N 116 0w
54 Paicheng, China 45 50N 122 53E
54 Paide, U.S.S.R. 58 57N 25 31E
51 Paignton, Eng. 50 26N 3 33w
51 Päijänne, Finland 61 30N 25 30E
45 Pailin, Khmer Rep. 12 46N 102 36E
18 Paimbœuf, France 47 17N 2 0w
18 Paimpol, France 48 48N 3 4w
72 Painan, Indonesia 1 15s 100 40E
112 Painesville, U.S.A. 41 42N 81 18w
119 Painted Desert, U.S.A. 36 40N 112 0w
117 Paintsville, U.S.A. 37 50N 82 50w
126 Paita, Colombia 4 7N 73 7w
14 Paisley, Scotland 55 51N 4 27w
118 Paisley, U.S.A. 42 43N 120 40w
112 Paisley, Canada 44 20N 81 28w
126 Paita, Peru 5 5s 81 0w
60 Paiva, R., Portugal 40 57N 7 55w
67 Paiyu, China 31 12N 98 45E
76 Paiyü Shan, mts., China 37 20N 100 0E
76 Paiyunopo, China 42 10N 109 28E
72 Pajakumbuh, Indonesia 0 20s 100 35E
30 Pajala, Sweden 67 13N 23 30E
30 Pajares, Spain 39 57N 1 48w
30 Pajares, Puerto de, Sp. 43 0N 5 46w
28 Pajeczno, Poland 51 5N 19 1E
71 Pak Lay, Laos 18 15N 101 27E
71 Pak Phanang, Thailand 8 21N 100 12E
71 Pak Sane, Laos 18 15N 103 36E
72 Pakala, India 13 29N 79 8E
72 Pakanbaru, Indonesia 0 30N 101 15E
126 Pakaraima, Mts., Guyana 6 0N 60 0w
91 Pakenham, Zambia 13 3s 29 58E
100 Pakenham, Australia 38 6s 145 30E
113 Pakenham, Canada 45 18N 76 18w
77 Pakhoi, China 21 30N 109 10E
66 Pakistan ■, S. Asia 30 0N 70 0E
67 Pakistan, East = Bangladesh ■, S. Asia 24 0N 90 0E
76 Pakokku, Burma 21 30N 95 0E
68 Pakpattan, Pakistan 30 25N 73 16E
42 Pakrac, Yugoslavia 45 27N 17 12E
71 Pakse, Laos 15 5N 105 52E
90 Pakwach, Uganda 2 28N 31 27E
81 Pala, Chad 9 25N 15 5E
88 Pala, Zaïre 6 45s 29 30E
90 Palabek, Uganda 3 22N 32 33E
117 Palacious, U.S.A. 28 44N 96 12w
30 Palafrugell, Spain 41 55N 3 10E
41 Palagiano, Italy 40 35N 17 0E
45 Palaiokastron, Greece 35 12N 26 18E
45 Palaiokhora, Greece 35 16N 23 39E
70 Palakoi, India 16 31N 81 46E

* Renamed Owambo

MAP

44 Palamás, Greece 39 26N 22 4E
32 Palamós, Spain 41 50N 3 10E
68 Palampur, India 32 10N 76 30E
59 Palana, U.S.S.R. 59 10N 160 10E
73 Palanan, Phil. 17 8N 122 29E
68 Palanpur, India 24 10N 72 25E
92 Palapye Rd., Botswana 22 30s 27 7E
70 Palar, R., India 12 27N 80 13E
115 Palatka, U.S.A. 29 40N 81 40w
59 Palatka, U.S.S.R. 60 6N 150 54E
94 Palau Is., Pac Ocean 7 30N 134 30E
73 Palauig, Philippines 15 26N 119 54E
71 Palauk, Burma 13 10N 98 40E
20 Palavas, France 43 32N 3 56E
72 Palawan, I., Philippines 10 0N 119 0E
72 Palayankottai, India 8 45N 77 45E
41 Palazzo San Gervásio, It. 40 53N 15 58E
41 Palazzolo Acreida, Italy 37 4N 14 43E
100 Palchewoflock, Austral. 35 20s 142 15E
54 Paldisk, U.S.S.R. 59 23N 24 9E
42 Pale, Yugoslavia 43 50N 18 38E
73 Paleleh, Indonesia 1 10N 121 50E
72 Palembang, Indonesia 3 0s 104 50E
30 Palencia, Spain 42 1N 4 34w
30 Palencia ♦, Spain 42 31N 4 33w
126 Palermo, Colombia 2 54N 75 26w
40 Palermo, Italy 38 8N 13 20E
118 Palermo, U.S.A. 39 30N 121 37w
62 Palestine = Israel & Jordan, Asia 32 0N 35 0E
117 Palestine, U.S.A. 31 42N 95 35w
40 Palestrina, Italy 41 50N 12 52E
67 Paletwa, Burma 21 30N 92 50E
68 Palghat, India 10 46N 76 42E
68 Pali, India 25 50N 73 20E
85 Palimé, Togo 6 57N 0 37E
41 Palinuro, C., Italy 40 1N 15 14E
76 Palinyuchi (Tapanshang), China 43 40N 118 20E
116 Palisade, U.S.A. 40 35N 101 10w
68 Palitana, India 21 32N 71 49E
120 Palizada, Mexico 18 18N 92 8w
41 Palizza, Italy 37 58N 15 59E
70 Palk Bay, India-Sri Lanka 9 30N 79 30E
70 Palk Strait, India-Sri Lanka 10 0N 80 0E
70 Palkonda, India 18 36N 83 48E
70 Palkonda Ra., India 13 50N 79 20E
55 Pallasovka, U.S.S.R. 50 4N 47 0E
70 Palleru, R., India 17 30N 79 40E
90 Pallisa, Uganda 1 12N 33 43E
68 Pallu, India 28 59N 74 14E
115 Palm Beach, U.S.A. 26 46N 80 0w
98 Palm I., Australia 18 45s 146 35E
119 Palm Springs, U.S.A. 33 51N 116 35w
32 Palma, Balearic Is. 39 33N 2 39E
8 Palma, Canary Is. 28 40N 17 50w
91 Palma, Mozambique 10 46s 40 29E
33 Palma, Bahia de, Balearic Is. 39 30N 2 39E
31 Palma del Rio, Spain 37 43N 5 17w
40 Palma di Montechiaro, Sicily 37 12N 13 46E
80 Palma, I., Can. Is. 28 45N 17 50w
121 Palma Soriano, Cuba 20 15N 76 0w
39 Palmanova, Italy 45 54N 13 18E
127 Palmares, Brazil 8 41s 35 36w
73 Palmarito, Venezuela 7 37N 70 10w
40 Palmarola, I., Italy 40 57N 12 50E
125 Palmas, Brazil 26 29s 52 0w
84 Palmas, C., Liberia 4 27N 7 46w
40 Pálmas, G. di, Italy 39 0N 8 30E
119 Palmdale, U.S.A. 34 36N 118 7w
88 Palmeirinhas, Pta. das, Angola 9 2s 12 57E
31 Palmela, Portugal 38 32N 8 57w
104 Palmer, Alaska, U.S.A. 61 35N 149 10w
113 Palmer, Mass., U.S.A. 42 9N 72 21w
5 Palmer Arch, Antarc. 64 15s 65 0w
116 Palmer Lake, U.S.A. 39 10N 104 52w
96 Palmer, R., N. Terr., Australia 24 30s 133 0E
98 Palmer, R., Queens., Australia 15 46s 143 30E
5 Palmer Pen., Antarc. 73 0s 60 0w
112 Palmerston, Canada 43 50N 80 40w
101 Palmerston, N.Z. 45 29s 170 43E
98 Palmerston, C., Australia 21 21s 149 20E
101 Palmerston North, N.Z. 40 21s 175 39E
113 Palmerton, U.S.A. 40 47N 75 36w
115 Palmetto, U.S.A. 27 33N 82 33w
41 Palmi, Italy 38 21N 15 51E
124 Palmira, Argentina 32 59s 68 25w
126 Palmira, Colombia 3 32N 76 16w
112 Palms, U.S.A. 43 37N 82 47w
64 Palmyra = Tadmor, Syria 34 30N 37 55E
117 Palmyra, Mo., U.S.A. 39 45N 91 30w
112 Palmyra, N.Y., U.S.A. 34 5N 77 18w
70 Palni, India 10 30N 77 30E
70 Palni Hills, India 10 14N 77 33E
119 Palo Alto, U.S.A. 37 25N 122 8w
41 Palo del Colle, Italy 41 4N 16 43E
73 Paloe, Indonesia 8 20s 121 43E
39 Palombara Sabina, It. 42 4N 12 45E
126 Palomino, Colombia 11 16N 73 34w
73 Palopo, Indonesia 3 0s 120 16E
33 Palos, Cabo de, Spain 37 38N 0 40w
118 Palouse, U.S.A. 46 59N 117 5w
100 Palparara, Australia 24 47s 141 22E
49 Pålsboda, Sweden 59 3N 15 22E
64 Palu, Turkey 38 45N 40 0E
73 Palu, Indonesia 1 0s 119 59E
73 Paluan, Philippines 13 35N 120 29E
68 Palwal, India 28 8N 77 19E
85 Pama, Upper Volta 11 19N 0 44E
100 Pamamaroo, I., Austral. 32 17s 142 28E
72 Pamanukan, Indonesia 6 16s 107 49E

MAP

70 Pamban I., Sri Lanka 9 24N 79 35E
73 Pamekasan, Indonesia 7 10s 113 29E
73 Pameungpeuk, Indon. 7 38s 107 44E
20 Pamiers, France 43 7N 1 39E
115 Pamlico, R., U.S.A. 35 25N 76 40w
115 Pamlico Sd., U.S.A. 35 20N 76 0w
117 Pampa, U.S.A. 35 35N 100 58w
124 Pampa de las Salinas, Argentina 32 1s 66 58w
73 Pampanua, Indonesia 4 22s 120 14E
73 Pamparato, Italy 44 16N 7 54E
128 Pampas, Arg. 34 0s 64 0w
126 Pampas, Peru 12 20s 74 50w
126 Pamplona, Colombia 7 23N 72 39w
30 Pamplona, Spain 42 48N 1 38w
106 Pampoenpoort, S. Afr. 31 3s 22 40E
43 Panagyurishte, Bulgaria 42 49N 24 15E
70 Panaji (Panjim), India 15 25N 73 50E
121 Panama ■, Cent. America 8 48N 79 55w
120 Panamá, Pan. Rep. 9 0N 79 25w
120 Panama Canal, Central America 9 10N 79 56w
120 Panama Canal Żone, Central America 9 10N 79 56w
115 Panama City, U.S.A. 30 10N 85 41w
121 Panamá, Golfo de, Panama 8 4N 79 20w
119 Panamint Mts., U.S.A. 36 15N 117 20w
126 Panão, Peru 9 55s 75 55w
38 Panarea, I., Italy 38 38N 15 3E
38 Panaro, R., Italy 44 48N 11 5E
73 Panarukan, Indonesia 7 40s 113 52E
73 Panay, G., Phillipines 11 0N 122 30E
73 Panay I., Philippines 11 0N 122 30E
119 Pancake Ra., U.S.A. 38 30N 116 0w
42 Pančevo, Yugoslavia 44 52N 20 41E
46 Panciu, Rumania 45 54N 27 8E
30 Pancorbo, Paso, Spain 42 32N 3 5w
42 Pancota, Rumania 46 20N 21 45E
73 Pandan, Philippines 11 45N 122 10E
73 Pandeglang, Indonesia 6 25s 106 0E
70 Pandharpur, India 17 41N 75 20E
68 Pandhurna, India 21 36N 78 35E
32 Pandilla, Spain 41 32N 3 43w
125 Pando, Uruguay 34 30s 56 0w
73 Pando, C., Indonesia 8 42s 118 30E
28 Pandyz, Poland 51 19N 20 2E
117 Panola, U.S.A. 36 5N 90 30w
44 Paramithiá, Greece 39 30N 20 35E
59 Panfilov, U.S.S.R. 44 30N 80 0E
58 Panfilov, U.S.S.R. 50 25N 42 46E
73 Pang-Long, Burma 23 11N 98 45E
67 Pang-Yang, China 22 7N 98 48E
93 Panga, Zaire 1 52N 26 18E
93 Pangalanes, Canal des, Malag. 22 48s 47 50E
44 Pangaion Óros, Gr. 40 50N 24 0E
90 Pangani, Tanzania 5 25s 38 58E
90 Pangani ♦, Tanzania 5 25s 39 0E
90 Pangani, R., Tanzania 4 40s 37 50E
71 Panghai, Burma 23 0N 97 25E
90 Pangi, Congo 3 10s 26 35E
72 Pangkalanberandan, Indonesia 4 1N 98 20E
72 Pangkalanbuun, Indonesia 2 41s 111 41E
72 Pangkalansusu, Indon. 4 2N 98 42E
72 Pangkoh, Indonesia 3 5s 114 8E
71 Pangkor, I., Malaysia 4 16N 100 30E
105 Pangnirtung, Canada 66 0N 66 0w
73 Pangrango, Indon. 6 46s 107 1E
119 Panguitch, U.S.A. 37 52N 112 30w
73 Pangutaran Group, Phil. 6 18N 120 34E
117 Panhandle, U.S.A. 35 23N 101 23w
68 Pani Mines, India 22 29N 73 50E
68 Panipat, India 29 25N 77 2E
100 Panitya, Australia 35 15s 141 0E
68 Panjal Range, India 32 30N 76 50E
65 Panjgur, Pakistan 27 0N 64 5E
65 Panjnad Barrage, Pakistan 29 22N 71 15E
73 Pankadjene, Indonesia 4 46s 119 34E
72 Pankal Pinang, Indon. 2 0s 106 0E
85 Pankshin, Nigeria 9 25N 9 25E
69 Panna, India 24 40N 80 15E
69 Panna Hills, India 24 40N 81 15E
70 Panruti, India 11 46N 79 35E
70 Pantano, U.S.A. 32 0N 110 32w
73 Pantar, I., Indonesia 8 28s 124 10E
40 Pantelleria, Italy 36 52N 12 0E
40 Pantelleria, I., Italy 36 52N 12 0E
73 Pantjo, Indonesia 8 42s 118 40E
30 Pantón, Spain 42 31N 7 37w
73 Pantuan, Philippines 7 17N 125 58E
120 Panuco, Mexico 22 0N 98 25w
85 Panyam, Nigeria 9 27N 9 8E
77 Paoking, China 31 57N 111 21E
77 Paoki, China 34 25N 107 15E
77 Paoko, China 34 22N 107 12E
41 Pàola, Italy 39 21N 16 2E
116 Paonia, U.S.A. 38 56N 107 37w
67 Paoshan, China 25 10N 99 5E
76 Paoteh, China 39 0N 110 45E
76 Paoting, China 38 50N 115 30E
76 Paotow, China 40 45N 110 0E
76 Paotsing, China 28 35N 109 35E
81 Paoua, Cent. Afr. Rep. 7 16N 16 20E
31 Pápa, Hungary 47 22N 17 30E
121 Papagayo, Golfo de, Costa Rica 10 4N 85 50w
120 Papagayo, R., Brazil 12 30s 58 10w
68 Papagni R., India 14 10N 78 30E
101 Papakura, New Zealand 37 4s 174 59E
120 Papalantla de Olarte, Mexico 20 30N 97 21w
120 Papaloapan, R., Mexico 18 2N 96 51w

MAP

120 Papantla, Mexico 20 45N 116 0E
73 Papar, Malaysia 5 45N 116 0E
45 Pápas, Akra, Greece 38 13N 21 6E
124 Papenburg, Germany 53 7N 7 25E
124 Paposo, Chile 25 0s 70 30w
98 Papua, Gulf of, Papua 9 0s 144 50E
*98 Papua, Terr. of, ♦ 8 0s 145 0E
Austral. N. Guin.
39 Papuča, Yugoslavia 44 22N 15 30E
124 Papudo, Chile 32 29s 71 27w
45 Papuk, mts., Yugoslavia 45 30N 17 30E
67 Papun, Burma 18 0N 97 30E
127 Para, R., Brazil 0 40s 48 30w
127 Pará ♦, Brazil 3 20s 52 0w
41 Parábita, Italy 40 3N 18 8E
72 Paracel Is., Asia 16 49N 111 2E
99 Parachilna, Australia 31 10s 138 21E
66 Parachinar, Pakistan 34 0N 70 10E
42 Paračin, Yugoslavia 43 54N 21 27E
31 Paradas, Spain 37 18N 5 29w
30 Paradela, Spain 42 44N 7 37w
70 Paradip, India 20 15N 86 35E
118 Paradise, U.S.A. 47 27N 114 54w
118 Paradise Valley, U.S.A. 41 30N 117 28w
73 Parado, Indonesia 8 42s 118 30E
28 Paradyz, Poland 51 19N 20 2E
117 Paragould, U.S.A. 36 5N 90 30w
126 Paragua, R., Venezuela 6 30N 63 30w
125 Paraguaçu Paulista, Brazil 22 22s 50 35w
127 Paraguaçu, R., Brazil 16 0s 57 52w
126 Paraguaipoa, Ven. 11 21N 71 57w
126 Paraguana, Pen. de, Venezuela 12 0N 70 0w
124 Paraguari, Paraguay 25 36s 57 0w
124 Paraguari ♦, Paraguay 26 0s 57 10w
124 Paraguay ■, S. America 23 0s 57 0w
124 Paraguay, R., Paraguay 24 30s 58 20w
127 Paraiba ♦, Brazil 7 0s 36 0w
127 Paraiba, R., São Paulo, Brazil 21 37s 41 3w
51 Parainen, Finland 60 18N 22 18E
54 Parakhino Paddubye, U.S.S.R. 58 46N 33 10E
85 Parakou, Dahomey 9 25N 2 40E
45 Paralion-Astrous, Gr. 37 25N 22 45E
91 Paramagudi, India 9 31N 78 39E
126 Paramaribo, Surinam 5 50N 55 10w
126 Paramillo, Nudo del, Col. 7 4N 75 55w
44 Paramithiá, Greece 39 30N 20 35E
59 Paramushir, Ostrov, U.S.S.R. 50 24N 156 0E
62 Paran, N., Israel 30 14N 34 48E
124 Paraná, Argentina 32 0s 60 30w
124 Paraná, Brazil 12 30s 47 40w
124 Paraná ♦, Argentina 33 43s 59 15w
127 Paraná, R., Brazil 22 25s 53 1w
125 Paraná ♦, Brazil 24 30s 51 0w
125 Paranaguá, Brazil 25 30s 48 30w
127 Paranaiba, Brazil 18 0s 49 12w
125 Paranapiacaba, Serra do, Brazil 24 31s 48 35w
125 Paranavaí, Brazil 23 4s 52 28w
73 Parang, Jolo, Phil. 5 55N 120 54E
73 Parang, Mindanao, Phil. 7 23N 124 16E
127 Paraopeba, Brazil 18 48s 44 10w
45 Parápola, I., Greece 36 55N 23 27E
45 Paraspóri, Akra, Gr. 35 55N 27 15E
124 Paratinga, Brazil 12 40s 43 10w
99 Paratoo, Australia 32 38s 139 15E
99 Parattah, Australia 42 22s 147 23E
20 Paray-le-Monial, Fr. 46 27N 4 7E
68 Parbati, R., India 24 0N 77 10E
73 Parbhani, India 19 8N 76 52E
24 Parchim, Germany 53 25N 11 50E
28 Parczew, Poland 51 9N 22 52E
62 Pardes Hanna, Israel 32 28N 34 57E
30 Pardilla, Spain 41 33N 3 43w
127 Pardo, R., Bahia, Brazil 15 40s 39 0w
127 Pardo, R., Mato Grosso, Brazil 21 0s 53 25w
127 Pardo, R., São Paulo, Brazil 20 45s 48 0w
26 Pardubice, Cz. 50 3N 15 45E
73 Pare, Indonesia 7 43s 112 12E
90 Pare ♦, Tanz. 4 10s 38 0E
90 Pare Mts., Tanzania 3 37s 37 45E
126 Parecis, Serra dos, Brazil 13 0s 60 0w
30 Paredes de Nava, Spain 42 9N 4 42w
59 Paren, U.S.S.R. 62 45N 163 0E
106 Parent, Canada 47 55N 74 35w
113 Parent, Canada 48 31N 77 1w
106 Parent, Lac., Canada 48 31N 77 1w
20 Parentis-en-Born, Fr. 44 21N 1 4w
73 Parepare, Indonesia 4 0s 119 40E
54 Parfino, U.S.S.R. 57 59N 31 34E
93 Parfuri, Mozam. 22 28s 31 17E
24 Parham, Canada 44 40N 76 40w
126 Paria, Golfo de, Venezuela 10 20N 62 0w
126 Paria, Pen. de, Venezuela 10 50N 62 30w
92 Pasto Zootécnico do Cunene, Angola 8 51N 64 43w
72 Pariaguán, Venezuela 0 47s 100 11E
72 Pariaman, Indonesia 0 50s 120 5E
126 Parigi, Indon. 6 50N 58 20w
126 Parika, Guyana 2 30N 64 0w
126 Parima, Serra, Brazil 4 35s 74 25w
126 Parinari, Peru 2 40s 56 50w
127 Parintins, Brazil 67 Paripárit Kyun, Burma 14 55s 93 45E
106 Paris, Canada 43 20N 80 25w
19 Paris, France 48 50N 2 20E
114 Paris, Idaho, U.S.A. 42 13N 111 30w
114 Paris, Ky., U.S.A. 38 12N 84 12w
115 Paris, Tenn., U.S.A. 36 20N 88 20w
117 Paris, Tex., U.S.A. 33 40N 95 30w
73 Pariti, Indonesia 9 55s 123 30E
118 Park City, U.S.A. 40 42N 111 35w

MAP

116 Park Falls, U.S.A. 45 58N 90 27E
112 Park Head, Canada 44 36N 81 10w
118 Park Range, U.S.A. 40 0N 106 30w
116 Park Rapids, U.S.A. 46 56N 95 0w
116 Park River, U.S.A. 48 25N 97 17w
93 Park Rynie, S. Africa 30 25s 30 35E
119 Park View, U.S.A. 36 45N 106 37w
119 Parker, Ariz., U.S.A. 34 8N 114 16w
116 Parker, S.D., U.S.A. 43 25N 97 7w
119 Parker Dam, U.S.A. 34 13N 114 5w
114 Parkersburg, U.S.A. 39 18N 81 31w
109 Parkerview, Can. 51 28N 103 18w
100 Parkes, Australia 33 9s 148 11E
116 Parkston, U.S.A. 43 25N 98 0w
108 Parksville, Can. 49 20N 124 21w
70 Parlakimedi, India 18 45s 84 5E
38 Parma, Italy 44 50N 10 20E
118 Parma, Idaho, U.S.A. 43 49N 116 59w
112 Parma, Ohio, U.S.A. 41 25N 81 42w
38 Parma, R., Italy 44 27N 10 3E
127 Parnaguá, Brazil 10 10s 44 10w
127 Parnaiba, Piauí, Brazil 3 0s 41 40w
127 Parnaiba, São Paulo, Brazil 19 34s 51 14w
127 Parnaiba, R., Brazil 3 35s 43 0w
45 Parnassós, mt., Greece 38 17N 21 30E
45 Párnis, mt., Greece 38 14N 23 45E
45 Párnon Oros, Gr. 37 15N 22 45E
54 Pärnu, U.S.S.R. 58 12N 24 33E
68 Parola, India 20 47N 75 7E
99 Paroo Chan., Australia 30 50s 143 35E
99 Paroo, R., Australia 30 0s 144 5E
65 Paropamisus Range = Fi roz Kohi, Afghan. 34 45N 63 0E
45 Páros, Greece 37 5N 25 9E
45 Páros, I., Greece 37 5N 25 12E
119 Parowan, U.S.A. 37 54N 112 56w
20 Parpaillon, mts., France 44 30N 6 40E
124 Parral, Chile 36 10s 72 0w
100 Parramatta, Australia 33 48s 151 1E
120 Parras, Mexico 25 30N 102 20w
13 Parrett, R., Eng. 51 7N 2 58w
115 Parris I., U.S.A. 32 20N 80 30w
107 Parrsboro, Canada 45 30N 64 10w
109 Parry, Canada 49 47N 104 41w
4 Parry Is., Canada 77 0N 110 0w
112 Parry Sound, Canada 45 20N 80 0w
116 Parshall, U.S.A. 47 56N 102 11w
117 Parsons, U.S.A. 37 20N 95 10w
70 Partabpur, India 20 0N 80 42E
40 Partanna, Italy 37 43N 12 51E
68 Partapgarh, India 24 2N 74 40E
18 Parthenay, France 46 38N 0 16w
49 Partille, Sweden 57 48N 12 1E
40 Partinico, Italy 38 3N 13 6E
70 Partur, India 19 40N 76 14E
127 Paru, R., Brazil 0 20s 53 30w
70 Parur, India 10 13N 76 14E
126 Paruro, Peru 13 45s 71 50w
66 Parvatipuram, India 18 50N 83 25E
66 Parwan ♦, Afghan. 35 0N 69 0E
43 Pavlikeni, Bulgaria 43 14N 25 20E
49 Päryd, Sweden 56 34N 15 55E
92 Parys, S. Africa 26 52s 27 29E
/19 Pas-de-Calais ♦, Fr. 50 30N 2 30E
55 Pavlovo, Gorkiy, U.S.S.R. 55 58N 43 5E
59 Pavlovo, Yakut A.S.S.R. 63 5N 115 25E
55 Pavlovsk, U.S.S.R. 50 26N 40 5E
55 Pavlovskiy Posad, U.S.S.R. 55 37N 38 42E
38 Pavullo nel Frignano, It. 44 20N 10 50E
117 Pawhuska, U.S.A. 36 40N 96 25w
113 Pawling, U.S.A. 41 35N 73 37w
116 Pawnee, U.S.A. 36 24N 96 50w
116 Pawnee City, U.S.A. 40 8N 96 10w
113 Pawtucket, U.S.A. 41 51N 71 22w
73 Paximádhia, Greece 35 0N 24 35E
44 Paxoi, I., Greece 39 14N 20 12E
114 Paxton, Ill., U.S.A. 40 25N 88 0w
116 Paxton, Nebr., U.S.A. 41 12N 101 27w
71 Paya Bakri, Malaysia 2 3N 102 44E
20 Payerne, Switzerland 46 49N 6 56E
118 Payette, U.S.A. 44 0N 117 0w
31 Paymogo, Spain 37 44N 7 21w
105 Payne L., Canada 59 30N 74 30w
60 Payne, U.S.A. 60 0N 70 0w
84 Paynesville, Liberia 6 20N 10 45w
119 Paynesville, U.S.A. 45 21N 94 44w
126 Payo, Ecuador 1 25s 78 20w
124 Paysandú, Uruguay 32 19s 58 8w
119 Payson, Ariz., U.S.A. 34 17N 111 15w
118 Payson, Utah, U.S.A. 40 8N 111 41w
120 Paz, Bahia de la, Mexico 24 15N 110 25w
64 Pazar, Turkey 41 10N 40 50E
43 Pazardzhik, Bulgaria 42 12N 24 20E
21 Pazin, Yugoslavia 45 14N 13 56E
42 Pčinja, R., Yugoslavia 42 0N 21 45E
118 Pe Ell, U.S.A. 46 30N 122 59w
113 Peabody, U.S.A. 42 31N 70 56w
108 Peace Point, Canada 59 15N 112 30w
108 Peace River, Canada 56 15N 117 18w
108 Peace, R., Canada 59 0N 111 25w
108 Peace River Res., Canada 55 50N 123 40w
119 Peach Springs, U.S.A. 35 36N 113 30w
98 Peak Downs, Australia 22 55s 148 0E
100 Peak Hill, N.S.W., Austral. 32 39s 148 11E
96 Peak Hill, W. A., Austral. 25 35s 118 43E
98 Peak Range, Australia 22 50s 148 20E
12 Peak, The, U.K. 53 24N 1 53w
96 Peake, Australia 35 25s 140 0E
119 Peale Mt., U.S.A. 38 25N 109 12w
70 Pearl Banks, Ceylon 8 45N 79 45E
110 Pearl City, Hawaii 2 21N 158 0w

MAP

117 Pearl, R., U.S.A. 31 50N 90 0w
117 Pearsall, U.S.A. 28 55N 99 8w
108 Pearse I., Canada 54 9N 130 4w
4 Peary Land, Greenland 82 40N 33 0w
117 Pease, R., U.S.A. 34 18N 100 15w
91 Pebane, Mozambique 17 10s 38 8E
126 Pebas, Peru 3 10s 71 55w
42 Peó, Yugoslavia 42 40N 20 17E
38 Péccioli, Italy 43 32N 10 43E
56 Pechenezhin, U.S.S.R. 48 30N 24 48E
52 Pechenga, U.S.S.R. 69 30N 31 25E
55 Pechnezhskoye Vdkhr., U.S.S.R. 50 0N 36 50E
52 Pechora, R., U.S.S.R. 62 30N 56 30E
52 Pechorskaya Guba, U.S.S.R. 68 40N 54 0E
54 Pechory, U.S.S.R. 57 48N 27 40E
42 Pecica, Rumania 46 10N 21 3E
42 Pečka, Yugoslavia 44 18N 19 33E
40 Pécora, C., Italy 39 28N 8 23E
117 Pecos, U.S.A. 31 25N 103 35w
117 Pecos, R., U.S.A. 31 22N 102 30w
27 Pécs, Hungary 46 5N 18 15E
70 Peddapalli, India 18 40N 79 24E
70 Peddapuram, India 17 6N 82 5E
70 Peddavagu, R., India 16 33N 79 8E
84 Pedembu, Sierra Leone 8 7N 10 48w
72 Pedjantan, I., Indonesia 0 5s 106 15E
126 Pedreg, Venezuela 9 48N 68 30w
127 Pedreiras, Brazil 4 32s 44 40w
127 Pedro Afonso, Brazil 9 0s 48 10w
126 Pedro Chico, Colombia 1 4N 70 25w
124 Pedro de Valdivia, Chile 22 33s 69 38w
125 Pedro Juan Caballero, Paraguay 22 30s 55 40w
120 Pedro Miguel Locks, Panama Canal Zone 9 1N 79 36w
33 Pedro Muñoz, Spain 39 25N 2 56w
30 Drógão Grande, Port. 39 55N 8 0w
99 Peebinga, S. Australia 34 52s 140 57E
14 Peebles, Scotland 55 40N 3 12w
† 14 Peebles ♦, Scot. 55 37N 3 4w
113 Peekshill, U.S.A. 41 18N 73 57w
12 Peel, I. of Man 54 14N 4 40w
104 Peel, R., Canada 67 0N 135 0w
24 Peene, R., Germany 53 53N 13 53E
99 Peera Peera Poolanna L., South Australia 26 30s 138 0E
101 Pegasus Bay, N.Z. 43 20s 173 10E
26 Peggau, Austria 47 12N 15 21E
33 Pego, Spain 38 51N 0 8w
67 Pegu, Burma 17 20N 96 29E
67 Pegu Yoma, mts., Burma 19 0N 96 0E
77 Peh K., China 24 20N 113 20E
76 Pehan, China 48 17N 120 31E
42 Pehčevo, Yugoslavia 41 41N 23 3E
77 Pehpei, China 29 44N 106 29E
124 Pehuajó, Argentina 36 0s 62 0w
24 Peine, Germany 52 19N 10 12E
76 Peiping, China 39 50N 116 20E
25 Peissenberg, Germany 47 48N 11 4E
24 Peitz, Germany 51 50N 14 23E
127 Peixe, Brazil 12 0s 48 40w
42 Pek, R., Yugoslavia 44 58N 21 55E
73 Pekalongan, Indonesia 6 53s 109 40E
71 Pekan, W. Malaysia 3 30N 103 25E
116 Pekin, U.S.A. 40 35N 89 40w
76 Peking = Peiping, China 39 50N 116 20E
73 Pelabuhanratu, Indon. 7 0s 106 32E
73 Pelabuhan Ratu, Teluk, Indonesia 7 5s 106 30E
44 Pélagos, I., Greece 39 17N 24 4E
39 Pelagruza, Is., Y.-slavia 42 24N 16 15E
72 Pelaihari, Indonesia 3 55s 114 45E
28 Peltzyce, Poland 53 3N 15 16E
46 Peleaga, mt., Rumania 45 22N 22 55E
106 Pelee I., Canada 41 40N 82 40w
121 Pelée, Mt., Martinique 14 40N 61 0w
90 Pelekech, mt., Kenya 3 52N 35 8E
71 Peleng, I., Indonesia 1 20s 123 30E
115 Pelham, U.S.A. 31 5N 84 6w
26 Pelhrimov, Cz. 49 24N 15 12E
109 Pelican Narrows, Can. 55 12N 102 55w
108 Pelican Portage, Can. 55 51N 113 0w
109 Pelican Rapids, Canada 52 38N 100 42w
121 Peligre, L. de, Haiti 19 1N 71 58w
115 Pella, U.S.A. 41 20N 93 0w
44 Pélla ♦, Greece 40 52N 22 0E
41 Pellaro, Italy 38 1N 15 40E
24 Pellworm, I., Germany 54 30N 8 40E
104 Pelly L., Canada 66 0N 102 0w
104 Pelly, R., Canada 62 15N 133 30w
105 Pelly Bay, Canada 68 0N 89 50w
45 Peloponnese = Pelopónnisos, Gr.
45 Pelopónnisos, Greece 37 10N 22 0E
41 Peloro, C., Italy 38 15N 15 40E
101 Pelorus Sound, N.Z. 40 59s 173 59E
125 Pelotas, Brazil 31 42s 52 23w
43 Pel'ovo, Bulgaria 43 26N 24 17E
73 Pelvoux, Massif de, Fr. 44 52N 6 20E
73 Pemalang, Indonesia 6 53s 109 23E
72 Pematang, I., Indonesia 2 50N 96 55E
72 Pematang Siantar, Indonesia 2 57N 99 5E
91 Pemba, Zambia 16 30s 27 28E
90 Pemba Channel, Tanz. 5 0s 39 37E
91 Pemba, I., Tanz. 5 0s 39 45E
96 Pemberton, Austral. 34 30s 116 0E
108 Pemberton, Canada 50 25s 122 50w
114 Pembine, U.S.A. 45 38N 87 59w
106 Pembroke, Canada 45 50N 77 15w
‡101 Pembroke, New Zealand 44 33s 169 10E
13 Pembroke, Wales 51 41N 4 57w
* 13 Pembroke ♦, Wales 51 40N 5 0w

113 Pen Argyl, U.S.A. 40 52N 75 17E
12 Pen-y-Ghent, mt., Eng. 54 10N 2 15w
30 Peña, Sierra de la, Spain 42 32N 0 45w
30 Peña de Francia, Sierra de, Spain 40 32N 6 10w
32 Peña Roya, mt., Spain 40 24N 0 40w
30 Peñafiel, Portugal 41 12N 8 17w
30 Peñaflor, Spain 37 43N 5 21w
30 Peñalara, Pico, Spain 40 51N 3 57w
30 Penamacôr, Portugal 40 10N 7 10w
71 Penang = Pinang, Malaysia 5 25N 100 15E
125 Penápolis, Brazil 21 30s 50 0w
30 Peñaranda de Bracamonte, Spain 40 53N 5 13w
100 Penarie, Austral. 34 30s 143 35E
31 Peñarroya-Pueblonuevo, Spain 38 19N 5 16w
126 Peñas, Pta., Ven. 11 17N 70 28w
30 Peñas, C. de, Spain 43 42N 5 52w
128 Peñas, G. de, Chile 47 0s 75 0w
33 Peñas de San Pedro, Sp. 38 44N 2 0w
118 Pend Oreille, L., U.S.A. 48 0N 116 30w
118 Pend Oreille, R., U.S.A. 48 30N 117 8w
44 Pendálofon, Greece 40 14N 21 12E
118 Pendleton, U.S.A. 45 35N 118 50w
97 Penedo, Brazil 10 15s 36 36w
106 Penetanguishene, Can. 44 50N 79 55w
73 Pengalengan, Indon. 7 9s 107 30E
77 Pengan, China 31 0N 106 18E
72 Pengchia Yu (Agincourt) Is., Taiwan 25 4N 122 2E
90 Penge, Kasai, Congo 5 30s 24 33E
90 Penge, Kivu, Congo 4 27s 28 25E
77 Penghu (Pescadores), Taiwan 23 34N 119 30E
76 Penglai (Tengchowfu), China 37 50N 120 50E
77 Pengpu, China 33 0N 117 25E
77 Pengshui, China 29 20N 108 15E
99 Penguin, Austral. 41 8s 146 6E
91 Penhalonga, Rhodesia 18 52s 32 40E
30 Peniche, Portugal 39 19N 9 22w
72 Penida, I., Indonesia 8 45s 115 30E
32 Peñiscola, Spain 40 22N 0 24E
76 Penki, China 41 20N 132 50E
18 Penmarch, France 47 49N 4 21w
18 Penmarch, Pte. de, Fr. 47 48N 4 22w
112 Penn Yan, U.S.A. 42 39N 77 7w
39 Pennabilli, Italy 43 50N 12 17E
39 Penne, Italy 42 28N 13 56E
70 Penner, R., India 14 50N 78 20E
12 Pennines, Eng. 54 50N 2 20w
39 Pennino, Mte., Italy 43 6N 12 54E
114 Pennsylvania ♦, U.S.A. 40 50N 78 0w
108 Penny, Canada 53 58N 121 1w
55 Peno, U.S.S.R. 57 2N 32 33E
100 Penola, Australia 37 12s 140 51E
98 Penong, Australia 31 59s 133 5E
95 Penrhyn Is., Pac. Oc. 9 0s 150 30w
12 Penrith, England 54 40N 2 45w
100 Penrith, Austral. 33 43s 150 38E
12 Pensacola, U.S.A. 30 30N 87 10w
5 Pensacola Mts., Antarc. 84 0s 40 0w
100 Penshurst, Austral. 37 49s 142 20w
108 Penticton, Canada 49 30N 119 30w
98 Pentland, Australia 20 32s 145 25E
14 Pentland Firth, Scot. 58 43N 3 10w
14 Pentland Hills, Scotland 55 48N 3 25w
70 Penukonda, India 14 5N 77 38E
55 Penza, U.S.S.R. 53 15N 45 5E
13 Penzance, Eng. 50 7N 5 32w
25 Penzberg, Germany 47 46N 11 23E
59 Penzhinskaya Guba, U.S.S.R. 61 30N 163 0E
24 Penzlin, Germany 53 32N 13 6E
119 Peoria, Ariz., U.S.A. 33 40N 112 15w
116 Peoria, Ill., U.S.A. 40 40N 89 40w
118 Pepperwood, U.S.A. 40 23N 124 0w
44 Peqini, Albania 41 4N 19 44E
62 Pequ'in, Israel 32 58N 35 20E
72 Perabumilih, Indonesia 3 27s 104 15E
126 Peraitepuy, Ven. 4 59N 60 54w
71 Peraki, R., W. Malaysia 5 10N 101 4E
45 Perakhóra, Greece 38 2N 22 56E
32 Perales de Alfambra, Sp. 40 38N 1 0w
30 Perales del Puerto, Sp. 40 10N 6 40w
32 Peralta, Spain 42 21N 1 49w
45 Pérama, Greece 34 55N 24 22E
42 Perast, Yugoslavia 42 31N 8 47E
18 Perche, France 48 31N 1 1E
18 Perche, Collines de la, Fr. 48 30N 2 5E
19 Percy, France 48 55N 1 11w
98 Percy Is., Australia 21 39s 150 16E
98 Percyville, Australia 19 2s 143 45E
32 Perdido, Mt., Spain 42 40N 0 5E
100 Perekerton, Australia 34 53s 143 49E
126 Pereira, Colombia 4 49N 75 43w
90 Pereira de Eça, Angola 16 48s 15 50E
54 Pereslavi-Zelesskiy, U.S.S.R. 56 45N 38 58E
54 Pereyaslav-Khmelnitskiy, U.S.S.R. 50 3N 31 28E
26 Perg, Austria 48 15N 14 38E
124 Pergamino, Argentina 33 52s 60 30w
39 Pergine Valsugano, It. 46 4N 11 15E
39 Pérgola, Italy 43 35N 12 50E
116 Perham, U.S.A. 46 36N 95 36w
71 Perhentian, Kepulauan, W. Malaysia 5 54N 102 42E
63 Peria, Jordan 30 0N 35 22E

126 Perija, Sierra de, Col. 9 30N 73 3w
63 Perim, I., Red Sea 12 39N 43 25E
127 Periperi, Serra do, Brazil 14 50s 40 30w
45 Peristera, I., Greece 39 15N 23 58E
70 Periyakulam, India 10 5N 77 30E
70 Periyar, L., India 9 25N 77 10E
70 Periyar, R., India 10 15N 78 10E
73 Perkam, Tg., Indonesia 1 35s 137 50E
39 Perkovió, Yugoslavia 43 41N 16 10E
121 Perlas, Arch. de las, Panama 8 41N 79 7w
121 Perlas, Punta de, Nic. 11 30N 83 30w
127 Perleberg, Germany 53 5N 11 50E
55 Perlevka, U.S.S.R. 51 56N 38 57E
42 Perlez, Yugoslavia 45 11N 20 22E
71 Perlis ♦, W. Malaysia 6 30N 100 15E
52 Perm (Molotov), U.S.S.R. 58 0N 57 10E
44 Përmeti, Albania 40 15N 20 21E
127 Pernambuco = Recife, Brazil 8 0s 35 0w
127 Pernambuco ♦, Braz. 8 0s 37 0w
19 Péronne, France 49 55s 2 57E
38 Perosa Argentina, Italy 44 57N 7 11E
20 Perpignan, France 42 42N 2 53E
18 Perros-Guirec, France 48 49N 3 28w
115 Perry, Fla., U.S.A. 30 9N 83 10w
115 Perry, Ga., U.S.A. 32 25N 83 41w
116 Perry, Iowa, U.S.A. 41 48N 94 5w
115 Perry, Maine, U.S.A. 44 59N 67 20w
112 Perry, N.Y., U.S.A. 42 44N 77 59w
117 Perry, Okla., U.S.A. 36 20N 97 20w
117 Perryton, U.S.A. 36 28N 100 48w
117 Perryville, Mo., U.S.A. 37 42N 89 50w
48 Persberg, Sweden 59 47N 14 15E
65 Persepolis, Iran 29 55N 52 50E
65 Persia = Iran, Asia 35 0N 50 0E
65 Persian Gulf, Asia 27 0N 50 0E
49 Perstorp, Sweden 56 10N 13 25E
96 Perth, Australia 31 57s 115 52E
106 Perth, N.B., Canada 46 43N 67 42w
114 Perth, Ont., Canada 44 55N 76 20w
14 Perth, Scotland 56 24N 3 27w
113 Perth, U.S.A. 40 33N 74 36w
*14 Perth ♦, Scot. 56 30N 4 0w
115 Phenix City, U.S.A. 32 30N 85 0w
20 Pertuis, France 43 42N 5 30E
20 Pertuis Breton, France 46 17N 1 25w
20 Pertuis d'Antioche, Fr. 46 4N 1 10w
116 Peru, Ill., U.S.A. 41 18N 89 12w
114 Peru, Ind., U.S.A. 40 42N 86 0w
126 Peru ■, S. America 8 0s 75 0w
39 Perúgia, Italy 43 6N 12 24E
39 Perušić, Yugoslavia 44 40N 15 22E
55 Pervomayskiy, U.S.S.R. 53 20N 40 10E
58 Pervouralsk, U.S.S.R. 56 55N 60 0E
39 Pésaro, Italy 43 55N 12 53E
38 Pescara, Italy 42 28N 14 13E
57 Peschanokopskoye, U.S.S.R. 46 14N 41 4E
55 Peski, U.S.S.R. 51 14N 42 12E
39 Pescina, Abruzzi, Italy 42 0N 13 39E
38 Pescina, Toscana, Italy 43 54N 10 40E
66 Peshawar, Pakistan 34 2N 71 37E
44 Peshkopia, Albania 41 41N 20 25E
43 Peshtera, Bulgaria 42 2N 24 18E
114 Peshtigo, U.S.A. 45 4N 87 46w
55 Peskovka, U.S.S.R. 59 23N 52 28E
55 Peski, U.S.S.R. 51 14N 42 12E
55 Pestovo, U.S.S.R. 58 33N 35 18E
55 Pestravka, U.S.S.R. 52 28N 49 57E
45 Péta, Greece 39 10N 21 2E
62 Petah Tiqwa, Israel 32 6N 34 53E
45 Petalidhion, Khóra, Greece 36 57N 21 55E
3 Petaling Jaya, Malaysia 3 4N 101 42E
118 Petaluma, U.S.A. 38 13N 122 45w
16 Petange, Luxembourg 49 33N 5 55E
126 Petare, Venezuela 10 29N 66 49w
120 Petatlán, Mexico 17 31N 101 16w
91 Petauke, Zambia 14 14s 31 12E
106 Petawawa, Canada 45 54N 77 17w
5 Peter 1st, I., S. Oc. 69 0s 91 0w
109 Peter Pond L., Canada 56 0N 109 0w
106 Peterbell, Canada 48 36N 83 21w
113 Peterboro, U.S.A. 42 55N 71 59w
112 Peterborough, Canada 44 20N 78 20w
13 Peterborough, Eng. 52 35N 0 14w
99 Peterborough, Austral. 33 0s 138 45E
14 Peterhead, Scot. 57 30N 1 49w
109 Petersburg, Alas., U.S.A. 56 50N 133 0w
114 Petersburg, Ind., U.S.A. 38 30N 87 15w
114 Petersburg, Va., U.S.A. 37 17N 77 26w
114 Petersburg, W. Va., U.S.A. 38 59N 79 10w
98 Petford, Australia 17 20s 144 50E
41 Petilia Policastro, It. 39 7N 16 48E
115 Petit Bois I., U.S.A. 30 16N 88 25w
107 Petit Cap, Canada 48 58N 63 58w
121 Petit Goâve, Haiti 18 27N 72 51w
107 Petitcodiac, Canada 45 57N 65 11w
107 Petite Saguenay, Can. 47 59N 70 1w
107 Petitsikapau, L., Can. 54 50N 66 30w
68 Petlad, India 22 30N 72 45E
120 Peto, Mexico 20 10N 88 53w
101 Petone, New Zealand 41 13s 174 53E
114 Petoskey, U.S.A. 45 21N 84 55w
63 Petra, Jordan 30 20N 35 22E
32 Petra, Spain 39 37N 3 6E
4 Petra, Ostrova, U.S.S.R. 76 15N 118 30E
41 Petralia, Italy 37 49N 14 4E
33 Petrel, Spain 38 30N 0 46w
43 Petrich, Bulgaria 41 24N 23 13E
39 Petrijanec, Yugoslavia 46 23N 16 17E

54 Petrikov, U.S.S.R. 52 11N 28 29E
46 Petrila, Rumania 45 29N 23 29E
39 Petrinja, Yugoslavia 45 28N 16 18E
127 Petrolândia, Brazil 9 5s 38 20w
106 Petrolia, Canada 42 54N 82 9w
127 Petrolina, Brazil 9 24s 40 30w
58 Petropavlovsk, U.S.S.R. 55 0N 69 0E
59 Petropavlovsk-Kamchatskiy, U.S.S.R. 53 16N 159 0E
127 Petrópolis, Brazil 22 33s 43 9w
46 Petroşani, Rumania 45 28N 23 20E
42 Petrova Gora, Y.-slav. 45 15N 15 45E
42 Petrovac, Yugoslavia 42 13N 18 57E
46 Petrovaradin, Y.-slav. 45 16N 19 55E
55 Petrovsk, Saratov, U.S.S.R. 52 22N 45 19E
59 Petrovsk-Zabaykalskiy, U.S.S.R. 51 26N 108 30E
57 Petrovskoye, U.S.S.R. 45 25N 42 58E
52 Petrozavodsk, U.S.S.R. 61 41N 34 20E
93 Petrus Steyn, S. Africa 27 38s 28 8E
92 Petrusburg, S. Africa 29 4s 25 26E
68 Phalodi, India 27 12N 72 24E
19 Phalsbourg, France 48 46N 7 15E
71 Phan Rang, S. Vietnam 11 40N 109 9E
71 Phan Thiet, S. Vietnam 11 1N 108 9E
71 Phangnga, Thailand 8 28N 98 30E
69 Pharenda, India 27 5N 83 17E
75 Pharo Dzong, China 27 45N 89 14E
71 Phatthalung, Thailand 7 39N 100 6E
112 Phelps, N.Y., U.S.A. 42 57N 77 5w
116 Phelps, Wis., U.S.A. 46 2N 89 2w
115 Phenix City, U.S.A. 32 30N 85 0w
71 Phetchabun, Thailand 16 25N 101 8E
71 Phetchaburi, Thailand 13 1N 99 55E
71 Phichai, Thailand 17 22N 100 10E
117 Philadelphia, Miss., U.S.A. 32 47N 89 5w
113 Philadelphia, N.Y., U.S.A. 44 9N 75 40w
114 Philadelphia, Pa., U.S.A. 40 0N 75 10w
116 Philip, U.S.A. 44 4N 101 42w
83 Philippe Thomas, Tun. 34 21N 8 28E
16 Philippeville, Belgium 50 12N 4 33E
92 Philippi, L., Australia 24 0s 138 55E
92 Philippi, U.S.A. 33 35N 25 16E
42 Philippopolis = Plovdiv, Bulgaria 42 8N 24 44E
118 Philipsburg, Mont., USA 46 20N 113 21w
112 Philipsburg, Pa., U.S.A. 40 53N 78 10w
92 Philipstown, S Africa 30 28s 24 30E
100 Phillip I., Austral. 38 20s 145 15E
117 Phillips, Texas, U.S.A. 35 48N 101 17w
116 Phillips, Wis., U.S.A. 45 41N 90 22w
116 Phillipsburg, Kans., U.S.A. 39 48N 99 20w
113 Phillipsburg, Penn., U.S.A. 40 43N 75 12w
99 Phillott, Australia 27 53s 145 50E
113 Philmont, U.S.A. 42 14N 73 37w
114 Philomath, U.S.A. 44 28N 123 21w
71 Phitsanulok, Thailand 16 50N 100 12E
71 Phnom Penh, Khmer Rep. 11 33N 104 55E
71 Phnom Thbeng, Khmer Rep. 13 50N 104 56E
119 Phoenix, Ariz., U.S.A. 33 30N 112 10w
113 Phoenix, N.Y., U.S.A. 43 13N 76 18w
95 Phoenix Is., Pac. Oc. 3 30s 172 0w
113 Phoenixville, U.S.A. 40 12N 75 29w
67 Phongdo, China 30 14N 91 14E
71 Phra Chedi Sam Ong, Thailand 15 16N 98 23E
71 Phra Nakhon Si Ayutthaya, Thailand 14 25N 100 30E
71 Phrae, Thailand 18 7N 100 9E
71 Phrao, Thailand 19 23N 99 15E
71 Phu Doan, N. Vietnam 21 40N 105 10E
71 Phu Loi, Laos 20 14N 103 14E
71 Phu Ly (Ha Nam), N. Vietnam 20 35N 105 50E
71 Phu Qui, Vietnam 19 20N 105 20E
71 Phuket, Thailand 8 0N 98 28E
68 Phulera (Phalera), India 26 52N 75 16E
71 Phuoc Le (Baria), S. Vietnam 10 39N 107 19E
71 Pi Ho, China 32 0N 116 20E
98 Piabia, Austral. 22 12s 152 45E
38 Piacenza, Italy 45 2N 9 42E
39 Piádena, Italy 45 8N 10 22E
98 Pialba, Australia 25 20s 152 45E
99 Pian Cr., Austral. 30 2s 149 0E
38 Pianella, Italy 42 24N 14 5E
100 Piangil, Australia 35 3s 143 20E
39 Pianoro, Italy 44 20N 11 20E
39 Pianosa, I., Puglia, Italy 42 12N 15 44E
38 Pianosa, I., Toscana, Italy 42 12N 10 4E
109 Piapot, Canada 49 59N 109 8w
31 Pias, Portugal 38 1N 7 29w
28 Piaseczno, Poland 52 5N 21 2E
28 Piastów, Poland 52 12N 20 48E
46 Piatra, Rumania 43 51N 25 9E
46 Piatra Neamţ, Rum. 46 56N 26 21E
127 Piauí ♦, Brazil 7 0s 43 0w

39 Piave, R., Italy 45 50N 13 9E
41 Piazza Armerina, Italy 37 21N 14 20E
87 Pibor, Sudan 6 52N 33 0E
87 Pibor Post, Sudan 6 47N 33 3E
124 Pica, Chile 20 35s 69 25w
19 Picard, Plaine de, France 50 0N 2 0E
19 Picardie, France 50 0N 2 15E
19 Picardy = Picardie, France 50 0N 2 15E
117 Picayune, U.S.A. 30 40N 89 40w
91 Piccadilly, Zambia 14 0s 29 30E
41 Picerno, Italy 40 40N 15 37E
77 Pichieh, China 27 20N 105 20E
124 Pichilemu, Chile 34 22s 72 9w
126 Pichincha, vol., Ec. 0 10s 78 30w
106 Pickerel L., Canada 48 40N 91 25w
106 Pickle Crow, Canada 51 30N 90 0w
8 Pico, Azores 38 28N 28 18w
128 Pico Truncado, Arg. 46 40s 68 10w
30 Picos Ancares, Sierra de, 42 51N 6 52w
19 Picquigny, France 49 56N 2 10E
120 Picton, Austral. 34 12s 150 34E
106 Picton, Canada 44 1N 77 9w
101 Picton, New Zealand 41 18s 174 3E
107 Pictou, Canada 45 41N 62 42w
108 Picture Butte, Canada 49 55N 112 45w
70 Pidurutalagala, mt., Sri Lanka 7 10N 80 50E
126 Piedecuesta, Col. 6 59N 73 3w
38 Piedicavallo, Italy 45 41N 7 57E
38 Piedmont = Piemonte, Italy 45 0N 7 30E
115 Piedmont, U.S.A. 33 55N 85 39w
115 Piedmont Plat., U.S.A. 34 0N 81 30w
41 Piedmonte d'Alife, Italy 41 22N 14 22E
32 Piedra, R., Spain 41 10N 1 45w
41 Piedrabuena, Spain 39 0N 4 10w
30 Piedrahita, Spain 40 28N 5 23w
126 Piedras, R. de las, Peru 11 40s 70 50w
119 Piedras Blancas Pt., U.S.A. 35 45N 121 18w
120 Piedras Negras, Mexico 28 35N 100 35w
50 Pieksämäki, Finland 62 18N 27 10E
38 Piemonte, Italy 45 0N 7 30E
21 Piena, Corsica 42 15N 9 8E
28 Pieńsk, Poland 51 16N 15 2E
20 Pierre, France 46 54N 5 13E
116 Pierre, U.S.A. 44 23N 100 20w
38 Pierrefeu, France 43 8N 6 9E
19 Pierrefonds, France 49 20N 3 0E
19 Pierrefontaine, France 47 14N 6 32E
20 Pierrefort, France 44 55N 2 50E
21 Pierrelatte, France 44 23N 4 43E
28 Pieszyce, Poland 50 43N 16 33E
111 Piešťany, Cz. 48 35N 17 50E
27 Piesting, R., Austria 48 0N 16 19E
93 Piet Retief, S. Africa 27 1s 30 50E
50 Pietarsaari, Finland 63 41N 22 40E
93 Pietermaritzburg, South Africa 29 35s 30 25E
93 Pietersburg, S. Africa 23 54s 29 25E
41 Pietraperzia, Italy 37 26N 14 8E
38 Pietrasanta, Italy 43 57N 10 12E
46 Pietrosu, mt., Rumania 47 12N 25 8E
46 Pietrosul, mt., Rumania 47 35N 24 43E
39 Pieve di Cadore, Italy 46 25N 12 22E
38 Pieve di Teco, Italy 44 3N 7 54E
38 Pievepélago, Italy 44 12N 10 35E
41 Pigadia, Greece 35 30N 27 12E
44 Pigadhitsa, Greece 39 59N 21 23E
70 Pigeon I., India 14 2N 74 20E
106 Pigeon, R., Canada 48 1N 89 42w
117 Piggott, U.S.A. 36 20N 90 10w
27 Pigna, Italy 43 57N 7 40E
124 Pigüe, Argentina 37 36s 62 25w
69 Pihani, India 27 36N 80 15E
54 Pikalevo, U.S.S.R. 59 37N 34 0E
116 Pikes Peak, U.S.A. 38 50N 105 10w
92 Piketberg, S. Africa 32 54s 18 42E
114 Pikeville, U.S.A. 37 30N 82 30w
109 Pikwitonei, Canada 55 35N 97 11w
28 Piła, Poland 53 10N 16 48E
33 Piła, mte., Spain 38 16N 1 11w
44 Pilaia, Greece 40 32N 22 59E
68 Pilani, India 28 22N 75 33E
124 Pilar, Paraguay 26 50s 58 20w
73 Pilas, I., Philippines 6 39N 121 37E
90 Pilbara, Australia 21 14s 118 19E
124 Pilcomayo, R., Par. 25 21s 57 42w
69 Pili, Greece 36 50N 27 5E
69 Pilibhit, India 28 40N 79 50E
44 Pilion, mt. Greece 39 27N 23 7E
27 Pilis, Hungary 47 38N 18 56E
27 Pilisvörösvár, Hung. 47 38N 18 54E
45 Pilkhawa, India 28 43N 77 42E
45 Pilos, Greece 36 55N 21 42E
109 Pilot Mound, Canada 49 15N 98 54w
117 Pilot Point, U.S.A. 33 26N 97 0w
118 Pilot Rock, U.S.A. 45 30N 118 58w
26 Pilsen = Plzen, Czech. 49 45N 13 22E
39 Pilštanj, Yugoslavia 46 8N 15 39E
27 Pilzno, Poland 50 0N 21 16E
99 Pimba, Australia 31 18s 136 46E
126 Pimenta Bueno, Brazil 11 35s 61 10w
126 Pimentel, Peru 6 45s 79 55w
32 Pina, Spain 41 29N 0 33w
71 Pinang, I., W. Malaysia 5 25N 100 15E
121 Pinar del Rio, Cuba 22 26N 83 40w
105 Pinawa, Canada 50 9N 95 50w
107 Pince C., Canada 46 38N 53 45w
108 Pincher Creek, Canada 49 30N 113 57w
116 Pinckneyville, U.S.A. 38 5N 89 20w
68 Pind Dadan Khan, Pakistan 32 55N 73 47E
85 Pindiga, Nigeria 9 58N 10 53E

* Incorporated within the county of Dyfed
58 † Incorporated within the region of Borders
‡ Renamed Wanaka

* Incorporated within the regions of Tayside and Central

Pindos Óros INDEX Port Bergé Vaovao

MAP
44 Pindos Oros, Greece 40 0N 21 0E
44 Pindus Mts. = Pindos Oros, Greece 40 0N 21 0E
119 Pine, U.S.A. 34 27N 111 30W
117 Pine Bluff, U.S.A. 34 10N 92 0W
116 Pine City, U.S.A. 45 46N 93 0W
96 Pine Creek, Australia 13 51S 131 52E
109 Pine Falls, Canada 50 51N 96 11W
98 Pine Hill, Australia 23 42S 147 0E
108 Pine Point, Canada 60 50N 114 40W
108 Pine Point, Canada 61 0N 114 26W
116 Pine Ridge, U.S.A. 42 2N 102 35W
109 Pine River, Canada 51 45N 100 30W
116 Pine River, U.S.A. 46 40N 94 20W
119 Pinedale, U.S.A. 34 23N 110 16W
119 Pinetop, U.S.A. 34 10N 109 57W
26 Pinega, U.S.S.R. 64 45N 43 40E
52 Pinega, R., U.S.S.R. 64 20N 43 0E
38 Pinerolo, Italy 44 47N 7 21E
39 Pineto, Italy 42 36N 14 4E
93 Pinetown, S. Afr. 29 48S 30 54E
116 Pinetree, U.S.A. 43 42N 105 52W
115 Pineville, Ky., U.S.A. 36 42N 83 42W
117 Pineville, La., U.S.A. 31 22N 92 30W
109 Pinewood, Canada 48 45N 94 10W
109 Piney, Canada 49 5N 96 10W
19 Piney, France 48 22N 4 21E
71 Ping, R., Thailand 16 40N 99 30E
77 Pinghuo, China 24 14N 117 2E
77 Pingkiang, China 28 45N 113 30E
76 Pingliang, China 35 20N 106 40E
77 Pinglo, Kwangsi-Chuang, China 24 30N 110 45E
76 Pinglo, Ningsia Hui, China 38 58N 106 30E
77 Pingnam, China 23 30N 110 15E
77 Pingsiang, Kiangsi, China 27 43N 113 50E
77 Pingsiang, Kwangsi-Chuang, China 22 2N 106 55E
77 Pingtung, Taiwan 22 36N 120 30E
77 Pingyang, China 27 45N 120 25E
76 Pingyao, China 37 12N 112 0E
125 Pinhal, Brazil 22 10S 46 46W
30 Pinhel, Portugal 40 18N 7 0W
72 Pini, I., Indonesia 0 10N 98 40E
45 Piniós, R., Ilia, Greece 37 38N 21 20E
44 Piniós, R., Trikkala, Gr. 39 55N 22 10E
96 Pinjarra, Australia 32 37S 115 52E
27 Pinkafeld, Austria 47 22N 16 9E
100 Pinnaroo, Australia 35 13S 140 56E
120 Pinos, Mexico 22 20N 101 40W
121 Pinos, I. de, Cuba 21 40N 82 40W
119 Pinos Pt., U.S.A. 36 50N 121 57W
31 Pinos Puente, Spain 37 15N 3 45W
73 Pinrang, Indonesia 3 46S 119 34E
54 Pinsk, U.S.S.R. 52 10N 26 8E
126 Pintados, Chile 20 35S 69 40W
77 Pinyang, China 23 17N 108 47E
52 Pinyug, U.S.S.R. 60 5N 48 0E
38 Pinzolo, Italy 46 9N 10 45E
119 Pioche, U.S.A. 38 0N 114 35W
38 Piombino, Italy 42 54N 10 30E
59 Pioner, I., U.S.S.R. 79 50N 92 0E
28 Pionki, Poland 51 29N 21 28E
126 Piorini, L., Brazil 3 15S 62 35W
28 Piotrków Trybunalsk, Poland 51 23N 19 43E
39 Piove di Sacco, Italy 45 18N 12 1E
65 Pip, Iran 26 45N 60 10E
68 Pipar, India 26 25N 73 31E
68 Pipariya, India 22 45N 78 23E
44 Pipéri, I., Greece 39 20N 24 19E
116 Pipestone, U.S.A. 44 0N 96 20W
107 Pipmuacan Res., Canada 49 40N 70 25W
18 Pipriac, France 47 49N 1 58W
114 Piqua, U.S.A. 40 10N 84 10W
125 Piquiri, R., Brazil 24 3S 54 14W
127 Piracicaba, Brazil 22 45S 47 30W
127 Piracuruca, Brazil 3 50S 41 50W
45 Piraeuis = Piraiévs, Greece 37 57N 23 42E
45 Piraiévs, Greece 37 57N 23 42E
45 Piraiévs ♦, Greece 37 0N 23 30E
41 Piráino, Italy 38 10N 14 52E
39 Piran (Pirano), Y.-slav. 45 31N 13 33E
124 Pirane, Argentina 25 25S 59 30W
127 Pirapora, Brazil 17 20S 44 56W
54 Piratyin, U.S.S.R. 50 15N 32 25E
43 Pirdop, Bulgaria 42 40N 24 10E
69 Pirganj, Bangladesh 25 51S 88 24E
45 Pirgos, Ilia, Greece 37 40N 21 27E
45 Pirgos, Messinia, Greece 36 50N 22 16E
43 Pirgovo, Bulgaria 43 44N 25 43E
18 Piriac, France 47 23N 2 31W
124 Piribebuy, Paraguay 25 26S 57 2W
73 Pirimapun, Indonesia 6 45S 138 10E
43 Pirin Planina, Bulg. 41 40N 23 30E
32 Pirineos, mts., Sp. 42 40N 1 0E
127 Piripiri, Brazil 4 15S 41 46W
126 Piritu, Venezuela 9 23N 69 12W
25 Pirmasens, Germany 49 12N 7 30E
24 Pirna, Germany 50 57N 13 57E
69 Pirojpur, Bangladesh 22 35N 90 1E
42 Pirot, Yugoslavia 43 9N 22 39E
57 Pirsagat, R., U.S.S.R. 40 15N 48 45E
119 Pirtleville, U.S.A. 31 25N 109 35W
45 Piryi, Greece 38 13N 25 59E
38 Pisa, Italy 43 43N 10 23E
126 Pisagua, Chile 19 40S 70 15W
39 Pisarovina, Yugoslavia 45 35N 15 50E
41 Pisciotta, Italy 40 7N 15 12E
126 Pisco, Peru 13 50S 76 5W
46 Piscu, Rumania 45 30N 27 43E
26 Pisek, Czechoslovakia 49 19N 14 10E
73 Pising, Indonesia 5 8S 121 53E
20 Pissos, France 44 19N 0 49W
41 Pisticci, Italy 40 24N 16 33E
38 Pistoia, Italy 43 57N 10 53E
30 Pisuerga, R., Spain 42 10N 4 15W

MAP
28 Pisz, Poland 53 38N 21 49E
126 Pitalito, Colombia 1 51N 76 2W
100 Pitarpunga, L., Austral. 34 24S 143 30E
95 Pitcairn I., Pac. Oc. 25 5S 130 5W
50 Pite älv, Sweden 65 44N 20 50W
50 Piteå, Sweden 65 20N 21 25E
44 Piteşti, Rumania 44 52N 24 54E
70 Pithapuram, India 17 10N 82 15E
44 Píthion, Greece 41 24N 26 40W
19 Pithiviers, France 48 10N 2 13E
39 Pitigliano, Italy 42 38N 11 40E
14 Pitlochry, Scot. 56 43N 3 43W
108 Pitt I., Canada 53 30N 129 50W
118 Pittsburg, Calif., U.S.A. 38 1N 121 50W
117 Pittsburg, Kans., U.S.A. 37 21N 94 43W
117 Pittsburg, Tex., U.S.A. 32 59N 94 58W
112 Pittsburgh, U.S.A. 40 25N 79 55W
116 Pittsfield, Ill., U.S.A. 39 35N 90 46W
113 Pittsfield, Mass., U.S.A. 42 28N 73 17W
113 Pittsfield, N.H., U.S.A. 43 17N 71 18W
113 Pittston, U.S.A. 41 19N 75 50W
99 Pittsworth, Australia 27 41S 151 37E
126 Piura, Peru 5 5S 80 45W
42 Piva, R., Yugoslavia 43 15N 18 50E
126 Pivijay, Colombia 10 28N 74 37W
27 Piwniczna, Poland 49 27N 20 42E
45 Pixariá Oros, Gr. 38 42N 23 39E
44 Piyai, Greece 39 17N 21 25E
25 Piz Bernina, Switz. 46 23N 9 45E
126 Pizarro, Colombia 4 58N 77 22W
41 Pizzo, Italy 38 44N 16 10E
107 Placentia, Canada 47 20N 54 0W
107 Placentia B., Canada 47 0N 54 40W
118 Placerville, U.S.A. 38 47N 120 51W
121 Placetas, Cuba 22 15N 79 44W
42 Plačkovica, mts., Y.-slavia 41 45N 22 30E
117 Plain Dealing, U.S.A. 32 56N 93 41W
113 Plainfield, U.S.A. 40 37N 74 28W
117 Plains, Kans., U.S.A. 37 20N 100 35W
118 Plains, Mont., U.S.A. 47 27N 114 57W
117 Plains, Tex., U.S.A. 33 11N 102 50W
116 Plainview, Nebr., U.S.A. 42 25N 97 48W
117 Plainview, Tex., U.S.A. 34 10N 101 40W
116 Plainville, U.S.A. 39 18N 99 19W
114 Plainwell, U.S.A. 42 28N 85 40W
20 Plaisance, France 43 36N 0 3E
45 Pláka, Greece 36 45N 24 26E
58 Plakhino, U.S.S.R. 67 45N 86 5E
72 Plampang, Indonesia 8 48S 117 46E
26 Planá, Czechoslovakia 49 50N 12 44E
127 Planaltina, Brazil 15 30S 47 45W
18 Plancoët, France 48 32N 2 13W
42 Plandište, Yugoslavia 45 16N 21 10E
126 Planeta Rica, Colombia 8 25N 75 36W
39 Planina, Slovenija, Yugoslavia 45 47N 14 19E
39 Planina, Slovenija, Yugoslavia 46 10N 15 12E
116 Plankinton, U.S.A. 43 45N 98 27W
117 Plano, U.S.A. 33 0N 96 45W
115 Plant City, U.S.A. 28 0N 82 15W
117 Plaquemine, U.S.A. 30 20N 91 15W
30 Plasencia, Spain 40 3N 6 8W
39 Plaški, Yugoslavia 45 4N 15 22E
48 Plassen, Norway 61 9N 12 30E
107 Plaster Rock, Canada 46 53N 67 22W
128 Plata, Rio de la, South America 35 30S 56 0W
40 Platani, R., Italy 37 28N 13 23E
5 Plateau, Antarctica 70 55S 40 0E
116 Plateau du Coteau du Missouri, U.S.A. 47 9N 101 5W
44 Platí, Akra, Greece 40 27N 24 0E
126 Plato, Colombia 9 47N 74 47W
57 Platrand, S. Afr. 27 8S 29 29E
116 Platte, U.S.A. 43 28N 98 50W
116 Platte, R., U.S.A. 41 0N 98 0W
116 Platteville, U.S.A. 40 18N 104 47W
25 Plattling, Germany 48 46N 12 53E
113 Plattsburgh, U.S.A. 44 41N 73 30W
116 Plattsmouth, U.S.A. 41 0N 96 0W
24 Plau, Germany 53 27N 12 16E
24 Plauen, Germany 50 29N 12 9E
42 Plav, Yugoslavia 42 38N 19 57E
42 Plavnica, Yugoslavia 42 10N 19 20E
55 Plavsk, U.S.S.R. 53 40N 37 18E
31 Playa de Castilla, Spain 41 25N 0 12W
109 Playgreen L., Canada 53 20N 98 0W
116 Pleasant Bay, Canada 46 51N 60 43W
116 Pleasant Hill, U.S.A. 38 48N 94 14W
100 Pleasant Hills, Austral. 35 28S 146 50E
117 Pleasanton, U.S.A. 29 0N 98 30W
114 Pleasantville, U.S.A. 39 25N 74 30W
20 Pléaux, France 45 8N 2 13E
71 Pleiku (Gia Lai), South Vietnam 14 3N 108 0E
18 Plélan-le-Grand, France 48 0N 2 7W
18 Plémet, France 48 11N 2 36W
18 Pléneuf, France 48 37N 2 32W
46 Pleniţa, Rumania 44 14N 23 10E
101 Plenty, Bay of, N.Z. 37 45S 177 0E
116 Plentywood, U.S.A. 48 45N 104 35W
52 Plesetsk, U.S.S.R. 62 40N 40 10E
107 Plessisville, Canada 46 14N 71 46W
18 Plestin-les-Grèves, Fr. 48 40N 3 39W
28 Pleszew, Poland 51 53N 17 47E
42 Pleternica, Yugoslavia 45 17N 17 48E
107 Pletipi L., Canada 51 45N 70 12W
43 Pleven, Bulgaria 43 26N 24 37E
42 Plevlja, Yugoslavia 43 21N 19 21E
28 Płock, Poland 52 32N 19 40E
39 Plöcken Passo, Italy 46 37N 12 57E
18 Ploëmeur, France 47 44N 3 26W
18 Ploërmel, France 47 55N 2 26W
46 Ploieşti, Rumania 44 57N 26 5E
45 Plomárion, Greece 43 58N 26 24E
20 Plomb du Cantal, Fr. 45 2N 2 48E
19 Plombières, France 47 59N 6 27E
39 Plomin, Yugoslavia 45 8N 14 10E

MAP
24 Plön, Germany 54 8N 10 22E
24 Plöner See, Germany 53 9N 15 5E
28 Płonsk, Poland 52 37N 20 21E
28 Płoty, Poland 53 48N 15 18E
18 Plouay, France 47 55N 3 21W
18 Ploudalmézeau, France 48 34N 4 41W
18 Plougasnou, France 48 42N 3 49W
18 Plouha, France 48 41N 2 57W
18 Plouhinec, France 48 0N 4 29W
43 Plovdiv, Bulgaria 42 8N 24 44E
113 Plum I., U.S.A. 41 10N 72 12W
118 Plummer, U.S.A. 47 21N 116 59W
91 Plumtree, Rhodesia 20 27S 27 55E
54 Plunge, U.S.S.R. 55 53N 21 51E
18 Pluvigner, France 47 46N 3 1W
13 Plymouth, Eng. 50 23N 4 9W
114 Plymouth, Ind., U.S.A. 41 20N 86 19W
113 Plymouth, Mass., U.S.A. 41 58N 70 40W
115 Plymouth, N.C., U.S.A. 35 54N 76 55W
113 Plymouth, N.H., U.S.A. 43 44N 71 41W
113 Plymouth, Pa., U.S.A. 41 17N 76 0W
114 Plymouth, Wis., U.S.A. 43 42N 87 58W
13 Plymouth Sd., Eng. 50 20N 4 10W
13 Plynlimon = Pumlum-on Fawr, U.K. 52 29N 3 47W
54 Plyussa, U.S.S.R. 47 40N 29 0E
54 Plyussa, R., U.S.S.R. 58 40N 28 30E
26 Plzen, Czechoslovakia 49 45N 13 22E
24 Plöner See, Germany 53 9N 15 5E
28 Pniewy, Poland 52 31N 16 16E
85 Pô, Upper Volta 11 14N 1 5W
38 Po, R., Italy 45 0N 10 45E
76 Po Hai, China 38 30N 119 0E
85 Pobé, Dahomey 7 0N 2 38E
58 Pobedino, U.S.S.R. 49 51N 142 49E
58 Pobedy Pik, U.S.S.R. 40 45N 79 58E
28 Pobiedziska, Poland 52 29N 17 19E
32 Pobla de Segur, Spain 42 15N 0 58E
30 Pobladura de Valle, Sp. 42 6N 5 44W
116 Pocahontas, Iowa, U.S.A. 42 41N 94 42W
117 Pocahontas, Va., U.S.A. 37 18N 81 20W
118 Pocatello, U.S.A. 42 50N 112 25W
26 Počátky, Cz. 49 15N 15 14E
54 Pochep, U.S.S.R. 52 58N 33 15E
55 Pochinki, U.S.S.R. 54 41N 44 59E
54 Pochinok, U.S.S.R. 54 28N 32 29E
26 Pöchlarn, Austria 48 12N 15 12E
108 Pochontas, Canada 53 0N 117 51W
120 Pochutla, Mexico 15 50N 96 31W
114 Pocomoke City, U.S.A. 38 4N 75 32W
125 Pocos de Caldas, Brazil 21 50S 46 45W
28 Poddebice, Poland 51 54N 18 58E
26 Poděbrady, Cz. 50 9N 15 8E
20 Podensac, France 44 40N 0 22W
42 Podgorac, Yugoslavia 45 28N 18 13E
59 Podkamennaya Tunguska, U.S.S.R. 61 50N 90 26E
39 Podlapac, Yugoslavia 44 45N 15 47E
26 Podmokly, Cz. 50 48N 14 10E
46 Podoleni, Rumania 46 46N 26 39E
27 Podolinec, Czechoslovakia 49 16N 20 31E
55 Podolsk, U.S.S.R. 55 25N 37 30E
84 Podor, Senegal 16 40N 14 50W
52 Podporozhy, U.S.S.R. 60 55N 34 2E
42 Podravska Slatina, Y.-slav. 45 42N 17 45E
39 Podsreda, Yugoslavia 45 42N 17 41E
46 Podu Turcului, Rum. 46 11N 27 25E
42 Podujevo, Yugoslavia 42 54N 21 10E
24 Poel, I., Germany 54 0N 11 25E
92 Pofadder, S. Africa 29 10S 19 22E
106 Pogamasing, Canada 46 55N 81 50W
41 Poggiardo, Italy 40 3N 18 21E
39 Poggibonsi, Italy 43 27N 11 8E
46 Pogoanele, Rumania 44 55N 27 0E
28 Pogorzela, Poland 51 50N 17 12E
44 Pogradeci, Albania 40 57N 20 48E
76 Pogranichnyy, U.S.S.R. 44 21N 131 23E
73 Poh, Indonesia 0 46S 122 51E
76 Pohang, S. Korea 36 1N 129 23E
27 Poherelá, Cz. 48 50N 20 2E
27 Poherelice, Cz. 48 59N 16 31E
39 Pohorje, mts., Y.-slavia 46 30N 15 7E
46 Poiana Mare, Rumania 43 57N 23 5E
46 Poiana Ruscăi, Munţii, Rumania 45 45N 22 25E
106 Point Edward, Canada 43 10N 82 30W
121 Point Fortin, Trinidad 10 9N 61 46W
70 Point Pedro, Ceylon 9 50N 80 15E
114 Point Pleasant, U.S.A. 38 50N 82 7W
117 Point Rock, U.S.A. 31 30N 99 56W
117 Pointe-à-la Hache, U.S.A. 29 35N 89 55W
88 Pointe-Noire, Congo 4 48S 12 0E
121 Pointe-à-Pitre, Guadeloupe 16 10N 61 30W
38 Poirino, Italy 44 55N 7 50E
19 Poissy, France 48 55N 2 0E
18 Poitiers, France 46 35N 0 20W
20 Poitou, Plaines du, Fr. 46 30N 0 1W
19 Poix, France 49 47N 2 0E
19 Poix-Terron, France 49 38N 4 38E
119 Pojoaque, U.S.A. 35 55N 106 0W
99 Pokataroo, Australia 29 30S 148 34E
90 Poko, Zaïre 3 7N 26 52E
87 Poko, Sudan 5 41N 31 55E
76 Pokotu, China 48 47N 122 7E
77 Pokpak, China 22 20N 109 45E
59 Pokrovsk, U.S.S.R. 61 29N 129 6E
30 Pol, Spain 43 9N 7 20W
54 Pola, R., U.S.S.R. 57 30N 32 0E
30 Pola de Allande, Spain 43 16N 6 37W
30 Pola de Lena, Spain 43 10N 5 49W
30 Pola de Siero, Spain 43 24N 5 39W
30 Pola de Someido, Spain 43 5N 6 15W
119 Polacca, U.S.A. 35 52N 110 25W
65 Polan, Iran 25 30N 1 10E

MAP
28 Poland ■, Europe 52 0N 20 0E
28 Polanów, Poland 54 7N 16 41E
124 Polcura, Chile 37 10S 71 50W
28 Polcyn Zdrój, Poland 53 47N 16 5E
13 Polden Hills, Eng. 51 7N 2 50W
54 Polessk, U.S.S.R. 54 50N 21 8E
73 Polewali, Sulawesi, Indonesia 3 21S 119 31E
73 Polewali, Sulawesi, Indonesia 4 8S 119 43E
27 Polgar, Hungary 47 54N 21 6E
76 Poli, China 45 43N 130 28E
88 Poli, Cameroon 8 34N 12 54E
45 Poliaigos, I., Greece 36 45N 24 38E
41 Policastro, Golfo di, Italy 39 55N 15 35E
28 Police, Poland 53 33N 14 33E
27 Polička, Czechoslovakia 49 43N 16 15E
41 Polignanoa Mare, Italy 41 0N 17 12E
19 Poligny, France 46 50N 5 42E
45 Polikhnitas, Greece 39 4N 26 10E
73 Polillo I., Philippines 14 56N 122 0E
64 Polis, Cyprus 35 3N 32 30E
41 Polistena, Italy 38 25N 16 4E
44 Políyiros, Greece 40 23N 23 25E
112 Polk, U.S.A. 41 22N 79 57W
28 Polkowice, Poland 51 29N 16 3E
41 Polla, Italy 40 31N 15 27E
70 Pollachi, India 10 35N 77 0E
32 Pollensa, Spain 39 54N 3 2E
32 Pollensa, B. de, Spain 39 55N 3 5E
41 Póllica, Italy 40 13N 15 3E
41 Pollino, Mte., Italy 39 54N 16 13E
116 Pollock, U.S.A. 45 58N 100 18W
54 Polna, U.S.S.R. 58 31N 28 0E
58 Polnovat, U.S.S.R. 63 50N 66 5E
116 Polo, U.S.A. 42 0N 89 38W
56 Pologi, U.S.S.R. 47 29N 36 15E
54 Polonnoye, U.S.S.R. 50 6N 27 30E
54 Polotsk, U.S.S.R. 55 30N 28 50E
43 Polski Trŭmbesh, Bulg. 43 20N 25 38E
43 Polsko Kosovo, Bulg. 43 23N 25 38E
118 Polson, U.S.A. 47 45N 114 12W
56 Poltava, U.S.S.R. 49 35N 34 35E
70 Polur, India 12 32N 79 11E
52 Polyarny, U.S.S.R. 69 8N 33 20E
95 Polynesia, Pac. Oc. 10 0S 162 0W
38 Pomarance, Italy 43 18N 10 51E
41 Pomarico, Italy 40 31N 16 33E
127 Pombal, Brazil 6 55S 37 50W
30 Pombal, Portugal 39 55N 8 40W
45 Pómbia, Greece 35 0N 24 51E
114 Pomeroy, Ohio, U.S.A. 39 0N 82 0W
118 Pomeroy, Wash., U.S.A. 46 30N 117 33W
119 Pomona, U.S.A. 34 2N 117 49W
43 Pomorie, Bulgaria 42 26N 27 41E
48 Pomosnjaja, U.S.S.R. 48 13N 31 36E
115 Pompano, U.S.A. 26 12N 80 6W
41 Pompei, Italy 40 45N 14 30E
25 Pompey, France 48 50N 6 2E
118 Pompeys Pillar, U.S.A. 46 0N 108 0W
94 Ponape I., Pac. Oc. 6 55N 158 10E
106 Ponask, L., Canada 54 0N 92 30W
116 Ponca, U.S.A. 42 38N 96 41W
117 Ponca City, U.S.A. 36 40N 97 5W
121 Ponce, Puerto Rico 18 1N 66 37W
117 Ponchatoula, U.S.A. 30 27N 90 25W
21 Poncin, France 46 6N 5 25E
4 Pond Inlet, Canada 72 30N 75 0W
70 Pondicherry, India 11 59N 79 50E
93 Pondoland, S. Afr. 31 10S 29 30W
107 Ponds, I. of, Canada 53 27N 55 52W
30 Ponferrada, Spain 42 32N 6 35W
87 Pongo, W., Sudan 8 0N 27 20E
28 Poniatowa, Poland 51 11N 22 3E
28 Poniec, Poland 51 48N 16 50E
70 Ponnalyar, R., India 11 50N 79 45E
70 Ponnani, India 10 45N 75 59E
70 Ponnani, R., India 10 45N 75 59E
70 Ponneri, India 13 20N 80 15E
67 Ponnyadaung, Burma 22 0N 94 10E
52 Ponoi, U.S.S.R. 67 0N 41 0E
52 Ponoi, R., U.S.S.R. 67 10N 39 0E
108 Ponoka, Canada 52 35N 113 40W
73 Ponorogo, Indonesia 7 52S 111 29E
20 Pons, France 45 35N 0 34W
32 Pons, Spain 41 55N 1 12E
31 Ponsul, R., Portugal 39 54N 8 45E
18 Pont Audemer, France 49 21N 0 30E
18 Pont Aven, France 47 51N 3 47W
38 Pont Canavese, Italy 45 24N 7 33E
18 Pont Château, France 47 26N 2 8W
18 Pont-l'Eveque, France 49 18N 0 11E
107 Pont Lafrance, Canada 47 40N 64 58W
21 Pont-St.-Esprit, France 44 16N 4 40E
125 Ponta Grossa, Brazil 25 0S 50 10W
125 Ponta Pora, Brazil 22 20S 55 35W
93 Ponta São Sebastião, Mozam. 22 2S 35 25E
20 Pontacq, France 43 11N 0 8W
19 Pontailler, France 47 18N 5 24E
19 Pont-à-Mousson, France 45 54N 6 1E
19 Pontarlier, France 46 54N 6 20E
39 Pontassieve, Italy 43 47N 11 25E
18 Pontaubault, France 48 40N 1 20W
20 Pontaumur, France 45 52N 2 40E
21 Pontcharra, France 45 26N 6 1E
38 Pontcharra, Fr. 45 22N 5 1E
117 Pontchartrain, L., U.S.A. 30 12N 90 0W
19 Pont-de-Roide, France 47 23N 6 45E
20 Pont-de-Salars, France 44 18N 2 44E
21 Pont-de-Vaux, France 46 26N 4 56E
21 Pont-de-Veyle, France 46 17N 4 53E
30 Ponte da Barca, Port. 41 48N 8 25W
30 Ponte de Lima, Portugal 41 43N 8 39W
31 Ponte de Sor, Portugal 39 17N 7 57W
38 Ponte dell 'Olio, Italy 44 52N 9 39E
38 Ponte di Legno, Italy 46 15N 10 30E
30 Ponte do Lima, Port. 41 46N 8 35W

MAP
91 Ponte do Pungué, Mozam. 19 30S 34 33E
21 Ponte Leccia, Corsica 42 28N 9 13E
39 Ponte nell' Alpi, Italy 46 10N 12 18E
125 Ponte Nova, Brazil 20 25S 42 54W
38 Ponte San Martino, It. 45 36N 7 47E
38 Ponte San Pietro, Italy 45 42N 9 35E
39 Pontebba, Italy 46 30N 13 17E
40 Pontecorvo, Italy 41 28N 13 40E
38 Pontedera, Italy 43 40N 10 37E
12 Pontefract, Eng. 53 42N 1 19W
109 Ponteix, Canada 49 46N 107 29W
41 Pontelandolfo, Italy 41 17N 14 41E
73 Pontemacassar Naikliu, Indonesia 9 30S 123 58E
30 Pontevedra, Spain 42 26N 8 40W
30 Pontevedra, R. de, Sp. 42 22N 8 45W
30 Pontevedra ♦, Sp. 42 25N 8 39W
38 Pontevico, Italy 45 16N 10 6E
90 Ponthierville = Ubundi, Zaïre 0 22S 25 30E
116 Pontiac, Ill., U.S.A. 40 50N 88 40W
114 Pontiac, Mich., U.S.A. 42 40N 83 20W
71 Pontian Kechil, Malay. 1 29N 103 23E
72 Pontianak, Indonesia 0 3S 109 15E
40 Pontine Is. = Ponziane, Isole, Italy 40 55N 13 0E
64 Pontine Mts. = Karadeniz D., Turkey 41 30N 35 0E
40 Pontínia, Italy 41 25N 13 2E
18 Pontivy, France 48 5N 3 0W
19 Pontoise, France 49 3N 2 5E
18 Pontorson, France 48 34N 1 30W
38 Pontrémoli, Italy 44 22N 9 52E
18 Pontrieux, France 48 42N 3 10W
21 Pont-sur-Yonne, France 48 18N 3 10E
112 Pontypool, Canada 44 6N 78 36W
13 Pontypool, Wales 51 42N 3 1W
13 Pontypridd, Wales 51 36N 3 21W
40 Ponza, I., Italy 40 55N 12 57E
40 Ponziane, Isole, Italy 40 55N 13 0E
13 Poole, England 50 42N 2 2W
70 Poona, India 18 29N 73 57E
70 Poonamallee, India 13 3N 80 10E
100 Pooncarie, Australia 33 22S 142 31E
126 Poopó, Lago de, Bolivia 18 30S 67 35W
71 Popak, China 22 15N 109 56E
126 Popayán, Colombia 2 27N 76 36W
16 Poperinge, Belgium 50 51N 2 42E
59 Popigay, U.S.S.R. 71 55N 110 47E
100 Popio, L., Austral. 33 10S 141 52E
116 Poplar, U.S.A. 48 3N 105 9W
117 Poplar Bluff, U.S.A. 36 45N 90 22W
117 Poplarville, U.S.A. 30 55N 89 30W
120 Popocatepetl, vol., Mex. 19 10N 98 40W
88 Popokabaka, Zaïre 5 49S 16 40E
127 Popakai, Surinam 3 20N 55 30W
127 Popakai, Austral. 32 12S 141 46E
39 Pópoli, Italy 42 12N 13 50E
39 Popovaca, Yugoslavia 45 30N 16 41E
43 Popovo, Bulgaria 43 21N 26 18E
27 Poprád, Czechoslovakia 49 3N 20 18E
27 Poprád, R., Cz. 49 15N 20 30E
68 Porbandar, India 21 44N 69 43E
108 Porcher I., Canada 53 50N 130 30W
31 Porcuna, Spain 37 52N 4 11W
104 Porcupine, R., Alaska 67 0N 143 0W
109 Porcupine, R., Can. 59 40N 104 0W
39 Pordenone, Italy 45 58N 12 40E
43 Pordim, Bulgaria 43 23N 24 51E
126 Pore, Colombia 5 43N 72 0W
39 Poreč, Yugoslavia 45 14N 13 36E
55 Poretskoye, U.S.S.R. 55 9N 46 21E
51 Pori, Finland 61 29N 21 48E
51 Pori, I., Greece 37 31N 23 29E
50 Porjus, Sweden 66 57N 19 50E
54 Porkhov, U.S.S.R. 57 45N 29 38E
51 Porkkala, Uudenmaan, Finland 59 59N 24 26E
126 Porlamar, Venezuela 10 57N 63 51W
38 Porlezza, Italy 46 2N 9 8E
30 Porma, R., Spain 42 45N 5 21W
18 Pornic, France 47 7N 2 5W
59 Poronaysk, U.S.S.R. 49 20N 143 0E
45 Póros, Greece 37 30N 23 30E
45 Póros, I., Greece 37 30N 23 30E
27 Poroszló, Hungary 47 39N 20 40E
91 Poroto Mts., Tanzania 9 0S 33 30E
25 Porrentruy, Switzerland 47 25N 7 6E
32 Porreras, Spain 39 29N 3 2E
50 Porsangen, Norway 70 40N 25 40E
47 Porsgrunn, Norway 59 10N 9 40E
19 Port, France 47 43N 6 4E
99 Port Adelaide, Australia 34 46S 138 30E
108 Port Alberni, Can. 49 15N 124 50W
100 Port Albert, Australia 38 42S 146 42E
68 Port Albert Victor, India 21 0N 71 30E
92 Port Alfred, Canada 48 18N 70 53W
108 Port Alice, Canada 50 25N 127 25W
112 Port Allegany, U.S.A. 41 49N 78 17W
117 Port Allen, U.S.A. 30 30N 91 15W
98 Port Alma, Australia 23 38S 150 53E
118 Port Angeles, U.S.A. 48 0N 123 30W
121 Port Antonio, Jamaica 18 10N 76 30W
117 Port Aransas, U.S.A. 27 49N 97 4W
99 Port Arthur, Australia 43 7S 147 50E
106 Port Arthur = Thunder Bay, Canada 48 25N 89 10W
117 Port Arthur, U.S.A. 30 0N 94 0W
107 Port au Port B., Can. 48 40N 58 50W
121 Port-au-Prince, Haiti 18 40N 72 20W
99 Pt. Augusta, S.A., Austral. 32 30S 137 50E
99 Pt. Augusta, W.A., Austral. 32 30S 137 45E
112 Port Austin, U.S.A. 44 3N 82 59W
107 Port aux Basques, Can. 47 32N 59 8W
90 Port Bell, Uganda 0 18N 32 35E
93 Port Bergé Vaovao, Malagasy Rep. 15 33S 47 40E

Port Blair INDEX Puebla de Don Fadrique

MAP
71 Port Blair, Andaman Is. 11 40N 92 30E
107 Port Blandford, Canada 48 30N 53 50W
117 Port Bolivar, U.S.A. 29 20N 94 40W
32 Port Bou, Spain 42 25N 3 9E
84 Port Bouet, Ivory C. 5 16N 4 57W
97 Port Bradshaw, Austral. 12 30S 137 0E
106 Port Burwell, Canada 42 40N 80 48W
69 Port Canning, India 22 17N 88 48E
107 Port Cartier, Canada 50 10N 66 50W
101 Port Chalmers, N.Z. 45 49S 170 30E
113 Port Chester, U.S.A. 41 0N 73 41W
108 Port Clements, Canada 53 40N 132 10W
98 Port Clinton, Australia 22 30S 150 46E
114 Port Clinton, U.S.A. 41 30N 83 0W
106 Port Colborne, Canada 42 50N 79 10W
108 Port Coquitlam, Can. 49 20N 122 45W
112 Port Credit, Canada 43 34N 79 35W
98 Port Curtis, Australia 24 0S 151 34E
112 Port Dalhousie, Canada 43 13N 79 17W
128 Port Darwin, Falk. Is. 51 50S 59 0W
99 Port Davey, Australia 43 16S 145 55E
38 Port-de-Bouce, Fr. 43 19N 4 58E
121 Port de Paix, Haiti 19 50N 72 50W
71 Port Dickson, Malaysia 2 30N 101 49E
98 Port Douglas, Australia 16 30S 145 30E
112 Port Dover, Canada 42 45N 80 10W
108 Port Edward, Canada 54 12N 130 10W
112 Port Elgin, Canada 44 25N 81 25W
92 Port Elizabeth, S. Afr. 33 58S 25 40E
99 Port Elliott, Austral. 35 32S 138 41E
12 Port Erin, I. of M. 54 5N 4 45W
80 Port Etienne = Nouadhibou, Mauritania 21 0N 17 0W
100 Port Fairy, Australia 38 13S 142 14E
86 Port Fouâd = Bûr Fuad, Egypt 31 15N 32 20E
88 Port Francqui, Congo 4 17S 20 47E
88 Port-Gentil, Gabon 0 47S 8 40E
117 Port Gibson, U.S.A. 31 57N 91 0W
14 Port Glasgow, Scot. 55 57N 4 40W
96 Port Gregory, Australia 27 40S 114 0E
85 Port Harcourt, Nigeria 4 40N 7 10E
108 Port Hardy, Canada 50 41N 127 30W
105 Port Harrison, Canada 58 25N 78 15W
107 Port Hawkesbury, Can. 45 36N 61 22W
96 Port Hedland, Austral. 20 25S 118 35E
113 Port Henry, U.S.A. 44 0N 73 30W
107 Port Hood, Canada 46 0N 61 32W
106 Port Hope, Canada 44 0N 78 20W
114 Port Huron, U.S.A. 43 0N 82 28W
117 Port Isabel, U.S.A. 26 12N 97 9W
100 Port Jackson, Australia 33 53S 151 12E
113 Port Jefferson, U.S.A. 40 58N 73 5W
113 Port Jervis, U.S.A. 41 22N 74 42W
18 Port Joinville, France 46 45N 2 23W
126 Port Kaituma, Guyana 8 3N 59 58W
57 Port Katon, U.S.S.R. 46 27N 38 56E
71 Port Kelang, Malaysia 3 0N 101 23E
100 Port Kembla, Australia 34 29S 150 56E
20 Port La Nouvelle, France 43 1N 3 3E
15 Port Laoise, Ireland 53 2N 7 20W
117 Port Lavaca, U.S.A. 28 38N 96 38W
96 Port Lincoln, Austral. 34 42S 135 52E
84 Port Loko, Sierra Leone 8 48N 12 46W
18 Port Louis, France 47 42N 3 22W
82 Port Lyautey = Kenitra, Morocco 34 15N 6 40W
99 Port Macquarie, Austral. 31 25S 152 54E
107 Port Maitland, N.S., Canada 44 0N 66 2W
112 Port Maitland, Ont., Can. 42 53N 79 35W
108 Port Mellon, Canada 49 32N 123 31W
107 Port Menier, Canada 49 51N 64 15W
98 Port Moresby, Papua 9 24S 147 8E
107 Port Mouton, Canada 43 58N 64 50W
98 Port Musgrave, Austral. 11 55S 141 50E
18 Port Navalo, France 47 34N 2 54W
109 Port Nelson, Canada 57 5N 92 56W
92 Port Nolloth, S. Africa 29 17S 16 52E
105 Port Nouveau-Quebec (George R.), Canada 58 30N 65 50W
117 Port O'Connor, U.S.A. 28 26N 96 24W
121 Port of Spain, Trinidad 10 40N 61 20W
118 Port Orchard, U.S.A. 47 31N 122 47W
118 Port Oxford, U.S.A. 42 45N 124 28W
96 Port Patterson, Austral. 12 40S 130 30E
101 Port Pegasus, N.Z. 47 12S 167 41E
112 Port Perry, Canada 44 6N 78 56W
100 Port Phillip B., Austral. 38 0S 145 0E
99 Port Pirie, Australia 33 10S 137 58E
113 Port Pleasant, U.S.A. 40 5N 74 4W
104 Port Radium, Canada 66 10N 117 40W
108 Port Renfrew, Canada 48 30N 124 20W
112 Port Rowan, Canada 42 40N 80 30W
112 Port Ryerse, Canada 42 47N 80 15W
86 Port Safaga = Bûr Safâga, Egypt 26 43N 33 57E
86 Port Said = Bûr Sa'îd, Egypt 31 16N 32 18E
115 Port St. Joe, U.S.A. 29 49N 85 20W
93 Port St. Johns, S. Africa 31 38S 29 33E
21 Port-St. Louis, France 43 23N 4 50E
93 Port St. Louis, Malag. 13 7S 48 48E
107 Port St. Servain, Can. 51 21N 58 0W
112 Port Sanilac, U.S.A. 43 26N 82 33W
107 Port Saunders, Canada 50 40N 57 18W
112 Port Severn, Canada 44 47N 79 43W
93 Port Shepstone, S. Afr. 30 44S 30 28E
108 Port Simpson, Canada 54 30N 130 20W
106 Port Stanley, Canada 42 40N 81 10W
100 Port Stephens, Austral. 32 38S 152 12E
86 Port Sudan = Bôr Sôdân, Sudan 19 32N 37 9E
13 Port Talbot, Wales 51 35N 3 48W
86 Port Taufiq = Bôr Taufiq, Egypt 29 54N 32 32E
118 Port Townsend, U.S.A. 48 0N 122 50W
20 Port-Vendres, France 42 32N 3 8E

MAP
114 Port Washington, U.S.A. 43 25N 87 52W
71 Port Weld, Malaysia 4 50N 100 38E
126 Portachuelo, Bolivia 17 10S 63 20W
15 Portadown (Craigavon), N. Ire. 54 27N 6 26W
107 Portage, Canada 46 40N 64 5W
116 Portage, U.S.A. 43 31N 89 25W
109 Portage la Prairie, Can. 49 58N 98 18W
108 Portage Mt. Dam, Canada 56 0N 122 0W
117 Portageville, U.S.A. 36 25N 89 40W
31 Portalegre, Portugal 39 19N 7 25W
31 Portalegre ♦, Portugal 39 20N 7 40W
117 Portales, U.S.A. 34 12N 103 25W
15 Portarlington, Ireland 53 10N 7 10W
31 Portel, Portugal 38 19N 7 41W
92 Porterville, S. Africa 33 0S 18 57E
119 Porterville, U.S.A. 36 5N 119 0W
20 Portet, France 43 34N 0 11W
118 Porthill, U.S.A. 49 0N 116 30W
46 Portile de Fier, Rumania-Y.-slav. 44 42N 22 30E
31 Portimão, Port. 37 8N 8 32W
100 Portland, N.S.W., Austral. 33 13S 149 59E
100 Portland, Victoria, Australia 38 15S 141 45E
113 Portland, Canada 44 42N 76 11W
113 Portland, Conn., U.S.A. 41 34N 72 39W
107 Portland, Me., U.S.A. 43 40N 70 15W
114 Portland, Mich., U.S.A. 42 52N 84 58W
118 Portland, Oreg., U.S.A. 45 35N 122 40W
100 Portland B., Australia 38 15S 141 45E
13 Portland Bill, Eng. 50 31N 2 27W
99 Portland, C., Australia 40 46S 148 0E
94 Portland I., N.Z. 39 20S 177 51E
94 Portland, I. of, England 50 32N 2 25W
105 Portland Prom., Can. 59 0N 78 0W
107 Portneuf, Canada 46 43N 71 55W
30 Pôrto, Portugal 41 8N 8 40W
21 Porto, G. de, Corsica 42 17N 8 34E
30 Pôrto ♦, Portugal 41 8N 8 20W
125 Pôrto Alegre, Rio Grande do Sul, Braz. 30 5S 51 3W
127 Pôrto Alegre, Mato Grosso, Brazil 21 40S 53 30W
92 Porto Alexandre, Angola 15 55S 11 55E
88 Porto Amboim, Angola 10 50S 13 50E
*91 Porto Amelia, Mozam. 12 58S 40 30E
38 Porto Argentera, Italy 44 15N 7 27E
38 Porto Azzurro, Italy 42 46N 10 24E
40 Porto Botte, Italy 39 3N 8 33E
39 Porto Civitanova, Italy 43 19N 13 44E
127 Pôrto de Moz, Brazil 1 41S 52 22W
40 Porto Empédocle, Sicily 37 18N 13 30E
126 Pôrto Esperança, Brazil 19 37S 57 29W
127 Pôrto Franco, Brazil 6 20S 47 24W
39 Porto Garibaldi, Italy 44 41N 12 14E
44 Pôrto Lago, Greece 41 1N 25 6E
125 Pôrto Mendes, Brazil 24 30S 54 15W
126 Pôrto Murtinho, Brazil 21 45S 57 55W
127 Pôrto Nacional, Brazil 10 40S 48 30W
85 Porto Novo, Dahomey 6 23N 2 42E
70 Porto Novo, India 11 30N 79 38E
39 Porto Recanati, Italy 43 26N 13 40E
125 Pôrto São José, Brazil 22 43S 53 10W
39 Porto San Giorgio, Italy 43 11N 13 49E
44 Porto San Stéfano, It. 42 26N 11 6E
80 Porto Santo, I., Madeira 33 45S 16 25W
125 Pôrto São José, Brazil 22 43S 53 10W
127 Pôrto Seguro, Brazil 16 26S 39 5W
39 Porto Tolle, Italy 44 57N 12 20E
40 Porto Tórres, Italy 40 50N 8 23E
125 Pôrto União, Brazil 26 10S 51 10W
126 Pôrto Válter, Brazil 8 5S 72 40W
126 Pôrto Velho, Brazil 8 46S 63 54W
121 Portobelo, Panama 9 35N 79 42W
38 Portoferráio, Italy 42 50N 10 20E
39 Portogruaro, Italy 45 47N 12 50E
118 Portola, U.S.A. 39 49N 120 28W
39 Portomaggiore, Italy 44 41N 11 47E
40 Portoscuso, Italy 39 12N 8 22E
38 Portovénere, Italy 44 2N 9 50E
126 Portoviejo, Ecuador 1 0S 80 20W
14 Portpatrick, Scot. 54 50N 5 7W
14 Portree, Scot. 57 25N 6 11W
15 Portrush, N. Ire. 55 13N 6 40W
18 Portsall, France 48 37N 4 45W
113 Portsmouth, Canada 44 14N 76 34W
13 Portsmouth, Eng. 50 48N 1 6W
113 Portsmouth, N.H., U.S.A. 43 5N 70 45W
114 Portsmouth, Ohio, U.S.A. 38 45N 83 0W
113 Portsmouth, R.I., U.S.A. 41 35N 71 44W
114 Portsmouth, Va., U.S.A. 36 50N 76 20W
50 Porttipahta, Finland 68 5N 26 30E
30 Portugal ■, Europe 40 0N 7 0W
32 Portugalete, Spain 43 19N 3 4W
88 Portugalia, Angola 7 23S 20 48E
126 Portuguesa ♦, Venezuela 9 10N 69 15W
†84 Portuguese Guinea ■, West Africa 12 0N 15 0W
73 Portuguese Timor ■, E. Indies 8 0S 126 30E
15 Portumna, Ireland 53 5N 8 12W
112 Portville, U.S.A. 42 3N 78 21W
128 Porvenir, Chile 53 10S 70 30W
51 Porvoo, Finland 60 24N 25 40E
31 Porzuna, Spain 39 9N 4 9W
40 Posada, R., Italy 40 40N 9 35E
31 Posadas, Spain 37 47N 5 11W
25 Poschiavo, Switzerland 46 19N 10 4E
77 Poseh, China 23 50N 106 0E
32 Posets, mt., Spain 42 39N 0 25E
44 Posidhio, Akra, Gr. 39 57N 23 30E
43 Poski Trûmbesh, Bulg. 43 20N 25 38E
28 Poslek, Poland 54 3N 19 41E
73 Poso, Indonesia 1 20S 120 55E
73 Poso, D., Indonesia 1 20S 120 55E

MAP
124 Poso Colorado, Paraguay 23 30S 58 45W
127 Posse, Brazil 14 4S 46 18W
5 Possession I., Antarctica 72 4S 172 0E
24 Pössneck, Germany 50 42N 11 34E
117 Post, U.S.A. 33 13N 101 21W
118 Post Falls, U.S.A. 47 50N 116 59W
54 Postavy, U.S.S.R. 55 4N 26 58E
106 Poste de la Baleine, Canada 55 20N 77 40E
82 Poste Maurice Cortier (Bidon 5), Algeria 22 14N 1 2E
73 Postiljon, Kepulauan, Indonesia 6 30S 118 50E
92 Postmasburg, S. Africa 28 18S 23 5E
39 Postojna, Yugoslavia 45 46N 14 12E
45 Potamós, Greece 39 38N 19 53E
92 Potchefstroom, S. Afr. 26 41S 27 7E
46 Potcoava, Rumania 44 30N 24 39E
117 Poteau, U.S.A. 35 5N 94 37W
117 Poteet, U.S.A. 29 4N 98 35W
46 Poteiu, Lacul, Rum. 43 44N 24 20E
41 Potenza, Italy 40 40N 15 50E
39 Potenza Picena, Italy 43 22N 13 37E
101 Poteriteri, L., N.Z. 46 5S 167 10E
30 Potes, Spain 43 15N 4 42W
93 Potgietersrus, S. Africa 24 10S 29 3E
57 Poti, U.S.S.R. 42 10N 41 38E
85 Potiskum, Nigeria 11 39N 11 2E
46 Potlogi, Rumania 44 34N 25 34E
114 Potomac, R., U.S.A. 39 40N 78 25W
126 Potosi, Bolivia 19 38S 65 50W
126 Potosí ♦, Bolivia 20 31S 67 0W
124 Potrerillos, Chile 26 20S 69 30W
124 Potros, Cerro del, Chile 28 32S 69 0W
24 Potsdam, Germany 52 23N 13 4E
113 Potsdam, U.S.A. 44 40N 74 59W
24 Potsdam ♦, E. Ger. 52 40N 12 50E
116 Potter, U.S.A. 41 15N 103 20W
86 Pottery Hill = Abu Ballas, Egypt 24 26N 27 36E
113 Pottstown, U.S.A. 40 17N 75 40W
113 Pottsville, U.S.A. 40 39N 76 12W
18 Pouancé, France 47 44N 1 10W
108 Pouce Coupé, Canada 55 40N 120 10W
113 Poughkeepsie, U.S.A. 41 40N 73 57W
19 Pouilly, France 47 18N 2 57E
15 Poulaphouca Res., Ire. 53 8N 6 30W
18 Pouldu, le, France 47 41N 3 36W
118 Poulsbo, U.S.A. 47 45N 122 45W
127 Pouso Alegre, Mato Grosso, Brazil 11 55S 57 0W
125 Pouso Alegre, Minas Gerais, Brazil 22 14S 45 57W
20 Pouzages, France 46 40N 0 50W
50 Povenets, U.S.S.R. 62 50N 34 50E
101 Poverty Bay, N.Z. 38 43S 178 2E
30 Póvoa de Lanhosa, Port. 41 33N 8 15W
30 Póvoa de Varzim, Port. 41 25N 8 46W
55 Povorino, U.S.S.R. 51 12N 42 28E
106 Powassan, Canada 46 5N 79 25W
116 Powder, R., U.S.A. 46 47N 105 12W
118 Powell, U.S.A. 44 45N 108 45W
96 Powell Creek, Austral. 18 6S 133 46E
108 Powell River, Canada 49 48N 125 20W
114 Powers, Mich., U.S.A. 45 40N 87 32W
118 Powers, Oreg., U.S.A. 42 53N 124 2W
116 Powers Lake, U.S.A. 48 37N 102 38W
77 Poyang Hu, China 29 10N 116 10E
59 Poyarkovo, U.S.S.R. 49 36N 128 41E
27 Poysdorf, Austria 48 40N 16 37E
32 Poza de la Sal, Spain 42 35N 3 31W
120 Poza Rica, Mexico 20 33N 97 27W
42 Požarevac, Yugoslavia 44 35N 21 18E
42 Požega, Yugoslavia 45 21N 17 41E
28 Poznań, Poland 52 25N 17 0E
28 Poznań ♦, Poland 52 30N 18 0E
33 Pozo Alcón, Sp. 37 42N 2 56W
126 Pozo Almonte, Chile 20 10S 69 50W
31 Pozoblanco, Spain 38 23N 4 51W
125 Pozzallo, Italy 36 44N 15 40E
85 Pra, R., Ghana 5 30N 1 38W
28 Prabuty, Poland 53 47N 19 15E
42 Prača, Yugoslavia 43 47N 18 43E
26 Prachatice, Cz. 49 1N 14 0E
71 Prachin Buri, Thailand 14 0N 101 25E
72 Prachuap Khiri Khan, Thailand 11 49N 99 48E
20 Pradelles, France 44 46N 3 52E
126 Pradera, Colombia 3 25N 76 15W
20 Prades, France 42 38N 2 23E
127 Prado, Brazil 17 20S 39 13W
31 Prado del Rey, Spain 36 48N 5 33W
49 Praestö, Denmark 55 8N 12 2E
49 Prasto Amt ♦, Denmark 55 15N 12 0E
39 Pragersko, Yugoslavia 46 27N 15 42E
26 Prague = Praha, Cz. 50 5N 14 22E
26 Praha, Cz. 50 5N 14 22E
20 Prahecq, France 46 19N 0 26W
70 Prahita, R., India 19 0N 79 55E
46 Prahova, Reg., Rumania 44 50N 25 50E
46 Prahova, R., Rumania 44 50N 25 50E
46 Prahova ♦, Rumania 45 10N 26 0E
42 Prahovo, Yugoslavia 44 18N 22 39E
46 Praid, Rumania 46 32N 25 10E
126 Prainha, Amazonas, Braz. 7 10S 60 30W
127 Prainha, Pará, Brazil 1 45S 53 30W
98 Prairie, Australia 20 50S 144 35E
117 Prairie, R., U.S.A. 34 45N 101 15W
118 Prairie City, U.S.A. 45 27N 118 44W
116 Prairie du Chien, U.S.A. 43 1N 91 9W
72 Praja, Indonesia 8 39S 116 27E
28 Prajeczno, Poland 51 10N 19 0E
44 Pramánda, Greece 39 32N 21 8E
85 Prang, Ghana 8 1N 0 56W
72 Prapat, Indonesia 2 41N 98 58E
127 Prappia, Brazil 10 15S 37 1W
28 Praszka, Poland 51 32N 18 31E
127 Prata, Minas Gerais, Brazil 19 25S 49 0W

MAP
127 Prata, Pará, Brazil 1 10S 47 35W
40 Prática di Mare, Italy 41 40N 12 26E
38 Prato, Italy 43 53N 11 5E
39 Prátola Peligna, Italy 42 7N 13 51E
39 Pratovécchio, Italy 43 44N 11 43E
20 Prats-de-Molló, France 42 25N 2 27E
117 Pratt, U.S.A. 37 40N 98 45W
115 Prattville, U.S.A. 32 30N 86 28W
70 Pravara, R., India 19 30N 74 28E
55 Pravdinsk, U.S.S.R. 56 29N 43 28E
30 Pravia, Spain 43 30N 6 12W
73 Pre Pare, Indonesia 3 59S 119 45E
38 Pré St. Didier, Italy 45 45N 7 0E
124 Precordillera, Argentina 30 0S 69 1W
39 Predáppio, Italy 44 7N 11 58E
39 Predazzo, Italy 46 19N 11 37E
42 Predejane, Yugoslavia 42 51N 22 9E
109 Preeceville, Canada 52 0N 102 50W
18 Pré-en-Pail, France 48 28N 0 12W
18 Préfailles, France 47 9N 2 11W
126 Pregonero, Venezuela 8 1N 71 46W
39 Pregrada, Yugoslavia 46 11N 15 45E
39 Preko, Yugoslavia 44 7N 15 14E
39 Prelog, Yugoslavia 46 18N 16 32E
100 Premer, Austral. 31 29S 149 56E
96 Premier Downs, Australia 30 30S 126 30E
117 Premont, U.S.A. 27 19N 91 8W
39 Premuda, I., Yugoslavia 44 20N 14 36E
42 Prenj, mt., Yugoslavia 43 33N 17 53E
44 Prenjasi, Albania 41 6N 20 32E
116 Prentice, U.S.A. 45 31N 90 19W
24 Prenzlau, Germany 53 19N 13 51E
44 Prepansko Jezero, Yugoslavia 40 45N 21 0E
67 Preparis I., Burma 14 55N 93 45E
71 Preparis North Channel, Andaman Islands 15 12N 93 40E
71 Preparis South Channel, Andaman Islands 14 36N 93 40E
27 Prerov, Czechoslovakia 49 28N 17 27E
106 Prescott, Canada 44 45N 75 30W
119 Prescott, Ariz., U.S.A. 34 35N 112 30W
117 Prescott, Ark., U.S.A. 33 49N 93 22W
101 Preservation Inlet, N.Z. 46 8S 166 35E
42 Preševo, Yugoslavia 42 19N 21 39E
116 Presho, U.S.A. 43 56N 100 4W
41 Presicce, Italy 39 53N 18 13E
124 Presidencia de la Plaza, Argentina 27 0S 60 0W
124 Presidencia Roque Sáenz Peña, Arg. 26 45S 60 30W
124 Presidente Jayes ♦, Paraguay 24 0S 59 0W
126 Presidente Hermes, Brazil 11 0S 61 55W
125 Presidente Prudente, Brazil 22 5S 51 25W
124 Presidente Rogue Saena Peña, Arg. 34 33S 58 30W
117 Presidio, U.S.A. 29 30N 104 20W
43 Preslav, Bulgaria 43 10N 26 52E
43 Prespa, mt., Bulgaria 41 44N 25 0E
107 Presque Isle, U.S.A. 46 40N 68 0W
84 Prestea, Ghana 5 22N 2 7W
13 Presteigne, Wales 52 17N 3 0W
26 Preštice, Czechoslovakia 49 34N 13 20E
112 Preston, Canada 43 25N 80 20W
12 Preston, England 53 46N 2 42W
118 Preston, Idaho, U.S.A. 42 0N 112 0W
116 Preston, Minn., U.S.A. 43 39N 92 3W
118 Preston, Nev., U.S.A. 38 59N 115 2W
14 Prestonpans, Scot. 55 58N 3 0W
14 Prestwick, Scot. 55 30N 4 38W
93 Pretoria, S. Afr. 25 44S 28 12E
45 Préveza, Greece 38 57N 20 47E
44 Préveza ♦, Greece 39 20N 20 40E
71 Prey-Veng, Khmer Rep. 11 35N 105 29E
56 Priazovskoye, U.S.S.R. 46 22N 35 28E
4 Pribilof Is., Bering Sea 56 0N 170 0W
42 Priboj, Yugoslavia 43 35N 19 32E
26 Pribram, Cz. 49 41N 14 2E
118 Price, U.S.A. 39 40N 110 48W
57 Prichalnaya, U.S.S.R. 48 57N 44 33E
32 Priego, Spain 40 38N 2 21W
31 Priego de Córdoba, Sp. 37 27N 4 12W
54 Priekule, U.S.S.R. 57 27N 21 45E
92 Prieska, S. Afr. 29 40S 22 42E
118 Priest L., U.S.A. 48 30N 116 55W
118 Priest River, U.S.A. 48 11N 117 0W
27 Prievidza, Cz. 48 46N 18 36E
39 Prijedor, Yugoslavia 44 58N 16 41E
42 Prijepolje, Yugoslavia 43 27N 19 40E
42 Prilep, Yugoslavia 41 21N 21 37E
54 Priluki, U.S.S.R. 50 30N 32 15E
43 Primorsko, Bulgaria 42 15N 27 44E
56 Primorsko-Akhtarsk, U.S.S.R. 46 2N 38 10E
109 Primrose L., Canada 54 55N 109 40W
109 Prince Albert, Canada 53 15N 105 50W
104 Prince Albert Pen., Can. 72 0N 116 0W
4 Prince Alfred C., Can. 74 0N 124 0W
105 Prince Charles I., Can. 68 0N 76 0W
3 Prince Edward Is., Indian Oc. 45 15S 39 0E
107 Prince Edward I. ♦., Canada 44 2N 77 20W
108 Prince George, Canada 53 50N 122 50W
104 Prince of Wales, I., Alaska 53 30N 131 30W
98 Prince of Wales I., Austral. 10 35S 142 0E
4 Prince Patrick I., Can. 77 0N 120 0W
4 Prince Regent Inlet, Can. 73 0N 90 0W
108 Prince Rupert, Canada 54 20N 130 20W
98 Princess Charlotte B., Australia 14 15S 144 0E
108 Princess Royal I., Can. 53 0N 128 40W
108 Princeton, Can. 49 27N 120 30W

MAP
116 Princeton, Ill., U.S.A. 41 25N 89 25W
114 Princeton, Ind., U.S.A. 38 20N 87 35W
114 Princeton, Ky., U.S.A. 37 6N 87 55W
116 Princeton, Mo., U.S.A. 40 23N 93 35W
113 Princeton, N.J., U.S.A. 40 18N 74 40W
114 Princeton, W. Va., U.S.A. 37 21N 81 8W
78 Principe, I. de, Gulf of Guinea 1 37N 7 27E
126 Principe da Beira, Brazil 12 20S 64 30W
118 Prineville, U.S.A. 44 17N 120 57W
92 Prins Albert, S. Africa 33 12S 22 2E
5 Prins Harald Kyst, Ant. 70 0S 35 1E
121 Prinzapolca, Nicaragua 13 20N 83 35W
30 Prior, C., Spain 43 34N 8 17W
54 Pripet Marshes = Polesye, U.S.S.R. 52 0N 28 10E
54 Pripet, R. = Pripyat, R., U.S.S.R. 51 30N 30 0E
54 Pripyat, R., U.S.S.R. 51 30N 30 0E
46 Prislop, Pasul, Rumania 47 37N 25 15E
55 Pristen, Italy 41 47N 12 40E
42 Priština, Yugoslavia 42 40N 21 13E
115 Pritchard, U.S.A. 30 47N 88 5W
24 Pritzwalk, Germany 53 10N 12 11E
21 Privas, France 44 45N 4 37E
40 Priverno, Italy 41 29N 13 10E
55 Privolzhsk, U.S.S.R. 57 9N 14 9E
55 Privolzhskaya Vozvyshennest, U.S.S.R. 51 0N 46 0E
55 Privolzhskiy, U.S.S.R. 51 25N 46 3E
55 Privolzhye, U.S.S.R. 52 52N 48 33E
57 Privutnoye, U.S.S.R. 47 12N 43 30E
42 Prizren, Yugoslavia 42 13N 20 45E
40 Prizzi, Italy 37 44N 13 24E
42 Prnjavor, Yugoslavia 44 52N 17 43E
73 Probolinggo, Indonesia 7 46S 113 13E
28 Prochowice, Poland 51 17N 16 20E
40 Procida, I., Italy 40 46N 14 0E
70 Proddatur, India 14 45N 78 30E
31 Proença-a-Nova, Port. 37 45N 7 54W
120 Progreso, Mex. 21 20N 89 40W
57 Prokhladnyy, U.S.S.R. 43 50N 44 2E
44 Prokletije, Alb. 42 30N 19 45E
58 Prokopyevsk, U.S.S.R. 54 0N 87 3E
42 Prokuplje, Yugoslavia 43 16N 21 36E
57 Proletarskaya, U.S.S.R. 46 42N 41 50E
67 Prome, Burma 18 45N 95 30E
21 Propriano, Corsica 41 41N 8 52E
98 Proserpine, Australia 20 21S 148 36E
118 Prosser, U.S.A. 46 11N 119 52W
27 Prostějov, Cz. 49 30N 17 9E
28 Prostki, Poland 53 45N 22 25E
99 Proston, Australia 26 14S 151 32E
27 Proszowice, Poland 50 13N 20 16E
117 Protection, U.S.A. 37 16N 99 30W
45 Próti, I., Greece 37 5N 21 32E
43 Provadija, Bulgaria 43 12N 27 30E
21 Provence, Fr. 43 40N 5 46E
114 Providence, Ky., U.S.A. 37 25N 87 46W
113 Providence, R.I., U.S.A. 41 41N 71 15W
106 Providence Bay, Can. 45 41N 82 15W
87 Providence C., N.Z. 45 59S 166 29E
119 Providence Mts., U.S.A. 35 0N 115 30W
126 Providencia, Ecuador 0 28S 76 28W
121 Providencia, I. de, Colombia 13 25N 81 26W
59 Provideniya, U.S.S.R. 64 23N 173 18W
71 Province Wellesley, Malaysia 5 15N 100 20E
114 Provincetown, U.S.A. 42 5N 70 11W
19 Provins, France 48 33N 3 15E
118 Provo, U.S.A. 40 16N 111 37W
109 Provost, Canada 52 25N 110 20W
42 Prozor, Yugoslavia 43 50N 17 34E
96 Prudhoe Bay, Australia 21 30S 149 30W
98 Prudhoe I., Australia 21 23S 149 45E
4 Prudhoe Land, Green. 78 1N 65 0W
28 Prudnik, Poland 50 20N 17 38E
25 Prüm, Germany 50 14N 6 22E
28 Pruszcz, Poland 54 17N 19 40E
28 Pruszków, Poland 52 9N 20 49E
46 Prut, R., Rumania 46 3N 28 10E
39 Prvič, I., Yugoslavia 44 55N 14 47E
5 Prydz B., Antarctica 69 0S 74 0E
117 Pryor, U.S.A. 36 17N 95 20W
28 Przasnysz, Poland 53 2N 20 45E
28 Przedbórz, Poland 51 6N 19 53E
28 Przedecz, Poland 52 20N 18 53E
27 Przemysl, Poland 49 50N 22 45E
27 Przeworsk, Poland 50 6N 22 32E
28 Przewóz, Poland 51 28N 14 57E
58 Przhevalsk, U.S.S.R. 42 30N 78 20E
28 Przysucha, Poland 51 22N 20 38E
45 Psakhná, Greece 38 34N 23 35E
45 Psará, I., Greece 38 37N 25 38E
45 Psathoúra, I., Greece 39 30N 24 12E
56 Psel, R., U.S.S.R. 49 25N 33 50E
45 Pserimos, I., Greece 36 56N 27 12E
54 Pskov, U.S.S.R. 57 50N 28 25E
42 Psunj, mt., Yugoslavia 45 25N 17 19E
27 Pszczyna, Poland 49 59N 18 58E
45 Pteleón, Greece 39 3N 22 57E
54 Ptich, R., U.S.S.R. 52 30N 28 45E
44 Ptolemais, Greece 40 30N 21 43E
39 Ptuj, Yugoslavia 46 28N 15 50E
39 Ptujska Gora, Y.-slav. 46 23N 15 47E
124 Puán, Argentina 37 30S 63 0W
107 Pubnico, Canada 43 47N 65 50W
126 Pucallpa, Peru 8 25S 74 30W
77 Pucheng, China 28 0N 118 30E
46 Pucheni, Rumania 45 12N 25 17E
77 Puchi, China 29 42N 113 54E
39 Pucisce, Yugoslavia 43 22N 16 43E
28 Puck, Poland 54 45N 18 23E
70 Pudukkottai, India 10 28N 78 47E
120 Puebla, Mexico 19 0N 98 10W
120 Puebla ♦, Mexico 18 30N 98 0W
31 Puebla de Alcocer, Sp. 38 59N 5 14W
33 Puebla de Don Fadrique, Spain 37 58N 2 25W

* Renamed Pemba
† Renamed Guinea-Bissau

MAP

31 Puebla de Don Rodrigo, Spain, 39 5N 4 37w
31 Puebla de Guzmán, Sp. 37 37N 7 15w
30 Puebla de Sanabria, Sp. 42 4N 6 38w
30 Puebla de Trives, Spain 42 20N 7 10w
30 Puebla del Caramiñal. Sp. 42 37N 8 56w
116 Pueblo, U.S.A. 38 20N 104 40w
119 Pueblo Bonito, U.S.A. 36 4N 107 57w
31 Puebla de Guzmán, Sp. 37 37N 7 15w
124 Pueblo Hundido, Chile 26 20s 69 30w
126 Pueblo Nuevo, Venezuela 8 26N 71 26w
124 Puelches, Argentina 38 5s 66 0w
124 Puelén, Argentina 37 32s 67 38w
124 Puente Alto, Chile 33 32s 70 35w
30 Puente del Arzobispo, Sp. 39 48N 5 10w
31 Puente Genil, Spain 37 22N 4 47w
32 Puente la Reina, Sp. 42 40N 1 49w
30 Puentearas, Spain 42 10N 8 28w
30 Puentedeume, Spain 43 24N 8 10w
30 Puentes de García Rodríguez, Sp. 43 27N 7 51w
119 Puerco, R., U.S.A. 35 10N 109 45w
75 Puerh, China 23 11N 100 56E
128 Puerto Aisén, Chile 45 10s 73 0w
121 Puerto Armuelles, Pan. 8 20N 83 10w
126 Puerto Ayacucho, Ven. 5 40N 67 35w
120 Puerto Barrios, Guat. 15 40N 88 40w
77 Puerto Belgrano, Arg. 38 50s 62 0w
124 Puerto Bermejo, Arg. 26 55s 58 34w
126 Puerto Bermúdez, Peru 10 20s 75 0w
126 Puerto Bolívar, Ec. 3 19s 79 55w
126 Puerto Cabello, Ven. 10 28N 68 1w
121 Puerto Cabezas, Nic. 14 0N 83 30w
82 Puerto Capaz = Jebha, Morocco 35 11N 4 43w
126 Puerto Carreño, Col. 6 12N 67 22w
124 Puerto Casado, Par. 22 19s 57 56w
121 Puerto Castilla, Hond. 16 0N 86 0w
126 Puerto Chicama, Peru 7 45s 79 20w
128 Puerto Coig, Argentina 50 54s 69 15w
120 Puerto Columbia, Col. 10 59N 74 58w
121 Puerto Cortés, C. Rica 8 20N 82 20w
120 Puerto Cortés, Hond. 15 51N 88 0w
126 Puerto Cuemani, Col. 0 5N 73 21w
126 Puerto Cumareño, Ven. 11 29N 69 21w
80 Puerto de Cabras, Canary Is. 28 40N 13 30w
120 Puerto de Morelos, Mex. 20 49N 86 52w
31 Puerto de Santa María, Sp. 36 36N 6 13w
128 Puerto Deseado, Arg. 47 45s 66 0w
126 Puerto Heath, Bolivia 12 25s 68 45w
126 Puerto Huitoto, Colombia 0 18N 74 3w
126 Puerto Juárez, Mexico 21 11N 86 49w
126 Puerto La Cruz, Ven. 10 13N 64 38w
126 Puerto Leguízamo, Col. 0 12s 74 46w
120 Puerto Libertad, Mex. 29 55N 112 41w
126 Puerto Limón, Meta, Colombia 3 23N 73 30w
126 Puerto Limón, Putumayo, Colombia 1 3N 76 30w
128 Puerto Lobos, Argentina 42 0s 65 3w
126 Puerto López, Colombia 4 5N 72 58w
33 Puerto Lumbreras, Sp. 37 34N 1 48w
128 Puerto Madryn, Arg. 42 48s 65 4w
126 Puerto Maldonado, Peru 12 30s 69 10w
33 Puerto Mazarrón, Spain 37 34N 1 15w
126 Puerto Mercedes, Col. 1 11N 72 54w
128 Puerto Montt, Chile 41 28s 73 0w
128 Puerto Natales, Chile 51 45s 72 25w
126 Puerto Nuevo, Colombia 5 53N 69 56w
126 Puerto Ordaz, Ven. 8 16N 62 44w
121 Puerto Padre, Cuba 21 13N 76 35w
126 Puerto Páez, Venezuela 6 13N 67 28w
124 Puerto Pinasco, Par. 22 43s 57 50w
128 Puerto Pirámides, Arg. 42 35s 64 20w
121 Puerto Plata, Dom. Rep. 19 40N 70 45w
68 Puerto Princesa, Phil. 9 44N 118 44E
121 Puerto Quepos, C. Rica 9 29N 84 6w
31 Puerto Real, Spain 36 33N 6 12w
126 Puerto Rico, Colombia 1 54N 75 10w
121 Puerto Rico ■, W. Indies 18 15N 66 45w
6 Puerto Rico Trough, North Atlantic Ocean 20 0N 63 0w
124 Puerto Sastre, Par. 22 25s 57 55w
126 Puerto Suárez, Bolivia 18 58s 57 52w
126 Puerto Tejada, Col. 3 14N 76 24w
126 Puerto Umbria, Col. 0 52N 76 33w
120 Puerto Vallarta, Mexico 20 26N 105 15w
126 Puerto Villamizar, Col. 8 25N 72 30w
126 Puerto Wilches, Col. 7 21N 73 54w
31 Puertollano, Spain 38 43N 4 7w
30 Puertomarín, Spain 42 48N 7 37w
46 Puești, Rumania 46 25N 27 33E
128 Pueyrredón, L., Argentina 47 20s 72 0w
55 Pugachev, U.S.S.R. 52 0N 48 55E
90 Puge, Tanzania 4 45s 33 11E
118 Puget Sd., U.S.A. 47 15N 123 30w
21 Puget-Théniers, France 43 58N 6 53E
41 Puglia, It. 41 0N 16 30E
90 Puguu, Tanzania 6 55s 39 4E
46 Pui, Rumania 45 30N 23 4E
32 Puig Mayor, Mte., Spain 39 49N 2 47E
32 Puigcerdá, Spain 42 24N 1 50E
32 Puigmal, Mt., Spain 42 23N 2 7E
19 Puisaye, Collines de, Fr. 47 34N 3 18E
19 Puiseaux, France 48 11N 2 30E
44 Puka, Albania 42 2N 19 53E
101 Pukaki L., N.Z. 44 4s 170 1E
109 Pukatawagan, Canada 55 45N 101 20w
101 Pukekohe, N.Z. 37 12s 174 55E
77 Pukow, China 32 15N 118 45E
40 Pula, Italy 39 0N 9 0E
39 Pula (Pola), Y.-slavia 44 54N 13 57E
113 Pulaski, N.Y., U.S.A. 43 32N 76 9w
115 Pulaski, Tenn., U.S.A. 35 10N 87 0w
114 Pulaski, Va., U.S.A. 37 4N 80 49w
28 Pulawy, Poland 51 23N 21 59E
70 Pulgaon, India 20 44N 78 21E
70 Pulicat, L., India 13 40N 80 15E
70 Puliyangudi, India 9 11N 77 24E
118 Pullman, U.S.A. 46 49N 117 10w
85 Pulmakong, Ghana 11 2N 0 2E
118 Pullman, U.S.A. 46 49N 117 10w
73 Pulog, Mt., Philippines 16 40N 120 50E
28 Pułtusk, Poland 52 43N 21 6E
75 Puluntohai (Bulun Tokhai), China 47 2N 87 29E
126 Puna, Bolivia 19 45s 65 28w
126 Puná, I., Ecuador 2 55s 80 5w
124 Puna de Atacama, Arg. 25 0s 67 0w
69 Punakha, Bhutan 27 42N 89 52E
70 Punalur, India 9 0N 76 56E
68 Punasar, India 27 6N 73 6E
126 Punata, Bolivia 17 25s 65 50w
69 Punch, Kashmir 33 48N 74 4E
91 POngOê, Ponte de, Mozam. 19 0s 34 0E
68 Punjab ♦, India 31 0N 76 0E
126 Puno, Peru 15 55s 70 3w
124 Punta Arenas, Chile 53 0s 71 0w
124 Punta de Díaz, Chile 28 0s 70 45w
124 Punta de Piedras, Ven. 10 54N 64 6w
124 Punta del Lago Viedma, Argentina 49 45s 72 0w
120 Punta Gorda, Br. Hond. 16 10N 88 45w
115 Punta Gorda, U.S.A. 26 55N 82 0w
124 Puntarenas, Costa Rica 10 0N 84 50w
30 Puntes de García Rodríguez, Sp. 43 27N 7 50w
126 Punto Fijo, Venezuela 11 42N 70 13w
112 Punxsutawney, U.S.A. 40 56N 79 0w
77 Punyu, China 22 58N 113 16E
126 Puquio, Peru 14 45s 74 10w
58 Pur, R., U.S.S.R. 65 30N 77 40E
126 Purace, vol., Colombia 2 21N 76 23w
42 Puračić, Yugoslavia 44 33N 18 28E
13 Purbeck, Isle of, England 50 40N 2 5w
117 Purcell, U.S.A. 35 0N 97 25w
33 Purchena Tetica, Spain 37 21N 2 21w
98 Purdy Is., Terr. of New Guinea 3 0s 146 0E
69 Puri, India 19 50N 85 58E
126 Purificación, Colombia 3 51N 74 55w
70 Purli, India 18 50N 76 35E
71 Purmerend, Neth. 52 30N 4 58E
70 Purna, R., India 19 55N 76 20E
70 Purnea, India 25 45N 87 31E
71 Pursat, Khmer Rep. 12 34N 103 50E
126 Puruey, Venezuela 7 35N 64 48w
69 Purulia, India 23 17N 86 33E
126 Purus, R., Brazil 5 25s 64 0w
43 Pŭrvomay, Bulgaria 42 8N 25 17E
73 Purwakarta, Indonesia 6 35s 107 29E
73 Purwodadi, Djawa, Indon. 7 7s 110 55E
73 Purwodadi, Djawa, Indon. 7 51s 110 0E
73 Purworedjo, Indonesia 7 43s 110 2E
70 Pus, R., India 19 50N 77 45E
70 Pusad, India 19 56N 77 36E
59 Pushchino, U.S.S.R. 54 20N 158 10E
59 Pushkin, U.S.S.R. 59 45N 30 25E
55 Pushkino, U.S.S.R. 51 16N 47 9E
108 Puskitamika L., Canada 49 20N 76 30w
27 Püspökladány, Hung. 47 19N 21 6E
93 Pussa, Mozambique 24 30s 33 55E
54 Pustoshka, U.S.S.R. 56 11N 29 30E
28 Puszczykowo, Poland 52 18N 16 49E
109 Putahow L., Canada 59 52N 101 28w
72 Putao, Burma 27 28N 97 30E
101 Putaruru, New Zealand 38 2s 175 50E
24 Putbus, Germany 54 19N 13 29E
76 Putehachi (Chalantun), China 48 4N 122 45E
46 Puteni, Rumania 45 49N 27 42E
71 Puthein Myit, R., Burma 15 56N 94 18E
77 Putien, China 25 28N 119 0E
41 Putignano, Italy 40 50N 17 5E
24 Putlitz, Germany 53 15N 12 3E
46 Putna, Rumania 47 50N 25 33E
46 Putna, R., Rumania 45 42N 27 26E
113 Putnam, U.S.A. 41 55N 71 55w
27 Putnok, Hungary 48 18N 20 26E
59 Putorana, Gory, U.S.S.R. 69 0N 95 0E
70 Puttalam Lagoon, Sri Lanka 8 15N 79 45E
16 Putten, Netherlands 52 16N 5 36E
24 Puttgarden, Germany 54 28N 11 15E
70 Puttur, India 12 46N 75 12E
126 Putumayo, R., Col. 1 30N 70 0w
126 Putumayo ♦, Colombia 1 30N 70 0w
73 Putussibau, G., Indon. 0 45N 113 50E
20 Puy-de-Dôme, Fr. 45 46N 2 57E
20 Puy-de-Dôme ♦, Fr. 45 47N 3 0E
20 Puy-de-Sancy, Fr. 45 32N 2 41E
20 Puy l'Evêque, France 44 31N 1 9E
20 Puy Guillaume, France 45 57N 3 28E
118 Puyallup, U.S.A. 47 10N 122 22w
20 Puylaurens, France 43 35N 2 0E
20 Puyôo, France 43 33N 0 56w
85 Pweto, Zaïre 8 25s 28 51E
12 Pwllheli, Wales 52 54N 4 17w
54 Pya Ozero, U.S.S.R. 66 8N 31 22E
55 Pyana, R., U.S.S.R. 55 30N 45 0E
67 Pyapon, Burma 16 5N 95 50E
59 Pyasina, R., U.S.S.R. 72 30N 90 30E
56 Pyatigorsk, U.S.S.R. 44 2N 43 0E
56 Pyatikhatki, U.S.S.R. 48 28N 33 38E
67 Pyinmana, Burma 19 45N 96 20E
76 Pyöngyang, N. Korea 39 0N 125 30E
117 Pyote, U.S.A. 31 34N 103 5w
100 Pyramid Hill, Australia 36 2s 144 6E
118 Pyramid L., U.S.A. 40 0N 119 30w
86 Pyramids, Egypt 29 58N 31 9E
20 Pyrenees, Europe 42 45N 0 18E
20 Pyrénées-Atlantiques ♦, France 43 15N 1 0w
20 Pyrénées-Orientales ♦, France 42 35N 2 26E
28 Pyrzyce, Poland 53 10N 14 55E
55 Pyshchug, U.S.S.R. 58 57N 45 27E
54 Pytalovo, U.S.S.R. 57 5N 27 55E
91 Python, Rhodesia 17 56s 29 10E
47 Pyttegga, Norway 13 2N 7 42E
67 Pyu, Burma 18 30N 96 35E
86 Qaar Zeitun, Egypt 29 58N 31 9E
62 Qabalan, Jordan 32 8N 35 17E
62 Qadam, Afghanistan 32 55N 66 45E
64 Qadhimah, Si. Arabia 22 20N 39 13E
68 Qadian, India 31 51N 74 19E
64 Qal'at al Akhdhar, Saudi Arabia 28 0N 37 10E
86 Qal'at Saura, Si. Arab. 26 10N 38 40E
86 Qal at Shajwa, Si. Arab. 25 2N 38 57E
68 Qala-i-Jadid (Spin Baldak), Afghanistan 31 1N 66 25E
65 Qala-i-Kirta, Afghan. 32 15N 63 0E
65 Qala Nau, Afghan. 35 0N 63 0E
65 Qala Punja, Afghan. 37 0N 72 40E
62 Qalqilya, Israel 32 12N 34 58E
86 Qalyûb, Egypt 30 12N 31 11E
62 Qam, Jordan 32 36N 35 43E
63 Qamar, Ghubbat al, Southern Yemen 16 20N 52 30E
68 Qamruddin Karez, Pak. 31 45N 68 20E
62 Qana, Lebanon 33 12N 35 17E
86 Qâra, Egypt 29 38N 26 30E
86 Qara, Saudi Arabia 29 55N 40 3E
86 Qarachuk, Syria 37 0N 42 2E
87 Qardud, Sudan 10 20N 29 56E
86 Qârsa, Ethiopia 9 28N 41 48E
83 Qaşr Bū Hadi, Libya 31 1N 16 45E
65 Qasr-e-Qand, Iran 26 15N 60 45E
86 Qasr Farâfra, Egypt 27 0N 28 1E
62 Qastina, Israel 31 44N 34 45E
65 Qatar ■, S.W. Asia 25 30N 51 15E
62 Qâttâra, Egypt 30 12N 27 3E
86 Qattâra Depression = Q., Munkhafed el 29 30N 27 30E
86 Qattâra, Munkhafed el, Egypt 29 30N 27 30E
65 Qayen, Iran 33 40N 59 10E
64 Qazvin, Iran 36 15N 50 0E
86 Qena, Egypt 26 10N 32 43E
86 Qena, Wadi, Egypt 26 57N 32 50E
44 Qendrevca, Albania 40 20N 19 48E
62 Qesari, Israel 32 30N 34 53E
65 Qeshm, Iran 26 55N 56 10E
65 Qeshm, I., Iran 26 50N 56 0E
66 Qila Safed, Pakistan 29 0N 61 30E
68 Qila Saifula, Pakistan 30 45N 68 17E
62 Qiryat 'Anivim, Israel 31 49N 35 7E
62 Qiryat Bialik, Israel 32 50N 35 5E
62 Qiryat 'Eqron, Israel 31 52N 34 49E
62 Qiryat Hayyim, Israel 32 49N 35 4E
62 Qiryat Shemona, Israel 33 13N 35 35E
62 Qiryat Yam, Israel 32 51N 35 4E
65 Qishan, R., Israel 32 51N 35 7E
86 Qishran, Saudi Arabia 20 14N 40 2E
65 Qizan, Saudi Arabia 16 57N 42 34E
65 Qom, Iran 34 40N 51 0E
87 Quabbo, Ethiopia 12 2N 39 56E
24 Quackenbrück, Ger. 52 40N 7 59E
113 Quakerstown, U.S.A. 40 27N 75 20w
100 Quambatook, Australia 35 49s 143 34E
99 Quambone, Australia 30 57s 147 53E
71 Quan Long, S. Vietnam 9 7N 105 8E
71 Quang Nam, S. Vietnam 15 55N 108 15E
71 Quang Ngai, S. Vietnam 15 13N 108 58E
71 Quang Yen, N. Vietnam 21 3N 106 52E
100 Quandialla, Australia 34 1s 147 47E
13 Quantock Hills, The, England 51 8N 3 10w
124 Quaraí, Brazil 30 15s 56 20w
20 Quarré les Tombes, Fr. 47 21N 4 0E
40 Quartu Sant' Elena, It. 39 15N 9 10E
119 Quartzsite, U.S.A. 33 44N 114 16w
91 Quatsino, Canada 50 30N 127 40w
108 Quatsino Sd., Canada 50 42N 127 58w
62 Qubab = Mishmar Aiyalon, Israel 31 52N 34 57E
62 Qubatiya, Jordan 32 25N 35 17E
65 Quchan, Iran 37 10N 58 27E
91 Que Que, Rhodesia 18 58s 29 48E
99 Queanbeyan, Australia 35 17s 149 14E
107 Québec, Canada 46 52N 71 13w
107 Québec ♦, Canada 50 0N 70 0w
24 Quedlinburg, Germany 51 47N 11 9E
5 Queen Alexandra Ra., Antarctica 85 0s 170 0E
108 Queen Bess Mt., Can. 51 13N 124 35w
108 Queen Charlotte, Can. 53 10N 132 0w
108 Qn. Charlotte Is., Can. 53 20N 132 10w
108 Qn. Charlotte Str., Can. 51 0N 128 0w
4 Qn. Elizabeth Is., Can. 75 0N 95 0w
90 Queen Elizabeth Nat. Pk., Uganda 0 0s 30 0E
5 Qn. Mary Coast, Antarc. 70 0s 95 0E
54 Queen Maud G., Can. 68 15N 102 30w
96 Queen's Chan., Austral. 15 0s 129 30E
100 Queenscliff, Australia 38 8s 144 27E
98 Queensland ♦, Australia 15 0s 142 0E
99 Queenstown, Australia 42 4s 145 35E
101 Queenstown, N.Z. 45 1s 168 40E
124 Queguay Grande, R., Uruguay 32 9s 58 9w
127 Queimadas, Brazil 11 0s 39 38w
88 Quela, Angola 9 10s 16 56E
91 Quelimane, Mozam. 17 53s 36 58E
128 Quellón, Chile 43 0s 73 50w
77 Quelpart = Cheju Do, S. Korea 33 29N 126 34E
119 Quemado, N. Mex., U.S.A. 34 17N 108 28w
117 Quemado, Tex., U.S.A. 28 58N 100 35w
77 Quemoy = Kinmen, China 24 25N 118 24E
124 Quemú-Quemú, Arg. 36 3s 63 36w
120 Querétaro, Mexico 20 40N 100 23w
120 Querétaro ♦, Mexico 20 30N 100 30w
24 Querfurt, Germany 51 22N 11 33E
33 Quesada, Spain 37 51N 3 4w
108 Quesnel, Canada 53 5N 122 30w
108 Quesnel L., Canada 52 30N 121 20w
119 Questa, U.S.A. 36 45N 105 35w
18 Questembert, France 47 40N 2 28w
106 Quetico, Canada 48 45N 90 55w
106 Quetico Prov. Park, Canada 48 15N 91 45w
66 Quetta, Pakistan 30 15N 66 55E
66 Quetta ♦, Pakistan 30 15N 66 55E
120 Quezaltenango, Guat. 14 40N 91 30w
73 Quezon City, Phil. 14 38N 121 0E
71 Qui Nhon, S. Vietnam 13 40N 109 13E
88 Quibaxi, Angola 8 24s 14 27E
126 Quibdó, Colombia 5 42N 76 40w
18 Quiberon, France 47 29N 3 9w
126 Quibor, Venezuela 9 56N 69 37w
24 Quickborn, Germany 53 42N 9 52E
108 Quiet L., Canada 61 0N 132 40w
124 Quiindy, Paraguay 25 58s 57 14w
124 Quilán, C., Chile 43 15s 74 30w
89 Quilengues, Angola 14 12s 14 12E
124 Quilimari, Chile 32 5s 70 30w
124 Quilino, Argentina 30 14s 64 29w
126 Quillabamba, Peru 12 50s 72 50w
124 Quillagua, Chile 21 40s 69 40w
124 Quillaicillo, Chile 31 17s 71 40w
20 Quillan, France 42 53N 2 10E
18 Quillebeuf, France 49 28N 0 30E
124 Quillota, Chile 32 54s 71 16w
124 Quilmes, Argentina 34 43s 58 15w
70 Quilon, India 8 50N 76 38E
99 Quilpie, Australia 26 35s 144 11E
124 Quilpué, Chile 33 5s 71 33w
91 Quiua, Mozambique 16 17s 39 54E
124 Quilimili, Argentina 27 40s 62 30w
18 Quimper, France 48 0N 4 9w
18 Quimperlé, France 47 53N 3 33w
118 Quincy, Calif., U.S.A. 39 56N 121 0w
115 Quincy, Fla., U.S.A. 30 34N 84 34w
116 Quincy, Ill., U.S.A. 39 55N 91 20w
113 Quincy, Mass., U.S.A. 42 14N 71 0w
118 Quincy, Wash., U.S.A. 47 22N 119 56w
124 Quines, Argentina 32 13s 65 48w
91 Quinga, Mozambique 15 49s 40 15E
19 Quingey, France 47 7N 5 52E
31 Quintana de la Serena, Spain 38 45N 5 40w
32 Quintana Roo ♦, Mexico 19 0N 88 0w
32 Quintanar de la Orden, Spain 39 36N 3 5w
33 Quintanar de la Sierra, Spain 41 57N 2 55w
33 Quintanar del Rey, Sp. 39 21N 1 56w
18 Quintin, France 48 26N 2 56w
32 Quinto, Spain 41 25N 0 32w
124 Quintero, Chile 32 45s 71 30w
100 Quinyambie, Austral. 30 15s 141 0E
33 Quipar, R., Spain 37 58N 2 3w
124 Quirihue, Chile 36 15s 72 35w
100 Quirindi, Australia 31 28s 150 40E
126 Quiriquire, Venezuela 9 59N 63 13w
30 Quiroga, Spain 42 28N 7 18w
107 Quirpon I., Canada 51 32N 55 28w
126 Quisiro, Venezuela 10 53N 71 17w
91 Quissanga, Mozam. 12 24s 40 28E
124 Quitilipi, Argentina 26 50s 60 13w
115 Quitman, Ga., U.S.A. 30 49N 83 35w
115 Quitman, Miss., U.S.A. 32 2N 88 42w
117 Quitman, Tex., U.S.A. 32 48N 95 25w
126 Quito, Ecuador 0 15s 78 35w
127 Quixadá, Brazil 4 55s 39 0w
91 Quixaxe, Mozambique 15 17s 40 4E
86 Qul'ān, Jazā'ir, Egypt 24 22N 35 31E
62 Qumran, Jordan 31 43N 35 27E
65 Quneitra, Syria 33 7N 35 48E
99 Quondong, Australia 33 4s 140 20E
99 Quoin Pt., S. Africa 34 46s 19 37E
99 Quorn, Australia 32 25s 138 0E
109 Quorn, Canada 49 25N 90 55w
87 Quo-oin, Sudan 13 30N 34 50E
86 Qûs, Egypt 25 55N 32 50E
86 Qusair, Egypt 26 7N 34 16E
62 Qusra, Jordan 32 5N 35 24E
44 Qyteti Stalin (Kuçove), Albania 40 47N 19 57E
20 Rabastens, Tarn, Fr. 43 50N 1 43E
36 Rabat, Malta 35 53N 14 25E
82 Rabat, Morocco 34 2N 6 48w
98 Rabaul, Terr. of New Guinea 4 24s 152 18E
49 Rabbalshede, Sweden 58 40N 11 27E
109 Rabbit L., Canada 47 0N 79 38w
64 Rabigh, Saudi Arabia 22 50N 39 5E
28 Rabka, Poland 49 37N 19 59E
41 Rácale, Italy 39 57N 18 6E
40 Racalmuto, Italy 37 25N 13 41E
41 Racconigi, Italy 44 47N 7 41E
42 Rácúșdia, Rumania 44 59N 21 36E
107 Race C., Canada 46 40N 53 18w
42 Rach Gia, S. Vietnam 10 5N 105 5E
28 Raciaz, Poland 52 46N 20 10E
28 Raciborz (Ratibor), Pol. 50 7N 18 18E
114 Racine, U.S.A. 42 41N 87 51w
93 Radama, Is., Malag. 14 0s 47 47E
93 Radama, Presqu'île d', Malag. 14 16s 47 53E
42 Radan, mt., Yugoslavia 42 59N 21 29E
46 Rădăuți, Rumania 47 50N 25 59E
28 Radbuza, R., Cz. 49 35N 13 5E
47 Rade, Norway 59 21N 10 53E
24 Radeburg, Germany 51 6N 13 55E
54 Radekhov, U.S.S.R. 50 25N 24 32E
114 Radford, U.S.A. 37 8N 80 32w
68 Radhanpur, India 23 50N 71 38E
42 Radika, R., Yugoslavia 41 38N 20 37E
109 Radisson, Canada 52 30N 107 20w
124 Radium Hill, Austral. 32 30s 140 42E
108 Radium Hot Springs, Canada 50 48N 116 12w
73 Radja Empat, Kepulauan, Indonesia 0 30s 129 40E
73 Radja, Udjung, Indonesia 3 40N 96 25E
28 Radków, Poland 50 30N 16 24E
27 Radlin, Poland 50 3N 18 29E
43 Radna, Rumania 46 7N 21 41E
43 Radnevo, Bulgaria 42 17N 25 58E
28 Radnice, Czechoslovakia 49 51N 13 35E
13 • Radnor ♦, Wales 52 20N 3 20w
13 Radnor Forest, Wales 52 17N 3 10w
28 Radom, Poland 51 23N 21 12E
42 Radomir, Bulgaria 42 37N 23 4E
28 Radomsko, Poland 51 5N 19 28E
54 Radomyshl, U.S.S.R. 50 30N 29 12E
27 Radomyśl Wielki, Pol. 50 14N 21 15E
28 Radoszyce, Poland 51 4N 20 15E
42 Radovljica, Yugoslavia 41 38N 22 28E
47 Radøy I., Norway 60 40N 4 55E
26 Radstadt, Austria 47 24N 13 28E
13 Radstock, Eng. 51 17N 2 25w
96 Radstock, C., Australia 32 4s 134 7E
46 Răducăneni, Rumania 46 58N 27 54E
54 Radviliškis, U.S.S.R. 55 49N 23 33E
109 Radville, Canada 49 30N 104 15w
28 Radzanów, Poland 52 56N 20 8E
28 Radzymin, Poland 52 40N 18 30E
28 Radzyń Chełminski, Poland 53 23N 18 55E
108 Rae, Canada 62 45N 115 50w
69 Rae Bareli, India 26 18N 81 20E
105 Rae Isthmus, Canada 66 40N 87 30w
101 Raeside, L., Austral. 29 20s 122 0E
101 Raetihi, New Zealand 39 25s 175 17E
124 Rafaela, Argentina 31 10s 61 30w
86 Rafah, Egypt 31 18N 34 14E
90 Rafai, Cent. Afr. Rep. 4 59N 23 58E
40 Raffadali, Italy 37 23N 13 29E
64 Rafha, Si. Arabia 29 35N 43 35E
65 Rafid, Syria 32 57N 35 52E
65 Rafsanjan, Iran 30 30N 56 5E
87 Ragag, Sudan 10 59N 24 40E
99 Ragalia, Australia 23 48s 150 45E
107 Ragueneau, Canada 49 11N 68 18w
49 Ragunda, Sweden 63 6N 16 23E
41 Ragusa, Italy 36 56N 14 42E
73 Raha, Indonesia 8 20s 118 40E
87 Rahad el Berdi, Sudan 11 20N 23 40E
87 Rahad, Nahr er, Sudan 12 40N 35 30E
24 Rahden, Germany 52 26N 8 36E
87 Raheita, Ethiopia 12 46N 43 4E
68 Rahimyar Khan, Pak. 28 30N 70 25E
70 Raichur, India 16 10N 77 20E
73 Raidnesia, Indonesia 10 57s 121 36E
69 Raiganj, India 25 37N 88 10E
69 Raigarh, Madhya Pradesh, India 21 56N 83 25E
70 Raigarh, Orissa, India 19 51N 82 6E
68 Raiis, Saudi Arabia 23 33N 38 43E
99 Railton, Austral. 41 25s 146 28E
100 Rainbow, Australia 35 55s 142 0E
108 Rainbow Lake, Canada 58 30N 119 30w
118 Rainier, U.S.A. 46 4N 123 0w
118 Rainier, Mt., U.S.A. 46 50N 121 50w
109 Rainy L., Canada 48 30N 92 30w
106 Rainy River, Canada 48 50N 94 30w
69 Raipur, India 21 17N 81 45E
70 Rajahmundry, India 17 1N 81 48E
49 Raja-Joseppi, Finland 68 28N 28 29E
72 Rajang, R., Malaysia 2 30N 113 30E
69 Rajapalaiyarm, India 9 25N 77 35E
68 Rajasthan ♦, India 26 45N 73 30E
68 Rajasthan Canal, India 30 31N 71 0E
68 Rajgarh, Mad. P., India 24 2N 76 45E
68 Rajgarh, Raj., India 28 40N 75 25E
28 Rajgród, Poland 53 42N 22 42E
39 Rajhenburg, Y.-slavia 46 1N 15 29E
68 Rajkot, India 22 15N 70 56E

* Incorporated within the county of Powys

MAP

69 Rajmahal Hills, India 24 30N 87 30E
69 Rajnandgaon, India 21 5N 81 5E
68 Rajpipla, India 21 50N 73 30E
30 Rajpura, India 30 32N 76 32E
68 Rajshahi, Bangladesh 24 22N 88 39E
69 Rajshahi ♦, Bangladesh 25 0N 89 0E
101 Rakaia, New Zealand 43 45S 172 1E
101 Rakaia, R., N.Z. 43 26S 171 47E
65 Rakan, Ras, Qatar 26 10N 51 20E
66 Rakaposhi, Kashmir 36 10N 74 0E
86 Rakha, Saudi Arabia 18 25N 41 30E
68 Rakhni, Pakistan 30 4N 69 56E
43 Rakitovo, Bulgaria 41 59N 24 5E
47 Rakkestad, Norway 59 25N 11 21E
28 Rakoniewice, Poland 52 10N 16 16E
92 Rakops, Botswana 21 1S 24 28E
27 Rákospalota, Hungary 47 30N 19 5E
39 Rakovica, Yugoslavia 44 59N 15 38E
26 Rakovník, Cz. 50 6N 13 42E
43 Rakovski, Bulgaria 42 21N 24 57E
106 Raleigh, Canada 49 30N 92 5w
106 Raleigh, U.S.A. 35 46N 78 38w
115 Raleigh B., U.S.A. 34 50N 76 15w
42 Ralja, Yugoslavia 44 33N 20 34E
117 Ralls, U.S.A. 33 40N 101 20w
62 Rām Allāh, Jordan 31 55N 35 10E
62 Rama, Israel 32 56N 35 21E
41 Ramacca, Italy 37 24N 14 40E
70 Ramachandrapuram, India 16 50N 82 4E
64 Ramadi, Iraq 33 28N 43 15E
32 Ramales de la Victoria, Spain 43 15N 3 28w
70 Ramanathapuram, India 9 25N 78 55E
93 Ramanetaka, B. de, Malag. 14 13S 47 52E
70 Ramas C., India 15 5N 73 55E
62 Ramat Gan, Israel 32 4N 34 48E
32 Ramatayim, Israel 32 9N 34 54E
92 Ramatlhabama, Bots. 25 37S 25 33E
19 Rambervillers, France 48 20N 6 38E
73 Rambipudji, Indonesia 8 12S 113 37E
19 Rambouillet, France 48 40N 1 48E
67 Rambree Kyun, Burma 19 0N 94 0E
70 Ramdurg, India 15 58N 75 22E
67 Ramechhap, Nepal 27 25N 86 10E
73 Ramelau, Mte., Port. Tim. 8 55S 126 22E
55 Ramenskoye, U.S.S.R. 55 32N 38 15E
69 Ramgarh, Bihar, India 23 40N 85 35E
68 Ramgarh, Jaisalmer, Rajasthan, India 27 30N 70 36E
68 Ramgarh, Sikar, Rajasthan, India 27 16N 75 14E
64 Ramhormoz, Iran 31 15N 49 35E
62 Ramla, Israel 31 55N 34 52E
83 Ramlat Zaltan, Libya 28 30N 19 30E
87 Ramlu Mt., Ethiopia 13 32N 41 40E
49 Ramme, Denmark 56 30N 8 11E
62 Rammun, Jordan 31 55N 35 17E
70 Ramnad = Ramanathapuram, India 9 25N 78 55E
48 Ramnäs, Sweden 59 46N 16 12E
55 Ramon, U.S.S.R. 52 8N 39 21E
119 Ramona, U.S.A. 33 1N 116 56w
106 Ramore, Canada 48 30N 80 25w
120 Ramos Arizpe, Mexico 23 35N 100 59w
92 Ramoutsa, Botswana 24 50S 25 52E
68 Rampur, H.P., India 31 26N 77 43E
68 Rampur, M.P., India 23 25N 73 53E
69 Rampur, Orissa, India 21 48N 83 58E
68 Rampur, U.P., India 28 50N 79 5E
69 Rampurhat, India 24 10N 87 50E
68 Rampura, India 24 30N 75 27E
50 Ramsele, Sweden 63 31N 16 27E
106 Ramsey, Canada 47 25N 82 20w
13 Ramsey, U.K. 54 20N 4 21w
13 Ramsgate, England 51 20N 1 25E
48 Rämshyttan, Sweden 60 17N 15 15E
48 Ramsjö, Sweden 62 11N 15 37E
48 Ramvik, Sweden 62 49N 17 51E
69 Ranaghat, India 23 15N 88 35E
68 Ranahu, West Pakistan 25 55N 69 45E
72 Ranau, Malaysia 6 2N 116 40E
124 Rancagua, Chile 34 10S 70 50w
18 Rance, R., France 48 34N 1 59w
118 Ranchester, U.S.A. 44 57N 107 12w
69 Ranchi, India 23 19N 85 27E
46 Rancu, Rumania 44 32N 24 15E
100 Rand, Austral. 35 33S 146 32E
20 Randan, France 46 2N 3 21E
41 Randazzo, Italy 37 53N 14 56E
49 Randböl, Denmark 55 43N 9 17E
49 Randers, Denmark 56 29N 10 1E
49 Randers Fjord, Denmark 56 37N 10 20E
93 Randfontein, S. Africa 26 8S 27 45E
112 Randolph, N.Y., U.S.A. 42 10N 78 59w
118 Randolph, Utah, U.S.A. 41 43N 111 10w
113 Randolph, Vt., U.S.A. 43 55N 72 39w
119 Randsburg, U.S.A. 35 26N 117 44w
47 Randsfjord, Norway 60 15N 10 25E
50 Ranea, Sweden 65 53N 22 18E
101 Rangaunu B., N.Z. 34 51S 173 15E
49 Rangedala, Sweden 57 47N 13 9E
113 Rangeley, U.S.A. 44 58N 70 33w
118 Rangely, U.S.A. 40 3N 108 53w
117 Ranger, U.S.A. 32 30N 98 42w
67 Rangia, India 26 15N 91 20E
101 Rangiora, N.Z. 43 19S 172 36E
94 Rangitaiki, N.Z. 38 52S 176 23E
101 Rangitaiki, R., N.Z. 37 54S 176 49E
101 Rangitata, R., N.Z. 43 45S 171 15E
73 Rangkasbitung, Indon. 6 22S 106 16E
67 Rangon, Burma 16 45N 96 20E
67 Rangon, R., Burma 16 28N 96 40E
67 Rangoon = Rangon, Burma 16 45N 96 20E
90 Rangpur, Bangladesh 25 42N 89 22E
70 Ranibennur, India 14 35N 75 30E
69 Raniganj, India 23 40N 87 15E

MAP

70 Ranipet, India 12 56N 79 23E
117 Rankin, U.S.A. 31 16N 101 56w
104 Rankin Inlet, Canada 62 30N 93 0w
100 Rankin's Springs, Austral. 33 49S 146 14E
98 Rannes, Australia 24 6S 150 11E
14 Rannoch, Scotland 56 41N 4 20w
93 Ranobe, B. de, Malag. 23 3S 43 33E
93 Ranohira, Malagasy Republic 22 29S 45 24E
93 Ranomafana, Tamatave, Malag. 18 57S 48 50E
93 Ranomafana, Tuléar, Malag. 24 34S 47 0E
71 Ranong, Thailand 9 56N 98 40E
72 Ransiki, Indonesia 1 30S 134 5E
72 Rantau, Indonesia 4 15N 98 5E
73 Rantauprapat, Indonesia 2 15N 99 50E
73 Rantemario, Indon. 3 15S 119 57E
62 Rantis, Jordan 32 4N 35 3E
114 Rantoul, U.S.A. 40 18N 88 10w
49 Ranum, Denmark 56 54N 9 14E
92 Ranwanlenau, Bots. 19 37S 22 49E
19 Raon-l' Etape, France 48 24N 6 50E
82 Raoui, Erg er, Algeria 29 0N 2 0w
95 Rapa Iti, I., Pac. Oc. 27 35S 144 20w
38 Rapallo, Italy 44 21N 9 12E
73 Rapang, Indonesia 3 45S 119 55E
65 Rāpch, Iran 25 40N 59 15E
116 Rapid City, U.S.A. 44 0N 103 0w
114 Rapid River, U.S.A. 45 55N 87 0w
106 Rapides des Joachims, Canada 46 13N 77 43w
54 Rapla, U.S.S.R. 58 88N 24 52E
64 Raqqa, Syria 36 0N 38 55E
91 Raquete, Mozambique 14 8S 38 13E
95 Rarotonga, I., Pac. Oc. 21 30S 160 0w
65 Ras al Khaima, Trucial Oman 25 50N 56 5E
83 Ra's Al-Unūf, Libya 30 25N 18 15E
64 Ra's at Tannurah, Saudi Arabia 26 40N 50 10E
86 Ras Banâs, Egypt 23 57N 35 50E
87 Ras Dashen, Mt., Ethiopia 13 8N 37 45E
82 Ras el Ma, Algeria 34 26N 0 50w
86 Ras Gharib, Egypt 28 6N 33 18E
86 Ras Mallap, Egypt 29 18N 32 50E
128 Rasa, Punta, Argentina 40 50S 62 15w
48 Rasboda, Sweden 60 8N 16 58E
87 Raseiniai, U.S.S.R. 55 25N 23 5E
87 Rashad, Sudan 11 55N 31 0E
86 Rashîd, Egypt 31 21N 30 22E
86 Rashîd, Masabb, Egypt 31 22N 30 17E
64 Rasht, Iran 37 20N 49 40E
70 Rasipuram, India 11 30N 78 25E
42 Raška, Yugoslavia 43 19N 20 39E
46 Rásnov, Rumania 45 35N 25 27E
127 Raso, C., Brazil 1 50N 50 0w
98 Rason, L., Austral. 28 45S 124 25E
46 Raşova, Rumania 44 15N 27 55E
43 Rasovo, Bulgaria 43 42N 23 17E
68 Rasra, India 25 50N 83 50E
82 Rass el Oued, Algeria 35 57N 5 2E
55 Rasskazovo, U.S.S.R. 52 35N 41 50E
25 Rastatt, Germany 48 50N 8 12E
46 Rastu, Rumania 43 53N 23 16E
28 Raszków, Poland 51 43N 17 40E
104 Rat Is., Alaska 51 50N 178 15w
71 Rat Buri, Thailand 13 30N 99 54E
108 Rat, R., Canada 56 0N 99 30w
68 Ratangarh, India 28 5N 74 35E
68 Rath, India 25 36N 79 37E
15 Rathdrum, Ireland 52 57N 6 13w
114 Rathdrum, U.S.A. 47 50N 116 58w
24 Rathenow, Germany 52 38N 12 23E
15 Rathkeale, Ireland 52 32N 8 57w
15 Rathlin I., N. Ire. 55 18N 6 14w
15 Rathlin O'Birne I., Ire. 54 40N 8 50w
24 Ratlam, India 23 20N 75 0E
70 Ratnagiri, India 16 57N 73 18E
70 Ratnapura, Sri Lanka 6 40N 80 20E
117 Raton, U.S.A. 37 0N 104 30w
26 Ratten, Austria 47 28N 15 44E
14 Rattray Hd., Scot. 57 38N 1 50w
48 Rättvik, Sweden 60 52N 15 7E
25 Ratzeburg, Germany 53 41N 10 46E
71 Raub, Malaysia 3 47N 101 52E
124 Rauch, Argentina 36 45S 59 5w
50 Raufarhöfn, Iceland 66 27N 15 57w
47 Raufoss, Norway 60 44N 10 37E
101 Raukumara Ra., N.Z. 38 5S 177 55E
47 Rauland, Norway 59 43N 8 0E
47 Rauma, Finland 61 10N 21 30E
47 Rauma, R., Norway 62 34N 7 43E
47 Raundal, Norway 60 40N 6 37E
73 Raung, Mt., Indonesia 8 8S 114 4E
69 Raurkela, India 22 14N 84 50E
54 Rava Russkaya, U.S.S.R. 50 15S 23 42E
40 Ravanusa, Italy 37 16N 13 58E
64 Ravar, Iran 31 20N 56 51E
113 Ravena, U.S.A. 42 28N 73 49w
39 Ravenna, Italy 44 28N 12 15E
116 Ravenna, Nebr., U.S.A. 41 3N 98 58w
112 Ravenna, Ohio, U.S.A. 41 11N 81 15w
25 Ravensburg, Germany 47 48N 9 38E
98 Ravenshoe, Australia 17 43S 145 35E
98 Ravensthorpe, Australia 33 35S 120 2E
98 Ravenswood, Australia 20 5S 146 55E
114 Ravenswood, U.S.A. 38 58N 81 47w
126 Raventasón, Peru 6 10S 81 0w
68 Ravi, R., Pakistan 31 0N 73 0E
42 Ravna Gora, Y.-slavia 45 24N 14 50E
42 Ravna Reka, Y.-slavia 43 59N 21 35E
49 Ravnsborg, Denmark 54 57N 11 9E
28 Rawa Mazowiecka, Pol. 51 46N 20 12E
68 Rawalpindi, Pak. 33 38N 73 8E
64 Rawanduz, Iraq 36 40N 44 30E
71 Rawang, Malaysia 3 20N 101 35E

MAP

106 Rawdon, Canada 46 3N 73 40w
101 Rawene, New Zealand 35 25S 173 32E
28 Rawicz, Poland 51 36N 16 52E
96 Rawlinna, Austral. 30 58S 125 28E
118 Rawlins, U.S.A. 41 50N 107 20w
96 Rawlinson Range, Australia 24 40S 128 30E
128 Rawson, Argentina 43 15S 65 0w
85 Rawuya, Nigeria 12 10N 6 50E
117 Ray, N. Mex., U.S.A. 35 57N 104 8w
116 Ray, N.D., U.S.A. 48 21N 103 6w
107 Ray, C., Canada 47 33N 59 15w
70 Rayachoti, India 14 4N 78 50E
70 Rayadrug, India 14 40N 76 50E
70 Rayagada, India 19 15N 83 20E
59 Raychikhinsk, U.S.S.R. 49 46N 129 25E
65 Rayin, Iran 29 40N 57 22E
108 Raymond, Canada 49 30N 112 35w
118 Raymond, U.S.A. 46 45N 123 48w
117 Raymondville, U.S.A. 26 30N 97 50w
117 Rayne, U.S.A. 30 16N 92 16w
71 Rayong, Thailand 12 40N 101 20E
117 Rayville, U.S.A. 32 30N 91 45w
18 Raz, Pte. du, France 48 2N 4 47w
42 Razana, Yugoslavia 44 6N 19 55E
42 Razanj, Yugoslavia 43 40N 21 31E
43 Razdelna, Bulgaria 43 13N 27 41E
46 Razelm, Lacul, Rumania 44 50N 29 0E
43 Razgrad, Bulgaria 43 33N 26 34E
43 Razlog, Bulgaria 41 53N 23 28E
68 Razmak, Pakistan 32 45N 69 50E
70 Razole, India 16 56N 81 48E
108 Razor Back Mt., Can. 51 32N 125 0w
20 Ré, Ile de, France 46 12N 1 30w
13 Reading, Eng. 51 27N 0 57w
113 Reading, U.S.A. 40 20N 75 53w
124 Realicó, Argentina 35 0S 64 15w
20 Réalmont, France 43 48N 2 10E
71 Ream, Khmer Rep. 10 34N 103 39E
14 Reay, Scotland 58 33N 3 48w
19 Rebais, France 48 50N 3 10E
73 Rebi, Indonesia 5 30S 134 7E
83 Rebiana, Libya 24 12N 22 10E
60 Rebun-jima, Japan 44 40N 142 45E
39 Recanati, Italy 43 24N 13 32E
42 Recaş, Rumania 45 46N 21 30E
96 Recherche, Arch. of the, Austral. 34 0S 124 30E
52 Rechitsa, U.S.S.R. 52 13N 30 15E
127 Recife, Brazil 8 0S 35 0w
124 Reconquista, Argentina 29 10S 59 45w
124 Recreo, Argentina 29 25S 65 10w
28 Recz, Poland 53 16N 15 31E
116 Red L., U.S.A. 48 0N 95 0w
116 Red, R., Minn., U.S.A. 48 10N 97 0w
117 Red, R., U.S.A. 33 57N 95 30w
113 Red Bank, U.S.A. 40 21N 74 4w
117 Red Bluff, U.S.A. 40 11N 122 11w
117 Red Bluff L., U.S.A. 31 59N 103 58w
116 Red Cloud, U.S.A. 40 8N 98 33w
108 Red Deer, Canada 52 20N 113 50w
108 Red Deer, L., Canada 52 55N 101 30w
100 Red Hill South, Australia 38 25S 145 2E
107 Red Indian L., Canada 48 35N 57 0w
109 Red Lake, Canada 51 1N 94 1w
116 Red Lake Falls, U.S.A. 47 54N 96 30w
118 Red Lodge, U.S.A. 45 10N 109 10w
116 Red Oak, U.S.A. 41 0N 95 10w
114 Red Rock, L., U.S.A. 41 30N 93 15w
63 Red Sea, Africa-Asia 25 0N 36 0E
116 Red Wing, U.S.A. 44 32N 92 35w
28 Reda, Poland 54 40N 18 19E
71 Redang, I., Malaysia 5 46N 103 2E
13 Redbridge, Eng. 51 35N 0 7E
12 Redcar, Eng. 54 37N 1 4w
108 Redcliff, Canada 50 10N 110 50w
99 Redcliffe, Australia 27 12S 153 0E
99 Redcliffs, Australia 34 16S 142 10E
92 Reddersburg, S. Africa 29 41S 26 10E
117 Redding, U.S.A. 40 30N 122 25w
13 Redditch, Eng. 52 18N 1 57w
100 Redesdale, Australia 37 2S 144 31E
119 Redfield, U.S.A. 45 0N 98 30w
119 Redlands, U.S.A. 34 0N 117 0w
118 Redmond, U.S.A. 44 19N 121 11w
18 Redon, France 47 40N 2 6w
32 Redondela, Spain 42 15N 8 38w
31 Redondo, Portugal 38 39N 7 37w
119 Redondo Beach, U.S.A. 33 52N 118 26w
99 Redpa, Australia 40 48S 144 49E
13 Redruth, Eng. 50 14N 5 14E
109 Redvers, Canada 49 35N 101 40w
108 Redwater, Canada 53 55N 113 0w
119 Redwood City, U.S.A. 37 30N 122 15w
116 Redwood Falls, U.S.A. 44 30N 95 2w
15 Ree, Lough, Ireland 53 35N 8 0w
107 Reed, Mt., Canada 52 5N 68 5w
116 Reed City, U.S.A. 43 52N 85 30w
116 Reeder, U.S.A. 46 7N 102 52w
116 Reedley, U.S.A. 36 36N 119 27w
116 Reedsburg, U.S.A. 43 34N 90 5w
118 Reedsport, U.S.A. 43 45N 124 4w
101 Reef Pt., New Zealand 35 10S 173 5E
101 Reefton, N.Z. 42 6S 171 51E
47 Refsnes, Norway 61 9N 7 14E
49 Reftele, Sweden 57 11N 13 35E
119 Refugio, U.S.A. 28 18N 97 17w
28 Rega, R., Poland 54 10N 15 18E
41 Regalbuto, Italy 37 40N 14 38E
62 Regavim, Israel 32 32N 35 2E
25 Regensburg, Germany 49 1N 12 7E
38 Réggio di Calábria, It. 38 7N 15 38E
38 Réggio nell' Emilia, It. 44 42N 10 38E
109 Regina, Canada 50 30N 104 35w
66 Registan ♦, Afghanistan 30 15N 65 0E
125 Registro, Brazil 24 29S 47 49w

MAP

46 Regnin, Rumania 46 46N 24 41E
31 Reguengos de Monsaraz, Portugal 38 25N 7 32w
69 Rehar, India 23 36N 82 52E
92 Rehoboth, Damaraland, S.W. Africa 23 15S 17 4E
92 Rehoboth, Ovamboland, S.W. Africa 17 55S 15 5E
62 Rehovot, Israel 31 54N 34 48E
24 Reichenbach, Germany 50 36N 12 19E
98 Reid River, Australia 19 40S 146 48E
115 Reidsville, U.S.A. 36 21N 79 40w
13 Reigate, Eng. 51 14N 0 11w
32 Reillo, Spain 39 54N 1 53w
19 Reims, France 49 15N 4 0E
128 Reina Adelaida, Arch., Chile 52 20S 74 0w
116 Reinbeck, U.S.A. 42 18N 92 40w
109 Reindeer I., Canada 52 30N 98 0w
109 Reindeer L., Canada 57 20N 102 20w
101 Reinga, C., New Zealand 34 25S 172 43E
32 Reinosa, Spain 43 2N 4 15w
32 Reinosa, Paso, Spain 42 56N 4 10w
87 Reira, Sudan 15 25N 34 50E
93 Reitz, S. Africa 27 48S 28 29E
92 Reivilo, S. Africa 27 36S 24 8E
49 Rejmyra, Sweden 58 50N 15 55E
39 Reka, R., Yugoslavia 45 40N 14 0E
42 Rekovac, Yugoslavia 43 51N 21 3E
82 Remad, Ouedber, Algeria 33 28N 1 20w
127 Remanso, Brazil 9 41S 42 4w
32 Remarkable Mt., Australia 32 52S 138 0E
73 Rembang, Indonesia 6 42S 111 21E
82 Remchi, Algeria 35 2N 1 26w
126 Remedios, Colombia 7 2N 74 41w
26 Remeshk, Iran 26 55N 58 50E
46 Remetea, Rumania 46 45N 29 29E
16 Remich, Luxembourg 49 32N 6 22E
19 Remiremont, France 48 0N 6 36E
87 Remo, Ethiopia 6 48N 41 20E
47 Remontnoye, U.S.S.R. 47 44N 43 37E
21 Remoulins, France 43 55N 4 35E
24 Remscheid, Germany 51 11N 7 12E
47 Rena, Norway 61 8N 11 20E
41 Rende, Italy 39 19N 16 11E
24 Rendina, Greece 39 4N 21 58E
24 Rendsburg, Germany 54 18N 9 41E
109 Renfrew, Canada 45 30N 76 40w
14 Renfrew, Scotland 55 52N 4 24w
14 Renfrew ♦, Scotland 55 50N 4 30w
72 Rengat, Indonesia 0 30S 102 45E
54 Reni, U.S.S.R. 45 28N 28 15E
70 Renigunta, India 13 38N 79 30E
16 Renkum, Netherlands 51 58N 5 43E
99 Renmark, Australia 34 5S 140 46E
108 Rennell Sd., Canada 53 32N 133 28w
96 Renner Springs Teleg. Off., Austral. 18 20S 133 47E
18 Rennes, France 48 7N 1 41w
47 Rennesöy, Norway 59 6N 5 43E
100 Rennie, Australia 35 49S 146 8E
118 Reno, U.S.A. 39 30N 119 50w
39 Reno, R., Italy 44 45N 11 40E
112 Renovo, U.S.A. 41 20N 77 47w
114 Rensselaer, Ind., U.S.A. 41 0N 87 10w
113 Rensselaer, N.Y., U.S.A. 42 38N 73 41w
32 Renteria, Spain 43 19N 1 54w
112 Renton, U.S.A. 47 30N 122 9w
84 Réo, Upper Volta 12 28N 2 35E
69 Reotipur, India 25 33N 83 45E
16 Repalle, India 16 2N 80 45E
27 Répcelak, Hungary 47 24N 17 1E
112 Republic, Mich., U.S.A. 46 25N 87 59w
118 Republic, Wash., U.S.A. 48 38N 118 42w
116 Republican, R., U.S.A. 40 0N 98 30w
116 Republican City, U.S.A. 40 9N 99 20w
105 Repulse Bay, Canada 66 30N 86 30w
99 Repulse B., Antarctica 64 30S 99 30E
99 Repulse B., Australia 20 31S 148 45E
126 Requena, Peru 5 5S 73 52w
32 Requena, Spain 39 30N 1 4w
42 Resen, Yugoslavia 41 5N 21 0E
118 Reserve, U.S.A. 33 50N 108 54w
64 Resht, Iran 37 20N 49 40E
124 Resistencia, Argentina 27 30S 59 0w
46 Reşiţa, Rumania 45 18N 21 53E
28 Resko, Poland 53 47N 15 25E
101 Resolution I., Canada 61 30N 65 0w
101 Resolution I., N.Z. 45 40S 166 40E
126 Ressano Garcia, Mozam. 25 25S 32 0E
126 Restrepo, Colombia 4 15N 73 33w
28 Reszel, Poland 54 4N 21 10E
120 Retalhuleu, Guatemala 14 33N 91 46w
46 Reteag, Rumania 47 10N 24 0E
91 Retenue, Lac de, Zaïre 11 0S 27 0E
19 Rethel, France 49 30N 4 20E
24 Rethem, Germany 52 47N 9 25E
45 Réthimnon, Greece 35 18N 24 30E
45 Réthimnon ♦, Greece 35 23N 24 28E
18 Rétiers, France 47 55N 1 25w
124 Retiro, Chile 35 59S 71 47w
30 Retortillo, Spain 40 48N 6 21w
27 Retság, Hungary 47 58N 19 10E
3 Réunion, I., Indian Oc. 22 0S 56 0E
32 Reus, Spain 41 10N 1 5E
25 Reuss, R., Switzerland 48 58N 8 24E
24 Reuterstadt-Stavenhagen, Ger. 53 41N 12 54E
25 Reutlingen, Germany 48 28N 9 13E
26 Reutte, Austria 47 29N 10 42E
20 Revel, France 43 28N 2 0E
69 Revelganj, India 25 50N 84 40E

MAP

108 Revelstoke, Canada 51 0N 118 0w
19 Revigny, France 48 50N 5 0E
95 Revilla Gigedo, Is. de, Pacific Ocean 18 40N 112 0w
109 Revillagigedo I., Alaska 55 50N 131 20w
19 Revin, France 49 55N 4 39E
91 Revuè, R., Mozambique 19 30S 33 35E
69 Rewa, India 24 33N 81 25E
68 Rewari, India 28 15N 76 40E
118 Rexburg, U.S.A. 43 45N 111 50w
81 Reÿ Bouba, Cameroon 8 40N 14 15E
50 Reykjahlið, Iceland 65 40N 16 55w
50 Reykjanes, Iceland 63 48N 22 40w
50 Reykjavík, Iceland 64 10N 21 57E
96 Reynolds Ra., Austral. 22 30S 133 0E
112 Reynoldsville, U.S.A. 41 5N 78 58w
120 Reynosa, Mexico 26 5N 98 18w
64 Rezā'iyeh, Iran 37 40N 45 0E
64 Rezā'iyeh, Daryâchech-ye, Iran 37 30N 45 30E
54 Rēzekne, U.S.S.R. 56 30N 27 17E
47 Rezina, U.S.S.R. 47 45N 29 0E
43 Rezovo, Bulgaria 42 0N 28 0E
43 Rgotina, Yugoslavia 44 1N 22 18E
83 Rharis, O., Algeria 26 30N 5 4E
13 Rhayader, Wales 52 19N 3 30w
16 Rheden, Netherlands 52 0N 6 3E
109 Rhein, Canada 51 25N 102 15w
24 Rhein, R., Germany 51 42N 6 20E
24 Rheinbach, Germany 50 38N 6 54E
24 Rheine, Germany 52 17N 7 25E
25 Rheinland-Pfalz ♦, Germany 50 0N 7 0E
24 Rheinsberg, Germany 53 6N 12 52E
24 Rheydt, Germany 51 10N 6 24E
24 Rhin, R., France 51 42N 6 20E
18 Rhinau, France 48 19N 7 43E
16 Rhine, R. = Rhein, Ger. 51 42N 6 20E
116 Rhinelander, U.S.A. 45 38N 89 29w
90 Rhino Camp, Uganda 3 0N 31 22E
38 Rho, Italy 45 31N 9 2E
113 Rhode Island ♦, U.S.A. 41 38N 71 37w
45 Rhodes = Ródhos, Greece 36 15N 28 10E
91 Rhodes' Tomb, Rhod. 20 30S 28 30E
91 Rhodesia ■, Africa 20 0S 30 0E
43 Rhodope Mts. = Rhodopi Planina, Bulgaria
43 Rhodopi Planina, Bulgaria 41 40N 24 20E
13 Rhondda, Wales 51 39N 3 30w
21 Rhône, R., France 43 28N 4 42E
21 Rhône ♦, France 45 54N 4 35E
14 Rhum, I., Scot. 57 0N 6 20w
13 Rhyl, Wales 53 19N 3 29w
127 Riachão, Brazil 7 20S 46 37w
32 Riaño, Spain 42 59N 5 0w
21 Rians, France 43 37N 5 44E
32 Riansares, R., Spain 40 0N 3 0w
66 Riasi, Kashmir 33 10N 74 50E
72 Riau, Kepulauan, Indonesia 0 30N 104 20E
72 Riau ♦, Indonesia 0 0N 102 35E
32 Riaza, Spain 41 18N 3 30w
32 Riaza, R., Spain 41 16N 3 29w
32 Riba de Saelices, Spain 40 55N 2 18E
30 Ribadavia, Spain 42 17N 8 8w
32 Ribadeo, Spain 43 35N 7 5w
30 Ribadesella, Spain 43 30N 5 7w
32 Ribas, Spain 42 19N 2 15E
13 Ribble, R., Eng. 54 13N 2 20w
49 Ribe, Denmark 55 19N 8 44E
49 Ribe Amt ♦, Denmark 55 34N 8 30E
19 Ribeauville, France 48 10N 7 20E
19 Ribécourt, France 49 30N 2 55E
93 Ribeira, Spain 36 8N 8 58w
125 Ribeirão Prêto, Brazil 21 10S 47 50w
19 Ribémont, France 49 47N 3 27E
40 Ribera, Italy 37 30N 13 13E
21 Ribérac, France 45 15N 0 20E
126 Riberalta, Bolivia 11 0S 66 0w
39 Ribnica, Yugoslavia 45 45N 14 45E
24 Ribnitz-Dangarten, Ger. 54 14N 12 24E
26 Ričany, Czechoslovakia 50 0N 14 40E
101 Riccarton, New Zealand 43 32S 172 37E
41 Riccia, Italy 41 30N 14 50E
39 Riccione, Italy 44 0N 12 39E
112 Rice L., Canada 44 10N 78 10w
116 Rice Lake, U.S.A. 45 30N 91 42w
82 Rich, Morocco 32 16N 4 30w
117 Rich Hill, U.S.A. 38 5N 94 22w
93 Richards B., S. Afr. 28 48S 32 6E
128 Richards Deep, Pac. Oc. 25 0S 73 0w
18 Richelieu, France 47 0N 0 20E
47 Richey, U.S.A. 47 42N 105 5w
118 Richfield, Idaho, U.S.A. 43 2N 114 5w
118 Richfield, Utah, U.S.A. 38 50N 112 0w
113 Richford, U.S.A. 45 0N 72 40w
107 Richibucto, Canada 46 42N 64 54w
115 Richland, Ga., U.S.A. 32 7N 84 40w
118 Richland, Oreg., U.S.A. 44 49N 117 9w
118 Richland, Wash., U.S.A. 46 15N 119 15w
114 Richland Center, U.S.A. 43 21N 90 22w
114 Richlands, U.S.A. 37 7N 81 49w
100 Richmond, N.S.W., Australia 33 35S 150 42E
98 Richmond, Queens., Australia 20 43S 143 8E
101 Richmond, N.Z. 41 4S 173 12E
13 Richmond, Surrey, Eng. 51 28N 0 18w
12 Richmond, Yorks., Eng. 54 24N 1 43w
119 Richmond, Calif., U.S.A. 37 58N 122 21w
114 Richmond, Ind., U.S.A. 39 50N 84 50w
114 Richmond, Ky., U.S.A. 37 40N 84 20w
112 Richmond, Mich., U.S.A. 42 47N 82 45w
116 Richmond, Mo., U.S.A. 39 15N 93 58w
113 Richmond, N.Y., U.S.A. 40 35N 74 6w

MAP
117 Richmond, Tex., U.S.A. 29 32N 95 42w
114 Richmond, Va., U.S.A. 37 33N 77 27w
106 Richmond Gulf, Canada 56 20N 75 50w
115 Richton, U.S.A. 31 23N 88 58w
114 Richwood, U.S.A. 38 17N 80 32w
32 Ricla, Spain 41 31N 1 24w
48 Riddarhyttan, Sweden 59 49N 15 33E
109 Ridgedale, Canada 53 0N 104 10w
115 Ridgeland, U.S.A. 32 30N 80 58w
98 Ridgelands, Australia 23 16s 150 17E
106 Ridgetown, Canada 42 26N 81 52w
112 Ridgway, U.S.A. 41 25N 78 43w
26 Ried, Austria 48 14N 13 30E
39 Rienza, R., Italy 46 49N 11 47E
24 Riesa, Germany 51 19N 13 19E
41 Riesi, Italy 37 16N 14 4E
92 Rietfontein, S. Africa 26 44s 20 1E
39 Rieti, Italy 42 23N 12 50E
20 Rieupeyroux, France 44 19N 2 12E
21 Riez, France 43 49N 6 6E
118 Rifle, U.S.A. 39 40N 107 50w
50 Rifstangi, Iceland 66 32N 16 12w
90 Rift Valley, Kenya 0 20N 36 0E
81 Rig Rig, Chad 14 13N 14 25E
54 Riga, U.S.S.R. 56 53N 24 8E
54 Riga, G. of = Rīgas Jūras Licis, U.S.S.R. 57 40N 23 45E
54 Rīgas Jūras Licis, U.S.S.R. 57 40N 23 45E
113 Rigaud, Canada 45 28N 74 20w
118 Rigby, U.S.A. 43 41N 111 58w
118 Riggins, U.S.A. 45 29N 116 26w
20 Rignac, France 44 25N 2 16E
98 Rigo, Terr. of Papua 9 41s 147 31E
107 Rigolet, Canada 54 10N 58 23w
51 Riihimäki, Finland 60 45N 24 48E
5 Riiser-Larsen halvöya, Ant. 68 0s 35 0E
74 Riishiri-tô, Japan 45 10N 140 17E
85 Rijau, Nigeria 11 8N 5 17E
42 Rijeka Crnojevica, Yugoslavia 42 24N 19 1E
39 Rijeka (Fiume), Y.-slav. 45 20N 14 21E
16 Rijn, R., Netherlands 52 5N 4 50E
16 Rijssen, Netherlands 52 19N 6 30E
16 Rijswijk, Netherlands 52 4N 4 22E
87 Rike, Ethiopia 10 50N 39 53E
87 Rikita, Sudan 5 5N 28 29E
43 Rila, Bulgaria 42 7N 23 7E
42 Rila Planina, Bulg. 42 10N 23 30E
19 Rilly, France 49 11N 4 3E
67 Rima, China 28 35N 97 5E
85 Rima, R., Nigeria 13 5N 5 15E
27 Rimavská Sobota, Cz. 48 22N 20 2E
108 Rimbey, Canada 52 35N 114 15w
48 Rimbo, Sweden 59 44N 18 21E
49 Rimforsa, Sweden 58 8N 15 42E
85 Rimi, Nigeria 12 58N 7 43E
39 Rimini, Italy 44 3N 12 33E
46 Rimna, R., Rumania 45 36N 27 3E
46 Rimnicu Sărat, Rum. 45 26N 27 3E
46 Rimnicu Vilcece, Rum. 45 9N 24 21E
107 Rimouski, Canada 48 27N 68 30w
134 Rinconada, Argentina 22 26s 66 10w
41 Rindjani, Mt., Indon. 8 20s 116 30E
15 Rineanna, Ire. 52 42N 85 7w
18 Ringarum, Sweden 58 21N 16 26E
49 Ringe, Denmark 55 13N 10 28E
85 Ringim, Nigeria 12 13N 9 10E
49 Ringkøbing, Denmark 56 5N 8 15E
49 Ringkøbing Amt ♦, Denmark 56 15N 8 30E
118 Ringling, U.S.A. 46 16N 110 56w
47 Ringmoen, Norway 60 21N 10 6E
47 Ringsaker, Norway 60 54N 10 45E
49 Ringsjön L., Sweden 55 55N 13 30E
49 Ringsted, Denmark 55 25N 11 46E
50 Ringvassøy, Norway 69 36N 19 15E
45 Rinia, I., Greece 37 23N 25 13E
24 Rinteln, Germany 52 11N 9 3E
73 Rintja, I., Indonesia 8 45s 119 35E
33 Rio, Punta del, Spain 36 49N 2 24w
126 Rio Arica, Peru 1 35s 75 30w
126 Rio Branco, Brazil 19 58s 67 49w
125 Rio Branco, Uruguay 32 40s 53 40w
125 Rio Brilhante, Brazil 21 48s 54 33w
126 Rio Chico, Venezuela 10 19N 65 59w
125 Rio Claro, Brazil 22 19s 47 35w
121 Rio Claro, Trinidad 10 20N 61 25w
128 Rio Colorado, Argentina 39 0s 64 0w
124 Rio Cuarto, Argentina 33 10s 64 25w
117 Rio Grande City, U.S.A. 26 30N 91 55w
93 Rio das Pedras, Mozam. 23 8s 35 28w
125 Rio de Janeiro, Brazil 23 0s 43 12w
125 Rio de Janeiro ♦, Brazil 22 50s 43 0w
85 Rio del Rey, Cameroon 4 42N 8 37E
125 Rio do Sul, Brazil 27 95s 49 37w
128 Rio Gallegos, Arg. 51 35s 69 15w
128 Rio Grande, Argentina 53 50s 67 45w
125 Rio Grande, Brazil 32 0s 52 20w
119 Rio Grande, R., U.S.A. 37 47N 106 15w
117 Rio Grande City, U.S.A. 26 30N 91 55w
110 Rio Grande del Norte, R., North America 26 0N 97 0w
125 Rio Grande do Sul ♦, Brazil 30 0s 53 0w
127 Rio Largo, Brazil 9 28s 35 50w
31 Rio Maior, Portugal 39 19N 8 57w
38 Rio Marina, Italy 42 48N 10 25E
126 Rio Mulatos, Bolivia 19 40s 66 50w
88 Rio Muni ♦, Eq. Guinea 1 30N 10 0E
125 Rio Negro, Brazil 26 0s 50 0w
127 Rio Pardo, Minas Gerais, Brazil 15 55s 42 30w
125 Rio Pardo, Rio Grande do Sul, Brazil 30 0s 52 30w
124 Rio Segundo, Arg. 31 40s 63 59w
124 Rio Tercero, Argentina 32 15s 64 8w
30 Rio Tinto, Portugal 41 11N 8 34w

120 Rio Verde, Mexico 21 56N 99 59w
118 Rio Vista, U.S.A. 38 11N 121 44w
126 Riobamba, Ecuador 1 50s 78 45w
126 Riohacha, Colombia 11 33N 72 55w
20 Riom, France 45 54N 3 7E
20 Riom-ès-Montagnes, Fr. 45 17N 2 39E
126 Rionegro, Colombia 6 9N 75 22w
41 Rionero in Vúlture, It. 40 55N 15 40E
30 Rios, Spain 41 58N 7 16w
126 Riosucio, Caldas, Colombia 5 30N 75 40w
126 Riosucio, Choco, Colombia 7 27N 77 7w
38 Riparia, Dora, R., It. 45 7N 7 24E
39 Ripatransone, Italy 43 0N 13 45E
112 Ripley, Canada 44 4N 81 32w
112 Ripley, N.Y., U.S.A. 42 16N 79 44w
117 Ripley, Tenn., U.S.A. 35 43N 89 34w
32 Ripoll, Spain 42 15N 2 13E
12 Ripon, England 54 8N 1 31w
114 Ripon, U.S.A. 43 51N 88 50w
41 Riposto, Italy 37 44N 15 12E
42 Risan, Yugoslavia 42 32N 18 42E
20 Riscle, France 43 39N 0 5w
62 Rishon Le Zion, Israel 31 58N 34 48E
62 Rishpon, Israel 32 12N 34 49E
47 Risløkka, Norway 58 56N 5 52E
18 Risle, R., France 48 55N 0 41E
46 Risnov, Rumania 45 35N 25 27E
117 Rison, U.S.A. 33 57N 92 11w
47 Risör, Norway 58 43N 9 13E
47 Risör, Norway 58 43N 9 13E
71 Ritchie's Archipelago, Andaman Islands 12 5N 94 0E
85 Riti, Nigeria 7 57N 9 41E
112 Rittman, U.S.A. 40 57N 81 48w
118 Ritzville, U.S.A. 47 10N 118 21w
73 Riung, Indonesia 8 22s 121 7E
18 Riva Bella Ouistreham, France 49 17N 0 18w
38 Riva del Garda, It. 45 53N 10 50E
124 Rivadavia, Buenos Aires, Argentina 35 29s 62 59w
124 Rivadavia, Mendoza, Arg. 33 13s 68 30w
124 Rivadavia, Salta, Arg. 24 5s 63 0w
124 Rivadavia, Chile 29 50s 70 35w
38 Rivarolo Canavese, It. 45 20N 7 42E
121 Rivas, Nicaragua 11 30N 85 50w
21 Rive-de-Gier, France 45 32N 4 37E
84 River Cess, Liberia 5 30N 9 25w
112 River Rouge, U.S.A. 42 16N 83 9w
125 Rivera, Uruguay 31 0s 55 50w
113 Riverhead, U.S.A. 40 53N 72 40w
109 Riverhurst, Canada 50 55N 106 50w
108 Rivers Inlet, Canada 51 40N 127 20w
92 Riversdal, S. Africa 34 7s 21 15E
112 Riverside, Canada 42 17N 82 59w
119 Riverside, Calif., U.S.A. 34 0N 117 15w
118 Riverside, Wyo., U.S.A. 41 5N 106 50w
98 Riversleigh, Australia 19 5s 138 48E
109 Riverton, Canada 51 5N 97 0w
101 Riverton, New Zealand 46 21s 168 0E
118 Riverton, U.S.A. 43 1N 108 27w
20 Rivesaltes, France 42 47N 2 50E
38 Riviera, Italy & France 44 0N 8 30E
36 Riviera di Levante, It. 44 23N 9 15E
36 Riviera di Ponente, It. 43 50N 7 58E
107 Rivière à Pierre, Canada 46 57N 72 12w
107 Rivière Bleue, Canada 47 26N 69 2w
107 Rivière du Loup, Can. 47 50N 69 30w
107 Rivière Pontecôte, Can. 49 57N 67 1w
38 Rivoli, Italy 45 3N 7 31E
99 Rivoli B., Australia 37 25s 140 0E
92 Rivungo, Angola 16 9s 21 51E
64 Riyadh = Ar Riyad, Saudi Arabia 24 41N 46 42E
64 Rize, Turkey 41 0N 40 30E
47 Rizzuto, C., Italy 38 54N 17 5E
47 Rjukan, Norway 59 54N 8 33E
47 Roa, Norway 60 17N 10 37E
30 Roa, Spain 41 41N 3 56w
14 Roag, L., Scotland 58 10N 6 55w
91 Roan Antelope, Zam. 13 2s 28 19E
21 Roanne, France 46 3N 4 4E
115 Roanoke, Ala., U.S.A. 33 9N 85 23w
114 Roanoke, Va., U.S.A. 37 19N 79 55w
115 Roanoke I., U.S.A. 35 55N 75 40w
115 Roanoke, R., U.S.A. 36 15N 77 20w
115 Roanoke Rapids, U.S.A. 36 36N 77 42w
99 Robbins I., Australia 40 42s 145 0E
100 Robe, Mt., Australia 31 40s 141 20E
15 Robe, R., Ire. 53 38N 9 10w
24 Röbel, East Germany 53 24N 12 37E
117 Robert Lee, U.S.A. 31 55N 100 26w
118 Roberts, U.S.A. 43 44N 112 8w
69 Robertsganj, India 24 44N 83 4E
100 Robertson, Australia 34 37s 150 36E
92 Robertson, S. Africa 33 46s 19 50E
5 Robertson I., Antarc. 68 0s 75 0w
96 Robertson Ra., Australia 23 15s 121 0E
84 Robertsport, Liberia 6 45N 11 26w
106 Roberval, Canada 48 32N 72 15w
4 Robeson Chan., Canada 82 0N 61 30w
4 Robeson Kanal, Greenland 82 0N 61 30w
96 Robinson Ranges, Australia 25 40s 118 0E
100 Robinvale, Australia 34 40s 142 45E
109 Roblin, Canada 51 21N 101 25w
126 Roborée, Bolivia 18 10s 59 45w
108 Robson Mt., Canada 53 10N 119 10w
117 Robstown, U.S.A. 27 47N 97 40w
31 Roca, C. da, Portugal 38 40N 9 31w
92 Roçadas, Angola 16 45s 15 0E
127 Rocas, I., Brazil 4 0s 34 1w
41 Rocca d'Aspide, Italy 40 27N 15 10E
39 Rocca San Casciano, It. 44 3N 11 30E
39 Roccabegna, Italy 42 47N 11 30E
39 Roccastrada, Italy 43 0N 11 10E

41 Rocella, Iónica, Italy 38 20N 16 24E
125 Rocha, Uruguay 34 30s 54 25w
12 Rochdale, Eng. 53 36N 2 10w
20 Rochechouart, France 45 50N 0 49E
20 Rochefort, Belgium 50 9N 5 12E
20 Rochefort, France 45 56N 0 57w
20 Rochefort-en-Terre, Fr. 47 42N 2 22w
116 Rochelle, U.S.A. 41 55N 89 5w
108 Rocher River, Canada 61 12N 114 0w
106 Rocheserviere, France 46 57N 1 30w
100 Rochester, Austral. 36 22s 144 41E
13 Rochester, England 51 22N 0 30E
114 Rochester, Ind., U.S.A. 41 5N 86 15w
113 Rochester, N.H., U.S.A. 43 19N 70 57w
113 Rochester, N.Y., U.S.A. 43 10N 77 40w
112 Rochester, Pa., U.S.A. 40 41N 80 17w
46 Rociu, Rumania 44 43N 25 2E
115 Rock Hill, U.S.A. 34 55N 81 2w
116 Rock Island, U.S.A. 41 30N 90 35w
116 Rock Lake, U.S.A. 48 50N 99 13w
116 Rock Rapids, U.S.A. 43 25N 96 10w
118 Rock River, U.S.A. 41 49N 106 0w
119 Rock Sprs., Ariz., U.S.A. 34 2N 112 11w
118 Rock Sprs., Mont., U.S.A. 46 55N 106 11w
117 Rock Sprs., Tex., U.S.A. 30 2N 100 11w
118 Rock Sprs., Wyo., U.S.A. 41 40N 109 10w
116 Rock Valley, U.S.A. 43 10N 96 17w
4 Rockall I., North Atlantic Ocean 57 37N 13 42w
117 Rockdale, U.S.A. 30 40N 97 0w
5 Rockefeller Plat., Ant. 84 0s 130 0w
112 Rockford, U.S.A. 42 20N 89 0w
98 Rockhampton, Austral. 23 22s 150 32E
98 Rockingham B., Australia 18 5s 146 10E
13 Rockingham For., England 52 28N 0 42w
113 Rockland, Canada 45 30N 75 19w
118 Rockland, Idaho, U.S.A. 42 37N 112 57w
107 Rockland, Me., U.S.A. 44 0N 69 0w
116 Rockland, Mich., U.S.A. 46 40N 89 10w
116 Rockmart, U.S.A. 34 1N 85 2w
116 Rockport, Mo., U.S.A. 40 26N 95 30w
117 Rockport, Tex., U.S.A. 28 2N 97 3w
113 Rockville, Conn., U.S.A. 41 51N 72 27w
116 Rockville, Md., U.S.A. 39 7N 77 0w
117 Rockwall, U.S.A. 32 55N 96 30w
100 Rockwell, Australia 32 3s 141 32E
116 Rockwell City, U.S.A. 42 20N 94 35w
115 Rockwood, U.S.A. 35 52N 84 40w
116 Rocky Ford, U.S.A. 38 7N 103 45w
108 Rocky Lane, Canada 58 29N 116 30w
115 Rocky Mount, U.S.A. 35 55N 77 48w
104 Rocky Mts., N. Amer. 48 0N 113 0w
96 Rocky Pt., Austral. 33 30s 123 57E
112 Rockyford, Canada 51 20N 113 10w
19 Rocroi, France 49 55N 4 30E
68 Rod, Pakistan 28 10N 63 5E
47 Rödberg, Norway 60 17N 8 56E
49 Rödby, Denmark 54 41N 11 23E
49 Rödby Havn, Denmark 54 39N 11 22E
107 Roddickton, Canada 50 51N 56 8w
49 Rödding, Denmark 55 23N 9 3E
49 Rödekro, Denmark 55 4N 9 20E
47 Rödenes, Norway 59 35N 11 34E
24 Rodenkirchen, Ger. 53 24N 8 26E
20 Rodez, France 44 21N 2 33E
44 Rodholivas, Greece 40 10N 25 30E
44 Rodhópi ♦, Greece 41 10N 25 30E
45 Rodhos, Greece 36 15N 28 10E
45 Rodhos, I., Greece 36 15N 28 10E
49 Rödjenäs, Sweden 57 33N 14 50E
46 Rodna, Rumania 47 25N 24 50E
112 Rodney, Canada 42 34N 81 43w
101 Rodney, C., New Zealand 36 17s 174 50E
55 Rodniki, U.S.S.R. 57 7N 41 37E
3 Rodriguez, I., Ind. Oc. 20 0s 65 0E
15 Roe, R., N. Ire. 55 0N 6 56w
113 Roebling, U.S.A. 40 7N 74 45w
96 Roebourne, Austral. 20 44s 117 9E
96 Roebuck B., Austral. 18 5s 122 20E
16 Roermond, Netherlands 51 12N 6 0E
16 Roes Welcome Sd., Can. 65 0N 87 0w
16 Roeselare, Belgium 50 57N 3 7E
54 Rogachev, U.S.S.R. 53 8N 30 5E
42 Rogaóica, Yugoslavia 44 4N 19 40E
126 Rogagua, L., Bolivia 14 0s 66 50w
39 Rogaška Slatina, Yugoslavia 46 15N 15 42E
39 Rogatec, Yugoslavia 46 15N 21 46E
54 Rogatin, U.S.S.R. 29 24N 24 36E
7 Rogers, U.S.A. 36 20N 94 0w
114 Rogers City, U.S.A. 45 25N 83 49w
118 Rogerson, U.S.A. 42 10N 114 40w
115 Rogersville, U.S.A. 36 27N 83 1w
107 Roggan River, Canada 54 24N 78 5w
92 Roggeveldberge, S. Afr. 32 10s 20 10E
41 Roggiano Gravina, Italy 39 37N 16 9E
39 Rogliano, France 42 57N 9 30E
41 Rogliano, Italy 39 11N 16 20E
126 Rogoaguado, L., Bolivia 13 0s 65 30w
28 Rogowo, Poland 52 43N 17 38E
28 Rogozno, Poland 52 45N 16 59E
118 Rogue, R., U.S.A. 42 30N 124 0w
68 Rohan, France 48 4N 2 45w
19 Rohrbach, France 49 3N 7 15E
68 Rohri, Pakistan 27 45N 68 51E
68 Rohri Canal, Pakistan 26 15N 68 27E
68 Rohtak, India 28 55N 76 43E
71 Roi Et, Thailand 15 56N 103 40E
19 Roisel, France 49 58N 3 6E
124 Rojas, Argentina 34 10s 60 45w
72 Rokan, R., Indonesia 1 30N 100 50E
54 Rokiskis, U.S.S.R. 55 55N 25 35E

55 Rokitnoye, U.S.S.R. 50 57N 35 56E
26 Rokycany, Cz. 49 43N 13 35E
125 Rolándia, Brazil 23 5s 52 0w
47 Röldal, Norway 59 47N 6 50E
116 Rolette, U.S.A. 48 42N 99 50w
49 Rollstorp, Sweden 57 11N 12 27E
117 Rolla, Missouri, U.S.A. 38 0N 91 42w
116 Rolla, Kansas, U.S.A. 37 10N 101 40w
116 Rolla, N. Dak., U.S.A. 48 50N 99 36w
47 Rollag, Norway 60 2N 9 18E
98 Rollingstone, Australia 19 0s 146 15E
87 Rom, Sudan 9 54N 32 16E
26 Roma, Australia 26 32s 148 49E
40 Roma, Italy 41 54N 12 30E
49 Roma, Sweden 57 32N 18 26E
46 Roman, Rumania 46 57N 26 55E
73 Romang, I., Indonesia 7 30s 127 20E
86 Români, Egypt 30 59N 32 38E
43 Romanija planina, Y.-slav. 43 50N 18 45E
121 Romano, Cayo, Cuba 22 0N 77 30w
38 Romano di Lombardia, Italy 45 32N 9 45E
38 Romans, France 45 3N 5 3E
25 Romanshorn, Switz. 47 33N 9 22E
40 Rome = Roma, Italy 41 54N 12 30E
115 Rome, Ga., U.S.A. 34 20N 85 0w
113 Rome, N.Y., U.S.A. 43 14N 75 29w
49 Romeleåsen, Swed. 55 34N 13 33E
21 Romenây, France 46 30N 5 1E
107 Romeo, Canada 47 28N 57 4w
47 Romerike, Norway 60 7N 11 10E
19 Romilly, France 48 31N 3 44E
46 Romini, Rumania 44 59N 24 11E
82 Rommani, Morocco 33 31N 6 40w
112 Romney, Canada 42 9N 82 23w
114 Romney, U.S.A. 39 21N 78 45w
13 Romney Marsh, England 51 0N 1 0E
54 Romny, U.S.S.R. 50 48N 33 28E
49 Römö, Denmark 55 10N 8 30E
54 Romodan, U.S.S.R. 50 0N 33 15E
54 Romodanovo, U.S.S.R. 54 26N 45 23E
25 Romont, Switzerland 46 42N 6 54E
19 Romorantin, France 47 20N 1 44E
19 Romorantin-Lanthenay, France 47 21N 1 45E
47 Romsdal, R., Norway 62 25N 8 0E
118 Ronan, U.S.A. 47 30N 114 11w
127 Roncador, Serra do, Brazil 12 30s 52 30w
32 Roncesvalles, Paso, Spain 43 1N 1 19w
114 Ronceverte, U.S.A. 37 45N 80 28w
41 Ronciglione, Italy 42 18N 12 12E
39 Ronco, R., Italy 44 26N 12 15E
30 Ronda, Spain 36 46N 5 12w
31 Ronda, Serrania de, Sp. 36 44N 5 3w
47 Rondane, Nor. 61 57N 9 50E
126 Rondón, Colombia 6 17N 71 6w
126 Rondônia ♦, Brazil 11 0s 63 0w
126 Rondonópolis, Brazil 16 28s 54 38w
49 Rönne, Denmark 55 6N 14 44E
5 Ronne Land, Antarctica 83 0s 70 0w
49 Ronneby, Sweden 56 12N 15 17E
16 Ronse, Belgium 50 45N 3 35E
119 Roof Butte, U.S.A. 36 29N 109 5w
68 Roorkee, India 29 52N 77 59E
118 Roosevelt, Minn., U.S.A. 48 51N 95 2w
118 Roosevelt, Utah, U.S.A. 40 19N 110 1w
5 Roosevelt I., Antarctica 79 0s 161 0w
108 Roosevelt, Mt., Canada 58 20N 125 20w
118 Roosevelt Res., U.S.A. 33 46N 111 0w
16 Roosendaal, Neth. 51 32N 4 29E
27 Ropczyce, Poland 50 4N 21 38E
99 Roper, R., Australia 14 30s 134 20E
115 Ropesville, U.S.A. 33 25N 102 10w
124 Roque Pérez, Arg. 35 25s 59 24w
21 Roquefort, France 44 2N 0 20w
20 Roquefort-sur-Souizon, France 43 58N 2 59E
21 Roquemaure, France 44 3N 4 48E
32 Roquetas, Spain 40 50N 0 30E
21 Roquevaire, France 43 20N 5 36E
126 Roraima ♦, Brazil 2 0N 61 30w
126 Roraima, Mt., Venezuela 5 10N 60 40w
47 Röros, Norway 62 35N 11 23E
25 Rorschach, Switz. 47 28N 9 30E
47 Rörvik, Norway 64 54N 11 15E
118 Rosa, U.S.A. 38 15N 122 16w
91 Rosa, Zambia 9 33N 31 15E
83 Rosa, C., Algeria 37 0N 8 16E
25 Rosa, Monte, Switzerland-Italy 45 57N 7 53E
30 Rosal, Spain 41 57N 8 51w
31 Rosal de la Frontera, Sp. 37 59N 7 13w
118 Rosalia, U.S.A. 47 26N 117 25w
21 Rosans, France 44 24N 5 29E
124 Rosario, Argentina 33 0s 60 50w
128 Rosário, Maran., Brazil 3 0s 44 15w
128 Rosário, Rio Grande do Sul, Brazil 30 15s 55 0w
120 Rosario, Baja California, Mexico 30 0N 116 0w
120 Rosario, Durango, Mex. 26 30N 105 35w
120 Rosario, Sinaloa, Mex. 23 0N 106 0w
126 Rosario, Venezuela 10 19N 72 19w
124 Rosario de Lerma, Arg. 24 59s 65 35w
124 Rosario de la Frontera, Argentina 25 50s 65 0w
124 Rosario del Tala, Arg. 32 20s 59 10w
128 Rosário do Sul, Brazil 30 15s 54 55w
32 Rosas, Spain 42 19N 3 10E
18 Roscoff, France 48 44N 4 0w
15 Roscommon, Ireland 53 38N 8 11w
114 Roscommon, U.S.A. 44 27N 84 35w
124 Roscommon ♦, Ireland 53 40N 8 15w

107 Rose Blanche, Canada 47 38N 58 45w
108 Rose Harbour, Canada 52 15N 131 10w
109 Rose Valley, Canada 52 19N 103 49w
121 Roseau, Dominica 15 20N 61 30w
116 Roseau, U.S.A. 48 56N 96 0w
117 Rosebud, U.S.A. 31 5N 97 0w
118 Roseburg, U.S.A. 43 10N 123 10w
98 Rosedale, Queens., Australia 24 38s 151 53E
100 Rosedale, Vic., Austral. 38 11s 146 48E
33 Rosedale, Spain 33 51N 91 0w
117 Rosedale, U.S.A. 29 30N 95 48w
51 Rosenberg, U.S.A. 2 2 24E
19 Rosendaël, France 51 3N 2 24E
25 Rosenheim, Germany 47 51N 12 9E
39 Roseto degli Abruzzi, It. 42 40N 14 2E
109 Rosetown, Canada 51 35N 108 3w
86 Rosetta = Rashid, Egypt 31 21N 30 22E
118 Roseville, U.S.A. 38 46N 121 41w
99 Rosewood, Australia 27 39s 152 36E
62 Rosh Haniqra, Kefar, Israel 33 5N 35 5E
62 Rosh Pinna, Israel 32 58N 35 32E
62 Rosh Ze'ira, Israel 31 14N 35 15E
49 Roshage C., Denmark 57 7N 8 35E
21 Rosières, France 48 36N 6 20E
38 Rosignano Marittimo, It. 43 23N 10 28E
126 Rosignol, Guyana 6 15N 57 30w
46 Roşiorï-de-Vede, Rum. 44 9N 25 0E
43 Rositsa, Bulgaria 43 57N 27 57E
43 Rositsa, R., Bulgaria 43 10N 25 30E
49 Roskilde, Denmark 55 38N 12 3E
49 Roskilde Amt ♦, Denmark 55 35N 12 5E
49 Roskilde Fjord, Denmark 55 50N 12 2E
54 Roslavl, U.S.S.R. 53 57N 32 55E
100 Roslyn, Austral. 34 31s 149 46E
31 Rosmaninhal, Portugal 39 44N 7 5w
49 Rösnaes, Denmark 55 44N 10 55E
41 Rosolini, Italy 36 49N 14 58E
18 Rosporden, France 47 57N 3 50w
101 Ross, New Zealand 42 53s 170 49E
13 Ross, Eng. 51 55N 2 34w
•14 Ross and Cromarty ♦, Scotland 57 43N 4 50w
5 Ross Dependency, Ant. 70 0s 170 5w
5 Ross Ice Shelf, Antarc. 80 0s 180 0w
5 Ross I., Antarctica 77 30s 168 0E
118 Ross L., U.S.A. 48 50N 121 0w
98 Ross River, Australia 19 20s 146 37E
5 Ross Sea, Antarctica 74 0s 178 0E
15 Rossan Pt., Ireland 54 42N 8 47w
41 Rossano Cálabro, Italy 39 36N 16 39E
112 Rosseau, Canada 45 26N 79 39w
98 Rossel I., Terr. of Papua 11 30s 154 30E
106 Rossignol, Lac, Canada 52 43N 74 0w
107 Rossignol, L., Canada 44 12N 65 0w
92 Rossing, S.W. Africa 22 30s 14 50E
108 Rossland, Canada 49 6N 117 50w
15 Rosslare, Ireland 52 17N 6 23w
24 Rosslau, Germany 51 52N 12 15E
84 Rosso, Mauritania 16 40N 15 45w
57 Rossosh, U.S.S.R. 50 15N 39 20E
106 Rossport, Canada 48 50N 87 30w
98 Rossville, Australia 15 48s 145 15E
109 Rosthern, Canada 52 40N 106 20w
24 Rostock, East Germany 54 4N 12 9E
24 Rostock ♦, E. Germany 54 10N 12 0E
55 Rostov, U.S.S.R. 57 14N 39 25E
57 Rostov, U.S.S.R. 47 15N 39 45E
18 Rostrenen, France 48 14N 3 21w
47 Rostvollen, Norway 65 45N 14 0E
117 Roswell, U.S.A. 33 26N 104 32w
14 Rosyth, Scotland 56 2N 3 26w
31 Rota, Spain 36 37N 6 20w
48 Rotälven, Sweden 61 30N 14 10E
117 Rotan, U.S.A. 32 52N 100 30w
24 Rotenburg, Germany 53 6N 9 24E
51 Rothaargebirge, Germany 51 0N' 8 20E
25 Rothenburg ob der Tauber, Germany 49 21N 10 11E
13 Rother, R., Eng. 50 59N 0 40w
12 Rotherham, Eng. 53 26N 1 21w
14 Rothes, Scotland 57 31N 3 12w
107 Rothesay, Canada 45 23N 66 0w
14 Rothesay, Scot. 55 50N 5 3w
73 Roti, I., Indonesia 10 50s 123 0E
92 Rotkop, S.W. Africa 26 44s 15 27E
100 Roto, Austral. 33 0s 145 30E
41 Rotondella, Italy 40 10N 16 30E
101 Rotoroa Lake, N.Z. 41 55s 172 39E
101 Rotorua, New Zealand 38 9s 176 16E
101 Rotorua, L., New Zealand 38 5s 176 18E
25 Rottenburg, Germany 48 28N 8 56E
26 Rottenmann, Austria 47 31N 14 22E
16 Rotterdam, Netherlands 51 55N 4 30E
25 Rottweil, Germany 48 9N 8 38E
19 Roubaix, France 50 40N 3 10E
16 Roudnice, Cz. 50 25N 14 15E
20 Rouen, France 49 27N 1 4E
21 Rouergue, France 44 20N 2 20E
20 Rouillac, France 45 47N 0 4w
109 Roulaeau, Canada 50 10N 104 50w
99 Round Mt., Australia 30 30s 152 7E
118 Round Mountain, U.S.A. 38 46N 117 3w
118 Roundup, U.S.A. 46 25N 108 35w
14 Rousay, I., Scot. 59 10N 3 2w
113 Rouses Point, U.S.A. 44 58N 73 22w
21 Rousillon, Fr. 45 24N 4 49E
92 Rouxville, S. Afr. 30 11s 26 50E
106 Rouyn, Canada 48 20N 79 0w
50 Rovaniemi, Finland 66 29N 25 41E
38 Rovato, Italy 45 34N 10 0E
57 Rovenki, U.S.S.R. 48 5N 39 27E
38 Rovereto, Italy 45 53N 11 3E

MAP

39 Rovigo, Italy 45 4N 11 48E
46 Rovinari, Rumania 46 56N 23 10E
39 Rovinj, Yugoslavia 45 18N 13 40E
126 Rovira, Colombia 4 15N 75 20W
54 Rovno, U.S.S.R. 50 40N 26 10E
55 Rovnoye, U.S.S.R. 50 52N 46 3E
91 Rovuma, R., Mozambique 11 30S 36 10E
100 Rowes, Australia 36 59S 149 12E
96 Rowley Shoals, Australia 17 40S 119 20E
119 Rowood, U.S.A. 32 18N 112 54W
84 Roxa, Port. Guinea 11 15N 15 45W
73 Roxas, Philippines 11 36N 122 49E
115 Roxboro, U.S.A. 36 24N 78 59W
98 Roxborough Downs, Australia 22 20S 138 45E
101 Roxburgh, New Zealand 45 33S 169 19E
14 Roxburgh, Scotland 55 34N 2 30W
•14 Roxburgh ♦, Scotland 55 30N 2 30W
49 Roxen, Sweden 58 30N 15 40E
118 Roy, U.S.A. 47 17N 109 0W
32 Roya, Peña, Sp. 40 25N 0 40W
114 Royal Oak, U.S.A. 42 30N 83 5W
20 Royan, France 45 37N 1 2W
19 Roye, France 47 40N 6 31E
47 Röyken, Norway 59 45N 10 23E
42 Rozaj, Yugoslavia 42 50N 20 15E
28 Rozan, Poland 52 52N 21 25E
54 Rozdol, U.S.S.R. 49 30N 24 1E
27 Roznava, Cz. 48 37N 20 35E
19 Rozoy, France 48 40N 2 56E
19 Rozoy-sur-Serre, Fr. 49 40N 4 8E
28 Rozwadów, Poland 50 37N 22 2E
44 Rrësheni, Albania 41 47N 19 49E
42 Rtanj, mt., Yugoslavia 43 45N 21 50W
82 Rtem, Oued el, Alg. 33 40N 5 34E
55 Rtishchevo, U.S.S.R. 52 35N 43 50E
30 Rúa, Spain 42 24N 7 6W
92 Ruacaná, S.W. Afr. 17 20S 14 12E
101 Ruahine Ra., N.Z. 39 55S 176 2E
101 Ruapehu, New Zealand 39 17S 175 35E
101 Ruapuke I., N.Z. 46 46S 168 31E
83 Ruáus, W., Libya 30 14N 15 0E
90 Rubeho, mts., Tanzania 6 50S 36 25E
56 Rubezhnoye, U.S.S.R. 49 6N 38 25E
39 Rubicone, R., Italy 44 0N 12 20E
84 Rubino, Ivory Coast 6 4N 4 18W
126 Rubio, Venezuela 7 43N 72 22W
90 Rubona, Uganda 0 29N 30 9E
58 Rubtsovsk, U.S.S.R. 51 30N 80 50E
118 Ruby, L., U.S.A. 40 10N 115 28W
118 Ruby Mts., U.S.A. 40 30N 115 30W
98 Rubyvale, Australia 23 25S 147 45E
54 Rucava, U.S.S.R. 56 9N 20 32E
28 Ruciane-Nida, Poland 53 40N 21 32E
47 Rud, Buskerud, Norway 60 1N 10 1E
49 Ruda, Sweden 57 6N 16 7E
27 Ruda Slaska, Poland 50 16N 18 50E
65 Rudbar, Afghanistan 30 0N 62 30E
14 Ruden, I., E. Germany 54 13N 13 47E
24 Rüdersdorf, Germany 52 28N 13 48E
91 Ruderata, Tanzania 10 7S 34 47E
14 Rudh a'Mhail, C., Scotland 55 55N 6 25W
49 Rudkøbing, Denmark 54 56N 10 41E
28 Rudna, Poland 51 30N 16 17E
52 Rudnichny, U.S.S.R. 59 40N 52 20E
43 Rudnik, Bulgaria 42 36N 27 30E
43 Rudnik, Yugoslavia 44 7N 20 35E
43 Rudnik, mt., Yugoslavia 44 7N 20 35E
59 Rudnogorsk, U.S.S.R. 57 15N 103 42E
54 Rudnya, U.S.S.R. 54 55N 31 13E
58 Rudnyy, U.S.S.R. 52 57N 63 7E
42 Rudo, Yugoslavia 43 41N 19 23E
75 Rudok, China 33 30N 79 40E
†90 Rudolf, L., Kenya 4 10N 36 10E
24 Rudolstadt, Germany 50 44N 11 20E
43 Rudozem, Bulgaria 41 29N 24 51E
114 Rudyard, U.S.A. 46 14N 84 35E
19 Rue, France 50 15N 1 40E
20 Ruelle, France 45 41N 0 14E
87 Rufa'a, Sudan 14 44N 33 12E
20 Ruffec Charente, Fr. 46 2N 0 12W
87 Rufi, Sudan 5 58N 30 8E
124 Rufino, Argentina 34 20S 62 50W
84 Rufisque, Senegal 14 40N 17 15W
91 Rufunsa, Zambia 15 4S 29 34E
13 Rugby, England 52 23N 1 16W
116 Rugby, U.S.A. 48 21N 100 0W
24 Rügen, I., Germany 54 22N 13 25E
90 Rugezi, Tanzania 2 6S 33 18E
18 Rugles, France 48 50N 0 40E
62 Ruhama, Israel 31 31N 34 43E
90 Ruhengeri, Rwanda 1 30S 29 36E
24 Ruhla, Germany 50 53N 10 21E
24 Ruhland, Germany 51 27N 13 52E
24 Ruhr, R., Germany 51 25N 7 15E
91 Ruhuhu, R., Tanzania 10 15S 34 55E
117 Ruidosa, U.S.A. 29 59N 104 39W
119 Ruidoso, U.S.A. 33 19N 105 39W
42 Ruj, mt., Bulgaria 42 52N 22 42E
42 Rujen, mt., Yugoslavia 42 9N 22 26E
68 Ruk, Pakistan 27 50N 68 42E
91 Rukwa, L., Tanzania 7 50S 32 10E
96 Rum Jungle, Australia 13 1S 131 0E
42 Ruma, Yugoslavia 45 8N 19 50E
64 Rumah, Saudi Arabia 25 35N 47 10E
35 Rumania ■, Europe 46 0N 25 0E
87 Rumbek, Sudan 6 54N 29 37E
26 Rumburk, Cz. 50 57N 14 32E
113 Rumford, U.S.A. 44 30N 70 30W
28 Rumia, Poland 54 37N 18 25E
21 Rumilly, France 45 53N 5 56E
90 Rumonge, Burundi 3 59S 29 26E
108 Rumsey, Canada 51 51N 112 48W
98 Rumula, Australia 16 28S 145 20E
90 Rumuruti, Kenya 0 17N 36 32E
101 Runanga, N.Z. 42 25S 171 15E
101 Runaway, C., N.Z. 37 32S 178 2E
13 Runcorn, England 53 20N 2 44W

90 Rungwa, Tanzania 6 55S 33 32E
90 Rungwa, R., Tanzania 7 15S 33 10E
91 Rungwe, Tanz. 9 11S 33 32E
91 Rungwe ♦, Tanz. 9 25S 33 32E
85 Runka, Nigeria 12 28N 7 20E
100 Runton Ra., Austral. 23 35S 123 15E
67 Rupa, India 27 15N 92 30E
100 Rupanyup, Australia 36 39S 142 39E
68 Rupar, India 31 2N 76 38E
121 Rupat, I., Indonesia 1 45N 101 40E
106 Rupert House = Fort Rupert, Canada 51 30N 78 40W
69 Rupsa, Bangladesh 21 44N 87 20E
127 Rupununi, R., Guyana 3 30N 59 30W
67 Ruquka Gie La, China 31 35N 97 55E
126 Rurrenabaque, Bolivia 14 30S 67 32W
32 Rus, R., Spain 39 30N 2 30W
91 Rusambo, Rhodesia 16 30S 32 4E
43 Ruschuk = Ruse, Bulg. 43 48N 25 59E
43 Ruse, Bulg. 43 48N 25 59E
46 Rusetu, Rumania 44 57N 27 14E
13 Rushden, Eng. 52 17N 0 37W
116 Rushford, U.S.A. 43 48N 91 46W
116 Rushville, Ill., U.S.A. 40 6N 90 35W
114 Rushville, Ind., U.S.A. 39 38N 85 22W
116 Rushville, Nebr., U.S.A. 42 43N 102 35W
49 Rusken, Sweden 57 15N 14 20E
113 Russell, Que., Canada 45 16N 75 21W
116 Russell, U.S.A. 38 56N 98 55W
69 Russellkonda, India 19 57N 84 42E
115 Russellville, Ala., U.S.A. 34 30N 87 44W
117 Russellville, Ark., U.S.A. 35 15N 93 0W
115 Russellville, Ky., U.S.A. 36 50N 86 50W
39 Russi, Italy 44 21N 12 1E
59 Russian S.F.S.R. ♦, U.S.S.R. 62 0N 105 0E
4 Russkoye Ustie, U.S.S.R. 71 0N 149 0E
27 Rust, Austria 47 49N 16 42E
57 Rustavi, U.S.S.R. 40 45N 44 30E
92 Rustenburg, S. Africa 25 41S 27 14E
117 Ruston, U.S.A. 32 30N 92 40W
90 Rutana, Burundi 3 55S 30 0E
64 Rutba, Iraq 33 4N 40 15E
31 Rute, Spain 37 19N 4 29W
73 Ruteng, Indonesia 8 26S 120 30E
112 Ruth, Mich., U.S.A. 43 42N 82 45W
118 Ruth, Nev., U.S.A. 39 15N 115 1W
14 Rutherglen, Australia 36 5S 146 29E
14 Rutherglen, Scot. 55 50N 4 11W
41 Rutigliano, Italy 41 1N 17 0E
113 Rutland, U.S.A. 43 38N 73 0W
•13 Rutland ♦, Eng. 52 38N 0 40W
71 Rutland I., Andaman Is. 11 25N 92 40E
109 Rutledge L., Canada 61 58N 110 58W
90 Rutshuru, Zaïre 1 13S 29 25E
16 Ruurlo, Netherlands 52 5N 6 24E
41 Ruvo di Púglia, Italy 41 7N 16 27E
90 Ruvu, Tanzania 6 49S 38 43E
90 Ruvu, R., Tanzania 7 25S 38 15E
91 Ruvuma, R., Tanzania 11 30S 36 10E
91 Ruvuma ♦, Tanz. 11 0S 36 30E
91 Ruwaidha, Si. Arabia 23 40N 44 40E
64 Ruwandiz, Iraq 36 40N 44 32E
90 Ruwenzori Mts., Africa 0 30N 29 55E
90 Ruyigi, Burundi 3 29S 30 15E
55 Ruzayevka, U.S.S.R. 54 10N 45 0E
43 Ruzhevo Konare, Bulg. 42 23N 24 46E
27 Ruzomberok, Cz. 49 3N 19 17E
90 Rwanda ■, Africa 2 0S 30 0E
49 Ryabacge, Sweden 56 47N 13 15E
43 Ryakhovo, Bulgaria 44 0N 26 18E
14 Ryan, L., Scot. 55 0N 5 2W
55 Ryazan, U.S.S.R. 54 50N 39 40E
55 Ryazhsk, U.S.S.R. 53 45N 40 3E
58 Rybache, U.S.S.R. 46 40N 81 20E
52 Rybachi Poluostrov, U.S.S.R. 69 43N 32 0E
55 Rybinsk (Shcherbakov), U.S.S.R. 58 5N 38 50E
55 Rybinsk Vdkhr., U.S.S.R. 58 30N 38 0E
27 Rybnik, Poland 50 6N 18 32E
56 Rybnitsa, U.S.S.R. 47 45N 29 0E
28 Rychwał, Poland 52 4N 18 10E
49 Ryd, Sweden 56 27N 14 42E
13 Rydal, England 50 44N 1 9W
49 Rydö, Sweden 56 58N 13 10E
49 Rydsnäs, Sweden 57 47N 15 9E
28 Rydułtowy, Poland 50 4N 18 23E
28 Rydzyna, Poland 51 47N 16 39E
13 Rye, England 50 57N 0 46E
13 Rye, R., Eng. 54 12N 0 53W
118 Rye Patch Res., U.S.A. 40 45N 118 20W
13 Ryegate, U.S.A. 46 21N 109 27W
54 Rylsk, U.S.S.R. 51 30N 34 51E
100 Rylstone, Austral. 32 46S 149 58E
28 Rymanów, Poland 49 35N 21 51E
28 Ryn, Poland 53 57N 21 34E
49 Ryningsnäs, Sweden 57 17N 15 58E
28 Rypin, Poland 53 3N 19 32E
77 Ryūjō-rettō, Asia 26 0N 127 0E
28 Rzepin, Poland 52 20N 14 49E
27 Rzeszow, Poland 50 0N 22 0E
27 Rzeszów ♦, Poland 50 0N 22 0E
54 Rzhev, U.S.S.R. 56 20N 34 20E

54 Saaremaa, U.S.S.R. 58 30N 22 30E
95 Saarland, Germany 49 20N 7 0E
25 Saarlouis, Germany 49 19N 6 45E
121 Saba I., Leeward Is. 17 30N 63 10W
32 Sabac, Yugoslavia 44 48N 19 42E
32 Sabadell, Spain 41 28N 2 7E
72 Sabagalel, Indonesia 1 36S 98 40E
72 Sabah ♦, Malaysia 6 0N 117 0E
121 Sábana de la Mar, Dom. Rep. 19 7N 69 40W
126 Sábanalarga, Colombia 10 38N 74 55W
72 Sabang, O., Indonesia 5 50N 95 15E
73 Sabará, Brazil 19 55S 43 55W
73 Sabarania, Indonesia 2 5S 138 18E
70 Sabari, R., India 18 0N 81 25E
62 Sabastiya, Jordan 32 17N 35 12E
113 Sabattis, U.S.A. 44 6N 74 40W
87 Sabderat, Ethiopia 15 26N 36 42E
83 Sabhah, Libya 27 9N 14 29E
93 Sabie, S. Africa 25 4S 30 48E
30 Sabinal, Mexico 30 50N 107 25W
33 Sabinal, Punta del, Sp. 36 43N 2 44W
30 Sabinas, Mexico 27 50N 101 10W
120 Sabinas Hidalgo, Mex. 26 40N 100 10W
117 Sabine, U.S.A. 29 42N 93 54W
117 Sabine, R., U.S.A. 31 30N 93 35W
36 Sabine, Monti, Italy 42 15N 12 50E
27 Sabinov, Czechoslovakia 49 6N 21 5E
57 Sabirabad, U.S.S.R. 40 0N 48 30E
87 Sabkhat Tawurgha, Lib. 31 48N 15 30E
73 Sablayan, Philippines 12 5N 120 50E
18 Sable, France 47 50N 0 21W
107 Sable C., Canada 43 29N 65 38W
107 Sable, C., U.S.A. 25 5N 81 0W
13 Sable I., Canada 44 0N 60 0W
20 Sables-d'Olonne, les, France 46 30N 1 45W
30 Sabor, R., Portugal 41 16N 7 10W
84 Sabou, Upper Volta 12 1N 2 28W
83 Sabrátah, Libya 32 47N 12 29E
5 Sabrina Coast, Antarc. 67 0S 120 0E
73 Sabtang I., Philippines 20 15N 121 30E
30 Sabugal, Portugal 40 20N 7 5W
49 Saeby, Denmark 57 21N 10 30E
65 Sabzevar, Iran 36 15N 57 40E
65 Sabzvaran, Iran 28 45N 57 50E
116 Sac City, U.S.A. 42 26N 95 0W
32 Sacedón, Spain 40 29N 2 41W
106 Sachigo, L., Canada 53 50N 92 12W
26 Sachkhere, U.S.S.R. 42 25N 43 28E
39 Sacile, Italy 45 58N 12 30E
113 Sackett's Harbor, U.S.A. 43 56N 76 25W
25 Säckingen, W. Germany 47 34N 7 56E
114 Saco, Me., U.S.A. 43 30N 70 27W
118 Saco, Mont., U.S.A. 48 28N 107 19W
118 Sacramento, U.S.A. 38 39N 121 30W
119 Sacramento Mts., U.S.A. 32 30N 105 30W
118 Sacramento, R., U.S.A. 39 30N 122 0W
33 Sacratif, Cabo, Spain 36 42N 3 28W
46 Săcueni, Rumania 47 20N 22 5E
30 Sada, Spain 43 22N 8 15W
32 Sádaba, Spain 42 19N 1 12W
70 Sadao, Thailand 6 38N 100 26E
91 Sadimi, Zaïre 9 25S 23 32E
30 Sado, R., Portugal 38 10N 8 22W
74 Sado, Shima, Japan 38 15N 138 30E
67 Sadon, Burma 25 28N 98 0E
68 Sadra, India 23 21N 72 45E
86 Sadd el Aali, Egypt 24 5N 32 54E
85 Sade, Nigeria 11 22N 10 45E
92 Sadiba, Botswana 18 53S 23 1E
91 Sadimi, Zaïre 9 25S 23 32E
30 Sado, R., Portugal 38 10N 8 22W
74 Sado, Shima, Japan 38 15N 138 30E
67 Sadon, Burma 25 28N 98 0E
42 Sagág, Norway 59 46N 5 25E
86 Safaga, Egypt 26 42N 34 0E
86 Safaha, Saudi Arabia 26 25N 39 0E
64 Safaniya, Saudi Arabia 28 5N 48 42E
65 Safárikovo, Cz. 48 25N 20 20E
65 Safed Koh, Mts., Afghan. 34 15N 64 0E
48 Säffle, Sweden 59 8N 12 55E
117 Safford, U.S.A. 32 54N 109 52W
13 Saffron Walden, England 52 2N 0 15E
62 Safi, Jordan 31 2N 35 28E
84 Safi, Morocco 32 18N 9 14W
18 Safiah, Israel 31 27N 34 46E
54 Safonovo, U.S.S.R. 65 40N 47 50E
64 Safranbolu, Turkey 41 15N 32 34E
113 Sag Harbor, U.S.A. 40 59N 72 17W
73 Saga, Indonesia 2 40S 132 55E
74 Saga-ken ♦, Japan 33 15N 130 20E
67 Sagaing, Burma 22 0N 96 0E
84 Sagala, Mali 14 9N 6 38W
68 Sagar, India 23 50N 78 50E
70 Sagara, India 14 14N 75 6E
90 Sagara, L., Tanz. 5 20S 31 0E
48 Sågen, Sweden 60 17N 14 10E
114 Saginaw, U.S.A. 43 26N 83 55W
75 Sagil, Mongolia 50 15N 91 15E
121 Sagiennie, Liberia 7 0N 8 52W
48 Sagleipie, Liberia 7 0N 8 52W
105 Saglouc (Sugluk), Canada 62 30N 74 15W
21 Sagone, France 42 7N 8 42E
21 Sagone, G. de, Fr. 42 4N 8 40E
31 Sagres, Portugal 37 0N 8 58W
121 Sagua la Grande, Cuba 22 50N 80 10W
107 Saguenay, R., Canada 48 22N 70 30W
32 Sagunto, Spain 39 42N 0 18W
86 Sahaba, Sudan 18 57N 30 25E
126 Sahagún, Colombia 8 57N 75 27W
31 Sahagún, Spain 42 18N 5 2W
62 Saham, Jordan 32 42N 35 46E
84 Sahara, Africa 23 0N 5 0W
82 Saharien Atlas, Algeria 34 9N 3 29E

68 Saharanpur, India 29 58N 77 33E
82 Saharien Atlas, Algeria 34 9N 3 29E
68 Sahaswan, India 28 5N 78 45E
84 Sahel, Canal du, Mali 14 20N 6 0W
69 Sahibganj, India 25 12N 87 55E
68 Sahiwal, Pakistan 30 45N 73 8E
62 Sahl Arraba, Jordan 32 26N 35 12E
120 Sahuaripa, Mexico 29 30N 109 0W
119 Sahuarita, U.S.A. 31 58N 110 59W
120 Sahuayo, Mexico 20 4N 102 43W
27 Sahy, Czechoslovakia 48 4N 18 55E
81 Sa'id Bundas, Sudan 8 24N 24 48E
65 Sa'idabad, Iran 29 30N 55 45E
82 Saïda, Algeria 34 50N 0 11E
70 Saidapet, India 13 0N 80 15E
68 Saidu, Pakistan 34 50N 72 15E
65 Saighan, Afghanistan 35 10N 67 55E
20 Saignes, France 45 20N 2 31E
63 Saihut, S. Yemen 15 12N 51 10E
71 Saigon, S. Vietnam 10 58N 106 40E
65 Saih-al-Malih, Oman 23 37N 58 31E
63 Saihut, S. Yemen 15 12N 51 10E
74 Saijō, Japan 34 0N 133 5E
74 Saiki, Japan 32 35N 131 50E
68 Saikhoa Ghat, India 27 50N 95 40E
74 Saikū, Japan 32 35N 131 50E
21 Saillans, France 44 42N 5 12E
52 Saimaa, L., Finland 61 15N 28 15E
14 St. Abbs Head, Scotland 55 55N 2 10W
26 St. Aegyd, Austria 47 52N 15 33E
20 St. Affrique, France 43 57N 2 53E
18 St.-Aignan, France 47 16N 1 22E
98 St. Albans, Australia 24 43S 139 56E
107 St. Albans, Canada 47 51N 55 50W
13 St. Albans, Eng. 51 44N 0 19W
113 St. Albans, Vt., U.S.A. 44 49N 73 7W
114 St. Albans, W. Va., U.S.A. 38 21N 81 50W
13 St. Albans Head, England 50 34N 2 3W
107 St. Albert, Canada 53 37N 113 40W
19 St. Amand, France 50 25N 3 6E
20 St.-Amand-Mont- Rond, France 46 43N 2 30E
19 St.-Amarin, France 47 54N 7 0E
21 St.-Amour, France 46 26N 5 21E
26 St. Andrä, Austria 46 46N 14 50E
18 St. André de l'Eure, Fr. 48 54N 1 16E
20 St.-André-de- Cubzac, France 44 59N 0 26W
21 St. André-les-Alpes, Fr. 43 58N 6 30E
93 St. André, C., Malag. 16 11S 44 27E
107 St. Andrews, Canada 45 15N 59 15W
101 St. Andrews, Scot. 56 20N 2 48W
113 St. Anicet, Canada 45 9N 74 23W
118 St. Ann B., Canada 46 22N 60 25W
13 St. Anne, U.K. 49 43N 2 11W
118 St. Anthony, U.S.A. 44 0N 111 49W
20 St.-Antonin-Noble- Val, France 44 10N 1 45E
107 St. Arnaud, Australia 36 32S 143 16E
107 St. Arthur, Canada 47 32N 67 28W
93 St. Augustin, Malag. 23 33S 43 46E
115 St. Augustine, U.S.A. 29 52N 81 20W
13 St. Austell, Eng. 50 20N 4 48W
19 St. Avoed, France 49 7N 6 40E
121 St. Barthélemy, I., W.I. 17 50N 62 50W
12 St. Bee's Hd., Eng. 54 30N 3 38E
20 St.-Benoît-du-Sault, France 46 26N 1 24E
25 St. Bernard, Col du Grand, Fr.-Switz. 45 53N 7 11E
109 St. Boniface, Canada 49 50N 97 10W
21 St. Bonnet, France 44 40N 6 5E
18 St.-Brévin-les-Pins, France 47 14N 2 10W
18 St.-Brice-en-Coglès, France 48 25N 1 22W
107 St. Bride's, Canada 46 56N 54 10W
13 St. Bride's B., Wales 51 48N 5 15W
18 St.-Brieuc, France 48 30N 2 46W
18 St.-Cast, France 48 37N 2 18W
115 St. Catharines, Canada 43 10N 79 15W
115 St. Catherine's I., U.S.A. 31 35N 81 10W
13 St. Catherine's Pt., U.K. 50 34N 1 18W
20 St.-Céré, France 44 51N 1 54E
25 St. Cergue, Switzerland 46 27N 6 10E
20 St. Cernin, France 45 5N 2 25E
21 St.-Chamond, France 45 28N 4 31E
114 St. Charles, Ill., U.S.A. 41 55N 88 21W
116 St. Charles, Mo., U.S.A. 38 46N 90 30W
20 St.-Chély-d'Apcher, France 44 48N 3 17E
121 St. Christopher (St. Kitts), Leeward Is. 17 20N 62 40W
20 St.-Ciers-sur-Gironde, France 45 17N 0 37W
112 St. Clair, Mich., U.S.A. 42 47N 82 27W
113 St. Clair, Pa., U.S.A. 40 42N 76 12W
31 St. Clair, R., N. Amer. 42 40N 82 20W
112 St. Clairsville, U.S.A. 40 5N 80 53W
21 St.-Claude, France 46 22N 5 52E
16 St.-Claud, France 45 54N 0 28E
115 St. Cloud, Fla., U.S.A. 28 15N 81 15W
116 St. Cloud, Minn., U.S.A. 45 30N 94 11W
18 St. Coeur de Marie, Can. 48 39N 71 43W
116 St. Croix, U.S.A. 45 18N 92 22W
116 St. Croix Falls, U.S.A. 45 18N 92 22W
20 St. Cyprien, France 42 37N 3 0E

21 St.-Cyr, France 43 11N 5 43E
13 St. David's, Wales 51 54N 5 16W
13 St. David's Head, Wales 51 54N 5 16W
19 St.-Denis, France 48 56N 2 22E
18 St.-Denis-d'Orques, France 48 2N 0 17W
19 St. Dié, France 48 17N 6 56E
19 St. Dizier, France 48 40N 5 0E
21 St.-Egrève, France 45 14N 5 41E
104 St. Elias, Mt., Alaska 60 20N 141 59W
20 St. Eloy, France 46 10N 2 51E
20 St. Emilon, France 44 53N 0 9W
21 St. Étienne, Fr. 45 27N 4 22E
21 St.-Etienne-de- Tinée, France 44 16N 6 56E
113 Ste. Eugene, Canada 45 30N 74 28W
106 Ste. Félicien, Canada 48 40N 72 25W
107 Ste. Fintan's, Canada 48 10N 58 50W
21 St.-Florent, France 42 41N 9 18E
19 St.-Florent-sur- Cher, France 46 59N 2 15E
21 St.-Florentin, France 48 0N 3 45E
20 St.-Flour, France 45 2N 3 6E
21 St.-Fons, France 45 42N 4 52E
116 St. Francis, U.S.A. 39 48N 101 47W
92 St. Francis, C., S. Africa 34 14S 24 49E
113 St. Francis L., Canada 45 10N 74 20W
117 St. Francis, R., U.S.A. 32 25N 90 36W
18 St.-Fulgent, France 46 50N 1 10W
106 St. Gabriel de Brandon, Canada 46 17N 73 24W
20 St.-Guedens, France 43 6N 0 44E
18 St.-Gualtier, France 46 39N 1 26E
21 St.-Gengoux-le- National, France 46 37N 4 40E
20 St.-Geniez-d'Olt, France 44 27N 2 58E
121 St. George, Bermuda 32 24N 64 42W
107 St. George, Canada 45 11N 66 57W
119 St. George, Utah, U.S.A. 37 10N 113 35W
98 St. George, Austral. 28 1S 148 35E
107 St. George, C., Canada 48 30N 59 16W
115 St. George, C., U.S.A. 29 36N 85 2W
100 St. George Hd., Australia 35 11S 150 45E
109 St. George West, Can. 50 33N 96 7W
107 St. George's, Canada 48 26N 58 31W
106 St. Georges, Canada 46 8N 70 40W
106 St. Georges, Canada 46 42N 72 35W
127 St. Georges, Fr. Gui. 4 0N 52 0W
121 St. George's, Grenada 12 5N 61 43W
110 St. George's Channel, U.K. 52 0N 6 0W
19 St. Georges, France 45 36N 1 0W
19 St. Germain, France 48 53N 2 5E
20 St.-Germain-de- Calberte, France 44 13N 3 48E
20 St.-Germain-des- Fossés, France 46 12N 3 26E
19 St.-Germain-du- Plain, France 46 42N 4 58E
21 St.-Germain-Laval, France 45 50N 4 1E
20 St.-Germain- Lembron, France 45 27N 3 14E
21 St. Gervais, Haute Savoie, France 45 53N 6 42E
20 St. Gervais, Puy de Dôme, France 46 4N 2 50E
18 St.-Gildas, Pte. de, Fr. 47 8N 2 14W
18 St.-Gilles, Gard, France 43 40N 4 26E
18 St. Gilles Croix-de- Vie, France 46 41N 1 55W
20 St.-Girons, Ariège, France 42 59N 1 8E
48 St. Gla, L., Sweden 59 35N 12 30E
25 St. Goar, Germany 50 31N 7 43E
25 St. Gotthard P. = San Gottardo, Switz. 46 33N 8 33E
49 St. Heddinge, Denmark 55 9N 12 26E
7 St. Helena, I., Atl. Oc. 15 55S 5 44W
34 St. Helena, U.S.A. 38 29N 122 30W
92 St. Helenabaai, S. Africa 32 40S 18 10E
12 St. Helens, England 53 28N 2 44W
118 St. Helens, U.S.A. 45 55N 122 50W
18 St. Helier, U.K. 49 11N 2 6W
18 St. Hilaire, France 48 35N 1 7W
19 St. Hippolyte, France 47 20N 6 50E
20 St. Hippolyte-du- Fort, France 43 58N 3 52E
16 St. Honoré, France 46 54N 3 50E
16 St.-Hubert, Belgium 50 2N 5 23E
106 St. Hyacinthe, Canada 45 40N 72 58W
25 St. Ignace, U.S.A. 45 53N 84 43W
21 St. Ignace, I., Canada 48 45N 88 0W
112 St. Ignatius, U.S.A. 47 25N 114 2W
25 St.-Imier, Switzerland 47 9N 6 58E
13 St. Ives, Cornwall, England 50 13N 5 29W
13 St. Ives, Hunts., England 52 20N 0 5W
18 St.-James, France 48 31N 1 20W
116 St. James, U.S.A. 43 57N 94 40W
13 St. James, U.S.A. 51 55N 131 0W
49 St. Jean Baptiste, Can. 49 15N 97 20W
88 St. Jean, C., Eq. Guinea 1 5N 9 20E
20 St.-Jean-de-Luz, France 43 23N 1 39W
21 St.-Jean-de- Maurienne, France 45 16N 6 28E
18 St.-Jean-de-Monts, France 46 47N 2 4W
20 St.-Jean-du-Gard, Fr. 47 7N 3 52E
21 St.-Jean-en-Royans, France 45 1N 5 18E
107 St. Jean-Port-Joli, Can. 47 15N 70 13W
107 St. Jerome, L. St. John, Canada 48 26N 71 53W
106 St. Jerone, Canada 45 55N 74 0W

MAP
107 St. John, Canada 45 20N 66 8W
117 St. John, Kans., U.S.A. 37 59N 98 45W
116 St. John, N.D., U.S.A. 48 58N 99 40W
77 St. John I., China 21 45N 112 45E
107 St. John L., Canada 48 40N 72 0W
116 St. John, R., Canada 46 30N 67 40W
107 St. John's, Canada 47 35N 52 40W
119 St. Johns, Ariz., U.S.A. 34 31N 109 26W
114 St. Johns, Mich., U.S.A. 43 0N 84 38W
115 St. Johns, R., U.S.A. 30 20N 81 30W
113 St. Johnsbury, U.S.A. 44 25N 72 1W
113 St. Johnsville, U.S.A. 43 0N 74 43W
117 St. Joseph, La., U.S.A. 31 55N 91 15W
116 St. Joseph, Mo., U.S.A. 39 40N 94 50W
106 St. Joseph I., Canada 46 12N 83 58W
106 St. Joseph L., Canada 51 10N 90 50W
114 St. Joseph, R., U.S.A. 42 0N 86 30W
114 St. Joseph's, U.S.A. 42 5N 86 30W
106 St. Jovite, Canada 46 8N 74 38W
20 St. Juéry, France 43 55N 2 42E
21 St. Julien, France 46 8N 6 5E
21 St.-Julien- Chapteuil, France 45 2N 4 4E
19 St.-Julien-de-Sault, France 48 2N 3 18E
20 St.-Junien, France 45 53N 0 55E
19 St.-Just-en- Chaussée, France 49 30N 2 25E
20 St.-Just-en- Chevalet, France 45 55N 3 50E
20 St.-Justin, France 43 59N 0 14W
49 St. Karlsö, I., Sweden 57 17N 17 58E
101 St. Kilda, New Zealand 45 53s 170 31E
121 St. Kitts, I., Leeward Is. 17 20N 62 40W
109 St. Laurent, Canada 50 25N 97 58W
21 St. Laurent, Fr. 46 35N 5 56E
21 St.-Laurent-du-Pont, France 45 23N 5 45E
98 St. Lawrence, Australia 22 16s 149 31E
107 St. Lawrence, Canada 46 54N 55 23W
107 St. Lawrence, Gulf of, Canada 48 25N 62 0w
107 St. Lawrence, Canada 46 54N 55 23W
98 St. Lawrence, Australia 22 16s 149 31E
104 St. Lawrence, I., U.S.A. 63 0N 170 0w
107 St. Lawrence, R., Canada 49 30N 66 0w
107 St. Leonard, Canada 47 12N 67 58W
20 St.-Léonard-de- Noblat, France 45 49N 1 29E
106 St. Lin, Canada 45 44N 73 46W
18 St.-Lô, France 49 7N 1 5W
84 St. Louis, Senegal 16 8N 16 27W
114 St. Louis, Mich., U.S.A. 43 27N 84 38W
116 St. Louis, Mo., U.S.A. 38 40N 90 20W
116 St. Louis, R., U.S.A. 47 15N 92 45W
19 St.-Loup-sur- Semouse, France 47 53N 6 16E
93 St. Lucia, C., S. Africa 28 32s 32 29E
121 St. Lucia, I., Wind. Is. 14 0N 60 50W
93 St. Lucia, Lake, S. Afr. 28 5s 32 30E
121 St. Maarten, I., Leeward Is. 18 0N 63 5W
20 St.-Maixent-l'École, France 46 24N 0 12W
18 St.-Malo, France 48 39N 2 1W
18 St. Malo, G. de, France 48 50N 2 30W
21 St. Mandrier, France 43 4N 5 56E
121 St. Marc, Haiti 19 10N 72 50W
21 St.-Marcellin, France 45 9N 5 20E
18 St. Marcouf, Is., France 49 30N 1 10W
118 St. Maries, U.S.A. 47 17N 116 34W
19 St. Martin, France 50 42N 1 38E
121 St. Martin, I., Leeward Is. 18 0N 63 0W
109 St. Martin L., Canada 51 40N 98 30W
21 St. Martin-Tende- Vésubie, France 44 4N 7 15E
107 St. Martins, Canada 45 22N 65 38W
117 St. Martinsville, U.S.A. 30 10N 91 50W
20 St.-Martory, France 43 9N 0 56E
107 St. Mary B., Canada 46 50N 53 50W
84 St. Mary C., Gambia 13 24N 13 10E
70 St. Mary Is., India 14 0N 74 35E
99 St. Mary's, Australia 41 32s 148 11E
107 St. Mary's, Newf., Canada 46 56N 53 34W
112 St. Mary's, Ont., Canada 43 20N 81 10W
114 St. Mary's, Ohio, U.S.A. 40 33N 84 20W
112 St. Mary's, Pa., U.S.A. 41 30N 78 33W
107 St. Mary's, Bay, Canada 46 50N 53 45W
107 St. Mary's, C., Canada 46 50N 54 12W
13 St. Mary's I., U.K. 49 55N 6 17W
99 St. Mary's Pk., Australia 31 30s 138 33E
18 St.-Mathieu, Pte. de, France 48 20N 4 45W
71 St. Matthew's I. = Zadetkyi Kyon, Burma 10 0N 98 25E
19 St.-Maur-des- Fosses, France 48 48N 2 30E
106 St. Maurice R., Canada 47 20N 72 50W
20 St.-Médard-de- Guizières, France 45 1N 0 4W
18 St.-Méen-le-Grand, France 48 11N 2 12W
119 St. Michaels, U.S.A. 35 45N 109 5W
13 St. Michael's Mt., England 50 7N 5 30W
21 St. Michel, Fr. 45 15N 6 29E
19 St. Mihiel, France 48 54N 5 30E
19 St.-Nazaire, France 47 17N 2 12W
9 St. Neots, Eng. 52 14N 0 16W
19 St.-Nicholas-de- Port, France 48 38N 6 18E
112 St. Ola Sta., Canada 44 50N 77 38W
49 St. Olaf, Sweden 55 40N 14 12E
19 St.-Omer, France 50 45N 2 15E
19 St. Ouen, France 48 50N 2 20E
107 St. Pacome, Canada 47 24N 69 58W
20 St. Palais, France 45 40N 1 8W

MAP
107 St. Pamphile, Canada 46 58N 69 48W
20 St.-Pardoux-la- Rivière, France 45 29N 0 45E
107 St. Pascal, Canada 47 32N 69 48W
109 St. Paul, Canada 54 0N 111 17W
20 St. Paul, France 43 44N 1 3W
116 St. Paul, Minn., U.S.A. 44 54N 93 5W
116 St. Paul, Nebr., U.S.A. 41 15N 98 30W
6 St. Paul, I., Atlantic Oc. 0 50N 31 40W
107 St. Paul, I., Canada 47 12N 60 9W
3 St. Paul I., Ind. Oc. 30 40s 77 34E
20 St. Paul-de- Fenouillet, France 42 50N 2 28E
107 St. Paul's B., Canada 49 48N 57 58W
21 St.-Peray, France 44 57N 4 50E
18 St.-Père-en-Retz, France 47 11N 2 2W
91 St. Peter, U.S.A. 44 15N 93 57W
18 St. Peter Port, Channel Is. 49 27N 2 31W
107 St. Peters, N.S., Can. 45 40N 60 53W
107 St. Peters, P.E.I., Can. 46 20N 62 25W
115 St. Petersburg, U.S.A. 27 45N 82 40W
18 St.-Philbert-de- Grand-Lieu, France 47 2N 1 39W
20 St.-Pierre-d'Oleron, France 45 57N 1 19W
18 St.-Pierre-Église, France 49 40N 1 24W
18 St.-Pierre-en-Port, France 49 48N 0 30E
18 St.-Pierre-sur-Dives, Fr. 49 2N 0 1W
107 St. Pierre Miquelon ♦, N. Amer. 46 49N 56 15W
19 St. Pol, France 50 21N 2 20E
18 St.-Pol-de-Léon, France 48 41N 4 0W
19 St.-Pol-sur-Mer, France 51 1N 2 20E
20 St. Pons, France 43 30N 2 45E
19 St.-Pourçain-sur- Sioule, France 46 18N 3 18E
19 St.-Quentin, France 49 50N 3 16E
21 St. Rambert-d'Albon, Fr. 45 17N 1 35E
21 St.-Raphaël, France 43 25N 6 46E
118 St. Regis, Mont., U.S.A. 47 20N 115 3w
113 St. Regis, N.Y., U.S.A. 44 39N 74 34W
21 St.-Rémy-de- Provence, France 43 48N 4 50E
18 St.-Renan, France 48 26N 4 37w
18 St.-Saëns, France 49 41N 1 16E
19 St.-Sauveur-en- Puisaye, France 47 37N 3 12E
18 St.-Sauveur-le- Vicomte, France 49 23N 1 32w
20 St. Savin, France 46 34N 0 50E
20 St.-Savinien, France 45 53N 0 42W
93 St. Sebastien, C., Malag. 12 26s 48 44E
19 St.-Seine-l'Abbaye, France 47 26N 4 47E
20 St. Sernin, France 43 54N 2 35E
18 St.-Servan-sur-Mer, France 48 38N 2 0E
18 St.-Sever-Calvados, France 48 50N 1 3w
107 St. Siméon, Canada 47 51N 69 54W
107 St. Stephen, Canada 45 16N 67 17W
20 St.-Sulpice, France 43 46N 1 41E
20 St.-Sulpice- Laurière, France 46 3N 1 29E
18 St.-Thegonnec, France 48 31N 3 57w
106 St. Thomas, Canada 42 45N 81 10W
106 St. Tite, Canada 46 45N 72 40W
16 St. Troud, Belgium 50 48N 5 10E
21 St. Tropez, France 43 17N 6 38E
18 St.-Vaast-la-Hougue, France 49 35N 1 17W
18 St. Valéry, France 50 10N 1 38E
18 St.-Valéry-en-Caux, France 49 52N 0 43E
21 St.-Vallier, Drôme, France 45 11N 4 50E
21 St.-Vallier-de- Thiey, France 43 42N 6 51E
18 St.-Varent, France 46 53N 0 13W
6 St. Vincent, C., Verde Is. 16 10N 26 1W
89 St. Vincent, C., Malag. 21 58s 43 20E
31 St. Vincent, C. = São Vincente, Port. 37 0N 9 0W
99 St. Vincent, G., Austral. 35 0s 138 0E
121 St. Vincent, I., Wind. Is. 13 10N 61 10W
20 St. Vincent-de- Tyrosse, France 43 39N 1 18W
20 St.-Yrieux-la- Perche, France 45 31N 1 12E
18 Ste.-Adresse, France 49 31N 0 5E
107 Ste. Anne de Beaupré, Canada 47 2N 70 58W
107 Ste. Anne de Portneuf, Canada 48 38N 69 8W
19 Ste. Benoîte, France 49 47N 3 30E
107 Ste. Cecile, Canada 47 56N 64 34W
19 Ste.-Croix, Switzerland 46 49N 6 34W
20 Ste.-Foy-la-Grande, France 44 50N 0 13E
116 Ste. Geneviève, U.S.A. 37 59N 90 2W
107 Ste. Germaine, Canada 46 24N 70 24W
20 Ste.-Hermine, France 46 32N 1 4W
20 Ste.-Livrade-sur-Lot, France 44 24N 0 36E
121 Ste. Marie, Martinique 14 48N 61 1w
93 Ste. Marie, C., Malag. 25 36s 45 8E
93 Ste. Marie, I., Malag. 16 50s 49 55E
19 Ste.-Marie-aux- Mines, France 48 10N 7 12E
107 Ste. Marie de la Madeleine, Canada 46 26N 71 0W
18 Ste.-Maure-de- Touraine, France 47 7N 0 37E
21 Ste.-Maxime, France 43 19N 6 39E
19 Ste.-Menehould, France 49 5N 4 54E
18 Ste.-Mère-Eglise, France 49 24N 1 19W
121 Ste. Rose, Guadalupe 16 20N 61 45W
109 Ste. Rose du lac, Can. 51 10N 99 30W

MAP
124 Ste. Teresa, Argentina 33 33s 60 54W
20 Saintes, France 45 45N 0 37W
127 Saintonge, Fr. 45 40N 0 50W
67 Sairang, India 23 50N 92 45E
74 Saitama-ken ♦, Japan 36 25N 137 0E
42 Sajan, Yugoslavia 45 50N 20 58E
27 Sajószentpéter, Hung. 48 12N 20 44E
66 Saka Ilkalat, Pakistan 27 20N 64 7E
74 Sakai, Japan 34 30N 135 30E
74 Sakai Shimane, Japan 35 30N 133 25E
74 Sakaimachi, Japan 35 30N 133 15E
74 Sakaide, Japan 34 32N 133 50E
64 Sakaka, Saudi Arabia 30 0N 40 8E
106 Sakami, L., Canada 53 10N 77 0W
82 Sakâne, 'Erg i-n, Mali 20 30N 1 30W
91 Sakania, Zaïre 12 43s 28 30E
98 Sakar, I., Terr. of New Guinea 5 30s 148 0E
56 Sakarya, R., Turkey 40 5N 31 0E
74 Sakata, Japan 38 55N 139 56E
93 Sakeny, R., Malag. 20 0s 45 25E
59 Sakhalin, Ostrov, U.S.S.R. 51 0N 143 0E
69 Sakhi Gopal, India 19 58N 85 50E
62 Sakhnin, Israel 32 52s 35 12E
54 Saki, U.S.S.R. 45 16N 33 34E
54 Sakiai, U.S.S.R. 54 59N 23 0E
74 Sakishima-guntō, Japan 24 30N 124 0E
28 Sakołow Małopolski, Poland 50 10N 22 9E
71 Sakon Nakhon, Thailand 17 0N 104 0E
66 Sakrand, Pakistan 26 10N 68 15E
68 Sakri, India 21 2N 74 40E
49 Sakskøbing, Denmark 54 49N 11 39E
57 Sal, R., U.S.S.R. 47 25N 42 20E
49 Säkylä, Finland 61 4N 22 20E
57 Sal, R., U.S.S.R. 47 25N 42 20E
27 Sal'a, Czechoslovakia 48 10N 17 50E
48 Sala, Sweden 59 58N 16 35E
41 Sala Consilina, Italy 40 23N 15 35E
113 Sala-y-Gomez, I., Pacific Ocean 26 28s 105 28W
124 Saladas, Argentina 28 15s 58 40W
124 Saladillo, Argentina 35 40s 59 55W
124 Saladillo, R., Buenos Aires, Argentina 35 40s 58 10W
124 Salado R., Santa Fe, Argentina 27 0s 63 40W
85 Salaga, Ghana 8 31N 0 31W
46 Sălaj ♦, Rumania 47 15N 23 0E
73 Salajar, I., Indonesia 6 15s 120 30E
84 Salala, Liberia 6 42N 10 7W
81 Salala, Sudan 21 17N 36 16E
63 Salalah, Oman 16 56N 53 59E
62 Salama, Israel 32 3N 34 48E
124 Salamanca, Chile 32 0s 71 25W
124 Salamanca, Spain 40 58s 5 39W
112 Salamanca, U.S.A. 42 10N 78 42W
30 Salamanca ♦, Spain 40 57N 5 40W
98 Salamaua, Terr. of New Guinea 7 10s 147 0E
126 Salamina, Colombia 5 25N 75 29W
45 Salamis, Greece 37 56N 23 30E
124 Salar de Atacama, Chile 23 30s 68 25W
126 Salar de Uyuni, Bolivia 20 30s 67 45W
46 Salard, Rumania 47 12N 22 3E
30 Salas, Spain 43 25N 6 15W
32 Salas de los Infantes, Sp. 42 2N 3 17W
76 Salatu, Mongolia 44 25N 107 58E
126 Salaverry, Peru 8 15s 79 0W
58 Salawati, Indonesia 1 7s 130 52E
98 Salayar, I., Indonesia 6 15s 120 30E
32 Salazar, R., Spain 42 45N 1 8W
48 Salbohed, Sweden 59 55N 16 22E
19 Salbris, France 47 25N 2 3E
46 Salcia, Rumania 43 56N 24 55E
30 Saldaña, Spain 42 32N 4 48W
92 Saldanha, S. Afr. 33 0s 17 58E
92 Saldanhabaai, S. Africa 33 6s 18 0E
54 Saldus, U.S.S.R. 56 45N 22 37E
100 Sale, Australia 38 7s 147 0E
9 Sale, England 53 26N 2 19W
82 Salé, Morocco 34 3N 6 48W
84 Saléa-koïra, Mali 16 54N 0 46W
73 Salebabu, Indonesia 3 45N 125 55E
58 Salehabad, Iran 35 40N 61 2E
58 Salekhard, U.S.S.R. 66 30N 66 25E
68 Salem, India 11 40N 78 11E
114 Salem, Ind., U.S.A. 38 38N 86 0w
113 Salem, Mass., U.S.A. 42 29N 70 53W
116 Salem, Mo., U.S.A. 37 40N 91 30W
114 Salem, N.J., U.S.A. 39 34N 75 29W
114 Salem, Ohio, U.S.A. 40 52N 80 50W
118 Salem, Oreg., U.S.A. 45 0N 123 0W
114 Salem, Va., U.S.A. 37 19N 80 8W
41 Salemi, Italy 37 49N 12 47E
21 Salernes, France 43 34N 6 15E
41 Salerno, Italy 40 40N 14 44E
41 Salerno, G. di, Italy 40 35N 14 45E
62 Salfit, Jordan 32 5N 35 11E
9 Salford, England 53 30N 2 17W
56 Salgir, R., U.S.S.R. 45 30N 34 30E
27 Salgótarján, Hungary 48 5N 19 47E
20 Salies-de-Béarn, France 43 28N 0 56W
62 Salima = Shomron, Jordan 32 15N 35 13E
58 Salimanca, U.S.S.R. 39 40N 67 0E
69 Samastipur, India 25 50N 85 50E
124 Salinas, Chile 23 31s
124 Salinas, Ecuador 2 10s 80 50W
121 Salinas, B. de, Nicaragua 11 4N 85 45W
30 Salinas, Cabo de, Spain 39 16N 3 4E
124 Salinas, Pampa de las, Arg. 31 58s 66 42W
119 Salinas, R., U.S.A. 36 10N 121 10W
124 Salinas Ambargasta, Arg. 29 0s 65 30W
120 Salinas (de Hidalgo), Mexico 22 30N 101 40w

MAP
116 Salinas Grandes, Arg. 30 0s 65 0w
116 Saline, R., U.S.A. 39 10N 99 5w
127 Salinópolis, Brazil 0 40s 47 20W
31 Salines-les-Bains, France 46 58N 5 52E
31 Salir, Portugal 37 14N 8 2W
91 Salisbury, Rhodesia 17 50s 31 2E
115 Salisbury, Md., U.S.A. 38 20N 75 38W
115 Salisbury, N.C., U.S.A. 35 42N 80 29W
13 Salisbury Plain, England 51 13N 2 0W
46 Salişte, Rumania 45 45N 23 56E
85 Salka, Nigeria 10 20N 4 58E
32 Sallent, Spain 41 49N 1 54E
20 Salles-Curan, France 44 11N 2 48E
49 Salling, Denmark 56 40N 8 55E
117 Sallisaw, U.S.A. 35 26N 94 45W
86 Sallom Junc., Sudan 19 23N 37 6E
32 Salmerón, Spain 40 33N 2 29W
108 Salmo, Canada 49 0N 117 20W
118 Salmon, U.S.A. 45 12N 113 56W
118 Salmon, R., U.S.A. 46 0N 116 30W
108 Salmon Arm, Canada 50 40N 119 15W
118 Salmon Falls, U.S.A. 42 55N 114 59W
107 Salmon Res., Canada 48 05N 56 00w
118 Salmon River Mts., U.S.A. 45 0N 114 30W
51 Salo, Finland 60 22N 23 3E
38 Saló, Italy 45 37N 10 32E
31 Salobreña, Spain 36 44N 3 35W
119 Salome, U.S.A. 33 51N 113 37W
21 Salon-de-Provence, France 43 39N 5 6E
44 Salonica = Thessaloníki, Greece 40 38N 22 58E
46 Salonta, Rumania 46 49N 21 42E
31 Salor, R., Spain 39 39N 7 3W
32 Salou, Cabo, Spain 41 3N 1 10E
124 Salsacate, Argentina 31 20s 65 5W
48 Salsaker, Sweden 62 59N 18 20E
20 Salses, France 42 50N 2 55E
48 Salsette I., India 19 5N 72 50E
57 Salsk, U.S.S.R. 46 28N 41 30E
41 Salso, R., Italy 37 6N 13 55E
38 Salsomaggiore, Italy 44 48N 9 59E
62 Salt, Jordan 32 2N 35 43E
119 Salt, R., U.S.A. 33 50N 110 25W
68 Salt Range, Pakistan 32 30N 72 25E
99 Salt Creek Telegraph Office, S. Australia 36 0s 139 35E
117 Salt Fork, R., U.S.A. 37 25N 98 40W
118 Salt Lake City, U.S.A. 40 45N 111 58W
124 Salta, Argentina 24 47s 65 25W
124 Salta ♦, Argentina 24 48s 65 30W
14 Saltcoats, Scot. 55 38N 4 47W
50 Saltee Is., Ireland 52 7N 6 37W
50 Saltfjorden, Norway 67 15N 14 20E
50 Saltholm, Denmark 55 38N 12 43E
50 Salthólmavik, Iceland 65 24N 21 57W
120 Saltillo, Mexico 25 30N 100 57W
124 Salto, Argentina 34 20s 60 15W
124 Salto ♦, Uruguay 31 20s 57 59W
124 Salto Augusto, falls, Brazil 8 30s 58 0w
119 Salton Sea, U.S.A. 33 20N 116 0w
85 Saltpond, Ghana 5 15N 1 3W
48 Saltsjöbaden, Sweden 59 15N 18 20E
108 Saltspring, Canada 48 54N 123 37E
115 Salula, U.S.A. 34 12N 81 45W
86 Salûm, Egypt 31 31N 25 7E
86 Salûm, Khâlig el, Egypt 31 30N 25 9E
70 Salur, India 18 27N 83 18E
38 Saluzzo, Italy 44 39N 7 29E
127 Salvador, Brazil 13 0s 38 30W
109 Salvador, Canada 52 10N 109 32W
120 Salvador ■, Central America 13 50N 89 0W
117 Salvador, L., U.S.A. 29 46N 90 16W
31 Salvaterra de Magos, Portugal 39 1N 8 47W
30 Sálvora, Isla, Spain 42 30N 8 58W
65 Salwa, Qatar 24 45N 50 55E
67 Salween, R. = Thanlwin Myit, Burma 20 0N 98 0E
26 Salza, R., Austria 47 43N 15 0E
26 Salzach, R., Austria 47 15N 12 25E
26 Salzburg, Austria 47 48N 13 2E
26 Salzgitter, Germany 52 2N 10 22E
24 Salzwedel, Germany 52 50N 11 11E
68 Sam Neua, Laos 20 29N 104 0E
71 Sam Ngao, Thailand 17 18N 99 0E
117 Sam Rayburn Res., U.S.A. 31 15N 94 20W
58 Sama, U.S.S.R. 60 10N 60 15E
30 Sama de Langreo, Sp. 43 18N 5 40W
73 Samak, Indonesia 4 40s 122 26E
73 Samales Group, Phil. 6 0N 122 0E
70 Samalkota, India 17 3N 82 13E
86 Samâlût, Egypt 28 20N 30 42E
68 Samana, India 30 10N 76 13E
126 Samanco, Peru 9 10s 78 30W
91 Samangwa, Zaïre 4 23s 24 10E
59 Samar, I., Philippines 12 0N 125 0E
98 Samarai, Terr. of Papua 10 32s 150 35E
58 Samarkand, U.S.S.R. 39 40N 67 0E
64 Samarra, Iraq 34 16N 43 55E
69 Samastipur, India 25 50N 85 50E
90 Samba, Zaïre 4 38s 26 22E
93 Sambava, Malagasy Rep. 14 16s 50 10E
91 Sambawizi, Rhodesia 18 24s 26 13E
68 Sambhal, India 28 35N 78 37E
68 Sambhar, India 26 52N 11 16E
38 Sambonifacio, Italy 45 24N 11 16E

MAP
71 Samoor, Khmer Rep. 12 46N 106 0E
54 Sambor, U.S.S.R. 49 30N 23 10E
124 Samoorombón, Bahía, Argentina 36 5s 57 20W
16 Samore, R., Belg.-Fr. 50 27N 4 52E
40 Sambuca, Italy 37 39N 13 6E
92 Sambusu, S.W. Afr. 17 55s 19 37E
19 Samer, France 50 38N 1 44E
91 Sámfi, Zambia 11 16s 29 31E
45 Sámi, Greece 38 15N 20 39E
86 Samna, Saudi Arabia 25 12N 37 17E
60 Samnager, Norway 60 23N 5 39E
83 Samnu, Libya 27 15N 14 55E
2 Samo Alto, Chile 30 22s 71 0W
2 Samoan Is., Pac. Ocean 14 0s 171 0w
39 Samobor, Yugoslavia 45 47N 15 44E
21 Samoëns, France 46 5N 6 45E
84 Samorogouan, Upper Volta 11 21N 4 57W
30 Samos, Spain 42 44N 7 20W
45 Samoš, Yugoslavia 45 13N 20 49E
45 Sámos, I., Greece 37 45N 26 50E
72 Samosir, P., Indonesia 2 35N 98 50E
44 Samothráki, Greece 40 28N 25 38E
45 Samothráki, I., Greece 40 25N 25 40E
85 Sampa, Ghana 8 0N 2 36W
124 Sampacho, Argentina 33 20s 64 50W
73 Sampang, Indonesia 7 11s 113 13E
32 Samper de Calanda, Sp. 41 11N 04 2w
44 Sampit, Indonesia 2 20s 113 0E
72 Sampit, Teluk, Indonesia 3 10s 113 20E
85 Samra, Saudi Arabia 25 35N 41 0E
84 Samreboi, Ghana 5 34N 7 28E
23 Samshui, China 23 7N 112 58E
49 Samsö, Denmark 55 50N 10 35E
49 Samsö Baelt, Denmark 55 45N 10 45E
56 Samsun, Turkey 41 15N 36 15E
45 Samsun Daği, Tur. 37 45N 27 10E
54 Samtredia, U.S.S.R. 42 7N 42 24E
57 Samur, R., U.S.S.R. 41 30N 48 0E
91 Samusole, Zaïre 10 2s 24 0E
71 Samut Prakan, Thailand 13 32N 100 40E
71 Samut Sakhon, Thai. 13 31N 100 24E
71 Samut Songkhram (Mekong), Thailand 13 24N 100 1E
68 Samwari, Pakistan 28 5N 66 46E
67 Samyo La, China 29 55N 84 46E
84 San, Mali 13 15N 4 43W
126 San Agustín, Colombia 1 53N 76 16W
73 San Agustin, C., Phil. 6 20N 126 13E
124 San Agustin de Valle Fértil, Arg. 30 35s 67 30W
95 San Ambrosio, I., Pac. Oc. 26 35s 79 30W
118 San Andreas, U.S.A. 38 17N 120 39W
121 San Andres, I. de, Caribbean 12 42N 81 46W
119 San Andres Mts., U.S.A. 33 0N 106 45W
119 San Andrés Tuxtla, Mex. 18 30N 95 20W
79 San Angelo, U.S.A. 31 30N 100 30W
124 San Antonio, Chile 33 40s 71 40W
119 San Antonio, N. Mex., U.S.A. 33 58N 106 57W
117 San Antonio, Tex., U.S.A. 29 30N 98 30W
124 San Antonio, Venezuela 3 30N 66 44W
124 San Antonio, C., Arg. 36 15s 56 40W
121 San Antonio, C., Cuba 21 50N 84 57W
33 San Antonio, C. de, Sp. 38 48N 0 12E
117 San Antonio, R., U.S.A. 28 30N 97 14W
33 San Antonio Abad, Sp. 38 59N 1 19E
126 San Antonio de Caparo, Ven. 7 35N 71 27W
121 San Antonio de los Baños, Cuba 22 54N 82 31W
124 San Antonio de los Cobres, Arg. 24 16s 66 2W
128 San Antonio Oeste, Arg. 40 40s 65 0W
38 San Benedetto, Italy 45 2N 10 57E
39 San Benedetto del Tronto, Italy 42 57N 13 52E
117 San Benito, U.S.A. 26 5N 97 32W
119 San Bernardino, U.S.A. 34 7N 117 18W
41 San Bernardo, Chile 33 40s 70 50W
126 San Bernardo, I. de, Col. 9 45N 75 50W
120 San Blas, Mex. 26 10N 108 40W
115 San Blas, C., U.S.A. 29 40N 85 25W
121 San Blas, Cord. de, Pan. 9 15N 78 30W
126 San Borja, Bolivia 15 0s 67 12W
124 San Carlos, Argentina 33 50s 69 0W
76 San Carlos, Chile 36 25s 72 0W
+85 San Carlos, Eq. Guinea 3 29N 8 33E
120 San Carlos, Mexico 29 0N 101 10W
121 San Carlos, Nicaragua 11 12N 84 50W
73 San Carlos, Philippines 10 29N 123 25E
125 San Carlos, Uruguay 34 46s 54 58W
119 San Carlos, U.S.A. 33 24N 110 27W
126 San Carlos, Amazonas, Venezuela 1 55N 67 4W
126 San Carlos, Cojedes, Venezuela 9 40N 68 36W
119 San Carlos L., U.S.A. 33 20N 110 10W
128 San Carlos de Bariloche, Argentina 41 10s 71 25W
32 San Carlos de la Rápita, Spain 40 37N 0 35E
126 San Carlos del Zulia, Ven. 9 1N 71 55W
40 San Cataldo, Italy 37 30N 13 58E
32 San Celoni, Spain 41 42N 2 30E
124 San Clemente, Chile 35 30s 71 39W
33 San Clemente, Spain 39 24N 2 25W
119 San Clemente, U.S.A. 33 29N 117 45W

* Renamed Butuku-Luba

65

MAP

119 San Clemente I., U.S.A. 33 0N 118 30W
39 San Constanzo, Italy 43 46N 13 5E
124 San Cristóbal, Argentina 30 20S 61 10W
126 San Cristóbal, Ven. 7 46N 72 14W
120 San Cristóbal de las Casas, Mexico 16 50N 92 33W
38 San Damiano d'Asti, It. 44 51N 8 4E
39 San Daniele del Friuli, It. 46 10N 13 0E
41 San Demétrio Corone, It. 39 34N 16 22E
119 San Diego, Calif., U.S.A. 32 50N 117 10W
117 San Diego, Tex., U.S.A. 27 47N 98 15W
128 San Diego, C., Arg. 54 40S 65 10W
39 San Doná di Piave, It. 45 38N 12 34E
39 San Elpídio a Mare, It. 43 16N 13 41E
124 San Estanislao, Paraguay 24 39S 56 26W
32 San Esteban de Gormaz, Spain 41 34N 3 13W
38 San Felice sul Panaro, Italy 44 51N 11 9E
124 San Felipe, Chile 32 43S 70 50W
126 San Felipe, Venezuela 10 20N 68 44W
32 San Feliu de Guixols, Sp. 41 45N 3 1E
32 San Feliu de Llobregat, Spain 41 23N 2 2E
126 San Félix, Venezuela 8 20N 62 35W
95 San Felíx, I., lac. Oc. 26 30S 80 0W
124 San Fernando, Chile 34 30S 71 0W
120 San Fernando, Mexico 30 0N 115 10W
73 San Fernando, Luzon, Phil. 15 5N 120 37E
73 San Fernando, Luzon, Phil. 16 40N 120 23E
31 San Fernando, Spain 36 22N 6 17W
121 San Fernando, Trinidad 10 20N 61 30W
119 San Fernando, U.S.A. 34 15N 118 29W
42 San Fernando, Ven. 8 0N 67 30W
120 San Fernando, R., Mex. 25 0N 99 0W
126 San Fernando de Apure, Ven. 7 54N 67 28W
126 San Fernando de Atabapo, Venezuela 4 3N 67 42W
41 San Fernando di Puglia, Italy 41 18N 16 5E
124 San Francisco, Córdoba, Arg. 31 30S 62 5W
124 San Francisco, San Luis, Arg. 32 45S 66 10W
119 San Francisco, U.S.A. 37 35N 122 30W
124 San Francisco, Paso de, Arg.-Chile 35 40S 70 24W
119 San Francisco, R., U.S.A. 33 30N 109 0W
121 San Francisco de Macorís, Dom. Rep. 19 19N 70 15W
124 San Francisco del Monte de Oro, Arg. 32 36S 66 8W
120 San Francisco del Oro, Mexico 26 52N 105 50W
33 San Francisco Javier, Sp. 38 40N 1 25E
126 San Francisco Solano, Pta., Col. 6 18N 77 29W
117 San Francisville, U.S.A. 30 48N 91 22W
41 San Fratello, It. 38 1N 14 33E
126 San Gabriel, Ecuador 0 36N 77 49W
40 San Gavino Monreale, It. 39 33N 8 47E
126 San Gil, Colombia 6 33N 73 8W
38 San Gimignano, Italy 43 28N 11 3E
39 San Giórgio di Nogaro, Italy 45 50N 13 13E
41 San Giórgio Iónico. It. 40 27N 17 23E
38 San Giovanni Bianco, It. 45 52N 9 40E
41 San Giovanni in Fiore, Italy 39 16N 16 42E
41 San Giovanni in Persiceto, Italy 44 39N 11 12E
41 San Giovanni Rotondo, Italy 41 41N 15 42E
39 San Giovanni Valdarno, It. 43 32N 11 30E
38 San Giuliano Terme, It. 43 45N 10 26E
25 San Gottardo, Paso del, Switz. 46 33N 8 33E
125 San Gregorio, Uruguay 32 37S 55 40W
40 San Guiseppe Iato, It. 37 57N 13 11E
126 San Ignacio, Bolivia 16 20S 60 55W
124 San Ignacio, Paraguay 26 52S 57 3W
73 San Ildefonso, C., Phil. 16 0N 122 10E
124 San Isidro, Argentina 34 29S 58 31W
126 San Jacinto, Col. 9 50N 75 8W
125 San Javier, Misiones, Argentina 27 55S 55 5W
124 San Javier, Santa Fe, Argentina 30 40S 59 55W
124 San Javier, Santa Cruz, Bolivia 16 18S 62 30W
124 San Javier, Chile 35 40S 71 45W
33 San Javier, Spain 37 49N 0 50W
126 San Jerónimo, Sa. de, Col. 8 0N 75 50W
126 San Joaquín, Venezuela 10 16N 67 47W
119 San Joaquin R., U.S.A. 37 0N 120 0W
124 San Jorge, Argentina 31 54S 61 50W
120 San Jorge, Bahía de, Mexico 31 20N 113 20W
128 San Jorge, Golfo de, Argentina 46 0S 66 0W
32 San Jorge, G. de, Spain 40 50N 0 55W
126 San José, Bolivia 17 45S 60 50W
120 San José, Guatemala 14 0N 90 50W
73 San Jose, Luzon, Philippines 15 45N 120 55E
73 San Jose, Mindoro, Philippines 10 50N 122 5E
33 San José, Spain 38 55N 1 18E
119 San Jose, Calif., U.S.A. 37 20N 122 0W

117 San Jose, N. Mex., U.S.A. 35 26N 105 30W
124 San José de Feliciano, Argentina 30 26S 58 46W
124 San José de Jáchal, Arg. 30 5S 69 0W
124 San José de Mayo, Urug. 34 27S 56 27W
126 San José de Ocuné, Col. 4 15N 70 20W
120 San José del Cabo, Mex. 23 0N 109 50W
126 San José del Guaviare, Col. 2 35N 72 38W
124 San Juan, Argentina 31 30S 68 30W
126 San Juan, Antioquia, Colombia 8 46N 76 32W
126 San Juan, Meta, Colombia 3 26N 73 50W
121 San Juan, Dom. Rep. 18 49N 71 12W
120 San Juan, Coahuila, Mex. 29 34N 101 53W
120 San Juan, Jalisco, Mex. 21 20N 102 50W
120 San Juan, Querétaro, Mex. 20 25N 100 0W
73 San Juan, Philippines 8 35N 126 20E
119 San Juan Mts., U.S.A. 38 30N 108 30W
120 San Juan, Presa de, Mexico 17 45N 95 15W
124 San Juan, R., Argentina 32 20S 67 25W
126 San Juan, R., Colombia 4 0N 77 20W
121 San Juan, R., Nicaragua 11 0N 84 30W
119 San Juan, R., U.S.A. 37 20N 110 20W
124 San Juan ♦, Arg. 31 9S 69 0W
33 San Juan Bautista, Sp. 39 5N 1 31E
124 San Juan Bautista, Par. 26 37S 57 6W
119 San Juan Capistrano, U.S.A. 33 29N 117 46W
126 San Juan de los Cayos, Ven. 11 10N 68 25W
126 San Juan de los Morros, Venezuela 9 55N 67 21W
121 San Juan de Norte, B. de, Nicaragua 11 30N 83 40W
31 San Juan del Puerto, Sp. 37 20N 6 50W
121 San Juan del Sur, Nic. 11 20N 86 0W
128 San Julián, Argentina 49 15S 68 0W
32 San Just, Sierra de, Spain 40 45N 0 41W
124 San Justo, Argentina 30 55S 60 30W
120 San Lázaro, Sa. de, Mex. 23 25N 110 0W
119 San Leandro, U.S.A. 37 40N 122 6W
32 San Leonardo, Spain 41 51N 3 5W
124 San Lorenzo, Argentina 32 45S 60 45W
126 San Lorenzo, Ecuador 1 15N 78 50W
124 San Lorenzo, Paraguay 25 20S 57 32W
126 San Lorenzo, Venezuela 9 47N 71 4W
126 San Lorenzo, I., Peru 12 7S 77 15W
128 San Lorenzo, Mt., Arg. 47 40S 72 20W
32 San Lorenzo de la Parilla, Spain 39 51N 2 22W
32 San Lorenzo de Morunys, Spain 42 8N 1 35E
126 San Lucas, Bolivia 20 5S 65 0W
120 San Lucas, C. de, Mexico 22 50N 110 0W
41 San Lucido, Italy 39 18N 16 3E
124 San Luis, Argentina 33 20S 66 20W
119 San Luis, U.S.A. 37 14N 105 26W
126 San Luis, Venezuela 11 7N 69 42W
120 San Luis Río Colorado, Mexico 32 29N 114 48W
34 Sao Marcelino, Braz. 1 0N 67 12W
41 San Marco Argentano, It. 39 34N 16 8E
41 San Marco dei Cavoti, It. 41 20N 14 50E
41 San Marco in Lámis, It. 41 43N 15 38E
120 San Marcos, Guatemala 14 59N 91 52W
117 San Marcos, U.S.A. 29 53N 98 0W
39 San Marino, San Marino 43 56N 12 25E
39 San Marino ■, Europe 43 56N 12 25E
124 San Martín, Argentina 33 5S 68 28W
126 San Martín, Colombia 3 42N 73 42W
128 San Martín, L., Arg. 48 50S 72 50W
30 San Martín de Valdeiglesias, Spain 40 21N 4 24W
38 San Martino de Calvi, It. 45 57N 9 41E
32 San Mateo, Spain 40 28N 0 10E
119 San Mateo, U.S.A. 37 32N 122 25W
126 San Matías, Bolivia 16 25S 58 20W
128 San Matías, Golfo de, Argentina 41 30S 64 0W
124 San Miguel, Salvador 13 30N 88 12W
33 San Miguel, Spain 39 3N 1 26E
126 San Miguel, Venezuela 9 40N 65 11W
124 San Miguel, R., Bolivia 16 0S 62 45W
124 San Miguel, Ec./Col. 0 25N 76 30W
33 San Miguel de Salinas, Sp. 37 59N 0 47W
124 San Miguel de Tucumán, Arg. 26 50S 65 20W
124 San Miguel del Monte, Arg. 35 23S 58 50W
38 San Miniato, Italy 43 40N 10 50E
73 San Narciso, Phil. 15 2N 120 3E
124 San Nicolás de los Arroyas, Argentina 33 17S 60 10W
110 San Nicolas I., U.S.A. 33 16N 119 30W
126 San Onofre, Colombia 9 44N 75 32W
124 San Pablo, Bolivia 21 43S 66 38W
126 San Pablo, Colombia 7 28N 70 56W
41 San Paolo di Civitate, It. 41 44N 15 16E
125 San Pedro, Buenos Aires, Argentina 33 43S 59 45W
124 San Pedro, Jujuy, Argentina 24 12S 64 55W
124 San Pedro, Chile 21 58S 68 30W
126 San Pedro, Colombia 4 56N 71 53W
121 San Pedro, Dom. Rep. 18 30N 69 18W

84 San Pedro, Ivory Coast 4 50N 6 33W
124 San Pedro, Pta., Chile 25 30S 70 38W
120 San Pedro, R., Chihuahua, Mexico 28 20N 106 10W
119 San Pedro, R., U.S.A. 32 45N 110 35W
31 San Pedro, Sierra de, Spain 39 18N 6 40W
124 San Pedro ♦, Paraguay 24 0S 57 0W
126 San Pedro de Arimena, Col. 4 37N 71 42W
124 San Pedro de Atacama, Chile 22 55S 68 15W
124 San Pedro de Jujuy, Paraguay 24 12S 64 55W
120 San Pedro de las Colonias, Mexico 25 50N 102 59W
125 San Pedro de Lloc, Peru 7 15S 79 28W
125 San Pedro del Paraná, Paraguay 26 43S 56 13W
33 San Pedro del Pinatar, Spain 37 50N 0 50W
120 San Pedro Mártir, Sierra, Mexico 31 0N 115 30W
120 San Pedro Mixtepec, Mexico 16 2N 97 0W
120 San Pedro Ocampo, Mex. 24 52N 101 40W
120 San Pedro Sula, Hond. 15 30N 88 0W
40 San Pietro, I., Italy 39 9N 8 17E
41 San Pietro Vernotico, It. 40 28N 18 0E
73 San Quintín, Philippines 16 1N 120 56E
124 San Rafael, Argentina 34 40S 68 30W
126 San Rafael, Colombia 6 2N 69 45W
118 San Rafael, Calif., U.S.A. 38 0N 122 40W
119 San Rafael, N. Mex., U.S.A. 35 6N 107 58W
126 San Rafael, Venezuela 10 42N 71 46W
124 San Ramón de la Nueva Orán, Arg. 23 10S 64 20W
38 San Remo, Italy 43 48N 7 47E
124 San Román, C., Ven. 12 12N 70 0W
124 San Roque, Argentina 28 15S 58 45W
31 San Roque, Spain 36 17N 5 21W
124 San Rosendo, Chile 37 10S 72 50W
117 San Saba, U.S.A. 31 12N 98 45W
124 San Salvador, Salvador 13 40N 89 20W
121 San Salvador (Watlings) I., Bahamas 24 0N 74 40W
124 San Salvador de Jujuy, Arg. 23 30S 65 40W
128 San Sebastián, Arg. 53 10S 68 30W
32 San Sebastián, Spain 43 17N 1 58W
126 San Sebastián, Ven. 9 57N 67 11W
39 San Serverino, Italy 43 13N 13 10E
39 San Severo, Italy 41 41N 15 23E
119 San Simon, U.S.A. 32 14N 109 16W
39 San Stéfano di Cadore, It. 46 34N 12 33E
128 San Valentin, Mte., Chile 46 30S 73 30W
31 San Vicente de Alcántara, Spain 39 22N 7 8W
30 San Vicente de la Barquera, Spain 43 30N 4 29W
126 San Vicente del Caguán, Col. 2 7N 74 46W
65 San Vicenzo, Italy 43 9N 10 32E
40 San Vito, C., Italy 38 11N 12 41E
39 San Vito al Tagliamento, Italy 45 55N 12 50E
39 San Vito Chietino, Italy 42 19N 14 27E
41 San Vito dei Normanni, Italy 40 40N 17 40E
126 San Yanaro, Colombia 2 47N 69 42W
117 San Ygnacio, U.S.A. 27 6N 92 24W
119 San Ysidro, U.S.A. 32 33N 117 5W
63 San'a, Yemen 15 27N 44 12E
44 Sana, R., Yugoslavia 44 40N 16 43E
84 Sanaba, Upper Volta 12 25N 3 47W
86 Sanáfir, Saudi Arabia 27 49N 34 37E
72 Sanana, Indonesia 2 5S 125 50E
68 Sanand, India 22 59N 72 25E
21 Sanandaj, Iran 35 25N 47 7E
21 Sanary, France 43 7N 5 48E
68 Sanawad, India 22 11N 76 5E
19 Sancergues, France 47 10N 2 54E
19 Sancerre, France 47 20N 2 50E
77 Sancha Ho, China 26 20N 105 30E
68 Sanchor, India 24 52N 71 49E
73 Sanco, Pt., Philippines 8 15N 126 24E
19 Sancoins, France 46 47N 2 55E
93 Sancti-Spíritus, Cuba 21 52N 79 33W
49 Sand, R., S. Afr. 22 25S 30 5E
106 Sand Lake, Canada 47 46N 84 31W
119 Sand Springs, U.S.A. 36 12N 96 5W
86 Sanḍah, Saudi Arabia 20 35N 39 32E
72 Sandai, Indonesia 1 15S 110 31E
72 Sandakan, Malaysia 5 53N 118 10E
72 Sandan, Khmer Rep. 12 46N 106 0E
43 Sandanski, Bulgaria 41 35N 23 16E
84 Sandaré, Mali 14 40N 10 15W
14 Sanday I., Scotland 59 15N 2 30W
47 Sande, Möre og Romsdal, Norway 62 15N 5 27E
47 Sande, Sogn og Fjordane, Norway 61 20N 5 47E
47 Sandefjord, Norway 59 10N 10 15E
47 Sandnar, Norway 59 33N 5 52E
119 Sanders, U.S.A. 35 12N 109 25W
50 Sandfell, Iceland 63 57N 16 48W
99 Sandgate, Australia 27 18S 153 3E
99 Sandhammaren, C., Sweden 55 23N 14 14E
126 Sandiá, Peru 14 10S 69 30W
64 Sandikli, Turkey 38 30N 30 20E
47 Sandnes, Norway 58 50N 5 45E
88 Sandoa, Zaïre 9 48S 23 0E
28 Sandomierz, Poland 50 40N 21 43E

126 Sandona, Colombia 1 17N 77 28W
67 Sandoway, Burma 18 20N 94 30E
118 Sandpoint, U.S.A. 48 20N 116 40W
12 Sandringham, Eng. 52 50N 0 30E
96 Sandstone, W. Australia 28 0S 119 15E
112 Sandusky, Mich., U.S.A. 43 26N 82 50W
112 Sandusky, Ohio, U.S.A. 41 25N 82 40W
92 Sandveld, S. Afr. 32 0S 18 15E
49 Sandvig, Denmark 55 18N 14 48E
47 Sandvika, Akershus, Norway 59 54N 10 29E
47 Sandviken, Sweden 60 38N 16 46E
107 Sandwich B., Canada 53 40N 57 15W
92 Sandwich B., S. Afr. 23 25S 14 20E
5 Sandwich Group, Falkland Is. Dep. 57 0S 27 0W
67 Sandwip Chan., Bangladesh 22 35N 91 35E
99 Sandy C., Australia 24 41S 153 8E
106 Sandy L., Canada 52 10N 94 30W
106 Sandy Lake, Canada 53 0N 93 0W
118 Sandy Cr., R., U.S.A. 42 20N 109 30W
100 Sandy Hollow, Austral. 32 36S 150 15E
113 Sandy Hook, U.S.A. 40 22N 74 0W
115 Sanford, Fla., U.S.A. 28 45N 81 20W
115 Sanford, Me., U.S.A. 43 28N 70 47W
115 Sanford, N.C., U.S.A. 35 30N 79 10W
104 Sanford Mt., Alas. 62 30N 143 0W
96 Sanford, R., Australia 27 22S 115 53E
91 Sanga, Mozam. 12 22S 35 21E
88 Sanga, R., Congo 1 0N 16 30E
59 Sanga Tolon, U.S.S.R. 61 50N 149 40E
70 Sangamner, India 19 30N 74 15E
59 Sangar, U.S.S.R. 63 55N 127 31E
72 Sangasanga, Indonesia 0 29S 117 13E
77 Sangchen La, China 31 30N 84 40E
77 Sangchih, China 29 25N 109 30E
90 Sange, Zaïre 6 58S 28 21E
73 Sangeang, I., Indonesia 8 12S 119 6E
119 Sanger, U.S.A. 36 47N 119 35W
24 Sangerhausen, Germany 51 28N 11 18E
73 Sanggau, Indonesia 0 5N 110 30E
73 Sanghe, Kep., Indonesia 3 0N 126 0E
73 Sanghe, P., Indonesia 3 45N 125 30E
72 Sangkapura, Indonesia 5 52S 112 40E
72 Sangkulirang, Indonesia 1 0N 118 0E
70 Sangli, India 16 55N 74 33E
85 Sangmélina, Cameroon 2 57N 12 1E
33 Sangonera, R., Spain 37 39N 2 0W
117 Sangre de Cristo Mts., U.S.A. 37 0N 105 0W
39 Sangro, R., Italy 42 10N 14 30E
75 Sangsang, China 29 30N 86 0E
108 Sangudo, Canada 53 50N 115 0W
19 Sangüesa, Spain 42 37N 1 17W
21 Sanguinaires, I., France 41 51N 8 36E
84 Sanhala, Ivory Coast 10 3N 6 51W
116 Sanish, U.S.A. 48 0N 102 30W
90 Sanje, Uganda 0 49S 31 30E
70 Sankaranayinarkovil, India 9 10N 77 35E
68 Sankeshwar, India 16 23N 74 23E
88 Sankuang, China 25 39N 109 30E
26 Sankt Andra, Austria 46 46N 14 50E
25 Sankt Blasien, Germany 47 47N 8 7E
25 Sankt Gallen, Switzerland 47 26N 9 22E
25 Sankt Gallen ♦, Switzerland 47 25N 9 22E
25 Sankt Ingbert, Germany 49 16N 7 6E
26 Sankt Johann, Austria 47 22N 13 12E
25 Sankt Moritz, Switzerland 46 30N 9 50E
49 Sankt Olof, Sweden 55 37N 14 8E
26 Sankt Pölten, Austria 48 12N 15 38E
25 Sankt Valentin, Austria 48 11N 14 33E
26 Sankt Veit, Austria 46 54N 14 22E
25 Sankt Wendel, Germany 49 27N 7 9E
25 Sankt Wolfgang, Austria 47 43N 13 27E
31 Sanlúcar de Barrameda, Spain 37 26N 6 18W
31 Sanlúcar la Mayor, Sp. 37 26N 6 18W
41 Sanluri, Italy 39 35N 8 55E
46 Sanmartin, Rumania 46 19N 25 58E
77 Sanmen Wan, China 29 10N 121 45E
77 Sanmenhsia, China 34 46N 111 30E
92 Sannaspos, S. Afr. 29 6S 26 34E
41 Sannicandro Gargánico, Italy 41 50N 15 34E
47 Sännicolaul-Maré, Rum. 46 5N 20 39E
47 Sannidal, Norway 58 55N 9 15E
92 Sanniehof, S. Africa 26 30S 25 47E
28 Sanok, Poland 49 35N 22 10E
84 Sanokwelle, Liberia 7 19N 8 38W
14 Sanquhar, Scot. 55 21N 3 56W
84 Sansanding Dam, Mali 13 37N 6 0W
85 Sansanné-Mango, Togo 10 20N 0 30E
39 Sansepolcro, Italy 43 34N 12 8E
84 Sanski Most, Yugoslavia 44 46N 16 40E
41 Sant' Agata di Gati, It. 41 6N 14 30E
41 Sant' Agata di Militello, It. 38 2N 14 40E
126 Santa Ana, El Beni, Bolivia 13 50S 65 40W
126 Santa Ana, Ecuador 1 10S 80 20W
120 Santa Ana, Mexico 30 31N 111 8W
124 Santa Ana, Salvador 14 0N 89 40W
119 Santa Ana, U.S.A. 33 48N 117 55W
38 Sant' Angelo Lodigiano, Italy 45 14N 9 25E
40 Sant' Antioco, Italy 39 2N 8 30E
40 Sant' Antioco, I., Italy 39 2N 8 30E
39 Sant' Arcángelo di Romagna, Italy 44 4N 12 26E

32 Santa Bárbara, Spain 40 42N 0 29E
119 Santa Bárbara, U.S.A. 34 25N 119 40W
126 Santa Bárbara, Venezuela 7 47N 71 10W
33 Santa Bárbara, Mt., Sp. 37 23N 2 50W
119 Santa Barbara Is., U.S.A. 33 31N 119 0W
124 Santa Catalina, Colombia 10 36N 75 17W
119 Santa Catalina, G. of, U.S.A. 33 0N 118 0W
119 Santa Catalina, I., U.S.A. 33 20N 118 30W
125 Santa Catarina, I. de, Braz. 27 30S 48 40W
125 Santa Catarina ♦, Brazil 27 25S 48 30W
41 Santa Caterina, Italy 37 37N 14 1E
125 Santa Cecilia, Brazil 26 56S 50 27W
121 Santa Clara, Cuba 22 20N 80 0W
119 Santa Clara, Calif., U.S.A. 37 21N 122 0W
119 Santa Clara, Utah, U.S.A. 37 10N 113 38W
125 Santa Clara de Olimar, Uruguay 32 50S 54 54W
125 Santa Clotilde, Peru 2 25S 73 45W
32 Santa Coloma de Farnés, Spain 41 50N 2 39E
32 Santa Coloma de Gramanet, Spain 41 27N 2 13E
30 Santa Comba, Spain 43 2N 8 49W
41 Santa Croce Camerina, It. 36 50N 14 30E
128 Santa Cruz, Argentina 50 0S 68 50W
124 Santa Cruz, Chile 34 38S 71 27W
121 Santa Cruz, Costa Rica 10 15N 85 41W
73 Santa Cruz, Philippines 14 20N 121 30E
119 Santa Cruz, Calif., U.S.A. 36 55N 122 10W
35 Santa Cruz, N. Mexico, U.S.A. 35 59N 106 1W
110 Santa Cruz I., U.S.A. 34 0N 119 45W
128 Santa Cruz, R., Arg. 50 0S 70 0W
126 Santa Cruz ♦, Bolivia 17 43S 63 10W
33 Santa Cruz de Mudela, Sp. 38 39N 3 28W
48 Santa Cruz de Tenerife 28 10N 17 20W
30 Santa Cruz del Retamar, Spain 40 8N 4 14W
121 Santa Cruz del Sur, Cuba 20 50N 78 0W
125 Santa Cruz do Rio Pardo, Brazil 22 54S 49 37W
125 Santa Cruz do Sul, Braz. 29 42S 52 25W
124 Santa Elena, Argentina 30 58S 59 47W
121 Santa Elena, Costa Rica 10 54N 85 56W
126 Santa Elena, Ecuador 2 16S 80 52W
20 Santan Enimie, France 44 24N 3 26E
41 Sant' Eufémia, Golfo di, Italy 38 50N 16 10E
33 Santa Eulalia, Spain 40 34N 1 20W
124 Santa Fe, Argentina 31 35S 60 41W
32 Santa Fe, Spain 37 11N 3 43W
119 Santa Fe, U.S.A. 35 40N 106 0W
127 Santa Filomena, Brazil 9 0S 45 50W
41 Santa Groce di Magliano, Italy 41 43N 14 59E
128 Santa Inés, I., Chile 54 0S 73 0W
31 Santa Inés, Mt., Spain 38 32N 5 37W
124 Santa Isabel, Arg. 36 10S 67 0W
⁕85 Santa Isabel, Eq. Guinea 3 45N 8 50E
85 Santa Isabel, Pico, Eq. Guinea 3 43N 8 49E
124 Santa Lucía, Corrientes, Argentina 28 58S 59 5W
124 Santa Lucía, San Juan, Argentina 31 30S 68 45W
33 Santa Lucía, Spain 37 7N 0 58W
125 Santa Lucía, Uruguay 34 27S 56 24W
119 Santa Lucía Range, U.S.A. 36 0N 121 30W
124 Santa Margarita, Arg. 38 18S 61 35W
120 Santa Margarita, I., Mex. 24 30N 112 0W
38 Santa Margherita, Italy 44 20N 9 11E
124 Santa María, Argentina 26 40S 66 0W
125 Santa María, Brazil 29 40S 53 40W
41 Santa María, Italy 41 3N 14 29E
120 Santa María, Mexico 27 40N 114 40W
32 Santa María, Spain 39 39N 2 45E
119 Santa María, U.S.A. 34 58N 120 29W
91 Santa María, Zambia 11 5S 29 58E
120 Santa María, Bahía de, Mexico 25 0N 108 40W
31 Santa María, Cabo de, Portugal 36 39N 7 53W
127 Santa María da Vitória, Brazil 13 24S 44 12W
120 Santa María del Oro, Mexico 25 30N 105 20W
41 Santa Maria di Leuca, C., Italy 39 48N 18 20E
30 Santa María la Real de Nieva, Sp. 41 4N 4 24W
126 Santa Marta, Colombia 11 15N 74 13W
31 Santa Marta, Spain 38 37N 6 39W
110 Santa Marta, Sierra Nevada de, Colombia 10 55N 73 50W
30 Santa Marta, Ría de, Sp. 43 44N 7 45W
125 Santa Marta Grande, C., Brazil 28 43S 48 50W
119 Santa Monica, U.S.A. 34 0N 118 30W
118 Santa Napa, U.S.A. 38 28N 122 45W
31 Santa Olalla, Huelva, Sp. 37 54N 6 14W
31 Santa Olalla, Toledo, Sp. 40 2N 4 43W
41 Sant' Onofrio, Italy 38 42N 16 10E
119 Santa Paula, U.S.A. 34 20N 119 2W

⁕ *Renamed Rey Malabo*

MAP
33 Santa Pola, Spain 38 13N 0 35W
119 Santa Rita, U.S.A. 32 50N 108 0W
126 Santa Rita, Guarico, Venezuela 8 8N 66 16W
126 Santa Rita, Zulia, Venezuela 10 32N 71 32W
124 Santa Rosa, La Pampa, Argentina 36 40s 64 30W
124 Santa Rosa, San Luis, Argentina 32 30s 65 10W
126 Santa Rosa, Bolivia 10 25s 67 20W
125 Santa Rosa, Brazil 27 52s 54 29W
126 Santa Rosa, Colombia 3 32N 69 48W
120 Santa Rosa, Honduras 14 40N 89 0W
118 Santa Rosa, Calif., U.S.A. 38 20N 122 50W
117 Santa Rosa, N. Mexico, U.S.A. 34 58N 104 40W
126 Santa Rosa, Amazonas, Venezuela 1 29N 66 55W
126 Santa Rosa, Apure, Venezuela 6 37N 67 57W
119 Santa Rosa I., Calif., U.S.A. 34 0N 120 15W
115 Santa Rosa I., Fla., U.S.A. 30 23N 87 0W
118 Santa Rosa Mts., U.S.A. 41 45N 117 30W
126 Santa Rosa de Cabal, Col. 4 52N 75 38W
126 Santa Rosa de Osos, Col. 6 39N 75 28W
124 Santa Rosa de Rio Primero, Arg. 31 8s 63 20W
126 Santa Rosa de Viterbo, Col. 5 53N 72 59W
120 Santa Rosalia, Mexico 27 20N 112 30W
39 Santa Sofia, Italy 43 57N 11 55E
124 Santa Sylvina, Arg. 27 50s 61 10W
120 Santa Tecla = Nueva San Salvador, Sal. 13 40N 89 25W
124 Santa Teresa, Arg. 33 25s 60 47W
126 Santa Teresa, Ven. 4 43N 61 4W
39 Santa Teresa di Riva, It. 37 58N 15 21E
40 Santa Teresa Gallura, It. 41 14N 9 12E
125 Santa Vitória do Palmar, Brazil 33 32s 53 25W
40 Santadi, Italy 39 5N 8 42E
125 Santana, Coxilha de, Brazil 30 50s 55 35W
125 Santana do Livramento, Brazil 30 55s 55 30W
126 Santander, Colombia 3 1N 76 28W
30 Santander, Spain 43 27N 3 51W
30 Santander ♦, Spain 43 25N 4 0W
120 Santander Jiménez, Mex. 24 11N 98 29W
33 Santañy, Spain 39 20N 3 5E
118 Santaquin, U.S.A. 40 0N 111 51W
127 Santarém, Brazil 2 25s 54 42W
31 Santarém, Portugal 39 12N 8 42W
31 Santarém ♦, Portugal 39 10N 8 40W
41 Santèramo in Colle, It. 40 48N 16 45E
39 Santerno, R., Italy 44 10N 11 38E
24 Santhia, Italy 45 20N 8 10E
125 Santiago, Brazil 29 11s 54 52W
124 Santiago, Chile 33 24s 70 50W
121 Santiago, Dom. Rep. 19 30N 70 40W
121 Santiago, Panama 8 0N 81 0W
85 Santiago, Punta de, Eq. Guinea 3 12N 8 40E
128 Santiago ♦, Chile 33 30s 70 50W
30 Santiago de Compostela, Spain 42 52N 8 37W
121 Santiago de Cuba, Cuba 20 0N 75 49W
124 Santiago del Estero, Arg. 27 50s 64 15W
124 Santiago del Estero ♦, Argentina 27 50s 64 20W
31 Santiago do Cacém, Portugal 38 1N 8 42W
120 Santiago Ixcuintla, Mex. 21 50N 105 11W
120 Santiago Papasquiaro, Mexico 25 0N 105 20W
30 Santillana del Mar, Sp. 43 24N 4 6W
69 Santipur, India 23 17N 88 25E
33 Santisteban del Puerto, Spain 38 17N 3 15W
127 Santo Amaro, Baia, Brazil 12 30s 38 50W
125 Santo André, Brazil 23 39s 46 29W
125 Santo Angelo, Brazil 28 15s 54 15W
127 Santo Antonio, Mato Grosso, Brazil 15 50s 56 0W
88 Santo Antonio do Zaire, Angola 6 7s 12 20E
126 Santo Corazón, Bolivia 18 0s 58 45W
121 Santo Domingo, Dominican Republic 18 30N 70 0W
121 Santo Domingo, Nic. 12 14N 84 59W
32 Santo Domingo de la Calzada, Spain 42 26N 2 27W
41 Santo Stéfano di Camastro, Italy 38 1N 14 22E
39 Santo Stino di Livenza, Italy 45 45N 12 40E
30 Santo Tirso, Portugal 41 29N 8 18W
126 Santo Tomás, Peru 14 34s 72 30W
125 Santo Tomé, Argentina 28 40s 56 5W
30 Santoña, Spain 43 29N 3 20W
125 Santos, Brazil 24 0s 46 20W
31 Santos, Sierra de los, Spain 38 7N 5 12W
125 Santos Dumont, Brazil 22 55s 43 10W
77 Santu, China 25 59N 113 3E
77 Santuhao, China 26 36N 119 42E
62 Sanur, Jordan 32 22N 35 15E
19 Sanvignes-les-Mines, France 46 40N 4 18E
88 Sanza Pombo, Angola 7 18s 15 56E
125 São Anastacio, Brazil 22 0s 51 40W
31 São Bartolomeu de Messines, Portugal 37 15N 8 17W
125 São Borja, Brazil 28 45s 56 0W
31 São Bras d'Alportel, Portugal 37 8N 7 58W
125 São Carlos, Brazil 22 0s 47 50W
127 São Cristóvão, Brazil 11 15s 37 15W
127 São Domingos, Brazil 13 25s 46 10W
127 São Domingos, Port. Guin. 12 22N 16 8W
127 São Francisco, Brazil 16 0s 44 50W
127 São Francisco do Sul, Brazil 26 15s 48 36W
125 São Gabriel, Brazil 30 10s 54 30W
125 São Gonçalo, Brazil 22 48s 43 5w
91 São Hill, Tanz. 8 20s 35 18E
30 São João da Pesqueira, Portugal 41 8N 7 24W
125 São João del Rei, Braz. 21 8s 44 15W
127 São João do Piaui, Braz. 8 10s 42 50W
127 São José do Rio Prêto, Brazil 20 50s 49 20W
125 São José dos Campos, Brazil 23 7s 45 52W
125 São Leopoldo, Brazil 29 50s 51 10W
127 São Lourenço, Mato Grosso, Brazil 16 30s 55 5W
127 São Lourenço, R., Brazil 16 40s 56 0W
127 São Luís (Maranhão), Brazil 2 39s 44 15W
125 São Luis Conzaga, Braz. 28 25s 55 0W
125 São Marcelino, Brazil 1 0N 67 12W
127 São Marcos, B. de, Brazil 2 0s 44 0W
30 São Martinho, Portugal 39 30N 9 8W
127 São Mateus, Brazil 18 44s 39 50W
8 São Miguel, Azores 37 33N 25 27W
125 São Paulo, Brazil 23 40s 46 50W
125 São Paulo ♦, Brazil 22 0s 49 0W
30 São Pedro do Sul, Port. 40 46N 8 4W
126 São Romão, Amazonas, Brazil 5 53s 67 50W
127 São Roque, C. de, Brazil 5 30s 35 10W
88 São Salvador do Congo, Angola 6·18s 14 16E
125 São Sebastião do Paraiso, Brazil 20 54s 46 59W
31 São Teotónio, Portugal 37 30N 8 42W
125 São Tomé, C. de, Brazil 22 0s 41 10W
78 São Tomé, I., G. of Guin. 0 10N 7 0E
125 São Vicente, Brazil 23 57s 46 23W
31 São Vicente, Cabo de, 37 0N 9 0W
19 Sáone, R., France 46 25N 4 50E
19 Saône-et-Loire ♦, France 46 25N 4 50E
82 Saonek, Indonesia 0 28s 130 47E
82 Saoura, O., Algeria 29 55N 1 50W
73 Sapai, Greece 41 2N 25 43E
73 Saparua, I., Indonesia 3 33s 128 40E
85 Sapele, Nigeria 5 50N 5 40E
115 Sapelo I., U.S.A. 31 28N 81 15W
45 Sapiëntza I., Greece 36 33N 21 43E
59 Sapodnyy Sayan, U.S.S.R. 52 30N 94 0E
85 Saponne, Upper Volta 12 3N 1 35W
126 Saposoa, Peru 6 55s 76 30W
55 Sapozhok, U.S.S.R. 53 59N 40 51E
74 Sapporo, Japan 43 0N 141 15E
41 Sapri, Italy 40 5N 15 37E
73 Spudi, I., Indonesia 7 2s 114 17E
117 Sapulpa, U.S.A. 36 0N 96 40W
87 Saqota, Ethiopia 12 40N 39 1E
64 Saqqez, Iran 36 15N 46 20E
42 Sar Planina, Yugoslavia 42 10N 21 0E
65 Sar-i-Pul, Afghanistan 36 10N 66 0E
84 Sara, Upper Volta 11 40N 3 53W
65 Sarab, Iran 38 0N 47 30E
32 Saragossa, Spain 41 39N 0 53W
126 Saraguro, Ecuador 3 35s 79 16W
46 Sarai, Rumania 44 43N 28 10E
69 Saraipalli, India 21 20N 82 59E
42 Sarajevo, Yugoslavia 43 52N 18 26E
86 Saran, Saudi Arabia 19 35N 40 30E
82 Saran, G., Indonesia 0 30s 111 25E
113 Saranac Lake, U.S.A. 44 20N 74 10W
44 Saranda, Albania 39 59N 19 55E
90 Saranda, Tanzania 5 45s 34 59E
124 Sarandi Grande, Uruguay 33 20s 55 50W
73 Sarangani B., Phil. 6 0N 125 13E
73 Sarangani Is., Phil. 5 25N 125 25E
55 Saransk, U.S.S.R. 54 10N 45 10E
115 Sarasota, U.S.A. 27 10N 82 30W
118 Saratoga, U.S.A. 41 30N 106 56W
113 Saratoga Springs, U.S.A. 43 5N 73 47W
58 Saratok, Malaysia 3 5s 110 50E
55 Saratov, U.S.S.R. 51 30N 46 2E
71 Saravane, Laos 15 42N 106 3E
72 Sarawak ♦, Malaysia 2 0s 113 0E
84 Saraya, Senegal 12 50N 11 45W
65 Sarbaz, Iran 26 38N 61 19E
65 Sarbisheh, Iran 32 30N 59 40E
27 Sárbogárd, Hungary 46 55N 18 40E
38 Sarca, R., Italy 46 5N 10 68E
83 Sardalas, Libya 25 50N 10 54E
69 Sardarshahr, India 28 30N 74 29E
40 Sardegna, I., Italy 39 57N 9 0E
68 Sardhana, India 29 9N 77 39E
126 Sardinata, Colombia 8 5s 20 48W
40 Sardinia = Sardegna, Italy 39 57N 9 0E
87 Sardo, Ethiopia 11 56N 41 14E
50 Sarektjákká, Sweden 67 27N 17 43E
42 Sarengrad, Yugoslavia 45 14N 19 16E
84 Saréyamou, Mali 16 25N 3 00W
116 Sargent, U.S.A. 41 42N 99 24W
68 Sargodha, Pakistan 32 10N 72 40E
68 Sargodha ♦, Pakistan 31 50N 72 0E
6 Sargasso Sea, Atlan. Oc. 27 0N 72 0W
82 Sarhro, Jebel, Morocco 31 6N 5 0W

65 Sári, Iran 36 30N 53 11E
45 Sária, I., Greece 35 54N 27 17E
62 Sarida, R., Jordan 32 4N 35 3E
72 Sarikamis, Turkey 40 22N 42 35E
72 Sarikei, Malaysia 2 8N 111 30E
99 Sarina, Austral. 21 22s 149 13E
32 Sariñena, Spain 41 47N 0 10W
83 Sarir Tibasti, Libya 22 50N 18 30E
72 Sarita, U.S.A. 27 14N 90 49W
43 Sariyer, Turkey 41 10N 29 3E
18 Sark, I., Channel Is. 49 25s 2 20W
27 Sarkad, Hungary 46 47N 21 17E
20 Sarlat-la-Canéda, Fr. 44 54N 1 13E
116 Sarles, U.S.A. 48 58N 98 57W
46 Sărmasu, Rumania 46 45N 25 13E
48 Särna, Sweden 61 41N 12 58E
39 Sarnano, Italy 43 2N 13 17E
32 Sarnen, Switzerland 46 53N 8 13E
106 Sarnia, Canada 43 0N 82 30W
41 Sarno, Italy 40 48N 14 35E
54 Sarnowa, Poland 51 39N 16 53E
54 Sarny, U.S.S.R. 51 17N 26 40E
49 Särö, Sweden 57 31N 11 57E
72 Sarolangun, Indonesia 2 30s 102 30E
45 Saronikós Kólpos, Greece 37 45N 23 45E
44 Saros Körfezi, Turkey 40 30N 26 15E
27 Sárospatak, Hungary 48 18N 21 33E
42 Sarosul Romanesc, Rum. 45 34N 21 43E
47 Sarpsborg, Norway 59 16N 11 12E
32 Sarracin, Spain 42 15s 3 45W
20 Sarralbe, France 48 55N 7 1E
19 Sarre, R., France 48 49N 7 0E
20 Sarrebourg, France 48 43N 7 3E
19 Sarreguemines, France 49 1N 7 4E
30 Sarriá, Spain 42 41N 7 29W
32 Sarrión, Spain 40 9N 0 49W
84 Sarro, Mali 13 40N 5 5W
24 Sarstedt, Germany 52 13N 9 50E
18 Sartène, Corsica 41 38N 9 0E
18 Sarthe, R., France 47 33N 0 31W
18 Sarthe ♦, France 47 58N 0 10E
18 Sartilly, France 48 45N 1 28W
58 Sartynya, U.S.S.R. 63 30N 62 50E
86 Sarum, Saudi Arabia 21 11N 39 10E
65 Sarúr, Oman 23 17N 58 4E
27 Sárvár, Hungary 47 15N 16 56E
65 Sarveston, Iran 29 20N 53 10E
48 Särvfjället, Sweden 62 42N 13 30E
27 Sárviz, R., Hungary 46 40N 18 40E
58 Sary Tash, U.S.S.R. 39 45N 73 40E
56 Sarych, Mys., U.S.S.R. 44 25N 33 25E
58 Saryshagan, U.S.S.R. 46 12N 73 48E
46 Sarzana, Italy 44 7N 9 57E
18 Sarzeau, France 47 31N 2 48W
62 Sasa, Israel 33 2N 35 23E
69 Sasabeneh, Ethiopia 7 59N 44 43E
69 Sasaram, India 24 57N 84 5E
42 Sasca Montană, Rum. 44 41N 21 45E
74 Sasebo, Japan 33 15N 129 50E
65 Saser Mt., Kashmir 34 50N 77 50E
109 Saskatchewan, R., Can. 53 40N 103 30W
109 Saskatchewan ♦, Canada 52 10N 106 45W
93 Sasolburg, S. Afr. 26 46s 27 49E
55 Sasovo, U.S.S.R. 54 25N 41 55E
84 Sassandra, Ivory Coast 5 0N 6 8W
84 Sassandra, R., Ivory Coast 5 0N 6 8W
40 Sássari, Italy 40 44N 8 33E
24 Sassnitz, Germany 54 29N 13 39E
39 Sasso Marconi, Italy 44 22N 11 12E
39 Sassocorvaro, Italy 43 47N 12 30E
39 Sassoferrato, Italy 43 26N 12 51E
39 Sassuolo, Italy 44 31N 10 47E
42 Sástago, Spain 41 19N 0 21W
84 Sastown, Liberia 4 45N 8 27W
90 Sasumua Dam, Kenya 0 54s 36 46E
84 Sasyk, Ozero, U.S.S.R. 45 45N 30 0E
84 Satadougou, Mali 12 40N 11 25W
117 Satanta, U.S.A. 37 30N 101 0W
70 Satara, India 17 44N 73 58E
70 Satilla, R., U.S.A. 31 15N 81 50W
69 Satkhira, Bangladesh 22 43N 89 8E
69 Satmala Hills, India 20 15N 74 40E
69 Satna, India 24 35N 80 50E
39 Sator, mt., Yugoslavia 44 11N 16 43E
68 Satpura Ra., India 21 40N 75 0E
21 Satrup, Germany 54 39N 9 38E
70 Sattenpalle, India 16 25N 80 6E
46 Satu Mare, Rumania 47 46N 22 55E
72 Satui, Indonesia 3 50s 115 20E
46 Satumare ♦, Rumania 47 45N 23 0E
71 Satun, Thailand 6 43N 100 2E
124 Sauce, Argentina 30 5s 58 46W
47 Sauda, Norway 59 38N 6 21E
50 Sauðarkrókur, Iceland 65 45N 19 40W
63 Saudi Arabia ■, Asia 26 0N 44 0E
24 Sauerland, Ger. 51 0N 8 0E
112 Saugeen, R., Canada 44 20N 81 15W
113 Saugerties, U.S.A. 42 4N 73 58W
20 Saugues, France 44 58N 3 32E
47 Sauherad, Norway 59 25N 9 15E
82 Sauid el Amia, Maur. 25 57N 6 8W
20 Saujon, France 45 41N 0 55W
116 Sauk Center, U.S.A. 45 42N 94 56W
116 Sauk Rapids, U.S.A. 45 35N 94 10W
25 Saulgau, Germany 48 4N 9 32E
19 Saulieu, France 44 6N 5 24E
21 Sault, France 44 6N 5 24E
107 Sault Ste. Marie, Can. 46 30N 84 20W
114 Sault Ste. Marie, U.S.A. 46 27N 84 22W
98 Saumarez Reef, Australia 21 50s 153 40E
82 Saumlaki, Indonesia 7 55s 131 20E
18 Saumur, France 47 15N 0 5W
106 Saunders C., N.Z. 45 53s 170 45E
5 Saunders I., Falkland Is. 57 30s 27 30W
Dependencies

50 Saurbaer, Borgarfjarðarsýsla, Iceland 64 24N 21 35W
50 Saurbaer, Eyjafjarðarsýsla, Iceland 65 27N 18 13W
85 Sauri, Nigeria 11 50N 6 44E
126 Sautatá, Colombia 7 50N 77 4W
20 Sauveterre, B., France 43 25N 0 57W
20 Sauzé-Vaussais, France 46 8N 0 8E
41 Sava, Italy 40 28N 17 32E
39 Sava, R., Yugoslavia 44 40N 19 50E
116 Savage, U.S.A. 47 43N 104 20W
85 Savalou, Dahomey 7 57N 2 4E
98 Savannah Downs, Australia 19 30s 141 30E
91 Savane, Mozambique 19 37s 35 8E
116 Savanna, U.S.A. 42 5N 90 10W
121 Savanna la Mar, Jam. 18 10N 78 10w
115 Savannah, Ga., U.S.A. 32 4N 81 4W
116 Savannah, Mo., U.S.A. 39 55N 94 46W
115 Savannah, Tenn., U.S.A. 35 12N 88 18W
115 Savannah, R., U.S.A. 33 0N 81 30W
71 Savannakhet, Laos 16 30N 104 49E
106 Savant Lake, Canada 50 20N 90 40W
106 Savant Lake, Canada 50 16N 90 44W
70 Savantvadi, India 15 55N 73 54E
70 Savanur, India 14 59N 75 28E
68 Savda, India 21 9N 75 56E
85 Savé, Dahomey 8 2N 2 17E
64 Saveh, Iran 35 2N 50 20E
55 Savelovo, U.S.S.R. 56 51N 37 20E
85 Savelugu, Ghana 9 38N 0 54W
18 Savenay, France 47 20N 1 55W
20 Saverdun, France 43 14N 1 34E
19 Saverne, France 48 39N 7 20E
38 Savigliano, Italy 44 39N 7 40E
47 Savignac, Spain 42 53N 7 38W
18 Savigny-sur-Braye, Fr. 47 53N 0 49E
39 Savinao, Spain 42 35N 7 38W
39 Savio, R., Italy 43 58N 12 10E
42 Savnik, Yugoslavia 42 59N 19 10E
24 Savoie ♦, France 45 26N 6 35E
38 Savona, Italy 44 19N 8 29E
52 Savonlinna, Finland 61 55N 28 55E
49 Sävsjö, Sweden 57 20N 14 40E
49 Sävsjöström, Sweden 57 1N 15 25E
73 Savu, I., Indonesia 10 35s 121 50E
73 Savu Sea, E. Indies 9 30s 121 50E
24 Saxony, Lower = Niedersachsen, Germany
112 Saxton, U.S.A. 40 12N 79 18W
85 Say, Niger 13 8N 2 22E
85 Saya, Nigeria 9 30N 3 18E
107 Sayabec, Canada 48 35N 67 41W
59 Sayan, Vostochnyy, U.S.S.R. 54 0N 96 0E
59 Sayan, Zapadnyy, U.S.S.R. 52 30N 94 0E
126 Sayán, Peru 11 0s 77 25W
57 Sayansk, U.S.S.R. 42 56N 46 15E
64 Sayda, Lebanon 33 35N 35 25E
100 Sayer's Lake, Australia 32 40s 143 30E
76 Saynshand, Mongolia 44 55N 110 11E
117 Sayre, Okla., U.S.A. 35 20N 99 40W
113 Sayre, Pa., U.S.A. 42 0N 76 30W
120 Sayula, Mexico 19 50N 103 40W
113 Sayville, U.S.A. 40 45N 73 7W
44 Sazan, Albania 40 30N 19 20E
42 Sázava, R., Cz. 49 50N 15 0E
66 Sazin, Kashmir 35 35N 73 30E
83 Sazlika, R., Bulgaria 42 15N 25 50E
12 Sca Fell, Mt., Eng. 54 27N 3 14W
41 Scalea, Italy 39 49N 15 47E
108 Scandia, Canada 50 20N 112 0W
38 Scandiano, Italy 44 36N 10 40E
39 Scandinavia, Eur. 64 0N 12 0E
39 Scansano, Italy 42 40N 11 20E
12 Scapa Flow, Scot. 58 52N 3 0W
12 Scarborough, Eng. 54 17N 0 24W
121 Scarborough, Tobago 11 11N 60 42W
14 Scarpe, R., France 50 31N 3 27E
63 Scebeli, Uebi, Somali Rep. 2 0N 44 0E
112 Scenic, U.S.A. 43 49N 102 32W
24 Schaal See, Germany 53 40N 10 57E
32 Schaffhausen ♦, Switzerland 47 42N 8 36E
16 Schagen, Netherlands 52 49N 4 48E
24 Schärding, Austria 48 27N 13 27E
24 Scharhörn, I., Germany 53 58N 8 24E
24 Scharnitz, Austria 47 23N 11 15E
24 Scheessel, Germany 53 10N 9 33E
24 Scheibbs, Austria 48 1N 15 9E
16 Schelde, R., Belgium 51 10N 4 20E
113 Schenectady, U.S.A. 42 50N 73 58W
24 Scherfede, Germany 51 32N 9 2E
16 Schiedam, Netherlands 51 55N 4 25E
16 Schiermonnikoog, I., Neths. 53 30N 6 15E
25 Schifferstadt, Germany 49 22N 8 23E
19 Schiltigheim, France 48 35N 7 45E
73 Schio, Italy 45 42N 11 21E
19 Schirmeck, France 48 29N 7 12E
25 Schladming, Austria 47 23N 13 41E
24 Schlei, R., Germany 54 40N 9 52E
24 Schleiden, Germany 50 32N 6 26E
24 Schleswig, Germany 54 32N 9 34E
24 Schleswig-Holstein, Germany 54 10N 9 40E

MAP
24 Schleswig-Holstein ♦, Germany 54 10N 9 40E
25 Schlüchtern, Germany 50 20N 9 32E
24 Schmalkalden, Germany 50 43N 10 28E
26 Schmölln, Germany 50 54N 12 22E
26 Schneeberg, Germany 50 35N 12 39E
26 Schneeberg, Aust. 47 53N 15 55E
116 Schofield, U.S.A. 44 54N 89 39W
24 Schönberg, Rostock, Ger. 53 50N 10 55E
24 Schönberg, Schleswig-Holstein, Germany 54 23N 10 20E
24 Schönebeck, Germany 52 2N 11 42E
24 Schöningen, Germany 52 8N 10 57E
24 Schortens, Germany 53 37N 7 51E
73 Schouten, Kepulauan, Indonesia 1 0s 136 0E
16 Schouwen, I., Neth. 51 43N 3 45E
24 Schramberg, Germany 48 12N 8 24E
24 Schrankogl, Aust. 47 3N 11 7E
106 Schreiber, Canada 48 45N 87 20W
26 Schruns, Austria 47 5N 9 56E
106 Schumacher, Canada 48 30N 81 16W
118 Schurz, U.S.A. 38 59N 118 57W
113 Schuylkill Haven, U.S.A. 40 37N 76 11W
25 Schwabach, Germany 49 19N 11 3E
25 Schwäbisch Gmünd, West Germany 48 49N 9 48E
25 Schwäbisch Hall, West Germany 49 7N 9 45E
25 Schwäbischer Alb, West Germany 48 30N 9 30E
72 Schwaner, Pegunungan, Indonesia 1 0s 112 30E
76 Schwangcheng, China 45 27N 126 27E
76 Schwangyashan, China 46 35N 131 15E
26 Schwarzach, R., Austria 50 30N 11 30E
24 Schwarzenberg, Ger. 50 31N 12 49E
24 Schwarzwald, Germany 48 0N 8 0E
26 Schwaz, Austria 47 20N 11 44E
24 Schwedt, Germany 53 4N 14 18E
25 Schweinfurt, Germany 50 3N 10 12E
92 Schweizer Reneke, S. Africa 27 11s 25 18E
24 Schwenningen, Ger. 48 3N 8 32E
24 Schwerin, Germany 53 37N 11 22E
24 Schwerin ♦, Germany 53 35N 11 20E
24 Schweriner See, Ger. 53 45N 11 26E
25 Schwetzingen, Germany 49 22N 8 35E
25 Schwyz, Switzerland 47 2N 8 39E
25 Schwyz ♦, Switzerland 47 2N 8 39E
40 Sciacca, Italy 37 30N 13 3E
41 Scicli, Italy 36 48N 14 41E
116 Scioto, R., U.S.A. 39 0N 83 0W
116 Scobey, U.S.A. 48 47N 105 30W
99 Scone, Austral. 32 0s 150 52E
14 Scone, Scot. 56 25N 3 26W
4 Scoresby Sund, Green. 70 20N 23 0W
40 Scorno, Punta dello, Italy 41 7N 8 23E
118 Scotia, U.S.A. 40 36N 124 4W
5 Scotia Sea, Antarctica 56 5s 56 0W
25 Scotland ♦, U.K. 57 0N 4 0W
116 Scotland, U.S.A. 43 10N 97 45W
116 Scotland Neck, U.S.A. 36 6N 77 24W
5 Scott, Antarctica 77 0s 165 0E
5 Scott, C., Antarctica 71 30s 168 0E
118 Scott, C., Antarctica 67 0s 179 0E
105 Scott Inlet, Canada 71 0N 71 30W
109 Scott, L., Canada 60 0N 106 0W
108 Scott City, U.S.A. 38 30N 100 52W
93 Scottburgh, S. Afr. 30 15s 30 47E
112 Scottdale, U.S.A. 40 8N 79 35W
115 Scottsboro, U.S.A. 34 40N 86 0W
115 Scottsburg, U.S.A. 38 40N 85 46W
115 Scottsville, Ky., U.S.A. 36 48N 86 10W
113 Scottsville, N.Y., U.S.A. 43 2N 77 47W
98 Scottville, Australia 20 35s 147 40E
114 Scottville, U.S.A. 43 57N 86 18W
113 Scranton, U.S.A. 41 22N 75 41W
112 Scugog L., Canada 44 8N 78 53W
12 Scunthorpe, Eng. 53 35N 0 38W
63 Scusciuban, Somali Rep. 10 28N 50 5E
124 Sea Breeze, U.S.A. 43 12N 77 32W
100 Sea Lake, Austral. 35 28s 142 55E
118 Seaford, Australia 38 10s 145 11E
114 Seaford, U.S.A. 38 37N 75 36W
106 Seaforth, Canada 43 35N 81 25W
126 Seagraves, U.S.A. 32 56N 102 30W
109 Seal, R., Canada 58 50N 97 30W
107 Seal Cove, Can. 49 57N 56 22W
117 Sealy, U.S.A. 29 46N 96 9W
119 Searchlight, U.S.A. 35 31N 111 57W
117 Searcy, U.S.A. 35 15N 91 45W
119 Searles, L., U.S.A. 35 47N 117 17W
118 Searles L., U.S.A. 45 59N 124 0W
100 Seaspray, Austral. 38 25s 147 15E
98 Seaview Ra., Australia 19 0s 146 10E
120 Sebastián Vizcaino, Bahia, Mexico 28 0N 114 30W
118 Sebastopol, U.S.A. 38 16N 122 56W
82 Sebderat, Ethiopia 15 26N 36 42E
82 Sebdou, Algeria 34 38N 1 19W
46 Sebeşului, Mții., Rumania 45 56N 23 40E
114 Sebewaing, U.S.A. 43 45N 83 27W
54 Sebezh, U.S.S.R. 56 14N 28 22E
56 Sebi, Mali 15 50N 4 12W
56 Sebinkarahisar, Tur. 40 22N 38 28E
46 Sebiş, Rumania 46 23N 22 13E

MAP

82 Sebkra Azzel Mati. Alg. 26 10N 0 43E
82 Sebkra Mekerghene, Alg. 26 21N 1 30E
82 Sebou, Oued, Morocco 34 16N 6 40w
115 Sebring, Fla., U.S.A. 27 36N 81 47w
112 Sebring, Ohio, U.S.A. 40 55N 81 2w
112 Sebringville, Canada 43 25N 81 4w
82 Sebta = Ceuta, 35 52N 5 26w
   Morocco
72 Sebuku, I., Indonesia 3 30s 116 25E
72 Sebuku, Teluk, Sabah 4 0N 118 10E
42 Sečanj, Yugoslavia 45 25N 20 47E
38 Secchia, R., Italy 44 30N 10 40E
108 Sechelt, Canada 49 25N 123 42w
126 Sechura, Desierto de, 6 0s 80 30w
   Peru
19 Seclin, France 50 33N 3 2E
18 Secondigny, France 46 37N 0 26w
27 Sečovce, Cz. 48 42N 21 40E
101 Secretary I., N.Z. 45 15s 166 56E
70 Secunderabad, India 17 28N 78 30E
31 Seda, R., Portugal 39 6N 7 53w
116 Sedalia, U.S.A. 38 40N 93 18w
19 Sedan, France 49 43N 4 57E
99 Sedan, Australia 34 35s 139 29E
117 Sedan, U.S.A. 37 10N 96 11w
32 Seddon, Spain 42 43N 3 49w
101 Seddon, New Zealand 41 40s 174 7E
101 Seddonville, N.Z. 41 33s 172 1E
62 Sede Ya'aqov, Israel 32 43N 35 7E
92 Sederberg, Mt., S. Afr. 32 22s 19 7E
108 Sedgewick, Canada 52 48N 111 41w
84 Sedhiou, Senegal 12 50N 15 30w
39 Sédico, Italy 46 8N 12 6E
26 Sedičany, Cz. 49 40N 14 25E
43 Sedinenie, Bulgaria 42 16N 24 33E
109 Sedley, Canada 50 10N 104 0w
62 Sedom, Israel 31 5N 35 20E
58 Sedova, Pik, U.S.S.R. 73 20N 55 10E
83 Sédrata, Algeria 36 7N 7 31E
118 Sedro Woolley, U.S.A. 48 30N 122 15w
54 Seduva, U.S.S.R. 55 45s 23 45E
27 Sedziszów Małapolski, 50 5N 21 45E
   Poland
24 Seebad Ahlbeck, 53 56N 14 10E
   Germany
26 Seefeld, Germany 51 53N 13 17E
24 Seehausen, Germany 52 52N 11 43E
92 Seeheim, S.W. Africa 26 32s 17 52E
24 Seekoe, R., S. Afr. 30 34s 24 45E
24 Seelaw, Germany 52 32N 14 22E
18 Sées, France 48 38N 0 10E
24 Seesen, Germany 51 53N 10 10E
84 Sefadu, Sierra Leone 8 35N 10 58w
84 Séfeto, Mali 14 8N 9 49w
82 Sefrou, Morocco 33 52N 4 52w
84 Sefwi Bekwai, Ghana 6 10N 2 25w
58 Seg-ozero, U.S.S.R. 63 0N 33 10E
71 Segamat, Malaysia 2 30N 102 50E
46 Segarcea, Rumania 44 6N 23 43E
84 Segbwema, Sierra Leone 8 0N 11 0w
73 Seget, Indonesia 1 24s 130 58E
82 Seggueur, O., Algeria 32 4N 2 4E
87 Segid, Saudi Arabia 16 55N 42 0E
20 Segonzac, France 45 36N 0 14w
32 Segorbe, Spain 39 50N 0 30w
84 Ségou, Mali 13 30N 6 10w
30 Segovia, Spain 40 57N 4 10w
30 Segovia ◆, SPain 40 55N 4 10w
18 Segré, France 47 40N 0 52w
32 Segre, R., Spain 41 40N 0 43E
84 Ségéla, Ivory Coast 7 55N 6 40w
117 Segundo, U.S.A. 37 12N 104 50w
124 Segundo, R., Argentina 30 53s 62 44w
33 Segura, R., Spain 38 9N 0 40w
33 Segura, Sierra de, Spain 38 5N 2 45w
68 Sehore, India 23 10N 77 5E
68 Sehwan, Pakistan 26 28N 67 53E
46 Seica Mare, Rumania 46 1N 24 7E
117 Seiling, U.S.A. 36 10N 99 5w
21 Seille, R., France 46 31N 4 57E
18 Seine, R., France 49 28N 0 15E
19 Seine ◆, France 49 0N 3 0E
19 Seine-et-Marne ◆, 48 45N 3 0E
   France
18 Seine- Maritime ◆, 49 40N 1 0E
   France
19 Seine-Saint-Denis ◆, 48 58N 2 24E
   France
46 Seini, Rumania 47 44N 23 21E
65 Seistan, Iran 30 50N 61 0E
86 Seiyala, Egypt 22 57N 32 41E
126 Sejal, Colombia 2 45N 68 0w
49 Sejerby, Denmark 55 54N 11 10E
49 Sejerø, Denmark 55 54N 11 15E
49 Sejerø Bugt, Denmark 55 53N 11 9E
87 Seka, Ethiopia 8 10N 36 52E
72 Sekaju, Indonesia 2 58s 103 58E
90 Seke, Tanzania 3 20s 33 31E
90 Sekenke, Tanz. 4 18s 34 11E
77 Sekibi-shō, Japan 25 45N 124 35E
118 Sekiu, U.S.A. 48 30N 124 29w
82 Sekkane, Erg in, Mali 20 30N 1 30w
84 Sekondi, Ghana 5 2N 1 48w
92 Sekuma, Botswana 24 36s 23 57E
87 Sela Dingay, Ethiopia 9 58N 39 32E
118 Selah, U.S.A. 46 44N 120 30w
71 Selama, Malaysia 5 12N 100 42E
71 Selangor ◆, Malaysia 3 20N 101 30E
40 Selargius, Sardinia 39 14N 9 14E
73 Selaru, I., Indonesia 8 18s 131 0E
72 Selat Bangka, Indonesia 2 30s 105 30E
72 Seletan, Tg., Indon. 4 10s 114 40E
25 Selb, Germany 50 9N 12 9E
116 Selby, England 53 47N 1 5w
116 Selby, U.S.A. 45 34N 99 55w
39 Selce, Yugoslavia 45 10N 14 41E
116 Selden, U.S.A. 39 24N 100 39w
41 Sele, R., Italy 40 27N 15 0E
76 Selenga, R. = Selenge 49 25N 103 45E
   Mörön, Mongolia

76 Selenge, Mongolia 49 25N 103 59E
76 Selenge Mörön, 52 16N 106 16E
   Mongolia
44 Selenica, Albania 40 33N 19 39E
24 Selenter See, Germany 54 19N 10 26E
19 Selestat, France 48 10N 7 26E
48 Selet, Sweden 63 15N 15 45E
46 Seletin, Rumania 47 50N 25 12E
42 Selevac, Yugoslavia 44 44N 20 52E
116 Selfridge, U.S.A. 46 3N 100 57w
84 Sélibaby, Mauritania 15 20N 12 15w
58 Seliger, Oz., U.S.S.R. 57 15s 33 0E
119 Seligman, U.S.A. 35 17N 112 56w
90 Selim, Cen. Africa 5 31N 23 48E
57 Selim, Turkey 40 15N 42 58E
86 Selima, El Wâhât el, 21 28N 29 31E
   Sudan
92 Selinda Spillway, Bots. 18 35s 23 10E
45 Selinoús, Greece 38 57N 21 34E
69 Selipuk Gompa, Tibet 31 23N 82 49E
54 Selizharovo, U.S.S.R. 57 1N 33 17E
47 Selje, Norway 62 3N 5 22E
47 Seljord, Norway 59 30N 8 40E
109 Selkirk, Canada 50 10N 97 20w
14 Selkirk, Scotland 55 33N 2 50w
14 Selkirk ◆, Scotland 55 30N 3 0w
108 Selkirk Mts., Canada 51 0N 117 10w
19 Selles-sur-Cher, France 47 16N 1 33E
19 Sellières, France 46 50N 5 32E
119 Sells, U.S.A. 31 57N 111 57w
27 Sellye, Hungary 45 52N 17 51E
115 Selma, Ala., U.S.A. 32 30N 87 0w
119 Selma, Calif., U.S.A. 36 39N 119 39w
115 Selma, N.C., U.S.A. 35 32N 78 15w
115 Selmer, U.S.A. 35 9N 88 36w
44 Sélo, Oros, Greece 41 10N 126 0E
19 Selongey, France 47 36N 5 10E
91 Selowandoma Falls, 21 15s 31 50E
   Rhod.
73 Selpele, Indonesia 0 1s 130 5E
13 Selsey Bill, Eng. 50 44N 0 47w
19 Seltz, France 48 48N 8 4E
73 Selu, I., Indonesia 7 26s 130 55E
91 Selukwe, Rhodesia 19 40s 30 0E
18 Sélune, R., France 48 38N 1 22w
124 Selva, Argentina 29 50s 62 0w
32 Selva, Spain 41 13N 1 8E
126 Selvas, Brazil 6 30s 67 0w
98 Selwyn, Australia 21 30s 140 29E
109 Selwyn L., Canada 60 0N 104 30w
98 Selwyn Ra., Australia 21 10s 140 0E
44 Semani, R., Albania 40 45N 19 50E
73 Semarang, Indonesia 7 0s 110 26E
87 Sembabule, Ugan. 0 4s 31 25E
55 Semenov, U.S.S.R. 56 43N 44 30E
56 Semenovka, U.S.S.R. 49 37N 33 2E
73 Semeru, Mt., Indonesia 8 4s 113 4E
84 Sémi, Senegal 15 4N 13 41w
55 Semiluki, U.S.S.R. 51 41N 39 10E
118 Seminoe Res., U.S.A. 42 0N 107 0w
117 Seminole, Okla., U.S.A. 35 15N 96 45w
117 Seminole, Tex., U.S.A. 32 41N 102 38w
58 Semiozernoye, U.S.S.R. 52 35N 64 0E
58 Semipalatinsk, U.S.S.R. 50 30N 80 10E
73 Semirara Is., Phil. 12 0N 121 20E
72 Semitau, Indonesia 0 29N 111 57E
58 Semiyarskoye, U.S.S.R. 50 55N 78 30E
26 Semmering Pass., Aust. 47 41N 15 45E
65 Semnan, Iran 35 55s 53 25E
65 Semnan ◆, Iran 36 0N 54 0E
65 Semois, R., Belgium 49 53N 4 44E
73 Semporna, Malaysia 4 30N 118 33E
2 Semuda, Indonesia 2 51s 112 58E
19 Semur-en-Auxois, Fr. 47 30N 4 20E
71 Sen. R., Khmer Rep. 13 45N 105 12E
126 Sena Madureira, Brazil 9 5s 68 45w
127 Senador Pompeu, Brazil 5 40s 39 20w
71 Senai, Malaysia 1 38N 103 38E
72 Senaja, Malaysia 6 49s 117 2E
92 Senanga, Zambia 16 2s 23 14E
117 Senatobia, U.S.A. 34 38N 89 57w
87 Sendafa, Ethiopia 9 11N 39 3E
74 Sendai, Kagoshima, Jap. 31 50N 130 20E
74 Sendai, Miyagi, Japan 38 15N 141 0E
70 Sendamangalam, India 11 17N 78 17E
92 Sendeling's Drift, S.W. 28 12s 16 52E
   Afr.
24 Sendenhorst, Germany 51 50N 7 49E
68 Sendurjana, India 21 32N 78 24E
72 Senduruhan, Indonesia 0 1s 110 46E
27 Senec, Czechoslovakia 48 12N 17 23E
118 Seneca, Oreg., U.S.A. 44 10N 119 2w
115 Seneca, S.C., U.S.A. 34 43N 82 59w
112 Seneca, L., U.S.A. 42 40N 76 58w
112 Seneca Falls, U.S.A. 42 55N 76 50w
84 Senegal ■, W. Africa 14 30N 14 30w
84 Senegal, R., W. Africa 16 30N 15 30w
93 Senekal, S. Afr. 28 18s 27 36E
24 Senftenberg, Germany 51 30N 13 51E
91 Senga Hill, Zam. 9 19s 31 11E
68 Senge Khambab (Indus), 28 40N 70 10E
   R., Pak.
55 Sengiley, U.S.S.R. 53 58N 48 54E
91 Sengwa, R., Rhod. 17 10s 28 15E
127 Senhor-do-Bonfim, Braz. 10 30s 40 10w
27 Senica, Czechoslovakia 48 41N 17 25E
39 Senigállia, Italy 43 42N 13 12E
39 Senio, R., Italy 44 35N 12 15E
39 Senj, Yugoslavia 45 0N 14 58E
50 Senja, Norway 69 25N 17 20E
77 Senkaku-guntō, Japan 25 30N 123 30E
19 Senlis, France 49 13N 2 35E
71 Senmonorom, Khmer 12 50N 107 15E
   Rep.

18 Senonches, France 48 34N 1 2E
40 Senorbi, Sardinia 39 33N 9 8E
39 Senozeče, Yugoslavia 45 43N 14 3E
19 Sens, France 48 11N 3 15E
42 Senta, Yugoslavia 45 55N 20 3E
20 Sentein, France 42 53N 0 58E
90 Sentery, Zaïre 5 17s 25 42E
119 Sentinel, U.S.A. 32 56N 113 13w
71 North Sentinel, I., 11 35N 92 15E
   Andaman Is.
71 South Sentinel, I., 11 1N 92 16E
   Andaman Is.
73 Sentolo, Indonesia 7 55s 110 13E
85 Senya Beraku, Ghana 5 28N 0 31w
32 Seo de Urgel, Spain 42 22N 1 23E
68 Seohara, India 29 15N 78 33E
68 Seoni, India 22 5N 79 30E
69 Seorinayan, India 21 45N 82 34E
107 Separation Point, Can. 53 40N 57 16w
98 Sepik, R., Terr. of New 4 5s 143 0E
   Guinea
28 Sepólno Krajeńskie, 53 26N 17 30E
   Poland
71 Sepone, Laos 16 45N 106 13E
92 Sepopa, Botswana 18 49s 22 12E
28 Sepopol, Poland 54 16N 21 2E
107 Sept Iles, Canada 50 13N 66 22w
43 Septemvri, Bulgaria 42 13N 24 6E
31 Septimus, Australia 21 20s 148 35E
30 Sepúlveda, Spain 41 18N 3 45w
30 Sequeros, Spain 40 31N 6 2w
119 Sequoia Nat. Park, 36 20N 118 30w
   U.S.A.
57 Serafimovich, U.S.S.R. 49 30N 42 50E
16 Seraing, Belgium 50 35N 5 32E
73 Seram, I., Indonesia 3 10s 129 0E
73 Serampore, India 22 44N 88 30E
73 Serang, Indonesia 6 8s 106 10E
21 Seravezza, I., Indonesia 2 29N 109 4E
38 Seravezza, Italy 43 59N 10 13E
42 Serbia = Srbija, Y.-slav. 43 30N 21 0E
46 Sercaia, Rumania 45 49N 25 9E
87 Serdo, Ethiopia 11 56N 41 14E
54 Serdobsk, U.S.S.R. 52 28N 44 10E
71 Seremban, Malaysia 2 43N 101 53E
90 Serengeti Plain, Tanz. 2 40s 35 0E
72 Sergach, U.S.S.R. 55 30N 45 30E
32 Serge, R., Spain 42 5N 1 21E
72 Sergievsk, U.S.S.R. 54 0N 51 10E
72 Seria, Brunei 4 37N 114 30E
72 Seriate, Italy 45 42N 9 43E
19 Sérifontaine, France 49 20N 1 45E
44 Sérifos, I., Greece 37 9N 24 30E
20 Sérignan, France 43 17N 3 17E
64 Serik, Turkey 36 55N 31 10E
19 Sermaize-les-Bains, Fr. 48 47N 4 54E
21 Sermata, I., Indonesia 8 15s 128 50E
39 Sérmide, Italy 45 0N 11 17E
84 Sero, Mali 14 42N 10 59w
32 Serón, Spain 37 20N 2 29w
32 Serós, Spain 41 27N 0 24E
58 Serov, U.S.S.R. 59 40N 60 20E
92 Serowe, Botswana 22 25s 26 43E
31 Serpa, Portugal 37 57N 7 38E
89 Serpa Pinto, Angola 14 48s 17 52E
40 Serpeddi, Punta, Italy 39 19N 9 28E
40 Serpentara, Italy 39 8N 9 38E
126 Serpent's Mouth, 10 0N 61 30w
   Trinidad
31 Serpis, R., Spain 38 45N 0 21w
54 Serpukhov, U.S.S.R. 54 55N 37 28E
89 Sa. da Canastra, Brazil 19 30s 46 5w
41 Serra Capriola, Italy 41 47N 15 12E
127 Serra do Salitre, Brazil 19 6s 46 41w
30 Serradilla, Spain 39 50N 6 9w
44 Sérrai ◆, Greece 41 5s 23 37E
40 Serramanna, Sard. 39 26N 8 56E
30 Serrania de Cuenca, Sp. 40 10N 1 50w
83 Serrat, C., Tunisia 37 14N 9 10E
124 Serrezuela, Argentina 30 40s 65 20w
127 Serrinha, Brazil 11 39s 39 0w
31 Sersale, Italy 39 1N 16 44E
30 Sertã, Portugal 39 48N 8 6w
83 Sertânia, Brazil 8 5s 37 20w
127 Sertão, Brazil 10 0s 40 20w
73 Serui, P., Indonesia 6 18s 130 1E
73 Serui, Indonesia 1 45s 136 10E
92 Serule, Botswana 21 57s 27 11E
44 Sérvia, Greece 40 9N 21 58E
100 Serviceton, Austral. 36 25s 141 55E
3 Sesajap Lama, Indon. 3 32N 117 11E
90 Sese Is., Uganda 0 30s 32 30E
73 Sesepe, Indonesia 1 30s 127 59E
19 Sesfontein, S. Africa 19 7s 13 39E
41 Sesia, R., Italy 45 35N 8 23E
31 Sesimbra, Portugal 38 28N 9 0w
39 Sessa Aurunca, Italy 41 14N 13 55E
76 Sessy, China 42 40N 110 30E
32 Sestao, Spain 43 18N 3 0w
38 Sesto S. Giovanni, Italy 45 32N 9 14E
38 Sestri Levante, Italy 44 17N 9 22E
38 Sestrières, Italy 44 58N 6 56E
40 Sestu, Sardinia 39 18N 9 6E
20 Sète, France 43 25N 3 42E
55 Sete Lagoas, Brazil 19 27s 44 16w
82 Sétif, Algeria 36 9N 5 26E
19 Settat, Morocco 33 0N 7 40w
88 Setté Cama, Gabon 2 32s 9 57E
39 Séttimo Tor, Italy 45 9N 7 46E
12 Settle, England 54 5N 2 18w
115 Settlement Pt., Bahamas 26 40N 79 0w
38 Setto Calende, Italy 45 44N 8 37E

31 Setúbal, Portugal 38 30N 8 58w
31 Setúbal, B. de, Port. 38 40N 8 56w
31 Setúbal ◆, Portugal 38 25N 8 35w
106 Seul L., Canada 50 25N 92 30w
72 Seulimeum, Indonesia 5 27N 95 15E
56 Sevastopol, U.S.S.R. 44 35N 33 30E
31 Sever, R., Sp. -Port. 39 40N 7 32w
106 Severn, R., Canada 44 52N 79 30w
13 Severn, R., Eng. 52 35N 2 38w
59 Severnaya Zemlya, 79 0N 100 0E
   U.S.S.R.
52 Severnye Uvaly, 58 0N 48 0E
   U.S.S.R.
59 Severo-Kurilsk, U.S.S.R. 50 40N 156 8E
57 Severodonetsk, U.S.S.R. 48 50N 38 30E
58 Severodvinsk, U.S.S.R. 64 27N 39 58E
27 Severomoravsky ◆, 49 38N 17 40E
   Czechoslovakia
119 Sevier, U.S.A. 38 39N 112 11w
118 Sevier L., U.S.A. 39 0N 113 20w
119 Sevier, R., U.S.A. 39 10N 112 50w
126 Sevilla, Colombia 4 16N 75 57w
31 Sevilla, Spain 37 23N 6 0w
31 Sevilla ◆, Spain 37 0N 6 0w
31 Seville = Sevilla, Spain 37 23N 6 0w
39 Sevnica, Yugoslavia 46 2N 15 19E
54 Sevsk, U.S.S.R. 52 10N 34 30E
104 Seward, U.S.A. 60 0N 149 40w
104 Seward Pen., Alaska 65 0N 164 0w
101 Shannon, N.Z. 40 33s 175 25E
128 Sewell, Chile 34 10s 70 45w
73 Sewer, Indonesia 5 46s 134 40E
119 Sequim, U.S.A. 48 3N 123 9w
3 Seychelles, Is., Indian 5 0s 56 0E
   Ocean
50 Sey ðisfjörður, Iceland 65 16N 14 0w
65 Seym, R., U.S.S.R. 51 45N 35 0E
59 Seymchan, U.S.S.R. 62 40N 152 30E
13 Seymour, Austral. 36 58s 145 10E
113 Seymour, Conn., U.S.A. 41 23N 73 5w
114 Seymour, Ind., U.S.A. 39 0N 85 50w
117 Seymour, Tex., U.S.A. 33 35N 99 18w
114 Seymour, Wis., U.S.A. 44 30N 88 20w
21 Seyne, France 44 21N 6 22E
39 Sezana, Yugoslavia 45 43N 13 41E
19 Sézanne, France 48 40N 3 40E
21 Sezze, Italy 41 30N 13 3E
83 Sfax, Tunisia 34 49N 10 48E
46 Sfîntu Gheorghe, Rum. 45 52N 25 48E
16 's-Gravenhage, Neth. 51 47N 4 37E
16 's-Gravenhage, Neth. 52 7N 4 17E
67 Shaba Gamba, Tibet, 32 8N 88 55E
   China
91 Shabani, Rhodesia 20 17s 30 2E
43 Shabla, Bulgaria 43 31N 28 32E
107 Shabogama L., Canada 48 40N 77 0w
90 Shabunda, Zaïre 2 40s 27 16E
5 Shackleton, Antarctica 78 30s 36 1w
5 Shackleton Inlet, Ant. 83 0s 160 0E
86 Shaddad, Saudi Arabia 21 25N 40 2E
85 Shadwan, Egypt 27 30N 34 0E
85 Shaffa, Nigeria 10 30N 12 6E
119 Shafter, U.S.A. 35 32N 119 14w
13 Shaftesbury, Eng. 51 0N 2 12w
85 Shagamu, Nigeria 6 51N 3 39E
68 Shah Bunder, Pakistan 24 13N 67 56E
70 Shahabad, And. P., India 17 10N 78 11E
68 Shahabad, Raj., India 25 15N 77 11E
68 Shahabad, Punjab, India 30 10N 76 55E
27 Shahabad, Uttar Pradesh, 27 36N 79 56E
   India
65 Shahābād, Iran 37 40N 56 50E
70 Shahapur, India 11 33N 74 34E
65 Shāhbâd, Iran 15 50N 74 34E
76 Shahcheng, China 40 18N 115 27E
65 Shāhdād, Iran 30 30N 57 40E
70 Shahdadkot, Pakistan 27 50N 67 55E
68 Shahdadpur, Pakistan 25 55N 68 35E
69 Shahganj, India 26 3N 82 44E
81 Shahhat (Cyrene), Libya 32 40N 21 35E
69 Shahjahanpur, India 27 54N 79 57E
76 Shahcheng, China 28 29N 113 2E
70 Shahpur, Mysore, India 16 40N 76 48E
70 Shanpur, Mad. P., India 22 12N 77 58E
68 Shahpur, India 32 12N 44 45E
68 Shahpur, Pakistan 28 46N 68 27E
65 Shahr Kord, Iran 32 15N 50 55E
65 Shahr-e Babak, Iran 30 7N 55 0E
64 Shahraban, Iraq 34 0N 45 0E
65 Shahreza, Iran 32 0N 51 55E
68 Shahrig, Pakistan 30 15N 67 40E
65 Shahrud, Iran 32 0N 51 50E
65 Shahrukh, Iran 33 50N 60 10E
77 Shahsien, China 26 25N 117 50E
65 Shahsavar, Iran 36 45N 51 12E
65 Shaibara, Saudi Arabia 25 26N 36 47E
65 Shaikhabad, Afghan. 34 0N 68 45E
68 Shajapur, India 23 20N 76 15E
68 Shakargarh, Pakistan 32 17N 75 43E
92 Shakawe, Botswana 18 28s 21 49E
55 Shakhty, U.S.S.R. 47 40N 40 0E
85 Shaki, Nigeria 8 40N 3 21E
116 Shakopee, U.S.A. 44 45N 93 30w
87 Shala Lake, Ethiopia 7 30N 38 30E
112 Shallow Lake, Canada 44 37N 81 6w
77 Shalu, Taiwan 24 24N 120 26E
82 Sham, J. esh, Oman 23 10N 57 5E
85 Shama, Ghana 5 1N 1 42w
65 Shamar, Jabal, Si. 27 40N 41 0E
   Arabia
7 Shambe, Sudan 7 8N 30 46E
8 Shambu, Ethiopia 9 32N 37 3E
68 Shamil, India 29 32N 77 18E

65 Shamil, Iran 27 30N 56 55E
57 Shamkhor, U.S.S.R. 40 56N 46 0E
75 Shamo (Gobi), Asia 44 0N 111 0E
87 Shamo, L., Ethiopia 5 45N 37 30E
113 Shamokin, U.S.A. 40 47N 76 33w
117 Shamrock, U.S.A. 35 15N 100 15w
67 Shan ◆, Burma 21 30N 98 30E
87 Shanan, R., Ethiopia 8 0N 40 20E
85 Shanga, Nigeria 11 9N 5 2E
91 Shangalowe, Zaïre 10 50s 26 30E
91 Shangani, Rhod. 19 1s 28 51E
91 Shangani, R., Rhod. 18 35s 27 45E
77 Shangch'eng, China 31 44N 115 22E
76 Shangchih, (Chuho), 45 10N 127 59E
   China
77 Shangchwan Shan, China 21 35N 112 45E
77 Shanghai, China 31 10N 121 25E
77 Shanghsien, China 33 30N 109 58E
77 Shangkiu, China 34 28N 115 42E
77 Shangshui, China 33 42N 115 .4E
77 Shangtse, China 22 0N 107 45E
76 Shangtu, China 41 31N 113 35E
77 Shangyu, China 25 59N 114 29E
76 Shanh, Mongolia 47 5N 103 5E
85 Shani, Nigeria 10 14N 12 2E
118 Shaniko, U.S.A. 45 0N 120 15w
4 Shannon, Greenland 75 10N 18 30E
101 Shannon, N.Z. 40 33s 175 25E
4 Shannon I., Greenland 75 0N 18 0w
15 Shannon, R., Ireland 53 10N 8 10w
59 Shantar, Ostrov Bolshoi, 55 9N 137 40E
   U.S.S.R.
77 Shantow, (Swatow), 23 25N 116 40E
   China
77 Shanyang, China 33 3N 110 2E
77 Shaohsing, China 30 0N 120 32E
77 Shaowu, China 27 25N 117 30E
77 Shaoyang, China 27 10N 111 30E
14 Shapinsay I., Scot. 59 2N 2 50w
64 Shaqra, Saudi Arabia 25 15N 45 16E
87 Sharafa (Ogr), Sudan 11 59N 27 7E
70 Sharavati, R., India 14 32N 5 0E
113 Sharbot Lake, Canada 44 47N 76 41w
65 Sharhjui, Afghanistan 32 30N 67 22E
65 Shari, Saudi Arabia 27 0N 43 45E
76 Sharin Gol, Mongolia 49 12N 106 27E
96 Shark B., Australia 25 15s 133 20E
86 Sharm el Sheikh, Egypt 27 53N 34 15E
112 Sharon, U.S.A. 41 18N 80 30w
62 Sharon, Plain of = 32 12N 34 49E
   Hasharon, Israel
106 Sharpe, L., Canada 54 10N 93 21w
112 Sharpsburg, U.S.A. 40 30N 79 56w
112 Sharpsville, U.S.A. 41 16N 80 28w
5 Sharya, U.S.S.R. 58 12N 45 40E
87 Shasha, Ethiopia 6 29N 35 59E
87 Shashemene, Ethiopia 7 13N 38 33E
91 Shashi, R., Rhod. & 21 40s 28 40E
   Botswana
77 Shasi, China 30 16N 112 20E
118 Shasta, Mt., U.S.A. 41 45N 122 0w
118 Shasta Res., U.S.A. 40 50N 122 15w
55 Shatsk, U.S.S.R. 54 0N 41 45E
117 Shattuck, U.S.A. 36 17N 99 55w
109 Shaunavon, Canada 49 35N 108 40w
98 Shaw I., Australia 20 30s 149 10E
96 Shaw, R., Australia 20 30s 119 15E
75 Shawan, China 44 34N 85 48E
112 Shawanaga, Canada 45 31N 80 14w
114 Shawano, U.S.A. 44 45N 88 38w
106 Shawinigan, Can. 46 35N 72 50w
117 Shawnee, U.S.A. 35 15N 97 0w
119 Shaziz, China 33 10N 82 43E
58 Shchékino, U.S.S.R. 54 1N 37 28E
58 Shcherbakov = Rybinsk, 58 5N 38 50E
   U.S.S.R.
55 Shchigri, U.S.S.R. 51 55N 36 58E
55 Schors, U.S.S.R. 51 48N 31 56E
52 Shchuchinsk, U.S.S.R. 52 56N 70 12E
55 Shchurovo, U.S.S.R. 55 0N 38 51E
87 Shebele, Wabi, Ethiopia 2 0N 44 0E
114 Sheboygan, U.S.A. 43 46N 87 45w
32 Shechem, Jordan 32 13N 35 21E
107 Shediac, Canada 46 14N 64 32w
15 Sheelin Lough, Ireland 53 48N 7 20w
15 Sheep Haven, Ireland 55 12N 7 55w
13 Sheerness, Eng. 51 26N 0 47E
107 Sheet Harbour, Canada 44 56N 62 31w
62 Shefar'am, Israel 32 48N 35 10E
101 Sheffeiya, Israel 32 35N 34 58E
12 Sheffield, Eng. 53 23N 1 28w
101 Sheffield, New Zealand 43 23s 172 2E
115 Sheffield, Ala., U.S.A. 34 45N 87 42w
112 Sheffield, Mass., U.S.A. 42 6N 73 23w
112 Sheffield, Pa., U.S.A. 41 42N 79 3w
117 Sheffield, Tex., U.S.A. 30 42N 101 49w
87 Shehojele, Ethiopia 10 40N 35 27E
69 Sheikhpura, India 25 9N 85 53E
87 Shek Hasan, Ethiopia 12 5N 35 58E
69 Shekar Dzong, China 28 45N 87 0E
68 Shekhupura, Pakistan 31 42N 73 58E
77 Sheki, China 41 10N 47 5E
77 Shekki, China 22 30N 113 15E
77 Sheklung, China 23 5N 113 55E
55 Sheksna, R., U.S.S.R. 59 30N 38 30E
107 Shelburne, Ont., Canada 44 4N 80 15w
107 Shelburne, N.S., Canada 43 47N 65 20w
99 Shelburne B., Australia 11 50s 143 0E
113 Shelburne Falls, U.S.A. 42 36N 72 45w
114 Shelby, Mich., U.S.A. 43 34N 86 27w
118 Shelby, Mont., U.S.A. 48 30N 111 59w
115 Shelby, N.C., U.S.A. 35 18N 81 34w
112 Shelby, Ohio, U.S.A. 40 52N 82 40w

Shelbyville INDEX Sivand

MAP
116 Shelbyville, Ill., U.S.A. 39 25N 88 45W
114 Shelbyville, Ind., U.S.A. 39 30N 85 42W
115 Shelbyville, Tenn., U.S.A. 35 30N 86 25W
116 Sheldon, S. Afr. 32 59S 25 55E
116 Sheldon, U.S.A. 43 6N 95 51W
107 Sheldrake, Canada 50 20N 64 51W
59 Shelikhova, Zaliv, U.S.S.R. 59 30N 157 0E
109 Shell Lake, Canada 53 19N 107 6W
100 Shellharbour, Australia 34 31S 150 51E
54 Shelon, R., U.S.S.R. 58 10N 30 30E
107 Shelter Bay, Canada 50 30N 67 20W
113 Shelton, Conn., U.S.A. 41 18N 73 7W
118 Shelton, Wash., U.S.A. 47 15N 123 6W
57 Shemakha, U.S.S.R. 40 50N 48 28E
116 Shenandoah, Iowa, U.S.A. 40 50N 95 25W
113 Shenandoah, Pa., U.S.A. 40 49N 76 13W
114 Shenandoah, Va., U.S.A. 38 30N 78 38W
114 Shenandoah, R., U.S.A. 38 30N 78 38W
76 Shenchih, China 39 12N 112 2E
70 Shencottah, India 8 59N 77 18E
85 Shendam, Nigeria 9 10N 9 30E
87 Shendi, Sudan 16 46N 33 33E
68 Shendurni, India 20 39N 75 36E
44 Shëngjergj, Albania 41 2N 20 10E
44 Shëngjini, Albania 41 50N 19 35E
44 Shenmëria, Albania 42 7N 20 13E
75 Shentsa, China 30 56N 88 25E
76 Shenyang (Mukden), China 41 35N 123 30E
54 Shepetovka, U.S.S.R. 50 10N 27 0E
62 Shephelah = Hashefela, Israel 31 30N 34 43E
100 Shepparton, Australia 36 18S 145 25E
113 Sheppton, U.S.A. 40 52N 76 10W
87 Sherada, Ethiopia 7 25N 36 30E
13 Sherborne, Eng. 50 56N 2 31W
84 Sherbro I., Sierra Leone 7 30N 12 40W
107 Sherbrooke, Canada 45 24N 71 57W
83 Sherda, Chad 20 7N 16 46E
86 Shereik, Sudan 18 52N 33 40E
117 Sheridan, Ark., U.S.A. 34 20N 92 25W
116 Sheridan, Col., U.S.A. 39 44N 105 3W
118 Sheridan, Wyo., U.S.A. 44 50N 107 0W
68 Sherkot, India 29 22N 78 35E
117 Sherman, U.S.A. 33 40N 96 35W
69 Sherpur, India 25 1N 90 3E
109 Sherridon, Canada 55 10N 101 5W
116 Sherwood, N.D., U.S.A. 48 59N 101 36W
117 Sherwood, Tex., U.S.A. 31 18N 100 45W
12 Sherwood For., Eng. 53 5N 1 5W
108 Sheslay, Canada 58 25N 131 45W
14 Shetland Is., Scot. 60 30N 1 30W
70 Shevaroy Hills, India 11 58N 78 12E
57 Shevchenko, U.S.S.R. 44 25N 51 20E
87 Shewa ♦, Ethiopia 9 33N 38 10E
117 Sheyenne, U.S.A. 47 52N 99 8W
116 Sheyenne, R., U.S.A. 47 40N 98 15W
63 Shibam, South Yemen 16 0N 48 36E
66 Shiberghan ♦, Afghanistan 35 45N 66 0E
86 Shibin El Kôm, Egypt 30 31N 30 55E
74 Shibushi, Japan 31 25N 131 0E
14 Shiel, L., Scot. 56 48N 5 32W
14 Shifnal, England 52 40N 2 23W
74 Shiga-ken ♦, Japan 35 20N 136 0E
81 Shigaib, Sudan 15 5N 23 35E
75 Shigatse, China 29 10N 89 0E
77 Shih Ho, China 31 45N 115 50E
76 Shihkiachwang, China 38 0N 114 32E
77 Shihlu, China 19 15N 109 0E
77 Shihpu, China 29 12N 121 58E
77 Shihtsien, China 27 28N 108 3E
76 Shihwei, China 51 28N 119 59E
44 Shijaku, Albania 41 21N 19 33E
68 Shikarpur, India 28 17N 78 7E
68 Shikarpur, Pakistan 27 57N 68 39E
68 Shikohabad, India 27 6N 78 38E
74 Shikoku-Sanchi, Japan 33 30N 133 30E
59 Shilka, U.S.S.R. 52 0N 115 55E
59 Shilka, R., U.S.S.R. 57 30N 93 18E
15 Shillelagh, Ireland 52 46N 6 32W
67 Shillong, India 25 30N 92 0E
62 Shiloh, Jordan 32 4N 35 10E
55 Shilovo, U.S.S.R. 54 25N 40 57E
74 Shimabara, Japan 32 48N 130 20E
74 Shimada, Japan 34 49N 138 19E
74 Shimane-ken ♦, Japan 35 0N 132 30E
74 Shimano-gawa, Japan 36 50N 138 30E
59 Shimenovsk, U.S.S.R. 52 15N 127 30E
74 Shimizu, Japan 35 0N 138 30E
74 Shimodate, Japan 36 20N 139 55E
70 Shimoga, India 13 57N 75 32E
90 Shimoni, Kenya 4 38S 39 20E
74 Shimonoseki, Japan 33 58N 131 0E
58 Shimpek, U.S.S.R. 44 50N 74 10E
92 Shimpuru Rapids, Angola 17 45S 19 55E
70 Shimsha, R., India 13 15N 76 54E
54 Shimsk, U.S.S.R. 58 15N 30 50E
14 Shin L., Scot. 58 7N 4 30W
65 Shin Dand, Afghanistan 33 12N 62 8E
74 Shingu, Japan 33 40N 135 55E
76 Shinankow, China 48 40N 121 32E
85 Shinkafe, Nigeria 13 8N 6 29E
76 Shinkiachwang, China 38 0N 114 31E
90 Shinyanga, Tanz. 3 45S 33 27E
90 Shinyanga ♦, Tanz. 3 30S 33 30E
74 Shio-no-Misaki, Japan 33 25N 135 45E
117 Ship I., U.S.A. 30 16N 88 55W
107 Shippegan, Canada 47 45N 64 45W
112 Shippensburg, U.S.A. 40 4N 77 32W
119 Shiprock, U.S.A. 36 51N 108 45W
65 Shir Kûh, Iran 31 45N 53 30E
90 Shirati, Tanzania 1 10S 34 0E
65 Shiraz, Iran 29 42N 52 30E
91 Shire, R., Malawi 16 30S 35 0E
55 Shiringushi, U.S.S.R. 42 54N 53 56W
MAP
74 Shiriya-Zaki, Japan 41 25N 141 30E
70 Shirol, India 16 47N 74 41E
68 Shirpur, India 21 21N 74 57E
65 Shirvan, Iran 37 30N 57 50E
43 Shishmanova, Bulgaria 42 58N 23 12E
77 Shiukwah, China 24 58N 113 3E
70 Shivali, (Sirkall) India 11 15N 79 41E
68 Shivpuri, India 25 18N 77 42E
62 Shivta, Israel 30 53N 34 40E
91 Shiwele Ferry, Zambia 11 25S 28 31E
86 Shiyata, Egypt 29 25N 25 7E
74 Shizuoka, Japan 35 0N 138 30E
74 Shizuoka-ken ♦, Japan 35 15N 138 40E
54 Shklov, U.S.S.R. 54 10N 30 15E
44 Shkodra, Albania 42 6N 19 20E
44 Shkodra ♦, Albania 42 5N 19 20E
44 Shkumbini, R., Albania 41 5N 19 50E
59 Shmidt, O., U.S.S.R. 81 0N 91 0E
87 Shoa Ghimirra, (Wota), Ethiopia 7 4N 35 51E
109 Shoal Lake, Canada 50 30N 100 35W
100 Shoalhaven, R., Austral. 34 55S 150 5E
98 Shoalwater B., Austral. 22 15S 150 20E
13 Shoeburyness, Eng. 51 31N 0 49E
76 Shohsien, China 39 30N 112 25E
70 Sholapur, India 17 43N 75 56E
59 Shologontsy, U.S.S.R. 66 13N 114 14E
62 Shomera, Israel 33 4N 35 17E
62 Shômrôn, Jordan 32 15N 35 13E
119 Shongopovi, U.S.A. 35 49N 110 37W
70 Shoranur, India 10 46N 76 19E
70 Shorapur, India 16 31N 76 48E
118 Shoshone, U.S.A. 43 0N 114 27W
118 Shoshone L., U.S.A. 44 0N 111 0W
118 Shoshone Mts., U.S.A. 39 30N 117 30W
118 Shoshoni, U.S.A. 43 13N 108 5W
54 Shostka, U.S.S.R. 51 57N 33 32E
119 Show Low, U.S.A. 34 16N 110 0W
56 Shpola, U.S.S.R. 49 1N 31 30E
117 Shreveport, U.S.A. 32 30N 93 50W
12 Shrewsbury, Eng. 52 42N 2 45W
70 Shrivardhan, India 18 10N 73 3E
• 13 Shropshire ♦, England 52 36N 2 45W
77 Shucheng, China 31 25N 117 2E
67 Shugden Gomba, China 29 35N 96 55E
91 Shuguri Falls, Tanz. 8 33S 37 22E
77 Shuikiahu, China 32 14N 117 4E
68 Shujalpur, India 23 43N 76 40E
76 Shulan, China 44 27N 126 57E
104 Shumagin Is., Alaska 55 0N 159 0W
55 Shumerlya, U.S.S.R. 55 30N 46 10E
58 Shumikha, U.S.S.R. 55 15N 63 30E
77 Shunan, China 29 37N 119 0E
77 Shunchang, China 26 52N 117 48E
57 Shungay, U.S.S.R. 48 30N 46 45E
67 Shunning, China 24 35N 99 50E
77 Shuntak, China 22 54N 113 8E
63 Shuqra, S. Yemen 13 22N 45 34E
65 Shur, R., Iran 28 30N 55 0E
65 Shusf, Iran 31 50N 60 5E
64 Shūshtar, Iran 32 0N 48 50E
62 Shuweika, Jordan 32 20N 35 1E
55 Shuya, U.S.S.R. 56 50N 41 28E
76 Shwangliao, China 43 39N 123 40E
67 Shwebo, Burma 22 30N 95 45E
67 Shwegu, Burma 24 15N 96 50E
67 Shweli Myit, Burma 23 45N 96 45E
66 Shyok, Kashmir 34 15N 78 5E
66 Shyok, R., Kashmir 34 30N 78 15E
71 Si Racha, Thailand 13 20N 101 10E
64 Siah, Saudi Arabia 22 0N 47 0E
66 Siahan Range, Pakistan 27 30N 64 40E
72 Siaksriinderapura, Indon. 0 51N 102 0E
75 Siakwan, China 25 45N 100 10E
68 Sialkot, Pakistan 32 32N 74 30E
71 Siam, G. of, Asia 11 30N 101 0E
77 Sian, China 34 2N 109 0E
77 Siang K., Hunan, China 27 10N 112 45E
77 Siang K., Kwangsi-chuang, China 23 20N 107 40E
77 Siangfan, China 32 15N 112 2E
77 Siangsiang, China 27 50N 112 30E
77 Siangtan, China 28 0N 112 55E
77 Siangyang, China 32 18N 111 0E
77 Siangyin, China 28 45N 113 0E
72 Siantan, I., Indonesia 3 14N 106 5E
76 Siao Hingan Ling, China 49 0N 127 0E
76 Siaohaotze, China 46 52N 124 22E
77 Siapu, China 26 53N 120 0E
65 Siareh, Iran 28 5N 60 20E
73 Siargao, I., Philippines 9 52N 126 3E
73 Siasi, Philippines 5 34N 120 50E
44 Siátista, Greece 40 15N 21 33E
73 Siau, I., Indonesia 2 50N 125 25E
90 Siaya ♦, Kenya 0 0N 34 20E
54 Siauliai, U.S.S.R. 55 56N 23 15E
57 Siazan, U.S.S.R. 41 3N 48 7E
86 Sibâi, Gebel el, Egypt 25 45N 34 10E
41 Sibari, Italy 39 47N 16 27E
93 Sibaya, L., S. Afr. 27 20S 32 45E
109 Sibbald, Canada 51 24N 110 10W
39 Sibenik, Yugoslavia 43 48N 15 54E
50 Siberia, N. Asia 60 0N 100 0E
72 Siberut, I., Indonesia 1 30S 99 0E
68 Sibi, Pakistan 29 30N 67 48E
73 Sibil, Indonesia 4 59S 140 35E
88 Sibiti, Congo 3 38S 13 19E
46 Sibiu, Rumania 45 45N 24 9E
46 Sibiu ♦, Rumania 45 50N 24 15E
116 Sibley, Iowa, U.S.A. 43 21N 95 43W
117 Sibley, La., U.S.A. 32 34N 93 16W
72 Sibolga, Indonesia 1 50N 98 45E
67 Sibsagar, India 27 0N 94 36E
73 Sibuco, Phil. 7 20N 122 10E
73 Sibuguey B., Phil. 7 50N 122 45E
73 Sibuko, Philippines 7 20N 122 10E
73 Sibutu, Philippines 4 45N 119 30E
73 Sibutu Passage, E. Ind. 4 50N 120 0E
73 Sibuyan, I., Philippines 12 25N 122 40E
108 Sicamous, Canada 50 49N 119 0W

* *Renamed Salop*

MAP
73 Sicapoo, Philippines 18 9N 121 34E
110 Sicasica, Bolivia 17 20S 67 45W
75 Sichang, China 28 0N 102 10E
40 Sicilia, Canale di, Italy 37 25N 12 30E
41 Sicilia, I., Italy 37 30N 14 30E
41 Sicily = Sicilia, Italy 37 30N 14 30E
126 Sicuani, Peru 14 10S 71 10W
40 Siculiana, Italy 37 20N 13 23E
39 Sid, Yugoslavia 45 6N 19 16E
87 Sidamo ♦, Ethiopia 5 0N 37 50E
85 Sidaouet, Niger 18 34N 8 3E
70 Siddipet, India 18 0N 79 0E
48 Sidensjo, Sweden 63 20N 18 20E
84 Sidéradougou, Upper Volta 10 42N 4 12W
41 Siderno Marina, Italy 38 16N 16 17E
45 Sidheros, Akra, Gr. 35 19N 26 19E
44 Sidhirókastron, Greece 37 20N 21 46E
68 Sidhpur, India 23 56N 71 25E
86 Sidi Abd el Rahman, Egypt 30 55N 28 41E
86 Sîdi Barrâni, Egypt 31 32N 25 58E
82 Sidi-Bel-Abbès, Algeria 35 13N 0 10W
82 Sidi Bennour, Morocco 32 40N 9 26W
86 Sidi Haneish, Egypt 31 10N 27 35E
82 Sidi Ifni, Morocco 29 29N 10 3W
82 Sidi Kacem, Morocco 34 11N 5 40W
83 Sīdī Miftāh, Libya 31 8N 16 58E
82 Sidi Moussa, O., Morocco 33 0N 8 50W
86 Sidi Omar, Egypt 31 24N 24 57E
82 Sidi Smil, Morocco 32 50N 9 31W
83 Sīdī Yahya, Libya 30 55N 16 30E
14 Sidlaw Hills, Scot. 56 32N 3 10W
13 Sidmouth, Eng. 50 40N 3 13W
116 Sidney, Mont., U.S.A. 47 51N 104 7W
113 Sidney, N.Y., U.S.A. 42 18N 75 20W
114 Sidney, Ohio, U.S.A. 40 18N 84 6W
73 Sidoardjo, Indonesia 7 30S 112 46E
64 Sidon, (Saida), Lebanon 33 38N 35 28E
35 Sidra, G. of = Khalī j Surt, Libya 31 40N 18 30E
28 Siedlce, Poland 52 10N 22 20E
24 Siegburg, Germany 50 48N 7 12E
24 Siegen, Germany 50 52N 8 2E
71 Siem Reap, Khmer Rep. 13 20N 103 52E
39 Siena, Italy 43 20N 11 20E
77 Sienfeng, China 29 45N 109 10E
77 Sienyang, China 34 20N 108 48E
27 Sieniawa, Poland 50 11N 22 38E
28 Sieradz, Poland 51 37N 18 41E
28 Sieraków, Poland 52 39N 16 2E
19 Sierck-les-Bains, France 49 26N 6 20E
28 Sierpc, Poland 52 55N 19 43E
126 Sierpe, Bocas de la, Ven. 10 0N 61 30W
32 Sierra Alta, Spain 40 31N 1 30W
119 Sierra Blanca, U.S.A. 31 11N 105 17W
119 Sierra Blanca, mt., U.S.A. 33 20N 105 54W
118 Sierra City, U.S.A. 39 42N 120 42W
128 Sierra Colorado, Arg. 40 35S 67 50W
33 Sierra de Gádor, Spain 36 57N 2 45W
33 Sierra de Yeguas, Spain 37 7N 4 52W
124 Sierra Gorda, Chile 23 0S 69 15W
84 Sierra Leone ■, W. Afr. 9 0N 12 0W
120 Sierra Majada, Mexico 27 19N 103 42W
25 Sierre, Switzerland 46 17N 7 31E
45 Sífnos, Greece 37 0N 24 45E
82 Sig, Algeria 35 32N 0 12W
73 Sigaboy, Philippines 6 39N 126 10E
47 Sigdal, Norway 60 4N 9 38E
20 Sigean, France 43 2N 2 58E
46 Sighet, Rumania 47 57N 23 52E
46 Sighişoara, Rumania 46 12N 24 50E
72 Sigli, Indonesia 5 25N 96 0E
50 Siglufjörður Iceland 66 12N 18 55W
73 Sigma, Philippines 11 29N 122 40E
25 Sigmaringen, Germany 48 5N 9 13E
57 Signakhi, U.S.S.R. 40 52N 45 57E
5 Signy I., Antarctica 60 45S 46 30W
19 Signy-l'Abbaye, France 49 40N 4 25E
126 Sigsig, Ecuador 3 0S 78 50W
48 Sigtuna, Sweden 59 36N 17 44E
32 Sigüenza, Spain 41 3N 2 40W
84 Siguiri, Guinea 11 31N 9 10W
54 Sigulda, U.S.S.R. 57 10N 24 55E
119 Sigurd, U.S.A. 38 57N 112 0W
71 Sihanoukville = Kompong Som, Khmer Rep. 10 40N 103 30E
77 Siho, China 34 0N 105 0E
76 Sihsien, Anwhei, China 29 55N 118 23E
62 Si'ir, Jordan 31 35N 35 9E
64 Siirt, Turkey 37 57N 41 55E
91 Sijarira, Ra., Rhodesia 17 36S 27 45E
5 Sijsele, Belgium 51 12N 3 20E
68 Sikandarabad, India 28 30N 77 39E
68 Sikandra Rao, India 27 43N 78 24E
68 Sikar, India 27 39N 75 10E
84 Sikasso, Mali 11 7N 5 35W
92 Sikerete, S.W. Afr. 19 0S 20 48E
117 Sikeston, U.S.A. 36 52N 89 35W
59 Sikhote Alin, Khrebet, U.S.S.R. 46 0N 136 0E
44 Sikiá, Greece 40 2N 23 56E
45 Sikinos, I., Greece 36 40N 25 8E
45 Sikionia, Greece 38 0N 22 44E
•69 Sikkim ■, India 27 50N 88 50E
27 Siklós, Hungary 45 50N 18 19E
84 Sikoro, Sudan 12 19N 7 8W
77 Siku, China 33 48N 104 18E
30 Sil, R., Spain 42 23N 7 30W
76 Silamulun Ho, China 43 30N 123 35E
38 Silandro, Italy 46 38N 10 48E
62 Silat adh Dhahr, Jordan 32 19N 35 11E
39 Silba, Yugoslavia 44 24N 14 41E
39 Silba, I., Yugoslavia 44 24N 14 41E
64 Silchar, India 24 45N 93 0E
109 Silcox, Canada 57 14N 94 0W
115 Siler City, U.S.A. 35 44N 79 30W

• *Now an administrative subdivision of India*

MAP
70 Sileru, R., India 18 0N 82 0E
22 Silesia, Poland 51 0N 16 30E
82 Silet, Algeria 22 44N 4 37E
69 Silgarhi Doti, Nepal 29 15N 82 0E
67 Silghat, India 26 35N 93 0E
64 Silifke, Turkey 36 22N 33 58E
69 Siliguri, India 26 45N 88 25E
77 Silin, China 24 10N 105 36E
40 Siliqua, Italy 39 20N 8 49E
43 Silistra, Bulgaria 44 6N 27 19E
48 Siljan, L., Sweden 60 55N 14 45E
49 Silkeborg, Denmark 56 10N 9 32E
126 Sillajhuay, Cordillera, Chile 19 40S 68 40W
18 Sillé-le Guillaume, Fr. 48 10N 0 8W
117 Siloam Springs, U.S.A. 36 15N 94 31W
72 Silogui, Indonesia 1 10S 98 46E
117 Silsbee, U.S.A. 30 20N 94 8W
54 Silute, U.S.S.R. 55 21N 21 33E
89 Silva Porto, Angola 12 22S 16 55E
118 Silver Cr., R., U.S.A. 43 30N 119 30W
120 Silver City, Panama Canal Zone 9 21N 79 53W
118 Silver City, Calif., U.S.A. 36 19N 119 44W
119 Silver City, N. Mex., U.S.A. 32 50N 108 18W
112 Silver Creek, U.S.A. 42 33N 79 9W
118 Silver Lake, U.S.A. 43 9N 121 4W
48 Silverhojden, Sweden 60 2N 15 0E
100 Silverton, Australia 31 52S 141 10E
119 Silverton, Colo., U.S.A. 37 51N 107 45W
117 Silverton, Tex., U.S.A. 34 30N 101 16W
31 Silves, Portugal 37 11N 8 26W
126 Silvia, Colombia 2 37N 76 21W
118 Silvies, R., U.S.A. 43 57N 119 5W
25 Silvretta Gruppe, Switz. 46 50N 10 6E
86 Silwa Bahari, Egypt 24 45N 32 55E
62 Silwan, Jordan 31 59N 35 15E
68 Silwani, India 23 18N 78 27E
26 Silz, Austria 47 16N 10 56E
82 Sim, C., Morocco 31 26N 9 51W
72 Simanggang, Malaysia 1 15N 111 25E
106 Simard, Lac, Canada 47 40N 78 40W
46 Simărtin, Rumania 46 19N 25 58E
65 Simarun, Iran 31 16N 51 40E
90 Simba, Tanzania 1 41S 34 12E
25 Simbach, Germany 48 16N 13 3E
90 Simbo, Tanzania 4 51S 29 41E
106 Simcoe, Canada 42 50N 80 20W
59 Simenga, U.S.S.R. 62 50N 107 55E
72 Simeulue, I., Indonesia 2 45N 95 45E
56 Simferopol, U.S.S.R. 44 55N 34 3E
45 Simi, Greece 36 35N 27 50E
45 Simi, I., Greece 36 35N 27 50E
69 Simikot, Nepal 30 0N 81 50E
126 Simiti, Colombia 7 58N 73 57W
43 Simitli, Bulgaria 41 52N 23 7E
68 Simla, India 31 2N 77 15E
46 Simleu-Silvaniei, Rum. 47 17N 22 50E
24 Simmern, Germany 49 59N 7 32E
109 Simmie, Canada 49 56N 108 6W
50 Simojoki, Finland 65 46N 25 15E
50 Simojärvi, Finland 66 5N 27 10E
92 Simonstown, S. Africa 34 14S 18 26E
27 Simontornya, Hungary 46 45N 18 33E
72 Simpang, Indonesia 1 3S 110 6E
72 Simpang, Malaysia 4 50N 100 40E
25 Simplon Pass, Switzerland 46 15N 8 0E
25 Simplontunnel, Switz. 46 15N 8 7E
97 Simpson Des., Austral. 25 0S 137 0E
49 Simrishamn, Sweden 55 33N 14 22E
72 Simunjan, Malay. 1 25N 110 45E
59 Simushir, Ostrov, Kuril Is. 46 50N 152 30E
70 Sina, R., India 18 25N 75 28E
72 Sinabang, Indonesia 2 30N 46 30E
63 Sinadogo, Somali Rep. 5 40N 46 33E
86 Sinai, Mt., Egypt 28 32N 33 59E
86 Sinai = Es Sînâ', Egypt 29 0N 34 0E
46 Sinaia, Rumania 45 21N 25 38E
120 Sinaloa, Mexico 25 50N 108 20W
120 Sinaloa ♦, Mexico 25 0N 107 30W
39 Sinalunga, Italy 43 12N 11 43E
126 Sinamaica, Ven. 11 5N 71 51W
46 Sînandrei, Rumania 45 52N 21 13E
83 Sīnāwan, Libya 31 0N 10 30E
126 Sincé, Colombia 9 15N 75 9W
126 Sincelejo, Colombia 9 18N 75 24W
77 Sincheng, China 34 25N 113 56E
77 Sinchengtu, China 23 55N 108 30E
118 Sinclair, U.S.A. 41 47N 107 35W
108 Sinclair Mills, Canada 54 5N 121 40E
127 Sincorá, Serra do, Brazil 13 30S 41 0W
68 Sind Sagar Doab, Pakistan 32 0N 71 30E
91 Sinda, Zambia 17 28S 25 51E
49 Sindal, Denmark 57 28N 10 10E
73 Sindangan, Phil. 8 10N 123 5E
73 Sindangbarang, Indon. 7 27S 107 9E
73 Sindjai, Indonesia 5 0S 120 20E
56 Sinelnikovo, U.S.S.R. 48 25N 35 30E
31 Sines, Portugal 37 56N 8 51E
31 Sines, Cabo de, Portugal 37 58N 8 53W
32 Sineu, Spain 39 39N 3 0E
77 Sinfeng, Kiangsi, China 25 28N 114 40E
77 Sinfeng, Kweichow, China 26 59N 106 55E
84 Sinfra, Ivory Coast 6 35N 5 56W
87 Singa, Sudan 13 10N 33 57E
70 Singanallurt, India 11 2N 77 1E
73 Singaparna, Indonesia 7 23S 108 4E
71 Singapore ■, Asia 1 17N 103 51E
71 Singapore, Straits of, Asia 1 10N 103 40E
72 Singaradja, Indonesia 8 15S 115 10E
25 Singen, Germany 47 45N 8 50E
90 Singida, Tanzania 4 49S 34 48E
90 Singida ♦, Tanz. 5 30S 34 30E
MAP
44 Singitikós, Kólpos, Greece 40 6N 24 0E
67 Singkaling Hkamti, Burma 26 0N 95 45E
73 Singkang, Indonesia 4 8S 120 1E
72 Singkawang, Indonesia 1 0N 109 5E
72 Singkep, I., Indonesia 0 30S 104 20E
48 Singö, Sweden 60 12N 18 45E
68 Singoli, India 25 0N 75 16E
76 Singtai, China 37 2N 114 30E
77 Singtze, China 29 30N 116 4E
77 Singyang, China 32 10N 114 0E
77 Sinhailien, China 34 31N 119 0E
76 Sinhsien, China 38 25N 112 45E
77 Sinhwa, China 27 36N 111 6E
44 Siniatsikon, Oros, Gr. 40 25N 21 35E
75 Sining, China 36 35N 101 50E
40 Siniscóla, Italy 40 35N 9 40E
39 Sinj, Yugoslavia 43 42N 16 39E
42 Sinjajevina, Planina, Y.-slav. 42 57N 19 22E
62 Sinjil, Jordan 32 3N 35 15E
77 Sinkan, China 27 45N 115 30E
86 Sinkat, Sudan 18 55N 36 49E
75 Sinkiang-Uigur, China 42 0N 85 0E
40 Sinnai Sardinia, Italy 39 18N 9 13E
70 Sinnar, India 19 48N 74 0E
41 Sinni, R., Italy 40 6N 16 15E
46 Sinnicolau-Maré, Rumania 46 5N 20 39E
86 Sinnûris, Egypt 29 26N 30 31E
46 Sinoe, L., Rumania 44 35N 28 50E
91 Sinoia, Rhodesia 17 20S 30 8E
64 Sinop, Turkey 42 1N 35 11E
56 Sinop, R., Turkey 42 1N 35 2E
77 Sinsiang, China 35 15N 113 55E
59 Sinskoye, U.S.S.R. 61 8N 126 48E
16 Sint Niklaas, Belgium 51 10N 4 9E
16 Sint Truiden, Belgium 50 48N 5 12E
77 Sintai, China 30 59N 105 0E
72 Sintang, Indonesia 0 5N 111 35E
46 Sintana Ano, Rum. 46 20N 21 30E
77 Sinti, (Hunghu), China 29 49N 113 30E
117 Sinton, U.S.A. 28 1N 97 30W
31 Sintra, Portugal 38 47N 9 25W
76 Sinŭiju, North Korea 40 5N 124 24E
77 Sinyang, China 32 6N 114 2E
56 Sinyukha, R., U.S.S.R. 48 31N 30 31E
27 Siófok, Hungary 46 54N 18 4E
92 Sióma, Zambia 16 25S 23 28E
25 Sion, Switzerland 46 14N 7 20E
86 Sioua, El Wâhât es, Egypt 29 10N 25 30E
116 Sioux City, U.S.A. 42 32N 96 25W
116 Sioux Falls, U.S.A. 43 35N 96 40W
106 Sioux Lookout, Canada 50 10N 91 50W
77 Sipa, China 33 34N 118 59E
42 Sipan, Yugoslavia 42 45N 17 52E
72 Sipera, I., Indonesia 2 18S 99 40E
77 Siping, China 33 25N 114 10E
98 Sipul, Terr. of N. Guin. 5 50S 148 28E
121 Siquia, R., Nicaragua 12 30N 84 30W
73 Siquijor, I., Philippines 9 12N 123 45E
126 Siquisique, Venezuela 10 34N 69 42W
97 Sir Edward Pellew Group, Australia 15 40S 137 10E
70 Sira, India 13 41N 76 49E
47 Sira, R., Norway 58 43N 6 40E
41 Siracusa, Italy 37 4N 15 17E
69 Sirajganj, Bangladesh 24 25N 89 47E
98 Sirake, Terr. of Papua 9 1S 141 2E
84 Sirakoro, Mali 12 41N 9 14W
84 Sirasso, Ivory Coast 9 16N 6 6W
46 Siret, Rumania 47 55N 26 5E
46 Siret, R., Rumania 47 58N 26 5E
42 Siria, Rumania 46 16N 21 38E
70 Sirkall (Shivali), India 11 15N 79 41E
45 Sirna, I., Greece 36 22N 26 42E
68 Sirohi, India 24 52N 72 53E
42 Siroki Brijeg, Y.-slavia 43 21N 17 36E
68 Sironj, India 24 5N 77 45E
45 Siros, Greece 37 28N 24 57E
45 Siros, I., Greece 37 28N 24 57E
68 Sirsa, India 29 33N 75 4E
70 Sirsi, India 14 40N 74 49E
31 Siruela, Spain 38 58N 5 3W
39 Sisak, Yugoslavia 45 30N 16 21E
71 Sisaket, Thailand 15 8N 104 23E
33 Sisante, Spain 39 25N 2 12W
30 Sisargas, Islas, Spain 43 21N 8 50W
109 Sisipuk I., Canada 55 40N 102 0W
71 Sisophon, Khmer Rep. 13 31N 102 59E
116 Sisseton, U.S.A. 45 43N 97 3W
19 Sissonne, France 49 34N 3 51E
65 Sistan-Baluchistan ♦, Iran 27 0N 62 0E
30 Sistema Central, Spain 40 40N 5 55W
32 Sistema Ibérico, Spain 41 0N 2 10W
21 Sisteron, France 44 12N 5 57E
118 Sisters, U.S.A. 44 21N 121 32W
69 Sitamarhi, India 26 37N 85 30E
69 Sitapur, India 27 38N 80 45E
93 Siteki, Swaziland 26 32S 31 58E
32 Sitges, Spain 41 17N 1 47E
44 Sithoniá, Greece 40 0N 23 45E
45 Sitia, Greece 35 13N 26 6E
104 Sitka, Alaska 57 9N 134 58W
87 Sitona, Ethiopia 14 25N 37 23E
92 Sitoti, Botswana 23 15S 23 40E
86 Sitra, Egypt 28 40N 26 53E
67 Sittang Myit, R., Burma 18 20N 96 45E
16 Sittard, Netherlands 51 0N 5 52E
24 Sittensen, Germany 53 17N 9 32E
73 Situbondo, Indonesia 7 45S 114 0E
77 Siuwu, China 35 10N 113 30E
76 Siuyen, China 40 20N 123 15E
70 Sivaganga, India 9 50N 78 28E
70 Sivagiri, India 9 16N 77 26E
70 Sivakasi, India 9 24N 77 45E
65 Sivand, Iran 30 5N 52 55E

Sivas INDEX Soúnion, Ákra

MAP
64 Sivas, Turkey 39 43N 36 58E
64 Siverek, Turkey 37 50N 39 25E
64 Sivrihisar, Turkey 39 30N 31 35E
86 Siwa, Egypt 29 11N 25 31E
69 Siwalik Range, Nepal 28 0N 83 0E
69 Siwan, India 26 13N 84 27E
86 Siyâl, Jazâ'ir, Egypt 22 49N 36 6E
68 Siyana, India 28 37N 78 6E
13 Sizewell, Eng. 52 13N 1 38E
49 Sjaelland, Denmark 55 30N 11 30E
49 Sjaellands Odde, Denmark 56 0N 11 15E
48 Själevad, Sweden 63 19N 18 40E
42 Sjarinska Banja, Y.-slav. 42 45N 21 38E
42 Sjenica, Yugoslavia 43 16N 20 0E
47 Sjernaröy, Norway 59 15N 5 50E
47 Sjoa, Norway 61 41N 9 40E
49 Sjöbo, Sweden 55 37N 13 45E
47 Sjöholt, Norway 62 27N 6 52E
50 Sjönsta, Norway 67 10N 16 3E
49 Sjösa, Sweden 58 47N 17 4E
48 Själevad, Sweden 63 18N 18 36E
56 Skadovsk, U.S.S.R. 46 17N 32 52E
49 Skagen, pt., Denmark 57 43N 10 35E
48 Skagern, Sweden 59 0N 14 20E
49 Skagerrak, Denmark 57 30N 9 0E
104 Skagway, U.S.A. 59 30N 135 20W
56 Skala Podolskaya, U.S.S.R. 48 50N 26 15E
54 Skalat, U.S.S.R. 94 23N 25 55E
28 Skalbmierz, Poland 56 22N 12 30E
27 Skalicd, Cz. 48 50N 17 15E
43 Skalni Dol = Kamenyak, Bulg. 43 24N 26 57E
49 Skals, Denmark 56 34N 9 24E
49 Skalderviken, Sweden 56 22N 12 30E
49 Skallingen, Odde, Denmark 55 32N 8 13E
49 Skanderborg, Denmark 56 2N 9 55E
47 Skånevik, Norway 59 43N 5 53E
49 Skanninge, Sweden 58 24N 15 5E
49 Skanor, Sweden 55 24N 12 50E
45 Skantzoúra I., Greece 39 5N 24 6E
49 Skanör, Sweden 55 24N 12 50E
49 Skara, Sweden 58 25N 13 30E
49 Skaraborgs län ♦, Swed. 58 20N 13 30E
49 Skarblacka, Sweden 58 36N 15 50E
47 Skardhö, Norway 62 30N 8 47E
66 Skardu, Kashmir 35 20N 75 35E
49 Skaresta, Sweden 58 26N 16 22E
28 Skarszewy, Poland 54 4N 18 25E
47 Skarvane, Mt., Norway 63 18N 11 27E
28 Skarzysko Kamienna, Poland 51 7N 20 52E
47 Skatöy, Norway 50 50N 9 30E
48 Skattungbyn, Sweden 61 10N 14 56E
49 Skaw (Grenen), Den. 57 46N 10 34E
48 Skebo, Sweden 59 58N 18 37E
48 Skebokvarn, Sweden 59 7N 16 45E
108 Skeena Mts. Canada 56 40N 128 0W
108 Skeena, R., Canada 54 20N 129 20W
50 Skeggjastadir, Iceland 66 3N 14 50W
12 Skegness, Eng. 53 9N 0 20E
126 Skeldon, Guyana 6 0N 57 20W
50 Skellefteå, Sweden 64 45N 20 59E
50 Skelleftehamn, Sweden 64 41N 21 14E
50 Skellefte älv, Sweden 65 30N 18 30E
50 Skelleftea, Sweden 64 45N 20 58E
42 Skender Vakuf, Y.-slav. 44 29N 17 22E
49 Skene, Sweden 57 30N 12 37E
45 Skhíza, I., Greece 36 41N 20 40E
45 Skhoinoúsa, I., Greece 36 53N 25 31E
47 Ski, Norway 59 43N 10 52E
45 Skiathos, I., Greece 39 12N 23 30E
15 Skibbereen, Ireland 51 33N 9 16W
12 Skiddaw, Mt., Eng. 54 39N 3 9W
24 Skidegate, Inlet, Canada 53 20N 132 0W
47 Skien, Norway 59 12N 9 35E
28 Skierniewice, Poland 51 58N 20 19E
83 Skikda, Algeria 36 50N 6 58E
48 Skillingmark, Sweden 59 48N 120 1E
49 Skillingaryd, Sweden 57 27N 14 5E
49 Skillinge, Sweden 55 30N 14 16E
45 Skinari, Akra, Gr. 37 56N 20 40E
100 Skipton, Australia 37 39S 143 21E
12 Skipton, Eng. 53 57N 2 1W
49 Skirild, Denmark 55 58N 8 53E
45 Skiropoúla, I., Greece 38 50N 24 21E
45 Skíros, Greece 38 55N 24 34E
45 Skíros, I., Greece 38 55N 24 34E
49 Skivarp, Sweden 55 26N 13 34E
49 Skive, Denmark 56 33N 9 2E
47 Skják, Norway 61 52N 8 22E
50 Skjálfandafljót, Iceland 65 15N 17 25W
50 Skjálfandi, Iceland 66 5N 17 30W
47 Skjeberg, Norway 59 12N 11 12E
49 Skjern, Denmark 55 57N 8 30E
47 Skjönne, Norway 60 16N 9 1E
27 Skoczów, Poland 49 49N 18 45E
47 Skodje, Norway 62 30N 6 43E
39 Skofja Loka, Y.-slavia 46 9N 14 19E
47 Skoger, Norway 59 42N 10 16E
48 Skoghall, Sweden 59 20N 13 30E
49 Skoghult, Sweden 56 59N 15 55E
28 Skoki, Poland 52 40N 17 11E
54 Skole, U.S.S.R. 49 3N 23 30E
48 Skonsberg, Sweden 62 25N 17 21E
45 Skópelos, Greece 39 9N 23 47E
45 Skópelos, I., Greece 39 9N 23 47E
55 Skopin, U.S.S.R. 53 55N 39 32E
42 Skopje, Yugoslavia 42 1N 21 32E
28 Skorcz, Poland 43 47N 18 30E
48 Skorped, Sweden 63 23N 17 55E
47 Skotfoss, Norway 59 12N 9 30E
54 Skoudas, U.S.S.R. 56 21N 21 45E
107 Skowhegan, U.S.A. 44 49N 69 40W
109 Skowman, Canada 51 58N 99 35W
39 Skradin, Yugoslavia 43 52N 15 53E
49 Skreanäs, Sweden 56 52N 12 35E
47 Skudeneshavn, Norway 59 10N 5 10E

MAP
15 Skull, Ireland 51 32N 9 40W
49 Skultorp, Sweden 58 24N 13 51E
56 Skulyany, U.S.S.R. 47 19N 27 39E
116 Skunk, R., U.S.A. 41 10N 91 45W
49 Skurup, Sweden 55 28N 13 30E
49 Skutskär, Sweden 60 37N 17 25E
56 Skvira, U.S.S.R. 49 44N 29 32E
28 Skwierzyna, Poland 52 46N 15 30E
14 Skye, I., Scot. 57 15N 6 10W
118 Skykomish, U.S.A. 47 43N 121 16W
45 Skyros (Skiros), L., Gr. 38 52N 24 37E
49 Slagelse, Denmark 55 23N 11 19E
72 Slamet, G., Indonesia 7 16S 109 8E
100 Slammannon, Australia 32 1S 143 41E
15 Slaney, R., Ireland 52 52N 6 45W
49 Slangerup, Denmark 55 50N 12 11E
46 Slânic, Rumania 45 14N 25 58E
42 Slankamen, Yugoslavia 45 8N 20 15E
42 Slano, Yugoslavia 42 48N 17 53E
54 Slantsy, U.S.S.R. 59 7N 28 5E
26 Slany, Czechoslovakia 50 13N 14 6E
77 Slaokan, China 30 57N 114 2E
49 Slatbaken, Swed. 58 28N 16 30E
106 Slate Is., Canada 48 40N 87 0W
46 Slatina, Rumania 44 28N 24 22E
117 Slaton, U.S.A. 33 27N 101 38W
85 Slave Coast, W. Africa 6 0N 2 30E
108 Slave Lake, Canada 55 25N 114 50W
108 Slave Pt., Canada 61 15N 116 0W
108 Slave, R., Canada 60 40N 112 50W
58 Slavgorod, U.S.S.R. 53 10N 78 50E
42 Slavinja, Yugoslavia 43 14N 22 50E
27 Slavkov (Austerlitz), Cz. 49 10N 16 52E
54 Slavnoye, U.S.S.R. 54 24N 29 15E
42 Slavonski Brod, Y.-Slav. 45 11N 18 0E
42 Slavonski Pozega, Y.-slav. 45 20N 17 40E
54 Slavuta, U.S.S.R. 50 15N 27 2E
56 Slavyans, U.S.S.R. 48 55N 37 30E
56 Slavyansk, U.S.S.R. 45 15N 38 11E
28 Sława, Poland 51 52N 16 2E
28 Sławno, Poland 54 20N 16 41E
28 Sławoborze, Poland 53 55N 15 42E
12 Sleaford, Eng. 53 0N 0 22W
14 Sleat, Sd. of, Scot. 57 5N 5 47W
105 Sleeper, Is., Canada 56 50N 80 30W
105 Sleepers, The, Canada 58 30N 81 0W
116 Sleepy Eye, U.S.A. 44 15N 94 45W
73 Sleman, Indonesia 7 40S 110 20E
47 Slemmestad, Norway 59 47N 10 30E
28 Slesin, Poland 52 22N 18 14E
49 Sletterhage, Kap, Den. 56 7N 10 31E
117 Slidell, U.S.A. 30 20N 89 48W
16 Sliedrecht, Netherlands 51 50N 4 45E
15 Slieve Aughty, Ireland 53 4N 8 30W
15 Slieve Bloom, Ireland 53 4N 7 40W
15 Slieve Donard, Northern Ireland 54 10N 5 57W
15 Slieve Gullion, Northern Ireland 54 8N 6 26W
15 Slieve Mish, Ireland 52 12N 9 50W
15 Slievenamon Mt., Ire. 52 25N 7 37W
15 Sligo, Ire. 54 17N 8 28W
15 Sligo B., Ire. 54 20N 8 40W
51 Slite, Sweden 57 42N 18 48E
43 Sliven, Bulgaria 42 42N 26 19E
42 Slivnitsa, Bulgaria 42 50N 23 0E
39 Sljeme, mt., Y.-slavia 45 57N 15 58E
113 Sloansville, U.S.A. 42 45N 74 22W
55 Slobodskoy, U.S.S.R. 58 40N 50 6E
46 Slobozia, Ialomiţa, Rum. 44 34N 27 23E
46 Slobozia, Valahia, Rum. 44 30N 25 14E
49 Slöinge, Sweden 56 51N 12 42E
28 Słomniki, Poland 50 16N 20 4E
54 Slonim, U.S.S.R. 53 4N 25 19E
13 Slough, England 51 30N 0 35W
27 Slovakia, Czechoslovakia 48 30N 19 0E
39 Slovenia = Slovenija, Y.-slav. 45 58N 14 30E
39 Slovenija Nar ♦, Yugoslavia 45 58N 14 30E
39 Slovenska Bistrica, Yugoslavia 46 24N 15 35E
27 Slovenská Socialistická Republica ♦, Cz. 48 40N 19 0E
27 Slovenske Krusnohorie, Cz. 48 45N 20 0E
26 Slovenské Rhudhori, Cz. 50 25N 13 0E
28 Słubice, Poland 52 22N 14 35E
16 Sluis, Netherlands 51 18N 3 23E
43 Slunchev Bryag, Bulg. 42 40N 27 41E
39 Slunj, Yugoslavia 45 6N 15 33E
28 Słupca, Poland 52 15N 17 52E
28 Slupsk, Poland 54 30N 17 3E
92 Slurry, S. Africa 25 49S 25 42E
15 Slyne Hd., Ireland 53 25N 10 10W
59 Slyudyanka, U.S.S.R. 51 40N 103 30E
49 Smälandstarvandet, Denmark 55 10N 11 20E
49 Smål-Taberg, Sweden 57 42N 14 5E
49 Smalandsstenar, Swed. 57 9N 13 24E
82 Smara, Spanish Sahara 26 48N 11 31W
39 Smarje, Yugoslavia 46 15N 15 34E
92 Smart Syndicate Dam, S. Afr. 30 45S 23 10E
49 Smedberg, Sweden 58 35N 12 0E
42 Smederevo, Yugoslavia 44 40N 20 57E
49 Smedstorp, Sweden 55 38N 13 58E
56 Smela, U.S.S.R. 49 30N 32 0E
112 Smethport, U.S.A. 41 50N 78 28W
59 Smidovich, U.S.S.R. 48 36N 133 49E
43 Smilyan, Bulgaria 41 29N 24 46E
108 Smith, Canada 55 10N 114 0W
108 Smith Arm, Canada 66 30N 123 0W
116 Smith Center, U.S.A. 39 50N 98 50W
4 Smith Sound, Canada 78 0N 75 0W
4 Smith Sund, Greenland 78 30N 74 0W
108 Smithers, Canada 54 45N 127 10W
115 Smithfield, N.C., U.S.A. 35 31N 78 16W
106 Smith's Falls, Canada 44 55N 76 0W

MAP
99 Smithton, N.S.W., Austral. 31 0S 152 48E
99 Smithton, Tas., Austral. 40 53S 145 6E
112 Smithville, Canada 43 7N 79 32W
117 Smithville, U.S.A. 30 2N 97 12W
106 Smoky Falls, Canada 50 10N 82 10W
116 Smoky Hill, R., U.S.A. 38 45N 98 0W
108 Smoky Lake, Canada 54 10N 112 30W
47 Smola, Norway 63 23N 8 3E
54 Smolensk, U.S.S.R. 54 45N 32 0E
44 Smolikas, Oros, Greece 40 9N 20 58E
27 Smolník, Czechoslovakia 48 43N 20 44E
43 Smolyan, Bulgaria 41 36N 24 38E
106 Smooth Rock Falls, Can. 49 17N 81 37W
54 Smorgon, U.S.S.R. 54 28N 26 24E
46 Smulţi, Rumania 45 57N 27 44E
43 Smyadovo, Bulgaria 43 2N 27 1E
49 Smålandsfarvandet, Denmark 55 10N 11 20E
12 Snaefell, United Kingdom 54 18N 4 26W
100 Snake I., Australia 38 47S 146 33E
118 Snake, R., U.S.A. 46 31N 118 50W
118 Snake Ra., Mts., U.S.A. 39 0N 114 30W
118 Snake River Plain, U.S.A. 43 13N 113 0W
47 Snarum, Norway 60 1N 9 54E
48 Snasahogarha, Sweden 63 10N 12 20E
49 Snedsted, Denmark 56 55N 8 32E
16 Sneek, Netherlands 53 2N 5 40E
49 Snejbjerg, Denmark 56 8N 8 54E
26 Sněka, Cz. – Pol. 50 41N 15 50E
57 Snezhnoye, U.S.S.R. 48 0N 38 58E
39 Sneznik, mt. Y.-slavia 45 36N 14 35E
56 Snigirevka, U.S.S.R. 47 2N 32 35E
27 Snina, Czechoslovakia 49 0N 22 9E
14 Snizort L., Scot. 57 33N 6 28W
47 Snohetta, Norway 62 19N 9 16E
118 Snohomish, U.S.A. 47 53N 122 0W
47 Snonuten, Norway 59 31N 6 50E
114 Snow Hill, U.S.A. 38 10N 75 21W
109 Snowbird L., Canada 60 45N 103 0W
12 Snowdon, Mt., Wales 53 4N 4 8W
109 Snowdrift, Canada 62 10N 110 0W
109 Snowdrift, R., Canada 62 10N 110 0W
119 Snowflake, U.S.A. 34 30N 110 4W
108 Snowshoe, Canada 53 43N 121 0W
118 Snowville, U.S.A. 41 59N 112 47W
100 Snowy Mts., Australia 36 15S 148 20E
100 Snowy, R., Austral. 36 13S 148 30E
117 Snyder, Okla., U.S.A. 34 4N 99 0W
117 Snyder, Tex., U.S.A. 32 45N 100 57W
126 Soacha, Colombia 4 35N 74 13W
93 Soahanina, Malag. 18 42S 44 13E
93 Soalala, Malagasy Rep. 16 6S 45 20E
93 Soanierana-Ivongo, Malag. 16 55S 49 35E
118 Soap Lake, U.S.A. 47 29N 119 31W
87 Sobat, Nahr, Sudan 8 32N 32 40E
26 Soběslav, Cz. 49 16N 14 45E
68 Sobhapur, India 22 47N 78 17E
55 Sobinka, U.S.S.R. 56 0N 40 0E
28 Sobótka, Poland 50 54N 16 44E
30 Sobrado, Spain 43 2N 8 2W
127 Sobral, Brazil 3 50S 40 30W
31 Sobreira Formosa, Port. 39 46N 7 51W
71 Soc Trang = Khonh Hung, S. Vietnam 9 37N 105 50E
39 Soča, R., Yugoslavia 46 20N 13 40E
46 Socariclu, Rumania 44 15N 27 35E
126 Socha, Colombia 6 0N 72 41W
28 Sochaczew, Poland 52 15N 20 13E
75 Soche (Yarkand), China 38 24N 77 20E
57 Sochi, U.S.S.R. 43 35N 39 40E
95 Société, Is. de la, Pacific 17 0S 151 0W
124 Socompa, Portezuelo de, Chile 24 27S 68 18W
126 Socorro, Colombia 6 29N 73 16W
113 Socorro, U.S.A. 34 3N 106 58W
63 Socotra, I., Ind. Oc. 12 30N 54 0E
33 Socúellmos, Spain 39 16N 2 47W
108 Soda Creek, Canada 52 25N 122 10W
119 Soda L., U.S.A. 35 7N 116 2W
78 Soda Springs, U.S.A. 42 4N 111 40W
50 Sodankylä, Finland 67 29N 26 40E
48 Söderfjärden, Sweden 62 3N 17 25E
48 Söderfors, Sweden 60 23N 17 25E
48 Söderhamn, Sweden 61 18N 17 10E
48 Söderköping, Sweden 58 31N 16 35E
48 Södermanlands län ♦, Sweden 59 10N 16 30E
48 Södertälje, Sweden 59 12N 17 50E
92 Sodium, S. Afr. 30 15S 15 45E
87 Sodo, Ethiopia 7 0N 37 57E
49 Södra Vi, Sweden 57 45N 15 45E
39 Sodrażica, Yugoslavia 45 45N 14 39E
112 Sodus, U.S.A. 43 13N 77 5W
112 Sodus Pt., U.S.A. 43 15N 77 0W
93 Soekmekaar, S. Africa 23 30S 29 55E
24 Soest, Germany 51 34N 8 7E
16 Soest, Netherlands 52 9N 5 19E
44 Sofádhes, Greece 39 28N 22 4E
84 Sofara, Mali 13 59N 4 9W
43 Sofia = Sofiya, Bulgaria 42 45N 23 20E
93 Sofia, R., Malagasy Rep. 15 25S 48 40E
56 Sofievka, U.S.S.R. 47 58N 34 14E
58 Sofiiski, U.S.S.R. 52 20N 133 55E
45 Sofikón, Greece 37 47N 23 3E
43 Sofiya, Bulgaria 42 45N 23 20E
73 Sogad, Philippines 10 30N 125 0E
85 Sogakofe, Ghana 6 2N 0 39E
126 Sogamoso, Colombia 5 43N 72 56W
24 Sögel, Germany 52 50N 7 32E
47 Sogn og Fjordane fylke ♦, Norway 61 40N 6 0E
47 Sogndal, Norway 58 20N 6 15E
47 Sognefjord, Norway 61 10N 5 50E
86 Sohâg, Egypt 26 27N 31 43E
16 Soignies, Belgium 50 35N 4 5E

MAP
87 Soira, Mt., Ethiopia 14 45N 39 30E
19 Soissons, France 49 25N 3 19E
27 Soitava, R., Cz. 49 30N 16 37E
68 Sojat, India 25 55N 73 38E
55 Sok, R., U.S.S.R. 53 30N 50 30E
54 Sokal, U.S.S.R. 50 31N 24 15E
45 Söke, Turkey 37 48N 27 28E
44 Sokhós, Greece 40 48N 23 22E
65 Sokhta Chinar, Afghan. 35 5N 67 35E
47 Sokna, Norway 60 16N 9 50E
47 Soknedal, Norway 62 57N 10 13E
42 Soko Banja, Y.-slavia 43 40N 21 51E
85 Sokodé, Togo 9 0N 1 11E
55 Sokol, U.S.S.R. 59 30N 40 5E
28 Sokółka, Poland 53 25N 23 30E
26 Sokolov, Czechoslovakia 50 12N 12 40E
27 Sokołów Matopolski, Poland 50 12N 22 7E
28 Sokołów Podlaski, Pol. 52 25N 22 15E
85 Sokoto, Nigeria 13 2N 5 16E
85 Sokoto, R., Nigeria 12 30N 6 10E
52 Sol Iletsk, U.S.S.R. 51 20N 54 50E
47 Sola, Norway 58 53N 5 36E
90 Sola, R., Poland 49 38N 19 8E
90 Solai, Kenya 0 2N 36 12E
73 Solano, Philippines 16 25N 121 15E
30 Solares, Spain 43 23N 3 43W
49 Solberga, Sweden 57 45N 14 43E
28 Solec Kujawski, Poland 53 5N 18 14E
49 Solojärg, Den. 56 50N 10 8E
46 Solca, Rumania 47 40N 25 50E
126 Soledad, Colombia 10 55N 74 46W
119 Soledad, U.S.A. 36 27N 121 16W
126 Soledad, Venezuela 8 10N 63 34W
13 Solent, The, Eng. 50 45N 1 25W
21 Solenzara, Corsica 41 53N 9 23E
19 Solesmes, France 50 10N 3 30E
47 Solfonn, Mt., Norway 60 2N 6 57E
55 Soligalich, U.S.S.R. 59 5N 42 10E
52 Solikamsk, U.S.S.R. 59 38N 56 50E
93 Solila, Malagasy Rep. 21 25S 46 37E
82 Soliman, Tunisia 36 42N 10 30E
126 Solimões, R., Brazil 2 15S 66 30W
24 Solingen, Germany 51 10N 7 4E
49 Sollebrunn, Sweden 58 8N 12 32E
48 Sollefteå, Sweden 63 12N 17 20E
48 Sollentuna, Sweden 59 26N 17 56E
32 Soller, Spain 39 43N 2 45E
48 Sollerön, Sweden 60 54N 14 38E
48 Solna, Sweden 59 22N 18 1E
55 Solnechnogorsk, U.S.S.R. 56 10N 36 57E
47 Sölnkletten, Mt., Norway 61 55N 10 18E
33 Sologne, France 47 40N 2 0E
72 Solok, Indonesia 0 55S 100 40E
120 Sololá, Guatemala 14 49N 91 10E
116 Solomon, N. Fork, R., U.S.A. 39 45N 99 0W
116 Solomon, S. Fork, R., U.S.A. 39 25N 99 12W
62 Solomon's Pools = Burak Sulayman, Jordan 31 42N 35 7E
116 Solon Springs, U.S.A. 46 19N 91 47W
73 Solor, I., Indonesia 8 27S 123 0E
55 Solotcha, U.S.S.R. 54 48N 39 53E
25 Solothurn, Switzerland 47 13N 7 32E
25 Solothurn ♦, Switz. 47 18N 7 40E
32 Solsona, Spain 42 0N 1 31E
27 Solt, Hungary 46 45N 19 1E
39 Solta, I., Yugoslavia 43 24N 16 15E
65 Soltanabad, Iran 36 29N 58 5E
64 Soltaniyeh, Iran 36 20N 48 55E
24 Soltau, Germany 52 59N 9 50E
54 Soltsy, U.S.S.R. 58 10N 30 10E
76 Solun, China 46 40N 120 40E
47 Solund, Norway 61 5N 4 50E
47 Solund I., Norway 61 7N 4 50E
42 Solunska Glava, Yugoslavia 41 44N 21 31E
113 Solvay, U.S.A. 43 5N 76 17W
49 Solvesborg, Sweden 56 5N 14 35E
14 Solway Firth, Br. Isles 54 45N 3 38W
91 Solwezi, Zambia 12 20S 26 21E
63 Somali Rep. ■, E. Africa 7 0N 47 0E
87 Somaliland, Fr = Fr. Terr. Afars & Issas 12 0N 43 0E
69 Sombe Dzong, Bhutan 27 13N 89 8E
19 Sombernon, France 47 20N 4 40E
42 Sombor, Yugoslavia 45 46N 19 17E
112 Sombra, Canada 42 43N 82 28W
120 Sombrerete, Mexico 23 40N 103 40W
121 Sombrero I., Leeward Is. 18 30N 63 30W
118 Somers, U.S.A. 48 4N 114 18W
98 Somerset, Australia 10 45S 142 25E
121 Somerset, & I., Bermuda 32 20N 64 55W
119 Somerset, Colo., U.S.A. 38 55N 107 30W
114 Somerset, Ky., U.S.A. 37 5N 84 40W
113 Somerset, Mass., U.S.A. 41 45N 71 10W
112 Somerset, Pa., U.S.A. 40 1N 79 4E
13 Somerset ♦, United Kingdom 51 9N 3 0W
92 Somerset East, S. Afr. 32 42S 25 35E
92 Somerset West, S. Afr. 34 8S 18 50E
104 Somerset, Is., Canada 73 30N 93 0W
113 Somersworth, U.S.A. 43 15N 70 51W
119 Somerton, U.S.A. 32 41N 114 47W
113 Somerville, U.S.A. 40 34N 74 36W
46 Someş, R., Rumania 47 15N 23 45E
46 Someşul Mare, R., Rum. 47 18N 24 30E
38 Somma Lombardo, It. 45 41N 8 42E
41 Somma Vesuviana, It. 40 52N 14 23E
41 Sommatino, It. 37 20N 14 0E
18 Somme, B. de la, France 5 22N 1 30E
19 Somme ♦, France 50 0N 2 20E
49 Sommen, Sweden 58 12N 15 0E
49 Sommen, L., Sweden 58 0N 15 15E
19 Sommepy-Tahure, France 49 15N 4 31E
24 Sömmerda, Germany 51 10N 11 8E
49 Sommersted, Denmark 55 19N 9 18E

MAP
19 Sommesous, France 48 44N 4 12E
21 Sommières, Fr. 43 47N 4 6E
27 Somogy ♦, Hungary 46 19N 17 30E
27 Somogyszob, Hungary 46 18N 17 20E
28 Sompolno, Poland 52 26N 18 45E
32 Somport, Paso, Spain 42 48N 0 31W
32 Somport, Puerto de, Spain 42 48N 0 31W
47 Son, Norway 59 32N 10 42E
30 Son, Spain 42 43N 8 58W
71 Son La., N. Vietnam 21 20N 103 50E
69 Sonamukhi, India 23 18N 87 27E
38 Soncino, Italy 45 24N 9 52E
92 Sondags, R., S. Africa 32 10N 24 40E
38 Sóndala, Italy 46 20N 10 20E
49 Sönder Hornum, Den. 56 32N 9 38E
49 Söonder Nissum, Den. 56 19N 8 11E
49 Sönder Omme, Den. 55 50N 8 54E
49 Sönderborg, Denmark 54 55N 9 49E
24 Sonderhausen, Germany 51 22N 10 50E
49 Sonderjyllands Amt ♦, Denmark 55 10N 9 10E
47 Sondre Höland, Nor. 59 44N 11 30E
47 Sondre Land, Norway 60 44N 10 21E
4 Söndre Stromfjord, Greenland 66 30N 50 52W
38 Sóndrio, Italy 46 10N 9 53E
91 Sone, Mozambique 17 23S 34 55E
68 Sonepat, India 29 0N 77 5E
69 Sonepur, India 20 55N 83 50E
71 Song Cau, S. Vietnam 13 20N 109 18E
47 Songa, R., Norway 59 57N 7 30E
91 Songea, Tanzania 10 40S 35 40E
91 Songea ♦, Tanzania 10 42S 35 35E
19 Songeons, France 49 32N 1 50E
71 Songkhla, Thailand 7 13N 100 37E
91 Songwe, Zaïre 3 20S 26 16E
91 Songwe, Malawi 9 44S 33 58E
55 Sonkovo, U.S.S.R. 57 50N 37 5E
66 Sonmiani, Pakistan 25 25N 66 40E
40 Sonnino, Italy 41 25N 13 13E
119 Sonora, Calif., U.S.A. 37 59N 120 27W
117 Sonora, Texas, U.S.A. 30 33N 100 37W
118 Sonora P., U.S.A. 38 17N 119 35W
120 Sonora ♦, Mexico 28 0N 111 0W
92 Sonskyn, S. Afr. 30 47S 26 28E
25 Sonthofen, Germany 47 31N 10 16E
114 Soo Junction, U.S.A. 46 20N 85 14W
77 Soochow, China 31 18N 120 41E
73 Sopi, Indonesia 2 40N 128 28E
87 Sopo, Nahr, Sudan 8 40N 26 30E
28 Sopot, Poland 54 27N 18 31E
42 Sopot, Yugoslavia 44 29N 20 30E
42 Sopotnica, Yugoslavia 41 23N 21 13E
25 Sopron, Hungary 47 41N 16 37E
107 Sop's Arm, Canada 49 46N 56 56W
31 Sor, R., Portugal 39 7N 9 52E
47 Sör-Fron, Norway 61 35N 9 59E
5 Sör-Rondane, Ant. 72 0S 25 0E
47 Sör Tröndelag fylke ♦, Norway 63 0N 11 0E
40 Sora, Italy 41 45N 13 36E
69 Sorada, India 19 32N 84 45E
68 Sorah, Pakistan 27 13N 68 56E
48 Söråker, Sweden 62 30N 17 32E
39 Sorano, Italy 42 40N 11 42E
126 Sorata, Bolivia 15 50S 68 50W
33 Sorbas, Spain 37 6N 2 7W
18 Sordeval, France 48 44N 0 55W
106 Sorel, Canada 46 0N 73 10W
38 Soresina, Italy 45 17N 9 51E
50 Sörfold, Norway 67 5N 14 20E
21 Sorgues, France 44 1N 4 53E
32 Soria, Spain 41 43N 2 32W
32 Soria ♦, Spain 41 46N 2 28W
124 Soriano, Uruguay 33 24S 58 19W
128 Soriano ♦, Uruguay 33 30S 58 0W
49 Sorö, Denmark 55 26N 11 32E
84 Soro, Guinea 10 9N 9 48W
125 Sorocaba, Brazil 23 31S 47 35W
56 Soroki, U.S.S.R. 48 8N 28 12E
27 Soroksár, Hungary 47 24N 19 9E
68 Soron, India 27 55N 78 45E
73 Sorong, Indonesia 0 55S 131 15E
126 Sororoca, Brazil 0 43N 61 31W
90 Soroti, Uganda 1 43N 33 35E
50 Soröy Sundet, Norway 70 25N 23 0E
47 Soroyane, Norway 62 25N 5 32E
31 Sorraia, R., Portugal 38 55N 8 35W
41 Sorrento, Italy 40 38N 14 23E
92 Sorris Sorris, S.W. Afr. 21 0S 14 46E
50 Sorsele, Sweden 65 31N 17 30E
40 Sorso, Italy 40 50N 8 34E
73 Sorsogon, Philippines 13 0N 124 0E
41 Sortino, Italy 37 9N 15 1E
32 Sos, Spain 42 30N 1 13W
49 Sosdala, Sweden 56 2N 13 41E
106 Soseumica, L., Canada 50 15N 77 30W
55 Sosna, R., U.S.S.R. 52 30N 38 0E
28 Sosnowiec, Poland 50 20N 19 10E
21 Sospel, France 43 52N 7 27E
39 Šoštanj, Yugoslavia 46 23N 15 4E
120 Soto la Marina, R., Mex. 23 40N 97 40W
30 Soto y Amío, Spain 42 46N 5 53W
47 Sotra I., Norway 60 15N 5 0E
18 Sotteville, France 49 24N 1 5E
88 Souanke, Congo 2 10N 14 10E
84 Soufi, Mauritania 15 13N 12 17W
44 Souflíon, Greece 41 12N 26 18E
121 Soufrière, vol., St. Vincent 13 10N 61 10W
20 Souillac, France 44 53N 1 29E
83 Souk-Ahras, Algeria 36 17N 7 57E
82 Souk el Arba du Rharb, Morocco 34 50N 5 59W
83 Souk el Khemis, Tunisia 36 36N 8 58E
20 Soulac-sur-Mer, France 45 30N 1 7W
19 Soultz, France 48 57N 7 52E
45 Soúnion, Akra, Gr. 37 37N 24 1E

Sour el Ghozlane INDEX Stour, R.

MAP
83 Sour el Ghozlane, Alg. 36 10N 3 45E
93 Sources, Mt. aux, Les. 28 45S 28 50E
127 Soure, Brazil 0 35S 48 30W
30 Soure, Portugal 40 4N 8 38W
107 Souris, Canada 49 40N 100 20W
116 Souris, R., U.S.A. 48 35N 101 29W
45 Soúrpi, Greece 39 6N 22 54E
82 Sous, R., Morocco 30 31N 9 27W
127 Sousa, Brazil 6 45S 38 10W
127 Sousel, Brazil 2 38S 52 29W
31 Sousel, Portugal 38 57N 7 40W
82 Souss, O., Morocco 30 23N 8 24W
83 Sousse, Tunisia 35 50N 10 38E
20 Soustons, France 43 45N 1 19W
107 South Pt., Canada 49 6N 62 11W
89 South Africa, Rep. of, ■, Afr. 30 0S 25 0E
122 South America, cont. 10 0S 60 0W
96 South Australia ♦, Australia 32 0S 139 0E
119 South Baldy, Mt., U.S.A. 34 6N 107 27W
114 South Bend, Indiana, U.S.A. 41 38N 86 20W
118 South Bend, Wash., U.S.A. 46 44N 123 52W
113 South Berwick, U.S.A. 43 15N 70 47W
98 South Blackwater, Australia 24 00S 148 35E
115 South Boston, U.S.A. 36 42N 78 58W
107 South Branch, U.S.A. 44 30N 83 55W
115 South Carolina ♦, U.S.A. 33 45N 81 0W
114 South Charleston, U.S.A. 38 20N 81 40W
77 South China Sea, Asia 20 0N 115 0E
116 South Dakota ♦, U.S.A. 45 0N 100 0W
13 South Downs, Eng. 50 53N 0 10W
99 South East Cape, Australia 43 39S 146 50E
14 South Esk, R., Scot. 56 44N 2 40W
13 South Foreland, Eng. 51 7N 1 23E
118 South Fork, R., U.S.A. 47 54N 113 15W
120 South Gamboa, Panama Canal Zone 9 4N 79 40W
5 South Georgia, Falk. Is. Dep. 54 30S 37 0W
114 South Haven, U.S.A. 42 22N 86 20W
109 South Henik, L., Can. 61 30N 98 0W
90 South Horr, Kenya 2 12N 36 56E
90 South I., Kenya 2 35N 36 35E
101 South Invercargill, N.Z. 46 26N 168 23E
90 South Island, L. Rudolf, Kenya 2 40N 26 25E
76 South Korea ■, Asia 36 0N 128 0E
5 South Magnetic Pole (1965) 66 30S 139 30E
114 South Milwaukee, U.S.A. 42 50N 87 52W
5 South Orkney Is., Falk. Is. Dep. 63 0S 45 0W
118 South Pass, U.S.A. 42 20N 108 58W
96 South Passage, Australia 26 07S 113 09E
115 South Pines, U.S.A. 35 10N 79 25W
116 South Platte, R., U.S.A. 40 50N 102 45W
5 South Pole, Antarctica 90 0S 0 0E
106 South Porcupine, Can. 48 30N 81 12W
14 South Ronaldsay I., Scotland 58 46N 2 58W
7 S. Sandwich Is., Falk. Is. Dep. 57 0S 27 0W
109 South Saskatchewan, R., Canada 51 0N 109 0W
5 South Shetland Is., Ant. 62 0S 59 0W
12 South Shields, Eng. 54 59N 1 26W
116 South Sioux City, U.S.A. 42 30N 96 30W
101 South Taranaki Bight, N.Z. 39 40S 174 5E
106 South Twin I., Canada 53 0N 79 50W
12 South Tyne, R., England 54 46N 2 25W
14 South Uist, I., Scot. 57 10N 7 10W
48 South Ulvön, I., Swed. 63 0N 18 45E
71 South Vietnam ■, Asia 14 0N 108 40E
101 South West Cape, N.Z. 47 16S 167 31E
92 South West Africa ■, South Africa 22 0S 18 9E
63 South Yemen ■, Asia 15 0N 48 0E
106 Southampton, Canada 44 30N 81 25W
13 Southampton, Eng. 50 54N 1 23W
113 Southampton, U.S.A. 40 54N 72 22W
105 Southampton I., Can. 64 30N 84 0W
101 Southbridge, N.Z. 43 48S 172 16E
113 Southbridge, U.S.A. 42 4N 72 2W
109 Southend, Canada 56 28N 103 14W
13 Southend-on-Sea, England 51 32N 0 43E
91 Southern ♦, Malawi 15 0S 35 0E
84 Southern ♦, Sierra Leone 0 8N 12 30E
101 Southern Alps, N.Z. 43 41S 170 11E
96 Southern Cross, Austral. 31 12S 119 15E
109 Southern Indian Lake, Canada 57 0N 99 0W
5 Southern Ocean 62 0S 160 0W
91 Southern ♦, Zambia 16 20S 26 20E
14 Southern Uplands, Scotland 55 30N 4 0W
113 Southington, U.S.A. 41 37N 72 53W
113 Southold, U.S.A. 41 4N 72 26W
99 Southport, Australia 28 0S 153 25E
12 Southport, Eng. 53 38N 3 1W
115 Southport, U.S.A. 33 55N 78 0W
13 Southwold, Eng. 52 19N 1 41E
93 Soutpansberge, S. Africa 23 0S 29 30E
20 Souvigny, France 46 33N 3 10E
46 Sovata, Rumania 46 35N 25 3E
54 Sovetsk, Lithuania, U.S.S.R. 55 6N 21 50E
55 Sovetsk, R.S.F.S.R., U.S.S.R. 57 38N 48 53E
59 Sovetskaya Gavan, U.S.S.R. 48 50N 140 0E
39 Sovicille, Italy 43 16N 11 12E
42 Sovra, Yugoslavia 42 44N 17 34E
74 Sōya-Misaki, Japan 45 30N 142 0E
54 Sozh, R., U.S.S.R. 53 50N 31 50E
43 Sozopol, Bulgaria 42 23N 27 42E
16 Spa, Belgium 50 29N 5 53E
29 Spain ■, Europe 40 0N 5 0W
12 Spalding, England 52 47N 0 9W
116 Spalding, U.S.A. 41 45N 98 27W
49 Spandet, Denmark 55 15N 8 54E
48 Spånga, Sweden 59 23N 17 55E
49 Spångenäs, Sweden 57 36N 16 7E
47 Spangereid, Norway 58 3N 7 9E
112 Spangler, U.S.A. 40 39N 78 48W
107 Spaniard's Bay, Canada 47 38N 53 20W
106 Spanish, Canada 46 12N 82 20W
118 Spanish Fork, U.S.A. 40 10N 111 37W
•80 Spanish Sahara ♦, Africa 25 0N 13 0W
121 Spanish Town, Jamaica 18 0N 77 20W
118 Sparks, U.S.A. 39 30N 119 45W
45 Sparta = Spárti, Greece 37 5N 22 25E
115 Sparta, Ga., U.S.A. 33 18N 82 59W
116 Sparta, Wis., U.S.A. 43 55N 91 10W
112 Spartanburg, Pa., U.S.A. 41 48N 79 43W
115 Spartanburg, S.C., U.S.A. 35 0N 82 0W
82 Spartel, C., Morocco 35 47N 5 56W
45 Spárti, Greece 37 5N 22 25E
41 Spartivento, C., Calabria, It. 37 56N 16 4E
41 Spartivento, C., Sard., It. 38 52N 8 50E
54 Spas-Demensk, U.S.S.R. 54 20N 34 0E
55 Spas-Klepiki, U.S.S.R. 54 34N 40 2E
59 Spassk-Dalniy, U.S.S.R. 44 40N 132 40E
55 Spassk-Ryazanskiy, U.S.S.R. 54 30N 40 25E
45 Spatha Akra., Greece 35 42N 23 43E
116 Spearfish, U.S.A. 44 32N 103 52W
117 Spearman, U.S.A. 36 15N 101 10W
100 Speed, Australia 35 21S 142 27E
90 Speke Gulf, L. Victoria 2 20S 32 50E
104 Spenard, Alaska 61 5N 149 50W
118 Spencer, Idaho, U.S.A. 44 18N 112 8W
116 Spencer, Iowa, U.S.A. 43 5N 95 3W
116 Spencer, Nebr., U.S.A. 42 52N 98 43W
113 Spencer, N.Y., U.S.A. 42 14N 76 13W
114 Spencer, W. Va., U.S.A. 38 47N 81 24W
104 Spencer B., Canada 69 30N 94 0W
92 Spencer B., S.W. Afr. 25 30S 14 47E
99 Spencer, C., Austral. 35 20S 136 45E
99 Spencer G., Austral. 34 30S 137 0E
113 Spencerville, Canada 44 51N 75 34W
101 Spenser Mts., N.Z. 42 15S 172 45E
45 Sperkhiós, R., Greece 38 57N 22 3E
15 Sperrin Mts., U.K. 54 50N 7 0W
25 Spessart, Germany 50 0N 9 20E
45 Spetsai, Greece 37 16N 23 9E
45 Spétsai, I., Greece 37 15N 23 10E
14 Spey, R., Scotland 57 26N 4 30W
25 Speyer, Germany 49 19N 8 26E
17 Speyer, R., Germany 49 18N 7 52E
38 Spezia (La Spezia), Italy 44 7N 9 49E
41 Spezzano Albanese, It. 39 41N 16 19E
24 Spiekeroog, I., Germany 53 45N 7 42E
39 Spielfeld, Austria 46 43N 15 38E
25 Spiez, Switzerland 46 40N 7 40E
45 Spili, Greece 35 13N 24 31E
39 Spilimbergo, Italy 46 7N 12 53E
108 Spillimacheen, Canada 51 6N 117 0W
65 Spin Baldak, Afghan. 31 3N 66 16E
41 Spinazzola, Italy 40 58N 16 5E
19 Spincourt, France 49 20N 5 39E
47 Spind, Norway 58 6N 6 53E
46 Spineni, Rumania 44 43N 24 37E
118 Spirit Lake, U.S.A. 47 56N 116 56W
55 Spirit River, Canada 55 45N 119 0W
109 Spiritwood, Canada 53 24N 107 33W
27 Spišská Nová Ves, Cz. 48 58N 20 34E
27 Spišské Podhradie, Cz. 49 0N 20 48E
26 Spittal, Austria 46 48N 13 31E
4 Spitzbergen (Svalbard), Norway 78 0N 17 0E
39 Split, Yugoslavia 43 31N 16 26E
109 Split L., Canada 56 15N 96 0W
39 Splitski Kan, Y.-slavia 43 31N 16 20E
25 Splügen Pass, Switz. 46 30N 9 20E
117 Spofford, U.S.A. 29 10N 100 27W
118 Spokane, U.S.A. 47 45N 117 25W
47 Sponvika, Norway 59 7N 11 15E
116 Spooner, U.S.A. 45 49N 91 51W
45 Sporádhes, Greece 37 0N 27 0E
58 Sporyy Navolok, M., U.S.S.R. 75 50N 68 40E
106 Spragge, Canada 46 15N 82 40W
118 Sprague, U.S.A. 47 25N 117 59W
118 Sprague River, U.S.A. 42 49N 121 31W
•72 Spratly, I., S. China Sea 8 20N 112 0E
118 Spray, U.S.A. 44 56N 119 46W
24 Spree, R., Germany 52 23N 13 52E
119 Spring Mts., U.S.A. 36 20N 115 43W
118 Spring City, U.S.A. 39 31N 111 28W
116 Spring Valley, Minn., U.S.A. 43 40N 92 30W
113 Spring Valley, N.Y., U.S.A. 41 7N 74 4W
92 Springbok, S. Africa 29 42S 17 54E
101 Springburn, N.Z. 43 40S 171 32E
107 Springdale, Canada 49 30N 56 6W
117 Springdale, Ark., U.S.A. 36 10N 94 5W
118 Springdale, Wash., U.S.A. 48 1N 117 50W
24 Springe, Germany 52 12N 9 35E
119 Springerville, U.S.A. 34 10N 109 16W
112 Springfield, Canada 42 52N 80 57W
101 Springfield, N.Z. 43 19S 171 56E
117 Springfield, Colo., U.S.A. 37 26N 102 40W

* Renamed Western Sahara

116 Springfield, Ill., U.S.A. 39 58N 89 40W
113 Springfield, Mass., U.S.A. 42 8N 72 37W
117 Springfield, Mo., U.S.A. 37 15N 93 20W
114 Springfield, Ohio, U.S.A. 39 50N 83 48W
118 Springfield, Oreg., U.S.A. 44 2N 123 0W
115 Springfield, Tenn., U.S.A. 36 35N 86 55W
113 Springfield, Vt., U.S.A. 43 20N 72 30W
92 Springfontein, S. Africa 30 15S 25 40E
107 Springhill, Canada 45 40N 64 4W
108 Springhouse, Canada 51 56N 122 7W
100 Springhurst, Australia 36 12S 146 24E
93 Springs, S. Afr. 26 13S 28 25E
98 Springsure, Australia 24 8S 148 6E
113 Springvale, U.S.A. 43 28N 70 48W
112 Springville, N.Y., U.S.A. 42 31N 78 41W
118 Springville, Utah, U.S.A. 40 14N 111 35W
109 Springwater, Canada 51 58N 108 23W
112 Spruce-Creek, U.S.A. 40 36N 78 9W
117 Spur, U.S.A. 33 28N 100 50W
12 Spurn Hd., Eng. 53 34N 0 8W
42 Spuz, Yugoslavia 42 32N 19 10E
108 Spuzzum, Canada 49 37N 121 23W
47 Spydeberg, Norway 59 37N 11 4E
108 Squamish, Canada 49 45N 123 10W
107 Square Islands, Canada 52 47N 55 47W
41 Squillace, Golfo di, Italy 38 43N 16 35E
41 Squinzano, Italy 40 27N 18 1E
73 Sragen, Indonesia 7 28S 110 59E
42 Srbac, Yugoslavia 45 7N 17 30E
42 Srbija ♦, Y.-slavia 43 30N 21 0E
42 Srbobran, Yugoslavia 45 32N 19 48E
71 Sre Umbell, Khmer Rep. 11 8N 103 46E
42 Srebrnica, Yugoslavia 44 10N 19 18E
59 Sredinyy Khrebet, U.S.S.R. 57 0N 160 0E
39 Središce, Yugoslavia 46 24N 16 17E
43 Sredna Gora, Bulg. 42 40N 25 0E
55 Sredne Tambovskoye, U.S.S.R. 50 55N 137 45E
59 Srednekolymsk, U.S.S.R. 67 20N 154 40E
59 Srednevilyuysk, U.S.S.R. 63 50N 123 5E
43 Sredni Rodopi, Rum. 41 40N 24 45E
28 Srem, Poland 52 6N 17 2E
59 Sretensk, U.S.S.R. 52 10N 117 40E
70 Sri Lanka ■, S. Asia 7 30N 80 50E
70 Sriharikota, I., India 13 40N 81 30E
70 Srikakulam, India 18 14N 84 4E
66 Srinagar, Kashmir 34 12N 74 50E
69 Sripur, Bangladesh 24 14N 90 30E
70 Srirangam, India 10 54N 78 42E
70 Srirangapatnam, India 12 26N 76 43E
70 Śrivilliputtur, India 9 31N 77 40E
28 Środa Slaska, Poland 51 10N 16 35E
28 Środa Wlkp., Poland 52 15N 17 19E
42 Srpska Crnja, Y.-slav. 45 38N 20 44E
42 Srpska Itabej, Y.-slav. 45 35N 20 44E
24 Stade, Germany 53 35N 9 31E
50 Staðarhólskirkja, Iceland 65 23N 21 58W
49 Stadil, Denmark 56 12N 8 12E
48 Städjan, Sweden 61 56N 12 30E
47 Stadlandet, Norway 62 10N 5 10E
48 Stadsforsen, Swed. 63 0N 16 45E
24 Stadthagen, Germany 52 20N 9 14E
24 Stadtlohn, Germany 51 59N 6 52E
24 Stadtroda, E. Germany 50 51N 11 44E
50 Stafafell, Iceland 64 25N 14 52W
12 Staffa, I., Scot. 56 26N 6 21W
14 Stafford, England 52 49N 2 9W
12 Stafford ♦, Eng. 52 53N 2 10W
117 Stafford, U.S.A. 38 0N 98 35W
113 Stafford Springs, U.S.A. 41 58N 72 20W
40 Stagnone, I., Italy 37 50N 12 28E
13 Staines, England 51 26N 0 30W
26 Stainz, Austria 46 53N 15 17E
49 Stakkroge, Denmark 55 53N 8 51E
42 Stalač, Yugoslavia 43 43N 21 28E
57 Stalingrad = Volgograd, U.S.S.R. 48 40N 44 25E
57 Staliniri = Iskhinvali, U.S.S.R. 42 14N 44 1E
56 Stalino = Donetsky, U.S.S.R. 48 0N 37 45E
55 Stalinogorsk = Novomoskovsk, U.S.S.R. 54 5N 38 15E
28 Stalowa Wola, Poland 50 34N 22 3E
12 Stalybridge, Eng. 53 29N 2 2W
98 Stamford, Australia 21 15S 143 46E
13 Stamford, Eng. 52 39N 0 29W
113 Stamford, Conn., U.S.A. 41 5N 73 30W
117 Stamford, Tex., U.S.A. 32 58N 99 50W
117 Stamps, U.S.A. 33 22N 93 30W
116 Stanberry, U.S.A. 40 12N 94 32W
93 Standerton, S. Africa 26 55S 29 13E
114 Standish, U.S.A. 43 58N 83 57W
118 Stanford, U.S.A. 47 11N 110 10W
47 Stange Hedmark, Norway 60 43N 11 11E
93 Stanger, S. Africa 29 18S 31 21E
27 Stanišic, Yugoslavia 45 53N 19 12E
54 Stanislav = Ivano-Frankovsk, U.S.S.R. 49 0N 24 40E
42 Stanke Dimitrov, Bulg. 42 27N 23 9E
99 Stanley, Australia 40 46S 145 19E
107 Stanley, N.B., Canada 46 20N 66 50W
109 Stanley, Sask., Canada 55 20N 104 40W
118 Stanley, U.S.A. 44 10N 114 59W
128 Stanley, Falkland Is. 51 40S 58 0W
118 Stanley, Idaho, U.S.A. 44 10N 114 59W
116 Stanley, N.D., U.S.A. 48 20N 102 23W
112 Stanley, N.Y., U.S.A. 42 48N 77 6W
116 Stanley, Wis., U.S.A. 44 57N 91 0W
•90 Stanley, Chutes, Congo 0 12N 25 25E
70 Stanley Res., India 11 50N 77 40E
90 Stanleyville = Kisangani, Zaïre 0 35N 25 15E
120 Stann Creek, Br. Hond. 17 0N 88 20W

* Renamed Chutes Boyoma

59 Stanovoy Khrebet, U.S.S.R. 55 0N 130 0E
99 Stanthorpe, Australia 28 36S 151 59E
104 Stanton, Canada 69 45N 128 52W
117 Stanton, U.S.A. 32 8N 101 45W
116 Stapleton, U.S.A. 41 30N 100 31W
28 Staporkow, Poland 51 9N 20 31E
109 Star City, Canada 52 55N 104 20W
57 Stara-minskaya, U.S.S.R. 46 33N 39 0E
42 Stara Moravica, Y.-slav. 45 50N 19 30E
42 Stara Pazova, Y.-slavia 45 0N 20 10E
43 Stara Planina, Bulgaria 43 15N 23 0E
43 Stara Zagora, Bulgaria 42 26N 25 39E
28 Starachowice- Wierzbnik, Poland 51 3N 21 2E
54 Staraya Russa, U.S.S.R. 57 58N 31 10E
95 Starbuck I., Pac. Oc. 5 37S 155 55W
24 Stargard, Germany 53 29N 13 19E
28 Stargard Szczecinski, Pol. 53 20N 15 0E
42 Stari Bar, Yugoslavia 42 7N 19 13E
39 Stari Trg., Y.-slavia 45 29N 15 7E
54 Staritsa, U.S.S.R. 56 33N 35 0E
115 Starke, U.S.A. 30 0N 82 10W
117 Starkville, Colo., U.S.A. 37 10N 104 31W
115 Starkville, Miss., U.S.A. 33 26N 88 48W
25 Starnberg, Germany 48 0N 11 20E
25 Starnberger See, Ger. 48 0N 11 0E
57 Starobelsk, U.S.S.R. 49 27N 39 0E
54 Starodub, U.S.S.R. 52 30N 32 50E
28 Starogard, Poland 53 55N 18 30E
13 Start Pt., Scotland 59 17N 2 25W
27 Stary Sacz, Poland 49 33N 30 26E
57 Staryy Biryuzyak, U.S.S.R. 44 46N 46 50E
59 Staryy Kheydzhan, U.S.S.R. 60 0N 144 50E
56 Staryy Krym, U.S.S.R. 44 48N 35 8E
55 Staryy Oskol, U.S.S.R. 51 12N 37 55E
24 Stassfurt, Germany 51 51N 11 34E
112 State College, U.S.A. 40 47N 77 49W
128 Staten, I. = Los Estados, I. de, Arg. 54 40S 64 0W
113 Staten I., U.S.A. 40 35N 74 10W
115 Statesboro, U.S.A. 32 26N 81 46W
115 Statesville, U.S.A. 35 48N 80 51W
47 Stathelle, Norway 59 3N 9 41E
116 Staunton, Ill., U.S.A. 39 0N 89 49W
114 Staunton, Va., U.S.A. 38 7N 79 4W
117 Stavanger, Norway 58 57N 5 40E
16 Stavelot, Belgium 50 23N 5 55E
47 Stavern, Norway 59 0N 10 1E
47 Stavfjord, Norway 61 30N 5 0E
16 Stavoren, Netherlands 52 53N 5 21E
48 Stavre, Sweden 62 51N 15 19E
57 Stavropol, U.S.S.R. 45 5N 42 0E
44 Stavroúpolis, Greece 41 12N 24 45E
49 Stavsjö, Sweden 48 42N 16 30E
100 Stawell, Australia 36 58S 142 47E
28 Stawiszyn, Poland 51 56N 18 4E
112 Stayner, Canada 44 25N 80 5W
118 Steamboat Springs, U.S.A. 40 30N 106 58W
28 Stebark, Poland 53 30N 20 10E
44 Stebleva, Albania 41 18N 20 33E
116 Steele, U.S.A. 46 56N 99 52W
112 Steelton, U.S.A. 40 17N 76 50W
117 Steelville, U.S.A. 37 57N 91 21W
108 Steen River, Canada 59 40N 117 12W
19 Steenvoorde, France 50 48N 2 33E
96 Steep Pt., Australia 26 08S 113 8E
109 Steep Rock, Can. 51 30N 98 40W
106 Steep Rock Lake, Can. 48 50N 91 38W
46 Stefănesti, Rumania 47 44N 27 15E
87 Stefanie L. = Chew Bahir, Ethiopia 4 40N 30 50E
46 Stefănesti, Rumania 47 44N 27 15E
49 Stege, Denmark 55 0N 12 18E
42 Steierdorf Anina, Rum. 45 6N 21 51E
26 Steiermark ♦, Austria 47 26N 15 0E
25 Steigerwald, West Germany 49 45N 10 30E
109 Steinbach, Canada 49 32N 96 40W
16 Steinfort, Luxembourg 49 39N 5 55E
24 Steinheim, Germany 51 50N 9 6E
50 Steinkjer, Norway 63 59N 11 31E
92 Stella Land, S. Africa 26 45S 24 50E
92 Stellenbosch, S. Africa 33 58S 18 50E
47 Stemshaug, Norway 63 19N 8 44E
24 Stendal, Germany 52 36N 11 50E
49 Stenmagle, Denmark 55 49N 11 39E
50 Stensele, Sweden 65 3N 17 8E
49 Stenstorp, Sweden 58 17N 13 45E
49 Stenungsund, Sweden 58 6N 11 50E
53 Stepanakert, U.S.S.R. 40 0N 46 25E
116 Stephan, U.S.A. 48 30N 96 53W
100 Stephens Creek, Austral. 31 50S 141 30E
107 Stephenville, Canada 48 31N 58 30W
117 Stephenville, U.S.A. 32 12N 98 12W
28 Stepnica, Poland 53 38N 14 36E
57 Stepnoi = Elista, U.S.S.R. 46 25N 44 17E
45 Stereáellas, Greece 38 55N 22 0E
92 Sterkstroom, S. Africa 31 32S 26 32E
4 Sterlego, Mys, U.S.S.R. 80 30N 90 0E
116 Sterling, Colo., U.S.A. 40 40N 103 15W
116 Sterling, Ill., U.S.A. 41 45N 89 45W
116 Sterling, Kans., U.S.A. 38 17N 98 13W
117 Sterling City, U.S.A. 31 50N 100 59W
112 Sterling Run, U.S.A. 41 25N 78 12W
52 Sterlitamak, U.S.S.R. 53 40N 56 0E
24 Sternberg, Germany 53 42N 11 48E
27 Šternberk, Cz. 49 45N 17 15E
28 Stettin = Szczecin, Poland 53 27N 14 27E
24 Stettiner Haff, Germany 53 50N 14 25E
108 Stettler, Canada 52 25N 112 40W
112 Steubenville, U.S.A. 40 21N 80 39W
116 Stevens Port, U.S.A. 44 32N 89 34W
96 Stevenson, R., Australia 46 15S 134 10E
49 Stevns Klint, Den. 55 17N 12 28E
128 Stewart, I., Chile 54 50S 71 30W
101 Stewart I., N.Z. 46 58S 167 54E
107 Stewiacke, Canada 45 9N 63 22W
92 Steynsburg, S. Africa 31 15S 25 49E
26 Steyr, Austria 48 3N 14 25E
26 Steyr, R., Austria 48 57N 14 15E
92 Steytlerville, S. Africa 33 17S 24 19E
39 Stia, Italy 43 48N 11 41E
117 Stigler, U.S.A. 35 19N 95 6W
41 Stigliano, Italy 40 24N 16 13E
49 Stigsnaes, Denmark 55 13N 11 18E
49 Stigtomta, Sweden 58 47N 16 48E
104 Stikine Mts., Canada 59 30N 129 30W
104 Stikine, R., Canada 58 0N 131 0W
92 Stilfontein, S. Africa 26 50S 26 50E
45 Stilis, Greece 38 55N 22 37E
116 Stillwater, Minn., U.S.A. 45 3N 92 47W
113 Stillwater, N.Y., U.S.A. 42 55N 73 41W
117 Stillwater, Okla., U.S.A. 36 5N 97 3W
118 Stillwater Mts., U.S.A. 39 45N 118 6W
117 Stilwell, U.S.A. 35 52N 94 36W
45 Stimfalias, L., Greece 37 51N 22 27E
106 Stimson, Canada 48 58N 80 30W
42 Stip, Yugoslavia 41 42N 22 10E
45 Stira, Greece 38 9N 24 14E
19 Stiring Wendel, France 49 12N 6 57E
96 Stirling, Australia 17 12S 141 35E
108 Stirling, Canada 49 30N 112 30W
14 Stirling, Scotland 56 17N 3 57W
•14 Stirling ♦, Scot. 56 3N 4 10W
113 Stittsville, Canada 45 15N 75 58W
49 Stjärneborg, Sweden 57 53N 14 45E
48 Stjarnsfors, Sweden 60 2N 13 45E
47 Stjördalshalsen, Nor. 63 29N 10 51E
49 Stockaryd, Sweden 57 19N 14 36E
27 Stockerau, Austria 48 24N 16 12E
118 Stockett, U.S.A. 47 23N 111 7W
48 Stockholm, Sweden 59 20N 18 3E
48 Stockholms län ♦, Sweden 59 30N 18 20E
100 Stockinbingal, Austral. 34 30S 147 53E
12 Stockport, Eng. 53 25N 2 11W
100 Stockton, Australia 32 56S 151 47E
118 Stockton, Calif., U.S.A. 38 0N 121 20W
116 Stockton, Kans., U.S.A. 39 30N 99 20W
117 Stockton, Mo., U.S.A. 37 40N 93 48W
12 Stockton-on-Tees, England 54 34N 1 20W
48 Stockvik, Sweden 62 17N 17 23E
28 Stoczek Łukowski, Poland 51 58N 22 22E
48 Stode, Sweden 62 28N 16 35E
42 Stogovo, mts., Y.-slavia 41 31N 20 38E
12 Stoke-on-Trent, England 53 1N 2 11W
106 Stokes Bay, Canada 45 0N 81 22W
47 Stokke, Norway 59 13N 10 17E
47 Stokken, Norway 58 31N 8 53E
50 Stokksnes, Iceland 64 14N 14 58W
42 Stolac, Yugoslavia 43 8N 17 59E
24 Stolberg, E. Germany 51 33N 11 0E
24 Stolberg, W. Germany 50 48N 6 13E
55 Stolbovaya, R.S.F.S.R., U.S.S.R. 55 10N 37 32E
59 Stolbovaya, R.S.F.S.R., U.S.S.R. 64 50N 153 50E
54 Stolbtsy, U.S.S.R. 53 22N 26 43E
54 Stolin, U.S.S.R. 51 53N 26 50E
46 Stolnici, Rumania 44 31N 24 48E
42 Ston, Yugoslavia 42 51N 17 43E
106 Stonecliffe, Canada 46 13N 77 56W
14 Stonehaven, Scot. 56 58N 2 11W
13 Stonehenge, Eng. 51 9N 1 45W
109 Stonewall, Canada 50 10N 96 50W
47 Stongfjord, Norway 61 28N 14 0E
112 Stony L., Canada 44 35N 78 15W
109 Stony Rapids, Canada 59 15N 105 55W
28 Stopnica, Poland 50 27N 20 57E
47 Stor Elvdal, Norway 61 30N 11 1E
24 Stora Borge Fjell, Mt., Norway 65 12N 14 0E
48 Stora Gla, Sweden 59 30N 12 30E
49 Stora Karlsö, Sweden 57 17N 17 59E
50 Stora Lulevatten, Swed. 67 10N 19 30E
50 Stora Sjöfallet, Sweden 67 29N 18 40E
50 Storavan, Sweden 65 45N 18 10E
47 Stord Leirvik, I., Nor. 59 48N 5 27E
49 Store Baelt, Den. 55 20N 11 0E
100 Store Creek, Australia 32 54S 149 6E
49 Store Heddinge, Denmark 55 18N 12 23E
47 Storen, Norway 63 3N 10 18E
47 Storfjorden, Möre og Romsdal, Norway 62 7N 6 34E
47 Storfjorden, Möre og Romsdal, Norway 62 25N 6 30E
99 Storm B., Austral. 43 10S 147 30E
116 Storm Lake, U.S.A. 42 35N 95 5W
92 Stormsrivier, S. Africa 33 59S 23 52E
14 Stornoway, Scot. 58 12N 6 23W
56 Storozhinets, U.S.S.R. 48 14S 25 45E
48 Storsjö, Sweden 62 49N 13 5E
47 Storsjöen, Hedmark, Norway 60 20N 11 40E
47 Storsjöen, Hedmark, Norway 61 30N 11 14E
48 Storsjön, Gavleborg, Sweden 60 35N 16 45E
48 Storsjön, Jämtland, Sweden 62 50N 13 8E
49 Storstroms Amt ♦, Denmark 49 50N 11 45E
50 Storuman, Sweden 65 5N 17 10E
48 Storvätteshagna, Mt., Sweden 62 6N 12 30E
48 Storvik, Sweden 60 35N 16 33E
109 Stoughton, Canada 49 40N 103 0W
13 Stour, R., Dorset, England 50 48N 2 7W
13 Stour, R., Kent, Eng. 51 15N 0 57E

* Incorporated within the regions of Central and Strathclyde

Stour, R. INDEX Sym

MAP
13 Stour, R., Suffolk, England 52 7N 0 28E
13 Stour, R., Worcs., England 52 25N 2 13W
13 Stourbridge, Eng. 52 28N 2 8W
109 Stout, L., Canada 52 0N 94 40W
13 Stowmarket, Eng. 52 11N 1 0E
15 Strabane, N. Ire. 54 50N 7 28W
42 Stracin, Yugoslavia 42 13N 22 2E
38 Stradella, Italy 45 4N 9 20E
99 Strahan, Australia 42 8S 145 24E
26 Stralkonice, Cz. 49 15N 13 53E
43 Straldzha, Bulgaria 42 35N 26 40E
24 Stralsund, Germany 54 17N 13 5E
92 Strand, S. Afr. 34 9S 18 48E
47 Strand, Hedmark, Nor. 61 18N 11 15E
47 Strand, Rogaland, Nor. 59 3N 5 56E
47 Stranda, Möre og Romsdal, Norway 62 19N 6 58E
47 Stranda, Norway 62 19N 6 58E
49 Strandby, Denmark 56 47N 9 13E
47 Strandebarm, Norway 60 17N 6 0E
47 Strandvik, Norway 60 9N 5 41E
15 Strangford, N. Ire. 54 23N 5 34W
15 Strangford, L., Northern Ireland 54 30N 5 37W
48 Strängnäs, Sweden 59 23N 17 8E
14 Stranraer, Scot. 54 54N 5 0W
109 Strasbourg, Canada 51 10N 104 55W
19 Strasbourg, France 48 35N 7 42E
24 Strasburg, Germany 53 30N 13 44E
116 Strasburg, U.S.A. 46 12N 101 9W
100 Stratford, Austral. 37 59S 147 5E
106 Stratford, Canada 43 23N 81 0W
101 Stratford, New Zealand 39 20S 174 19E
119 Stratford, Calif., U.S.A. 36 10N 119 55W
113 Stratford, Conn., U.S.A. 41 13N 73 8W
117 Stratford, Tex., U.S.A. 36 20N 102 3W
13 Stratford-on-Avon, Eng. 52 12N 1 42W
14 Strath Spey, Scot. 57 15N 3 40W
99 Strathalbyn, Australia 35 13S 138 53E
98 Strathmore, Australia 17 50S 142 35E
108 Strathmore, Canada 51 5N 113 25W
14 Strathmore, Scot. 56 40N 3 4W
106 Strathroy, Canada 42 58N 81 38W
14 Strathy Pt., Scot. 58 35N 4 0W
116 Stratton, U.S.A. 39 20N 102 36W
25 Straubing, Germany 48 53N 12 35E
50 Straumnes, Iceland 66 26N 23 8W
47 Stramsnes, Norway 63 4N 8 2E
24 Strausberg, Germany 52 40N 13 52E
118 Strawberry Res., U.S.A. 40 0N 111 0W
117 Strawn, U.S.A. 32 36N 98 30W
27 Strážnice, Cz. 48 54N 17 19E
96 Streaky B., S. Austral. 32 51S 134 18E
100 Streatham, Austral. 37 43S 143 5E
116 Streator, U.S.A. 41 9N 88 52W
26 Středočeský ♦, Cz. 49 55N 14 30E
27 Stredoslovenský ♦, Cz. 48 30N 19 15E
112 Streetsville, Canada 43 36N 79 43W
46 Strehaia, Rumania 44 37N 23 10E
43 Strelcha, Bulgaria 42 30N 24 19E
59 Strelka, U.S.S.R. 58 5N 93 10E
50 Strengelvåg, Norway 68 58N 15 11E
58 Strezhevoy, U.S.S.R. 60 42N 77 34E
58 Strezhnoye, U.S.S.R. 57 45N 84 2E
100 Strezlecki, Austral. 38 16S 145 50E
26 Stribro, Czechoslovakia 49 44N 13 0E
98 Strickland, R., Papua 7 0S 141 45E
44 Strimón, R., Greece 41 0N 23 30E
44 Strimonikós Kólpos, Greece 40 33N 24 0E
45 Strofadhes, I., Greece 37 15N 21 0E
47 Strom, Norway 60 17N 11 44E
48 Ström, Sweden 61 52N 17 20E
48 Strombacka, Sweden 61 58N 16 44E
41 Strómboli, I., Italy 38 48N 15 12E
14 Stromeferry, Scot. 57 20N 5 33W
48 Stromsberg, Sweden 60 28N 17 44E
49 Strömsnäsbruk, Sweden 56 35N 13 45E
48 Strömstad, Sweden 58 55N 11 15E
48 Stromsund, Sweden 63 51N 15 35E
41 Strongoli, Italy 39 16N 17 2E
14 Stronsay I., Scot. 59 8N 2 38W
27 Stropkov, Cz. 49 13N 21 39E
100 Stroud, Austral. 32 25S 152 9E
13 Stroud, England 51 44N 2 12W
100 Stroud Road, Australia 32 21S 151 48E
113 Stroudsburg, U.S.A. 40 59N 75 15W
49 Struer, Denmark 56 30N 8 35E
42 Struga, Yugoslavia 41 13N 20 44E
54 Strugi Krasnye, U.S.S.R. 58 21N 28 51E
43 Struma, R., Bulgaria 41 50N 23 18E
42 Strumica, Yugoslavia 41 28N 22 41E
42 Strumica, R., Y.-slavia 41 26N 27 46E
47 Strusshamn, Norway 60 24N 5 10E
112 Struthers, U.S.A. 41 6N 80 38W
43 Stryama, Bulgaria 42 16N 24 54E
54 Stryi, U.S.S.R. 49 16N 23 48E
108 Stryker, U.S.A. 48 40N 114 44W
28 Stryków, Poland 51 55N 19 33E
28 Strzegom, Poland 50 58N 16 20E
28 Strzelce Krajeńskie, Pol. 52 52N 15 33E
99 Strzelecki Creek, Australia 29 37S 139 59E
28 Strzelin, Poland 50 46N 17 2E
28 Strzelno, Poland 52 35N 18 9E
28 Strzybnica, Poland 50 29N 18 48E
27 Strzyżów, Poland 49 52N 21 47E
48 Strömstad, Sweden 58 56N 11 10E
115 Stuart, Fla., U.S.A. 27 11N 80 12W
116 Stuart, Nebr., U.S.A. 42 39N 99 8W
108 Stuart L., Canada 54 40N 124 40W
100 Stuart Town, Australia 32 47S 149 10E
96 Stuart's Ra., Australia 29 10S 135 0E
49 Stubbekøbing, Denmark 54 53N 12 9E
26 Stuben, Austria 46 58N 10 31E
24 Stuberhuk, Germany 54 23N 11 18E
48 Stugsund, Sweden 61 16N 17 18E
48 Stugun, Sweden 63 10N 15 40E
109 Stull, L., Canada 54 26N 92 20W
71 Stung-Treng, Khmer Rep. 13 26N 106 0E
55 Stupino, U.S.S.R. 54 57N 38 2E
109 Sturgeon B., Canada 52 0N 98 0W
106 Sturgeon Falls, Canada 46 25N 79 57W
112 Sturgeon L., Can. 44 30N 78 45W
114 Sturgeon Bay, U.S.A. 44 52N 87 20W
114 Sturgis, Mich., U.S.A. 41 50N 85 25W
116 Sturgis, S.D., U.S.A. 44 25N 103 30W
49 Sturko, I., Sweden 56 5N 15 42E
27 Stúrovo, Czechoslovakia 47 48N 18 41E
96 Sturt Cr., Australia 19 0S 128 15E
92 Stutterheim, S. Africa 32 33S 27 28E
25 Stuttgart, Germany 48 46N 9 10E
117 Stuttgart, U.S.A. 34 30N 91 33W
113 Stuyvesant, U.S.A. 42 23N 73 45W
50 Stykkishólmur, Iceland 65 2N 22 40W
54 Styr, R., U.S.S.R. 51 4N 25 20E
26 Styria = Steiermark, Austria 47 26N 15 0E
86 Suakin, Sudan 19 0N 37 20E
77 Suancheng, China 30 58N 118 57E
77 Süanen, China 30 0N 109 30E
77 Suanhan, China 31 17N 107 46E
76 Suanhwa, China 40 35N 115 0E
77 Suao, Taiwan 24 32N 121 42E
71 Suay Rieng, Cambodia 11 9N 105 45E
73 Subang, Indonesia 7 30S 107 45E
72 Subi, I., Indonesia 2 58N 108 50E
39 Subiaco, Italy 41 56N 13 5E
42 Subotica, Yugoslavia 46 6N 19 29E
109 Success, Canada 50 28N 108 6W
46 Suceava, Rumania 47 38N 26 16E
46 Suceava, R., Rumania 47 38N 26 16E
46 Suceava ♦, Rumania 47 37N 26 18E
27 Sucha-Beskidzka, Poland 49 44N 19 35E
28 Suchan, Poland 53 18N 15 18E
28 Suchedniów, Poland 51 3N 20 49E
120 Suchitoto, Salvador 13 56N 89 0W
77 Süchow, China 34 10N 117 20E
28 Suchowola, Poland 53 33N 23 3E
126 Sucio, R., Colombia 6 40N 77 0W
15 Suck, R., Ire. 53 17N 8 10W
126 Sucre, Bolivia 19 0S 65 15W
126 Sucre, Venezuela 10 25N 64 5W
126 Sucre, est., Venezuela 10 25N 63 30W
126 Sucre ♦, Colombia 8 50N 75 40W
126 Sucre ♦, Venezuela 10 25N 63 30W
126 Sucunduri, R., Brazil 6 20N 58 35W
39 Sučuraj, Yugoslavia 43 10N 17 8E
55 Suda, R., U.S.S.R. 59 40N 36 30E
56 Sudak, U.S.S.R. 44 51N 34 57E
81 Sudan ■, E. Africa 15 0N 30 0E
78 Sudan, The, Africa 11 0N 9 0E
55 Suday, U.S.S.R. 59 0N 43 15E
106 Sudbury, Canada 46 30N 81 0W
87 Sûdd, Sudan 8 20N 29 30E
24 Süderbrarup, W. Ger. 54 38N 9 47E
24 Süderlügum, W. Ger. 54 50N 8 46E
27 Sudety, Pol.-Cz. 50 20N 16 45E
91 Sudi, Tanzania 10 11S 39 57E
73 Sudirman, Pengunungan, Indonesia 4 30N 137 0E
46 Suditi, Rumania 44 35N 27 38E
55 Sudogda, U.S.S.R. 55 55N 40 50E
86 Sudr, Egypt 29 40N 32 42E
54 Sudzha, U.S.S.R. 51 14N 34 25E
33 Sueca, Spain 39 12N 0 21W
86 Suez = Suweis, Egypt 28 40N 33 0E
62 Suf, Jordan 32 19N 35 49E
64 Sufaina, Saudi Arabia 23 6N 40 44E
114 Suffolk, U.S.A. 36 47N 76 33W
13 Suffolk ♦, Eng. 52 16N 1 0E
• 13 Suffolk, East, ♦, England 52 16N 1 10E
• 13 Suffolk, West, ♦, England 52 16N 0 45E
75 Sufu, China 39 44N 75 53E
65 Sufuk, Trucial States 23 50N 51 50E
46 Sugag, Rumania 45 47N 23 37E
116 Sugar City, U.S.A. 38 18N 103 38W
90 Sugarloaf Pt., Australia 32 22S 152 30E
105 Sugluk = Saglout, Canada 62 10N 75 40W
46 Suhaia, L., Rum. 43 45N 25 15E
65 Suhār, Oman 24 20N 56 40E
76 Suhbaatar, Mongolia 50 17N 106 10E
24 Suhl, Germany 50 35N 10 40E
24 Suhl ♦, Germany 50 37N 10 43E
85 Suhum, Ghana 6 5N 0 27W
42 Suica, Y.-slav. 43 52N 17 11E
76 Suifenho, China 44 30N 131 2E
77 Suihsien, China 31 58N 113 20E
76 Suihwa, China 46 40N 126 57E
77 Suiknai, China 21 17N 110 19E
77 Suining, China 26 11N 109 5E
19 Suippes, France 49 8N 4 30E
15 Suir, R., Ire. 52 31N 7 59W
76 Suiteh, China 37 35N 110 5E
68 Sujangarh, India 27 42N 47 31E
73 Sukabumi, Indonesia 6 56S 106 57E
72 Sukadana, Indonesia 1 10S 110 0E
72 Sukandja, Indonesia 2 28S 110 25E
73 Sukarnapura = Djajapura, Indonesia 2 28N 140 38E
73 Sukarno G., Indonesia 3 57S 137 17E
54 Sukhinichi, U.S.S.R. 54 8N 35 10E
52 Sukhona, R., U.S.S.R. 60 30N 45 0E
57 Sukhumi, U.S.S.R. 43 0N 41 0E
68 Sukkur, Pakistan 27 50N 68 46E
70 Sukma, India 18 24N 81 37E
42 Sukovo, Yugoslavia 43 4N 22 37E
73 Sula, Kepulauan, Indonesia 1 45S 125 0E
54 Sula, R., U.S.S.R. 50 0N 33 0E
68 Sulaiman Range, Pakistan 30 30N 69 50E
68 Sulaimanke Headworks, Pakistan 30 27N 73 55E

* *United to form the county of Suffolk*

57 Sulak, R., U.S.S.R. 43 20N 47 20E
62 Sulam Tsor, Israel 33 4N 35 6E
73 Sulawesi, I., Indon. 2 0S 120 0E
73 Sulawesi ♦, Indon. 2 0S 120 0E
28 Sulechów, Poland 52 5N 15 40E
28 Sulecin, Poland 52 26N 15 10E
28 Sulejów, Poland 51 26N 19 53E
28 Sulejówek, Poland 52 13N 21 17E
84 Sulima, Sierra Leone 6 58N 11 32W
46 Sulina, Rumania 45 10N 29 40E
24 Sulingen, Germany 52 41N 8 47E
46 Sulita, Rumania 47 39N 20 59E
50 Sulitälma, Sweden 67 17N 17 28E
27 Sułkowice, Poland 49 50N 19 49E
126 Sullana, Peru 5 0S 80 45W
116 Sullivan, Ill., U.S.A. 39 40N 88 40W
114 Sullivan, Ind., U.S.A. 39 5N 87 26W
116 Sullivan, Mo., U.S.A. 38 10N 91 10W
108 Sullivan Bay, Canada 50 55N 126 50W
19 Sully-sur-Loire, France 47 45N 2 20E
28 Sulmierzyce, Poland 51 36N 17 30E
39 Sulmona, Italy 42 3N 13 55E
117 Sulphur, La., U.S.A. 30 20N 93 22W
117 Sulphur, Okla., U.S.A. 34 35N 97 0W
108 Sulphur Pt., Canada 60 50N 114 50W
117 Sulphur Springs, U.S.A. 33 5N 95 30W
117 Sulphur Springs, Cr., U.S.A. 32 50N 102 8W
106 Sultan, Canada 47 36N 82 47W
69 Sultanpur, India 26 18N 82 10E
73 Sulu Arch., Philippines 6 0N 121 0E
73 Sulu Sea, E. Indies 8 0N 120 0E
87 Sululta, Ethiopia 9 10N 38 43E
83 Suluq, Libya 31 44N 20 14E
25 Sulzbach, Germany 49 30N 11 46E
25 Sulzbach-Rosenburg, West Germany 49 30N 11 46E
73 Sumalata, Indonesia 1 0N 122 37E
124 Sumampa, Argentina 29 25S 63 29W
72 Sumatera, I., Indonesia 0 40N 100 20E
72 Sumatera Selatan ♦, Indonesia 3 30S 104 0E
72 Sumatera Tengah ♦, Indonesia 1 0S 100 0E
72 Sumatera Utara ♦, Indonesia 2 0N 99 0E
72 Sumatra = Sumatera, Indonesia 0 40N 100 20E
118 Sumatra, U.S.A. 46 45N 107 37W
73 Sumba, I., Indonesia 9 45S 119 35E
73 Sumba, Selat, Indonesia 9 0S 118 40E
72 Sumbawa, Indonesia 8 26S 117 30E
73 Sumbawa, I., Indonesia 8 34S 117 17E
73 Sumbing, mt., Indonesia 7 19S 110 3E
90 Sumbawanga ♦, Tanzania 8 0S 30 50E
14 Sumburgh Hd., Scotland 59 52N 1 17W
73 Sumedang, Indonesia 6 49S 107 56E
27 Sümeg, Hungary 46 59N 17 20E
73 Sumenep, Indonesia 7 3S 113 51E
57 Sumgait, U.S.S.R. 40 34N 49 10E
118 Summer L., U.S.A. 42 50N 120 50W
107 Summerside, Canada 46 29N 63 41W
115 Summerville, Ga., U.S.A. 34 30N 85 20W
115 Summerville, S.C., U.S.A. 33 2N 80 11W
106 Summit, Canada 47 50N 72 20W
108 Summit L., Canada 54 20N 122 40W
119 Summit Pk., U.S.A. 37 20N 106 48W
116 Sumner, U.S.A. 42 49N 92 7W
27 Šumperk, Cz. 49 59N 17 0E
115 Sumter, U.S.A. 33 55N 80 10W
54 Sumy, U.S.S.R. 50 57N 34 50E
90 Suna, Tanzania 5 23S 34 48E
14 Sunart, L., Scot. 56 42N 5 35W
118 Sunburst, U.S.A. 48 56N 111 59W
100 Sunbury, Australia 37 30S 144 40E
113 Sunbury, U.S.A. 40 50N 76 46W
124 Sunchales, Argentina 30 58S 61 35W
124 Suncho Corral, Arg. 27 55S 63 14W
77 Sunchön, South Korea 34 52N 127 31E
113 Suncook, U.S.A. 43 8N 71 27W
47 Sund, Store Sotra, Norway 60 13N 5 10E
72 Sunda Ketjil, Kepulauan, Indonesia 7 30S 117 0E
116 Sundance, U.S.A. 44 27N 104 27W
69 Sundarbans, The, India and Pakistan 22 0N 89 0E
92 Sundays, R., S. Africa 32 10S 24 40E
49 Sundby, Denmark 56 53N 8 40E
48 Sundbyberg, Sweden 59 22N 17 58E
112 Sunderland, Canada 44 16N 79 3W
12 Sunderland, Eng. 54 54N 1 22W
113 Sunderland, U.S.A. 42 27N 72 36W
108 Sundre, Canada 51 49N 114 46W
106 Sundridge, Canada 45 45N 79 25W
49 Sunds, Denmark 56 13N 9 1E
48 Sundsjö, Sweden 62 59N 15 9E
48 Sundsvall, Sweden 62 23N 17 17E
68 Sungaianjar, Indonesia 2 53S 116 14E
72 Sungaipakning, Indon. 1 19N 102 0E
72 Sungaipenuh, Indonesia 2 1S 101 20E
72 Sungaitiram, Indonesia 0 45S 117 8E
71 Sungei Lembing, Malay 2 53N 103 4E
71 Sungei Patani, Malaysia 5 38N 100 29E
71 Sungei Siput, Malaysia 4 51N 101 6E
73 Sungguminasa, Indon. 5 17S 119 30E
77 Sunghsien, China 34 10N 112 10E
76 Sung-hua Kiang (Sungari), China 47 0N 130 50E
87 Sungikai, Sudan 12 20N 29 51E
77 Sungkiang, China 31 0N 121 20E
75 Sungpan, China 32 50N 103 20E
77 Sungtao, China 28 12N 109 12E
77 Sungtzu, China 30 25N 111 46E
77 Sungtzu Hu, China 30 10N 111 45E
93 Sungüé, Mozambique 21 18S 32 28E
56 Sungurlu, Turkey 40 12N 34 21E
77 Sungyang, China 28 16N 119 29E
39 Sunja, Yugoslavia 45 21N 16 35E
48 Sunnäsbruk, Sweden 61 10N 7 12E
47 Sundalsöra, Norway 62 40N 8 36E
48 Sunne, Jamtland, Sweden 63 7N 14 25E
48 Sunne, Varmland, Swed. 59 52N 13 12E
47 Sunnfjord, Norway 61 25N 5 18E
47 Sunnhordland, Nor. 59 50N 5 30E
47 Sunnmöre, Nor. 62 15N 6 30E
118 Sunnyside, Utah, U.S.A. 39 40N 110 24W
118 Sunnyside, Wash., U.S.A. 46 24N 120 2W
117 Sunray, U.S.A. 36 1N 101 47W
100 Sunshine, Australia 37 48S 144 52E
85 Sunson, Ghana 9 35N 0 2W
59 Suntar, U.S.S.R. 62 15N 117 30E
84 Sunyani, Ghana 7 21N 2 22W
50 Suolahti, Finland 62 34N 25 52E
50 Suonenjoki, Finland 62 37N 27 7E
119 Supai, U.S.A. 36 14N 112 44W
69 Supaul, India 26 10N 86 40E
87 Supe, Ethiopia 8 34N 35 35E
119 Superior, Ariz., U.S.A. 33 19N 111 9W
118 Superior, Mont., U.S.A. 47 15N 114 57W
116 Superior, Nebr., U.S.A. 40 3N 98 2W
116 Superior, Wis., U.S.A. 46 45N 92 0W
111 Superior, L., Canada-U.S.A. 47 40N 87 0W
39 Supetar, Yugoslavia 43 25N 16 32E
71 Suphan Buri, Thailand 14 30N 100 10E
28 Supraśl, Poland 53 13N 23 19E
77 Supu, China 27 57N 110 15E
76 Supung Hu, China 40 40N 125 0E
83 Suq al Jumah, Libya 32 58N 13 12E
62 Sūr, Lebanon 33 19N 35 16E
65 Sūr, Oman 22 34N 59 32E
77 Sur, Pt., U.S.A. 36 12N 121 55W
55 Sura, R., U.S.S.R. 55 30N 46 20E
73 Surabaja, Indonesia 7 17S 112 45E
48 Surahammar, Sweden 59 43N 16 13E
46 Suraia, Rumania 45 40N 27 25E
73 Surakarta, Indonesia 7 35S 110 48E
57 Surakhany, U.S.S.R. 40 13N 50 1E
70 Surandai, India 8 58N 77 26E
27 Surany, Czechoslovakia 48 6N 18 10E
68 Surat, India 21 12N 72 55E
99 Surat, Austral. 27 10S 149 6E
83 Surat, Khalīj, Libya 31 40N 18 30E
71 Surat Thani, Thailand 9 3N 99 28E
68 Suratgarh, India 29 18N 73 55E
54 Surazh, U.S.S.R. 53 5N 32 27E
46 Surduc, Rumania 47 15N 23 25E
46 Surduc Pasul, Rumania 45 21N 23 23E
42 Surdulica, Yugoslavia 42 41N 22 11E
16 Sûre, R., Luxembourg 49 51N 6 6E
68 Surendranagar, India 22 45N 71 40E
108 Surf Inlet, Canada 53 8N 128 50W
20 Surgères, France 46 7N 0 47W
58 Surgut, U.S.S.R. 61 20N 73 28E
69 Suri, India 23 50N 87 34E
46 Surianu, mt., Rumania 45 33N 23 31E
70 Suriapet, India 17 10N 79 40E
62 Surif, Jordan 31 40N 35 4E
71 Surin, Thailand 14 50N 103 34E
127 Surinam ■, S. America 4 0N 56 15W
127 Suriname, R., Guyana 4 30N 55 30W
57 Sürmene, Turkey 41 0N 40 1E
57 Surovikino, U.S.S.R. 48 32N 42 55E
13 Surrey ♦, England 51 16N 0 30W
25 Sursee, Switzerland 47 11N 8 6E
55 Sursk, U.S.S.R. 53 3N 45 40E
83 Surt, Libya 31 11N 16 46E
83 Surt, Al Hammādah al, Libya 30 0N 17 50E
50 Surtsey, Iceland 63 20N 20 30W
74 Suruga-Wan, Japan 34 45N 138 30E
73 Surup, Philippines 6 27N 126 17E
65 Surur, Oman 23 20N 58 10E
38 Susa, Italy 45 8N 7 3E
49 Susaa, R., Denmark 55 20N 11 42E
39 Sušac, I., Yugoslavia 42 46N 16 30E
39 Susak, I., Yugoslavia 44 30N 14 28E
64 Susangerd, Iran 31 35N 48 20E
59 Susanino, U.S.S.R. 52 50N 140 14E
118 Susanville, U.S.A. 40 28N 120 40W
26 Sušice, Czechoslovakia 49 17N 13 30E
113 Susquehanna, R., U.S.A. 41 50N 76 20W
113 Susquehanna Depot, U.S.A. 41 55N 75 36W
124 Susques, Argentina 23 35S 66 25W
107 Sussex, Canada 45 45N 65 37W
113 Sussex, U.S.A. 41 12N 74 38W
13 Sussex, E. ♦, U.K. 51 0N 0 0E
13 Sussex, W. ♦, U.K. 51 0N 0 30W
59 Susuman, U.S.S.R. 62 47N 148 10E
73 Susuna, Indonesia 3 20S 133 25E
28 Susz, Poland 53 44N 19 20E
46 Suţeşti, Rumania 45 13N 27 27E
109 Sutherland, Canada 52 15N 106 40W
116 Sutherland, U.S.A. 41 12N 101 11W
• 14 Sutherland ♦, Scot. 58 10N 4 30W
101 Sutherland Falls, N.Z. 44 48S 167 46E
99 Sutherland Pt., Australia 28 15S 153 35E
118 Sutherlin, U.S.A. 43 28N 123 16W
39 Sutivan, Yugoslavia 43 23N 16 30E
68 Sutlej, R., India 29 50N 72 20E
68 Sutlej, R., Pakistan 30 0N 73 0E
113 Sutton, Canada 45 8N 72 36W
116 Sutton, U.S.A. 40 40N 97 50W
12 Sutton-in-Ashfield, Eng. 52 8N 1 16W
101 Suva, Fiji Islands 17 40S 178 8E
42 Suva Gora, Yugoslavia 41 45N 21 3E
42 Suva Planina, Y.-slavia 43 10N 22 5E
42 Suva Reka, Yugoslavia 42 21N 20 50E
95 Suvarov Is., Pac. Oc. 13 15S 163 30W
42 Suvo Rudište, Yugoslavia 43 17N 20 49E
43 Suvorovo, Bulgaria 43 20N 27 35E
28 Suwałki, Poland 54 8N 22 59E
115 Suwannee, R., U.S.A. 30 0N 83 0W
74 Suwanose Jima, Japan 29 26N 129 30E

* *Incorporated with the region of Highland*

86 Suweis, El, Egypt 29 58N 32 31E
86 Suweis, Khalig es, Egypt 28 40N 33 0E
86 Suweis, Qanâl es, Egypt 31 0N 32 20E
77 Suwen, China 20 27N 110 2E
76 Suwŏn, S. Korea 37 17N 127 1E
77 Suyung, China 28 12N 105 10E
55 Suzdal, U.S.S.R. 56 29N 40 26E
74 Suzuka, Japan 34 55N 136 36E
38 Suzzara, Italy 45 0N 10 45E
50 Svalbard, Nordurpingeyjarsýsla, Iceland 66 12N 15 43W
49 Svalöv, Sweden 55 57N 13 8E
48 Svanå, Sweden 59 46N 15 23E
50 Svanvik, Norway 69 38N 30 3E
50 Svappavaari, Sweden 67 40N 21 03E
47 Svarstad, Norway 59 27N 9 56E
50 Svartisen, Norway 66 40N 14 16E
48 Svartvik, Sweden 62 19N 17 24E
56 Svatovo, U.S.S.R. 49 35N 38 5E
49 Svedala, Sweden 55 30N 13 15E
48 Sveg, Sweden 62 2N 14 21E
47 Sveio, Norway 59 33N 5 23E
47 Svelvik, Norway 59 37N 10 24E
49 Svendborg, Denmark 55 4N 10 35E
49 Svendborg Amt ♦, Den. 55 11N 10 25E
47 Svene, Norway 59 45N 9 31E
49 Svenljunga, Sweden 57 29N 13 29E
49 Svensbro, Sweden 58 15N 13 52E
48 Svenstavik, Sweden 62 45N 14 26E
49 Svenstrup, Denmark 56 58N 9 50E
58 Sverdlovsk, U.S.S.R. 56 50N 60 30E
4 Sverdrup Is., Canada 79 0N 97 0W
39 Svetac, Yugoslavia 43 3N 15 43E
39 Sveti Ivan Zelina, Yugoslavia 45 57N 16 16E
39 Sveti Jurij, Yugoslavia 46 14N 15 24E
39 Sveti Lenart, Y.-slavia 46 36N 15 48E
42 Sveti Nikola, Y.-slavia 41 51N 21 56E
39 Sveti Trojica, Y.-slavia 46 37N 15 33E
54 Svetlogorsk, U.S.S.R. 52 38N 29 46E
57 Svetlograd, U.S.S.R. 45 25N 42 58E
54 Svetlovodsk, U.S.S.R. 49 2N 33 13E
42 Svetozarevo, Y.-slavia 44 0N 21 15E
27 Svidník, Czechoslovakia 49 20N 21 37E
39 Svilaja Pl., Yugoslavia 43 49N 16 31E
42 Svilajnac, Yugoslavia 44 15N 21 11E
43 Svilengrad, Bulgaria 41 49N 26 12E
49 Svinö, Denmark 55 6N 11 44E
52 Svir, R., U.S.S.R. 61 2N 34 50E
54 Svisloch, U.S.S.R. 53 26N 24 2E
43 Svishov, Bulgaria 43 36N 25 23E
27 Svitavy, Czechoslovakia 49 47N 16 28E
59 Svobodnyy, U.S.S.R. 51 20N 128 0E
43 Svoge, Bulgaria 42 59N 23 23E
50 Svolvaer, Norway 68 15N 14 34E
27 Svratka, R., Cz. 49 27N 16 12E
42 Svrljig, Yugoslavia 43 25N 22 6E
25 Swabian Alps, Germany 48 30N 9 30E
98 Swain Reefs, Australia 21 45S 152 20W
115 Swainsboro, U.S.A. 32 38N 82 22W
92 Swakopmund, S.W. Africa 22 37S 14 30E
12 Swale R., Eng. 54 18N 1 30W
121 Swan Islands, W. Ind. 17 22N 83 57W
109 Swan L., Canada 52 30N 100 50W
96 Swan, R., Australia 32 3S 115 45E
100 Swan Hill, Austral. 35 15S 143 31E
108 Swan Hills, Canada 54 42N 115 49W
109 Swan River, Canada 52 10N 101 25W
13 Swanage, Eng. 50 36N 1 59W
100 Swansea, Austral. 33 3S 151 35E
13 Swansea, Wales 51 37N 3 57W
92 Swartberg, S. Africa 30 15S 29 23E
92 Swartberge, S. Afr. 33 20S 22 0E
92 Swartruggens, S. Africa 25 39S 26 42E
28 Swarzedz, Poland 52 25N 17 4E
106 Swastika, Canada 48 7N 80 6W
77 Swatow = Shantow, China 23 25N 116 40E
93 Swaziland ■, Africa 26 30S 31 30E
50 Sweden ■, Eur. 67 0N 15 0E
85 Swedru, Ghana 5 32N 0 41W
118 Sweet Home, U.S.A. 44 26N 122 38W
117 Sweetwater, U.S.A. 32 30N 100 28W
118 Sweetwater, R., U.S.A. 42 31N 107 30W
92 Swellendam, S. Africa 34 1S 20 26E
28 Świdnica, Poland 50 50N 16 30E
28 Swidin, Poland 53 47N 15 49E
28 Swidnik, Poland 51 13N 22 39E
28 Swiebodzice, Poland 50 51N 16 20E
28 Swiebodzin, Poland 52 15N 15 37E
28 Swiecie, Poland 53 25N 18 30E
28 Swietorkrzyskie, Góry, Poland 51 0N 20 30E
109 Swift Current, Canada 50 20N 107 45W
15 Swilly L., Ireland 55 12N 7 35W
108 Swindle, I., Canada 52 30N 128 35W
28 Swinemünde = Swinoujscie, Poland 53 54N 14 16E
28 Swinoujscie, Poland 53 54N 14 16E
24 Switzerland ■, Eur. 46 30N 8 0E
15 Swords, Ireland 53 27N 6 15W
54 Syasstroy, U.S.S.R. 60 5N 32 15E
54 Sychevka, U.S.S.R. 55 45N 34 10E
28 Syców, Poland 51 19N 17 40E
100 Sydney, Austral. 33 53S 151 10E
107 Sydney, Canada 46 7N 60 7W
116 Sydney, U.S.A. 41 12N 103 0W
107 Sydney Mines, Canada 46 18N 60 15W
4 Sydproven, Greenland 60 30N 45 35W
24 Syke, Germany 52 55N 8 50E
52 Syktyvkar, U.S.S.R. 61 45N 50 40E
115 Sylacauga, U.S.A. 33 10N 86 15W
48 Sylarna, Mt., Sweden 63 2N 12 11E
67 Sylhet, Bangladesh 24 43N 91 55E
24 Sylt, I., Germany 54 50N 8 20E
108 Sylvan Lake, Canada 52 20N 114 10W
115 Sylvania, U.S.A. 32 45N 81 37W
115 Sylvester, U.S.A. 31 31N 83 50W
58 Sym, U.S.S.R. 60 20N 87 50E

MAP
58 Syr Darya, U.S.S.R. 45 0N 65 0E
117 Syracuse, Kans., U.S.A. 38 0N 101 40W
113 Syracuse, N.Y., U.S.A. 43 4N 76 11W
64 Syria ■, Asia 35 0N 38 0E
71 Syriam, Burma 16 44N 96 19E
64 Syrian Des., S.W. Asia 31 30N 40 0E
59 Syuldzhyukyor, U.S.S.R. 63 25N 113 40E
43 Syutkya, mt., Bulgaria 41 50N 24 16E
55 Syzran, U.S.S.R. 53 12N 48 30E
27 Szabolcs-Szatmár ♦, Hungary 48 2N 21 45E
28 Szamocin, Poland 53 2N 17 7E
28 Szamotuły, Poland 52 35N 16 34E
28 Szaraz, R., Hungary 46 28N 20 44E
27 Szárvas, Hungary 46 50N 20 38E
28 Szazhalombatta, Hungary 47 20N 18 58E
27 Szczara, R., U.S.S.R. 53 15N 25 10E
28 Szczebrzeszyn, Poland 50 42N 22 59E
28 Szczecin, Pol. 53 27N 14 27E
28 Szczecin ♦, Poland 53 25N 14 32E
28 Szczecinek, Poland 53 43N 16 41E
28 Szczekociny, Poland 50 38N 19 48E
28 Szczrk, Poland 49 42N 19 1E
28 Szczuczyn, Poland 53 36N 22 19E
28 Szczytno, Poland 53 33N 21 0E
27 Szechwan ♦, China 30 15N 103 15E
27 Szécsény, Hungary 48 7N 19 30E
27 Szeged, Hungary 46 16N 20 10E
27 Szeghalom, Hungary 47 1N 21 10E
27 Székesfehérvár, Hung. 47 15N 18 25E
27 Szekszárd, Hungary 46 22N 18 42E
75 Szemao, China 22 50N 101 0E
27 Szenan, China 27 50N 108 25E
27 Szendrö, Hungary 48 24N 20 41E
77 Szengen,
  Kwangsi-Chuang. China 23 0N 108 5E
  Szengen,
  Kwangsi-Chuang. China 24 50N 108 0E
27 Szentendre, Hungary 47 39N 19 4E
27 Szentes, Hungary 46 39N 20 21E
27 Szentgotthárd, Hung. 46 58N 16 19E
27 Szentlörinc, Hungary 46 3N 18 1E
76 Szeping, China 43 10N 124 18E
27 Szerencs, Hungary 48 10N 21 12E
27 Szewui, China 23 30N 112 35E
27 Szigetvár, Hungary 46 3N 17 46E
27 Szlichtygowa, Poland 51 42N 16 15E
27 Szob, Hungary 47 48N 18 53E
27 Szolnok, Hungary 47 10N 20 15E
27 Szolnok ♦, Hungary 47 15N 20 30E
27 Szombathely, Hungary 47 14N 16 38E
28 Szprotawa, Poland 51 33N 15 35E
28 Sztuto, Poland 54 20N 19 15E
28 Szydłowiec, Poland 51 15N 20 51E
28 Szypliszki, Poland 54 17N 23 2E
76 Ta Fengman, China 43 45N 126 35E
76 Ta Hinghan Ling, China 48 0N 121 0E
50 Taalintehdas, Finland 60 2N 22 30E
51 Taavetti, Finland 60 56N 27 32E
64 Taba, Saudi Arabia 26 55N 42 30E
124 Tabacal, Argentina 23 15s 64 15W
73 Tabaco, Philippines 13 22N 123 44E
84 Tabagné, Ivory Coast 7 59N 3 4W
98 Tabar Is., Terr. of New Guinea 3 0s 152 20E
33 Tabarca, Isla de, Spain 38 17N 0 30W
83 Tabarka, Tunisia 36 56N 8 46E
33 Tabarra, Spain 38 37N 1 44E
65 Tabas, Khorasan, Iran 32 48N 60 12E
65 Tabas, Khorasan, Iran 33 35N 56 55E
121 Tabasará, Serranía de, Panama 8 35N 81 40W
120 Tabasco ♦, Mexico 17 45N 93 30W
126 Tabatinga, Brazil 4 11s 69 58W
127 Tabatinga, Serra da, Braz. 10 30s 44 0W
82 Tabelbala, Kahal de, Algeria 28 47N 2 0W
33 Tabernas, Spain 37 4N 2 26W
33 Tabernas de Valldigna, Spain 39 5N 0 13W
62 Tabigha, Israel 32 53N 35 33E
12 Tablas, I., Philippines 12 25N 122 2E
107 Table B., Canada 53 40N 56 15W
92 Table Mt., S. Africa 34 0s 18 22E
98 Table Top Mt., Austral. 23 30s 147 0E
26 Tábor, Czechoslovakia 49 25N 14 39E
62 Tabor, Israel
90 Tabora, Tanzania 5 2s 32 57E
90 Tabora ♦, Tanzania 6 0s 32 0E
84 Tabou, Ivory Coast 4 30N 7 20W
82 Tabouda, Morocco 34 44N 5 14W
64 Tabriz, Iran 38 7N 46 20E
64 Tabūk, Saudi Arabia 28 30N 36 25E
48 Tåby, Sweden 59 29N 18 4E
126 Tacarigua, L. de, Venezuela 11 3N 68 25W
126 Tachira, Venezuela 8 7N 72 21W
126 Tachira ♦, Venezuela 8 7N 72 15W
26 Tachov, Czechoslovakia 49 47N 12 39E
77 Tachu, China 30 45N 107 13E
41 Tacina, R., Italy 39 5N 16 51E
73 Tacloban, Philippines 11 15N 124 58E
126 Tacna, Peru 18 0s 70 20W
118 Tacoma, U.S.A. 47 15N 122 30W
125 Tacuarembó, Uruguay 31 45s 56 0W
82 Tademaït, Plateau du, Algeria 28 30N 2 30E
83 Tadent, O., Algeria 22 30N 7 0E
83 Tadjerdjert, O., Algeria 26 0N 8 0E
83 Tadjerouna, Algeria 33 31N 2 3E
83 Tadjettaret, O., Algeria 21 0N 7 30W
82 Tadjmout, O., Alg. 25 37N 3 6E
87 Tadjoura, T.F.A.I. 11 50N 42 55E
87 Tadjoura, Golfe de, T.F.A.I. 11 50N 43 0E
101 Tadmor, New Zealand 41 27s 172 45E
126 Tado, Colombia 5 16N 76 32W
107 Tadoussac, Canada 48 11N 69 42W

MAP
58 Tadzhikistan S.S.R. ♦, U.S.S.R. 35 30N 70 0E
76 Taegu, South Korea 35 50N 128 37E
76 Taerh Hu, China 43 25N 116 40E
32 Tafalla, Spain 42 30N 1 41W
124 Tafi Viejo, Argentina 26 43s 65 17W
84 Tafirë, Ivory Coast 9 4N 5 10W
82 Tafnidilt, Morocco 28 47N 10 58W
82 Tafraout, Morocco 29 50N 8 58W
73 Taft, Philippines 11 57N 125 30E
119 Taft, Ala., U.S.A. 35 10N 119 28W
117 Taft, Tex., U.S.A. 27 58N 97 23W
69 Taga Dzong, Bhutan 27 5N 90 0E
57 Taganrog, U.S.S.R. 47 12N 38 50E
56 Taganrogskiy Zaliv, U.S.S.R. 47 0N 38 30E
84 Tagant, Mauritania 18 20N 11 0W
73 Tagbilaran, Philippines 9 39N 123 51E
38 Tággia, Italy 43 52N 7 50E
82 Taghrifat, Libya 29 5N 17 26E
82 Taghzout, Morocco 33 30N 4 49W
123 Tagish L., Canada 60 15N 134 30W
39 Tagliacozzo, Italy 42 4N 13 13E
39 Tagliamento, R., Italy 45 38N 13 5E
38 Táglio di Po, Italy 45 0N 12 12E
33 Tagomago, Isla de, Sp. 39 2N 1 39E
126 Taguatinga, Brazil 12 26s 46 26W
98 Tagula I., Papua 11 40s 153 15E
98 Tagum (Hijo), Phil. 7 33N 125 53E
29 Tagus = Tajo, R., Spain 39 44N 5 50W
72 Tahabhala, I., Indon. 0 30s 98 30E
101 Tahakopa, N.Z. 46 30s 169 23E
82 Tahala, Morocco 34 0N 4 28W
71 Tahan, Gunong, Malaysia 4 45N 102 25E
83 Tahat Mt., Algeria 23 18N 5 21E
75 Tahcheng, China 46 50N 83 1E
72 Taheiho, China 50 10N 127 20E
65 Tahëri, Iran 27 43N 52 20E
91 Tahiti, I., Pacific Ocean 17 37s 149 27W
118 Tahoe, U.S.A. 39 12N 119 54W
118 Tahoe, L., U.S.A. 39 6N 120 0W
85 Tahoua, Niger 14 57N 5 16E
86 Tahta, Egypt 26 44N 31 32E
73 Tahulandang, I., Indon 2 27N 125 23E
72 Tahuna, Indonesia 3 45N 125 30E
84 Taï, Ivory Coast 5 55N 7 30W
77 Tai Hu, China 31 10N 120 0E
77 Taichow, China 32 30N 119 50E
77 Taichow Wan., China 28 55N 121 10E
77 Taichung, Taiwan 24 10N 120 35E
101 Taieri, R., N.Z. 45 30s 170 18E
76 Taiga Madema, Libya 23 46N 15 25E
76 Taihan Shan, China 36 0N 114 0E
101 Taihape, N.Z. 39 41s 175 48E
77 Taiho, China 26 50N 114 54E
77 Taihu, China 30 30N 116 25E
77 Taikang, China 34 3N 115 0E
77 Taikiang, China 26 45N 108 44E
77 Taikkyi, Burma 17 20N 96 0E
77 Taikung, China 26 50N 108 48E
76 Tailagein Shara, Mongolia 44 10N 106 0E
99 Tailem Bend, Australia 35 12s 139 29E
25 Tailfingen, Germany 48 15N 9 1E
64 Taïma, Saudi Arabia 27 35N 38 45E
59 Taimyr, O., U.S.S.R. 74 20N 102 0E
77 Tain, Scotland 57 49N 4 4W
77 Tainan, Taiwan 23 0N 120 15E
45 Taïnaron, Akra, Gr. 36 22N 22 27E
77 Taining, China 27 0N 117 15E
77 Taipei, Taiwan 25 2N 121 30E
71 Taiping, Malaysia 5 51N 100 45E
90 Taita ♦, Kenya 4 0s 38 30E
90 Taita Hills, Kenya 3 25s 38 15E
128 Taitao, Pen. de, Chile 46 30s 75 0W
77 Taitung, Taiwan 22 43N 121 4E
77 Taiwan (Formosa) ■, Asia 23 30N 121 0E
65 Taiwara, Afghanistan 33 30N 64 24E
45 Taïyetos Oros, Gr. 37 0N 22 23E
62 Taiyiba, Israel 32 36N 35 27E
62 Taiyiba, Jordan 31 55N 35 17E
76 Taiyüan, China 38 0N 112 30E
72 Tajan, Indonesia 0 6s 110 2E
65 Tajarhï, Afghan. 24 15N 14 46E
120 Tajicaringa, Mexico 23 15N 104 44W
29 Tajimi Gifu, Japan 35 25N 137 5E
31 Tajo, R., Spain 40 35N 1 52W
120 Tajumulco, Volcán de, Guat. 15 20N 91 50W
83 Tájürã, Libya 32 51N 13 27E
71 Tak, Thailand 17 0N 99 10E
74 Takada, Japan 37 7N 138 15E
101 Takaka, New Zealand 40 51s 172 50E
74 Takamatsu, Japan 34 20N 134 5E
74 Takaoka, Japan 36 40N 137 0E
101 Takapuna, N.Z. 36 47s 174 47E
74 Takasaki, Japan 36 20N 139 0E
74 Takatsuki, Japan 34 40N 135 37E
90 Takaungu, Kenya 3 38s 39 52E
74 Takayama, Japan 36 18N 137 11E
74 Takefu, Japan 35 50N 136 10E
71 Takeo, Khmer Rep. 10 59N 104 47E
49 Tåkern, Sweden 58 21N 14 45E
64 Takestan, Iran 36 0N 49 50E
77 Takhing, China 23 10N 111 45E
72 Takingeun, Indonesia 4 45N 96 50E
108 Takla Landing, Canada 55 30N 125 50W
75 Takla Makan, China 39 0N 83 0E

MAP
84 Takoradi, Ghana 4 58N 1 55W
85 Takum, Nigeria 7 18N 9 36E
76 Takushan, China 39 55N 123 30E
59 Tala, U.S.S.R. 72 40N 113 30E
125 Tala, Uruguay 34 21s 55 46W
76 Talai, China 45 30N 124 20W
82 Talaint, Morocco 29 37N 9 45W
85 Talak, Niger 18 0N 5 0E
121 Talamanca, Cordillera de, Cent. Amer. 9 20N 83 20W
30 Talangbetutu, Indon. 2 50s 104 35E
126 Talara, Peru 4 30s 81 10E
98 Talasea, Terr. of New Guinea 5 14s 150 5E
85 Talata Mafara, Nigeria 12 38N 6 4E
73 Talaud, Kepulauan, Indonesia 4 30N 127 10E
30 Talavera de la Reina, Spain 39 55N 4 46W
73 Talayan, Philippines 6 52N 124 24E
96 Talbot C., Australia 13 56s 125 49E
100 Talbragar, R., Australia 32 11s 148 39E
124 Talca, Chile 35 20s 71 46W
124 Talca ♦, Chile 35 20s 71 46W
124 Talcahuano, Chile 36 40s 73 10W
85 Talcho, Niger 14 35N 3 22E
55 Taldom, U.S.S.R. 56 45N 37 29E
58 Taldy Kurgan, U.S.S.R. 45 10N 78 45E
66 Taleqan ♦, Afghan. 36 40N 69 30E
64 Talesh, Kúlhä-Ye, Iran 39 0N 48 30E
62 Talfit, Jordan 32 5N 35 17E
77 Tali, Shensi, China 34 48N 109 48E
75 Tali, Yunnan, China 25 45N 100 5E
73 Tali Post, Sudan 5 55N 30 44E
73 Taliabu, I., Indonesia 1 45s 125 0E
73 Taliang Shan, China 28 0N 103 0E
73 Talibon, Philippines 10 4N 124 17E
76 Talien, (Dairen), China 38 53N 121 37E
117 Talihina, U.S.A. 34 45N 95 1W
70 Talikoti, India 16 29N 76 17E
72 Taling Sung, Thailand 15 5N 99 11E
72 Taliwang, Indonesia 8 50s 116 55E
104 Talkeetna Mts., Alaska 62 40N 28 37E
62 Tall 'Asūr, Jordan 31 59N 35 17E
86 Talla, Egypt 28 5N 30 43E
115 Talladega, U.S.A. 33 28N 86 2W
115 Tallahassee, U.S.A. 30 25N 84 15W
100 Tallangatta, Australia 36 10s 147 14E
100 Tallarook, Austral. 37 5s 145 6E
48 Tallåsen, Sweden 62 3N 16 2E
48 Tällberg, Sweden 60 51N 15 2E
96 Tallering Peak, Australia 28 6s 115 37E
54 Tallinn (Reval), U.S.S.R. 59 29N 24 58E
117 Tallulah, U.S.A. 32 25N 91 12W
46 Tálmaciu, Rumania 45 38N 24 19E
109 Talmage, Canada 49 46N 103 40W
100 Talmalmo, Australia 35 51s 148 58E
82 Talmest, Morocco 31 48N 9 21W
20 Talmont, France 46 27N 1 37W
56 Talnoye, U.S.S.R. 48 57N 30 35E
68 Taloda, India 21 34N 74 19E
87 Talodi, Sudan 10 35N 30 22E
55 Talovaya, U.S.S.R. 51 13N 40 38E
82 Talsinnt, Morocco 32 33N 3 27W
124 Taltal, Chile 25 23s 70 40W
72 Talu, Indonesia 0 12N 99 50E
99 Talwood, Australia 28 27s 149 20E
100 Talyawalka Cr., Austral. 32 20s 143 0E
116 Tama, U.S.A. 41 56N 92 37W
72 Taman Abu, Pegunungan, Malay. 3 10N 115 0E
120 Tamalameque, Col. 8 52N 73 49W
85 Tamale, Ghana 9 22N 0 50W
56 Taman, U.S.S.R. 45 14N 36 41E
82 Tamanar, Morocco 31 1N 9 46W
74 Tamano, Japan 34 35N 133 59E
83 Tamanrasset, Algeria 22 56N 5 30E
82 Tamanrasset, O., Alg. 22 0N 2 0E
113 Tamaqua, U.S.A. 40 46N 75 58W
13 Tamar, R., Eng. 50 33N 4 15W
126 Tamara, Colombia 5 50N 72 10W
32 Tamarite de Litera, Sp. 41 52N 0 25E
27 Tamási, Hungary 46 40N 18 18E
85 Tamaské, Niger 14 55N 5 55E
93 Tamatave ♦, Malagasy Republic 18 10s 49 25E
93 Tamatave ♦, Malag. 18 0s 49 0E
120 Tamaulipas ♦, Mexico 24 0N 99 0W
120 Tamaulipas, Sierra de, Mexico 23 30N 98 20W
120 Tamazula, Mexico 24 55N 106 58W
84 Tambacounda, Senegal 13 55N 13 45W
82 Tambai, Ethiopia 16 32N 37 13E
72 Tambelan, Kepulauan, Indon. 1 0N 107 30E
98 Tambo, Australia 24 54s 146 14E
126 Tambo de Mora, Peru 13 30s 76 20W
93 Tambohorano, Malag. 17 30s 43 58E
72 Tambora, G., Indon. 8 12s 118 5E
55 Tambov, U.S.S.R. 52 45s 41 20E
30 Tambre, R., Spain 42 55N 8 30W
72 Tambuku, G., Indon. 7 8s 113 40E
87 Tamburá, Sudan 5 40N 27 25E
84 Tamchaket, Mauritania 17 25N 10 40W
69 Tamchok Khambab (Brahmaputra), China 29 25N 88 0E
126 Tame, Colombia 6 28N 71 44W
30 Tamega, R., Portugal 41 12N 8 5W
82 Tamelelt, Algeria 35 50N 4 30E
82 Temelelt, Morocco 31 50N 7 32W
83 Tamerza, Tunisia 34 23N 7 58E
85 Tamgak, Monts., Niger 19 12N 1 35E
120 Tamiahua, Laguna de, Mexico 21 30N 97 30W
70 Tamil Nadu ♦, India 11 0N 77 0E
76 Taming, China 36 20N 115 10E

MAP
69 Tamluk, India 22 18N 87 58E
51 Tammisaari (Ekenäs), Finland 60 0N 23 26E
62 Tammun', Jordan 32 18N 35 23E
48 Tamnaren, Sweden 60 10N 17 25E
85 Tamou, Niger 12 45N 2 11E
115 Tampa, U.S.A. 27 57N 82 30W
115 Tampa B., U.S.A. 27 40N 82 40W
51 Tampere, Finland 61 30N 23 50E
120 Tampico, Mexico 22 20N 97 50W
71 Tampin, Malaysia 2 28N 102 13E
82 Tamri, Morocco 30 49N 9 50W
99 Tamworth, Australia 31 0s 150 58E
13 Tamworth, Eng. 52 38N 1 2W
77 Tan Kiang, China 33 25N 111 0E
50 Tana, Norway 70 7N 28 5E
50 Tana Fd., Norway 70 35s 28 30E
87 Tana, L., Ethiopia 13 5N 37 30E
90 Tana, R., Kenya 0 50s 39 45E
24 Tana, R., Norway 69 50N 26 0E
104 Tanacross, Alaska 63 40N 143 30W
41 Tanagro, R., Italy 40 35N 15 25E
72 Tanahdjampea, I., Indon. 7 10s 120 35E
72 Tanahgrogot, Indon. 1 55s 116 15E
72 Tanahmasa, I., Indon. 0 5s 98 29E
72 Tanahmerah, Indonesia 6 0s 140 7E
25 Tanami Des., Australia 23 15s 132 20E
104 Tanana, Alaska 65 10N 152 15W
104 Tanana, R., Alas. 64 25N 145 30W
93 Tananarive, Malag. 18 55s 47 31E
93 Tananarive ♦, Malag. 19 0s 47 0E
47 Tananger, Norway 58 57N 5 37E
21 Tanaro, R., Italy 44 9N 8 8E
82 Tánaro, R., Italy 44 9N 7 50E
40 Tanaunelia, Italy 40 42N 9 45E
99 Tanbar, Australia 25 55s 142 0E
18 Tancarville, France 49 29N 0 28E
77 Tanchai, China 25 58N 107 49E
77 Tanchow, China 19 33N 109 22E
69 Tanda, U.P., India 28 57N 78 56E
69 Tanda, U.P., India 26 33N 82 35E
84 Tanda, Ivory Coast 7 48N 3 10W
73 Tandag, Philippines 9 4N 126 9E
91 Tandala, Tanzania 9 25s 34 15E
46 Tándárei, Rumania 44 39N 27 40E
124 Tandil, Argentina 37 15s 59 6W
124 Tandil, Sierra del, Arg. 37 20s 59 5W
72 Tandjung, Indonesia 2 10s 115 25E
72 Tandjung Balai, Indon. 2 55N 99 44E
72 Tandjungbatu, Indon. 2 23N 118 3E
72 Tandjungenim, Indon. 3 51s 103 35E
72 Tandjungkarang, Indon. 5 20s 105 10E
72 Tandjungpandan, Indon. 2 43s 107 38E
72 Tandjungpinang, Indon. 1 5N 104 30E
73 Tandjungpriok, Indon. 6 8s 106 55E
72 Tandjungpura, Indon. 3 59N 98 21E
72 Tandjungredeb, Indon. 2 12N 117 35E
72 Tandjungselor, Indon. 2 55N 117 25E
68 Tandlianwald, Pakistan 31 3N 73 9E
68 Tando Adam, Pakistan 25 45N 68 40E
100 Tandou L., Australia 32 40s 142 0E
48 Tandsbyn, Sweden 63 0N 14 45W
68 Tandur, India 19 11N 79 30E
101 Taneatua, New Zealand 38 4s 177 1E
74 Tane-ga-Shima, Japan 30 30N 131 0E
71 Tanen Range, Thailand 16 30N 98 30E
67 Tanen Tong Dan, Burma 16 30N 98 30E
82 Tanezrouft, Algeria 23 9N 0 11E
77 Tang La, China 32 59N 92 17E
67 Tang Pass, China 32 59N 92 17E
90 Tanga, Tanzania 5 5N 39 2E
90 Tanga ♦, Tanzania 5 20s 38 0E
98 Tanga Is., N. Guin. 3 45s 148 17E
69 Tangail, East Pakistan 24 15N 90 0E
90 Tanganyika, L., E. Afr. 6 40s 30 0E
82 Tanger, Morocco 35 50N 5 49W
73 Tangerang, Indonesia 6 12s 106 39E
24 Tangerhütte, Germany 52 32N 11 50E
24 Tangermünde, Germany 52 32N 11 57E
77 Tanghing, China 21 30N 108 2E
77 Tangho, China 32 40N 112 50E
76 Tanghsien, China 38 48N 114 54E
82 Tangier = Tanger, Mor. 35 50N 5 49W
71 Tangkak, Malaysia 2 18N 102 34E
77 Tanglha Shan, China 33 0N 90 0E
98 Tangorin, Australia 21 45s 144 9E
77 Tangshan, Hopei, China 39 40N 118 10E
77 Tangtu, China 31 37N 118 39E
85 Tanguiéta, Dahomey 10 40N 1 21E
77 Tangyang, China 30 50N 111 45E
77 Tanhsien (Nata), China 19 30N 109 17E
72 Tanimbar, Kepulauan, Indon. 7 30s 131 30E
77 Taning = Wuki, China 31 28N 109 46E
73 Tanjay = Philippines 9 30N 123 5E
70 Tanjore, India 10 48N 79 12E
68 Tank, Pakistan 32 14N 70 25E
48 Tanndalen, Sweden 62 33N 12 18E
49 Tannis B., Denmark 57 40N 10 15E
77 Tannu Ola, Asia 51 0N 94 0E
84 Tano, R., Ghana 6 0N 2 30W
82 Tanout, Niger 14 50N 8 55E
85 Tanout, Niger 14 50N 8 55E
77 Tanshui, Taiwan 25 10N 121 28E
86 Tanta, Egypt 30 45N 30 57E
82 Tantan, Morocco 28 29N 11 1W
120 Tantoyuca, Mexico 21 21N 98 10W
62 Tantura = Dor, Israel 32 37N 34 55E

MAP
70 Tanuku, India 16 45N 81 44E
49 Tanum, Sweden 58 42N 11 20E
99 Tanunda, Australia 34 30s 139 0E
72 Tanur, India 11 1N 75 46E
20 Tanus, France 44 8N 2 19E
90 Tanzania ■, E. Afr. 6 40s 34 0E
77 Taohsien, China 25 37N 111 24E
77 Taonan, China 45 30N 122 20E
41 Taormina, Italy 37 52N 15 16E
82 Taoudenni, Mali 22 40N 3 55W
82 Taounate, Morocco 34 32N 4 41W
82 Taourirt, Algeria 26 37N 0 8E
82 Taourirt, Morocco 34 20N 2 47W
82 Taouz, Morocco 31 2N 4 0W
54 Tapa, U.S.S.R. 59 15N 26 0E
31 Tapa Shan, China 31 45N 109 30E
71 Tapah, Malaysia 4 12N 101 15E
77 Tapaktuan, Indonesia 3 30N 97 10E
125 Tapanshang, China 43 40N 118 20E
101 Tapanui, New Zealand 45 56s 169 18E
126 Tapauá, Brazil 5 40s 64 20W
126 Tapauá, R., Brazil 6 0s 65 40W
84 Tapeta, Liberia 6 36N 8 52W
31 Tapia, Spain 43 34N 6 56W
27 Tápiószele, Hungary 47 45N 19 55E
126 Tapirapecó, Serra, Ven. 1 10N 65 0W
114 Tappahannock, U.S.A. 37 56N 76 50W
77 Tapsing, China 30 22N 96 25E
21 Tapti, R., India 21 25N 75 0E
101 Tapuaenuku, Mt., New Zealand 41 55s 173 50E
73 Tapul Group, Is., Phil. 5 35N 120 50E
125 Taquara, Brazil 29 36s 50 46W
126 Taquari, R., Brazil 18 10s 56 0W
59 Tara, U.S.S.R. 56 55N 74 30E
91 Tara, Zambia 16 58s 26 45E
42 Tara, R., Yugoslavia 43 10N 19 20E
64 Tarābulus, Lebanon 34 31N 35 50E
83 Tarābulus, Libya 32 49N 13 7E
100 Tarago, Austral. 35 6s 149 39E
83 Tarahouahout, Algeria 22 47N 5 59E
72 Tarakan, Indonesia 3 20N 117 35E
90 Tarakit, Mt., Kenya 2 2N 35 10E
100 Taralga, Austral. 34 26s 149 52E
100 Tarana, Austral. 33 31s 149 52E
68 Taranagar, India 28 43N 75 9E
101 Taranaki ♦, N.Z. 39 5s 174 51E
32 Tarancón, Spain 40 1N 3 1W
68 Taranga, India 23 56N 72 43E
68 Taranga Hill, India 24 0N 72 40E
41 Taranto, Italy 40 30N 17 11E
41 Táranto, G. di, Italy 40 0N 17 15E
126 Tarapacá, Colombia 2 56s 69 46W
124 Tarapacá ♦, Chile 20 45s 69 30W
21 Tarare, France 45 54N 4 26E
101 Tararua Range, N.Z. 40 45s 175 25E
20 Tarascon, Ariège, Fr. 42 50N 1 37E
21 Tarascon, France 43 48N 4 39E
56 Tarashcha, U.S.S.R. 49 30N 30 31E
83 Tarat, Bj., Algeria 26 4N 9 7E
126 Tarauacá, Brazil 8 6s 70 48W
126 Tarauacá, R., Brazil 7 30s 70 30W
21 Taravo, R., Corsica 41 48N 8 52E
73 Tarawasi, Indonesia 2 19s 139 32E
101 Tarawera, N.Z. 39 2s 176 36E
101 Tarawera Lake, N.Z. 38 13s 176 27E
85 Tarazat, Massif de, Niger 20 2N 8 30E
32 Tarazona, Spain 41 55N 1 43W
32 Tarazona de la Mancha, Spain 39 16N 1 55W
75 Tarbagatai, Mong. 48 30N 99 0E
14 Tarbat Ness, Scot. 57 52s 3 48W
14 Tarbert, Scotland 57 54N 6 49W
20 Tarbes, France 43 15N 0 3E
115 Tarboro, U.S.A. 35 55N 77 3W
83 Tarbū, Libya 26 0N 15 5E
46 Tarcău, Munţii, Rumania 46 39N 26 7E
39 Tarcento, Italy 46 12N 13 12E
99 Tarcoola, Australia 30 15s 134 36E
99 Tarcoon, Austral. 30 15s 146 35E
20 Tardets-Sorholus, France 43 17N 0 52W
20 Tardin, France 37 16N 92 30E
100 Taree, Austral. 31 50s 152 30E
21 Tarentaise, Fr. 45 30N 6 35E
86 Tarf Shaqq al Abd, Saudi Arabia 26 50N 36 6E
86 Tarfa, Wadi el, Egypt 28 16N 31 15E
82 Tarfaya, Morocco 55 25N 12 55W
20 Targon, France 44 44N 0 16W
46 Târgu Neamţ, Rum. 47 12N 26 25E
82 Targuist, Morocco 34 59N 4 14W
82 Tarhbalt, Morocco 30 48N 5 10W
83 Tarhit, Algeria 30 58N 2 0W
83 Tarhünah, Libya 32 15N 13 28E
84 Tarib, Wadi, Si. Arabia 18 30N 43 23E
126 Táriba, Venezuela 7 49N 72 13W
31 Tarifa, Spain 36 1N 5 36W
126 Tarija, Bolivia 21 30s 64 40W
124 Tarija ♦, Bolivia 21 30s 63 30W
77 Tarim, R., China 40 40N 85 20E
73 Taritoe, R., Indon. 3 0s 138 5E
58 Tarko Sale, U.S.S.R. 64 55N 77 50E
84 Tarkwa, Ghana 5 20N 2 0W
73 Tarlac, Phil. 15 29N 120 35E
108 Tarlsland, Canada 57 03N 111 40W
49 Tarm, Denmark 55 56N 8 31E

Renamed Hadibu

MAP
126 Tarma, Peru 11 25s 75 45w
20 Tarn, R., France 44 5N 1 2E
20 Tarn ♦, France 43 49N 2 8E
20 Tarn-et-Garonne ♦, France 44 8N 1 20E
50 Tärna, Sweden 65 45N 15 10E
27 Tarna, R., Hungary 48 0N 20 5E
49 Tårnby, Denmark 55 37N 12 36E
27 Tarnów, Poland 50 3N 21 0E
28 Tarnowskie Góry, Pol. 50 27N 18 54E
38 Táro, R., Italy 44 37N 9 58E
99 Tarong, Australia 26 48s 151 45E
99 Taroom, Australia 25 36s 149 48E
82 Taroudannt, Morocco 30 30N 8 52w
24 Tarp Germany 54 40N 9 25E
115 Tarpon Springs, U.S.A. 28 8N 82 42w
39 Tarquinia, Italy 42 15N 11 45E
62 Tarqumiyah, Jordan 31 35N 35 1E
32 Tarragona, Spain 41 5N 1 17E
32 Tarragona ♦, Spain 41 0N 1 0E
99 Tarraleah, Australia 42 9s 146 14E
32 Tarrasa, Spain 41 26N 2 1E
32 Tárrega, Spain 41 39N 1 9E
113 Tarrytown, U.S.A. 41 5N 73 52w
62 Tarshiha = Me'ona, Israel 33 1N 35 15E
83 Tarso Emissi, Chad 21 27N 18 36E
83 Tarso Ovrari, Chad 21 27N 17 27E
64 Tarsus, Turkey 36 58N 34 55E
124 Tartagal, Argentina 22 30s 63 50w
20 Tartas, France 43 50N 0 49w
100 Tartna Point, Australia 32 54s 142 24E
54 Tartu, U.S.S.R. 58 25N 26 58E
64 Tartus, Syria 34 55N 35 55E
55 Tarussa, U.S.S.R. 54 44N 37 10E
71 Tarutao, Ko, Thailand 6 33N 99 40E
72 Tarutung, Indonesia 2 0N 99 0E
39 Tarvisio, Italy 46 31N 13 35E
83 Tarz Ulli, Algeria 25 46N 9 44E
83 Tasāwah, Libya 26 0N 13 7E
106 Taschereau, Canada 48 40N 78 40w
70 Tasgaon, India 17 2N 74 39E
87 Ta'shan, Saudi Arabia 16 31N 42 33E
58 Tashauz, U.S.S.R. 42 0N 59 20E
69 Tashi Chho Dzong, Bhutan 27 31N 89 45E
75 Tashigong, China 33 0N 79 30E
58 Tashkent, U.S.S.R. 41 20N 69 10E
58 Tashkumyr, U.S.S.R. 41 40N 72 10E
75 Tashkurgan, China 37 51N 74 57E
75 Tashkurghan, Afghan. 36 45N 67 40E
58 Tashtagol, U.S.S.R. 52 47N 87 53E
77 Tasi Ho, China 28 20N 119 40E
73 Tasikmalaja, Indonesia 7 18s 108 12E
77 Tasin (Yangli), China 22 57N 107 15E
50 Tasjon, öar, Sweden 64 15N 15 45E
56 Taşköpru, Turkey 41 30N 34 15E
101 Tasman Bay, N.Z. 40 59s 173 25E
101 Tasman Glacier, N.Z. 43 45s 170 20E
101 Tasman Mts., N.Z. 41 3s 172 25E
99 Tasman Pen., Australia 43 10s 147 52E
99 Tasmania, I., ♦, Australia 49 0s 146 30E
46 Tăşnad, Rumania 47 30N 22 33E
83 Tassil n-Ajjer, Algeria 25 47N 8 1E
82 Tassil Tin-Rerhoh, Alg. 20 5N 3 55E
83 Tassili-Oua-Ahaggar, Algeria 20 41N 5 30E
27 Tata, Hungary 47 37N 18 19E
82 Tata, Morocco 29 46N 7 50w
27 Tatabánya, Hungary 47 32N 18 25E
55 Tatar A.S.S.R., U.S.S.R. 55 30N 51 30E
58 Tatarsk, U.S.S.R. 55 20N 75 50E
74 Tateyama, Japan 35 0N 139 50E
108 Tathlina L., Canada 60 30N 117 30w
77 Tatien, China 25 45N 118 0E
77 Tating, China 27 0N 105 35E
109 Tatinnai L., Canada 60 50N 97 50w
108 Tatlayoka Lake, Can. 51 35N 124 24w
108 Tatnam C., Canada 57 20N 91 0w
100 Tatong, Australia 36 43s 146 9E
27 Tatra = Tatry, Cz. 49 20N 20 0E
27 Tatry, Cz. 49 20N 20 0E
77 Tatsatsankou, China 37 55N 95 0E
77 Tatsu, China 29 40N 105 45E
68 Tatta, Pakistan 24 42N 67 55E
125 Tatuí, Brazil 23 25s 48 0w
117 Tatum, U.S.A. 33 16N 103 16w
76 Tatung, Anhwei, China 30 50N 117 45E
100 Tatura, Australia 36 29s 145 16E
64 Tatvan, Turkey 38 28N 42 27E
125 Taubaté, Brazil 23 5s 45 30w
25 Tauberbischofsheim, Germany 49 37N 9 40E
24 Taucha, Germany 51 22N 12 31E
26 Tauern-tunnel, Austria 47 0N 13 12E
87 Taufikia, Sudan 9 24N 31 37E
101 Taumarunui, N.Z. 38 53s 175 15E
125 Taumaturgo, Brazil 9 0s 73 50w
92 Taung, S. Afr. 27 33s 24 47E
67 Taungdwingyi, Burma 20 1N 95 40E
67 Taungup, Burma 18 48N 94 20E
67 Taungup Tanggya, Burma 18 20N 93 40E
69 Taunsa Barrage, Pakistan 31 0N 71 0E
13 Taunton, Eng. 51 1N 3 7w
24 Taunus, W. Ger. 50 15N 8 20E
101 Taupo, N.Z. 38 41s 176 7E
101 Taupo L., N.Z. 38 46s 175 55E
64 Tauq, Iraq 35 12N 44 29E
124 Tauramena, Colombia 5 1N 72 45w
101 Tauranga, N.Z. 37 35s 176 11E
101 Tauranga Harb., N.Z. 37 30s 176 5E
54 Taurage, U.S.S.R. 55 14N 22 28E
106 Taureau, Lac, Canada 46 50N 73 40w
41 Taurianova, Italy 38 22N 16 1E
64 Taurus Mts. = Toros Dağlari, Turkey 37 0N 35 0E

MAP
32 Táuste, Spain 41 58N 1 18w
57 Tauz, U.S.S.R. 41 0N 45 40E
77 Tava Wan, China 22 35N 114 35E
109 Tavani, Canada 62 10N 93 30w
64 Tavas, Turkey 37 35N 29 8E
58 Tavda, U.S.S.R. 58 7N 65 8E
58 Tavda, R., U.S.S.R. 59 30N 63 0E
19 Taverny, France 49 2N 2 13E
21 Tavignano, R., France 42 7N 9 33E
31 Tavira, Portugal 37 8N 7 40w
112 Tavistock, Canada 43 21N 80 53w
13 Tavistock, Eng. 50 33N 4 9w
40 Tavolara, I., Italy 40 55N 9 40E
30 Távora, R., Portugal 41 0N 7 30w
67 Tavoy, Burma 14 7N 98 18E
13 Taw, R., Eng. 50 58N 3 58w
114 Tawas City, U.S.A. 44 16N 83 31w
72 Tawau, E. Malaysia 4 20N 117 55E
77 Tawu, Taiwan 22 30N 120 50E
83 Tăwurghā', Libya 32 1N 15 2E
14 Tay, Firth of, Scot. 56 25N 3 8w
14 Tay, L., Scot. 56 30N 4 10w
14 Tay, R., Scot. 56 37N 3 58w
71 Tay Ninh, S. Vietnam 11 20N 106 5E
126 Tayabamba, Peru 8 15s 77 10w
69 Tayaparva La, China 31 35N 83 20E
77 Tayen, China 30 4N 115 0E
113 Taylor, Pa., U.S.A. 41 23N 75 43w
117 Taylor, Tex., U.S.A. 30 30N 97 30w
116 Taylorville, U.S.A. 39 32N 89 20w
74 Taymyr, Oz., U.S.S.R. 74 50N 102 0E
59 Taymyr, P-ov., U.S.S.R. 75 0N 100 0E
14 Tayport, Scot. 56 27N 2 52w
62 Tayr Zebna, Lebanon 33 14N 35 23E
59 Tayshet, U.S.S.R. 55 58N 97 25E
73 Taytay, Philippines 10 45N 119 30E
77 Tayu, China 25 38N 114 9E
75 Tayulehsze, China 29 15N 98 1E
77 Tayung, China 29 8N 110 30E
58 Taz, R., U.S.S.R. 65 40N 82 0E
82 Taza, Morocco 34 10N 4 0w
82 Tazenakht, Morocco 30 46N 7 3w
109 Tazin L., Canada 59 40N 109 0w
83 Tazoult, Algeria 35 29N 6 11E
58 Tazovskiy, U.S.S.R. 67 30N 78 30E
57 Tbilisi (Tiflis), U.S.S.R. 41 50N 44 50E
81 Tchad (Chad) ■, Afr. 12 30N 17 15E
81 Tchad, Lac, Chad 13 30N 14 30E
85 Tchaourou, Dahomey 8 58N 2 40E
88 Tchibanga, Gabon 2 45s 11 12E
85 Tchien Tabaraden, Niger 15 58N 5 56E
77 Tchpao (Tienpao), China 23 25N 106 47E
28 Tczew, Poland 54 8N 18 50E
101 Te Anau L., N.Z. 45 15s 167 45E
101 Te Aroha, N.Z. 37 32s 175 44E
101 Te Awamutu, N.Z. 38 1s 175 20E
101 Te Horo, N.Z. 40 48s 175 6E
101 Te Kuiti, N.Z. 38 20s 175 11E
101 Te Puke, N.Z. 37 46s 176 22E
101 Te Waewae B., N.Z. 46 13s 167 33E
46 Teaca, Rumania 46 55N 24 30E
117 Teague, U.S.A. 31 40N 96 20w
41 Teano, Italy 41 15N 14 1E
120 Teapa, Mexico 17 35N 92 56w
31 Teba, Spain 36 59N 4 55w
57 Teberda, U.S.S.R. 43 30N 43 54E
83 Tebessa, Algeria 35 22N 8 8E
124 Tebicuary, R., Paraguay 26 36s 58 16w
72 Tebing Tinggi, Indon. 3 38s 102 1E
83 Tébourba, Tunisia 36 49N 9 51E
83 Téboursouk, Tunisia 36 29N 9 10E
57 Tebulos, U.S.S.R. 42 36N 45 25E
84 Techiman, Ghana 7 35N 1 58w
46 Techirghiol, Rumania 44 4N 28 32E
46 Tecuci, Rumania 45 51N 27 27E
114 Tecumseh, U.S.A. 42 1N 83 59w
87 Tedesa, Ethiopia 5 10N 37 40w
58 Tedzhen, U.S.S.R. 37 23N 60 31E
12 Tees, R., Eng. 54 36N 1 25w
12 Teesside, Eng. 54 37N 1 13w
112 Teeswater, Canada 43 59N 81 17w
126 Tefé, Brazil 3 25s 64 50w
73 Tegal, Indonesia 6 52s 109 8E
16 Tegelen, Netherlands 51 20N 6 9E
41 Teggiano, Italy 40 24N 15 32E
69 Teghra, India 25 30N 85 34E
85 Tegina, Nigeria 10 5N 6 11E
121 Tegucigalpa, Honduras 14 10N 87 0w
119 Tehachapi, U.S.A. 35 11N 118 29w
119 Tehachapi Mts., U.S.A. 35 0N 118 40w
86 Tehamiyam, Sudan 18 26N 36 45E
86 Tehilla, Sudan 17 42N 36 6E
84 Téhini, Ivory Coast 9 39N 3 32w
65 Tehrān, Iran 35 44N 51 30E
75 Tehtsin (Atuntze), China 28 45N 98 58E
120 Tehuacán, Mexico 18 20N 97 30w
120 Tehuantepec, Mexico 16 15N 95 19w
120 Tehuantepec, Golfo de, Mexico 15 50N 95 0w
120 Tehuantepec, Istmo de, Mexico 17 0N 94 30w
13 Teifi, R., Wales 52 4N 4 14w
13 Teign, R., Eng. 50 41N 3 52w
13 Teignmouth, Eng. 50 33N 3 30w
24 Teisendorf, W. Ger. 47 51N 12 49E
54 Teishyai, U.S.S.R. 55 59N 22 14E
46 Teius, Rumania 46 12N 23 40E
88 Teixeira de Sousa, Angola 10 40s 22 10E
84 Teixeira Pinto, Port. Guinea 12 10N 13 55E
31 Tejo, R., Portugal 39 15N 8 35w
116 Tekamah, U.S.A. 41 48N 96 14w
101 Tekapo, L., N.Z. 43 53s 170 33E
120 Tekax, Mexico 20 11N 89 18w
58 Tekeli, U.S.S.R. 44 50N 79 0E
87 Tekeze, W., Ethiopia 13 50N 37 50E

MAP
42 Tekija, Yugoslavia 44 42N 22 26E
64 Tekirdağ, Turkey 40 58N 27 30E
70 Tekkali, India 18 43N 84 24E
118 Tekoa, U.S.A. 47 19N 117 4w
22 Tekoulât, O., Algeria 22 30N 2 20E
62 Tel Adashim, Israel 32 39N 35 17E
62 Tel Aviv-Yafo, Israel 32 4N 34 48E
62 Tel Hanan, Israel 32 47N 35 3E
62 Tel Hazor, Israel 33 2N 35 2E
62 Tel Lakhish, Israel 31 34N 34 51E
62 Tel Malhata, Israel 31 13N 35 2E
62 Tel Megiddo, Israel 32 35N 38 11E
62 Tel Mond, Israel 32 15N 34 56E
120 Tela, Honduras 15 40N 87 28w
82 Télagh, Algeria 34 51N 0 32w
72 Telanaipura, Indonesia 1 38s 103 30E
57 Telavi, U.S.S.R. 42 0N 45 30E
46 Telciu, Rumania 47 25N 24 24E
46 Telega, Rumania 45 17N 25 45E
108 Telegraph Cr., Canada 58 0N 131 10w
54 Telekhany, U.S.S.R. 52 30N 25 46E
47 Telemark fylke ♦, Norway 59 25N 8 30E
124 Telén, Argentina 36 15s 65 31w
46 Teleneshty, U.S.S.R. 47 35N 28 24E
30 Teleño, Spain 42 23N 6 22w
46 Teleorman, R., Rum. 44 15N 25 20E
46 Teleorman ♦, Rumania 44 0N 25 0E
126 Teles Pires (São Manuel), R., Brazil 8 40s 57 0w
119 Telescope Peak, Mt., U.S.A. 36 6N 117 7w
85 Teletaye, Mali 16 31N 1 30E
12 Telford = Wellington, U.K. 52 42N 2 31w
26 Telfs, Austria 47 19N 11 4E
24 Telgte, Germany 51 59N 7 46E
99 Telichie, S. Australia 31 45s 139 59E
108 Télimélé, Guinea 10 54N 13 2w
108 Telkwa, Canada 54 41N 126 56w
62 Tell, Jordan 32 12N 35 12E
114 Tell City, U.S.A. 38 0N 86 44w
13 Telicherry, India 11 45N 75 30E
119 Telluride, U.S.A. 37 58N 107 54w
71 Telok Anson, Malaysia 4 3N 101 0E
71 Telom, R., Malaysia 4 20N 101 46E
52 Telpos Iz., U.S.S.R. 63 35N 57 30E
128 Telsen, Argentina 42 30s 66 50w
24 Teltow, Germany 52 24N 13 15E
72 Telukbetung, Indon. 5 29s 105 17E
72 Telukbutun, Indonesia 4 5N 108 7E
72 Telukdalem, Indonesia 0 45N 97 50E
85 Tema, Ghana 5 41N 0 0E
106 Temagami L., Canada 47 0N 80 10w
73 Temanggung, Indonesia 7 18s 110 10E
120 Temax, Mexico 21 10N 88 50w
90 Tembe, Zaïre 0 30s 28 25E
71 Tembeling, R., Malaysia 4 20N 102 23E
32 Tembleque, Spain 39 41N 3 30w
93 Tembuland ♦, S. Afr. 31 35s 28 0E
13 Teme, R., England 52 23N 3 5w
119 Temecula, U.S.A. 33 26N 117 6w
71 Temerloh, Malaysia 3 27N 102 25E
58 Temir Tau, U.S.S.R. 53 10N 87 20E
58 Temirtau, U.S.S.R. 50 5N 72 56E
106 Témiskaming, Canada 46 44N 79 5w
99 Temma, Australia 41 17s 144 50E
55 Temnikov, U.S.S.R. 54 40N 43 11E
40 Temo, R., Italy 40 20N 8 30E
100 Temora, Austral. 34 30s 147 30E
120 Temosachic, Mexico 28 58N 107 50w
119 Tempe, S. Africa 29 1s 26 13E
119 Tempe, U.S.A. 33 26N 111 59w
126 Tempestad, Peru 1 20s 74 56w
72 Tempino, Indonesia 1 55s 103 23E
40 Tempio Pausania, Italy 40 53N 9 6E
117 Temple, U.S.A. 31 5N 97 28w
98 Temple B., Australia 12 15s 143 3E
15 Templemore, Ireland 52 48N 7 50w
98 Templeton, R., Austral. 21 0s 138 40E
24 Templin, Germany 53 8N 13 31E
112 Temuka, Canada 43 5N 81 15w
128 Temuco, Chile 38 50s 72 50w
101 Temuka, N.Z. 44 14s 171 17E
126 Tena, Ecuador 0 59s 77 49w
117 Tenaha, U.S.A. 31 57N 94 15w
70 Tenali, India 16 15N 80 35E
120 Tenancingo, Mexico 19 0N 99 33w
120 Tenango, Mexico 19 7N 99 40w
71 Tenasserim, Burma 12 6N 99 3E
21 Tenasserim ♦, Burma 14 0N 98 30E
21 Tenay, France 45 55N 5 30E
13 Tenby, Wales 51 40N 4 42w
21 Tenda, France 44 9N 7 34E
21 Tenda, Col de, France 44 9N 7 32E
87 Tendaho, Ethiopia 11 39N 40 54E
86 Tendelti, Sudan 13 1N 31 55E
83 Tendjedi, Adrar, Alg. 23 41N 7 32E
82 Tendrara, Morocco 33 3N 1 58w
86 Teneida, Egypt 25 30N 29 19E
83 Ténéré, Sahara 23 2N 16 0E
82 Tenerife, I., Canary Is. 28 20N 16 40w
82 Ténés, Algeria 36 31N 1 14E
77 T'eng Ch'ung, China 25 9N 98 22E
77 Teng, R., Burma 20 30N 98 10E
72 Tengah Kepulauan, Indonesia 7 5s 118 15E
75 Tengchung, China 24 58N 98 30E
71 Tenggol, I., Malaysia 4 48N 103 39E
77 Tenghsien, Kwangsi-Chuang, China
77 Tenghsien, Shantung, China 35 10N 117 10E
58 Tengiz, Ozero, U.S.S.R. 50 30N 69 0E
67 Tengyoeh, China 25 0N 98 28E
115 Tenille, U.S.A. 32 58N 82 50w
120 Teniztlán, Mexico 19 50N 97 30w

MAP
91 Tenke, Zaïre 10 32s 26 7E
11 Tenke, Congo 11 22s 26 40E
85 Tenkodogo, Upper Volta 12 0N 0 10w
96 Tennant Creek, Austral 19 30s 134 0E
111 Tennessee ♦, U.S.A. 36 0N 86 30w
82 Tennsift, Oued, Morocco 32 3N 9 28w
72 Tenom, Malaysia 5 4N 115 38E
120 Tenosique, Mexico 17 30N 91 24w
74 Tenryū-Gawa, Japan 35 30N 91 24w
127 Teófilo Otôni, Brazil 17 50s 41 30w
84 Tepa, Ghana 6 57N 20 3w
82 Ter, R., Spain 42 0N 2 30E
16 Ter Apel, Netherlands 52 53N 7 5E
85 Téra, Niger 14 0N 0 57E
30 Tera, R., Spain 41 54N 5 44w
39 Téramo, Italy 42 40N 13 40E
100 Terang, Australia 38 3s 142 59E
64 Tercan, Turkey 39 50N 40 30E
124 Tercero, R., Argentina 32 58s 61 47w
32 Terdal, India 16 33N 75 9E
54 Terebovlya, U.S.S.R. 49 18N 25 44E
46 Teregova, Rumania 45 10N 22 16E
71 Terengganu ♦, Malaysia 4 55N 103 0E
55 Tereshka, R., U.S.S.R. 52 0N 46 36E
125 Teresina, Brazil 5 2s 42 45w
126 Terezinha, Colombia 0 44N 69 27w
31 Terges, R., Portugal 37 49N 7 41w
57 Terhazza, Mali 23 45N 4 59w
19 Tergnier, France 49 40N 3 17E
81 Terkezi, Chad 18 27N 21 40E
41 Terlizzi, Italy 41 8N 16 32E
124 Termas de Chillan, Chile 36 50s 71 31w
56 Terme, Turkey 41 11N 37 0E
58 Termez, U.S.S.R. 37 0N 67 15E
39 Términi Imerese, Italy 37 59N 13 51E
120 Términos, Laguna de, Mexico 18 35N 91 30w
39 Termoli, Italy 42 0N 15 0E
72 Ternate, Indonesia 0 45N 127 25E
16 Terneuzen, Netherlands 51 20N 3 50E
74 Terney, U.S.S.R. 45 3N 136 37E
39 Terni, Italy 42 34N 12 38E
27 Ternitz, Austria 47 43N 16 2E
54 Ternopol, U.S.S.R. 49 30N 25 40E
99 Terowie, Australia 38 10s 138 50E
7 Terra Nova B., Antarc. 74 50s 164 40E
108 Terrace, Canada 54 30N 128 35w
41 Terracina, Italy 41 17N 13 12E
40 Terralba, Italy 39 42N 8 38E
40 Terranuova, Italy 43 31N 11 35E
114 Terre Haute, U.S.A. 46 30N 75 13w
117 Terrebonne B., U.S.A. 29 15s 90 28w
117 Terrecht, Mali 20 10N 0 10w
117 Terrell, U.S.A. 32 44N 96 19w
116 Terry, U.S.A. 46 47N 105 20w
16 Terschelling, I., Neth. 53 25N 5 20E
57 Terter, R., U.S.S.R. 40 5N 46 15E
32 Teruel, Spain 40 22N 1 8w
32 Teruel ♦, Spain 40 48N 1 0w
42 Tervel, Bulgaria 43 45N 27 28E
50 Tervola, Finland 66 6N 24 49E
42 Tešanj, Yugoslavia 44 38N 17 59E
87 Teseney, Ethiopia 15 5N 36 42E
74 Teshio gawa, Japan 44 45N 142 0E
75 Tesiyn Gol, Mongolia 50 40N 93 20E
42 Teslió, Yugoslavia 44 37N 17 54E
104 Teslin, Canada 60 2N 132 45w
108 Teslin L., Canada 60 13N 132 50w
109 Tessier, Canada 51 48N 107 26w
24 Tessin, Germany 54 2N 12 28E
85 Tessit, Mali 15 13N 0 18E
13 Test, R., Eng. 51 7N 1 30w
41 Testa del Gargano, It. 41 50N 16 10E
27 Tét, Hungary 47 30N 17 33E
124 Tetas, Pta., Chile 23 1s 70 38w
91 Tete, Mozambique 16 13s 33 33E
91 Tete ♦, Mozam. 15 15s 32 40E
55 Teterev, R., U.S.S.R. 50 30N 29 30E
24 Teterow, Germany 53 45N 12 34E
43 Teteven, Bulgaria 42 58N 24 17E
58 Tetiyev, U.S.S.R. 49 22N 29 38E
118 Teton, R., U.S.A. 47 58N 111 0w
82 Tétouan, Morocco 35 35N 5 21w
42 Tetovo, Yugoslavia 42 1N 21 2E
82 Tetuán = Tétouan, Morocco 35 30N 5 25w
† 59 Tetyukhe, U.S.S.R. 44 45N 135 40E
124 Teuco, R., Argentina 25 30s 60 25w
40 Teulada, Italy 38 59N 8 47E
109 Teulon, Canada 50 30N 97 20w
22 Teutoburger Wald, Germany 52 5N 8 20E
39 Tevere, R., Italy 42 30N 12 20E
14 Teviot, R., Scot. 55 21N 2 51w
99 Tewantin, Australia 26 27s 153 3E
13 Tewkesbury, Eng. 51 59N 2 8w
117 Texarkana, Ark., U.S.A. 33 25N 94 0w
117 Texarkana, Tex., U.S.A. 33 25N 94 3w
99 Texas, Austral. 28 49s 151 15E
117 Texas ♦, U.S.A. 31 40N 98 30w
117 Texas City, U.S.A. 29 20N 95 20w
16 Texel, I., Netherlands 53 5N 4 50E
117 Texhoma, U.S.A. 36 32N 101 47w
117 Texoma L., U.S.A. 34 0N 96 38w
58 Teykovo, U.S.S.R. 56 55N 40 30E
62 Teyr Zebna, Lebanon 33 14N 35 23E
55 Teza, R., U.S.S.R. 56 41N 41 45E
120 Teziutlán, Mexico 19 50N 97 30w

MAP
67 Tezpur, India 26 40N 92 45E
71 Tha Nun, Thailand 8 12N 98 17E
93 Thaba Putsoa, mt., Lesotho 29 45s 28 0E
93 Thabana Ntlenyana, Mt., Lesotho 29 30s 29 9E
93 Thabazimbi, S. Africa 24 40s 26 4E
71 Thai Nguyen, N. Vietnam 21 35N 105 46E
71 Thailand (Siam) ■, Asia 16 0N 101 0E
71 Thakhek, Laos 17 25N 104 45E
66 Thal, Pakistan 33 28N 70 33E
66 Thal Desert, Pakistan 31 0N 71 30E
83 Thala, Tunisia 35 35N 8 40E
67 Thala La, Burma 28 25N 97 23E
99 Thallon, Australia 28 30s 148 57E
25 Thalwil, Switzerland 47 17N 8 35E
13 Thame, R., Eng. 51 52N 0 47w
112 Thames, Canada 42 35N 82 1w
112 Thames, R., Canada 42 25N 82 15w
13 Thames, R., Eng. 51 24N 0 24w
101 Thames, R., N.Z. 37 32s 175 45E
13 Thames, R., U.S.A. 41 25N 72 9w
112 Thamesford, Canada 43 5N 81 0w
12 Thämit, W., Libya 30 51N 16 14E
70 Thana, India 19 12N 72 59E
68 Thanesar, India 30 1N 76 52E
13 Thanet, I. of, Eng. 51 21N 1 20E
71 Thang Binh, S. Vietnam 15 50N 108 20E
98 Thangool, Australia 24 29s 150 35E
71 Thanh Hoa, N. Vietnam 19 35N 105 40E
70 Thanjavur (Tanjore), India 10 48N 79 12E
67 Thanlwin myit, R., Burma 20 0N 98 0E
19 Thann, France 47 48N 7 5E
19 Thaon, France 48 15N 6 25E
68 Thar (Great Indian) Desert, India 28 25N 72 0E
68 Tharad, India 24 30N 71 30E
67 Thargomindah, Austral. 27 58s 143 46E
67 Tharrawaddy, Burma 17 38N 95 48E
64 Tharthâr, Bahr ath, Iraq 34 0N 43 0E
44 Thasopoúla, I., Greece 40 49N 24 45E
44 Thásos, Greece 40 50N 24 50E
44 Thásos, I., Greece 40 50N 24 50E
119 Thatcher, Ariz., U.S.A. 32 54N 109 46w
119 Thatcher, Colo., U.S.A. 37 38N 104 6w
67 Thatón, Burma 16 55N 97 39E
67 Thaungdut, Burma 24 30N 94 40E
117 Thayer, U.S.A. 36 34N 91 34w
67 Thayetmyo, Burma 19 20N 95 18E
67 Thazi, Burma 21 0N 96 5E
118 The Dalles, U.S.A. 45 40N 121 11w
99 The Diamantina, Australia 26 45s 139 30E
100 The Entrance, Australia 33 21s 151 30E
121 The Flatts, Bermuda 32 19N 64 45w
100 The Grampians, Mts., Australia 37 0s 142 30E
96 The Granites, Australia 20 35s 130 21E
100 The Great Divide, Australia 35 0s 149 17E
16 The Hague (s'Gravenhage), Neth. 52 7N 4 14E
121 The Lake, Bahamas 21 7N 73 30w
109 The Pas, Canada 53 45N 101 15w
91 The Range, Rhodesia 19 2s 31 2E
100 The Rock, Australia 35 15s 147 2E
99 The Round Mountain, Australia 30 1s 151 47E
100 The Vale, Austral. 33 34s 143 49E
86 Thebes, Egypt 25 40N 32 35E
112 Thedford, Canada 43 10N 81 50w
116 Thedford, U.S.A. 41 59N 100 31w
99 Theebine, Australia 26 1s 152 30E
109 Thekulthili L., Canada 61 3N 110 0w
67 Thelon, R., Canada 62 35N 104 3w
18 Thénezay, France 46 44N 0 2w
19 Thenon, France 45 9N 1 4E
99 Theodore, Australia 24 55s 150 3E
18 Thérain, R., France 49 15N 2 27E
113 Theresa, U.S.A. 44 13N 75 50w
44 Thermaïkos Kólpos, Greece 40 15N 22 45E
45 Thermopilai P., Greece 38 48N 22 45E
118 Thermopolis, U.S.A. 43 14N 108 10w
44 Thesprotia ♦, Gr. 39 30N 20 22E
44 Thessalia ♦, Greece 39 30N 22 0E
106 Thessalon, Canada 46 20N 83 30w
44 Thessaloníki, Greece 40 38N 22 58E
44 Thessaloníki ♦, Gr. 40 45N 23 0E
44 Thessaly = Thessalia, Greece 39 30N 22 0E
13 Thetford, Eng. 52 25N 0 44E
107 Thetford Mines, Canada 46 8N 71 18w
93 Theunissen, S. Africa 28 26s 26 43E
44 Thiámis, R., Greece 39 34N 20 18E
18 Thiberville, France 49 8N 0 27E
109 Thicket Portage, Can. 55 25N 97 45w
117 Thief River Falls, U.S.A. 48 15N 96 10w
39 Thiene, Italy 45 42N 11 29E
18 Thierache, France 49 51N 3 45E
20 Thiers, France 45 52N 3 33E
84 Thiès, Senegal 14 50N 16 51w
87 Thiet, Sudan 7 37N 28 49E
90 Thika, Kenya 1 1s 37 5E
90 Thika ♦, Kenya 1 1s 37 5E
101 Thikombia, I., Fiji 15 44s 179 55w
84 Thille-Boubacar, Senegal 16 31N 15 5w
69 Thimphu (Tashi Chho Dzong), Bhutan 27 31N 89 45E
50 þingvallavatn, Iceland 64 11N 21 9w
20 Thionville, France 49 20N 6 10E
45 Thirá, Greece 36 23N 25 27E
45 Thirasiá, I., Greece 36 26N 25 21E
100 Thirlmere, Australia 34 11s 150 35E
12 Thirsk, England 54 15N 1 20w
25 Thistle I., Australia 35 0s 136 8E

* Incorporated within the new Eastern Province

† Renamed Dalnegorsk

Thiu Khao Petchabun INDEX Tondibi

MAP
71 Thiu Khao Phetchabun, Thailand 16 20N 100 55E
20 Thiviers, France 45 25N 0 54E
21 Thizy, France 46 2N 4 18E
50 Þjorsa, Iceland 63 47N 20 48W
21 Thoissey, France 46 12N 4 48E
117 Thomas, Okla., U.S.A. 35 48N 98 48W
114 Thomas, W. Va., U.S.A. 39 10N 79 30W
15 Thomastown, Ireland 52 32N 7 10W
115 Thomasville, Ala., U.S.A. 31 55N 87 42W
115 Thomasville, Fla., USA 30 50N 84 0W
115 Thomasville, N.C., USA 35 5N 80 4W
109 Thompson, Canada 55 50N 97 34W
98 Thompson, R., Austral. 24 30N 142 50E
108 Thompson, R., Canada 50 30N 121 14W
116 Thompson, R., U.S.A. 40 25N 93 43W
118 Thompson Falls, U.S.A. 47 37N 115 26W
109 Thompson Landing, Canada 62 45N 111 7W
119 Thompsons, U.S.A. 39 0N 109 50W
113 Thompsonville, U.S.A. 42 0N 72 37W
* 90 Thompson's Falls, Kenya 0 2N 36 27E
71 Thonburi, Thailand 13 50N 100 36E
21 Thônes, France 45 54N 6 18E
71 Thongwa, Burma 16 45N 96 33E
21 Thonon-les-Bains, Fr. 46 22N 6 29E
57 Thorez, U.S.S.R. 48 4N 38 34E
50 Þorlákshöfn, Iceland 63 51N 21 22W
12 Thornaby on Tees, England 54 36N 1 19W
98 Thornborough, Austral. 16 54S 145 2E
112 Thornbury, Canada 44 34N 80 28W
5 Thorne Glacier, Antarc. 87 30N 150 0E
112 Thorold, Canada 43 8N 79 13W
100 Thorpedale, Australia 38 19S 146 13E
50 Þórshöfn, Iceland 66 12N 15 20W
19 Thouarcé, France 47 17N 0 30W
44 Thrace = Thráki, Greece 41 10N 25 30E
44 Thráki, Greece 41 9N 25 30E
44 Thrakikón Pélagos, Gr. 40 30N 25 0E
118 Three Forks, U.S.A. 45 5N 111 40W
108 Three Hills, Canada 51 43N 113 15W
98 Three Hummock I., Austral. 40 30S 144 59E
101 Three Kings Is., N.Z. 34 10S 172 10E
116 Three Lakes, U.S.A. 45 41N 89 10W
84 Three Points, C., Ghana 4 42N 2 6W
117 Three Rivers, U.S.A. 28 30N 98 10W
118 Three Sisters, Mt., U.S.A. 44 10N 121 52W
113 Throop, U.S.A. 41 24N 75 39W
96 Throssell Ra., Australia 22 0S 121 45E
14 Thrumster, Scotland 58 24N 3 38E
100 Thuddungra, Australia 34 8S 148 8E
21 Thueyts, France 44 41N 4 9E
16 Thuin, Belgium 50 20N 4 17E
20 Thuir, France 42 38N 2 45E
4 Thule, Greenland 77 30N 69 0W
25 Thun, Switzerland 46 45N 7 38E
112 Thunder B., U.S.A. 45 0N 83 20W
106 Thunder Bay, Canada 48 20N 89 10W
108 Thunder River, Canada 52 13N 119 20W
25 Thunersee, Switz. 46 43N 7 39E
71 Thung Song, Thailand 8 10N 99 40E
69 Thunkar, Bhutan 27 55N 91 0E
25 Thur, R., Switzerland 47 32N 9 10E
25 Thurgau ♦, Switz. 47 34N 9 10E
24 Thüringer Wald, Germany 50 35N 11 0E
15 Thurles, Ireland 52 40N 7 53W
99 Thurloo Downs, Australia 29 15S 143 30E
25 Thurn P., Austria 47 20N 12 15E
98 Thursday I., Austral. 10 30S 142 3E
106 Thurso, Canada 45 36N 75 15W
14 Thurso, Scotland 58 34N 3 31W
14 Thurso, R., Scot. 58 3N 3 30W
112 Thurston, U.S.A. 39 50N 82 33W
5 Thurston I., Antarctica 72 0S 100 0W
18 Thury-Harcourt, Fr. 49 0N 0 30W
91 Thyolo, Malawi 16 7S 35 5E
† 88 Thysville, Zaïre 5 12S 14 53E
99 Tia, Australia 31 15S 151 40E
120 Tiahualilo, Mexico 26 20N 103 30W
84 Tiankoura, Upper Volta 10 47N 3 17W
82 Tiaret (Tagdent), Algeria 35 28N 1 21E
84 Tiassalé, Ivory Coast 5 58N 4 57W
87 Tibari, Sudan 5 2N 31 48E
85 Tibati, Cameroon 6 22N 12 30E
39 Tiber = Tevere, R., Italy 42 30N 12 20E
118 Tiber Res., U.S.A. 48 20N 111 15W
62 Tiberias, Israel 32 47N 35 32E
62 Tiberias, L. = Kinneret, Yam, Is. 32 49N 35 36E
83 Tibesti, Chad 21 0N 17 30E
67 Tibet, China 32 30N 86 0E
85 Tibiri, Niger 13 34N 7 4E
46 Tibleş, mt., Rumania 47 32N 24 15E
46 Tibleş, Mţii, Rum. 47 41N 24 6E
62 Tibnīn, Lebanon 33 12N 35 24E
99 Tibooburra, Australia 29 26S 142 1E
49 Tibro, Sweden 58 28N 14 10E
126 Tibugá, Golfo de, Colombia 5 45N 77 20W
120 Tiburón, I., Mexico 29 0N 112 30W
84 Tichit, Mauritania 18 35N 9 20W
38 Ticino, R., Italy 45 23N 8 47E
25 Ticino ♦, Switzerland 46 20N 8 45E
113 Ticonderoga, U.S.A. 43 50N 73 28W
120 Ticul, Mexico 20 20N 89 50W
49 Tidaholm, Sweden 58 12N 13 55E
67 Tiddim, Burma 23 20N 93 45E
82 Tideridjaouine, Adrar, Algeria 23 0N 2 15E
82 Tidikelt, Algeria 26 58N 1 30E
84 Tidjikja, Mauritania 18 4N 11 35W
73 Tidore, Indonesia 0 40N 127 25E
84 Tidra, I., Mauritania 19 45N 16 20W
85 Tiébélé, Upper Volta 11 6N 0 59W
84 Tiébissou, Ivory Coast 7 9N 5 18W
83 Tiéboro, Chad 21 20N 17 7E
84 Tiego, Upper Volta 12 6N 2 38E
16 Tiel, Netherlands 51 53N 5 26E
16 Tielt, Belgium 51 0N 3 20E
65 Tien Shan, Aisa 42 0N 80 0E
16 Tienen, Belgium 50 48N 4 57E
77 Tienho, China 24 58N 108 35E
84 Tiénigbé, Ivory Coast 8 11N 5 43W
45 Tienkianghsien, China 30 25N 107 30E
77 Tieno, China 25 3N 107 3E
77 Tienpao, China 23 25N 106 47E
76 Tientsin, China 39 10N 117 0E
77 Tientu, China 18 12N 109 33E
77 Tientung, China 23 47N 107 2E
48 Tierp, Sweden 60 20N 17 30E
126 Tierra Alta, Colombia 8 11N 76 4W
124 Tierra Amarilla, Chile 27 28S 70 18W
31 Tierra de Barros, Sp. 38 40N 6 30W
30 Tierra de Campos, Spain 42 10N 4 50W
128 Tierra del Fuego, I., Gr. de, Arg.-Chile 54 0S 69 0W
30 Tiétar, R., Spain 39 55N 5 50W
114 Tiffin, U.S.A. 41 8N 83 10W
87 Tifi, Ethiopia 6 12N 36 55E
82 Tiflèt, Morocco 33 54N 6 20W
57 Tiflis = Tbilisi, U.S.S.R. 41 50N 44 50E
62 Tifrah, Israel 31 19N 34 42E
115 Tifton, U.S.A. 31 28N 83 32W
73 Tifu, Indonesia 3 39S 126 18E
59 Tigil, U.S.S.R. 58 0N 158 10E
107 Tignish, Canada 46 58N 63 57W
126 Tigre, R., Colombia 3 30S 74 58W
87 Tigre ♦, Ethiopia 13 35N 39 15E
67 Tigu, China 29 48N 91 38E
83 Tiguentourine, Algeria 28 8N 8 58E
85 Tiguila, Mali 14 44N 1 50W
46 Tigveni, Rumania 45 10N 24 31E
67 Tigyaing, Burma 23 45N 96 10E
86 Tih, Gebel el, Egypt 29 32N 33 26E
83 Tihodaine, Dunes de, Algeria 25 15N 7 15E
75 Tihua, China 43 40N 87 50E
83 Tiji, Libya 32 0N 11 18E
73 Tijiamis, Indonesia 7 16S 108 29E
73 Tijibadok, Indonesia 6 53S 106 47E
84 Tijirit, O., Mauritania 19 30N 6 15W
120 Tijuana, Mexico 32 30N 117 10W
68 Tikamgarh, India 24 44N 78 57E
98 Tikan, New Guinea 5 58S 149 2E
77 Tikang, China 31 7N 118 2E
57 Tikhoretsk, U.S.S.R. 45 56N 40 5E
54 Tikhvin, U.S.S.R. 59 35N 33 30E
82 Tikkadouine, Adrar, Alg. 24 28N 1 30E
85 Tiko, Cameroon 4 4N 9 20E
64 Tikrit, Iraq 34 35N 43 37E
59 Tiksi, U.S.S.R. 71 50N 129 0E
73 Tilamuta, Indonesia 0 40N 122 15E
16 Tilburg, Netherlands 51 31N 5 6E
106 Tilbury, Canada 42 17N 84 23W
13 Tilbury, England 51 27N 0 24E
124 Tilcara, Argentina 23 30S 65 23W
116 Tilden, U.S.A. 42 3N 97 45W
85 Tilemsès, Niger 15 37N 4 44E
85 Tilemsi, Vallée du, Mali 17 42N 0 15E
69 Tilhar, India 28 0N 79 45E
82 Tilia, O., Algeria 27 32N 0 55E
59 Tilichiki, U.S.S.R. 61 0N 166 5E
56 Tiligul, R., U.S.S.R. 47 35N 30 30E
82 Tililane, Algeria 27 49N 0 6W
45 Tilissos, Greece 38 15N 25 0E
12 Till, R., Eng. 55 35N 2 3W
118 Tillamook, U.S.A. 45 29N 123 55E
48 Tillberga, Sweden 59 42N 16 39E
108 Tilley, Canada 50 28N 111 38W
85 Tillia, Niger 16 8N 4 47E
112 Tillsonburg, Canada 42 53N 80 55W
45 Tilos, I., Greece 36 27N 27 27E
99 Tilpa, Australia 30 58S 144 30E
82 Tilrhemt, Algeria 33 9N 3 22E
54 Tilsit = Sovetsk, U.S.S.R. 55 6N 21 50E
14 Tilt, R., Scotland 56 50N 3 50W
113 Tilton, U.S.A. 43 25N 71 36W
52 Timanskiy Kryazh, U.S.S.R. 65 58N 50 5E
101 Timaru, New Zealand 44 23S 171 14E
57 Timashevsk, U.S.S.R. 45 35N 39 0E
90 Timau, Kenya 0 4N 37 15E
45 Timbákion, Greece 35 4N 24 45E
84 Timbédra, Mauritania 16 17N 8 16W
116 Timber L., U.S.A. 45 29N 101 0W
100 Timbilica, Australia 37 22S 149 42E
126 Timbío, Colombia 2 20N 76 40W
126 Timbiqui, Colombia 2 46N 77 42W
100 Timboon, Austral. 38 31S 143 0E
84 Timbuktu = Tombouctou, Mali 16 50N 3 0W
82 Timdjaouine, Algeria 21 47N 4 30E
85 Timétrine Montagnes, Mali 19 25N 1 0W
44 Timfi Oros, Greece 39 59N 20 45E
45 Timfristós, Óros, Greece 38 57N 21 50E
82 Timhadite, Morocco 33 15N 5 4W
82 Timimoun, Algeria 29 14N 0 16E
82 Timimoun, Sebkha de, Algeria 28 50N 0 46E
46 Timiş, R., Rumania 45 30N 21 0E
42 Timiş ♦, Rumania 45 40N 21 30E
42 Timişoara, Rumania 45 43N 21 15E
106 Timmins, Canada 48 28N 81 25W
82 Timmoudi, Algeria 29 20N 1 8W
42 Timok, R., Yugoslavia 44 10N 22 40E
127 Timon, Brazil 5 8S 42 52W
73 Timor, I., East Indies 9 0S 125 0E
96 Timor Sea, Ind. Oc. 10 0S 127 0E
73 Timur ♦, Indonesia 9 0S 125 0E
83 Tin Alkoum, Algeria 24 30N 10 17E
85 Ti-n-Amzi, O., Algeria-Niger 17 35N 4 20E
85 Tin Gornai, Mali 16 38N 0 38W
86 Tîna, Khalig el, Egypt 31 20N 32 42E
73 Tinaca Pt., Philippines 5 30N 125 25E
126 Tinaco, Venezuela 9 42N 68 26W
83 Tinafak, O., Algeria 27 10N 7 0W
73 Tinambacan, Phil. 12 5N 124 32E
99 Tinapagee, Australia 29 25S 144 15E
126 Tinaquillo, Venezuela 9 55N 68 18W
98 Tinaroo Falls, Austral. 17 5S 145 4E
85 Ti-n-Barraouene, O., Algeria-Mali 18 40N 4 5E
46 Tinca, Rumania 46 46N 21 58E
18 Tinchebray, France 48 47N 0 45W
70 Tindivanam, India 12 15N 79 35E
82 Tindouf, Algeria 27 50N 8 4W
69 Tindzhe Dzong, China 28 20N 88 8E
82 Ti-n-Emensan, Algeria 22 59N 4 45E
30 Tineo, Spain 43 21N 6 27W
82 Tinerhir, Morocco 31 29N 5 31W
82 Tinfouchi, Algeria 28 58N 5 54W
82 Ti-n-Geloulet, Algeria 25 58N 4 2E
77 Tinghai, China 30 0N 122 10E
49 Tinglev, Denmark 54 57N 9 13E
77 Tingnan, China 24 45N 114 50E
126 Tingo María, Peru 9 10S 76 0W
76 Tingsi, China 35 50N 104 17E
49 Tingsryd, Sweden 56 31N 15 0E
49 Tingvalla, Sweden 58 47N 12 2E
85 Tinié, Upper Volta 14 17N 1 30W
82 Tinioulig, Sebkra, Mauritania 22 30N 6 45W
82 Tinjoub, Algeria 29 45N 5 40W
82 Ti-n-Medjerdam, O., Algeria 25 45N 1 30W
124 Tinnia, Argentina 27 0S 62 45W
47 Tinnoset, Norway 59 45N 9 3E
47 Tinnsjö, Norway 59 55N 8 54E
124 Tinogasta, Argentina 28 0S 67 40W
45 Tinos, Greece 37 33N 25 8E
33 Tiñoso, C., Spain 37 32N 1 6W
77 Tinpak, China 21 40N 111 15E
83 Ti-n-Tarabine, O., Alg. 21 37N 7 11E
124 Tintina, Argentina 27 2S 62 45W
99 Tintinara, Australia 35 48S 140 2E
31 Tinto, R., Spain 37 30N 5 33W
82 Ti-n-Zaouatene, Algeria 48 55S 77 9W
112 Tioga, U.S.A. 41 54N 77 9W
71 Tioman, I., Malaysia 2 50N 104 10E
106 Tionaga, Canada 48 0N 82 0W
38 Tione di Trento, Italy 46 3N 10 44E
112 Tionesta, U.S.A. 41 29N 79 28W
87 Tior, Sudan 6 26N 31 11E
82 Tioulilin, Algeria 27 1N 0 2W
67 Tipongpani, India 27 20N 95 55E
15 Tipperary, Ireland 52 28N 8 10W
15 Tipperary ♦, Ireland 52 37N 7 55W
13 Tipton, England 52 32N 2 4W
119 Tipton, Calif., U.S.A. 36 3N 119 0W
114 Tipton, Ind., U.S.A. 40 17N 86 30W
116 Tipton, Iowa, U.S.A. 41 45N 91 12W
117 Tiptonville, U.S.A. 36 22N 89 30W
70 Tiptur, India 13 15N 76 26E
62 Tira, Israel 32 14N 34 56E
82 Tirahart, O., Algeria 23 55N 2 0W
65 Tiran, Iran 32 45N 51 0E
86 Tirān, Saudi Arabia 27 56N 34 35E
44 Tirana, Albania 41 18N 19 49E
44 Tirana-Durrësi ♦, Albania 41 35N 20 0E
38 Tirano, Italy 46 13N 10 11E
85 Tirarer, Mont, Mali 19 35N 1 10W
56 Tiraspol, U.S.S.R. 46 55N 29 35E
62 Tirat Carmel, Israel 32 46N 34 58E
62 Tirat Tsevi, Israel 32 26N 35 31E
62 Tirat Yehuda, Israel 32 1N 34 56E
82 Tiratimine, Algeria 25 56N 3 37E
85 Tirdout, Mali 16 7N 1 5W
64 Tire, Turkey 38 5N 27 50E
64 Tirebolu, Turkey 40 58N 38 45E
14 Tiree, I., Scot. 56 31N 6 49W
46 Tîrgovişte, Rumania 44 55N 25 27E
46 Tîrgu Frumos, Rumania 47 12N 27 2E
46 Tîrgu-Jiu, Rumania 45 5N 23 19E
46 Tîrgu Mureş, Rumania 46 31N 24 38E
46 Tîrgu Ocna, Rumania 46 16N 26 39E
46 Tîrgu Săcuesc, Rumania 46 0N 26 10E
66 Tirich Mir Mt., W. Pak. 36 15N 71 35E
41 Tiriola, Italy 38 57N 16 32E
70 Tirna, R., India 18 5N 76 30E
46 Tîrnava, Rumania 44 8N 25 32E
46 Tîrnava Mare, R., Rumania 46 15N 24 30E
46 Tîrnava Mica, R., Rumania 46 17N 24 30E
46 Tîrnăveni, Rumania 46 19N 24 13E
44 Tîrnavos, Greece 39 45N 22 18E
46 Tîrnova, Rumania 45 23N 22 1E
26 Tirol ♦, Austria 47 3N 10 43E
25 Tirschenreuth, Ger. 49 51N 12 20E
40 Tirso, L., Italy 40 8N 8 56E
40 Tirso, R., Italy 40 33N 9 12E
49 Tirstrup, Denmark 56 18N 10 42E
70 Tiruchchirappalli, India 10 45N 78 45E
70 Tiruchendur, India 8 30N 78 11E
70 Tiruchengodu, India 11 23N 77 56E
70 Tirumangalam, India 9 49N 77 58E
70 Tirunelveli (Tinnevelly), India 8 45N 77 45E
70 Tirupati, India 13 45N 79 30E
70 Tiruppattur, India 12 30N 78 30E
70 Tiruppur, India 11 12N 77 22E
70 Tiruturaipundi, India 10 32N 79 41E
70 Tiruvadaimarudur, India 11 2N 79 27E
70 Tiruvallar, India 13 9N 79 57E
70 Tiruvannamalai, India 12 10N 79 12E
70 Tiruvarur (Negapatam), India 10 46N 79 38E
70 Tiruvatipuram, India 12 39N 79 33E
70 Tiruvottiyur, India 13 10N 80 22E
42 Tisa, R., Yugoslavia 45 30N 20 20E
109 Tisdale, Canada 52 50N 104 0W
82 Tiseirhatène, Mares de, Mauritania 22 51N 9 30W
117 Tishomingo, U.S.A. 34 14N 96 38W
48 Tisjön, Sweden 60 56N 13 0E
48 Tisnaren, Sweden 58 58N 15 56E
39 Tisno, Yugoslavia 44 45N 15 41E
27 Tišnov, Czechoslovakia 49 21N 16 25E
27 Tisovec, Czechoslovakia 48 41N 19 56E
82 Tissemsilt, Algeria 35 35N 1 50E
83 Tissit, O., Alg.-Libya 27 28N 9 58W
49 Tissö, Denmark 55 35N 11 18E
69 Tista, R., India 27 33N 88 30E
49 Tisted, Denmark 56 58N 8 40E
27 Tisza, R., Hungary 47 38N 20 44E
27 Tiszaföldvár, Hungary 47 0N 20 14E
27 Tiszafüred, Hungary 47 38N 20 50E
27 Tiszalök, Hungary 48 0N 21 10E
27 Tiszavasvári, Hungary 47 58N 21 18E
83 Tit, Algeria 23 0N 5 10E
82 Tit, Algeria 27 0N 1 37E
59 Tit-Ary, U.S.S.R. 71 50N 126 30E
32 Titaguas, Spain 39 53N 1 6W
87 Titai Damer, Ethiopia 16 43N 37 25E
42 Titel, Yugoslavia 45 29N 20 18E
126 Titicaca, L., Bolivia-Peru 15 30S 69 30W
69 Titilagarh, India 20 15N 83 5E
85 Titiwa, Nigeria 12 14N 12 53E
42 Titograd, Yugoslavia 42 30N 19 19E
42 Titov Veles, Y.-slavia 41 46N 21 47E
39 Titova Korenica, Y.-slav. 44 45N 15 41E
42 Titovo Užice, Y.-slav. 43 55N 19 50E
90 Titule, Zaïre 3 15N 25 31E
126 Titumate, Colombia 8 19N 77 5W
112 Titusville, U.S.A. 41 35N 79 39W
84 Tivaouane, Senegal 14 56N 16 45W
42 Tivat, Yugoslavia 42 28N 18 43E
49 Tiveden, Sweden 58 50N 14 30E
13 Tiverton, Eng. 50 54N 3 30W
39 Tívoli, Italy 41 58N 12 45E
65 Tiwi, Oman 22 45N 59 12E
87 Tiyo, Ethiopia 14 41N 40 57E
82 Tizga, Morocco 32 1N 5 9W
82 Tizi n'Isly, Morocco 32 28N 5 47W
82 Tizi Ouzou, Algeria 36 42N 4 3E
120 Tizmin, Mexico 21 0N 88 1W
126 Tiznados, R., Venezuela 8 50N 67 50W
82 Tiznit, Morocco 29 48N 9 45W
73 Tjabangbungin, Indonesia 5 59S 107 5E
73 Tjalang, Indonesia 4 30N 95 43E
72 Tjangkuang, Tg., Indonesia 7 0S 105 0E
73 Tjareme, G., Indonesia 6 55S 108 27E
50 Tjeggelvas, Sweden 66 37N 17 45E
73 Tjepu, Indonesia 7 12S 111 31E
16 Tjeukemeer, Netherlands 52 53N 5 48E
73 Tjiandjur, Indonesia 6 51S 107 7E
73 Tjibatu, Indonesia 7 8S 107 59E
73 Tjidulang, Indonesia 7 42S 108 27E
73 Tjikadjang, Indonesia 7 25S 107 48E
73 Tjikampek, Indonesia 6 23S 107 28E
73 Tjilatjap, Indonesia 7 43S 109 0E
73 Tjimahi, Indonesia 6 53S 107 33E
73 Tjipatudjan, Indonesia 7 42S 108 2E
73 Tjirebon, Indonesia 6 45S 108 32E
47 Tjöllong, Norway 59 6N 10 3E
47 Tjöme, Norway 59 8N 10 26E
49 Tjörn, Sweden 58 0N 11 35E
49 Tjuls, Sweden 57 30N 18 15E
72 Tjurup, Indonesia 4 26S 102 13E
50 Tjörnes, Iceland 66 12N 17 9W
57 Tkibuli, U.S.S.R. 42 26N 43 0E
57 Tkvarcheli, U.S.S.R. 42 47N 41 52E
120 Tlaxcala, Mexico 19 20N 98 14W
120 Tlaxcala ♦, Mexico 19 30N 98 20W
120 Tlaxiaco, Mexico 17 10N 97 40W
82 Tlemcen, Algeria 34 52N 1 15W
82 Tleta di Sidi Bouguedra, Morocco 32 16N 8 58W
82 Tleta Sidi Bouguedra, Mor. 32 16N 9 59W
54 Tlumach, U.S.S.R. 48 46N 25 0E
28 Tłuszcz, Poland 52 25N 21 25E
57 Tlyarata, U.S.S.R. 42 9N 46 26E
83 Tmassah, Libya 26 19N 15 51E
83 Tmisan, Libya 27 23N 13 30E
124 Toay, Argentina 36 50S 64 30W
74 Toba, Japan 34 30N 136 45E
72 Toba, L., Indonesia 2 40N 98 50E
68 Toba Kakar, Pakistan 31 30N 69 0E
68 Toba Tek Singh, Pakistan 30 55N 72 25E
121 Tobago, I., W. Indies 11 10N 60 30W
33 Tobarra, Spain 38 35N 1 41W
73 Tobelo, Indon. 1 25N 127 56E
98 Tobermorey, Australia 22 12S 138 0E
112 Tobermory, Canada 45 12N 81 40W
14 Tobermory, Scot. 56 37N 6 4W
109 Tobin L., Canada 53 35N 103 30W
72 Toboali, Indonesia 3 0S 106 25E
73 Toboli, Indonesia 0 38S 120 12E
58 Tobolsk, U.S.S.R. 58 0N 68 10E
81 Tobruk = Tubruq, Libya 32 7N 23 55E
113 Tobyhanna, U.S.A. 41 10N 75 15W
127 Tocantinópolis, Brazil 6 20S 47 25W
127 Tocantins, R., Brazil 14 30S 49 0W
115 Toccoa, U.S.A. 34 6N 83 17W
38 Toce, R., Italy 46 5N 8 29E
14 Tochigi, Japan 36 25N 139 45E
74 Tochigi-ken ♦, Japan 36 45N 139 45E
31 Tocina, Spain 37 37N 5 44W
124 Toconao, Chile 34 35N 83 19W
126 Tocópero, Venezuela 11 30N 69 16W
124 Tocopilla, Chile 22 5S 70 10W
100 Tocumwal, Australia 35 45S 145 31E
126 Tocuyo, R., Venezuela 10 50N 69 0W
73 Todeli, Indonesia 1 38S 124 34E
90 Todenyang, Kenya 4 35N 35 56E
39 Todi, Italy 42 47N 12 24E
73 Todjo, Indonesia 1 20S 121 15E
25 Todtnau, Germany 47 50N 7 56E
85 Toecé, Upper Volta 11 50N 1 16W
108 Tofield, Canada 53 25N 112 50W
48 Töfsingdalems National Park, Sweden 62 15N 12 44E
49 Tofta, Hallands, Sweden 57 11N 12 20E
49 Toftlund, Denmark 55 11N 9 2E
101 Tofua I., Tonga 19 45S 175 05W
84 Togba, Mauritania 17 26N 10 25W
75 Toghral Ombo, China 35 10N 81 40E
73 Togian, Kepulauan, Indonesia 0 20S 121 50E
55 Togliatti, U.S.S.R. 53 37N 49 18E
85 Togo ■, West Africa 6 15N 1 35E
74 Tohoku ♦, Japan 38 40N 142 16E
87 Toinya, Sudan 6 17N 29 46E
76 Toirim, Mongolia 46 0N 106 50E
27 Tokaj, Hungary 48 8N 21 27E
73 Tokala, G., Indonesia 1 30S 121 40E
74 Tokamachi, Japan 37 8N 138 43E
101 Tokanui, New Zealand 46 34S 168 56E
74 Tokara-gunto, Japan 29 0N 129 0E
74 Tokara Kaikyō, Japan 30 0N 130 0E
101 Tokarahi, New Zealand 44 56S 170 39E
64 Tokat, Turkey 40 22N 36 35E
94 Tokelau Is., Pac. Oc. 9 0S 172 0W
58 Tokmak, Kirgizia, U.S.S.R. 42 55N 75 45E
56 Tokmak, Ukraine, U.S.S.R. 47 16N 35 42E
85 Tokombere, Nigeria 11 18N 3 30E
27 Tókomlós, Hungary 46 24N 20 45E
71 Tokong, Malaysia 5 27N 100 23E
76 Tokoto, China 40 18N 111 0E
87 Tokule, Ethiopia 14 54N 38 26E
77 Tokuno-shima, Japan 27 50N 129 2E
74 Tokushima, Japan 34 0N 134 45E
74 Tokushima-ken ♦, Japan 35 50N 134 30E
74 Tokuyama, Japan 34 0N 131 50E
74 Tōkyō, Japan 35 45N 139 45E
74 Tōkyō-to ♦, Japan 35 40N 139 30E
101 Tolaga Bay, N.Z. 38 21S 178 20E
43 Tolbukhin, Bulgaria 43 37N 27 49E
30 Toledo, Spain 39 50N 4 2W
114 Toledo, Ohio, U.S.A. 41 37N 83 33W
118 Toledo, Oreg., U.S.A. 44 40N 123 59W
118 Toledo, Wash., U.S.A. 42 29N 122 58W
31 Toledo, Montes de, Sp. 39 33N 4 20W
39 Tolentino, Italy 43 12N 13 17E
108 Tolfino, Canada 49 6N 125 54W
82 Tolga, Algeria 34 46N 5 22E
47 Tolga, Norway 62 26N 11 1E
126 Tolima ♦, Colombia 3 45N 75 15W
126 Tolima, Vol., Colombia 4 40N 75 19W
73 Tolitoli, Indonesia 1 5N 120 50E
28 Tolkmicko, Poland 54 19N 19 31E
49 Tollarp, Sweden 55 55N 13 58E
119 Tolleson, U.S.A. 33 29N 112 10W
54 Tolmachevo, U.S.S.R. 58 56N 29 57E
39 Tolmezzo, Italy 46 23N 13 0E
39 Tolmino, Yugoslavia 46 11N 13 45E
27 Tolna, Hungary 46 25N 18 48E
27 Tolna ♦, Hungary 46 30N 18 30E
49 Tolne, Denmark 57 28N 10 20E
88 Tolo, Zaïre 2 50S 18 40E
73 Tolo, Teluk, Indonesia 2 20S 122 10E
98 Tolokiwa I., Terr. of New Guinea 5 30S 147 30E
85 Tolon, Ghana 9 26N 1 3W
32 Tolosa, Spain 43 8N 2 5W
31 Tolox, Spain 36 41N 4 54W
120 Toluca, Mexico 19 20N 99 50W
76 Tolun, China 42 22N 116 30E
93 Tom Burke, S. Africa 23 5S 28 4E
116 Tomahawk, U.S.A. 45 28N 89 40W
31 Tomar, Portugal 39 36N 8 25W
44 Tómaros Oros, Greece 39 29N 20 48E
28 Tomaszów Lubelski, Poland 50 29N 23 23E
28 Tomaszów Mazowiecki, Poland 51 30N 19 57E
127 Tombodor, Serra do, Brazil 12 0S 41 30W
87 Tombe, Sudan 5 53N 31 40E
115 Tombigbee, R., U.S.A. 32 0N 88 6W
84 Tombouctou, Mali 16 50N 3 0W
119 Tombstone, U.S.A. 31 40N 110 4W
124 Tomé, Chile 36 36S 73 6W
49 Tomelilla, Sweden 55 33N 13 58E
33 Tomelloso, Spain 39 10N 3 2W
100 Tomerong, Australia 34 58S 150 30E
100 Tomingley West, Australia 32 34S 148 12E
73 Tomini, Indonesia 0 30N 120 30E
73 Tomini, Teluk, Indonesia 0 10S 122 0E
84 Tominian, Mali 13 17N 4 35W
30 Tomiño, Spain 41 59N 8 46W
59 Tommot, U.S.S.R. 58 50N 126 20E
126 Tomo, Colombia 2 38N 67 32W
100 Tomorong, Australia 35 0S 151 9E
113 Toms River, U.S.A. 39 59N 74 12W
58 Tomsk, U.S.S.R. 56 30N 85 12E
49 Tomtabacken, Sweden 57 30N 14 30E
120 Tonalá, Mexico 16 8N 93 41W
119 Tonalea, U.S.A. 36 17N 110 58W
126 Tonantins, Brazil 2 45S 67 45W
118 Tonasket, U.S.A. 48 45N 119 30W
112 Tonawanda, U.S.A. 43 0N 78 54W
13 Tonbridge, Eng. 51 12N 0 18E
73 Tondano, Indonesia 1 35N 124 54E
30 Tondela, Portugal 40 31N 8 5W
49 Tönder, Denmark 54 58N 8 50E
49 Tönder Amt ♦, Den. 55 8N 8 50E
70 Tondi, India 9 45N 79 4E
85 Tondi Kiwindi, Niger 14 28N 2 02E
85 Tondibi, Mali 16 39N 0 14W

* Renamed Nyahururu
† Renamed Mbanza Ngungu

MAP
74 Tone gawa, Japan 36 15N 139 30E
101 Tonga Is. ■, Pacific 20 0s 173 0w
  Ocean
101 Tonga Trench, Pac. Oc. 18 0s 175 0w
93 Tongaat, S. Afr. 29 33s 31 9E
93 Tongaland, S. Afr. 27 0s 32 0E
101 Tongatapu I., Tonga I. 21 10s 174 0w
16 Tongeren, Belgium 50 47N 5 28E
71 Tongking = Bac-Phan, 21 30N 105 0E
  North Vietnam
71 Tongking, G. of, Asia 20 0N 108 0E
93 Tongobory, Malagasy 23 32s 44 20E
  Rep.
124 Tongoy, Chile 30 25s 71 40w
16 Tongres = Tongeren, 50 47N 5 28E
  Belg.
118 Tongue, R., U.S.A. 48 30N 106 30w
87 Tonj, Sudan 7 20N 28 44E
68 Tonk, India 26 6N 75 54E
117 Tonkawa, U.S.A. 36 44N 67 22w
71 Tonlé Sap, Cambodia 13 0N 104 0E
20 Tonnay-Charente, Fr. 45 56N 0 55w
20 Tonneins, France 44 24N 0 20E
19 Tonnerre, France 47 51N 3 59E
24 Tönning, Germany 54 18N 8 57E
119 Tonopah, U.S.A. 38 4N 117 12w
47 Tonsberg, Norway 59 19N 10 25E
47 Tonstad, Norway 58 40N 6 45E
35 Tonto Basin, U.S.A. 33 58N 111 15w
118 Tooele, U.S.A. 40 30N 112 20w
99 Toompine, Australia 27 15s 144 19E
100 Toongi, Austral. 32 28s 148 30E
98 Toonpan, Australia 19 28s 146 48E
59 Toora-Khem, U.S.S.R. 52 28N 96 9E
99 Toowong, Australia 27 30s 152 58E
99 Toowoomba, Austral. 27 32s 151 56E
52 Top Ozero, U.S.S.R. 65 35N 32 0E
46 Topalu, Rumania 44 31N 28 3E
116 Topeka, U.S.A. 39 3N 95 40w
58 Topki, U.S.S.R. 55 25N 85 20E
27 Topla, R., Cz. 49 0N 21 36E
108 Topley, Canada 54 32N 126 5w
42 Toplica, R., Yugoslavia 43 15N 21 30E
46 Toplița, Rumania 46 55N 25 27E
124 Topocalma, Pta., Chile 34 10s 72 2w
119 Topock, U.S.A. 34 46N 114 29w
42 Topola,-Yugoslavia 44 17N 20 32E
27 Topol'čany, Cz. 48 35N 18 12E
57 Topoli, U.S.S.R. 47 59N 51 45E
43 Topolnitsa. R., Bulg. 42 21N 24 0E
120 Topolobampo, Mexico 25 40N 109 10w
43 Topolovgrad, Bulgaria 42 5N 26 20E
43 Topolvăț Mare, Rum. 45 46N 21 41E
118 Toppenish, U.S.A. 46 27N 120 16w
39 Topusko, Yugoslavia 45 18N 15 59E
96 Tor Bay, Australia 35 5s 117 50E
32 Torá, Spain 41 49N 1 25E
87 Tora Kit, Sudan 11 2N 32 30E
126 Torata, Peru 17 3s 70 1w
65 Torbat-e Heydarïyeh, 35 15N 59 12E
  Iran
65 Torbat-e Jām, Iran 35 8N 60 35E
107 Torbay, Canada 47 40N 52 42w
13 Torbay, U.K. 50 26N 3 31w
100 Torbreck Mt., Austral. 37 10s 145 57E
54 Torchin, U.S.S.R. 50 45N 25 0E
47 Tordal, Norway . 59 10N 8 45E
30 Tordesillas, Spain 41 30N 5 0w
30 Tordoya, Spain 43 6N 8 36w
50 Töre, Sweden 65 55N 22 40E
49 Töreboda, Sweden 58 41N 14 7E
50 Torfajökull, Iceland 63 54N 19 0w
24 Torgau, Germany 51 32N 13 0E
24 Torgelow, Germany 53 40N 13 59E
16 Torhout, Belgium 51 5N 3 7E
87 Tori, Ethiopia 7 53N 33 35E
18 Torigni-sur-Vire, France 49 3N 0 58w
32 Torija, Spain 40 44N 3 2w
120 Torín, Mexico 27 33N 110 5w
30 Toriñana, C., Spain 43 9N 9 17w
38 Torino, Italy 45 4N 7 40E
87 Torit, Sudan 4 20N 32 55E
54 Torkovichi, U.S.S.R. 58 51N 30 30E
42 Tormac, Rumania 45 30N 21 30E
107 Tormentine, Canada 46 6N 63 46w
30 Tormes, R., Spain 41 7N 6 0w
108 Tornado Mt., Canada 49 55N 114 40w
49 Tornby, Denmark 57 32N 9 56E
50 Torne älv, Sweden 65 50N 24 12E
50 Torneträsk, Sweden 68 24N 19 15E
50 Torneå = Tornio, 65 50N 24 12E
  Finland
50 Tornio, Finland 65 50N 24 12E
50 Tornionjoki, Finland 65 50N 24 12E
124 Tornquist, Argentina 38 0s 62 15w
30 Toro, Spain 41 35N 5 24w
49 Torö, Sweden 58 48N 17 50E
120 Toro, Pta., Panama 9 22N 79 57w
  Canal Zone
• 90 Toro ♦, Uganda 0 20N 30 15E
124 Toro, Cerro del, Chile 29 0s 69 50w
27 Törökszentmiklós, 47 11N 20 27E
  Hungary
44 Toronáios Kólpos, 40 5N 23 30E
  Greece
100 Toronto, Austral. 33 0s 151 30E
106 Toronto, Canada 43 39N 79 20w
112 Toronto, U.S.A. 40 27N 80 36w
120 Toronto, L., Mexico 27 40N 105 30w
54 Toropets, U.S.S.R. 56 30N 31 40E
90 Tororo, Uganda 0 45N 34 12E
64 Toros Dağlari, Turkey 37 0N 35 0E
48 Torpshammar, Sweden 62 29N 16 20E
100 Torquay, Australia 38 20s 144 19E
13 Torquay, U.K. 50 27N 3 31w
30 Torquemada, Spain 42 2N 4 19w
31 Torralba de Calatrava, 39 1N 3 44w
  Spain
31 Torrão, Portugal 38 16N 8 11w
40 Torre Annunziata, Italy 40 45N 14 26E

MAP
30 Tôrre de Moncorvo, 41 12N 7 8w
  Port.
41 Torre del Greco, Italy 40 47N 14 22E
31 Torre del Mar, Spain 36 44N 4 6w
38 Torre Pellice, Italy 44 49N 7 13E
30 Torreblanca, Spain 40 14N 0 12E
31 Torrecampo, Spain 38 29N 4 41w
32 Torrecilla en Cameros, 42 15N 2 38w
  Spain
32 Torredembarra, Spain 41 9N 1 24w
31 Torredonjimeno, Spain 37 46N 3 57w
30 Torrejoncillo, Spain 39 54N 6 28w
32 Torrelaguna, Spain 40 50N 3 38w
30 Torrelavega, Spain 43 20N 4 5w
41 Torremaggiore, Italy 41 42N 15 17E
31 Torremolinos, Spain 36 38N 4 30w
98 Torrens Creek, Austral. 20 48s 145 3E
99 Torrens, L., S. Austral. 31 0s 137 45E
33 Torrente, Spain 39 27N 0 28w
33 Torrenueva, Spain 38 38N 3 22w
120 Torreón, Mexico 25 33N 103 25w
33 Torreperogil, Spain 38 2N 3 17w
30 Torres, Spain 41 6N 5 0w
31 Tôrres Novas, Portugal 39 27N 8 33w
98 Torres Strait, Austral. 10 20s 142 0E
31 Torres Vedras, Portugal 39 5N 9 15w
33 Torrevieja, Spain 37 59N 0 42w
119 Torrey, U.S.A. 38 12N 111 30w
13 Torridge, R., Eng. 50 57N 4 10w
14 Torridon, L., Scot. 57 35N 5 50w
30 Torrijos, Spain 39 59N 4 18w
49 Torring, Denmark 55 52N 9 29E
113 Torrington, Conn., 41 50N 73 9w
  U.S.A.
116 Torrington, Wyo., U.S.A. 42 5N 104 8w
32 Torroella de Montgri, 42 2N 3 8E
  Spain
100 Torrowangee, Australia 31 22s 141 30E
31 Torrox, Spain 36 46N 3 57w
49 Torsås, Sweden 56 24N 16 0E
48 Torsby, Sweden 60 7N 13 0E
48 Torsjok, U.S.S.R. 57 5N 34 55E
49 Torsö, Sweden 58 48N 13 45E
30 Tórtoles de Esgueva, Sp. 41 49N 4 2w
38 Tortona, Italy 44 53N 8 54E
39 Tortoreto, Italy 42 50N 13 55E
41 Tortorici, Italy 38 2N 14 48E
32 Tortosa, Spain 40 49N 0 31E
32 Tortosa C., Spain 40 41N 0 52E
30 Tortosendo, Portugal 40 15N 7 31w
121 Tortue, I. de la, Haiti 20 5N 72 57w
121 Tortuga, Isla la, 11 8N 67 2w
  Venezuela
65 Torud, Iran 35 25N 55 5E
28 Toruń, Poland 53 0N 18 39E
49 Torup, Sweden 56 57N 13 5E
47 Torvastad, Norway 59 23N 5 15E
112 Tory Hill, Canada 44 56N 78 18w
27 Torysa, R., Cz. 48 50N 21 15E
54 Torzhok, U.S.S.R. 57 5N 34 55E
74 Tosa-Wan, Japan 33 15N 133 30E
38 Toscana, Italy 43 30N 11 5E
54 Tosno, U.S.S.R. 59 30N 30 58E
32 Tossa, Spain 41 43N 2 56E
124 Tostado, Argentina 29 15s 61 50w
24 Tostedt, Germany 53 17N 9 42E
28 Toszek, Poland 50 27N 18 32E
47 Totak, Norway 59 40N 7 45E
33 Totana, Spain 37 45N 1 30w
47 Toten, Norway 60 37N 10 53E
92 Toteng, Botswana 20 22s 22 58E
55 Totma, U.S.S.R. 60 0N 42 40E
120 Totonicapán, Guat. 14 50N 91 20w
100 Tottenham, Australia 32 15s 147 15E
112 Tottenham, Canada 44 2N 79 48w
74 Tottori, Japan 35 30N 134 15E
74 Tottori-ken ♦, Japan 35 30N 134 12E
82 Touat, Algeria 27 30N 0 30E
84 Touba, Ivory Coast 8 15N 7 40w
82 Toubkal, Djebel, 31 0N 8 0w
  Morocco
19 Toucy, France 47 44N 3 15E
84 Tougan, Upper Volta 13 11N 2 58w
83 Touggourt, Algeria 33 10N 6 0E
84 Tougué, Guinea 11 25N 11 50w
83 Toukmatine, Algeria 24 49N 7 11E
19 Toul, France 48 40N 5 53E
21 Toulon, France 43 10N 5 55E
20 Toulouse, France 43 37N 1 27E
83 Toummo, Niger 22 45N 14 8E
83 Toummo Dhoba, Niger 22 30N 14 31E
84 Toumodi, Ivory Coast 6 32N 5 4w
82 Tounassine, Hamada, 28 48N 5 0w
  Algeria
67 Toungoo, Burma 19 0N 96 30E
84 Touques, R., France 49 22N 0 8E
18 Touraine, France 47 20N 0 30E
19 Tourcoing, France 50 42N 3 10E
85 Tourcoingbam, Upper 13 23N 1 33w
  Volta
16 Tournai, Belgium 50 35N 3 25E
19 Tournan-en-Brie, France 48 44N 2 46E
20 Tournay, France 43 13N 0 13E
21 Tournon, France 45 4N 4 50E
18 Tournon-St.-Martin, 46 45N 0 58E
  France
21 Tournus, France 46 35N 4 54E
18 Tours, France 47 22N 0 40E
83 Touside, Pic, Chad 21 1N 16 18E
92 Toutsrivier, S. Africa 33 20s 20 0E
126 Tovar, Venezuela 8 20N 71 46w
55 Tovarkovskiy, U.S.S.R. 53 40N 38 5E
47 Tovdal, Norway 58 47N 8 10E
47 Tovdalselva, Nor. 58 20N 8 16E
100 Towanda, Australia 37 6s 149 55E
113 Towanda, U.S.A. 41 46N 76 30w
116 Tower, U.S.A. 47 49N 92 17w
116 Towner, U.S.A. 48 25N 100 26w
118 Townsend, U.S.A. 46 25N 111 32w

MAP
100 Townsend Mt., Austral. 36 25s 148 16E
98 Townshend, C., 22 18s 150 30E
  Australia
98 Townshend, I., Austral. 22 16s 150 31E
98 Townsville, Australia 19 15s 146 45E
100 Towong, Australia 36 8s 147 59E
77 Towshan, China 22 5N 112 50E
114 Towson, U.S.A. 39 26N 76 34w
7 Toyah, Indonesia 2 40s 121 30E
117 Toyah, U.S.A. 31 20N 103 48w
117 Toyahvale, U.S.A. 30 58N 103 45w
74 Toyama, Japan 36 40N 137 15E
74 Toyama ♦, Japan 36 45N 137 30E
74 Toyama-Wan, Japan 37 0N 137 30E
74 Toyohashi, Japan 34 45N 137 25E
74 Toyokawa, Japan 34 48N 137 27E
74 Toyonaka, Japan 34 50N 135 28E
74 Toyooka, Japan 35 35N 134 55E
83 Tozeur, Tunisia 33 56N 8 8E
30 Trabancos, R., Spain 41 0N 5 3E
64 Trabzon, Turkey 41 0N 39 45E
107 Tracadie, Canada 47 30N 64 55w
119 Tracy, Calif., U.S.A. 37 46N 121 27w
116 Tracy, Minn., U.S.A. 44 12N 95 3w
38 Tradate, Italy 45 43N 8 54E
77 Tradom, China 30 0N 83 59E
100 Trafalgar, Australia 38 14s 146 12E
30 Trafalgar, C., Spain 36 10N 6 2w
83 Traghan, Libya 26 0N 14 30E
100 Tragowel, Austral. 35 51s 143 59E
46 Traian, Rumania 45 2N 28 15E
108 Trail, Canada 49 5N 117 40w
15 Tralee, Ireland 52 16N 9 42w
15 Tralee B., Ireland 52 17N 9 55w
15 Tramore, Ireland 52 10N 7 10w
71 Tran Ninh, Cao 19 30N 103 10E
  Nguyen, Laos
49 Tranas, Sweden 58 3N 14 59E
124 Trancas, Argentina 26 20s 65 20w
30 Trancoso, Portugal 40 49N 7 21w
49 Tranebjerg, Denmark 55 51N 10 36E
49 Tranemo, Sweden 57 30N 13 20E
71 Trang, Thailand 7 33N 99 38E
93 Trangahy, Malagasy 19 7s 44 43E
  Rep.
7 Trangan, I., Indonesia 6 40s 134 20E
100 Trangie, Austral. 32 4s 148 0E
48 Trångsviken, Sweden 63 19N 14 0E
41 Trani, Italy 41 17N 16 24E
93 Tranoroa, Malag. 24 42s 45 4E
11 Tranquebar, India 11 1N 79 54E
125 Tranqueras, Uruguay 31 8s 56 0w
90 Trans Nzoia ♦, Kenya 1 0N 35 0E
109 Transcona, Canada 49 50N 97 0w
46 Transilvania, Rum. 46 19N 25 0E
43 Transkei ♦, S. Afr. 32 15s 28 15E
49 Träslöv, Sweden 57 8N 12 21E
48 Transtrand, Sweden 61 6N 13 20E
92 Transvaal ♦, S. Africa 25 0s 29 0E
46 Transylvania = 46 19N 25 0E
  Transilvania, Rum.
46 Transylvanian Alps, 45 30N 25 0E
  Rumania
49 Tranås, Sweden 55 37N 13 59E
41 Trápani, Italy 38 1N 12 30E
118 Trappe Peak, Mt., 45 56N 114 29w
  U.S.A.
100 Traralgon, Austral. 38 6s 146 31E
84 Trarza ♦, Mauritania 17 30N 15 0w
39 Trasacco, Italy 41 58N 13 30E
46 Trăscău, Muntii, 46 14N 23 14E
  Rumania
39 Trasimeno, L., Italy 43 10N 12 5E
71 Trat, Thailand 12 14N 102 33E
26 Traun, Austria 48 14N 14 15E
26 Traun-see, Austria 47 48N 13 45E
25 Traunstein, Germany 47 52N 12 40E
49 Tråvad, Sweden 58 15N 13 5E
101 Travers, Mt., N.Z. 42 1s 172 45E
118 Traverse City, U.S.A. 44 45N 85 39w
5 Traverse I., Falk. Is. 48 0s 28 0E
  Dep.
42 Travnik, Yugoslavia 44 17N 17 39E
107 Traynor, Canada 52 20N 108 32w
30 Trazo, Spain 43 0N 8 30w
39 Trbovlje, Yugoslavia 46 12N 15 5E
38 Trebbia, R., Italy 44 52N 9 30E
24 Trebel, R., Germany 54 0N 12 50E
41 Trebinje, Yugoslavia 42 44N 18 22E
42 Trebisacce, Italy 39 52N 16 32E
42 Trebišnica, R., Y.-slavia 42 47N 18 8E
27 Trebišov, Cz. 48 38N 21 41E
42 Trebizat, Yugoslavia 43 15N 17 30E
27 Trebon, Czechoslovakia 48 59N 14 48E
31 Trebujena, Spain 36 52N 6 11w
38 Trecate, Italy 45 29N 8 42E
27 Trnava, Czechoslovakia 48 23N 17 35E
18 Trédegar, U.K. 51 47N 3 16w
18 Trégastel-Plage, France 48 49N 3 31w
39 Tregnago, Italy 45 31N 11 10E
97 Tregosse Is., Australia 17 41s 150 50E
18 Tréguier, France 48 47N 3 16w
109 Treherne, Canada 49 39N 98 41w
39 Tréia, Italy 43 30N 13 20E
20 Treignac, France 45 32N 1 48E
125 Treinta y Tres, Uruguay 33 10s 54 50w
25 Treis, Germany 50 9N 7 19E
92 Trekveld, S. Africa 30 35s 19 45E
128 Trelew, Argentina 43 10s 65 20w
49 Trelleborg, Sweden 55 20N 13 10E
19 Trélon, France 50 5N 4 6E
117 Trementina, U.S.A. 35 27N 105 30w
118 Tremonton, U.S.A. 41 45N 112 10w
32 Tremp, Spain 42 10N 0 52E
114 Trenary, U.S.A. 46 12N 86 59w
27 Trenčín, Czechoslovakia 48 52N 18 4E

MAP
73 Trenggalek, Indonesia 8 5s 111 44E
124 Trenque Laquen, Arg. 36 0s 62 45w
12 Trent, R., Eng. 53 33N 0 44w
38 Trentino-Alto Adige ♦, 46 5N 11 0E
  Italy
38 Trento, Italy 46 5N 11 8E
106 Trenton, Canada 44 10N 77 40w
116 Trenton, Mo., U.S.A. 40 5N 93 37w
116 Trenton, Nebr., U.S.A. 40 14N 101 4w
113 Trenton, N.J., U.S.A. 40 15N 74 41w
117 Trenton, Tenn., U.S.A. 35 58N 88 57w
107 Trepassey, Canada 46 43N 53 25w
24 Treptow, Germany 53 42N 13 15E
41 Trepuzzi, Italy 40 26N 18 4E
124 Tres Arroyos, Argentina 38 20s 60 20w
125 Três Corações, Brazil 21 30s 45 30w
82 Tres Fourches, C. de, 35 26N 3 0w
  Mor.
128 Três Lagoas, Brazil 20 50s 51 50w
128 Três Montes, C., Chile 47 0s 75 35w
125 Três Pontas, Brazil 21 23s 45 29w
124 Tres Puentes, Chile 27 50s 70 15w
119 Tres Puntas, C., Arg. 47 0s 66 0w
125 Tres Rios, Brazil 22 20s 43 30w
42 Treska, R., Yugoslavia 41 45N 21 11E
42 Treskavika Planina, 43 40N 18 20E
  Yugoslavia
30 Trespaderne, Spain 42 47N 3 24w
27 Trets, France 43 27N 5 41E
25 Treuchtlingen, Ger. 48 58N 10 55E
24 Treuenbrietzen, Ger. 52 6N 12 51E
30 Trevinca, Peña, Spain 42 15N 6 46w
30 Treviso, Italy 45 40N 12 15E
21 Trévoux, France 45 57N 4 47E
42 Trgovište, Yugoslavia 42 20N 22 10E
99 Triabunna, Australia 42 28s 148 0E
45 Triánda, Greece 36 25N 28 10E
71 Triang, Malaysia 3 13N 102 27E
19 Triaucourt-en-Argonne, 48 59N 5 2E
  France
24 Tribsees, Germany 54 4N 12 46E
98 Tribulation, C., Australia 16 10s 145 50E
116 Tribune, U.S.A. 38 30N 101 45w
41 Tricárico, Italy 40 37N 16 9E
41 Tricase, Italy 39 56N 18 20E
70 Trichinopoly = 10 45N 78 45E
  Tiruchchirappalli, India
70 Trichur, India 10 30N 76 18E
100 Trida, Austral. 33 2s 144 57E
25 Trier, Germany 49 45N 6 37E
39 Trieste, Italy 45 39N 13 45E
39 Trieste, G. di, Italy 45 37N 13 40E
41 Triggiano, Italy 41 4N 16 58E
39 Triglav, Y.-slavia 46 30N 13 45E
39 Trigno, R., Italy 41 55N 14 37E
31 Trigueros, Spain 37 24N 6 50w
45 Trikeri, Greece 39 6N 23 5E
45 Tríkhonis, Límni, Gr. 38 34N 21 30E
44 Tríkkala, Greece 39 34N 21 47E
44 Tríkkala ♦, Greece 39 41N 21 30E
73 Trikora, G., Indonesia 4 11s 138 0E
39 Trilj, Yugoslavia 43 38N 16 42E
32 Trillo, Spain 40 42N 2 35w
15 Trim, Ireland 53 34N 6 48w
70 Trincomalee, Sri Lanka 8 38N 81 15E
7 Trindade, I., Southern 20 20s 29 50w
  Atlantic Ocean
126 Trinidad, Bolivia 14 54s 64 50w
76 Trinidad, Colombia 5 25N 71 40w
121 Trinidad, Cuba 21 40N 80 0w
117 Trinidad, U.S.A. 37 15N 104 30w
125 Trinidad, Uruguay 33 30s 56 50w
128 Trinidad, I., Argentina 39 10s 62 0w
121 Trinidad & Tobago ■, 10 30N 61 20w
  West Indies
41 Trinitápoli, Italy 41 22N 16 5E
107 Trinity, Canada 48 22N 53 29w
117 Trinity, U.S.A. 30 50N 95 20w
98 Trinity B., Australia 16 30s 146 0E
107 Trinity B., Canada 48 20N 53 10w
117 Trinity Mts., U.S.A. 40 20N 118 50w
117 Trinity, R., U.S.A. 30 30N 95 0w
38 Trino, Italy 45 10N 8 18E
115 Trion, U.S.A. 34 35N 85 18w
41 Trionto C., Italy 34 38N 16 47E
38 Trítora, Italy 40 40N 7 46E
84 Tripoli = Tarābulus, 32 49N 13 7E
  Libya
45 Trípolis, Greece 37 31N 22 25E
116 Tripp, U.S.A. 43 16N 97 58w
67 Tripura ♦, India 24 0N 92 0E
24 Trischen, I., W. Ger. 54 3N 8 32E
7 Tristan da Cunha, I., 37 6s 12 20w
  Atlantic Ocean
70 Trivandrum, India 8 31N 77 0E
41 Trivento, Italy 41 48N 14 31E
27 Trnava, Czechoslovakia 48 23N 17 35E
98 Trobriand, Papua 8 40s 151 0E
108 Trochu, Canada 51 50N 113 20w
106 Trodely I., Canada 52 20N 79 20w
39 Trogir, Yugoslavia 43 32N 16 15E
47 Trögstad, Norway 59 37N 11 16E
39 Troia, Italy 41 22N 15 19E
87 Troina, Italy 37 47N 14 34E
107 Trois Pistoles, Canada 48 5N 69 10w
106 Trois Rivières, Canada 46 25N 72 40w
57 Troitsk, U.S.S.R. 54 10N 61 35E
52 Troitsko-Pechorsk, 62 40N 56 10E
  U.S.S.R.
49 Trollhättan, Sweden 58 17N 12 20E
46 Trollheimen, Nor. 62 46N 9 1E
47 Tromsø, Norway 58 28N 8 53E
50 Troms fylke ♦, Norway 68 56N 19 0E
50 Tromsö, Norway 69 40N 18 56E
128 Tronador, Mt., Arg. 41 53s 71 0w
50 Tröndelag, N. ♦, Nor. 65 0N 12 0E

MAP
47 Tröndelag, S. ♦, Nor. 62 0N 10 0E
47 Trondheim, Norway 63 25N 10 25E
50 Trondheimsfjorden, Nor. 63 35N 10 30E
49 Trönninge, Sweden 56 38N 12 59E
48 Trönö, Sweden 61 22N 16 54E
39 Tronto, R., Italy 42 50N 13 46E
92 Troodos, mt., Cyprus 34 58N 32 55E
41 Tropea, Italy 38 40N 15 53E
119 Tropic, U.S.A. 37 44N 112 4w
44 Tropoja, Albania 42 23N 20 10E
14 Trossachs, The, Scotland 56 14N 4 24w
15 Trostan Mt., N. Ireland 55 4N 6 10w
25 Trostberg, Germany 48 2N 12 33E
117 Troup, U.S.A. 32 10N 95 3w
108 Trout L., N.W. Terr., 60 40N 121 40w
  Canada
109 Trout L., Ont., Canada 51 20N 93 15w
118 Trout Peak, Mt., U.S.A. 44 37N 109 30w
18 Trouville, France 49 21N 0 5E
13 Trowbridge, Eng. 51 18N 2 12w
64 Troy, Turkey 39 55N 26 20E
115 Troy, Alabama, U.S.A. 31 50N 85 58w
39 Troy, Kans., U.S.A. 39 47N 95 2w
116 Troy, Mo., U.S.A. 38 56N 90 59w
118 Troy, Montana, U.S.A. 48 30N 115 58w
113 Troy, N.Y., U.S.A. 42 45N 73 39w
114 Troy, Ohio, U.S.A. 40 0N 84 10w
112 Troy, Tur. 39 55N 26 20E
43 Troyan, Bulgaria 42 57N 24 43E
19 Troyes, France 48 19N 4 3E
43 Trpanj, Yugoslavia 43 1N 17 15E
27 Trstena, Czechoslovakia 49 21N 19 37E
42 Trstenik, Yugoslavia 43 36N 21 0E
54 Trubchevsk, U.S.S.R. 52 33N 33 47E
65 Trucial States ■, Asia 24 0N 54 30E
118 Truckee, U.S.A. 39 20N 120 11w
126 Trujillo, Colombia 4 10N 76 19w
121 Trujillo, Honduras 16 0N 86 0w
126 Trujillo, Peru 8 0s 79 0w
31 Trujillo, Spain 39 28N 5 55w
117 Trujillo, U.S.A. 35 34N 104 44w
126 Trujillo, Venezuela 9 22N 70 26w
95 Truk Is., U.S. Pac. Is. 7 25N 151 46E
  Trust Terr.
117 Trumann, U.S.A. 35 42N 90 32w
119 Trumbull, Mt., U.S.A. 36 25N 113 32w
42 Trún, Bulgaria 42 51N 22 38E
18 Trun, France 48 50N 0 2E
100 Trundle, Austral. 32 52s 147 35E
107 Truro, Canada 45 21N 63 14E
13 Truro, England 50 17N 5 2w
49 Trustrup, Denmark 56 20N 10 46E
119 Truth or Consequences, 33 9N 107 16w
  U.S.A.
26 Trutnov, Cz. 50 37N 15 54E
20 Truyère, R., France 44 38N 2 34E
42 Tryavna, Bulgaria 42 54N 25 25E
115 Tryon, U.S.A. 35 15N 82 16w
112 Tryonville, U.S.A. 41 42N 79 48w
28 Trzcianka, Poland 53 3N 16 25E
28 Trzciel, Poland 52 23N 15 50E
28 Trzcinsko-Zdroj, Poland 52 58N 14 35E
54 Trzebiatów, Poland 54 3N 15 18E
28 Trzebinia, Poland 50 11N 19 30E
28 Trzebiez, Poland 53 38N 14 31E
28 Trzebnica, Poland 51 20N 17 1E
28 Trzemeszno, Poland 52 33N 17 48E
39 Trzič, Yugoslavia 46 22N 14 18E
50 Trölladyngia, Iceland 64 54N 17 15w
62 Tsafriya, Israel 31 59N 34 51E
76 Tsagaan-Oür, Mongolia 50 20N 105 3E
75 Tsaidam, China 37 0N 95 0E
44 Tsamandás, Greece 39 46N 20 21E
67 Tsana Dzong, China 28 0N 91 55E
75 Tsangpo, China 30 43N 100 32E
77 Tsaohsien, China 34 50N 115 45E
93 Tsaratanana, Malg. 16 47s 47 39E
93 Tsaratanana, Mt. de, 14 0s 49 0E
  Malag.
43 Tsarevo = Michurin, 42 9N 27 51E
  Bulgaria
77 Tsaring Nor, China 35 0N 97 0E
44 Tsaritsáni, Greece 39 53N 15 14E
92 Tsau, Botswana 20 8s 22 29E
92 Tsaukaib, S.W. Afr. 26 37s 15 39E
58 Tsebrikovo, U.S.S.R. 47 9N 30 10E
58 Tselinograd, U.S.S.R. 51 10N 71 30E
53 Tskhinali, U.S.S.R. 42 22N 43 52E
77 Tsetserling, Mongolia 47 29N 101 10E
76 Tsetserleg, Mongolia 47 36N 101 32E
92 Tshabong, Botswana 26 2s 22 29E
88 Tsheka, Zaïre 5 4s 13 0E
93 Tshesebe, Botswana 20 43s 27 32E
92 Tshibeke, Zaïre 2 40s 28 35E
88 Tshibinda, Zaïre 6 17s 21 0E
88 Tshikapa, Zaïre 6 17s 21 0E
88 Tshilenge, Zaïre 6 2s 23 40E
91 Tshinsenda, Congo 12 15s 28 0E
93 Tshombe, Malagasy Rep. 25 18s 45 29E
92 Tshwane, Botswana 22 24s 22 1E
76 Tsian, China 41 12N 126 5E
77 Tsiaotso, China 35 11N 113 37E
92 Tsigara, Botswana 20 22s 25 54E
87 Tsihombe, Ethiopia 4 5N 43 10E
57 Tsimlyansk, U.S.S.R. 47 45N 42 0E
57 Tsimlyanskoye Vdkhr., 48 0N 43 0E
  U.S.S.R.
77 Tsinan, China 36 41N 116 59E
92 Tsineng, S. Africa 27 5s 23 5E
44 Tsinga, mt., Greece 41 23N 24 44E
75 Tsinghai, China 36 0N 98 0E
77 Tsinghsien, China 26 30N 109 0E
77 Tsingliu, China 26 10N 116 50E
77 Tsingshih, China 29 43N 112 13E
76 Tsinghsuiho, China 39 56N 111 55E
77 Tsingsi (Kweishun), 23 6N 106 25E
  China

* Incorporated within the
  new Western Province

MAP

76 Tsingsi, China 38 1N 114 42E
76 Tsingtung Hu, China 37 34N 105 40E
76 Tsingyuan, China 37 43N 104 35E
77 Tsingyun, China 23 45N 112 55E
77 Tsining, China 35 30N 116 35E
93 Tsinjomitondraka, Malag. 15 40S 47 8E
93 Tsiroanomandidy, Malag. 18 46S 46 2E
76 Tsitsihar, China 47 20N 124 0E
55 Tsivilsk, U.S.S.R. 55 50N 47 25E
93 Tsivory, Malagasy Rep. 24 4S 46 5E
57 Tskhinali, U.S.S.R. 42 14N 44 1E
92 Tsodilo Hill, Botswana 18 49S 21 43E
67 Tsona Dzong, China 28 0N 91 55E
74 Tsu, Japan 34 45N 136 25E
74 Tsuchiura, Japan 36 12N 140 15E
74 Tsugaru-Kaikyo, Japan 41 30N 140 30E
76 Tsuiluan, China 47 58N 28 27E
92 Tsumeb, S.W. Africa 19 9S 17 44E
92 Tsumis, S.W. Africa 23 39S 17 29E
77 Tsunga, China 23 35N 113 05E
77 Tsungming Tao, China 31 40N 121 30E
77 Tsungtso, China 22 26N 107 34E
77 Tsunyi, China 27 40N 107 0E
74 Tsuruga, Japan 35 35N 136 0E
74 Tsushima, Japan 34 20N 129 20E
74 Tsushima-kaikyō, Japan 34 20N 130 0E
74 Tsuyama, Japan 35 0N 134 0E
56 Tsvetkovo, U.S.S.R. 49 15N 31 33E
93 Tswana ✴ S. Africa 24 0S 27 50E
71 Tu, R., Burma 22 50N 97 15E
31 Tua, R., Portugal 41 19N 7 15W
73 Tual, Indonesia 5 30S 132 50E
15 Tuam, Ireland 53 30N 8 50W
95 Tuamotu Arch = Touamotou, Pac. Oc. 17 0S 144 0W
73 Tuao, Philippines 17 47S 121 30E
57 Tuapse, U.S.S.R. 44 5N 39 10E
101 Tuatapere, N.Z. 48 7S 167 41E
119 Tuba City, U.S.A. 36 8N 111 12W
119 Tubac, U.S.A. 31 45N 111 2W
95 Tubai Is. = Toubouai, Iles. Pac. Oc. 25 0S 150 0W
72 Tuban, Indonesia 6 57S 112 4E
125 Tubarão, Brazil 28 30S 49 0W
62 Tubas, Jordan 32 20N 35 22E
72 Tubau, Malaysia 3 10N 113 40E
86 Tubayq, Jabal at. Jordan 29 30N 37 30E
24 Tübingen, Germany 48 31N 9 4E
86 Tubja, W., Si-Arabia 25 27N 38 55E
81 Tubruq, (Tobruk), Libya 32 7N 23 55E
126 Tucacas, Venezuela 10 48N 68 19W
77 Tuchang, China 29 15N 116 15E
28 Tuchola, Poland 53 33N 17 52E
27 Tuchów, Poland 49 54N 21 1E
121 Tucker's Town, Bermuda 32 19N 64 43W
119 Tucson, U.S.A. 32 14N 110 59W
124 Tucumán, Argentina 26 50S 65 20W
124 Tucumán ♦, Arg. 26 48S 66 2W
117 Tucumcari, U.S.A. 35 12N 103 45W
126 Tucupido, Venezuela 9 17N 65 47W
126 Tucupita, Venezuela 9 14N 62 3W
126 Tucuracas, Colombia 11 45N 72 22W
28 Tuczno, Poland 53 13N 16 10E
32 Tudela, Spain 42 4N 1 39W
30 Tudela de Duero, Spain 41 37N 4 39W
107 Tudor, Lac, Canada 55 50N 65 0W
46 Tudora, Rumania 47 31N 26 45E
30 Tuella, R., Portugal 41 50N 7 10W
9 Tuen, Austral. 28 33S 145 37E
98 Tufi, Terr. of Papua 9 3S 149 16E
73 Tuguegarao, Philippines 17 35N 121 42E
59 Tugur, U.S.S.R. 53 50N 136 45E
92 Tugwa, Angola 17 7S 18 33E
77 Tuhshan, China 25 40N 107 30E
73 Tukangbesi, Kepulauan, Indonesia 6 0S 124 0E
106 Tukarak I. Canada 56 15N 78 10W
84 Tukobo, Ghana 5 1N 2 47W
83 Tūkrah, Libya 32 30N 20 37E
87 Tuku, mt., Ethiopia 9 10N 36 43E
54 Tukums, U.S.S.R. 57 2N 23 3E
91 Tukuyu, Tanzania 9 17S 33 35E
120 Tula, Hidalgo, Mexico 20 0N 99 20W
126 Tula, Colombia 23 0N 99 40W
85 Tula, Nigeria 9 51N 11 27E
55 Tula, U.S.S.R. 54 13N 37 32E
65 Tulak, Afghanistan 33 55N 63 40E
75 Tulan, China 37 24N 98 1E
119 Tulare, U.S.A. 36 15N 119 26W
119 Tulare Lake, U.S.A. 36 0N 119 53W
119 Tularosa, U.S.A. 33 4N 106 1W
92 Tulbagh, S. Africa 33 16S 19 6E
126 Tulcán, Ecuador 0 48N 77 43W
46 Tulcea, Rumania 45 13N 28 46E
46 Tulcea ♦, Rumania 45 0N 29 0E
56 Tulchin, U.S.S.R. 48 41N 28 55E
93 Tuléar, Malagasy Rep. 23 21S 43 40E
93 Tuléar ♦, Malag. 21 0S 45 0E
109 Tulemalu L., Canada 62 50N 100 0W
46 Tulgheş, Rumania 46 58N 25 45E
73 Tuli, Indonesia 1 24S 122 26E
91 Tuli, Rhodesia 21 58S 29 13E
62 Tulkarm, Jordan 32 19N 35 2E
115 Tullahoma, U.S.A. 35 23N 86 12W
100 Tullamore, Australia 32 39S 147 36E
15 Tullamore, Ireland 53 17N 7 30W
20 Tulle, France 45 16N 1 46E
100 Tullibigeal. Australia 34 19S 146 20E
21 Tullins, France 45 18N 5 29E
26 Tulln, Austria 48 20N 16 4E
15 Tullow, Ireland 52 48N 6 45W
87 Tully, Austral. 17 56S 145 55E
81 Tulmaythah, Libya 32 40N 20 55E
98 Tulmur, Australia 22 40S 142 20E
46 Tulnici, Rumania 45 51N 26 38E
43 Tulovo, Bulgaria 42 33N 25 32E
117 Tulsa, U.S.A. 36 10N 96 0W
108 Tulsequah, Canada 58 39N 133 35W

MAP

87 Tulu Milki, Ethiopia 9 55N 38 14E
87 Tulu Welel, Mt., Ethiopia 8 56N 35 30E
126 Tulua, Colombia 4 6N 76 11W
59 Tulun, U.S.S.R. 54 40N 100 10E
73 Tulungagung, Indon. 8 5S 111 54E
73 Tum, Indonesia 3 28S 130 21E
55 Tuma, U.S.S.R. 55 10N 40 30E
121 Tuma, R., Nicaragua 13 18N 84 50W
126 Tumaco, Colombia 1 50N 78 45W
126 Tumatumari, Guyana 5 20N 58 55W
48 Tumba, Sweden 59 12N 17 48E
88 Tumba, L., Zaïre 0 50S 18 0E
100 Tumbarumba, Australia 35 44S 148 0E
124 Tumbaya, Argentina 23 50S 65 20W
91 Tumbes, Peru 3 30S 80 20W
91 Tumbwe, Zaïre 11 25S 27 15E
96 Tumby B., S. Australia 34 21S 136 8E
76 Tumen K., China 42 30N 130 0E
126 Tumeremo, Venezuela 7 18N 61 30W
49 Tumkur, India 13 18N 77 12E
49 Tumleberg, Sweden 58 16N 12 52E
66 Tummel L., Scot. 56 43N 3 55W
66 Tump, Pakistan 26 7N 62 16E
69 Tumpat, Malaysia 6 11N 102 10E
69 Tumsar, India 21 26N 79 45E
84 Tumu, Ghana 10 56N 1 56E
127 Tumucumaque, Serra de, Brazil 2 0N 55 0W
100 Tumut, Austral. 35 16S 148 13E
118 Tumwater, U.S.A. 47 0N 122 58W
99 Tunbridge, Australia 42 5S 147 28E
13 Tunbridge Wells, England 51 7N 0 16E
100 Tuncurry, Australia 32 9S 152 29E
91 Tunduru, Tanzania 11 0S 37 25E
91 Tunduru ♦, Tanz. 11 5S 37 22E
43 Tundzha, R., Bulgaria 42 0N 26 35E
47 Tune, Norway 59 16N 11 2E
59 Tung-Pei, China 44 0N 126 0E
67 Tunga La, India-China 29 0N 94 14E
72 Tunga, R., India 13 42N 75 20E
70 Tungabhadra Dam, India 15 21N 76 23E
70 Tungabhadra, R., India 15 30N 77 0E
77 Tungcheng, China 31 0N 117 3E
76 Tungfanghsien, (Paso), China 18 50N 108 33E
76 Tunghwa, China 41 46N 126 0E
77 Tungjen, China 27 45N 109 3E
77 Tungjen, China 27 40N 109 10E
76 Tungkang, Taiwan 22 18N 120 29E
76 Tungkiang, Heilungkiang, China 47 40N 132 30E
77 Tungkiang, Szechwan, China 31 55N 107 30E
77 Tungkun, China 23 0N 113 45E
77 Tungkwan, China 37 50N 116 35E
77 Tungkwan, China 34 40N 110 10E
120 Tungla, Nicaragua 13 24N 84 15W
76 Tungliao, China 43 42N 122 11E
77 Tungliu, China 31 0N 117 54E
77 Tunglu, China 29 50N 119 35E
50 Tungnafellsjökull, Iceland 64 45N 17 55E
76 Tungping, China 35 50N 116 20E
67 Tungpu, China 31 42N 98 19E
77 Tungshan, Fukien, China 23 40N 117 31E
77 Tungshan, Hupeh, China 29 36N 114 28E
108 Tungsten, Canada 61 52N 128 01W
77 Tungsten, U.S.A. 40 50N 118 10W
77 Tungtao, China 26 15N 109 25E
77 Tungting Hu, China 29 15N 112 30E
77 Tungtze, China 27 59N 106 56E
60 Tunguska, Nizhmaya, R., U.S.S.R. 64 0N 95 0E
59 Tunguska, Podkammenaya, R., U.S.S.R. 61 0N 98 0E
77 Tungyang, China 29 12N 120 12E
76 Tunhwa, China 43 27N 128 16E
75 Tunhwang, China 40 5N 94 46E
70 Tuni, India 17 22N 82 43E
126 Tunia, Colombia 2 41N 76 31W
117 Tunica, U.S.A. 34 43N 90 23W
83 Tunis, Tunisia 36 50N 10 11E
83 Tunis, Golfe de, Tunisia 37 0N 10 30E
83 Tunisia ■, Africa 33 30N 9 10E
126 Tunja, Colombia 5 40N 73 25W
113 Tunkhannock, U.S.A. 41 32N 75 56W
77 Tunki, China 29 44N 118 4E
77 Tunliu, China 36 15N 112 54E
50 Tunnsjöen, Norway 64 45N 13 25E
49 Tuno I., Denmark 55 58N 10 27E
124 Tunungayualuk I., Can. 56 0N 61 0W
124 Tunuyán, Argentina 33 55S 69 0W
124 Tunuyán, R., Argentina 33 33S 67 30W
119 Tuolumne, U.S.A. 37 59N 120 16W
59 Tuoy-Khaya, U.S.S.R. 62 32N 111 18E
125 Tupá, Brazil 21 57S 50 28W
115 Tupelo, U.S.A. 34 15N 88 42W
59 Tupik, U.S.S.R. 54 26N 119 57E
127 Tupinambaranas, I., Brazil 3 0S 58 0W
124 Tupiza, Bolivia 21 30S 65 40W
113 Tupper L., U.S.A. 44 18N 74 30W
124 Tupungato, Cerro, Arg.-Chile 33 15S 69 50W
126 Túquerres, Colombia 1 5N 77 37W
62 Tura, Jordan 31 47N 35 14E
69 Tura, India 25 30N 90 16E
59 Tura, U.S.S.R. 64 20N 99 30E
86 Turaba, W., Si. Arabia 21 15N 41 32E
126 Turagua, Serrania, Ven. 7 20N 64 35W
70 Turaiyur, India 11 9N 78 38E
65 Tūrān, Iran 35 45N 56 50E
48 Tureburg, Sweden 59 30N 17 58E
30 Turégano, Spain 41 9N 4 1W

MAP

28 Turek, Poland 52 3N 18 30E
126 Turen, Venezuela 9 17N 69 6w
43 Turfan, China 43 6N 89 24E
75 Turfan Depression, China 43 0N 88 0E
43 Turgovishte, Bulgaria 43 17N 26 38E
64 Turgutlu, Turkey 38 30N 27 48E
56 Turhal, Turkey 40 24N 36 19E
32 Turia, R., Spain 39 43N 1 0W
127 Turiaçu, Brazil 1 40S 45 28W
127 Turiaçu, R., Brazil 3 0S 46 0W
37 Turiec, R., Cz. 48 52N 18 30E
38 Turin (Torino), Italy 45 3N 7 40E
108 Turin Taber, Canada 49 47N 112 24w
54 Turka, U.S.S.R. 49 10N 23 0E
90 Turkana ♦, Kenya 3 0N 35 30E
58 Turkestan, U.S.S.R. 43 10N 68 10E
27 Türkeve, Hungary 47 6N 20 44E
64 Turkey ■, Europe & Asia 39 0N 36 0E
55 Turki, U.S.S.R. 52 0N 43 15E
58 Turkmenistan (Turkmen S.S.R.), U.S.S.R. 39 0N 59 0E
121 Turks Is., West Indies 21 20N 71 20W
121 Turks Island Passage, West Indies 21 30N 71 20W
51 Turku (Abo), Finland 60 27N 22 14E
51 Turku-Pori ♦, Fin. 60 27N 22 14E
90 Turkwell, R., Kenya 2 30N 35 20E
119 Turlock, U.S.A. 37 30N 120 55w
101 Turnagain, C., N.Z. 40 28S 176 38E
109 Turnberry, Canada 53 25N 101 45W
120 Turneffe Is., Br. Hond. 17 20N 87 50W
118 Turner, U.S.A. 48 52N 108 25W
108 Turner Valley, Canada 50 40N 114 30W
113 Turners Falls, U.S.A. 42 36N 72 34W
16 Turnhout, Belgium 51 19N 4 57E
26 Türnitz, Austria 47 55N 15 29E
109 Turnor L., Canada 56 35N 108 50W
26 Turnov, Czechoslovakia 50 34N 15 10E
43 Turnovo, Bulgaria 43 5N 25 41E
43 Turnovo ♦, Bulg. 43 4N 25 39E
46 Turnu Măgurele, Rum. 43 46N 24 56E
46 Turnu Roşu Pasul, Rum. 45 33N 24 17E
46 Turnu-Severin, Rum. 44 39N 22 41E
49 Turö, Denmark 55 2N 10 40E
117 Turon, U.S.A. 37 48N 98 27w
14 Turriff, Scot. 57 32N 2 28W
55 Tursha, U.S.S.R. 56 55N 47 0E
41 Tursi, Italy 40 15N 16 27E
98 Turtle Hd. I., Austral. 10 50S 142 37E
116 Turtle L., N.D., U.S.A. 47 30N 100 55w
118 Turtle L., Wis., U.S.A. 45 22N 92 10W
109 Turtleford, Canada 53 30N 108 50w
64 Turubah, Saudi Arabia 28 20N 43 15E
59 Turukhansk, U.S.S.R. 65 50N 87 50E
51 Turun ja Porin lääni ♦, Finland 60 27N 22 15E
27 Turzovka, Cz. 49 25N 18 41E
119 Tuscaloosa, U.S.A. 33 13N 87 31W
39 Tuscánia, Italy 42 25N 11 53E
38 Tuscany = Toscana, Italy 43 28N 11 15E
15 Tuscar Rock, Ire. 52 10N 6 15W
114 Tuscola, Ill., U.S.A. 39 48N 88 15w
117 Tuscola, Tex., U.S.A. 32 15N 99 48W
115 Tuscumbia, U.S.A. 34 42N 87 42W
55 Tushino, U.S.S.R. 55 44N 37 29E
115 Tuskegee, U.S.A. 32 24N 85 39w
47 Tustna, Norway 63 10N 8 5E
28 Tuszyn, Poland 51 36N 19 33E
49 Tutaryd, Sweden 56 54N 13 59E
70 Tutikorin, India 8 50N 78 12E
42 Tutin, Yugoslavia 43 0N 20 20E
127 Tutóia, Brazil 2 45S 42 20W
72 Tutong, Brunei 4 47N 114 34E
46 Tutova, R., Rumania 46 20N 27 30E
43 Tutrakan, Bulgaria 44 2N 26 40E
25 Tuttlingen, Germany 47 59N 8 50E
73 Tutuala, Portuguese Timor 8 25S 127 15E
101 Tutuila, I., Amer. Samoa 14 19S 170 50W
76 Tuul Gol, R., Mongolia 48 30N 104 25E
59 Tuva, U.S.S.R. ♦, U.S.S.R. 51 30N 95 0E
120 Tuxpan, Mexico 20 50N 97 30W
120 Tuxtla Gutiérrez, Mex. 16 50N 93 10W
30 Tuy, Spain 42 3N 8 39W
71 Tuy Hoa, S. Vietnam 13 5N 109 17E
71 Tuyen Hoa, S. Vietnam 17 55N 106 3E
59 Tuyun, China 26 15N 107 32E
64 Tuz Gölü, Turkey 38 45N 33 30E
64 Tuz Khurmati, Iraq 34 52N 44 41E
64 Tuz Khurmatu, Iraq 34 50N 44 45E
42 Tuzla, Yugoslavia 44 34N 18 41E
57 Tuzlov, R., U.S.S.R. 47 28N 39 45E
49 Tvåaker, Sweden 57 4N 12 25E
49 Tvaerested, Denmark 57 36N 10 12E
49 Tvarskog, Sweden 56 34N 16 0E
49 Tved, Denmark 56 12N 10 25E
47 Tvedestrand, Norway 58 38N 8 58E
47 Tveit, Norway 60 30N 7 11E
47 Tveitsund, Norway 59 2N 8 31E
43 Tvyrditsa, Bulgaria 42 42N 25 53E
28 Twardogóra, Poland 51 23N 17 28E
112 Tweed, Canada 44 30N 77 20W
12 Tweed, R., Scot. 55 42N 2 10W
108 Tweedsmuir Prov. Park, Canada 53 10N 126 20W
15 Twelve Pins, Ire. 53 32N 9 50W
119 Twentynine Palms, U.S.A. 34 10N 116 4w
107 Twillingate, Canada 49 42N 54 45W
28 Twin Bridges, U.S.A. 45 33N 112 20W
118 Twin Falls, U.S.A. 42 30N 114 30W
28 Twin Valley, U.S.A. 47 18N 96 13W
118 Twisp, U.S.A. 48 21N 120 5w
24 Twistringen, Germany 52 48N 8 38E
116 Two Harbors, U.S.A. 47 6N 91 30W

MAP

114 Two Rivers, U.S.A. 44 10N 87 31w
98 Two Tree, Australia 18 25S 140 3E
100 Twofold B., Australia 37 8S 149 59E
87 Twong, Sudan 5 18N 28 29E
49 Ty, Denmark 56 27N 8 32E
49 Tyborön, Denmark 56 42N 8 12E
28 Tychy, Poland 50 9N 18 59E
28 Tyczyn, Poland 49 58N 22 2E
28 Tykocin, Poland 53 13N 22 46E
47 Tyldal, Norway 62 8N 10 48E
116 Tyler, Minn., U.S.A. 44 18N 96 15w
117 Tyler, Tex., U.S.A. 32 18N 95 18W
47 Tylldal, Norway 62 7N 10 45E
48 Tylösand, Sweden 56 33N 12 40E
59 Tyndinskiy, U.S.S.R. 55 10N 124 43E
12 Tyne, R., Eng. 54 58N 1 56w
12 Tynemouth, Eng. 55 1N 1 27W
47 Tynset, Norway 62 17N 10 47E
62 Tyre = Sûr, Lebanon 33 19N 35 16E
100 Tyrell Creek, Australia 35 22S 143 0E
100 Tyrell L., Austral. 35 22S 143 0E
100 Tyrendarra, Australia 38 12S 141 50E
50 Tyrifjorden, Nor. 60 2N 10 8E
49 Tyringe, Sweden 56 9N 13 35E
60 Tyristrand, Norway 60 5N 10 5E
76 Tyrma, U.S.S.R. 50 0N 132 2E
57 Tyrnyauz, U.S.S.R. 43 21N 42 45E
26 Tyrol = Tirol, Austria 46 50N 11 20E
*15 Tyrone ♦, N. Ire. 54 40N 7 15W
112 Tyrone, U.S.A. 40 39N 78 10W
34 Tyrrhenian Sea, Europe 40 0N 12 30E
50 Tysfjörden, Norway 68 10N 16 10E
47 Tyssedal, Norway 60 7N 6 35E
49 Tyssedse, Sweden 58 51N 17 15E
54 Tysmenitsa, U.S.S.R. 48 58N 24 50E
58 Tyumen, U.S.S.R. 57 0N 65 18E
47 Tyvoll, Norway 62 43N 11 21E
13 Tywi, R., Wales 52 2N 3 53W
47 Tywyn, R., Wales 52 9N 4 30W
93 Tzaneen, S. Afr. 23 47S 30 9E
62 Tzefa, Israel 31 7N 35 12E
77 Tzeki, China 27 40N 117 5E
77 Tzekung, China 29 25N 104 30E
77 Tzekwei, China 31 0N 110 46E
77 Tzepo, China 36 28N 117 58E
45 Tzermiadhes Neapolis, Greece 35 11N 25 29E
77 Tzetung, China 31 31N 105 1E
44 Tzoumérka, Oros, Greece 39 30N 21 26E
77 Tzuchien, China 27 43N 98 34E
77 Tzuyang, China 34 5N 116 51E
82 Uad Erni, O., Spanish Sahara 26 30N 9 30W
126 Uainambi, Colombia 1 43N 69 51W
63 Uarsciek, Somali Rep. 2 28N 45 55E
126 Uasadi-jidi, Sierra, Ven. 4 54N 65 18W
90 Uasin ♦, Kenya 0 30N 35 20E
62 Uassem, Syria 32 59N 36 2E
73 Uato-Udo, Port Timor 4 3S 126 6E
126 Uatumã, R., Brazil 1 30S 59 25W
126 Uaupés, Brazil 0 8S 67 5W
42 Ub, Yugoslavia 44 28N 20 6E
125 Ubá, Brazil 21 0S 43 0W
126 Ubaté, Colombia 5 19N 73 49W
68 Ubauro, Pakistan 28 15N 69 45E
74 Ube, Japan 34 6N 131 20E
32 Ubeda, Spain 38 3N 3 23W
127 Uberaba, Brazil 19 50S 47 55W
127 Uberlândia, Brazil 19 0S 48 20W
85 Ubiaja, Nigeria 6 41N 6 22E
93 Ubombo, S. Africa 27 31S 32 4E
71 Ubon Ratchathani, Thailand 15 15N 104 50E
88 Ubondo, Zaïre 0 55S 25 42E
54 Ubort, R., U.S.S.R. 51 45N 28 30E
31 Ubrique, Spain 36 41N 5 27W
88 Ubundi, Zaïre 0 22S 25 30E
126 Ucayali, R., Peru 6 0S 75 0W
109 Uchi Lake, Canada 51 10N 92 40W
74 Uchiura-Wan, Japan 42 25N 140 40E
24 Uchte, Germany 52 29N 8 52E
24 Uckerath, W. Germany 50 44N 7 22E
108 Ucluelet, Canada 48 57N 125 32w
46 Ucuriş, Rumania 46 41N 21 58E
59 Uda, R., U.S.S.R. 54 42N 135 14E
68 Udaipur, India 24 36N 73 44E
69 Udaipur Garhi, Nepal 27 0N 86 35E
70 Udamalpet, India 10 35N 77 15E
43 Udbina, Yugoslavia 44 31N 15 47E
48 Uddeholm, Sweden 60 1N 13 38E
49 Uddevalla, Sweden 58 21N 11 55E
50 Uddjaur, Sweden 65 55N 17 50E
68 Udgir, India 18 25N 77 5E
68 Udhampur, Kashmir 33 0N 75 5E
85 Udi, Nigeria 6 23N 7 21E
39 Udine, Italy 46 3N 13 14E
39 Udine ♦, Italy 46 5N 13 10E
68 Udipi, India 13 25N 74 42E
52 Udmurt, A.S.S.R. ♦, U.S.S.R. 57 30N 52 30E
71 Udon Thani, Thailand 17 29N 102 46E
85 Udubo, Nigeria 11 52N 10 35E
43 Udvoj Balken, Bulgaria 42 50N 26 50E
91 Udzungwa Range, Tanz. 11 15S 35 10E
24 Ueckermünde, Ger. 53 45N 14 1E
74 Ueda, Japan 36 30N 138 10E
88 Uedineniya, O., U.S.S.R. 78 0N 85 0E
59 Uelen, U.S.S.R. 66 10N 170 0W
24 Uelzen, Germany 52 58N 10 30E
88 Uere, R., Zaïre 3 45N 24 45E
52 Ufa, U.S.S.R. 54 45N 55 55E
52 Ufa, R., U.S.S.R. 56 30N 58 10E
90 Ugalla, R., Tanzania 6 0S 32 0E
92 Uganus, S.W. Africa 19 41S 16 0E
90 Uganda ■, E. Africa 2 0N 32 0E
41 Ugento, Italy 39 55N 18 10E
85 Ugep, Nigeria 5 53N 8 2E

MAP

93 Ugie, S. Africa 31 10S 28 13E
33 Ugijar, Spain 36 58N 3 7W
21 Ugine, France 45 45N 6 25E
86 Ugla, Saudi Arabia 25 40N 37 42E
55 Uglich, U.S.S.R. 57 33N 38 13E
39 Ugljane, Yugoslavia 43 35N 16 46E
54 Ugra, R., U.S.S.R. 54 45N 35 30E
43 Ugurchin, Bulgaria 43 6N 24 26E
27 Uh, R., Czechoslovakia 48 40N 22 0E
27 Uherske Hradiště, Cz. 49 4N 17 30E
27 Uhersky Brod, Cz. 49 1N 17 40E
112 Uhrichsville, U.S.A. 40 23N 81 22W
88 Uíge ♦, Angola 7 0S 15 30E
76 Uiji, North Korea 40 15N 124 35E
118 Uinta Mts., U.S.A. 40 45N 110 30W
92 Uitenhage, S. Africa 33 40S 25 28E
16 Uithuizen, Netherlands 53 24N 6 41E
27 Ujda = Oujda, Morocco 34 45N 2 0W
27 Ujfehértó, Hungary 47 49N 21 41E
28 Uji, India 22 0N 79 6E
74 Uji-guntô, Japan 31 15N 129 25E
49 Ujjain, India 23 9N 75 43E
27 Újpest, Hungary 47 22N 19 6E
27 Ujszász, Hungary 47 19N 20 7E
59 Uka, U.S.S.R. 57 50N 162 0E
90 Ukara I., Tanzania 1 44S 33 0E
85 Ukehe, Nigeria 6 40N 7 24E
91 Ukerewe ♦., Tanzania 2 0S 33 0E
90 Ukerewe ♦, Tanzania 2 0S 32 30E
55 Ukholovo, U.S.S.R. 54 47N 40 30E
67 Ukhrul, India 25 10N 94 25E
52 Ukhta, U.S.S.R. 63 55N 54 0E
118 Ukiah, U.S.A. 39 10N 123 9W
56 Ukmerge, U.S.S.R. 55 15N 24 45E
56 Ukraine S.S.R. ♦, U.S.S.R. 48 0N 35 0E
92 Ukwi, Botswana 23 29S 20 30E
76 Ulaanbaatar, Mongolia 47 54N 106 52E
76 Ulaangom, Mongolia 50 0N 92 10E
91 Ulambua, Zaïre 9 3S 23 38E
76 Ulan-Bator = Ulaanbaatar, Mongolia 47 54N 106 52E
59 Ulan Ude, U.S.S.R. 52 0N 107 30E
91 Ulanga ♦, Tanzania 8 40S 36 50E
76 Ulanhot, China 46 5N 122 1E
28 Ulanów, Poland 50 30N 22 16E
90 Ulaya, Shinyanga, Tanzania 4 25S 33 30E
90 Ulaya, Morogoro, Tanzania 7 3S 36 55E
42 Ulcinj, Yugoslavia 41 58N 19 10E
92 Ulco, S. Africa 28 21S 24 15E
76 Uldz Gol, Mongolia 49 30N 114 0E
47 Ulefoss, Norway 59 17N 9 16E
49 Ulëza, Albania 41 46N 19 57E
49 Ulfborg, Denmark 56 16N 8 20E
70 Ulhasnagar, India 19 15N 73 10E
42 Uljma, Yugoslavia 45 2N 21 10E
32 Ulla, R., Spain 42 45N 8 30W
100 Ulladulla, Australia 35 21S 150 29E
48 Ullånger, Sweden 62 58N 18 10E
49 Ullapool, Scot. 57 54N 5 10W
49 Ullared, Sweden 57 8N 12 42E
12 Ullswater, L., Eng. 54 35N 2 52W
76 Ullung Do, S. Korea 37 30N 130 30E
48 Ullvättern, L., Sweden 59 30N 14 21E
25 Ulm, Germany 48 23N 10 0E
100 Ulmarra, Australia 29 31S 153 6E
46 Ulmeni, Rumania 45 4N 46 40E
46 Ulmeni, Rumania 44 16N 27 0E
127 Ulricehamn, Sweden 57 46N 13 26E
47 Ulsberg, Norway 62 45N 9 59E
47 Ulsteinvik, Norway 62 21N 5 53E
15 Ulster ♦, N. Ire. 54 45N 6 30W
43 Ulstrem, Bulgaria 42 1N 26 27E
100 Ultima, Australia 35 22S 143 18E
69 Ulubaria, India 22 31N 88 4E
69 Ulugh Muztagh, China 36 40N 87 30E
91 Ulungur Mts., Tanzania 7 15S 37 30E
12 Ulverston, Eng. 54 13N 3 7W
99 Ulverstone, Australia 41 11S 146 11E
47 Ulvik, Norway 60 35N 6 54E
49 Ulvo, Sweden 56 40N 14 37E
59 Ulya, U.S.S.R. 59 10N 142 0E
55 Ulyanovsk, U.S.S.R. 54 25N 48 25E
75 Ulyasutay, (Javhlant), Mongolia 47 56N 97 28E
119 Ulysses, U.S.A. 37 39N 101 25W
62 Um Qeis, Jordan 32 40N 35 41E
39 Umag, Yugoslavia 45 26N 13 31E
124 Uman, Bolivia 17 25S 68 5W
126 Uman, U.S.S.R. 48 40N 30 12E
4 Umánaé, Greenland 70 40N 52 10W
2 Umánaé Fjord, Greenland 70 40N 52 0W
70 Umarkhed, India 19 37N 77 38E
68 Umarkot, Pakistan 25 15N 69 40E
118 Umatilla, U.S.A. 45 58N 119 17W
39 Umbertide, Italy 43 18N 12 20E
98 Umboi I., Terr. of New Guinea 5 59S 148 0E
101 Umbrella Mts., N.Z. 45 35S 169 5E
41 Umbria ♦, Italy 42 53N 12 30E
50 Ume, R., Sweden 64 45N 18 30E
50 Umeå, Sweden 63 45N 20 20E
73 Umera, Indonesia 0 12S 129 30E
91 Umfuli, R., Rhodesia 17 30S 29 23E
91 Umgusa, Rhodesia 19 29S 27 52E
44 Umka, Yugoslavia 44 40N 20 19E
93 Umkomaas, S. Africa 30 13S 30 48E
65 Umm al Qaiwain, Trucial States 25 30N 55 35E
87 Umm Arda, Sudan 15 17N 32 31E
65 Umm az Zamul, Muscat & Oman 22 35N 55 18E
87 Umm Bel, Sudan 13 35N 28 0E
87 Umm Digulgulaya, Sud. 10 28N 24 58E
87 Umm Dubban, Sudan 15 23N 32 52E
83 Umm al Aranib, Libya 26 10N 14 54E

In April 1973 districts replaced counties in N. Ireland

MAP
62 Umm el Fahm, Israel 32 31N 35 9E
87 Umm Hagar, Ethiopia 14 20N 36 41E
87 Umm Koweika, Sudan 13 10N 32 16E
64 Umm Lajj, Saudi Arabia 25 0N 37 23E
86 Umm Merwa, Sudan 18 4N 32 30E
87 Umm Qurein, Sudan 16 3N 28 49E
86 Umm Rumah, Saudi 25 50N 36 30E
  Arabia
87 Umm Ruwaba, Sudan 12 50N 31 10E
65 Umm Said, Qatar 25 0N 51 40E
87 Umm Sidr, Sudan 14 29N 25 10E
24 Ummanz I., Germany 54 29N 13 9E
104 Umnak I., Aleutian Is. 53 0N 168 0w
91 Umniati, R., Rhodesia 18 0s 29 0E
71 Umpang, Thailand 16 3N 98 54E
118 Umpqua, R., U.S.A. 43 30N 123 30w
68 Umrer, India 20 51N 79 18E
68 Umreth, India 22 41N 73 4E
91 Umshandige Dam, 20 10s 30 40E
  Rhodesia
91 Umtali, Rhodesia 18 58s 32 38E
93 Umtata, S. Africa 31 36s 28 49E
85 Umuahia-Ibeku, Nigeria 5 33N 7 29E
91 Umvukwe Ra.., Rhod. 16 45s 30 45E
91 Umvuma, Rhodesia 19 16s 30 30E
93 Umzimkulu, S. Africa 30 15s 30 45E
68 Una, India 20 46N 71 8E
39 Una, R., Yugoslavia 44 50N 16 15E
39 Unac,·R., Yugoslavia 44 42N 16 15E
113 Unadilla, U.S.A. 42 20N 75 17w
104 Unalanaska I., Alaska 54 0N 164 30w
32 Uncastillo, Spain 42 21N 1 8w
126 Uncia, Bolivia 18 25s 66 40w
119 Uncompahgce Pk., Mt., 38 5N 107 32w
  U.S.A.
49 Unden, Sweden 58 45N 14 25E
100 Underbool, Australia 35 10s 141 51E
48 Undersaker, Sweden 63 19N 13 21E
48 Undersvik, Sweden 61 36N 16 20E
124 Undlöse, Denmark 55 37N 11 35E
47 Undredal, Norway 60 57N 7 6E
54 Unecha, U.S.S.R. 52 50N 32 37E
100 Ungarie, Australia 33 38s 146 56E
105 Ungava B., Canada 59 30N 67 0w
56 Ungeny, U.S.S.R. 47 11N 27 51E
87 Ungwatiri, Sudan 16 52N 36 10E
55 Uni, U.S.S.R. 56 44N 51 47E
127 União, Brazil 4 50s 37 50w
125 União da Vitória, Brazil 26 5s 51 0w
28 Uniejow, Poland 51 59N 18 46E
39 Unije, I., Yugoslavia 44 40N 14 15E
104 Unimak I., Alaska 54 30N 164 30w
104 Unimak Pass., Alaska 53 30N 165 15w
116 Union, Mo., U.S.A. 38 25N 91 0w
113 Union, N.J., U.S.A. 40 47N 74 3w
115 Union, S.C., U.S.A. 34 49N 81 39w
119 Union, Mt., U.S.A. 34 34N 112 21w
113 Union City, N.J., U.S.A. 40 47N 74 5w
114 Union City, Ohio, 40 11N 84 49w
  U.S.A.
112 Union City, Pa., U.S.A. 41 53N 79 50w
113 Union City, Tenn., 36 25N 89 0w
  U.S.A.
115 Union Gap, U.S.A. 46 38N 120 29w
59 Union of Soviet Soc. 47 0N 100 0E
  Rep. ■. Eurasia
115 Union Springs, U.S.A. 32 9N 85 44w
92 Uniondale Road, S. 33 39s 23 7E
  Africa
114 Uniontown, U.S.A. 39 54N 79 45w
79 United Arab Republic 27 5N 30 0E
  ■. N. Africa
11 United Kingdom ■. 55 0N 3 0w
  Europe
111 United States of 37 0N 96 0w
  America ■. N. America
109 Unity, Canada 52 30N 109 5w
68 Unjha, India 23 46N 72 24E
69 Unnao, India 26 35N 80 30E
84 Uno, Ilha, Port. Guinea 11 15N 16 13w
14 Unst, I. Scot. 60 50N 0 55w
24 Unstrut, R., Germany 51 16N 11 29E
25 Unterwalden ob dem 46 55N 8 15E
  Wald ◆, Switz.
25 Unterwalden nid dem 46 50N 8 15E
  Wald ◆, Switz.
126 Unturán, Sierra de, Ven. 1 35N 64 40w
56 Unye, Turkey 41 5N 37 15E
55 Unzha, U.S.S.R. 57 40N 44 8E
55 Unzha, R., U.S.S.R. 58 0N 43 40E
27 Upa, R., Czechoslovakia 50 45N 16 12E
87 Upal, Sudan 6 56N 34 12E
126 Upata, Venezuela 8 1N 62 24w
91 Upemba, L., Zaïre 8 30s 26 20E
4 Upernavik, Greenland 72 49N 56 7w
92 Upington, S. Africa 28 25s 21 15E
68 Upleta, India 21 46N 70 16E
101 Upolu, I., Samoa 13 58s 172 0w
108 Upper Arrow L., Can. 50 30N 117 50w
26 Upper Austria = 48 15N 14 10E
  Oberösterreich, Austria
15 Upper L. Erne, N. Ire. 54 14N 7 22w
101 Upper Hutt, N.Z. 41 8s 175 5E
42 Upper Klamath L., 42 16N 121 55w
  U.S.A.
118 Upper Lake, U.S.A. 39 10N 122 55w
118 Upper Lake (Alkali), 41 47N 120 0w
  U.S.A.
107 Upper Musquodoboit, 45 10N 62 58w
  Canada
114 Upper Sandusky, U.S.A. 40 50N 83 17w
84 Upper Volta ■. Africa 12 0N 0 30w
49 Upphärad, Sweden 58 9N 12 19E
48 Uppsala, Sweden 59 53N 17 38E
48 Uppsala län ◆, Swed. 60 0N 17 30E
116 Upton, U.S.A. 44 8N 104 35w
64 Ur, Iraq 30 55N 46 25E
126 Urabá, Golfo de, 8 25N 76 53w
  Colombia

MAP
126 Uracará, Brazil 2 20s 57 50w
25 Urach, Germany 48 29N 9 25E
100 Ural, Mt., Australia 33 21s 146 12E
52 Ural Mts. = Uralskie 60 0N 59 0E
  Gory, U.S.S.R.
57 Ural, R., U.S.S.R. 49 0N 52 0w
99 Uralla, Australia 30 37s 151 29E
52 Uralsk, U.S.S.R. 51 20N 51 20E
52 Uralskie Gory, U.S.S.R. 60 0N 59 0E
90 Urambo, Tanzania 5 4s 32 47E
100 Urana, Australia 35 15s 146 21E
100 Urana, L., Australia 35 15s 146 21E
99 Urandangi, Australia 21 32s 138 14E
100 Uranium City, Canada 59 28N 108 40w
100 Uranquinty, Australia 35 6s 147 12E
126 Uraricaá, R., Brazil 3 20N 61 56w
70 Uravakonda, India 14 57N 77 12E
71 Urawa, Japan 35 50N 139 40E
58 Uray, U.S.S.R. 60 5N 65 15E
114 Urbana, Ill., U.S.A. 40 7N 88 12w
114 Urbana, Ohio, U.S.A. 40 9N 83 44w
39 Urbánia, Italy 43 40N 12 31E
32 Urbel, R., Spain 42 30N 3 49w
39 Urbino, Italy 43 43N 12 38E
32 Urbión, Picos de, Spain 42 1N 2 52w
126 Urcos, Peru 13 30s 71 30w
31 Urda, Spain 39 25N 3 43w
57 Urda, U.S.S.R. 48 52N 47 23E
124 Urdinarrain, Argentina 32 37s 58 52w
20 Urdos, France 42 51N 0 35w
58 Urdzhar, U.S.S.R. 47 5N 81 38E
12 Ure, R., Eng. 54 20N 2 17w
57 Uren, U.S.S.R. 57 35N 45 55E
120 Ures, Mexico 29 30N 110 30w
64 Urfa, Turkey 37 12N 38 50E
26 Urfahr, Austria 48 19N 14 17E
58 Urgench, U.S.S.R. 41 40N 60 30E
65 Urgun, Afghanistan 32 55N 69 12E
25 Uri ◆, Switzerland 46 43N 8 35E
126 Uribante, R., Venezuela 7 25N 71 50w
126 Uribe, Colombia 3 13N 74 24w
126 Uribia, Colombia 11 43N 72 16w
62 Urim, Israel 31 18N 34 32E
16 Urk, Netherlands 52 39N 5 36E
64 Urla, Turkey 38 20N 26 55E
64 Urlati, Rumania 44 59N 26 15E
64 Urmia (Rezā'iyeh), Iran 37 40N 45 0E
64 Urmia, L., Iran 37 30N 45 30E
42 Urosevac, Yugoslavia 42 23N 21 10E
126 Urrao, Colombia 6 20N 76 11w
49 Urshult, Sweden 56 31N 14 50E
87 Urso, Ethiopia 9 35N 41 33E
28 Ursus, Poland 52 12N 20 53E
120 Uruapán, Mexico 19 30N 102 0w
126 Urubamba, Peru 13 5s 72 10w
126 Urubamba, R., Peru 11 0s 73 0w
127 Uruçui, Brazil 7 20s 44 28w
125 Uruguai, R., Brazil 24 0s 53 30w
124 Uruguaiana, Brazil 29 50s 57 0w
124 Uruguay ■, South 32 30s 55 30w
  America
124 Uruguay, R., S. Amer. 28 0s 56 0w
75 Urumchi = Wulumuchi, 43 40N 87 50E
  China
75 Urumqi, China 46 30N 88 50E
59 Urup, I., U.S.S.R. 43 0N 151 0E
57 Urup, R., U.S.S.R. 44 19N 41 30E
59 Uruyén, Venezuela 5 41N 62 25w
66 Uruzgan ◆, Afghan. 33 30N 66 0E
55 Uryupinsk, U.S.S.R. 50 45N 42 3E
55 Urzhum, U.S.S.R. 57 10N 49 56E
46 Urziceni, Rumania 44 46N 26 42E
52 Usa, R., U.S.S.R. 66 20N 56 0E
64 Uşak, Turkey 38 43N 29 28E
92 Usakos, S.W. Africa 22 0s 15 31E
90 Usambara Mts., Tanz. 4 50s 38 20E
42 Ušče, Yugoslavia 43 43N 20 39E
24 Usedom, Germany 53 50N 13 55E
86 Usfan, Saudi Arabia 21 58N 39 27E
58 Ush-Tobe, U.S.S.R. 45 16N 78 0E
58 Ushakova, O., U.S.S.R. 82 0N 80 0E
18 Ushant = Oessant, Ile 48 25N 5 5w
  d', France
90 Ushashi, Tanzania 1 59s 33 57E
87 Ushat, Sudan 7 59N 29 28E
128 Ushuaia, Argentina 54 50s 68 23w
59 Ushumun, U.S.S.R. 52 47N 126 32E
13 Usk, R., Wales 51 37N 2 56w
64 Uskedal, Norway 59 56N 5 53E
64 Usküdar, Turkey 41 0N 29 5E
24 Uslar, Germany 51 39N 9 39E
52 Usman, U.S.S.R. 52 5N 39 48E
90 Usoke, Tanzania 5 7s 32 19E
59 Usolye Sibirskoye, 52 40N 103 40E
  U.S.S.R.
85 Usoro, Nigeria 5 33N 6 11E
124 Uspallata, P. de, Arg. 32 30s 69 28w
58 Uspenskiy, U.S.S.R. 48 50N 72 55E
20 Ussel, France 45 32N 2 18E
57 Ussuri, Czechoslovakia 50 41N 14 2E
59 Ust Aldan = Batamay, 63 30N 129 15E
  U.S.S.R.
59 Ust Amginskoye = 62 30N 134 50E
  Khandyga, U.S.S.R.
59 Ust-Bolsheretsk, U.S.S.R. 52 40N 156 30E
55 Ust Buzulukskaya, 50 8N 42 11E
  U.S.S.R.
57 Ust Donetskiy, U.S.S.R. 47 35N 40 55E
59 Ust Ilga, U.S.S.R. 55 5N 104 55E
59 Ust Ilimpeya = Yukti, 63 20N 105 0E
  U.S.S.R.
59 Ust-Ilimsk, U.S.S.R. 58 3N 102 39E
58 Ust Ishim, U.S.S.R. 57 45N 71 10E
58 Ust Kamchatsk, U.S.S.R. 56 10N 162 0E
58 Ust Kamenogorsk, 50 0N 82 20E
  U.S.S.R.
59 Ust Karenga, U.S.S.R. 54 40N 116 45E
59 Ust Khayryuzova, 57 15N 156 55E
  U.S.S.R.
59 Ust Kut, U.S.S.R. 56 50N 105 10E

MAP
59 Ust Kuyga, U.S.S.R. 70 1N 135 36E
57 Ust Labinsk, U.S.S.R. 45 15N 39 50E
54 Ust Luga, U.S.S.R. 59 35N 28 26E
59 Ust Maya, U.S.S.R. 60 30N 134 20E
59 Ust Mil, U.S.S.R. 59 50N 133 0E
64 Ust Nera, U.S.S.R. 64 35N 193 15E
59 Ust Olenek, U.S.S.R. 73 0N 120 10E
59 Ust-Omchug, U.S.S.R. 61 9N 149 38E
58 Ust Port, U.S.S.R. 70 0N 84 10E
52 Ust Tsilma, U.S.S.R. 65 25N 52 0E
58 Ust-Tungir, U.S.S.R. 55 25N 120 15E
52 Ust Usa, U.S.S.R. 66 0N 56 30E
58 Ust Vorkuta, U.S.S.R. 67 7N 63 35E
47 Ustaoset, Norway 60 30N 8 2E
20 Ustaritz, France 43 24N 1 27w
55 Uste, U.S.S.R. 59 35N 39 40E
27 Ustí na Orlici, Cz. 49 58N 16 38E
26 Ustí nad Labem, Cz. 50 41N 14 3E
40 Ustica, I., Italy 38 42N 13 10E
28 Ustka, Poland 54 35N 16 55E
27 Ustroń, Poland 49 45N 18 48E
27 Ustrzyki Dolne, Poland 49 27N 22 40E
58 Ustye, U.S.S.R. 55 30N 97 30E
58 Ustyurt, Plato, U.S.S.R. 44 0N 55 0E
55 Ustyuzhna, U.S.S.R. 58 50N 36 32E
74 Usuki, Japan 33 5N 131 40E
120 Usulután, Salvador 13 25N 88 28w
120 Usumacinta, R., Mex. 17 0N 91 0w
42 Uta, Rumania 45 24N 21 13E
118 Utah, L., U.S.A. 40 10N 111 58w
118 Utah ◆, U.S.A. 39 30N 111 30w
117 Ute, Cr., U.S.A. 36 5N 103 45w
54 Utena, U.S.S.R. 55 27N 25 40E
24 Utersen, Germany 53 40N 9 40E
71 Uthai Thani, Thailand 15 22N 100 3E
64 Uthmaniyah, Si. Arab. 25 5N 49 6E
126 Utiariti, Brazil 13 0s 58 10w
113 Utica, N.Y., U.S.A. 43 5N 75 18w
114 Utica, Ohio, U.S.A. 40 13N 82 26w
32 Utiel, Spain 39 37N 1 11w
108 Utik L., Canada 55 20N 96 5w
108 Utikuma L., Canada 55 50N 115 30w
93 Utrecht, S. Afr. 27 38s 30 20E
16 Utrecht, Netherlands 52 3N 5 8E
16 Utrecht ◆, Neth. 52 6N 5 7E
31 Utrera, Spain 37 12N 5 48w
50 Utsjoki, Finland 69 51N 26 59E
69 Utsunomiya, Japan 36 30N 139 50E
69 Uttar Pradesh ◆, India 27 0N 80 0E
71 Uttaradit, Thailand 17 36N 100 5E
48 Uttersberg, Sweden 59 45N 15 36E
49 Uttersley, Denmark 54 56N 11 11E
112 Utterson, Canada 45 13N 79 20w
12 Uttoxeter, Eng. 52 53N 1 50w
24 Utze, Germany 52 28N 10 11E
51 Uudenmaan lääni ◆, 60 25N 25 0E
  Fin.
76 Uldza, Mongolia 49 8N 112 10E
51 Uusikaupunki, Finland 60 47N 21 25E
42 Uvac, R., Yugoslavia 43 35N 19 40E
117 Uvalde, U.S.A. 29 15N 99 48w
55 Uvarovo, U.S.S.R. 51 59N 42 14E
58 Uvat, U.S.S.R. 59 5N 68 50E
90 Uvinza, Tanzania 5 5s 30 24E
90 Uvira, Zaïre 3 22s 29 3E
75 Uvs Nuur, Mongolia 50 20N 92 30E
64 Uwainhid, Saudi Arabia 24 50N 46 0E
74 Uwajima, Japan 33 10N 132 35E
112 Uxbridge, Canada 44 10N 79 9w
120 Uxmal, Mexico 20 22N 89 46w
85 Uyo, Nigeria 5 1N 7 53E
124 Uyuni, Bolivia 20 35s 66 55w
124 Uyuni, Salar de, Bolivia 20 10s 68 0w
58 Uzbekistan S.S.R. ◆, 40 5N 65 0E
  U.S.S.R.
50 Uzen, Bol., U.S.S.R. 50 0N 49 30E
50 Uzen, Mal., U.S.S.R. 50 0N 48 30E
20 Uzerche, France 45 25N 1 35E
21 Uzès, France 44 1N 4 26E
54 Uzh, R., U.S.S.R. 51 15N 29 45E
54 Uzhgorod, U.S.S.R. 48 36N 22 18E
90 Uzice, Tanzania 4 40s 34 22E
55 Uzlovaya, U.S.S.R. 54 0N 38 5E
64 Uzunköprü, Turkey 41 16N 26 43E

MAP
21 Vaison, France 44 14N 5 4E
68 Vajpur, India 21 24N 73 45E
43 Vakarel, Bulgaria 42 35N 23 40E
47 Vaksdal, Norway 60 29N 5 45E
47 Vál, Hungary 47 22N 18 40E
106 Val d'Or, Canada 48 7N 77 47w
109 Val Marie, Canada 49 15N 107 45w
92 Valadares, Portugal 41 5N 8 38w
46 Valahia, Rumania 44 35N 25 0E
25 Valais, can., Switz. 46 8N 7 40E
25 Valais ◆, Switz. 46 12N 7 45E
27 Valandovo, Yugoslavia 41 19N 22 34E
45 Valaxa, I., Greece 38 50N 24 29E
48 Válcani, Rumania 46 0N 20 26E
128 Valcheta, Argentina 40 40s 66 20w
128 Valdagno, Italy 45 38N 11 18E
54 Valdajy, U.S.S.R. 57 58N 31 9E
54 Vakdayskaya 57 0N 33 40E
  Vozvyshennost, U.S.S.R.
31 Valdeazogues, R., Sp. 38 45N 4 55w
19 Val-de-Marne ◆, France 48 45N 2 28E
49 Valdemarsvik, Sweden 58 14N 16 40E
31 Valdepeñas, Ciudad 38 43N 3 25w
  Real, Spain
31 Valdepeñas, Jaén, Sp. 37 33N 3 47w
30 Valderaduey, R., Spain 42 30N 5 0w
32 Valderrobres, Spain 40 53N 0 9E
128 Valdes Pen., Argentina 42 30s 63 45w
15 Valdezia, S. Afr. 23 5s 30 14E
31 Valdivia, Chile 39 50s 73 14w
39 Valdobbiádene, Italy 45 53N 12 0E
19 Val-d'Oise ◆, France 49 5N 2 0E
15 Valdosta, U.S.A. 30 50N 83 48w
47 Valdres, Norway 60 55N 9 28E
118 Vale, U.S.A. 44 0N 117 15w
47 Vale, U.S.S.R. 41 30N 42 58E
57 Valea lui Mihai, Rum. 47 32N 22 11E
127 Valença, Brazil 13 20s 39 5w
92 Valença, Portugal 42 1N 8 34w
127 Valença do Piauí, Brazil 6 20s 41 45w
21 Valence, France 44 57N 4 54E
20 Valence-d'Agen, France 44 8N 0 54E
33 Valencia, Spain, £ 39 27N 0 23w
33 Valencia ◆, Spain 39 20N 0 40w
126 Valencia, Venezuela 10 11N 68 0w
33 Valencia, G. de, Spain 39 30N 0 20E
121 Valencia, L. de, 10 13N 67 40w
  Venezuela
33 Valencia, Albufera de, 39 20N 0 27w
  Spain
30 Valencia de Alcántara, 39 25N 7 14w
  Spain
30 Valencia de Don Juan, 42 17N 5 31w
  Spain
31 Valencia des Ventoso, 38 15N 6 29w
  Spain
21 Valenciennes, France 50 20N 3 34E
46 Văleni, Rumania 44 15N 24 45E
43 Valensole, France 43 50N 5 59E
116 Valentine, Nebr., U.S.A. 42 50N 100 35w
117 Valentine, Tex., U.S.A. 30 36N 104 28w
118 Valenton, France 48 45N 2 28E
26 Valenza, Italy 45 2N 8 39E
47 Våler, Norway 60 41N 11 50E
126 Valera, Venezuela 9 19N 70 37w
41 Valguarnera Caropepe, 37 30N 14 22E
  Italy
118 Valier, U.S.A. 48 15N 112 9w
42 Valinco, G. de, France 41 40N 8 52E
42 Valjevo, Yugoslavia 44 18N 19 53E
16 Valkenswaard, Neth. 51 21N 5 29E
33 Vall de Uxó, Spain 40 49N 0 15E
48 Valla, Sweden 59 2N 16 20E
120 Valladolid, Spain 41 38N 4 43w
120 Valladolid, Mexico 20 30N 88 20w
30 Valladolid ◆, Spain 41 38N 4 43w
41 Vallata, Italy 41 3N 15 16E
47 Valldalssaeter, Norway 59 56N 6 57E
47 Valle, Norway 59 13N 7 33E
38 Valle d'Aosta ◆, Italy 45 45N 7 22E
30 Valle de Arán, Sp. 42 50N 0 55E
126 Valle de la Pascua, Ven. 9 13N 66 0w
30 Valle de Cabuérniga, Sp. 43 14N 4 18w
120 Valle de Santiago, Mex. 20 25N 101 15w
30 Valle del Cauca ◆, Col. 3 45N 76 30w
124 Valle Fértil, Sierra del, 30 20s 68 0w
  Arg.
120 Valle Hermoso, Mexico 25 35N 102 25E
30 Vallecas, Spain 40 23N 3 41w
30 Valledupar, Colombia 10 29N 73 15w
118 Vacaville, U.S.A. 38 21N 122 0w
124 Vallenar, Chile 28 30s 70 50w
21 Valleraugue, France 44 6N 3 39E
18 Vallet, France 47 10N 1 15w
116 Valley City, U.S.A. 46 57N 98 0w
117 Valley Falls, U.S.A. 42 33N 120 8w
117 Valley Okolona, U.S.A. 34 0N 88 45w
15 Valleyfield, Canada 45 15N 74 8w
108 Valleyview, Canada 55 5N 117 25w
31 Valli di Comácchio, It. 44 40s 12 15E
124 Vallimanca, Arroyo, Arg. 35 40s 59 10w
41 Vallo della Lucánia, It. 40 14N 15 16E
21 Vallon, France 44 25N 4 23E
25 Vallorbe, Switzerland 46 42N 6 20E
32 Valls, Spain 41 18N 1 15E
48 Vallsta, Sweden 61 31N 16 22E
43 Valmaseda, Spain 43 11N 3 12w
54 Valmiera, U.S.S.R. 57 37N 25 38E
41 Valmont, France 49 45N 0 30E
19 Valmy, France 49 5N 4 45E
18 Valognes, France 49 30N 1 28w
32 Valonga, Mte., Spain 41 43N 0 18w
44 Valona (Vlorë), Albania 40 32N 19 28E
30 Valongo, Portugal 41 8N 8 27w
30 Valpaços, Portugal 41 36N 7 17w

MAP
124 Valparaiso, Chile 33 2s 71 40w
120 Valparaiso, Mexico 22 50N 103 32w
114 Valparaiso, U.S.A. 41 27N 87 2w
124 Valparaiso ◆, Chile 33 2s 71 40w
42 Valpovo, Yugoslavia 45 39N 18 25E
21 Valréas, France 44 24N 5 0E
25 Vals, Switzerland 46 39N 10 11E
92 Vals, R., S. Africa 27 28s 26 52E
73 Vals, Tandjung, 8 32s 137 32E
  Indonesia
21 Vals-les-Bains, France 44 42N 4 24E
92 Valsbaai, S. Africa 34 15s 18 40E
48 Valskog, Sweden 59 27N 15 57E
44 Valta, Greece 40 3s 23 25E
38 Valtellina, Italy 46 9N 10 2E
55 Valyiki, U.S.S.R. 50 10N 38 5E
31 Valverde del Camino, 37 35N 6 47w
  Spain
30 Valverde del Fresno, Sp. 40 15N 6 51w
46 Vama, Rumania 47 34N 25 42E
48 Vammala, Finland 61 20N 22 55E
45 Vámos, Greece 35 24N 24 13E
70 Vamsadhara, R., India 18 22N 84 15E
64 Van, Turkey 38 30N 43 20E
117 Van Alstyne, U.S.A. 33 25N 96 36E
117 Van Buren, Ark., U.S.A. 35 28N 94 18w
115 Van Buren, Me., U.S.A. 47 10N 68 1w
117 Van Buren, Mo., U.S.A. 37 0N 91 0w
92 Van der Kloof Dam, S. 30 04s 24 40E
  Afr.
98 Van Diemen C., Austral. 16 30s 139 46E
96 Van Diemen G., Austral. 12 0s 132 0E
64 Van Gölü, Turkey 38 30N 43 0E
119 Van Horn, U.S.A. 31 3N 104 55w
93 Van Reenen P., S. Afr. 28 22s 29 27E
73 Van Rees, Pegunungan, 2 30s 138 0E
  Indon.
116 Van Tassell, U.S.A. 42 40N 104 3w
70 Van Tivu, I., India 8 51N 78 15E
114 Van Wert, U.S.A. 40 52N 84 31w
108 Vancouver, Canada 49 20N 123 10w
118 Vancouver, U.S.A. 45 44N 122 41w
108 Vancouver I., Canada 49 50N 126 30w
114 Vandalia, Ill., U.S.A. 38 57N 89 4w
116 Vandalia, Mo., U.S.A. 39 18N 91 30w
70 Vandeloos Bay, Sri 8 0N 81 45E
  Lanka
92 Vanderbijlpark, S. Afr. 26 42s 27 54E
112 Vandergrift, U.S.A. 40 36N 79 33w
108 Vanderhoof, Canada 54 0N 124 0w
97 Vanderlin I., Australia 15 59s 138 1E
98 Vandyke, Australia 24 8s 142 45E
49 Vänern, Sweden 58 47N 13 30E
49 Vänersborg, Sweden 58 26N 12 27E
71 Vang Vieng, Laos 18 58N 102 32E
90 Vanga, Kenya 4 35s 39 12E
79 Vangaindrano, Malag. 23 21s 47 36E
109 Vanguard, Canada 49 55N 107 20w
92 Vanimo, North East 2 50s 141 25E
  New Guinea
70 Vanivilasa Sagara, India 13 45N 76 30E
70 Vaniyambadi, India 12 46N 78 44E
106 Vankleek Hill, Canada 45 32N 74 40w
50 Vanna, Norway 70 6N 19 50E
50 Vannas, Sweden 63 58N 19 48E
18 Vannes, France 47 40N 2 47w
21 Vanoise, Massif de la, 45 25N 6 40E
  France
92 Vanrhynsdorp, S. Afr. 31 36s 18 44E
48 Vansbro, Sweden 60 32N 14 15E
47 Vanse, Norway 58 6N 6 41E
96 Vansittart B., Australia 14 3s 126 17E
68 Vänthli, India 21 28N 70 25E
101 Vanua Levu, I., Fiji Is. 16 45s 179 10E
101 Vanua Mbalavu, I., Fiji 17 40s 178 57w
92 Vanwyksvlei, S. Africa 30 18s 21 49E
47 Vanylven, Norway 62 5N 5 33E
47 Vapnyarka, U.S.S.R. 48 32N 28 45E
21 Var ◆, France 43 27N 6 18E
50 Vara, Sweden 58 16N 12 55E
70 Varada, R., India 14 46N 75 15E
18 Varades, France 47 25N 1 1w
38 Varaita, R., Italy 44 35N 7 15E
47 Varaldsøy, Norway 60 6N 5 59E
38 Varallo, Italy 45 49N 8 15E
69 Varanasi (Benares), India 25 22N 83 8E
47 Varangerfjorden, Norway 70 3N 29 25E
38 Varazza, Yugoslavia 46 20N 16 20E
38 Varazze, Italy 44 21N 8 36E
49 Varberg, Sweden 57 17N 12 20E
42 Vardar, R., Yugoslavia 41 25N 22 20E
24 Varde, Denmark 55 38N 8 29E
49 Varde A, Denmark 55 35N 8 19E
24 Varel, Germany 53 2N 8 12E
54 Varena, U.S.S.R. 54 12N 24 30E
47 Värendseke, Sweden 57 4N 15 0E
20 Varennes-sur-Allier, Fr. 49 12N 5 0E
47 Vareš, Yugoslavia 44 12N 18 23E
38 Varese, Italy 45 49N 8 50E
38 Varese Ligure, Italy 44 22N 9 33E
125 Varginha, Brazil 21 33s 45 25w
47 Vargön, Sweden 58 22N 12 20E
47 Varhaug, Norway 58 37N 5 41E
124 Varillas, Chile 24 0s 70 10w
49 Varing, Sweden 58 30N 14 0E
48 Värmdö, I., Sweden 59 18N 18 45E
47 Värmeln, Sweden 59 35N 13 20E
48 Värmlands län ◆, 59 45N 13 20E
  Sweden
48 Värmlandssaby, Swed. 59 7N 14 15E
43 Varna, Bulgaria 43 13N 27 56E
70 Varna, R., India 17 13N 73 50E
49 Varnamo, Sweden 57 10N 14 3E
26 Varnsdorf, Cz. 50 54N 14 38E
49 Värö, Sweden 51 16N 12 15E
24 Varpelev, Denmark 55 22N 12 20E
113 Vars, Canada 45 22N 75 22w
49 Värsjö, Sweden 56 23N 13 27E

Varteig
INDEX
Villalón de Campos

MAP
47 Varteig, Norway 59 23N 11 12E
64 Varto, Turkey 39 10N 41 28E
49 Vartofta, Sweden 58 6N 13 40E
42 Varvarin, Yugoslavia 43 43N 21 20E
65 Varzaneh, Iran 32 25N 52 40E
38 Varzi, Italy 44 50N 9 12E
38 Varzo, Italy 46 12N 8 15E
19 Varzy, France 47 22N 3 20E
27 Vas ♦, Hungary 47 10N 16 55E
27 Vásárosnamény, Hung. 48 9N 22 19E
49 Väsby, Sweden 56 13N 12 37E
31 Vascão, R., Portugal 37 44N 8 15W
46 Vaşcău, Rumania 46 28N 22 30E
32 Vascongadas, Sp. 42 50N 2 45W
48 Väse, Sweden 59 23N 13 52E
65 Vasht = Khāsh, Iran 28 20N 61 6E
43 Vasil Levski, Bulgaria 43 23N 25 26E
54 Vasilevichi, U.S.S.R. 52 15N 29 50E
45 Vasilikón, Greece 38 25N 23 40E
54 Vasilkov, U.S.S.R. 50 7N 30 28E
46 Vaslui, Rumania 46 38N 27 42E
47 Vaslui ♦, Rumania 46 30N 27 30E
48 Väsman, Sweden 60 9N 15 5E
109 Vassar, Canada 49 10N 95 55W
114 Vassar, U.S.A. 43 23N 83 33W
48 Vast Silen, L., Sweden 59 15N 12 15E
49 Västerås, Sweden 59 37N 16 38E
50 Västerbottens län ♦, Swed. 64 58N 18 0E
48 Västerdalälven, Swed. 60 50N 13 25E
48 Västernorrlands län ♦, Sweden 63 30N 17 40E
49 Västervik, Sweden 57 43N 16 43E
48 Västmanland ♦, Swed. 59 55N 16 30E
39 Vasto, Italy 42 8N 14 40E
27 Vasvár, Hungary 47 3N 16 47E
19 Vatan, France 47 4N 1 50E
45 Vathí, Greece 37 46N 27 1E
45 Váthia, Greece 36 29N 22 29E
39 Vatican City, Italy 41 54N 12 27E
42 Vatin, Yugoslavia 45 12N 21 20E
50 Vatnajökull, Ice. 64 30N 16 48W
47 Vatne, Norway 62 33N 6 38E
50 Vatneyri, Iceland 65 35N 24 0W
47 Vatnås, Norway 59 58N 9 37E
101 Vatoa, I., Fiji 19 50S 178 13W
93 Vatoloha, Mt., Malag. 17 52S 47 48E
93 Vatomandry, Malag. 19 20S 48 59E
46 Vatra-Dornei, Rum. 47 22N 25 22E
47 Vats, Norway 59 29N 5 45E
49 Vättern, L., Sweden 58 25N 14 30E
21 Vaucluse ♦, France 44 3N 5 10E
19 Vaucouleurs, France 48 37N 5 40E
25 Vaud ♦, Switzerland 46 35N 6 30E
119 Vaughan, U.S.A. 34 37N 105 12W
118 Vaughn, U.S.A. 47 37N 111 36W
126 Vaupés, R., Colombia 1 0N 71 0W
126 Vaupés ♦, Colombia 1 0N 71 0W
21 Vauvert, France 43 42N 4 17E
108 Vauxhall, Canada 50 5N 112 9W
101 Vavāu, I., Tonga 18 36S 174 0W
19 Vavincourt, France 48 49N 5 12E
84 Vavoua, Ivory Coast 7 23N 6 29W
48 Vaxholm, Sweden 59 25N 18 20E
49 Växjö, Sweden 56 52N 14 50E
58 Vaygach, Ostrov, U.S.S.R. 70 0N 60 0E
127 Vaza Barris, R., Brazil 10 0S 37 30W
24 Vechta, Germany 52 47N 8 18E
16 Vechte, R., Netherlands 52 34N 6 6E
27 Vecsés, Hungary 47 26N 19 19E
70 Vedaraniam, India 10 25N 79 50E
49 Vedbaek, Denmark 55 50N 12 33E
49 Veddige, Sweden 57 17N 12 20E
46 Vedea, R., Rumania 44 0N 25 20E
124 Vedia, Argentina 34 30S 61 31W
33 Vedra, Isla del, Spain 38 52N 1 12E
16 Veendam, Netherlands 53 5N 6 52E
16 Veenendaal, Neth. 52 2N 5 34E
50 Vefsna, Norway 65 48N 13 10E
50 Vega, Norway 65 40N 11 55E
117 Vega, U.S.A. 35 18N 102 26W
50 Vega Fd., Norway 65 37N 12 0E
30 Vegadeo, Spain 43 27N 7 4W
24 Vegesack, Germany 53 10N 8 38E
50 Vegfjorden, Norway 65 37N 12 0E
49 Veggerby, Denmark 56 54N 9 39E
47 Veggli, Norway 60 3N 9 9E
16 Veghel, Netherlands 51 37N 5 32E
44 Vegorritis, Limni, Gr. 40 45N 21 45E
108 Vegreville, Canada 53 30N 112 5W
47 Vegusdal, Norway 58 32N 8 10E
39 Veii, Italy 42 0N 12 24E
124 Veinticino de Mayo, Arg. 38 0S 67 40W
49 Vejen, Denmark 55 30N 9 9E
31 Vejer de la Frontera, Spain 36 15N 5 59W
49 Vejle, Denmark 55 43N 9 30E
49 Vejle Amt ♦, Den. 55 2N 11 22E
49 Vejle Fjord, Denmark 55 40N 9 50E
49 Vejlo, Denmark 55 10N 11 45E
39 Vela Luka, Yugoslavia 42 59N 16 44E
70 Velanai I., Sri Lanka 9 45N 79 45E
119 Velarde, U.S.A. 36 11N 106 1W
117 Velasco, U.S.A. 29 0N 95 20W
124 Velasco, Sierra de., Arg. 29 20S 67 10W
20 Velay, Mts. du, France 45 0N 3 40E
92 Velddrif, S. Africa 32 42S 18 11E
39 Velebit Planina, Y.-slav. 44 50N 15 20E
39 Velebitski Kanal, Yugoslavia 44 45N 14 55E
43 Veleka, R., Bulgaria 42 4N 27 30E
39 Velenje, Yugoslavia 46 23N 15 8E
44 Velestínon, Greece 39 23N 22 43E
126 Vélez, Colombia 6 1N 73 41W
42 Velez, mt., Yugoslavia 43 19N 18 2E
31 Vélez Blanco, Spain 37 41N 2 5W
31 Vélez Málaga, Spain 36 48N 4 5W
33 Vélez Rubio, Spain 37 41N 2 5W

MAP
127 Velhas, R., Brazil 17 13S 44 49W
42 Velika, Yugoslavia 45 27N 17 40E
39 Velika Goricá, Y.-slavia 45 44N 16 5E
39 Velika Kapela, Y.-slav. 45 10N 15 5E
39 Velika Kladuša, Y.-slav. 45 11N 15 48E
42 Velika Morava, R., Yugoslavia 44 30N 21 9E
42 Velika Plana, Y.-slavia 44 20N 21 1E
54 Velikaya, R., U.S.S.R. 56 40N 28 40E
27 Veliké Kapušany, Cz. 48 34N 22 5E
39 Velike Lašče, Y.-slavia 45 49N 14 45E
44 Veliki Backa Kanal, Yugoslavia 45 45N 19 15E
42 Veliki Jastrebac, Yugoslavia 43 25N 21 30E
52 Veliki Ustyug, U.S.S.R. 60 47N 46 20E
54 Velikiye Luki, U.S.S.R. 56 25N 30 32E
43 Veliko Turnovo, Bulgaria 43 5N 25 41E
70 Velikonda Range, India 14 45N 79 10E
55 Velikoye, Oz., U.S.S.R. 55 15N 40 0E
43 Velingrad, Bulgaria 42 4N 23 58E
39 Velino, Mt., Italy 42 10N 13 20E
54 Velizh, U.S.S.R. 55 30N 31 11E
27 Velké Karlovice, Cz. 49 20N 18 17E
26 Velke Mezirici, Cz. 49 21N 16 1E
27 Velký ostrov Zitný, Cz. 48 5N 17 20E
70 Vellar, R., India 11 30N 79 36E
40 Velletri, Italy 41 43N 12 43E
49 Velling, Denmark 56 2N 8 20E
49 Vellinge, Sweden 55 29N 13 0E
50 Vellir, Iceland 65 55N 18 28W
70 Vellore, India 12 57N 79 10E
16 Velsen, Netherlands 52 27N 4 40E
52 Velsk, U.S.S.R. 61 10N 42 5E
24 Velten, Germany 52 40N 13 11E
116 Velva, U.S.A. 48 6N 100 56W
44 Velvendós, Greece 40 15N 22 6E
49 Vem, Denmark 56 21N 8 21E
70 Vembanad Lake, India 9 36N 76 15E
47 Veme, Norway 60 14N 10 7E
49 Ven, Sweden 55 55N 12 45E
49 Vena, Sweden 57 31N 16 0E
120 Venado, Mexico 22 50N 101 10W
124 Venado Tuerto, Arg. 33 50S 62 0W
41 Venafro, Italy 41 28N 14 3E
19 Venarey, France 47 32N 4 26E
38 Venaria, Italy 45 12N 7 39E
42 Venčane, Yugoslavia 44 24N 20 28E
21 Vence, France 43 43N 7 6E
31 Vendas Novas, Portugal 38 39N 8 27W
18 Vendée, France 46 50N 1 35W
18 Vendée, Collines de, France 46 35N 0 45W
18 Vendée, R., France 46 30N 0 45W
20 Vendée ♦, France 46 40N 1 20W
19 Vendeuvres, France 48 14N 4 27E
18 Vendôme, France 47 47N 1 3E
32 Vendrell, Spain 41 10N 1 30E
49 Vendsyssel, Den. 57 22N 10 0E
39 Veneta, Laguna, Italy 45 19N 12 13E
39 Véneto ♦, Italy 45 30N 12 0E
55 Venev, U.S.S.R. 54 22N 38 17E
39 Venézia, Italy 45 27N 12 20E
39 Venézia, Golfo di, Italy 45 20N 13 0E
126 Venezuela ■, S. Amer. 8 0N 65 0W
126 Venezuela, Golfo de, Ven. 11 30N 71 0W
70 Vengurla, India 15 53N 73 45E
70 Vengurla Rocks, India 15 50N 73 22E
39 Venice = Venézia, Italy 45 27N 12 20E
21 Vénissieux, France 45 43N 4 53E
49 Venjansjön, Sweden 60 58N 14 2E
70 Venkatagiri, India 14 0N 79 35E
70 Venkatapuram, India 18 20N 80 30E
16 Venlo, Netherlands 51 22N 6 11E
47 Vennesla, Norway 58 15N 8 0E
49 Venö, Is., Denmark 56 33N 8 38E
16 Venraij, Netherlands 51 31N 6 0E
31 Venta de Cardeña, Sp. 38 16N 4 20W
30 Venta de San Rafael, Spain 40 42N 4 12W
120 Ventana, Punta de la, Mexico 24 4N 109 48W
92 Ventersburg, S. Africa 28 7S 27 9E
38 Ventimíglia, Italy 43 50N 7 39E
13 Ventnor, Eng. 50 35N 1 12W
70 Ventotene, I., Italy 40 48N 13 25E
54 Ventspils, U.S.S.R. 57 25N 21 32E
126 Ventuari, R., Venezuela 5 20N 66 0W
119 Ventura, U.S.A. 34 16N 119 25W
47 Veoy, Norway 62 45N 7 30E
47 Veoy Is., Norway 62 45N 7 30E
124 Vera, Argentina 29 30S 60 20W
33 Vera, Spain 37 15N 1 15W
120 Veracruz, Mexico 19 10N 96 10W
120 Veracruz ♦, Mexico 19 0N 96 15W
68 Veraval, India 20 53N 70 27E
38 Verbánia, Italy 45 50N 8 55E
41 Verbicaro, Italy 39 46N 15 54E
38 Vercelli, Italy 45 19N 8 25E
128 Verde, R., Argentina 41 55S 66 0W
120 Verde, R., Veracruz, Mexico 21 10N 102 50W
124 Verde, R., Paraguay 23 9S 57 37W
44 Verdhikoúsa, Greece 39 47N 21 59E
30 Veriña, Spain 43 32N 5 43W
116 Verdigre, U.S.A. 42 38N 98 0W
19 Verdun, France 49 12N 5 24E
19 Verdun-sur-le Doubs, Fr. 46 54N 5 0E
93 Vereeniging, S. Africa 26 38S 27 57E
32 Vergara, Spain 43 9N 2 28W
38 Vergato, Italy 44 18N 11 8E
113 Vergennes, U.S.A. 44 9N 73 15W
20 Vergt, France 45 2N 0 43E
30 Verin, Spain 41 57N 7 27W
30 Veriña, Spain 43 32N 5 43W
54 Verkhnedvinsk, U.S.S.R. 55 45N 27 58E
59 Verkhneye Kalinino, U.S.S.R. 60 0N 108 15E

MAP
57 Verkhniy Baskunchak, U.S.S.R. 48 5N 46 50E
55 Verkhovye, U.S.S.R. 52 55N 37 15E
59 Verkhoyansk, U.S.S.R. 67 50N 133 50E
59 Verkhoyanskiy Khrebet, U.S.S.R. 66 0N 129 0E
109 Verlo, Canada 50 25N 108 35W
47 Verma, Norway 62 21N 8 3E
19 Vermenton, France 47 40N 3 42E
109 Vermilion, Canada 53 20N 110 50W
109 Vermilion Bay, Canada 49 50N 93 20W
117 Vermilion, B., U.S.A. 29 45N 91 55W
116 Vermillion, U.S.A. 42 50N 96 56W
118 Vernal, U.S.A. 40 28N 109 35W
106 Verner, Canada 46 25N 80 8W
18 Verneuil, France 48 45N 0 56E
108 Vernon, Canada 50 20N 119 15W
18 Vernon, France 49 5N 1 30E
117 Vernon, U.S.A. 34 0N 99 15W
115 Vero Beach, U.S.A. 27 39N 80 23W
44 Véroia, Greece 40 34N 22 18E
38 Verolanuova, Italy 45 20N 10 5E
40 Véroli, Italy 41 43N 13 24E
38 Verona, Italy 45 27N 11 0E
59 Veropol, U.S.S.R. 66 0N 168 0E
19 Versailles, France 48 48N 2 8E
84 Vert, C., Senegal 14 45N 17 30W
18 Vertou, France 47 10N 1 28W
19 Vertus, France 48 54N 4 0E
93 Verulam, S. Afr. 29 38S 31 2E
16 Verviers, Belgium 50 37N 5 52E
19 Vervins, France 49 50N 3 53E
109 Verwood, Canada 49 30N 105 40W
39 Verzej, Yugoslavia 46 34N 16 13E
26 Veselí nad Luznici, Cz. 49 12N 14 15E
43 Veselie, Bulgaria 42 18N 27 38E
57 Veselovskoye Vdkhr., U.S.S.R. 47 0N 41 0E
57 Veselyy Res., U.S.S.R. 47 0N 41 0E
57 Veshenskaya, U.S.S.R. 49 35N 41 44E
19 Vesle, R., France 49 17N 3 50E
19 Vesoul, France 47 40N 6 11E
49 Vessigebro, Sweden 56 58N 12 40E
47 Vest-Agder fylke ♦, Norway 58 30N 7 15E
47 Vest Fjorden, Norway 68 0N 15 0E
47 Vestby, Norway 59 37N 10 45E
49 Vester Hassing, Den. 57 4N 10 8E
50 Vestfjorden, Norway 67 55N 14 0E
47 Vestfold fylke ♦, Norway 59 15N 10 0E
49 Vestjaellands Amt ♦, Denmark 55 30N 11 20E
50 Vestmannaeyjar, Ice. 63 27N 20 15W
47 Vestmarka, Norway 59 56N 11 59E
47 Vestnes, Norway 62 39N 7 5E
38 Vestone, Italy 45 43N 10 25E
4 Vestspitsbergen, Svalbard 78 40N 17 0E
50 Vestvågöy, Norway 68 18N 13 50E
41 Vesuvio, Italy 40 50N 14 22E
27 Veszprém, Hungary 47 8N 17 57E
27 Veszprém ♦, Hungary 47 5N 17 55E
27 Vésztő, Hungary 46 55N 21 16E
70 Vetapalam, India 15 47N 80 18E
49 Vetlanda, Sweden 57 24N 15 3E
55 Vetluga, U.S.S.R. 57 53N 45 45E
55 Vetluzhskiy, U.S.S.R. 57 17N 45 12E
43 Vetovo, Bulgaria 43 42N 26 16E
39 Vetralia, Italy 42 20N 12 2E
43 Vetren, Bulgaria 42 15N 24 3E
39 Vettore, Mte., Italy 44 38N 7 5E
16 Veurne, Belgium 51 5N 2 40E
25 Vevey, Switzerland 46 28N 6 51E
44 Vévi, Greece 40 47N 21 38E
64 Veys, Iran 31 30N 49 0E
19 Vézelise, France 48 30N 6 5E
43 Vezhen, mt., Bulgaria 42 50N 24 20E
126 Viacha, Bolivia 16 30S 68 5W
38 Viadana, Italy 44 55N 10 30E
127 Viana, Brazil 3 0S 44 40W
32 Viana, Spain 42 31N 2 22W
30 Viana do Castelo, Port. 41 42N 8 50W
30 Vianna do Castelo ♦, Portugal 41 50N 8 30W
127 Vianópolis, Brazil 16 40S 48 35W
30 Viar, R., Spain 37 45N 5 54W
38 Viaréggio, Italy 43 52N 10 13E
109 Vibank, Canada 50 25N 104 0W
32 Vibey, R., Spain 42 21N 7 15E
41 Vibo Valéntia, Italy 38 40N 16 5E
49 Viborg, Denmark 56 27N 9 23E
49 Viborg Amt ♦, Den. 56 30N 9 20E
20 Vic Fézensac, France 43 47N 0 19E
20 Vic-en-Bigorre, France 43 24N 0 3E
39 Vicenza, Italy 45 32N 11 31E
32 Vich, Spain 41 58N 2 19E
126 Vichada ♦, Col. 5 0N 69 30W
55 Vichuga, U.S.S.R. 57 25N 41 55E
20 Vichy, France 46 9N 3 26E
114 Vicksburg, Mich., U.S.A. 42 10N 85 30W
117 Vicksburg, Miss., U.S.A. 32 22N 90 56W
39 Vico, L. di, Italy 42 20N 12 10E
127 Viçosa, Min. Ger., Brazil 20 45S 42 53W
127 Viçosa, Pernambuco, Brazil 9 28S 36 14W
20 Vic-sur-Cère, France 44 59N 2 38E
19 Vic-sur-Seille, France 48 45N 6 33E
116 Victor, Col., U.S.A. 38 43N 105 7W
112 Victor, N.Y., U.S.A. 42 58N 77 24W
99 Victor Harbour, Austral. 35 30S 138 37E
124 Victoria, Argentina 32 40S 60 10W
98 Victoria, Australia 21 16S 149 3E
85 Victoria, Cameroon 4 1N 9 10E
108 Victoria, Canada 48 30N 123 25W
128 Victoria, Chile 38 13S 72 20W
77 Victoria, Hong Kong 22 25N 114 15E
72 Victoria, Malaysia 5 20N 115 20E
117 Victoria, Tex., U.S.A. 28 50N 97 0W
116 Victoria, Va., U.S.A. 38 52N 99 8W
104 Victoria I., Canada 71 0N 11 0W

MAP
90 Victoria, L., E. Africa 1 0S 33 0E
100 Victoria, L., Australia 38 0S 147 35E
98 Victoria, Mt., Territory of New Guinea 8 40S 147 20E
96 Victoria, R., Australia 15 30S 131 0E
100 Victoria ♦, Australia 37 0S 144 0E
91 Victoria ♦, Rhodesia 21 0S 31 30E
109 Victoria Beach, Canada 50 45N 96 32W
121 Victoria de las Tunas, Cuba 20 58N 76 59W
91 Victoria Falls, Rhodesia 17 58S 25 45E
106 Victoria Harbour, Canada 44 45N 79 45W
5 Victoria Ld., Antarctica 75 0S 160 0E
90 Victoria Nile R., Uganda 2 25N 31 50E
107 Victoria Res., Canada 48 20N 57 27W
96 Victoria R. Downs, Austral. 16 30S 131 20E
67 Victoria Taungdeik, Burma 21 15N 93 55E
92 Victoria West, S. Africa 31 25S 23 4E
107 Victoriaville, Canada 46 4N 71 56W
124 Victorica, Argentina 36 20S 65 30W
126 Victorino, Venezuela 2 48N 67 50W
124 Vicuña, Chile 30 0S 70 50W
124 Vicuña Mackenna, Arg. 33 53S 64 25W
115 Vidalia, U.S.A. 32 13N 82 25W
21 Vidauban, France 43 25N 6 27E
47 Videlv, R., Norway 58 50N 8 32E
31 Vidigueira, Portugal 38 12N 7 48W
30 Vidio, Cabo, Spain 43 35N 6 14W
68 Vidisha (Bhilsa), India 23 28N 77 53E
49 Vidöstern, Sweden 57 5N 14 0E
46 Vidra, Rumania 45 56N 26 55E
42 Viduša, mts., Y.-slavia 42 55N 18 21E
54 Vidzy, U.S.S.R. 54 40N 26 37E
128 Viedma, Argentina 40 50S 63 0W
128 Viedma, L., Argentina 49 30S 72 30W
30 Vieira, Portugal 41 38N 8 8W
32 Viella, Spain 42 43N 0 44E
71 Vien Pou Kha, Laos 20 45N 101 5E
24 Vienenburg, W. Ger. 51 57N 10 35E
27 Vienna = Wien, Austria 48 12N 16 22E
117 Vienna, U.S.A. 37 29N 88 54W
21 Vienne, France 45 31N 4 53E
18 Vienne, R., France 47 5N 0 30E
20 Vienne ♦, France 45 53N 0 42E
71 Vientiane, Laos 18 7N 102 35E
24 Viersen, Germany 51 15N 6 23E
25 Vierwaldstättersee, Switzerland 47 0N 8 30E
19 Vierzon, France 47 13N 2 5E
20 Vieux-Boucau-les- Bains, France 43 48N 1 23W
21 Vif, France 45 5N 5 41E
73 Vigan, Philippines 17 35N 120 28E
38 Vigevano, Italy 45 18N 8 50E
127 Vigia, Brazil 0 50S 48 5W
19 Vignacourt, France 50 1N 2 15E
20 Vignemale, Pic du, Fr. 42 47N 0 10W
19 Vigneulles, France 48 59N 5 40E
38 Vignola, Italy 44 29N 11 0E
30 Vigo, Spain 42 12N 8 41W
30 Vigo, Ria de, Spain 42 15N 8 45W
18 Vihiers, France 47 10N 0 30W
70 Vijayadurg, India 16 30N 73 25E
70 Vijayawada (Bezwada), India 16 31N 80 39E
47 Vikedal, Norway 59 30N 5 55E
49 Viken, sjö, Skaraborgs, Sweden 58 40N 14 20E
49 Viken, L., Sweden 58 40N 10 2E
47 Vikersund, Norway 59 58N 10 2E
108 Viking, Canada 53 7N 111 50W
50 Vikna, Norway 64 52N 10 57E
70 Vikramasingapuram, India 8 40N 76 47E
48 Viksjö, Sweden 62 45N 17 26E
58 Vikulovo, U.S.S.R. 56 50N 70 40E
93 Vila Alferes Chamusca, Mozam. 24 27S 33 0E
89 Vila Arriaga, Angola 14 35S 13 30E
126 Vila Bittencourt, Brazil 1 20S 69 20W
† 91 Vila Cabral, Mozam. 13 13S 35 11E
91 Vila Caldas Xavier, Mozambique 14 28S 33 0E
91 Vila Coutinho, Mozam. 14 37S 34 19E
91 Vila da Maganja, Mozambique 17 18S 37 30E
89 Vila da Ponte, Angola 14 35S 16 40E
89 Vila de Aljustrel, Ang. 13 30S 19 45E
* 93 Vila de João Belo, Mozambique 25 6S 33 31E
73 Vila de Liquica, Portuguese Timor 8 40S 125 20E
31 Vila de Rei, Portugal 39 41N 8 9W
91 Vila de Sena, Mozam. 17 25S 35 0E
31 Vila do Bispo, Portugal 37 5N 8 53W
30 Vila do Conde, Portugal 41 21N 8 45W
91 Vila Fontes Velha, Mozam. 17 51S 35 24E
31 Vila Franca de Xira, Portugal 38 57N 8 59W
91 Vila Gamito, Mozam. 14 12S 33 0E
89 Vila General Machado, Angola 11 58S 17 22E
93 Vila Gomes da Costa, Mozambique 24 20S 33 37E
88 Vila Henrique de Carvalho, Angola 9 40S 20 12E
91 Vila Junqueiro, Mozam. 15 25S 36 58E
93 Vila Luiza, Mozam. 25 45S 32 35E
89 Vila Luso, Angola 11 53S 19 55E
91 Vila Machado, Mozam. 19 15S 34 14E
88 Vila Marechal Carmona, Angola 7 30S 14 40E
89 Vila Mariano Machado, Angola 13 3S 14 35E
91 Vila Moatize, Mozambique 16 11S 33 40E

* *Renamed Xai-Xai*
† *Renamed Lichinga*

MAP
91 Vila Mouzinho, Mozam. 14 48S 34 25E
126 Vila Murtinho, Brazil 10 20S 65 20W
30 Vila Nova de Fozcôa, Port. 41 5N 7 9W
31 Vila Nova de Ourém, Portugal 39 40N 8 35W
30 Vila Novo de Gaia, Port. 41 4N 8 40W
89 Vila Nova do Seles, Angola 11 35S 14 22E
89 Vila Paiva Couceiro, Angola 14 37S 14 40E
91 Vila Paiva de Andrada, Mozam. 18 37S 34 2E
† 91 Vila Pery, Mozambique 19 4S 33 30E
30 Vila Pouca de Aguiar, Portugal 41 30N 7 38W
30 Vila Real, Portugal 41 17N 7 48W
31 Vila Real de Santo Antonio, Portugal 37 10N 7 28W
89 Vila Robert Williams, Angola 12 46S 15 30E
88 Vila Salazar, Angola 9 12S 14 48E
73 Vila Salazar, Port. Timor 5 25S 123 50E
89 Vila Teixeira da Silva, Angola 12 10S 15 50E
91 Vila Vasco da Gama, Mozambique 14 54S 32 14E
88 Vila Verissimo Sarmento, Angola 8 15S 20 50E
31 Vila Viçosa, Portugal 38 45N 7 27W
30 Vilaboa, Spain 42 21N 8 39W
18 Vilaine, R., France 47 35N 2 10W
93 Vilanculos, Mozam. 22 1S 35 17E
30 Vilar Formosa, Portugal 40 38N 6 45W
30 Vilareal ♦, Portugal 41 36N 7 35W
54 Vileyka, U.S.S.R. 54 30N 27 0E
50 Vilhelmina, Sweden 64 35N 16 39E
126 Vilhena, Brazil 12 30S 60 0W
59 Viliga, U.S.S.R. 60 2N 156 56E
54 Viliya, R., U.S.S.R. 54 57N 24 35E
54 Viljandi, U.S.S.R. 58 28N 25 30E
124 Villa Abecia, Bolivia 21 0S 68 18W
120 Villa Ahumada, Mexico 30 30N 106 40W
124 Villa Ana, Argentina 28 28S 59 40W
124 Villa Angela, Argentina 27 34S 60 45W
126 Villa Bella, Bolivia 10 25S 65 30W
80 Villa Bens (Tarfaya), Morocco 27 55N 12 55W
124 Villa Cañás, Argentina 34 0S 61 35W
* 80 Villa Cisneros, Spanish Sahara 23 50N 15 53W
* 80 Villa Cisneros ♦, Span. Sahara 25 0N 13 30W
124 Villa Colón, Argentina 31 38S 68 20W
124 Villa Constitución, Arg. 33 15S 60 20W
126 Villa de Cura, Ven. 10 2N 67 29W
124 Villa de Maria, Arg. 30 0S 63 43W
124 Villa de Rosario, Par. 24 30S 57 35W
124 Villa Dolores, Argentina 31 58S 65 15W
124 Villa Franca, Paraguay 26 14S 58 20W
124 Villa Guillermina, Arg. 28 15S 59 29W
124 Villa Hayes, Paraguay 25 0S 57 20W
124 Villa Iris, Argentina 38 12S 63 12W
121 Villa Julia Molina, Dominican Republic 19 5N 69 45W
120 Villa Madero, Mexico 24 28N 104 10W
124 Villa Maria, Argentina 32 20S 63 10W
124 Villa Mazán, Arg. 28 40S 66 30W
124 Villa Mentes, Bolivia 21 10S 63 30W
38 Villa Minozzo, Italy 44 21N 10 30E
124 Villa Montes, Bolivia 21 10S 63 30W
124 Villa Ocampo, Argentina 28 30S 59 20W
124 Villa Ojo de Agua, Argentina 29 30S 63 44W
124 Villa San Agustín, Arg. 30 35S 67 30W
41 Villa San Giovanni, It. 38 13N 15 38E
124 Villa San José, Argentina 32 12S 58 15W
124 Villa San Martín, Arg. 28 9S 64 9W
39 Villa Santina, Italy 46 25N 12 55E
30 Villablino, Spain 42 57N 6 19W
63 Villabruzzi, Somali Rep. 3 3N 45 18E
30 Villacampo, Pontano de, Spain 41 31N 6 0W
32 Villacañas, Spain 39 38N 3 20W
32 Villacarlos, Spain 39 53N 4 17E
32 Villacarriedo, Spain 43 14N 3 48W
33 Villacarrillo, Spain 38 7N 3 3W
30 Villacastín, Spain 40 46N 4 25W
26 Villach, Austria 46 37N 13 51E
40 Villaciaro, Italy 39 27N 8 45E
30 Villada, Spain 42 15N 4 59W
30 Villadiego, Spain 42 31N 4 1W
38 Villadossóla, Italy 46 4N 8 16E
32 Villafeliche, Spain 41 10N 1 30W
32 Villafranca, Spain 42 17N 1 46W
31 Villafranca de los Barros, Spain 38 35N 6 18W
33 Villafranca de los Caballeros, Spain 39 26N 3 21W
30 Villafranca del Bierzo, Spain 42 38N 6 50W
32 Villafranca del Cid, Sp. 40 26N 0 16W
32 Villafranca del Panadés, Spain 41 21N 1 40E
38 Villafranca di Verona, Italy 45 20N 10 51E
30 Villagarcia de Arosa, Spain 42 34N 8 46W
124 Villaguay, Argentina 32 0S 58 45W
31 Villaharta, Spain 38 9N 4 54W
120 Villahermosa, Mexico 17 45N 92 50W
33 Villahermosa, Spain 38 46N 2 52W
18 Villaines-la-Juhel, Fr. 48 21N 0 20W
33 Villajoyosa, Spain 38 30N 0 12W
30 Villalba, Spain 40 36N 3 59W
30 Villalba de Guardo, Sp. 42 42N 4 49W
30 Villalón de Campos, Sp. 42 5N 5 4W

* *Renamed Dakhla*
† *Renamed Chimoio*

Villalpando INDEX Wairarapa I.

MAP
30 Villalpando, Spain 41 51N 5 25W
30 Villaluenga, Spain 40 2N 3 54W
30 Villamañán, Spain 42 19N 5 35W
30 Villamartín, Spain 36 52N 5 38W
32 Villamayor, Spain 41 42N 0 43W
20 Villamblard, France 45 2N 0 32E
40 Villanova Monteleone, Italy 40 30N 8 28E
126 Villanueva, Col. 10 37N 72 59W
119 Villanueva, U.S.A. 35 16N 105 31W
33 Villanueva de Castellón, Spain 39 5N 0 31W
31 Villanueva de Córdoba, Spain 38 20N 4 38W
33 Villanueva de la Fuente, Spain 38 42N 2 42W
31 Villanueva de la Serena, Spain 38 59N 5 50W
30 Villanueva de la Sierra, Spain 40 12N 6 24W
31 Villanueva de los Castillejos, Spain 37 30N 7 15W
33 Villanueva del Arzobispo, Spain 38 10N 3 0W
31 Villanueva del Duque, Spain 38 20N 4 38W
31 Villanueva del Fresno, Spain 38 23N 7 10W
32 Villanueva y Geltrú, Sp. 41 13N 1 40E
30 Villaodrid, Spain 43 20N 7 11W
40 Villaputzu, Italy 39 28N 9 33E
32 Villar del Arzobispo, Sp. 39 44N 0 50W
31 Villar del Rey, Spain 39 7N 6 50W
32 Villarcayo, Spain 42 56N 3 34W
21 Villard, France 45 4N 5 33E
21 Villard-Bonnot, France 45 14N 5 53E
30 Villarino de los Aires, Sp. 41 18N 6 23W
41 Villarosa, Italy 37 36N 14 9E
30 Villarramiel, Spain 42 2N 4 55W
32 Villarreal, Spain 39 55N 0 3W
128 Villarrica, Chile 39 15S 72 30W
124 Villarrica, Paraguay 25 40S 56 30W
33 Villarrobledo, Spain 39 18N 2 36W
32 Villarroya de la Sierra, Spain 41 27N 1 46W
33 Villarrubia de los Ojos, Spain 39 14N 3 36W
21 Villars, France 46 0N 5 2E
33 Villarta de San Juan, Spain 39 15N 3 25W
32 Villasayas, Spain 41 24N 2 39W
30 Villaseca de los Gamitos, Spain 41 2N 6 7W
32 Villastar, Spain 40 17N 1 9W
32 Villatobas, Spain 39 54N 3 20W
124 Villavicencio, Argentina 32 28S 69 0W
126 Villavicencio, Colombia 4 9N 73 37W
30 Villaviciosa, Spain 43 32N 5 27W
124 Villazón, Bolivia 22 0S 65 35W
19 Ville de Paris ♦, France 48 50N 2 20E
106 Ville Marie, Canada 47 20N 79 30W
117 Ville Platte, U.S.A. 30 45N 92 17W
18 Villedieu, France 48 50N 1 12W
20 Villefort, France 44 28N 3 56E
19 Villefranche, France 47 19N 146 0E
20 Villefranche-de-Lauragais, France 43 25N 1 44E
20 Villefranche-de-Rouergue, France 44 21N 2 2E
20 Villefranche-du-Périgord, France 44 38N 1 5E
21 Villefranche-sur- Saône, France 45 59N 4 43E
32 Villel, Spain 40 14N 1 12W
19 Villemaur, France 48 14N 3 40E
20 Villemur, France 43 52N 1 31E
33 Villena, Spain 38 39N 0 52W
19 Villenauxe, France 48 36N 3 30E
20 Villenave, France 44 46N 0 33W
19 Villeneuve, France 48 42N 2 25E
38 Villeneuve, Italy 45 40N 7 10E
19 Villeneuve- l'Archevèque, France 48 14N 3 32E
21 Villeneuve- lès-Avignon, France 43 57N 4 49E
20 Villeneuve-sur- Allier, Fr. 46 40N 3 13E
20 Villeneuve-sur- Lot, Fr. 44 24N 0 42E
20 Villeréal, France 44 38N 0 45E
18 Villers Bocage, France 49 3N 0 40W
19 Villers Bretonneux, Fr. 49 50N 2 30E
19 Villers-Cotterets, France 49 15N 3 4E
18 Villers-sur-Mer, France 49 21N 0 2W
19 Villersexel, France 47 33N 6 26E
49 Villerslev, Denmark 56 49N 8 29E
19 Villerupt, France 49 28N 5 55E
18 Villerville, France 49 26N 0 5E
21 Villeurbanne, France 45 46N 4 55E
93 Villiers, S. Africa 27 2S 28 36E
25 Villingen, Germany 48 3N 8 29E
116 Villisca, U.S.A. 40 55N 94 59W
70 Villupuram, India 11 59N 79 31E
54 Vilnius, U.S.S.R. 54 38N 25 25E
26 Vils, Austria 47 33N 10 37E
25 Vilsbiburg, Germany 48 27N 12 23E
49 Vilslev, Denmark 55 24N 8 42E
42 Vilusi, Yugoslavia 42 44N 18 34E
16 Vilvoorde, Belgium 50 56N 4 26E
59 Vilyuy, R., U.S.S.R. 63 58N 125 0E
59 Vilyuysk, U.S.S.R. 63 40N 121 20E
38 Vimercate, Italy 45 38N 9 25E
30 Vimioso, Portugal 41 35N 6 13W
49 Vimmerby, Sweden 57 40N 15 55E
48 Vimo, Sweden 60 50N 14 20E
18 Vimoutiers, France 48 57N 0 10E
26 Vimperk, Cz. 49 3N 13 46E
124 Viña del Mar, Chile 33 0S 71 30W
32 Vinaroz, Spain 40 30N 0 27E
114 Vincennes, U.S.A. 38 42N 87 29W
124 Vinchina, Argentina 28 45S 68 15W
50 Vindel älv, Sweden 64 20N 19 20E
50 Vindeln, Sweden 64 12N 19 43E
49 Vinderup, Denmark 56 29N 8 45E
68 Vindhya Ra., India 22 50N 77 0E
114 Vineland, U.S.A. 39 30N 75 0W
42 Vinga, Rumania 46 0N 21 14E
47 Vingnes, Norway 61 7N 10 26E
71 Vinh, North Vietnam 18 45N 105 38E
71 Vinh Loi, S. Vietnam 9 20N 104 45E
30 Vinhais, Portugal 41 50N 7 0W
39 Vinica, Yugoslavia 45 28N 15 16E
117 Vinita, U.S.A. 36 40N 95 12W
42 Vinkovci, Yugoslavia 45 19N 18 48E
56 Vinnitsa, U.S.S.R. 49 15N 28 30E
47 Vinstra, Norway 61 37N 9 44E
116 Vinton, Iowa, U.S.A. 42 8N 92 1W
117 Vinton, La., U.S.A. 30 13N 93 35W
46 Vintu de Jos, Rum. 46 0N 23 30E
24 Viöl, Germany 54 32N 9 12E
100 Violet Town, Australia 36 19S 145 37E
39 Vipava, Yugoslavia 45 51N 13 38E
39 Vipiteno, Italy 46 55N 11 25E
73 Viqueque, Port. Timor 8 42S 126 30E
39 Vir, I., Yugoslavia 44 17N 15 3E
73 Virac, Philippines 13 30N 124 20E
70 Virajpet, India 12 15N 75 50E
68 Viramgam, India 23 5N 72 0E
70 Virarajendrapet (Virajpet), India 12 10N 75 50E
70 Viravanallur, India 8 40N 79 30E
109 Virden, Canada 49 50N 101 0W
18 Vire, France 48 50N 0 53W
128 Virgenes, C., Argentina 52 19S 68 21W
121 Virgin Gorda, I., Virgin Islands, W.I. 18 45N 64 26W
121 Virgin Is., W. Indies 18 40N 64 30W
119 Virgin, R., U.S.A. 36 50N 114 10W
92 Virginia, S. Afr. 28 8S 26 55E
116 Virginia, U.S.A. 47 30N 92 32W
114 Virginia ♦, U.S.A. 37 45N 78 0W
114 Virginia Beach, U.S.A. 36 54N 75 58W
118 Virginia City, Mont., U.S.A. 45 25N 111 58W
118 Virginia City, Nev., U.S.A. 39 25N 119 48W
106 Virginiatown, Canada 48 9N 79 36W
128 Virgins, C., Argentina 52 10S 68 30W
21 Virieu-le-Grande, Fr. 45 51N 5 39E
42 Virje, Yugoslavia 46 4N 16 59E
116 Viroqua, U.S.A. 43 33N 90 57W
42 Virovitica, Yugoslavia 45 51N 17 21E
42 Virpaza, R., Yugoslavia 42 14N 19 6E
49 Virserum, Sweden 57 20N 15 35E
16 Virton, Belgium 49 35N 5 32E
54 Virtsu, U.S.S.R. 58 32N 23 33E
70 Virudhunagar, India 9 30N 78 0E
39 Vis, Yugoslavia 43 0N 16 10E
39 Vis, I., Yugoslavia 43 0N 16 10E
39 Vis Kanal, Yugoslavia 43 4N 16 5E
119 Visalia, U.S.A. 36 25N 119 18W
73 Visayan Sea, Phil. 11 30N 123 30E
49 Visby, Sweden 57 37N 18 18E
4 Viscount Melville Sd., Canada 78 0N 108 0W
16 Visé, Belgium 50 44N 5 41E
42 Višegrad, Yugoslavia 43 47N 19 17E
127 Viseu, Brazil 1 10S 46 20W
30 Viseu, Portugal 40 40N 7 55W
30 Viseu ♦, Portugal 40 40N 7 55W
46 Vişeu, Rumania 47 45N 24 25E
70 Vishakhapatnam, India 17 45N 83 20E
69 Vishnupur, India 23 8N 87 20E
5 Visikoi I., Falkland Is. 56 30S 26 40E
49 Visingsö, Sweden 58 2N 14 20E
49 Viskafors, Sweden 57 37N 12 50E
49 Vislanda, Sweden 56 46N 14 30E
28 Vislinskil Zaliv (Zalew Wislany), Poland 54 20N 19 50E
68 Visnagar, India 23 45N 72 32E
39 Višnja Gora, Y.-slavia 45 58N 14 45E
38 Viso, Mte., Italy 44 38N 7 5E
33 Viso del Marqués, Sp. 38 32N 3 34W
42 Visoko, Yugoslavia 43 58N 18 10E
25 Visp, Switzerland 46 17N 7 52E
24 Visselhovde, Germany 52 59N 9 36E
44 Vistonis, Limni, Gr. 41 0N 25 7E
28 Vistula, R. = Wisła, R., Pol. 53 38N 18 47E
43 Vit, R., Bulgaria 43 30N 24 30E
39 Vitanje, Yugoslavia 46 40N 15 18E
54 Vitebsk, U.S.S.R. 55 10N 30 15E
39 Viterbo, Italy 42 25N 12 8E
101 Viti Levu, I., Fiji Is. 17 30S 177 30E
98 Vitiaz Str., Territory of New Guinea 5 46S 147 0E
30 Vitigudino, Spain 41 1N 6 35W
59 Vitim, U.S.S.R. 59 45N 112 25E
59 Vitim, R., U.S.S.R. 58 40N 112 50E
45 Vitina, Greece 37 40N 22 10E
42 Vitina, Yugoslavia 43 17N 17 29E
127 Vitória, Brazil 20 20S 40 22W
32 Vitoria, Spain 42 50N 2 41W
127 Vitória da Conquista, Brazil 14 51S 40 51W
127 Vitória de São Antão, Brazil 8 10S 37 20W
18 Vitré, France 48 8N 1 12W
19 Vitry-le-François, Fr. 48 43N 4 33E
44 Vitsi, Mt., Greece 40 40N 21 25E
50 Vittangi, Sweden 67 41N 21 40E
19 Vitteaux, France 47 24N 4 30E
19 Vittel, France 48 12N 5 57E
112 Vittoria, Canada 42 48N 81 21W
41 Vittória, Italy 36 58N 14 30E
39 Vittório Véneto, Italy 45 59N 12 18E
32 Viver, Spain 39 55N 0 36W
30 Vivero, Spain 43 39N 7 38W
21 Viviers, France 44 30N 4 40E
20 Vivonne, France 46 36N 0 15E
48 Vivsta, Sweden 62 30N 17 18E
120 Vizcaíno, Desierto de, Mex. 27 40N 113 50W
120 Vizcaíno, Sierra, Mex. 27 30N 114 0W
32 Vizcaya ♦, Spain 43 15N 2 45W
70 Vizianagram, India 18 6N 83 10E
21 Vizille, France 45 5N 5 46E
39 Vizinada, Yugoslavia 45 20N 13 46E
46 Viziru, Rumania 45 0N 27 43E
27 Vizovice, Cz. 49 12N 17 56E
41 Vizzini, Italy 37 9N 14 43E
44 Vjosa, R., Albania 40 35N 19 30E
16 Vlaardingen, Neth. 51 55N 4 21E
46 Vlădeasa, mt., Rumania 46 47N 22 50E
42 Vladicin Han, Y.-slav. 42 42N 22 1E
55 Vladimir, U.S.S.R. 56 0N 40 30E
54 Vladimir Volynskiy, U.S.S.R. 50 50N 24 18E
42 Vladimirci, Yugoslavia 44 36N 19 45E
42 Vladimirovac, Y.-slav. 45 1N 20 53E
57 Vladimirovka, U.S.S.R. 48 27N 46 5E
57 Vladimirovka, U.S.S.R. 44 37N 44 41E
43 Vladimirovo, Bulg. 43 32N 23 22E
56 Vladislavovka, U.S.S.R. 45 15N 35 15E
43 Vladimirovo, Bulg. 43 32N 23 22E
56 Vladivostok, U.S.S.R. 43 10N 131 53E
42 Vlasenica, Yugoslavia 44 11N 18 59E
42 Vlašió, mt., Yugoslavia 44 19N 17 37E
26 Vlasim, Czechoslovakia 49 40N 14 53E
42 Vlasinsko Jezero, Yugoslavia 42 44N 22 37E
42 Vlasotinci, Yugoslavia 42 59N 22 7E
16 Vlieland, I., Neth. 53 30N 4 55E
16 Vlissingen, Netherlands 51 26N 3 34E
44 Vlora, Albania 40 32N 19 28E
44 Vlora ♦, Albania 40 12N 20 0E
26 Vltava, R., Cz. 49 35N 14 10E
38 Vobarno, Italy 45 38N 10 30E
42 Vočin, Yugoslavia 45 37N 17 33E
39 Vodice, Yugoslavia 43 47N 15 47E
26 Vodnany, Cz. 49 9N 14 11E
39 Vodnjan, Yugoslavia 44 59N 13 52E
85 Voga, Togo 6 23N 1 30E
73 Vogelkop, Indonesia 1 25S 133 0E
73 Vogelkop = Doberai, Djazirah, Indon. 1 25S 133 0E
38 Voghera, Italy 44 59N 9 1E
93 Vohémar, Malagasy Rep. 13 25S 50 0E
93 Vohipeno, Malagasy Rep. 22 22S 47 51E
90 Voi, Kenya 3 25S 38 32E
19 Void, France 48 40N 5 36E
46 Voineşti, Rumania 47 5N 27 27E
46 Voineşti, Rumania 45 5N 25 14E
45 Voiotia ♦, Greece 38 20N 23 0E
21 Voiron, France 45 22N 5 35E
107 Voiseys B., Canada 56 15N 61 0W
26 Voitsberg, Austria 47 3N 15 9E
44 Voiviis Limni, L., Gr. 39 30N 22 45E
49 Vojens, Denmark 55 16N 9 18E
50 Vojmsjön, Sweden 64 55N 16 40E
39 Vojnió, Yugoslavia 45 19N 15 43E
42 Vojvodina, Auton. Pokragina, Y-slav. 45 20N 20 0E
55 Vokhma, U.S.S.R. 59 0N 46 45E
55 Vokhma, R., U.S.S.R. 59 0N 46 44E
55 Vokhtoga, U.S.S.R. 58 46N 41 8E
110 Volary, Czechoslovakia 48 54N 13 52E
116 Volborg, U.S.A. 45 50N 105 44W
55 Volchansk, U.S.S.R. 50 17N 36 58E
56 Volchya, R., U.S.S.R. 48 0N 37 0E
47 Volda, Norway 62 9N 6 5E
55 Volga, U.S.S.R. 57 58N 38 16E
57 Volga, R., U.S.S.R. 52 20N 48 0E
53 Volga Hts. = Privolzhskaya V.S., U.S.S.R. 51 0N 46 0E
57 Volgodonsk, U.S.S.R. 47 33N 42 5E
57 Volgograd, U.S.S.R. 48 40N 44 25E
55 Volgogradskoye Vdkhr., U.S.S.R. 50 0N 45 20E
55 Volgorechensk, U.S.S.R. 57 28N 41 14E
45 Volissós, Greece 38 29N 25 54E
26 Völkermarkt, Austria 46 39N 14 39E
54 Volkhov, U.S.S.R. 59 55N 32 15E
54 Volkhov, R., U.S.S.R. 59 30N 32 0E
25 Völklingen, Germany 49 15N 6 50E
54 Volkovysk, U.S.S.R. 53 9N 24 30E
93 Volksrust, S. Africa 27 24S 29 53E
16 Vollenhove, Neth. 52 40N 5 58E
56 Volnovakha, U.S.S.R. 47 35N 37 30E
100 Volo, Australia 31 37S 143 0E
59 Volochayevka, U.S.S.R. 48 40N 134 30E
55 Volodary, U.S.S.R. 56 12N 43 15E
55 Vologda, U.S.S.R. 59 25N 40 0E
55 Volokolamsk, U.S.S.R. 56 5N 36 0E
55 Volokonovka, U.S.S.R. 50 33N 37 58E
56 Volontirovka, U.S.S.R. 46 28N 29 28E
44 Vólos, Greece 39 24N 22 59E
54 Volosovo, U.S.S.R. 59 27N 29 32E
45 Volozhin, U.S.S.R. 54 3N 26 30E
55 Volsk, U.S.S.R. 52 5N 47 28E
49 Volstrup, Denmark 57 19N 10 27E
85 Volta, L., Ghana 7 30N 0 15E
85 Volta, R., Ghana 8 0N 0 10W
125 Volta Redonda, Brazil 22 31S 44 5W
38 Volterra, Italy 43 24N 10 50E
38 Voltri, Italy 44 25N 8 43E
41 Volturara Appula, It. 41 30N 15 2E
41 Volturno, R., Italy 41 18N 14 20E
82 Volubilis, Morocco 34 2N 5 33W
44 Vólvi, L., Greece 40 40N 23 34E
55 Volzhsk, U.S.S.R. 55 57N 48 23E
57 Volzhskiy, U.S.S.R. 48 56N 44 46E
93 Vondrozo, Malag. 22 49S 47 20E
45 Vónitsa, Greece 38 53N 20 58E
16 Voorburg, Netherlands 52 5N 4 24E
50 Vopnafjör ð ur, Iceland 65 45N 14 40W
26 Vorarlberg ♦, Aust. 47 20N 10 0E
44 Vóras Oros, Gr. 40 57N 21 45E
49 Vorbasse, Denmark 55 39N 9 6E
25 Vorderrhein, R., Switzerland 46 49N 9 25E
49 Vordingborg, Denmark 55 0N 11 54E
45 Voriai Sporádhes, Greece 39 15N 23 30E
45 Vórios Evvoïkós Kólpos, Greece 38 45N 23 15E
52 Vorkuta, U.S.S.R. 67 48N 64 20E
47 Vorma, Norway 60 9N 11 27E
55 Vorona, R., U.S.S.R. 52 0N 42 20E
55 Voronezh, R.S.S.R., U.S.S.R. 51 40N 39 10E
54 Voronezh, Ukraine, U.S.S.R. 51 47N 33 28E
55 Voronezh, R., U.S.S.R. 52 30N 39 30E
57 Voroshilovgrad, U.S.S.R. 48 38N 39 15E
57 Voroshilovsk = Kommunarsk, U.S.S.R. 48 3N 38 40E
59 Vorovskoye, U.S.S.R. 54 30N 155 50E
56 Vorskla, R., U.S.S.R. 49 30N 34 31E
49 Vorupör, Denmark 56 58N 8 22E
19 Vosges, France 48 20N 7 10E
19 Vosges ♦, France 48 12N 6 20E
44 Voskopoja, Albania 40 40N 20 33E
55 Voskresensk, U.S.S.R. 55 27N 38 31E
55 Voskresenskoye, U.S.S.R. 56 51N 45 30E
47 Voss, Norway 60 38N 6 26E
95 Vostok I., Pacific Ocean 10 5S 152 23W
59 Vostotnyy Sayan, U.S.S.R. 54 0N 96 0E
26 Votice, Czechoslovakia 49 38N 14 39E
52 Votkinsk, U.S.S.R. 57 0N 53 55E
52 Votkinskoye Vdkhr., U.S.S.R. 57 30N 55 0E
30 Vouga, R., Portugal 40 46N 8 10W
45 Voúxa, Akra, Greece 35 37N 20 32E
30 Vouzela, Portugal 40 43N 8 7W
19 Vouziers, France 49 22N 4 40E
19 Voves, France 48 15N 1 38E
48 Voxna, Sweden 61 20N 15 30E
52 Vozhe Oz., U.S.S.R. 60 45N 39 0E
55 Vozhgaly, U.S.S.R. 58 24N 50 1E
56 Voznesensk, U.S.S.R. 47 35N 31 15E
52 Voznesenye, U.S.S.R. 61 0N 35 45E
27 Vráble, Czechoslovakia 48 15N 18 16E
42 Vrácevšnica, Y.-slavia 44 2N 20 34E
47 Vrådal, Norway 59 20N 8 25E
56 Vradiyevka, U.S.S.R. 49 56N 30 38E
44 Vraka, Albania 42 8N 19 28E
45 Vrakhnéika, Greece 38 10N 21 40E
46 Vrancea ♦, Rumania 45 50N 26 45E
46 Vrancei, Munţi, Rumania 46 0N 26 30E
59 Vrangelja, Ostrov, U.S.S.R. 71 0N 180 0E
48 Vrangtjarn, Sweden 62 14N 16 37E
42 Vranica, mt., Y.-slavia 43 59N 18 0E
42 Vranje, Yugoslavia 42 34N 21 54E
42 Vranjska Banja, Y.-slav. 42 34N 22 1E
27 Vranov, Czechoslovakia 48 53N 21 40E
39 Vransko, Yugoslavia 46 17N 14 58E
43 Vratsa, Bulgaria 43 13N 23 30E
43 Vratsa ♦, Bulgaria 43 30N 23 30E
42 Vrbas, Yugoslavia 45 0N 17 27E
42 Vrbas, R., Yugoslavia 44 30N 17 10E
39 Vrbnik, Yugoslavia 45 4N 14 32E
39 Vrboviec, Yugoslavia 45 53N 16 28E
39 Vrbovsko, Yugoslavia 45 24N 15 5E
26 Vrchlabí, Cz. 49 38N 15 37E
93 Vrede, S. Africa 27 24S 29 6E
92 Vredefort, S. Afr. 27 0S 26 58E
92 Vredenburg, S. Africa 32 51S 18 0E
92 Vredendal, S. Africa 31 41S 18 35E
49 Vrena, Sweden 58 54N 16 41E
42 Vrgorac, Yugoslavia 43 12N 17 20E
39 Vrhnika, Yugoslavia 45 58N 14 15E
70 Vriddhachalam, India 11 30N 79 10E
84 Vridi, Ivory Coast 5 15N 4 3W
84 Vridi Canal, Ivory Coast 5 15N 4 3W
68 Vrindaban, India 27 37N 77 40E
39 Vrnograč, Yugoslavia 43 12N 17 20E
45 Vrondádhes, Greece 38 25N 26 7E
42 Vrpolje, Yugoslavia 43 42N 16 1E
42 Vršac, Yugoslavia 45 8N 21 18E
42 Vršački Kanal, Y.-slav. 45 15N 21 0E
92 Vryburg, S. Africa 26 55S 24 45E
93 Vryheid, S. Afr. 27 54S 30 47E
27 Vsetin, Cz. 49 20N 18 0E
43 Vǔcha, R., Bulg. 41 53N 24 26E
42 Vučitrn, Yugoslavia 42 49N 20 59E
16 Vught, Netherlands 51 38N 5 20E
42 Vuka, R., Yugoslavia 45 28N 18 30E
42 Vukovar, Yugoslavia 45 21N 18 59E
108 Vulcan, Canada 50 25N 113 15W
46 Vulcan, Rumania 45 23N 23 17E
114 Vulcan, U.S.A. 45 46N 87 51W
41 Vulcano, I., Italy 38 25N 14 58E
43 Vǔlchedrǔma, Bulgaria 43 42N 23 16E
39 Vulci, Italy 42 23N 11 37E
56 Vulkaneshty, U.S.S.R. 45 35N 28 30E
91 Vunduzi, R., Mozam. 18 0S 33 45E
71 Vung Tau, S. Vietnam 10 28N 107 10E
43 Vǔrbitsa, Bulgaria 42 59N 26 40E
43 Vǔrsheto, Bulgaria 43 15N 23 23E
46 Vutcani, Rumania 46 26N 27 59E
70 Vuyyuru, India 16 28N 80 50E
68 Vyara, India 21 8N 73 28E
55 Vyasniki, U.S.S.R. 56 10N 42 10E
55 Vyatka, R., U.S.S.R. 56 30N 51 0E
55 Vyatskiye Polyany, U.S.S.R. 56 5N 51 0E
59 Vyazemskiy, U.S.S.R. 47 32N 134 45E
54 Vyazma, U.S.S.R. 55 10N 34 15E
52 Vychegda R., U.S.S.R. 61 50N 52 30E
27 Vychodné Beskydy, Europe 49 30N 22 0E
26 Východočeský ♦, Cz. 50 20N 15 45E
27 Východoslovenský ♦, Cz. 48 50N 21 0E
52 Vyg-ozero, U.S.S.R. 63 30N 34 0E
55 Vyja, R., Bulgaria 41 53N 24 26E
70 Vypin, I., India 10 10N 76 15E
12 Vyrnwy, L., Wales 52 48N 3 30W
54 Vyshniy Volochek, U.S.S.R. 57 30N 34 30E
27 Vyškov, Czechoslovakia 49 17N 17 0E
27 Vysoké Mýto, Cz. 49 58N 16 23E
27 Vysoké Tatry, Europe 49 30N 20 0E
55 Vysokovsk, U.S.S.R. 56 22N 36 30E
54 Vysotsk, U.S.S.R. 51 43N 36 32E
64 Vyssi Brod, Cz. 48 36N 14 20E
26 Vytegra, U.S.S.R. 61 15N 36 40E
85 Wa, Ghana 10 7N 2 25W
16 Waal, R., Netherlands 51 59N 4 8E
16 Waalwijk, Netherlands 51 42N 5 4E
107 Wabana, Canada 47 40N 53 0W
108 Wabasca, Canada 55 57N 113 45W
114 Wabash, U.S.A. 40 48N 85 46W
114 Wabash, R., U.S.A. 39 10N 87 30W
114 Wabeno, U.S.A. 45 25N 88 40W
87 Wabi, R., Ethiopia 7 35N 40 5E
87 Wabi Gestro, R., Ethiopia 6 0N 41 35E
87 Wabi Shaballe, R., Ethiopia 8 0N 40 45E
109 Wabigoon, L., Canada 49 44N 92 34W
109 Wabowden, Canada 54 55N 98 35W
28 Wabrzezno, Poland 53 16N 18 57E
106 Wabuk Pt., Canada 55 30N 85 30W
107 Wabush City, Canada 52 40N 67 0W
118 Wabuska, U.S.A. 39 16N 119 13W
117 Waco, U.S.A. 31 33N 97 5W
106 Waconichi, L., Canada 50 0N 74 0W
64 Wad ar Rimsa, Si. Arab. 26 5N 41 30E
87 Wad Ban Naqa, Sudan 16 32N 33 9E
87 Wad Banda, Sudan 13 10N 27 50E
87 Wad el Haddad, Sudan 13 50N 33 30E
87 Wad en Nau, Sudan 14 10N 33 34E
87 Wad Hamid, Sudan 16 20N 32 45E
87 Wâd Medani, Sudan 14 28N 33 30E
99 Waddamana, Australia 41 59S 146 34E
83 Waddān, Libya 29 9N 16 45E
83 Waddān, Jabal, Libya 29 0N 16 15E
113 Waddington, U.S.A. 44 51N 75 12W
108 Waddington Mt., Can. 51 10N 125 20W
109 Wadena, Canada 52 0N 103 50W
116 Wadena, U.S.A. 46 25N 95 2W
25 Wädenswil, Switzerland 47 14N 8 30E
115 Wadesboro, U.S.A. 35 2N 80 2W
108 Wadhams, Canada 51 30N 127 30W
85 Wadi, Nigeria 13 5N 11 40E
83 Wādī ash Shāfi', Libya 27 30N 15 0E
83 Wādī Banī Walīd, Libya 31 49N 14 0E
86 Wadi Gemâl, Egypt 24 35N 35 10E
86 Wadi Halfa, Sudan 21 53N 31 19E
63 Wadi Masila, S. Arabia 16 30N 49 0E
64 Wadi Sabha, Si. Arab. 23 50N 48 30E
28 Wadlew, Poland 51 31N 19 23E
27 Wadowice, Poland 49 52N 19 30E
118 Wadsworth, U.S.A. 39 44N 119 22W
64 Wafra, Saudi Arabia 28 33N 48 3E
16 Wageningen, Neth. 51 58N 5 40E
105 Wager Bay, Canada 66 0N 91 0W
105 Wager B., Canada 65 50N 88 0W
100 Wagga Wagga, Austral. 35 7S 147 24E
73 Waghete, Indonesia 4 10S 135 50E
96 Wagin, Australia 33 17S 117 25E
85 Wagin, Nigeria 12 42N 7 10E
117 Wagon Mound, U.S.A. 36 10N 105 0W
117 Wagoner, U.S.A. 36 0N 95 20W
28 Wagrowiec, Poland 52 48N 17 19E
100 Wahgunyah, Australia 35 57S 146 25E
73 Wahai, Indonesia 2 48S 129 35E
116 Wahoo, U.S.A. 41 15N 96 35W
116 Wahpeton, U.S.A. 46 20N 96 35W
70 Wai, India 17 56N 73 57E
110 Waianae, Oahu I., Hawaii 21 25N 158 8W
101 Waiau, R., New Zealand 42 44S 173 10E
70 Waiawe Ganga, Cey. 6 15N 81 0E
73 Waibeem, Indonesia 0 30S 132 50E
25 Waiblingen, Germany 48 49N 9 20E
26 Waidhofen, Niederösterreich, Austria 48 49N 15 17E
26 Waidhofen, Niederösterreich, Austria 47 57N 14 46E
73 Waigeo, I., Indonesia 0 20S 130 40E
101 Waihi, New Zealand 37 23S 175 52E
101 Waihou, R., New Zealand 37 15S 175 40E
90 Waika, Zaïre 2 22S 25 42E
73 Waikabubak, Indonesia 9 45S 119 25E
101 Waikaremoana, N.Z. 38 42S 177 12E
101 Waikari, New Zealand 42 58S 172 41E
101 Waikato, R., N.Z. 37 32S 174 45E
101 Waikawa Harbour, N.Z. 46 39S 169 9E
99 Waikerie, S. Australia 34 9S 140 0E
101 Waikokopu, N.Z. 39 3S 177 52E
101 Waikouaiti, N.Z. 45 36S 170 41E
95 Waikoati, N.Z. 45 36S 170 41E
101 Waimakahiri, R., N.Z. 43 17S 171 59E
110 Waimanola, Oahu I., Hawaii 21 19N 157 43W
101 Waimarino, N.Z. 40 40S 175 20E
101 Waimate, N.Z. 44 53S 171 3E
110 Waimea, Kauai I., Hawaii 21 57N 159 39W
69 Wainganga, R., India 21 0N 79 45E
73 Waingapu, Indonesia 9 35S 120 11E
109 Wainwright, Canada 52 50N 110 50W
101 Waiouru, N.Z. 39 28S 175 41E
101 Waipara, N.Z. 43 3S 172 46E
101 Waipawa, N.Z. 39 56S 176 38E
101 Waipiro, New Zealand 38 2S 176 22E
95 Waipori, New Zealand 45 50S 169 52E
101 Waipu, New Zealand 35 59S 174 29E
101 Waipukurau, N.Z. 40 1S 176 33E
101 Wairakei, New Zealand 38 37S 176 6E
101 Wairarapa L., N.Z. 41 14S 175 15E

MAP
101 Wairoa, New Zealand 39 3s 177 25E
101 Waitaki, R., N.Z. 44 23s 169 55E
101 Waitara, New Zealand 38 59s 174 15E
118 Waitsburg, U.S.A. 46 15N 118 10w
101 Waiuku, New Zealand 37 15s 174 45E
73 Wajabula Rau, Indon. 2 29N 128 17E
74 Wajima, Japan 37 30N 137 0E
90 Wajir, Kenya 1 42N 40 20E
90 Wajir ♦, Kenya 1 42N 40 20E
74 Wakamatsu, Japan 33 50N 130 45E
74 Wakasa-Wan, Japan 34 45N 135 30E
101 Wakatipu. L., N.Z. 45 5s 168 33E
74 Wakayama, Japan 34 15N 135 15E
74 Wakayama-ken ♦, Jap. 33 50N 135 30E
115 Wake Forest, U.S.A. 35 58N 78 30w
94 Wake I., Pacific Ocean 19 18N 166 36E
12 Wakefield, Eng. 53 41N 1 31w
101 Wakefield, N.Z. 41 24s 173 5E
113 Wakefield, Mass., U.S.A. 42 30N 71 3w
116 Wakefield, Mich., U.S.A. 46 28N 89 53w
71 Wakema, Burma 16 40N 95 18E
65 Wakhan ♦, Afghan. 37 0N 73 0E
74 Wakkanai, Japan 45 28N 141 35E
93 Wakkerstroom, S. Afr. 27 24s 30 10E
106 Wako, Canada 49 50N 91 22w
100 Wakool, R., Australia 32 25s 144 15E
73 Wakre, Indonesia 0 30s 131 5E
107 Wakuach L., Canada 55 20N 67 10w
46 Walachia ♦, Rum. 44 40N 25 0E
91 Walamba, Zambia 13 30s 28 42E
28 Wałbrzych, Poland 50 45N 16 18E
99 Walcha, Australia 30 55s 151 31E
16 Walcheren, I., Neth. 51 30N 3 35E
118 Walcott, U.S.A. 41 50N 106 55w
28 Walcz, Poland 53 17N 16 27E
25 Wald, Switzerland 47 17N 8 56E
24 Waldbröl, Germany 50 52N 7 36E
24 Waldeck, Germany 51 12N 9 4E
118 Walden, Colo., U.S.A. 40 47N 106 20w
113 Walden, N.Y., U.S.A. 41 32N 74 13w
118 Waldport, U.S.A. 44 30N 124 2w
109 Waldron, Canada 50 53N 102 35w
117 Waldron, U.S.A. 34 52N 94 4w
25 Waldshut, Germany 47 37N 8 12E
87 Waldya, Ethiopia 11 50N 39 34E
84 Walembele, Ghana 10 1N 1 14w
13 Wales ♦, U.K. 52 30N 3 30w
85 Walewale, Ghana 10 21N 0 50w
99 Walgett, Australia 30 0s 148 5E
100 Walhalla, Australia 37 50s 146 25E
87 Waliso, Ethiopia 8 33N 38 1E
116 Walker, U.S.A. 47 4N 94 35w
107 Walker L., Canada 50 20N 67 11w
118 Walker, U.S.A. 38 56N 118 46w
98 Walkerston, Australia 21 11s 149 8E
112 Walkerton, Canada 44 10N 81 10w
116 Wall, U.S.A. 44 0N 102 14w
118 Walla Walla, U.S.A. 46 3N 118 25w
98 Wallabadah, Australia 17 57s 142 15E
112 Wallace, Canada 45 12N 78 9w
118 Wallace, Idaho, U.S.A. 47 30N 116 0w
116 Wallace, Nebr., U.S.A. 40 51N 101 12w
115 Wallace, N.C., U.S.A. 34 50N 77 59w
106 Wallaceburg, Canada 42 40N 82 30w
46 Wallachia = Valahia, 44 35N 25 0E
  Rumania
99 Wallal, Australia 26 32s 146 7E
99 Wallangarra, Australia 28 56s 151 58E
99 Wallaroo, Australia 33 55s 137 33E
12 Wallasey, Eng. 53 26s 3 2w
25 Walldürn, Germany 49 34N 9 23E
100 Wallerawang, Australia 33 25s 150 4E
113 Wallingford, Eng. 51 36N 1 7w
113 Wallingford, U.S.A. 43 27N 72 58w
100 Wallis, L., Australia 32 15s 152 28E
118 Wallowa, U.S.A. 45 40N 117 35w
118 Wallowa, Mts., U.S.A. 45 20N 117 30w
12 Wallsend, England 54 59N 1 30w
100 Wallsend, Australia 32 55s 151 40E
118 Wallula, U.S.A. 46 3N 118 59w
99 Wallumbilla, Australia 26 33s 149 9E
92 Walmer, S. Africa 33 57s 25 35E
109 Walmsley, L., Canada 63 25N 109 0w
12 Walney, Isle of, England 54 5s 3 15w
117 Walnut Ridge, U.S.A. 36 7N 90 58w
100 Walpeup, Australia 35 10s 142 2E
13 Walsall, England 52 36N 1 59w
117 Walsenburg, U.S.A. 37 42N 104 45w
98 Walsh, Australia 16 40s 144 0E
117 Walsh, U.S.A. 37 28N 102 15w
24 Walsrode, Germany 52 51N 9 37E
70 Waltair, India 17 44N 83 23E
115 Walterboro, U.S.A. 32 53N 80 40w
117 Walters, U.S.A. 34 25N 98 20w
24 Waltershausen, Ger. 50 53N 10 33E
106 Waltham, Canada 45 57N 76 57w
117 Waltham, U.S.A. 42 22N 71 12w
118 Waltman, U.S.A. 43 8N 107 15w
113 Walton, U.S.A. 42 12N 75 9w
7 Walvis Ridge, South 30 0s 3 0E
  Atlantic Ocean
92 Walvisbaai, S. Africa 23 0s 14 28E
90 Wamaza, Zaïre 4 12s 27 2E
90 Wamba, Zaïre 0 58N 37 19E
85 Wamba, Nigeria 8 58N 8 34E
90 Wamba, Zaïre 2 10N 27 57E
100 Wamberra, Australia 33 52s 142 21E
116 Wamego, U.S.A. 39 14N 96 22w
73 Wamena, Indonesia 3 58s 138 50E
67 Wampo, China 31 30N 86 38E
73 Wamsasi, Indonesia 3 27s 126 7E
76 Wan Ta Shan, China 46 20N 132 20E
68 Wana, Pakistan 32 20N 69 32E
101 Wanaka L., N.Z. 44 33s 169 7E
77 Wanan, China 26 5N 114 50E
73 Wanapiri, Indonesia 4 30s 135 50E
106 Wanapitei, Canada 46 30N 80 45w
106 Wanapitei L., Canada 46 45N 80 40w
99 Wanbi, S. Australia 34 46s 140 21E

MAP
76 Wanchuan, China 40 53N 114 32E
91 Wanderer, Rhodesia 19 36s 30 1E
70 Wandiwash, India 12 30N 79 30E
99 Wandoan, Australia 26 5s 149 55E
87 Wang Kai (Ghâbat el 9 3N 29 23E
  Arab), Sudan
71 Wang Saphung, Thailand 17 29N 101 33E
90 Wanga, Zaïre 2 58N 29 12E
73 Wangal, Indonesia 6 8s 134 9E
100 Wanganella, Australia 35 6s 144 49E
101 Wanganui, N.Z. 39 35s 175 3E
100 Wangaratta, Australia 36 21s 146 7E
76 Wangching, China 43 15N 129 37E
24 Wangerooge I., Ger. 53 47N 7 52E
90 Wangi, Kenya 1 58s 40 58E
73 Wangiwangi, I., 5 22s 123 37E
  Indonesia
77 Wangkiang, China 30 6N 116 59E
77 Wanhsien, Szechwan, 30 50N 108 30E
  China
76 Wanhsien, Kansu, China 36 45N 107 24E
68 Wankaner, India 22 42N 71 0E
92 Wankie Nat. Park, 19 0s 26 30E
  Rhodesia
91 Wankie, Rhod. 18 18s 26 30E
91 Wankie ♦, Rhod. 18 18s 26 30E
109 Wanless, Canada 54 11N 101 21w
77 Wanning, China 18 45N 110 28E
100 Wannon, R., Australia 37 40s 141 53E
77 Wantsai, China 28 5N 114 22E
77 Wanyüan, China 32 4N 108 5E
83 Wanzarik, Libya 27 3N 13 30E
114 Wapakoneta, U.S.A. 40 35N 84 10w
118 Wapato, U.S.A. 46 30N 120 25w
106 Wapikopa L., Canada 42 50N 88 10w
106 Wapiti, R., Canada 55 5N 119 0w
113 Wappingers Fs., U.S.A. 41 35N 73 56w
116 Wapsipinicon, R., U.S.A. 42 10N 91 30w
63 Warandab, Ethiopia 7 20N 44 2E
100 Waranga Res., Austral. 36 38s 145 4E
70 Warangal, India 17 58N 79 45E
99 Waratah, Austral. 41 30s 145 30E
100 Waratah B., Australia 38 45s 146 8E
24 Warburg, Germany 51 29N 9 10E
100 Warburton, Australia 37 41s 145 42E
101 Warburton, R., Austral. 27 30s 138 30E
101 Ward, New Zealand 41 49s 174 11E
108 Ward Cove, Alas. 55 25N 132 10w
93 Warden, S. Afr. 27 50s 29 0E
68 Wardha, India 20 45N 78 39E
108 Wardlow, Canada 50 56N 111 31w
99 Wardoan, Australia 25 59s 149 59E
108 Ware, Canada 57 26N 125 41w
113 Ware, U.S.A. 42 16N 72 15w
113 Wareham, U.S.A. 41 45N 70 44w
24 Waren, Germany 53 30N 12 41E
99 Warialda, Australia 29 29s 150 33E
73 Warkopi, Indonesia 1 12s 134 9E
101 Warkworth, Eng. 55 22N 1 38w
13 Warley, Eng. 52 30N 2 0w
118 Warm Springs, Mont., 46 11N 112 56w
  U.S.A.
119 Warm Springs, Nev., 38 16N 116 32w
  U.S.A.
109 Warman, Canada 52 19N 106 30w
92 Warmbad, S.W. Africa 28 25s 18 42E
92 Warmbad, S.W. Afr. 19 14s 13 51E
92 Warmbad, S. Africa 24 51s 28 19E
19 Warmeriville, France 49 20N 4 13E
100 Warnambool, Australia 38 12s 142 31E
98 Warnambool Downs, 24 30s 142 45E
  Australia
100 Warncoort, Australia 38 30s 143 45E
24 Warnemünde, Germany 54 9N 12 5E
118 Warner Range, Mts., 41 30s 120 20w
  U.S.A.
115 Warner Robins, U.S.A. 32 41N 83 36w
24 Warnow, R., Germany 54 9N 12 1E
70 Warora, India 20 14N 79 1E
100 Warracknabeal, Austral. 36 9s 142 26E
100 Warragul, Australia 38 1s 145 57E
87 Warrayelu, Ethiopia 10 40N 39 28E
98 Warrego R., Australia 25 15s 146 0E
99 Warrego, R., Australia 26 30s 146 0E
100 Warren, Austral. 31 42s 147 51E
117 Warren, Ark., U.S.A. 33 35N 92 3w
112 Warren, Ohio, U.S.A. 41 18N 80 52w
112 Warren, Pa., U.S.A. 41 52N 79 10w
113 Warren, R.I., U.S.A. 41 43N 71 19w
15 Warrenpoint, Northern 54 7N 6 15w
  Ireland
109 Warrens Landing, Can. 53 40N 98 0w
116 Warrensburg, U.S.A. 38 45N 93 45w
92 Warrenton, S. Africa 28 9s 24 47E
118 Warrenton, U.S.A. 46 11N 123 59w
99 Warrenville, Australia 25 48s 147 22E
85 Warri, Nigeria 5 30N 5 41E
96 Warrina, Australia 28 12s 135 50E
12 Warrington, Eng. 53 25N 2 38w
115 Warrington, U.S.A. 30 22N 87 16w
116 Warroad, U.S.A. 49 0N 95 20w
28 Warsaw = Warszawa, 52 13N 21 0E
  Poland
114 Warsaw, Ind., U.S.A. 41 14N 85 50w
113 Warsaw, N.Y., U.S.A. 42 46N 78 10w
112 Warsaw, Ohio, U.S.A. 40 20N 82 0w
28 Warszawa, Poland 52 13N 21 0E
28 Warszawa ♦, Poland 52 35N 21 0E
24 Warstein, Germany 51 26N 8 20E
28 Warta, Poland 51 43N 18 38E
28 Warta, R., Poland 52 40N 16 10E
73 Waru, Indonesia 3 30s 130 36E
68 Warud, India 21 30N 78 16E
99 Warwick, Australia 28 10s 152 1E
13 Warwick, Eng. 52 17N 1 36w
13 Warwick ♦, Eng. 52 20N 1 30w
108 Wasa, Canada 49 45N 115 50w
112 Wasaga Beach, Canada 44 31N 80 0w

MAP
118 Wasatch, Mt., Ra., 40 30N 111 15w
93 Wasbank, S. Afr. 28 15s 30 9E
119 Wasco, Calif., U.S.A. 35 37N 119 16w
118 Wasco, Oreg., U.S.A. 45 45N 120 46w
116 Waseca, U.S.A. 44 3N 93 31w
112 Washago, Canada 44 46N 79 21w
116 Washburn, N.D., U.S.A. 47 23N 101 0w
116 Washburn, Wis., U.S.A. 46 38N 90 55w
114 Washington, D.C., 38 52N 77 0w
  U.S.A.
115 Washington, Ga., U.S.A. 33 45N 82 45w
116 Washington, Ind., U.S.A. 38 40N 87 8w
116 Washington, Iowa, 41 20N 91 45w
  U.S.A.
116 Washington, Miss., 38 35N 91 20w
  U.S.A.
115 Washington, N.C., 35 35N 77 1w
  U.S.A.
113 Washington, N.J., U.S.A. 40 45N 74 59w
114 Washington, Ohio, 39 34N 83 26w
  U.S.A.
112 Washington, Pa., U.S.A. 40 10N 80 20w
119 Washington, Utah, 37 10N 113 30w
  U.S.A.
118 Washington ♦, U.S.A. 47 45N 120 30w
114 Washington Court 39 34N 83 26w
  House, U.S.A.
95 Washington I., Pac. Oc. 4 43N 160 25w
87 Washington I., U.S.A. 45 24N 86 54w
113 Washington Mt., U.S.A. 44 15N 71 18w
73 Wasian, Indonesia 1 47s 133 19E
28 Wasilków, Poland 53 12N 23 13E
73 Wasior, Indonesia 2 43s 134 30E
109 Waskaiowaka, L., Can. 56 35N 96 40w
86 Wasm, Saudi Arabia 18 2N 41 32E
82 Wassenaar, Netherlands 52 8N 4 24E
25 Wasserburg, Germany 48 4N 12 15E
19 Wassy, France 48 30N 4 58E
106 Waswanipi L., Canada 49 35N 76 40w
73 Watampone, Indonesia 4 29s 120 25E
73 Watawaha, P., Indon. 6 30s 122 20E
113 Water Valley, U.S.A. 34 9N 89 38w
93 Waterberg, S. Africa 24 14s 28 0E
92 Waterberg, S.W. Africa 20 30s 17 18E
92 Waterberg, mt., S.W. 20 26s 17 13E
  Afr.
113 Waterbury, Conn., 41 32N 73 0w
  U.S.A.
113 Waterbury, Vt., U.S.A. 44 22N 72 44w
109 Waterbury, L., Canada 58 16N 105 0w
112 Waterdown, Canada 43 21N 79 53w
92 Waterford, S. Afr. 33 6s 25 0E
15 Waterford ♦, Ireland 51 10N 7 40w
15 Waterford Harb., Ire. 52 10N 6 58w
109 Waterhen L., Canada 52 10N 99 40w
16 Waterloo, Belgium 50 43N 4 25E
113 Waterloo, Que., Canada 45 22N 72 32w
106 Waterloo, Ont., Canada 43 30N 80 32w
84 Waterloo, Sierra Leone 8 26N 13 8w
116 Waterloo, Ill., U.S.A. 38 22N 90 6w
116 Waterloo, Iowa, U.S.A. 42 27N 92 20w
112 Waterloo, N.Y., U.S.A. 42 54N 76 53w
112 Waterpoint, U.S.A. 43 19N 78 15w
116 Watermeet, U.S.A. 46 15N 89 12w
113 Watertown, Conn., 41 36N 73 7w
  U.S.A.
113 Watertown, N.Y., U.S.A. 43 58N 75 57w
116 Watertown, S.D., U.S.A. 44 57N 97 5w
116 Watertown, Wis., U.S.A. 43 15N 88 45w
93 Waterval-Boven, Africa 25 40s 30 18E
113 Waterville, Canada 45 17N 71 53w
112 Waterville, Me., U.S.A. 44 35N 69 40w
113 Waterville, N.Y., U.S.A. 42 56N 75 23w
113 Waterville, Pa., U.S.A. 41 19N 77 21w
118 Waterville, Wash., USA 47 45N 120 1w
113 Watervliet, U.S.A. 42 46N 73 43w
73 Wates, Indonesia 7 53s 110 6E
112 Watford, Canada 42 58N 81 52w
13 Watford, England 51 38N 0 23w
116 Watford City, U.S.A. 47 50N 103 23w
113 Watkins Glen, U.S.A. 42 25N 76 55w
110 Watonga, U.S.A. 35 51N 98 24w
109 Watrous, Canada 51 40N 105 25w
116 Watrous, U.S.A. 35 50N 104 55w
90 Watsa, Zaïre 3 4N 29 30E
114 Watseka, U.S.A. 40 45N 87 45w
96 Watson, Australia 30 19s 131 41E
109 Watson, Canada 52 10N 104 30w
104 Watson Lake, Canada 60 12N 129 0w
119 Watsonville, U.S.A. 37 58N 121 49w
100 Wattle Hill, Australia 38 42s 143 1E
25 Wattwil, Switzerland 47 18N 9 6E
73 Watubela, Kepulauan, 4 28s 131 54E
  Indonesia
98 Wau, New Guinea 7 25s 146 42E
112 Waubamik, Canada 45 29N 80 3w
100 Waubay, U.S.A. 45 42N 97 17w
100 Waubra, Australia 37 21s 143 39E
115 Wauchula, U.S.A. 27 35N 81 50w
109 Waugh, Canada 49 40N 95 20w
114 Waukegan, U.S.A. 42 22N 87 54w
116 Waukon, U.S.A. 43 16N 91 8w
116 Waukon, U.S.A. 43 14N 91 33w
116 Wauneta, U.S.A. 40 27N 101 25w
116 Waupaca, U.S.A. 44 22N 89 8w
116 Waupun, U.S.A. 43 38N 88 44w
117 Waurika, U.S.A. 34 12N 98 0w
116 Wausau, U.S.A. 44 57N 89 40w
116 Wautoma, U.S.A. 44 5N 89 20w
114 Wauwatosa, U.S.A. 43 6N 87 59w
13 Waveney, R., Eng. 52 24N 1 20E
101 Waverley, N.Z. 39 46s 174 37E
116 Waverly, Iowa, U.S.A. 42 40N 92 30w
113 Waverly, N.Y., U.S.A. 42 0N 76 33w
16 Wavre, Belgium 50 43N 4 38E
87 Wâw, Sudan 7 45N 28 1E

MAP
83 Waw an Namus, Libya 24 24N 18 11E
85 Wawa, Nigeria 9 54N 4 27E
86 Wawa, Sudan 20 30N 30 22E
109 Wawanesa, Canada 49 30N 99 40w
117 Waxahachie, U.S.A. 32 22N 96 53w
90 Way Way, Australia 33 30s 151 18E
99 Wayatinah, Australia 42 15s 146 15E
115 Waycross, U.S.A. 31 12N 82 25w
116 Wayne, Mich., U.S.A. 42 16N 97 0w
114 Wayne, W. Va., U.S.A. 38 15N 82 27w
115 Waynesboro, Miss., 31 40N 88 39w
  U.S.A.
114 Waynesboro, Pa., U.S.A. 39 46N 77 32w
114 Waynesboro, Va., U.S.A. 38 4N 78 57w
114 Waynesburg, U.S.A. 39 54N 80 12w
114 Waynoka, U.S.A. 36 38N 98 53w
83 Wäzin, Libya 31 58N 10 51E
65 Wazirabad, Afghanistan 36 44N 66 47E
68 Wazirabad, Pakistan 32 30N 74 8E
72 Wé, Indonesia 6 3N 95 56E
13 Weald, The, Eng. 51 7N 0 9E
114 Wear, R., Eng. 54 55N 1 58w
117 Weatherford, Okla., 35 30N 98 45w
  U.S.A.
117 Weatherford, Tex., 32 45N 97 48w
  U.S.A.
117 Webb City, U.S.A. 37 9N 94 30w
87 Webera, Bale, Ethiopia 6 29N 40 33E
87 Webera, Shewa, Ethiopia 9 40N 39 0E
113 Webster, Mass., U.S.A. 42 4N 71 54w
116 Webster, N.Y., U.S.A. 43 11N 77 27w
116 Webster, S.D., U.S.A. 45 24N 97 33w
116 Webster, Wis., U.S.A. 45 53N 92 25w
116 Webster City, U.S.A. 42 30N 93 50w
116 Webster Green, U.S.A. 38 38N 90 20w
116 Webster Springs, U.S.A. 38 30N 80 25w
28 Wecliniec, Poland 51 18N 15 10E
73 Weda, Indonesia 0 30N 127 50E
73 Weda, Teluk, Indonesia 0 30N 127 50E
91 Wedza, Rhodesia 18 40s 31 33E
100 Wedderburn, Australia 36 20s 143 33E
100 Wedge I., Australia 30 50s 115 11E
24 Wedel, Germany 53 35N 9 41E
100 Wee Elwah, Australia 32 56s 145 20E
99 Wee Waa, Australia 30 11s 149 26E
113 Weedsport, U.S.A. 43 3N 76 35w
112 Weedville, U.S.A. 41 17N 78 28w
93 Weenen, S. Afr. 28 48s 30 7E
24 Weener, Germany 53 10N 7 23E
16 Weert, Netherlands 51 15N 5 43E
27 Wegierska-Gorka, Poland 49 36N 19 7E
28 Wegorzewo, Poland 54 13N 21 43E
28 Wegrów, Poland 52 24N 22 0E
77 Wei Ho, China 35 45N 114 30E
76 Weichow Tao, China 21 0N 109 1E
24 Weida, Ger. 50 47N 12 3E
25 Weiden, Germany 49 40N 12 10E
25 Weifang, China 36 47N 119 10E
76 Weihai, China 37 30N 122 10E
24 Weilburg, Germany 50 28N 8 17E
24 Weilheim, Germany 47 50N 11 9E
25 Weimar, Germany 51 0N 11 20E
27 Weiner Neustadt, Aust. 47 50N 16 15E
25 Weingarten, Germany 47 49N 9 39E
25 Weinheim, Germany 49 33N 8 40E
25 Weipa, Austral. 12 24s 142 0E
109 Weir River, Canada 56 54N 94 10w
112 Weirton, U.S.A. 40 22N 80 35w
118 Weiser, U.S.A. 44 10N 117 0w
67 Wei-si, China 27 18N 99 8E
25 Weissenfels, Germany 51 11N 11 58E
24 Weisswasser, Germany 51 30N 14 36E
27 Weitra, Austria 48 41N 14 54E
76 Weiyüan, China 35 10N 104 10E
27 Weiz, Austria 47 13N 15 39E
28 Wejherowo, Poland 54 35N 18 12E
109 Wekusko, Canada 54 40N 99 45w
109 Wekusko L., Canada 54 40N 99 45w
109 Welby, Canada 50 33N 101 29w
114 Welch, U.S.A. 37 29N 81 36w
98 Welcome, Australia 15 20s 144 40E
87 Welega ♦, Ethiopia 9 25N 34 20E
87 Welkite, Ethiopia 8 15N 37 42E
92 Welkom, S. Afr. 28 0s 26 50E
106 Welland, Canada 43 0N 79 10w
12 Welland, R., Eng. 52 43N 0 10w
100 Wellesley Is., Australia 17 20s 139 30E
16 Wellin, Belgium 50 5N 5 6E
13 Wellingborough, England 52 18N 0 41w
100 Wellington, N.S.W., 32 30s 149 0E
  Austral.
106 Wellington, Canada 43 57N 77 20w
12 Wellington (Telford), 52 42N 2 31w
  England
101 Wellington, N.Z. 41 19s 174 46E
116 Wellington, Col., U.S.A. 40 43N 105 0w
117 Wellington, Kans., 37 15N 97 25w
  U.S.A.
118 Wellington, Nev., U.S.A. 38 47N 119 28w
112 Wellington, Ohio, U.S.A. 41 9N 82 12w
117 Wellington, Okla., 34 55N 100 13w
  U.S.A.
101 Wellington, dist., N.Z. 40 8s 175 36E
11 Wellington, I., Chile 49 30s 75 0w
100 Wellington, I., Austral. 38 5s 147 22E
13 Wells, Somerset, Eng. 51 12N 2 39w
113 Wells, Me., U.S.A. 43 18N 70 35w
116 Wells, Minn., U.S.A. 43 44N 93 45w
118 Wells, Nev., U.S.A. 41 8N 115 0w
108 Wells Gray Prov. Park,
  Canada

MAP
96 Wells L., Australia 26 44s 123 15E
113 Wells River, U.S.A. 44 9N 72 4w
112 Wellsboro, U.S.A. 41 46N 77 20w
112 Wellsburg, U.S.A. 40 15N 80 36w
117 Wellsville, Mo., U.S.A. 39 4N 91 30w
112 Wellsville, N.Y., U.S.A. 42 9N 77 53w
112 Wellsville, Ohio, U.S.A. 40 36N 80 40w
118 Wellsville, Utah, U.S.A. 41 35N 111 59w
119 Wellton, U.S.A. 32 46N 114 6w
87 Welmel, W., Ethiopia 6 0N 40 20E
87 Welo ♦, Ethiopia 11 50N 39 48E
26 Wels, Austria 48 9N 14 1E
100 Welshpool, Australia 38 42s 146 26E
13 Welshpool, Wales 52 40N 3 9w
92 Welwitschia, S.W. Afr. 20 16s 14 59E
109 Welwyn, Canada 50 20N 101 30w
12 Wem, England 52 52N 2 45w
90 Wembere, R., Tanzania 4 45s 34 0E
77 Wenchi, China 7 46N 2 8w
77 Wenchow, China 28 0N 120 35E
118 Wendell, U.S.A. 42 50N 114 51w
73 Wendesi, Indonesia 2 30s 134 10E
87 Wendo, Ethiopia 6 40N 38 27E
118 Wendover, U.S.A. 40 49N 114 1w
90 Wenge, Zaïre 0 3N 24 0E
76 Wengtsung, China 37 15N 122 10E
98 Wenlock, R., Australia 12 15s 142 0E
75 Wensu, China 41 6N 80 3E
76 Wenteng, China 37 10N 122 0E
100 Wentworth, Australia 34 2s 141 54E
73 Wenut, Indonesia 3 11s 133 19E
118 Weott, U.S.A. 40 19N 123 56w
92 Wepener, S. Afr. 29 42s 27 3E
24 Werdau, Germany 50 45N 12 20E
92 Werda, Botswana 25 24s 23 15E
63 Werder, Ethiopia 6 58N 45 1E
24 Werder, Germany 52 23N 12 56E
24 Werdohl, Germany 51 15N 7 47E
73 Weri, Indonesia 3 10s 132 30E
24 Werne, Germany 51 38N 7 38E
24 Wernigerode, Germany 51 49N 0 45E
100 Werribee, Austral. 37 54s 144 40E
100 Werrimull, Austral. 34 22s 143 30E
99 Werris Creek, Australia 31 18s 150 38E
73 Wersar, Indonesia 1 30s 131 55E
25 Wertheim, Germany 49 44N 9 32E
24 Wesel, Germany 51 39N 6 34E
24 Weser, R., Germany 53 33N 8 30E
24 Wesselburen, Germany 54 11N 8 53E
24 Wesselburen, Germany 54 11N 8 53E
116 Wessington, U.S.A. 44 30N 98 40w
116 Wessington Springs, 44 10N 98 35w
  U.S.A.
117 West, U.S.A. 31 50N 97 5w
108 West B., Canada 45 53N 82 8w
117 West, B., U.S.A. 29 5N 89 27w
114 West Bend, U.S.A. 43 25N 88 10w
69 West Bengal ♦, India 25 0N 90 0E
114 West Branch, U.S.A. 44 16N 84 13w
13 West Bromwich, 52 32N 2 1w
  England
113 West Chazy, U.S.A. 44 49N 73 28w
113 West Chester, U.S.A. 39 58N 75 36w
117 West Columbia, U.S.A. 29 10N 95 38w
116 West Des Moines, 41 30N 93 45w
  U.S.A.
128 West Falkland Island, 51 30s 60 0w
  Falkland Islands
116 West Frankfort, U.S.A. 37 56N 89 0w
95 West Harbour, N.Z. 45 51s 170 33E
113 West Hartford, U.S.A. 45 72N 72 45w
113 West Haven, U.S.A. 41 18N 72 57w
117 West Helena, U.S.A. 34 30N 90 40w
116 West Indies, Atlantic 15 0N 70 0w
  Ocean
90 West Lake ♦, Tanzania 2 5s 31 20E
14 West Lothian ♦, Scot. 55 55N 3 35w
112 West Lorne, Canada 42 37N 81 41w
91 West Lunga, R., Zam. 13 35s 24 45E
94 West Malling, Eng. 51 16N 0 25E
117 West Memphis, U.S.A. 35 5N 90 3w
‡ 90 West Mengo ♦, Uganda 0 15N 32 15E
117 West Monroe, U.S.A. 32 32N 92 7w
114 West Newton, U.S.A. 40 14N 79 46w
91 West Nicholson, Rhod. 21 2s 29 20E
66 West Pakistan ■, Asia 27 0N 67 0w
115 West Palm Beach, 26 44N 80 3w
  U.S.A.
113 West Paris, U.S.A. 44 18N 70 30w
117 West Pittston, U.S.A. 19 11N 75 49w
114 West Plains, U.S.A. 36 45N 91 50w
107 West Point, Canada 49 55N 64 30w
121 West Point, Jamaica 18 14N 78 30w
115 West Point, Ga., U.S.A. 32 54N 85 10w
116 West Point, Miss., 33 36N 88 38w
  U.S.A.
116 West Point, Nebr., 41 50N 96 43w
  U.S.A.
114 West Point, Va., U.S.A. 37 35N 76 47w
90 West Pokot ♦, Kenya 1 30N 35 40E
* 12 West Riding ♦, England 53 50N 1 30w
16 West Schelde = 51 25N 4 0E
  Westerschelde, Neth.
16 West Schelde = 51 25N 3 50E
  Westerschelde, Neth.
4 West Spitsbergen, 78 40N 17 0E
  Spitsbergen
16 West-Terschelling, Neth. 53 22N 5 13E
114 West Virginia ♦, U.S.A. 39 0N 81 0w
100 West Wyalong, Austral. 33 56s 147 10E
118 West Yellowstone, 44 47N 111 4w
  U.S.A.
108 Westbank, Canada 49 50N 119 25w
113 Westbrook, Maine, 43 40N 70 22w
  U.S.A.

* Incorporated within the counties of North, West and South Yorkshire
† Incorporated within the region of Lothian
‡ Incorporated within the new N. Buganda Province

Westbrook INDEX **Wrightson, Mt.**

MAP
117 Westbrook, Tex., U.S.A. 32 25N 101 0W
99 Westbury, Australia 41 30S 146 51E
100 Westby, Australia 35 30S 147 24E
116 Westby, U.S.A. 48 52N 104 3W
24 Westerland, Germany 54 51N 8 20E
96 Western Australia ♦, Australia 25 0S 118 0E
107 Western Bay, Canada 46 50N 52 30W
24 Western Germany ■, Europe 50 0N 8 0E
70 Western Ghatis, mts., India 15 30N 74 30E
90 Western ♦, Kenya 0 30N 34 30E
91 Western ♦, Zambia 13 15N 27 30E
101 Western Samoa ■, Pacific Ocean 14 0S 172 0W
114 Westernport, U.S.A. 30 30N 79 5W
16 Westerschelde, R., Neth. 51 25N 4 0E
24 Westerstede, Germany 51 15N 7 55E
24 Westerwald, mts., Ger. 50 39N 8 0E
113 Westfield, Mass., U.S.A. 42 9N 72 49W
112 Westfield, N.Y., U.S.A. 42 20N 79 38W
112 Westfield, Pa., U.S.A. 41 54N 77 32W
116 Westhope, U.S.A. 48 55N 101 0W
101 Westland ♦, N.Z. 43 33S 169 59E
101 Westland Bight, N.Z. 42 55S 170 5E
108 Westlock, Canada 54 20N 113 55W
15 Westmeath, co., Ire. 53 30N 7 30W
114 Westminster, U.S.A. 39 34S 77 1W
•12 Westmorland ♦, Eng. 54 28N 2 40W
72 Weston, Malaysia 5 10N 115 35E
118 Weston, Oreg., U.S.A. 45 50N 118 30W
114 Weston, W. Va., U.S.A. 39 3N 80 29W
106 Weston I., Canada 52 30N 79 50W
13 Weston-super-Mare, England 51 20N 2 59W
113 Westport, Canada 44 38N 76 28W
15 Westport, Ireland 53 44N 9 31W
101 Westport, N.Z. 41 46S 171 37E
118 Westport, U.S.A. 46 48N 124 4W
14 Westray I., Scot. 59 18N 3 0W
106 Westree, Canada 47 26N 81 34W
108 Westview, Canada 49 50N 124 31W
114 Westville, Ill., U.S.A. 40 3N 87 36W
117 Westville, Okla., U.S.A. 36 0N 94 33W
118 Westwood, U.S.A. 40 26N 121 0W
73 Wetar, I., Indonesia 7 30S 126 30E
108 Wetaskiwin, Canada 52 55N 113 24W
16 Wetteren, Belgium 51 0N 3 53E
100 Wetupoa, Australia 35 16S 143 46E
24 Wetzlar, Germany 50 33N 8 30E
98 Wewak, N. Guinea 3 29S 143 28E
117 Wewaka, U.S.A. 35 10N 96 35W
15 Wexford, Ireland 52 20N 6 28W
15 Wexford Harb., Ireland 52 20N 6 25W
109 Weyburn, Canada 49 40N 103 50W
26 Weyer, Austria 47 51N 14 40E
106 Weymont, Canada 47 50N 73 50W
107 Weymouth, Canada 44 30N 66 1W
13 Weymouth, Eng. 50 36N 2 28W
113 Weymouth, U.S.A. 42 13N 70 53W
98 Weymouth, C., Australia 12 37S 143 27E
101 Whakatane, N.Z. 37 57S 177 1E
105 Whale, R., Canada 57 40N 67 0W
104 Whale Cove, Canada 62 10N 93 0W
5 Whales, B. of Antarc. 78 0S 165 0W
14 Whalsay I., Scot. 60 22N 1 0W
77 Whampoa, China 23 5N 113 20E
101 Whangamomona, N.Z. 39 8S 174 44E
101 Whangarei, N.Z. 35 43S 174 21E
101 Whangarei Harbour, N.Z. 35 45S 174 28E
101 Whangaroa Harbour, N.Z. 35 4S 173 46E
12 Wharfe, R., Eng. 53 55N 1 30W
113 Wharton, N.J., U.S.A. 40 53N 74 36W
112 Wharton, Pa., U.S.A. 41 31N 78 1W
117 Wharton, Tex., U.S.A. 29 20N 96 6W
99 Whayjonta, Australia 29 40S 142 35E
116 Wheatland, U.S.A. 42 4N 105 58W
112 Wheatley, Canada 42 7N 82 29W
116 Wheaton, U.S.A. 45 50N 96 29W
118 Wheeler, Oreg., U.S.A. 45 45N 123 57W
117 Wheeler, Tex., U.S.A. 35 29N 100 15W
118 Wheeler Peak, Mt., U.S.A. 38 57N 114 15W
112 Wheeling, U.S.A. 40 2N 80 41W
12 Whernside, Mt., England 54 14N 2 24W
96 Whidbey Is., S. Austral. 34 30S 135 3E
108 Whiskey Gap, Canada 49 0N 113 3W
109 Whiskey Jack, L., Canada 58 25N 101 55W
115 Whistler, U.S.A. 30 50N 88 10W
112 Whitby, Canada 43 50N 78 50W
12 Whitby, England 54 29N 0 37W
95 Whitcombe, Mt., New Zealand 43 12S 171 0E
95 Whitcombe, P., New Zealand 43 12S 171 0E
107 White B., Canada 50 0N 56 35W
101 White I., N.Z. 37 30S 177 13E
113 White L., Canada 45 17N 76 35W
117 White L., U.S.A. 29 45N 92 30W
119 White Mts., Calif., U.S.A. 37 30N 118 6W
113 White, Mts., N.H., U.S.A. 44 15N 71 15W
117 White, R., Ark., U.S.A. 36 28N 93 55W
118 White, R., Colo., U.S.A. 40 8N 108 52W
114 White, R., Ind., U.S.A. 39 25N 86 30W
116 White, R., S.D., U.S.A. 43 10N 102 52W
107 White Bear Res., Canada 48 10N 57 05W
118 White Bird, U.S.A. 45 46N 116 21W
118 White Butte, U.S.A. 46 23N 103 25W
114 White City, U.S.A. 38 50N 96 45W
99 White Cliffs, Australia 30 50S 143 10E
101 White Cliffs, N.Z. 43 26S 171 55E
117 White Deer, U.S.A. 35 30N 101 8W
116 White Hall, U.S.A. 39 25N 90 27W

MAP
113 White Haven, U.S.A. 41 3N 75 47W
13 Whitehorse, Vale of, Eng. 51 37N 1 30W
87 White Nile = Nîl el Abyad, Bahr, Sudan 9 30N 31 40E
87 White Nile Dam, Sudan 15 24N 32 30E
106 White Otter L., Canada 49 5N 91 55W
104 White Pass, Canada 59 40N 135 3W
84 White Plains, Liberia 6 28N 10 40W
113 White Plains, U.S.A. 41 2N 73 44W
106 White River, Canada 48 35N 85 20W
93 White River, S. Africa 25 20S 31 00E
116 White River, U.S.A. 43 48N 100 5W
113 White River Junc., U.S.A. 43 38N 72 20W
54 White Russia = Byelorussia, SSR, USSR 53 30N 27 0E
52 White Sea = Beloye More, U.S.S.R. 66 30N 38 0E
118 White Sulphur Springs, Mont., U.S.A. 46 35N 111 0W
118 White Sulphur Springs, W. Va., U.S.A. 37 50N 80 16W
85 White Volta, R., (Volta Blanche), Ghana 10 0N 1 0W
108 Whitecourt, Canada 54 10N 115 45W
117 Whiteface, U.S.A. 33 35N 102 40W
113 Whitefield, U.S.A. 44 23N 71 37W
118 Whitefish, U.S.A. 48 25N 114 22W
109 Whitefish L., Canada 62 35N 107 20W
114 Whitefish Pt., U.S.A. 46 45N 85 0W
107 Whitegull, L., Canada 55 30N 64 40W
114 Whitehall, Mich., U.S.A. 43 21N 86 20W
118 Whitehall, Mont., U.S.A. 45 52N 112 4W
113 Whitehall, N.Y., U.S.A. 43 32N 73 28W
116 Whitehall, Wis., U.S.A. 44 20N 91 19W
12 Whitehaven, Eng. 54 33N 3 35W
104 Whitehorse, Canada 60 45N 135 10W
13 Whitehorse, Vale of, Eng. 51 37N 1 30W
98 Whiteman Ra., Territory of New Guinea 5 54S 149 56E
109 Whitemouth, Canada 50 0N 96 10W
108 Whitesail, L., Canada 53 35N 127 45W
113 Whitesboro, N.Y., U.S.A. 43 8N 75 20W
117 Whitesboro, Tex., U.S.A. 33 40N 96 58W
116 Whitetail, U.S.A. 48 54N 105 15W
115 Whiteville, U.S.A. 34 20N 78 40W
114 Whitewater, U.S.A. 42 50N 88 45W
119 Whitewater Baldy, Mt., U.S.A. 33 20N 108 44W
106 Whitewater L., Canada 50 50N 89 10W
98 Whitewood, Australia 21 28S 143 30E
109 Whitewood, Canada 50 20N 102 20W
100 Whitfield, Austral. 36 42S 146 24E
14 Whithorn, Scot. 54 55N 4 25W
101 Whitianga, N.Z. 36 47S 175 41E
113 Whitman, U.S.A. 42 4N 70 55W
115 Whitmire, U.S.A. 34 33N 81 40W
112 Whitney, Canada 45 31N 78 14W
119 Whitney, Mt., U.S.A. 36 35N 118 14W
113 Whitney Pt., U.S.A. 42 19N 75 59W
13 Whitstable, Eng. 51 21N 1 2E
98 Whitsunday I., Austral. 20 15S 149 4E
104 Whittier, Alaska 60 46N 148 48W
107 Whittle, C., Canada 50 11N 60 8W
100 Whittlesea, Australia 37 27S 145 9E
100 Whitton, Australia 34 30S 146 6E
115 Whitwell, U.S.A. 35 15N 85 30W
109 Wholdaia L., Canada 60 40N 104 20W
99 Whyalla, S. Australia 33 2S 137 30E
112 Wiarton, Canada 44 50N 81 10W
84 Wiawso, Ghana 6 10N 2 25W
28 Wiazow, Poland 50 50N 17 10E
116 Wibaux, U.S.A. 47 0N 104 13W
117 Wichita, U.S.A. 37 40N 97 29W
117 Wichita Falls, U.S.A. 33 57N 98 30W
14 Wick, Scotland 58 26N 3 5W
119 Wickenburg, U.S.A. 33 58N 112 45W
117 Wickett, U.S.A. 31 37N 102 58W
112 Wickliffe, U.S.A. 41 46N 81 29W
15 Wicklow, Ireland 53 0N 6 2W
15 Wicklow ♦, Ireland 52 59N 6 25W
15 Wicklow Hd., Ireland 52 59N 6 3W
28 Widawa, Poland 51 27N 18 51E
98 Wide B., Territory of New Guinea 4 52S 152 0E
12 Widnes, England 53 22N 2 44W
24 Wiek, Germany 54 37N 13 17E
28 Wielbark, Poland 53 24N 20 55E
28 Wielén, Poland 52 53N 16 9E
27 Wieliczka, Poland 50 0N 20 5E
28 Wielun, Poland 51 15N 18 40E
27 Wien, Austria 48 12N 16 22E
27 Wiener Neustadt, Aust. 47 49N 16 16E
28 Wieprz, R., Koszalin, Poland 54 26N 16 35E
28 Wieprz, R., Lublin, Pol. 51 15N 22 50E
16 Wierden, Netherlands 52 22N 6 35E
28 Wieruszów, Poland 51 19N 18 9E
25 Wiesbaden, Germany 50 7N 8 17E
25 Wiesental, Germany 49 15N 8 30E
12 Wigan, England 53 33N 2 38W
116 Wiggins, Colo., U.S.A. 40 16N 104 3W
117 Wiggins, Miss., U.S.A. 30 53N 89 9W
•13 Wight, I. of, Eng. 50 40N 1 20W
14 Wigtown, Scot. 54 52N 4 27W
†14 Wigtown ♦, Scot. 54 53N 4 45W
14 Wigtown B., Scot. 54 46N 4 15W
25 Wil, Switzerland 47 28N 9 3E
27 Wilamowice, Poland 49 55N 19 9E
116 Wilber, U.S.A. 40 34N 96 59W
112 Wilberforce, Canada 45 0N 78 15W
117 Wilburton, U.S.A. 34 55N 95 15W
100 Wilcannia, Australia 31 30S 143 26E
112 Wilcox, U.S.A. 41 34N 78 43W
25 Wildbad, Germany 48 44N 8 32E
24 Wildeshausen, Germany 52 54N 8 25E
26 Wildon, Austria 46 52N 15 31E

MAP
116 Wildrose, U.S.A. 48 36N 103 17W
26 Wildspitze, Austria 46 53N 10 53E
114 Wildwood, U.S.A. 39 5N 74 46W
98 Wilhelm Mt., North East New Guinea 5 57S 145 0E
24 Wilhelm-Pieck-Stadt Guben, Ger. 51 59N 14 48E
5 Wilhelm II Coast, Antarctica 67 0S 90 0E
127 Wilhelmina, Mt., Surinam 3 50N 56 30W
26 Wilhelmsburg, Austria 48 6N 15 36E
24 Wilhelmsburg, Germany 53 28N 10 1E
24 Wilhelmshaven, Ger. 53 30N 8 9E
92 Wilhelmstal, S.W. Afr. 21 58S 16 21E
5 Wilkes Land, Antarc 69 0S 120 0E
113 Wilkes-Barre, U.S.A. 41 15N 75 52W
115 Wilkesboro, U.S.A. 36 10N 81 9W
109 Wilkie, Canada 52 27N 108 42W
112 Wilkinsburg, U.S.A. 40 26N 79 50W
118 Willamina, U.S.A. 45 9N 123 32W
118 Willapa, B., U.S.A. 46 44N 124 0W
119 Willard, N.M., U.S.A. 34 35N 106 1W
118 Willard, Utah, U.S.A. 41 28N 112 1W
98 Willaumez Pen., Territory of New Guinea 5 3S 150 3E
119 Willcox, U.S.A. 32 13N 109 53W
121 Willemstad, Curacao 12 5N 69 0W
100 William Mt., Australia 37 11S 142 33E
119 Williams, U.S.A. 35 16N 112 11W
108 Williams Lake, Canada 52 20N 122 10W
115 Williamsburg, Ky., U.S.A. 36 45N 84 10W
112 Williamsburg, Pa., U.S.A. 40 27N 78 14W
114 Williamsburg, Va., U.S.A. 37 17N 76 44W
112 Williamson, N.Y., U.S.A. 43 14N 77 15W
114 Williamson, W. Va., U.S.A. 37 46N 82 17W
112 Williamsport, U.S.A. 41 18N 77 1W
115 Williamston, U.S.A. 35 50N 77 5W
100 Williamstown, Austral. 37 46S 144 58E
113 Williamstown, Mass., U.S.A. 42 41N 73 12W
113 Williamstown, N.Y., U.S.A. 43 25N 75 54W
117 Williamsville, U.S.A. 37 0N 90 33W
113 Willimantic, U.S.A. 41 45N 72 12W
92 Williston, S. Africa 31 20S 20 53E
115 Williston, Fla, U.S.A. 29 25N 82 28W
116 Williston, N.D., U.S.A. 48 10N 103 35W
118 Willits, U.S.A. 39 28N 123 17W
116 Willmar, U.S.A. 45 5N 95 0W
112 Willoughby, U.S.A. 41 38N 81 26W
109 Willow Bunch, Canada 49 20N 105 35W
116 Willow Lake, U.S.A. 44 40N 97 40W
108 Willow River, Canada 54 6N 122 28W
117 Willow Springs, U.S.A. 37 0N 92 0W
100 Willow Tree, Australia 31 40S 150 45E
92 Willowmore, S. Africa 33 15S 23 30E
98 Willows, Australia 23 45S 147 25E
118 Willows, U.S.A. 39 30N 122 10W
117 Wills Pt., U.S.A. 32 42N 95 57W
99 Willunga, Australia 35 15S 138 30E
114 Wilmete, U.S.A. 42 6N 87 44W
114 Wilmington, Del., U.S.A. 39 45N 75 32W
114 Wilmington, Ill., U.S.A. 41 19N 88 10W
115 Wilmington, N.C., U.S.A. 34 14N 77 54W
114 Wilmington, Ohio, U.S.A. 39 29N 83 46W
118 Wilsall, U.S.A. 45 59N 110 4W
115 Wilson, U.S.A. 35 44N 77 54W
119 Wilson, Mt., U.S.A. 37 55N 105 3W
100 Wilson's Prom., Austral. 39 5S 146 28E
24 Wilster, Germany 53 55N 9 23E
116 Wilton, U.S.A. 47 12N 100 53W
13 Wiltshire ♦, Egn. 51 20N 2 0W
16 Wiltz, Luxembourg 49 57N 5 55E
96 Wiluna, Australia 26 40S 120 25E
19 Wimereux, France 50 45N 1 37E
100 Wimmera, Austral. 36 30S 142 0E
100 Wimmera, R., Australia 36 48S 142 50E
92 Winburg, S. Afr. 28 30S 27 2E
113 Winch, U.S.A. 42 26N 71 9W
100 Winchelsea, Australia 38 10S 144 1E
113 Winchendon, U.S.A. 42 40N 72 3W
13 Winchester, Eng. 51 4N 1 19W
113 Winchester, Conn., U.S.A. 41 53N 73 9W
118 Winchester, Idaho, U.S.A. 46 11N 116 32W
114 Winchester, Ind., U.S.A. 40 10N 84 56W
114 Winchester, Ky., U.S.A. 38 0N 84 8W
113 Winchester, N.H., U.S.A. 42 47N 72 22W
115 Winchester, Tenn., U.S.A. 35 11N 86 8W
114 Winchester, Va., U.S.A. 39 14N 78 8W
118 Wind, R., U.S.A. 43 30N 109 30W
118 Wind River Range, Mts., U.S.A. 43 0N 109 30W
112 Windber, U.S.A. 40 14N 78 50W
115 Winder, U.S.A. 34 0N 83 40W
99 Windera, Australia 26 17S 151 51E
12 Windermere, Eng. 54 24N 2 56W
108 Windfall, Canada 54 12N 116 25W
92 Windhoek, S.W. Africa 22 35S 17 4E
26 Windischgarsten, Aust. 47 42N 14 21E
116 Windom, U.S.A. 43 48N 95 3W
99 Windorah, Australia 25 24S 142 36E
119 Window Rock, U.S.A. 35 47N 109 4W
13 Windrush, R., Eng. 51 48N 1 35W
100 Windsor, Austral. 33 34S 150 44E
107 Windsor, N.S., Canada 44 59N 64 5W
106 Windsor, Ont., Canada 42 25N 83 0W
13 Windsor, England 51 28N 0 36W
116 Windsor, Col., U.S.A. 40 33N 104 55W

MAP
113 Windsor, Conn., U.S.A. 41 50N 72 40W
116 Windsor, Miss., U.S.A. 38 32N 93 31W
113 Windsor, N.Y., U.S.A. 42 5N 75 37W
113 Windsor, Vt., U.S.A. 43 30N 72 25W
92 Windsorton, S. Africa 28 16S 24 44E
121 Windward Is., W. Ind. 13 0N 63 0W
121 Windward Passage, Caribbean 20 0N 74 0W
109 Winefred L., Canada 55 30N 110 30W
87 Winejok, Sudan 9 1N 27 30E
117 Winfield, U.S.A. 37 15N 97 0W
100 Wingen Mt., Australia 31 50S 150 58E
100 Wingham, Australia 31 48S 152 22E
106 Wingham, Canada 43 55N 81 25W
118 Winifred, U.S.A. 47 30N 109 28W
106 Winisk, Canada 55 20N 85 15W
106 Winisk L., Canada 52 55N 87 40W
106 Winiski, R., Canada 54 40N 87 0W
117 Wink, U.S.A. 31 49N 103 9W
109 Winkler, Canada 49 15N 98 0W
26 Winklern, Austria 46 52N 12 52E
85 Winneba, Ghana 5 25N 0 36W
116 Winnebago, U.S.A. 43 43N 94 8W
114 Winnebago L., U.S.A. 44 0N 88 20W
118 Winnemucca, U.S.A. 41 0N 117 45W
118 Winnemucca, L., U.S.A. 40 25N 19 21W
116 Winner, U.S.A. 43 23N 99 52W
114 Winnetka, U.S.A. 42 8N 87 46W
118 Winnett, U.S.A. 47 2N 108 28W
117 Winnfield, U.S.A. 31 57N 92 38W
116 Winnibigoshish L., U.S.A. 47 25N 94 12W
109 Winnipeg, Canada 49 50N 97 15W
109 Winnipeg, L., Canada 52 30N 98 0W
109 Winnipeg, R., Canada 50 25N 95 30W
109 Winnipeg Beach, Can. 50 30N 96 58W
109 Winnipegosis, Canada 52 40N 100 0W
109 Winnipegosis L., Can. 52 40N 100 0W
117 Winnsboro, Lou, U.S.A. 32 10N 91 41W
115 Winnsboro, S.C., U.S.A. 34 23N 81 5W
116 Winnsboro, Tex., U.S.A. 32 56N 95 15W
107 Winokapau, L., Canada 53 15N 62 50W
117 Winona, Miss., U.S.A. 33 30N 89 42W
116 Winona, Wis., U.S.A. 44 2N 91 45W
113 Winooski, U.S.A. 44 31N 73 11W
16 Winschoten, Neth. 53 9N 7 3E
24 Winsen, Germany 52 40N 9 54E
24 Winsen, Ger. 53 21N 10 11E
119 Winslow, U.S.A. 35 2N 110 41W
113 Winstead, U.S.A. 41 55N 73 5W
115 Winston-Salem, U.S.A. 36 7N 80 15W
115 Winter Garden, U.S.A. 28 33N 81 35W
115 Winter Haven, U.S.A. 28 0N 81 42W
115 Winter Park, U.S.A. 28 34N 81 19W
24 Winterberg, Germany 51 12N 8 30E
117 Winters, U.S.A. 31 58N 99 58W
116 Winterset, U.S.A. 41 18N 94 0W
112 Wintersville, U.S.A. 40 23N 80 38W
16 Winterswijk, Neth. 51 58N 6 43E
25 Winterthur, Switzerland 47 30N 8 44E
116 Winthrop, U.S.A. 44 31N 94 25W
118 Winthrop, U.S.A. 48 27N 120 6W
98 Winton, Australia 22 21S 143 0E
101 Winton, New Zealand 46 8S 168 20E
115 Winton, N.C., U.S.A. 36 25N 76 58W
113 Winton, Pa., U.S.A. 41 27N 75 33W
12 Wirral, Eng. 53 25N 3 0W
12 Wisbech, England 52 39N 0 10E
116 Wisconsin ♦, U.S.A. 44 30N 90 0W
116 Wisconsin, R., U.S.A. 45 25N 89 45W
116 Wisconsin Dells, U.S.A. 43 38N 89 45W
116 Wisconsin Rapids, U.S.A. 44 25N 89 50W
14 Wishaw, Scot. 55 46N 3 55W
116 Wishek, U.S.A. 46 20N 99 35W
27 Wisła, Poland 49 38N 18 53E
28 Wisła, R., Poland 53 38N 18 47E
28 Wiślany, Zalew, Poland-U.S.S.R. 54 20N 19 50E
27 Wisłok, R., Poland 50 7N 22 25E
27 Wisłoka, R., Poland 49 50N 21 28E
24 Wismar, Germany 53 53N 11 23E
24 Wismar B., Germany 54 0N 11 15E
116 Wisner, U.S.A. 42 0N 96 46W
19 Wissant, France 50 52N 1 40E
19 Wissembourg, France 48 57N 7 57E
93 Witbank, S. Afr. 25 51S 29 14E
117 Witchita, U.S.A. 37 40N 97 22W
92 Witdraai, S. Africa 26 58S 20 48E
12 Witham, R., Eng. 53 3N 0 8W
12 Withernsea, Eng. 53 43N 0 2W
28 Witkowo, Poland 52 26N 17 45E
13 Witney, England 51 47N 1 29W
28 Witnica, Poland 52 41N 14 55E
92 Witnossob, R., S.W. Africa 23 0S 18 40E
24 Wittdün, Germany 54 38N 8 23E
24 Witten, Germany 51 26N 7 19E
24 Wittenberg, Germany 51 51N 12 39E
24 Wittenberge, Germany 53 0N 11 44E
24 Wittenburg, Germany 53 30N 11 4E
96 Wittenoom, Australia 22 15S 118 20E
24 Wittingen, Germany 52 43N 10 43E
25 Wittlich, Germany 50 0N 6 54E
24 Wittmund, Germany 53 39N 7 35E
24 Wittow, Germany 54 37N 13 21E
24 Wittstock, Germany 53 10N 12 30E
24 Witzenhausen, Ger. 51 20N 9 50E
87 Wiyeb, W. Ethiopia 7 15N 40 15E
28 Władysławowo, Poland 52 6N 18 28E
28 Wlen, Poland 51 0N 15 39E
73 Wlingi, Indonesia 8 5S 112 25E
28 Włocławek, Poland 52 40N 19 3E
28 Włodawa, Poland 51 33N 23 31E
28 Włoszczowa, Poland 50 50N 19 55E
113 Woburn, U.S.A. 42 31N 71 7W
100 Wodonga, Austral. 36 5S 146 50E
27 Wodzisław Sl., Poland 50 1N 18 26E
19 Woerth, France 48 57N 7 45E
19 Woevre, France 49 15N 5 45E

MAP
73 Wokam, I., Indonesia 5 45S 134 28E
108 Woking, Canada 55 35N 118 50W
28 Wolbrom, Poland 50 24N 19 45E
24 Woldegk, Germany 53 27N 13 35E
118 Wolf Creek, U.S.A. 47 1N 112 2W
116 Wolf Point, U.S.A. 48 6N 105 40W
113 Wolfe I., Canada 44 7N 76 27W
24 Wolfenbüttel, Germany 52 10N 10 33E
108 Wolfenden, Canada 52 0N 119 25W
98 Wolfram, Australia 17 6S 145 0E
26 Wolfsberg, Austria 46 50N 14 52E
24 Wolfsburg, Germany 52 27N 10 49E
24 Wolgast, Germany 54 3N 13 46E
25 Wolhusen, Switzerland 47 4N 8 4E
28 Wolin, Poland 53 40N 14 37E
128 Wollaston, Islas, Chile 55 40S 67 30W
109 Wollaston L., Canada 58 20N 103 30W
104 Wollaston Pen., Canada 69 30N 113 0W
100 Wollondilly, R., Austral. 34 0S 150 27E
100 Wollongong, Australia 34 25S 150 54E
92 Wolmaransstad, S. Afr. 27 12S 26 13E
24 Wolmirstedt, Germany 52 15N 11 35E
28 Wołomin, Poland 52 19N 21 15E
28 Wołow, Poland 51 20N 16 38E
99 Wolseley, Australia 36 14S 140 58E
109 Wolseley, Canada 50 25N 103 15W
92 Wolseley, S. Africa 33 26S 19 7E
4 Wolstenholme Sound, Greenland 74 30N 75 0W
28 Wolsztyn, Poland 52 8N 16 5E
13 Wolverhampton, England 52 35N 2 6W
87 Wombera, Ethiopia 10 45N 35 49E
100 Won Wron, Australia 38 23S 146 45E
99 Wondai, Australia 26 20S 151 49E
91 Wonder Gorge, Zam. 14 40S 29 0E
100 Wongalloroo L., Australia 31 35S 144 2E
76 Wŏnjui, South Korea 37 30N 127 59E
73 Wonosari, Indonesia 7 38S 110 36E
76 Wŏnsan, North Korea 39 11N 127 27E
100 Wonthaggi, Australia 38 29S 145 31E
109 Wood, Mt., Canada 49 13N 106 13W
108 Wood Buffalo Pk., Can. 59 30N 113 0W
116 Wood Lake, U.S.A. 42 38N 100 14W
112 Woodbridge, Canada 43 48N 79 35W
100 Woodend, Austral. 37 20S 144 33E
118 Woodland, U.S.A. 38 40N 121 50W
98 Woodlark I., Territory of Papua 9 1S 148 0E
108 Woodpecker, Canada 53 30N 122 40W
109 Woodridge, Canada 49 20N 96 20W
96 Woodroffe, Mt., Australia 26 20S 131 45E
119 Woodruff, Ariz., U.S.A. 34 51N 110 1W
118 Woodruff, Utah, U.S.A. 41 30N 111 4W
100 Woodside, Australia 38 28S 146 53E
96 Woods, L., Australia 17 50S 133 30E
107 Woods, L., Canada 54 30N 65 0W
109 Woods, Lake of the, Canada-U.S.A. 49 30N 94 30W
100 Woodside, Australia 38 28S 146 53E
98 Woodstock, Australia 19 22S 142 45E
107 Woodstock, N.B., Can. 46 11N 67 37W
106 Woodstock, Ont., Can. 43 10N 80 45W
13 Woodstock, Eng. 51 51N 1 20W
116 Woodstock, Ill., U.S.A. 42 17N 88 30W
65 Woodstock, N.H., U.S.A. 43 59N 71 41W
113 Woodstock, Vt., U.S.A. 43 37N 72 31W
113 Woodsville, U.S.A. 44 10N 72 0W
101 Woodville, N.Z. 40 20S 175 53E
117 Woodville, U.S.A. 30 45N 94 25W
117 Woodward, U.S.A. 36 24N 99 28W
100 Woolamai, C., Austral. 38 30S 145 23E
100 Woomargama, Austral. 35 45S 147 15E
99 Woombye, Australia 26 40S 152 55E
100 Woomelang, Australia 35 37S 142 40E
99 Woomera, Australia 31 9S 136 56E
100 Woonona, Australia 34 32S 150 49E
113 Woonsocker, U.S.A. 42 0N 71 30W
116 Woonsockett, U.S.A. 44 5N 98 15W
96 Wooramel, R., Austral. 25 30S 114 30E
100 Woorinen, Australia 35 14S 143 27E
99 Wooroorooka, Austral. 29 0S 145 41E
112 Wooster, U.S.A. 40 38N 81 55W
13 Worcester, Eng. 52 12N 2 12W
113 Worcester, Mass., U.S.A. 42 14N 71 49W
113 Worcester, N.Y., U.S.A. 42 35N 74 45W
•13 Worcestershire ♦, Eng. 52 13N 2 10W
26 Wörgl, Austria 47 29N 12 3E
85 Worikambo, Ghana 10 43N 0 11W
12 Workington, Eng. 54 39N 3 34W
12 Worksop, Eng. 53 19N 1 9W
16 Workum, Netherlands 52 59N 5 26E
118 Worland, U.S.A. 44 0N 107 59W
19 Wormhoudt, France 50 52N 2 28E
25 Worms, Germany 49 37N 8 21E
117 Wortham, U.S.A. 31 48N 96 27W
26 Wörther See, Aust. 46 37N 14 19E
13 Worthing, Eng. 50 49N 0 21W
116 Worthington, U.S.A. 43 35N 95 30W
73 Wosi, Indonesia 0 15S 128 0E
87 Wota (Shoa Ghimirra), Ethiopia 7 4N 35 51E
83 Wour, Chad. 21 14N 16 0E
73 Wowoni, I., Indonesia 4 5S 123 5E
28 Woźniki, Poland 50 36N 19 2E
104 Wrangell, Alaska 56 30N 132 25W
14 Wrath, C., Scot. 58 38N 5 0W
116 Wray, U.S.A. 40 8N 102 18W
12 Wrekin, The, Mt., England 52 41N 2 35W
115 Wrens, U.S.A. 33 13N 82 23W
12 Wrexham, Wales 53 5N 3 0W
24 Wriezen, Germany 52 43N 14 9E
108 Wright, Canada 51 45N 121 30W
73 Wright, Philippines 11 42N 125 2E
107 Wright, Mt., Canada 52 40N 67 25W
119 Wrightson, Mt., U.S.A. 31 49N 110 56W

• Incorporated within the county of Cumbria

• Created a county, separate from Hampshire

† Incorporated within the region of Dumfries & Galloway

• Incorporated within the county of Hereford and Worcester

MAP
104 Wrigley, Canada 63 0N 123 30W
28 Wrocław, Pol. 51 5N 17 5E
28 Wrocław ♦, Poland 51 0N 77 0E
28 Wronki, Poland 52 41N 16 21E
28 Września, Poland 52 21N 17 36E
28 Wschowa, Poland 51 48N 16 20E
77 Wu K., China 27 30N 107 45E
76 Wuchang, Heilungkiang, China 44 51N 127 10E
77 Wuchang, China 41 10N 108 32E
77 Wuchow, China 23 26N 111 19E
77 Wuchung, China 38 4N 106 12E
75 Wulang K., China 32 0N 100 0E
58 Walutorovsk, U.S.S.R. 56 30N 65 40E
77 Wuhan, China 30 35N 114 15E
77 Wuhu, China 31 18N 118 20E
77 Wukang, Chekiang, China 30 35N 119 50E
77 Wukang, Hunan, China 26 50N 110 15E
85 Wukari, Nigeria 7 57N 9 42E
77 Wuki (Taning), China 31 27N 109 46E
85 Wulehe, Ghana 3 42N 0 0E
43 Wuliaru, I., Indonesia 7 10s 131 0E
75 Wulumuchi, China 43 40N 87 50E
85 Wum, Cameroon 6 40N 10 2E
87 Wuneba, Sudan 4 49N 30 22E
77 Wuning, China 29 16N 115 0E
106 Wunnummin L., Can. 52 50N 89 20W
25 Wunsiedel, Germany 50 2N 12 0E
24 Wunstorf, Germany 52 26N 9 29E
67 Wuntho, Burma 23 55N 95 45E
77 Wuping, China 25 5N 116 20E
24 Wuppertal, Germany 51 15N 7 8E
92 Wuppertal, S. Africa 32 13s 19 12E
25 Würzburg, Germany 49 46N 9 55E
24 Wurzen, Germany 51 21N 12 45E
77 Wushan, China 31 3N 109 57E
77 Wusih, China 31 30N 120 30E
24 Wustrow, Germany 54 4N 11 33E
77 Wusu, China 44 27N 84 37E
75 Wutunghliao, China 29 25N 104 0E
75 Wuwei, China 38 0N 102 30E
77 Wuyi, China 28 45N 119 56E
77 Wuyi Shan, China 26 40N 116 30E
76 Wuying, China 48 10N 129 20E
85 Wuyo, Nigeria 10 23N 11 50E
100 Wyalong, Australia 35 4s 147 50E
113 Wyalusing, U.S.A. 41 40N 76 16W
114 Wyandotte, U.S.A. 42 14N 83 13W
99 Wyandra, Australia 27 12s 145 56E
100 Wyangala Res., Austral. 34 6s 149 22E
100 Wycheproof, Australia 36 0N 143 17E
13 Wye, R., England 52 0N 2 36W
24 Wyk, W. Germany 54 41N 8 33E
100 Wymlet, Austral. 34 52s 142 10E
13 Wymondham, England 52 34N 1 7E
116 Wymore, U.S.A. 40 10N 97 8W
92 Wynberg, S. Africa 34 2s 18 28E
96 Wyndham, Australia 15 33s 128 3E
101 Wyndham, N.Z. 46 20s 168 51E
117 Wynne, U.S.A. 35 15N 90 50W
99 Wynnum, Australia 27 29s 152 58E
99 Wynyard, Australia 40 59s 145 45E
109 Wynyard, Canada 51 45N 104 10W
112 Wyoming ♦, U.S.A. 42 46N 78 4W
110 Wyoming ♦, U.S.A. 42 48N 109 0W
100 Wyong, Austral. 33 14s 151 24E
28 Wyrzysk, Poland 53 10N 17 17E
28 Wysoka, Poland 53 13N 17 2E
28 Wyszków, Poland 52 36N 21 25E
28 Wyszogród, Poland 52 23N 20 9E
114 Wytheville, U.S.A. 37 0N 81 3W
24 Xanten, Germany 51 40N 6 27E
44 Xanthi, Greece 41 10N 24 58E
44 Xanthi ♦, Greece 41 10N 24 58E
126 Xapuri, Brazil 10 35s 68 35W
92 Xau, Botswana 21 15s 24 44E
125 Xavantina, Brazil 21 15s 52 48W
114 Xenia, U.S.A. 39 42N 83 57W
71 Xieng Khouang, Laos 19 17N 103 25E
45 Xilókastron, Greece 38 4N 22 43E
93 Xinavane, Mozambique 25 2s 32 47E
45 Xiniás, L. Greece 39 2N 22 12E
127 Xingu, R., Brazil 2 25s 52 35W
127 Xique-Xique, Brazil 10 50s 42 40W
98 Yaamba, Australia 23 8s 150 22E
75 Yaan, China 30 0N 102 59E
100 Yaapeet, Australia 35 38s 142 0E
85 Yabassi, Cameroon 4 30N 9 57E
87 Yabelo, Ethiopia 4 57N 38 8E
43 Yablanitsa, Bulgaria 43 2N 24 5E
59 Yablonovyy Khrebet, U.S.S.R. 53 0N 114 0E
64 Yabrin, Saudi Arabia 23 7N 48 52E
62 Ya 'Bud, Jordan 32 27N 35 10E
124 Yacuiba, Bolivia 22 0s 63 25W
70 Yadgir, India 16 45N 77 5E
115 Yadkin, R., U.S.A. 36 15N 81 0W
55 Yadrin, U.S.S.R. 55 57N 46 6E
74 Yayama-rettō, Ryukyu Is. 24 30N 123 40E
85 Yagaba, Ghana 10 14N 1 20W
88 Yagoua, Cameroon 10 20N 14 58E
62 Yagur, Israel 32 45N 35 4E
74 Yahatashama, Japan 33 25N 132 40E
108 Yahk, Canada 49 15N 116 10W
88 Yahuma, Zaïre 1 0N 22 5E
77 Yaicheng, China 18 14N 109 7E
85 Yajua, Nigeria 11 27N 12 49E
67 Yakiang, China 30 4N 101 15E
118 Yakima, U.S.A. 46 42N 120 30W
118 Yakima, R., U.S.A. 46 15N 81 0W
84 Yako, Upper Volta 12 59N 2 15W
43 Yakoruda, Bulgaria 42 1N 23 39E
76 Yakoshih, China 49 13N 120 35E
74 Yaku-Shima, Japan 30 20N 130 30E
104 Yakutat, Alaska 59 50N 139 44W
59 Yakutsk, U.S.S.R. 62 5N 129 40E
73 Yala, Thailand 6 33N 101 12E
117 Yalabusha, R., U.S.A. 33 53N 89 50W
98 Yalboroo, Australia 20 50s 148 30E

MAP
112 Yale, U.S.A. 43 9N 82 47W
96 Yalgoo, Australia 28 16s 116 39E
45 Yalikavak, Turkey 37 6N 27 18E
81 Yalinga, Cent. Afr. Rep. 6 20N 23 10E
120 Yalkubul, Punta, Mex. 21 32N 88 37W
86 Y'allaq, G., Egypt 30 21N 33 31E
98 Yalleroi, Australia 24 3s 145 42E
100 Yallourn, Austral. 38 10s 146 18E
46 Yalpukh, Oz., U.S.S.R. 45 30N 28 41E
56 Yalta, U.S.S.R. 44 30N 34 10E
76 Yalu K., China-Korea 41 30N 126 30E
76 Yalu Kiang, China 47 45N 122 40E
75 Yalung K., China 32 0N 100 0E
58 Yalutorovsk, U.S.S.R. 56 30N 65 40E
62 Yam Kinneret, Israel 32 49N 35 36E
74 Yamagata, Japan 37 55N 140 20E
74 Yamagata-ken ♦, Japan 38 30N 140 0E
74 Yamaguchi, Japan 34 10N 131 32E
74 Yamaguchi-ken ♦, Japan 34 20N 131 40E
58 Yamal, Poluostrov, U.S.S.R. 71 0N 70 0E
52 Yaman Tau, U.S.S.R. 54 20N 57 40E
64 Yamana, Saudi Arabia 24 5N 47 30E
74 Yamnashi-ken ♦, Ja-. 35 40N 138 40E
57 Yamankhalinka, U.S.S.R. 47 43N 49 21E
99 Yamba, Austral. 29 30s 153 22E
87 Yâmbiô, Sudan 4 35N 28 16E
43 Yambol, Bulgaria 42 30N 26 36E
75 Yamdrok Tso, China 29 0N 90 40E
77 Yamhsien, China 21 45N 108 31E
85 Yamil, Nigeria 12 53N 8 4E
99 Yamma-Yamma L., Australia 26 16s 141 20E
118 Yampa, R., U.S.A. 40 37N 108 0W
96 Yampi Sd., Austral. 15 15s 123 30E
56 Yampol, U.S.S.R. 48 15N 28 15E
85 Yamrat, Nigeria 10 11N 9 55E
43 Yamrukohal, Mt., Bulg. 42 44N 24 52E
62 Yamun, Jordan 32 29N 35 14E
68 Yamuna (Jumna), R., India 27 0N 78 30E
85 Yan, Nigeria 10 5N 12 11E
70 Yan Oya, Ceylon 9 0N 81 10E
59 Yana, R., U.S.S.R. 69 0N 134 0E
100 Yanac, Australia 36 0s 141 15E
70 Yanam, India 16 47N 82 15E
52 Yanaul, U.S.S.R. 56 25N 55 0E
64 Yanbu 'al Bahr, Saudi Arabia 24 0N 38 5E
99 Yancannia, Australia 30 12s 142 35E
100 Yanco, Austral. 34 38s 146 27E
85 Yanda Bayo, Nigeria 11 32N 10 48E
98 Yandabome, New Guinea 7 1s 145 46E
84 Yanfolila, Mali 11 11N 8 9W
90 Yangambi, Zaïre 0 47N 24 20E
77 Yangchow, China 32 25N 119 25E
76 Yangchuan, China 38 0N 113 29E
58 Yangi-Yer, U.S.S.R. 40 17N 68 48E
76 Yangkao, China 40 20N 113 40E
77 Yangshui (Hinghwa), China 29 53N 115 3E
75 Yangso, China 24 36N 110 32E
77 Yangtze Kiang, China 31 40N 122 0E
71 Yanhee Res., Thailand 17 30N 98 45E
116 Yankton, U.S.A. 42 55N 97 25W
99 Yanna, Australia 26 58s 146 0E
88 Yanonge, Zaïre 0 35N 24 38E
77 Yanping, China 22 25N 112 0E
43 Yantra, R., Bulgaria 43 35N 25 37E
81 Yao, Chad 12 56N 17 33E
77 Yao Shan, China 24 0N 110 0E
76 Yaomen, China 44 31N 125 8E
85 Yaoundé, Cameroon 3 50N 11 35E
73 Yap Is., J.S. Pac. Is. Trust Terr. 9 30N 138 10E
126 Yapo, R., Ecuador 0 30s 77 0W
120 Yaqui, R., Mexico 28 28N 109 30W
55 Yar, U.S.S.R. 58 14N 52 5E
58 Yar-Sale, U.S.S.R. 66 50N 70 50E
126 Yaracuy ♦, Venezuela 10 20N 68 45W
98 Yaraka, Australia 24 53s 144 3E
55 Yaransk, U.S.S.R. 57 13N 47 56E
54 Yaratishky, U.S.S.R. 54 3N 25 52E
81 Yarda, Chad 18 35N 19 0E
13 Yare, R., England 52 36N 1 28E
52 Yarensk, U.S.S.R. 61 10N 49 8E
86 Yarfa, Saudi Arabia 24 40N 38 35E
126 Yari, R., Colombia 1 0N 73 40W
75 Yarkand (Soche), China 38 24N 77 20E
113 Yarker, Canada 44 23N 76 26W
66 Yarkhun, R., W. Pak. 36 30N 72 45E
107 Yarmouth, Canada 43 53N 65 45W
55 Yaroslavl, U.S.S.R. 57 35N 39 55E
100 Yarra, R., Australia 37 45s 143 21E
98 Yarraden, Australia 14 28s 143 15E
99 Yarram, Australia 38 29s 146 40E
99 Yarraman Cr., Austral. 26 46s 152 1E
99 Yarrawonga, Australia 26 50s 145 20E
100 Yarrawonga, Australia 36 0s 146 0E
100 Yarto, Australia 35 28s 142 16E
126 Yarumal, Colombia 6 58N 75 24W
101 Yasawa Group, Fiji 17 00s 177 23E
54 Yaselda, R., U.S.S.R. 52 26s 25 30E
85 Yashi, Nigeria 12.23N 7 54E
56 Yasinovataya, U.S.S.R. 48 7N 37 57E
106 Yasinski, L., Canada 53 10N 77 0W
59 Yasnogorsk, U.S.S.R. 54 32N 37 38E
71 Yasothon, Thailand 15 50N 104 10E
100 Yass, Australia 34 49s 148 54E
100 Yass, Res., Australia 34 50s 149 0E
62 Yas'ur, Israel 32 54N 35 10E
45 Yatağan, Turkey 37 20N 28 10E
117 Yates Center, U.S.A. 37 53N 95 45W
109 Yathkyed L., Canada 63 0N 98 0W
74 Yatsushiro, Japan 32 30N 130 40E
62 Yatta, Jordan 31 27N 35 6E
90 Yatta Plat., Kenya 2 0s 38 0E
62 Yattah, Jordan 31 27N 35 6E

MAP
12 Yauyos, Peru 12 10s 75 50W
21 Yaval, India 21 10N 75 42E
126 Yavari R., Peru 4 50s 72 0W
84 Yawri B., Sierra Leone 8 22N 13 0W
65 Yazdan, Iran 33 30N 60 50E
117 Yazoo City, U.S.A. 32 48N 90 28W
26 Ybbs, Austria 48 12N 15 4E
83 Yebbi-Souma, Chad 21 7N 17 54E
83 Yebbigué, Chad 22 30N 17 30E
82 Yebel Jarris Tighzert, O., Morocco 28 10N 9 37W
67 Yebyu, Burma 14 15N 98 13E
33 Yecla, Spain 38 35N 1 5W
82 Yeddou, Spanish Sahara 28 5N 9 2W
55 Yefremov, U.S.S.R. 53 15N 38 3E
55 Yegorlyk, R., U.S.S.R. 46 15N 41 30E
55 Yegorlykskaya, USSR 46 5N 40 35E
55 Yegoryevsk, U.S.S.R. 55 27N 38 55E
124 Yegros, Paraguay 26 20s 56 25W
62 Yehsien, China 37 12N 119 58E
62 Yehud, Israel 32 3N 34 53E
62 Yehuda, Midbar, Israel 31 35N 34 57E
87 Yei, Sudan 4 3N 30 40E
87 Yei, Nahr, Sudan 5 50N 30 20E
55 Yelan, U.S.S.R. 50 55N 43 43E
55 Yelan Kolenovski, U.S.S.R. 51 16N 40 45E
70 Yelandur, India 12 6N 77 0E
55 Yelanskoye, U.S.S.R. 61 25N 128 0E
99 Yelarbon, Australia 28 33s 150 49E
55 Yelatma, U.S.S.R. 55 0N 41 52E
55 Yelets, U.S.S.R. 52 40N 38 30E
84 Yélimané, Mali 15 9N 22 49E
14 Yell I., Scotland 60 35N 1 5W
14 Yell Sd., Scotland 60 33N 1 15W
70 Yellamanchilli (Elamanchili), India 17 26N 82 50E
77 Yellow River = Hwang Ho, China 38 0N 117 20E
108 Yellowhead P., Canada 53 0N 118 30W
109 Yellowknife, Canada 62 30N 114 10W
104 Yellowknife, R., Canada 63 30N 113 30W
116 Yellowstone L., U.S.A. 44 30N 110 20W
116 Yellowstone, R., U.S.A. 46 35N 105 45W
118 Yellowstone National Park, U.S.A. 44 35N 110 0W
54 Yelnya, U.S.S.R. 54 35N 33 15E
54 Yelsk, U.S.S.R. 51 50N 29 3E
86 Yelwa, Nigeria 10 49N 8 41E
12 Yemen ■, Arabia 15 0N 44 0E
50 Yemen, South ■, Arabia 15 0N 48 0E
56 Yenakiyevo, U.S.S.R. 48 15N 38 5E
67 Yenangyaung, Burma 20 30N 95 0E
67 Yenchang, China 36 44N 110 2E
100 Yenda, Australia 34 13s 146 14E
84 Yendéré, Ivory Coast 10 12N 4 59W
85 Yendi, Ghana 9 29N 0 1W
77 Yengchun, China 22 10N 111 27E
58 Yengisar, China 38 0N 76 12E
55 Yenisey, R., U.S.S.R. 68 0N 86 30E
59 Yeniseysk, U.S.S.R. 58 39N 92 4E
59 Yeniseyskiy Zaliv, U.S.S.R. 72 20N 81 0E
76 Yenki, China 43 12N 129 30E
21 Yenne, France 45 43N 5 44E
57 Yenotayevka, U.S.S.R. 47 15N 47 0E
77 Yentai, China 37 30N 121 22E
59 Yenyuka, U.S.S.R. 58 20N 121 30E
28 Yeo, L., Australia 28 0s 124 30E
13 Yeo, R., England 51 1N 2 46W
70 Yeola, India 20 0N 74 30E
68 Yeotmal, India 20 20N 78 15E
100 Yeoval, Australia 32 41s 148 39E
13 Yeovil, England 50 57N 2 38W
30 Yepes, Spain 39 55N 3 39W
98 Yeppoon, Australia 23 5s 150 47E
45 Yeraki, Greece 37 0N 22 42E
57 Yerbogachen, U.S.S.R. 61 16N 108 0E
57 Yerevan, U.S.S.R. 40 10N 44 20E
118 Yerington, U.S.A. 39 0N 119 11W
70 Yerla, R., India 17 35N 74 30E
57 Yermakovo, U.S.S.R. 52 35N 126 20E
119 Yermo, U.S.A. 34 58N 116 13W
59 Yerofey Pavlovich, U.S.S.R. 54 0N 122 0E
55 Yershov, U.S.S.R. 51 15N 48 27E
62 Yerushalayim, Israel 31 47N 35 10E
18 Yerville, France 49 40N 0 53E
13 Yes Tor, Mt., Eng. 50 41N 3 59W
45 Yesilirmak, Turkey 41 0N 36 40E
117 Yeso, U.S.A. 34 29N 104 37W
57 Yessentuki, U.S.S.R. 44 0N 42 45E
57 Yessey, U.S.S.R. 68 29N 102 10E
18 Yeu, I. d', France 46 42N 2 20W
77 Yeungchun, China 22 15N 111 40E
77 Yeungkong, China 21 55N 112 0E
77 Yeungshan, China 24 27N 112 15E
56 Yevlakh, U.S.S.R. 40 39N 47 7E
56 Yevpatoriya, U.S.S.R. 45 15N 33 20E
56 Yevstratovskiy, U.S.S.R. 50 11N 39 2E
57 Yeya, R., U.S.S.R. 46 40N 39 0E
56 Yeysk, U.S.S.R. 46 40N 38 12E
124 Yhati, Paraguay 25 45s 56 35W
125 Yhú, Paraguay 25 0s 56 0W
125 Yi, R., Uruguay 33 7s 57 8W
45 Yialí, I., Greece 36 41N 27 11E
45 Yianisádhes, I., Greece 35 20N 26 10E
63 Yibal, Oman 22 10N 56 8E
81 Yihsien, China 34 50N 117 50E
77 Yilan, Taiwan 24 47N 121 44E
76 Yilan, Australia 35 10s 118 10E
86 Yuli, Nigeria 9 44N 10 12E
76 Yinchwan, China 38 30N 106 20E
77 Yingcheng, China 31 0N 113 44E

MAP
76 Yingchow, China 39 45N 113 30E
30 Yingshan, China 50N 115 45E
77 Yingshang, China 32 36N 116 16E
77 Yingtak, China 24 10N 113 5E
77 Yingkiang, China 28 10N 108 40E
44 Yioura, I., Greece 39 23N 24 10E
45 Yithion, Greece 36 46N 22 34E
88 Yirga Alem, Ethiopia 6 34N 38 29E
45 Yithion, Greece 36 46N 22 34E
76 Yixian, Liaoning, China 41 32N 121 15E
77 Yiyang, China 28 45N 112 15E
62 Yizre'el, Israel 32 34N 35 19E
50 Ylitornio, Finland 66 19N 23 39E
49 Ylivieska, Finland 64 4N 24 28E
49 Yngaren, Sweden 58 50N 16 35E
59 Ynykchanskiy, U.S.S.R. 60 15N 137 43E
117 Yoakum, U.S.A. 29 20N 97 10W
73 Yog Pt., Philippines 13 55N 124 20E
88 Yokadouma, Cameroon 3 35N 14 50E
74 Yokkaichi, Japan 35 0N 136 30E
85 Yoko, Cameroon 5 50N 12 20E
74 Yokohama, Japan 35 30N 139 32E
74 Yokosuka, Japan 35 20N 139 40E
85 Yola, Nigeria 9 10N 12 29E
121 Yolaina, Cordillera de, Nicaragua 11 30N 84 0W
100 Yolgali, Australia 34 20s 146 7E
71 Yom Mae Nam, Thailand 15 15N 100 20E
74 Yonago, Japan 35 25N 133 19E
71 Yonaguni, Japan 24 28N 122 59E
71 Yong Peng, Malaysia 2 0N 103 3E
76 Yŏngchŏn, South Korea 35 55N 138 55E
76 Yŏngwŏl, South Korea 37 18N 128 20E
84 Yonibana, Sierra Leone 8 30N 12 19W
109 Yonker, Canada 52 40N 109 40W
113 Yonkers, U.S.A. 40 57N 73 51W
19 Yonne ♦, France 48 23N 2 58E
19 Yonne, R., France 48 23N 2 58E
85 Yonov, Nigeria 7 33N 8 42E
62 Yoqueam, Israel 32 40N 35 6E
96 York, Australia 31 52s 116 47E
115 York, Ala., U.S.A. 32 30N 88 18W
116 York, Nebr., U.S.A. 40 55N 97 35W
114 York, Pa., U.S.A. 39 57N 76 43W
98 York, C., Australia 10 35s 142 30E
4 York, C., Greenland 75 55N 66 25W
4 York, Kap, Greenland 75 55N 66 25W
109 York Factory, Canada 57 0N 92 30W
96 York Sd., W. Australia 14 30s 125 0E
12 York Wolds, Eng. 54 0N 0 30W
99 Yorke Pen., Austral. 34 40s 137 35E
12 Yorkshire ♦, Eng. 54 54N 1 0W
109 Yorkton, Canada 51 11N 102 28W
117 Yorktown, U.S.A. 29 0N 97 29W
100 Yorketown, Australia 34 13s 146 14E
119 Yosemite National Park, U.S.A. 37 50N 119 30W
55 Yoshkar Ola, U.S.S.R. 56 49N 47 10E
76 Yŏsu, South Korea 34 47N 127 45E
77 Yotsing, China 28 10N 120 55E
15 Youghal, Ireland 51 58N 7 51W
15 Youghal Har., Ireland 51 55N 7 50W
84 Youkounkoun, Guinea 12 35N 13 11W
100 Young, Austral. 34 19s 148 18E
119 Young, U.S.A. 34 9N 110 56W
124 Young, Uruguay 32 44s 57 36W
99 Younghusband Pen., Australia 34 45s 139 15E
109 Youngstown, Canada 51 35N 111 10W
112 Youngstown, N.Y., U.S.A. 43 16N 79 2W
112 Youngstown, Ohio, U.S.A. 41 7N 80 41W
112 Youngsville, U.S.A. 41 51N 79 21W
82 Youssoufia, Morocco 32 16N 8 31W
77 Yoyang, China 29 27N 113 10E
45 Yozgat, Turkey 39 51N 34 47E
124 Ypané, R., Paraguay 23 29s 57 19W
18 Yport, France 49 45N 0 15E
17 Ypres, Belgium 50 50N 2 52E
114 Ypsilanti, U.S.A. 42 18N 83 40W
118 Yreka, U.S.A. 41 44N 122 40W
119 Ysleta, U.S.A. 31 45N 106 24W
21 Yssingeaux, France 45 9N 4 8E
49 Ystad, Sweden 55 26N 13 50E
14 Ythan, R., Scotland 57 26N 1 12W
47 Ytre Adal, Norway 60 15N 10 14E
48 Ytterhogdal, Sweden 62 12N 14 56E
85 Ytyk-Kel, U.S.S.R. 62 30N 133 28E
77 Yu Shan, Mt., Taiwan 23 30N 121 0E
77 Yuan Kiang, China 28 30N 110 0E
75 Yuanyang, China 23 10N 102 58E
118 Yuba City, U.S.A. 39 12N 121 45W
74 Yubetsu, Japan 44 15N 143 40E
120 Yucatán ♦, Mexico 21 30N 86 30W
6 Yucatán Basin, Caribbean Sea 20 0N 84 0W
121 Yucatán Channel, Caribbean Sea 22 0N 86 30W
119 Yucca, U.S.A. 34 56N 114 6W
77 Yucheng, China 36 55N 116 40E
58 Yuchow, U.S.S.R. 51 5N 67 55E
37 Yugoslavia ■, Eur. 44 0N 20 0E
77 Yühsien, Honan, China 34 10N 113 30E
77 Yukan, China 28 1N 121 12E
54 Yukhnov, U.S.S.R. 54 44N 35 15E
77 Yukikow, China 31 29N 118 17E
104 Yukon ♦, Canada 63 0N 135 0W
104 Yukon, R., Alas./Canada 65 30N 150 0W
59 Yukti, U.S.S.R. 63 20N 105 0E
76 Yuli, Australia 9 35s 118 10E
86 Yuli, Nigeria 9 44N 10 12E
76 Yulin, Hainan, China 18 10N 109 31E
77 Yülin (Watlam), Kwangsi-Chuang, China 22 30N 110 50E

MAP
100 Yuluma, Austral. 35 6s 146 15E
119 Yuma, Ariz., U.S.A. 32 45N 114 45W
116 Yuma, Colo., U.S.A. 40 10N 102 43W
90 Yumbe, Uganda 3 28N 31 15E
90 Yumbi, Zaïre 1 12s 26 15E
126 Yumbo, Colombia 3 35N 76 28W
75 Yumen, China 41 13N 96 55E
75 Yun Ho, China 35 0N 117 0E
77 Yungan, China 25 50N 117 25E
126 Yungas, Bolivia 17 0s 66 0W
77 Yungay, Chile 37 10s 72 5W
77 Yungchun, China 25 20N 118 15E
100 Yungera, Austral. 34 42s 143 3E
77 Yuigfu, China 24 59N 109 59E
77 Yunghing, China 26 12N 113 3E
77 Yungshun, China 29 3N 109 50E
77 Yungsin, China 26 55N 114 10E
77 Yungyun, China 24 31N 113 28E
77 Yunhsien, China 32 30N 111 0E
77 Yuhwo, China 28 0N 119 32E
77 Yunlin, Taiwan 23 45N 120 30E
77 Yunlung, China 25 50N 99 25E
75 Yunnan ♦, China 25 0N 102 30E
32 Yunquera de Henares, Spain 40 47N 3 11W
77 Yunsiao, China 24 0N 117 20E
59 Yur, U.S.S.R. 59 52s 137 49E
58 Yurga, U.S.S.R. 55 42N 84 51E
58 Yuribei, U.S.S.R. 71 20N 76 30E
126 Yurimaguas, Peru 5 55s 76 0W
55 Yurya, U.S.S.R. 59 1N 49 13E
55 Yuryev Polskiy, U.S.S.R. 56 30N 59 47E
55 Yuryevets, U.S.S.R. 57 25N 43 2E
121 Yuscarán, Honduras 13 58N 86 51W
62 Yusha, Jebel, Jordan 32 4N 35 41E
75 Yushu = Fyekundo, China 33 6N 96 48E
77 Yütu, China 26 0N 115 24E
76 Yutze, China 37 45N 112 45E
77 Yuyang, China 28 44N 108 46E
77 Yuyao, China 30 0N 121 20E
55 Yuzha, U.S.S.R. 56 40N 42 10E
59 Yuzhno-Sakhalinsk, U.S.S.R. 47 5N 142 5E
19 Yvelines ♦, France 48 40N 1 45E
25 Yverdon, Switzerland 46 47N 6 39E
18 Yvetot, France 49 37N 0 44E
82 Za, O., Morocco 34 5s 2 30W
16 Zaandam, Netherlands 52 26N 4 49E
82 Zab, Monts du, Algeria 34 55N 5 0E
42 Zabalj, Yugoslavia 45 21N 20 5E
42 Zabari, Yugoslavia 44 21N 21 15E
42 Zabarj, Yugoslavia 45 2N 20 5E
86 Zabarjad, Egypt 23 40N 36 12E
59 Zabaykalskiy, U.S.S.R. 49 40N 117 10E
28 Zabkowice Slaskie, Pol. 50 22N 19 17E
42 Zabljak, Yugoslavia 42 19N 19 10E
65 Zābol, Iran 31 0N 61 25E
65 Zābolī, Iran 27 10N 61 35E
28 Zabludow, Poland 53 0N 23 19E
27 Zabno, Poland 50 9N 20 53E
85 Zabré, Upper Volta 11 12N 0 36W
28 Zabrze, Poland 50 24N 18 50E
120 Zacapa, Guatemala 14 59N 89 31W
120 Zacatecas, Mexico 22 49N 102 34W
120 Zacatecas ♦, Mexico 23 30N 103 0W
120 Zacatecolua, Salvador 13 29N 88 51W
120 Zacoalco, Mexico 20 10N 103 40W
39 Zadar, Yugoslavia 44 8N 15 8E
85 Zadawa, Nigeria 11 33N 10 19E
71 Zadetkyi' Kyun, Burma 10 0N 98 25E
52 Zadonsk, U.S.S.R. 52 25N 38 56E
62 Zafed, Israel 32 58N 35 29E
45 Zafora, I., Greece 36 5N 26 24E
30 Zafra, Spain 38 26N 6 30W
28 Zagan, Poland 51 39N 15 22E
86 Zagazig, Egypt 30 40N 31 12E
83 Zaghouan, Tunisia 36 23N 10 10E
44 Zaglivérion, Greece 40 36N 23 15E
85 Zagnanado, Dahomey 7 18N 2 28E
82 Zagora, Greece 39 27N 23 6E
82 Zagora, Morocco 30 14N 5 51W
28 Zagórów, Poland 52 10N 17 54E
27 Zagórz, Poland 49 30N 22 14E
37 Zagreb, Yugoslavia 45 50N 16 0E
42 Zagros, Kudha-ye, Iran 33 45N 47 0E
42 Zagubica, Yugoslavia 44 15N 21 47E
84 Zaguinaso, Ivory Coast 10 1N 6 14W
65 Zāhedān, Iran 29 30N 60 50E
70 Zahirabad, India 17 43N 77 37E
72 Zahlah, Lebanon 33 52N 35 50E
24 Zahna, Germany 51 54N 12 47E
82 Zahrez Chergui, Algeria 35 0N 3 30E
82 Zahrez Rharbi, Algeria 34 50N 2 55E
88 Zaïre, Rep. of ■, Africa 3 0s 23 0E
42 Zaječar, Yugoslavia 43 53N 22 18E
59 Zakamensk, U.S.S.R. 50 23N 103 17E
62 Zakariya, Israel 31 43N 34 57E
57 Zakataly, U.S.S.R. 41 38N 46 35E
57 Zakavkazye, U.S.S.R. 42 0N 44 0E
64 Zakho, Iraq 37 10N 42 50E
45 Zákinthos, Greece 37 47N 20 54E
45 Zákinthos, I., Greece 37 45N 27 45E
27 Zakopane, Poland 49 18N 19 57E
27 Zala ♦, Hungary 46 53N 17 0E
27 Zala, R., Hungary 46 53N 16 47E
27 Zalaegerszeg, Hungary 46 53N 16 47E
27 Zalakomár, Hungary 46 33N 17 9E
27 Zalalővő, Hungary 46 51N 16 35E
31 Zalamea de la Serena, Spain 38 40N 5 38W
31 Zalamea la Real, Spain 37 41N 6 38W
46 Zalău, Rumania 47 12N 23 5E
85 Zalina, Nigeria 10 30N 8 58E
39 Zalec, Yugoslavia 46 16N 15 10E

MAP	Name	Lat	Long
56	Zaleshchiki, U.S.S.R.	48 45N	25 45E
28	Zalewo, Poland	53 55N	19 41E
81	Zalingei, Sudan	13 5N	23 10E
83	Zaltan, Jabal, Libya	28 46N	19 45E
90	Zambeke, Zaïre	2 8N	25 17E
91	Zambèze, R., Africa	18 46s	36 16E
91	Zambezi, R., Africa	18 46s	36 16E
91	Zambezia ♦, Mozam.	16 15s	37 30E
89	Zambia ■, Africa	15 0s	28 0w
73	Zamboanga, Philippines	6 59N	122 3E
126	Zambrano, Colombia	9 45N	74 49w
55	Zametchino, U.S.S.R.	53 30N	42 30E
120	Zamora, Mexico	20 0N	102 21w
30	Zamora, Spain	41 30N	5 45w
30	Zamora ♦, Spain	41 30N	5 46w
28	Zamość, Poland	50 50N	23 22E
126	Zamuro, Sierra del. Ven.	4 0N	62 30w
83	Zamzam, W., Libya	31 0N	14 30E
85	Zan, Ghana	9 26N	0 17w
32	Záncara, R., Spain	39 20N	3 0w
16	Zandvoort, Netherlands	52 22N	4 32E
112	Zanesville, U.S.A.	39 56N	82 2w
91	Zangue, R., Mozambique	18 5s	35 10E
64	Zanjan, Iran	36 40N	48 35E
40	Zannone, I., Italy	40 58N	13 2E
45	Zante = Zákinthos, Greece	37 47N	20 54E
96	Zanthus, Australia	30 55s	123 29E
90	Zanzibar, Tanzania	6 12s	39 12E
90	Zanzibar I., Tanzania	6 12s	39 12E
83	Zanzūr, Libya	32 55N	13 1E
83	Zaouatalaz, Algeria	24 57N	8 16E
82	Zaouiet Reggane, Algeria	26 32N	0 3E
42	Zapadna Morava, R., Yugoslavia	43 50N	20 15E
54	Zapadnaya Dvina, U.S.S.R.	56 15N	32 3E
27	Západné Beskydy, Eur.	49 30N	19 0E
26	Západočesky ♦, Cz.	49 35N	13 0E
27	Západoslovenský ♦, Cz.	48 30N	17 30E
128	Zapala, Argentina	39 0s	70 0w
117	Zapata, U.S.A.	26 56N	92 17w
31	Zapatón, R., Spain	39 0N	6 49w
56	Zaporozhye, U.S.S.R.	47 50N	35 10E
41	Zapponeta, Italy	41 27N	15 57E
64	Zara, Turkey	39 58N	37 43E
126	Zaragoza, Colombia	7 30N	74 52w
32	Zaragoza, Spain	41 39N	0 53w
32	Zaragoza ♦, Spain	41 35N	1 0w
120	Zaragoza, Coahuila, Mexico	28 30N	101 0w
120	Zaragoza, Nuevo León, Mexico	24 0N	99 36w
65	Zarand, Iran	30 46N	56 34E
46	Zărandului, Rumania	46 14N	22 7E
54	Zarasai, U.S.S.R.	55 40N	26 12E
55	Zaraysk, U.S.S.R.	54 48N	38 53E
126	Zaraza, Venezuela	9 21N	65 19w
109	Zarembo I., Alaska	56 20N	132 50w
49	Zari, Nigeria	13 8N	12 17E
85	Zaria, Nigeria	11 0N	7 40E
92	Zarisberge, S.W. Africa	24 30s	16 15E
28	Zarki, Poland	50 38N	19 21E
28	Zarnów, Poland	51 16N	20 9E
62	Zarnuqa, Israel	31 53N	34 47E
28	Zaróv, Poland	50 56N	16 29E
62	Zarqa, R., Jordan	32 10N	35 37E
126	Zaruma, Ecuador	3 40s	79 30w
28	Zary, Poland	51 37N	15 10E
31	Zarza de Alange, Spain	38 49N	6 13w
30	Zarza de Granadilla, Sp.	40 14N	6 3w
83	Zarzaïtine, Algeria	28 32N	9 5E
126	Zarzal, Colombia	4 24N	76 4w
83	Zarzis, Tunisia	33 31N	11 2E
30	Zas, Spain	43 4N	8 53w
59	Zashiversk, U.S.S.R.	67 25N	142 40E
66	Zaskar Mountains, Kashmir	33 15N	77 30E
92	Zastron, S. Africa	30 18s	27 7E
26	Zatec, Czechoslovakia	50 20N	13 32E
27	Zator, Poland	49 59N	19 28E
32	Zavala, Yugoslavia	42 50N	17 59E
65	Zavareh, Iran	33 35N	52 28E
57	Zavetnoye, U.S.S.R.	47 13N	43 50E
42	Zavidovici, Yugoslavia	44 27N	18 13E
54	Zavitinsk, U.S.S.R.	50 10N	129 20E
5	Zavodoski, I., Falk. Is.	56 0s	27 45w
55	Zavolzhye, U.S.S.R.	56 37N	43 18E
28	Zawadzkie, Poland	50 37N	18 28E
28	Zawidów, Poland	51 1N	15 1E
28	Zawiercie, Poland	50 30N	19 13E
86	Zâwyet Shammâs, Egypt	31 30N	26 37E
86	Zâwyet Um el Rakham, Egypt	31 18N	27 1E
28	Zawyet Ungeila, Egypt	31 23N	26 42E
65	Zayandeh, R., Iran	32 35N	32 0E
59	Zayarsk, U.S.S.R.	56 20N	102 55E
58	Zaysan, U.S.S.R.	47 28N	84 52E
58	Zaysan, Oz., U.S.S.R.	48 0N	83 0E
83	Zazamt, W., Libya	30 29N	14 30E
83	Zazir, O., Algeria	22 0N	5 40E
27	Zázrivá, Czechoslovakia	49 16N	19 7E
54	Zbarazh, U.S.S.R.	49 43N	25 44E
28	Zbaszyn, Poland	52 14N	15 56E
28	Zbaszynek, Poland	52 16N	15 51E
28	Zblewo, Poland	53 56N	18 19E
54	Zdolbunov, U.S.S.R.	50 30N	26 15E
42	Zdrelo, Yugoslavia	44 16N	21 28E
28	Zdunska Wola, Poland	51 37N	18 59E
28	Zduny, Poland	51 39N	17 21E
108	Zebediela, S. Africa	24 20s	29 17E
16	Zeebrugge, Belgium	51 19N	3 12E
99	Zeehan, Australia	41 52s	145 25E
16	Zeeland ♦, Neth.	51 30N	3 50E
62	Ze'elim, Israel	31 13N	34 32E
92	Zeerust, S. Afr.	25 31s	26 4E
62	Zefat, Israel	32 58N	35 29E
82	Zegdou, Algeria	29 51N	4 53w
87	Zege, Ethiopia	11 43N	37 18E
84	Zegoua, Mali	10 32N	5 35w
52	Zehdenick, Germany	52 59N	13 20E
63	Zeila, Somali Republic	11 15N	43 30E
16	Zeist, Netherlands	52 5N	5 15E
62	Zeita, Jordan	32 23N	35 2E
24	Zeitz, Germany	51 3N	12 9E
42	Zelengora, mts., Y.-slav.	43 22N	18 30E
42	Zelenika, Yugoslavia	42 27N	18 37E
55	Zelendolsk, U.S.S.R.	55 55N	48 30E
54	Zelenogradsk, U.S.S.R.	54 53N	20 29E
57	Zelenokumsk, U.S.S.R.	44 30N	44 1E
16	Zelhem, Netherlands	52 0N	6 21E
57	Zelenovski, U.S.S.R.	48 6N	50 45E
26	Zell, Baden, Germany	47 42N	7 50E
26	Zell am See, Austria	47 19N	12 47E
24	Zella Mehlis, Germany	50 40N	10 41E
60	Zelouane, Morocco	35 1N	2 58w
16	Zelzate, Belgium	51 13N	3 47E
83	Zemora, I., Tunisia	37 5N	10 56E
90	Zémio, Cen. Afr.	5 2N	25 5E
82	Zemmora, Algeria	35 44N	0 51E
82	Zemoul, W., Algeria	29 15N	7 30w
42	Zenica, Yugoslavia	44 10N	17 57E
82	Zenina, Algeria	34 30N	2 37E
42	Zepce, Yugoslavia	44 28N	18 2E
24	Zerbst, Germany	51 59N	12 8E
82	Zerhamra, Algeria	29 58N	2 30w
28	Zerków, Poland	52 4N	17 32E
25	Zermatt, Switzerland	46 2N	7 46E
57	Zernograd, U.S.S.R.	46 52N	40 11E
83	Zeroud, O.,·Tusisia	35 30N	9 30E
44	Zerqani, Albania	41 30N	20 20E
57	Zestafoni, U.S.S.R.	42 6N	43 0E
24	Zetel, Germany	53 33N	7 57E
14	Zetland ♦, Scot.	60 30N	0 15w
24	Zeulenroda, Germany	50 39N	12 0E
24	Zeven, Germany	53 17N	9 19E
38	Zévio, Italy	45 23N	11 10E
59	Zeya, U.S.S.R.	54 2N	127 20E
59	Zeya, R., U.S.S.R.	53 30N	127 0E
62	Zeyse, Ethiopia	5 44N	37 23w
30	Zêzere, R., Portugal	40 0N	7 55w
28	Zgierz, Poland	51 45N	19 27E
28	Zgorzelec, Poland	51 10N	15 0E
54	Zhabinka, U.S.S.R.	52 13N	24 2E
58	Zhailma, U.S.S.R.	51 30N	61 50E
54	Zhamensk, U.S.S.R.	54 37N	21 17E
58	Zhanatas, U.S.S.R.	43 11N	81 18E
54	Zharkovskiy, U.S.S.R.	55 56N	32 19E
56	Zhashkov, U.S.S.R.	49 15N	30 5E
56	Zhdanov, U.S.S.R.	47 5N	37 31E
59	Zheleznogorsk- Ilimskiy, U.S.S.R.	56 34N	104 8E
55	Zherdevka, U.S.S.R.	51 56N	41 21E
55	Zhigansk, U.S.S.R.	66 35N	124 10E
53	Zhigulevsk, U.S.S.R.	53 28N	49 45E
55	Zhirhovsk, U.S.S.R.	50 57N	44 49E
54	Zhitomir, U.S.S.R.	50 20N	28 40E
54	Zhizdra, U.S.S.R.	53 45N	34 40E
54	Zhlobin, U.S.S.R.	52 55N	30 0E
56	Zhmerinka, U.S.S.R.	49 2N	28 10E
54	Zhodino, U.S.S.R.	54 5N	28 17E
56	Zhovtnevoye, U.S.S.R.	47 54N	32 2E
54	Zhukovka, U.S.S.R.	53 35N	33 50E
59	Zhupanovo, U.S.S.R.	51 59N	15 9E
68	Ziarat, Pakistan	30 25N	67 30E
28	Ziebice, Poland	50 37N	17 2E
86	Ziel, Mt., Australia	23 20s	132 30E
28	Zielona Góra, Poland	51 57N	15 31E
28	Zielona Góra ♦, Pol.	51 57N	15 30E
16	Zierikzee, Netherlands	51 40N	3 55E
24	Ziesar, Germany	52 16N	12 19E
86	Zifta, Egypt	30 43N	31 14E
81	Zigey, Chad	14 50N	15 50E
84	Ziguinchor, Senegal	12 35N	16 20w
62	Zikhron Ya'Aqov, Israel	32 34N	34 56E
64	Zile, Turkey	40 15N	36 0E
64	Zilfi, Saudi	26 12N	44 52E
27	Zilina, Czechoslovakia	49 12N	18 42E
83	Zillah, Libya	28 40N	17 41E
26	Zillertaler Alpen, Aust.	47 6N	11 45E
75	Zilling Tso, China	31 40N	89 0E
83	Zima, U.S.S.R.	54 0N	102 5E
82	Zimane, Adrar in, Alg.	22 10N	4 30E
120	Zimapán, Mexico	20 40N	99 20w
91	Zimba, Zambia	17 20s	26 25E
91	Zimbabwe, Rhod.	20 16s	31 0E
57	Zimovniki, U.S.S.R.	47 10N	42 25E
85	Zind, Niger	13 48N	9 0E
91	Zinga, Tanzania	9 16s	38 41E
82	Zini, Yebel, Morocco	28 0N	11 0w
63	Zinjibar, S. Yemen	13 5N	46 0E
49	Zinkgruvan, Sweden	58 50N	15 6E
119	Zion Nat. Park, U.S.A.	37 25N	112 50w
62	Zippori, Israel	32 64N	35 16E
39	Zirc, Hungary	47 17N	17 42E
39	Ziri, Yugoslavia	47 17N	11 14E
39	Zirje, I., Yugoslavia	43 39N	15 42E
26	Zirl, Austria	47 17N	11 14E
27	Zisterdorf, Austria	48 33N	16 45E
120	Zitácuaro, Mexico	19 20N	100 30w
27	Zitava, R., Cz.	48 14N	18 21E
16	Zitiste, Yugoslavia	45 30N	2 32E
44	Zitsa, Greece	39 47N	20 40E
24	Zittau, Germany	50 54N	14 47E
93	Zitundo, Mozam.	26 48s	32 47E
87	Ziway, L., Ethiopia	8 0N	38 50E
82	Ziz, Oued, Morocco	31 40N	4 15w
64	Zizip, Turkey	37 5N	37 50E
39	Zlarin, Yugoslavia	43 42N	15 49E
42	Zlatar, Yugoslavia	46 5N	16 3E
42	Zlatar, mts., Yugoslavia	42 55N	25 59E
43	Zlataritsa, Bulgaria	43 2N	24 55E
42	Zlatibor, Y.-slavia	43 45N	19 43E
43	Zlatista, Bulgaria	42 41N	24 7E
46	Zlatna, Rumania	46 8N	23 11E
43	Zlatograd, Bulgaria	41 22N	25 7E
52	Zlatoust, U.S.S.R.	55 10N	59 30E
119	Zlin, U.S.S.R.	41 59N	22 17E
83	Zlitan, Libya	32 25N	14 35E
28	Złocieniec, Poland	53 30N	16 1E
28	Złoczew, Poland	51 24N	18 35E
42	Zlot, Yugoslavia	44 1N	22 0E
28	Złotoryja, Poland	51 8N	15 55E
28	Złotów, Poland	53 22N	17 2E
28	Złoty Stok, Poland	50 27N	16 53E
55	Zmeinogorsk, U.S.S.R.	51 10N	82 13E
28	Zmigród, Poland	51 28N	16 53E
56	Zmiyev, U.S.S.R.	49 45N	36 27E
56	Znamenka, U.S.S.R.	48 45N	32 30E
27	Znojmo, Czechoslovakia	48 50N	16 2E
92	Zobia, Zaïre	3 0N	25 50E
38	Zogno, Italy	45 49N	9 41E
56	Zolochev, U.S.S.R.	49 45N	24 58E
56	Zolotonosha, U.S.S.R.	49 45N	32 5E
91	Zomba, Malawi	15 30s	35 19E
90	Zombi, Zaïre	3 35N	29 10E
56	Zonguldak, Turkey	41 28N	31 50E
82	Zorgo, Upper Volta	12 22N	0 35w
31	Zorita, Spain	39 17N	5 39w
46	Zorleni, Rumania	46 14N	27 44E
43	Zornitsa, Bulgaria	42 23N	26 58E
120	Zorra Island, Panama Canal Zone	9 18N	79 52w
84	Zorzor, Liberia	7 46N	9 28w
126	Zorritos, Peru	3 50s	80 40w
27	Zory, Poland	50 3N	18 44E
83	Zouar, Chad	20 30N	16 32E
82	Zousfana, O., Algeria	31 51N	1 30w
16	Zoutkamp, Netherlands	53 20N	6 18E
28	Zgorzelec, Poland	51 9N	15 0E
85	Zuarungu, Ghana	10 49N	0 52w
85	Zuba, Nigeria	9 11N	7 12E
87	Zubair, Jazāir, Yemen	15 0N	42 10E
31	Zubia, Spain	37 8N	3 33w
52	Zubtsov, U.S.S.R.	56 10N	34 34E
83	Zueitina, Libya	30 58N	20 7E
84	Zuénoula, Ivory Coast	7 34N	6 3w
32	Zuera, Spain	41 51N	0 49w
25	Zug, Switzerland	47 10N	8 31E
57	Zugdidi, U.S.S.R.	42 30N	41 48E
25	Zugersee, Switzerland	47 7N	8 35E
25	Zugspitze, Ger.	47 25N	10 59E
16	Zuid-Holland ♦,	52 0N	4 35E
16	Zuid-horn, Netherlands	53 15N	6 23E
33	Zújar, Spain	37 34N	2 50w
33	Zújar, R., Spain	38 30N	5 30E
31	Zújar, Pantano del, Sp.	38 55N	5 35w
87	Zula, Ethiopia	15 17N	39 40E
126	Zulia ♦, Venezuela	10 0N	72 10w
24	Zülpich, Germany	50 41N	6 38E
93	Zululand, S. Africa	28 2s	2 15w
32	Zumaya, Spain	43 19N	2 15w
91	Zumbo, Mozambique	15 35s	30 26E
85	Zummo, Nigeria	9 51N	12 59E
42	Zupania, Yugoslavia	45 4N	18 43E
87	Zugar, Yemen	14 0N	42 40E
42	Zur, Yugoslavia	42 13N	20 34E
25	Zürich, Switzerland	47 22N	8 32E
25	Zürich ♦, Switz.	47 26N	8 40E
25	Zürichsee, Switz.	47 18N	8 40E
28	Zuromin, Poland	53 4N	19 57E
85	Zuru, Nigeria	11 27N	5 4E
39	Zut, I., Yugoslavia	43 52N	15 17E
16	Zutphen, Netherlands	52 9N	6 12E
83	Zuwárrah, Libya	32 58N	12 1E
55	Zuyevka, U.S.S.R.	58 27N	51 10E
39	Zuzemberk, Yugoslavia	45 52N	14 56E
58	Zvenigorodka, U.S.S.R.	49 4N	30 56E
58	Zverinogolovskoye, U.S.S.R.	55 0N	62 30E
43	Zvezdets, Bulgaria	42 6N	27 26E
27	Zvolen, Czechoslovakia	48 33N	19 10E
42	Zvonce, Yugoslavia	42 57N	22 34E
42	Zvornik, Yugoslavia	44 26N	19 7E
84	Zwedru (Tchien), Liberia	5 59N	8 15w
25	Zweibrücken, Germany	49 15N	7 20E
24	Zwenkau, Germany	51 13N	12 19E
26	Zwettl, Austria	48 35N	15 9E
24	Zwickau, Germany	50 43N	12 30E
16	Zwolle, Netherlands	52 31N	6 6E
28	Zychlin, Poland	52 13N	19 36E
28	Zyrardów, Poland	52 3N	20 35E

The following are new or considerably enlarged counties in England and Wales and new regions in Scotland created by the Local Government Act 1972. In Northern Ireland 26 new districts were created. The co-ordinates will help to locate these new areas on the maps on pages 12-13, 14 and 15.

England and Wales

	Lat	Long
Avon	51 25N	2 35W
Cambridge	52 20N	0 0
Cleveland	54 35N	1 5W
Clwyd	53 5N	3 20W
Cumbria	54 35N	2 55W
Dyfed	52 0N	4 30W
East Sussex	50 55N	0 20E
Greater Manchester	53 30N	2 20W
Gwent	51 45N	2 55W
Gwynedd	53 0N	4 0W
Hereford & Worcester	52 10N	2 30W
Humberside	53 50N	0 30W
Isle of Wight	50 40N	1 20W
Merseyside	53 25N	2 55W
Mid Glamorgan	51 40N	3 35W
North Yorkshire	54 15N	1 25W
Powys	52 20N	3 20W
Salop	52 40N	2 40W
South Glamorgan	51 30N	3 20W
South Yorkshire	53 30N	1 20W
Suffolk	52 10N	1 0E
Tyne & Wear	54 55N	1 35W
West Glamorgan	51 40N	3 55W
West Midlands	52 30N	1 55W
West Sussex	50 55N	0 30W
West Yorkshire	53 45N	1 40W

Scotland

	Lat	Long
Borders	55 30N	2 50W
Central	56 10N	4 15W
Dumfries & Galloway	55 0N	4 0W
Grampian	57 30N	2 50W
Highland	57 40N	5 10W
Shetland	60 20N	1 30W
Strathclyde	55 45N	4 50W
Tayside	56 30N	3 35W
Western Isles	57 35N	7 10W

Northern Ireland

	Lat	Long
Antrim	54 45N	6 15W
Ards	54 30N	5 35W
Armagh	54 20N	6 35W
Ballymena	54 55N	6 15W
Ballymoney	55 5N	6 25W
Banbridge	54 20N	6 10W
Belfast	54 35N	5 55W
Carrickfergus	54 45N	5 50W
Castlereagh	54 35N	5 50W
Coleraine	55 5N	6 40W
Cookstown	54 40N	6 40W
Craigavon	54 30N	6 25W
Down	54 20N	5 45W
Dungannon	54 30N	6 55W
Fermanagh	54 20N	7 40W
Larne	54 55N	5 55W
Limavady	55 0N	6 55W
Lisburn	54 30N	6 9W
Londonderry	54 55N	7 15W
Magherafelt	54 50N	6 40W
Moyle	55 10N	6 15W
Newry & Mourne	54 10N	6 15W
Newtownabbey	54 45N	6 0W
North Down	54 40N	5 45W
Omagh	54 35N	7 15W
Strabane	54 45N	7 25W